91% — eText

93% — Study Plan

93% — Dynamic Study Modules

% of students who found learning tool helpful

Pearson eText enhances student learning—both in and outside the classroom. Take notes, highlight, and bookmark important content, or engage with interactive lecture and example videos that bring learning to life (available with select titles). Accessible anytime, anywhere via MyLab or the app.

The **MyLab Gradebook** offers an easy way for students and instructors to view course performance. Item Analysis allows instructors to quickly see trends by analyzing details like the number of students who answered correctly/incorrectly, time on task, and median time spend on a question-by-question basis. And because it's correlated with the AACSB Standards, instructors can track students' progress toward outcomes that the organization has deemed important in preparing students to be **leaders.**

84%

of students would tell their instructor to keep using MyLab Marketing

For additional details visit: www.pearson.com/mylab/marketing

Advertising & IMC

PRINCIPLES & PRACTICE

11e

Advertising & IMC

PRINCIPLES & PRACTICE

11e

Sandra Moriarty
University of Colorado Boulder

Nancy Mitchell
University of Nebraska–Lincoln

Charles Wood
University of Tulsa

William Wells
University of Minnesota

New York, NY

Vice President, Business, Economics, and UK Courseware:
  Donna Battista
Director of Portfolio Management: Stephanie Wall
Executive Portfolio Manager: Lynn M. Huddon
Editorial Assistant: Luis Gonzalez
Vice President, Product Marketing: Roxanne McCarley
Senior Product Marketer: Becky Brown
Product Marketing Assistant: Marianela Silvestri
Manager of Field Marketing, Business Publishing:
  Adam Goldstein
Field Marketing Manager: Nicole Price
Vice President, Production and Digital Studio, Arts and Business:
  Etain O'Dea
Director of Production, Business: Jeff Holcomb
Managing Producer, Business: Melissa Feimer
Content Producer: Michelle Zeng

Operations Specialist: Carol Melville
Design Lead: Kathryn Foot
Manager, Learning Tools: Brian Surette
Content Developer, Learning Tools: Sarah Peterson
Managing Producer, Digital Studio and GLP, Media Production
  and Development: Ashley Santora
Managing Producer, Digital Studio: Diane Lombardo
Digital Studio Producer: Monique Lawrence
Digital Studio Producer: Alana Coles
Project Managers: Susan McNally, Mary Sanger,
  Cenveo® Publisher Services
Interior Design: Cenveo® Publisher Services
Cover Design: Cenveo® Publisher Services
Cover Art: Cenveo® Publisher Services
Printer/Binder: LSC Communications
Cover Printer: LSC Communications

Library of Congress Cataloging-in-Publication Data
Names: Moriarty, Sandra E. (Sandra Ernst) author. | Mitchell, Nancy, author.
Title: Advertising & IMC: principles & practice/Sandra Moriarty, University of Colorado, Nancy Mitchell, University of Nebraska-
    Lincoln, Charles Wood, University of Tulsa, William Wells, University of Minnesota.
Other titles: Advertising and IMC
Description: Eleventh Edition. | New York: Pearson, [2017] | Revised edition of Advertising & IMC, [2015] | Includes bibliographical
    references and index.
Identifiers: LCCN 2017044442 | ISBN 9780134480435 | ISBN 0134480430
Subjects: LCSH: Advertising.
Classification: LCC HF5823 .W455 2017 | DDC 659.1—dc23
LC record available at https://lccn.loc.gov/2017044442

ISBN 10:   0-13-448043-0
ISBN 13: 978-0-13-448043-5

The Eleventh Edition is dedicated to all the students who have inspired us with their questions and ideas and all the colleagues who have challenged us with new thoughts and new findings. Most of all we dedicate this book to all our many contributors—the students, graduates, professors, and professionals who have contributed their thoughts, creative work, and professional experience to this edition.

Sandra Moriarty, Nancy Mitchell, and Charles Wood

BRIEF CONTENTS

CONTENTS

PART 3   Principle: Great Creative Communicates a Truth about a Brand

PART 4   Principle: Media in a World of Change

PART 5   Principle: IMC and Total Communication

ABOUT THE AUTHORS

Sandra Moriarty, Ph.D., *Professor Emerita, University of Colorado Boulder*

Sandra Moriarty is the cofounder of the Integrated Marketing Communication (IMC) graduate program at the University of Colorado. Now retired, she has also taught at Michigan State University, the University of Kansas, and Kansas State University, where she earned her Ph.D. in education. She specialized in teaching the campaign course and courses on the creative side—both writing and design. She has worked in government public relations, owned an advertising and public relations agency, directed a university publications program, and edited a university alumni magazine. She has been a consultant on IMC with agencies such as BBDO and Dentsu, the largest advertising agency in the world, and with their clients in the United States, Europe, and Asia. She has published widely in scholarly journals on marketing communication and visual communication topics and has authored 12 books on advertising, IMC, marketing, visual communication, and typography. A classic book on integrated marketing, *Driving Brand Value*, was written with coauthor Tom Duncan. Most recently she has authored the *Science and Art of Branding* with Giep Franzen, University of Amsterdam. International versions of her books include Spanish, Chinese, Taiwanese, Korean, Japanese, and an English-language version for India. She has spoken to groups and presented seminars in most European countries as well as Mexico, Japan, Korea, India, New Zealand, and Turkey.

Nancy Mitchell, Ph.D., *Professor, University of Nebraska–Lincoln*

Nancy Mitchell is professor of advertising in the College of Journalism and Mass Communications at the University of Nebraska–Lincoln, where she has taught since 1990. She served as chair of the advertising department for 11 years before heading the graduate program in her college. Prior to her tenure at the University of Nebraska, she taught at West Texas A&M University. She has taught a variety of courses, including advertising principles, design, copywriting, research and strategy, and campaigns and media ethics. She worked as an advertising professional for 15 years before entering academe. She gained experience as a copywriter, designer, editor, fund-raiser, and magazine editor in an array of businesses, including a large department store, a publishing company, an advertising agency, a newspaper, and a Public Broadcasting System affiliate. Her research focuses on creating effective advertising messages to underrepresented groups, ethical issues, and assessment of student learning. Nationally, she served as Advertising Division Head for the Association for Education in Journalism and Mass Communications. She serves on the editorial boards for *Journal of Advertising Education* and *Journalism and Mass Communication Educator*.

Charles Wood, Ph.D., *Professor, University of Tulsa*

Charles M. Wood is an associate professor of marketing at the University of Tulsa. He has academic degrees in engineering, journalism, and business, worked for a dozen years in industry as an engineer for a Fortune 10 firm, and started up a successful stage production company and creative agency. He previously served as faculty at Mississippi State University and the University of Missouri, where he earned his Ph.D. in marketing. His scholarly work has been published in leading journals such as the *Journal of Advertising, Journal of Retailing, Journal of Business Ethics, Business Horizons,* and *Journal of Marketing Education.* His research and teaching have received national and international recognition, including a Fulbright Scholar Award. He has taught courses at universities in Austria, India, Ireland, and Italy; traveled across Cuba before it was open to U.S. tourism; and had the unique experience of conducting business in the former Soviet Union. He enjoys developing and implementing fresh approaches to higher education and helping students work on a variety of creative and applied projects for small businesses and nonprofit organizations. He is a reviewer for numerous marketing conferences and journals and serves on the editorial review boards of the *Journal of Marketing Education* and *Journal of Business Market Management.*

William Wells, Ph.D., *Professor Emeritus, University of Minnesota, and former Executive Vice President, DDB, Chicago*

One of the industry's leading market and research authorities, William Wells is a retired professor of advertising at the University of Minnesota's School of Journalism and Mass Communication. Formerly executive vice president and director of marketing services at DDB Needham Chicago, he is the only representative of the advertising business elected to the Attitude Research Hall of Fame. He earned a Ph.D. from Stanford University and was formerly professor of psychology and marketing at the University of Chicago. He joined Needham, Harper, Chicago as director of corporate research. He is author of the Needham Harper Lifestyle study as well as more than 60 books and articles, including *Planning for ROI: Effective Advertising Strategy* (Prentice Hall, 1989).

A Wrinkle in Time: Reimagining Intelligence and Insights

When you take a foreign language class, you find yourself not only struggling with words, but also with how you think and how you live your life and relate to other people. Your experience studying marketing communication may be similar in some ways to studying a foreign language. A course or text in marketing communication where you study advertising, public relations, direct marketing, and promotions opens a new world of language. There are new words for old ideas, new terms for hard-to-explain concepts, new phrases for behind-the-scenes practices, and new words for world-shaking theories.

Today's marketing communication is more than just a new language. There also are new ways of talking: to yourself, to your mother, to your best friend, in class, on the phone, or in a text message. Because of the new shapes of media and forms of interaction—and the opportunities they open up—the heart of marketing communication also is being reshaped and reimagined both as a profession and as an academic area. This 11th edition of *Advertising & IMC: Principles & Practice* will help you acquire this new language and the intelligence and insights driving these changes.

But we're not just reimagining new ways of conversing, using new media and old media in new ways. We're also adjusting our ways of thinking and behaving based on computers, online devices, and information systems that extend, connect, and reshape our talking as well as our thinking. When you speak on the telephone or send a tweet on Twitter, don't you shape each conversation differently? And aren't your thoughts either condensed or expanded to fit the form of the medium?

Behind those patterns of talking, however, is additional intelligence you bring to the conversation: what you know about the people you are talking to and with. More important, however, are the insights you have into these people's beliefs and behavior.

This computer-driven transformation of our communication patterns is occurring in marketing communication. Hot topics such as artificial intelligence (AI), virtual reality (VR), and the Internet of Things (IoT) are being used to create conversational interactions that are more personalized and more personally relevant. They have the potential to reshape how we study, work, travel, and play as well as organize and manage the world around us.

AI is the mechanism that mines data and searches for patterns that drive consumer relevance. VR is a graphic system, also based on compilation of massive numbers of data points, to provide real-life images and experiences. Imagine driving a new car without leaving the showroom—just by putting on a set of glasses. The IoT refers to all the communication and connections between tiny computers that are embedded in things we wear and in our homes, cars, offices, and shops, like a Fitbit, Siri, your in-home climate control system, or the GPS device in your car.

The Amazon Echo placed in your room is a personal hands-free, voice-activated "digital assistant," like an electronic concierge. It can help you find the best restaurant and make your reservation, call a friend and leave a message, find sports scores, control the room temperature, or play your favorite music.

These systems accumulate data as they provide information and feedback. For the consumer, it simplifies tasks. Ask Alexa to order your Starbucks coffee, for example, and Alexa remembers what you like and places the order based on where you are, what time it is, and whether it is the same thing you ordered the last time. For the organization, these information-driven experiences make it easier to deliver a product or service that customers want—the way they want it.

The term *big data* describes the practice of compiling these massive databases of consumer information, interactions, preferences, and experiences that can be used to create or deepen brand relationships. Mining the data to see patterns is how information is turned into insights and insights into relevant messages and responses. You do that intuitively as you navigate conversations and personal experiences based on your own set of insights.

On the commercial level these tools and practices are used to talk to and with customers, prospective customers, and other important people in a brand's corporate life. The goal is to increase the relevancy of each contact and each conversation. Although these new tools open up new opportunities, it's important to remember that there are enduring principles that also drive effective communication. This 11th edition continues to focus on principles as well as practices of effective marketing communication.

So reimagine your idea of advertising or public relations or other areas of marketing communication. These professional areas teem with possibilities as their practitioners learn how to reshape their practices and the principles of their professions. It's a wrinkle in time, but it's a marvelous time to get involved in this reimagining.

What's New in the 11th Edition

1. *A New Author Added to the Team* As you may have noticed when you read the "About the Authors" section, a new team member has been added to this 11th edition. Charles Wood, an associate professor of marketing in the Collins College of Business at the University of Tulsa, brings his business and marketing insights to this edition.

2. *A Greater Emphasis on IMC* This 11th edition provides an even stronger focus on integrated marketing communication (IMC), which is accomplished by substantial revisions in chapter order, chapter revisions, and updated material. All the marketing communication chapters have been grouped with advertising at the front of the text to provide more comprehensive presentations of the professional areas and functions of IMC. This change has involved a major reorganization of the chapters, which reflects feedback that students need to know what these professional areas are and how they work (public relations, direct response, promotion, and advertising) before moving into the Part 2 discussion of strategy and planning how these areas work together.

3. *Strategic Brand Communication* In previous editions the book led off with an advertising chapter followed by a marketing chapter. The basics of marketing chapter had been revised some editions ago to function as an introduction to the field of marketing communication (also referred to as *strategic communication*). In the 11th edition this chapter now becomes Chapter 1, the introductory chapter to the book. It focuses on brands and the marketing practices that provide the communication foundation of branding. Included in this chapter is an introduction to the marketing mix and how the marketing mix sends messages. Additional concepts include an introduction to the concept and practice of IMC and an explanation of how branding is shaped by communication.

4. *Advertising* Previously Chapter 1, advertising now becomes Chapter 2, the first of three chapters detailing the basics of the most important functional areas of marketing communication. The chapter introduces the basic functions, components, and roles of advertising. It also explains the evolution of current practices through advertising's eras and ages as well as the contemporary world of advertising's key players, types of agencies, and agency jobs.

5. *Public Relations* Previously Chapter 15, in this edition public relations is moved to Chapter 3, emphasizing the integral role it plays in IMC and that many of our student readers are enrolled in strategic communication programs that combine public relations with advertising. The

chapter introduces public relations' basic roles, functions, and tools as well as different types of public relations programs.

6. ***Direct Response and Promotion*** The decision to start with the marketing communication professional areas, specifically advertising and public relations, also meant that the other two areas covered in previous editions needed to move forward as well. We recognize that both direct response and promotions (previously Chapters 16 and 17), although important, are not typically majors (or a curriculum of courses) in our adopters' schools. Therefore, we decided to combine these two topics into one chapter. The merger is anchored by an emphasis on action and interaction, both being characteristics and objectives of direct-response and promotion efforts. This new Chapter 4 introduces the elements and media of direct-response communication and provides an introduction to both consumer and trade promotions. In addition, this chapter includes an explanation of various types of multiplatform promotions and explains the important role of databases in both direct-response communication and promotions.

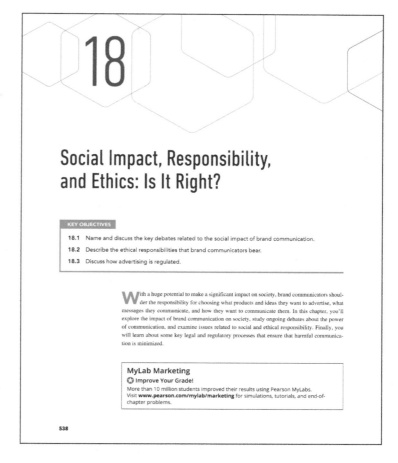

7. ***Social Impact, Responsibility, and Ethics: Is It Right?*** Chapter 3 in the previous edition was titled "Brand Communication and Society." This edition revises what is now Chapter 18 to increase the focus on the ethical and social responsibilities of all IMC professionals. The emphasis on social responsibility and ethics makes a strong conclusion for the book, particularly because it is paired with the evaluation and effectiveness discussion ("Does It Work?") in Chapter 17. Chapter 18 focuses on the ethical and social responsibility issues across all areas of marketing communication, broadening the focus from advertising in previous editions.

8. ***New Topics, New Media*** Every time this book is revised, we have to acknowledge the changes brought about by new media. Since the last edition, managers are confronting new ways of communicating centered on AI, VR, and the IoT. Other new terms popping up in the professional press include *native advertising*, *programmatic buying*, and *beacons*. All these innovations are driven by new ways of collecting, manipulating, and using data, and all are discussed in this 11th edition.

9. ***New Examples of Award-Winning Brand Communication Campaigns from Around the World*** Part of the added value of this textbook lies in the cohesive story it tells about effective brand communication. New and updated case studies open each chapter in the 11th edition to illustrate basic principles and best practices and show students how professionals design and execute effective strategies that work.

10. ***A Wealth of Contributions from Experts*** The philosophy of this textbook is to invite contributions from many people—academics and professionals from around the world. These contributions aren't just quotes from speeches or articles; rather, they are pieces written specifically for this book, with experts sharing stories about campaigns they've worked on as well as research they've conducted. This book was guided by the insights and direction of the professionals on the book's Advisory Board. In addition, stories, essays, and examples of the work of a group of young professionals who were nominated by their professors are featured in this textbook.

A MATTER OF PRACTICE

Branding Billings

John Brewer, *President and CEO, Billings (Montana) Chamber of Commerce and Visitors Bureau*

What do yo
you think of N
right? That's
incredibly su
campaign for
What do
you think of E
Probably not
That's th
when our sto
took on the p
ing Billings. So this is a story of our
create a brand identity campaign for t
You can check out the results of
.brandbillings.com. In addition to b
the first thing you may notice on t
with the slogan "Billings—Montana's
how the city arrived at that theme line
The campaign began with researc
than a thousand online surveys, comr

A MATTER OF PRINCIPLE

Ivory: It's Pure and It Floats

Soap is soap, right?
A basic principle of branding is that a brand takes
on meaning when it makes
its product category. Procto
plished that by creating ide
brand Ivory before anyon
soap a distinctive product
system also called attentio
the product. Here's the ba
Ivory came to be one of th
brands of all time.
Before the Civil War, ho
soap from lye, fats (cooking
It was a soft, jelly-like, yello
things adequately, but if it fe
dissolved into mush. In Vict
for quality soap was the hig
pure white soap imported fi
made from the finest olive o

A DAY IN THE LIFE

A View from the Marcom Front Line

Peter Stasiowski, *Director of Communications, Interprint USA, Pittsfield, MA*

There's a big difference between working
agency, where the focus is on promoting n
and becoming an individual company's lon
professional, where the focus is on promotir
pany that signs your paycheck.
The most obvious changes, such as fine
marketing plan instead of juggling several,
more subtle and important differences. When
agency title of art director and creative directo
rent position as marketing and communicatic
for an industrial printing company, I went fr
with a group of people dedicated to prac
marketing communications to working with a
cated to printing good decor paper for its c
the laminate industry.

A PRINCIPLED PRACTICE

PAUSE FOR THE CAUSE: Boosting Brand Value with Cause Marketing

Scott Hamula, *Ithaca College*

Things are really tough out there
for brands: lots of competition, savvier consumers, media
messages that just don't break
through the clutter like they used
to, and occasional pieces of bad
publicity. Today, though, some
brands are turning to corporate social responsibility not only
because it is the right thing to
do, but also as a way for brands
to more clearly differentiate themselves in this dynamic
marketplace.

vehicles to an earthquake-ravaged disaster area in
China, brands act as good corporate citizens.
This socially responsible promotional strategy
occurs when a brand or company aligns itself with a
nonprofit organization to generate both sales and
charitable donations at the same time. Simply put, it's
"buy my product, and I'll donate to your cause." This
approach tends to make a lot of sense. Surveys continue
to show that, given two very similar products, consumers are more likely to purchase the brand that is associated with a cause they care about.
American Express Company is often credited with
starting cause-related marketing in the early 1980s
when it pledged to donate 5 cents to the arts in San
Francisco whenever a member used their American
Express card to make a purchase, and $2 for each new
card member.
To launch and sustain a successful cause-related
marketing program, a brand must first know what
issues are important to its customers so as to align
itself with a cause that's a good match. An example
is Yoplait yogurt's "Save Lids to Save Lives" campaign. Because this brand's primary target market is
women, Yoplait linked itself with the Susan G. Komen

The Central Themes

Although the introduction to this preface highlighted changes, the important thing in a textbook project of this size and scale is that there are central threads that weave key ideas across the chapters and throughout the book. So let's consider the foundational themes that make this book different from other introductory textbooks in advertising and marketing communication.

Brand Communication and IMC

This book started out many years ago as an introduction to advertising textbook, although it acknowledged the role of other areas. Over the years the scope of advertising has changed. Now we use the phrase *brand communication* (or *marketing communication*) because what used to be known as *advertising* has expanded beyond the familiar ads in print media and commercials on radio and television to include public relations, direct marketing, and other forms of promotion. The emphasis then shifts to the brand and the communication activities that surround it.

Electronic and social media have opened up new ways to communicate online with consumers about a brand. Alternative and nontraditional forms, such as *guerilla marketing* that reaches people in surprising ways in unexpected places, have opened up new opportunities to engage people with brand messages through memorable experiences.

Creating buzz and dialogue now accompany the practice of targeting messages at consumers. A new goal is to enlist word-of-mouth conversations to reinforce and extend the power of the more traditional marketing communication forms.

This wider view of *brand communication* includes an array of communication tools used by a variety of organizations—nonprofit as well as for-profit—promoting their brands, consumer as well as business-to-business products and services. We mention public relations, direct marketing, and sales promotion, but those are just a few of the tools in the brand communication tool kit.

We describe the use of these various forms of brand communication as *integrated marketing communication* (IMC), which refers to the strategic use of multiple forms of communication to engage different types of consumers who have an interest in or connection to a brand. The key word is integration, which means the various tools are strategically employed to work together. The title of this book changed in the previous edition to recognize the importance of IMC in modern brand communication.

Effectiveness

During a Super Bowl some years ago, an ad for Anheuser-Busch called "Applause" showed people in an airport spontaneously applauding a group of American troops returning home. Even the audience watching from their living rooms was inclined to join in with applause as part of this graceful display of respect and appreciation. It was touching and memorable, and it might have nudged a few viewers to think well of Anheuser-Busch.

But was it an effective ad? What was it trying to accomplish? Did the viewers remember it as an Anheuser-Busch ad? If so, did it affect their opinions of that company and its brands?

What is effective? Is it marketing communication that gets talked about? Is it a message like the Anheuser-Busch commercial that touches your emotions and inspires you to applaud? What, exactly, does it mean to say that a brand message "works"?

Our answer is that brand communication is effective if it creates a desired response in the audience. A brand message that *works* is one that affects people; it gets intended results that can be measured.

Effective messages move people to like, love, laugh, dance, squirm in their seats, or even shed tears. But they can also cause you to stop and watch or even to stop and think. Commercial communication can't make you do something you don't want to do, but it can inspire you to read about a new product or remember a favorite brand when you're walking down the aisle in a supermarket or applaud a service member or first responder.

Advertising & IMC: Principles & Practice uses the *Facets Model of Effects* to better explain brand communication strategies, consumer responses, and effectiveness. The facets model is like a diamond or a crystal whose surfaces represent the different types of responses generated by a brand message. This model and the ideas it represents are used throughout the book to help explain such things as how objectives are decided on, what strategies deliver what kind of effects, and how an advertisement and other forms of marketing communication are evaluated based on their objectives.

That's why this textbook, *Advertising & IMC: Principles & Practice*, is dedicated not only to explaining advertising and other areas of brand communication—such as public relations, direct marketing, and sales promotion—but also to make you think about what works in all commercial communication efforts.

Enduring Principles and Best Practices

To help you better understand how effective communication is created, this textbook will highlight the principles and practices of the industry.

The Facets Model of Effects

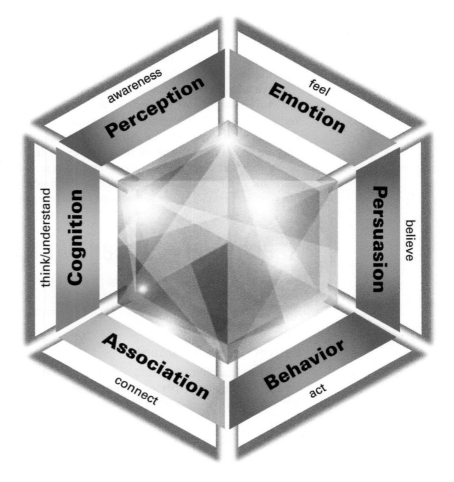

Marketing communication messages are part inspiration and part hard work, but they are also a product of clear and logical thinking. In most cases, consumers have little idea what the objectives are because that information generally isn't made public—and sometimes you can't tell from the communication itself. But think about the "Applause" ad. From what we've told you, what do you think the ad's objectives were? To sell beer? To get viewers to run out and buy the brand? Actually, the ad seems to be a bit removed from a straight sales pitch.

An educated guess—and that's what you will be better able to make after reading this book—is that perhaps its objective is simply to make people feel good—to see the goodness in a simple patriotic gesture and ultimately associate that feeling of goodness and warmth with the brand. Does it work? How did you feel when you read over the description of the ad?

This book presents both principles and practices of effective brand communication. You will find principles in the margins of the text in every chapter. In addition, boxes and other features elaborate on both the principles and practices related to the topic of each chapter.

In this 11th edition, we take you behind the scenes of many award-winning campaigns, such as the "Gatorade," "#LikeAGirl," "REI," "Old Spice," "TOMS," and "Fearless Girl" campaigns, to uncover the hard work and explain the objectives, the inspiration, and the creative ideas behind them. You'll see how the ideas come together, you'll analyze the decision making, and you'll understand the risks the message creators faced.

We also have contributions from highly experienced professionals as well as our Ad Stars, graduates from advertising, public relations, and marketing communication programs around the United States who were nominated by their professors to be featured in this book. We showcase their work throughout the book. These Ad Stars have also written "Inside Stories" that explain strategies and what they have learned on the job as well as "A Day in the Life" features that provide insight into various career opportunities in marketing communication.

The Proof It Works

Advertisers and marketers want proof their marketing communication is effective and efficient. Likewise, you should want proof about the value of your textbooks. You will learn in this book that all claims in messages need to be supported. That's why we make the claim—and, yes, this is an advertisement—that *Advertising & IMC: Principles & Practice* is the book to read to learn about effective brand communication. We are making a bold claim, but here is how we back it up.

Advertising & IMC: Principles & Practice is time-tested. It has continued as one of the market leaders since 1989. It continues to be in touch with the most current practices in the industry, but it also presents the fundamental principles in ways that will give you a competitive edge. That's why students keep this textbook on their shelves as an important reference book as they move through their major. One thing we hear from our young professional Ad Stars is that they continue to rely on this book as they make their transition to professional life. The principles in this book are enduring, and your understanding of the language and effective practices of the field can jump-start your career.

Reach Every Student with MyLab Marketing

MyLab is the teaching and learning platform that empowers you to reach *every* student. By combining trusted author content with digital tools and a flexible platform, MyLab personalizes the learning experience and improves results for each student. Learn more about MyLab Marketing at www.pearson.com/mylab/marketing.

Deliver Trusted Content

You deserve teaching materials that meet your own high standards for your course. That's why we partner with highly respected authors to develop interactive content and course-specific resources that you can trust—and that keep your students engaged.

- **Mini Sims** put your students in business professional roles and give them the opportunity to apply course concepts as they make decisions about real-world business challenges. The simulations branch based on each decision, creating various scenario paths and helping students understand the impact of their decisions on an organization—strengthening their critical thinking skills.

Empower Each Learner

Each student learns at a different pace. Personalized learning pinpoints the precise areas where each student needs practice, giving all students the support they need—when and where they need it—to be successful.

- The **Study Plan** acts as a tutor, providing personalized recommendations for each of your students based on his or her ability to master the learning objectives in your course.

Teach Your Course Your Way

Your course is unique. So whether you'd like to build your own assignments, teach multiple sections, or set prerequisites, MyLab gives you the flexibility to easily create *your* course to fit *your* needs.

Improve Student Results

When you teach with MyLab, student performance improves. That's why instructors have chosen MyLab for over 15 years, touching the lives of over 50 million students.

Instructor Teaching Resources

Advertising & IMC: Principles & Practice comes with the following teaching resources.

Supplements available to instructors at www.pearsonhighered.com	Features of the supplement
Instructor's Manual authored by Stephanie Bibb from Chicago State University	• Chapter-by-chapter summaries • Examples and activities not in the main book • Teaching outlines • Teaching tips • Solutions to all questions and problems in the book
Test Bank authored by Bonnie Flaherty	2000 multiple-choice, true/false, short-answer, and graphing questions with these annotations: • Difficulty level (1 for straight recall, 2 for some analysis, 3 for complex analysis) • Type (multiple-choice, true/false, short-answer, essay) • Topic (the term or concept the question supports) • Learning outcome • AACSB learning standard (Written and Oral Communication; Ethical Understanding and Reasoning; Analytical Thinking; Information Technology; Interpersonal Relations and Teamwork; Diverse and Multicultural Work; Reflective Thinking; Application of Knowledge)
Computerized TestGen	TestGen allows instructors to: • Customize, save, and generate classroom tests • Edit, add, or delete questions from the Test Item Files • Analyze test results • Organize a database of tests and student results.
PowerPoints authored by James Andrew Lingwall from Clarion University of Pennsylvania	Slides include all the graphs, tables, and equations in the textbook. PowerPoints meet accessibility standards for students with disabilities. Features include, but not limited to: • Keyboard and Screen Reader access • Alternative text for images • High color contrast between background and foreground colors

ADVISORY BOARD VIPS

Shawn M. Couzens
Sole Proprietor and CCO, AbbaSez, Bucks County, Pennsylvania

Constance Cannon Frazier
Chief Operating Officer, AAF, Washington, DC

Larry Kelley
Professor, University of Houston, Texas, and former Partner, Media Director, and Chief Planning Officer, The Company of Others, Houston

Regina Lewis
Associate Professor, University of Alabama, Tuscaloosa

Ingvi Logason
Principal, H:N Marketing Communications, Reykjavík, Iceland

Harley Manning
Vice President, Research Director Serving Customer Experience Professionals, Forrester Research

Susan Mendelsohn
President, Susan Mendelsohn Consultants, Chicago, Illinois

David Rittenhouse
Representative Director, Neo@Ogilvy, Tokyo, Japan

William H. Weintraub
Chief Marketing Officer (Retired), Coors Inc., Professor at University of Colorado Boulder

Karl Weiss
President, Market Perceptions & Healthcare Research, Denver, Colorado

Robert Witeck
CEO, Witeck Communications, Washington, DC

Charles E. Young
Founder and CEO, Ameritest/CY Research, Albuquerque, New Mexico

FEATURE CONTRIBUTORS

Glenda Alvarado
Assistant Professor, University of South Carolina, Columbia

Masaru Ariga
Group Account Director, Dentsu Inc., Tokyo, Japan

Bill Barre
Professor Emeritus, University of Wisconsin–Eau Claire

Fred Beard
Professor, Gaylord College of Journalism and Mass Communication, University of Oklahoma, Norman

Heather Beck
Owner/Photographer, Beck Impressions Photography, Lewisburg, Tennessee

Daryl Bennewith
Strategic Director, TBWA Group, Durban, South Africa

John Brewer
President and CEO, Billings Chamber of Commerce/Convention and Visitors Bureau, Billings, Montana

Edoardo Teodoro Brioschi
Professor and Chair of Economics and Techniques of Business Communication, Università Cattolica del Sacro Cuore, Milan, Italy

Sheri Broyles
Professor, Mayborn School of Journalism, University of North Texas, Denton

Clarke Caywood
Professor, Medill School of Journalism, Northwestern University, Evanston, Illinois

Ed Chambliss
CEO, The Phelps Group, Santa Monica, California

Nick Ciffone
Creative Director, TBWA\Media Arts Lab, Los Angeles

Michael Dattolico
Owner, Musion Creative, LLC, Gainesville, Florida

Tammie DeGrasse-Cabrera
Senior Account Director, CP+B, Miami, Florida

Graham Douglas
Head of Creative, Vimeo, New York City

Bonnie Drewniany
Professor and Advertising Sequence Head, University of South Carolina, Columbia

Rusty Duncan
COO and Partner, Insight Creative Group

Tom Duncan
Professor Emeritus, University of Colorado Boulder

Steve Edwards
Distinguished Chair, Professor, and Director, Temerlin Advertising Institute, Southern Methodist University, Dallas, Texas

Gary Ennis
Creative Director, The Baiocco and Maldari Connection, Brooklyn, New York

Kristin Ewing
Corporate Communication and Public Relations Specialist, Express Employment Professionals, Oklahoma City

Nate Folbrecht
Producer, CP + B, Boulder, Colorado; Integrated Producer, Intel's Global Production Labs, San Francisco

Eric Foss
Vice President, Consulting Services, North America, Pcubed, Ann Arbor, Michigan

Jami Fullerton
Peggy Welch Chair in Integrated Marketing Communications, Oklahoma State University School of Media and Strategic Communication, Stillwater, Oklahoma

Rachel Gallen
Division Manager, Beverage Distributors, Aurora, Colorado

Arlene Gerwin
Marketing Consultant and President, Bolder Insights, Boulder, Colorado

Thomas Groth
Professor Emeritus, University of West Florida, Pensacola

Jean M. Grow
Professor and Chair, Strategic Communication, Diederich School of Communication, Marquette University, Milwaukee, Wisconsin

Anastasia Guletsky
Senior Copywriter and Content Strategist, Rise Interactive, Chicago

Scott R. Hamula
Associate Professor and Chair, Strategic Communication, Roy H. Park School of Communications, Ithaca College, New York

Michael Hanley
Associate Professor, Department of Journalism, Ball State University, Muncie, Indiana

Valerie Jones
Assistant Professor of Advertising, College of Journalism and Mass Communications, University of Nebraska–Lincoln

Alice Kendrick
Professor of Advertising, Temerlin Advertising Institute, Southern Methodist University, Dallas, Texas

Jooyoung Kim
Associate Professor, Grady College of Communications and Journalism, University of Georgia, Athens

Su Jung Kim
Assistant Professor, Greenlee School of Journalism and Communication, Iowa State University, Ames

Amanda Koone
Director of Communications, Fredericksburg Convention & Visitor Bureau, Fredericksburg, Texas

Meg Lauerman
Director of University Communication Emeritus, University of Nebraska–Lincoln

Melissa Lerner
Partner, EnPlay Media, New York City

Hairong Li
Professor of Advertising, Michigan State University, East Lansing

Elisabeth Loeck
Learning Support Specialist, Ewing Marion Kauffman School, Kansas City, Missouri

Qing Ma
Assistant Professor, Zhejiang University City College, Hangzhou, China

Sara Mahmood
Senior Strategist/Analyst, GTB, Dearborn, Michigan

Karen Mallia
Associate Professor, University of South Carolina, Columbia

Galit Marmor-Lavie
Professor, Stan Richards School of Advertising and Public Relations, University of Texas at Austin

James Maskulka
Associate Professor of Marketing, Lehigh University, Bethlehem, Pennsylvania

Robert Meeds
Associate Professor, Department of Communications, California State University, Fullerton

George Milne
Director of Doctoral Program and Professor of Marketing, University of Massachusetts, Amherst

Anthony Morrison
Owner and CEO, MYP Training, Houston, Texas

Keith Murray
Professor, Department of Marketing, Bryant University, Smithfield, Rhode Island

Mary Nichols
Founder and Chief Community Builder, Karmic Marketing, Portland, Oregon

Amy Niswonger

Design Instructor, School of Advertising Art, Dayton, Ohio; President, Ninth Cloud Creative and Little Frog Prints, Lebanon, Ohio

Connie Pechmann

Professor, Paul Merage School of Business, University of California, Irvine

Jimmy Peltier

Professor, Department of Marketing, University of Wisconsin–Whitewater

Joseph E. Phelps

Professor and Chair, Department of Advertising and Public Relations, University of Alabama, Tuscaloosa

James Pokrywczynski

Associate Professor, Strategic Communication, Diederich College of Communication, Marquette University, Milwaukee, Wisconsin

Ben Preston

Cofounder, Hereditary Cancer Foundation, Omaha; Digital Marketing Manager, EDG Architecture and Engineering, Life Coded, and Bond Development Partners, New York City

Herbert Rotfeld

Professor, Department of Marketing, Auburn University, Alabama

Karl Schroeder

Copy Director, Nike, Portland, Oregon

Brian Sheehan

Professor, S. I. Newhouse School of Public Communications, Syracuse University, New York

Kim Sheehan

Professor and Director, Honors Program at the University of Oregon School of Journalism and Communication, Eugene

Peter Stasiowski

Director of Communications, Interprint USA, Pittsfield, Massachusetts

Aaron Stern

Creative Director/Consultant, Stern & Co., New York City

Mark Stuhlfaut

Associate Professor, Department of Integrated Strategic Communication, University of Kentucky, Lexington

John Sweeney

Director of Advertising and Public Relations, University of North Carolina at Chapel Hill

Ronald E. Taylor

Professor, School of Advertising and Public Relations, University of Tennessee, Knoxville

Joe Tougas

Professor, Evergreen State College, Olympia, Washington

Wan-Hsiu Sunny Tsai

Associate Professor, School of Communication, University of Miami, Florida

Bruce G. Vanden Bergh

Professor Emeritus, Department of Advertising and Public Relations, Michigan State University, East Lansing

Trent Walters

Brand Management Principal, The Richards Group, Dallas, Texas

Philip Willet

Assistant Professor, University of Oklahoma, Norman

Joyce M. Wolburg

Associate Dean, Diederich College of Communication, and Professor, Strategic Communication, Marquette University, Milwaukee, Wisconsin

Leo Wong

Account Manager, Droga5, New York City

Lisa Yansura

Supervisor, Client Engagement, VML, Kansas City, Missouri

Wende Zomnir

Cofounder, Urban Decay, Costa Mesa, California

Advertising & IMC

PRINCIPLES & PRACTICE

11e

1

PRINCIPLE
All Communications
One Voice

▲ ED CHAMBLISS
is CEO of Phelps.

"People crave consistency. Predictability. To know what's going to happen before it does so they can minimize risk," said Ed Chambliss, CEO of IMC agency Phelps and a member of this book's Advisory Board. He explained: "That's one reason why McDonald's remains the world's largest hamburger chain. Not because they have the *best* burger you've ever had, but because you can depend on them to deliver a burger that is consistently *good enough*."

Chambliss explains that his agency is a leader in "defining our clients' brands and aligning their communications." That's summarized in the agency's slogan: "All Communications. One Voice."

To accomplish consistency, today's companies intend that the experiences and communications you have with them are aligned. Whether it's in advertising, public relations, direct marketing, sales marketing, special events, sports marketing, digital marketing, loyalty programs, customer service, or personal selling, they want to ensure that you have a consistent brand experience.

These experiences involve communication about a brand with a customer—or potential customer. Sometimes it's a river or even torrent of communication, usually from a company to a customer or prospective customer, but sometimes the communication involves a brand conversation to and from a customer. The customer may receive a message or may send it; likewise, the brand may send a message or may receive it.

Fractured Communication

The problem is that all these areas that deliver and receive messages about the brand may not be on the same page. Ideally, there's some corporate concept of what the brand is and stands for, but sometimes a special promotion or some other communication program may not reflect that brand vision. The brand's communication landscape becomes fractured.

In the old days, these specialist areas operated like silos, and managers rarely talked with one another. Today, though, there's pressure from the brand client that there be more coordination among these communication areas. The solution is a process called integrated marketing communication (IMC), which is a major theme of this textbook.

What Do You Call It?

There's also a blurring among the tools these communication areas use. Public relations, for example, may use advertising, and an advertising campaign may use public relations techniques such as publicity or special promotions.

The promise, and now reality, of interactivity (brand conversations) through social media, mobile media, and real-time online communication is shutting some doors and opening others. When someone makes a brand contact, mentions a brand to a friend online, or searches for information related to a brand, how does the brand or company respond? Is it an ad? A press release? A direct-response piece? Customer service? A website? Who's involved in this customer interaction, and how is it aligned with other messages about the brand? Who's in charge?

In the past, all these platforms and tools were often called advertising, and in many cases, advertising had the biggest budget and led the communication effort. Coming from that viewpoint, Rance Crain, publisher of industry magazine *Advertising Age*, explained that "everything a brand does, really, is advertising."[1] Northwestern professor Don Schultz, a leader in the development of IMC, believes, however, that "we're no longer in the advertising business (or whatever you want to call it)."[2]

In this textbook we call it strategic communication or integrated marketing communication.

The challenge to a student of strategic communication is pointed out by Maurice Levy, CEO of communication giant Publicis, who calls for a system of services that "is seamless and fully integrated in one single platform."[3]

Chambliss summarized the rationale for the Phelps IMC system of "All Communications. One Voice." He said, "IMC delivers far more impact and effectiveness from every precious marketing communication dollar because it ties together everything you do into ONE consistent, cohesive message that is much more noticeable and memorable."

1

Strategic Brand Communication

KEY OBJECTIVES

1.1 What is the marketing mix, and how does it send messages?

1.2 What is integrated marketing communication?

1.3 Understand how this text will prepare you for your career.

In today's marketplace, new forms of communication and promotion are changing all areas of marketing and strategic communication. Intensive competition for the minds and money of people who buy products and support organizations has brought us so many choices that a text like this one is constantly challenged to have a focus. We believe the focus should be on the brand, the one constant in the shifting sands of strategic communication. By strategic communication we mean the principles and practices used in advertising, public relations, direct response communication, sales promotion, online communication, and other areas of promotion.

Category	Brand	Agency	Awards
Long-Term Brand Development	New Pig	In-house	Since 2005: *Telly Award for Christmas video; Automotive Communications Award (Direct Mail, Campaign, Newsletter); Multichannel Merchant Gold Award for Pigalog, three times); Multichannel Merchant "Catalog of the Year" award for UK Pigalog (twice); Multichannel Silver International award for BV Pigalog; Catalog Age Gold Industrial Supplies Category for Pigalog; Catalog Age Gold International Category for UK Pigalog; WebAward Standard of Excellence*

New Pig: Partners in Grime

Photo: Courtesy New Pig Corporation, www.newpig.com

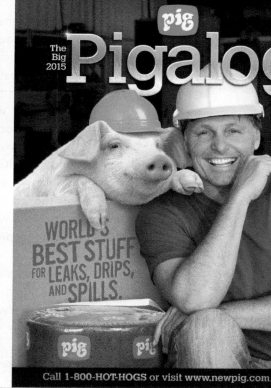

Photo: Courtesy New Pig Corporation, www.newpig.com

New Pig Corporation, an international business-to-business (B2B) company, has built a unique brand position in the often-dull niche markets of industrial absorbent products and workplace safety. New Pig reaches its markets through its award-winning Pigalog® catalog, direct marketing program, and distributors. The company is also recognized for its innovative product line and legendary customer service.

Its fun brand personality has transformed the dirty world of the factory into a clean, pig-focused theme park. The "pig" theme is integrated throughout the company. Here are a few examples:

- Catalog name: **Pigalog®**
- Employees are **Piggers**
- Address: **One Pork Avenue**
- Phone: **1-800-HOT HOGS®**
- Fax: **1-800-621-PIGS**
- Intranet: **OINKX** (**O**nline **IN**formation & **K**nowledge **X**change)
- Cafeteria: **Pig Trough**
- Promotional item: **PIG® Snout Hat, PIG® Pen, PIG® Note Pad, etc.**
- The founder is **Chairman of the Boar . . . d**
- The president/chief executive officer (CEO) is the **Head Hog**
- Vocabulary: **Swine-cerely, Boarthday, Hamiversary, ThOINKs, Boar-B-Q, etc.**

Historically, oil spills, as well as other liquids, were absorbed by spreading around dirt or clay. The process may have soaked up most of the spill, but it created its own mess. The solution was an invention: the Original PIG® Absorbent Sock, the first contained absorbent sock that changed leak and spill management forever.

All the products project the light-hearted pig brand image. For example, a mat commonly used around machinery to soak up spills has been marketed as the PIG® Ham-O® Mat with a colorful piggy pattern as well as slogans that carry the brand theme, such as "Scuff-resistant top layer is tough as a pig's hide!" (New Pig Corporation). A scratchy sketch of a friendly pig face ("Mr. Pig") pops up from time to time in the Pigalog, on the website, or on special promotions to add surprise and fun to its pig-themed personality.

Although the company avoided industrial distribution in the early stages of its growth, the demand for PIG® products was such that select distributors like Grainger, Caterpillar, Safety-Kleen, Motion Industries, and NAPA are now "partners in grime." Today the company is a multichannel, multibrand manufacturer and merchandiser offering the world's largest selection of absorbent products and other industrial maintenance products to help workplaces maintain a clean, safe environment.

It all began in the corner of a warehouse in Altoona, Pennsylvania, aptly nicknamed the *Pig Pen*. With rounds of experimentation and product testing in constant progress, it was always messy. As the sausage-sized socks wallowed in pools of dirty oil, it's easy to understand why the founders started calling them *Pigs*.

When it came time to register an official name, it made perfect sense to name the world's first contained absorbent, the PIG® Absorbent Sock, in honor of its birthplace, the *Pig Pen*. However, a top ad agency warned that the "Pig" name would never do as a commercial name because it conjured up too many negative connotations. For example, angry protestors called police "pigs," overeaters are called "pigs," and some religions have strong precepts about pigs.

The founders nevertheless realized that many "pig" references are positive as well: think of Porky Pig, piggy banks, and hog heaven, for example. "Pigs are really a lot of fun," said the company's public relations director, Carl DeCaspers.

The founders also chose *Pig Corporation* as the company's new name, but company chairman and cofounder Ben Stapelfeld discovered that *Pig Corporation* had already been registered. Undaunted, Stapelfeld simply added the word *new* at the beginning to create *New Pig Corporation*, and the company with the funny name was born. His compromise name, New Pig, was a stroke of genius because it reflected the nature of the product as well as the innovativeness of the company.

Because customers had so much fun with the name and remembered it so easily, the founders decided to stick with it as the corporate name, despite the experts' advice. The success of the company has proved the power of the brand vision. The leak and spill experts serve more than 200,000 industrial, commercial, utility, institutional, military, and government facilities in more than seventy countries. Headquartered in Tipton, Pennsylvania, the company employs 570 people worldwide.

New Pig has kept its sense of fun intact while continuing to expand its reach globally. Listed as the sixty-fourth-fastest-growing private company in the United States by *Inc.* magazine in 1990, New Pig's growth has continued uninterrupted. It currently maintains ten facilities in the United States consisting of manufacturing, warehousing, and sales operations. International development continues as New Pig has expanded operations with headquarters in the United Kingdom and Holland to serve continental Europe. In 2007, New Pig continued its Asia growth by founding Shanghai-based New Pig China. Its most recent foreign subsidiary, New Pig India, opened its doors in March 2015 with headquarters in New Delhi and warehousing and sales operations in Mumbai.

New Pig's sales are driven by direct marketing and rely heavily on its award-winning catalogs. The Big Pigalog® (annual January edition) is a colorful 450-page catalog showcasing more than 3,100 industrial maintenance solutions for a clean and safe workplace.

New Pig's customer service is legendary. Customers contact the company by phone, by Internet, and in person through sales representatives. Every interaction reflects the personality of the company's corporate culture.

New Pig has successfully branded what some might think is the unbrandable by selling mundane industrial absorbents and workplace safety products with a pig theme and pig-related product and promotion paraphernalia.

This chapter will give you a foundation for thinking about marketing and the role of communication. The New Pig story demonstrates how imaginative strategic communication can help establish a brand and bring a product to life. This chapter starts with an explanation of the basic principles of marketing and relates marketing to strategic communication and integrated marketing communication. We explain the concept of branding and why it is so heavily dependent on strategic communication.

The brand is the anchor for our thoughts, feelings, and experiences with a product or organization. It's the name we use, the image we have in our minds, and the way we organize and perceive the marketplace. To understand brands and how they work, however, we first need an understanding of marketing, which is the corporate function most likely to manage an organization's brand or brands.

1.1 What is the marketing mix, and how does it send messages?

The Marketing Foundation

Because many advertising, public relations, and marketing communication majors are expected to take an introductory course in marketing, we won't try to present Marketing 101 here. Instead, we will review some of marketing's basic concepts in terms of how they affect or give direction to strategic communication.

Photo: Courtesy Urban Decay Cosmetics. Used with permission.

SHOWCASE

The Urban Decay line of cosmetics projects is designed to lead the market with edgy product designs and formulations that appeal to fashion-conscious young women. Its street-smart attitude is embodied in its packaging and product names.

Wende Zomnir, co-founder, Urban Decay, Costa Mesa, California, is a graduate of the University of North Texas advertising program. She was nominated to be featured here by Professor Sheri Broyles.

Marketing is designed to build brand and customer relationships that generate sales and profits or, in the case of non-profit organizations, memberships, volunteers, and donations. Traditionally, the goal of most marketing programs has been to sell products, defined as *goods*, *services*, or *ideas*. Marketing's sales goals respond to the marketplace, ideally matching a product's availability—and the company's production capabilities—to the consumer's need, desire, or demand for the product.

Sometimes the challenge is to build demand for a product, as the Showcase feature illustrates. Urban Decay is a line of cosmetics with a street-smart attitude that markets to fashionable young women. The *Wall Street Journal* says Urban Decay caught its market's attention with its edgy packaging and product names, such as "Perversion" and "Stray Dog."[1]

The Marketing Mix

Marketing accomplishes its goal by managing a set of operations and strategic decisions referred to as the **marketing mix** (or the **Four Ps**). They are the design and performance of the *product*, its *place* (where it's available, distribution), its *pricing* strategies, and its *promotion*. These Four Ps all deliver messages about the brand. In other words, what do the design and construction of the product say about the brand; what does the price suggest about the quality of the product; what does the store or online site contribute to the brand image; and what do the more formal marketing communication messages (such as advertising, public relations, direct communication, events and sponsorships, packaging, sales promotion, and other planned messages) say about the brand?

Marketing also focuses on managing customer relationships to benefit a brand's **stakeholders**. By stakeholders, we mean all the individuals and groups who have a stake in the success of the brand, including employees, investors, the community, media, business partners, as well as customers. As we'll explain later in the section on branding, positive stakeholder relationships create value for a brand.

Marketing and Messages

What we call **marketing communication** (marcom for short) involves the use of a variety of tools and functions, such as advertising, public relations, sales promotion, direct response, events and sponsorships, point of sale, digital media, and the communication aspects of packaging as well as personal sales and new forms of online communication that are constantly being developed. They are pieces of a planned effort that strategically delivers specific messages to promote a brand or organization, such as New Pig.

On a more general level, **brand communication** includes all the various marketing communication messages from marketing communication. It also includes personal experiences that create and maintain a coherent brand image.

For example, consider the Puma brand. The same creative spirit that drives Puma's cutting-edge product design also drives its marketing communication, which includes advertising. Puma also uses nontraditional ways to connect with customers, such as **word of mouth**; the Internet; eye-catching in-store merchandising displays; and other marcom programs that promote the brand on the street and on the feet of its devotees. Clever brand communication ideas include promotions, such as one during the World Cup held in Japan and South Korea that featured a special Puma sushi roll served in select Japanese restaurants in cities around the world. These restaurants also discretely announced the sponsorship through Puma-branded chopsticks, sake cups, and napkins. At the same time, Puma partnered with a UK-based design shop to sell an exclusive version of its World Cup soccer boot. It also held weekend sushi-making events at a home furnishings store. In other words, Puma's brand communication extends well beyond advertising and traditional media.

The management challenge, then, is to plan and monitor all the messages delivered by all the various types of marketing communication so that they work together to present the brand in a coherent and consistent way[2] as a coordinated basket of messages.

> **● Principle**
> The challenge is to manage all the messages delivered by all aspects of marketing communication so that they work together to present the brand in a coherent and consistent way.

Who Are the Key Players?

The marketing industry is a complex network of professionals, all of whom are involved in creating, producing, delivering, and promoting something to customers. They are involved both as audiences for marcom messages and as partners in delivering brand messages. The four categories of key players are (1) marketers; (2) marketing partners, such as advertising and public relations agencies; (3) suppliers and vendors; and (4) distributors and retailers. These positions represent jobs, so this review also describes careers should you be interested in working in marketing.

The marketer is any company or organization behind the brand—that is, the organization or company producing the product or service and offering it for sale—or promoting a good cause or nonprofit organization to its supporters. To marketing communication partners (advertising agencies and other marketing communication firms), the company or firm behind the brand is referred to as the *client*. The product or brand manager is the key contact within the market organization for marketing communication partners. This person gives direction to the agencies about the brand strategy, budget, and schedule. As one brand manager explained, the effective manager is one who lets his or her market communications experts do the work: "I finally figured out that I never had to solve the problems. I just gave them my problems to solve."[3]

As a *Wall Street Journal* article explained, the relationship between marketers and their agencies can be a complicated one because of pressures to cut costs as well as changing strategies and technologies, particularly in the digital arena.[4] Achieving an effective "partner" relationship between agency and client is sometimes challenging, as the Inside Story explains.

The materials and ingredients used in producing a product or managing a nonprofit organization are obtained from other companies, referred to as *suppliers* or *vendors*. The phrase **supply chain** is used to refer to this complex network of suppliers who produce components and ingredients that are then sold to the manufacturer. The **distribution chain** or **channel of distribution** refers to the various companies involved in moving a product from its manufacturer to its buyers. Suppliers and distributors may also be used in nonprofit organizations, where they are also partners in the communication process.

What Are the Most Common Types of Markets?

The word **market** originally meant the place where the exchange between seller and buyer took place. Today, we speak of a market not only as a place (for example, the New England market), but also as a particular type of buyer (for example, the youth market or the motorcycle market). The phrase **share of market** refers to the percentage of the total sales in a product category belonging to a particular brand.

As Figure 1.1 shows, the four main market types are (1) consumer, (2) business-to-business (industrial), (3) institutional, and (4) channel markets. We can further divide each of these markets by size or geography (local, regional, national, or international).

- **Consumer markets** (business-to-consumer or B2C) refer to businesses selling to consumers who buy goods and services for personal or household use. As a student, you are considered a member of the consumer market for companies that sell jeans, athletic shoes, sweatshirts,

Dos and Don'ts of an Insatiable Client

Anthony Morrison, *Owner and CEO, MYP Training, Houston, Texas*

Advertising is a very exciting, fast-paced, and rewarding industry. Many look at advertising as a way to deliver client needs and wants and develop tangible materials out of intangible concepts and ideas. All that is true, and for a young advertiser, there are so many columns, stories, mentors, and examples of how to succeed in the advertising industry.

A good skill to pick up as a young advertiser is how to deal with a client who is not ideal. A client might have a strong personality but not the industry knowledge to develop the concept. I like to call them "Good but not good enough" clients. Handled the wrong way, this type of client can make or break a young advertiser's career. This client can even have a young advertiser thinking of a career change. Before that happens, here are some important "Dos" and "Don'ts" to dealing with this type of client.

Do

- **Do understand the full scope of the deliverable.** Never start a project without knowing the end result.
- **Do keep the client abreast at every step in the process.** Doing so makes the client feel involved.
- **Do stay within the budget and time line initially scoped out.** If you are in danger of going over budget or falling behind, say something immediately. If not, the client will lose trust in you.
- **Do reach out for help from colleagues.** Coworkers may have had some of the same experiences.

Don't

- **Don't deliver a product that is out of scope.** Even if the product is better than originally scoped, it needs to be discussed first.
- **Don't get frustrated with the client.** The client is just as passionate about the product as you are. Everyone just wants the best deliverable product.
- **Don't talk to the client when you are upset.** Some communications may come off as angry and will hurt the relationship.

Note: A graduate of the University of Houston, Morrison was nominated to be featured here by Professor Larry Kelley, a member of this book's advisory board.

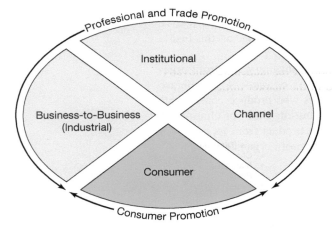

FIGURE 1.1

Four Types of Markets
The consumer market, which is the target of consumer advertising, public relations, and promotion, is important, but it is only one of the four types of markets. The other three are reached through professional and trade marketing communication.

pizza, music, textbooks, backpacks, computers, education, checking accounts, bicycles, and a multitude of other products.

- **Business-to-business (B2B) markets** consist of companies, such as New Pig, that buy products or services to use in their own businesses or in making other products. General Electric, for example, buys computers to use in billing and inventory control, steel and wiring to use in the manufacture of its products, and cleaning supplies to use in maintaining its buildings. In 2016, the three biggest B2B marketers were Microsoft, IBM, and Wells Fargo.[5] Promotion in this category tends to be heavy on factual content and information.
- **Institutional markets** include a wide variety of nonprofit organizations, such as hospitals, government agencies, and museums. Universities, for example, are in the market for furniture, cleaning supplies, computers, office supplies, groceries, audiovisual material, paper towels, and toilet paper. Such ads are similar to B2B ads in that they are generally heavy on facts.
- **Channel markets** include members of the distribution chain, which is made up of businesses we call **resellers** or intermediaries. **Channel marketing**, the process of targeting messages to the distribution channel, is more important now that manufacturers consider their distributors to be partners in their marketing programs.

Most marketing communication dollars are spent on consumer markets, although B2B marketing is becoming almost as strong. What's important, however, is that marketing communication is used to reach customers in all four types of markets. The type of marketing communication and the way it is directed to the audience might differ, but strategic communication is essential to all four types of marketing.

How Does the Marketing Mix Send Messages?

Marketing managers construct the *marketing mix*, the Four Ps, to accomplish marketing objectives. As shown in Figure 1.2, these marketing mix decisions are key elements of marketing strategy. To a marketing manager, marketing communication is just one part of the marketing mix, but to a marcom manager, all these marketing mix elements send messages that can sometimes contradict planned marcom messages or even confuse consumers. The following sections explain these three other components of the marketing mix as providers of communication cues.

> ● **Principle**
> Every part of the marketing mix—not just marketing communication—sends a message.

Product   Design, performance, and quality are key elements of a product's success. When a product performs well, its performance sends a positive message that this brand is okay to repurchase or revisit. (The opposite is also true: poor performance sends a negative message.) A positive brand experience also motivates the buyer to recommend the brand to others, extending the reach of the positive experience through word of mouth.

Some brands, such as Apple, are known for their design, which becomes a major **point of differentiation** from competitors. When this point of difference is also of significant importance to customers, it becomes a **competitive advantage**. Apple's personal digital products, such as the iPod, iPhone, and iPad, have built a fanatical following because of their innovativeness. The iPhone, for example, was characterized in the *Wall Street Journal* as "the defining consumer item of its age."[6]

A *product launch* for a new brand such as Apple's iWatch depends on announcements in the media usually involving publicity and advertising as well as trade promotion. The communication is designed to build awareness of the new brand and to explain how this new product works and how it differs from competitors. Performance is important for launching innovative and technical products, such as the iWatch, that are introduced to the market through ads and publicity that explain how to use this new technology.

Photo: Justin Sullivan/Getty Images

The Apple Watch launched in 2015 has a clean design and is a well-constructed smartwatch with hundreds of apps and the ability to send and receive calls, similar to an iPhone. It's also like a super iPod combined with a fitness device that's worn on the wrist.

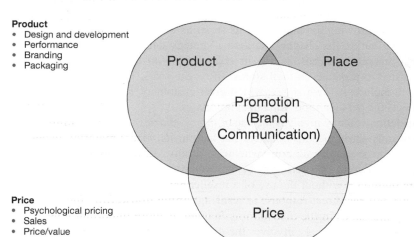

Product
- Design and development
- Performance
- Branding
- Packaging

Place (Distribution)
- Channels
- Market coverage
- Push–pull
- Co-op advertising

Promotion (Brand Communication)
- Personal selling
- Advertising
- Sales promotion
- Point of purchase
- Customer service
- Public relations
- Direct marketing
- Merchandising
- Packaging
- Events, sponsorships

Price
- Psychological pricing
- Sales
- Price/value

Product   Place   Promotion (Brand Communication)   Price

FIGURE 1.2
The Marketing Mix
The four marketing mix elements and their related tools and marketing communication techniques are basic components of marketing. Brand communication is shown in the middle and overlaps the other three Ps—product, place/distribution, and price—because all have communication effects.

● Principle

Product performance sends the loudest message about a product or brand and determines whether it will be purchased again.

Product performance—how it handles or is used—sends the loudest messages about a product or brand and determines whether the product is purchased again or whether the buyer recommends it to others. Buyers of computers, for example, will assess performance by asking the following: Is the computer easy to use? Does it crash? How big is its memory? Quality is another product feature that is often linked to upscale brands, such as Mercedes and Rolex. The idea is that if the product is well engineered and its manufacturer maintains a high standard of quality, the brand will perform at a high level.

Related to product performance is product adaptation, particularly when innovation is driven by consumer needs. An example comes from Avon's bath oil, Skin So Soft, which has long been used as a bug repellent. Avon figured that out and launched Skin So Soft Bug Guard.

● Principle

The treatment of the price in marketing communication cues a meaning that puts the price/value proposition in perspective.

Pricing   The price that a seller sets for a product sends a "quality" or "status" message. The higher the price relative to the competition, the higher—supposedly—the quality or status will be. The price is based not only on the cost of making and marketing the product, but also on the seller's expected margin of profit as well as the effect of the price on the brand image. Ultimately, the price of a product is based on what the market will bear, the competition, the relative value of the product, and the consumer's ability to gauge that value, which is referred to as the *price/value proposition*. **Psychological pricing** strategies use marketing communication to affect the customer's judgment of value. For example, ads showing *prestige pricing* in which a high price seems to make the product worthy or valuable may be illustrated by photographs of the "exceptional product" in luxury settings or by ad copy explaining the reasons for a high price. The meaning of the price is often dependent on the context provided by the marketing communication, which puts the price in perspective.

With the exception of price information delivered at the point of sale, marketing communication is often the primary vehicle for telling the consumer about price. The term **price copy**, which is the focus of much retail advertising, refers to copy devoted primarily to the price and its relation to value. During the Great Recession, fast-food chains as well as Walmart and, of course, discount and dollar stores depended on a *value pricing* strategy using the $1 price to signal money-saving offers. *Promotional pricing* is used to communicate a dramatic or temporary price reduction through terms such as *sale*, *special*, and *today only*.

Place/Distribution   It does little good to offer a good or service that will meet customers' needs unless you have a mechanism for making the product or service available and handling the exchange of payment. Where or how a brand is made available also sends a message. The image of a watch, like Swatch, can be quite different if it's sold in Walmart as opposed to Nordstrom. The objective is to match the distribution to the product quality, brand personality, and price.

Puma, for example, is growing the market for its shoes and athletic apparel because of its unusual approach to distribution. Its channel marketing strategy delivers Puma products both to exclusive and mass-market audiences, selling its edgy designs to trendy retailers and then placing its more mainstream products in mall stores. In recent years, Puma has expanded its distribution program to include its own stores, which greet customers with a unique shopping environment that reflects the personality of the Puma brand.

A common distribution strategy involves the use of *intermediaries* such as retailers. Apple, for example, sells not only through other retailers but also in its very popular Apple stores. "Clicks or bricks" is a phrase used to describe whether a product is sold online (clicks) or in a traditional store (bricks). **Direct marketing (DM)** companies, such as Lands' End and Dell, distribute their products directly without the use of a reseller. The sale is totally dependent on the effectiveness of catalogs and direct-response advertising. New Pig has some resellers, but it depends primarily on direct marketing.

Another distribution-related strategy involves the distinction between push and pull strategies. A **push strategy** offers promotional incentives, such as discounts and money for advertising, to retailers. Distribution success depends on the ability of these intermediaries to promote the product, which they often do with their own advertising. In contrast, a **pull strategy** directs marketing communication efforts at the consumer and attempts to pull the product through the channel by intensifying consumer demand.

Other Functions in the Mix   The Four Ps concept is useful in identifying the key marketing strategy decisions that support communication about a brand. Other areas, such as personal sales and customer service, are also important in the brand's communication mix.

Personal sales rely on face-to-face contact between the marketer and a prospective customer rather than contact through media. It's particularly important in B2B marketing and high-end retail. In contrast, self-service retailers (grocery stores, drugstores, and big-box stores like Costco) rely on customers to know what they want and where in the store to find it.

In contrast to most advertising, whose effects are often delayed, marketers use *personal selling* to create immediate sales to people who are shopping for a product. The different types of personal selling include sales calls at the place of business by a field representative (field sales), assistance at an outlet by a sales clerk (retail selling), and calls by a representative who goes to customers' offices. Marketing communication supports sales programs to develop leads, the identification of potential customers, or **prospects**. **Lead generation** is a common objective for trade promotion and advertising. Personal sales are even more important in B2B marketing for reaching key decision makers within a company who can authorize a purchase.

Customer service refers to the help provided to a customer before, during, and after a purchase. It also refers to the company's willingness to provide such help. Most manufacturers have a customer service operation that provides follow-up services for many goods and also answers questions and deals with complaints about products. It's more than just traditional face-to-face customer service, though. Many companies now provide more assistance to customers through online connections than through face-to-face communication.

What Is the Added Value of Marcom?

Information from the marketing mix and marketing communication can add value to a product both for consumers and for marketers. **Added value** refers to a strategy or activity that makes the product more useful or appealing to the consumer as well as to distribution partners. The three Ps of product, price, and place add more tangible value. For example, the more convenient the product is to buy, the more valuable it is to the customer. Likewise, the lower the price, the more useful features a product has, or the higher its quality, the more a customer may value it.

Marketing communication adds psychological value by creating a brand that people remember, by delivering useful information, and by making a product appealing, as in the "Classic" ad for Lydia Pinkham's Vegetable Compound. With no added value, why pay more for one brand over the competition? A motorcycle is a motorcycle, but a Harley-Davidson is a highly coveted bike because of the brand image created by its marketing communication and relationship with its customers. Advertising and other marketing communication not only showcase the product's inherent

Photo: National Library of Medicine

CLASSIC

Ads for Lydia Pinkham's Vegetable Compound appeared in newspapers in the 1870s with claims that the product "goes to the very root of all female complaints." Other turn-of-the-century concoctions made even more dramatic and extreme claims. How do products and advertising like this one compare with modern-day pharmaceutical advertising?

value but also may add value by making the product more attractive and getting the attention of potential customers, members, or donors.

On the other hand, not all marketing mix decisions send positive messages and add value to products. Netflix found that a clumsy plan that split its streaming video service and DVD-via-mail services so that it could add a more expensive alternative system called Quickster enraged its customers and drove its share price down. Nothing in the proposal was seen as adding value for Netflix customers, who instead saw the move as a way for Netflix to get more money for a more inconvenient form of the video service.

1.2 What is integrated marketing communication?

⬤ Principle
IMC is like a musical score that helps various instruments play together. The song is the meaning of the brand.

What Is Integrated Marketing Communication?

The form of strategic communication called **integrated marketing communication (IMC)** is the practice of coordinating messages from all marketing communication tools as well as the messages from the marketing mix decisions. One important IMC goal is to send a consistent message about the brand. IMC is like a musical score that helps all the various instruments play together, but before you decide what tune each individual instrument will play, you have to decide what the song is all about. We say that the song is the brand: it is its strategy and meaning. This concept will be developed in more detail in Chapter 16, where we explain the challenge of managing IMC campaigns and programs.

IMC is still evolving, and both professionals and professors are engaged in defining the field and explaining how it works. *Integration* is a key; it means that every message is focused and that all messages work together to create a coherent and attractive brand image, as the Day in the Life feature about the varied marketing communication program of a B2B company explains. Coordination creates *synergy*, which is expressed in the common saying that "2 plus 2 equals 5." In other words, when the pieces are effectively coordinated, the whole has more effect than the sum of its parts. A simple example is McDonald's brand identity, where the "M" in the name is reflected in the shape of McDonald's iconic arches. A name, a logo, a building design, and signage all work together to create the face of this familiar and highly successful brand.

How Does New Pig Use IMC?

New Pig's marketing has been successful because of an unforgettable brand image supported by a highly creative approach to marketing communication. New Pig operates a sophisticated IMC program using multiple marketing communication tools. Its award-winning B2B direct marketing program incorporates not only its flagship Big Pigalog® January edition but also product-focused monthly "mini-catalogs" ranging from 52 to 148 pages. The program includes daily customer and prospect mailers, email and fax blasts, and Internet and telesales efforts as well as advertising in trade publications (print and digital) and directories. New Pig also produces a series of videos that tell the company's story and serve as video catalogs and employee and sales training materials.

Interactive face-to-face contact is also important, so New Pig not only boasts an outstanding customer service operation, but it also attends several major trade shows each year. Customers respond to the quirky "pig personality" and have come to expect a certain level of fun in their dealings with the company. New Pig soon discovered that the name also appealed to customers who were testing the product in research and development. Not only did the *Pig* name tickle them pink, but they also enjoyed adding a "piggy" comment or joke when talking about the product. Frequently, they would "oink" or ask about Miss Piggy or Boss Hog in conversations. These kinds of responses, unusual in typical buyer/seller relationships, made the product development process a lot more fun.

In addition, a proactive public relations/media program—corporate and technical articles, press releases, and awards, for example—strengthens New Pig's brand. It also helps reinforce the company's reputation as the world's leading expert and resource for keeping

A View from the Marcom Front Line

Peter Stasiowski, *Director of Communications, Interprint USA, Pittsfield, MA*

There's a big difference between working for an ad agency, where the focus is on promoting many clients, and becoming an individual company's lone marketing professional, where the focus is on promoting the company that signs your paycheck.

The most obvious changes, such as fine-tuning one marketing plan instead of juggling several, give way to more subtle and important differences. When I traded my agency title of art director and creative director for my current position as marketing and communications manager for an industrial printing company, I went from working with a group of people dedicated to practicing good marketing communications to working with a group dedicated to printing good decor paper for its customers in the laminate industry.

In my case, the opportunities to expand my marketing skills beyond commercial art into areas like copywriting and financial planning came with the responsibility to make good marketing decisions without the security of an ad agency's team behind me.

At its core, a day in my life as the marketing and communications manager for Interprint is spent communicating clear messages to the right markets as efficiently as possible. For example, to the broad laminate market, I write 90 percent of the articles for Interprint's promotional magazine about everything from our latest printing technologies to our environmental stewardship programs.

I'm also responsible for speaking with newspaper reporters, either to answer their questions or to promote a press release. Then there's coordinating the construction of trade show exhibits, planning press conferences, and, yes, designing print advertising. It's all meant to get the good word out to the right eyes and ears.

At the end of the day, my reward is knowing that as I dive deeper into the fabric of one company and learn what messages and media resonate with its customers, I gain both a broader skill set and the unfiltered feedback that ensures increasingly successful marketing efforts into the future.

For more about Interprint, check out the company's fact sheet at https://www.interprint.com/interprint/facts#facts.

Note: Peter Stasiowski is a graduate of the advertising program at the University of West Florida. He started his career as an art director at Gargan Communications in Massachusetts before moving to the client side. He and his work were nominated to be featured here by Professor Tom Groth.

Photo: Courtesy Interprint, Inc. Used with permission.

Photo: Courtesy Interprint, Inc. Used with permission.

workplace environments clean, safe, more productive, and in compliance with safety practices and regulations.

Marketing communication is at the center of brand communication and marketing planning. Those relationships are depicted in Figure 1.3. The problem arises when the marcom tools are not aligned with other marketing mix communication messages that deliver

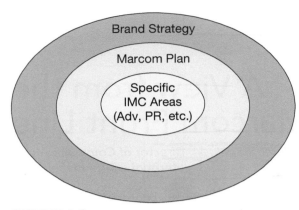

FIGURE 1.3

The Hierarchy of Brand Communication
Brand communication begins with a brand strategy that is outlined in a marketing plan. Then specific plans are developed for the relevant marcom areas that are needed to implement the marketing and brand strategy.

⬤ **Principle**
An organization cannot *not* communicate. People form brand impressions whether or not the branding process is managed by the organization.

brand communication. For example, how well do the activities of a function such as sales promotion reflect the brand image? Does it distract from the pricing strategy and the relationship of price to value? A high-priced status product, such as a Lexus or Tiffany jewelry, can be undercut by poorly created sales promotions. Likewise, direct-response messages, whether by mail or online, can raise issues of privacy that can make a brand seem insensitive to its customers.

One thing that makes the practice of IMC different from traditional advertising or public relations is its focus on branding and the totality of brand communication, including experiences. Tom Duncan and Frank Mulhern, authors of a symposium report on IMC, explain that "IMC is, among other things, a process for doing advertising and promotion better and more effectively in the process of building brands."[7] Through IMC that considers all possible brand messages, marketing communication managers are able to ensure that the perception of their brand is clear and sharp rather than confused and mushy.

Why Focus on Brands?

We've mentioned brands throughout this chapter, so let's take a minute to explain the importance of that concept. A brand is more than a product or an organization. Hamburgers are products, but the Big Mac and Whopper are brands. Toothpaste is a product (also the *product category*), but Colgate and Crest are brands of toothpaste. Branding applies to organizations (McDonald's) and products (the Big Mac) as well as to services (State Farm and the US Postal Service). Branding is also important to nonprofit organizations, such as United Way and Habitat for Humanity.

Organization brands may or may not be distinct from product brands, as in the New Pig example. International branding expert Giep Franzen and his team of Dutch researchers found that "organizations should be aware that simply by existing and interacting with others, an organization is branding itself. So branding the organization is inevitable. It is going to happen whether the process is managed or not."[8] In other words, an organization cannot *not* communicate.

Branding is a management function that uses communication to create the intangible aspects of a brand that make it memorable and meaningful to a consumer. Effective marketing communication establishes the unique identity by which the brand engages the hearts and minds of consumers. Here's how we would define a **brand**: *a perception, often imbued with emotion, that results from experiences with and information about a company, an organization, or a line of products*. Other definitions include the identity elements, such as the brand name and the trademark, that stand for the brand.

A brand is a complex bundle of feelings, promises, and experiences. In other words, a brand lives in the heads and hearts of consumers and other stakeholders. Their heads hold brand information (promises), and their hearts hold brand emotions and feelings (like or dislike, high or low status, sexy or boring, and so forth).

In fact, all organizations with a name can be considered brands. For many brands, specifically smaller ones like cosmetic company Urban Decay, the communication decisions lie with the owner, founder, or partners in the business. Wende Zomnir is not only a founding partner and creative director of the street-smart Urban Decay brand of cosmetics, but also an advertising graduate and a marketing communication professional who used her creativity to shape a distinctive brand presence in the highly competitive cosmetics market.

Branding Differentiates Products and Organizations

Branding also differentiates similar products and organizations from one another. Sometimes the difference between brands in the same product category lies in product features—the quality of the meat in the hamburger or the chemistry of the toothpaste—but often we choose one brand over another because of a difference in the brand impressions we carry. Companies make products, but they promote brands. A brand differentiates a product from its competitors and makes a promise to its customers, as the Keds ad demonstrates.

Product brands are not just about "goods" for sale; they apply to services and nonprofit organizations as well. You may have heard of a hospice program in your community, but did you know that there are many different for-profit and nonprofit hospice programs sometimes competing in the same community? That's why many of these programs are trying to develop distinctive brand identities.

How Does a Brand Acquire Meaning?

A brand is more than a name or logo; in fact, it is a perception: an identification or impression that we assign to the products we know and use. In their book on the science and art of branding, Giep Franzen and Sandra Moriarty explain that the meaning of a brand is "an integrated perception that is derived from experiences with and messages about the brand."[9] What do we mean by that?

Why does one brand sell twice the number of products as another when there is no basic difference in product attributes or performance and when both brands sell for the same price? The answer is that there is a difference in the brand meaning. Meaning-making cues and images are what marketing communication delivers to brands. This *brand meaning* is the one thing a brand has that can't be copied. Competitors can make a similar product, but it's difficult for them to make the same brand because brand meaning is built on a collection of personal experiences.

A brand, then, is a perception, an impression loaded with emotions and feelings (intangible elements) as well as tangible elements, such as a trademark or package design. Tangible features are things you can observe or touch, such as a product's design, ingredients, components, size, shape, and performance. Intangibles include the product's perceived value, its brand image, positive and negative impressions and feelings, and experiences customers have with the brand, product, or company. Intangibles are just as important as the tangible features because they create the emotional bonds people have with their favorite brands.

An example of a campaign that attempts to imbue a city with a distinctive brand meaning comes from Billings, Montana, a story that is showcased in the Matter of Practice feature.

The meaning of a brand, then, is an aggregation of everything a customer (or other stakeholder) sees, hears, reads, or experiences about an organization or a product brand. This meaning cannot be totally controlled by management, however. A company can *own* a **brand name** and brand symbol and *influence* to some degree what people think about the brand, but it can't dictate brand impressions because those exist in people's minds and are derived from their personal experiences.

Brand meaning affects more than just customers or consumers. Employees often say that they are searching for meaningful work. Sometimes that involves the job description—what they do—but more likely it comes from the mission of the organization, that is, what the company does and what it stands for. Even Harley-Davidson's marketing chief admitted at an investor event that "there is a higher purpose to the Harley-Davidson brand that is more than motorcycles."[10]

carson pirie scott . keds.com

freewheeling in keds stretch⁓

keds
every wear⁓

Photo: Ilan Rubin/Art Department

There are many different types of tennis shoes, and the advertising challenge is to create a distinctive brand image for the product. What do you think this ad says about the Keds brand?

● Principle
A brand is an integrated perception derived from personal experiences with and messages about the brand.

Branding Billings

John Brewer, *President and CEO, Billings (Montana) Chamber of Commerce/Convention and Visitors Bureau*

What do you think of when you think of Montana? Big Sky, right? That's an example of an incredibly successful branding campaign for a place.

What do you think of when you think of Billings, Montana? Probably not much, right?

That's the problem I faced when our steering committee took on the problem of branding Billings. So this is a story of our two-year effort to create a brand identity campaign for the city.

You can check out the results of this plan at www .brandbillings.com. In addition to beautiful scenery, the first thing you may notice on the site is a logo with the slogan "Billings—Montana's Trailhead." Here's how the city arrived at that theme line.

The campaign began with research, including more than a thousand online surveys, community workshops, and presentations to clubs and service groups, followed by countless hours of strategic envisioning sessions. The research and analysis determined that Billings is a very special place that merges its location with an attitude, a position that combines "open space" and "western pace."

The important brand characteristics begin with its location, which is shaped by the Yellowstone River and sheltered by the Rims geographic formation. The community is progressive and a regional center for finance, health care, transportation, arts and culture, and diverse educational opportunities. Its hardworking citizens have a unique Montana perspective that combines warmth with an appreciation of scenery and history, but what defines them most is a lifestyle that loves the adventure of an untamed wilderness right outside the door.

Those characteristics translated into a statement of Billings brand essence as "Montana's city connects you to the authentic historical West." The "trailhead" idea springs from the recognition that Billings is a starting point for business growth and development as well as a gateway for opportunities to explore the wonders of Montana. The starting point idea was supported in the "trail" graphic with its "X marks the spot" symbol. The "Where Ya Headin'?" tagline expresses the idea that Billings is the gateway for adventure.

The campaign's objective was to create a position that expresses this brand essence. In addition, the campaign aimed to create a consistent and cohesive brand message that unifies the city's efforts to encourage business and workforce development, individual and family relocation, tourism, and community pride.

Photo: Billings Chamber of Commerce/Convention and Visitors' Bureau

The Travel Planner is the primary piece sent to visitors by the Billings Chamber of Commerce/Convention and Visitors Bureau. Its cover uses an appealing photo of Billings, the new logo and Trailhead slogan, and the "trail" graphics.

An ongoing identity development project, the campaign is spreading out to local businesses and community events. For example, the airport etched the brand logo into its five main terminal entryways. Newspaper ads by local merchants proclaimed Billings as the trailhead for great shopping. The local Walmart carries Trailhead apparel with the new logo. Pepsi branded half a million Pepsi cans with a picture of Trailhead hats for a joint promotion with the chamber of commerce.

To sustain the campaign, a Trailhead Marketing Committee meets regularly. Using the brand standards website and tool kit as a guide, this committee encourages

1. Businesses to adopt the brand.
2. General local awareness.
3. Individual and family relocation.
4. Community pride through public relations and other marketing opportunities.

Success will be determined on an annual basis from media clips and the increased number of businesses that are using the brand in their messaging and the frequency of that use. In terms of results, in the first eight months of the campaign following the brand launch, the site www.brandbillings.com had 7,913 visitors and a daily average total of 33 per day.

Note: John Brewer graduated from the University of West Florida. He was nominated to be featured here by Professor Tom Groth.

How Does Brand Transformation Work?

A basic principle of branding is that brand communication transforms a product—goods as well as services—into something more meaningful than the product itself. A brand adds personality and creates a brand identity that separates similar products and makes them unique. That simplifies shopping and adds value for the consumer. A Tiffany watch is more than a timepiece; it is also different from a Swatch even if both have the same basic components, and both are different from a generic Kmart watch with an unknown brand name. **Brand transformation** creates this difference by enriching the brand meaning through symbolic brand cues. The Tiffany brand symbolizes quality, sophistication, and luxury; a Swatch brand is fun and fashionable; and a generic watch from Walmart is inexpensive and utilitarian.

> **Principle**
> A brand transforms a product into something more meaningful than the product itself.

There are many elements in branding, but for our discussion here, we will focus on four: identity, position and promise, image and personality, and reputation.

Brand Identity   A critical function of branding is to create a separate **brand identity** for a product within a product category, and that starts with the name we use. Analyze the language you use when talking about things you buy: chips or Doritos? A soft drink or a Pepsi? Tennis shoes or Nikes? And do you call it a discount store or Walmart? If branding works, you refer to a specific brand by name rather than its generic category.

> **Principle**
> If branding is successful, you refer to a specific brand by name rather than its general category label.

The choice of a brand name for new products is tested for memorability and relevance. The idea is that the easier it is to recognize, the easier it will be to create awareness of the brand. That also makes it easy to find and repurchase a brand, which is an important factor in brand loyalty. Successful brand names have several characteristics.

- *Distinctive* A common name that is unrelated to a product category, such as Apple for a computer, ensures there will be no similar names creating confusion. It can also be provocative, as in the Virgin line.
- *Association* Subaru, for example, chose Outback as the name for its rugged SUV, hoping the name would evoke the adventure of the Australian wilderness.
- *Benefit* Some brand names relate to the brand promise, such as Slim-Fast for weight loss and Head & Shoulders for dandruff control shampoo.
- *Heritage* Some brand names reflect the maker, such as H&R Block, Kellogg's, and Dr. Scholl's. The idea is that there is credibility in a product when makers are proud to put their names on it, particularly in some international markets, such as Japan, where the company behind the brand is an important part of the brand image.
- *Simplicity* To make a brand name easy to recognize and remember, they are often short and easy to pronounce, such as Tide, Bic, and Nike. Because of the increase in multinational marketing, it is also important that names properly translate into other languages.

When Coke moved into the Chinese market in the late 1970s, it faced the immediate problem of translating its well-known brand name into Chinese. There are no equivalent Chinese words for *Coca* and *Cola*, and phonetic-based translations were meaningless. The ingenious solution was to use a group of four characters—可口可乐—the first half meaning "tasty" or "delicious" and the next two characters together meaning "really happy." Although it has come to stand as a generic phrase for cola, the name for Coke in Chinese is roughly "tasty happy" cola. So Coke owns the category. The effectiveness of the Chinese trademark has been an important factor in making Coca-Cola the leading soft drink in China.

Photo: Michele and Tom Grimm/Alamy Stock photo

Although the distinctive logo is known around the world, Coca-Cola's brand name needed to be represented in Chinese characters that had meaning for the Chinese market.

Brand identity cues are generally the brand name, but they can also be visual symbols—think of the "swoosh" graphic that symbolizes Nike and the leaping cat for Puma. A number of elements contribute to the visual identity: logos, trademarks, characters, and other visual cues such as color and distinctive typefaces. For organizations, such things as building design, delivery trucks, packaging, shopping bags, and even the clothing worn by employees are also part of the brand identity. A **logo** is similar to a cattle brand in that it stands for the product's source.

If a trademark is misused it could come undone.

If you didn't know zipper was a trademark, don't worry, it's not. But it used to be. It was lost because people misused the name. And the same could happen to ours. Xerox. Please help us ensure it doesn't. Use Xerox only as an adjective to identify our products and services, such as Xerox copiers, not a verb, "to Xerox," or a noun, "Xeroxes." Something to keep in mind that will help us keep it together.

xerox.com   Ready For Real Business **xerox** 🔴

Photo: Xerox Corporation

Xerox has a long-running campaign that seeks to protect its name as a brand. Ads such as this one warn against using *Xerox* as a general term for a copy machine or as a verb for making a copy. The zipper is a reminder that the Zipper brand lost the rights to its name when the term became used as a category label.

A **trademark** is a legal sign that indicates ownership. Originally, trademarks were simple symbols or initials that silversmiths etched into their products, the "mark of the trade." Today, trademarks include logos, other graphic symbols, and even unusual renderings of the brand name, such as the distinctive Coca-Cola script. A trademark is registered with the government, and the company has exclusive use of its trademark as long as it is used consistently for that product alone.

Problems can arise when a brand name dominates a product category, such as Kleenex and Xerox. In such situations, the brand name becomes a substitute label for the category label. Refrigerator, laundromat, zipper, and aspirin lost the legal right to their names when they became generic category names. Band-Aid and Q-tips, although legally registered as indicated by their use of the registration symbol ®, have also crept into common usage as generic names—"It's a band-aid for the budget"—so they, too, are in danger of having their brand names become generic category labels.

Brand names and logos are important to brand identity, but some brands have anchored their identity in association with an iconic figure. The Pillsbury Doughboy, the Keebler Elves, McDonald's Ronald McDonald, Procter & Gamble's Mr. Clean, among many others, also lend personality to a brand.

Sounds, too, can be strong brand cues, such as Apple computer's start-up noise, which sound expert Joel Beckerman calls a "sonic signature."[11] He also points to Intel's four-note audio logo ad something customers on four continents now recognize. The most common audio identity element, of course, is a jingle.

We use the word *cues* in talking about branding because a brand name is essentially a reminder of a product or organization that is familiar; it brings to mind some information, an impression, or an experience. Brand cues also set up expectations about what we get when we buy or affiliate with that brand. As Charles Young, president of the Ameritest research firm and a member of this book's advisory board, explained, "A brand memory is about the future not the past—consumers buy future memories."[12]

Brand Position and Promise   Beyond the basic identification elements, another strategic decision in brand development involves deciding on an authentic **brand position**. *Positioning* is a way to identify the location a product or brand occupies in consumers' minds relative to its competitors, such as higher, lower, bigger, or more expensive. It's authentic to the degree that it represents the way people actually see the brand, not the desired position the brand manager hopes it might achieve.

Related to position is the **brand promise**. From a consumer viewpoint, the value of a brand lies in the promise it makes. In other words, the brand through its communication sets expectations for what customers believe will happen when the product is used. The development of the Ivory Soap brand by Procter & Gamble in 1879 represented a major advance in branding because of the way its makers built a meaningful brand concept to transform a **parity product** (a product with few distinguishing characteristics)—soap—into a powerful brand—Ivory. Its two slogans, "It floats" and "99 and 44/100 percent pure," are promises that identify key selling points for Ivory Soap, as explained in the Matter of Principle feature. Ivory represents one of the all-time great marketing and branding stories.

Consistency is the backbone of a promise. The promise needs to be delivered at all points of contact with a brand. Furthermore, the brand has to deliver on the promise. Many weak brands suffer from overpromising. Using hype and exaggeration, they promise more than they can deliver, and consumers end up disappointed. If a cough drop promises relief from throat irritation, it better deliver that relief. If it also promises good taste, it better not disappoint with a bitter medicinal flavor.

Brand Image   Another aspect of brand meaning is brand image, which refers to something more complex than a brand impression. More specifically, a **brand image** is a mental picture or

Ivory: It's Pure and It Floats

Soap is soap, right?

A basic principle of branding is that a brand takes on meaning when it makes a product distinctive within its product category. Procter & Gamble (P&G) accomplished that by creating identity elements for its soap brand Ivory before anyone had thought of making soap a distinctive product. The Ivory brand identity system also called attention to innovative features of the product. Here's the background story about how Ivory came to be one of the first and most successful brands of all time.

Before the Civil War, homemakers made their own soap from lye, fats (cooking grease), and fireplace ashes. It was a soft, jelly-like, yellowish soap that would clean things adequately, but if it fell to the bottom of a pail, it dissolved into mush. In Victorian times, the benchmark for quality soap was the highly expensive castile bar, a pure white soap imported from the Mediterranean and made from the finest olive oil.

William Procter and James Gamble, who were partners in a candle-making operation, discovered a formula that produced a uniform, predictable bar soap, which they provided in wooden boxes to both armies during the Civil War. They introduced the concept of mass production and opened up a huge market when

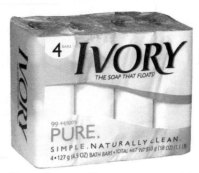

Photo: Courtesy The Procter & Gamble Company. Used with permission.

the soldiers returned to their homes with a demand for the bars of soap. Back at home, though, the bars of soap were still yellow and sunk to the bottom.

P&G hired a chemist to create a white-bar equivalent to the legendary castile bar. The chemist's work represented the first time that scientific-based research and development was used to design a product. In 1878, P&G white soap was invented. It was only a modest success until the company began getting requests for the "soap that floats." One legend is that a worker in 1879 accidentally left the soap-mixing machine operating during lunch, resulting in an unusually frothy mixture. Recent research, however, has found that James Gamble may have always intended for Ivory to float. Whether accident or intention, it led to one of the world's greatest statements of a product benefit: "It floats."

Other decisions also helped make it a branding breakthrough. In 1879, one of the P&G family was in church listening to a scripture about ivory palaces and proposed that the white bar be renamed Ivory Soap. Now the great product had a great name as well as a great product benefit. Rather than asking for soap—soap was soap—and taking a bar from the barrel, customers could now ask for a specific product they liked by name.

That wasn't the end of P&G's branding innovations. A grandson who was determined to match the quality of the legendary castile soap again turned to chemists and independent laboratories to determine the purity of both castile and Ivory. In 1882, the research found that the total impurities in Ivory added up to only 0.56 percent, which was actually lower than that of the castile bars. By turning that into a positive, Harley Procter wrote the legendary slogan that Ivory is "99 and 44/100 percent pure." Thus was born a pledge of quality that became one of the most famous brand slogans in marketing history.

For more about the history of this famous brand, check out http://news.pg.com and search on "Birth of an icon: Ivory."

Sources: Charles Goodrum and Helen Dalrymple, *Advertising in America* (New York: Harry N. Abrams, 1990); Laurie Freeman, "The House That Ivory Built: 150 Years of Procter & Gamble," *Advertising Age*, August 20, 1987, 4–18, 164–220; "P&G History: History of Ivory," June 2004.

Photo: Courtesy The Procter & Gamble Company. Used with permission.

Photo: Courtesy Celestial Seasonings. Used with permission.

Celestial Seasonings uses its distinctive packages to send messages to consumers about its brand image. In what way do packages like this one reinforce the brand personality?

● **Principle**
Brands speak to us through their distinctive images and personalities.

idea about a brand that contains visual associations and cues for such qualities as luxury, durability, or cheapness as well as emotions and past experiences with the brand. These associations and feelings result primarily from the content of advertising and other marketing communication, as Ivory illustrates. For other examples, what comes to your mind when you think of the Marines, Ben & Jerry's ice cream, the Chicago Cubs, or Celestial Seasonings teas?

Part of the image is **brand personality**, which humanizes an organization or a brand. It symbolizes the personal qualities of people you know: bold, fun, exciting, studious, geeky, daring, boring, and so on. Probably the greatest brand personality ever created was for Harley-Davidson. How do you describe it? Partly it's the people who you associate with the brand, people you may think of as black-leather, devil-may-care individuals who are a little on the outlaw side. It doesn't matter that in their real lives Harley owners may be doctors, lawyers, or professors. When they put on that black jacket and climb on the bike, they are renegades of the road. The Harley brand personality reflects the people who ride it, and the people who ride it reflect—or aspire to—the Harley brand personality. Brands speak to us through their distinctive images and personalities.

Reputation and Integrity   A brand takes on a distinctive meaning as the branding elements—identity, position, promise, image, and personality—come together to create a coherent and unified perception.[13] Most of the brand identity elements are managed by the organization, but it's important to know that, ultimately, a brand is an impression in a consumer's mind. It's what and how people think of the brand based on what the brand does, how it performs, and how it lives up to its brand promises. It's also what people say about the brand, and that's the measure of its reputation.

Effective communication across the brand's communication spectrum builds a brand's reputation to the degree that it reflects the brand's integrity. Integrity means that the brand stands for something, has a coherent presence, and has a brand reputation that honestly reflects the promise that the brand signals to stakeholders. Effective strategic communication programs deliver cohesive images and coordinated messages that lead to measurable brand integrity as well as equity.

Brand Value and Brand Equity

Brand value comes in two forms: the brand's value to a consumer and its value to the corporation. The first is a result of the experiences a customer has had with a brand, and the second is a financial measure, which we call brand equity.

Consumer Brand Value   On the customer side, the decision to buy or use a product or affiliate with an organization is made easier by the familiar face of a known brand. There is less risk in committing to a known brand, particularly if you have previous experience with it, you liked it, and it is highly promoted. The impression of convenience and confidence from familiarity are derived from past experience and marketing communication.

Another type of added value comes from associating the brand with a good cause, a practice called **cause marketing** as explained by Scott Hamula (Ithaca College). The primary goals, he said, are "to help communities and nonprofit organizations while generating goodwill, positive word of mouth, and the hope that people will look more favorably on these brands when making their next purchase decision." Customers feel good about themselves because they support a company or brand that is aligned with a good cause. Hamula explains how cause marketing contributes to the value of a brand in the eyes of its customers in the Principled Practice feature.

The added value that comes from brand communication and goodwill-building activities, such as cause marketing, makes a brand more valuable to a consumer. Brands also carry financial value, however.

PAUSE FOR THE CAUSE:
Boosting Brand Value with Cause Marketing

Scott Hamula, *Ithaca College*

Things are really tough out there for brands: lots of competition, savvier consumers, media messages that just don't break through the clutter like they used to, and occasional pieces of bad publicity. Today, though, some brands are turning to corporate social responsibility not only because it is the right thing to do, but also as a way for brands to more clearly differentiate themselves in this dynamic marketplace.

"Values-driven marketing is the next generation of business and an evolution of society," states Liz Brenna, founder of Socially Good Business. "Business practices that companies are implementing under the corporate responsibility or 'values-led business' umbrella are becoming more important to consumers, especially younger ones, and by adopting 'values-driven' strategies, like responsible sourcing initiatives and 'buy one, give one' (to an underserved population or charity), brands can connect with consumers' core values and create unparalleled brand loyalty."

An increasingly popular form of customer engagement is called cause-related marketing. From a local pizzeria donating money to pay for a neighborhood Little League team's baseball shirts to Ford Motor Company donating vehicles to an earthquake-ravaged disaster area in China, brands act as good corporate citizens.

This socially responsible promotional strategy occurs when a brand or company aligns itself with a nonprofit organization to generate both sales and charitable donations at the same time. Simply put, it's "buy my product, and I'll donate to your cause." This approach tends to make a lot of sense. Surveys continue to show that, given two very similar products, consumers are more likely to purchase the brand that is associated with a cause they care about.

American Express Company is often credited with starting cause-related marketing in the early 1980s when it pledged to donate 5 cents to the arts in San Francisco whenever a member used their American Express card to make a purchase, and $2 for each new card member.

To launch and sustain a successful cause-related marketing program, a brand must first know what issues are important to its customers so as to align itself with a cause that's a good match. An example is Yoplait yogurt's "Save Lids to Save Lives" campaign. Because this brand's primary target market is women, Yoplait linked itself with the Susan G. Komen Fight for the Cure organization, which is dedicated to fighting against breast cancer worldwide and is often recognized by its pink ribbon symbol. During Yoplait's annual drive, for every pink lid sent in, the brand donated 10 cents, up to $1.5 million. Some brands, like Pier 1 Imports, go as far as creating specific products for its annual partnership with Komen, including a candle whose design is remodeled every August, a pink jewelry box, and a pink shawl. For more information on these and other cause-related marketing programs, visit the Cause Marketing Forum at www.engageforgood.com.

What do you think? Is cause marketing limited to certain types of industries, or is it a strategy with more universal appeal for brands in a variety of categories?

Celestial Seasonings supports the "Red Dress" campaign for women's heart health, which is part of the bigger American Heart Association's "Go Red for Women" campaign. The herbal tea company links its brand to the "Go Red" campaign using the symbol of the dress on its tea packages.

Photo: Courtesy of Celestial Seasonings

Brand Equity On the corporate financial side, a brand and what it symbolizes can affect how much people are willing to pay for it. That's true for computers as well as cars, cornflakes, and colleges. Brand studies consistently find that in blind taste tests, people perceive the recognizable brand as tasting better than an unknown brand, even when the sample is identical. When identical products carry different labels, people will pay more for the recognizable brand.

Effective branding brings in the dollars. CNN's Fareed Zakaria wrote in a *Washington Post* column that "you can make a sneaker equally well in any part of the world, but you can't sell it for $300 unless you've built a story around it." He explained, "The value added is in the brand—how it is imagined, presented, sold, and sustained."[14]

Successful brands have loyal users who purchase the brand repeatedly. **Brand relationship** programs leading to *loyalty* are important brand strategies and indicators of financial performance. A MediaPost.com article reported that 48 percent of people between 18 and 44 say that their brand loyalty is determined by the types of experiences brands create for them. How do brands do that? They do so by being transparent and considerate, creating content that's actually needed and wanted by the audience, investing empathy in each message, and creating special moments.[15] **Brand loyalty** programs can also offer rewards for repeat business. The frequent-flyer and frequent-buyer programs, for example, provide incentives to loyal customers to keep them coming back.

● **Principle**
Brand relationships drive brand value.

Another principle, then, is that *brand relationships drive brand value.* Positive brand experiences and truthful brand communication lead to a positive reputation, which is the focus of many public relations programs. The part of brand equity that is based on relationships is also referred to as **goodwill**. It lies in the accumulation of positive brand relationships, which can be measured as a level of personal attachment to the brand that can be analyzed as revenue-producing potential.

An example of a marketing effort designed to drive positive customer relationships comes from Volvo, which promises that it will provide a personal service technician for every customer. The senior marketing vice president explained that "when customers buy a Volvo they are buying a relationship—the personal service technician is like your butler."[16]

To summarize, **brand equity** is the intangible value of the brand based on the strength of its relationships with stakeholders, the effectiveness of its identity elements, its reputation and perceived performance, and its intellectual property, such as product formulations.

Google was the first $100 billion brand and has been in one of the top positions for years. Now there are many brands valued in the billions. The managing director of Landor, a branding firm, explains that brand value "is about how much would a consumer pay for a caramel-colored soda versus how much they would pay for a Coke."[17] Here is the 2016 BrandZ Top 10 list by Millward Brown, a brand consulting firm that calculates the value of global brands.[18]

Most Valuable Global Brands

1. Google, $229,198 billion
2. Apple, $228,460 billion
3. Microsoft, $121,824 billion
4. AT&T, $107,387 billion
5. Facebook, $102,551 billion
6. Visa, $100,800 billion
7. Amazon, $98,988 billion
8. Verizon, $93,220 billion
9. McDonald's, $88,654 billion
10. IBM, $86,206 billion

What you don't see on this list are any Chinese brands. Consider that three of the top five smartphone makers globally are Chinese (Huawei, Lenovo, Xiaomi), but few Western consumers know these brands other than maybe Lenovo for laptops. Alibaba, a giant e-commerce site, also has low awareness outside China.[19] Many of these huge companies do business outside China, so it's only a matter of time before their brands begin to crack the Top 20 and Top 10 brand value lists. First, though, they have to use the techniques of brand communication to build global brand awareness.

Leveraging Brand Equity Brand marketing and communication managers, who we call **brand stewards,** will sometimes leverage brand equity through a **brand extension** strategy, which is the use of an established brand name on a related line of products. In effect, they launch new products with a recognized and respected brand name. Because the brand is known and has a good reputation, it carries with it associations and feelings as well as a certain level of trust. The disadvantage is that the extension may dilute the meaning of the brand or may even boomerang negatively if the extension performance is not comparable to the original brand.

Another practice is **cobranding**, which is a strategy that uses two brand names owned by two separate companies to create a partnership offering. Cobranding is a common practice for credit cards, such as Visa and United Airlines on their cobranded Mileage Plus card. The Doritos Locos Taco, which paired Taco Bell and Frito-Lay's research and development teams, has been praised as one of the most successful product launches in the fast-food industry.[20] The idea is that the partnership provides customers with value from both brands.

A strong brand may also be attractive to other business partners through a practice called **brand licensing**. In effect, a partner company rents the brand name and transfers some of its brand equity to another product. For example, California's Milk Industry licenses the use of its famous "Got Milk?" slogan to other brands, including Oreo, Wheaties, and Pillsbury, as well as cookies, granola, and other products.[21] The most common example comes from sports teams whose names and logos are licensed to makers of all kinds of goods: shirts, caps, mugs, and other memorabilia. You may also be aware of the practice of brand licensing for your own school. Universities and colleges generate revenue by licensing their names, logos, and mascots to apparel makers, among many others.

Another way to leverage a brand is through **ingredient branding**, which refers to the use of a brand name of a manufacturing component in another product's advertising and promotion. The most well-known example is the "Intel Inside" phrase and logo used by other computer makers to call attention to the quality of the chips they use in manufacturing their own products. Other examples of promoting the quality of components are found in advertising for outdoor wear that announces the use of Gore-Tex, a lightweight, warm, and water-resistant fabric, and in food advertising that promotes the use of NutraSweet or Hershey's chocolate. For ingredient branding to be successful, the ingredient must have a high level of awareness and be known as a premium product.

The point of this review of branding practices is that the way a product is made or how it performs its services may not be the primary differentiating point. Marketing strategy isn't as much about promoting product features as it is about creating brand meanings. It isn't about gaining new customers but rather about building strong brand relationships. Ultimately, the stronger a brand is, the more value it has to all its stakeholders. Most of the added value that comes from an effective brand strategy is driven by marketing communication. In other words, advertising, public relations, and other marketing communication tools are the drivers of strong brands and create marketing success stories.

Photo: TP/Alamy Stock Photo

Intel Inside is an example of ingredient branding, in which a computer manufacturer advertises that it is using Intel chips as a testimony to the product's quality. On what brands have you seen this Intel Inside logo exhibited?

● **Principle**
Most of the added value that comes from an effective brand strategy is driven by marketing communication.

Brand Communication in a Time of Change

Marketing and integrated marketing communication are dynamic fields and are subject to challenges and change. The new digital technologies, as well as consumer-generated brand messages, and shared brand experiences through social media have opened up new worlds of communication possibilities. Let's consider ways in which the practice of marketing is changing, particularly in this new social media period.

Accountability Marketing managers are challenged by senior management to prove that their decisions lead to the most effective marketing strategies and their programs are accountable. Business results are traditionally measured in terms of sales increases, the percentage share of the market the brand holds, and **return on investment (ROI)**. The calculation of ROI determines how much money the brand made compared to its expenses. In other words, what did the marketing program cost, and what did it deliver in revenue?

Brand managers today are moving away from some of these standard measures and employing metrics that study the effect of brand communication in terms of such factors as engagement. One theorist developed an ROE^2 model, which stands for return on experience × engagement. He sees as a longer-term, more holistic measure of brand relationships.[22]

Another writer pointed out that marketing is messy and numbers may not tell the whole story. A mediapost.com columnist noted, "Marketing is all about trying to decipher the mangled mess of living just long enough to shoehorn in a message that maybe, just maybe, will catch the right person at the right time."[23] He called marketing an "ill-defined problem," which is a problem because if you can't define it, you can't measure it. That's the messiness in modern marketing.

Brand Relationship Strategies Relationship-building communication programs have strategic implications because they shift the marketing strategy from focusing on one-time purchases to emphasizing repeat purchases and the maintenance of long-term brand loyalty. It depends on the category, but many areas, particularly in the services, have become much more concerned about strong relationships than about quarterly sales. You can see the results in the repeat business New Pig enjoys from its loyal customers.

Brand relationship programs involve all the brand's critical stakeholders, such as employees, shareholders, distributors and suppliers, the community, and, of course, customers. All stakeholders are communicators who send personal messages—either positive or negative—about a brand. Therefore, it is important to plan for multiaudience interactions and encourage fans of a brand to talk to their friends. In social media, this advocacy strategy means using a network of fans to create a lot of "likes" for a brand.

Word-of-Mouth Marketing   A powerful new force in marketing communication, **word-of-mouth communication**, is a partner to relationship programs. Word-of-mouth strategies have emerged because of its inherent persuasiveness—you tend to believe what you hear from a friend, family member, or other important person in your life. In addition, comments from influential friends and family are more believable than most planned marketing communication messages, such as advertising, which is often seen by consumers as self-serving. The goal is to get the right people talking about the brand and having them say things in support of the brand strategy.

The power and reach of personal communication has been driven in the 21st century by the emergence of social media. Today, marketing messages are spread not only in face-to-face conversations but also online. If the messages are spread quickly on the Internet through a wide network of contacts, the phenomenon is referred to as **viral marketing**. Brands can instigate the viral process but can't control it.

Global Marketing   Marketers have moved into global markets. In some cases, it is a deliberate strategy; in other cases, they found themselves involved in global marketing because international competitors have moved into their own markets. Even a B2B marketer such as New Pig is a strong global marketer selling its products in more than 40 countries.

What makes global marketing different from national marketing? In most countries, markets are composed of local, regional, international, and global brands. A *local brand* is one marketed in a single country. A *regional brand* is one marketed throughout a region (e.g., North America, Europe, Asia). An *international brand* is available in a number of different countries in various parts of the world. A *global brand* is available virtually everywhere in the world, such as Coke.

The communication strategy for international marketing depends in part on whether the brand's messages are *standardized* across all markets or *localized* to accommodate cultural differences. If the company wants to take a highly standardized approach in international markets, it is likely to favor international agencies that can handle marketing communication for the product in both domestic and international markets. A localized effort, in contrast, favors use of local agencies for planning and implementation in all the countries where the product is distributed. We'll discuss the role of various types of communication agencies in the following chapters.

Convergence   Another trend that is affecting marketing and particularly marketing communication is convergence. As the CEO of global marcom agency Publicis said, "Convergence of business models, convergence of digital, convergence of tools, everything is changing quite radically the way we are doing business."[24] Consumers are empowered and engage in both sending and receiving messages. Media forms are becoming blurred, and it's hard to know what a newspaper is when its content appears not only in print, but also on television, online, on cell

Photo: Andy Kropa/Redux Pictures

Photo: imageBROKER/Alamy Stock photo

Photo: Jim Wileman/Alamy Stock Photo

Here are a few brands that represent different types of geographical marketing strategies. Sainsbury's, an example of regional marketing, is the largest grocery retailer in the United Kingdom, with stores in Great Britain, Wales, Scotland, and Northern Ireland. IKEA furniture stores are found in various countries, but the company keeps its base and image firmly anchored in Sweden and represents Scandinavian functional design and craftsmanship. McDonald's, of course, is one of the best-known brands in the world, and its logo is recognized everywhere.

phones, and now on our watches. Advertising, public relations, and other marcom areas are blurring their functions as well as integrating their programs. Agencies that used to be identified as advertising, or public relations, or media shops are taking on different kinds of responsibilities, and they all promise to do many of the same things, including digital communication.

Diversity Marketing programs and marketing communication are becoming more complicated as they are challenged to be more socially inclusive. Lisa Donohue, CEO of the Starcom Mediavest agency, pointed to diversity as a key trend in the submissions to the annual Cannes Lions International Festival of Creativity.[25] In particular, she mentioned marketing to young women with heartfelt advertising such as the "Like a Girl" campaign for Always. The gender issue is the focus of the 3% Conference, a San Francisco and New York event dedicated to assisting women who work in advertising, whose numbers are particularly low in management.

Ethnicity is also important. Toymaker Mattel announced in 2015 a new Barbie Fashionistas line with 23 dolls featuring eight skin tones, among many other variations. The Advertising Educational Foundation launched a Race & Ethnicity project in 2014 that explores the history of diverse populations in the United States from 1890 to current times (see aef.com). A study by Google in 2015 concludes that data from Google and YouTube show that messages about diversity and equality, particularly for the lesbian, gay, bisexual, and transgender (LGBT) community, have widespread impact. It reports that "brands are held accountable not only for the quality of their products and services but, increasingly, for their stance on political and social issues." That is especially true when it comes to LGBT marketing.[26]

The traditional blond Barbie has become more culturally diverse after Mattel launched its Fashionista line with 23 dolls in 8 skin tones, 14 different facial styles, 18 eye colors, 22 hairstyles, and 23 hair colors, along with a variety of different fashions.

Photo: Sam Simmonds/Polaris/Newscom

Looking Ahead

Marketing and marketing communication begin with coordination across a variety of communication functions and tools, but that coordination is complicated by changes in the industry. We will continue to track these changes in the next three chapters, which will present the basic functions of advertising and public relations as well as supporting marcom areas, such as direct response and promotion.

1.3 Understand how this text will prepare you for your career.

Developing Skills for Your Career

If you're not an advertising, public relations, or marketing major, you may be thinking that this section isn't relevant to you. Whether or not you plan on a career in some field of integrated marketing communication, the lessons you learn in this course will help you in your chosen profession and in your life. In this course, you will have the opportunity to acquire many of the skills that employers have identified as critical to success in the workplace. This text will help you develop and practice these skills, which will contribute to your employability.

Think about some of the skills you'll gain. You'll sharpen your ability to be a *creative problem solver*. You'll think about how creativity can contribute to brand communication in any form. You'll develop your ability to be a *critical thinker*. In other words, you'll be asked to think about all sorts of issues related to brands and apply what you know to contemporary issues facing strategic marketing so that you can come up with opinions based on substantial evidence. You'll be more *analytical* as you look at components of complex issues and problems.

How will you demonstrate what you know? We assume that your professors will share in the goal of improving your *written, oral,* and *visual communication skills* by assigning meaningful assignments so that you have opportunities to practice communicating effectively. By dedicating yourself to this work, you will also develop a good work ethic and earn a reputation as someone who is a *dependable* and *professional team member*. Above all, you'll have the opportunity to see examples of brands that define what it means to be *socially responsible* in a business context and to develop strategies to accomplish those ends. These skills and abilities are characteristics that employers across many disciplines value highly in the workplace.

Kiss a Pig and Hug a Sock

Innovation may be an overused word, but it's part of New Pig's DNA. When it comes to marketing and product innovation, New Pig has excelled. New Pig has won the coveted *Plant Engineering* Magazine's Product of the Year Award 29 times, more than any other company. Recognized for its entrepreneurial successes as well as one of the best places to work in Pennsylvania, Pig's marketing team has been delighting customers with award-winning catalogs, advertisements, videos, and other communications for 30 years.

In terms of marketing communication, the New Pig catalog (Pigalog) has been the recipient of numerous *MultiChannel Merchant* Gold Awards, including the 2006 Catalog of the Year Award, beating out such household names as LL Bean and Victoria's Secret. The UK version earned that same recognition in 2009. In a 1995 MCM article titled "The Ten Best Catalog Covers," catalog/direct marketing guru Glenda Shasho Jones cited New Pig's Pigalog cover among the best ever.

In the end, the accountability of marketing and marketing communication is obvious from the success of the brand. New Pig now fights grime all over the world. And it does so with a clever marketing communication strategy designed to make dull products fun.

Logo: Courtesy New Pig Corporation, www.newpig.com

1.1. **What is the marketing mix, and how does it send messages?** The *marketing mix*, also known as the Four Ps, are the product, its pricing, its place/distribution, and the marketing communication, all of which send messages. In other words, what do the design and construction of the product say about the brand; what does the price suggest about the quality of the product; what does the store or online site contribute to the brand image; and what do the more formal marketing communication messages (such as advertising, public relations, direct communication, events and sponsorships, packaging, sales promotion, and other planned messages) say about the brand?

1.2. **What is integrated marketing communication (IMC)?** IMC can be described as total communication, which means that everything that sends a message is monitored for its impact on the brand image. Central to IMC is the practice of unifying all marketing communication messages and tools, as well as the marketing mix messages, to send a consistent brand message. Doing so not only maximizes consistency, but it also creates *synergy* such that a group of coordinated messages has more impact than marketing communications that are independent of one another. IMC recognizes a variety of *stakeholders* who contribute to the brand conversation as well as a multitude of *touch points* where messages are delivered, including marketing mix messages and more formal planned marketing communication.

lead generation, p. 13
leads, p. 13
logo, p. 19
market, p. 9
marketing, p. 8
marketing communication,
    p. 8

marketing mix, p. 8
parity products, p. 20
personal sales, p. 13
point of differentiation,
    p. 11
price copy, p. 12
prospects, p. 13

psychological pricing, p. 12
pull strategy, p. 13
push strategy, p. 12
resellers, p. 10
return on investment (ROI),
    p. 25
share of market, p. 9

stakeholders, p. 8
supply chain, p. 9
trademark, p. 20
viral marketing, p. 26
word of mouth, p. 8
word-of-mouth
    communication, p. 26

MyLab Marketing

Go to **www.pearson.com/mylab/marketing** for MyLab discussion questions (⭐) as well as the following assisted-graded writing questions:

1-1. This chapter stressed integration of advertising with other components of the marketing mix. A classmate argues that advertising is a small part of the marketing process and relatively unimportant; another says advertising is the most important communication activity and needs to get the bulk of the budget. If you were in marketing management for Kellogg's cereals, how would you see advertising supporting the marketing mix? Does advertising add value to each of these functions for Kellogg's? Do you think it is a major responsibility for the marketing manager? What would you say either in support of or in opposition to your classmates' views?

1-2. Explain why two brands in the same category—such as Pepsi and Coke—that are essentially the same can have customers that are fanatically loyal to one or the other.

REVIEW QUESTIONS

1-3. What is the difference between marketing communication and brand communication?

1-4. What is the definition of marketing, and where does marketing communication fit within the operation of a marketing program?

1-5. Outline the general structure of the marketing industry and identify the key players.

1-6. Explain how marketing communication relates to the four key marketing concepts and to the marketing mix.

1-7. Define integrated marketing communication and explain what integration contributes to brand communication.

⭐ **1-8.** Explain how brand meaning and brand value are created and how they relate to brand equity.

DISCUSSION QUESTIONS

⭐ **1-9.** Apple is one of the most recognized brands in the world. How did the company achieve this distinction? What has the company done in its marketing mix in terms of product, price, distribution, and marketing communications that has created such tremendous brand equity and loyalty? How have advertising and other forms of marketing communication aided in building the brand?

1-10. When identical products carry different labels, people will pay more for the recognized brand. Explain why that is so.

1-11. List your favorite brands and, from that list, do the following analyses:

a. Think about the categories where it is important to you to buy your favorite brand. For which categories does the brand not make a difference? Why is that so?

b. In those categories where you have a favorite brand, what does that brand represent to you? Is it something that you've used and liked? Is it comfortable familiarity—you know it will be the same every time? Is it a promise—if you use this brand, something good will happen? Is it something you have always dreamed about owning? Why are you loyal to this brand?

⭐ **1-12.** *Portfolio Project:* Look through the ads in this book or in other publications and find an example of an advertisement that you think is strongly focused on building a strong brand and another ad that you think does not effectively focus on the brand. Compare the two and explain why you evaluated them as you did. Copy both ads and mount them and your analysis in your portfolio.

1-13. *Mini-Case Analysis:* Explain how New Pig's marketing communication helps support and build the brand image. In what ways do the other elements of the marketing mix communicate messages about the New Pig brand?

TRACE North America Case

Multicultural Millennials

Read the TRACE case in the Appendix before coming to class.

1-14. What aspects of the marketing mix are relevant to a campaign to Multicultural Millennials (ages 18–29)?

1-15. Why do you think TRACE would want a campaign directed to Multicultural Millennials?

1-16. Prepare a one-page statement explaining how the "Hard to Explain, Easy to Experience" campaign will actually help TRACE sales among Multicultural Millennials.

2

Advertising

In this chapter, we will define advertising and its role in marketing communication. We'll also explain how advertising's basic concepts and practices evolved. Then we'll describe the agency world. We'll conclude by analyzing the changes facing the larger area of marketing communication.

MyLab Marketing

⭐ **Improve Your Grade!**

More than 10 million students improved their results using Pearson MyLabs. Visit **www.pearson.com/mylab/marketing** for simulations, tutorials, and end-of-chapter problems.

IT'S A WINNER

Campaign	**Company**	**Agency**	**Awards**
"Sweat it to get it"	*Gatorade*	*TBWA\Chiat\Day\ Los Angeles*	*Gold Clio Sports 2015, USA Today Sports Best Commercial, 2015 D&D Wood Pencil (British Design and Art Direction); Number 2 on Adweek's Top 10 Advertising Stories of 2014; 2015 Cannes Awards: Silver Lion for Promo & Activation, Bronze Lion for Branded Entertainment, Bronze Lion for Promo & Activation*

Burn Some to Earn Some

Photo: Courtesy of The Gatorade Company and TBWA\Chiat\ Day. Used with permission.

No sweat. You just don't make the cut.

That's the reason customers who don't reek of athleticism are cut from the Gatorade team and denied the privilege of downing their favorite drink.

So says the guy behind the counter at the convenience store, Rob Belushi (a son of Jim). And when he calls his uber-athlete boss, Peyton Manning appears and confirms the "sweat it to get it" policy.

The dumbfounded customers were caught on hidden-camera style videos that recorded this exchange as Belushi and a deadpan Manning deny sales of the sports beverage to people who obviously aren't sweating. Instead of walking away empty-handed, customers perform jumping jacks, push-ups, and even a little yoga to break a sweat and earn their Gatorade.

The "C-Store" campaign by TBWA\Chiat\Day was written by one of this book's featured Ad Stars, senior copywriter Nick Ciffone, and his partner, senior art director Dave Estrada. Ciffone observed, "Dave and I got to sit with director Jody Hill and write lines that went right into Peyton Manning's earpiece during filming. Definitely a career highlight."

When your body is working hard and burning carbs, it's obvious: you sweat. That's the idea. Sweat. You sweat it, you get it. You don't sweat it, you don't get it. It's simple.

Gatorade was invented as a replacement for the fluids and electrolytes that athletes sweat out in tough workouts and competitions. According to the executive creative director, "The intent of the campaign is to cause someone who reaches for a Gatorade to think, 'Hold on. Have I earned this?'" In other words, it's not for everyone. The humorous "sweat it to get it" campaign reinforces Gatorade's long-time reputation as the brand for serious athletes as it drives understanding of the functional benefit among athletes, committed exercisers, and sports fans, making the drink a prestige badge of athletic prowess.

The eight episodes in this campaign were shot on location at an actual convenience store. In six of the spots, the prank campaign features well-known pitchman Manning as the immovable manager who says you have to earn it to get it. But in an unexpected hand-off, Cam Newton, quarterback with the Carolina Panthers and a rising spokesperson star, appears in two commercials as a fellow customer who also repeats the theme of "sweat it to get it" to surprised folks in line with him at the counter. You can view them all at Gatorade.com/sweat-it-get-it.

The campaign was launched as a web campaign, which means that the content had to be entertaining enough to capture attention of internet-savvy consumers and drive viewing as well as sharing. The focus was on creating a real experience for unsuspecting customers from all walks of life. The idea was to catch them by surprise and capture their honest reactions.

The honest reactions and hilarious interactions reached the target audience of athletes, exercisers, and fans who are interested in sports and comedy. The on-screen interactions lured in millions of people on YouTube and Facebook who shared the convenience store moments. MTV created a three-minute behind-the-scenes vignette on the filming of the C-Store campaign, which was broadcast as an MTV News Hit at the launch. Comedy Central also featured a behind-the-scenes look at Cam Newton's shoot. The social media encouraged binge-viewing of all eight episodes.

Most viewers loved the series of ads, but the deprivation strategy is not without risk. Do you really want to tell your best customers that they don't qualify to buy the product? The strategy worked for Burger King some years ago when the fast-food chain announced to passionate fans that the famous Whopper had been removed from the menu. The burger's fans were videotaped at the drive-in windows as they reacted with disbelief. The "freakout" campaign for the Whopper's 50th anniversary demonstrated both the power of consumer demand and the loyalty strength of a carefully crafted brand identity.

In this case, the "sweat it" angle works once Peyton Manning is on camera. Most viewers, and the surprised customers, recognize the football superstar. Their reactions are classic: amazed, a little befuddled, and a bit awkward. In your role as a viewer, you can't help wonder if you, too, would qualify for a Gatorade in the eyes of such a superstar athlete.

The commercials are the heart of the campaign, but the "sweat it to get it" theme is supported in signage in most convenience stores selling Gatorade. The campaign's playbook also employs earned media through public relations and social media viral video as well as the more traditional purchased media for the advertising campaign, all working together seamlessly.

Did it work? At the end of this chapter, the "It's a Wrap" section will report the results.

Sources: Nick Ciffone, personal correspondence, March 10 and 11, 2015; Marc Johns, personal correspondence, March 27, 2015, March 31, 2015, and April 13, 2015; Kim Ashby MacColeman, "No Sweat, Gatorade Gets It. New Branding Campaign with Peyton Manning Leads to Publicity Gold," August 20, 2014, Hope-Beckham newsletter; Jarvis Holliday, "Gatorade Debuts 'Sweat It to Get It' Commercials with Peyton Manning and Cam Newton…and 'Customers,'" August 19, 2014, www.Grownpeopletalking.com; Tim Nudd, "Adweek.com's Top 10 Advertising Stories of 2014," August 18, 2014, www.adweek.com; and Josh Sanchez, "Gatorade Unveils 'Sweat It. Get It.' Campaign with Lionel Messi, David Luiz, and Usain Bolt," June 12, 2014, Fansided blog on www.SI.com.

The Practice of Advertising

2.1 Describe the practice of advertising.

Jerry Della Femina, one of the great advertising icons who was known for his colorful witticisms, answered the question "What is advertising?" by saying, "Advertising is the most fun you can have with your clothes on."[1] Della Femina, who lived the *Mad Men* life and inspired the television series of that name, was at the height of his creativity in the 1960s. Advertising in the 21st century is a lot more focused on strategy and business results than it was in his time, but it's still an exciting area.

You've seen thousands, maybe millions, of commercial messages. Some of them are advertising. Others are different types of promotional messages, such as the design of a package or a sporting event sponsorship, but the heavyweight promotional tool in terms of dollars and impact is advertising. It's also the most visible of all the forms of marketing communication, and that's why we will start this series of chapters with advertising.

At its most basic, the purpose of advertising has always been to sell a **product,** which can be *goods*, *services*, or *ideas*. Although there have been major changes in recent years, the basic premises of advertising remain unchanged even in the face of economic downturns and media convulsions. How do we define it now, realizing that advertising is dynamic and its forms are constantly changing to meet the demands of society and the marketplace? We can summarize a modern view of advertising with the following definition:

> **Advertising** is a paid form of persuasive communication that uses mass and interactive media to reach broad audiences so as to connect an identified sponsor with buyers (a target audience), provide information about products (goods, services, and ideas), and interpret the product features in terms of the customer's needs and wants.

This definition has a number of elements, and as we review them, we will also point out where the definition is changing because of new technology, media shifts, and cultural changes.

Advertising is usually *paid* for by the advertiser (e.g., Gatorade) who has a product to *sell*, although some forms of advertising, such as public service announcements, use donated space and time. Not only is the message paid for, but the sponsor is identified. The Inside Story explains how the "paid" characteristic affects regulation.

Advertising began as *one-way* communication, from an advertiser to a targeted audience. It generally reaches a *broad audience* of *potential customers*, either as a *mass audience* or in smaller *targeted* groups. However, *direct-response* advertising, particularly those practices that involve digital communication, has the ability to address individual members of the audience. So, some advertising can deliver *one-to-one* communication, but with a large group of people.

In traditional advertising, the message is conveyed through different kinds of **mass media**, which are largely *nonpersonal* messages. This nonpersonal characteristic, however, is changing with the introduction of more *interactive* types of media, as the buzz around Gatorade's "sweat it" campaign illustrates. Digital, interactive media, such as word-of-mouth conversations on social media or consumer-generated messages sent to a company, have opened the door to interesting new forms of *two-way* and *multiple-way* brand-related communication.

The Importance of a Definition

Herbert Jack Rotfeld, *Auburn University*

In the beginning, there is a definition.

Modern language often uses *advertising* to describe any communications that might influence consumer purchase decisions. Business planning often places all mass communications under the advertising budget. However, the American Marketing Association definition below makes an important statement about financial relations between different businesses and provides a distinction that implicitly guides US communications laws:

> "Any paid form of non-personal presentation and promotion of ideas, goods or services by an identified sponsor."*

The key is that advertising is "paid" media content: the advertiser pays the vehicle for the time or space in which the message is run. This practice would also apply to sponsored journalism or paid product placements or any other business-funded messages. Publicity is the content generated or purchased by the media vehicle without any payments to it from the marketing company; examples are news, opinions, or entertainment. If the advertiser does not pay the vehicle for the message to appear, it is publicity.

The distinction is not trivial.

Although no laws or regulations say it directly, government regulations implicitly use this distinction. The focus has been on paid messages to assert sales efforts as having limited free speech rights under the United States Constitution. Only paid commercial messages have been regulated to limit potential consumer deception. And regulatory efforts have not tried to limit consumers being misled by bona fide news stories or other publicity.

The validity for regulating sponsor-paid messages and not publicity might seem strained at times. From a marketing point of view, thinking in terms of consumer effects, it matters not if a product placement is the result of advertisers paying the broadcaster or moviemakers for the brand mention.

But it should be said for the start of the class that even though every textbook starts with a definition, it is not just an academic exercise (although it can be on your tests).

The trade magazine Advertising Age once ran a reader contest to come up with a definition of advertising, and a judge then combined what he considered the best elements of the submissions. Charles Sandage's first advertising textbook in 1936 was combined with the first efforts of definitions that the National Association of Marketing Teachers reported in their NATMA Bulletin. A final form of the definition was then published in the Journal of Marketing as the American Marketing Association's 1948 Report of Definitions Committee. (Yes, the largest trade association for marketing had a definitions committee. It still does.)

Most advertising has a defined strategy and seeks to *inform* consumers or make them *aware* of a brand, company, or organization. In many cases, it also tries to *persuade* or influence consumers to do something, such as buy a product or check out a brand's website. Persuasion may involve *emotional* messages as well as information. The "sweat it to get it" strategy was designed to associate the brand's athletic credentials with the aspirations of everyday fans.

Keep in mind that a *product* can be a *good*, a *service*, or an *idea*. Some nonprofit organizations, for example, use ads to "sell" memberships, inform about a cause and its need for donations and volunteers, or advocate on behalf of a position or point of view.

What Are Advertising's Basic Functions?

To summarize the key parts of the definition and to better understand advertising's development as a commercial form of communication, it helps to see how advertising's definition has evolved in terms of three critical functions.

1. ***Identification*** *Advertising identifies a product, the store where the product is sold, or both the product and the store.* In its earliest years, advertising focused on identifying a product and where you could buy it. Some of the earliest ads were simply signs with the name or graphic image of the type of store, such as cobbler, grocer, or blacksmith.

2. **Information** *Advertising provides information about a product*. Advances in printing technology at the beginning of the Renaissance spurred literacy and brought an explosion of printed materials in the form of posters, handbills, and newspapers. Literacy was no longer the badge of the elite, and it was possible to reach a general audience with more detailed information about products. The word **advertisement** first appeared around 1655, and by 1660, publishers were using the word as a heading in newspapers for commercial information. These messages announced land for sale, runaways (slaves and indentured servants), transportation (ships arriving, stagecoach schedules), and goods for sale from local merchants. Because of the importance of commercial information, these ads were considered news and in many cases occupied more space in early newspapers than what today we would call news stories.

3. **Persuasion** *Advertising may persuade people to buy things*. The Industrial Revolution accelerated social change as well as mass production. It brought the efficiency of machinery not only to the production of goods but also to their distribution. Efficient production plus wider distribution meant that manufacturers could offer more products than their local markets could consume. With the development of trains and national roads, manufacturers could move their products around the country. For widespread marketing of products, it became important to have a recognizable **brand name**, such as Ivory or, more recently, Gatorade. Also, large groups of people needed to know about these goods, so along with industrial mechanization and the opening of the frontier came the use of new communication media, such as magazines, catalogs, and billboards, that reached more people with enticing forms of persuasion. P. T. Barnum and patent medicine makers were among the advertising pioneers who moved promotion from identification and information to a flamboyant version of persuasion with graphics and language characterized by exaggeration, or hyperbole.

What Are the Key Components of Advertising?

In this brief review of how advertising developed over some 300 years, a number of key concepts were introduced, all of which will be discussed in more detail in the chapters that follow. But let's summarize these concepts in terms of a simple set of key components that describe the practice of advertising: strategy, message, media, and evaluation (Figure 2.1).

- **Strategy** The logic or **strategy** behind an advertisement or any type of marketing communication message is stated in measurable objectives that focus on areas such as sales, news, psychological appeals, emotion, branding, and brand reputation; the position and differentiation of the product from the competition; and segmenting and targeting the best prospects.
- **Message** The concept behind a message and how that message is expressed are based on research and consumer insights, with an emphasis on creativity and artistry.
- **Media** Various media, including print (handbills, newspapers, and magazines), outdoor (signs and posters), broadcast (radio and television), and now digital media, have been used

Photo: Collection of the John and Mable Ringling Museum of Art Tibbals Collection.

CLASSIC

P. T. Barnum was a pioneer in advertising and promotion. His flamboyant circus posters were more than just hype. What other roles did they perform?

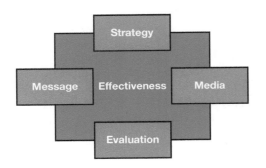

FIGURE 2.1
Four Components of Advertising

🔵 **Principle**
Effectiveness means meeting the stated objectives, which can be determined only if evaluation is built into the strategy.

by advertisers over the centuries. Targeting ads to prospective buyers is done by matching their profiles to media audiences. Advertising agency compensation was originally based on the cost of buying time or space in the media.

- *Evaluation* Effectiveness means meeting the stated objectives. To determine if that has happened, evaluation methods must be planned into the strategy. Standards also are set by professional organizations and companies that rate the size and makeup of media audiences as well as advertising's social responsibility.

Marketing and advertising face many challenges, and images of both are changing due to new media and strategies that focus on reaching individual consumers with personalized messages. Some even question if advertising, as we have known it, still exists. A 2016 *Advertising Age* article argued that the advertising agency role is still critical for brand leaders, not simply as the generator of the big idea but also as the steward of the brand and consumer brand experiences.[2]

What Are the Common Types of Advertising?

Advertising is not only a large industry but also a varied one. Different types of advertising have different roles. Considering all the different advertising situations, we can identify eight major types of advertising:

1. **Brand advertising**, the most visible type of advertising, is referred to as *national* or *consumer* advertising. Brand advertising, such as that for Gatorade, focuses on developing and reinforcing a long-term brand identity and image.
2. **Retail advertising** or **local advertising** focuses on retailers, distributors, or dealers who sell their merchandise in a certain geographical area; retail advertising has information about products that are available in local stores. The objectives focus on stimulating store traffic and creating a distinctive image for the retailer. Local advertising can refer to a local store, such as T. J. Maxx, a service provider, such as KFC, or a manufacturer or distributor that offers products in a fairly restricted geographic area.
3. **Direct-response advertising** tries to stimulate an immediate response by the customer to the message. It can use any advertising medium, particularly direct mail and the internet. The consumer can respond by telephone, by mail, or over the internet, and the product is delivered directly to the consumer by mail or some other carrier.
4. **Business-to-business (B2B) advertising**, or *trade advertising*, is sent from one business to another. It includes messages directed at companies distributing products as well as industrial purchasers and professionals, such as lawyers and physicians. Advertisers place business advertising in professional publications that reach these audiences.
5. **Institutional advertising**, sometimes called **corporate advertising**, focuses on establishing a corporate identity or winning the public over to the organization's point of view. The ads for a pharmaceutical company showcasing leukemia treatment adopt that focus.
6. **Nonprofit advertising** is used by not-for-profit organizations, such as charities, foundations, associations, hospitals, orchestras, museums, and religious institutions, to reach customers (e.g., hospital patients), members (e.g., Sierra Club), and volunteers (e.g., Red Cross). It is also used to solicit donations and other forms of program participation. The **"Truth"** campaign for the American Legacy Foundation, which tries to reach teenagers with antismoking messages, is an example of nonprofit advertising.
7. **Public service advertising** provides messages on behalf of a good cause, such as stopping drunk driving (as in ads from Mothers Against Drunk Driving) or preventing child abuse. Also called **public service announcements (PSAs)**, advertising and public relations professionals usually create them **pro bono** (free of charge), and the media donate the space and time.
8. Specific advertising areas, such as health care, green marketing, agribusiness, and international advertising, address specific situations or issues and have developed specialized advertising techniques and agencies.

Retail Retailers sometimes advertise nationally, but much of their advertising is targeted to a specific market, such as Loft's appeal to women who wear petite sizes.

Photo: Patti McConville/Alamy Stock Photo

Photo: Courtesy Procter & Gamble Company. Used with permission.

Brand Advertising This ad promotes a brand, Crest Whitestrips, and provides information about the product as well as reasons to buy it.

Photo: © 2004 The Pharmaceutical Research and Manufacturers of America (PhRMA). All rights reserved

Institutional This ad for a pharmaceutical trade association uses a heart-tugging visual and copy to show consumers the value of the organization's activities: producing drugs that help save lives.

Photo: Courtesy of Aflac Incorporated

Business-to-Business (B2B) Most people buy Aflac policies through payroll deduction at their workplace. Aflac used its memorable, quirky duck in B2B advertising to create a brand identity and help businesspeople understand how Aflac insurance can be part of an employee benefit package at no direct cost to the company.

⬤ **Principle**
All types of advertising demand creative, original messages with a sound strategy delivered through some form of media.

Although these eight categories identify characteristics of various types of advertising, they share many common features. In practice, all types of advertising demand creative, original messages that are strategically sound and well executed, and all of them are delivered through some form of media. Furthermore, advertisements can be developed as single ads largely unrelated to other ads by the same advertiser, such as the "leukemia" ad for the pharmaceutical industry, or as a **campaign**, a term that refers to a set of related ads that are variations on a theme. Campaigns are often used in different media at different times for different segments of the audience and to keep attracting the attention of the target audience over a period of time.

What Roles Does Advertising Perform?

Advertising obviously plays a role in both communication and marketing, as we've been discussing. In addition to marketing communication, advertising also has a role in the functioning of the economy and society. Consider the launch of the Apple Macintosh in 1984, which was successful because of the effect of one advertisement, a television commercial generally considered to be the greatest ever made. As you read about this "1984" commercial in the Matter of Practice feature, notice how this commercial demonstrated these marketing communication, social, and economic roles.

Marketing Communication Role In its marketing communication role, advertising provides information about a product. It can also transform a product into a distinctive brand by creating a **brand image** that goes beyond straightforward information about product features. The "1984" commercial demonstrated how a personality could be created for a computer (innovative), one that showcased it as a creative tool that breaks through the rigid systems of other computer brands (such as IBM). Advertising also creates consumer brand awareness and demand (lines of customers the following day at stores where the Macintosh was sold) and makes statements that reflect social issues and trends (opening up the new category of personal computers for nonexperts).

Branded entertainment and brand content are similar terms used to emphasize the recent trend in building brand relationships. Marc Johns, director of branded content at TBWA\CHIAT\DAY and a member of the agency's Gatorade team, described the trend as "stories told through the brand lens." The term highlights the ability of brand message to inspire, engage, and develop long-term brand relationships. Johns admits that there is some blurring with traditional advertising, but he sees the differences as follows:[3]

- Drive product awareness (traditional) versus Drive brand equity/affinity (content)
- Impressions (traditional) versus Engagement (content)
- Paid networks (traditional) versus People networks (content)
- On media time (traditional) versus On consumers' time (content)

In addition to marketing and brand communication, advertising also has economic and social roles.

Economic and Societal Roles Advertising flourishes in societies that enjoy economic abundance in which supply exceeds demand. In these societies, advertising extends beyond a primarily informational role to create a demand for a particular brand. In the case of the Gatorade

The Greatest Commercial Ever Made

The advertiser was Apple, the product was its new Macintosh, and the client—the person handling the advertising responsibility and making decisions—was Steve Jobs, Apple's CEO, who wanted a "thunderclap" ad. The agency was California-based Chiat\Day (now TBWA\Chiat\Day) with its legendary creative director Lee Clow (now global director for media arts at TBWA worldwide). The medium was the Super Bowl. The "supplier" was legendary British film director Ridley Scott of *Alien* and *Blade Runner* fame. The audience was the 96 million people watching Super Bowl XVIII that winter day in January 1984, and the target audience was all those in the audience who were trying to decide whether to buy a personal computer, a relatively new type of product for consumers.

It's a basic principle in advertising: the combination of the right product at the right time in the right place with all the right people involved can create something magical—in this case, Jobs's thunderclap. It also required a cast of 200 and a budget of $900,000 for production and $800,000 for the 60-second time slot. By any measure, it was a big effort.

The story line was a takeoff on *1984*, George Orwell's science-fiction novel about the sterile mind-controlled world predicted by Orwell for that year. An audience of mindless, gray-skinned drones (who were actually skinheads from the streets of London) watches a massive screen image of "Big Brother" spouting an ideological diatribe. Then an athletic young woman in bright red shorts runs in, chased by helmeted storm troopers, and throws a sledgehammer at the screen. The destruction of the image is followed by a burst of fresh air blowing over the open-mouthed drones as they "see the light." In the last shot, the announcer reads the only words in the commercial as they appear on screen:

> On January 24th, Apple Computer will introduce Macintosh. And you'll see why 1984 won't be like "1984."

Was it an easy idea to sell to the client?
First of all, some Apple executives who first saw the commercial were terrified that it wouldn't work because it didn't look like any commercial they had ever seen. After viewing it, several board members put their heads in their hands. Another said, "Who would like to move on firing Chiat/Day immediately?" Legend has it that Apple's other founder, Steve Wozniak, took out his checkbook and told Jobs, "I'll pay for half if you pay for the other half." The decision to air the commercial finally came down to Jobs, whose confidence in the Chiat/Day creative team gave him the courage to run the ad. Clow and Steve Hayden, copywriter on "1984," have said that Steve Jobs "put a stake in the ground," referring to how he wanted "technology in the hands of everybody."

Was it effective?
On January 24, long lines formed outside computer stores carrying the Macintosh, and the entire inventory sold out in one day. The initial sales goal of 50,000 units was easily surpassed by the 72,000 units sold in the first 100 days. More would have been sold if production had been able to keep up with demand.

The "1984" commercial is one of the most talked about and most remembered commercials ever made. Every time someone draws up a list of best commercials, it sits at the top, and it continues to receive accolades even today. If you haven't seen it, check it out and decide for yourself.

Remember that the commercial ran only once, as an expensive spot on the year's most watched television program. The commercial turned the Super Bowl from just another football game into the advertising event of the year. What added to its impact was the hype before and after it ran. People knew about the spot because of press coverage prior to the game, and they were watching for it. Coverage after the game was as likely to talk about the "1984" spot as the football score. Advertising became news, and watching Super Bowl commercials became an event. That's why *Advertising Age* critic Bob Garfield called it "the greatest TV commercial ever made."

You can watch "1984" online on YouTube as well as an interview with Ridley Scott about making "1984."

Sources: "The Breakfast Meeting: What Olbermann Wrought, and Recalling Apple's '1984,'" *New York Times* Media Decoder, April 2, 2012, http://mediadecoder.blogs.nytimes.com; Kevin Maney, "Apple's '1984' Super Bowl Commercial Still Stands as Watershed Event," *USA Today*, January 28, 2004, 3B; Liane Hansen (host), "Steve Hayden Discusses a 1984 Apple Ad Which Aired during the Super Bowl," National Public Radio Weekend Edition, February 1, 2004; Bradley Johnson, "10 Years after '1984': The Commercial and the Product That Changed Advertising," *Advertising Age*, June 1994.

online campaign, the strategy was to engage viewers and generate **buzz** as well as reinforce the brand reputation. Creating buzz—word of mouth or getting people to talk about the brand—has become an important goal of marketing communication in this era of social media.

Most economists presume that because it reaches large groups of potential consumers, advertising brings cost efficiencies to marketing and thus lower prices to consumers. The more people know about a product, the higher the sales, and the higher the level of sales, the less expensive the product. Think about the initial high price of new products, such as HDTVs, the iWatch, or other new technologies. As demand—as well as competition—grows, prices begin to drop. David Bell, retired CEO of the Interpublic Group, told a group of advertising educators that "advertising is the motor of a successful economy.... But it isn't effective without trust...and ethics is critical to trust." In his view, the economic importance of advertising is a function of its social acceptance.[4] We'll talk about the critical role of trust in Chapter 5 and ethics in Chapter 18.

Two contrasting points of view explain how advertising creates economic impact. In the first, the rational view, advertising is seen as a vehicle for helping consumers assess value through price cues and other information, such as quality, location, and reputation. Advocates of this viewpoint see the role of advertising as a means to objectively provide price/value information, thereby creating more *rational economic decisions*. By focusing on images and emotional responses, the second approach appeals to consumers making a decision on *nonprice, emotional appeals*. This emotional view explains how images and psychological appeals influence consumer decisions. This type of advertising is believed to be so persuasive that it decreases the likelihood that a consumer will switch to an alternative product, regardless of the price charged.

In addition to informing us about new and improved products, advertising also mirrors fashion and design trends and adds to our aesthetic sense. Advertising has an educational role in that it teaches about new products and their use. It may also expose social issues—some say the "1984" commercial symbolically proclaimed the value of computer literacy "for the rest of us," those who weren't slaves to the hard-to-operate PC systems of the time. It helps us shape an image of ourselves by setting up role models with which we can identify (a woman athlete liberating the gray masses), and it gives us a way to express ourselves in terms of our personalities (smash the screen image of Big Brother) and sense of style (red shorts, the only color in the drab environment) through the things we wear and use. It also presents images capturing the diversity of the world in which we live. These social roles have both negative and positive dimensions, which we will discuss in Chapter 18.

2.2 Explain the evolution of the key concepts of advertising.

Evolution of the Key Concepts of Advertising

As illustrated in the time line in Figure 2.2, the advertising industry is dynamic and is affected by changes in technology, media, and the economic and social environment. But this history is far more than names and dates. The time line reflects how the principles and practices of a multibillion-dollar industry have evolved.[5]

Eras and Ages

The time line divides the evolution of advertising into six stages that reflect historical eras and changes that led to different philosophies and styles of advertising. As you read through the time line, notice how changing environments—in particular, media advancements—have changed the way advertising functions. (For more historical information, check out the extensive time line at http://adage.com/century/timeline/index.html or http://library.duke.edu/digitalcollections/eaa. Another source for classic ads is www.vintageadbrowser.com.)

The Early Age of Print   Industrialization and mechanized printing spurred literacy, which encouraged businesses to advertise beyond just their local place of business. Ads of the early years look like what we call **classified advertising** today. Their objective was to *identify products* and *deliver information* about them, including where they were being sold. The primary medium of this age was *print*, particularly newspapers, although handbills and posters were also important, as were hand-painted signs. The first newspaper ad appeared in 1704 for Long Island real estate, and Benjamin Franklin's *Pennsylvania Gazette* ran the first advertising section in 1729. The first *magazine* ads appeared in 1742 in Franklin's *General Magazine*.

The Early Age of Agencies   The 19th century brought the beginning of what we now recognize as the advertising industry. Volney Palmer opened the *first ad agency* in 1848 in Philadelphia. The J. Walter Thompson agency formed in 1864 and is the oldest advertising

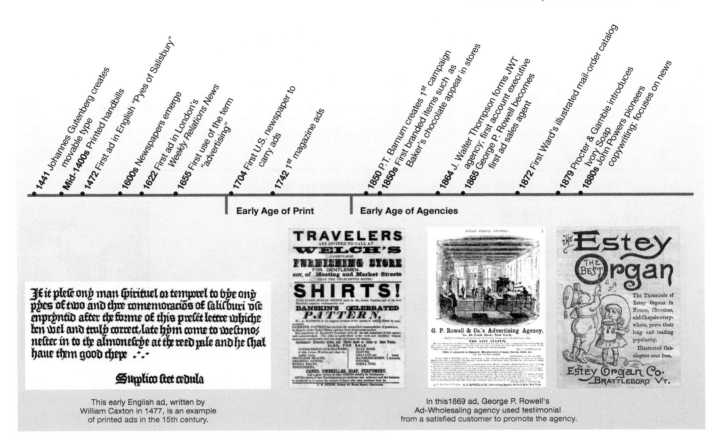

This early English ad, written by William Caxton in 1477, is an example of printed ads in the 15th century.

In this 1869 ad, George P. Rowell's Ad-Wholesaling agency used testimonial from a satisfied customer to promote the agency.

agency still in existence. P. T. Barnum brought a Swedish singer to the United States and used a blitz of newspaper ads, handbills, and posters, one of the first *campaigns.* In 1868, the N. W. Ayer agency began the **commission system** for placing ads; advertising professionals initially were agents or brokers who bought space and time on behalf of the client for which they received a commission, a percentage of the media bill. The J. Walter Thompson agency invented the **account executive** position, a person who acts as a liaison between the client and the agency.

As advertisers and marketers became more concerned about creating ads that worked, professionalism in advertising began to take shape. Here, also, is when it became important to have a definition or a theory of advertising. In the 1880s, advertising was referred to by advertising legend Albert Lasker as *"salesmanship in print* driven by a *reason why."* Those two phrases became the model for stating an ad *claim* and explaining the *support* behind it.

On the retail side, department store owner John Wanamaker hired John E. Powers in 1880 as the store's full-time **copywriter,** and Powers crafted an advertising strategy of *"ads as news."* The McCann agency, which began in 1902, also developed an agency philosophy stated as *"truth well told"* that emphasized the agency's role in crafting the ad message. *Printer's Ink,* the advertising industry's first trade publication, appeared in 1888. In the early 1900s, the J. Walter Thompson agency began publishing its "Blue Books," which explained how advertising works and compiled media data as an industry reference.

By the end of the 19th century, advertisers began to give their goods brand names, such as Baker's Chocolate and Ivory Soap. The purpose of advertising during this period was to create demand as well as a visual identity for these new brands. Inexpensive brand-name products, known as *packaged goods,* began to fill the shelves of grocers and drugstores. The questionable ethics of hype and *puffery,* or exaggerated promises, came to a head in 1892 when *Ladies Home Journal* banned advertising of patent medicines. Yet another aspect of hype was the use of powerful graphics that dramatized the sales message.

In Europe, the visual quality of advertising improved dramatically as artists who were also *illustrators,* such as Toulouse-Lautrec, Aubrey Beardsley, and Alphonse Mucha, brought their craftsmanship to posters and print ads as well as magazine illustrations. Because of the artistry,

FIGURE 2.2
Time Line

Photos (left to right): Lebrecht Music and Arts Photo Library/Alamy Stock Photo; Danskins; George P. Rowell (1838–1908); Jay Paull/Getty Images; Photography © New-York Historical Society. Used with permission. http://www .nyhistory.org; Artokoloro Quint Lox Limited/Alamy Stock Photo; Printers' Ink Magazine, Vol CXII, No. 1. July 1, 1920; The Thompson Blue Book of Advertising, 1906; Pictorial Press Ltd/Alamy Stock Photo; Courtesy The Procter & Gamble Company. Used with permission; The Protected Art Archive/Alamy Stock Photo; Steve Allen/ Liaison/Getty Images; Brand Z/Alamy Stock Photo; Courtesy Kraft Heinz Company. Used with permission.

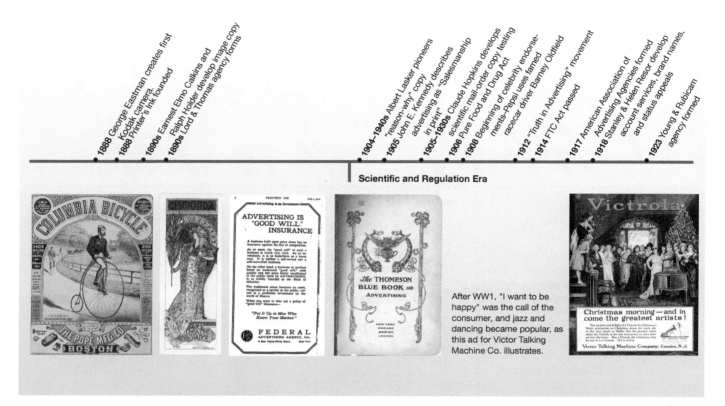

1888 George Eastman creates first Kodak camera

1888 Printer's Ink founded

1890s Earnest Elmo Calkins and Ralph Holden develop image copy

1890s Lord & Thomas agency forms

1904–1940s Albert Lasker pioneers "reason-why" copy

1905 John E. Kennedy describes advertising as "Salesmanship in print"

1905–1930s Claude Hopkins develops scientific mail-order copy testing

1906 Pure Food and Drug Act

1908 Beginning of celebrity endorsements–Pepsi uses famed racecar driver Barney Oldfield

1912 "Truth in Advertising" movement

1914 FTC Act passed

1917 American Association of Advertising Agencies formed

1918 Stanley & Helen Resor develop account services, brand names, and status appeals

1923 Young & Rubicam agency formed

Scientific and Regulation Era

After WW1, "I want to be happy" was the call of the consumer, and jazz and dancing became popular, as this ad for Victor Talking Machine Co. illustrates.

FIGURE 2.2
(continued)

this period is known as the *Golden Age*. The artist role moved beyond illustration to become the *art director* in 20th-century advertising.

The Scientific Era   In the early 1900s, professionalism in advertising was reflected in the beginnings of a professional organization of large agencies, which was officially named the American Association of Advertising Agencies in 1917 (www.aaaa.org). In addition to getting the industry organized, this period also brought a refining of professional practices. As 19th-century department store owner John Wanamaker commented, "Half the money I spend on advertising is wasted and the trouble is I don't know which half." That statement partly reflected a need to know more about how advertising works, but it also recognized the need to better target the message.

In the early 20th century, modern professional advertising adopted scientific *research* techniques. Advertising experts believed they could improve advertising by blending science and art. Two leaders were Claude Hopkins and John Caples. At the height of his career, Hopkins was Lord & Thomas's best-known copywriter. Highly analytical, he conducted *tests of his copy* to refine his advertising methods, an approach explained in his 1923 book, *Scientific Advertising*. Caples, vice president of Batten, Barton, Durstine and Osborn (BBDO), published *Tested Advertising Methods* in 1932. His theories about the *pulling power of headlines* also were based on extensive tests. Caples was known for changing the style of advertising writing, which had been wordy and full of exaggerations. During the 1930s and 1940s, Daniel Starch, A. C. Nielsen, and George Gallup founded research organizations that are still part of today's advertising industry.

During and after the Great Depression, Raymond Rubicam emerged as an advertising power and launched his own agency with John Orr Young, a Lord & Thomas copywriter, under the name of Young and Rubicam. Their work was known for intriguing headlines and fresh, original approaches to advertising ideas.

The idea that messages should be directed at particular groups of prospective buyers, a practice called **targeting**, evolved as media became more complex. Advertisers realized they could spend their budgets more efficiently by identifying those most likely to purchase a product as well as the best ways to reach them. The scientific era helped media better identify their audiences. In 1914, the Audit Bureau of Circulation, now known as Alliance for Audited Media, was formed to

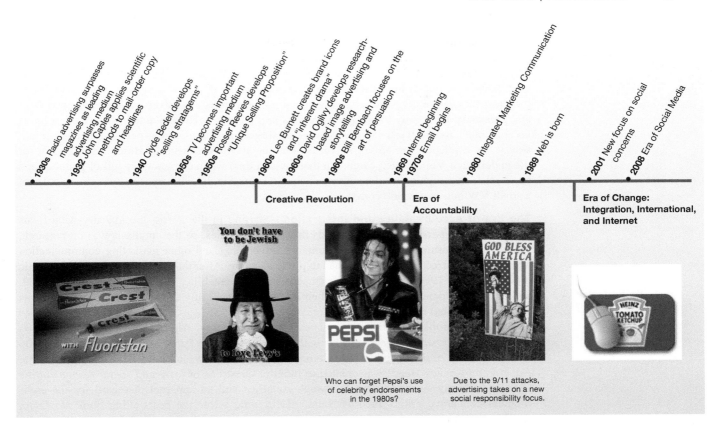

Creative Revolution

Era of
Accountability

Era of Change:
Integration, International,
and Internet

Who can forget Pepsi's use
of celebrity endorsements
in the 1980s?

Due to the 9/11 attacks,
advertising takes on a new
social responsibility focus.

standardize the definition of paid circulation for magazines and newspapers. Media changes saw print being challenged by *radio advertising* in 1922. Radio surpassed print in ad revenue in 1938.

The world of advertising agencies and management of advertising developed rapidly in the years after World War II. The J. Walter Thompson agency led the boom in advertising during this period. The agency's success was due largely to its *creative copy* and the *management* style of the husband-and-wife team of Stanley and Helen Resor. Stanley developed the concept of **account services** and expanded the account executive role into strategy development; Helen developed innovative copywriting techniques. The Resors also coined the brand-name concept as a strategy to associate a unique identity with a particular product as well as the concept of *status appeal* to persuade nonwealthy people to imitate the habits of rich people (www.jwt.com).

Television commercials came on the scene in the early 1950s and brought a huge new revenue stream to the advertising industry. In 1952, the Nielsen rating system for television advertising became the primary way to measure the reach of *television commercials*.

This period also saw marketing practices, such as *product differentiation* and *market segmentation* (identifying groups of people who would likely buy the product) incorporated into advertising strategy. The idea of **positioning**, or carving out a unique spot in people's minds for the brand relative to its competition, was developed by Al Ries and Jack Trout in 1969.

The Creative Era   The creative power of agencies exploded in the 1960s and 1970s, a period celebrated by the *Mad Men* television show and marked by the resurgence of art, inspiration, and intuition. Largely in reaction to the emphasis on research and science, this revolution was inspired by three creative geniuses: Leo Burnett, David Ogilvy, and William Bernbach.

Burnett was the leader of what came to be known as the *Chicago school of advertising*. He believed in finding the "*inherent drama*" in every product. He also believed in using *cultural archetypes* to create mythical characters who represented American values, such as the Jolly Green Giant, Tony the Tiger, the Pillsbury Doughboy, and his most famous campaign character, the Marlboro Man (www.leoburnett.com).

Ogilvy, founder of the Ogilvy & Mather agency, is in some ways a paradox because he married both the *image school* of Rubicam and the *claim school* of Lasker and Hopkins.

He created enduring brands with *symbols*, such as the Hathaway Man and his mysterious eye patch for the Hathaway shirt maker, and handled such quality products as Rolls-Royce, Pepperidge Farm, and Guinness with product-specific and information-rich claims (www.ogilvy.com).

The Doyle, Dane, and Bernbach (DDB) agency opened in 1949. From the beginning, Bernbach—with his acute sense of words, design, and creative concepts—was considered to be the most innovative advertising creative person of his time. His advertising touched people—and persuaded them—by focusing on *feelings and emotions.* He explained: "There are a lot of great technicians in advertising. However, they forget that advertising is persuasion, and persuasion is not a science, but an art. Advertising is the art of persuasion."[6] Bernbach is known for the understated Volkswagen campaign that ran at a time when car ads were full of glamour and bombast. The campaign used headlines such as "Think Small" with an accompanying picture of a small VW bug (www.ddb.com).

The Era of Accountability and Integration   Starting in the 1970s, the industry-wide focus was on *effectiveness*. Clients wanted ads that produced sales, so the emphasis was on research, testing, and measurement. To be accountable, advertising and other marketing communication agencies recognized that their work had to prove its value. After the dot-com boom and economic downturn in the 1980s and 1990s, this emphasis on accountability became even more important, and advertisers demanded proof that their advertising was truly effective in accomplishing its *objectives* as stated in the strategy.

Social responsibility is another aspect of accountability. Although advertising regulation has been in place since the early 1900s with the passage of the Pure Food and Drug Act in 1906 and the creation of the Federal Trade Commission in 1914, it wasn't until 1971 that the National Advertising Review Board was created to monitor questions of *taste and social responsibility*. Charges of using sweatshops in low-wage countries and an apparent disregard for the environment concerned critics such as Naomi Klein, who wrote the best-selling book *No Logo*, and Marc Gobe, who wrote *Citizen Brands*. One powerful campaign that demonstrates social responsibility is the SORPA effort from Iceland.

As the *digital era* brought nearly instantaneous means of communication, spreading *word of mouth* among a social network of consumers, companies became even more concerned about their practices and brand or corporate reputation. The recession that began in December 2007 and subsequent headlines about bad business practices, such as the Bernard Madoff "Ponzi" scheme and bank lending practices, made consumers even more concerned about *business ethics*.

We also characterize this time as the era when integrated marketing communication became important. *Integrated marketing communication* (IMC) is another technique that managers began to adopt in the 1980s as a way to better coordinate their brand communication. Integration leading to consistency makes marketing communication more efficient and thus more financially accountable.

The Social Media Era   Advertising and marketing communication practices have been turned upside down in the years since 2008 because of the widespread use of **social media** and the word-of-mouth practices it fostered. Digital and online communication became important in brand communication even earlier in the new century, with most brands and companies setting up websites and experimenting with online advertising worldwide. With the launch of Facebook, Twitter, YouTube, and other vehicles for sharing thoughts, photos, and even videos, however, the structure of consumer communication was radically altered.

No longer are brand messages dependent on planned and managed marketing communication programs with their targeted messages and one-way communication. In this new interactive world, consumers are generating brand messages and posting them to YouTube as well as sharing their thoughts and experiences with brands on Facebook, Snapchat, and Instagram, and in tweets. Brands set up their own Facebook and Twitter accounts, but the exciting dialogue is happening beyond their control in person-to-person conversations, as Mountain Dew found out when one of its ads featuring a battered woman and a lineup of black men had to be pulled because of vociferous criticism. Companies and organizations are hard pressed to keep up with changing technology and consumers as they search for new ways to listen, respond, and engage their customers in conversations.

This time line has briefly identified how various jobs and professional concepts emerged and changed over time. Let's now put the advertising world under a microscope and look deeper at the structure of the industry.

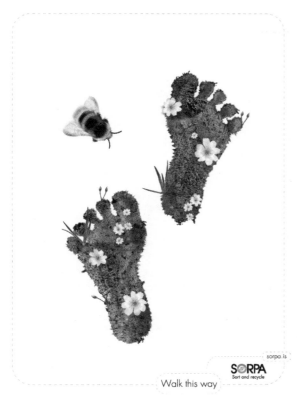

Photo: Courtesy Ingvi Jökull Logason. Used with permission.   Photo: Courtesy Ingvi Jökull Logason. Used with permission.

SHOWCASE

Contributed by Ingvi Logason, this work by his agency H:N Marketing Communication in Reykjavík, Iceland, for the local SORPA recycling center urged people to participate in recycling. He explained, "From day one the marketing strategy, concept and platform have been very consistent—always positive, encouraging, and built around light colors." These two print ad examples were part of an overall image/reminder campaign that has the company aiming for even higher positive ratings. SORPA is now maintaining a positive rating of more than 90 percent.

A graduate of the University of West Florida, Logason, who is a member of this book's Advisory Board, was nominated to be featured here by Professor Tom Groth.

Ingvi Jökull Logason CEO and Strategy Director, H:N Marketing Communication, Reykjavík, Iceland

The Advertising World

2.3 Identify the key players and jobs within agencies.

In the discussion of definitions and the evolution of advertising practices, we briefly introduced agencies, but as a student of advertising and marketing communication, you need to know more about how the advertising industry and agencies are organized and how they operate. One way to get a peek at the field is through the lens of television, such as the *Mad Men* show, which was based on the creative era in advertising history. Professor Bruce Vanden Bergh analyzes the cultural relevance of the popular award-winning drama *Mad Men* in the Matter of Practice feature.

Who Are the Key Players?

As we discuss the organization of the industry, consider that all the key players also represent job opportunities you might want to consider if you are interested in working in advertising. The players include the advertiser (referred to by the agency as the *client*) who sponsors the message, the agency, the media, and the *suppliers*, who provide expertise. The feature about "1984" introduced a number of these key players and illustrated how they all make different contributions to the final advertising.

Mad Men: An Unsentimental Education*

Bruce Vanden Bergh, *Michigan State University*

In episode eight of the first season of *Mad Men*, Sterling Cooper ad agency cofounder Bert Cooper gives Don Draper a $2,500 bonus and suggests that he read Ayn Rand's novel *Atlas Shrugged*. In Rand's 1957 novel, she espoused her philosophy of objectivism, which emphasizes rationality, self-interest, and an unsentimental attitude toward the people (e.g., clients) who depend on our work. This philosophy provides a counterpoint throughout *Mad Men* as Roger Sterling, Bert Cooper, and Don Draper respond to the changes in the workplace and society during the 1960s. They are largely unmoved by these changes until Don finds a way of using them in an objective way in a Coca-Cola commercial at the end of the series.

Don Draper's entire demeanor toward his relationships with coworkers, clients, family, and women with whom he had affairs is characterized by a detachment and lack of sentimental involvement. The irony is that his creative job within the ad agency is to create sentimental connections through advertising. For example, in Don's pitch for the Kodak slide projector business, he says that the purpose of advertising is to create a sentimental bond between the brand and consumer, and this bond for the slide projector, that he renames the carousel, is nostalgia. Yet he says all that in a confident, calculated, and unsentimental manner.

Peggy Olson, who rose from a secretarial position to become a creative force, demands more recognition from Don as they work late on the Samsonite account on her birthday. Don shouts at her, "That is what the money is for." In the end of season seven, we find out that Peggy chooses a romantic relationship with coworker and art director Stan Rizzo over her career, thus demonstrating her real sentimental difference with Don.

Joan Harris started as an office manager and head of the secretarial pool at Sterling Cooper and eventually used her natural business sense to become a partner in the agency, Sterling Cooper & Partners. She ultimately decided to start her own production company, Holloway Harris, thus choosing the unsentimental career choice after a series of harassment experiences at McCann-Erickson when it took over Sterling Cooper & Partners.

Photo: Moviestore collection Ltd/Alamy Stock Photo

Season seven saw Don Draper leave McCann-Erickson, the large agency that acquired Sterling Cooper & Partners, to go on an odyssey that finds him at the end of the series at the Esalen Institute in Big Sur, California, doing yoga. As he sits among the Esalen members on the cliffs overlooking the Pacific Ocean, he conjures up the idea for the iconic Coca-Cola commercial, "I'd Like to Teach the World to Sing," and grins at the camera. (It is a fictional account of how the song was created. Bill Backer of McCann-Erickson came up with the idea while sitting in an airport in London.) And we wonder what that means. I find it an unsentimental grin because he realizes that he can use, in an objective way, this pop culture hippie experience to create a sentimental bond with Coke drinkers worldwide. In doing so, he finds his way back to what he does best.

Mad Men is a seven-season odyssey of a self-made man who invented an identity so that he could become successful and achieve all the financial and social status that goes along with it. This success could only do the things for Don that success can do. He can get tickets to the Beatles Concert (season five), but he cannot cure his former wife Betty's cancer. He cannot save the world, but he can take care of himself. Realizing these things in the ending episode, Don went back to his unsentimental business attitude and found that it had to be sufficient.

*With homage to Gustave Flaubert's *A Sentimental Education*.

The Organization   Advertising begins with the organization behind the promotion message, or the **advertiser**. The company sponsors advertising and other promotional messages about its business. In the "1984" story, Apple Computer was the advertiser, and Steve Jobs, the company's CEO, made the final decision to run the then-controversial commercial. The advertiser is the number one key player. Management of the advertising function usually lies with the organization's marketing or **advertising department**.

In terms of the top advertisers in the United States, the list usually begins with Procter & Gamble. The next leaders in 2014 were General Motors, Toyota, AT&T, Ford, Comcast, Berkshire Hathaway, Pfizer, Loreal, and Fiat.[7] Other companies that periodically show up in the Top 10 include Verizon, News Corp, Time Warner, and Johnson & Johnson. The top categories these companies represent include automotive, telecom, media, pharmaceuticals, and personal care and cosmetics. Other important categories are retail, financial services, food and candy, beverages, and restaurants.

Most advertisers have an executive or department that initiates the advertising effort by identifying a marketing problem advertising can solve. For example, Apple executives knew that the Macintosh easy-to-use computer platform needed to be explained and that information about the launch of the new computer would need to reach a large population of potential computer buyers. Advertising was essential to the success of this new product.

The marketing executive (with input from the corporate officers and others on the marketing team) also hires the advertising agency—for Gatorade, the agency was TBWA\Chiat\Day—and other marketing communication agencies as needed. As the client, the advertiser is responsible for monitoring the work and paying the agency for its work on the account. That use of the word *account* is the reason agency people refer to the advertiser as the *account* and the agency person in charge of that advertiser's business as the *account manager*.

The clients' marketing team, sometimes in conjunction with the agency account people, makes the final decisions about strategy, including the target audience and the size of the advertising budget. The client team approves the advertising or marketing communication plan, which contains details outlining the message and media strategies.

Big companies may have hundreds of agencies working for them, although they normally have an **agency of record**, a lead agency that handles most of their advertising business and may even manage or coordinate the work of other agencies.

The Agency   The second player is the **advertising agency** that creates, produces, and distributes the messages. Agency styles, philosophies, and cultures are different in some cases because of the types of products they handle, but also because of the personalities of the agency founders. One agency with an unusual culture is Japan's Dentsu, which has a ritual that started in 1925 for all its young hires and newly promoted executives to climb Mount Fuji. Ranked fifth in size in the world, the agency literally and metaphorically asks its employees to climb mountains on behalf of its clients.[8]

The working arrangement between advertiser and agency is known as the *agency-client partnership*. The "1984" story demonstrated how important it is to cultivate a strong sense of trust between the agency and its clients because the commercial involved risky ideas. Partnerships are important on the media side as well. Amazon, for example, has developed a training program for ad agencies to help them better understand Amazon's ad formats and services.[9]

An advertiser uses an outside agency because it believes the agency will be more efficient in creating advertising messages than the advertiser would be on its own. Successful agencies typically have strategic and creative expertise, media knowledge, workforce talent, and the ability to negotiate good deals for clients.

Not all advertising professionals work in agencies. Large advertisers, either companies or organizations, manage the advertising process either by setting up an advertising department (sometimes called **marketing services**) that oversees the work of agencies or by setting up their own in-house agency, as Figure 2.3 illustrates. Tasks performed by the company's marketing services department include the following: set the budget and select the agencies; coordinate activities with vendors, such as media, production, and photography; make sure the work gets done as scheduled; and determine whether the work has achieved prescribed objectives.

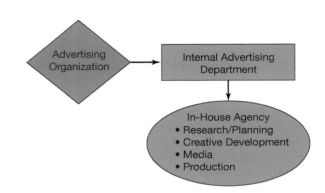

FIGURE 2.3
Two Advertising Organization Structures

The Media   The third player in the advertising world is the media, the systems used to deliver messages and engage audiences. The emergence of mass media has been a central factor in the development of advertising because the use of mass media offers a way to reach a widespread audience. In traditional advertising, the term **media** refers to all the channels of communication that carry the message from the advertiser to the audience and from consumers back to companies. We refer to these media as **channels** because they deliver messages, but they are also companies, such as your local newspaper or radio station.

Some of these media conglomerates are huge, such as Time Warner and Viacom. Time Warner, for example, is a $40 billion company with some 38,000 employees. It owns HBO, Time Inc., Turner Broadcasting, and Warner Brothers, among other media companies. You can learn more about this media conglomerate at www.timewarner.com. **Media vehicles** are the specific programs, such as *60 Minutes* or *The Simpsons*, or magazines, such as the *New Yorker*, *Advertising Age*, and *Woman's Day*.

Note *media* is plural when it refers to various channels, but singular—*medium*—when it refers to only one form, such as newspapers.

Each medium (newspaper, radio or television station, billboard company, and so on) has a department that is responsible for selling ad space or time. These departments specialize in assisting advertisers in comparing the effectiveness of various media as they try to select the best mix of media to use. Many media organizations will assist advertisers in the design and production of advertisements. That's particularly true for local advertisers using local media, such as a retailer preparing an advertisement for the local newspaper.

The primary advantage of advertising's use of *mass media* is that the costs to buy time in broadcast media, space in print media, and time and space in digital media are spread over the tremendous number of people that these media reach. For example, $3 million may sound like a lot of money for one Super Bowl ad, but when you consider that the advertisers are reaching more than 100 million people, the cost is not so extreme. One of the big advantages of mass-media advertising is that it can reach a lot of people with a single message in a very cost-efficient form.

⬤ **Principle**
Advertising is most cost efficient when it uses mass media to reach large numbers of prospective consumers.

Professional Suppliers and Consultants   The fourth player in the world of advertising includes artists, writers, photographers, directors, producers, printers, and self-employed freelancers and consultants. In the "1984" story, movie director Ridley Scott was a supplier in that Chiat/Day contracted with him to produce the commercial.

This array of suppliers mirrors the variety of tasks required to put together an ad. Other examples include freelance copywriters (see the Inside Story) and graphic artists, songwriters, printers, market researchers, direct-mail production houses, telemarketers, and public relations consultants.

Freelancing: Two Sides of the Coin

Aaron Stern, *Creative Director/Consultant, Stern & Co., New York City*

When I tell people I'm a freelance creative director, I usually get the same vaguely concerned look. In a time of economic uncertainty, many people assume that what I'm actually saying is, "I can't find a real job." But for the past five years, I've been consistently freelancing and turning down full-time job offers along the way. Freelancing has some wonderful benefits. And it definitely has drawbacks.

One of the biggest benefits of being a freelancer is that, for the most part, I get to choose the projects I work on. If I get a call for a project that doesn't sound appealing to me, I can simply turn it down. If I were on staff, I probably wouldn't have that luxury.

Another nice aspect of freelance is that I have the opportunity to work with many different agencies on a variety of clients. In any given year, I may work at 10 agencies or more. It's a great way to learn about the range of approaches agencies use to tackle problems. In some cases, the best creative agencies aren't necessarily the best places to work. And sometimes I'm pleasantly surprised by agencies that are smaller and lesser known.

Freelancing also gives me a lot more flexibility with my time. I can take time off when I want to work on other projects. A lot of freelancers I know have personal projects in art, writing, or music that they are able to pursue more easily because freelance allows for that kind of flexibility.

As a rule of thumb, freelance pays better in the short term than staff jobs, which means that, say, in a month of freelance I'll make more than I would in a month of a salaried job. And if I work over a weekend, I get paid for that time.

Of course, there's always a flip side. Moving from agency to agency, project to project, means that I constantly have to acclimate to a new environment. It's like starting a new job every time. I have to figure out how to navigate the politics, who to listen to, and what the new process is. Also, because the agency is paying me at an additional cost to them, I have to prove to them on a daily basis that I'm worth it.

Another drawback is that the projects often given to freelancers aren't always the most exciting ones in the agency. Usually, those are given to the staff creatives. And freelancers are often brought in to help pitch new business, which can mean long hours and a lower chance of actually producing the work you do.

Finally, one of the hardest things for a freelancer to get used to is not knowing when the next job is going to come along. Even after five years, at the end of a project I still get a little nervous that I'll never work again. Fortunately, I've always proved myself wrong.

Freelancing isn't for everyone. Some people prefer the routine, teamwork, and security that come with a full-time job. And if you're just starting out in the business, it may make more sense to find a staff job that will give you the experience and portfolio you need to establish yourself. But I encourage you to try freelancing at some point in your career. After all, you can always go back to a "real" job.

A graduate of the University of Colorado, Stern was an award-winning copywriter at Goodby, Silverstein & Partners; Black Rocket; and Venables Bell & Partners in San Francisco before moving to New York to work on an MFA in creative writing at New York University. He was nominated to be featured here by Professor Brett Robbs.

Why would the other advertising players hire an outside supplier? There are many reasons. The advertiser or the agency may not have expertise in a specialized area, their people may be overloaded with work, or they may want a fresh perspective. They also may not want to incur the overhead of full-time employees.

In the new world of digital media, another type of supplier has emerged, and that is the consumer, people who supply what we call **consumer-generated content**. They do so through YouTube contributions and contests sponsored by advertisers such as Doritos, which has sponsored a competition for the best commercial to be used on the Super Bowl.

Types of Agencies

We are concerned primarily with advertising agencies here, but other disciplines, such as public relations, direct marketing, sales promotion, and internet marketing, have agencies that provide specialized promotional help as well. Many of the practices discussed in this chapter apply to those agencies too.

Photos (left to right): Peter Atkins/Fotolia; JackF/Fotolia; ID1974/Fotolia; vukas/Fotolia; Stockbyte/ Getty Images.

Advertising relies on the expertise of many different people, such as television producers, graphic designers, photographers, printers, and musicians.

The A-List awards by *Advertising Age* recognize cutting-edge agencies that rank high in three areas. First, they are creative—*Ad Age* calls them "widely imaginative"—in developing brand strategies and executions. Second, they are fast growing and are the winners of some of the biggest new business pitches. Finally, they are recognized for their effectiveness and results. Notice that the agencies in the following list represent big and small agencies as well as full-service and a variety of specialized agencies.

Advertising Age's 2017 A-List of Agencies[10]

1. **Anomaly** Recognized by *Advertising Age* as the Agency of the Year in 2017, Anomaly pushed the boundaries of mainstream creative agencies with its work in data analytics, intellectual property and multicultural insights. The revenue skyrocketed 44%, as the agency attracted lots of new business, including Apple's Beats by Dre, Campbell Soup and Coca-Cola.
2. **McCann** Century-old McCann earned the No. 2 spot by delivering exciting ideas effectively across multiple platforms for clients like Lockheed Martin, MasterCard, Chevrolet and NYC Pride.
3. **R/GA** R/GA's specializes in business transformation and consults with Fortune 500 companies such as Walmart and Campbell Soup on innovations strategy, as they meld technology and creativity
4. **Droga5** This agency has become the "go-to agency for attention-grabbing work in surprising of categories from sausages (Johnsonville Sausages) and sports apparel to pizza (Pizza Hut) and politics (Hillary Clinton)," according to AdAge.
5. **VML** This Kansas-City, Missouri-based agency has built its reputation on its digital work but has increasingly added creative accounts for big-name clients like Sprint, Wendy's, New Balance, Tyson, and Miami tourism.
6. **BBDO** Shattering the perception of an agency that focused mainly as a creative TV house, BBDO concentrated on understanding consumer behavior and delivering great work where the consumers are going. Outstanding examples include GE's podcasts and "Unimpossible Missions" film series, Snapchat-centric Lowe's campaign, and Snickers messaging and packaging.
7. **Weiden & Kennedy** The shop that created Nike's "Just Do It" and Procter & Gamble's "Proud Sponsor of Moms" campaigns has proven it has staying power through consistently producing quality creative. Point in case: W&K made KFC relevant again by updating the brand's iconic founder-mascot in its "Re-Colonelization" campaign.
8. **The Community** Founded in 2001 in Miami and Buenos Aires, the agency has experienced a meteoric rise, landing such prized new clients as Verizon and General Mills and growing existing clients like BMW.
9. **Laundry Service** For an agency that started in 2010, Laundry Service has an impressive client roster. As the social agency-of-record, it scored wins for T-Mobile, BMW, Twitter, GrubHub to name a few by creating content and distributing it from the same place. As the agency has evolved as some clients like LG, Jordan Brand, and Freixenet, have asked the agency to repurpose their content for more traditional formats of TV, print, out-of-home, and more.

Content Management: Making It Happen

Tammie DeGrasse-Cabrera; *Senior Account Director, CP+B, Miami*

"So what exactly do you do in advertising?" That is by far the most common question I am asked once someone finds out I'm in content management. "Do you create the ads?" "Do you choose the actors?" "Do you decide which magazines to run in?" To be honest, I don't think my own mother has it figured out yet.

I've since realized that the best way to define what we, as account people, do in advertising is [that we] make it all happen. To use a simple analogy, an account person is like the supervisor in a car factory's assembly line. We don't physically connect part A to part B, but we do make sure every department fully understands what the car is supposed to look like, work with them on what drivers want and how it should run, and ensure it's built effectively and efficiently to make the sale.

We wear many hats in this job. I act like a train conductor, leading the team to keep all our projects moving forward, and at times as a translator, decoding consumers' responses on a new campaign idea to help solve for any issues and make the work even more powerful. I'm always a problem solver, whether it's working with the clients on product innovations, offers, or promotions to help boost sales or with a producer and creative team on how to create the next best spot, app, event, or social media effort. It is a very creative and ever-evolving role that entails anything and everything to get the job done.

For those of you considering entering the advertising industry, deciding which area to concentrate in can be difficult. Each department—whether creative, technology, production, strategic planning, or media—is so equally interesting that anyone would have trouble figuring out what the best fit for him or her might be.

Because I possess leadership qualities, enjoy strategizing, and like to get my hands in just about everything, content management was the perfect fit for me. For others it may not be so easy, so I strongly suggest learning more about the specifics of every group. Keep in mind that there are pros and cons to each, and only you can decipher on which end of the factory assembly line you would be best to work.

That's all for now. Have to run and prep for our next television shoot. Best of luck to you all!

DeGrasse-Cabrera was nominated to be featured here by Kartik Pashupti from the advertising program at Florida State University, where DeGrasse-Cabrera graduated. Since then, she has worked for McCann Erickson New York and is currently with CP+B.

10. **Tongal** An agency that is really more a confederation of 125,000 freelancers or production firms (aka Tongalers), Tongal uses its distributed workforce to create low-budget, fast-turnover "content." The creative network spans more than 150 countries and produces work for some big clients like Johnson & Johnson, Disney, and General Motor, helping the agency grow six-fold in three years with revenue of about $30 million in 2016.

The advertising professionals working for an agency, such as TBWA\Chiat\Day, the agency behind the Gatorade "sweat it" story, or Crispin Porter + Bogusky (CP+B), are experts in interpreting the client's marketing research and strategy as well as in managing the varied areas of advertising and marketing communication. The Inside Story by Tammie DeGrasse-Cabrera explains her work at CP+B coordinating the many pieces of a campaign; it also provides an overview of what an agency does for its clients.

Ad Age's A-List is based on its analysis of those agencies doing the most innovative work and having the most success in attracting new business. There are other indicators of quality performance. As one of this book's Advisory Board members, David Rittenhouse, managing director at Neo@Ogilvy in Japan, found from research and his experiences judging the Asian-Pacific Effie Awards, an international effectiveness competition: "In 2015, the most effective brand marketers were Coca-Cola, Unilever, Procter & Gamble, Mondelez, and PepsiCo. The most effective Holding Group is WPP. The most effective Agency Network is BBDO. They are the ones to observe and learn from."[11]

Full-Service Agencies In advertising, a **full-service agency** such as Crispin Porter + Bogusky (CP+B) includes the four major staff functions of account management, creative services, media planning, and account planning, which includes research. A full-service advertising agency also has its own finance and accounting department, a **traffic department** to handle internal tracking on completion of projects, a department for *broadcast* and *print production* (sometimes organized within the creative department), and a human resources department.

Let's take a minute to look inside CP+B, which has been named agency of the year in the past by *Adweek* and *Advertising Age* as well as *Ad Age*'s sister publication *Creativity*. CP+B celebrates some $140 million in revenue and employs nearly 900 in its two offices in Miami and Boulder, Colorado. The agency is known for its edgy, pop-culture approach to strategy. You may remember Burger King's weird "king" character. That's the kind of provocative work *Ad Age* calls "culturally primal."[12] It infiltrates the social scene and creates buzz. Although known for its creative work, CP+B also has an innovative product design think tank that has come up with such ideas as a public bike rental program, a portable pen version of WD-40, and Burger King's popular Burger Shots sliders.

In-House Agencies   Like a regular advertising agency, an **in-house agency** produces ads and places them in the media, but the agency is a part of the advertiser's organization rather than an outside company. Companies that need closer control over their advertising have their own internal in-house agencies. An in-house agency performs most—and sometimes all—of the functions of an outside advertising agency and produces materials, such as point-of-sale displays, sales team literature, localized ads and promotions, and coupon books, that larger agencies have a hard time producing in a cost-effective manner. Retailers, for example, find that doing their own advertising and media placement provides cost savings as well as the ability to meet fast-breaking deadlines. Some fashion companies, such as Ralph Lauren, also create their own advertising in-house to maintain complete control over the brand image and the fashion statement it makes. Check out that in-house agency at http://about.ralphlauren.com/campaigns/default.asp.

Specialized Agencies   Many agencies specialize in certain functions (writing copy, producing art, or creating digital ads), audiences or markets (youth or minority groups such as Asian, African American, or Hispanic), or industries (health care, computers, agriculture, or B2B communication). In addition, some agencies specialize in other marketing communication areas, such as branding, direct marketing, sales promotion, public relations, events and sports marketing, packaging, and point-of-sale promotions. Sometimes one-client agencies are created to handle the work of one large client. In addition to agencies that specialize in advertising and other areas of marketing communication, there are also consulting firms in marketing research and branding that offer specialized services to other agencies as well as advertisers. Because these various types of marketing communication areas are all part of an integrated marketing communication approach, we cover many of these functions in separate chapters later in the book.

Let's take a look at two special types of agencies:

- **Creative boutiques** are agencies, usually small (two or three people to a dozen or more), that concentrate entirely on preparing the creative execution of the idea or the creative product. A creative boutique has one or more writers or artists on staff but generally no staff for media, research, or strategic planning. Typically, these agencies can prepare advertising to run in print and broadcast media as well as in out-of-home (such as outdoor and transit advertising), internet, and alternative media. Creative boutiques usually serve companies directly but are sometimes retained by full-service agencies that are overloaded with work.
- **Media-buying services** specialize in the purchase of media for clients. They are in high demand for many reasons, but three reasons stand out: complexity of the media environment, increased staffing costs, and the cost efficiencies of bulk buying across a group of clients. Reviews of media operations by giant marketers, such as Coca-Cola, Unilever, and Procter & Gamble, are also getting headlines as advertisers look for agencies that can better handle new tools,[13] such as programmatic buying and "big data," or computer-driven analysis that relies on massive databanks of consumer information.

The types of agencies mentioned above are traditional ways of viewing agency structure and focus. New ideas about organization also are getting headlines. Tom Goodwin, senior VP-strategy and innovation at Havas Media, imagines a new set of roles:[14]

- *Visionary agencies* are those with innovators, technologists, futurists, and business strategists who do future planning for clients.
- *Brand agencies*, which would focus on telling brand stories and building brand equity, are similar to the current model of advertising agencies.

- *Performance agencies* would concentrate on short-term sales and immediate action using the tools of retail and out-of-home advertising, short-term public relations and publicity, and sales promotion.

Agency Networks and Holding Companies   Finally, let's talk about **agency networks**, which are large conglomerations of agencies under a central ownership. Agency networks are all the offices that operate under one agency name, such as DDB Worldwide (200 offices in 90 countries) or BBDO Worldwide (287 offices in 79 countries). You can read more about these agencies and their networks at www.ddb.com and www.bbdoworldwide.com.

McCann Worldwide is another large worldwide group. When Harris Diamond took over as president, he found a group of "jumbled agencies that didn't work particularly well together." The new chairman and CEO inspired the network of agencies to collaborate; they were so successful that the company won the massive global Microsoft business as part of a larger Interpublic holding company team.[15]

Holding companies include one or more advertising agency networks as well as other types of marketing communication agencies and marketing services consulting firms. The four largest are WPP Group, Interpublic, Omnicom, and Publicis. WPP, for example, includes the J. Walter Thompson Group, Ogilvy & Mather Worldwide, Young & Rubicam, Grey Global Group, and Bates advertising networks as well as the Berlin Cameron creative agency; public relations agencies Hill and Knowlton, Ogilvy Public Relations, and Burson-Marsteller; direct-response company Wunderman; research firms Millward Brown and Research International; media firms Mindshare and Mediaedge:cia; and branding and corporate identity firms Landor and Lambie-Naim, to name a few. Most of those firms are also networks with multiple offices. For an inside look at a big holding company, check out WPP at www.wpp.com.

How Are Agencies Paid?

Advertising agencies are a big business. Procter & Gamble, for example, spends nearly $5 billion annually on global advertising. With that kind of money on the table, you can imagine that the agency-client relationship is under pressure from both sides. Agencies want to get more work and get paid more; clients want to cut costs and make their advertising as cost effective as possible.

Agencies derive their revenues and profits from four main sources: commissions, fees, retainers, and performance incentives. For years, a 15 percent *commission* on media billings was the traditional form of compensation. That's how agencies got started in the 19th century. For those few accounts still using a commission approach, the rate is rarely 15 percent; it is more likely lower and subject to negotiation between agency and client.

Because of changes in the media, which now are fragmented and much less dominated by traditional "paid" media such as television, many advertisers now use a fee system or hourly rates[16] either as the primary compensation tool or in combination with a commission system. The **fee system** is comparable to the system by which advertisers pay their lawyers and accountants. During the 1990s, it replaced commissions as the main compensation method.[17] The client and agency agree on an hourly fee or rate or may negotiate a charge for a specific project. Charges are also included for out-of-pocket expenses, travel, and other standard items.

An agency also may be put on a monthly or a yearly **retainer**. The amount billed per month is based on the projected amount of work and the hourly rate charged. This system is most commonly used by public relations agencies.

A more recent trend in agency compensation is for advertisers to pay agencies on the basis of their performance. One consultant recommends that this **performance incentive** approach be based on paying the agency either a percentage of the client's sales or a percentage of the client's marketing budget. Another approach is that agencies share in the profits of their client when they create a successful campaign, but that also means that they have a greater financial risk in the relationship should the advertising not create the intended effect.

Another performance-related compensation innovation is **value billing**, which means that the agency is paid for its creative and strategic ideas rather than for executions and media placements. Sarah Armstrong, Coke's director of worldwide media and communication, urged the industry to shift to "value-based" forms of compensation that reward agencies based on effectiveness; that is, agencies' compensation is based on whether or not they make the objectives they set for their advertising.[18]

Account Management: A Priceless Feeling

Leo Wong, *Account Manager, Droga5, New York*

The alarm rings at 7:45 A.M. I get ready and am at the Droga5 office by 9 A.M. I hit the ground running and spend time catching up on emails, browsing advertising trade publications, and checking my calendar to see the day's events.

Before I know it, it's time for my weekly Scion client status meeting to update them and the partner agencies on our progress for the upcoming integrated campaign launch for two new vehicles. We talk about how we're tracking with the TV scripts, website designs, dealership display pieces, and digital banners.

I have a short break before heading into a meeting to discuss website updates for my other client, Toyota, which is launching a new hydrogen fuel-cell vehicle called the Mirai. It's time to push some updates live with new content, so I work with our creative team to get client approval on designs and digital production to see how to get it live.

Noon hits and I grab a quick bite and sit with our brand strategist to finalize a brief that we will be presenting to clients later that day to kick off another project.

As I step into an internal meeting to review TV scripts for Scion, I get a frantic note from my Toyota account director to help with something as soon as possible.

I step out and have to do a deep dive on the celebrity host we are using for a project because the client found some foul material on the celebrity's social account.

Once I finish, I have 20 unread emails in my inbox to tend to. I respond to the emails, schedule some meetings, and book upcoming travel for an in-person client meeting.

Switching gears back to Scion, I get the approval from the internal team to send the brief to clients for our upcoming call. The call goes well, and we await feedback.

The day's wrapping up, and I decide to stay for our daily dinner at the office. As I eat dinner, I make my to-do list for tomorrow and catch up on social media before heading home around 7:00 P.M.

Things can certainly get busy on any given day and the hours may get crazy from time to time, but I love my job because the feeling I get when the campaign goes live is priceless.

Leo Wong is currently an Account Manager at Droga5, a creative advertising agency based in New York City. In addition to creating influential campaigns for brands like Dos Equis, Google Pixel, and Scion, he is also an advocate for diversity and inclusion by spearheading efforts for Droga5 and industry organizations such as the 4A's. He is a proud alum of Syracuse University's S.I. Newhouse School of Public Communications.

Jobs within Agencies

If the agency is large enough, it usually has one or more vice presidents in addition to the CEO as well as department heads for the different functional areas. We will concentrate on five of those areas: account management; account planning and research; creative development and production; media research, planning, and buying; and internal operations.

Account Management The **account management** function (sometimes called account services) acts as a liaison between the client organization and the agency. The account team summarizes the client's communication needs and develops the basic "charge to the agency," which the account manager presents to the agency's creative and media team as well as other marcom areas involved in the campaign. Once the client and agency together establish the general guidelines for a campaign, the account management team supervises the day-to-day development of the strategy.

Account management in a major agency typically has three levels: the *management supervisor*, who provides leadership on strategic issues and looks for new business opportunities; the *account supervisor*, who is the key executive working on a client's business and the primary liaison between the client and the agency; and the *account executive* (as well as *assistant account executives*), who is responsible for day-to-day activities and operates like a project manager. A smaller agency will combine some of these levels.

Account Planning and Research Full-service agencies often have a separate department specifically devoted to planning and sometimes to research as well. Today the emphasis in agency research is on gaining insights into consumer thinking and behaviors so as to develop messages that focus on the consumer's perspective and relationship with the brand. The **account planning** group gathers all available intelligence on the market and consumers and acts as the voice of the consumer. Account planners are strategic specialists who prepare comprehensive information about consumers' wants, needs, and relationship to the client's brand and recommendations on how the advertising should work to satisfy those elements based on insights they derive from consumer research.

Creative Development and Production   A creative group includes people who write (copywriters), people who design ideas for print ads or television commercials (**art directors**), and people who convert these ideas into television or radio commercials (**producers**). Shawn Couzens, who is on this book's Advisory Board, prefers the title "conceptual engineer" for his work, which focuses on generating big ideas or concepts around which promotional campaigns may be built. Many agencies build a support group around a team of an art director and copywriter who work well together. Two other areas where creative personnel can apply their skills are the broadcast production department and the art studio.

Media Research, Planning, and Buying   Agencies that don't rely on outside media specialists have a media department that recommends to the client the most efficient means of delivering the message to the target audience. That department has three functions: research, planning, and buying. Because the media world is so complex, it is not unusual for some individuals to become experts in certain markets or types of media.

Internal Operations   The departments that serve the operations within the agency include the traffic department and print production department as well as the more general financial services and human resources (personnel) departments. The traffic department is the lifeblood of the agency, and its personnel keep track of everything that happens.

Collaboration   Agencies may have people in specialized roles, but collaboration is still the basic organizing principle. On the creative side, teams of copywriters and art directors can be long-term and incredibly prolific. Brainstorming sessions and "war rooms" for major project planning are common. An *Advertising Age* columnist called for more focus on agency-wide creative culture. He said that successful agencies need employees who collaborate across disciplines to ensure that every aspect of a client's business is considered in planning strategies and searching for new marketing and advertising ideas.[19]

Changes in the Practice of Advertising

2.4 Discuss changes in the practice of advertising.

Let's end this review of advertising basics by talking about the changes and issues in the advertising industry. Because of the recent Great Recession and the impact of online communication, advertising is clearly at a point in time when things will never be quite the same again for the industry.

Advertising Age columnist Bob Garfield wrote a controversial article in 2005 called "The Chaos Scenario" that predicted the end of mass media marketing and advertising. A book by that title followed in 2009. That was in the early days of online marketing and predates most of what we know as social media. At the time, many in the industry were skeptical, but in his book, Garfield pointed out all the changes that had happened in media—the weakening of print and TV networks and the dominance of online media—to underline the significance of his predictions. He explained, "We are not only facing an utter collapse of all of the media infrastructure we've so come to love and depend on for going on 350 years, we're in the middle of it."[20] The marketing world is now multichannel, multiaudience, and consumer-controlled interactive communication, and the industry has little resemblance to the old world of *Mad Men* advertising. Let's analyze some of those changes.

Consumer Takes Control

As Jim Stengel, Procter & Gamble's former global marketing officer said, "The customer is boss." The keys to the marketplace lie in the minds and hearts of those who use the brands.[21] This change, which was referred to in the Figure 2.2 time line, is causing major shifts in the way the advertising business operates. We mentioned user-generated content, which illustrates how consumers are even taking charge of the ads they see.

For example, the East Coast grocery store Wegmans found itself the focus of a YouTube musical tribute, "Wegmans the Musical," written and produced by students at a high school in Northborough, Massachusetts, who were celebrating the opening of a new Wegmans store. You can see it on YouTube.

That trend is occurring with the help of advertisers. It started in 2009 when CareerBuilder dismissed one of the most creative agencies—Portland-based Wieden + Kennedy, which had created five great Super Bowl ads for the job-posting website—and took its advertising in-house. The reason was that the company wanted ordinary consumers to create its commercials. Doing so would not only bring publicity, but would also save bucks. CareerBuilder, through its in-house agency, still paid for production of the winning ad and bought the ad time. Not only did this move bring more opportunities for *consumer-generated advertising* (user-generated content), but the company estimated that it saved money on its advertising costs.

Consumer involvement in advertising is a bigger issue than just ad agencies losing clients. In fact, consumers have been taking control of media and marketing for a number of years through Wikipedia, Twitter, and other newly democratized information sources. YouTube, Instagram, and Facebook have invited everyone into the ad distribution game.

Weakened Media and Blurred Lines

One of the biggest changes affecting the advertising industry is the changing media environment. Television used to be the big gun, and it still eats up the biggest part of the budget, but the old networks (CBS, NBC, ABC, and Fox) are only half as important as they used to be as the number of cable channels has exploded. The spending on advertising has been down since the beginning of the recession in 2007, but in 2015, *Advertising Age* reported that the global advertising expenditure of $520 billion was predicted to pass its prerecession level. Although television spending continues to decline, the difference is made up in the increasing use of digital media.[22]

The big bomb that has fragmented the media world is digital media, which appear in so many different forms that it's impossible to keep up with them. The newspaper industry has been particularly hurt as it has realized that much, if not most, of its content can be accessed more easily and quickly in a digital format. Are newspapers dead?

Traditional media are trying to adjust by transforming themselves into new digital formats as well. So what do you call online versions of newspapers and magazines? Are they still considered print when they appear on a screen? And new personal media—iPhones, iPods, iPads, BlackBerrys, and Kindles—are real shape changers. They can be phones, music players, calendars, and sources of local and national information as well as cameras, video viewers, book readers, web surfers, and video game players. Commercials that used to be the province of television are now just as likely to appear online (on social media such as Facebook) as well as on mobile devices. An analyst at eMarketer said that there's now a "perfect storm of consumer behavior, technology, development, and content availability."[23] Changes such as these need to be considered when putting together media plans, a challenge that will be discussed in Part 4.

Blurring also relates to marketing communication functions. For example, a Washington, DC, public relations firm, APCO Worldwide, bought Strawberry Frog, a small boutique New York ad agency. The reason is because public relations firms are now being challenged to make more creative content for the clients in a variety of areas other than just public relations. The line is even blurring between traditional marketing communication functions and tools.

Interactive Communication and Real-Time Advertising

The original philosophy of advertising was essentially one-way communication, with a brand sending a message to a prospective customer. The brand was the sender of the message; the consumer was the receiver. It took time to prepare and produce the message, and it took even more time before the consumer responded, if there was any response at all.

As Garfield noted, that's all different now. Brands do still send messages, but so do consumers. If brand stewards are smart, they are now listeners and responders as well as senders. They are truly communication managers, and the communication is much more interactive than in the *Mad Men* days. Managers listen through research, customer service comments, and, more importantly, the new social media that operates online independently of companies and agencies. It's not just business to consumer, but also consumer to business and consumer to consumers. And, because of interactive online delivery, messages can be sent, received, and responded to in real time, just like a personal conversation.

Effectiveness

Given the 2007–2009 recession and its aftermath, you can guess that efficiency is an advantage in this new marketing communication world. The other critical client concern is effectiveness, which is another way to look at accountability in advertising and marketing communication. A survey by the Association of National Advertisers found that 52 percent of marketers will challenge their agencies to cut costs and share more of the burden of cost efficiency.[24] As mentioned, CareerBuilder took its advertising in-house partly to save costs, which is critical in an economic downturn. Agencies that are creative in finding new ways to deliver cost efficiencies have a real advantage in their client dealings.

Along with the ongoing need for efficiencies, there's also a concern about effectiveness. The recession forced the advertising industry to become even more serious about creating advertising that delivers results and then proving the effectiveness of the advertising work once it's completed. Effectiveness is a theme that you will see discussed throughout this book.

Effective ads are ads that work. That is, they deliver the message the advertiser intended—as stated in its objectives—and consumers respond as the advertiser hoped they would. Ultimately, advertisers such as Procter & Gamble want consumers to buy and keep buying their goods and services. To get to that point, ads must first effectively communicate a message that motivates consumers to respond.

The Effie Awards, named for a shortened form of the word *effective*, are given by the New York chapter of the American Marketing Association to advertising and other forms of marketing communication that have been proven to be not only creative, but also, more importantly, effective. That means that the campaigns were guided by measurable *objectives*, and evaluation after the campaign determined that the effort did, in fact, meet or exceed the objectives. (Check out the Effies at www.effie.org.)

The Effie Awards recognize advertising and marketing communication effectiveness around the world. The awards cover a range of business categories, from Beauty and Wellness to Travel and Tourism, plus new areas like prosocial Good Works and forward-leaning Media Innovation. As one of this book's Advisory Board members, David Rittenhouse, managing director at Neo@Ogilvy in Japan, said: "To win an Effie is to receive affirmation from the industry that your advertising idea worked, though it is not the idea alone that is judged. In fact Effie jurists review multiple aspects of each entry including the difficulty of the marketing challenge, the strategic insight behind the execution, the campaign execution, and most importantly, the outcome." He details his experiences as a judge in the Matter of Principle feature.

Other award shows that focus on effectiveness are the Advertising and Marketing Effectiveness Awards by the New York Festivals company, Canada's Cassie Awards, and the London-based Institute of Practitioners Awards. Check out these award programs at their respective websites.

Award shows may also focus on other aspects of advertising, such as creative ideas. Examples are the Clios, a private award-show company; the One Show, sponsored by a New York–based advertising association; and the Cannes Lions Awards, an international competition from France. Awards are also given for media plans (*Adweek*'s Media Plan of the Year) and art direction (New York–based Art Directors Club award show). These awards can be found at www.clioawards.com, www.oneshow.org, www.canneslions.com, www.adweek.com, and www.adcglobal.org/awards/annual, respectively. Other professional areas also have award shows that reward such things as clever promotional ideas. For example, the Reggies are given by the Promotion Marketing Association, and outstanding public relations efforts are recognized by the Public Relations Society of America's Silver Anvil Award.

Integrated Marketing Communication

Although effectiveness is a central theme for this book, another central concept we will discuss throughout this book is *integration*. As mentioned earlier in the discussion about the time line in Figure 2.2, the search for effective communication has led many companies to focus on the consistency of their brand communication so as to more efficiently establish a coherent brand. As explained in Adage.com, the advertising business used to be fairly simple, but now, agencies must manage marketing communication across multiple devices as well as media and marcom platforms, and they must advertise to mass media audiences as well as design customized messages for specific, perhaps individual targets, based on real-time and constantly changing communication opportunities. The article asks who will be the partner to manage this mash-up of

● Principle
Advertising is effective when it achieves its objectives and consumers respond as the advertiser hoped they would.

If It Isn't Effective, It Isn't Creative

David Rittenhouse, *Representative Director, Neo@Ogilvy Japan*

Recently I served as an Effie Awards jury member for the Asia-Pacific region. It was one of the most inspiring experiences I have ever had in advertising. It dramatically expanded my understanding of how committed we are as an industry to making an impact.

You could say that Effies come from effectiveness because they recognize and reward marketing communication that works. Or it could be the other way around because they incentivize the industry to prioritize marketing effectiveness in addition to creativity.

Either way, they are organized each year by Effie Worldwide to, as the Effies website says, "spotlight marketing ideas that work and encourage thoughtful dialogue about the drivers of marketing effectiveness."

So what is effectiveness?

In this context, it means measuring outcomes and comparing them with marketing goals to see how well they were met (or not).

What do we mean by outcomes? We don't market for the sake of marketing. We do it to achieve goals, such as drive brand engagement, generate sales, increase market share, launch new products, increase brand loyalty, and gain new customers.

Measuring outcomes is simply quantifying the effects of marketing activities to determine their impact on the stated goals.

Performance indicators must be chosen carefully to reflect what is important and what represents progress toward strategic goals. By capturing this information, we can validate the claim that a campaign has been successful against its objective(s).

As mentioned, I was on the jury of the Asia-Pacific Effie Awards. This is the regional competition for the Asia-Pacific region and included campaigns from Australia, China, India, Japan, Singapore, New Zealand, and more—nearly 20 markets in total.

My contribution was to review entries from a number of business categories and score them based on how well the entrants understood their challenge, articulated their idea, executed that idea, and ultimately measured the impact of the message.

Although I cannot share the specifics of any entries I reviewed, a study was published that profiled the cases submitted in the Asia-Pacific region and described the shared characteristics of award winners. I found this survey broadly reflective of the entries I read and scored. Here's a summary:

- The top objective for the winners was to "Increase Sales Volume."
- The top target audience for winners was "Young Audiences/Youth."
- Winning entries used an average of seven or more communication touchpoints.
- "Interactive" and "Social Networking" were the most-used touchpoints by winners.
- Nearly all winners used either their own website or Facebook as a channel.
- Winners used research for planning their campaigns twice as often as those that did not use research.

It's interesting to note how clearly success is associated with driving sales, being present for new buyers coming into the market, communicating via a mix of channels, fully embracing new channels, and making plans on fact-based insights (not opinions or intuitions).

The title of this essay plays forward an idea from David Ogilvy, who died in 1999. The quotable Ogilvy once said, "If it doesn't sell, it isn't creative." It is in that spirit that I am sharing my thoughts on effectiveness.

As a student of marketing communication, no matter what role you aspire to—chief marketing officer, marketing data scientist, strategic planner, creative director, media strategist—I implore you to be persistent about making "work that works,"

Without this fixation on effectiveness, our industry would unravel. Creativity for the sake of itself has no value from a marketing standpoint. It is mere campaignery.

So there it is. If it isn't effective, it isn't creative.

---

business operations and predicts a "rebundling" of previous sign-off agencies for greater consolidation of services.[25]

As explained in Chapter 1, we call that practice *integrated marketing communication (IMC)*, the primary approach for total brand communication. To be effective, these brand messages need to complement one another and present the same basic brand strategy.

The need for coordinated strategic communication has also changed the way agencies function. No longer are they operating in silos; rather, they operate through comprehensive programs and services that include many marcom disciplines or through the coordination of a team of agencies that all specialize in different areas. Notice how few of the A-List of agencies

Manning Says You Don't Get It If You Don't Sweat It

At the beginning of this chapter, you read about Gatorade's "Sweat It to Get It" campaign. The unusual deprivation strategy depicts exaggerated customer disbelief when they are told that they can't buy Gatorade unless they "burn some to earn some." The idea might seem far-fetched at first, but it does reinforce the brand's position as a drink for serious athletes and exercisers.

Did it work?

The "Sweat It to Get It" campaign broke Gatorade viewership records and became the most watched Gatorade online series with more than 23 million views across all eight episodes. Other measures explained why it was so effective:

- The campaign drove a significant increase in Gatorade brand awareness with an increase of 11 points in ad recall. The "sweat it" message had a recall level that was 10 times stronger than Google's CPG message recall benchmarks.
- In terms of persuasion, athletes and committed exercisers who watched the campaign were also more likely to identify Gatorade as a performance-improving sports drink (an increase of 17 points) and a "go-to" brand (an increase of 13 points).
- In terms of favorability, the campaign delivered 14,000 social mentions and a 97 percent positive-neutral sentiment in social mentions.
- The engagement factor led to a 147 percent increase in online searches for Gatorade.

So why was this online campaign so effective for Gatorade? In addition to the celebrity power of Peyton Manning and Cam Newton, the humorous content worked well with teen and young adult athlete audiences. They got it.

Logo: Courtesy The Gatorade Company and TBWA\Chiat\Day. Used with permission.

mentioned in the early pages of this chapter were traditional full-service advertising agencies and how many identified themselves as "multidiscipline" or even specialists in some other area, such as public relations or digital media.

Looking Ahead

The focus on effectiveness and results is the theme of this book, and throughout, we will introduce you to practices that generate effectiveness. We'll end each chapter with the results of the campaign that introduced the chapter; in this case, it's the "Sweat It to Get It" campaign for Gatorade. This chapter has provided an introduction to many of the basic concepts of advertising. We'll continue that introduction of principles and practices in public relations in Chapter 3.

2.1. Describe the practice of advertising. The definition of advertising has evolved over time from identification to information and persuasion leading to selling. In modern times, advertising is persuasive communication that uses mass and interactive media to reach broad audiences to connect an identified sponsor with buyers and provide information about products. It performs communication, marketing, economic, and societal roles. Seven types of advertising define the industry: brand, retail or local, direct response, B2B, institutional, nonprofit, and public service.

2.2. Explain the evolution of the key concepts of advertising. A review of the evolution of advertising practice identifies the source of many of the key concepts currently used in advertising. These concepts can be grouped into the four key components of advertising: *strategy* (objectives, appeals, branding, positioning and differentiation, and segmenting and targeting), *message* (creative concept based on research and consumer insight, creativity, and artistry), *media* (the evolution of print, broadcast, outdoor, and digital as well as the practice of matching targets to media audiences and compensation based on the media buy), and *evaluation* (effectiveness in terms of meeting objectives, testing, and standards). A time line from the earliest ages of print to the current era of social media illustrates how these components have developed and changed over time.

2.3. Identify the key players and jobs within agencies. The key players begin with the advertiser, the organization, or the brand behind the advertising effort.

Other players include the agency that prepares the advertising, the media that run it, and the professional suppliers and consultants who contribute expertise. The three types of agencies are full-service, in-house, and specialized agencies. Agency jobs are varied in expertise and provide a number of career opportunities for all kinds of skill sets: account management, planning and research, creative (writing, art direction, and production), media (research, planning, and buying) and internal operations.

2.4. Discuss changes in the practice of advertising. A number of changes are creating new forms of advertising, such as the consumer-controlled communication that has emerged with the new social media; weakened media and a blurring of lines between marcom areas and tools; media that are changing shape and merging with other media forms; and more accountable and effective advertising practices that emerged from the recession, including more emphasis on integrated marketing communication (IMC).

KEY TERMS

account executive, p. 43
account management, p. 56
account planning, p. 57
account services, p. 45
advertisement, p. 37
advertiser, p. 49
advertising, p. 35
advertising agency, p. 49
advertising department, p. 49
agency networks, p. 55
agency of record, p. 49
art director, p. 57
brand advertising, p. 38
brand content, p. 40
branded entertainment, p. 40

brand image, p. 40
brand name, p. 37
business-to-business (B2B) advertising, p. 38
buzz, p. 41
campaign, p. 40
channels, p. 50
classified advertising, p. 42
commission system, p. 43
consumer-generated content, p. 51
copywriter, p. 43
corporate advertising, p. 38
creative boutique, p. 54

direct-response advertising, p. 38
fee system, p. 55
full-service agency, p. 53
holding companies, p. 55
in-house agency, p. 54
institutional advertising, p. 38
local advertising, p. 38
marketing services, p. 49
mass media, p. 35
media, p. 50
media-buying services, p. 54
media vehicles, p. 50
nonprofit advertising, p. 38
performance incentive, p. 55

positioning, p. 45
pro bono, p. 38
producer, p. 57
product, p. 35
public service advertising, p. 38
public service announcements (PSAs), p. 38
retail advertising, p. 38
retainer, p. 55
social media, p. 46
social responsibility, p. 46
strategy, p. 37
targeting, p. 44
traffic department, p. 54
value billing, p. 55

MyLab Marketing

Go to **www.pearson.com/mylab/marketing** for MyLab discussion questions (⚙) as well as the following assisted-graded writing questions.

2-1. Look through the ads in this book and find examples that focus on each of the three definitional orientations: identification, information, and persuasion. Explain how each ad works and why you think it demonstrates that focus. Which ad do you think is most effective, and why do you think so?

2-2. You belong to an organization that wants to advertise a special event it is sponsoring. You are really concerned that the group not waste its limited budget on advertising that doesn't work. Outline a presentation you would make to the group's board of directors that explains advertising strengths and why advertising is important for this group. Then explain the concept of advertising effectiveness. In this situation, what would be effective, and what wouldn't? Why is it important to determine whether an ad works?

⭐ **2-3.** Analyze the Gatorade campaign discussed in this chapter and compare it to key aspects of the modern definition of advertising.

2-4. Advertising plays four general roles in society. Define and explain each one in the context of the "1984" commercial featured in this chapter.

2-5. What are the four components of advertising, and what key concepts and practices do they represent?

2-6. Trace the evolution of advertising and the current developments that shape the practice of advertising. In your opinion, what are the five most important changes that have shaped advertising as we know it today?

2-7. Who are the four key players in the world of advertising, and what are the responsibilities of each?

2-8. We discussed five categories of agency jobs. Explain each one and identify where your own personal skills might fit.

⭐ **2-9.** What challenges are affecting the current practice of advertising? Discuss why effectiveness is important to advertisers.

⭐ **2-10.** Many industry experts believe that Apple's "1984" commercial is the best television commercial ever made. Watch it online on YouTube and analyze how it works. How many of the basic advertising practices and concepts that we introduced in the historical time line in Figure 2.2 does it demonstrate? Why do you think the experts are so impressed with this ad?

⭐ **2-11.** In class, Mark tells the instructor that all this "history of advertising" stuff is irrelevant. The instructor asks the class to consider why it is important to understand the historical review of advertising definitions and practices. What would you say either in support of Mark's view or to change his mind?

2-12. *Portfolio Project:* Leo Burnett, a giant of the advertising industry, always kept a file he called "Ads Worth Saving," ads that struck him as effective for some reason. It was his portfolio of ideas. He explained that he would go through that file, not looking for ideas to copy but because these great ads would trigger thoughts about how to solve some problem. So, throughout this book, we will invite you to start your own portfolio. In some cases, the assignments will ask you to find examples of good (or bad) work and explain why you evaluate them as you do. In other cases, we'll ask you to actually do something—write, design, or propose—or create something that you could take to an interview that demonstrates your understanding of the principles we talk about in this book.

    A Facebook Profile (for your advertising portfolio): For this first assignment, choose one of the people from the historical discussions in this chapter (or some other advertising history article or book), someone you believe you would like to have met. Research this person on the internet and build a personal profile, including samples of work if you can find some. Present your report as if it were a Facebook page. Make sure your presentation explains why you believe this person was important.

2-13. *Mini-Case Analysis:* Every chapter in this book opens with an award-winning case. For this assignment, you will be asked to analyze why it was effective and, in many cases, come up with ideas for how that campaign could be extended to another year or another market.

    Reread the Gatorade campaign that was introduced at the beginning of this chapter and wrapped up at the end of the chapter. Go online and see if you can find any other information about this campaign. What are the strong points of this campaign? What are its weak points? Why was it deemed effective? If you were on the Gatorade team, would you recommend that this campaign be continued, or is it time to change it? In other words, what happens next? Is there a spin-off? Develop a one-page analysis and your proposal for the next year.

A Multicultural Campaign

Read the TRACE case in the Appendix before coming to class.

2-14. In class, discuss the following:

    a. In what ways does the TRACE case reflect the expanded definition of what advertising is?

    b. How does the case illustrate the various roles that advertising campaigns can perform as well as the role of advertising in the broader area of marketing communication?

2-15. Write a one-page explanation of the campaign.

3

Public Relations

3.1 Explain what public relations is.

3.2 Describe how public relations works.

3.3 List common public relations tools and their functions.

3.4 Name and discuss what is trending in public relations.

Did you find yourself engaged in thinking about how you would interpret "like a girl" as you read the following case study? The story illustrates how Procter & Gamble generated a positive emotional connection between the Always brand and its intended audience.

In Chapter 1, you learned the fundamentals of marketing: the selling of a product or service through price, product, promotion, or distribution. Chapter 2 introduced you to the basics of advertising, a part of marketing that is paid nonpersonal communication from an identified sponsor using media to persuade or influence an audience about an idea, product, or service. In this chapter, you'll learn about the role public relations (PR) plays in integrated marketing communication (IMC) and will explore how relationships—like those developed between Always and girls—can develop goodwill effectively in a marketing communication program. You'll find out what the terms *publics* and *relations* mean in public relations. You'll read about essential skills and tools you need as well as current issues you may face if you want to work in public relations.

Campaign	**Corporation**	**Agencies**	**Awards**
Always #LikeAGirl	*Procter & Gamble*	*MSLGROUP; Leo Burnett Chicago, London, Toronto; SMG; Holler*	*PRSA Silver Anvil Award, Grand Clio Award, Cannes Grand Prix, a Black Pencil and a White Pencil at D&AD, multiple Webby Awards, and an Emmy Award for Outstanding Commercial*

Always Runs #LikeAGirl

Procter & Gamble faced a formidable challenge in its competition to reach a new generation of girls with its feminine care product Always. Although Always was the global leader in the feminine care category, promotion lagged behind some of its leading rivals, which had replaced their focus on product benefits with building an emotional connection between their brands and girls via social media. Not wanting to lose any ground in the pursuit of new customers, the brand needed a strategy to update its approach and outpace its competitors to develop stronger brand loyalty among millennials.

Procter & Gamble recognized that one of the strengths of the Always brand was its decades-long commitment to empowering girls through puberty education. It commissioned research that pro-

Photo: Courtesy The Procter & Gamble Company. Used with permission.

vided evidence to support continuing in this strategic direction. A survey revealed more than half the girls interviewed expressed a drop in confidence when they hit puberty. Enhancing its core commitment to build confidence in girls during the vulnerable time in puberty could just prove the key insight to strengthen the brand and win more girls as consumers.

To be effective, the message had to be authentic and simple. One account of the campaign described the creative idea that launched the campaign. Judy John, CEO and chief creative officer of Leo Burnett Canada, explained the breakthrough idea: "We explored different factors that influence girls during the vulnerable time in puberty. During this exploration someone taped a piece of paper to the board that read 'like a girl.' The idea was explained as: 'like a girl' has been around forever and is used in derogatory ways, let's change the meaning of it."

Eureka! The writing on the piece of paper held the germ of an idea that had the potential to change the way girls thought about themselves and connect emotionally to the brand—and win lots of recognition for the campaign's effectiveness in the process.

How did the agencies—MSLGROUP, Leo Burnett Toronto, SMG, and Holler—manage to redefine confidence, turning an insult into empowerment? The centerpiece was a captivating video in which people of all ages were asked to demonstrate how they interpreted actions "like a girl." It became evident that "like a girl" was associated with weakness and vanity. Then the video showed viewers what it could mean to do things such as run like a girl. Viewers quickly got the point, which was relevant to the brand and the product.

To disseminate the idea, a social hashtag #LikeAGirl was created to engage girls and invite them to let others know what inspiring things they were doing. The video was launched on the Always YouTube site. MSLGROUP sparked interest prior to the launch by asking key influencers and bloggers to use their social platforms to generate word-of-mouth interest and start making the video go viral. These efforts were augmented with paid media coverage, including a 60-second spot that ran during the Super Bowl. A combination of tactics strategically designed and executed connected audiences with Always. Media producers recognized the sensation and ran stories about the campaign on *Good Morning America* and a host of other outlets. Adding to the impact, celebrities including Sarah Silverman, Chelsea Clinton, and Melinda Gates tweeted about the campaign.

Did Always emerge with a winning campaign that accomplished its goals? It won the Silver Anvil Award—the most distinguished honor—from the Public Relations Society of America for its efforts. Find out more about the impact of this campaign in the It's a Wrap section at the end of this chapter.

Sources: always.com; "Always #LikeAGirl: Turning an Insult into a Confidence Movement" Case Study, www.prsa .org, 2015; Case Study: Always #LikeAGirl, http://www.dandad.org/en/d-ad-leo-burnett-holler-always-likeagirl-campaign-case-study/, 2015 (retrieved June 15, 2016); Jillian Berman, "Why That 'Like A Girl' Super Bowl Ad Was So Groundbreaking," February 2, 2015, www.huffingtonpost.com; Alexandra Bruell, "Like A Girl" Wins PR Grand Prix," June 23, 2015, www.adage.com; Benjamin F. Mitchell, "Girl Power Wins Big at Cannes Ad Festival, June 23, 2015, www.usatoday.com; Jack Neff, "REI and Swedish Tourism Win Promo and Direct Grand Prix for Taking Unusual Risks," June 20, 2016, www.adage.com.

3.1 Explain what public relations is.

What Is Public Relations?

Public relations is a fundamental communication discipline covering a wide range of functions that help an organization connect with the audiences it touches. (In public relations, audiences are also known as publics.) In essence, public relations is used to generate goodwill for an organization. The opening case study illustrates how Always generated goodwill by making consumers feel good about themselves and the brand.

The mission of generating goodwill is as broad in scope as the definition offered by the Public Relations Society of America suggests: "**Public relations** is a strategic communication process that builds mutually beneficial relationships between organizations and their publics."[1] Public relations focuses on all the relationships an organization has with its various publics. By **publics**, we mean all the groups of people with which a company or organization interacts: employees, members, customers, local communities, shareholders, other institutions, and society at large. Another term for publics is **stakeholders**, which refers more specifically to people who have a stake, financial or otherwise, in a company or organization. Its publics may be external (customers, the news media, the investment community, the general public, and government bodies) and internal (shareholders and employees). The "#LikeAGirl" campaign reaches multiple publics, including consumers, stockholders in Procter & Gamble (the parent company), and employees.

Public relations is practiced by a wide range of organizations: companies, governments, trade and professional associations, nonprofit organizations, the travel and tourism industry, educational systems, labor unions, politicians, organized sports, and the media. Most organizations have in-house public relations departments that handle the organizations' public relations work, although many also hire outside public relations agencies.

Public relations is a dynamic, global profession. The US Bureau of Labor Statistics projects that the public relations field will see significant growth in employment opportunities, particularly in light of the growing impact of social media. As of 2014, more than 240,000 jobs existed for public relations specialists, and the outlook for employment in this area is projected to grow 6 percent by 2024.[2] What do these experts do?

On one level, public relations is a tactical function in that public relations staff produce a variety of communication tools to achieve corporate image objectives. On a higher level, it is a management function that monitors public opinion and advises senior corporate executives on how to achieve positive relationships with various audiences (publics) to effectively manage the organization's image and reputation. Before explaining how public relations functions, we need to explain some concepts fundamental to the practice.

Public Opinion

Public relations programs are built on an understanding of public opinion on issues critical to the organization, such as the company's impact on the environment and its local community or workers' rights and how a company deals with its employees. **Public opinion** is a consensus of what a group of people who share a common interest think about a particular issue.

To design effective public relations programs, the public relations strategist researches the answers to two primary questions about public opinion. First, which publics are most important to the organization, now and in the future? Second, what do these publics think? Particular emphasis falls on understanding the role for each of the publics of **opinion leaders**, important people who influence the opinions of others.

Reputation: Goodwill, Trust, and Integrity

Public **goodwill** is the greatest asset any organization can have. A well-informed public with a positive attitude toward an organization is critical to the organization's survival. That is why creating goodwill is the primary goal of most public relations programs.

Sometimes a totally unexpected crisis can threaten an organization's respect and trust. Credibility for the Wounded Warrior Project, a nonprofit organization dedicated to helping injured service members, took a hit when the CEO was accused of misspending funds and was forced to resign.[3] More than 5,000 employees who secretly created millions of unauthorized bank and credit card accounts damaged Wells Fargo's reputation and were later fired.[4]

● **Principle**
Public relations is the conscience of the company, with the objective of creating trust and maintaining the organization's integrity.

Photo: Jim West/Alamy Stock Photo

Volunteers build picnic tables for a park in Detroit and help build goodwill for their company, Home Depot.

Consumer perception of United Airlines dropped to its lowest level in 10 years less than a week after a video surfaced showing a passenger being forcibly removed from an overbooked flight.[5]

Beyond responding to immediate issues, a public relations program that is tuned to creating goodwill operates as the conscience of the organization. Creating goodwill demands that both public relations professionals and the clients they represent act with integrity. Howard Rubenstein, an elder statesman in public relations, has a paperweight in his office at his agency to remind him, "If you tell the truth, you don't have to remember anything."[6] He said: "Corporate executives ask me, 'How do I prevent bad things from happening to me—like bad publicity, bad headlines?' And my answer always is, 'Well, you don't prevent these things by deception. You need to look at the substance of your situation and say, 'How do I make things right?'"[7]

To underscore the importance of acting with integrity as a prerequisite for creating goodwill, public relations organizations have created codes of ethics, which encourage ethical behavior of industry members. The Public Relations Society of America's *Code of Ethics* spells out core values of conduct, such as advocacy, honesty, expertise, independence, loyalty, and fairness. It also includes specific provisions regarding the free flow of information, fair competition, disclosure of information, safeguarding confidences, and avoidance of conflicts of interest.[8] Other industry organizations, such as the Public Relations Council and the International Public Relations Association, offer similar guidelines.

A reputation for integrity involves more than image. Image is a perception based on messages delivered by advertising and other marketing communication tools. Reputation, however, is based on an organization's actual behavior. Image mirrors what a company says about itself, but reputation reflects what other people say about the company.[9]

● Principle
Reputation is earned based on what you do, not on what you say about yourself.

The value of a good reputation is difficult to measure. Although considered a soft asset, one that is not usually included in a company's financial statement, it can be significant in determining company and brand value. The lack of a good reputation can be devastatingly costly, as Volkswagen discovered as a result of an emissions cheating scandal that cost the company $14.7 billion to settle claims in the United States and a tainted reputation among consumers.[10] Research has shown that in the face of bad publicity, advertising only fans the flames and makes the company appear unconcerned.[11] Communicators must find ways to authentically connect with their audiences.

Thomas L. Harris of Thomas L. Harris & Company and former president/partner of Golin Harris, who was named one of the 100 Most Influential Public Relations People of the 20th Century by PR Week, reflected on the importance of integrity after practicing public relations for nearly a half century: "Truth is what we are all about. Not hype. Not spin. But truth. If public relations is to retain its position as the credible source, we must not blur the line between information and propaganda, between advocacy and salesmanship. The old description of public relations as 'the conscience of the corporation' is more relevant than ever in today's complex society. The highest calling of PR is to keep our organization on straight paths, to counsel the powers-that-be not just to say the right thing but to do the right thing."[12]

The Arthur W. Page Society, a professional association for senior public relations and corporate communications executives and educators, offers seven principles, known as the Page Principles,[13] to guide the actions and ethical behavior of public relations and all communications professionals:

1. Tell the truth.
2. Prove it with action.
3. Listen to stakeholders.
4. Manage for tomorrow.
5. Conduct public relations as if the whole enterprise depends on it.
6. Realize an enterprise's true character is expressed by its people.
7. Remain calm, patient, and good-humored.

How Public Relations Contributes to Brand Perception

Public relations, like advertising, contributes significantly to brand perceptions. In integrated programs, advertising and public relations aim at selected targets with different but complementary messages. Advertising and public relations specialists share a joint responsibility to promote a brand, and at times their efforts converge. Sponsorships of a charitable cause, such as Häagen-Dazs's efforts with honeybee research, illustrate such an effort.

Photo: © HDIP, Inc.

Demonstrating its corporate responsibility, Häagen-Dazs ice cream has donated more than $1,000,000 to support honeybee research since 2008.

Recognizing the important role honeybees play in food production, Häagen-Dazs teamed with researchers in a campaign to help determine why honeybee colonies in the United States are disappearing.[14] To help find a solution to what is known as honeybee colony collapse disorder, Häagen-Dazs's ad agency, Goodby, Silverstein & Partners, and public relations firm Ketchum created the "Häagen-Dazs Loves Honey Bees" program. Häagen-Dazs kicked off its multifaceted efforts to help solve the honeybee mystery by funding research with more than $1 million. An expert advisory "Bee Board" of scientists and beekeepers served as sources for news media. Häagen-Dazs created *advertorials*, advertising that looks like editorial matter in newspapers or magazines, about the bee problem, which ran in key magazines, such as *National Geographic* and *Gourmet*. Häagen-Dazs even created a new flavor, Vanilla Honey Bee, and earmarked the profits for research into colony collapse disorder. Elements of public relations integrated with advertising to help solve a common problem and build brand image for the client.

To understand public relations better, let's consider how the role of public relations differs from advertising. Advertisers create the consumer awareness and motivation that deliver sales for a brand, and they do so by designing ads, preparing written messages, and buying time or space. The goals of public relations specialists are to communicate with various stakeholders, manage the organization's image and reputation, create positive public attitudes, and build strong relationships between the organization and its constituents.

Ultimately, the difference between advertising and public relations is that public relations takes a longer, broader view of the importance of image and reputation as a corporate competitive asset and addresses more target audiences. Public relations and advertising also differ in how they use the media, the level of control they have over message delivery, and their perceived credibility. Here are some specific differences between public relations and advertising, although the boundaries between them are less distinct as the digital media evolve.

- *Media use* In contrast to buying advertising time and space, public relations people seek to persuade media gatekeepers to carry stories about their company. **Gatekeepers** include writers, producers, editors, talk-show coordinators, and newscasters. Although public relations has a distinguished tradition, people often mistake it for **publicity**, which refers to getting news media coverage. Publicity, however, is focused on the news media and their audiences, which is just one aspect of public relations, and it carries no direct media costs. Even when public relations uses paid-for media like advertising, the message focuses on the organization, with little or no attempt to sell a brand or product line.
- *Control* In the case of news stories that appear in traditional media (also known as legacy media such as newspapers, radio, and television), the public relations strategist is at the mercy of the media gatekeeper. There is no guarantee that all or even part of a story will appear. Public relations writers write the story, send it to the media, and cross their fingers that this story will appear. In fact, there is the real risk that a story may be rewritten or reorganized by an editor so that it no longer means what the strategist intended. In our current digital, mobile, multiplatform world, however, organizations are no longer totally dependent on traditional media to reach desired stakeholders. To exert more control, some organizations use **brand journalism**, in which they can create content in media they own using journalism-style stories about their brand or organization. In contrast, advertising runs exactly as the client who paid for it has approved, and it runs as scheduled. Corporations cannot control messages generated by consumers and communicated through social media. Public relations specialists can play a significant part in online reputation management. See the Matter of Practice feature for information about what contributor and Northwestern University professor Clarke Caywood sees as an emerging opportunity for employment in the public relations field.
- *Credibility* The public tends to trust the media more than they do advertisers. This consumer tendency to confer legitimacy on information simply because it appears in the news is called the **implied third-party endorsement** factor. Harris, in his book *Value-Added Public Relations*, observes that today's sophisticated and skeptical consumers know when they are being informed and when they are being "sold to." He explains that public relations "closes the marketing credibility gap because it is the one marketing communication tool devoted to providing information, not salesmanship."[15]

Content Management as a Career in Public Relations

Clarke Caywood, *Northwestern University*

An emerging trend suggests that those with skills in public relations and journalism have new career opportunities. Internet search engine trend spotter Technorati reports that those who can bring journalism-style content and credibility represent 18 percent of the professional bloggers on the subjects of business and technology. Corporate bloggers make up another 8 percent of the blogosphere. It also comes as no surprise that employers seek employees skilled in blogging, Twitter, Facebook, LinkedIn, Avatar sites, and even newspapers, magazines, and broadcast. Such skill paves the way for new career paths for those who can combine public relations and journalism as modern content managers and providers.

Identifying "who will provide content" as the number of traditional news organizations declines is a contemporary topic that is argued by surviving members of the press, by researchers in the automated delivery of journalism, and by investors in new media systems. If a precipitous decline in the numbers of traditional news hunters and gatherers means a relative decline in content, new sources for news content, information, and even entertainment content will have to be developed, staffed, and supported.

Journalists and public relations practitioners have always experimented in new media. Both fields have served the public and their audiences with useful content and often-credible communication standards. These new public relations journalists are poised to contribute content to a wide range of organizations, from hospitals, to nongovernmental organizations, to churches, to government and politics, and to the largest potential content provider: business.

All institutions are loved, abhorred, or not noticed by one stakeholder group or another at some point. Who will speak credibly about the missions of our social, economic, political, and governmental organizations? It seems reasonable to suggest that the students from journalism/advertising/public relations programs with their long tradition of credibility and content development through journalistic knowledge and skills can provide an educated and trained source of institutional credibility and content.

Caywood is author of The Handbook of Strategic Public Relations and Integrated Marketing Communications *(2012).*

The Edelman Trust Barometer is an annual global study of trust in institutions, including business, media, government, and **nongovernment organizations (NGOs)**, which are non-profit, voluntary citizens' groups. An analysis of the more than 33,000 respondents reported in the 2016 survey indicated that the most trusted media source was online search engines and the most trusted content creators were friends and family.[16] Furthermore, it identified an emerging gap in trust between elite and mass populations. That is, the more informed elite respondents trusted institutions of government, business, NGOs, and the media more than did the mass populations.

How Does Public Relations Work?

3.2 Describe how public relations works.

The word *relations* in *public relations* refers to relationships with various stakeholders. In fact, the main subspecialties in the field—public affairs, media relations, employee relations, and financial relations (community relations)—call attention to important relationships with such groups as the general public, media, employees, and the financial community. Figure 3.1 outlines the various publics, partners, or stakeholders for a multinational company. The term **relationship marketing** introduces a point of view in marketing planning that evolved from public relations.[17] The work done by Always to build relationships with girls in the opening case study is an example of relationship marketing.

Aspects of Public Relations That Focus on Relationships

The key publics addressed by relationship programs in public relations are the media, employees, members, shareholders and others in the financial community, government,

FIGURE 3.1

Twenty Key Publics
Of the 20 key publics of a typical multinational corporation, relationship management programs focus on the media, employees, the financial community, government, and the general public.

Source: SEITEL, FRASER P., THE PRACTICE OF PUBLIC RELATIONS, 13th Ed., © 2017. Reprinted and Electronically reproduced by permission of Pearson Education, Inc., New York, NY.

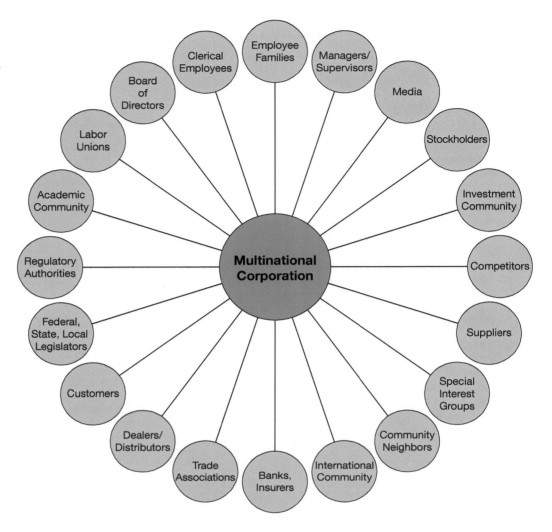

and the general public. Here are the specialty areas that focus on these relationship programs.

- *Media relations* The area that focuses on developing media contacts—that is, knowing who in the media might be interested in the organization's story—is called **media relations**. When you say *public relations*, most people immediately think about publicity, which indicates the importance of this media function. The organization initiates publicity and provides pertinent information to the media. A successful relationship between a public relations person and editors and producers is built on a public relations person's reputation for honesty, accuracy, and professionalism. Once this reputation is tarnished or lost, the public relations person cannot function effectively as a liaison between a company and the media.

- *Employee relations* Programs that communicate information to employees are called **employee relations**. This function may belong to public relations, although it may also be the responsibility of human resources. A related program is called **internal marketing**, which deals with communication efforts aimed at informing employees about marketing programs and encouraging their support. Public relations professionals are sometimes involved in employee recruitment, working with human resources and also membership recruitment for organizations. This role may involve preparing ads, websites, and literature on the company or organization as well as arranging events.

- *Financial relations* All the communication efforts aimed at the financial community, such as press releases sent to business publications, meetings with investors and analysts, and the annual report that the federal government requires of publicly held companies, are referred to as **financial relations**.

- *Public affairs* Corporate communication programs with government and with the public on issues related to government and regulation are called **public affairs**. For example, a company building a new plant may need to gain the approval of government health and public safety regulators. Public affairs also includes **lobbying**, which occurs when a company provides information to legislators to get their support and vote on a particular bill, as well as communication efforts with consumer or activist groups that seek to influence government policies. In addition to government relations, public affairs programs also monitor public opinion about issues central to the organization's interest and develop programs to communicate to and with the public about these issues. **Issue management** is another function under the purview of public affairs in which practitioners proactively manage issues to prevent escalation to a crisis.
- *Community relations* The scope of **community relations** has grown from a focus on the local community to encompass a larger meaning, including communities in broader society, both geographic and ethnic. This focus has expanded to include consideration of diverse communities, especially the underrepresented and underserved, no matter what ethnicity, age, sexual orientation, ability, class, and so on. Public relations plays a large role in nonprofit organizations that serve the diverse needs of the communities around them. Demonstrating social responsibility, which we cover in more detail in Chapter 18, is a core value of public relations.

    One way companies can build community relations is through **cause marketing**. The practice of companies associating themselves with a good cause by providing assistance and financial support, such as Häagen-Dazs and honeybee populations, is called cause marketing. Another example of cause marketing is the ubiquitous pink ribbon associated with breast cancer awareness that has been adopted by many organizations and companies, including the NFL and Yoplait. The pink ribbon campaign, along with the related areas of cause marketing and mission marketing, will be discussed in more detail in Chapter 16.
- *Consumer relations* One area where advertising and public relations overlap is the growing field of consumer relations. Simply stated, **consumer relations** is defined as building relationships with people who buy things in the United States and elsewhere around the globe. Building sales and building the brand are core objectives, and key activities to accomplish these goals include attracting and keeping customers, marketing new products or services, handling customer communication (often complaints), and educating customers. Because we live in a global society, public relations can be instrumental in helping organizations communicate with diverse consumers in their different cultures and locations.

The greatest strength public relations contributes to an integrated marketing communication program is its potential to help organizations establish credibility in the eyes of consumers. Public relations uses an unbiased, implied third-party endorsement to communicate information about an organization's products and practices.[18]

Chobani illustrates a brand that is increasingly dependent on public relations efforts as it competes with rivals with more money. Peter McGuinness, chief marketing officer for the Greek yogurt brand, said, "The growing importance of PR is not only a Chobani development, but a 'macro-category trend' because of highly curious consumers and the increasing need to reach them with brand information."[19]

Aspects of Public Relations That Focus on Particular Functions

Other areas of public relations, such as corporate reputation management, crisis management, marketing public relations, and public communication campaigns, are distinctive because of their unique functions rather than their target audience.

- *Corporate reputation management* The area that focuses on an organization's image and reputation is called **corporate relations**. The overriding goal of **reputation management** in a corporate relations program is to strengthen the trust that stakeholders have in an organization. Public relations expert Fraser Seitel offers advice about the importance of managing corporate image in *The Practice of Public Relations*:

    Most organizations and individuals in the spotlight today understand, first, that credibility is a fragile commodity, and second, to maintain and improve public support they must operate with the "implicit trust" of the public. That means that for a corporation in the 21st century, winning favorable public opinion isn't an option—it's a necessity, essential for continued long-term success.[20]

Photo: © Dave and Les Jacobs/AGE Fotostock

General Electric demonstrates its commitment to meet environmental challenges using green technology while spurring economic growth.

Because corporate reputation is a perception, it is earned through deeds, not created by advertising. Check out the website for Starbucks to learn about its efforts to do good works in the community and environment and look for other examples of **corporate social responsibility**, or companies working to create positive perceptions. Cause marketing, which we just mentioned, is another way corporations demonstrate their social responsibility.

John Paluszek, senior counsel at Ketchum, an expert in the area of public relations corporate social responsibility, said, "One of the great growth areas for PR is corporate social responsibility/sustainable development/corporate citizenship."[21] Many examples confirm this trend of doing well by doing good. Bill Gates's philanthropic efforts boosted public opinion of Microsoft and generated goodwill for his corporation in the process, and General Electric's "Ecomagination" campaign helps raise awareness of sustainability issues (http://ge.ecomagination.com).

- *Crisis management* There is no greater test for an organization than how it deals with a crisis. The key to **crisis management** is to anticipate the possibility of a disaster and plan how to deal with the bad news and all the affected publics. A crisis can be anything from an infestation of bedbugs in a residence hall on a college campus to a natural disaster. The cyanide-laced Tylenol crisis (1982) and the BP Deepwater Horizon oil disaster (2010) are examples of crises that public relations professionals would handle or at least consult with the corporations' top executives. Sometimes the stars of the campaign cause the crisis. Lance Armstrong's doping scandal caused a crisis for the brands like Nike, Trek, and RadioShack, who had hired him as a spokesperson. It cost Armstrong an estimated $30 million in potential earnings.[22] He also lost his seven Tour de France titles and is banned from cycling for life.

  Preparing for a potential crisis helps organizations weather the storm. By analyzing the potential for emerging crises and identifying resources to cope with them, an organization can be ready to respond quickly and meaningfully.[23] A quick response is essential. Public relations experts believe that unnecessary damage was done to FIFA, the governing body for world soccer, when its president and other top officials were involved in a corruption case and were forced to resign in 2015 after an investigation that lasted several years.

  Effective crisis plans can help both avoid crises and ease the damage if one occurs. A plan outlines who contacts the various stakeholders who might be affected (employees, customers, suppliers, civic and community leaders, and government agencies), who speaks to the news media, and who sets up and runs an on-site disaster management center. Crisis preparation can include, for example, contingency plans to educate consumers prior to an outbreak of the Zika virus or a natural disaster such as a hurricane.

- *Public communication campaigns* Used as a way to change public opinion, **public communication campaigns** also discourage socially harmful behaviors, such as driving in areas with high levels of air pollution. Sometimes they are engaged in countermarketing as they try to argue against other advertising messages. For example, the *truth*® campaign was designed to counter big tobacco companies' advertising that may appeal to teenagers.

- *Fund-raising* The practice of raising money by collecting donations is called **fund-raising (or development)**. It is used by nonprofit organizations, such as museums, hospitals, and emergency groups such as the Red Cross, and is directed to potential donors. Professional fundraisers know how to make the initial contacts that inspire other people to participate, how to use other marketing communication tools such as advertising, and how to make the best use of special events and public recognition. Sometimes fund-raising is called **strategic philanthropy**.

This review of some of the key types of public relations programs should give you a sense of the breadth of the activities as well as the variety of career opportunities in this field. The short exercise below might help you decide if public relations is the career for you.

TEST YOURSELF: WOULD YOU LIKE TO WORK IN PUBLIC RELATIONS?

Here's a list of 10 skills needed for public relations managers and specialists:

1. A knowledge of the role public relations and public affairs play in supporting business goals both locally and globally.
2. The ability to understand the "big picture" of communication and how to integrate all communication functions effectively.
3. The know-how to leverage traditional and social media to control key messages.
4. An aptitude for information technology and the determination to stay current with emerging trends in such areas as mobile, social content creation/curation, and search engine optimization.
5. The flexibility to work with a range of challenges and people and a knack for discerning which opponents to take seriously.
6. Strong verbal and written communication skills.
7. A talent for synthesizing, filtering, and validating information and the ability to apply analytics to help sort data.
8. Strong organizational skills for multitasking and managing time.
9. An ability to work with teams both face to face and remotely.
10. A willingness to be bold and the resilience to bounce back from disappointment or failure.

Sources: Doug Pinkham, "What It Takes to Work in Public Affairs and Public Relations," *Public Relations Quarterly,* Spring 2004, 15, www.prsa.org; Anik Hanson, "10 Skills PR Professionals Will Need in 2020," June 2012, www.prdaily.com; "Top 7 Skills Needed for a Public Relations Career," www.prcrossing.com, retrieved July 21, 2017; Ken Jacobs, "7 Skills PR Leaders Need to Succeed in the Coming Years: Do You Have What It Takes?," *Public Relations Strategist,* April 8, 2014, www.prsa.org.

What Are Common Public Relations Tools?

3.3 List common public relations tools and their functions.

Public relations uses a variety of marketing communication tools just as advertising does. Advertising is particularly useful in corporate image and reputation programs. Direct marketing is sometimes useful in sending out corporate or institutional publications. The internet is important because the corporate website is one of the primary ways to disseminate information about an organization. Public relations activities, such as publicity and corporate advertising, can help drive traffic to the corporate website. Sales promotion is used in support of public relations activities, such as special events. In some cases, it's hard to know whether an event is a sales promotion or public relations effort. But it's not just the use of these tools that makes public relations a viable function of brand communication; it's also that public relations can contribute valuable effects, such as credibility.

Planning how to use these tools for a public relations campaign is similar to planning an advertising or IMC campaign and will be covered in Chapter 8. The plan should complement the marketing and marcom strategies so that the organization communicates with one clear voice to various publics. An acronym for the parts of a strategic plan for public relations is **RPIE**, short for Research, Planning, Implementation, and Evaluation. The plan also identifies the various key publics and public relations activities that public relations specialists use to address the interests of its various publics. In addition to identifying key targets, public relations plans also specify the objectives and strategies that give direction to the public relations program or campaign. Assessing the effectiveness of the campaign in achieving its objectives is important, just as it is for all IMC campaigns.

As the media landscape has evolved in the digital age, so has the role of public relations in integrated marketing. Moving away from marketing that considered traditional public relations

A Communications Manager Juggles Responsibilities

Amanda Koone, *Communications Manager, Fredericksburg Convention & Visitors Bureau, Texas*

As the communications manager at the Fredericksburg Convention and Visitors Bureau (FCVB), I'd say that my major responsibility is to "just make it all happen." The role of the FCVB is to promote our small Texas town as a tourism destination, which is where I come in. My function as communications manager leaves me as part brand shepherd, part social media strategist, part social media and digital content creator/strategist, and so much more.

My previous agency experience comes in handy on a daily basis. There are days when I'm very "project manager" oriented, others where I'm writing search engine optimization custom content for the launch of a new digital campaign, others where I'm leading media familiarization tours (press junkets), writing press releases, working on various marketing tasks like writing e-newsletters and external communications, days I'm working with contract videographers and photographers to develop new editorial and advertising collateral, days where I'm the actual photographer, and other times where I'm spending hours scrutinizing our latest results in Google Analytics and running reports, or spending time planning with our PR firm, web development company, or full-service ad agency. Although my job functions are typically marketing and PR oriented, being on a somewhat small team, at the end of the day I just do whatever it is that needs to be done to reflect our destination in a positive light and achieve our marketing and PR goals.

Needless to say, there is no typical "day in the life" for a communications manager. The ability to prioritize projects, stay organized, and be flexible is of utmost importance. Insider tip: I highly recommend investing in a good planner and getting into good time-management routines as soon as you can! In this field, you can easily start the day with one set of "to-dos" and end the day with a totally different objective and task list.

To give you a better idea, here's a glance into my planner last week:

Monday:

10 A.M. meeting with local event organizer to discuss and plan upcoming media event showcasing 2015 horse racing

11 A.M. status meeting with Communications Associate to discuss weekend social media activity, action items for the week

2 P.M. conference call with CISION media software on recent upgrades

Tuesday:

9 A.M. meeting with San Antonio area TV station to discuss potential summer media buy and PR initiatives

11 A.M. conference call with advertising agency regarding launch of upcoming digital marketing campaign

2 P.M. webinar on culinary travel trends

4 P.M. call regarding high-res images for use in upcoming regional travel story

Wednesday:

9 A.M. sales and marketing meeting

11 A.M. final prep for monthly visitor newsletter distribution

4 P.M. conference call with PR firm to review recent media FAM

Thursday:

Welcome to International Media FAM, accompany media group to various attractions based on a culinary themed itinerary that highlights Texas Wine

Friday:

Continue to accompany International Media FAM until their departure at approximately 3 P.M.

3:30 P.M. call with editor of national publication regarding fact checking and images for upcoming editorial feature

In the day of the smartphone and iPad, I try to make myself available to media folks just about 24/7—this is just a snippet of my 9–5. After hours, I typically respond to emails, take calls from editors, and create content for various digital campaigns and platforms.

Koone was nominated to be featured here by Professor Larry Kelley, a member of this book's Advisory Board, a former executive at the FKM agency, and a professor at the University of Houston.

efforts as an afterthought to advertising campaigns, public relations now plays a central strategic role, especially integrating social media. Consider real estate company Coldwell Banker, which used its internal public relations team to talk about how smart home technology affects the buying and selling of residential real estate. As another example, H&R Block, partnered with the NBA and increased social media, has invested in cause marketing to improve the financial literacy of teenagers.[24]

The public relations practitioner has many tools, which we can divide into three categories: paid, owned, and earned media. We discuss the three types in depth in the media chapters in Part 4. Briefly, the three types reflect varying levels of credibility as well as control over the message and placements.

Paid media are traditional measured media, primarily in the format of advertising such as print and broadcast, in which the sponsoring company or organization pays for the promotion. Public relations advertising typically combines advertising and editorial functions.[25] Examples include house ads, public service announcements, corporate (institutional) advertising, in-house publications, and visual presentations. Sponsoring organizations pay for these media and maintain total control over how and when the message is delivered. Credibility suffers, however, because media-savvy publics are skeptical of self-promotion messages.

Owned media are those channels owned and controlled by the sponsoring organizations such as websites, blogs, sponsored events, and publications about the brand, such as news releases. The company or organization controls the messages but does not control how or when the message is delivered. Communication from contributors to conversations can't be controlled on a brand's social media channels, such as blogs, Twitter accounts, YouTube channels, Facebook pages, and the latest new online media. Competition with the owned media also complicates brand communication. Corporations and businesses control their own websites, for example, but websites owned by others (particularly those that are set up by critics and disgruntled ex-employees, like I Hate McDonald's and GTE Sucks), blogs, and chat rooms about the company are not controlled. Likewise, companies set special events and put sponsorships in place, but participation by the press and other important publics is not under the control of the sponsoring company. Like the paid media of advertising, a downside to owned media is that they may not be trusted because publics know they're owned.

Consumers and mass media—not the brand owners—control the mentions and comments about the brand in what is known as **earned media**, which makes it the most credible media option. Media are "earned" when objective reporters turn the work of public relations writers (news releases, story pitches, and press conferences) into positive communication about the brand. The result is positive word of mouth, viral communication, and publicity hits and mentions. Word of mouth, or buzz, is important to public relations programs because of the credible persuasive power of personal conversation. An example of earned media is a video about a brand that goes viral and gains traction with audiences because it becomes newsworthy. The Always video mentioned in the opening case did just that, earning free coverage across the globe on ABC's *Good Morning America*, the BBC, *Huffington Post*, Mashable, BuzzFeed, and *Time*. It's hard to measure, but it's undeniably valuable, as long as the coverage is positive.

Sometimes the coverage damages the brand's reputation. When Motrin posted an online ad on a Saturday about mothers who carried their babies in slings that suggested that this fashion caused back pain, outraged mommy bloggers and tweeters wasted no time calling for boycotts. Makers of Motrin responded by the end of the weekend with an apology and removed the ad.[26]

Some companies monitor the internet to see what is being said about them so that they can respond to protect their reputations. Thousands of companies have hired eWatch, a firm that provides web monitoring services, to collect such information.

How should organizations respond to negative information on the internet or social media? Entrepreneur and venture capitalist Mark Suster warned about the dangers of overreacting. His advice: If you make a major mistake, own it early. If negative information is posted and you believe your company is in the right, see if the story "gets much reverberation." If it's not picked up repeatedly in the media, social or otherwise, resist the temptation to respond because the response itself might make people aware of the issue unnecessarily.[27]

Advertising

Public relations programs sometimes employ advertising as a way to create corporate visibility or strengthen relationships with various stakeholder audiences. The primary uses of advertising are house ads, public service announcements, and corporate advertising.

House Ads   An organization (or a medium, such as a newspaper, magazine, or broadcast station) may prepare a **house ad**, which is an ad for use in its own publication or programming. Consequently, no money changes hands. For instance, a local television station may run a house

CLASSIC

Since 1972, PSAs for the United Negro College Fund have helped raise more than $2.2 billion to fund college educations for more than 350,000 minority students.

ad within its evening news program announcing its new fall programming; likewise, a company may run an ad within its corporate magazine advocating a point of view or promoting a special employee benefit program. These house ads are often managed by the public relations department.

Public Service Announcements   The ads for charitable and civic organizations that run free of charge on television or radio or in print media are called **public service announcements (PSAs)**. The United Way, the American Heart Association, and local arts councils all rely on PSAs. These ads are prepared just like other print ads or commercials, and in most instances, ad agencies donate their expertise and media donate time and space to run the ads.

The Advertising Council represents a public relations effort for the entire advertising industry and has produced most of the PSAs you see on television and in print, such as the "Friends Don't Let Friends Drive Drunk" campaign and the "Keep America Beautiful" antilitter campaign. The classic United Negro College Fund campaign has become one of the best-recognized Advertising Council PSAs with its slogan, "A Mind Is a Terrible Thing to Waste" (see the Classic feature). Recent campaigns include those focusing on welcoming refugees, reducing food waste, and teen bullying prevention.

Getting donated time and space is not easy. The PSA directors at various media receive a barrage of public service campaigns every week on different issues, and they must choose which ones to run. There is no guarantee which markets will see the campaign elements, and there is no guarantee that the same people will see the print and television versions of a campaign. Some PSA campaigns do not get any airtime or print placements.

Corporate Advertising   With **corporate advertising**, a company focuses on its **corporate image** or viewpoint. There is less emphasis on selling a particular product unless it is tied in to a good cause. For that reason, the ad or other campaign materials may originate in the public relations department rather than the advertising department.

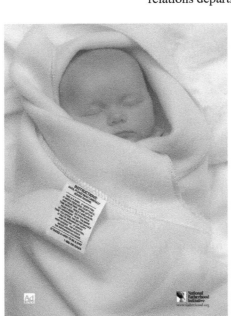

The Advertising Council has sponsored a number of public communication campaigns in support of good causes. The participating agencies donate their time and talent, and media donate the time and space to run the PSAs. This one is for new dads and encourages them to learn more about parenting.

An example of building goodwill through corporate advertising is Target's commitment to the communities it serves, donating more than $4 million every week to causes important to Target shoppers. Target's legacy of giving and service is explained on its website and reflects its customers' interests in supporting education, wellness, sustainability, and diversity and inclusion. Recognizing that education is the top social concern of Target's "guests" and critical to economic and national security, the company set and reached its goal to give $1 billion for education.[28]

Corporate identity advertising is another type of advertising that firms use to enhance or maintain their reputation among specific audiences or to establish a level of awareness of the company's name and the nature of its business. "The Johnson & Johnson Campaign for Nursing's Future" celebrates the nursing profession and helps recruit and retain nurses in one of its initiatives. Companies that have changed their names, such as Accenture (formerly Andersen Consulting) and KFC (formerly Kentucky Fried Chicken), have also used corporate identity advertising.

Sometimes companies deliver point-of-view messages called **advocacy advertising**. For example, the previously mentioned "Ecomagination" campaign of General Electric shows that the company wants to be a caretaker of the environment and is creating products in line with that philosophy. Another example comes from Procter & Gamble's Dawn brand, which has partnered with wildlife and rescue rehabilitation centers since 1975. Dawn's long-running campaign connects the dish soap known to be tough on grease yet gentle with the advocacy effort to rescue birds and marine mammals harmed by oil spills.[29]

Dawn's environmental cause-related campaign proved particularly timely in light of the massive BP oil spill in the Gulf of Mexico in 2010. Donating more than 12,000 bottles of Dawn to animal rescuers on the Gulf coast, Procter & Gamble enhanced its reputation and built goodwill based on its long-standing marketing relationship between wildlife rescue organizations and the brand.[30] The dawnsaveswildlife.com website features information about its continuing efforts to help rescue and release more than 75,000 wild animals affected by oil pollution.

Media Relations

Moving away from controlled messages, consider the various tools and techniques used by media relations specialists to get publicity in the news media on behalf of a company or brand. Consider these extreme examples. Human footwear maker Teva created sandals for an Asian elephant with foot problems. The result was an article and photo that ran as a news item. Red Bull took Felix Bumgartner to the edge of space in a stratospheric balloon where he returned to Earth after completing a free-fall jump at supersonic speeds, eventually parachuting safely to the ground. Red Bull's stunt resulted in massive social and mainstream media coverage.[31] Public relations expert Tom Harris calls this type of media coverage "an endorsement that money can't buy."[32]

Media relations is often seen as the most important core competency for public relations professionals. Media relations specialists know media would be interested in stories about their companies. They also develop personal contacts with reporters and editors who write regularly on topics related to their organization's industry. In addition to personal contact, the primary tool used in media relations is the news release, along with press conferences and media tours.

News Releases   The **news release** is the primary medium used to deliver public relations messages to the various external media. Although the company distributing the news release controls its original form and content, the media decide what to present and how to present it. What the public finally sees, then, is not necessarily what the originating company had in mind, so this form of publicity offers less control to the originating company than some other forms.

The decision to use any part of a news release is based on an editor's judgment of its news value. **News value** is based on such considerations as timeliness (something just happened or is about to happen), proximity (a local angle), impact (importance or significance), and human interest.

News releases must be written differently for each medium, accommodating space and time limitations. Traditional journalism form is followed, which means that the 5W format is standard; in other words, the release should lead with answers to questions of who, what, why, when, where, and how. The more carefully the news release is planned and written, the better the chance it has of being accepted and published as written. Notice the tight and simple writing style in the news release from the University of Nebraska–Lincoln. News releases can be accompanied in the digital age with associated media files, such as short videos, to help communicate the news.

News release: Courtesy University of Nebraska State Museum, University of Nebraska-Lincoln. Used with permission. *Photo within news release:* Courtesy NASA/JPL.

This piece from the University of Nebraska–Lincoln shows a typical news release format. It includes contact information at the top and a headline that summarizes the point of the news release.

The majority of news releases are delivered by email, although they can be delivered in a number of different ways. Sometimes a company that specializes in distribution, such as PR Newswire, U.S. Newswire, or Business Wire, is hired to provide targeted distribution to special-interest media outlets or handle mass distribution of news releases, photos, graphics, video, audio, and other materials.

Effective news releases for the internet should be brief and succinct. Recommendations for the format include the following:[33]

• Send to only one reporter in the "To" line.
• Limit the subject line headers to four to six words that entice the recipient to read the email.

- Write a strong headline for the news release to attract immediate interest in 10 words or less and use upper- and lowercase.
- Keep news releases short, writing fewer than 500 words.
- Observe the 5W format of traditional news release style, answering key questions of who, what, why, when, where, and how.
- Never add attachments.
- Keep email releases readable, using short paragraphs, bullets, numbers, and lists to make the release eye-friendly and able to be scanned.

Video news releases contain video footage for a television newscast. They are effective because they show target audiences the message in two different video environments: first as part of a news report and then reused later in an advertisement. Of course, there is no guarantee that such a release will be used.

Pitch Letters   Ideas for **feature stories**, which are human interest stories rather than hard news announcements, have to be "sold" to editors. That is done using a **pitch letter** that outlines the subject in an engaging way and encourages editors to cover the topic and distribute the information. Companies use this form to feature interesting research breakthroughs, employees, or corporate causes, hoping to receive positive coverage of their story. Not only is the distribution of news releases moving online, but so are the letters pitching editors with story ideas.

Press Conferences   A **press conference**—an event at which a company spokesperson makes a statement to media representatives—is one of the riskiest public relations activities because the media may not see the company's announcement as being real news. Companies often worry about whether the press will show up for a press conference. Will they ask the right questions, or will they ask questions the company cannot or does not want to answer?

To encourage reporters to cover press conferences, companies may issue a **media kit**, usually a folder that provides all important background information to members of the press, either before or when they arrive at the press conference. The risk in offering media kits (also called press kits) is that they give reporters all the necessary information so that the press conference itself becomes unnecessary.

Media Tours   A **media tour** is a press conference on wheels. The traveling spokesperson makes announcements and speeches, holds press conferences to explain a promotional effort, and offers interviews.

Publications

Organizations may provide employees and other publics with pamphlets, booklets, annual reports, books, bulletins, newsletters, inserts and enclosures, and position papers. The Securities and Exchange Commission requires that each publicly held company publish an **annual report**. A company's annual report is targeted to investors and may be the single most important document the company distributes. Millions of dollars are spent on the editing and design of annual reports. These reports are especially important to stockholders and potential investors.

Some companies publish material in print or online, often called **collateral material**, to support their marketing public relations efforts. Corporate publications, marketing, and sales promotion departments and their agencies also produce training materials and sales kits to support particular campaigns. Think about the high-quality brochures and booklets you can pick up at car dealerships when you go in to look at new cars. As another example, Owens Corning Fiberglass Insulation offers information on home insulation projects as an integral part of its promotion effort.

Zines provide another outlet for businesses. At the eZineArticles.com website, contributors write their own content and publish it online, making it available for others to publish on their own sites as well. The site doesn't like overtly promotional content, but a company can provide a service piece related to its business; any kind of "how-to" piece is welcome. For example, if you have a client that does faux painting, a general article on the art of faux painting and how to use it as a design element can also carry a short bio and link to your client's site.

FIGURE 3.2
The Impact of Banks
Regulations have become the standard for the banking industry. It is important for bankers to visit with their state and national representatives to leverage the impact community banks have as legislation is written and voted upon. Finding a way to communicate the importance of community banks was critical. The solution was to create an infographic to reach the target audience of busy elected officials and communicate quickly and powerfully.

SHOWCASE

This brochure was contributed by Kristin Ewing, a graduate of the University of Nebraska-Lincoln. She is a corporate communications and public relations specialist at Express Employment Professionals, Oklahoma City.

Photo: Kristin Ewing

Other Tools

In addition to advertising, publicity, and publications, public relations practitioners have various other types of materials and activities in their professional tool kits.

Videos, CDs, Podcasts, and Books   Videos and podcasts have become major public relations tools for many companies. Production costs can range widely depending on the quality of the production and size of the audience they'll reach. However, they are an ideal tool for distributing in-depth information about a company or program. With the advent of simplified electronic publication, corporate books have also become popular.

Speakers and Photos   Many companies have a **speakers' bureau** of articulate people who will talk about topics at the public's request. Organizations as varied as Apple Computer, Harvard University, and the Children's Hospital in Houston, Texas, all have speakers' bureaus that can arrange presentations to local groups and classes.

Photo: Paul Sakuma/AP Images

In one of his classic performances, the late Steve Jobs unveils the iPad, generating lots of buzz for the new Apple iPad.

Displays and Exhibits Displays and exhibits, along with special events and tours, may be important parts of both sales promotion and public relations programs. Displays include signage and booths, racks, and holders for promotional literature. Exhibits tend to be larger than displays; they may have moving parts, sound, or video and usually are staffed by a company representative. Booth exhibits are important at trade shows, where some companies may take orders for much of their annual sales.

Some brand communication tools, such as sales promotions, events, exhibits and displays, and brand clubs, are inherently more involving, particularly the ones that allow customers to have personal interaction with the brand.

Special Events and Tours Some companies stage events to get maximum publicity and generate positive attitudes toward the sponsors by celebrating milestones, such as key anniversaries and introductions of new products. A classic special event is the annual Macy's Thanksgiving Day parade, a tradition started in 1924. The event attracts more than 3.5 million people to watch it in New York City and more than 50 million viewers on television.[34] Corporate sponsorship of various sporting events like golf tournaments and car races has evolved into a favorite public relations tactic.

Steve Jobs, the late cofounder and CEO of Apple, was not only a master businessman; he was a showman without rival in his ability to create a frenzy around the launches of Apple's latest products, from Macintosh to the iPhone and iPad. Audiences eagerly anticipated the moment when he would go on stage to unveil the latest product.[35] Under the leadership of Jobs's successor, Tim Cook, these events have been transformed into showcases for corporate responsibility as well as news about new product introductions.[36]

Events can also be important for internal communication. Learning objectives and employee buy-in for a new campaign are often accomplished through meetings, seminars, and workshops sponsored by a company, typically in conjunction with training materials and other publications. To facilitate internal marketing, **town hall forums** are sometimes used. Forums provide management with an opportunity to make a presentation on some major project, initiative, or issue and invite employees to discuss it.

In addition to media tours, tours of all kinds are used in public relations programs, such as plant tours and trips by delegates and representatives. You are probably familiar with one form, the campus tour used by colleges in recruiting new students. Realizing the importance of these events, some colleges are hiring consulting companies to train the volunteer guides in appearance, presentation, and more relaxed "walks" designed to give a better sense of what makes a school distinctive.

Online Communication

Public relations practitioner and author Fraser Seitel says, "While those who predicted that the internet would change public relations thinking forever are wrong, it's still a 'relationship business'—seeking Internet outlets for publicity is an important complement to publicity in more traditional media."[37] Brand journalism, email, **intranets** (which connect people within an organization), **extranets** (which connect people in one business with its business partners), internet advertising and promotions, and websites and social media, such as blogs, Facebook, and Twitter, have opened up avenues for public relations activities.

Jason Cormier, cofounder of social media agency Room 214, points out that social media can be a useful tool in public relations because it stimulates word of mouth, which is one of the most powerful communication tools available to marketing communicators and particularly to public relations campaigns. Social media channels are powerful tools that magnify opportunities to spread the word about brands. Businesses like Room 214 offer a range of online monitoring and web-based business intelligence tools for gaining new insights about online conversations from blog and Twitter posts to online forums and mainstream media sites.

External Communication Corporate websites, which allow for communication directly between organizations and audiences, have become an important part of corporate communication. These sites can present information about the company and open up avenues of interactivity for stakeholders to contact the company and receive responses. Website newsrooms distribute a company's press releases to the media and other interested stakeholders.

A MATTER OF PRACTICE

APR: The Gold Standard

Kristin Ewing, *APR, Corporate Communications & Public Relations Specialist, Express Employment Professionals, Oklahoma City*

The Accredited in Public Relations (APR) credential was established in 1964 and is considered the gold standard for the profession of public relations. There are approximately 5,000 professionals worldwide with the APR credential. APRs are not only required to measure up to high standards of performance, to commit to continued education and give back to the industry, but more importantly, to be ethical.

Earning the APR is a challenging process. After earning my masters in marketing, communications, and advertising and with nearly a decade of work experience under my belt, I finally felt confident enough for the challenge. By submitting my application there was no turning back and it was time to focus, as you only have a year to earn your APR.

A year? You are thinking no problem; however, there are several steps required and if you don't accomplish a step the first time, you must wait a specified time before trying again. It can be a tad stressful. With the application submitted, it was time to focus on the first step—the readiness review panel.

The entire APR process focuses on KSAs— Knowledge, Skills, and Abilities. The three KSAs given the most importance are RPIE programs, ethics and law,

and communication models and theories. Those three KSAs account for more than half of what you will be tested on.

Prior to meeting with the panel, I had to submit answers to 16 questions. The first section of questions required me to take a close look at my current employer and my role there as well as my industry involvement. The second section focused on my professional experience. This section included one of my strategic communications plans. The third section was a personal assessment of how prepared I felt for the computer exam. The final document I submitted, including the strategic communications plan, was approximately 35 pages.

With the document submitted, I was off to meet with the panel consisting of three professionals who held the APR credential. No matter how confident you may be, it is a nerve-wracking experience. These professionals broke down every aspect of my answers and plan and proceeded to ask questions. The next morning I learned they had approved me to take the computer exam. One hurdle down, one to go.

Compared to the panel, the computer exam seemed easy, despite it taking four hours. The time between hitting the submit button and the results appearing on the screen felt as if it took twice as long as the exam. Finally, as I peered at the screen through my fingers, I saw the most glorious word possible— PASSED. I had done it. I could now be considered one of the best in the industry. Having those three letters behind your name may seem insignificant to those not in the industry, but those three letters are what I take the most pride in. The APR symbolizes tenacity, dedication, and professionalism. To learn more, visit www. praccreditation.org.

A graduate of the University of Nebraska–Lincoln advertising and public relations program, Ewing was nominated to be featured here by Professor Phyllis Larsen.

Internal Communication   Email is a great way for people at separate work sites to communicate. You can get a fast reply if people on the other end are checking their email regularly. It is also an inexpensive form of internal communication. Internal company email may have its public relations downside, however, in that it can be used in court. Some of the most damaging evidence that the federal government presented against Microsoft in its antitrust suit in 1998 came from email messages exchanged within the company.

Internal company networks have great benefits. Intranets and corporate portals (an extensive collection of databases and links that are important to people working in a company) encourage communication among employees in general and permit them to share data, such as customer records and client information. Some companies urge employees to set up personal home pages as part of the company portal, which allows them to customize the material they receive and set up their own links to crucial corporate information, such as competitor news, product information, and case histories.

3.4 Name and discuss what is trending in public relations.

What's Trending in Public Relations?

The public relations field is dynamic, presenting exciting opportunities for those pursuing careers in public relations. Aggregated from public relations publications,[38] watch for these trends, many of which are related to the impact of digital media on the practice of public relations:

1. Mobile communication will continue to grow as audiences access information increasingly on their smartphones.
2. Visual storytelling will be increasingly important, and news releases will include more visual content through infographics and videos and content that brand advocates can share across social media.
3. **Real-time marketing**, messages based on current events, will present opportunities to define brand personality, especially with the adoption of social media.
4. Educational video content will become more important, as research indicates that people don't want to be blatantly advertised to through videos.
5. Attempts to go viral will continue to try to get a crowd involved to replicate the success of other efforts, such as the ALS Ice Bucket Challenge.
6. Digital security will be a continuing concern as hacking endangers information collected through digital channels.
7. Twitter users (especially politicians and celebrities) need to become more sophisticated to avoid creating blunders that require public relations fixes.
8. Brand owners will continue to integrate their public relations, advertising, and marketing efforts to create one consistent voice.
9. The importance of social responsibility is paramount and will result in the increasing use of cause marketing to address challenging social and environmental issues. (Chapter 18 will cover social responsibility in greater depth.)
10. Measuring the effectiveness of public relations efforts continues to evolve, as traditional methods don't fit digital media.

Looking Ahead

In this chapter, we reviewed the practice of public relations as a fundamental discipline of integrated marketing communications. As you've seen, businesses and organizations have many ways to reach their publics and build positive images, reputations, and relationships for their brands. Chapter 4 will look at direct-response and promotions practices.

Running #LikeAGirl Wins Like a Champion

Earlier in this chapter, you read about the Always campaign. It won scads of awards, including the Silver Anvil Award from the Public Relations Society of America, the Cannes Grand Prix in the PR category, and an Outstanding Commercial Emmy, among other prizes. It's great to be recognized by peers for outstanding campaigns, but what really counts is the ability to reach business goals set by the client.

What makes a great PR campaign? It's the result of a great, well-executed idea that resonates with the consumer. How do we know that viewers connected with the message? Although measuring impact is sometimes hard to do, we can look at various indicators. Post-campaign research revealed that more than 80 percent of women age 16 to 24 viewed "like a girl" as a positive and inspiring statement. Initially, the video had 76 million total global views from 150 countries on YouTube. More than a million people shared the video. As of July 2017, the video had received more than 64 million views in the US. In addition, the campaign earned more than 1,880 media placements on influential media sites. The program received more than 290 million social impressions and 133,000 social mentions with #LikeAGirl. You'll learn more about what all this means in coming chapters.

Rob Reilly, Promo & Activation jury president at Cannes, summed up the victory for Always, which "took a stance on an issue and did a very good thing for young women, but is marketing at its finest. It sold a lot of product at the same time."[39] That's one way to stay ahead of the game and make a difference for your brand and your customers.

Logo: Courtesy The Procter & Gamble Company. Used with permission.

KEY OBJECTIVES SUMMARY

3.1. Explain what public relations is. Public relations is a strategic communication process that builds mutually beneficial relationships between organizations and their publics. Public relations aims to build goodwill, trust, and integrity for an organization or institution. Public relations professionals perform a wide range of functions that help an organization establish and maintain relationships with the people it touches.

3.2. Describe how public relations works. Practitioners in this field build relationships with a variety of publics. In addition to the key areas of government, media, employee, and investor relations, public relations programs also include corporate relations and reputation management, crisis management, public communication campaigns, and marketing public relations.

3.3. List common public relations tools and their functions. The public relations practitioner has many tools, classified in three categories: paid, owned, and earned media. These types reflect varying levels of credibility as well as control over the message and placements. The tools are used for advertising, media relations, publications, and a variety of other purposes. Online and external communication also aid in public relations programs.

3.4. Name and discuss what is trending in public relations. The public relations field is dynamic, presenting exciting opportunities for those pursuing careers in public relations. Some trends reflect the growing impact of digital on public relations, such as the increased use of mobile, real-time marketing, challenges in measuring the effectiveness of social media, and the security of information communicated online.

advocacy advertising, p. 78
annual report, p. 80
brand journalism, p. 70
cause marketing, p. 73
collateral material, p. 80
community relations, p. 73
consumer relations, p. 73
corporate advertising, p. 78
corporate identity advertising, p. 78
corporate image, p. 78
corporate relations, p. 73
corporate social responsibility, p. 74

crisis management, p. 74
earned media, p. 77
employee relations, p. 72
extranets, p. 82
feature stories, p. 80
financial relations, p. 72
fund-raising (or development), p. 74
gatekeepers, p. 70
goodwill, p. 67
house ad, p. 77
implied third-party endorsement, p. 70
internal marketing, p. 72
intranets, p. 82
issue management, p. 73
lobbying, p. 73

media kit, p. 80
media relations, p. 72
media tour, p. 80
news release, p. 79
news value, p. 79
nongovernment organizations (NGO), p. 71
opinion leaders, p. 67
owned media, p. 77
paid media, p. 77
pitch letter, p. 80
press conference, p. 80
public affairs, p. 73
public communication campaigns, p. 74
public opinion, p. 67
public relations, p. 66

public service announcements (PSAs), p. 78
publicity, p. 70
publics, p. 66
real-time marketing, p. 84
relationship marketing, p. 71
reputation management, p. 73
RPIE, p. 75
speakers' bureau, p. 81
stakeholders, p. 66
strategic philanthropy, p. 74
town hall forums, p. 82
video news releases, p. 80

MyLab Marketing

Go to **www.pearson.com/mylab/marketing** for MyLab discussion questions (⭐) as well as the following assisted-graded writing questions:

3-1. What is consumer relations, and what are the similarities to and differences from other forms of public relations, such as media relations and employee relations?

3-2. What is reputation management, and how does it intersect with advertising programs? Find a corporate reputation campaign and analyze its effectiveness.

3-3. Explain why public opinion is important to the success of public relations.

⭐ **3-4.** Compare and contrast the practice of advertising and the practice of public relations.

⭐ **3-5.** In analyzing public relations tools, compare the use of paid, owned, and earned media. Explain the difference between the three categories.

3-6. What are the primary tools of media relations?

3-7. What is the impact of digital and social media on public relations and IMC?

3-8. Why is public opinion so important to the success of public relations? In how many different ways does it affect the success of a program like the Always #LikeAGirl campaign?

3-9. In 2009, Oprah Winfrey suggested to her viewers that they could get a free meal at KFC if they printed out an internet coupon. Oprah's endorsement created demand from 4 million new customers that franchises couldn't meet. Is all publicity good publicity, or is this just a bad idea that hurt the client? Organize into a team, pick a point of view, and prepare to present it to your classmates. You might also propose how you would handle such a situation.

3-10. *Portfolio Project:* Identify a local organization that might benefit from a public relations plan. Study the organization's situation, identify a problem that can be addressed with public relations, and outline a plan to help the organization. Prepare your proposal in a three-page (maximum) paper.

⭐ **3-11.** *Mini-Case Analysis:* Study Häagen-Dazs's efforts to solve the problem of the disappearing honeybee colonies on its website. Look at the corporate social responsibility program on Ben & Jerry's website. Compare and contrast their efforts to be good corporate citizens.

TRACE North America Case

Multicultural Public Relations

Read the TRACE case in the Appendix before coming to class.

3-12. Reviewing the public relation tools in this chapter, identify at least two tools you could use effectively on a national basis to increase the impact of the "Hard to Explain, Easy to Experience" campaign.

4

Action and Interaction: Direct Response and Promotions

KEY OBJECTIVES

4.1 Identify the functions and key elements of direct-response communication.

4.2 Explain the importance of promotion.

4.3 Describe multiplatform promotions and explain how they are used.

4.4 Discuss databases and their importance to consumer and brand interaction.

The Katla Food's "Message in a Bottle" campaign is an example of an award-winning idea that reached a global market with a complex direct-response and promotion program. In this chapter, we will discuss the practice and process of direct-response communication and promotions: their functions and uses, the tools and media, and the principles of integrating direct response and promotions into the total brand communication effort. We'll start first with a review of direct-response communication.

MyLab Marketing

⭐ **Improve Your Grade!**

More than 10 million students improved their results using the Pearson MyLabs. Visit **www.pearson.com/mylab/marketing** for simulations, tutorials, and end-of-chapter problems.

Campaign

"A Message in a Bottle"

Organization

Katla Foods, Reykjavík, Iceland

Agency

H:N, Reykjavík, Iceland

Awards

IMARK: Best direct marketing piece in Iceland 2015

Fishing for Prospects around the Globe

Photos: Courtesy Ingvi Jökull Logason. Used with permission.

Pretend your assignment is to put together a strategic communication plan to market a shrimp bath cocktail that's used during the processing of raw shrimp. Your client is Katla Foods, one of three companies in Iceland that make this product. Your global business-to-business (B2B) market is some 200 shrimp processing companies in 12 countries.

So how do you reach this far-flung market with so many languages and locations? What communication tools are most appropriate for this campaign? Ingvi Logason, CEO of Iceland's award-winning agency H:N and member of this book's Advisory Board, explains in his own words how his agency solved this B2B problem.

You probably hadn't thought about it, but personal selling and dating have at least one thing in common: you only have one chance at a first impression. But how can you raise awareness and curiosity about your product and make sure your prospect will get a reminder of it in the weeks to come without becoming intrusive? By the way, you only have one chance, and your prospects are dispersed over six continents. No one said it would be easy.

One of our clients, Katla Food Inc., produces a very specific substance called *Katla AS One* for the shrimp and seafood industry—a billion-dollar market with relatively few large global manufacturers and a marketplace that is stretched around the globe.

Seafood and shrimp factories are often located in remote areas. Despite ever-improving transport and logistics, it is both costly and time consuming to pay them a visit. Shrimp is caught and processed in the far northern and southern regions—Greenland, Canada, Norway, Iceland, and the Faroe Islands, for example—as well as in Vietnam, Russia, and Chile. Finding prospects and making new business relationships through personal selling is therefore not an easy task and has its limitations, namely its cost.

Katla Food commissioned us to come up with creative solutions that would increase sales communication with possible prospects. Traditional ad campaigns were hindered by many languages and no trade media outlet (trade magazines, for example) that covered the broad geographic market. At the same time, the value of each possible sale for Katla Food was worth tens of millions of dollars. So, getting through and developing an advantage over the competition was very profitable.

The target market was well known, and we had the companies and the names of three to six decision makers within each company. We saw the challenge as a great opportunity to merge physical old-school direct mail with the in-depth capabilities and marketing options of newer digital marketing and personalized promotions. We designed an extremely trackable and traceable communication plan that gave us more touchpoints than previously available and that delivered a clear advantage over our competition.

So how did we do it?

Corks and Cocktails

We created a very simple-looking, but curious and elaborate, direct mail: a message in a bottle. The package was delivered by trackable carrier. The cork on that bottle was a USB stick carrying a digital message that drove the recipient to a microwebsite that was tailored to each region's primary language. Each USB had a unique code so that we knew when the "message" had been received—or if it was not received at all. From the microsite, users were led to Katla Food's website for more in-depth information.

Within three days from delivery of the direct mail, we followed up that contact with a phone call. The mailing piece was a great conversation starter and lead-in for product-driven sales conversation. That was true for all recipients, regardless of their interaction with the message.

At that point, the majority of all recipients had opened and interacted digitally with the mail, thus acquiring a deeper understanding of our unique selling points. But that meant that we also had the option of following up—we called it remarketing—through the Google Display Network (a personally targeted advertising system) with tailor-made messages (depending on how deep individuals experienced our message) to those who had seen any of our sites.

Usually we started the remarketing tactics about seven days after the phone call and ran it periodically over six to eight months. Within that timeframe, we could make a third follow-up call and schedule a sales meeting at the prospect's location. We also use sales promotion where we sit down with prospects at Katla Food's booth at key trade shows.

These interactions eventually lead to scheduling a visit with tailor-made demonstrations. The way the demos work is that a Katla sales representative and a prospect negotiate a contract. If the negotiation goes well and a contract is ready for signing, a demo cocktail is constructed and implemented to process a "batch" of shrimp. This test is a very costly proof of the product and concept for both buyer and seller. It is also a very important step because buyers don't want to risk a full season of production without proof that the cocktail works.

Each cocktail has to be adjusted and tailored to a specific production company over a period of few days. So, it is not a demo given away on a whim but a personalized demo designed only for clients on the verge of signing a lucrative contract. And the demo is an equal commitment by the client.

The lesson here is simple: Don't give up on old school methods. Enlarge them with new technology. In this case, combining the personal touch of physical direct mail with the options of online marketing and personalized demonstrations was the strategic magic. The totality of the idea has yielded positive results: the campaign has been running for three years now and is the focal point of all new business in the seafood industry for Katla Food.

We'll tell you more about the effectiveness of this case in the It's a Wrap conclusion at the end of this chapter.

Source: Case study written and provided by Ingvi Logason, September 2016.

Functions and Elements of Direct-Response Communication

4.1 Identify the functions and key elements of direct-response communication.

Direct-response communication (DRC) makes personal interaction between an organization and its customers or members possible. That interaction may deliver action, such as donating to a nonprofit organization (NGO), buying a product, or signing up for an activity. Because the response can be immediate, DRC makes it is easy to tell quickly if messages are meeting their objectives. In other words, unlike mass media advertising and public relations with their delayed effects, the effects of DRC are more immediate and more easily measured.

Because direct-response messaging can be designed to motivate an immediate sales response, it is also called **direct-response marketing**. We define direct-response marketing as a multichannel business practice that uses a variety of media to connect a company with customers and prospects who deal with each other directly (rather than through an intermediary, such as a wholesaler or retailer). Founded in 1917, the Direct Marketing Association is the professional association for this type of marketing.

The common thread that runs through all types of direct response is that of action. DRC is used by business and nonprofit organizations to reach important audiences with messages that encourage them to respond in some way, such as a purchase. NGOs use DRC to generate donations, memberships, and volunteers.

Another important function of DRC is to open opportunities for interactivity. Why is that important? Interactivity—two-way communication—is considered to be the most persuasive form of communication. It also drives engaging, relationship-building contacts that can lead to brand loyalty and repeated action.

Some managers see direct response as more limiting than brand or image advertising because it doesn't reach as many people, or if it does, the cost of reaching each individual is higher per impression. Proponents justify the higher costs by noting that action is a highly desired goal and probably the hardest impact to achieve—particularly in comparison to building awareness, which is usually the goal of advertising. As the Katla Foods story illustrated, today's digital and mobile media dramatically reduce the cost of message delivery, making DRC more efficient as well as effective.

Who Are the Key Players?

The main players in direct-response communication are (1) businesses such as Katla Foods and NGOs that use direct response to sell products or services or solicit participation; (2) agencies that produce DRC, such as Iceland's H:N; and (3) phone, mail, or internet media that deliver messages. Of course, the people who are the recipients of the information and sometimes initiators of the contact are also partners in the communication effort.

Traditionally, the types of companies that have made the greatest use of direct marketing have been book and record clubs, publishers, airlines and cruise lines, hotels, insurance companies, sellers of collectibles, gardening firms, and e-marketers, such as Amazon.com. Almost all nonprofit organizations, from university alumni groups to the United Way, use DRC for membership drives, fund-raising, soliciting volunteers, and promoting special events. B2B businesses such as Katla Foods also employ the tools of direct communication in their trade communication programs.

The four types of firms in the direct-response industry include advertising agencies, independent direct-marketing agencies, service firms, and fulfillment houses.

- *Advertising Agencies* Most major agencies whose main business is mass media advertising either have a department that specializes in direct response or own a separate direct-response company.
- *Direct-Marketing Agencies* Independent direct-marketing agencies create the DRC messages, arrange for their delivery to a target audience, and evaluate the results.
- *Service Firms* Service firms specialize in printing, mailing, list brokering, and data management.
- *Fulfillment Houses* Fulfillment houses are responsible for making sure that consumers receive whatever they request in a timely manner, be it a catalog, additional information, or the product itself.

In terms of media, there are thousands of telemarketing and web marketing firms that handle contact with consumers as well as a variety of other more traditional media companies. One of the most active direct-mail media organizations, for example, is the US Postal Service. We'll discuss these tools later in the section on DRC media.

Key Elements of DRC

Like a conversation, there are two sides to direct response. First, DRC involves communication sent in some form directly to the prospect. Second, the response (sales, sign-up, request for information, donation) comes directly back to the organization. Like a conversation, the original respondent can also initiate the conversation as well as respond.

As noted in Figure 4.1, direct response uses market research to guide strategy and databases to better identify prospects. A variety of media are available to deliver messages to and from a prospect. The initial contact hopes to elicit an immediate response, and it invites prospects to contact the organization. Because it's interactive, DRC also helps marcom planners listen to what people are saying as they respond.

The key elements of DRC are the offer and its response, the communication package that contains and delivers the message, testing and analysis of the effectiveness of the pieces of the package, and, finally, fulfillment of the order or follow-up on the response. Let's consider these elements in more detail.

All direct-marketing messages contain an **offer**, typically consisting of a description of the proposition (terms of sale, delivery, warranty information, membership, donation request) and

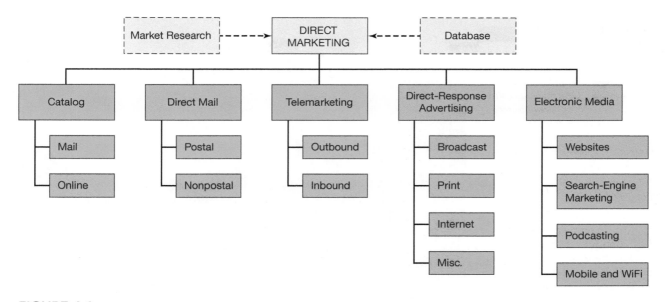

FIGURE 4.1
The Direct-Response Industry
Direct response begins with research and database development. The main tools of DRC are catalogs, direct mail, telemarketing, direct-response advertising, the internet, and other forms of social media.

its cost. In the offer, a successful message must communicate benefits by answering the enduring question, "What's in it for me?" Many DRC offers also include an incentive to respond quickly because organizations know that the longer people think about an offer, the less likely they will respond.

To maximize the response, the DRC message must make it as easy as possible for customers to respond. One way to do that is to offer a variety of ways to respond, such as online, mail, phone, and text. When customers respond, it is important that the company immediately acknowledge the response, thanking the customer for the order and advising when the product will arrive.

Similar to the steps in the sales process, the DRC message must move the reader from generating interest to creating conviction and inducing a sale. In mail media, it's all done with a strong offer conveyed through a complex package of printed pieces usually consisting of an outer envelope, a letter, a brochure, supplemental flyers or folders, and a reply card with a return envelope. Electronic versions of these pieces can also be seen in online appeals. As the Showcase story illustrates, a well-designed envelope (or opening screen shot online) is critical in grabbing the attention of readers and viewers to persuade them to open the piece.

The letter, brochure, or flyer (what's inside the envelope) is also a challenging element and therefore the focus of much research. Many techniques have proven effective in getting consumers to read a direct-response piece. Here are some tips: grab attention or generate curiosity with strong words and graphics, send a message to the right person, make it relevant and personal, and test everything.

The secret behind effective direct response lies in testing, both pretesting and posttesting. Offers are tested for the strength of their appeal, and materials are tested to evaluate attractiveness and impact. In posttesting, scale of the response is important because enough pieces need to be sent using various strategies to determine which techniques or versions (e.g., copy, visuals, offers) increase the response and which don't make a difference. By employing such measurement tools as tracking printed codes on responses that identify different offers, the organization can clearly identify those offers that are most attractive to different prospects.

The goal of the **fulfillment** operation is to respond quickly to customers' responses by getting the product (membership card, etc.) to those who respond. Fulfillment includes all the back-end activities of processing the transaction or interaction.

This envelope is used by the Billings Chamber of Commerce/ Convention and Visitors Bureau to send information about visitor, tourism, and relocation opportunities. It reinforces a new brand identity campaign, described in Chapter 1, and carries the campaign's "Trailhead" logo and slogan as well as the "explore" graphics.

The Billings, Montana, "Trailhead" brand identity campaign was provided by John Brewer, president and CEO of the Billings Chamber of Commerce/Convention and Visitors Bureau. An advertising graduate of the University of West Florida, Brewer was nominated to be featured here by Professor Tom Groth.

Photo: Courtesy Billings Chamber of Commerce/Convention and Visitors' Bureau.

● **Principle**

Marketers use interactive media forms to talk directly with, rather than at, customers and other stakeholders, thus creating higher levels of customer engagement.

What Are the Primary Media of DRC?

We'll review a number of the tools and media used in DRC, but we'll start with personal sales, the most involving and persuasive of all the DRC tools.

Personal Sales   Personal sales is the earliest and most effective—and also most expensive—form of direct marketing. Salespeople are found in stores, they make phone calls, and they call on business prospects. Personal sales are also found in home parties—the original form of social networking sales—which are sponsored by such companies as Mary Kay and Tupperware.

Fuller Brush, for example, is a cleaning products company founded in 1906 and known in its heyday for its small army of door-to-door salespeople. The Fuller Brush Man was a business icon, one that left its mark on popular culture with mentions in songs and appearances in movies and television shows. But times change, and the firm is now owned by Victory Park Capital, although its products will continue to be distributed online and through select retailers, such as Home Depot.[1] Its real contribution to business history, however, lies with its personal communication strategy that was memorialized in its "Ask the Fuller Brush Man" slogan.

Avon is one of the biggest direct-sales companies, with its millions of sales representatives and some $6 billion in revenue.[2] Amway's $8.8 billion in sales reflects its strong position in Latin America and Asia, where the personal sales opportunities are attractive to moonlighters and entrepreneurs.[3] But nothing in the direct-selling industry can compare with Holly Chen, a tiny Taiwanese woman who is a megastar for Amway. One of the most prolific salespeople on Earth, Chen motivates her multilevel commission-based network of thousands of salespeople with emotional presentations of her personal story.

Beyond personal sales, direct marketing employs five primary media tools to achieve its objectives: (1) direct mail, (2) catalogs, (3) direct-response advertising, (4) telemarketing, and (5) online e-marketing. All these forms offer an opportunity for in-depth information, and they all call for action.

Direct Mail   **Direct mail** is communication for a product, service, or nonprofit organization that is addressable, meaning that it can be delivered by mail or electronically to a specific person or business. If it is direct marketing or mail order, it allows business to be conducted between a firm and a customer without a middleman, such as a retailer. (Note: Direct mail is a form of communication, and mail order is a type of business model.)

Historically, the development of direct mail was a product of two innovations: the invention of movable type by Gutenberg in the mid-1400s, which made printing in quantity economically feasible, and the development of postal service. The 1700s saw the beginnings of direct response in the United States with William Penn publishing a pamphlet enticing Europeans to emigrate to Pennsylvania. Benjamin Franklin was appointed first US Postmaster General in 1775.

Most direct mail is sent using a third-class bulk mail permit, which requires a minimum of 200 identical pieces. The response rate for direct mail can vary, but it's typically in the 2 to 3 percent range. Because of the high level of nonresponse, direct mail is also a fairly costly tool in terms of cost per impression. However, it also is much easier to calculate the actual payout rate; that is, at what point do the returns on the investment begin to exceed the costs? That's why direct mail is considered more accountable than other forms of marketing communication.

Inside the envelope, the design of the direct-mail piece or pieces is important in getting the information read. Ideas about the creative use of direct mail are offered in the Inside Story. As Michael Dattolico, the designer, explained, "A synergistic message and visual can go a long way toward achieving your result." That's true with online messages as well as print.

The technology of the internet also has produced dramatic changes in the direct-mail industry. Much internet advertising is simply direct marketing in electronic form: emails are just another kind of "letter." The internet has made it easy to produce and distribute traditional direct mail by email. Email marketing software and advertising assistance are available from such companies as Constant Contact (www.constantcontact.com), which provide email templates.

Source: Courtesy Fuller Brush Company.

CLASSIC

"Dear Fuller Brush Man, I have a hard time reaching into the shower to clean it. What do you have that will make this job easier?" Sara from NC

The popular "Ask the Fuller Brush Man" feature, which draws on a century of door-to-door sales, continues to answer consumer cleaning questions as an important feature on the brand's "Ask" website.

Photo: Bygone Collection/Alamy Stock photo

Photo: Roger Tidman/Getty Images

It wasn't until 1863 when free postal delivery to cities began (the image on the left is from around 1908) and 1896 when service was brought to rural areas such as Ochopee, Florida, which still exists and is the smallest post office in the United States.

Thinking Outside the Mailbox

Michael Dattolico, *Musion Creative Marketing Agency, LLC*

The client, Microflex, Inc., has proven to be an innovative leader in US metal part manufacturing since 1975. Recently, it individually branded its automotive division, emphasizing the company's specialization in automotive parts. The majority of Microflex's marketing efforts focused on introducing this new branding (i.e., division of the company) and offering specific distinction over the competition and the company's dedication to the automotive industry.

The objective of this campaign was to introduce and reinforce awareness of the company's automotive specialization to current clients and to emphasize its experience and new facility dedicated to automotive parts. Although the campaign was originally intended for current clients, forethought was put in to make it a stand-alone piece for future leads gathered through internet sales or trade show follow-ups.

After doing market research, it was clear how to make this new division stand above the competition. The company focused on establishing its experience (although Microflex was newly branding this division individually, the company still had the years of

experience to back it up) and emphasizing its capabilities. Further research showed a distinct breakdown of capabilities among the competition, so it was easy to follow that as a guide and focus on Microflex's superior design, testing and development, manufacturing, and support.

At the agency, we used an attention-getting format—a double gatefold (which means both the inside front cover and the inside back cover fold out)—to draw the viewer to some dramatic visual cues as well as anticipate the flow of information to the viewer. We also viewed the dramatic opening of the brochure as an emphasis on the new chapter in the company's history: opening its doors on a 120,000-square-foot manufacturing facility dedicated to the automotive division.

The intense visuals, the folding path that leads readers through to the major content, and targeted copy focusing on establishing the company's new dedication to the automotive industry as well as the selling points above the competition all made this a powerful, effective direct-mail piece.

Owner of his own design studio, Musion Creative, LLC (www.musioncreative.com), Dattolico graduated from the advertising program at the University of Florida, where he was a student of Professor Elaine Wagner, and from a creative advertising program in England at University College Falmouth.

Photo: Courtesy Microflex Industries/Michael Dattalico

Another critical element in direct mail is the mailing list. Lists of customers, prospects, donors, volunteers, and other stakeholders engaged with an organization are built, updated, and employed to generate action and interaction. Of course, contact information is essential to direct-response programs. You have to know how to reach prospects—by mail, phone, or email—if you want to deliver a message. Promotions, such as events and loyalty programs, are often used to capure this information and build lists of participants. There are three types of lists:

- A **house list** is made up of the marketer's own customers or members, which is its most important target market and the most valuable list. These names often come from warranty cards.
- A **response list** is made up of people or households who have responded to some type of direct-response offer or promotion. The more similar the product to which they responded (dog food) is to the marketer's product (pet toys), the more valuable the list because these people should be similar to the company's current customers.

- A **compiled list** is a list of some specific category, such as association members or donors, sports car owners, new home buyers, graduating seniors, new mothers, or subscribers to a magazine, book club, or record club.

For example, you may want to develop a list of people who are in the market for fine furniture in your city. You could buy a list of new home buyers and combine that with a list of people who live in a desirable census tract. These two lists together—a compiled list—would let you find people who have bought new homes in upscale neighborhoods.

Issues and Ethics: Trees, Water, and Waste   Critics of direct mail cite its environmental impact. Production of direct mail uses millions of trees and billions of gallons of water annually.[4] And untold millions of dollars are spent for disposal and recycling.

Is there a need to ban direct mail? Consider local mailings. What would be the impact of such a ban on your local pizza restaurant, video store, or hair salon, which might rely on direct-mail offers? Do the waste and irritation factor of "junk mail" justify a ban on this form of marketing communication? On the other hand, might banning direct mail infringe on an organization's right to commercial free speech? What's fair, what's right, and what's a responsible organization to do?

Catalogs   A **catalog** is a multipage (in print) direct-mail publication that shows a variety of merchandise. Following the explosion of digital media, however, catalogs have also evolved into easy-to-use online publications with immense offerings, such as the Pigalog mail and online catalog published by New Pig, the B2B company featured in the Chapter 1 opening story.

Aaron Montgomery Ward was a direct-mail visionary who began his mail-order business in 1872 with a one-page catalog.[5] He made it possible for people to buy products without going through local retailers with their usually limited selection, particularly in rural towns. Richard Sears followed with his famous Sears catalogs that began in 1888 with a line of watches. In 1894, the offerings were expanded to include sewing machines, bicycles, saddles, musical instruments, and a host of new items. In 1896, the slogan "Cheapest Supply House on Earth" was added to the cover. For more on the history of this iconic catlog, visit www.searsarchives.com.

Like New Pig's Pigalog catalog, the growth is in specialty catalogs aimed at niche markets serving every business category, hobby, and interest. One of the most interesting catalogs is the Neiman Marcus Christmas Book, which features highly expensive fantasy gifts, such as a $250,000 two-seater plane complete with flying lessons, a $10 million Zeppelin, and a $10 million stable of racehorses.

Many large retailers are now multichannel, using catalogs, websites, and stores. Some catalog retailers have their own stores, such as Williams-Sonoma and Tiffany's. LL Bean also uses its catalog mailings to drive business to its websites. It expects that its online sales will soon overtake its catalog business, but it will still send out catalogs as a way to generate online sales.

A number of marketers use video or CD catalogs because they provide more information and because the message can be interactive and feature animated

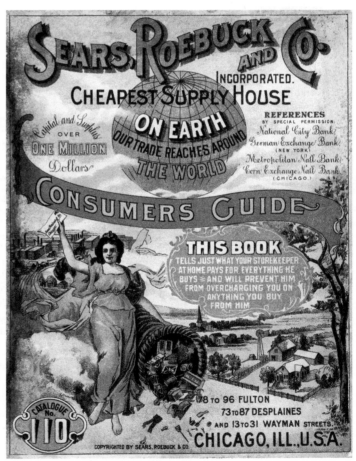

Photo: Bettmann/Contributor/Getty Images

CLASSIC

For most of its life, the Sears catalog was sent to homes via the US Postal Service, and shoppers could order directly from the "Wish Book" with their merchandise also delivered to them by mail. Some surprising offerings included the Sears motor buggy, sold from 1909 to 1912, and some 75,000 mail-order houses that Sears sold from its catalogs from 1908 to 1940.

Photo: Courtesy Microflex Industries/Michael Dattalico

SHOWCASE

This CD cover designed by Michael Dattolico for his client Microflex, a B2B company in the automotive industry.

Owner of his own design studio, Musion Creative, LLC (www .musioncreative.com), Dattolico graduated from the advertising program at the University of Florida, where he was a student of Professor Elaine Wagner, and from a creative advertising program in England at University College Falmouth.

illustrations. In the Inside Story, we saw the Microflex direct-mail design by Michael Dattolico. Here is an example of a CD design for that same client.

Direct marketers saw the internet's potential early. Actually, direct marketing—particularly catalog marketing—is the model for e-commerce. Amazon.com is the leader of the pack. Amazon.com's website, for example, operates like a direct-mail catalog, but interactivity and its unlimited breadth make it more useful than a print version.

Direct-Response Advertising   Direct-response advertising uses a variety of print, broadcast, and online media to deliver its offers. Even though they are mass media, ads in newspapers and magazines can carry a coupon, an order form, an online address, or a toll-free phone number, which make a direct response possible. In some cases, the desired response is a purchase, but it can also be an inquiry that becomes a sales lead for sales representatives or some other kind of follow-up contact.

A classic example of the power of direct-response advertising is the "97-Pound Weakling" ads for the Charles Atlas body-building mail-order courses. These ads featured a cartoon telling the story of a scrawny guy who decides to bulk up after a well-built lifeguard kicks sand in his face and steals his girlfriend. The business launched in 1928 when Atlas partnered with adman Charles Roman to promote the Charles Atlas exercise system and correspondence course. The campaign created a multi-million-dollar business, and the "97-pound weakling" who turned into a "he-man" became a pop-culture icon.

A direct-response commercial on radio or television can provide the necessary information (usually a simple, easy-to-remember toll-free phone number or web address) for the consumer to contact an organization. Direct-response advertising on television used to be the province of late-night television, with pitches for screwdrivers guaranteed to last a lifetime. As more national marketers move into the medium, the direct-response commercial is becoming more general in appeal, selling clothes and health products as well as insurance and financial services. The latest is the move into online or web-based advertising, which is often created using the techniques of such do-it-yourself media as YouTube, Pinterest, or Instagram. The Showcase feature describes how one production person found props for a light-hearted commercial for Microsoft's Bing.

Direct-response television also makes good use of **infomercials**, which have been around since the emergence of the cable industry (think Vegematics) and have become a multi-billion-dollar industry. Infomercials made George Foreman a marketing superstar. Marketers use the infomercial format if the product needs to be demonstrated, is not readily available through retail outlets, or has a relatively high profit margin. Cable television works for companies such as QVC because the medium is more tightly targeted to particular interests.

Telemarketing   Before telemarketing calls were limited by government-supported do-not-call lists, more direct-marketing dollars were spent on **telemarketing** phone calls than on any other DRC medium. That's because telemarketing is a form of personal sales but is a lot less expensive than the other forms. An in-person sales call may cost anywhere from $50 to $1,000 after factoring in time and transportation. In comparison, a telemarketing call ranges from $2 to

Basketball, Dolls, and Cat Outfits. March Really Is Madness

Nathan Folbrecht, *Integrated Producer, Digital Experience, Intel (formerly Producer, CP+B, Boulder)*

I was making my way through the normal responsibilities of a new Crispin Porter & Bogusky employee (a lot of expenses, coffee runs, and hard drive shipping) when I was suddenly entrusted with the task of helping find props for a Microsoft BING shoot. Naturally, I was thrilled. The general idea was having two puppets act as sports broadcasters for the NCAA March Madness.

A lot of the props were easy (tape, string, basketballs, etc.). However, others were much tougher, specifically cheerleading outfits and a Cinderella Dress. Feeling the pressure to succeed with my newly requested duty, I had to be creative about where to find these outfits, as our shoot was the next day (and there aren't many puppet clothing shops in Boulder). After exhausting my options at Toys-R-Us, while looking like a creep taking clothes off the dolls to see if they would fit a puppet, and Macy's, while asking for baby cheerleading outfits from the sweet, elderly lady, I was about to give up. Luckily, I thought of one last avenue to explore, PetSmart. As the doors opened to the retail chain, I realized that my commitment to not giving up, getting creative, and finding a solution had paid off. I walked out with an abundance of cat/puppet fashion.

As I marched back into the CP+B office, with my head and animal outfits held high, I realized that being a "good" producer is often determined by how well one can handle strange, uncomfortable situations. Whether a celebrity breaks his or her leg on a multi-million-dollar broadcast shoot or you need to explore most of

Photo: Courtesy Nathan Folbrecht and Crispin Porter & Bogusky. Used with permission.

Colorado for a puppet Cinderella Dress, fire drills will inevitably pop up. Handling them with a calm demeanor while always looking for solutions will be invaluable.

A graduate of the advertising program at the University of Colorado Boulder, Folbrecht was nominated to be featured here by Professor William Weintraub.

$15 per call. That is still expensive if you compare it to mass media advertising ($10 to $50 per thousand contacts), but the returns are much higher than those generated by mass advertising because they are more personalized and interactive.

A telemarketing campaign usually involves hiring a telemarketing company to make a certain number of calls using a prepared script. The callers work in **call centers**, rooms with large banks of phones and computers. Most calls are made from databases of prospects who were previously qualified on some factor, such as an interest in a related product or a particular profile of demographics and psychographics. Occasionally, a **cold call** (a term from personal sales) is used, which in this case means that the call center staff are calling random numbers, a practice that has a much lower response rate than calling previously qualified prospects. Perhaps the most universally despised telemarketing tool is **predictive dialing**, which makes it possible for telemarketing companies to call anyone using random dialing, even those with unlisted numbers. Many people consider these calls a nuisance.

There are two types of telemarketing: inbound and outbound. An **inbound telemarketing** call is initiated by a customer usually after seeing some other message. An **outbound**

Photo: ImagesBazaar/Getty Images

Call centers are large rooms with multiple stations for staff who make the calls (outbound) or answer calls from people placing orders (inbound).

telemarketing call originates from the firm. These calls typically generate the most consumer resistance because they are uninvited, intrusive, and unexpected.

Telemarketing messages need to be simple enough to be delivered over the telephone and be short; most people won't stay on the telephone longer than two to three minutes for a sales call. If the product requires a visual demonstration or a complicated explanation, the message might be better delivered by direct mail or online. The message also must be compelling. People resent intrusive telephone calls, so there must be a strong initial benefit to convince prospects to continue listening.

Issues and Ethics: Intrusion and Fraud
Telemarketing's reputation has been tarnished by fraudulent behavior, such as convincing consumers that they need some kind of financial or credit protection that they don't really need or enticing consumers to buy something by promising them prizes that are later discovered to be worthless. In response to these abuses, the Federal Trade Commission (FTC) enacted a regulation to protect consumers by imposing strict informational disclosure requirements and prohibiting misrepresentative or misleading statements.

The most serious restriction on telemarketing—a program that consumers love—is implemented by state and national do-not-call lists. The national Do Not Call Registry opened on June 27, 2003, and by July 27, 2010, 200 million numbers had been listed according to the FTC.[6] Telemarketing companies responded by challenging the legality of these lists based on what they believe to be an illegal restriction on commercial free speech. In 2004, however, the US Supreme Court let stand a lower-court ruling that the industry's free speech rights were not violated by the do-not-call list.

The do-not-call lists do not restrict companies from calling their own customers. They also allow nonprofit organizations to continue calling and market research firms to continue conducting phone surveys. Telemarketers subscribe to the database and check the list at least monthly for numbers they need to delete.

Internet Direct Response The most exciting advances in internet direct response are found in the areas of mobile marketing and social media. With mobile phones, marketers are also able to meet people "where they are," or, as a *Wall Street Journal* article explained, business owners can "meet their customers wherever their habits take them and integrate into that behavior."[7]

Social selling, also known as *network marketing*, utilizes the reach and persuasiveness of social media and its endless and continuous conversations. Network marketing has always been used in word-of-mouth campaigns enlisting friendship groups. The difference is that with social media, that network can include hundreds of Facebook and Twitter followers. The network can grow exponentially as messages zing through cyberspace.

Issues and Ethics: Spam Although email marketing has enjoyed increased success, the practice has received intense criticism for generating too much unwanted email, otherwise known as **spam**. But the problem is more than frequency. The FTC has determined that 90 percent of all spam involving business and investment opportunities as well as health products and travel contains false or misleading information. That is why Congress passed the CAN-SPAM Act in 2003.

Is spam cost effective? A spammer might send out 100,000 emails and get only two to five clients, which seems like a totally unacceptable number of responses. But a spammer who charges $300 to send out 100,000 messages or $900 for a million messages might make $14,000 to $15,000 on those few responses. That's not a bad return when you consider the cost of getting into the business—a computer and an internet connection.

Because spam is a huge problem for legitimate email marketers, many are now using an approach called **permission marketing**, which asks prospects for permission to send them email. There are two permission-marketing strategies for consumers to use to control their inclusion on lists. **Opt in** means that all bulk mailers have to get your permission before sending a promotion. Legitimate direct marketers use this permission form, which is tougher for spammers to abuse and more sensitive to consumer rage when they do. The concept at the heart of permission marketing is that every customer who opts in to a campaign is a qualified lead. **Opt out** means that emailers can send the first email but must give recipients the means to refuse any further emails from that business.

Direct-response marketing communication is an important tool in the IMC tool kit because it is uniquely designed to deliver action and interactivity. It is also important because of its ability to track effectiveness. Let's consider next the various ways people are engaged in brand experiences through promotions, another IMC area that also can deliver action and interactivity as well as measurable impact.

The Importance of Promotion

4.2 Explain the importance of promotion.

Promotion is about the fun, creative, and attention-getting ideas that the promotion industry uses to spur action and build strong brand relationships. Promotions build excitement for causes such as the Pink Ribbon but also for marketing events. Another example comes from a classic car event in Detroit where billboards were used to support the Chevy brand image.

Similar to direct-response communication, promotions engage customers and prospects on a personal level and encourage action. Promotions are used in marketing-oriented programs to build demand and stimulate immediate action and in public relations programs to create excitement and participation. An organization can increase the value of its brand by offering something special, such as an engaging sale or an extra incentive to purchase or affiliate with the organization.

The professional sales promotion industry, with annual revenues of about $12 billion, is estimated to include some 8,000 companies representing advertising and marketing firms that specialize in sales promotion. The Promotion Marketing Association is the professional organization that includes not only the professional companies but also marketers who use sales promotion. Founded in 1911, the organization promotes excellence in promotion marketing and showcases best practices in its Reggie Awards program.

A simple definition of **sales promotion** is activities and communication programs that build excitement in the market for a limited period of time to stimulate trial, increase consumer demand, or improve product availability. This definition recognizes that sales promotion is a set of techniques that prompts members of three audiences—consumers, sales representatives, and the trade (distributors,

Photo: Courtesy General Motors Media Archive

These three billboards were posted during an annual classic car event in Detroit. The series of billboards with their dramatic images and quirky headlines celebrates the history of GM's iconic Chevy brand. Their purpose was more event sponsorship than traditional brand advertising.

A Cross-Country Production for Best Buy

Nathan Folbrecht, *Integrated Producer, Digital Experience at Intel Corporation, San Francisco*

For a past Best Buy "Hinting Season" Production, our team was asked to surprise people around the country with gifts they had asked for via Twitter. We did six cities (Los Angeles, Fresno, Nashville, Lynchburg, Atlanta, and Brooklyn) in 13 days and had to do some crazy stuff (send in scouts at midnight to make sure the recipients were home, be covert with our caravan of five minivans and walkie-talkies to make sure we were all ready to move, set up the gifts at the same time, etc.), and everyone in our scrappy crew realized that we'd need to be willing to help with any and all tasks (creative directors helping wrap boxes, for example) to make the project a success. We recently won a Shorty Award for "Best in E-Commerce and Retail."

A graduate of the advertising program at the University of Colorado, Boulder, Folbrecht was nominated to be featured here by Professor William Weintraub.

Photos (top to bottom): Courtesy Nathan Folbrecht; Courtesy Best Buy; Courtesy Nathan Folbrecht

retailers, and dealers)—to take action. Simply put, sales promotion affects demand by making the brand more attractive or interesting.

Another traditional technique is to offer an incentive to act—a reward—sometimes in the form of price reductions, but incentives may also be additional amounts of the product, cash, prizes, and gifts, coupons, rebates, premiums, and so on. An example of a promotional reward was a $1 million offer by Netflix to consumers who could offer ideas for improving its movie recommendation production software. An example of an unusual incentive program was the delivery of Best Buy gifts during the pre-Christmas "hinting season" as described in the Showcase feature. The photo shows the producer, Nathan Folbrecht, setting up a screen shot for the online promotion.

Marketplace Changes

Before the 1980s, advertising was the dominant player in the marketing communication arena. During the 1980s, however, more marketers found themselves driving immediate bottom-line responses through the use of sales promotion.

Accountability is one reason. Similar to direct response communication, promotion delivers quick results that are easy to measure. Arlene Gerwin, a marketing expert who consults on promotional planning, explained, "Sales promotions deliver more immediate consumer response and a quicker payback than advertising." In Gerwin's view, it is relatively easy and quick to evaluate success because there is usually an immediate and measurable response of some kind.[8]

Other reasons for the move to sales promotion match changes in the marketplace; for example, consumers are less brand loyal and more willing to switch, particularly for a parity (largely undifferentiated) product. Also, dominant retailers such as Walmart demand promotional support for the products they carry and incentives for making shelf space available. Organizations are therefore exploring marketing communication forms that cost less and produce these immediate, tangible results. The proliferation of digital media and other new and novel media (see the Heinz bean promotion) has also made that goal easier to reach.

Promotional Big Ideas

Promotion planning and design is a highly creative area. Promotional plans start with a creative idea; in fact, a Big Idea such as Katla's message in a bottle is just as important for sales promotion as it is for advertising. In many cases, the promotion is part of a bigger IMC plan, and one of the requirements is that the promotion's Big Idea should support the campaign's creative idea. For example, Frontier Airlines' long-running position as "a different kind of animal" was reflected in a short-term promotional campaign to choose a favorite animal from the spokes-animals on the planes' tails.

The challenge is to come up with exciting, interesting promotional ideas that are involving and that capture the attention of the market while at the same time remaining true to the brand strategy. This challenge to be engaging as well as effective in terms of business results includes consumer as well as trade promotions.

Photo: Courtesy Kraft Heinz Company. Used with permission

An example of a novel promotional medium is the Heinz "personalized bean" social media promotion designed by UK-based We Are Social to launch the brand's new five-bean variety, Five Beanz. A contest based on a "Bean Personality" quiz let fans determine whether they're a pinto, red kidney, cannellini, haricot, or borlotti, which then enters them in a drawing. The 1,440 winners received their favorite bean engraved with their name.

The Functions of Promotion

As part of an integrated program, sales promotion has different functions than other marcom tools. Marketing consultant Gerwin explained: "The objective of advertising is quite different from that of sales promotion. Over time, advertising builds brand equity by establishing a consistent image or feeling for a brand." In contrast, she said, "Sales promotions are more immediate, involving a finite time period." In return for taking action, "sales promotions offer the consumer something more tangible."[9]

Promotions are often used with a new product launch to stimulate trial. Sales promotions can increase brand awareness and generate product trial as well as persuade consumers to buy the product again once they've tried it. It can push the product through the distribution channel by generating positive brand experiences among resellers and buyers in many places along the channel-and-purchase continuum. Promotions are also good at building traffic for a retailer. J.C. Penney, for example, has used free back-to-school haircuts for kids as part of its back-to-school promotion, which is a key selling period for the family retailer.[10]

Promotions are not effective in achieving all marketing objectives. For example, promotions cannot do much to change negative attitudes toward a product, overcome product problems, or reposition a brand in the minds of consumers. Brand building, however, is an interesting challenge, and promotional programs need to be designed to complement the brand's overall communication strategy. The most common sales promotion strategies are designed to motivate action among three audiences: consumer, trade, and sales force. The first two—consumer sales and trade support—have direct implications for marketing communication because many campaigns have separate message strategies for consumers or trade partners.

The third category, sales force promotions, is also important in building trade support. Two types of promotional activities are directed at the firm's salespeople to motivate them to increase and improve their sales performance. The first set of activities includes programs that better prepare salespeople to do their jobs, such as sales manuals, training programs, sales presentations, and supportive materials (training materials, videos, and visual aids). The second set of activities deals with incentives for retailers to use as in-store promotions and other programs, such as contests, that motivate retail salespeople to work harder.

An important dimension of sales promotion effectiveness is **payout planning** that calculates return on investment (ROI). This process means that the results derived from a promotion can be estimated and compared with the projected costs of the effort. If the promotion doesn't deliver more than it costs, it is not a good idea, at least financially.

The trade press is full of stories about poorly designed or performing promotions. Such failures hurt companies' reputations, waste money, and sometimes even hurt consumers. For example, Burger King once had to recall 400,000 toy boats given away with kids' meals after reports that children had been stuck with metal pins that came off the boats too easily.

Photo: Courtesy Billings Chamber of Commerce/Convention and Visitors Bureau

SHOWCASE

The Billings "Trailhead" campaign used weekly drawings, with the winners receiving caps and the grand prize winner receiving dinner and two nights at the Crowne Plaza Hotel.

John Brewer, president and CEO of the Billings Chamber of Commerce/Convention and Visitors Bureau, graduated from the University of West Florida. He was nominated to be featured here by Professor Tom Groth.

Consumer Promotions   Although trade promotion claims the greatest percent of the promotion budget, we'll start with consumer promotions because they are familiar to most people. Consumer sales promotions are directed at the ultimate user of the good or service or the general public for such things as membership appeals for nonprofit organizations. These promotions are intended to provide an incentive so that when people go into a store, they will look for a particular brand. The primary strengths of consumer sales promotions are their variety and flexibility as well as their accountability.

To maintain a brand's presence, increase its market share, or counter competitive actions, marketers use promotional tools such as coupons, premiums, special events, and contests and sweepstakes. Here's a summary of the most common types of consumer promotions.

- **Price Deals**   A **price deal** is a temporary price reduction, a sale price, or even a giveaway—pricing strategies that create excitement and drive demand. In 2015, Target advertised a special sale on a collection by high-end designer Lily Pulitzer. The demand was so great that the retailer had to take its website offline.[11] The Billings, Montana, "Trailhead" branding campaign that we discussed in Chapter 1 also used a drawing with prizes to build excitement for the community's new brand identity.

  The four common price deals used in consumer promotion include the following:

  1. A *cents-off deal* is a reduction in the normal price charged for a good or service (e.g., "was $1,000, now $500" or "50 percent off") announced at the point of sale or through mass or direct advertising.
  2. *Prize-pack deals* provide the consumer with something extra through the package itself, such as a prize in a cereal box.
  3. *Bonus packs* contain additional amounts of the product free when consumers purchase the standard size at the regular price. For example, Purina Dog Food may offer 25 percent more dog food in the bag.
  4. *Banded packs* are more units of a product sold at a lower price than if they were bought at the regular single-unit price. Sometimes, the products are physically packaged together, such as bar soap and six-packs of soft drinks.

- **Refunds and Rebates**   A **refund** or **rebate** is a marketer's offer to return a certain amount of money to the consumer who purchases the product. Sometimes, the refund is a check; at other times, it may be a coupon to encourage repeat use.

- **Sampling**   Allowing the consumer to try the product or service is called **sampling**. Advertisers can distribute samples to consumers in numerous ways, such as sampling tables for food products. Samples of products can also be distributed in newspapers, on house doorknobs, in doctors' and dentists' offices, and, most commonly, through the mail.

- *Premiums* A **premium** is a tangible reward for a desired behavior, such as trying a new product. The two general types of premiums are direct and mail. Direct premiums award the incentive immediately, at the time of purchase, such as store premiums given to customers at the retail site, in-pack premiums inserted in the package at the factory, on-pack premiums placed on the outside of the package at the factory, and container premiums in which the package is the premium. Mail premiums require the customer to take some action before receiving the premium.
- *Coupons* Coupons have always been popular, but since the beginning of the 2007 recession, research has found a 10 percent increase.[12] The two general types of **coupons** that provide a discount on the price of a product are retailer and manufacturer coupons. *Retailer-sponsored* coupons can be redeemed only at the specified store; *manufacturer-sponsored* coupons can be redeemed at any outlet distributing the product. Digital coupons such as Groupon are popular, not just because of their level of response, but because they also can track purchasing patterns of users and build brand loyalty.[13]

  The Old Navy "human coupon" is an example of a retail promotion. Manufacturers pay retailers a fee for handling their coupons.
- *Contests and Sweepstakes* Contest and sweepstake promotions create excitement by promising "something for nothing" and offering impressive prizes. **Contests** require participants to compete for a prize or prizes based on some sort of skill or ability. **Sweepstakes** require only that participants submit their names to be included in a drawing or other chance selection. A **game** is a type of sweepstakes that establishes continuity by requiring customers to return several times to acquire additional pieces (such as bingo-type games).
- *Specialties* **Specialty advertising** presents the brand's name on something that is given away in an attempt to remind consumers about the brand. Items include calendars, pens and pencils, T-shirts, mouse pads, tote bags, and water bottles, among many others. The ideal specialty item is one that is kept out in the open where other people can see it, such as a coffee mug.

Photo: Courtesy Gap, Inc.

When Old Navy gathered 5 million fans on Facebook, it celebrated with a coupon for 30 percent off its products. But to make the coupon idea come alive, Old Navy's agency, Crispin Porter + Bogusky, created a 120-foot by 60-foot "human coupon" using hundreds of Facebook friends and fans. The coupon is a scannable bar code of 88 placards that participants held above their heads.

Another type of freebie is the **swag** given to people who attend events. Gifts bags with low-cost promotional knickknacks are often given to conference and trade show attendees. The Academy Awards is known for its high-end gift bags filled with expensive and desirable branded items.

Consumer sales promotions can be delivered in various media, including print, broadcast, and online. In-store promotions using posters, shelf talkers, displays, and other types of signage are particularly effective at reaching people who are making a purchase decision. Many advertising campaigns include a campaign-dedicated website, such as a "microsite" designed as a tie-in. A Cheetos campaign, for example, was supported with an online website, Orangeunderground.com, which displayed the work of a social network of practical jokers committing Random Acts of Cheetos—in other words, using Cheetos to turn things orange.

How Are Consumer Promotions Used?

To demonstrate how these promotional tools are used in a new product launch, let's suppose that we are introducing a new corn chip named King Corn. Promotion is particularly useful for a new product launch because it has a number of tools designed to encourage trial, but it can also be used later in the brand's life to maintain or increase its share of market and to remind and reward loyal customers.

- *Awareness* Creating awareness of this new brand is the strength of advertising. However, sometimes awareness can be increased when advertising is supported by an appropriate promotion to call attention to the brand name to get people to try the product. Awareness-building promotion ideas for this new corn chip might include colorful point-of-purchase displays or a special event that will attract people in the target market.

- *Trial* Creating awareness will take the product only so far. Consumers must also perceive King Corn as offering some clear benefit compared to the competition. Trial is one of the most important objectives of promotion, but it is essential to get the right people, the targeted audience, involved with the product. An effective way to get people to try King Corn is sampling, which is most effective when reinforced with product coupons. To be successful, the product sampled must virtually sell itself with a simple trial experience.

  Another way sales promotion can motivate people to try a new product is to offer an initial price deal: you try this product, and we will give it to you cheaper than the usual price. These price deals are usually offered through coupons, refunds, rebates, or premiums. Refunds and rebates are effective because they encourage consumers to purchase a product before a deadline. In addition, refunds stimulate sales without the high cost and waste associated with coupons.

- *Market Share* In addition to encouraging trial of a new product, another purpose of price deals is to convince prospective users to switch from an established competing brand. Later, after the King Corn brand is established, a price deal can be used to reward loyal users and encourage their repeat business. Price deals are particularly effective in those situations where price is an important factor in brand choice or if consumers are not brand loyal.

- *Brand Reminder amd Loyalty* In addition to new product launches, promotions are also used in the reminder stage. After the initial purchase, you want the customer to remember the brand and repeat the purchase to build brand loyalty, so specialty items, such as a King Corn snack bowl, can serve as a brand reminder. Specialty advertising serves as a reminder to the consumer to consider the product. Specialties also build relationships, such as items given away as New Year or thank-you gifts (the calendar hanging in the kitchen). Organizations use specialty items to thank customers for patronage, to reinforce established products or services, to generate sales leads, and to build brand loyalty through repeat business.

Theses tyes of promotions can be delivered in various media, including print, broadcast, and online. Traditionally, direct mail has dominated the delivery; much of that has now moved online, however, as the Frontier "Bunny" promo illustrates. In-store promotions use posters, shelf talkers, displays, and other types of signage.

Trade Promotions Consumer awareness and desire mean nothing unless King Corn is available where the consumer thinks it should be. Somehow the trade must be convinced that the product will move off the shelves. In such programs, *trade* refers to all the people involved in the distribution channel, including buyers, brokers, distributors, wholesalers, dealers, franchisees, and retailers. Trade promotions are sometimes referred to as **channel marketing**.

An example comes from Kuni Automotive, a small group of auto dealerships that was pitching the smart car company to get dealerships in Portland, Seattle, and Denver. Karl Schroeder, then a copywriter at the Coates Kokes agency in Portland, explained the Big Idea behind the sales presentation kit his team designed to win the dealerships.

Kuni wanted to increase recognition and attention for its successful auto dealerships. A promotional kit was designed by the agency that included smart cars, dealership buildings, and interested prospects. The kit was sent to the smart car company before the official proposals to help Kuni create a presence against the competition. Kuni was successful in winning two smart centers in Portland and Denver with this promotion.

Save money with the bunny!

From $49-$299 each way

*Purchase by 2/24. Fly by 6/9/10.

Book Now >

Photo: Courtesy Frontier Airlines. Used with permission.

This piece is an example of an email price promotion sent to Frontier Airlines' frequent flyers. Even though it's promoting a sale price, it's still faithful to the Frontier image and "different kind of animal" slogan.

Typically, companies spend more than half of their total promotion budget on promotions directed at the trade, which is to say that although consumer promotion is highly visible, trade promotion is equally important as a marketing communication strategy. Let's look at the types of trade promotion.

Trade advertising directed at wholesalers and retailers provides trade members with information about the new product and its selling points. In addition, trade promotion techniques, especially price discounts, point-of-purchase displays, and advertising allowances, motivate retailers to provide shelf space for products and consumer promotions. The King Corn manufacturer in our fictional example will be encouraged that the product is acceptable if resellers are willing to carry and help promote it. Here are the most common types of trade promotion tools.

- *Retailer (Dealer) Kits* Materials that support retailers' selling efforts or that help representatives make sales calls on prospective retailing customers are often designed as sales kits. Sales kits contain supporting information, such as detailed product specifications, how-to display information, and ad slicks—print ads that are ready to be sent to the local print media as soon as the retailer or dealer adds identification, location, promotion price, or other information.
- *Trade Incentives and Deals* Similar to consumer price deals, a manufacturer may reward a reseller financially for purchase of a certain level of a product or support of a promotion. In return, retailers can receive special allowances, such as discounts, free goods, gifts, or cash from the manufacturer.
- *Contests* As in the case of consumer sales promotion, advertisers can develop contests and sweepstakes to motivate trade members, particularly salespeople. Sweepstakes are a random drawing, and contestants are required only to provide their names and contact information to enter. Contests are far more common than sweepstakes, mainly because resellers find it easy to tie contest prizes to the sale of the sponsor's product. A sales quota is set, for example, and the retailer or person who exceeds the quota by the largest percentage wins the contest.
- *Point-of-Purchase Promotions* According to the Point-of-Purchase Advertising International association, the industry includes manufacturer-designed displays distributed to retailers who sell their products. They are referred to as **point-of-purchase (PoP) materials** and include, among other tools, special racks, display cartons, banners, signs, price cards, and mechanical product dispensers.
- *Trade Shows and Exhibits* A **trade show** is a place where companies in the same industries gather to present and sell their merchandise and to demonstrate their products. Exhibits are the spaces that are designed to showcase the product.

How Are Trade Promotions Used?   The ultimate gauge of successful trade promotions is sales increases. There are two primary roles for a trade promotion:

1. *Trade Support* To stimulate in-store merchandising or other trade support (e.g., feature pricing, superior store location, or shelf space).
2. *Excitement* To create a high level of excitement about the product among those responsible for its sale.

In addition, trade promotion is used to accomplish other marketing objectives, such as manipulating levels of inventory held by wholesalers and retailers and expanding product distribution to new areas of the country or new markets and trade groups.

Demand: Push and Pull

To understand the role of trade promotion, consider how consumer and trade promotions interact through complementing push and pull strategies. If people really want to try King Corn based on what they have heard in advertising and publicity stories, they will ask their local retailers for it, which is called a *pull strategy*; that is, by asking for it or using a manufacturer promotion, consumer demand will pull the product through the distribution channel. However, you might use a *push strategy* to push the product through the channel by convincing (motivating or rewarding) members of the distribution network to carry King Corn and push its sales.

Here are the most common types of incentives and trade deals used with retailers as part of a push strategy: monetary bonuses to salespeople; dealer loader premiums that reward retailers for buying a certain amount; advertising allowances or cooperative advertising, where a

Planning Point-of-Purchase Promotions

Arlene Gerwin, *Marketing Consultant and President, Bolder Insights*

Ever since retail establishments came into existence, there has been some form of point-of-purchase (PoP) promotion. For example, carefully hand-painted signs announcing a sale can be seen in photos of 19th-century country general store windows. Inside the store, special displays of merchandise sometimes promoted seasonal prices or special deals.

Point-of-purchase promotions, also referred to as marketing-at-retail promotions, usually fall under the definition of marketing tactics; however, objectives, strategies, and tactics are as important in planning PoP promotions as they are in the development of the overall marketing plan:

- **SMART Plans** Effective PoP promotions support the marketing plan and deliver on its strategies by being Strategic, Measurable, Actionable, Realistic, and Timely—that is, SMART.
- **Objectives** The most successful PoP promotions are developed against a clear set of objectives, such as countering competitive actions. A PoP campaign should be long range and strategic.
- **Big Idea** The best PoP promotions develop from campaignable, ownable "Big Ideas" that extend over

a minimum of one year or more and should be in line with the overall marketing objectives. Many times, PoP promotions creatively echo the advertising campaign.

- **Brand Fit** When the promotion becomes intricately intertwined with the brand or service, it enhances the brand image.
- **Bridge** PoP displays serve as a bridge linking trade and consumer promotions. The most powerful offers are delivered directly to consumers in the retail environment, but they need retailer support to be strategically placed. Trade and consumer promotions should work in tandem often with a push–pull strategy: trade for push and consumer for pull.
- **Timing** PoP promotions should consider the consumer product-use cycle and not artificially inflate sales volume at the expense of short-term sales spikes.
- **Copromotions** Two brands that share PoP materials and link their products in a single promotion can make the shoppers' task easier if they have similar target audiences and consumer usage patterns. Copromotions may also be delivered via electronic media, many times in the store.
- **Realistic Tactics** The specific tools in a PoP promotional plan should be affordable, on strategy, and produced on time. These requirements are crucial for seasonal or specific holiday promotions.
- **Detailed Budgeting** Avoid Murphy's promotions law: designs that look great on paper often present unanticipated production complications, not to mention the unpredictability of natural disasters and ill-timed strikes. Whenever possible, test a prototype of the display in stores to work out the kinks before production.
- **ROI** Because PoP promotions are planned across a finite time period and their costs can be predicted, planners can evaluate the promotion's ROI and estimate the payback.
- **Flexibility** Use contingency planning and have an arsenal of tactics waiting in the wings in case of unplanned complications.

manufacturer agrees to pay a part or all of the retailer's advertising costs; and display allowances that reward retailers for using PoP displays.

In addition to affecting demand through push and pull strategies, trade promotions are also designed to get attention, motivate trade members, and provide information.

- *Attention* Point-of-purchase displays are designed to get the attention of shoppers when they are in the store and to stimulate impulse purchases. They are used by retailers but provided by manufacturers. Retailers appreciate point-of-purchase ideas that build store ambience. Club Med designed a floor display for travel agents that featured a beach chair with a surfboard on one side and a pair of skis on the other to show that Club Med has both snow and sun destinations. Retailers, who put a premium on their precious store space, will use a point-of-purchase display only if they are convinced that it will generate greater sales.
- *Motivation* Most trade promotions are designed to, in some way, motivate trade members to cooperate with the manufacturer's promotion. They encourage a higher quantity of purchases and create enthusiasm among trade members who are involved with the promotion.
- *Information* Trade shows, which are an information-rich environment, display products and provide an opportunity to sample and demonstrate products, particularly for trade

buyers, the people who buy for stores. The manufacturer of King Corn would want to sponsor an exhibit featuring the new corn chip at the appropriate food shows. Trade shows also permit companies to gather information about their competition. In an environment where all the companies are attempting to give a clear picture of their products to potential customers, competitors can easily compare quality, features, prices, and technology.

In the Practical Tips feature, marketing consultant Arlene Gerwin explains how to plan effective point-of-purchase promotions that deliver results.

Multiplatform Promotions

4.3 Describe multiplatform promotions and explain how they are used.

So far, we have looked at consumer and trade promotions. In this section, we focus on sponsorships, event marketing, loyalty programs, and comarketing or partnership promotions. Many of these promotion techniques, such as sponsorships and special events, cross over to other areas of marketing communication and blur the lines between promotions, advertising, and public relations. For example, the Wheaties box, which is hard to classify as a promotion, is a classic example of using a package to connect a brand to winning athletes who bring alive its "Breakfast of Champions" slogan.

Sponsorships

Sponsorships occur when companies support an event, such as a sporting event, concert, or charity, either financially or by donating supplies and services. Major sponsorships typically cost a lot of money, but they are used because they generate excitement for both consumer and trade audiences. Sponsors for major golf tournaments, for example, are expected to invest between $6 million and $8 million.

Sponsorships include sports (events, athletes, and teams); entertainment tours and attractions; festivals, fairs, and other annual events; and cause marketing (associating with an event that supports a good cause), including promotions that support the arts. Cause marketing sponsorship is a growth area, and it has been found by a Chicago research firm to be growing faster than sports sponsorships.[14] That kind of impact is what has made the Komen "Pink Ribbon" such a powerful symbol for brand sponsors. In contrast, popular Chinese search engine Baidu sparked a storm of criticism when it sought to get money from users of its previously free health forums that users consult for information about health care and medical issues.[15]

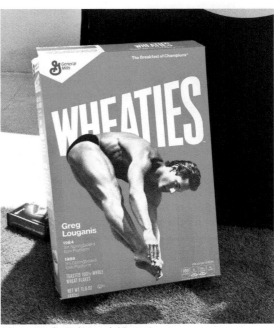

Photo: Rodin Eckenroth/Getty Images

Olympians have graced the Wheaties "Breakfast of Champions" box since 1958, when pole-vaulter Bob Richards was the first athlete to be featured on the box. Michael Phelps is a more contemporary example. You can see a long history of champions online. Just search for "classic Wheaties boxes."

Events

Events are used by brands and marketing programs and also by public relations programs for activities such as open houses, ribbon cuttings, and press conferences. **Event marketing** describes the practice of linking a brand to an event, either through sponsorship or by owning the event. Planners use related promotional events, such as a tour or the appearance of the product or its spokesperson at a mall or sporting event, to gain the attention and participation of people in the target audience who attend the event. The event showcases the brand, often with sampling, coupons, other incentives, and attention-getting stunts. To be successful, the event must match the brand to the target market's lifestyle.

Event Marketing and Special Events

Event marketing, which connects a sponsor with attendees of events like concerts, art exhibits, city and ethnic festivals, and sports (either as participants or viewers), is an increasingly important component in integrated marketing communication. More than $25 billion is spent annually in the United States on event marketing. Tactics include active engagement with attendees, such as distributing free samples or logo merchandise, supplying tickets and hospitality tents on-site

Active Engagement through Event Sponsorships

James Pokrywczynski, *Marquette University*

Can you remember the title sponsor of the last concert you attended? Can you name one sponsor of the last summer festival or sports event you attended? If your answer to either question is "I dunno," that's okay, because event and sports sponsors have a variety of goals for sponsorship beyond recall.

Sponsorship has moved beyond slapping a name on an event and hoping for the best. Events, sponsors, and especially sports teams have utilized social media to enhance engagement with participants and extend the impact of sponsorships. According to a 2011 *Sports Business Journal* study, game-day use of social media is highest for college football and basketball fans, with almost half using before, during, or after games. Professional sports leagues are not far behind.

As of mid-2012, pro basketball's Miami Heat had almost 6 million Facebook "likes," baseball's New York Yankees had 5.7 million, and pro football's Dallas Cowboys corralled 4.8 million. These numbers are key given a study of baseball's Milwaukee Brewers fans that shows that higher Facebook usage is correlated with both higher ticket-buying rates and projected merchandise buying. The 2011 Women's World Cup soccer final set a record for tweets per second (7,196), according to Twitter. The 2012 London Olympic Games are touted as the first "social media Olympics," as more sponsors provided interactive experiences around their brand's role in the games. These results mirror evidence in event marketing, where promotions on LinkedIn, Facebook, and Twitter for a Public Relations Society of America conference on health produced measurable, positive results related to attendance.

Of course, Twitter and other social media offer dangers when players and participants offer negative comments. A spring 2012 tweet from Miami Marlins manager Ozzie Guillen that caused enraged local Cubans to protest outside the ballpark led Guillen to later say, "Stop following me . . . Twitter is stupid."

for loyal customers or employees, and more passive efforts, such as signage on-site, logos on tickets or in event ads, and media mentions.

Goals of event marketing include building brand and top-of-mind awareness, enhancing brand attitudes, and, in some instances, generating sales. Lowe's has used special promotions during March Madness to reach its largely male customer base with plays on sports lingo, such as "throwing up the bricks," "dominating in the boards," and "let's hit the paint."[16]

In public relations programs, the term may be *special events* rather than event marketing. Special events are used to instill goodwill, as a holiday promotion by Yahoo! demonstrates. The online firm sent employees to airports to pay for airline customers' baggage fees. The stunt was described as "one small act of kindness," but it reinforced Yahoo!'s brand promise: "Yahoo! makes your life easier."[17] Beyond goodwill, the Komen organization uses its Race for the Cure to build active involvement and participation by friends and family of breast cancer sufferers and survivors. Other supporters engage with the Pink Ribbon cause through donations and corporate sponsorships.

Business-to-business promotions also use events to reach trade audiences. These stakeholders are invited to participate in the event as a reward for their support, and that's one of the big reasons why brands participate in the Super Bowl.

The granddaddy of all events is the Super Bowl, which is also an "Ad Bowl" because there is as much interest in the advertising as in the game. The ads are the most expensive on television; prices can top $4 million for a 30-second commercial, and that's just the cost of the time. The reason these costs make sense is because they also reach a huge audience. Generally, there is a significant budget tied up in the production of the commercials because they have to be highly professional so as to justify the costs. For another trend affecting costs, see the Matter of Principle feature.

It's not just the commercials, however, that get the attention of marketers. Brands buy a Super Bowl spot to participate in all the frenzy that surrounds the event, both before with pre-event teasers and in the postgame coverage. The television spots are the opportunity for wide-ranging promotional campaigns that involve publicity, point-of-purchase displays, video clips, websites and social media, search engine ads, and relationship programs with important partners, such as retailers and shareholders. YouTube, for example, gets involved by sponsoring

The Underdog Wins the Super Bowl Ad Championship

Bonnie Drewniany, *University of South Carolina*

Special effects. Expensive celebrities. Exotic locations. These are just some of the tactics advertising agencies use in the hopes of winning the Super Bowl advertising championship, the number-one spot in the *USA Today* Ad Meter. Once dominated by major agencies, the championship title has recently gone to the underdog: the average Joe (and Jane). And rather than spend upward of $1 million as the big agencies do, the winners spend a few thousand dollars or less to create their winning commercials.

It all began in 2007 when Doritos sponsored its first Crash the Super Bowl competition. A commercial created by a 22-year-old for less than $13 was the fourth most popular spot in the 2007 Ad Meter. The commercial, which shows a dorky guy trying to impress a woman while he's driving and munching on Doritos, beat out ads that cost upward of $1 million to produce.

Two years later, two unemployed brothers from Indiana created a Doritos commercial that won the ultimate coup: the number-one spot in the Ad Meter and a $1 million prize. The ad features a man trying to predict if he will get free Doritos chips for the office. He gets the answer he wants by throwing a snow globe at the vending machine. Impressed, a colleague uses the globe to predict if he'll get a raise. Not the best aim, the unlucky man hits his boss in a rather painful spot. "Promotion?" the first guy quips as he munches on a Doritos chip. "Not in your future."

A newly engaged couple won the 2011 Ad Meter and used part of the $1 million prize money on their wedding. Their commercial features a man, standing behind a storm door, taunting his girlfriend's pug with a Doritos chip. The pug beats the man at his own game by knocking over the door, pinning the man to the floor.

Two consumer-generated Doritos commercials came out on top in 2012. The *USA Today* panel's favorite spot features a man who sees his Great Dane burying the collar of a missing cat. To buy his silence, the dog slips his owner a bag of Doritos with a note "You didn't see nuthin'." Another spot, "Sling Baby," won the *USA Today*/Facebook online poll. Here, a grandmother uses a baby swing to catapult a baby to grab a bag of Doritos from an obnoxious boy.

Notice how none of these commercials used expensive celebrities or elaborate special effects? It's the idea that counts. Tell an engaging story that resonates with viewers, make your brand central to your message, and who knows? You may be the next underdog to win the Super Bowl advertising championship.

---

a Super Bowl Ad Blitz channel where viewers can vote for their favorite spots. Viewers are known to rewatch spots online on YouTube, AOL, Yahoo!, and other sites. They also pass along favorite commercials to friends and family.

The Matter of Principle feature makes the point that even in big-event advertising, it's still the Big Idea that counts. Check out Super Bowl commercials on www.superbowl-ads.com and www.youtube.com/superbowl. MSNBC has collected the 10 best of them at www.msnbc.msn.com/id/16691199 and the 10 worst at www.msnbc.msn.com/id/16790823.

Planners use blimps (Goodyear and MetLife's Snoopy blimps), balloons, inflatables, and skywriting planes to capture attention and create an aura of excitement at events. Inflatables—giant models of products, characters, and packages—are used at all kinds of events, including grand openings, sporting events, parades, trade shows, beaches, malls, and other places where they can make an impression for a new product rollout. A giant inflatable, such as Spider-Man on a building, demands attention and provides an entertaining and highly memorable product presentation.

Photo: Eric Risberg/AP Photo

To help promote the opening of the movie *Spider-Man*, inflatables like this one were placed along buildings in major cities throughout the world.

Loyalty Programs

Another type of program that crosses the line between advertising, public relatons, direct response, and promotion is a **loyalty program**, also called a **continuity program** or **frequency program**. The promotion's goal is to increase repeat business and customer retention.

If effective, one-on-one communication either from direct response or promotional programs leads to a customer retention strategy that ultimately increases brand loyalty. Direct response can be a highly targeted form of marketing communication that lets planners focus on their best customers and inform, encourage, or reward them in special ways for their brand loyalty. Frequent-flyer and frequent-buyer programs are examples of data-driven reward programs that help keep customers loyal.

Today, loyalty programs are synonymous with the word *frequent.* The frequent-flyer club, first created by United Airlines and American Airlines in 1981, is the model for a modern continuity program. These programs offer a variety of rewards, including seat upgrades, free tickets, and premiums based on the number of frequent-flyer miles accumulated. As a rewards program, people can earn miles through credit card purchases.

Continuity programs work in competitive markets in which the consumer has difficulty perceiving real differences between brands. Marketers like membership programs because they learn more about their customers and also generate information for customer databases. The problem is that shoppers are overwhelmed with loyalty programs, and a study of by eMarketer found that only 50 percent of members are active users. The conclusion is that the best programs offer rewards that are directly connected to their line of business, such as Amazon's free shipping.[18]

A concept called **lifetime customer value** is an efficiency metric that builds an estimate of how much purchase volume companies can expect to get over time from various markets. To put it formally, lifetime customer value is the financial contribution through sales volume of an individual customer or customer segment over a given length of time. By knowing your consumers' past behavior, you can decide how much you want to spend to get them to purchase and repurchase your product, and you can track your investment by measuring the response.

Partnership Programs

Another promotion tool that crosses the lines is the partnership program. **Comarketing** means that manufacturers develop marketing communication programs with their main retail accounts instead of for them. With this type of partnership, the advertising and sales promotions build equity for both the manufacturer and the retailer. For example, Procter & Gamble and Walmart might develop a spring cleaning promotion directed at Walmart shoppers that features Procter & Gamble cleaning products sold at reduced prices or with premium incentives.

When two companies come together to offer a product, the effort is called **cobranding**. That was a practice used by the Komen organization to immerse companies like Yoplait, with its pink lids, in the fund-raising and health care programming of the organization. Both companies are present in the product's design and promotion, and both get to build on the other company's brand equity. Another type of cooperative program is a **tie-in promotion** or **cross promotion**, which uses associations between complementary brands. For example, Doritos may develop a tie-in promotion with Pace salsa in which bottles of salsa are displayed next to the Doritos section in the chip aisle (and vice versa). The intent is to spur impulse sales of both products. Ads are designed to tie the two products together, and the sponsoring companies share the cost of the advertising.

Cross promotions are not only used by product marketers. For example, in its "Trailhead" rebranding campaign, Billings, Montana, used a tie-in promotion with Pepsi-Cola. A half a million special Pepsi cans with the campaign logo and slogan offered $5.00 off a "Trailhead" cap when visitors brought the can to the chamber of commerce. The promotion also was supported with a point-of-purchase poster in stores where Pepsi was sold.

Integrated Communication and Promotion

Historically, direct marketing was the first area of marketing communication that adopted an integrated marketing approach. In fact, some people refer to direct-response communication as *integrated direct marketing*. As technology has provided more and better ways to interact with customers, the challenge to direct marketers has been to integrate all the various media platforms and do so with a consistent brand voice that reflects brand integrity.

Instead of treating each medium separately, DRC programs seek to achieve precise, synchronized use of the right media at the right time, with a measurable return on dollars spent. For example, say you do a direct-mail campaign, which generates a 2 percent average response. If you include a toll-free phone number in your mailing as an alternative to the standard mail-in reply—with well-trained, knowledgeable people handling those incoming calls with a carefully thought-out script—you can achieve a 3 to 4 percent response rate. If you follow up your mailing with a phone call within 24 to 72 hours after your prospect receives the mailing, you can generate a response two to eight times as high as the base rate of 2 percent. So, by adding your toll-free number, you bring the response rate from 2 percent to 3 or 4 percent. By following up with phone calls and incentives, you can bring your total response rate as high as 10 to 18 percent.

Similar to direct-response and other marcom tools that we discuss in this book, promotions are strategically designed to work within a mix of brand messages and experiences to build brand strength and presence. As marketing consultant Gerwin explained: "When all the marketing tasks are driven by a common strategy and shared objectives, the company communicates with the consumer in a single voice with a consistent creative approach. For publicly held companies, this ultimately translates into building shareholder value and increasing the stock price."[19]

A common problem is that direct-marketing messages, promotions, and advertising messages often do not reinforce one another as well as they should because the three functions often are handled by different agencies who don't talk to one another. The Komen "Pink" campaign is a good example of how advertising and direct pieces can present a consistent brand message. The point is that, when planned strategically, direct marketing and promotions add impact to an IMC campaign and increase its efficiency.

Photo: Courtesy Billings Chamber of Commerce/Convention and Visitors' Bureau

SHOWCASE

Another element in the Billings, Montana, rebranding campaign that has been discussed throughout this book is a cross promotion that enlisted Pepsi-Cola to sponsor special cans with a premium offer on a "Trailhead" cap.

John Brewer, president and CEO of the Billings Chamber of Commerce/Convention and Visitors Bureau, graduated from the University of West Florida and was nominated for inclusion in this book by Professor Tom Groth. Brewer contributed a case study on the "Trailhead" campaign.

Databases and Why They Are Important to Interaction

4.4 Discuss databases and their importance to consumer and brand interaction.

At the heart of direct response communication and other types of promotion that support interaction with consumers are massive lists called **databases** that keep track of current customers and prospects, including their contact information as well as characteristics that predict their willingness to respond. A benefit for organizations that keep track of response behavior is that they are better able to personalize their messages. One goal of many promotions is to capture information and contribute to this database.

The practice of **behavioral targeting** means that messages are designed based on what people have done in the past, such as products they've bought, shows they've watched, and sites they've visited. Messages targeted on behavior are more than twice as effective as more general advertising in converting website visitors to buyers.[20]

The Smile Train organization sends out millions of pieces of direct mail each year and generates, in addition to donations, reams of data about which appeals and visuals generate the most money as well as information about which ZIP codes have the best responses. Volunteers in selected markets also host home parties to make personal appeals for donations.

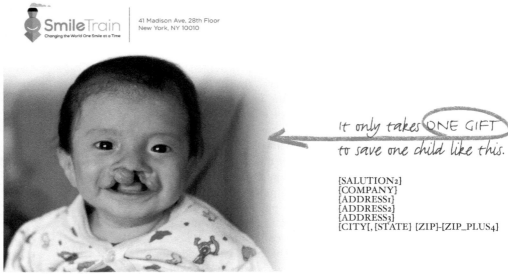

Photo: Courtesy Smile Train. Used with permission.

Databases tend to be huge data files that can be searched, compiled, merged, and purged to create a list that best matches the profile of an ideal prospect. According to Forrester Research, which has a program called Personal Identity Management, there are four categories of data being collected by organizations: individual identity data, behavorial data, compiled information (usually from other sources such as credit scores), and self-identified data such as likes.[21]

Big Data, a term that became popular in 2013, refers to using huge computer data storage capabilities combined with analytic software to do highly strategic identification of prospects. It is a characteristic of the Smile Train organization, which pays for cleft-palate operations in developing countries. It raises millions of dollars with its very sophisticated approach to research and analytics.[22] Smile Train uses direct mail as well as direct-response advertising and other promotional strategies, including sponsored home parties, to help some 1 million people get help for this type of surgery.

The circular database management process, which begins and ends with data collection, is illustrated in Figure 4.2. Initially, data are collected and entered into the database, and at the end of every campaign or communication effort, the response information goes back into the lists to update and extend the database.

Data Mining The practice of sifting through and sorting information captured in a company's database to maintain customer relationships is called **data mining.** Such information includes profiles based on demographics, lifestyle, and behavior as well as basic contact information.

How is data mining used? It's used for **prospecting** to find the most interested prospects. Instead of sending mass emails (spam) to everyone on a list, organizations can send information to people who might be really interested in the product, service, or cause based on profiles of key characteristics of current customers or members. If a grocery store that uses a loyalty card to track its customers' purchases notices that the young families in its customer pool live in certain neighborhoods, it can target family-oriented promotions to those particular neighborhoods rather than spraying

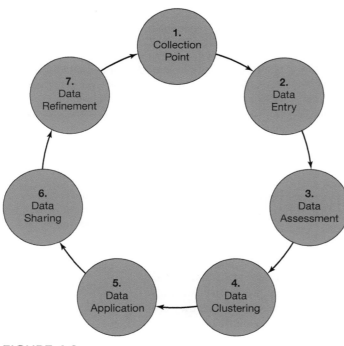

FIGURE 4.2
The Database Marketing Process
Database marketers continually improve the effectiveness of their marketing communication campaigns. Results feed back into planning, for a continual loop of improvement.

Privacy: *Use but Don't Abuse Consumer Information*

Joseph E. Phelps, *University of Alabama*
Jimmy Peltier, *University of Wisconsin, Whitewater*
George R. Milne, *University of Massachusetts, Amherst*

In your advertising and marketing communication classes (including this one), you will be encouraged to collect and examine all the information that is available so as to develop the consumer insights necessary to select the optimal audience and then develop and deliver messages that will move this audience to respond in the desired way.

To accomplish this task, marketing professionals are collecting and using more individual-level consumer information than ever before. Information such as names, addresses, demographic characteristics, lifestyle interests, shopping preferences, and purchase histories have been collected for many years. New information channels have emerged that provide marketers with the ability to capture more information and to capture that information in real time. For example, marketers can easily track online behaviors and use that information to deliver behavioral-based marketing communication.

Radio-frequency identification and video surveillance allow for the tracking of product and customer in-store movements. GPS-based functions in mobile devices also provide location-tracking abilities. Marketers have the ability to capture, store, and analyze tremendous amounts of consumer information.

This information helps marketers better understand and cater to the wants and needs of their customers and more effectively identify and communicate with prospective customers. However, because marketers have the ability to piece together personally identifying information from multiple sources, consumers have a real concern regarding their "digital dossier" and how their information dossiers are generated, utilized, and shared, particularly if there is a potential for their information to be used with negative personal and financial consequences.

As you become a marketing communicator, these consumer concerns should be important to you for multiple reasons, each of which revolves around your responsibilities to practice in the best interests of your customers, society, and the ongoing success of the organization for which you work. You need to understand consumer privacy concerns and privacy regulations because you will have the ethical and, in many cases, legal responsibility to thoughtfully protect consumers' personal information while using these data effectively. Your responsibility to the long-term success of your company is critical, and consumer privacy concerns represent an important yet too often ignored factor influencing the potential long-term success. Developing and maintaining long-term customer relationships require organizations to consider the negative impact that privacy concerns have on trust.

Thus, careful consideration of the amount and types of information collected and how that information will be used is critical. It is also essential to make sure that consumers are aware when information is being collected, what is being collected, and how that information will be used. This transparency is difficult to accomplish with emerging media that collect data in ways that are often invisible to the consumer. No one said the job would be easy.

Balancing the use of individual-level consumer information with consumer privacy is, however, a necessary task for which there are legal, ethical, and bottom-line business ramifications. You need consumer information to create great marketing communication, to direct it to the proper audience, and to build long-term relationships. Be sure to treat that information with the respect and protection it deserves.

them across its entire geographical market. Data mining can be used to spot trends and patterns; frequent flyers may also be buyers of international phone cards, for example.

Issues and Ethics: Privacy   One of the unexpected facts about life with social media is that your friends and associates can share information about you on all their online social networks. Say you have a party and some of the people attending post notes, photos, and tweets online, and then you start hearing from people you didn't invite. Even your friendly smartphone can tell tales about your comings and goings as it tracks your locations as well as your apps, your calls, and the sites you visit. It's a new life in the "nothing's private anymore" universe.

These practices have generated fierce debate among privacy advocates, marketing and advertising associations, and regulators in the United States and internationally. Companies are increasing the amount of data they collect on their customers, sometimes with their permission and knowledge but often without customers even being aware of the practice.

The lack of privacy on social media is an issue, particularly when it's combined with the gathering of marketing information. Larry Ellison, president of Oracle, explained the implications: "Now we can track not only what products you're buying, but what you're saying about those products. We know who your friends are. We know what you're saying to your friends. We know your friends' friends." His point is that when a company launches a product, it's easy to look at a Twitter or Facebook feed and find out what you and other users are saying about the product.[23] That may sound like good research being used to collect useful insights, but privacy activists see huge problems with these practices.

This unknown tracking is the problem with "cookies," files saved on users' computers without users' knowledge, to track their online behavior. Research at the University of California, Berkeley, found that 100 of the most popular sites had 6,485 cookies. Most of them are installed by third-party trackers, not the websites themselves. DoubleClick, Google's ad service, was the most prevalent tracker.[24]

David Rittenhouse, a member of this book's Advisory Board and an expert in digital marketing, observed that "at this moment, in my opinion, consumers have *no idea* how much data is being collected on them from their web browsing."[25] For example, a study in 2011 found that an average visit to a web page triggered 56 instances of data collection.

Privacy is particularly an issue with data mining. Giles D'Souza and Joseph Phelps call it the "privacy paradox,"[26] meaning that you can't do narrow targeting without collecting personal information. That may make direct-response targeting more efficient with consumers getting fewer unwanted contacts, but at what point is efficiency of targeting compromised by privacy concerns? This issue is discussed in the Principled Practice feature.

This introduction section of the book has reviewed the key strategic communication areas of advertising, public relations, direct response, and promotions. Now we will move on to Part 2, where we discuss the psychology and research behind marketing communication effectiveness and how this knowledge drives basic strategic planning decisions.

IT'S A WRAP

 # Hot Leads and Cold Shrimp

Iceland-based agency H:N developed an integrated campaign for its Katla client using trackable corks in a direct-mailed bottle as well as websites, personal sales, trade shows, and tailor-made demonstrations of the company's shrimp bath product. All these tools maximized opportunities for customer interaction.

The "Message in a Bottle" campaign initiated traceable delivery, signaled reception, and invited digital contact to tailored microwebsites. The campaign followed up with personalized ads and phone calls, invited more conversations at trade shows, and concluded with personalized on-site demonstrations.

Ingvi Logason, CEO of the marketing communication agency in Reykjavík, reports on the results of H:N's campaign after its first three years:

> The "Message in a Bottle" direct mail/digital approach has first and foremost generated more hot leads and loads more information than a direct effort alone would have done. And it opens up long-term possibilities like never before.
>
> Because of the scale of the client's business, a single sale as a result of all of these activities would more than pay for the entire campaign. But to close each sale takes greater effort than just the mail—the follow-up phone calls, visits, demo cocktails, and appearances at events.

The client's CEO doesn't disclose sales figures but says that the sales leads from the "Message in a Bottle" campaign are in the 10 to 20 percent range. In comparison, that outranks previous efforts by 10 to 1, thus catapulting Katla to the top of the list among the Icelandic competition.

The client's CEO has said that he will always argue over all invoices we send regarding all other projects—except this one. On this one, we can send whatever we want, and it will be paid. That clearly states that this project has been extremely effective in generating hot leads and has opened up avenues that otherwise would have been hard fought.

Suffice it to say that Katla Food is very happy with the project even though it was very expensive and time consuming in the initial stages. It has now been running for three years. We have sent, and the sales force has followed up on, close to 200 shipments. And we have been running ads for the same period of time.

Photo: Courtesy Ingvi Jökull Logason. Used with permission.

KEY OBJECTIVES SUMMARY

4.1.   Identify the functions and key elements of direct-response communication. Direct-response communication is personal and interactive and uses various media to effect a measurable response. The key elements are the offer and its response as well as the communication pieces or package, fulfillment, and pretesting and posttesting.

4.2.   Explain the importance of promotion. Sales promotion offers an extra incentive to take action. It gives the product or service additional value and motivates people to respond. Sales promotions directed at consumers include price deals, coupons, contests and sweepstakes, refunds, premiums, specialty advertising, continuity programs, and sampling. Their purpose is to pull the product through the distribution channel. Sales promotions directed at the trade include point-of-purchase displays, retailer merchandising kits, trade shows, and price deals, such as discounts, bonuses, and advertising allowances. These promotions are used to push the product through the channel.

4.3.   Describe multiplatform promotions and explain how they are used. Sponsorship is used to increase the perceived value of a brand by associating it with a cause or celebrity. Internet promotions can be used to drive people to a sponsor's web page. Licensing "rents" an established brand to other companies to use on their products. Loyalty programs are designed to increase customer retention. Partnership programs, such as cobranding and comarketing programs, are designed to build stronger relationships between manufacturers and retailers and between two brands that market related products to a similar target audience.

4.4.   Discuss databases and their importance to consumer and brand interaction. Direct-response communication and sales promotion have benefited from the development and maintenance of a database of customer names, addresses, telephone numbers, and demographic and psychographic characteristics. Organizations use this information to direct their campaigns to prospects who, based on demographics and other important characteristics, are likely to buy their products or affiliate with their organization.

KEY TERMS

behavioral targeting, p. 113
call centers, p. 99
catalog, p. 97
channel marketing, p. 106
cold call, p. 99
cobranding, p. 112
comarketing, p. 112
compiled list, p. 97
contest, p. 105
continuity program, p. 112
coupons, p. 105
cross promotion, p. 112
databases, p. 113

data mining, p. 114
direct mail, p. 94
direct-response
   communication, p. 91
direct-response marketing, p. 91
event marketing, p. 109
frequency program, p. 112
fulfillment, p. 93
game, p. 105
house list, p. 96
inbound telemarketing, p. 99
infomercial, p. 98
lifetime customer value, p. 112

loyalty program, p. 112
offer, p. 92
opt in, p. 101
opt out, p. 101
outbound telemarketing, p. 99
payout planning, p. 103
permission marketing, p. 101
point-of-purchase (PoP) materials, p. 107
predictive dialing, p. 99
premium, p. 105
price deal, p. 104
prospecting, p. 114

rebate, p. 104
refund, p. 104
response list, p. 96
sales promotion, p. 101
sampling, p. 104
spam, p. 100
specialty advertising, p. 105
sponsorships, p. 109
swag, p. 105
sweepstakes, p. 105
telemarketing, p. 98
tie-in promotion, p. 112
trade show, p. 107

MyLab Marketing

Go to **www.pearson.com/mylab/marketing** for MyLab discussion questions (⭐) as well as the following assisted-graded writing questions.

4-1. Discuss permission marketing and what strategies can be used to overcome the problems of spam.

4-2. How do push and pull marketing strategies relate to promotions targeted at consumers, and how do they relate to sales promotions targeted at trade audiences?

REVIEW QUESTIONS

4-3. What are the advantages and disadvantages of direct-response marketing communication?

4-4. What are the five primary tools of DRC media, and how are they used?

4-5. Define sales promotion and explain how it differs from other marcom areas.

⭐ **4-6.** Explain the three audiences for sales promotion and how they are reached.

4-7. Why are sponsorships and events used by marketers?

4-8. Define loyalty programs and explain why they are useful. How does lifetime customer value enter into the planning for such a program?

4-9. What is a database, and how and why is this tool used?

⭐ **4-10.** If you are using data mining to develop a prospecting program for a client, what would you be trying to accomplish?

⭐ **4-11.** Explain the privacy issues that involve direct-response communication.

⭐ **4-12.** Discuss permission marketing and strategies that can be used to overcome the problems of spam.

DISCUSSION QUESTIONS

⭐ **4-13.** Kali Johnson, a recent college graduate, is interviewing with a large garden product firm that relies on television for its direct-response advertising. "Your portfolio looks very good. I'm sure you can write," the interviewer said, "but let me ask you what is it about our copy that makes it more important than copy written for Ford, Pepsi, or Pampers?" What can Kali say that will help convince the interviewer that she understands the special demands of direct-response writing?

⭐ **4-14.** One of the smaller, privately owned bookstores on campus is considering a direct-response service to cut down on its severe in-store traffic problems at the beginning of each semester. What ideas do you have for setting up

some type of direct-response program to take the pressure off store traffic?

4-15. You have been named product manager for a new FDA-approved pharmaceutical, a diet pill that helps reduce hunger. Should you use a push or a pull strategy to introduce this new product? Prepare a short paper that explains your point of view.

⭐ **4-16.** How does the recent fervor surrounding personal privacy affect direct marketing and promotions, specifically email advertising and collecting information at events? You are designing a campaign for a local bookstore that employs email advertising and local promotions, but your client is concerned because of privacy issues. Argue either for or against the use of these tools in this situation.

TAKE-HOME PROJECTS

4-17. *Portfolio Project:* Pick a local business or nonprofit organization and find an ad or printed piece of some kind that represents the organization. Develop a Big Idea for a campaign for that organization. Then formulate a direct-response effort and a local promotion that supports the campaign. Explain your ideas in a one-page memo and sketch out how your direct-response and promotion ideas would look.

⭐ **4-18.** *Mini-Case Analysis:* Why do you think that Katla's "Message in a Bottle" campaign has been so successful? What lessons might you learn about direct response and promotional planning from this case? If you were on the Katla IMC team, what would you do next to continue the momentum? Come up with a Big Idea for a new campaign for the next year and explain how it would work and what it would accomplish.

Multicultural Direct-Response Communication

Read the TRACE case in the Appendix before coming to class.

4-19. What are the chief advantage and the chief disadvantage of direct response communication with this target audience? Of promotions and other multiplatform efforts?

4-20. Create a set of five direct-response materials, promotions, and multiplatform efforts that you believe will make this campaign more effective.

Authentically Green?

Increasingly, companies are attempting to align themselves with good causes, such as showing that they're caretakers of the environment. You may be familiar with "Ecomagination," a strategy created by General Electric to drive innovation and the growth of earth-friendly environmental solutions. It pledged a $25 billion investment in research and development of green technologies toward this effort, such as using wind energy, recovering wastewater, and exploring the use of compressed natural gas for vehicles. You don't have to look far to see examples of other corporations that are engaged in work to help sustain the environment.

Often criticized for the harm some of the ingredients do to the environment, corporations producing household cleaners are, well, trying to clean up their act.

Recently, the green niche has been a fast-growing segment of the $2.7 billion market for household cleaning products. In 2008, the Clorox Company, a century-old company known for its not-so-environmentally-friendly products, such as bleach, Pine-Sol, and Formula 409, launched a line of ecofriendly products it called Green Works®, in part to take advantage of this opportunity. The products contain 95 percent natural plant and mineral-based biodegradable cleaning ingredients. Packaging can be recycled, and the products are not tested on animals. The Sierra Club even endorsed it. Green Works® products received a seal from the Environmental Protection Agency's program Design for the Environment, which recognizes and promotes green chemistry and the health of humans and the environment.

Sales soared to $100 million. By 2011, though, they fell to $60 million. Do you wonder why? In the Part 1 opener, you read about seven enduring principles of marketing communication. The first of those principles stated that as a marketer, you should build and maintain distinctive brands that your customers love. Capitalizing on social trends can be good business and can connect your company with good causes that make consumers feel good about your brand. It can also backfire if they do not find the marketing to be sincere or the products inferior.

Some critics vented their opinions about Green Works® on blogs and other venues:

- This isn't green; it's greenwashing. How sincere can the Clorox Company be when it sells not only green products but other products that are highly toxic and environmentally unfriendly?
- Green isn't something a company is because it develops a new product line. Rather, it's about changing the inside culture of a company.
- Can Green Works® truly claim it's green on its labels when there are no industry standards defining "natural cleaners"?

Do you think Green Works is authentically green?

Consider This

P1-1. After reading about Green Works® in the case and on the Web, do you think this product line is a believable attempt by Clorox to improve the environment? Why or why not?

P1-2. Does Green Works® represent an attempt to mirror a trend in society or create one?

P1-3. Had you been the product manager, would you have put the Clorox name on the Green Works® products, as the company did? Explain your decision.

P1-4. Do you think that green marketing is an enduring movement? Why or why not?

Sources: http://ge.ecomagination.com. Retrieved September 17, 2017; www.greenworkscleaners.com; Jack Neff, "Has Green Stopped Giving? Seeds of Consumers Revolt Sprouting Against Some Environmentally Friendly Product Lines," November 8, 2010, www.adage.com.

2

PRINCIPLE
Be True to Thy Brand— and Thy Consumer

Part 1 introduced the basics of the professional areas of brand communication practice. Part 2 focuses on how brand communication strategy works, why and how consumers make the decisions they do, and how a winning strategy—one that reflects how consumers think and feel—can be developed.

No matter how much brand communication practices and media formats change, a basic principle is that brands must be true to themselves and to the consumers who buy them. Regina Lewis explains this principle in the Part 2 introduction below about how true branding works.

Brands Are Built on a Human Foundation

If there is one thing I have learned in igniting consumer passions across the United States for Dunkin' Brands and reigniting consumer passions around the world for Holiday Inn, it is that great brands are "human." Put another way, great brands are not created in a vacuum and then "marketed" successfully. Rather, great brands are built on the knowledge of consumers' deepest values and innermost feelings. Consumer loyalty is built when a brand seeks first to know everything possible about its consumer and then speaks to that consumer with a tone and message that emotionally resonates with him or her.

For example, consumers who are loyal to Dunkin' Donuts, which has built itself to be a down-to-earth, approachable brand, love the fact that carrying a Dunkin' cup says to others that they, personally, are down-to-earth and approachable. At Dunkin', success did not happen from

◄ REGINA LEWIS Dr. Regina Lewis has been vice president of consumer insights at InterContinental Hotels Group and vice president and director of the Consumer and Brand Insights Group at Dunkin' Brands. She is now a professor in the Department of Advertising and Public Relations at the University of Alabama and a member of this book's Advisory Board.

the "inside out." Success was made possible because the Dunkin' brand communication team and their agencies worked off the insight that a very large group of people, because of their "everyday Joe" love of everyday life, wanted an alternative to high-priced, status-oriented coffee brands. These people wanted a "brand for them," a brand that reflected their personally held value that authenticity trumps bells and whistles.

Another example: At Holiday Inn, the marketing team faced a real challenge because of the large number of similar midscale (mid-price-range) hotel brands on the market. Instead of simply copying others or advertising a tactic like "free Internet," the team spoke with consumers around the world to find out how guests really wanted to *feel* when staying in a hotel. They found that travelers are quite weary and just want to feel "at home" on the road, whether on business or with their families. Consumers told us over and over, "I just want to be able to be myself!" So, the successful "Stay You" campaign was launched.

When a brand fails to convey a soul or essence that matches personal characteristics that consumers value or when a brand fails to meet emotional needs, it lacks meaning. It blends in with all the other bland brands that lack charisma. On the other hand, when a brand meets a deep-seated need and becomes a badge that consumers are proud of displaying, it becomes interwoven into consumers' everyday lives.

The Enduring Principles

As I, along with my marketing and advertising agency teams, ensured that Holiday Inn retained its place in the hearts and minds of guests, I heeded the following set of principles:

1. *Feel* Because all human decisions involve some emotional component, no purely rational advertising approach can offer sustainable advantage. An advertisement must make folks "feel" something!
2. *Connect* All advertising must not only contain an emotional component but also get that emotion right. It must nail the way folks want to see their world or themselves.
3. *Identify* Although all consumers are individuals, we also can identify groups of consumers who think and feel the same way; identifying and understanding these groups is at the root of strategic planning.
4. *Understand* To effectively deliver emotion through advertising, we must avoid "group think"; sometimes, the most powerful idea can come from one consumer's story, and the most powerful message can be imagined by one brilliant creative mind that understands the minds of the target audience.
5. *Smile* It is critical to remember that people want to feel happy! Just as songs that made people smile were celebrated during the Great Depression, advertising that makes people smile will always be meaningful when life feels difficult.

These principles will be explained further in the chapters that make up Part 2. Chapter 5 answers the big picture question of "How does brand communication work?" Effectiveness factors are spelled out using the Facets Model of Effects. Building on that discussion as a foundation, Chapter 6 introduces the basics of research used to gather insights about consumers and the marketplace. Chapter 7 introduces the consumer audience and discusses how targeting works. Finally, Chapter 8 explains how brand communication and insights into how consumers think and behave come together in a strategic plan.

5

How Brand Communication Works

The "Save a Life" campaign is an example of an award-winning product and promotional idea that attracts attention, builds awareness, explains a somewhat complicated process, and at the same time tells a story that engages emotions. This chapter will first explain how communication works to create and support brands, and then it will look at various types of consumer responses to messages such as the "Save a Life" story to identify the key effects behind the concept of effectiveness. We organize and present these various aspects of message impact as the Facet Model of Effects. The communication role of brand experiences is a foundation for the discussions in the following chapters on consumer behavior, consumer research, and strategic planning. It's our view that you can't make intelligent decisions in those areas unless you understand how brand communication works.

Campaign	**Company**	**Agency**	**Awards**
Save a Life	*Help Remedies*	*Droga5*	*Cannes Grand Prix for Good, two Gold Lions*

A Tale of Brotherly Love and Sharp Thinking

 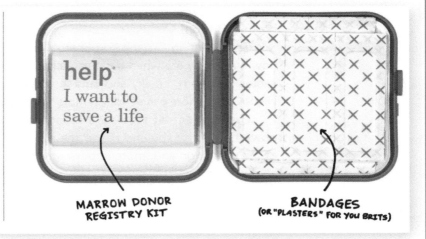

Photo: Courtesy of Graham Douglas.

In Chapter 2, you read about the four Ps of marketing (product, price, place, and promotion). Now we're going to switch gears and tell you about some "P" words that are significant to those on the creative side: problem solving, passion, perception, and powerful ideas.

As we discuss in this chapter, creativity isn't just about "ads" anymore. A creative idea can foster product development, and creative problem solving drives brand communication as well. We identify a problem, and we attempt to fix it by communicating a creative solution.

You'll see in this "Save a Life" case that the product, the message, and the media through which the fix is communicated demonstrate the creative thinking of ad wizard Graham Douglas, who describes himself as having grown up in Fort Worth, Texas, with an identical twin brother, Britton, and an obese beagle named Sam.

The Problem: More than 10,000 Americans need bone marrow transplants each year to help them win the battle against leukemia. Transplants are a last resort for those suffering from blood cancers, and only three of five people will receive the treatment they need because not enough donors have volunteered. How can you convince people to become donors?

The Passion: Graham's twin, Britton, fell ill with leukemia, and chemotherapy failed. Britton's hope for survival lay in finding a donor whose bone marrow matched his blood. The process is safe and relatively noninvasive; the risk to the donor is minimal, and bone marrow regenerates. Britton and Graham are identical twins, and Graham could not donate his bone marrow because their blood types were too similar. Inspired by his brother's plight and others in similar situations, Graham worked obsessively for almost a decade to find a creative solution to attract more donors.

The Perception: Graham imagined a simple concept, something that no one had ever done: create and market a product that would help convince people to become donors. He searched for and found a company, Help Remedies, to partner with him. The ingenious product sports an unusual name: "Help I've cut myself & I want to save a life." But it's what's inside that counts: bandage strips packaged with donor kits that let consumers swab their blood from a cut and send the sample to DKMS, the world's largest bone marrow donor center.

Powerful Ideas: Graham Douglas had already made a name for himself with his award-winning work as a copywriter at Droga5 and other agencies. Now he had to figure out how to grab the attention of potential donors to save lives like those of his brother, Britton.

The resulting "Thank You Sharp Objects" online video demonstrates to viewers how lucky they are when a cat scratches them, a cheese grater nicks their finger, or a cactus falls from the sky and cuts their arm. Why? Instead of letting the blood go to waste, consumers can send a sample to the DKMS registry.

Graham himself stars as a bloody blade. Weird? Yes. Effective? You bet. How powerful? Flip to the end of the chapter to the "It's a Wrap" feature to learn the fate of the campaign and, more importantly, what happened to Britton.

Note: Graham Douglas, one of this book's Ad Stars, shared this story about his award-winning "Save a Life" campaign. His work was nominated to be featured here by Professor Sheri Broyles.

5.1 Explain how communication works as a form of both mass communication and interactive communication.

It All Begins with Communication

Would you hire a doctor who doesn't understand how various parts of the body work? Wouldn't you expect a competent doctor to be able to diagnose ills and know what needs to be done to keep you healthy? Anatomy, chemistry, and biology are the fundamentals of medicine. So wouldn't you also expect brand communication professionals to understand the fundamental theories of their field—to know how communication and consumer psychology work as well as how to diagnose problems and keep consumer/brand relationships healthy? That was the challenge Wieden + Kennedy faced in turning around the brand image as well as the sales levels of Chrysler.

It all begins with communication. At its most basic, brand communication is a message to a consumer about a brand. It gets **attention** and provides information and sometimes even entertainment. It is purposeful in that it seeks to create some kind of response, such as an inquiry, a sale, a visit to a website, or a test drive.

The legendary David Ogilvy wanted advertising to be as relevant as a personal conversation. He would pretend he is at a dinner party and the woman next to him asks for advice. He explains, "I give her the facts, facts, facts. I try to make it interesting, fascinating, if possible, and personal—I don't write to the crowd."[1]

In reality, however, most traditional advertising is not as personal or as interactive as a conversation because it relies on mass communication. Although other forms of marketing communication, such as personal selling and telemarketing, can deliver the personal contact of a conversation, Ogilvy's comparison ignores the challenge of getting the attention of a largely disinterested audience when using mass media.

So let's look first at how *communication* works in general, and then we'll apply that analysis to mass media advertising and finally to the broader arena of brand communication, including newer forms of brand-related interaction.

The Mass Communication Foundation

Mass communication is a process, as depicted in the **SMCR model** in Figure 5.1a, which goes back to early work in the 1940s by Shannon and Weaver on the transmission of information.[2]

A Basic Communication Model

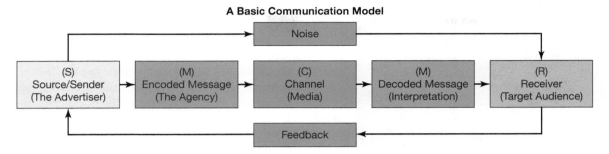

FIGURE 5.1
A Basic Mass Communication Model

There are seven key parts to this model. As it has been applied to mass communication, the communication process begins with (1) a **source**, a sender, who (2) **encodes**, or puts it in words and pictures as a **message**. The message is presented through (3) **channels of communication** or media, such as a newspaper, radio, or television. The message is (4) **decoded**, or interpreted, by the (5) **receiver**, who is the reader, viewer, or listener. The last step is (6) **feedback**, which is obtained by monitoring the response of the receiver to the message. The entire process is complicated by (7) **noise**, things that interrupt the sending and receiving of the message, such as a bad connection or words with unclear meanings. This model is sometimes referred to as the SMCR (source → message → channel → receiver) model.

In the chapter-opening "Save a Life" story, we translate this SMCR model to brand communication (Figure 5.2), where the *source* typically is the marketer (Graham Douglas and his new blood donor kit) or organization assisted by its agency (Graham Douglas) that encodes the information into various types of marketing communication. In other words, advertising professionals turn the marketer's information and objectives (a campaign to save lives of leukemia and blood marrow sufferers) into an interesting and attention-getting message ("Help I've cut myself & I want to save a life"). The *message*, of course, can be an advertisement or other marketing communication, such as an advertisement, press release, store banner, brochure, video, or web page.

Together, the marketer and its agency determine the *goals* and *objectives* for the campaign in terms of the effects they want the messages to have on the *receiver* (the audience). They also choose the *media* (*channels*), which are the vehicles that deliver the message. In advertising, the media tend to be newspapers and magazines in print and radio and television in broadcasting as well as the internet and cell phones and other forms of out-of-home vehicles, such as outdoor boards and posters. Other media include specialty items (mugs and T-shirts), in-store signs, brochures, catalogs, shopping bags, inflatables, and even sidewalks and toilet doors. For the "Save a

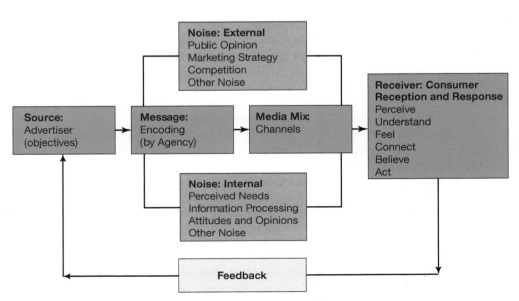

FIGURE 5.2
A Brand Communication Model

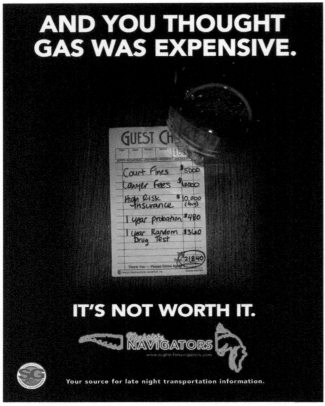

Photo: Adwerks

SHOWCASE

The "expensive gas" poster from the Nightlife Navigators campaign intends to create a negative feeling about the financial impact of a DUI ticket. This poster is one of a series of ads about drinking and driving by the Adwerks student advertising agency at the University of Florida.

Lisa Yansura, Supervisor, Client Engagement at VML, Kansas City, Missouri.

Life" campaign, Douglas used an online video, "Thank You Sharp Objects," that demonstrated how easy it was to provide a blood sample to a bone marrow donor center.

The end point of the communication process is the *receiver*, the consumers who make up the targeted audience. How the consumer responds to (decodes and interprets) the message determines the effectiveness of the brand communication. If the communication process fails to work and the consumer does not receive the message as intended by the advertiser, the communication effort is ineffective.

External noise, which hinders the consumer's reception of the message, includes technical and socioeconomic trends. Health trends, for example, often harm the reception of fast-food messages. External noise can also be related to media. It can be as simple as bad broadcast or cell phone reception. A more likely cause of noise is **clutter**, which is the multitude of messages all competing to get consumers' attention. It can even include any of the 3,000 or so commercial messages you see in your daily environment.

Internal noise includes personal factors that affect the reception of an advertisement, such as the receiver's needs and wants, language skills, purchase history, information-processing abilities, and other personal factors. If you are too tired to listen or your attention is focused elsewhere, your fatigue or disinterest creates noise that hinders your reception of the message. The Nightlife Navigators poster tries to overcome college students' feelings about being invincible when they drive after drinking too much.

Feedback is the reaction the audience has to a message. It can be obtained through research or through customer-initiated contact with the company, both of which are important tests of the effectiveness of marketing communication messages. An important thing to remember is that this communication process is not foolproof or even dependable. Instead, it's complicated.

Adding Interaction to Brand Communication

Mass communication, as we've been discussing it, is traditionally one-way communication with the message moving from the source to the receiver—from a company to a target audience (see Figures 5.1 and 5.2). However, **interactive communication** is two-way communication—a dialogue or conversation—and brand communication has moved in that direction with the emergence of social media and *word-of-mouth* communication strategies. Twitter is particularly good at starting conversations, and that feature has caught the attention of communication managers who would like to get influential Twitter users to tweet about their brands. Described as "conversational ads," these tweets contain a branded hashtag button that takes viewers to a brand message.[3]

The difference between one-way and two-way communication is that in two-way communication, the source and receiver change positions as the message bounces back and forth between them (think Ping-Pong): the source becomes the listener, and the receiver becomes the sender. It is different from simply acquiring feedback because in interactive communication, it's not just about the company contacting the consumer; in fact, the consumer may initiate the contact. And they talk to their network of friends, spreading the word about their experiences with a product or brand message. If advertisers want to overcome the impersonal nature of mass communication, they need to learn to receive (i.e., *listen to*) as well as send messages to customers. Figure 5.3 is a model of how two-way communication works.

Another way to describe interactive communication is to describe business-to-consumer communication as B → C and business-to-business communication as B → B. Consumer-initiated

An Interactive Communication Model

FIGURE 5.3

An Interactive Communication Model

The basic communication model is modified here to show how interactive communication works as a conversation or dialogue, including shared communication. Notice how the source and receiver change positions as the message bounces back and forth between them.

communication would turn around (C → B), which means that the customer is the sender and the company the receiver.

But communication is more complicated now because of the increasing use of social media and word of mouth, which we represent as B → C^2. We are using C^2 to refer to a network of messages with the communication shared among a network of friends. However, shared communication could also drive the communication, as in C^2 → B. In this case, people talk about a brand and then send messages to the company. *Group texts* are a form of shared text messages within a defined group that can be used to share messages to closest friends, such as within brand fan clubs. The point is that the communication situation becomes more complex as it becomes more interactive. Here's a summary that compares one-way and interactive communication:

	Company Initiated	**Consumer Initiated**
Targeted (one way)	B → C	C → B
Shared (two way)	B → C^2	C^2 → B

Marketers' use of *word of mouth*, *buzz marketing*, and online *social media* are indicators of the need for message integration. The important difference is that consumers are talking to one another in a circle of comments about products and brands. That raises the bar on the need for consistency in company-produced brand communication, whatever the format and medium.

Interactive communication is also making the classic two-step or multistep flow of communication model more relevant. Elihu Katz and Paul Lazarsfeld developed it in the 1940s as a theory of how persuasion works based on social influence.[4] In their view, people identified as opinion leaders talk to other people and influence the formation of attitudes and behaviors. As Professor Dennis DiPasquale noted, this model helps explain how word of mouth intersects with public relations and new media in brand communication.[5] For example, a report by the Burson-Marsteller agency called "Social Media Check-Up" noted that the *Fortune* Global 100 companies were mentioned a total of 10.4 million times online in one month in 2012. Most of this chatter was on Twitter.[6]

A final point is that interactive communication is the building block of the customer-brand experience, which can determine the likelihood of repeat business and brand loyalty. Harley Manning, a member of this book's advisory board, asked, "What qualifies as an interaction?" Manning, who is vice president of research and research director at Forrester Research, wrote a book with colleague Kerry Bodine titled *Outside In: The Power of Putting Customers at the Center of Your Business*, in which they explain:

> Here's how we think about interactions: they're reciprocal. Your customer takes an action like visiting your store or website. Your company responds in some way. Maybe an associate walks up to her or the website pops up an invitation to chat. Your customer then responds to your company's response—asking the associate a question or accepting the chat invitation—and so it goes until your customer achieves her goal, or gives up.[7]

The importance of interactions is the point of Manning's Inside Story about Office Depot. You can hear Manning and Bodine talk about customer service and the cases in their book at http://outsidein.forrester.com.

● **Principle**

In interactive communication, there are multiple conversations occurring in a network, with people contacting companies as well as talking to one another and companies listening and responding as well as sending messages.

What Went Wrong at Office Depot?

Harley Manning, *Vice President, Research Director Serving Customer Experience Professionals, Forrester Research*

When he was president of Office Depot's North American division, Kevin Peters visited stores all over the United States to get a firsthand look at how customers experienced his stores. In some cases, it was a painful experience.

He found that high mystery-shopping scores reflected clean floors and fully stocked shelves but not the things customers cared about. These customers are mostly small business owners who want to find the office products they came for, quickly and easily. In other words, they want to get in, buy, and get out.

But Office Depot stores didn't help them do that. They were large, and their signage was cluttered and confusing, making the stores hard for customers to navigate.

Employees were neither as empathetic nor as helpful as they should have been. They had been coached all along to focus on tasks, not on building relationships with customers by listening carefully and responding to their needs.

Wham, bam, thank you customer, and—oh, wait—did you forget to buy something? Sorry, I was so busy stocking the shelves that I missed that part.

Ultimately, Kevin knew that if he wanted to reverse the downward slide in sales, he needed to transform virtually every aspect of his in-store experience. Quickly.

He learned that customer experience goes to the heart of everything you do—how you conduct your business, the way your people behave when they interact with customers and each other. You literally can't afford to ignore any interaction because your customers take it personally each and every time they touch your products and interact with your support people.

Check out Forrester's website at www.forrester.com.

This Inside Story was contributed by Harley Manning, a master's graduate of the advertising program at the University of Illinois. He was nominated to be featured here by the late Kim Rotzell, former dean of the College of Communication.

Photo courtesy of Harley Manning

Other Aspects of Communication

So far, we've been discussing traditional communication based on words and conversations. It's important to recognize, however, that nonverbal communication can be just as powerful as word-based forms. As we mentioned earlier, many commercials are essentially nonverbal, relying on the impact of compelling visuals. Most billboards, packaging, posters, and ads rely on the power of visual imagery. With print advertising, most people look at the picture first in their decision about whether to stop and read the ad.

Brand signals include slogans, but they are dominated by logos, imagery, and color. Think about a Coca-Cola can. What comes to mind first? Brand identity operates through systems of *cues* that identify and signal brand personalities and strengths. *Signaling* is particularly important in the clutter and chaos of the internet, where attention is shortened and recognition happens in an instant.

Cues and signals are used in commercial communication to help structure a consumer's meaning-making process. We create personal brand meanings from formal communication (ads or conversations with friends) as well as from brand experiences. Events are an obvious form of experience-based communication, but experiences also include such things as finding the brand in the store, dealing with a sales clerk (or not), using the product, calling tech support, and visiting customer service. A big part of retailing involves managing the shopping experience and making it as painless as possible. Better yet, make it fun and memorable. McDonald's has recently added table service to its fast-food operations, hoping to improve interaction as well as the overall personal experience.[8] Navigating a website is another experience that can be challenging or rewarding and can color the impression of the brand.

Brand messages of all types contain layers of meaning. In most cases, particularly with advertising, there are obvious superficial or surface-layer meanings, but there may also be deeper layers of meaning that call for more interpretation (decoding) by the consumer. The "1984" commercial, for example, was obviously a product launch for the new Apple Macintosh.

A deeper meaning was the product comparison hinted at through Big Brother, who could be interpreted as representing IBM. **Semiotics** is a research tool used to uncover these layers of meaning.

The Effects behind Effectiveness

The most important characteristic of brand communication is that it is purposeful. Ads, for example, are created to have some effect on the people who read or see their message. We refer to this impact as **effects**, the idea being that effective brand communication will achieve the marketer's desired impact and the target audience will respond as the marketer intended. This desired impact is formally stated as a set of **objectives**, which are statements of the measurable goals or results that the message is intended to achieve. In other words, the brand message works if it achieves its objectives.

What are the effects that make brand communication effective? Consider your favorite commercials. Do they grip you emotionally? Do they have a compelling message ("1984")? How about learning something? Do you think about things because of something you heard or read in an ad ("Save a Life")? Does an ad need to be entertaining to work (think Apple's "1984" or New Pig from Chapter 1)?

The theme of this book is that good advertising—and brand communication—is effective when it achieves the advertiser's desired response. Thus, understanding what kinds of effects can be achieved with a marketing communication message is essential to anyone engaged in planning marketing communication. For example, a campaign for Detroit by Chrysler was designed to generate pride in Detroit-built Chryslers. This campaign started on the heels of Chrysler's bankruptcy during the recession when not only Chrysler was in crisis, but Detroit and American business as a whole were also in trouble. Since then, Chrysler has mounted a campaign, including a Super Bowl commercial, that contributed to Chrysler's turnaround and the way people think about the Motor City. The Super Bowl commercial featured rapper Eminem, who was believable because his story connected with Chrysler's. Eminem narrated the commercial with a backdrop of scenes of the Motor City, "a town that's been to hell and back," intercut with beauty shots of the Chrysler 200.

When we ask how it works, we are talking about the **impact** that communication has on receivers of the message—that is, how they respond to the message. What are the effects that

> **● Principle**
> The intended consumer response is the message's objective, and the message is effective to the degree that it achieves this desired response.

Photo: Courtesy FCA/Fiat Chrysler Automobiles. Used with permission.

Chrysler and its agency Wieden + Kennedy (the source) sought to convince American car buyers, particularly those who buy imports (the receivers), that they should buy Chrysler 200 and 300 sedans. In the words of the head of Chrysler brand communication, the message is that "you no longer have to cross oceans to get what you can have from these shores."

determine whether an advertisement works? Here are two of the traditional approaches used by professionals to outline the impact of advertising.[9]

- *AIDA* The most commonly used explanation of how advertising works is referred to as **AIDA**, which stands for attention, interest, desire, and action. This concept was first expressed around 1900 by advertising pioneer St. Elmo Lewis. Because AIDA assumes a predictable set of steps, it also is referred to as a **hierarchy of effects** model.
- *Think/Feel/Do* Another relatively simple answer to how advertising works is the **think/feel/do model** developed in the 1970s. Also referred to as the *FCB model* in honor of the agency where it was developed as a strategic planning tool, the idea is that advertising motivates people to think about the message, feel something about the brand, and then do something, such as try it or buy it.[10] This view is supported by recent research by Gergely Nyilasy and Leonard Reid, whose in-depth interviews found that "agency practitioners strongly believe that exposure to ads causes changes in human cognition, emotions, and behavior"—or think/feel/do.[11]

Principle

Not all purchases begin with a search for information. Some purchases are made out of habit or on impulse.

One problem with these approaches is that they are based on the concepts of a predictable process that consumers go through in making decisions, beginning with exposure to a brand message. The assumption is that consumers are engaged in systematic processing of information before they make a purchase. In reality, we know that consumers sometimes buy out of *habit*, such as people who are loyal drinkers of Coke or Pepsi. In other situations, consumers buy on *impulse*, such as when you are standing in line at a checkout counter and pick up a bar of candy. In both situations, you buy first and then think back on the purchase, if you give it any thought at all.

A different approach that attempts to eliminate the idea of predictable linear steps is found in Sandra Moriarty's domains model. It is based on the idea that messages have an impact on consumer responses, not in steps but at the same time. The three key effects, or domains, identified in this approach are (1) awareness, (2) learning, and (3) persuasion. The idea is that a message can engage consumers' perceptions (attention and interest), engage their thinking (learn), and persuade them (change attitude and behavior), and to some degree, all that occurs all at the same time.[12]

The Port of Vancouver USA ads are an example of how these effects interact. Even though the ads are in the business-to-business category, they get the attention of their audience with curiosity-provoking headlines: the "Vacancy" sign and "Part Specialist, Part Shepherd." The "vacancy" ad uses explanation to help readers understand ("858 acres to be exact"). It's also persuasive in that it makes the argument that the Port of Vancouver has room to grow and provide space to meet the needs of its customers.

A different approach to analyzing what works in brand communication is presented in J. Scott Armstrong's *Persuasive Advertising*, which identifies a set of 194 principles based on research findings over the years. Armstrong has reduced these principles to four categories that drive strategies: information, influence, emotion, and exposure. Other sets of categories describe tactics and media uses.[13]

How do we make sense of all these ideas about how brand communication works? One goal of this book is to organize these effects so that they are useful for setting objectives

Photo: Meinzahn/Getty Images.

In a world filled with commercial messages, understanding how to attract consumers' attention and engage them with the brand is key to effective communication.

and, ultimately, evaluating effectiveness. How do we do that? That's the question at the heart of this chapter, and we'll answer with our model of how brand communication works, a model we think you will find to be simple and easy to use in explaining the impact of a brand message.

The Facets of Impact

Our objective in this chapter is to present our Facets Model of Effects, which does a more complete job than previous models of explaining how advertising creates impact in terms of various types of consumer responses. Ultimately, we are guided by the kind of thinking that Regina Lewis expressed in the Part 2 opener: that consumers are loyal to brands that say something about them as human beings. Effective marketing communication speaks to us about things we want to know in ways we like.

The solution to our search for a new model is to build on the effects identified in the think/feel/do approach and add the missing categories, such as perception, association, and persuasion. It is interesting that these missing areas are also related to the three factors that the Ameritest research company uses in evaluating effective commercials: attention, brand linkage, and motivation (see www.ameritest.net).

Thus, we propose a six-factor model that is useful both in setting objectives and in evaluating the effectiveness of brand communication. Our answer to the question of how brand communication works is that effective brand messages create six types of consumer responses—(1) awareness, (2) feel, (3) think/understand, (4) connect, (5) believe, and (6) act/do—all of which work together to create the response to a brand message. These six consumer responses and the categories of effects to which they belong are represented in Figure 5.4.

5.2 Discuss how the idea of advertising effects developed and what problems exist in traditional approaches to advertising effects.

FIGURE 5.4
The Facets Model of Effects

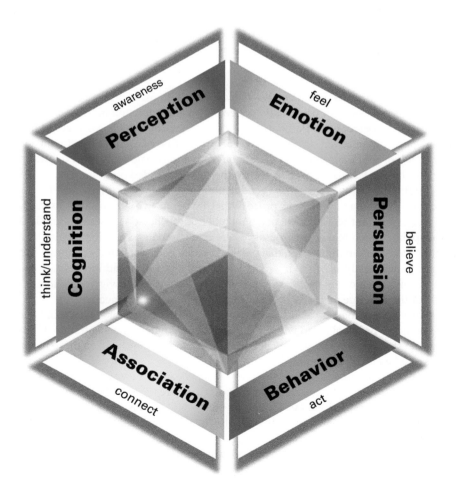

Think of these six effects as facets—polished surfaces like those of a diamond or crystal—that come together to make up a unique consumer response to a brand message. The effects are holistic in the sense that they lead to an impression, or what the late professor Ivan Preston calls an "integrated perception."[14] An effective message has a diamond-like quality that represents how the message effects work together to create the desired consumer response. The effects can vary in importance, with some campaigns more focused on one or several of the facets.

Here is a table to help you analyze impact in terms of the goal the message is trying to achieve and how that will be apparent in the way consumers respond to the message. The final column lists factors that can be measured to determine if you achieved the desired type of impact.

Communication Goal	Consumer Response	Factors That Drive a Response
Perception	Awareness	Exposure, selection and attention, interest, relevance, curiosity, recognition
Emotion	Feel	Wants and desires, excitement, feelings, liking, resonance
Cognition	Think/understand	Need, cognitive learning, comprehension, differentiation, recall
Association	Connect	Symbolism, conditioned learning, transformation
Persuasion	Believe	Motivation, influence, involvement, engagement, conviction, preference and intention, loyalty, believability and credibility
Behavior	Act/do	Mental rehearsal, trial, buying, contacting, advocating and referrals, prevention

Let's now explore these six categories of effects in more detail. We'll start with perception, which is where the consumer response to an advertisement begins.

The Perception Facet: Awareness

Principle
Breakthrough messages *grab* (get attention) and *stick* (lock in memory).

Every day, we are bombarded with stimuli—faces, conversations, scents, sounds, advertisements, and news announcements—yet we actually notice only a small fraction of those stimuli. Why?

The answer is perception. **Perception** is the process by which we receive information through our senses. If an advertisement is to be effective, first of all it must get noticed. It has to be seen or heard, even if the perception is minimal and largely below the level of awareness. We "see" commercials on television even as we zip through a recorded program. The challenge is to create breakthrough messages that *grab* (get attention) and *stick* (lock in memory).

Perception is a meaning-making process that involves two approaches, as explained by Charles Young, president of Ameritest and a member of this book's Advisory Board. One is the Gestalt viewpoint, which means that messages are understood as a unified whole. It is the way things come together as an impression that creates brand meanings. Another approach involves a moment-by-moment analysis of the interconnected string of words and images in a commercial or in a series of strategic messages. This process is used by active viewers who are trying to make sense of the message or messages in a process of constructing meaning.[15]

Principle
Breakthrough advertising breaks through perceptual filters, engages attention, and makes a lasting impression.

Either or both approaches lead to a brand impression in memory. Our minds are full of impressions that we have collected without much active thought or concentration. Of course, on occasion we do stop and read an ad or watch a commercial all the way through, so there are various degrees and levels of perception.

There are times when you know you have seen or heard a message before. In other words, **awareness** results when a brand message makes an impression—when something registers. New product campaigns, for example, seek to create high levels of brand awareness. Brand reminder ads on billboards and web pages are also designed to maintain a high level of awareness of familiar brands, as are logos on clothing.

The Eminem "Imported from Detroit" ad was particularly effective at breaking through inattention and building awareness. *Breakthrough advertising*, then, is brand communication that breaks through our perceptual filters, engages our attention, and makes a lasting impression on the audience.

Factors That Drive Perception   Consumers select messages to which they pay attention, a process called **selective perception**. Here's how perception works: Some ads for some product categories—personal hygiene products, for example—battle for attention because people don't choose to watch them. However, if the message breaks through the disinterest and is selected and attended to, the receiver may react to it with interest if it is relevant. An example comes from the media world, where a new service called Al Yenta uses algorithms based on massive databanks of information to send marketer's press releases only to the media outlets that really care about the subject rather than "carpet bombing" as many media outlets as possible.[16] The resulting relevance is a high level awareness of the ad or brand, which is filed in memory.

The key factors driving perception, then, are exposure, selection and attention, interest, relevance, curiosity, awareness, and recognition. Here is a brief review of these terms and how they relate to impact.

• **Exposure** The first test of perception is whether a brand communication message is seen or heard. In advertising, it is called **exposure**, which is an important goal of media planners who try to find the best way to reach consumers with a message.

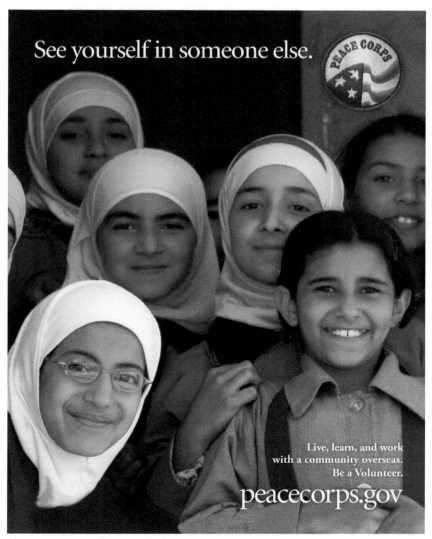

Photo: Courtesy of the Peace Corps

Messages that are personally relevant speak to a consumer's special interests.

- *Selection and Attention* The next factor that drives perception is **selective attention**, the process by which a receiver of a message chooses to attend to a message. Amid all the clutter in the media environment, selection is a huge problem. The ability to draw attention that brings visibility to a brand is one of advertising's greatest strengths. Advertisements, particularly television commercials, are often designed to be **intrusive**, which means that they intrude on people's perception so as to grab attention.

- *Interest* A factor in crossing the selection barrier is **interest**, which means that the receiver of the message has become mentally engaged in some way with the ad and the product. Ad messages are designed not only to get attention but also to hold the audience's interest long enough for the audience to register the point of the ad. That level of interest and attention is sometimes referred to as **stickiness**, particularly for websites.[17]

- *Relevance* One reason people are interested in something is **relevance**, which means that the message, such as the accompanying example for the Peace Corps, connects on some personal level. The Peace Corps launched a national recruiting campaign with the theme "See yourself in someone else." It was designed to address more relevant personal issues for potential volunteers and tell them how the volunteer experience would enrich their lives.

- *Curiosity* Another reason people pay attention is curiosity, which results from questioning, wanting to know more, or being intrigued by something. Curiosity also may be a problem for certain types of campaigns, such as antidrug and antismoking efforts.

- *Recognition* Advertisers are interested in two types of memory: **recognition**, which means that people remember seeing the ad, and **recall**, which means that they remember what the ad said. Recognition is a measure of perception and is used to determine awareness. Recall is a measure of understanding, which we will talk about in a later section on cognitive effects. Recognition relies on simple visuals that lock into memory, such as logos (Nike's swoosh), as well as colors (IBM's blue), jingles and sounds (Gershwin's "Rhapsody in Blue" for United Airlines), characters and key visuals (Polo's pony and the disbelieving look of the Aflac duck), and slogans (Altoids, "The Curiously Strong Mints"). Memory depends heavily on repetition to anchor an impression in the mind.

🔵 IMC Principle
People automatically integrate brand messages and experiences. Synergy occurs when all the messages work together to create a coherent brand perception.

The Synergy Requirement   As noted earlier, Ivan Preston wrote that the end result of effective marketing communication is an *integrated perception*. We call that a brand. In campaigns that use an integrated marketing communication (IMC) approach, marketers coordinate all the marketing communication messages to create **synergy**, which means that individual messages have more impact working jointly to promote a product than they would working on their own.[18] The reason is that people automatically integrate the messages and experiences they have with a brand to create their own personal brand perception. That happens whether or not the marketer plans for integrated communication. That's just how perception works. Sophistication managers understand this point and try to manage their communication programs so that all the messages work together to create Preston's coherent brand perception.

The Subliminal Issue   Before we leave the perception category, let's consider the controversial area of subliminal effects. **Subliminal** effects are message cues given below the threshold of perception. In other words, they don't register. As Professor Sheri Broyles explains in the Matter of Principle feature: "By definition, *subliminal* means the stimulus is below your threshold of consciousness. The first thing to know is that if you can see something, then it isn't subliminal." The idea is that subliminal messages are designed to get past your perceptual filters by talking directly to your subconscious. In contrast to the views of most professionals and even professors in advertising, critics who believe in subliminal advertising presume such messages to be intense enough to influence behavior, and they consider it to be unfair manipulation of unaware viewers. Broyles describes the research and thinking about the idea that unseen messages can be communicated in advertising.

The Emotion Facet: Feel

Can you remember any ads that you liked and why you liked them? **Affective responses** mirror our feelings about something: anger, love, fear, hate. The term *affective* describes something that stimulates wants, touches the emotions, establishes a mood, creates liking, and

Ice Cubes, Breasts, and Subliminal Ads

Sheri Broyles, *University of North Texas*

For more than 50 years, people have been looking for secret little subliminal messages carefully hidden in advertising we see every day. It began in 1957 in a movie theater experiment when James Vicary subliminally suggested people "eat popcorn" and "drink Coca-Cola" by projecting those words at 1/3,000th of a second on the screen during a movie. News media at the time widely reported his claims that sales of popcorn and soda increased as a result. Although he later admitted that these results were a hoax, it was as if Pandora had let subliminal advertising out of her box. A large majority of people have repeatedly said that they have heard of subliminal advertising (74 to 84 percent), they believe advertisers use this technique (68 to 85 percent), and they think it is effective (68 to 78 percent). Obviously, subliminal advertising continues to be an issue today.

Subliminal also has been misused to mean "suggestive" or "sexual." In the 1970s and 1980s, Wilson Bryan Key popularized this view in his books *Subliminal Seduction*, *Media Sexploitation*, and *The Clam-Plate Orgy*. He suggested that photographs were embedded (i.e., manipulated by airbrushing) with sexual or arousing images in ambiguous portions of the picture. He maintained that products ranging from alcoholic beverages to Ritz crackers used these sexual embeds. Key's self-proclaimed disciple, August Bullock, makes similar statements in his more recent book *The Secret Sales Pitch*.

There's been a continuing debate over the years about whether subliminal advertising actually exists. However, it's impossible to convince devout believers in subliminal advertising that what they *think* they see isn't there. Even more troubling is their assumption that presence implies effectiveness. Their belief is that because subliminal advertising exists—at least in their minds—it must be effective; otherwise, it wouldn't exist. Perhaps the more important question isn't whether subliminal advertising exists but whether it's an effective advertising tool. It should be noted that neither Key nor Bullock offers documentation that subliminal advertising actually works in any of the many examples in their books.

Several studies followed Vicary's theater experiment that explored whether subliminal advertising had an effect on consumers. Many different methodologies were used to test the effectiveness of subliminal stimuli. One 1959 study used early television to test subliminal persuasion. Another used a slide projector to subliminally superimpose a message. Others placed embeds in print ads. Most experiments showed no effect. Either those that did could not be replicated by the researchers or the effect was so weak that it would be canceled out by competing stimuli for the consumer's attention if it were not in a laboratory setting. There is no evidence to suggest that subliminal advertising would persuade real consumers to buy real products.

If subliminal advertising isn't effective, why are we still talking about it today? Although research has repeatedly shown that subliminal advertising doesn't work, the general public hasn't been persuaded, perhaps because they haven't been exposed to the decades of research. Subliminal advertising is like an urban legend or a good conspiracy theory: it's something that people want to believe. However, whether valid or not, it does affect the public's perception of advertising. That, in turn, reduces the credibility of advertisers and their agencies. And that's a concern for everyone in the advertising industry.

Photo: American Association of Advertising Agencies

A liquor advertising campaign showed ice cubes with shapes in them and deliberately called attention to these supposedly "subliminal" messages. Of course, they weren't subliminal because you could see the images. The whole campaign was a spoof on Key's theories.

elicits feelings. (*Affective* refers to emotional responses; *effective* refers to how well something works.) Young makes the point that feelings are emotions that make it into our consciousness;[19] in other words, we are aware of them.

Regina Lewis, a member of this book's Advisory Board, emphasized in the Part 2 opener that brands have a "human" quality, hence the importance of connecting with consumer's innermost feelings. Feelings and emotions can be positive or negative. Generally, brand communication seeks to wrap a positive halo around a brand and a purchase decision. Kevin Roberts, CEO of Saatchi & Saatchi, described the passion that loyal customers feel for their favorite brands in his books *Lovemarks* and *The Lovemarks Effect*. More recently, Brian Sheehan, a Saatchi executive who is now a Syracuse University advertising professor, has expanded this idea with the cases in his book, *Loveworks: How the World's Top Marketers Make Emotional Connections to Win in the Marketplace.*

The importance of positive responses has been institutionalized by Facebook with its famous "Like" button. Retailers are finding success with displays that allow customers to try such things as cosmetics or play with games before committing to a purchase. Entertainment has always had a positive value for commercial messages, and many commercials, such as the "Imported from Detroit" campaign, have high entertainment values that drive viewers' positive responses. For example, a hilarious YouTube ad in the 2016 US election featured Travis County (Texas) commissioner candidate Gerald Daugherty dominating parties and hanging around the house talking ad nauseam about the county's problems while his wife says that all he wants to do is fix things and that he doesn't have any hobbies. "Please re-elect Gerald," she says, rolling her eyes.[20]

Sometimes, however, a brand message arouses different emotions, such as dislike or anger. Ralph Lauren stumbled into negative territory with its ads promoting the uniforms that the firm designed for the US Olympic athletes. When the word got out that the outfits were made in China, angry Americans flooded Twitter and Ralph Lauren's Facebook page with negative comments.

Some ads are designed to make you feel negative about something (smoking, bugs in your home, or a political candidate). Negative messages are often used to alert consumers to problems that need to be solved, usually by applying or using the product being advertised. The "expensive gas" ad discussed earlier delivers a message about the dangers of drinking and driving.

In the case of irritating advertising, you may even respond by disliking a brand or an ad, which may be a sign of a failed campaign. Researchers have found that scaring people into action doesn't always work and that too much negativity can frighten people and make them turn against the brand.[21] Have you ever seen an ad that you positively disliked? How did that affect your attitude toward the brand?

Look back at the Facets Model of Effects in Figure 5.4. Notice how *perception* and emotion sit side by side at the top of the model. Although it isn't a linear process model, the perceptual process begins with perception, if a message registers at all. However, emotion is a driving factor because it is so closely related to perception. Erik du Plessis, the CEO of a global advertising research firm, makes the argument in his book *The Advertised Mind* that attention is driven by emotion.[22] He says our emotional responses to a message determine whether we pay attention. The key task of an ad, then, is initially to evoke an emotional response. It's generally thought that people respond to positive communication because they are more likely to like the subject of the message.

A question arises, however, about the power of a negative message, one that aims to generate negative responses such as dislike and loathing. Negative political advertising, for example, is a huge area for debate, particularly after the 2016 campaign with all its charges and countercharges by both Hillary Clinton and Donald Trump. In her research, Marilyn Roberts of Zayed University in the United Arab Emirates asked a key question: "Do negative ads work?" In her work, she has found that "almost in unison political media consultants for major US political parties say, 'Yes!'" That's the reason "the frequency of attack ads in presidential campaigns has risen steadily over the past decades, regardless of party affiliation," she said. She also pointed out that "exception is taken by consultants when referring to what they create as 'negative' advertising. Instead, many professionals prefer to use the term *contrast advertising* to underscore the differences between their candidate and his or her opponent."[23]

Factors That Drive Emotion   Emotional responses are powerful not only because they drive perception, but also because the ad breaks through disinterest. Furthermore, positive emotional responses drive memory as well as attention.

The affective response drivers are wants and desires, excitement, feelings, liking, and resonance. Emotion, then, causes us to "feel" something. A classic commercial that has generated positive responses for more than 40 years is the Coca-Cola "Hilltop" or "I want to teach the world to sing" commercial, which shows a multiethnic group of young people harmoniously singing the upbeat song. A product of the antiwar, peace movement, Woodstock generation, the 1972 commercial touched nerves as well as hearts, and it continues to get airtime, particularly on holidays. (Check out Coca-Cola's "Hilltop" commercial on YouTube.) The brand returned to "feelings" in 2016 with the "Taste the Feeling" campaign that showcased a new jingle, what some might call an emotional soundtrack for the brand.[24]

- *Wants and Desires* "I want something" implies desire. **Wants** are driven by emotions and based on wishes, longings, and cravings, such as teaching the world to sing, which is a metaphor for peace. Impulse buying is a good example of the motivational power of wants. When you are standing in line at a store and see a display of candy bars, you may want one, but that doesn't mean that you need it. It's strictly desire, and desire is driven by emotion. Consider Axe, which pioneered the new category of body spray for men in 2002 quickly dominating the market. Did guys know before 2002 that they would want scented body spray?
- *Excitement* A step above interest in terms of intensity of response (see the discussion of perception) is excitement, which means that our emotions or passions are aroused. If we are excited about something, we are agitated or energized and more willing to participate or make a commitment.
- *Feelings* Our passions and feelings are addressed in a number of ways in brand messages, such as humor, love, fear, or hate. Ads that rely on arousing feelings are referred to as using **emotional appeals**. The idea that emotional appeals may have more impact than rational approaches on both attitudes and behavior was supported by a University of Florida study that analyzed 23,000 consumer responses and found that the emotional response is more powerful than cognition in predicting action.[25]

Photo: Courtesy of The Gatorade Company and TBWA\Chiat\Day. Used with permission.

- *Liking* Two important affective responses to a message are liking the brand and liking the ad. On the opposite side, there's disliking the brand and the ad. *Liking* means having positive feelings, such as warmth, pleasure, enjoyment, and love. In brand communication, liking may reflect the personality of the brand or the entertainment power of the execution of the message. The assumption is that if you like the ad, that positive feeling will transfer to the brand, and if you feel positive about the brand, you will be more likely to buy it. A classic study of advertising testing methods by the Advertising Research Foundation found that liking—both the brand and the ad—was the best predictor of consumer behavior.[26]

Dislike, on the other hand, can lead to *aversion*, which means that people avoid buying a brand because they don't like the ads or what they associate with the brand. Avoidance is also a problem with messages and media; one example is zipping through commercials on television. We don't like to see condom ads, so they aren't often found in the mass media. Research has found that 75 percent of millennials dislike advertising

SHOWCASE

For the special occasion of Derek Jeter's retirement, Gatorade wanted to strike a more emotional chord with its audience. So, instead of just another TV spot, they created a moment and documented it.

"Made in New York" became a way for New York fans to see another side of their beloved legend in the final moments of his career. This content was specifically designed as a message from Jeter to be shared with all the fans who had supported him throughout his career.

Using the credibility of a 20-year relationship, Gatorade transformed its tribute to Jeter into a tribute from Jeter by giving him the chance to say good-bye his way. So, when it came to his final moments as a Yankee, Gatorade filmed him walking to Yankee Stadium thanking his fans in person. 90 minutes. 90 degrees. One take.

Ad Star Nick Ciffone, along with his art director partner Dave Estrada, created the spot that shows baseball great Derek Jeter saying farewell to his fans. Ciffone says, "Getting the chance to craft Derek Jeter's farewell spot was a once in 20 year opportunity. From what I could tell, Jeter was actually the kind of guy everyone thought he was." Watch the spot on the Gatorade or TBWA\Chiat\Day websites.

in general, which suggests that alternative forms of marketing communication are needed to communicate with this group.[27]

- *Resonance* Effective advertisements sometimes create **resonance**, or a feeling that the message "rings true." Like relevance, messages that resonate help the consumer identify with the brand on a personal level. Resonance is stronger than liking because it involves an element of self-identification. These sympathetic vibes amplify the emotional impact by engaging a consumer in a personal connection with a brand.

As described in the Showcase feature highlighting the work of copywriter Nick Ciffone, TBWA\CHIAT\DAY hit a home run when it put together the end-game commercial for Gatorade that bid farewell to New York Yankees superstar Derek Jeter. A touching tribute, the 90-second black-and-white commercial titled "My Way" showed the shortstop legend thanking Yankee fans to the tune of the famous Frank Sinatra song. Frank Sinatra's *My Way* became an anthem for Derek's retirement. As a legendary artist for the city of New York, Frank Sinatra's songs were played at the end of many Yankee games. The lyrics to *My Way* seemed to be written about Jeter's career. After the commercial played, *My Way* become so tied to Jeter that it played at Yankee stadium the last time he would be on the field in uniform.

The spot also showed him surprising kids and shocking patrons in a local sports bar as he made his way on foot to Yankee Stadium. The commercial was a true collaboration between TBWA\C\D and Jeter, who also appeared in an open letter tipping his cap to his fans in full-page advertisements that appeared in the *New York Daily News* and *Sports Illustrated*.

The spot was so successful it generated 846 stories representing more than 770 million impressions. It's estimated as being worth more than $16 million in ad value. There were also 10.5 million online views and it became Gatorade's most shared Facebook post ever.[28]

The Cognitive Facet: Think/Understand

How many ads that you have seen on television or noticed in print caused you to stop and think about the brand? Can you recall any instance where you learned something new about a product from an ad? Have you ever seen an ad you liked and then can't remember the name of the advertiser? Although perception and its partner, emotion, are the first effects of a brand message, messages may generate any of the other responses—cognition, association, persuasion, and behavior—nearly at the same time. For this discussion, we'll talk first about cognitive impact.[29]

Cognition refers to how consumers search for and make sense of information as well as how they learn and understand something. It's a rational response to a message that comes from thinking something through. Some call it a left-brain approach, based on the left brain–right brain ways of thinking that evolved from brain hemisphere research. Right-brain thinking is presumed to be more emotional, creative, and holistic than left-brain thinking. Cognitive neuroscientists continue to investigate hemispheric brain differences in humans to gain a better understanding of how and why the brain functions.

Traditionally, researchers have studied information processing as a way to understand how consumers think and learn about a product. Earlier we described Chrysler's "Keep Detroit Beautiful" campaign. At the same time this campaign ran, General Motors reported that its brand communication wasn't working. The reason: Despite spending some $4 billion on marketing and communication, "GM hasn't been able to dent the perception that other brands, particularly imports,

Photo: allanswart/Getty Images

The left side of this image represents left-brain cognitive thinking and the right side illustrates right-brain affective thinking that is more emotional, creative, and holistic.

are better."[30] In contrast, Chrysler linked its brand to the idea that imported cars are better quality with a twist on that idea in its "Imported from Detroit" campaign, an idea that takes some thought to understand. At the same time, General Motors was using such slogans as "Chevy Runs Deep," whatever that means.

The opposite of understanding is confusion and misunderstanding, which is equally of concern to brand communicators. Sometimes the information is oblique, as in "Chevy Runs Deep," or it might be too complex, such as the legal texts that are required to accompany pharmaceutical advertising. Critics of children's advertising are concerned that children cannot make rational decisions about advertisements. And sometimes there is brand confusion because too many messages from too many marcom functions are not consistent with one another.

Factors That Drive Cognition   Information processing—thinking things through—leads to a cognitive response. A consumer may need to know something so as to make a decision, and the information gathered in response to that need leads to understanding. The information has to be perceived and then filed in memory, but it can be recalled when needed. Advertising and other marketing communication often provide information about products, usually facts about product performance and features, such as size, price, construction, and design. In certain situations, such as the purchase of a big-ticket item (e.g., a computer or a car), consumers search for this kind of information and use it to compare one product with another.

The informative nature of brand communication is particularly important for product categories that are complex (e.g., appliances, cars, insurance, computers, and software) or that involve a high price or high risk (e.g., motorboats, vacations, and medical procedures). It is much less important for purchases bought out of habit, such as a favorite brand of soft drink, or impulse purchases made on the spot in the store. The key drivers of a consumer's cognitive response are need, cognitive learning, comprehension, differentiation, and recall.

- *Need* Brand stewards talk a lot about consumer needs and wants. Generally, **needs** are basic biological motivations, but they may also be something you think about; *wants* tend to be based more on feelings and desires. In other words, when we refer to needs, we are usually talking about a message that describes something lacking in consumers' lives and that often stimulates a cognitive response. Advertisers address consumer needs through informational ads that explain how a product works and what it can do for the user—in other words, the benefits it offers to the user. For example, consumers need a virus protection program for their personal computers, but they also may need an explanation of how the program works.

  Complicating our understanding of needs and wants is the impact of a major event, such as the recession that began in 2007. Consider the tug between *want* (a Cadillac Escapade specially designed on General Motor's website to a customer's order) and *need* (a used car that offers the best value in terms of miles and price) or between a want and a need that's simply postponed because it's of less significance than other, more compelling needs.

- *Cognitive Learning* Consumers learn about products and brands through two primary routes: cognitive learning and conditioned learning. (We'll talk about conditioned learning in the section on association.) **Cognitive learning** occurs when a presentation of facts, information, and explanations leads to understanding. Consumers who are trying to find information about a product before they buy it are taking the cognitive learning route. This route typically applies to large purchases, such as cars, computers, and major appliances. Learning is also a part of new product introductions. In recent years, we have had to learn to use computers, VCRs, the internet, and the iPod, and brand communication is the key tool used by marketers to teach prospective customers about these products and product innovations.

Photo: skhoward/Getty Images

In what ways can an emotional appeal like "craving" drive a cognitive response?

- *Comprehension* The process by which people understand, make sense of things, and acquire knowledge is called **comprehension**. Confusion, on the other hand, is the absence of understanding and is usually the result of logic problems. For example, it's difficult for consumers to understand why an outdoor board for the gas-guzzling Hummer would use a green marketing strategy. The headline "Thirst for adventure. Not gas." suggests a gas-efficient Hummer, and the logic doesn't follow from what people commonly know about this vehicle.
- *Differentiation* The consumer's ability to separate one brand from another in a product category is called **differentiation**. Distinguishing between competing brands is what happens when consumers understand the explanation of a competitive advantage. In a classic study of effective television commercials, researchers concluded that one of the most important effectiveness factors is a brand-differentiating message.[31]
- *Recall* We mentioned earlier that recognition is a measure of perception and that recall is a measure of learning or understanding. When you recall the ad message, you remember not only seeing the ad and, it is hoped, the brand, but also the copy points, or the information provided about the brand. To recall information presented in the ad, however, you must have concentrated on it and thought about it either as the information was being presented or afterward. Thinking about it—similar to mentally rehearsing the key points—is a form of information processing that helps anchor ideas in memory and makes recall easier.

Thinking and Feeling   Even though this section is on cognitive processing, notice that feeling and thinking work together. Psychologist and advertising professor Esther Thorson and her colleagues have developed a *memory model of advertising* to explain how commercials are stored in memory as traces that contain bits and pieces of the commercial's message, including the feelings elicited by the message. Recall of any of those elements—especially feelings—can serve as a cue to activate memory of the commercial.[32]

● **Principle**
In communication perception, emotion comes first, and thought comes second.

A frequent question asked by researchers is, "Which is more important in brand communication—thinking or feeling?" Young, the founder of the Ameritest research company, emphasized that "in all acts of perception and communication, emotion comes first, and thought comes second."[33] The important role of emotion in directing perception also structures our responses to brand messages, particularly those that engage us on a personal level. That, of course, completely contradicts the traditional information-processing–based models of effectiveness.

This view about the importance of emotion is supported by research in the neurosciences, which advertising professor Ann Marie Barry said, "acknowledges the primacy of emotions in processing all communication."[34] She explained in writing for this book that "perception, the process by which we derive meaning from what we see, is an elaborate symphony played first and foremost through the unconscious emotional system. Furthermore, emotion is the first path that perception takes. It is also the fastest, and most significant factor in perception." In terms of the relationship between thinking and feeling, Barry explained: "In fact, most of what we call the *thought process* in making decisions is actually trying to rationalize what we have already concluded through our emotional system. Marketers know that if they can convince us emotionally, we can rationalize away any objections by ourselves." According to Barry, here's how emotion and thinking work together:

● **Principle**
Communication that makes consumers both think and feel provides better support for a brand image; thought without emotion or emotion without thought makes it difficult to anchor the brand in memory.

> Every brand that we use in effect advertises who we are when we wear it or use it, telling people a little bit about us or just reinforcing how we feel about ourselves (or would like to feel). If the emotional appeal is missing, however, we lose a personal connection with the product or service. If the rational benefit is missing, we may not find enough reason to purchase an item where elements such as price, ease of use, or technological advantages play a major role. For an advertisement to be truly effective, the visual story implicit in it must seamlessly bring together both consumer image and brand image in a perfect integration of both thought and feeling.

Although researchers now recognize the significance of emotion in effective brand communication, it is important to note that the two responses of think and feel also work together. As Young said about his firms' research findings, "Images that made consumers simultaneously both *think and feel* were much more likely to be associated with the brand's current image.

These same images also better fit the brand's positioning in the marketplace." And the opposite is also true. He said, "Images that engendered a thought without an emotion—or an emotion without a thought—were not associated in their memories of the brand to any significant degree."[35]

The point is that brands live in the heads and hearts of users. A brand may be priced in the middle of the category, but if customers think it's high priced, that confusing misinformation (the head) muddies the brand impression. It may create a negative feeling (the heart). The communication has to change either the head by doing a better job of explaining the price relative to the competition or the heart by making customers feel better about the value of the brand.

The Association Facet: Connect

What do you think of when you see an ad for Nike, Viagra, or Mountain Dew? The things that come to your mind, such as athletes for Nike, older men for Viagra, and teenage guys having fun for Mountain Dew, are the brands' associations. **Association** is the technique of communicating through symbolism; we might say that symbolic meanings are transferred through the process of association. The transfer of meaning connects personal meanings to goods and other symbols, such as celebrities.[36] In the Matter of Practice feature, researcher Young analyzes the impact of a brand message in terms of its associations linking a Volkswagen Passat to the power of *Star Wars*'s Darth Vader.

> ● **Principle**
> Brand communication creates brand meaning through symbolism and association. These meanings transform a generic product into a specific brand with a distinctive image and personality.

A MATTER OF PRACTICE

May VW's Force Be with You

Charles Young, *Founder and CEO, Ameritest/CY Research*

A commercial for Volkswagen's Passat called "The Force" was created by the Deutsch agency and first aired on the 2011 Super Bowl. It was ranked by most commentators as the number one commercial shown during the game.

It opens with a pint-sized Darth Vader in costume marching through the house to *Star Wars* music. He is seen raising his hands to engage the power of The Force on home appliances and even his dog and a doll—with no effect. When his father returns home in a new Passat, Little Darth rushes outside to use "The Force" on this new machine. As he faces the car, the engine starts, and he jumps back, triumphant at having finally found "The Force." His father is shown looking out the window after pressing the start button on the radio key.

This commercial was analyzed by Steven Sands of Sands Research using brain wave metrics. He found that it was not only the highest-performing ad of that Super Bowl, but it was also one of the strongest commercials he's ever tested in terms of its ability to arouse viewers' brains.

I decided to test the ad using the Ameritest system, which uses information from an analysis of respondent's conscious reactions to a message. It includes classic measures of attention, branding, communication, and motivation.

Consistent with Sands's engagement ranking, we found that this ad is very strong in attracting attention, scoring in the 99th percentile of the thousands of ads we've tested. It's also significantly above the norm in motivation but below average in its brand linkage to Volkswagen.

The drivers of its attention score are its entertainment value, uniqueness, and the likability of the music. The drivers of its motivation score are its believable message and the relatability of the characters and the situation. The soft branding score is because, in part, it stretches brand perceptions, meaning that the message has to work harder to achieve good top-of-mind brand scores.

In terms of brand communication, the commercial did communicate the surface meaning that the new Passat is a "fun" car. The subtext, however, was that the new Volkswagen was "surprisingly powerful." This insight led Volkswagen to adopt the tagline "The Power of German Engineering" in the next evolution of this campaign.

See VW's "Force" ad at https://www.youtube.com/watch?v=9bPoD0f9Gas.

Association is an important tool used in brand communication and guides the process of making symbolic connections between a brand and desirable characteristics as well as people, situations, and lifestyles that cue the brand's image and personality. Young emphasizes the importance of association in creating brand images in his e-book *Branded Memory*. He defines a brand image as "the set of emotional and experiential association with the brand that is built up over time."[37]

You see association at work in brand communication in the practice of linking a brand with a positive experience, an idea, a personality type, or a lifestyle, such as Axe with cool young men or Coke with a mountaintop experience. The idea is to associate the brand with things that resonate positively with the customer. It's a three-way process: the (1) brand relates to (2) a quality that (3) customers value. Brands take on symbolic meaning through this association process. Preston, in his *association model of advertising*, believed that you can explain how advertising works by understanding association.[38]

● **Principle**
Brand communication employs both rational arguments and compelling emotions to create persuasive messages.

Sometimes associations can be powerful because they are unexpected. The Keebler cookie brand found a sweet spot in its partnership with the American Red Cross by encouraging consumers to donate blood. Keebler provided a much-needed sugary treat to those who did. Sometimes association can backfire, as it did in a 2013 ad for Nike that featured Oscar Pistorius with a picture of the double-amputee Olympian blasting from the starting line and a headline that read, "I am the bullet in the chamber." The symbolism was tragically ironic after Pistorius was arrested for, and later convicted of, the murder of his girlfriend.

Photo: winhorse/Getty Images

The Coke vending machine is decorated with the panda, a beloved symbol associated with China to help create a positive brand emotion.

Factors That Drive Association The goal of association is to use symbolic connections to define the brand and make it distinctive. **Brand linkage** reflects the degree to which the associations and ideas presented in the message, as well as the consumer's interest, are connected to the brand and transform it from a product to a recognizable and memorable brand image. For example, an ad for Bisquick Heart Smart mix shows a pancake in the shape of a heart. In this case, the brand name—Bisquick Heart Smart—is easily associated with the product use—your heart and healthy pancakes.

Linking a brand with an idea so as to build a brand image can be difficult to the degree that it involves cognition. The Darth Vader commercial, for example, is only effective to the degree that viewers understand and connect "the force is with you" concept from *Star Wars* with starting the VW Passat's engine.

The association drivers are symbolism, conditioned learning, and transformation.

- *Symbolism* Through association, a brand takes on a *symbolic meaning*, which means that the brand stands for certain qualities. It represents something, usually something abstract. Bisquick's pancakes shaped like hearts convey the heart-healthy message symbolically. The Port of Vancouver USA business-to-business ads use symbolism to catch attention and tell a story, such as the vacancy sign in the ad analyzed earlier. The panda, a symbol of China, is used on the vending machines, as the photo illustrates.
- *Conditioned Learning* Although advertisements sometimes use a cognitive strategy, they frequently are designed to elicit noncognitive associations through **conditioned learning**, the process by which a group of thoughts and feelings becomes linked to the brand through repetition of the message. Beer advertising directed at a young male audience, for example, often

uses images of sporting events, beach parties, and good-looking young women. People also learn by watching others, which is called **social learning**. We learn about fashion by watching how others dress and about manners by watching how other people interact. We connect their appearance and manners to certain situations reflected in the ads.

- *Transformation* The result of the brand association process is transformation. **Transformation,** as originally explained by former DDB research director Bill Wells, is what happens when a product takes on meaning and is transformed from a mere product into something special. It becomes differentiated from other products in the category by virtue of its brand-image symbolism and personality cues. Bisquick Heart Smart is more than just flour; it rises above the average product in the category and stands out as something unique and healthy. That transformation in a consumer's mind is a perceptual shift created by the associations cued through marcom messages.

Association Networks   You probably had a number of associations when we asked you to think about Nike. Athletes come to mind, but so do shoes, engineering, design, the "swoosh" logo, competition, sporting events, and maybe even a fun retail experience if you have ever visited a Nike store. The association process is built on a **network of associations**, called a **knowledge structure**, in which one thought cues other thoughts. Your thoughts and feelings about the Nike brand are elements linked in your own individual pattern of associative thinking. You might say that these association networks explain how our memories work. Researchers seeking to determine the meaning of a brand will ask people to talk about their associations with a brand and to re-create these association networks so as to understand how a brand's meaning comes together as an impression in people's minds.

The Persuasion Facet: Believe

When you see ads from the "Got Milk?" campaign with celebrities sporting a milk mustache, what do you think is the objective of the advertising? Is it providing information about milk? Is it trying to connect with you on an emotional level through feelings? Is it trying to get you to run down to the store and load up on milk? The real objective of these ads is to change your attitude toward milk. It aims to convince you that milk isn't just for kids and that attractive, interesting adults drink it, too. In other words, its goal is persuasion.

Persuasion is the conscious intent on the part of the source to influence or motivate the receiver of a message to believe or do something. Persuasive communication—creating or changing attitudes and creating conviction—is an important goal of most brand communication. An **attitude** is a state of mind: a tendency, inclination, or mental readiness to react to a situation in a given way. Because advertising rarely delivers immediate action, *surrogate* effects, such as changing an attitude that leads to a behavior, are often the goal of advertising. Attitudes are the most central factors in persuasion.

Attitudes can be positive, negative, or neutral. Both positive and negative attitudes, particularly those embedded in strong emotions, can motivate people to action or away from action. A negative attitude toward smoking, for example, may keep teenagers from trying cigarettes, and creating that negative attitude was the objective of the "Truth" campaign.

Attitudes are both rational and emotional. The rational element is confirmed by advertising pro Ogilvy, who said in his classic little book *Confessions of an Advertising Man*, "Very few advertisements contain enough factual information to sell the product." He was also quoted on the Advertising Hall of Fame website as saying that it needs to be informative to be persuasive.[39]

Rational *information processing* is important for certain types of ads. Consider, for example, the Canadian government's Citizenship Act, which was designed to restore citizenship to thousands of unsuspecting foreigners,

COUNTRIES
LOVE SET

Photo: Annykos/Getty Images

A visual filled with images that evoke the viewers' experience help create a positive attitude, in this case, for Canada.

many of them Americans, who were forced to renounce their Canadian citizenship when they became citizens of another country. Canada used ads on YouTube titled "Waking Up Canadian" to inform former Canadians about this situation. (Check it out at www.youtube.com/watch?v=eDeDQpIQFD0.)

When people are convinced of something, their attitudes are expressed as **beliefs**. Sometimes attitude strategies attempt to extinguish beliefs, such as that getting drunk is a badge of masculinity, that overeating is acceptable, or that racist and sexist comments are funny. Attitude change strategies often use the tools of logic and reasoning, along with arguments and counterarguments, to intensify the feelings on which beliefs are built. A successful belief change is called a *conversion*.

Persuasion, in other words, is an area where cognitive and affective factors are interrelated. Persuasion works both through rational arguments and by touching emotions in such a way that they create a compulsion to act. Negative political advertising campaigns, or attack ads, are a good example of how people form opinions at the same time that they process information that is presented within an emotional frame.

Factors That Drive Persuasion   Persuasion has many dimensions, but advertisers identify the following factors to explain how persuasion affects consumers: motivation, influence, involvement, engagement, conviction, preference and intention, loyalty, and believability and credibility.

- *Motivation* A factor in creating a persuasive message is **motivation**. Underlying motivation is the idea that something, such as hunger or a desire to be beautiful or rich, prompts a person to act in a certain way. How strongly does someone feel about acquiring something or about taking a certain kind of action, such as applying to graduate school or signing up for the Peace Corps? This feeling sets up a state of tension, and the product becomes a tool in achieving that goal and thus reducing the tension. A more current example of the power of motivation cropped up in the development of **carrot mobs**, a technique used by environmentalists to reward companies that support green marketing. It's a reverse boycott that uses positive action by getting large groups of people to shop at eco-friendly stores.

- *Influence* If you think that you need to lose weight or stop smoking, how much of that decision is based on your own motivations, and how much of your motivation results from messages from others? Some people, known as **opinion leaders**, may be able to influence other peoples' attitudes and convince them of the "right" decision. The idea is that these influencers—friends, family, teachers, and experts—may affect your decision making. Testimonies—from real people, celebrities (the "Got Milk?" campaign), and experts—are often used create or change attitudes. For example, Kellogg set up a "Breakfast Council" of dietitians and nutritional experts to advise on cereals. (The only problem, critics found, was that the council's tweets and other public comments were not identified as made by paid consultants.)[40]

   There's even a social media site that seeks to measure influence. Called Klout, the site estimates users' online influence based on their Facebook, Twitter, Foursquare, Google+, and LinkedIn activities. A +*K* button lets users vote on whether a person identified by Klout as having clout really is influential on a certain topic. In terms of promotional communication, **bandwagon appeals**—messages that suggest that everyone is doing it—are also used to influence people's decisions. Word-of-mouth communication has always been recognized as the most powerful form of persuasion, and that's why strategies that engage influencers are so important.

- *Involvement* Advertisers distinguish between products, messages, and media on the basis of the level of involvement they require from the buyer. Earlier, when we described reasons people don't always go through serious information processing such as habit and impulse purchases, we were referring to their level of involvement with the product decision. **Involvement** refers to the degree to which you are engaged in attending to a message and the process you go through in interacting with a product, including responding to a message and making a decision to buy. Some products, such as cosmetics, call for a more involving process than others, such as toothpaste. Products with **high involvement** demand more from consumers who may spend considerable time and effort searching for information and thinking before making decisions. These **considered purchases** include such products as cars, computers, and houses as well as things you care about a lot, like expensive clothing.

Examples of products with **low involvement** are aspirin, paper napkins, envelopes, paper clips, and lettuce. The idea is that with some products, you don't spend much time thinking about them before you buy them. Nor do you pay much attention to their brand messages, which you may ignore or file away without much thought.

In addition to product categories, some message strategies, such as dramas and humor, are more involving than others. Likewise, various types of media are intrinsically more or less involving. Television, for example, is considered to be less involving than print, which demands more concentration from its readers than television does of its viewers (although a gripping television drama can be involving because of the power of the story line).

- *Engagement* The idea of **engagement** is that a consumer is more than just interested in something; in other words, he or she is, in the words of the Advertising Research Foundation committee that investigated engagement, "turned on."[41] Participation and engagement cultivate passion and also drive people to be more involved in a brand experience.

Young explains what goes on in the mind of someone engaged with a brand message, such as a commercial or a promotion, as they ask themselves questions such as the following:[42]

"What's important here?"

"How does this point fit with that other point?"

"Where is this going?"

"How do I feel about this?"

"How is it relevant to me?"

Engagement with a brand or message is generally a good thing, but McDonald's had one engaging social media program blow up all over the web. The plan was to have McDonald's appear on the trend list on Twitter's home page with the hashtag #MeetTheFarmers that led to a series of ads with gritty farmers talking about real food born of the soil. But when viewers were led to #McDStories, a site where viewers were encouraged to continue the conversation, the site was overwhelmed with critics commenting about everything from health concerns to the "supersize-me" debate. The anti-McDonald's Twitter storm got all the media attention even if the positive comments were four to five times as frequent. Engagement is such an important concept for the new online media that there are companies today, such as sitecore. net, that specialize in measuring it. Sporting teams and events also are drivers of involvement, as the Matter of Principle feature explains.

- *Conviction* Effective persuasion results in **conviction**, which means that consumers agree with a persuasive message and achieve a state of certainty—a belief—about a brand. A factor in conviction is the power of the **argument**, which uses logic, reasons, and proof to make a point and build conviction. Understanding an argument is a complex cognitive process that demands the audience "follow through" on the reasoning to understand the point and reach a conclusion.

- *Preference and Intention* When consumers marry belief with a **preference** for or an **intention** to try or buy a product, they are motivated by conviction. Intention can be heightened with reward strategies, such as good deals, sale pricing, and gifts. Good intentions are the motivations behind cause marketing and social responsibility. Hewlett-Packard (HP), for example, promotes its computer recycling program to increase preference for HP products by its customers. Presumably the PC recycling program attracts consumers to HP products because the company assumes responsibility for recycling its old products. In other words, this consumer benefit leads to higher customer satisfaction and, thus, loyalty to the HP brand.

- *Loyalty* Is there any brand you buy, use, or visit on a regular basis? Do you have a favorite shampoo, restaurant, or beverage? Why is that? What we are referring to when we talk about a "favorite" brand is preference but also **brand loyalty**, which we mentioned in Chapter 2. Loyalty is an attitude (respect or preference), an emotion (liking), and an action (repeat purchases). As brands are connected to the internet through wearable devices and

The Engagement Strategy behind Sports Advertising

John Sweeney, *University of North Carolina at Chapel Hill*

The top 50 advertisers invested more than $5.68 billion in sports advertising in 2011. It is significant to note that the amount of spending on sports increased every year during the Great Recession.

Sports deliver a mass audience but also a passionate one. By associating with the emotional involvement of fans, a brand can win greater impact than traditional media, where the viewers have little or no loyalty.

The entire strategy that a brand brings to be part of sports also gives an insight into why this category has grown so prosperous. Let's look at a few years of McDonald's sponsorship of the Olympic Games. McDonald's became a top or global partner at the 1998 Nagano Olympics, and its sponsorship of the games has now been officially extended to the year 2020.

The Olympics are the world's most popular event, with the games being broadcast across the globe. It is one of the few opportunities in media for a company like McDonald's to involve not only the United States, but also—without hyperbole—the entire planet. And that is clearly valuable for a company with 35,000 locations in 119 countries.

McDonald's, as a partner for the 2016 Rio Summer Olympics, did far more than run commercials. Most companies use sponsorships in all aspects of their business, including bringing customers to the competitions and increasing company morale by involving employees. McDonalds' programs and stories that were highlighted during the Olympics include the following:

- The McDonald's Olympics Kids program brought 100 kids from 20 countries around the world to walk in the Parade of Nations during the opening ceremonies at Rio's famed Maracanã Stadium in front of 80,000 live spectators and billions of television viewers worldwide. The flag bearer of each of the country athlete delegations was accompanied by a McDonald's Olympics Kid (McDonald's, 2016).
- The McDonald's Olympics Kids from the United States and Canada were selected by Ronald McDonald House Charities as having overcome great adversity.
- Also, McDonald's received a great deal of positive publicity when stories emerged of athletes waiting in long lines at the McDonald's restaurant in the Olympic Village for their burgers, fries, and nuggets (Bariso, 2016; Partlow, 2016).

In a world of too many television channels with programming that gathers only modest interest, sports can deliver passionate involvement in a way that goes beyond a jingle or a catchphrase. That's why so many companies continue to invest in the leagues and events that we follow in sports.

Source: "McDonald's Olympics Kids Walk With Athletes in the Rio 2016 Olympic Games Opening Ceremony #friendswin," McDonald's Newsroom, August 5, 2016, www.news.mcdonalds.com/press-releases/mcdonald-s-olympics-kids-walk-with-athletes-in-the-rio-2016-olympic-games-openin-1271889, accessed August 22, 2017; "Why Do Olympic Athletes Love McDonald's So Much? It Comes Down to 2 Simple Reasons," Justin Bariso, *Inc Magazine*, August 5, 2016, www.inc.com/justin-bariso/the-2-simple-reasons-why-olympic-athletes-in-rio-are-eating-so-much-mcdonalds.html, accessed August 22, 2017; "Olympic athletes are gorging themselves on free McDonald's," Joshua Partlow, *The Washington Post*, August 12, 2016, www.washingtonpost.com/world/the_americas/olympic-athletes-are-gorging-themselves-on-free-mcdonalds/2016/08/12/25f0eb35-5a26-4bdb-8643-123855fb0430_story.html?utm_term=.a32deb80ad73, accessed August 22, 2017.

reward systems—a practice referred to as "the internet of things"—more opportunities develop for loyalty. For example, the Humana health care insurance company uses fitness brands to track the activity level of its Humana Vitality members to reward them for their fitness activities.[43]

It is a response to brand communication that crosses over between thinking, feeling, and doing, a response that is built on **customer satisfaction**. If you try a product and like it, you will be more likely to buy it again. Is there a return policy or guarantee that frees you from risk when you buy something for the first time in case you don't like it? Providing information about warranties, customer service, and technical support for technology products is an important part of preference and loyalty strategies. The idea is to reduce risk and put the customer's mind at ease. Incentives are also used in loyalty programs, such as frequent-flyer or frequent-buyer programs. In addition, social responsibility and cause marketing programs can build trust, respect, and preference that lead to loyalty.

- *Believability and Credibility* An important issue in persuasion is **believability**, which refers to the credibility of the arguments in a message. Puffery or unprovable claims, such as the common phrase "9 out of 10 doctors recommend . . . ," can strain believability. Related to believability is **credibility**, which is an indication of the trustworthiness of the source. **Source credibility** means that the person delivering the message, such as an expert, is respected, trusted, and believable. Believability and credibility are the two key ingredients in *trust*, which is essential to brand liking and loyalty. Trust took a hit during the recession as polls showed that people were much less likely to trust business leaders and believe that businesses would do the "right thing."[44]

Credibility is one of the big advantages of public relations because publicity stories delivered through a supposedly unbiased news medium have higher credibility than advertising, which is seen as self-serving. Using data to support or prove a claim, for example, gives consumers a **reason to believe** the advertising. Advertising can use a credibility strategy to intensify the believability of its message. After the 2010 Deepwater Horizon oil spill in the Gulf coast, BP used advertising to say that the company was committed to cleaning up the mess. The strategy hinges on the company's credibility.

The Behavior Facet: Act/Do

We introduced loyalty in the previous section on persuasion and noted that it intersects with behavior. Behavior can involve different types of action in addition to trying or buying the product, such as visit a store, return an inquiry card, call a toll-free number, join an organization, donate to a good cause, or click on a website.

Emotion is also linked closely to behavior. Conversion marketing, for example, often engages people with an emotional brand promise that drives action.[45] Seeing a new clothing line in a video on a smartphone or tablet can be exciting and can lead to an immediate purchase, and then tweets to friends can influence them to check it out. All that can be done in a matter of moments and a few keystrokes.

The Billings, Montana, "Trailhead" branding campaign that we discussed in Chapter 1 used a giveaway to build excitement for and community participation in the new community brand identity effort. Special promotions like that one are designed to engage and involve the audience.

We must distinguish, however, between **direct action**, which represents an immediate response (cut out the order form and send it back by return mail), and **indirect action**, which is a delayed response (recall the message later in the store and select the brand). Advertising almost by definition is characterized by indirect action; we're seldom at the store when we hear, see, or read an ad for the store's products. Mobile advertising, which means that targeted messages are sent to people in the neighborhood through their smartphones, is one way to better link a message and action.

The "I Want You" World War I poster by artist James Montgomery Flagg is a classic example of an advertising message that was designed to create action, although visiting a recruiting

Photo: Courtesy of the Billings Chamber of Commerce/ Convention and Visitors' Bureau

SHOWCASE

The Billings "Trailhead" campaign used weekly drawings, with the winners receiving "Trailhead" caps and the grand prize winner receiving dinner and two nights at the Crowne Plaza Hotel.

John Brewer, president and CEO of the Billings Chamber of Commerce/Convention and Visitors Bureau, graduated from the University of West Florida. He was nominated to be featured here by Professor Tom Groth.

● Principle
Advertising has delayed effects in that a consumer may see or hear an advertisement but not act on that message until later when in a store.

station would necessarily be indirect or delayed action. This image has been used many times by other organizations to replicate the power of this compelling message.

There is also purposeless action, which became a fad at the beginning of the twenty-first century when viral email messages would generate a sudden and conspicuous gathering of people. Called **flash mobs**, these public spectacles included concerts, marriage proposals, and even a worldwide day of pillow fights. Flash mobs demonstrate the power of the internet and buzz to engage people, involve them in something memorable, and drive them into action, even if the action is largely meaningless. For an example, find "Puttin' on the Ritz" in Moscow on YouTube.

In terms of media use, one behavior that worries marketers is the tendency to avoid brand messages. Ad skipping, which allows viewers to skip the ads in previously recorded television programs, is available through a number of technologies, such as Dish Network's Auto Hop. Millions of television viewers do it, and the industry recognizes the need to develop better or different programming to keep its audience in place.

Factors That Drive the Behavioral Response   The behavioral response involving action of some kind is often the most important goal of brand communication, particularly for tools such as sales promotion and direct marketing. Factors that drive a behavioral response include mental rehearsal, trial, buying, contacting, advocating and referrals, and prevention.

- *Mental Rehearsal* The **mental rehearsal** of behaviors is made possible by showing visuals of people doing things. As Young explained, one of the functions of brand messages is to create virtual memories—in other words, experiences that we can imagine ourselves doing.[46] Visualization is an imagined action, but one that is the predecessor to the behaviors with which the advertiser hopes the consumer will feel comfortable and familiar.
- *Trial* The first step in making a purchase is often to try the product. A **trial** is important for new products and expensive products because it lets a customer use the product without initially committing to a purchase. In other words, the risk is reduced. Sales promotion is particularly good at driving trials through special price deals, sampling, and incentive programs that motivate behavior, such as a free gift when you go to a dealer to test-drive a new car.
- *Buying* The objective of most marketing programs is sales. In advertising, sales are sometimes stimulated by the **call to action** at the end of an ad along with information on where to purchase the product. From a customer perspective, making a sale means making a purchase. In customer-focused marketing programs, the goal is to motivate people to try or buy a certain brand. In some marketing programs, such as those for nonprofit organizations, the marketing program may be designed to encourage the audience to sign up, volunteer, or donate. For many managers, however, sales volume is the gold standard for effective advertising. They believe that even if they are funny, memorable, or entertaining, ads are failures if they don't help sell the brand. The problem is that it may be difficult to prove that a brand communication message is the one factor in the marketing mix that delivered the sales. It could be the price, the distribution, the product design and performance, or some combination of the marketing mix elements. Effectiveness programs, such as the London-based Institute of Practitioners Award program, encourage advertisers to use research to prove that it was, in fact, the advertising that actually drove the sales.
- *Contacting* Trying and buying may be the marketer's dream response, but other actions can also be important measures of an advertisement's behavioral effectiveness. Responding by making contact with the advertiser can be an important sign of effectiveness. Initiating contact is also valuable, particularly in IMC programs designed to maintain brand relationships by creating opportunities for customer-initiated dialogue, such as encouraging customers with a complaint, compliment, or suggestion to contact the company.
- *Advocating and Referrals* One of the behavioral dimensions of brand loyalty is **advocacy**, or brand fans speaking out on a brand's behalf and referring to it when someone asks for a recommendation. Contacting other people is a valuable response, particularly when a satisfied customer brings in more business for the brand by providing testimonials to friends, family, and colleagues on behalf of the brand. In terms of the impact of **referrals**, when a satisfied customer recommends a favorite brand, this form of word of mouth can be

incredibly persuasive, more so than advertising, which is seen as self-serving. Apple's success is credited to its passionate customers who, as evangelists for the brand, spread the word among their friends and coworkers. Social media has intensified the importance of fans advocating on behalf of a brand to their friends.

This *advocacy level*, which Richard Cross and Janet Smith described in their book *Customer Bonding*,[47] represents the highest form of a brand relationship. A recommendation to buy a specific brand is the ultimate test of the bond between consumers and their favorite brands. The opposite—brand aversion—can be disastrous if the dissatisfied customer shares his or her dislike with other people.

- *Prevention* In some social action situations, brand messages are designed to deter behaviors, such as clean-air campaigns that hope to reduce car use. This complicated process involves *counterarguing* by presenting negative messages about an unwanted behavior and creating the proper incentives to stimulate the desired behavior. Because the effects are so complicated, the impact of such campaigns is not always clear. Earlier in the discussion of perception, we mentioned the national "Just Say No" campaign, which claims to have had an impact on teenagers' drug use. However, sometimes antidrug advertising can boomerang because it calls attention to the unwanted behavior.

The Power of Brand Communication

The six-factor Facets Model of Effects that we've been describing is our answer to the question of how brand communication works. These six factors, when they work together, can create a coherent brand perception. You should remember two things about how this model works: (1) the effects are interdependent, and (2) they are not all equal for all brand communication situations. In terms of impact, we recognize that different product situations call for different strategies. Sometimes more emphasis in a message strategy needs to be placed on emotion or image building than on reasons and facts.

In terms of effects interaction, we suggested in previous discussions that cognitive and emotional responses work together. Consider that memory is a function of both attention (the perception facet) and emotion (the affective facet). As du Plessis explained, "What we pay attention to, we remember."[48] The stronger the emotional hook, the more likely we'll attend to and remember the message. Even informative messages can be made more memorable if they are presented with an emotional story. Furthermore, recent ideas about how memory works suggest that an effective brand message helps consumers remember their best moments with a product, so it brings back emotion-laden brand experiences that encompass both feelings and thoughts.

Strong and Weak Effects

Some professionals believe that sales volume is the only true indication of message effectiveness. The power of advertising, for example, is determined by its ability to motivate consumers to buy a brand. Some professionals even believe that advertising is so powerful that it can motivate people to buy things they don't need, a perception counterargued by the American Association of Advertising Agencies.

Others, including the authors of this book, believe that communication effects include a wide range of consumer responses to a message, responses that may be just as important as sales because they lead to the creation of such things as brand liking and a long-term brand relationship. This debate over the power of brand communication is analyzed in terms of "strong" and "weak" effects.

This debate is the source of controversy in the analysis of what message effectiveness really represents. The sales-oriented philosophy suggests that advertising can move the masses to action. Those who believe in the "strong" theory reason along these lines:

Advertising increases people's knowledge and changes people's attitudes, and therefore it is capable of persuading people who had not formerly bought a brand to buy it, at first once and then repeatedly.

5.3 Describe the Facets Model of Effects, how it explains how brand communication works, and the key facets of brand communication effectiveness.

● **Principle**
Effects other than sales are important because they lead to long-term brand relationships.

A Principle of the Soul

Galit Marmor-Lavie, *University of Texas at Austin*

Every brand has a head, heart and soul that connect a product to its customers.

—John Osborn, *BBDO, New York*

Does a brand have a soul? What does it mean to connect with a brand on a soul level? Do we really need to talk about brands, products, marketing, and advertising in the context of soul and spirituality? Sure, we all realize that marketers and advertisers try to build and shape the personality of brands via various marketing techniques, but a soul?

Pause for a moment and ask yourself the following: what is it that you really want from life? Most likely, your answer lies in the realm of the intangible (I want health, fulfillment, abundance, meaning, etc.) more so than it lies in the realm of the tangible (I want a luxury car, beautiful dress, a pool, etc.). There is absolutely nothing wrong in owning tangible things, but when it comes to true happiness and fulfillment, the tangible things in our life are just the by-product of the consciousness and actions we put in it. For example, let's say that you really want to buy your first car but you don't have enough money to purchase one. You have two scenarios ahead of you: (1) your parents will pay and get the car for you next week, or (2) you will work for a year at a coffee shop, save money, and then purchase the car by yourself. Now, considering the situation, how can we connect between consciousness, a car (a tangible product), and fulfillment? Think about the first scenario, what will the car mean to you? You will possibly be happy because you received what you wanted, but that happiness is short-lived. Soon, you will ask yourself: "Is it really my car or my parents' car? Do I deserve it? Do I appreciate it enough?" The answer is probably not, and thus emotions and consciousness of insecurity will be attached to the car. Conversely, in the second scenario, the car would be very meaningful to you in the long term; after all, you have earned your independence and freedom in that process, you have also developed a healthy sense of ego in relation to the car, and it symbolizes a source of inspiration to others. Ultimately, two different scenarios—two different consciousnesses—are imbued into a product.

Businesspeople, marketers, and advertisers must realize that today, more than ever, people seek in life meaning, wisdom, sensitivity, growth, and connection, all things that are much more related to the world of spirituality (beyond religion) than the world of materialism. The challenge of practitioners today is to first truly understand and then carefully implement the bridge between these two worlds. People today would like to decipher the "soul" of the product before they are consuming or connecting with it. In other words, they are looking for the consciousness or energy behind the product. For instance, was it made under conditions of slavery or human dignity? Who is the owner of the company and what is his or her intention? Does the advertising message reflect the true nature of the brand or a false manipulation? What kind of advertising messages are attached to the brand: unity and positivity or separation and negativity?

The answers to these questions—the employees that shape the product, the owner's intention and implementation, the environment of the product, and the marketing message—and more are the various energetic dimensions, which constitute the "soul" of the product or brand. Now, as a consumer, you need to ask yourself: Do I choose to connect with that type of brand's energy, that type of brand's "soul"?

In contrast, those who believe in the "weak" theory of advertising think that advertising has only a limited impact on consumers and is best used to reinforce existing brand perceptions rather than change attitudes:

> *Consumers are not very interested in advertising. The amount of information communicated is limited. Advertising is not strong enough to convert people whose beliefs are different from those in the ad, overcome their resistance, or change their attitudes. Most advertising is more effective at retaining users rather than converting new ones.*

These differences explain why some experts believe that communication effects, such as emotion, knowledge, and persuasion, are merely "surrogate" effects; in other words, they are communication effects that can be measured more easily than sales but are less important to marketing managers. Others believe that these communication effects are important in and of themselves because of what they contribute to brand strength.

Complicating the issue is the recognition that the impact of traditional advertising is seldom immediate. In other words, advertising is a victim of **delayed effects**; that is, messages are seen and heard at one time (at home on the television, in the car on the radio, or in the doctor's office in a magazine ad) and may or may not come to mind at a later date when you are in a purchase situation (in a store or in a car looking for a place to eat). Advertisers must keep the delayed effects problem in mind when relying on the "surrogate effects," such as attention, interest, motivation, and memory, to bring a message to mind days or weeks later.

Long-term research by retired Syracuse professor John Philip Jones, who worked for many years at the J. Walter Thompson advertising agency, using extensive industry data, proves that there is a link between advertising and consumer behavior and that advertising can trigger sales. However, his research also led him to conclude that only 41 percent of advertising actually works in terms of producing sales.[49]

The problem has always been understanding *how it works* and, in many cases, *how it doesn't work*. The important conclusion to the bigger question about how brand messages work is that we know that advertising (and other marketing communication) does work when it's carefully planned and executed, and it can work in a variety of ways. It may not work in every situation, and every ad may not be equally effective, but if done right, brand communication can have an impact on consumer responses. That's why the Effie Awards and other award shows that recognize effectiveness are so valuable.

If you are interested in reading more about how advertising and other marketing communication work, see the Practical Tips feature by Professor Sheri Broyles at www.pearsonhighered.com/moriarty and consult some of the fascinating books that have been written about this industry, including Bob Garfield's *The Chaos Scenario: Amid the Ruins of Mass Media the Choice for Business Is Stark: Listen or Perish*. An excerpt from this provocative book can be found at the end of the interview transcript at www.npr.org/templates/story/story.php?storyid=111623614.

Looking Ahead

This chapter focused on the effects of brand communication. In other words, how does the consumer relate to the brand and respond to the brand message? In many cases, there is little or no connection because the brand, or the message, is irrelevant to that particular consumer. Women, for example, are less interested in shaving cream messages than are men, unless it's a product designed specifically for women, which is the strategy used by shaving cream manufacturers to create relevance for women.

The point is that many consumers, particularly young people, are constantly creating and adjusting their self-images. If a brand message connects, it probably does so because it connects with this innate search for personal identity. As Young said, "The mind of the consumer can be thought of as being continuously engaged in the process of defining the self and orienting it with respect to the outside world." Brand communication is just one small piece in the personal identity puzzle. He explained, "A brand's image is constructed in relationship to the consumer's concept of self."[50] Chapter 6 is on consumer insight and consumer behavior, which leads to targeting and segmenting the audience for a brand message.

IT'S A WRAP

help®   Creating Ideas That Stick

I want to save a life

Graham Douglas is on the cutting edge of saving lives. He came up with an idea that pierced the media environment to try to convince enough people to become bone marrow donors to save 10,000 lives a year.

Selling an idea is challenging enough. Convincing people to part with their blood defies their conventional behavior and makes the job seemingly impossible. Yet Douglas invented a product, found a pharmaceutical company that would sell it, and created a bizarre online video to market the bandages/donor combo kit.

The innovative product combined with the compelling story of one brother desperately helping both his blood relative and his unrelated brothers and sisters resulted in communication that took on a life of its own. Television reporters from *CBS News, ABC News, MSNBC,* and *CNN* picked up on the story and multiplied the impact by adding stories they told about people desperate for bone marrow matches. Some of the print and online highlights were the *Wall Street Journal, Bloomberg Businessweek, Fast Company,* and *Good Magazine,* and some big industry publications, such as *Creativity, AdWeek, Advertising Age, Creative Review,* and *Campaign Brief,* also helped educate the public about bone marrow donation. The number of media impressions has surpassed 75 million and continues to grow.

Graham's ability as a superior creative problem solver earned him the honor of the Grand Prix for Good plus two other Gold Lions at Cannes by age 27, and he was even named one of the "30 Under 30" for Marketing and Communication by *Forbes* magazine. Even better, as a result of receiving a bone marrow donation from a stranger, Britton Douglas, his twin brother, is a healthy, successful Dallas attorney.

Logo: Courtesy Graham Douglas

KEY OBJECTIVES SUMMARY

5.1. Explain how communication works as a form of both mass communication and interactive communication. By analyzing advertising as mass communication, we have a model for explaining how commercial messages work. In traditional mass media advertising, consider that the *source* typically is the advertiser assisted by its agency, and the *receiver* is the consumer who responds in some way to the message. The *message* is the advertisement or other marketing communication tool. The *medium* is the vehicle that delivers the message; in advertising, that tends to be newspapers and magazines in print, radio and television in broadcasting, the internet, and other forms of out-of-home vehicles, such as outdoor boards and posters. In integrated marketing communication, the media are varied and include all points of contact where a consumer receives an impression of the brand. *Noise* is both external and internal. *External noise* in advertising includes consumer trends that affect the reception of the message as well as problems in the brand's marketing mix and clutter in the channel. *Internal noise* includes personal factors that affect the reception of the message. If the communication process fails to work and the consumer does not receive the message as intended by the source, the communication effort is ineffective. Interactive communication is two way, such as a dialogue or conversation, and the source and receiver change positions as the message bounces back and forth; in other words, the source becomes the listener, and the receiver becomes the sender. Interactive communication also introduces the idea that consumers may initiate the conversation and, furthermore, that brand communication can occur within a network of social communication among friends.

5.2. Discuss how the idea of advertising effects developed and what problems exist in traditional approaches to advertising effects. The most common explanation of how advertising works is referred to as AIDA, which stands for attention, interest, desire, and action. This model in all its subsequent forms is described as a hierarchy of effects because it presumes a set of steps that consumers go through in responding to a message. A different approach, referred to as think/feel/do, recognizes that different marketing communication situations generate different patterns of responses. Two problems are inherent in these traditional approaches: (1) the idea of predictable steps and (2) missing effects, particularly those that govern other ways people respond to brand messages.

5.3. Describe the Facets Model of Effects, how it explains how brand communication works, and the key facets of brand communication effectiveness. The authors of this book believe that marketing communication works in six key ways: it is designed to help consumers (1) see and hear the message (perception), (2) feel something for the brand (emotional or affective response), (3) understand the point of the message (cognitive response), (4) connect positive qualities with the brand (association), (5) believe the message (persuasion), and (6) act in the desired ways (behavior). These ways all work together to create a brand perception and create the desired consumer response.

KEY TERMS

advocacy, p. 148
affective response, p. 134
AIDA, p. 130
argument, p. 145
association, p. 141
attention, p. 124
attitude, p. 143
awareness, p. 132
bandwagon appeals, p. 144
beliefs, p. 144
believability, p. 147
brand linkage, p. 142
brand loyalty, p. 145
call to action, p. 148
carrot mobs, p. 144
channels of communication, p. 125
clutter, p. 126
cognition, p. 138
cognitive learning, p. 139

comprehension, p. 140
conditioned learning, p. 142
considered purchase, p. 145
conviction, p. 145
credibility, p. 147
customer satisfaction, p. 146
decode, p. 125
delayed effects, p. 150
differentiation, p. 140
direct action, p. 147
effects, p. 129
emotional appeals, p. 137
encode, p. 125
engagement, p. 145
exposure, p. 133
feedback, p. 125
flash mob, p. 148
hierarchy of effects, p. 130
high involvement, p. 144
impacts, p. 129
indirect action, p. 147

intention, p. 145
interactive communication, p. 126
interest, p. 134
intrusive, p. 134
involvement, p. 144
knowledge structure, p. 143
low involvement, p. 145
mental rehearsal, p. 148
message, p. 125
motivation, p. 144
needs, p. 139
network of associations, p. 143
noise, p. 125
objectives, p. 129
opinion leaders, p. 144
perception, p. 132
persuasion, p. 143
preference, p. 145
reason to believe, p. 147

recall, p. 134
receiver, p. 125
recognition, p. 134
referrals, p. 148
relevance, p. 134
resonance, p. 138
selective attention, p. 134
selective perception, p. 133
semiotics, p. 129
SMCR model, p. 124
social learning, p. 143
source, p. 125
source credibility, p. 147
stickiness, p. 134
subliminal, p. 134
synergy, p. 134
think/feel/do model, p. 130
transformation, p. 143
trial, p. 148
wants, p. 137

MyLab Marketing

Go to **www.pearson.com/mylab/marketing** for MyLab discussion questions (⊛) as well as the following assisted-graded writing questions.

5-1. Differentiate between wants and needs. How are both of these concepts used in brand communication?

5-2. What is breakthrough advertising? What is engaging advertising? Look through this book, find an example of each, and discuss how they work.

5-3. Describe the Facets Model of Effects, how it explains how brand communication works, and the key facets of brand communication effectiveness.

REVIEW QUESTIONS

5-4. What are the key components of a communication model, and how do they relate to brand communication?

5-5. Why is it important to add interaction to the traditional communication model?

5-6. What are the six categories of effects identified in the Facets Model of Effects? What does each one represent

in terms of a consumer's response to an advertising message?

⊛ **5-7.** Explain the difference between recall and recognition. What facet does each represent?

5-8. Explain the difference between brand responses that involve thinking and feeling.

DISCUSSION QUESTIONS

5-9. This chapter identifies six major categories of effects or consumer responses. Find an ad in this book that you think is effective overall and explain how it works, analyzing the way it cultivates responses in these six categories.

5-10. Eva Proctor is a planner in an agency that handles a liquid detergent brand that competes with Lever's Wisk. Eva

is reviewing a history of the Wisk theme "Ring around the Collar." In its day, it was one of the longest-running themes on television, and Wisk's sales share indicated that it was successful. What is confusing Eva is that the Wisk history includes numerous consumer surveys that show consumers found "Ring around the Collar" to be a boring, silly, and irritating advertising theme. Discuss why Wisk was such a popular brand even though its advertising campaign was so disliked.

5-11. You have been asked to participate in a debate in your office about three different views on advertising effects. Your office has to introduce a new electric car. A copywriter says that informing consumers about the product's features is most important in creating effective advertising. An art director argues that creating an emotional bond with consumers is more important. One of the account managers says that the only advertising performance that counts is sales and that the message ought to focus on that. Your client wants to be single-minded and tells you to pick one of these viewpoints to guide the new marketing communication. Develop a position on one side or the other and discuss your point of view.

5-12. Your small agency has been invited to work on a new product called Wikicells, which are shell-like packaging systems that can be eaten. Milk, for example, could be packaged in a strawberry- or chocolate-flavored pouch that you could wash and eat, like the skin of an apple. Even if you decide to toss it, it's biodegradable. The first products to be introduced using this new packaging system will be yogurt and ice cream. Your assignment is to come up with a brand name and write a one-page brief on how to launch these new items. Consider the relevant facets in preparing your proposal. (This packaging system is from a list of new products published by the *New York Times* under the headline "Innovations That Will Change Your Tomorrow." It ran June 1, 2012. See www.nytimes.com.)

TAKE-HOME PROJECTS

5-13. *Portfolio Project:* From current magazines, identify one advertisement that has exceptionally high stopping power (attention), one that has exceptionally high pulling power (interest), and one that has exceptionally high locking power (memory). Make photocopies of these ads to turn in. Which of them are mainly information, and which are mainly emotional and focused on feelings? Which are focused on building a brand or creating associations? Do any of them do a great job of creating action? Choose what you believe to be the most effective ad in the collection. Why did you choose this one, and what can you learn from it about effective advertising?

5-14. *Mini-Case Analysis:* We discussed some aspects of the "Imported from Detroit" campaign for the Chrysler turnaround in the chapter. Briefly summarize the key decisions behind this campaign. Now apply the Facets Model of Effects to analyze how the campaign worked and explain your conclusions about what did or didn't make it an effective campaign. Write a short analysis (no more than one double-spaced page) that explains your thinking.

TRACE North America Case

Multicultural Communication Effectiveness

Read the TRACE case in the Appendix before coming to class.

5-15. Explain how brand communication works in the case of the "Hard to Explain, Easy to Experience" campaign.

5-16. How could you strengthen the target audience's participation in the campaign?

5-17. Analyze the campaign in terms of the Facets Model of Effects. Based on this model, what might be done to strengthen the campaign's desired effect?

6

Strategic Research

In our previous chapters on how to plan marketing communication that has a real impact on consumers, we noted that marketers need to do brand, market, and consumer research. This research effort becomes the foundation for setting objectives, segmenting the market, targeting the audience, and developing a brand communication plan. This chapter presents some key research concepts that lead to consumer insight, including an explanation of the major stages of the research process, how research can help advertising campaigns, the basic categories of research designs, and the most common research methods used in planning marketing communication. We also discuss the challenges facing advertising researchers.

MyLab Marketing

⭐ **Improve Your Grade!**

More than 10 million students improved their results using Pearson MyLabs. Visit **www.pearson.com/mylab/marketing** for simulations, tutorials, and end-of-chapter problems.

Campaign

Lean Cuisine #WeighThis

Company

Nestlé Lean Cuisine

Agencies

Nestlé Lean Cuisine & 360i MetaVision

Awards

Advertising Research Foundation, 2016 Grand Ogilvy Award

Gold Ogilvy for Best Use of Social Insights; Grand Prize

Nielsen Design Impact Awards: Grand Prize

Lean Cuisine Weighs in to Support What Really Matters to Its Customers

Photo: Keith Homan/Shutterstock

This is a story about the importance of listening to your customers, about being honest, about taking risks—and the role of research in creating positive brand communication. It is the tale of Lean Cuisine, which built its reputation helping people lose weight, but had rapidly lost relevance as "diet" became another four-letter word. The result—five years of sales declines. The amount of Lean Cuisine product purchased by the brand's core consumer base dropped by 70%.

Retailers reduced shelf space by 12%, indicating the frozen diet category was in trouble. "At the beginning of 2015 we were in double-digit decline. . . . The idea of dieting lost relevance and the brand lost relevance too. We lost over $400 million in sales over the last five years," Jeff Hamilton, president, Nestlé Prepared Foods told *Chief Marketer* at the time (Hamilton, 2016). The brand needed to pivot, fast.

Their first move? They listened to their customers. During the previous year, Lean Cuisine and their agency, 360i, spent months listening—in person and online—around the words *diet* and *healthy*, and found that conversations about Lean Cuisine were largely negative, and even when they were positive the chatter focused on function—that Lean Cuisine was a tool for dieting. The product was the butt of jokes, and the Lean Cuisine consumer was perceived to be a lonely single female. But when they listened more closely to Lean Cuisine's core target they found women who were succeeding (high income earners, college graduates, hard workers that provide for others) but were being judged by society based on their appearance, not by their accomplishments.

Lean Cuisine updated their product line and packaging, which gave consumers a rational reason to believe the product had changed, but they knew they needed to also give people a feeling to believe, and to become more aspirational and positive. They also looked at what Millennials were talking about, and found this group really wants a purpose-driven brand. Millennials considered the product their mom's Lean Cuisine, so the company set out to make the products more relevant to them as part of a healthy lifestyle. In short, their research revealed the need to shift Lean Cuisine's brand positioning from '80s-era diet and weight loss to modern health and wellness, and to support what really matters to their customers.

After listening to consumers, Lean Cuisine then set out to tap into the emotional drivers and accomplishments that fuel successful lifestyles for women. They did this through a moving social media campaign called #WeighThis, the centerpiece of which was an emotionally powerful series of videos featuring real women weighing their accomplishments—becoming a parent, making the Dean's List as a single mother, traveling the world—in lieu of weighing their bodies. Using an integrated marketing communication strategy, they redesigned the product's packaging to fit a more modern image, launched the videos on Facebook, Twitter, and YouTube, and utilized paid media, PR, and influencer marketing to expand and create buzz around the message. The campaign tagline was "Here to feed what really matters to you."

Throughout the campaign women were encouraged to share how they wanted to be weighed using the hashtag #WeighThis on Lean Cuisine's social channels. Responses included: "The miles I've run," "Feeding people in need," "Becoming a dentist," and "I'm 55 and back in college." The brand also partnered with artist Annica Lydenberg in a two-day interactive art event in New York City. Ms. Lydenberg took inspiring responses from women during the #WeighThis campaign and placed them on over 200 bathroom scales, which were then displayed as part of an art installation in Grand Central Station.

Did this gutsy move pay off? Turn to the It's a Wrap feature at the end of the chapter to find out!

Sources: "Winners—The Advertising Research Foundation David Ogilvie Awards," https://thearf.org/2016-arf-david-ogilvy-awards/finalists/; "360i & Lean Cuisine Awarded Grand Ogilvy in The ARF David Ogilvy Awards," 360ion, March 21, 2016, http://blog.360i.com/360i-news/360i-lean-cuisine-awarded-grand-ogilvy-arf-david-ogilvy-awards; "Lean Cuisine Mutes the 'Diet' Conversation to 'Weigh What Matters,'" 360ion, January 14, 2016, http://blog.360i.com/wp-content/uploads/2016/01/Lean-Cuisine-Weigh-This.png; "Lean Cuisine Celebrates Women's Accomplishments in NYC Art Installation," 360ion, October 29, 2015, http://blog.360i.com/social-marketing/lean-cuisine-celebrates-womens-accomplishments-with-art-installation; "Beyond dieting: Lean Cuisine shifts its messaging," by Tanya Dua, October 27, 2015, https://digiday.com/marketing/lean-cuisine-not-about-dieting/; "Lean Cuisine Eliminates the Word 'Diet'—Literally: Frozen-food company treats 'diet' as a four-letter word, offers software blocker," www.wsj.com/articles/lean-cuisine-eliminates-the-word-diet-literally-1452186000; "Nestlé Lean Cuisine wins Grand Ogilvy," Warc News, 16 March 2016, www.warc.com/NewsAndOpinion/news/Nestl%C3%A9_Lean_Cuisine_wins_Grand_Ogilvy/2c3c8069-1fe2-41e1-982b-4c817fbc7a60; "Lean Cuisine's Package Redseign Drives $58 Million Sales Increase in One Year," May 4, 2017, by Patty Odell, http://www.chiefmarketer.com/lean-cuisines-package-redesign-drives-58-million-sales-increase-in-one-year/, www.prnewswire.com/news-releases/more-than-a-pretty-package-nielsen-honors-package-redesigns-that-helped-to-remake-brands-bottom-lines-300449362.html; Jeff Hamilton, "Lean Cuisine's Double-Digit Turnaround," posted on April 6, 2016 by Patty Odell, www.chiefmarketer.com/lean-cuisines-double-digit-digital-turnaround/.

6.1 Understand the strategic research process and why brand communicators use it.

The Research Process

Whether you realize it or not, you were engaged in **strategic research** when you looked for the best college to attend. This means you actively sought reliable information to help you make an important decision. First, you recognized that you needed more information about college options. Then you probably began searching and sifting through several college websites and brochures, talked with friends, and perhaps you made personal visits to a few schools. You tried to gather enough objective information and insight to make an honest comparison of the schools. Then, you made your decision, and you have been evaluating your choice with each passing semester. Research for a brand communication plan goes through a similar process.

⬤ **Principle**
Listening is the first step in understanding customers.

In the Part 2 opener, Regina Lewis stressed that an effective brand communication program is totally dependent on consumer insight. Listening to your customers is the first step to knowing and understanding them. What does that mean? It means that brand strategy begins with **consumer research**—the tools of listening. Consumer research can help us effectively segment and target markets by better understanding consumer attitudes, motivations, perceptions, and behaviors. The research findings then lead to analysis and insights into why people think and behave as they do. But first we must understand the principles and practices of communication research and how to listen effectively to consumers.

The objective at all stages of the planning process is to answer this question: What do we need to know in order to make an informed decision about consumer behavior? In brand communication, this type of research covers all the factors and steps that lead to the creation of message strategies and media plans (Figure 6.1). Think of strategic research as collecting the information needed to make good decisions on advertising and marketing communication strategy.

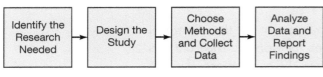

FIGURE 6.1
The Research Process

6.2 Discuss the main factors involved in designing a research study.

Why Do We Need Research?

Agencies and clients use research to make strategic decisions, as we have discussed, but agencies rarely *conduct* research. Most research has become so specialized that a client's in-house researchers or independent research companies usually handle a firm's market and consumer research. These firms and departments uncover and disseminate **secondary research** data that others have already collected, and conduct **primary research** to ask questions and collect data of their own so that the best information finds its way into brand communication efforts. DDB is one of the few large agencies that still does its own in-house research. Its annual Life Style Survey, which we will discuss in Chapter 7, is a major source of consumer information.

Whether you actually conduct research or not, it is important for advertising and marketing professionals to be familiar with the research process and understand how data are obtained and used to improve decision making. As markets have become more fragmented and saturated, and as consumers have become more demanding, the need for reliable research-based information in advertising planning has increased. Figure 6.2 summarizes the six ways research is used in marketing communication planning:

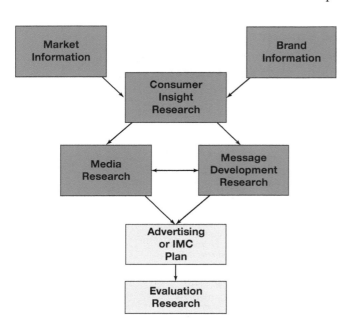

FIGURE 6.2
The Use of Research in Marketing Communication Planning

1. Market information
2. Consumer insight
3. Brand information
4. Media research
5. Message development
6. Evaluation research

Market Information

Formal research used by the marketing department for strategic planning is called **marketing research**. It includes surveys, in-depth interviews, observational methods, focus groups (which are like in-depth interviews with a group rather than individuals), and all types of primary and secondary data used to develop a marketing plan and ultimately improve brand communication plans. A subset of marketing research, **market research**, is research used to gather information about a particular market or segment of consumers, such as its size or ethnic makeup.

Photo: Courtesy Ingvi Jökull Logason. Used with permission.

SHOWCASE

To help cooks use less costly cuts of Iceland lamb, Ingvi Logason and his team at H:N Marketing Communications in Iceland created educational ads with great appetite appeal.

This ad was contributed by Ingvi Logason, principal at H:N Communications, Reykjavik, Iceland, and a member of this book's Advisory Board. A graduate of Western Florida University, his work was nominated to be featured here by Professor Tom Groth.

An example of marketing research comes from Iceland, a country hard hit by the global economic downturn several years ago that brought most of the world's economies to their knees. As explained by Ingvi Logason, a member of this book's Advisory Board and a principal in his own advertising firm in Reykjavik, "Iceland, with its over-expanded banking sector, was hit worse than any other Westernized country." This recession hit the Icelandic public suddenly and hard, obliterating purchasing power. One of his clients, Icelandic Lamb, had to react quickly to the changed market. Traditionally, lamb consumption was almost exclusively from one of the prime (and more expensive) parts of the lamb. In other words, lamb had become a luxury item, one that was dropped from the menu in tough times. How could the industry market less expensive cuts to consumers who were turning to cheaper meat products? Logason used clever probing in focus groups and found that the primary consumer problem was that consumers didn't know how to prepare these less costly cuts of lamb. The solution, of course, was to educate consumers with cooking shows and recipes that became viral ads.

Marketing information includes everything a planner can uncover about consumer perceptions of the brand, product category, and competitors' brands. Planners sometimes ride with the sales force and listen to sales pitches, tour manufacturing plants to see how a product is made, and work in a store or restaurant to evaluate employee interaction with customers. In terms of marketing communication, planners assess the brand's and its competitors' advertisements, promotions, retail displays, packaging, and other marketing communication efforts.

Brand information includes an assessment of the brand's role and performance in the marketplace: is it a leader, a follower, a challenger, or a sub-brand of a bigger and better-known brand? This research also investigates how people perceive brand personalities and images. Here are some common focal points and methods used to gather information about a brand and the marketplace.

- *The Brand Experience* When an agency gets a new client, the agency team first has to learn about the brand through brand research. That means learning where the brand has been in the past in terms of the market, its customers, and competitors. Also important is eliciting the corporate point of view regarding the brand's position within the company's line of products as well as corporate goals and plans for the brand. Another critical area of brand research is the brand's relationships with its customers. Researchers, for example, may go through all the experiences that a typical consumer has in buying and using the product. If you were taking on a pizza restaurant account, for example, you might work in the store, place an online order, or visit it as a customer. Brand buying is also a form of commitment to the client: the parking lots of agencies that have automotive accounts are usually full of cars made by their clients.
- *Competitive Analysis* It's also important to consider the brand's direct and indirect competitors, and how the brand is positioned relative to competitors. If you handle a soap account, you obviously want to use that brand of soap, but you may also buy the competing brands and substitute products and do your own comparative test just to add your experiences to your brand analysis.

• *Marketing Communication Audit* Either formally or informally, most planners will begin an assignment by collecting every possible piece of advertising and other forms of marketing communication for the brand and its competitors, as well as other relevant product categories that may have lessons for the brand. Often these pieces are attached to the walls in a "war room" where team members can immerse themselves in messages to stimulate new ideas. This step includes compiling a historical collection as well. There's nothing more embarrassing than proposing a great new advertising idea only to find out that it was used a couple of years ago by a competitor or, even worse, by your client.

• *Content Analysis* The marketing communication audit might include only informal summaries of the slogans, appeals, and images used most often, or it might include more formal and systematic tabulation of competitors' approaches, ads, and strategies, called a **content analysis**. By disclosing competitors' strategies and tactics, analysis of the content of competitive advertisements provides clues about how competitors are thinking and suggests ways to develop new and more effective campaigns. Planners also try to determine what mental territories or positions competitors claim and which are still available and relevant to the brand.

Photo: Courtesy of American Butter Institute and Dairy Management Inc. Used with permission.

The website for the trade association, DairyGood, offers many recipes which helps consumers solve the problem of how to cook great meals using cheese and other dairy products.

The DDB agency regularly conducts "Barriers to Purchase" research,[1] realizing that these barriers often create an opportunity for advertising and promotional messages to present information or change perceptions. The American Dairy Association, for example, asked DDB to find out why cheese consumption was declining. Similar to the Icelandic lamb story, the study identified one barrier that was most easily correctable through a marketing communication effort: the absence of simple cheese recipes for home cooks. A sister trade organization for the dairy industry, DairyGood, addressed this consumer hurdle by highlighting many such recipes at their website (https://dairygood.org/Recipes).

Consumer Insight

A basic principle in this book is that effective marketing communication rests on truly understanding the consumer. As Regina Lewis, a member of this book's Advisory Board, explained in the Part 2 opener, brands have to be true to the consumers who buy them. Both the creative team members (who create messages) and the media planners (who decide how and when to deliver the messages) need to know as much as they can, in as much depth and detail as possible, about their audience. That's the point of the story about selling Icelandic lamb during the recession. To turn the sales pattern around, the agency had to understand how its target market was adapting to the new economic situation.

Researchers often try to uncover the *whys of the buys*, but insight research may also uncover reasons people don't want to try or buy a product. Lewis explained that Dunkin' Donuts, when she was vice president of consumer and brand insights, found in its consumer research several reasons its customers were uncomfortable ordering fancy coffee drinks. Mostly, they were intimidated by the whole "barista" thing and the fancy coffee names.

Collecting Feedback   We mentioned earlier that *feedback* can be obtained from customers as a part of interactive customer contact: systematically recording information from customer service, technical service, inbound telemarketing calls, and online sites. Some businesses use the internet to involve customers in making decisions about product design, distribution, price, and company operations using online surveys, blogs, online communities, and other social media. Travel marketers, for example, have found that social media offer an opportunity to collect meaningful customer feedback on a mass scale; however, they have also found that conversation-oriented customers want to be the ones to start the conversation.[2]

You've probably heard the phrase "This call may be monitored for quality assurance." These recordings are used for training, but they also can be analyzed for marketing intelligence.[3] An indication that the sales offer or technical explanation isn't working right would be if customers say that they are confused or ask the representative to repeat a phrase. These calls can provide instant feedback about the strength of a brand's offering as well as competitors' offers. Specific questions such as "How have you heard about us?" are used to monitor brand contact points, word-of-mouth communication, and media performance.

Monitoring Buzz and Tracking Behavior　　The Internet has made it easier to track comments about a brand. Many marketers, such as IBM and Microsoft, monitor chats and blogs and also do more general scanning for key words to find out and perhaps respond to what people are saying about their brands and products. These findings can be incorporated back into other methods, such as focus groups, to verify and explain the sentiments expressed online.[4]

Monitoring buzz can also be used to monitor attitudes. For example, The *Wall Street Journal* followed the conversation on social networks about Twinkies after Hostess announced its bankruptcy. The study found that 25 percent of the comments focused on health issues (obesity), 33 percent were sad (an American icon going away), 35 percent were about unions (bankruptcy to break labor contracts), and 7 percent were jokes.[5] Social media, such as Facebook, can also be used to get consumer responses. Lay's Facebook app, for example, suggested new potato chip flavors and asked people to click on an "I'd Eat That" button.[6]

Pinterest, an online corkboard where people post pictures, articles, and videos, allows users to save images and group them. It's another online tool that can be used to unobtrusively monitor consumer thinking. As Kaila Strong explained, the Pinterest categories are a way to see what content is popular in a niche market. The "Popular" category lets users, and marketers, see the most popular of all pins on the site.[7]

Neuromarketing　　To get inside consumers' minds to see what they are really thinking, marketers have turned to neuroscience, which uses highly technical equipment to scan the brain as it processes information and makes decisions. Neuromarketing is the application of this research technology to consumer behavior. One study by a University of California Los Angeles researcher, for example, mapped how viewers responded to Super Bowl ads below the level of their awareness. This raises some ethical questions about just how private our thinking should be.[8]

Campbell's Soup has used neuromarketing and biometrics to analyze consumer responses to brand communication. As part of a major two-year study and redesign of the labels on its iconic red-and-white soup cans, Campbell's used neuromarketing techniques to see how consumers reacted to everything from pictures of bowls to the use of a spoon as well as other graphic cues, such as steam rising from the bowl. The objective was to find ways to help consumers connect on a deeper and more emotional level with the brand. Changes included color coding the different varieties; depicting steam to make the soup in the picture look warm; removing the spoon, which consumers said served no purpose; updating the look of the bowl; and moving the Campbell's logo to the bottom to better identify the varieties.[9]

Media Research

Media planning begins with consumer research and questions about media behavior that help with the media selection decision. Media planners often work in conjunction with account planners to decide which media formats (e.g., print, broadcast TV, cable TV, outdoor, web) make the most sense to accomplish the objectives. The goal is to activate consumer interest by reaching them through the media that most engage their attention.

Next, **media research** gathers information about the possible media and marketing communication tools that might be used in a campaign to deliver a message. Media researchers then match that information to what is known about the target audience. The MRI data shown in Figure 6.3 on page 167 illustrates the type of information media researchers consult to develop recommendations.

Message Development and Diagnostics

As planners, account managers, and people on the creative team begin to develop a message strategy, they involve themselves in various types of informal and formal message development research. They read all the relevant secondary research provided by the client and the planners to become better informed about the brand, the company, the competition, the media, and the product category.

Writers and art directors almost always conduct informal research of their own. They may do their own personal observational research and visit retail stores, talk to salespeople, and watch customers buy. In addition to reading, they will look at previous advertising, especially that of competitors, to see what others have done before. This personal backgrounding research is a source of insight and has a powerful influence on what happens later in the message development process.

The next step after personal backgrounding is to produce and test different Big Ideas both informally within the team and through more formal structured research. Big Ideas are strong brand messages that resonate with the target audience. Creative development research often uses qualitative methods to predict these ideas' effectiveness. Called **concept testing**, it can help evaluate the relative power of various creative approaches. It's a "work-in-progress" type of evaluation. The approach is to test the Big Idea to see if it communicates the strategy behind the message as well as test various *executions* of this Big Idea. These interviews are often conducted online or in malls where there are lots of people in the target in order to ask them to look at rough sketches of the ideas or ads and respond to them.

● **Principle**
Diagnostic research is used during the creative development of a brand message to find problems, make the communication clearer, and strengthen the impact of the execution.

After the Big Idea is agreed upon, the creative team will rough out the message across the integrated marketing communication (IMC) tools being used (e.g., sales promotion, television advertising, events), and they will test the executions to determine if there are any unexpected problems. For example, does the sales promotion catch attention? Does an ad take too long in the beginning to set up the problem? Will the event reinforce the key brand message and benefits? Does the brand get lost in an entertaining story line in a commercial? This diagnostic research is early enough in the creative process that it is still possible to find problems, adjust the Big Idea to make the branding and communication clearer, and make changes in the execution to strengthen its impact.

Another diagnostic technique used to analyze brand meaning is **semiotic analysis**, which is a way to take apart the signs and symbols in a message to uncover layers and types of meanings. The objective is to find deeper meanings in the symbolism that might relate to different groups of consumers. Its focus is on determining the meanings, even if they are not obvious or highly symbolic, that might relate to particular consumer motivations.

For example, the advertising that launched General Motors' OnStar global positioning system used a Batman theme. By looking at this commercial in terms of its signs and symbols, it is possible to determine if the obvious, as well as hidden, meanings of the message were on strategy. For example, the decision to use a comic book hero as the star created a heroic association for OnStar. However, Batman isn't a superhero; rather, he's more of a common person with a lot of great technology and cool gadgets—remember Jack Nicholson's line as the Joker when he said, "Where does he get all those wonderful toys?"[10] Batman is also ageless, appealing to young people who read comic books and watch movies as well as older people who remember Batman from their youth. A highly successful effort, this Batman OnStar campaign won a David Ogilvy Research Award.

Evaluation

After an advertisement or other type of marcom message has been developed and produced, it can be evaluated for its effectiveness both before and after it runs as part of a campaign. **Pretesting** is research on an execution in its finished stages but before it appears in media; it is the last step where diagnostics can generate change in the message. Whereas creative development research looks at the power of the advertising idea, pretesting looks at the way the idea is presented and received. The idea can be strong, but the target might hate the execution. This type of test elicits a *go or no-go* decision for a specific advertisement. Sometimes pretesting will also call into doubt the strength of the advertising idea, forcing the creative team to rethink its strategy.

Pretesting is also important for assessing other IMC tools. Special sales promotions such as discounts, contests, events, and rebates should be tested if the firm is unsure of the strength of the offer: the offer might be too weak (and receive little or no response), or the offer might be too strong (and cause too much consumer demand). A classic example is the Hoover company's sales promotion in the United Kingdom that offered two free airfares to the United States for a £100 purchase of a vacuum cleaner (about $150 at the time). This type of offer is classified as a "premium" (recall Chapter 4). What do you think the consumer response was? That's right: Hoover was totally overwhelmed by the demand to the point where Hoover could not fulfill all the airfares they promised, consumers began to sue the company, and senior executives were "sacked" (as the British like to say it). Yes, Hoover sold a lot of vacuum cleaners, but they lost consumer goodwill, lost a lot of money in the end, and received a great deal of negative publicity from news reports worldwide.[11] To avoid such problems, a company can simulate the promotional offer and pretest it with a variety of consumers to evaluate the strength of its appeal, perceived value, and the consumers' purchase intention. Adjustments to the offer can then be made as needed before launch.

Ameritest is a research company that specializes in pretesting the effectiveness of brand messages in print, television, and online. Charles Young, president of Ameritest and a member of this book's Advisory Board, explains how his firm's pretesting methodology diagnoses effectiveness of the execution of a brand message to identify, among other things, the high and low points of attention as well as the emotional structure of the message.

John Wanamaker, the famous industrialist from the 1800s, is credited with saying: "Half the money I spend on advertising is wasted; the trouble is I don't know which half."[12] The question remains alive today for companies of all types and sizes. How can we know if our advertising is working? To help answer this question, **evaluative research** is done during a campaign and afterward. During a campaign, the objective is diagnostic, to adjust the brand messages to make them stronger. This step is sometimes referred to as **copytesting**. After an ad or campaign has run, **posttesting** research helps determine the overall effectiveness in reaching objectives.

Many IMC tools can also be assessed over time as they run. For example, a firm can track: the number of coupons that have been redeemed, the number of people planning to attend a special event, the number of people who have entered a contest or sweepstakes, the number of follow-up sales visits from a trade show or trade promotion, the conversion rate from direct marketing efforts, and the number of positive news stories written about one of the company's new products.

Design the Study

New advertising assignments always begin with some kind of informal or formal background research into the marketing situation. This *secondary research* involves the regular collection and reporting of data by outside organizations. We'll compare it with *primary research*, which is original research tailored and conducted by the company or brand.

Secondary Research   Background research that uses available published information about a topic is secondary research. When advertising people get new accounts or new assignments, they start by reading everything they can find on the product, company, industry, and competition: sales reports, annual reports, complaint letters, and trade articles about the industry. They are looking for important facts and key insights. This kind of research is called secondary, not because it is less important, but because it has been collected and published by someone else.

A typical advertising campaign might be influenced, directly or indirectly, by information from many sources, including in-house agencies and outside research suppliers. The use of secondary information—finding information about the weight loss industry, in the case of Lean Cuisine—underscores the importance of reading widely. Here are a few of the more traditional sources of secondary information that are available to advertisers doing backgrounding.

- *Government Organizations* Governments, through their various departments, provide an astonishing array of statistics that can greatly enhance advertising and marketing decisions. Many of the statistics come from census records on the population's size, geographic distribution, age, income, occupation, education, and ethnicity. The US Census Bureau provides a wealth of information about the US population and economy, which is fundamental to making decisions about advertising targets and market segmentation. An advertiser cannot aim

Finding Moments of Truth

Charles E. Young, *Founder and CEO,*
Ameritest/CY Research

The most powerful search engine of all is the human eye, which scans advertising film, television commercials, and web videos, continuously deciding on an unconscious level whether the visual information streaming toward it is important enough to let into consciousness. Because our conscious minds have limited bandwidth or workspace, much of the imagery that advertisers are trying to communicate to consumers is ignored or deleted by our preconscious eye-brain filters as so much visual spam.

Ameritest's Picture Sorts® is a set of nonverbal research tools that have been developed for the Internet to survey the right-brained scanning and sorting processes involved in visual communication. These tools make use of the power of still photographs to capture an instant of time and store our fleeting emotions.

By sorting a randomized deck of pictures taken from the ad itself—which is like the visual vocabulary of the film—the ad researcher can reconstruct consumers' moment-by-moment attention and emotional response to an ad they just saw. Three different sorting exercises enable the advertiser to perform the equivalent of putting on 3-D glasses to see advertising through the eyes of its target audience.

The Flow of Attention® graph, the first of three measurement dimensions, is like a visual spell-checker that the researcher can use to analyze whether a piece of advertising film or web video has been put together well according to principles of proper film syntax or good visual grammar. The Flow of Attention graph reveals the hidden structure of audience attention to moving pictures, which, like music, follows a rhythmic beat of cognitive processing. The beat, or focal points of attention, is where the most important information in an ad, like the brand identity, is conveyed.

From the emotional hook at the beginning to the turning points in a story to the surprise ending of a funny commercial, engaging the emotions of consumers is essential to motivating them. The Flow of Emotion graph measures not only the volume of emotions pumping through ad film but also reveals which of four archetypal dramatic structures is being used in the creative design. Knowing this structure tells the advertiser when the timing is exactly right to first introduce the brand in the ad, which might be at the beginning, somewhere in the middle, or not until the end of a commercial.

The Flow of Meaning tool shows the researcher where key communication points or brand values are being cued visually. Meaning is created when thought and emotion come together, in a few memorable and emotionally charged moments in a commercial when memories are being created. Because there are three distinct memory systems in the mind, branding moments come in three flavors: (1) images that convey concepts or rational ideas go into our knowledge, or semantic, memory system; (2) images that evoke emotions go into our emotion, or episodic, memory system; and (3) images that rehearse or mirror the behavior the advertiser is trying to influence go into our action, or procedural, memory system (where memories of how you ride a bike or play a violin are stored). Taken together, this learn/feel/do imaging process is how the long-term work of advertising is performed, building a brand's image.

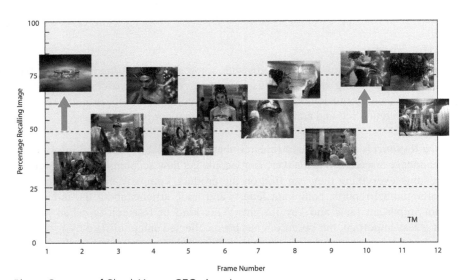

Photo: Courtesy of Chuck Young, CEO, Ameritest.

This diagram demonstrates the flow of attention across a commercial for Unilever's Thermasilk. The selected still frames represent those places in the commercial where the attention is high (above the red line) or low (below the red line). Notice the highest attention points, which are indicated with the red arrows. In this commercial, that tight shot of the face is the "moment of truth," the most highly attended to frame in this execution.

its advertising at a target audience without knowing that audience's size and major characteristics. In addition to census information, other government agencies generate reports that help advertisers make better decisions, such as the *Survey of Current Business* from the US Department of Commerce (www.bea.gov/scb).

- **Trade Associations** Many industries support trade associations— professional organizations whose members all work in the same field—that gather and distribute information of interest to association members. For instance, the American Frozen Food Institute and the Game Manufacturers Council are both organizations that assist members in conducting their business. The trade associations for marketing communication include the American Association of Advertising Agencies, which issues reports that help ad agencies monitor their performance and keep tabs on competitors; the Radio Advertising Bureau publishes *Radio Facts*, an overview of the commercial US radio industry; the American Marketing Assocation, which provides training, articles, and data resources to its members; the Account Planning Group conducts seminars and training sessions for account planners; and the American Association for Public Opinion Research serves the professional needs of opinion researchers.

- **Secondary Research Suppliers** Because of the overwhelming amount of information available through secondary research, specialized suppliers gather and organize that information around specific topic areas for other interested parties. Key secondary research suppliers are GfK, JD Power, Off-the-Shelf Publications, Dialog Information Services, FIND/SVP, Lexis-Nexis, and Dow Jones's Factiva.

- **Secondary Information on the Internet** For any given company, you're bound to find a website where you can learn about the company's history and philosophy of doing business, check out its complete product line, and discover who runs the company. These sites offer credible information for account planners and others involved in market research. Other sources of Internet information are blog and social media sites where you can learn about people's reactions to brands and products. There are also many industry-related sites for marketing that report on research, essays, and best practices:

  Advertising Age (http://adage.com/) is a global source of news, intelligence, and conversation for the marketing and media community.

  BrandEra (www.brandera.com) organizes its information by product category.

  Cluetrain (www.cluetrain.com) publishes new ways to find and share innovative marketing information and ideas.

  Forrester Research (www.forrester.com) provides industry research into technology markets.

  Greenbook.org (www.greenbook.org) is a worldwide directory of marketing research focus group suppliers.

  MarketPerceptions (http://marketperceptions.com) represents a research company that specializes in health care research, in particular, its focus group capabilities.

Primary Research If the needed information is not available through secondary sources, companies and their agencies may collect their own data. Information that is collected for the first time from original sources is called primary research.

DDB is a worldwide marketing communications agency that conducts the annual DDB Life Style Study, a form of primary research. According to its website: "The DDB Life Style Study® is the nation's

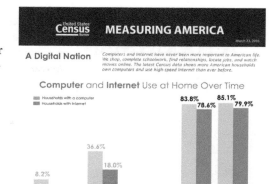

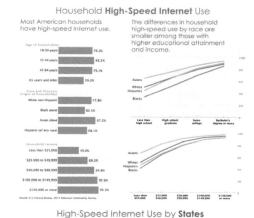

Demographic information, such as that available from the US Census Bureau, is fundamental to marketing and communication planning.
Source: From the U.S. Census Bureau. "A Digital Nation," March 23, 2016.

Photo: Image courtesy of Perdue

CLASSIC

"It takes a tough man to make a tender chicken" was the signature line for a long-running campaign that began in 1971 for Perdue Farms. It featured the owner, Frank Perdue, as the plain-spoken farmer who cared about the quality of his chickens. Scali, McCabe, and Sloves was the agency behind the campaign that created the first recognizable brand for an unlikely commodity product—chickens. But the reason the campaign was successful wasn't just the iconic, perhaps ironic, "tough man" line, but rather Frank Perdue's knowledge of his market. When he decided in the 1960s to eliminate brokers and sell directly to stores, he spent months on the road talking to butchers about what they wanted in chickens and identified 25 quality factors. Then he modified his operations to produce chickens that delivered on those 25 factors—a tough man who was obsessed with tender chickens.

🔷 **Principle**
Quantitative research is best used to count, predict, or draw conclusions about "how much" and "how often."

longest running and largest longitudinal study of attitudes and behaviors. This survey enables DDB to provide exceptional insight into American consumer attitudes and behaviors. Conducted annually since 1975, approximately 7000 men and women age 18+ are surveyed nationwide."[13] Former DDB strategy director Marty Horn says that "DDB believes that advertising—and all other forms of marketing communication—is really a personal conversation between the brand being advertised and the consumer, and the better we know the consumer with whom we are conversing, the more engaging and persuasive our message will be." The agency's Life Style Study is an important source of information that lets this conversation happen. Horn explained, "The DDB Life Style Study helps us get a more 'up close and personal' look at who our clients' customers are than what conventional research alone can provide."

An example of a company that took on its own research is Perdue Farms, which conducted consumer research to develop its classic "tough man" campaign.

Primary research suppliers (the firms that many clients and agencies hire) specialize in interviewing, observing, recording, and analyzing the behavior of those who purchase or influence the purchase of a particular good or service. The primary research supplier industry is extremely diverse. Companies range from Nielsen, the huge international tracker of TV viewing habits which employs more than 45,000 workers in the United States alone, to several thousand consultants who conduct focus groups and individual interviews, prepare reports, and provide advice on specific advertising and marketing problems for individual clients.

Many advertising agencies subscribe to large-scale surveys conducted by the Simmons Market Research Bureau (SMRB) or by Mediamark Research & Intelligence (MRI). These two organizations survey large samples of American consumers (approximately 30,000 for each survey) and ask questions about the consumption, possession, or use of a wide range of products, services, and media. The products and services covered in the MRI survey range from toothbrushes and dental floss to diet colas, camping equipment, and theme parks.

Both SMRB and MRI conduct original research and distribute findings tailored to their clients. The resulting reports are intended primarily for use in media planning, but because these surveys are so comprehensive, they also can be mined for other unique consumer information. Through a computer program called Gold-digger, for example, an MRI subscriber can select a consumer target and ask the computer to find all other products and services and all the media that members of the target segment use. This profile provides a vivid and detailed description of the target as a person, which is just the information creative teams need to help them envision their audiences. To give you an idea of what the media data look like, check out Figure 6.3 for a sample MRI report of the types of TV programs adults ages 18 to 34 watch.

Basic Research Designs

Primary research can be designed to collect both quantitative and qualitative data. Quantitative data is also collected through experimental research designs, another type of primary research.

Quantitative Research Design Research that delivers descriptive, numerical data such as number of users and purchases, their attitudes and knowledge, their exposure to ads, and other market-related information is called **quantitative research**. The MRI page is an example of data obtained through quantitative research. It also provides information on reactions to advertising, sometimes called *purchase intent*. Quantitative methods that investigate the responses of large numbers of people are useful in testing ideas to determine if their market is large enough or if most people really say or behave in a certain way.

Quantitative research is most often used either to accurately count something, such as sales levels, or to predict something, such as attitudes. To be predictive, however, this type of research

Base: Adults	Total U.S. 000	Respondent 18–34 1-Person Household				Respondent 18–34 and Married, no children				Respondent 18–34 and Married, Youngest Child <6				Respondent 18–34 and Married, Youngest Child 6+			
		A 000	B % Down	C % Across	D Index	A 000	B % Down	C % Across	D Index	A 000	B % Down	C % Across	D Index	A 000	B % Down	C % Across	D Index
All Adults	184274	5357	100.0	2.9	100	7559	100.0	4.1	100	18041	100.0	9.8	100	4978	100.0	2.7	100
Program-Types: Average Show																	
Adven/Sci Fi/West-Prime	19969	590	11.0	3.0	102	875	11.6	4.4	107	2303	12.8	11.5	118	694	13.9	3.5	129
Auto Racing-Specials	6590	*226	4.2	3.4	118	*242	3.2	3.7	90	634	3.5	9.6	98	*251	5.0	3.8	141
Awards-Specials	16490	397	7.4	2.4	83	514	6.8	3.1	76	1576	8.7	9.6	98	*451	9.1	2.7	101
Baseball Specials	28019	806	15.0	2.9	99	1128	14.9	4.0	98	2671	14.8	9.5	97	*506	10.2	1.8	67
Basketball-Weekend-College	7377	*222	4.1	3.0	104	*244	3.2	3.3	81	531	2.9	7.2	74	*183	3.7	2.5	92
Basketball Specials-College	17096	529	9.9	3.1	106	694	9.2	4.1	99	1459	8.1	8.5	87	*423	8.5	2.5	92
Basketball Specials-Pro.	32470	1057	19.7	3.3	112	1369	18.1	4.2	103	3128	17.3	9.6	98	886	17.8	2.7	101
Bowling-Weekend	16808	312	5.8	1.9	654	744	9.8	4.4	108	1476	8.2	8.8	90	*386	7.8	2.3	85
Comedy/Variety	26254	930	17.4	3.5	122	1150	15.2	4.4	107	3257	18.1	12.4	127	999	20.1	3.8	141
Daytime Dramas	7621	*192	3.6	2.5	87	*287	3.8	3.8	92	845	4.7	11.1	113	*343	6.9	4.5	167
Daytime Game Shows	7747	*97	1.8	1.3	43	*194	2.6	2.5	61	734	4.1	9.5	97	*235	4.7	3.0	112
Documen/Information-Prime	22514	532	9.9	2.4	81	504	6.7	2.2	55	1739	9.6	7.7	79	*454	9.1	2.0	75
Early Morning News	12226	280	5.2	2.3	79	*429	5.7	3.5	86	1065	5.9	8.7	89	*330	6.6	2.7	100
Early Morning Talk/Info/News	14681	258	4.8	1.8	60	580	7.7	4.0	96	1291	7.2	8.8	90	*268	5.4	1.8	68
Early Eve. Netwk News-M-F	25946	596	11.1	2.3	79	836	11.1	3.2	79	1822	10.1	7.0	72	*594	11.9	2.3	85
Early Eve. Netwk News-Wknd	11338	*197	3.7	1.7	60	*208	2.8	1.8	45	795	4.4	7.0	72	*187	3.8	1.6	61
Entertainment Specials	19630	408	7.6	2.1	71	701	9.3	3.6	87	1719	9.5	8.8	89	*494	9.9	2.5	93
Feature Films-Prime	17232	371	6.9	2.2	74	*538	7.1	3.1	76	1209	6.7	7.0	72	*475	9.5	2.8	102
Football Bowl Games-Specials	13322	369	6.9	2.8	95	*381	5.0	2.9	70	1512	8.4	11.3	116	*245	4.9	1.8	68
Football Pro.-Specials	44804	1471	27.5	3.3	113	1766	23.4	3.9	96	4555	25.2	10.2	104	1104	22.2	2.5	91
General Drama-Prime	19880	581	10.8	2.9	101	571	7.6	2.9	70	2095	11.6	10.5	108	*555	11.1	2.8	103
Golf	5161	*102	1.9	2.0	68	*152	2.0	2.9	72	*324	1.8	6.3	64	*15	.3	.3	11
Late Evening Netwk News Wknd	5146	*146	2.7	2.8	98	*114	1.5	2.2	54	*293	1.6	5.7	58	*104	2.1	2.0	75
Late Night Talk/Variety	9590	313	5.8	3.3	112	*297	3.9	3.1	75	1009	5.6	10.5	107	*198	4.0	2.1	76
News-Specials	14508	234	4.4	1.6	55	510	6.7	3.5	86	1297	7.2	8.9	91	*212	4.3	1.5	54
Pageants-Specials	22025	439	8.2	2.0	69	952	12.6	4.3	105	2503	13.9	11.4	116	547	11.0	2.5	92
Police Docudrama	23575	726	13.6	3.1	106	1179	15.6	5.0	122	2309	12.8	9.8	100	731	14.7	3.1	115
Pvt Det/Susp/Myst/Pol.-Prime	28183	673	12.6	2.4	82	763	10.1	2.7	66	1739	9.6	6.2	63	*493	9.9	1.7	65
Situation Comedies-Prime	19097	598	11.2	3.1	108	919	12.2	4.8	117	2737	15.2	14.3	146	688	13.8	3.6	133
Sports Anthologies-Weekend	4847	*218	4.1	4.5	155	*232	3.1	4.8	117	*403	2.2	8.3	85	*108	2.2	2.2	82
Sunday News/Interview	5809	*70	1.3	1.2	41	*116	1.5	2.0	49	*214	1.2	3.7	38	*97	1.9	1.7	62
Syndicated Adult General	10444	*271	5.1	2.6	89	462	6.1	4.4	108	766	4.2	7.3	75	*221	4.4	2.1	78
Tennis	10033	338	6.3	3.4	116	380	5.0	3.8	92	826	4.5	8.2	84	*105	2.1	1.0	39

FIGURE 6.3

MRI Page

This MRI report breaks down the 18 to 34 age market into four market segments based on size of household and age of children, if any, and describes their television viewing patterns. Here's a question: Where would you advertise to reach single adults in the 18 to 34 category? First look at the Index column under that category heading and find the two highest indexes. An index of 100 is average; thus, an index of 112 reflects a 12 percent above-average activity, and an index of 89 indicates activity 11 percent below the average. Then, for each high index, look across to column A and determine the size of that group. As a point of comparison, do the same analysis for the Married with the Youngest Child over 6 category. How do the two groups differ in their television viewing patterns?

Source: Gfk Mediamark Research & Intelligence, LLC

must follow careful scientific procedures. Two primary characteristics of quantitative research are (1) large sample sizes, typically from 100 to 1,000 people, and (2) random sampling. The most common quantitative research methods include surveys and studies that track such things as purchase behavior and opinions.

One of the biggest problems in using quantitative methods to study consumer decision processes is that consumers are often unable to articulate the reasons they do what they do because their reasons may not fit into answers provided in a survey. Furthermore, most people aren't tuned in to their own thoughts and thinking process so they may be uncomfortable saying yes or no or checking a space on a rating scale. Respondents also have a tendency to give the answers that they think the researcher wants to hear. All are reasons why qualitative research has become much more important in creating brand communication. It offers the ability to probe and move beyond the sometimes simplistic responses to a survey.

● **Principle**
Qualitative research provides insight into consumers' underlying reasons and motivations.

Qualitative Research   The goal of qualitative research methodologies is to move beyond the limitations of what consumers can explain through responses to preplanned questions. **Qualitative research** is considered exploratory and provides insight into the underlying reasons and motivations for how and why consumers behave as they do.

For example, when Pepsico/Frito Lay considered changing its target audience for Cheetos from kids to adults, this dramatic change in strategy called for in-depth research into the attitudes and behaviors of the new target. Researchers listened to what Cheetos fans said about the experience of eating the crunchy orange snack and found that these adults loved eating Cheetos and licking their fingers. They liked a food that was playful and that gave them permission to not act their age.[14]

Common qualitative research methods include such tools as observation, ethnographic studies, in-depth interviews, and case studies. They trade scientific predictions and generalizability of findings for greater richness and depth of insight. These exploratory research tools are useful for probing and gaining explanations and understanding of such questions as the following:

- What features do customers want?
- What are the motivations that lead to the purchase of a product?
- What do our customers think about our advertising?
- What are consumers' emotional links to the brand?

Qualitative methods often are used early in the process of developing a brand communication plan or message strategy for generating insights as well as questions and hypotheses for additional research. They are also good at confirming hunches, ruling out bad approaches and questionable or confusing ideas, and giving direction to the message strategy. However, because qualitative research is typically done with small groups, researchers cannot project their findings to the larger population. Rather than drawing conclusions, qualitative research is used to answer the "why" question as well as generate hypotheses that can be tested with quantitative methods.

As Sally Reinman, worldwide market planner at Saatchi & Saatchi, wrote for this book in an earlier edition, qualitative research can also be applied in cross-cultural marketing situations. "As consumers around the world become better informed and more demanding," she wrote, "advertisers that target different cultures need to find the 'commonalities' (or common ground) among consumer groups from these cultures." She used the example of research for Toyota's sport-utility vehicle (SUV), the RAV 4, which showed that consumers in all the targeted countries had three common desires: they all wanted an SUV to have style, safety, and economy. This makes developing an effective international campaign much easier.

Experimental Research Design   Tightly controlled scientific studies are sometimes used to puzzle out how people think and respond to different messages and incentives. **Experimental research** seeks to establish a cause-effect relationship between variables and uses formal hypothesis-testing techniques, such as comparing consumer response to different message treatments. The idea is to control for all factors except the one being tested; if there is a change in the results, the researcher can conclude that the variable being tested caused the difference. Experimental research may be used to test market a variety of factors: advertising appeals and executions, product features and design, price, and various creative ideas.

Does Advertising Make Smoking Cool?

Cornelia (Connie) Pechmann, *University of California, Irvine*

In 1991, I began a program of research on tobacco-use prevention through advertising and the mass media. I wondered how often people saw advertisements for products shortly before experiencing the products. It occurred to me that advertising exposure and product experience were perhaps most likely to occur concurrently in the case of cigarette advertising and encounters with smokers. In 1991, cigarette advertising on billboards was ubiquitous and 20 percent of high school seniors smoked daily, so I reasoned that adolescents might see cigarette advertisements and peers smoking concurrently. I also reasoned that encounters with smokers would often be ambiguous.

Looking at the literature, I could find few controlled experiments on cigarette advertising. However, surveys indicated there was a strong association between adolescents' perceptions of smokers and smoking initiation. With the assistance of coauthors, I completed two research projects that documented that cigarette advertisements can prime adolescents' positive beliefs about smokers and thus alter their social encounters with smokers. Specifically, cigarette advertisements serving as primes can favorably bias adolescents' perceptions of peers who smoke and thus increase their intent to smoke. One of our papers on this topic received the Best Paper Award from the *Journal of Consumer Research*. I continue to conduct research in this area.

I am told that my tobacco-related research has been cited by expert witnesses in legal cases such as the federal tobacco case, in legislative hearings, and in US Attorney General meetings. I believe that some academic research should be conducted to inform public policy and that if research is not designed for this purpose, it likely will not have this effect.

Sources: J. A. Bargh, M. Chen, and L. Burrows, "Automaticity of Social Behavior: Direct Effects of Trait Construct and Stereotype Activation on Action," *Journal of Personality and Social Psychology* 71, no. 2 (1996): 230–244; C. Pechmann and S. J. Knight, "An Experimental Investigation of the Joint Effects of Advertising and Peers on Adolescents' Beliefs and Intentions about Cigarette Consumption," *Journal of Consumer Research* 29, no. 1 (2002): 5–19; C. Pechmann and S. Ratneshwar, "The Effects of Antismoking and Cigarette Advertising on Young Adolescents' Perceptions of Peers Who Smoke," *Journal of Consumer Research* 21, no. 2 (1994): 236–251.

Do your professors and instructors talk about the research they conduct? Above is an example of one professor's research about cigarette advertising that has practical implications for the tobacco industry and policy makers. Of course, advertising can be used to either promote or discourage smoking. This research tests the idea that anti-cigarette advertising may unintentionally prime (or prepare) teens to think that smoking is cool. The Principled Practice feature explains how this researcher used experimental studies to determine the impact of advertising on behavior.

Sometimes in experimental research the measurements are electronically recorded using such instruments as MRI or EEG machines or eye-scan tracking devices. Electrodes can be used to monitor heart rate, pulse, and skin temperature to determine if people have a physical response to a message that they may not be able to put in words.

Emotional responses, in particular, are hard to verbalize but may be observable using these types of sensors. Hewlett-Packard Company, for example, wired a group of volunteers with electrodes to see how they reacted to photos of people smiling. The study found that there were obvious differences in brain activity in people looking at photos of smiling people, particularly pictures of children smiling. New *computer-vision* software attached to high-resolution cameras is trying to read expressions on faces to determine viewers' responses during such activities as watching a movie trailer or shopping online.[15] And *eye-tracking* technology, a retina-tracking camera hooked up to a computer screen that projects images, has long been used to watch how readers and viewers scan print and video. It is now being used to test shoppers' attention to shelf designs and store layouts.[16]

In practice, quantitative and qualitative methods are often used together in a complementary way to give researchers both the description and understanding of consumers that they need. The Lean Cuisine example showed how qualitative research may be used to help explain quantitative research insights. Likewise, because qualitative research is often exploratory, it may be used first to help develop quantitative tools such as surveys or experiments.

6.3 Understand how to choose appropriate research methods and collect data.

Choose Methods and Collect Data

This section focuses on the types of research used in message development and the research situations where these methods are typically used. Consumer research methodologies are often described in terms of the type of data they produce: numeric (quantitative) or verbal/behavioral communication (qualitative). Data for both of these methods might be collected in person, by telephone, by mail, through the Internet or cable TV, or by a computer kiosk in a mall or store.

Quantitative Methods

We have stated that most quantitative research in marketing communication is survey based; however, consumers can also be contacted in malls where they are invited to participate in experimental research.

Survey Research   In a survey, questionnaires are used to obtain information about a wide range of people's attitudes, knowledge, opinions, media use, and exposure to particular messages. **Survey research** is a quantitative method that uses structured interviews to ask large numbers of people the same set of questions. The questions at the end of the survey often include more personal information such as age, income, and education level. Surveys can be conducted in person, by phone, by mail, or online.

An example of a company doing its own survey research is Toyota, which undertook a huge two-year study of ultra-rich consumers in the United States to better market its upscale Lexus brand. A team of nine Lexus employees from various departments was designated the "superaffluent team" and was sent on the road to interview wealthy car buyers about why they live where they do, what they do for enjoyment, what brands they buy, and how they feel about car makes and models. One surprising finding was that these consumers don't just buy a car; rather, they buy a fleet of cars because they have multiple homes and offices.[17]

Incentives are important when doing surveys. As Karl Weiss explains in the Matter of Practice feature, you should choose an incentive that is appropriate for your audience, perhaps $5 or $10 in cash, a drawing for a Wii or iPhone, or even just a summary of the results. Different audiences have different interests, so make your incentive appealing to them. Be careful, however, not to bias your results in the process. If you are studying airline travel behavior and your incentive is a PlayStation, don't be surprised to find that most of those who complete the survey are

Photo: RON CHAPPLE/Getty Images

Photo: Janine Wiedel Photolibrary/Alamy Stock Photo

Survey research can be conducted in person and is often conducted in malls, supermarket aisles, or other public places.

Phone surveys are commonly used. Often they come from commercial call centers where many people hired by a research company staff a bank of phones. In recent years, the contact is made through electronic dialing, and when respondents answer, the call is transferred to an interviewer.

males under 35 years old. "Opinionators" are people who sign onto consumer market research survey sites as paid panelists. They are asked their opinions on everything from product design, to television commercials, to sales promotions.[18]

There are two big questions to consider in designing a survey: how to build a representative sample of people to be interviewed and what method is best to collect the data.

Sampling and Data Collection   A technique called sampling is used to find interviewees because, in most cases, it is cost prohibitive to try to interview everyone in the population or target market. Instead, the people interviewed are a representative **sample** of the larger group, a subset of the population that is representative of the entire population. For survey research to be an accurate reflection of the population, those who participate must be *selected at random*, which means every person who belongs to the population being surveyed has an equal likelihood (probability) of being chosen to participate. **Random sampling** also allows researchers to make valid use of statistical analyses on the data obtained and generalize the findings to the larger population. That is the main reason why random sampling is the basic requirement of opinion research and polling, which you hear about every time an election comes around.

For years, phone number lists in phone directories gave researchers the perfect source from which they could draw a random sample. However, phone lists have become much less reliable in recent years because many households have dropped their landlines in favor of cell phones.

A number of market research companies specialize in creating samples, particularly for online research. They try to identify appropriate groups based on the targeting decisions of a client—for example, certain demographics or usage rates—and then define the locations and size required as well as the methods for reaching these people. This method is used by Ameritest in doing online tests of commercials.

Online Survey Research   Since survey research first began, the way researchers have gone about collecting data from respondents has seen almost constant change as new technologies have made such research more cost efficient. Since the 1950s, research methods that involve personal interaction have moved from door-to-door interviews, to phone interviews, and now to online surveys. Online surveys now make up half of the $3.3 billion spent on market research.[19] As Karl Weiss explains and as his diagram shows, the internet has opened up new opportunities for collecting data (see the Matter of Practice feature on the next page).

A good example of how a company can gain significant benefits from online survey research is the QuikTrip Corporation (QT), an $11 billion privately held firm operating more than 700 convenience stores in 11 states (www.quiktrip .com). Because the company is very customer-centric in its thinking and decision-making, it developed a unique platform of its own for quickly and efficiently gathering customer research on a regular basis. The company calls it QT-Connect, and it allows the company to gather customers' opinions on new ideas, existing products, its advertising content, purchase frequency, store design, and even color preferences on QT's packaging. Nearly 80,000 of QT's customers are enrolled and complete short online surveys in exchange for free products and discounts. With QT-Connect, the research team can get feedback within a few days—or even a few hours—from thousands of QT's customers on virtually all aspects of its business. Throughout the process, QuikTrip ensures the data are valid and reliable so the results of the statistical analyses are objective, repeatable, and conclusive.[20]

In addition to survey research, the Internet can also be a useful tool for monitoring online behavior. Jason Cormier, cofounder of social-media agency Room 214, explains that marketing communication data can be based on interactions on social networks

Photo: Courtesy Billings Chamber of Commerce /Convention and Visitors Bureau

SHOWCASE

A rebranding campaign for Billings began with a broad survey of people involved in the business of supporting the city. For online surveys to work, they need to be supported by an invitation to participate that showcases an easy-to-use message.

The Billings, Montana, "Trailhead" brand identity campaign, which was described in more detail in Chapter 5, was provided by John Brewer.

Online Marketing Research

Karl Weiss, *President, Market Perceptions & Healthcare Research*

Remember when surveyors came to your door with clipboards in hand, asking to come into your home to ask you some questions about a new product idea or some different advertising approaches? Unless you're well over 50 years old, you probably don't.

Times have changed, and conducting surveys by going door to door was replaced by telephone interviewing in the 1960s. Someday you can tell your children, "When I was growing up, marketing researchers used to call people on the phone to do surveys," and that will seem about as foreign a concept to them as door-to-door interviewing does to most people today.

There are many reasons for the current shift from phone to online surveys, but they are largely the same as when door-to-door interviewing switched to phone. It was cheaper, it was faster, and the quality of the data was better. The Internet allows us to gather data so much faster because tens of thousands of requests can be sent out via email in a matter of seconds, and it's much less expensive because the data are all captured by computer rather than live interviewers. Although the quality of the data has been the greatest obstacle facing widespread acceptance of online surveying, the continued declines in people participating in telephone surveys have diminished the randomness (and representativeness) of telephone survey data.

So what does that mean for marketing research beyond an evolution in data collection methodology? Gathering data by telephone was an improvement in data randomness by being able to draw a better random sample. It also offered a reduction in cost because conducting surveys by phone is cheaper than going door to door, not to mention an improvement in timing. Although online surveying has further reduced both the cost of the data collection and even more dramatically reduced timing to gather the information, it has not been able to maintain the same quality when it comes to the representativeness of the data. With telephone surveying, almost every person in the United States has a phone number, and telephone directories provide a pretty good listing from which to draw a sample, and if you want to do even better, the phone numbers can be randomly generated so that even unlisted numbers are included.

For online surveys, there is no directory of all email addresses in the United States, but emails of various market segments can be purchased through list brokers. And even though most people today have an email address, there are significant differences between those who do and those who do not, representing not only the "digital divide" but even differences in how those who have computers with Internet access utilize this technology. Some only text and hardly ever check their email addresses. Some simply have not set up an email address to begin with.

Without a comprehensive directory from which marketing researchers can draw a sample, we cannot know how well our results reflect those of the larger population. And spamming people at random to complete a survey does not go over well in the Internet age, even if such a directory existed. The rules of the game have changed, and marketing research needs to adjust. Participants who do surveys online almost always have signed up to do so, joining an online panel where they get paid to do surveys. People who choose to join an online survey panel may be quite different from those who do not, likely thinking it is a fun way to make a little extra money on the side. Do you belong to a panel? How about your classmates? If there are different motivations for choosing whether or not to join a panel, those differences in thinking style will be reflected in the data gathered, creating a possible bias in the results.

But it's not all bad news—online surveying provides us with many new opportunities, such as the ability to present images, sounds, videos, and websites to participants for their review prior to answering questions. It's the new world of marketing research, and with the challenges come many new benefits.

such as Facebook. In Chapter 5, you read about the Billings, Montana, rebranding campaign, a campaign that was launched with an online survey of more than 1,000 people.

Qualitative Methods

Surveys are the most common quantitative research methods, but certain types of surveys both with individuals and groups can also be used for probing and to gather more insightful responses. In addition, qualitative methods take researchers into homes and stores to watch how consumers behave.

In-Depth Interviews   One qualitative method used to survey consumers is the **in-depth interview**, which is conducted one-on-one using **open-ended questions** that require respondents to generate their own answers. In a personal interview, the researcher asks questions to the consumer directly. The primary difference between an interview and a survey is the interviewer's use of a more flexible and unstructured questionnaire. This type of research method was used by the Lexus "superaffluent team" we discussed earlier. Interviewers use a discussion guide, which outlines the areas to be covered during the session.

The discussion guides tend to be longer than surveys, with questions that are usually very broad. Examples include "What do you like or dislike about this product?" and "What type of television programs do you like to watch?" Interviewers probe by responding to the answer with "Why do you say that?" or "Can you explain in more detail?" Interviews are considered qualitative, and because they use small sample sizes, their results cannot be generalized to the larger population.

Focus Groups   Another qualitative method is a **focus group**, which is a group interview of 6 to 10 users and potential users of a product who are gathered around a table to discuss some topic, such as a brand, product category, or marketing communication. The objective is to get participants talking in a conversational format so that researchers can observe the dialogue and interactions among the group. It's a *directed group interview*. A moderator supervises the group, providing direction through a set of carefully developed questions that stimulate conversation and elicit the group members' thoughts and feelings in their own words. Other qualitative tools can also be used with groups, such as asking participants to create posters, diaries, or poems or to complete exercises in day mapping or memory associations (i.e., what comes to mind when you think of something, such as a brand, situation, or location).

Focus groups can be used at any step in the planning process, but they are often used early in information gathering to probe for patterns of thought and behavior that are then tested using quantitative research tools, such as surveys. Focus groups are also useful in testing creative ideas, exploring a consumer problem or need, and exploring various alternatives in message strategy development.

A **friendship focus group** takes place in a comfortable setting, usually a private home, where the host has recruited the participants. This approach is designed to break down barriers and save time in getting to more in-depth responses. For example, one study of sensitive and

Photo: Robert Marmion/Alamy Stock Photo

In-depth interviews are conducted one-on-one with open-ended questions that permit the interviewee to give thoughtful responses. The informal structure of the questions allows the interviewer to follow up and ask more detailed questions to dig deeper into attitudes and motivations.

Photo: Spencer Grant/PhotoEdit

Focus groups are conducted around a conference table with a researcher serving as the moderator working from a list of prepared discussion questions. The session is usually held in a room with one-way glass so that the other team members from the agency and client can observe the way respondents answer the questions.

insensitive visuals used in advertising directed to African-American women found that a self-constructed friendship group was easier to assemble and yielded more honest and candid responses than a more traditional focus group where respondents are recruited by a research company.[21]

The web is not only a tool for online surveys, but also for online focus groups based on the idea of getting a group of brand loyalists together in a password-protected online community. Online research company Communispace has created some 225 online communities for marketers, including Kraft Foods, Unilever for its Axe brand, and Charles Schwab.

Online focus groups are sometimes considered to be **crowdsourcing**, which refers to aggregating the wisdom of Internet users in a type of digital brainstorming. In a search for "collective intelligence," crowdsourcing collects opinions and ideas from a digital community.

Customer Suggestions and Feedback   Dialogue creates new ways to listen to customers. In the traditional communication model we described in Chapter 5, customers' responses, or *feedback*, are gathered primarily through research. In newer approaches to communication, however, feedback is achieved by monitoring more interactive forms of marketing communication (personal selling, customer service, online marketing, social media) as well as the responses and customer-initiated dialogue that comes through response devices such as toll-free numbers and email addresses.

Informal feedback has always been available in stores through suggestion boxes and customer satisfaction cards and surveys. Target took that idea online by publishing an ad in the *Wall Street Journal* asking customers to "Tell us what more we can do for you." Some 627 respondents emailed suggestions. Target then published the suggestions and the company's responses to them in two-page ads. It was a novel way of eliciting comments, listening to them, and then responding. Starbucks, like many other companies, uses an online suggestion box incorporating the practices of crowdsourcing. MyStarbucks Idea is a website for Starbucks customers to contribute ideas, join the discussion, and vote on the ones they like best. Check it out at https://ideas.starbucks.com/.

Panels   An **expert panel** gathers experts from various fields into a focus group setting. This research tool can stimulate new ways of looking at a brand, product, or customer pattern. More commonly, however, a marketing panel or **consumer research panel** is an ongoing group of carefully selected people interested in a topic or product category. A standing panel can be maintained over time by a marketer as a proprietary source of information or by a research company whose clients provide topics for the panel members' consideration. Panels can gather in person or be contacted by phone, mail, or the Internet. An example of this type of research comes from "cool hunters" and trend watchers who may use proprietary panels to track new fashions and fads.

Observation Research   Like anthropologists, observation researchers study the actual behavior of consumers in settings where they live, work, shop, and play, acting as what Shay Sayre referred to as "professional snoops."[22] Direct **observation research** is closer and more personal than most other types of research. Researchers use video, audio, and cameras to record consumers' behavior at home (with consumer consent), in stores, or wherever people buy and use their products.

Lululemon, a women's athletic apparel chain, has built a mini-empire based on an unexpected strategy: it doesn't stock a lot of merchandise, and it cultivates a sense of scarcity. How does it work? The company doesn't use a lot of standard marketing research techniques, such as focus groups, but its executives spend hours each week observing customers, watching them shop, and listening to their comments and complaints so as to optimize and tweak the stores' offerings and merchandising.[23]

A marketer may rely on observation in the aisles of grocery, drug, and discount stores to watch people as they make product selections. Grocery shopping might seem like a mundane, mechanical activity, but look around next time you're in a store and watch how your fellow shoppers make their product choices.

Cool watchers, researchers who keep tabs on emerging trends, also use observational research when visiting places and events where their target market gathers. The Consumer

Behavior Odyssey was a classic observational research project that opened the door for this type of research in marketing. The Odyssey put a team of researchers in a Winnebago on a trip from Los Angeles to Boston. Along the way, the researchers used a variety of observational techniques to watch and record people behaving as consumers.[24]

A variation on observational research is **participant observation**. In this research method, the observer is a member of the group being studied and takes part in the activity. For example, research into television viewing behaviors sometimes uses friendship groups of the researcher, who unobtrusively records his or her friends' behavior as part of the viewing session. The idea is that by immersing themselves in the activity, observers have an inside view—perhaps a more empathetic view—of their groups' experiences.

Ethnographic Research Related to observation, **ethnographic research** involves the researcher in living the lives of the people being studied. Ethnographers have elevated people watching to a science. In ethnographic research, which combines anthropology and marketing, observers immerse themselves in a culture to study the meanings, language, interaction, and behavior of the people in the group.[25] The idea is that people's behavior tells you more than you can ever get in an interview or focus group. This method is particularly good at deriving a picture of a day in the life of a typical consumer. An example comes from a Walgreen's vice president who wore glasses that blurred his vision, taped his thumbs to his palms, and wore shoes containing unpopped popcorn. The exercise was designed to help him and other retail executives understand the difficulties facing elderly shoppers: confusing store layouts, eyesight problems, arthritis, and the inability to reach or stoop.[26]

Major companies like Harley-Davidson and Coca-Cola hire marketing experts trained in social science research to observe and interpret customer behavior. These participant observers then meet with the company's managers, planners, and marketing staff to discuss their impressions. The case of Eight O'Clock coffee is an example of the use of a video recorded ethnographic study. The brand's agency, New York–based Kaplan Thaler, got 14 families in Pittsburgh and Chicago to use video cameras to record their typical mornings so as to identify the various roles that coffee played in their morning rituals.

Direct observation and ethnographic research have the advantage of revealing what people actually do as distinguished from what people say they do. It can yield the correct answer when faulty memory, a desire to impress the interviewer, or simple inattention to details would cause an interview answer to be wrong. The biggest drawback to direct observation is that it shows what is happening but not *why*. Therefore, the results of direct observation often are combined with personal interviews afterward to provide a more complete and more understandable picture of attitudes, motives, and behavior.

The McCann agency has dedicated a $2.5 million research effort to understanding the lives of low-income Latinos from Mexico to Chile.[27] A new division named "Barrio" studies the marketing efforts of its clients, such as Nestlé and Danone. It has transformed conference rooms into bodegas (corner grocery shops) and sent employees to live with families, amassing some 700 hours of video recordings. The reason is that practical insights into low-income groups are hard to find, yet these people are consumers, too, and marketers need to understand their needs as emerging economies bring new lifestyles and products to the disadvantaged.

Diaries Sometimes, consumers are asked to record their activities through the use of diaries. These **diaries** are particularly valuable in media research because they tell media planners exactly what programs and ads the consumers watched. If comment lines are provided, the activities can also be accompanied by thoughts. *Beeper diaries* are used as a way to randomize the recording of activities. Consumers participating in the study are instructed to grab the diary and record what they are doing when the beeper goes off. Diaries are designed to catch the consumer in a more realistic, normal life pattern than you can derive from surveys or interviews that rely on consumers to remember their activities accurately. Diaries can also lead to a helpful reconstruction of a typical day in the life of a consumer.

An example comes from Regina Lewis and Dunkin' Donuts, where she used a young adult diary study to determine when this target audience starts drinking coffee. She recruited 20 people in five cities. From their records, Lewis and her team had hundreds of points of observations. At research centers, the participants were then asked to explain what was going on when

● Principle
Direct observation and ethnographic research methods reveal what people actually do rather than what they say they do, but they also lack the ability to explain why these people do what they do.

ADVICE FROM COLLEGE STUDENT BINGE DRINKERS: "Don't Be the One Who Drinks the Least, but Don't Be the One Who Drinks the Most"

Joyce M. Wolburg, *Professor and Associate Dean, Marquette University*

Binge drinking among college students continues to be a challenge for university administrators who are concerned about the consequences of heavy drinking. To that end, many universities promote moderation to reduce the harm to students. One approach attempts to convince students that excessive drinking is not the norm for their campus. For example, a social norms campaign might inform students that, contrary to popular opinion, only 35 percent of students on campus consume five or more drinks when they party. By setting the record straight, the theory predicts that students will model their behavior on consumption levels that fit the true norm for the campus instead of trying to match an overestimated, excessive level. Of course, this strategy can be problematic if the actual majority of students drink excessively.

As an intervention strategy, the use of social norms has worked well on some campuses but not all. To make sense of these findings, I began interviewing students about all aspects of drinking on campus: how alcohol fits their lives when transitioning to college life as freshmen; how the drinking culture changed when they had a stronger group of friends and were more accustomed to the course load as sophomores; how the drinking changed in their junior year when they moved out of the dorms and into apartments, away from the watchful eye of RAs; and how alcohol was part of their lives as 21-year-old seniors, who were legal drinkers beginning to focus on graduation and the next chapter in their lives. My goal was to help campaign strategists gain insights into students' lives and find out what is meaningful to them so that campaign messages would resonate well.

The students I interviewed generally felt entitled to drink and believed that the legal drinking age of 21 was unjust. As underage drinkers, they knew that they risked consequences if they were caught, but they focused on ways of drinking without getting caught. This strategy led to a complex system of avoiding detection in the dorms, avoiding bars that "card hard," and knowing how to get past the bouncer.

The one consistent piece of advice they offered is to avoid being the one who drinks the least as well as the one who drinks the most. As one student put it, "I don't want to be the drunkest guy in the room but I don't want to be the most sober. . . . Right or wrong, I want to be in that middle 50 or 75 percent." This statement may come as a surprise to people who think that anything goes, but there are norms in place and lines that shouldn't be crossed. Drinking the least is undesirable because most drinkers feel judged by nondrinkers, and the person drinking the least is often the object of intense peer pressure to drink. Furthermore, many find that being sober among people who are drunk is no fun. On the other hand, drinking the most makes students a liability to their friends because they may lose control, start a fight, need help getting home, or, in worst case scenarios, need to be taken to a hospital. As one student said, "People just don't want to go out with you. You've surpassed fun and gone into crazy."

So, what does it all mean? Drinkers may perceive a university-wide statistic as too abstract and irrelevant a social norm for modeling their behavior. Instead, they follow their own social norms based on their friends' level of consumption. Interventions based on social norms must be carefully designed to remain true to students' culture of friends.

Source: Joyce M. Wolburg, "Insights for Prevention Campaigns: The Power of Drinking Rituals in the College Student Experience from Freshman to Senior Year," *Journal of Current Issues and Research in Advertising, Vol. 37 (1),* 2016.

they thought about having coffee: what day, what time, why are they thinking about coffee, and so forth. From that research, the team learned that many young adults want "chuggable" coffee, particularly because they want an immediate caffeine hit. As a result, they drink iced coffee because hot coffee is too hot and they can't get their caffeine shot fast enough. Dunkin' responded with "Turbo Ice" coffee with an extra shot of espresso.[28]

Other Qualitative Methods As illustrated in the Principled Practice feature by Wolburg, marketing communication planners are always probing for reasons, feelings, and motivations behind what people say and do. To arrive at useful consumer insights, they may also use a variety of interesting and novel research methods. In particular, they may use stories and pictures. Cognitive psychologists have learned that human beings think more in images than in words.

Most research continues to use words to ask questions and obtain answers, but recent experiments with visual-based research open up new avenues of expression that may be better able to uncover people's deep thoughts.

Researchers use pictures as well as other tools to uncover mental processes that guide consumer behavior. Professor Larry Soley refers to these methods as **projective techniques**, which means that they ask respondents to generate impressions rather than respond to more controlled quantitative surveys and rating systems. He describes projective techniques as psychoanalytic.[29]

Harvard Business School professor Gerald Zaltman believes that the conventional wisdom about consumer research, such as using interviews and focus groups that rely on talking to people and grilling them about their tastes and buying habits, is only good for getting back predictable answers. If you ask people what they think about Coke, you'll learn that it is a "high-energy, thirst-quenching, fun-at-the-beach" kind of drink. But that may not be an adequate description of how people really feel about the soft drink.[30]

Word association is a projective technique that asks people to respond with thoughts or other words that come to mind when they are given a stimulus word. The idea is to uncover the **network of associations** in their thought patterns. Brand perceptions are tested this way to map the structure and logic of these association networks. For example, what do you think of when you think of Taco Bell? or Wendy's? or Arby's? Each restaurant should bring to mind some things in common (fast food, cheap food), but they also have distinct networks of associations based on type of food (Mexican, hamburgers, roast beef), restaurant design, logo and colors, brand characters, healthfulness, and so forth. Each restaurant, then, has a distinctive profile that can be determined from its associations network.

Here is a collection of some of the more imaginative ways qualitative researchers use projective techniques as games to gather insights about people's relationships with the brands they buy.

- *Fill in the blanks* is a form of attitude research in which people literally fill in the blanks in a story or balloons in a cartoon. Perceptions can come to the surface in the words that participants use to describe the action or situations depicted in the visuals.
- *Sentence completion* tests give respondents the beginning of a sentence and ask them to finish it. They are good at eliciting descriptions, causes, results, and the meanings in personal experiences.
- *Purpose-driven games* allow researchers to see how people solve problems and search for information.[31] Games can make the research experience more fun and involving for participants. They also uncover problem-solving strategies that may mirror the participants' approach to information searching or the kinds of problems they deal with in certain product situations.
- *Theater techniques* use games in a theater setting where researchers have people experience a variety of exercises to understand how they think about their brand. Some of these games have people tell stories about products or simulations where they have to convince others to use a brand.
- *Sculpting and movement techniques,* such as positioning the body as a statue, can be a source of insight in brainstorming for creative ideas and new product ideas. Sculpting involves physically putting product users in static positions that reflect how they think about or use a brand. Physical movements, such as dance movements and martial arts, can be added to increase the range of insight.
- *Story elicitation* asks consumers to explain the artifacts of their lives, such as the photos displayed in their homes and the objects they treasure. These stories can provide insights into how and why people use or do things.
- *Artifact creation* is a technique that uses such ideas as life collages, day mapping (tracking someone's activities across a day), and the construction of instruction books as ways to elicit stories that discuss brands and their role in daily life. These projects are also useful later in explaining to others—clients, the creative team, or other agencies—the triggers behind consumer insights.[32]
- *Photo elicitation* is similar to artifact research except that it uses visuals to elicit consumer thoughts and opinions. Emotions are elicited by asking consumers what they think people in various photos and situations are feeling. A form of photo-based interviewing, consumers

L'original

Photo: Courtesy Evian/Danone Waters of America, Inc.

This metaphoric ad equating Evian sparkling water with a mermaid tries to add a touch of originality, as well as meaning, to the Evian brand image.

can be asked to look at a set of visuals or instructed to visually record something with a camera, such as a shopping trip. Later, in reviewing the visuals, they are asked to explain what they were thinking or doing.

- *Photo sorts,* which is yet another visual technique, asks consumers to sort through a deck of photos and pick out visuals that represent something to them, such as typical users of the product or situations in which it might be used. In identifying typical users, consumers may be asked to sort the photos into specific piles, such as happy, sad, angry, excited, or innovative people.

- *Metaphors* can be used by researchers to enrich the language consumers use to talk about brands. (A **metaphor** compares one thing to another without using the actual words *like* or *as*.) The Evian ad, for example, uses a strong metaphor to define its product. The insight into how people perceive brands through such connections comes from exploring the link between the two concepts. Metaphor games are used in creativity to elicit new and novel ideas, but they can also be used to analyze cognitive patterns in people's thinking.

These methods can be combined. Zaltman is the creator of ZMET (pronounced ZEE-MET), the Zaltman Metaphor Elicitation Technique, which uses metaphors and visual images to uncover patterns in people's thinking. For a typical session, the respondents find images that they think relate to the product category or brand being studied. Then they create stories that describe their feelings about the product or brand.[33] For Coca-Cola in Europe, Zaltman asked volunteers to collect at least a dozen pictures that captured their feelings about Coca-Cola. Then they discussed the images in personal interviews. Finally, the volunteers created a summary image—a digital collage of their most important images—and recorded a statement that explained its meaning. The ZMET team found that Coke is not just about feelings of high energy and good times; it also has an element of calm, solitude, and relaxation.[34]

How Do You Choose a Research Method?

Determining the appropriate research method to use is an important planning decision. It might help to understand two basic research criteria, validity and reliability, that are derived from what is called the scientific method. **Validity** means that the research actually measures what it says it measures. Any differences that are uncovered by the research, such as different attitudes or purchasing patterns, really reflect differences among individuals, groups, or situations. **Reliability** means that you can run the same test again and get the same answer.

Quantitative researchers, particularly those doing experiments and surveys, are concerned about being faithful to the principles of science. Selecting a sample that truly represents the population, for example, increases the reliability of the research. Poorly worded questions and talking to the wrong people can hurt the validity of surveys. The problem with experiments is twofold: (1) experiments are limited by a small number of people in the experimental group, and (2) they are conducted under artificial conditions.

The information you get from surveys of a broad cross section of a population is limited to your ability to develop good clear questions that everyone can understand and answer. This tight control makes it harder to ask questions around the edges of a topic or elicit unexpected or unusual responses. On the other hand, focus groups and in-depth interviews that permit probing are limited by small numbers and possible problems with the representativeness of the sample.

Generally, quantitative methods are more useful for gathering numerical data (how many do this or believe that?), and qualitative methods are better at uncovering reasons and motives (why do they do this or believe that?). For these reasons, most researchers use a variety of

Embracing the Era of Big Data

Su Jung Kim, *Assistant Professor, Greenlee School of Journalism and Communication, Iowa State University*

The term *big data* has become part of everyday jargon in marketing industry and academia. Google searches for the keyword "big data" soared in 2013 and reached their peak in 2015, reflecting a fast-growing interest in this area. It is not uncommon to hear success stories of a waiter getting a six-figure-salary job as a data scientist or a magazine editor turning herself into a webpage developer after being trained in computer programming from a place like Galvanize (see *"As Tech Booms, Workers Turn to Coding for Career Change"* in *The New York Times*, July 28, 2015).

The concept still remains vague for many interested in big data's potential in strategic communication. A basic understanding involves its gigantic size, which cannot be handled by standard software tools. Instead of seeking a definitive meaning, we can discuss big data in terms of its unique "3 V" characteristics: volume, velocity, and variety. These characteristics show its massive size, fast streaming speed, and unstructured nature. Big data refers to data sets generated in seconds or even milliseconds on a massive scale. In addition, about 95 percent of big data are unstructured, meaning that the data exist in various formats such as text, photo, video, and various multimedia. Some add verification as the fourth V, emphasizing the need to validate the quality of big data before using it.

Common uses in marketing involve predictions and diagnostics. Many supermarket chains analyze customers' purchase records to identify shopping patterns and send out coupons to increase future purchases. In 2014, Amazon introduced an "anticipatory delivery" technique to determine whether a customer will purchase an item recently searched online based on previous search and purchase records. If it is likely that the customer will purchase the item, Amazon sends it to the customer's nearest inventory center so that it can be delivered as soon as the customer hits "Place your order." Telecommunication service carriers like AT&T analyze customer data to detect those unlikely to renew two-year contracts. These customers are given a more appealing contract before they make the switch to another carrier.

More recent, innovative uses of big data can be found in content creation. Johnson & Johnson's baby products division provides an app called "Hello, my name means," which helps soon-to-be parents with possible names. Once a user searches for a name, the app combs through big data sources and provides a summary of people having the same name, including their career paths, favorite music genres, and interests expressed on social media sites. This practice demonstrates how brands' use of big data can benefit companies and consumers.

What skill sets are needed to prepare for the big data era? As Davenport and Patil wrote in 2012 ("Data Scientist: The Sexiest Job of the 21st Century," *Harvard Business Review*, October issue), the most basic skill is the ability to code. Besides regular college courses, there are various online sources instructing how to code (e.g., CodeAcademy, Coursera, Lynda.com). That ability combined with statistical analytic skills provides the knowledge to identify, clean, and analyze large-scale data sets. Practitioners also should be able to work as a team and communicate findings effectively to multiple publics. It is also imperative to communicate the findings and their implications for business decisions. In the end, data don't speak. Analysts must transform data into meaningful stories. As Carly Fiorina, the former chief executive of Hewlett-Packard, said, "The goal is to turn data into information, and information into insight."

research methods, quantitative and qualitative and, occasionally, experimental designs. Which method should you choose when you conduct research? The answer depends on what questions you need to answer. In many cases, the answer may be multiple methods. As Weiss explains, sometimes the best way is to "triangulate," which means using a number of research methods to come at the research question from different directions.

A note of caution is in order here. Sometimes the biggest consumer research projects may not give reliable results. A classic example is the New Coke reformulation introduced in 1985 after some 200,000 consumers participated in blind taste tests. Based on this huge $4 million research effort, Coke managers decided to dump the old Coca-Cola formula, which had been in use since 1886, because researchers concluded that Coke drinkers preferred a new, sweeter taste. The reaction was overwhelming from loyal Coke drinkers who wanted the "Real Thing," an emotional bond that wasn't revealed in the consumer research.

Analyze Data and Report Findings

All types of data require additional steps that summarize the findings so that they can be interpreted and implemented. As mentioned earlier, a valid quantitative study can be summarized using a wide array of statistical techniques that allow researchers to generalize the findings to the larger population of interest. Qualitative studies produce data in the form of observations, verbal reports, and even images or collages. Verbal data from interviews or focus groups are often transcribed into documents to allow closer analysis and examination. Qualitative data are normally analyzed by categorizing or "coding" the responses so the researcher can consider the consumers' language, patterns in the data, and emergent themes. These types of analyses do not allow researchers to use statistical tools to generalize the findings to the population under study, but they often provide crucial insight and understanding to the research process. Finally, it is also important to report all findings objectively and in a manner that is easily understandable and useful to decision makers. As Dr. Su Jung Kim in the Matter of Practice feature states, enormous amounts of data are now available on consumer purchase, social media, and smartphone activities. To extract key insights and trends that can help firms better compete for the attention and loyalty of consumers, these "big data" require even more sophisticated analyses and creative reporting tools, including data visualization.

6.4 Describe current research trends and challenges.

Research Trends and Challenges

Marketing communication researchers face a number of challenges: globalization and new media technology are significantly reshaping the industry. Practices are also changing as the industry searches for ways to gain more insightful analyses and move into IMC planning. Let's briefly examine some of these trends and challenges.

Online Research Trends

Mobile surveys and online communities are two emerging market research methods that suppliers have most commonly adopted, according to the 2015 Greenbook Research Industry Trends Report.[35] Social media has also been developing into a source of research data. For example, Twitter developed a panel of 12,000 users into a quick-research panel for marketers. Major brands can use Twitter's panel of "Insiders" to gauge advertising campaigns before they run or as they run. Tim Perzyk, director of market insights and analytics at Twitter, told *Advertising Age*: "We select research methodologies based on the questions we'd like to answer on behalf of our clients. This includes a wide range of qualitative and quantitative techniques including forum-like environments and surveys as well as guided activities such as recording one's mobile video viewing and providing a voice-over of the experience."[36] Snapchat may soon consider a similar plan for its Millennial following, as the number of its users surpassed both Twitter and Pinterest in 2016, with most in the 18 to 24 age range.[37]

Sampling Challenges

We hinted at sampling challenges earlier in this chapter, but with the increasing use of new media and the Internet, research experts are struggling to find ways to find samples that are representative. As Weiss observed, "I wish I could fully support some mode of data collection but there's just nothing right now that is truly 'good.'"[38] The problem with online samples, for example, is representativeness. Weiss said, "If you are using an online panel there is no way to ever know if your results have any relationship to the population of interest." As mentioned earlier, he recommends triangulating to increase the effectiveness of the research design as well as sampling quality, using a variety of methods rather than relying on surveys. He concluded that "this is why the future of research cannot rely on survey data. Future researchers will be part mathematician and part philosopher. It will be a beautiful time."

Global Issues

The key issues that global researchers face include how to manage and communicate global brands in widely different localities and how to shift from studying differences to finding similarities around the world. The biggest problem is cross-cultural communication, including how to arrive at an intended message without cultural distortions or insensitivities.

Researchers are becoming more involved in puzzling out cultural meanings and testing marketing communication messages for cultural sensitivity in different countries. They struggle to determine how other cultures will interpret the elements of a campaign so that they convey the same brand message across cultures. Cultural differences complicate planning, as account planner Susan Mendelsohn, who is a member of this book's Advisory Board, discovered in planning for a new analgesic that contained caffeine. In test markets, the agency discovered that perceptions about caffeine vary widely (positive and negative) in different cultures.

IMC Research Challenges

The deluge of data complicates IMC planning, which requires research into many stakeholder groups and contact points. Instead of campaign planning, where messages are tweaked slightly to fit different media, *strategic consistency* in IMC planning suggests that different audiences, as well as media, need different messages. Mendelsohn calls it a more radical trend in planning research and points to the need for companies to be clear about the goals for their brands, recognizing that there might be multiple goals—a set of integrated goals—rather than one big underlying goal. This suggests multiple measurements of effectiveness be used as well.

Looking Ahead

Research and analysis that lead to insight into consumer thinking and behavior lead to brand communication plans and strategic decisions, which will be the topic of Chapter 8. The research findings also lead to message strategies, which we introduce in Part 3, and media strategies, which will follow in Part 4.

IT'S A WRAP

Lean Cuisine Weighs in to Support What Really Matters to Its Customers

Turning around a huge sales decline and giving a brand a fresh and meaningful connection to customers is both difficult and risky. Would the public accept Lean Cuisine's new message to "weigh what's important" or would the brand be forever stuck with the outdated "diet" label?

The #WeighThis videos were an instant and viral success, contributing to a 33% increase in positive brand perception. Within the first week of launch, their efforts earned Lean Cuisine the #9 spot in the Ad Age Viral Video chart and a 6.5 million reach. The campaign resonated emotionally with consumers describing how they wanted to be weighed and posts flooded into #WeighThis and Lean Cuisine's social channels. The responses also reduced share of negative conversations around Lean Cuisine on social media to just 4%—a stark decrease from the previous year's share of 25% negativity. Today, Lean Cuisine is no longer perceived as a lonely, single woman's quick-fix dinner, but rather an advocate for female empowerment, health, and wellness.

#WeighThis was an integral part of Lean Cuisine's holistic turnaround strategy and largely contributed to the brand seeing its first sales increase in six years despite a decline in media spend year-over-year. According to Jeff Hamilton, "In the second quarter we made the packaging changes and all the new communications and traditional media. Around July 1, business started to go positive. By the third quarter we were back to double-digit growth." The design makeover and #WeighThis campaign drove a sales increase of $58 million in the year following the campaign's launch. Clearly, listening to consumers pays off. #WeighThis made an impact, connected with its customers in a meaningful way, and Lean Cuisine was rewarded for it.

Sources: "#HyperMade: Re-Inventing "How To" at Millennial Speed" David Ogilvy Awards published case study, www.thearf.org; "Lowe's Releases the First Instagram Video Ad Timed to the Super Bowl," AdWeek, January 30, 2015; Jeff Hamilton, "Lean Cuisine's Double-Digit Digital Turnaround," posted on April 6, 2016 by Patty Odell, http://www.chiefmarketer.com/lean-cuisines-double-digit-digital-turnaround/.

Photo: Catherine Scola/Contributor/Getty Images

6.1. **Understand the strategic research process and why brand communicators use it.** Research is used to (1) develop an analysis of the marketing situation, (2) acquire consumer information and insights for making targeting decisions, (3) investigate past brand and competitors' activities, (4) identify information about available media to match the media to the target audience, (5) develop message strategies, and (6) evaluate the effectiveness of the brand communication.

6.2. **Discuss the main factors involved in designing a research study.** Secondary research is background research that gathers already published information, and primary research is original research findings collected for the first time from original sources. Quantitative research is statistical and uses numerical data to investigate how people think and behave; qualitative research is exploratory and uses probing techniques to gain insights and identify questions and hypotheses for further quantitative research. Experimental research tests hypotheses using carefully designed experiments.

6.3. **Understand how to choose appropriate research methods and collect data.** Survey research is used to amass quantities of responses from consumers about their attitudes

and behaviors. In-depth interviews probe the reasons and motivations consumers give to explain their attitudes and behavior. Focus groups are group interviews that operate like a conversation directed by a researcher. Panels are long-running consumer groups that permit tracking of attitude and behavior changes. Observation research happens in the store or home where researchers watch how consumers behave. Ethnographic research is an anthropological technique that involves the researcher in participating in the day-to-day lives of consumers. Diaries are records of consumers' behavior, particularly their media use. A number of other qualitative methods are used to creatively uncover patterns in the way consumers think and act.

6.4. **Describe current research trends and challenges.** Quantitative data from surveys and experiments, if collected properly, allow statistical analysis tools to be used so that the results can be generalized to a larger population. Qualitative data from focus groups, interviews, and observation are normally transcribed into documents. This method allows researchers to examine the verbal data more closely to uncover unique language, patterns with customers' brand experiences, and themes that are helpful in gaining more insight and empathy with the group being studied.

concept testing, p. 162
consumer research, p. 158
consumer research panel, p. 174
content analysis, p. 160
copytesting, p. 163
crowdsourcing, p. 174
diaries, p. 175
ethnographic research, p. 175
evaluative research, p. 163
experimental research, p. 168
expert panel, p. 174
focus group, p. 173
friendship focus group, p. 173

in-depth interview, p. 173
market research, p. 159
marketing research, p. 159
media research, p. 161
metaphor, p. 178
network of associations, p. 177
observation research, p. 174
open-ended questions, p. 173
participant observation, p. 175
posttesting, p. 163
pretesting, p. 162
primary research, p. 158
projective techniques, p. 177

qualitative research, p. 168
quantitative research, p. 166
random sampling, p. 171
reliability, p. 178
sample, p. 171
secondary research, p. 158
semiotic analysis, p. 162
strategic research, p. 158
survey research, p. 170
validity, p. 178
word association, p. 177

MyLab Marketing

Go to **www.pearson.com/mylab/marketing** for MyLab discussion questions (⬟) as well as the following assisted-graded writing questions.

6-1. Suppose you are developing a research program for a new bookstore serving your college or university. What kind of exploratory research would you recommend? Would you propose both qualitative and quantitative studies? Why or why not? Discuss what specific steps would you take.

6-2. Bottled water is an outgrowth of the health-and-fitness trend. It has recently moved into second place in the beverage industry behind wine and spirits, beating out beer and coffee. The latest twist on bottled water is the "enhanced" category, with designer waters that include such things as extra oxygen, vitamins, or caffeine. You have a client with a product that fits this new category. Go online and find secondary data about this market. Discuss how you would use this information to design a branding program for this product.

REVIEW QUESTIONS

6-3. Distinguish between marketing research and market research. Why is it important to understand the difference?

⭐ **6-4.** Discuss the difference between primary and secondary research.

6-5. What types of information are obtained from quantitative, qualitative, and experimental research designs? How are those three categories of research different?

6-6. What is survey research, and how is it conducted? How do in-depth interviews differ from surveys?

⭐ **6-7.** Discuss when each of the following research methods might be used: focus group, in-depth interviews, observational research, ethnographic research, panels, and diaries.

6-8. Explain the difference between validity and reliability and explain how these concepts affect brand communication research.

DISCUSSION QUESTIONS

⭐ **6-9.** Consult the MRI data reproduced in Figure 6.3 and do the following analysis. Look first at the four Index columns to find the highest viewing category of late evening weekend news and compare that with the highest viewers of early evening weekend news. If you were advertising a new hybrid car, which category and time slot would deliver the greatest *percentage* of viewers who might be in the market? Now analyze the size of the category to determine which of the high viewing categories delivers the greatest *number* of viewers.

6-10. You have been hired to develop and conduct a research study for a new upscale restaurant chain coming into your community. Your client wants to know how people in the community see the competition and what they think of the restaurant's offerings. It uses an unusual concept that focuses on fowl, such as duck, squab, pheasant, and other elegant meals in the poultry category. Given this specialty category, the restaurant would be somewhat like a seafood restaurant. One of your colleagues says that the best way to do this study is with a carefully designed survey. Another colleague says that what the client really needs is insight into the market; she believes that the best way to help the client with its advertising strategy is to use qualitative research. Review the strengths of the various research tools and match them to this new product launch. Be prepared to present your recommendations in a class discussion.

TAKE-HOME PROJECTS

6-11. *Portfolio Project:* Assume that you are working for Gerber Baby Foods. You have been asked to identify the relevant trends that are forecasted for US birthrates between 2020 and 2025. Identify internet sources that would provide that information. Gather as much information as you can from these sites and write a one-page report on the trends you find.

⭐ **6-12.** *Mini-Case Analysis:* What were the key research findings that led to Lean Cuisine's rebranding campaign? You have just been assigned to the Lean Cuisine team for the next year of the campaign. What research would you want to do before planning the next year's efforts? Identify a list of key research questions that have to be answered before the campaign can move forward.

TRACE North America Case

Multicultural Research

Read the TRACE case in the Appendix before coming to class.

6-13. How did the "Hard to Explain, Easy to Experience" team members use research to better understand the problem they were trying to solve?

6-14. How did the "Hard to Explain, Easy to Experience" team use research to inspire a creative solution to the Trace marketing challenge?

6-15. What other methodologies would you recommend to the team to better understand the success of their program in this market?

7

Segmenting and Targeting the Audience

KEY OBJECTIVES

7.1 Explain how the consumer decision process works.

7.2 Describe the cultural, social, psychological, and behavioral influences on consumer responses to marketing communication.

7.3 Discuss targeting and how it differs from segmenting.

7.4 List several characteristics that are used to segment markets and target consumers.

The success of brand communication, such as Dove's "Real Beauty" campaign, hinges on a critical consumer insight that gives direction to the advertising. By recognizing that the cultural obsession with idealized stick-thin models was impacting women's self-image, Dove was able to make the argument that real women were beautiful, too. Dove continues to extend this message to its audiences with its #MyBeautyMySay and #SpeakBeautiful campaigns and another effort that has focused attention on the shallowness of media portrayals of female athletes.[1]

This chapter explores drivers of consumer response to marketing messages, influences on consumers' behavior, what motivates them as they make purchasing decisions, and how these factors help define groups of people who might profitably be targeted with marketing communication or advertising messages.

MyLab Marketing

⭐ **Improve Your Grade!**

More than 10 million students improved their results using Pearson MyLabs. Visit **www.pearson.com/mylab/marketing** for simulations, tutorials, and end-of-chapter problems.

Campaign	**Company**	**Agency**	**Awards**
Dove's Campaign for Real Beauty	*Unilever*	*Ogilvy & Mather*	*Grand Effie*
			Grand Prix, Cannes International Advertising Festival
			Ad Age's Best Non-TV Campaigns of the Decade
			Festival of Media Awards

Dove Audiences Redefine Beauty

Source: Image courtesy of Ogilvy & Mather: Janet Kestin; Nancy Yonk; Tim Piper; Mike Kirkland; Aviva Groll; Coby Shuman.

Photo: Courtesy Janet Kestin; Nancy Vonk; Tim Piper; Mike Kirkland; Aviva Groll; Coby Shuman for Ogilvy & Mather, Toronto.

So far, you've read a lot about what makes brand communication effective. At the beginning of this book, we said that the most basic and important principle that should guide the practice of marketing communication is an understanding of your brand. So far, you've seen examples of companies that have done this exceptionally well in the opening case stories for each chapter, such as Gatorade and #LikeAGirl, and this chapter's opener, the Dove "Campaign for Real Beauty." As these cases demonstrate, a second fundamental principle of successful communication is the ability to understand how best to connect with the consumer.

Unilever's campaign for Dove, which won a Grand Effie Award and a Festival of Media Award for "branding bravery," showcases great advertising that recognized a truth held by consumers and then connected on a personal level with those consumers.

The "Campaign for Real Beauty" touched a nerve and punctured the cultural obsession with stick-thin bodies and Barbie-doll images. The Dove campaign was risky because it sought to literally redefine beauty in advertising and to acknowledge a change in the way women see themselves. It could have been a bomb, but it was a winner because it spoke to every woman's need to look and feel her best without promising or reinforcing impossible standards of beauty.

Unilever commissioned research that eventually drove the marketing campaign. Included in the findings from the study are these two startling statistics:

- Only 4 percent of the respondents believed that they were beautiful.
- Although 80 percent of women agree that every woman has something about her that is beautiful, each woman does not often see her own beauty.

Here's how the Dove "Campaign for Real Beauty" unfolded.

Dove recognized that it needed to reach every woman, and to do that strategically, it placed messages in many different media. The message of the Dove "Campaign for Real Beauty" provided a deliberate contrast with that of the competition in beauty and women's magazines like *Glamour*, *Allure*, and *Vogue*.

Dove didn't ignore broadcast media, however; it even ran an ad during the Super Bowl. Dove began its "Campaign for Real Beauty" by establishing websites and social media conversations (http://www.dove.com), urging a boost in self-esteem by defying stereotypes that define beautiful as perfect—and skinny. Part of the campaign, a web video titled *Evolution*, was a viral phenomenon, with more than 18 million views. Outdoor and transit advertisements were plastered on billboards and buses to generate public debate.

A similar strategy was used to launch Dove's ProAge line, which continued the counterintuitive strategy by celebrating older women with their silver hair, wrinkles, and age spots. Dove scored another viral megahit with "Real Beauty Sketches" in 2013, using a law-enforcement sketch artist to demonstrate that women see themselves as less beautiful than strangers do.

To launch Dove's new Nourishing Oil Care line for hair, Dove Canada extended the celebration of real women in its contemporary "Singin' in the Rain" campaign. Real women blogged about beauty and showcased their beautiful frizz-free hair as they sang and danced in a video shot in the rain. The social media effort was supported by paid media and included a partnership with the Weather Network, where ads reminded viewers that on "rainy days" or "humid days like today," the product worked to keep hair frizz-free.

Although the US culture seems to worship physical perfection, Dove is trying valiantly to broaden that definition. Is the definition of beauty universal? Does this message translate effectively to all women? Look for Professor Wanhsiu Sunny Tsai's explanation elsewhere in this chapter to discover why the Dove campaign flopped in Taiwan. At the end of the chapter, you'll read about the results of the Dove efforts.

Sources: "Singin' in the Rain" Effie Awards published case study, July 2012, www.effie.org; Effie brief supplied by Ogilvy & Mather; "Dove Campaign for Real Beauty Case Study: Innovative Marketing Strategies in the Beauty Industry," June 2005, www.datamonitor.com; Molly Prior, "Most Innovative Ad Campaign: Dove Campaign for Real Beauty," *Women's Wear Daily* 190, no. 122 (December 9, 2005): 36–39; Ann-Christine Diaz, "Book of Tens: Best Non-TV Campaigns of the Decade," www.adage.com, December 14, 2009; Michael Bush, "Unilever Wins Two Awards for Axe, Dove Media Campaigns," April 20, 2009, www.adage.com. www.unilever.com. www.dove.com, accessed November 22, 2016; "Let's Change the Way We Talk about Beauty on Social," http://www.dove.com, accessed November 22, 2016.

Starting the Conversation

7.1 Explain how the consumer decision process works.

There are more than 325 million people in the United States, and none of them are in the market for every product and every service. For every brand, some people are more likely to be interested than others. How do you find them, and then how do you start the conversation with them? Messages cost money both to send and to receive, so ideally, we want to have a brand conversation with existing and potential customers, and we don't want to waste money on others who aren't good prospects. How do you find those people?

Successful branding begins with connecting with your customers' priorities and values. Therefore, good marketing communication involves knowing everything possible about a brand's consumers and then speaking to them with a tone and message that resonates emotionally with them—like suggesting a candy bar when you're sitting on a bench. To target the best prospects, we first segment the market properly, and then we communicate with the segments most likely to respond well to the brand's benefits and message. Let's begin with some concepts about consumer decision making that build on the topics we discussed in Chapter 5.

Photo: Derek Hall @ White_Canvas

You have to understand the needs and wants of people to find the right prospect for a message at the right time.

How Do Consumers Make Brand Decisions?

The traditional view of consumer decision making, which is similar to the classic AIDA-based model of message impact that we discussed in Chapter 5, is based on a linear, information-processing approach. It suggests that for important decisions, most people follow a decision process with fairly predictable steps: (1) *need recognition*—the goal of brand communication at this stage is to activate or stimulate this need; (2) *information search*—marcom messages help the search process by providing information that is easy to find and remember; (3) *evaluation of alternatives*—brand communication helps buyers sort out products on the basis of tangible and intangible features; (4) *choice*—in-store promotions, such as packaging, point-of-purchase displays, price reductions, banners and signs, and coupon displays, help with purchase decisions; and (5) *postpurchase evaluation*—meeting customer expectations of the product as well as offering guarantees, warranties, and easy returns to reduce the fear of making a bad purchase.

This set of steps is hierarchical and suffers from the limitations we discussed in Chapter 5; however, it is useful in analyzing how consumers make decisions about major purchases, such as your choice of a college or university. The concept of **involvement** helps here. It is defined most simply as "personal relevance," and as we discussed in Chapter 5, when purchase decisions entail social or financial risk, they are considered higher involvement, and consumers are likely to work through each of the five stages in hopes of making the best decision possible. Likewise, purchases that involve little to no risk are considered lower involvement, and consumers skip some steps and are influenced more by emotions, image, and packaging.

Paths to a Brand Decision

The think/feel/do model of consumer response to a message can also be used to analyze various ways consumers make decisions. For example, the amount of information consumers need varies between low-involvement and high-involvement situations and products (Figure 7.1).

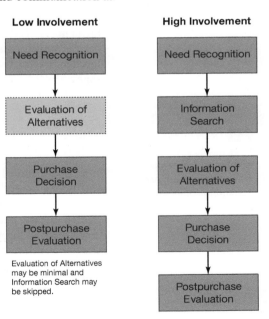

Low Involvement

Need Recognition → Evaluation of Alternatives → Purchase Decision → Postpurchase Evaluation

Evaluation of Alternatives may be minimal and Information Search may be skipped.

High Involvement

Need Recognition → Information Search → Evaluation of Alternatives → Purchase Decision → Postpurchase Evaluation

FIGURE 7.1

Low and High Involvement Decisions

The decision process for high involvement decisions involves all five stages, but low involvement decisions use just a few. What products have you purchased recently that could be considered low- or high-involvement? How did your decision process compare to these models?

The chart below summarizes six ways consumers make decisions relative to their need for information. Notice how the first step indicates whether the consumer thinks about the decision first (higher involvement), makes a decision based on feelings (feel), or just buys something without much thought (do).

Path	Goal	Example	Communication Objective
Think/feel/do	Learning, interest	Video game, DVD	Provide information, emotion
Think/do/feel	Learning, understanding	College search, a computer, a vacation	Provide information, arguments
Feel/think/do	Needs	A new suit, a motorcycle	Create desire
Feel/do/think	Wants	Cosmetics, fashion	Establish an emotional appeal
Do/feel/think	Impulse	A candy bar, a soft drink	Create brand familiarity
Do/think/feel	Habit	Cereal, shampoo	Remind of satisfaction

The point is that the path to a decision depends on the type of product and the buying situation. If you're hungry (and feeling drives the decision), you grab a candy bar without much information search. If you try a sample product and like it (behavior is the driver), you may buy the product without much evaluation of alternatives. In other words, not all responses begin with thinking about a product, nor do they follow the same route to a decision.

In business-to-business (B2B) marketing, decisions are almost always high-involvement. This is because businesses buy goods and services for two basic reasons: (1) they need ingredients for the products they manufacture, and (2) they need goods (such as computers, desks, and chairs) and services (legal, accounting, and maintenance) for their business operations. B2B buying decisions are usually made by committees, which include the decision maker, "influencers" (often the users of the products), and a buyer who will negotiate the final purchase arrangements. Department stores, for example, have a team of buyers who select the merchandise for their different departments. Because B2B purchases involve larger sums of money, the decision process resembles the full five-stage consumer model described earlier.

7.2 Describe the cultural, social, psychological, and behavioral influences on consumer responses to marketing communication.

What Influences Consumer Decisions?

Think about something you bought last week. How did the purchase process happen? Was it something you needed or just something you wanted? That is the kind of question marketers and advertisers ask about their customers. **Consumer behavior** describes how individuals or groups select, purchase, and use products as well as the needs and wants that motivate these behaviors. As we proceed through this chapter, keep asking yourself questions about your own consumer behavior and that of your friends and family.

Before we segment markets and target audiences, let's consider the various factors that influence consumers and their decisions: their cultural affinities, family and friends, personal needs, and experiences with a brand. Figure 7.2 is a general model highlighting a variety of influences on consumer behavior.

Cultural Influences

Marketing communication that grabs people's attention, sticks in their minds, and moves them to act often builds on or confronts deep-seated cultural values. **Culture** is made up of tangible items (art, literature, buildings, furniture, clothing, and music) and intangible concepts (history,

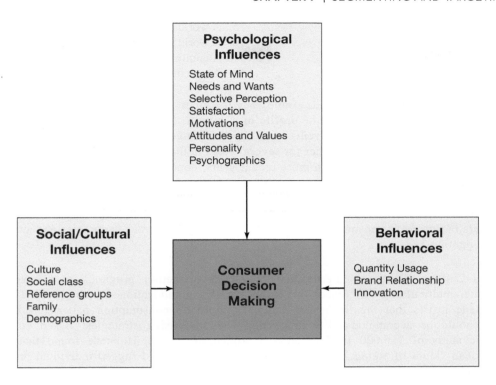

FIGURE 7.2
Influences on Consumer
Decision Making

knowledge, laws, morals, customs, and even standards of beauty) that together define a group of people or a way of life. We all had to learn our own culture's values and we pass them from one generation to the next. Culture generally is seen as providing a deep-seated context for marketing communication, but popular culture—what we see on television, sports, fashion, and music, among other areas—is more dynamic.

Norms and Values   The boundaries each culture establishes for "proper" behavior are **norms**, which are simple rules we learn through social interaction that specify or prohibit certain behaviors. The source of norms in a culture lies in its **values**, which represent its most fundamental guiding principles for behaviors and outcomes. For example, the United States has emphasized the values of freedom, independence, and individualism for many decades. In other countries, particularly some Asian and Latin countries, the priorities of values reflect the greater importance of family ties and group connections over individualism.

A culture's most important values are few in number, and their relative importance does not change much, even over a long period of time. These underlying **core values** govern people's attitudes and guide their behavior. A promotional message's primary appeal aims to match the core values of the brand to the core values of the audience (e.g., compassion, patriotism, community). Milton Rokeach developed a taxonomy of cultural values that researchers have used across a number of countries to help them create brand messages that are congruent with cultures.[2] Below is a list of Rokeach's 18 terminal values. In the country where you grew up, have any of these values received higher or lower priority in recent years? Would different generations rank these values differently? What would you rank highest and lowest for your own life?

1. True friendship
2. Mature love
3. Self-respect
4. Happiness
5. Inner harmony
6. Equality
7. Freedom
8. Pleasure
9. Social recognition
10. Wisdom

11. Salvation
12. Family security
13. National security
14. A sense of accomplishment

15. A world of beauty
16. A world at peace
17. A comfortable life
18. An exciting life

All the above values are desirable, but the ones which receive greater emphasis reveal the priorities and unique profile of a culture. Although value rankings do not change much over time, major events or crises can change them. One study revealed that "equality" was ranked much higher for several years in the United States during the years of the civil rights movement.[3] In more recent years, concerns about terrorism and weak economies have increased the emphasis on national security and family security. A Harris Poll found that in tight economic times, Americans save more and spend less, sacrificing comfort, pleasure, or excitement for family security. Likewise, a spendthrift mind-set appears in Europe as consumers scrimp under the pressure of weak economies and austerity budgeting.[4]

Cross-Cultural Factors   International or global marketing programs also have to consider multicultural differences that might derail communication. Dutch scholar Geert Hofstede insists that the impact of national culture on consumption patterns is huge and should be accommodated in marketing and advertising strategies. Based on his classic study of 116,000 IBM employees around the world, Hofstede found that the American values of taking initiative, personal competency, and rugged individualism are not universal values, and that some cultures prize collective thinking and group norms over independence.

Working with Hofstede's research and theories, Marieke de Mooij, a cross-cultural communication researcher and consultant, developed a set of principles for cross-national marketing communication.[5] One conclusion is that there is no one universal model for information processing. In the more collectivistic cultures in the south of Europe, for example, people do not search for information in a conscious way as do those in the north of Europe. Instead, information is gathered through social communication with friends and family. Her research also discredited the idea of a universality of emotions, finding that both expression and recognition of emotions vary across cultures. Likewise, personality cues are difficult. People in different countries attribute different personality traits to successful global brands and tend to attribute personalities to brands that fit their own cultural values, not the values of the producer.

An example of how difficult it is to manage brand communication across cultures comes from Tsai, who describes in the Matter of Principle feature how the Dove "Real Beauty" campaign was reworked for Taiwanese consumers. The point is that it may be necessary to localize a campaign to appeal to audiences in a different culture.

Corporate Culture   The concept of culture applies to B2B marketing as well as business-to-consumer marketing. **Corporate culture** is a term that describes how companies operate. Some are formal with lots of procedures, rigid work hours, and dress codes. Others are more informal in terms of their operations, office rules, and communication. The same patterns exist in the way businesses make purchasing decisions: some rigidly control and monitor purchases, others are loose and easygoing, and purchases may be less controlled or governed more by friendships and handshakes, as in Japan, than by rules. However, Hofstede, in his cross-cultural research on IBM, found that cultural differences were stronger than the legendary IBM corporate culture. He had assumed it would be a standardizing influence.

Social Influences

In addition to the culture in which you were raised, you also are a product of your social environment, which determines your social class or group. Reference groups, family, and friends also are important influences on opinions and consumer behavior and affect many of your

"There Are No Ugly Women, Only Lazy Ones": Why Dove's Real Beauty Campaign Flopped in Taiwan

Wanhsiu Sunny Tsai, *School of Communication, University of Miami*

Against the cultural backdrop of airbrushed supermodel perfection, Dove's "Campaign for Real Beauty" uses images of "real" women of different ages, races, and body shapes to empower female consumers. The campaign has won major awards and contributed to Dove's double-digit sales growth in North America and Europe.

Dove's international campaigns feature native models and address local beauty myths. For example, its pan-Asian campaign challenged the ideals of fair skin and larger eyes. However, consumer surveys and sales data revealed that women in Chinese societies were unmoved by the message, and Dove had to drop its ad campaign in the pan-Asian market.

As an international scholar, I was intrigued by this unexpected apathy toward the Dove campaign, and I visited Taiwan to conduct in-depth interviews with female consumers there. These women told me they did not think of beauty in media as promoting out-of-reach illusions; in fact, they appreciated glamorous images for their entertainment, aesthetic, and even fantasy value. They also expressed a strong desire for self improvement, reinforced by beauty magazines, television shows, and websites that featured women with common appearance "flaws" being transformed into glamour girls. The step-by-step instructions accompanying these makeovers assured consumers that high standards of beauty could indeed be achieved.

Every participant mentioned a popular Taiwanese saying, "There are no ugly women, only lazy ones." The cultural belief that any woman can be beautiful—if she tries hard enough—rendered Dove's message of embracing one's natural beauty irrelevant to local consumers' desires and concerns. The intended message of challenging idealized beauty stereotypes was lost on many participants, who only wanted to know how the product could *improve* their skin. Lesson learned: cultural differences really can make a difference in how an ad will be received.

Dove eventually found a solution for the Chinese version of its "real women" campaign by partnering with the Chinese version of the television show *Ugly Betty* based on the character "Ugly Wudi." Viewers were able to see the connection between Betty/Wudi and beauty and Dove's underlying message in this new version.[6]

habits and biases. For example, the Inside Story feature explains how a brand's character was developed based on insights into consumer attitudes and opinions about others in the neighborhood.

Social Class The position you and your family occupy within your society is called a **social class**, and it is determined by such factors as income, wealth, education, occupational prestige, family prestige, value of home, and neighborhood. In more rigid societies, such as those of India, people have a difficult time moving out of the class into which they were born. In the United States, although people may move into social classes that differ from their families', the country still has a class system consisting of upper, middle, and lower classes. Brand communication may segment consumers by social class, which assumes that people in one class buy different goods for different reasons than people in other classes.

Reference Groups A **reference group** is a group of people you use as a model for behavior in specific situations. Examples are teachers, family members, and religious leaders as well as members of political parties, religious groups, racial or ethnic organizations, hobby-based clubs, and informal affiliations, such as fellow workers or students—your peers. The ad for Virginia

Scotts Brand Comes Alive as Scott

Trent Walters, *Brand Management Principal, The Richards Group, Dallas, Texas*

As the Richards Group looked to develop a new advertising campaign for Scotts, the lawn care and gardening company, there were two key insights that came out of the consumer research to drive the campaign.

"OMG, It's Alive"

When consumers were reminded that their lawn was a living thing, it was very motivating. They felt a responsibility to care for the grass plants in their yards like they do for their houseplants. No longer could they sit back and do nothing. The lawn is alive and needs to be cared for. And if they didn't do it, who would?

Everyone Has a "Billy" in the Neighborhood

Billy is the guy that exists in every neighborhood who has the perfect lawn. He's the guy who loves to be out working in his yard. If you have any questions on what to do, you turn to ol' Billy. And when you see Billy doing something in his yard, that's your cue that it's probably time for you to do something in yours.

Those two insights were key in developing the new ad campaign for Scotts: "Scott the Scot for Scotts." Scott is basically Billy. He is the guy in his neighborhood who has the healthy lawn. His neighbors know they can turn to him for advice on what to do. Scott reminds them that their lawns are alive and points them back to Scotts' products to feed and care for them.

The campaign was designed to give Scotts a way to bring its brand personality to life. Scott is the embodiment of the Scotts brand personality: "An uncomplicated, optimistic expert." Scott helps the brand communicate in a way that is interesting, engaging, and does not lecture consumers. In addition, his name and his catch phrase, "Feed your lawn. Feed it!" help continuously reinforce the brand name and the activity that Scotts wants consumers to regularly engage in.

Photo: Used with permission of Scotts Miracle-Gro.
Writer: Mike Bales, Art Director: Jeff Hopler.

Photo: Used with permission of Scotts Miracle-Gro.
Writer: Mike Bales, Art Director: Jeff Hopler.

Trent Walters is a graduate of the University of North Texas, where he was selected by the American Advertising Federation as one of its "Most Promising Minority Students." He was nominated to be featured here by Professor Sheri Broyles.

Commonwealth University uses a reference-group strategy to describe the type of students the school wants to recruit.

Groups of people devoted to a particular brand are called **brand communities**, such as the Harley Owners Group (HOG). To get a sense of how HOG operates, check out www.hog.com. Apple is another company that has generated a brand community. One writer described a "Cult of Apple" with "fanboys" and "fangirls" who have Apple stickers on their briefcases and cars, wear Mac- or iPod-related clothing, and sport Mac tattoos. He observed, "It's not a brand, it's a lifestyle."[7] Check out www.CultofMac.com. The Internet has had a huge impact on the creation of reference groups in the form of online virtual communities that revolve around a wide range of interests, hobbies, and brands.

For consumers, reference groups have three functions: (1) provide information, (2) serve as a means of personal comparison, and (3) offer guidance. Ads that feature *typical users* in fun or pleasant surroundings are using a reference group strategy. The Dove campaign used a counterargument to say that the stick-thin women in glamor magazines and advertising are stereotypes that don't represent average women.

Sociologist David Reisman describes individuals in terms of their relationships to other people as *inner directed* (individualistic) or *outer directed* (peer group and society). Advertisers are particularly interested in the role of peers in influencing their outer-directed friends' wants and desires. Businesses such as BzzAgent (www.bzzagent.com) have helped brands receive personal recommendations from consumers' most important reference groups. What do you think of their pitch: "Try new products. Brag about them to your friends"?

Family   The family is the most important reference group for many people because of its formative role, small size, and the intensity of its relationships. According to the US Census definition, a **family** consists of two or more people who are related by blood, marriage, or adoption and live in the same household. A **household** differs from a family in that it consists of all those who occupy a dwelling whether they are related or not.

A compelling demographic trend in the 21st century is the rise of the one-person household. For the first time in US history, one-person households outnumber households with married couples and children.[8] With spending power over $2.3 trillion each year, singles have become an attractive market segment for many businesses including Coldwell Banker, Lowe's, Chevrolet, Keurig coffee makers, Kraft "single" portions, and even De Beers' diamond "right-hand rings."[9]

Psychological Influences

Personal characteristics also affect how you respond to brands as an individual in terms of both needs and wants as well as motivations.

Needs and Wants   In Chapter 4, we described needs and wants as two different types of responses that lead to different reactions to an advertising message. The basic driving forces that motivate us to do something that reflect basic survival, such as choose a motel (shelter) or restaurant (food) when traveling, are called primary needs. In the case of the needs pyramid

Courtesy of Virginia Commonwealth University. Used with permission.

Graduates of universities and colleges tend to identify themselves by their school affiliation, as this ad for the Virginia Commonwealth University demonstrates. What can you tell about this person's career choice and interests from these bumper stickers?

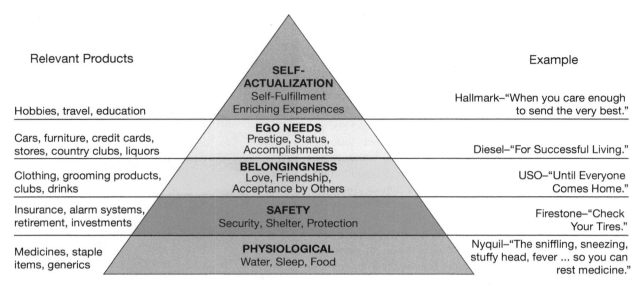

FIGURE 7.3
Maslow's Hierarchy of Needs

developed by psychologist Abraham Maslow (Figure 7.3), these are called physiological and safety needs.

Needs that we learn in response to our culture and environment are called **acquired needs**. They may include the need for esteem, prestige, affection, power, learning, and, yes, beauty. Because acquired needs are not necessary to your physical survival, they are also called secondary needs. Maslow called them *belonging* (social), *egoistic*, and *self-actualization*. The Dove campaigns have been directed to self-esteem and self-actualization.

A want occurs when we desire or wish for something: we won't die if we don't get it, but it can still provide a strong motivation to try or buy something new. Research has uncovered the power of new and novel. As account planner Susan Mendelsohn, who is a member of this book's advisory board, explained, "In some cases, we want things just for the sheer fun of newness—think about how many pairs of shoes or the amount of clothes people have."[10]

In his book *Breakthrough Advertising*, Schwartz describes the power of what he calls "mass desire." He explains that mass desire is the public spread of a private want; it can't be created by advertising, but advertising can address it and channel it to connect with a particular brand.[11] The trend toward more fuel-efficient cars has led to a demand for hybrid cars such as the Prius. If there weren't a mass desire for this type of vehicle, there would be no market for the Prius. On the other hand, there is also a market for the Cadillac Escalade.

Needs and wants can be characterized as a "gap" between a desired state of being and our actual state of being. The greater the gap is perceived to be, the greater the motivation to act in order to close that gap. Marketing communication can highlight the gaps in our lives by emphasizing an ideal state that a product can help us fulfill (e.g., a vacation exploring castles in Ireland; achieving greater fitness through a health club membership), or

> **Principle**
> An item we need is something we think is essential or necessary for our lives; an item we want is something we desire.

Photo: Courtesy Tourism Ireland/Fáilte Ireland/photographer John Miskelly. Used with permission.

This ad promotes an adventurous vacation in Ireland and suggests an ideal state that many consumers may feel the need to achieve.

by accentuating the pitfalls of maintaining the status quo that a product can help us avoid (e.g., a life insurance policy, a carbon monoxide detector, or a way to prevent the common cold).

Motivations   A **motive** is an internal force—like the desire to look good—that stimulates you to behave in a particular manner. This driving force is produced by the tension caused by an unfulfilled want or need. People strive to reduce the tension, as the Airborne ad demonstrates. At any given point, you are probably affected by a number of different motives. For example, your motivation to buy a new suit will be much higher if you have several job interviews scheduled next week.

Research into motivation uncovers the "why" questions. Why did you buy that brand and not another? What prompted you to go to that store? Interestingly, many motivations operate at a subconscious level. Some of the reasons may be apparent—you go to a restaurant because you are hungry. But what else governs that choice? Is it location, interior decoration, a favorite menu item, its image, a special memory, or the recommendation of a friend?

Photo: The Photo Works/Alamy Stock Photo. (AIRBORNE is a registered trademark of Reckitt Benckiser LLC. Trademark is used with permission.)

The motivation is obvious for a product that helps you avoid catching a cold when you travel. Do you think it is effective to also feature the motivation of the product's creator?

Repurchase behavior is influenced strongly by the final stage of the consumer-decision making process: postpurchase evaluation. This stage includes satisfaction and cognitive dissonance.

- *Satisfaction* Satisfaction is commonly viewed as the "gap" between our expectations of a product and our actual experience with it. Marketing communication helps create expectations in the minds of customers, and planners must be careful not to create unrealistically high expectations that a product cannot fulfill, or set expectations so low that customers will not be interested in the product. For example, when people hear publicity about a new film they form a set of expectations that they hope the film will meet or exceed. People may pay attention to a commercial for a product, buy it, and be disappointed. One reason is because advertising sometimes promises more than it can deliver. It is best to create expectations that are attractive but that the company knows it can meet or exceed.
- *Dissonance* **Cognitive dissonance** refers to a conflict between two thoughts: for example, you need a car but don't have the money. That creates a state of tension. Marketers must address this, and in auto marketing they do that by offering no-interest or low-interest plans to reduce the conflict and make it easier to rationalize the decision. *Buyer's remorse* is a related form of tension that occurs when there are discrepancies between what we thought we would receive and what we actually received. When there is a difference between reality and facts, people engage in a variety of activities to reduce cognitive dissonance. Most notably, we seek out information that supports our decisions—that's why we pay attention to ads for recent purchases—and ignore and distort information that does not.

Some consumer decisions are routine or habitual, and lack engaged, conscious thought. That is also true for decisions that are driven by emotions and feelings. **Neuromarketing**, the new brain-science approach to how people think, provides a deeper understanding of the way low-attention processing actually works and motivates people into unconscious, intuitive decision making. Ann Marie Barry reports that neurological research "reveals that visuals may be processed and form the basis of future action without passing through consciousness at all."[12] These studies are particularly useful in describing how emotion is the driving force behind motivations that can lead to largely unconscious brand decisions and behaviors.

Influences on B2B Decision Making

Many of the influences that affect consumer buying also are reflected in B2B marketing. We know that B2B decision making generally follows the same information path. Trade shows are important events in B2B marketing where buyers and sellers can meet, view new products, make demonstrations, and even close sales. Emotion may still be important in certain

Photo: Woodkern/Getty Images

Trade shows are an important activity where B2B buyers and sellers can meet. This exhibit for Casio watches was part of the 2016 Consumer Electronics Show (CES).

situations (e.g., the buyer wants to impress the boss), but ultimately these decisions are more rational than emotional for the following reasons:

- In organizational buying, many individuals are involved in reviewing the options, often with a buying committee making the final decision.
- Although the business buyer may be motivated by both rational and emotional factors, the use of rational and quantitative criteria dominates most decisions.
- The decision is sometimes made based on a set of specifications to potential suppliers who then bid on the contract. In these purchases, the lowest bid typically wins.
- Quality is hugely important, and repeat purchases are based on how well the product performs.

7.3 Discuss targeting and how it differs from segmenting.

How Do We Segment Markets and Target Audiences?

Cost efficiency—and effectiveness—demands that marketers (1) segment the market and (2) target the audience segment(s) most likely to respond to brand communication. First, let's discuss **segmenting**, which means dividing the market into groups of people who have similar characteristics in key product-related areas. Segmenting does two things: it identifies those people who are in the market, and it eliminates those who aren't.

There are various ways to segment markets. One way is to divide them by the type of market they represent, either business or consumer, which leads to B2B or B2C (business-to-consumer) marketing strategies. Another way is to refer to markets either as (1) those who shop for and purchase the product (*purchasers or customers*), (2) those who actually use the product (*users*), or (3) *influencers*, those people who help the buyer make a brand choice (children, trendsetters, family, and friends). Purchasers and users can have different needs and wants. In the case of children's cereals, parents (the purchasers) often look for nutritional value and a decent price. In contrast, children (the influencers and users) may look for a sweet taste and a package with a prize inside.

Segmentation Strategies

Political columnist David Brooks asked in 2012, "Are people more alike than they are different?" Despite a common history, currency, and national identity, he said the United States "has become more polarized, not less," and he sees that as a worldwide trend. Rather than a convergence of values, "people in different nations, even people within nations, have become less alike in at least as many ways as they have become more alike."[13] Why is that important to brand communication? Our era, as Brooks put it, is "the Segmentation Century." It's not about convergence of values, but rather about diverging opinions, interests, and tastes.

At one point in its history, Coca-Cola viewed the US market for its brand as homogeneous and used general appeals—such as "Coke is it!"—for all consumers, which is considered an **undifferentiated strategy**. But even Coke is sold in different types of places, and people hear about Coke through different types of media, particularly in international markets. Therefore, customers now are grouped based on their tastes as well as contact points with the product. Of course, there are also differences in age, such as between a longtime adult Coke drinker and a teenager.

Consumer differences as well as product variations determine how marketers address people in marketing communication and reach them using media. Few examples of homogeneous markets exist in contemporary marketing, so most strategies are based on a **market segmentation** strategy.

By using a segmentation strategy, a company can more precisely match the needs and wants of the customer with its products. That's why Coke and Pepsi introduced product variations to appeal to different consumer segments, such as diet, caffeine-free, diet caffeine-free, and flavored versions of their basic products.

Instead of marketing to a huge undifferentiated market, marketers target more narrow segments, such as single women in the international traveler category. Although marketing has gone global to reach large markets, at the same time many marketers have moved toward tighter and tighter **niche markets**, which are subsegments of a more general market segment. Individuals in a niche market, such as ecologically minded mothers who won't use disposable diapers, are defined by a distinctive interest or attitude. Niche marketers are companies that pursue market segments of sufficient size to be profitable although not large enough to be of interest to large marketers. Road Scholar, for example, markets to seniors who are interested in educationally oriented travel experiences.

Types of Segmentation

In general, marketers segment their markets using six key consumer characteristics (Figure 7.4). Which approach or combination of approaches is used varies with the market situation and product category.

- *Demographic segmentation* divides the market using such characteristics as age, gender, ethnicity, and income.
- *Life-stage segmentation* is based on the particular stage in consumers' life cycle, which includes such categories as children or young people living at home, college students, singles living on their own, couples, families with children, empty nesters, and senior singles living alone.
- *Geographic segmentation* uses location as a defining variable because consumers' needs sometimes vary depending on where they live: urban, rural, suburban, north, south. Defining variables typically are region, nation, state, city, or ZIP code. Geography affects both product distribution and marketing communication.
- *Psychographic segmentation* is based primarily on studies of how people spend their time and money, their patterns of work and leisure, their interest and opinions, and their views of themselves. This strategy is considered richer than demographic segmentation because it combines psychological information with lifestyle insights.
- *Behavioral segmentation* divides people into groups based on level of product and brand usage. "Heavy users" is a very important market segment for most products.

⬤ Principle
Segmenting is efficient and cost effective when it identifies those people who are in the market and also eliminates those who aren't.

⬤ Principle
Buyers may not be the users and users may not be the buyers. Buyers and users often have entirely different needs and wants.

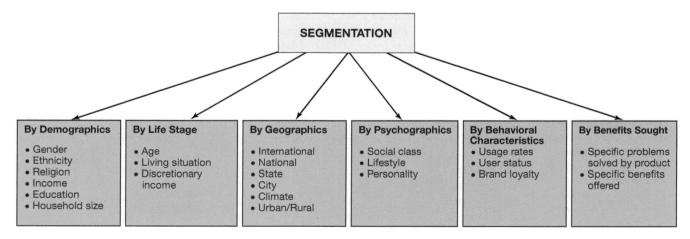

FIGURE 7.4
Market Segmentation Approaches

- *Values and benefits-based segmentation* groups people based on tangible and intangible factors. Values segmentation reflects consumers' underlying value system: spiritual, hedonistic, thrifty, ecological, and so forth. Benefit segmentation strategy is based on consumers' needs or problems. The idea is that people buy products for different benefits they hope to derive. Some cereals are purchased for their taste, others for their health benefits.

When companies consider international markets, they need to answer three basic segmentation questions:

- **What Countries?** This question can be answered with market research that helps determine if there is a match between the preferences of consumers in countries and a company's products.
- **Market Development Level** Countries, especially developing countries, vary greatly in market infrastructure, literacy levels, disposable income, and level of media development. For example, some countries' standard of living is such that luxury brands would not find a large enough segment of the population to cover the cost of setting up distribution and supporting the brand with marketing communication and a sales force.
- **Cultural Cohorts** A **cultural cohort** is a segment of customers from multiple countries sharing common characteristics that translate into common wants and needs. New mothers are an example. Regardless of their nationality, new mothers want their babies to be happy and healthy. Teenagers are another cultural cohort. Teens in Tokyo and teens in New York City may have more in common than a teen and his/her father in either country.

Targeting the Best Audiences

Regardless of whether the marketing communication uses one-way or two-way communication strategies, planners still need some sense of who they are talking to and with. Through **targeting**, the organization can design specific communication strategies to match the audience's needs and wants, and position the product in the most relevant way to match their interests.

Consider, for example, how Niman Ranch of Bolinas, California, built a luxury brand for its humanely raised beef and pork. The obvious target would be upscale consumers who value natural food and are willing to pay more for the best. But instead, Niman marketed directly to prestigious chefs whose restaurants featured the brand on their menus. By using an innovative targeting strategy, Niman moved from a commodity product to a cachet brand, bringing huge growth to the small company. With increasing interest in organic products and local farming, Niman also has knit together a network of hundreds of small-scale, organic farmers that leverages economies of scale while at the same time leaving farmers in control of their local operations.[14]

A target market is first identified using the segmentation characteristics that separate a group of prospective consumers from others who are not as likely to buy the brand, and then additional descriptive variables are added until an ideal consumer group is identified. Pretend you're launching a new diaper service. Consider your brand features and how important they may be to parents: e.g., price level, materials, ecological sensitiveness, and so forth. In the large market of parents of infants, who would most want the features that are distinctive for your brand? Mothers are primary caretakers of infants, but you know that mothers are not all alike. To narrow your target, what makes them different? Some are affluent, whereas others struggle to get by. Are these important factors for the brand (inexpensive or expensive?), or do factors other than income need to be considered (e.g., always rushed for time)?

You identify the target by starting with the most important characteristic that predicts which consumers are prospective customers: matching the key brand features to the interests and concerns of the market. In the diaper service example, that would be gender, primarily mothers and then age—say, women ages 18 to 35. Then you add other factors, such as income, urban versus rural dwellers, education, or whatever factors come up in research as important predictive variables for your brand.

As Figure 7.5 illustrates, each time you add a variable, you narrow the market as you come closer to the ideal target audience. The objective is to get the largest group that can be defined in such a way that you can direct a message that will resonate with people in that group, and that you can reach with specific media. Once these predictor variables have been sorted out, it should be possible to build an estimate of the size of this target market.

◆ Principle
Each time you add a variable to a target audience definition, you narrow the size of the target audience as you try to find the largest group to whom you can direct a relevant message and reach with specific media.

A targeting practice that has emerged from political campaigning is called **microtargeting**, which refers to using vast computer data banks of personal information to direct highly tailored messages to narrow slices of a segment. Marketers are also able to profile prospects by carefully analyzing data on their regular customers and then using this information to identify these revealing tendencies and characteristics in a group of prospects.[15] The practice of using data banks that contain collections of personal information is controversial; the privacy issues will be discussed in more detail in Chapter 18.

Another example of microtargeting based on location comes from retailers who use "geofencing"—defining a perimeter around a location—to reach customers via their cell phones who are in the neighborhood of the store. For example, promotional texting can be localized to announce a special on umbrellas when a storm is approaching, to engage with concertgoers, or provide a consumer in aisle 3 with a coupon for a product in aisle 4.[16]

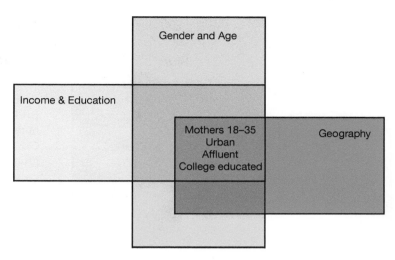

FIGURE 7.5
Narrowing the Target
As descriptors are added to the identification of the target, the number in the middle of the target gets smaller. As this target is defined, the size of the group can be predicted.

Profiling Markets and Target Audiences

7.4 List several characteristics that are used to segment markets and target consumers.

As our Dove opening story stressed, marketing communication planners need to describe prospective customers using characteristics that help predict the likelihood that they will respond to a brand message and, ultimately, buy the brand. Using these descriptions, profiles are built for typical customers or prospects to make the brand communication more personal and relevant. **Profiles** are descriptions of the target audience that read like a description of someone you know. Analyze how Clairol profiled its target in the classic "Does She or Doesn't She" campaign.

Another example of how consumers are profiled comes from Forrester Research, which uses a research approach called *personas*. Harley Manning, research director for customer experience and a member of this book's Advisory Board, described a persona as "a fictional character that embodies your target customers' key behaviors, attributes, motivations, and goals"—a vivid profile of a type of person. Unlike segmentation descriptions, "personas come to life with first and last names, photographs, and vivid narratives that describe day-in-the-life scenarios." For example, he referred to "Stanley," a person used by J. P. Morgan to model its active, savvy investors. He said that this type of person isn't satisfied with a simple account summary and instead wants advanced portfolio details.[17]

Targeting and Profiling Using Demographics

The statistical, social, and economic characteristics of a population, including such factors as age, education, occupation, gender and sexual orientation, income, family status, race, religion, and geography, are called **demographics**. Knowing these characteristics helps in message design and media selection for the **target audience**, the market segment(s) most likely to be interested in the product. The first place to start when analyzing and compiling demographics is the country's census data. In the United States, the Census Bureau compiles a huge collection of demographic information every 10 years; the most recent census was in 2010.

Age   The most important demographic characteristic used by marcom planners is age. People of different ages have different needs and wants. Age often determines product choice. How old are you? What products did you use 5 or 10 years ago that you don't use now? Look ahead 10 years.

Does she...
or doesn't she?

Hair color so natural only her hairdresser knows for sure!

Photo: The Advertising Archives/Alamy Stock Photo

CLASSIC

One of advertising's most familiar slogans—"Does she . . . or doesn't she?"—moved women who were tired of being told that there are things ladies don't do, such as color their hair. Legendary copywriter Shirley Polykoff understood these emotions and that it was okay to be a little bit naughty as long as you were nice. In 1967, Time magazine reported that the number of women who used hair color increased from 15 to 50 percent after this campaign began in 1956. The campaign also appears as number 9 on Advertising Age's list of the Top 100 Campaigns in history. What lesson can you learn from a successful ad like this even if it's 50 years old?

What products might you be interested in buying in the future that you don't buy now? The following list describes some of the other more common age-related population categories that are used by marketers:

- Referred to as the Greatest Generation by Tom Brokaw in his book by that name, this generation born in the 1910s through the late 1920s lived through the Great Depression and fought World War II. A small group, these older seniors are in their final years. This group opened up college education to the middle class after the war and lived frugal yet financially satisfying lives.
- Known as the Silent Generation or traditionalists, these people, born from the late 1920s through the World War II years, are now active seniors. They were described in a national poll as the generation having the most "positive impact" on the American economy for their role in fueling the postwar boom.
- Baby boomers, people born between 1946 and 1964, represent the second largest age-related category in the United States. The 79 million baby boomer consumers are now in the final years of their careers and moving into retirement, having made a huge population bulge as they moved through the life cycle. While they were growing up, boomers' numbers affected schools, the job market, and now retirement programs and health care. This generation has been influenced by significant societal movements and scientific breakthroughs, from the civil rights movement, to the anti–Vietnam War protests, to putting a person on the moon.
- A boomer subgroup called Generation Jones consists of the younger baby boomers who were born from the mid- to late 1950s through the mid-1960s. The "Jones" reference comes from their continuing need to chase the dream of affluence by trying to "keep up with the Joneses."
- Generation X, or Gen X, also known as baby busters, is the group whose 49 million members were born between 1962 and 1981. Now adults, they have been described as independent minded and somewhat cynical and also a generation that is most characterized by growing up in divorced households. They are concerned with their physical health (they grew up during the AIDS outbreak) and financial future (the job market became more difficult just about the time they reached their prime years).
- Sometimes referred to as the Me Generation because of their affluent younger years, those born in the 1970s to early 1990s are characterized as more self-absorbed and narcissistic than their parents, although that changed as they confronted the dot-com bust at the end of the 1990s and subsequent economic problems in the 2000s.
- Generation Y members were born between 1980 and 1996 and are also known as "echo boomers" because they are the children of baby boomers. They are important to marketers because they are next in size to the boomer generation, with more than 74 million members. This generation is also described as the Digital Generation or Net Generation because they are seen as more technologically savvy than their older siblings or parents. They are the first generation to grow up with email and cell phones. They are also environmentally conscious and more interested in "right-size" houses than the megamansions of Gen X.

- Millennials include the children and young people born from the late 1980s into the beginning decade of the new century. Also called the iGeneration, these young adults are digital natives and spend considerably more time texting and using social media than even the older Net Generation. Millennials recently overtook baby boomers as America's largest age cohort, so most marketers are desperately trying to understand them because they are also most unlike older generations in the ways they communicate and receive and interpret information.[18] You can bet that companies are already trying to understand the newest cohort, tentatively named Generation Z.

Age is a key factor in media plans because age usually determines what media you watch, listen to, or read. The older the age group, the more likely they are to use traditional media daily or several times a week, and the more likely they are to read newspapers. Kids ages 8 to 18 spend more than seven and a half hours a day with electronic devices, which include smartphones, computers, televisions, and video games.[19]

Age is driving a fundamental shift in US marketing strategy. Since the 1960s, marketers have focused on reaching young people not only because they are in the formative years of making brand choices, but also because the youth market was huge. As baby boomers move into retirement, marketers also realize that wealth and numbers belong to this active senior market.

Another interesting aspect of age is how we as individuals perceive it. **Cognitive age** is how old we feel that we are, and it is often quite different than our chronological age. Generally, older consumers will state a cognitive age that is 10 to 15 years *younger* than their actual age, and tweens and teens state a cognitive age that is 3 to 5 years *older* than their actual age. Because marketers try to address consumers in ways that are consistent with how they see themselves, advertisements targeted to these different ages often use models and messages that fit cognitive age. For example, ads for arthritis medication often use a younger model (in their 40s or 50s) and show activity that reflects the age that older consumers feel they are on the inside. Likewise, this ad for a toy uses a model that is much older-looking than the actual age of the 8- to 12-year-old target audience.

Photo: PA Images/Alamy Stock Photo

Ads and packaging often reflect the cognitive age of the buyers. Nerf uses an older-looking model for a product targeted to 8- to 12-year-olds.

Gender and Sexual Orientation An obvious basis for differences in marketing and advertising is gender. Many brands are either masculine or feminine in terms of use as well as brand personality. It is unlikely that men would use a brand of cologne called "White Shoulders." Women account for 85 percent of all consumer purchases in the United States, which makes them an important target for many marketers, and there are signs that the United States is evolving into a matriarchal society.[20] Other studies point to the increasing percentage of women in college,[21] which also may mean eventual changes in income and occupation patterns.

Gender stereotypes have been a problem in advertising for decades, and some believe that may be because the majority of the work has been created by men writing for women. Jessica Shank, a copywriter at Goodby, Silverstein & Partners, concluded, "If most of the work specifically aimed at women were any indication of modern life, we'd all be at home dancing with our mops and fretting about plastic food storage."[22]

Lesbian, gay, bisexual, transgender, and questioning (LGBTQ) households have recently become far more visible in the economy—as consumers, employees, shareholders, entrepreneurs, and business decision makers. According to the US Census Bureau's American Community Survey, same-sex households tend to be more concentrated in the West, Southwest, and Northeast than in other parts of the country. Washington, DC, has the highest rate of same-sex

Same-Sex Marriage: A Boon to the Economy?

Bob Witeck, *CEO, Witeck Communications, Inc., Washington, DC*

In 2015, the US Supreme Court ruled that the Constitution guarantees a nationwide right to same-sex marriage.

These social, cultural, and political changes are reshaping not only American households but also the economy itself. One year following the adoption of marriage equality in New York, New York City itself conducted an economic impact study that totaled up the travel, hospitality, and overall spending on weddings of gay and lesbian couples. They discovered that more than 10 percent, or 8,200, of the marriage licenses issued in the past year were for gay and lesbian couples. These weddings drew more than 201,000 guests from outside the city and booked more than 235,000 hotel rooms. Mayor Michael Bloomberg declared that New York City had earned $259 million of economic benefits from same-sex marriages in its very first year.

Many major corporations and multinational marketers welcome the trend, not just the short-lived wedding and honeymoon boomlet. They see the visibility and economic contributions of gay households as tangible evidence of new market and employment trends, too.

Not surprisingly, more leading corporations, including Starbucks, Nike, and household-friendly General Mills, have taken public positions in support of same-sex marriage. Whether as consumers or potential employees, corporations see these changes mirroring their own competitive objectives—especially since a majority of Americans, by almost all polling studies, now favor treating same-sex couples equally with their heterosexual counterparts.

households, with 21.3 out of every 1,000 households being headed by a same-sex couple. The survey also found that same-sex couples are more likely to have college degrees and earn slightly more money than opposite-sex couples.[23]

Bob Witeck, a member of this book's Advisory Board and president of Washington, DC–based Witeck Communications (www.witeck.com), explains that with nearly 20 years of expertise with this market, he estimates the buying power for LGBTQ consumers at $790 billion; he based his estimate on a population projection of approximately 6.7 percent of all adults, or roughly 15 million people.[24] He explains how that affects the wedding market in the Matter of Practice feature.

Education, Occupation, and Income   Generally, white US consumers attain higher levels of education than blacks and Latinos, and US males are falling behind females in higher levels of education. Education tends to correlate with media use—consumers with lower education are higher users of television, especially cable, than consumers with more education. Consumers with higher education prefer print media, the Internet, and selected radio and cable stations.

Likewise, education dictates the way promotional messages are written and a message's level of difficulty. Examine ads in *Fortune* or *Forbes*, and you will find different words, art, and products than you will in *People*. Advertisers don't make value judgments about these statistics. Their objective is to match advertising messages to the characteristics of the target audience.

Most people identify themselves by what they do for a living. In the United States, there has been a gradual trend from blue-collar occupations (e.g., manufacturing) to white-collar occupations (e.g., management and information). There have also been shifts within white-collar work from sales to other areas, such as professional, technical, and administrative positions. The number of service-related jobs continues to increase, especially in health care, education, and legal and business service sectors.

Another key demographic indicator for many advertisers is income, which relates to both education and occupation. You are more meaningful to marketers if you have the resources to buy their products or services or contribute to their causes. The updated census income data reported in 2011[25] showed a shift toward fewer people in the top third (6 percent, or around

7,000 households) and more people in the bottom third of the income distribution (72 percent, or 94,000 households), which reflected the impact of the recession that began in 2007. The remaining 21 percent (30,000 households) made up the shrinking middle class. But it's more than the size of the middle class that is worrisome to marketers. Federal Reserve statistics have shown that economic crises tend to fall disproportionately on the middle class.[26]

Although the demand for luxury goods continued to be healthy because of the increasing wealth of the top group, the retail winners for the rest of the population were dollar stores and low-price retailers, such as Walmart. A single word describes consumers when emerging from a recession—"cautious"—particularly in mortgages and borrowing for car loans as well as student loans. People are more conscious of debts and afraid that they will get overextended.[27]

European consumers are even more frugal, as many of their countries are in economic trouble and suffering from government austerity programs that have drastically increased unemployment and reduced income levels. In contrast, the middle class in China has been growing dramatically this century. Nevertheless, there has been a huge demand for major products, including everything from digitally controlled water heaters to big-screen televisions and washing machines. This generation is rapidly acquiring the furnishings of a modern **lifestyle** and learning how to use products that their parents never had.[28]

Advertisers track trends in income, especially **discretionary income**, which is the amount of money available to spend after paying for taxes and basic necessities, such as food and shelter. Some industries, such as movie theaters, travel, jewelry, and fashion, would be out of business if people didn't have discretionary income. Discretionary income has been found to be a more reliable predictor of spending than income, although it is most vulnerable in times of economic downturn.

● **Principle**
Income is a key demographic factor because consumers are more meaningful to a marketer if they have the resources needed to buy the product advertised.

Race, Ethnicity, and Immigration Status   In the United States, ethnicity is another major factor in segmenting markets. According to the 2011 census update, Latinos (or Hispanics) make up 16.3 percent of the population (up from 12.5 percent in 2000)[29] and have overtaken African Americans at 13 percent as the largest ethnic group. The Asian American segment represents 5 percent, but is growing quickly. African Americans, however, have seen a dramatic increase of more than 55 percent in their buying power since 2000.[30] The United States is more multicultural than ever.

Latinos, a category based on language rather than race, remain an important minority segment. Because of the size of this market, special brand communication programs are often designed for Hispanic as well as black consumers. Marketers are wise to note that Latinos are not a homogeneous group, but rather are one with widely varied backgrounds—from Mexico, Central or South America, or Cuba. Others trace their ancestry to Spain. In 2013, Coke, for example, began emphasizing its iconic contour bottle in packaging designed for Latino markets with Mexican backgrounds because soft drinks in Mexico traditionally are sold in glass bottles rather than cans.

Latinos and blacks make up more than half of the births in the US population, according to the Census Bureau, which announced in 2012 that whites now account for only 49.6 percent of all births.[31] The Census Bureau also revealed that minorities accounted for 92 percent of the nation's population growth in the decade that ended in 2010.[32]

The Census Bureau has found that about one in five US residents—mostly in California, New Mexico, and Texas—speaks a language other than English at home. In three metro areas—Miami, San Jose, and Los Angeles—more than a third of residents are foreign born. Research also found that of all Hispanics, most (56 percent) were born in the United States.[33]

Differences in media use may be based on ethnicity. For example, Latino viewers are more likely to watch commercials in their entirety than non-Hispanic viewers.

Photo: Courtesy Proctor & Gamble. Used with permission.

This ad for Tide targets the Hispanic market. The translation is "The salsa is something you dance, not what you wear." If you were on the Tide team, would you recommend continuing to use strategies like this one? Why or why not?

Also, Latino audiences are more influenced by advertising than other US consumers; they are more likely to base their purchasing decisions on advertisements, and they are less cynical about marketing.

Many marketers are employing multicultural strategies to better serve their customers. McDonald's chief marketing officer reported that 40 percent of the fast-food chain's customers come from the Latino, Asian, and African American markets, and 50 percent of customers under the age of 13 are from those segments. He observed that these ethnic segments are also McDonald's most loyal customers.[34]

Self-identity is also affected by race and ethnicity. That's another reason diversity is so important in advertising, both in the ads themselves and also in the minds of the professionals who create the advertising.

Geography   In targeting and profiling consumers, a retailer's first strategic concern is geography. Where do my customers live? How far will they drive to come to my store? In large market areas, individual retailers who only have one or two stores try to find media that just reach those within their stores' shopping area (generally a two- to five-mile radius).

Geographic segmentation is a basic strategy because marketers are often tied to locations where their products are sold. Beyond the distribution factor, marketers study the sales patterns of different parts of the country because people residing in different regions need certain products. For example, someone living in the Midwest or the Northeast is more likely to purchase products for removing snow and ice than a Floridian.

Differences also exist between urban areas and suburban or rural areas. Swimming pools that sell well in a residential suburban neighborhood would not be in demand in an urban neighborhood filled with apartment buildings. Another important role for geography is in media planning, where a **designated market area (DMA)** is used in describing media markets. A DMA is identified by the name of the dominant city in that area, and it generally aligns with the reach of local television signals. The Seattle-Tacoma DMA in Washington, for example, covers some 13 counties in the northwestern corner of the state.

Religion   One area that connects culture to demographics is religion. In terms of demographics, Christianity remains the largest religious group in the world, but because Muslims are younger and have more children than other religious groups globally, Islam is growing faster than any other major religion. By 2050, the number of Muslims will nearly equal the number of Christians in the world. In the United States, the Muslim population is currently relatively small (under 4 million), but is projected to grow rapidly.[35]

As an indication of that growth, *Mohammad* has become the top male name in England, many European cities, and also in the world.[36] There is also a large percentage of the population, both in the United States and worldwide, that is secular or unaffiliated with any organized religion.

Religion is sometimes an important factor because of product bans. Some religions forbid certain products. Mormons, for example, avoid tea, coffee, caffeinated soft drinks, alcohol, and tobacco. Muslims also avoid alcohol, and both Muslims and Jews avoid pork products as well as other food products that aren't certified as *halal* (Muslim) or *kosher* (Jewish). Religions sometimes affect people's choice of clothing and adornment. It depends on the product category, but religion can be a key factor in identifying those who are or are not in the market for a good, service, or idea.

Targeting and Profiling Using Psychographics

Just as demographics relates to social characteristics, psychographics summarize personal factors. **Psychographics** refers to lifestyle and psychological characteristics, such as activities, values, interests, attitudes, and opinions. Sometimes these complex psychographic factors are more relevant in explaining consumer behavior than are demographics. For example, two families living next door to each other with the same general income, education, and occupational profiles may have radically different buying patterns. One family may be obsessed with recycling, whereas their neighbors rarely bother to even keep their newspapers separate from their trash. One family is into hiking and other outdoor sports; the other watches sports on television.

One is saving money for a European vacation; the other is seriously in debt and can barely cover the monthly bills. The differences lie not in their demographics but in their personalities, interests, and lifestyles.

Advertisers use psychographics to depict fairly complex consumer patterns. Libraries of psychographic measures can be purchased from research firms, or a company and its agency can create their own set of psychographic measures to fit a particular product and market. These psychographic measures can then be used to describe customers (such as heavy users of gourmet coffee), their response to message strategies (taste comparison ads), or their media choices (heavy users of the Internet).

Attitudes   An **attitude** is a predisposition that reflects an opinion, emotion, or mental state directed at some object, person, or idea. Advertisers are interested in attitudes because of their impact on motivations. Because attitudes are learned and often based on our experiences, we can establish them, change them, reinforce them, or replace them with new ones. However, most attitudes are deeply set, reflect basic values, and tend to be resistant to change—you can hold an attitude for years or even decades. Attitudes also vary in direction and strength; that is, an attitude can be positive, negative, or neutral. Attitudes are important to advertisers because they influence how consumers evaluate products, institutions, retail stores, and brand communication.

One trend that depicts changing attitudes is what *Time* magazine editor Richard Stengel called "ethical consumerism," which refers to consumers who buy according to their conscience, whether it be a concern for supporting local businesses and ecology and energy efficiency or boycotting wasteful packaging and sweatshops. The *Time* poll found that 82 percent said they shop local, and 40 percent said that they purchased a product "because they liked the social or political values of the company that produced it." Stengel explained, "With global warming on the minds of many consumers, lots of companies are racing to 'outgreen' one another." This results in business practices that build a positive *"triple bottom line"*: profit, planet, and people.[37] *LOHAS* stands for Lifestyles of Health and Sustainability and defines a market segment that responds to "green" marketing strategies.

Lifestyles   Psychographic analysis looks at lifestyles in terms of patterns of consumption, personal relationships, interests, and leisure activities. Figure 7.6 illustrates the interactions between the person, the product, and the setting in which a product is used and how those three factors create a lifestyle.

The DDB advertising agency has been conducting lifestyle research annually in the United States since 1975. The agency surveys 5,000 men and women on nearly 1,000 questions pertaining to such diverse topics as health, financial outlook, raising kids, shopping, religion, hobbies, leisure activities, household chores, politics, and even their desired self-image. The survey also asks people about the products they use (from soup to nuts!) and their media habits. This wealth of information makes it possible to paint a vivid, detailed, multidimensional portrait of nearly any consumer segment that might be of interest to a client, and it also lets the agency spot changes and trends in people's lifestyles over time.

An example of the use of the Life Style Survey data to segment an audience comes from the Blood Center of Wisconsin when the center found itself low on donations. The DDB research team was able to describe frequent donors as sociable, doting parents, hard working, information seekers, and community leaders. The communication strategy was refined to appeal to a more professional working people audience, and the center saw a turnaround in its level of donations.

As part of their services to clients, some research firms create lifestyle profiles that collectively reflect a whole culture. We discuss three of these proprietary tools here: the Yankelovich

● **Principle**
Often, differences in consumer behavior lie in psychographics— consumers' interests and lifestyles—rather than in demographics.

● **Principle**
Strategies that are designed to affect attitudes focus on establishing, changing, reinforcing, or replacing them.

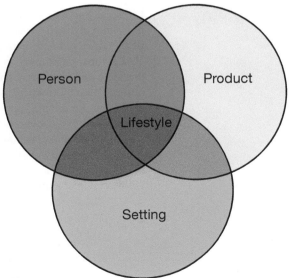

FIGURE 7.6
Lifestyle Components
Products are linked to lifestyles in the way they reflect the interests of people and the settings in which the products are used.

(renamed the Futures Company) MONITOR's MindBase, PRIZM Lifestage Groups, and the Values and Lifestyle Survey (VALS).

The MONITOR has been tracking consumer values and lifestyles since 1971. Its MindBase tool uses the MONITOR database to identify groups of people with distinctive attitudes, values, motivations, and lifestyles. (Check this company out at www.thefuturescompany.com.) Although the database can be used to custom design segments for individual clients, MindBase has identified eight general consumer groups:

- *"I Am Expressive"* Lives life to the fullest; not afraid to express my personality; active and engaged; "live in the now" attitude; believes that the future is limitless and I can do anything I put my mind to.
- *"I Am Down to Earth"* Cruising through life at my own pace; seek satisfaction where I can; hope to enhance my life; I like to try new things; I treat myself to novel things.
- *"I Am Driven"* Ambitious with a drive to succeed; self-possessed and resourceful; determined to show the world I'm on top of my game.
- *"I Am Sophisticated"* Intelligent, upstanding with an affinity for finer things; high expectations; dedicated to doing a stellar job, but I balance career with enriching experiences.
- *"I Am at Capacity"* Busy and looking for control and simplification; a demanding and vocal consumer; looking for convenience, respect, and a helping hand; want to devote more of my time to the important things in life.
- *"I Measure Twice"* Mature; like to think I'm on a path to fulfillment; live a healthy, active life; dedicated to a secure and rewarding future.
- *"I Am Rock Steady"* Positive attitude; draw energy from home and family; dedicated to an upstanding life; listen to my own instincts for decisions in life and in the marketplace.
- *"I Am Devoted"* Traditional; rooted in comforts of home; conventional beliefs; spiritual and content; like things the way they've always been; doesn't need novelty for novelty's sake or newfangled technology.

A second psychographic segmentation tool is called "PRIZM," which uses ZIP codes to classify consumers into 68 lifestyle segments and provides marketers with clusters of these segments across the United States. Figure 7.7 shows an example of the PRIZM system (acquired in 2017 by the Carlyle and Indian Hill Groups), which uses creative names for their lifestyle segments; examples are "Kids & Cul de Sacs," "New Melting Pot," "Connected Bohemians," and "Toolbelt Traditionalists."[38]

A third way to segment markets using psychographic factors comes from the Values and Lifestyle Survey (VALS), which categorizes US and Canadian adults age 18 years of age and older into distinctive consumer groups on the basis of an individual's responses to attitude questions validated to correspond to consumer behavior and a proprietary algorithm. Advertisers use VALS most commonly to identify targets, plan strategy, and develop communication for their products and services. "Thinkers" and "Believers" segments are motivated by ideals—abstract criteria such as tradition, quality, and integrity. "Achievers" and "Strivers" are motivated by achievement, seeking approval from a valued social group. "Experiencers" and "Makers" are motivated by self-expression and make value purchases that enable them to stand out from the crowd or make an impact on the physical world. In addition to the US framework, VALS frameworks are available for Japan, the United Kingdom, Venezuela, the Dominican Republic, Nigeria, and China. You can take the survey yourself and find out your own VALS type at www.strategicbusinessinsights.com/vals/presurvey.shtml.

Sociodemographic Segments

Age groups also connect with lifestyles. We've talked about the incredible impact baby boomers have had as an age cohort, so you can understand their importance as a market segment, but savvy marketers recognize many differences in lifestyles and attitudes among this huge population. Generations X and Y, as well as the echo boomers, are also important demographic segments, but their sociodemographic characteristics may represent more consistent lifestyle differences.

Some of the most common lifestyle patterns are described by familiar phrases, such as *yuppies* (young urban professionals) and *yuppie puppies* (their children). These terms are group

YOUNGER YEARS

FAMILY LIFE

MATURE YEARS

FIGURE 7.7
PRIZM Lifestage Groups Infographic
Source: Claritas PRIZM®
Premier 2017 (www.
MyBestSegments.com).
Used with permission.

◄──────────── LIFESTAGE GROUPS ────────────►

HIGH

Y1	MIDLIFE SUCCESS		F1	ACCUMULATED WEALTH		M1	AFFLUENT EMPTY NESTS
04	Young Digerati		02	Networked Neighbors		01	Upper Crust
13	Upward Bound		05	Country Squires		03	Movers & Shakers
21	The Cosmopolitans		06	Winner's Circle		07	Money & Brains
25	Up-and-Comers		10	Executive Suites		08	Gray Power
31	Connected Bohemians		11	Fast-Track Families		09	Big Fish, Small Pond
34	Young & Influential		14	Kids & Cul-de-Sacs		12	Cruisin' to Retirement
35	Urban Achievers		15	New Homesteaders			
			16	Beltway Boomers			

Y2	YOUNG ACHIEVERS		F2	YOUNG ACCUMULATORS		M2	CONSERVATIVE CLASSICS
40	Aspiring A-Listers		23	Township Travelers		17	Urban Elders
47	Striving Selfies		26	Home Sweet Home		18	Mayberry-ville
48	Generation Web		27	Big Sky Families		19	American Dreams
50	Metro Grads		29	White Picket Fences		20	Empty Nests
54	Struggling Singles		30	Pools & Patios		22	Middleburg Managers
						24	Pickup Patriarchs
						28	Country Casuals

$

Y3	STRIVING SINGLES		F3	MAINSTREAM FAMILIES		M3	CAUTIOUS COUPLES
55	Red, White & Blue		33	Second City Startups		32	Traditional Times
59	New Melting Pot		37	Bright Lights, Li'l City		36	Toolbelt Traditionalists
60	Small-Town Collegiates		39	Kid Country, USA		38	Hometown Retired
63	Low-Rise Living		44	Country Strong		41	Domestic Duos
64	Family Thrifts		51	Campers & Camo		43	City Roots
65	Young & Rustic					46	Heartlanders
66	New Beginnings					49	American Classics
						52	Simple Pleasures
						53	Lo-Tech Singles

			F4	SUSTAINING FAMILIES		M4	SUSTAINING SENIORS
			42	Multi-Culti Mosaic		57	Back Country Folks
			45	Urban Modern Mix		58	Golden Ponds
			56	Multi-Culti Families		62	Crossroad Villagers
			61	Second City Generations		67	Park Bench Seniors
			68	Bedrock America			

LOW

PREDOMINANTLY UNDER AGE 45, SINGLES AND COUPLES MOSTLY WITHOUT CHILDREN	**PREDOMINANTLY MIDDLE-AGED FAMILIES WITH CHILDREN IN THE HOUSEHOLD**	**PREDOMINANTLY AGE 55 AND ABOVE, EMPTY-NEST COUPLES AND MATURE SINGLES**

Segments in Younger Years (Y) consist of mostly singles and couples who are typically under 45 years old and generally have no children in the household. Residents may be too young to have children and/or are approaching middle age and choose not to have them.

At the household level, around age 45 is the cutoff for most segments. Among these younger segments, only those explicit in their definition for lack of children or with low indices for presence of children tend to be included in Younger Years.

Family Life (F) is composed of segments that are middle-aged and either defined by presence of children in the household or have high indices for households with children under age 18. They may be married couples or single parents.

At the household level, presence of children is the primary driver for many segments in this class. While this class also includes segments where the presence of children is not explicit at the household level, in general they do show high indices for that characteristic.

Mature Years (M) includes segments whose residents are primarily empty-nesters or those with children in their late teens, away at college or rebounding back to mom and dad's home.

At the household level, the primary driver is age, not necessarily the absence of children. Segments that are uniquely child-centered tend to be younger and are grouped under Family Years while those under age 45 and without children are grouped in Younger Years—leaving the last group of segments for the Mature Years.

identifiers, but they also refer to a set of products and the setting within which the products are used. For example, yuppies have been characterized as aspiring to an upscale lifestyle, so products associated with this lifestyle might include Cole Haan shoes, Hermes scarves, and BMW cars.

Seniors are sometimes referred to as the *gray market* and divided into two categories: young seniors (age 60–74) who are the *boomer-plus* group, and older seniors (age 75 and older). Seniors, both younger and older, make up a huge and often wealthy market. As baby boomers move into their retirement years, this senior market will become even larger relative to the rest of the population, although the recession has hurt their wealth profile. Other terms that have been used to describe demographic and lifestyle segments include the following:

- *Dinkies* Double-income young couples with no kids.
- *Guppies* Gay upwardly mobile professionals.
- *Skippies* School kids with purchasing power.
- *Ruppies* Retired urban professionals; older consumers with sophisticated tastes and generally affluent lifestyles.
- *Mini-Me* Infants and toddlers of affluent parents and grandparents who spend large amounts on luxury brands, with parents wanting their kids to reflect their taste and style.[39]

Courtesy of Michael Dattolico

SHOWCASE

This company is a nonprofit organization that is trying to reverse the momentum at which society is destroying the planet. Since no known external forces can stop this momentum, we are creating a new physics force variable. Ultimately, it is a spin on the "green" revolution, focusing on using yourself to power daily activities, but also the application of the mind to think differently. The physics reference is embedded in the logo above the "F" as well as in the "baggy man's" hair (the symbol for force). The second focus, the momentum of changing preconceptions and minds, is captured in the pushing movement of "baggy man."

Owner of his own design studio, Musion Creative LLC (www.musioncreative.com), Michael Dattolico graduated from the advertising program at the University of Florida and a creative advertising program in England at the University College of Falmouth. His work was nominated to be featured here by Professor Elaine Wagner.

Trends and Fads   The phenomenon of trends and fads is related to lifestyle and psychographic factors as well as the fascination with choice in a consumer culture. We've seen "acre homes" and fancy bathroom retreats as well as low-carb diets, healthy food (oat bran and antioxidants), natural products, fitness fads and personal trainers, hybrid cars, carbon trading, simple life (don't buy things), and local products (don't buy things that use a lot of gas in transportation to get to your local store). Sustainability and green marketing reach a population who are often passionate about the environment. The logo design for ForceHuman was created to reach this group. Michael Dattolico, its designer, explains the reasoning behind the design in the Showcase feature.

Young people are particularly involved in trends. For example, the way teenagers dress and talk and the products they buy are driven by a continuing search for coolness. **Trend spotters** are professional researchers hired by advertisers to identify trends that may affect consumer behavior. **Cool hunters** are trend spotters who specialize in identifying trendy fads that appeal to young people. They usually work with panels of young people in key trendsetting locations, such as New York, California, urban streets, and Japan. Loic Bizel, for example, hunts Japanese super-trendy fads as a consultant for many Western companies and designers. Through his website (www.fashioninjapan.com), you can get a taste of those cool ideas and fashion in Japan's streets and life.

Targeting and Profiling Using Behavioral Patterns

Behavioral targeting is a practice used by online marketers who track customers' activities—sites visited and products bought—to predict consumer interest in a product and design personalized brand communication. Google, for example, uses tracking to identify which advertisements to show to its viewers.[40] Another example of behavioral targeting comes from Orbitz, where Mac users were steered to more expensive accommodations than PC users. The *Wall Street Journal* reported that Orbitz's tracking data found that Mac users spend as much as 30 percent more on hotels than did PC users.[41]

Behavior is related to feelings (impulse) or thoughtful search. One area where such behaviors has been investigated is grocery shopping. An observational study by a University of Florida student, Kate Stein, found that grocery shoppers often buy food impulsively and irrationally. (Stein worked with Professor Brian Wansink, director of the Cornell University Food and Brand Lab.) Published as an op-ed piece in the *New York Times*, Stein reported that browsing slowly doesn't necessarily help you pick out the best products. She observed, "The shoppers I studied who took the longest, examining packages, stopping at whatever caught their eye, invariably spent more money." Furthermore, she noticed that these slow and thoughtful shoppers often loaded their shopping carts with unhealthy items that, when questioned, they couldn't give a reason for buying. In other words, the best shoppers use a grocery list, control their instincts, and move quickly through their product selections. For more tips on streamlining your grocery shopping endeavors, check out www.mindlesseating.org.[42]

Brand Usage and Experiences   There are two ways to classify **usage**: usage rates and brand relationship. *Usage rate* refers to quantity of purchase: light, medium, or heavy. Heavy users typically buy the most of a product category or a brand's share of the market. A rule of thumb called the Pareto rule states that 20 percent of the market typically buys 80 percent of the products. That explains why the heavy-user category is so important to marketers and why planners make special efforts to understand this key customer group. Heavy users and brand-loyal buyers are usually a brand's most important customers, and they are the most difficult for competitors to switch away from a brand. **Switchers** are people with low levels of brand loyalty who may be willing to try a new brand. Below is a chart that identifies consumer categories based on product usage.

Quantity	*Brand Relationship*	*Innovation*
Light users	Nonusers	Innovators
Medium users	Ex-users	Early adopters
Heavy users	Regulars	Early majority
	First-timers	Late majority
	Loyal users	Laggards
	Switchers	

● **Principle**
In many product categories, 20 percent of the users buy 80 percent of the products.

Innovation and Adoption   Another type of behavior has to do with how willing people are to try something new. Everett Rogers developed the classic system, called the *diffusion of innovation curve*, to identify adoption behaviors for new ideas. This **adoption process** is identified in terms of the speed with which people are willing to try something new, such as *innovators, early adopters*, *early majority*, *late majority*, and *laggards*.[43] This system reflects the speed of **diffusion** of new ideas. See Figure 7.8 for an interpretation of Rogers' diffusion of innovation model.

The innovator category, which is the group of brave souls willing to try something new, represents only about 2.5 percent of the population. Obviously, the early-adopter category is an important group for marketers launching new products because they become opinion leaders for their friends. *Risk taking* is a personality characteristic, but it drives behavior in the area of trying a new product. **Perceived risk** is your view of the relationship between what you gain by trying something new and what you lose if it doesn't work out—how important is the consequence of not making a good decision? Price is a huge barrier for high-involvement products; personal status and self-image may be a risk barrier for a fashion product.

FIGURE 7.8

The Diffusion of Innovation

This version of Rogers's diffusion of innovation model shows the usual bell curve with data estimating the percentage of people in the standard adaption categories; however, it also presents a percentage line that estimates the cumulative effect of successive groups of consumers adopting a new idea until it eventually reaches a saturation level.

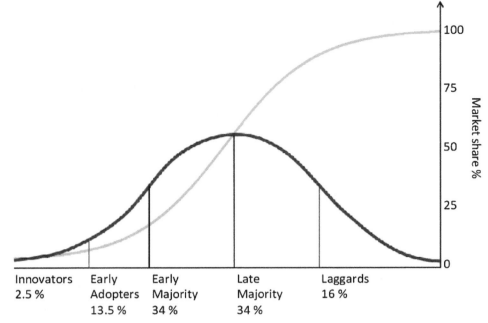

Source: Tungsten, http://en.wikipedia.org/wiki/Everett_Rogers. Based on E. Rogers, *Diffusion of Innovations* (London: Free Press, 1962).

Who are these people? SRI's research has found that, contrary to popular belief, there is no one innovator or early-adopter group; rather, adoption patterns vary with the product category. Early adopters are in different strata and roles in society and cannot be identified by demographics alone.

An example of a campaign targeting Latino innovators is found in the launch of the Sync technology in Ford's fuel-efficient Focus and Edge cars. Sync allows drivers to control cell phones and MP3 players at the touch of a button or a voice-activated command. An important feature is that the technology could understand various dialects of Spanish. Research found that many Latinos are technologically savvy and use their MP3 players during long commutes, so it was an ideal market to target with this new technology.[44]

Seeking Seekers

Segmenting and targeting strategies have evolved in recent years with developments in social media and Internet technology. This new more complex communication system recognizes the increased importance of word of mouth (C → C), where consumers talk among themselves about brands. Furthermore, companies are much more involved in listening and responding to consumers (C → B → C), rather than just targeting them. So, we not only need to rethink targeting, but also the way consumers interact with brands.

As we will see in Chapters 14 and 15, technological developments are allowing businesses to use ever more sophisticated targeting strategies. For example, Facebook allows advertisers to target their communication based on the user's location, gender, and interests. Twitter offers these options as well as targeting based on keywords used by Twitter users. The ideal of individual-level ad targeting is very near on Facebook, Twitter, and YouTube because they offer targeting based on our individual online behaviors.[45] Addressable TV is another technology that allows advertising messages to be tailored and selected for each household.

Don Schultz, founder of the IMC program at Northwestern University and a leading thinker on changes in brand communication, noted that consumers have evolved from having little to say and less control over marketing messages to a new model where customers are much more in control of the system. He explained that as customers get access to information through the internet, they can find, sort through, evaluate, make decisions, and share their thoughts with like-minded customers all over the world.[46]

This expansion of marketplace communication has, as Schultz argued, changed the dynamics of marketplace power, bringing a loss of control by marketers over marketing and marketing communication systems. More importantly, it makes the consumer more important as an agent using the new media to search for things they find relevant and important. We call them *Seekers*—people who search, share, and initiate marketing communication and brand relationships (Figure 7.9).

On one level, they seek traditional products, services, and ideas using powerful Internet search tools to find things that interest them—information, but also brand meanings and experiences that intersect with their self-esteem. They also are seeking pleasure, personal strokes, fellowship, and positive experiences. So, consider that when Seekers go online, they are looking for information and answers, but they are also looking for sensory stimulation, surprises, challenges, friends, things to like, happiness, belonging, respect and admiration, rewards, something to believe, something to talk about and share, the newest thing, and ways to be smarter or more attractive. The Seeker breed of consumer is personally independent but socially dependent: Seekers are frequently in contact and frequently in touch both with other people and with websites. It's a curious blend of individual search and communal sharing.

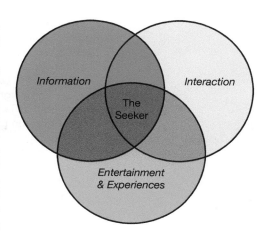

FIGURE 7.9
The Seeker Model

The challenge for a brand planner is to figure out where the brand fits in the Seeker's life. How can the brand help bring meaning, create experiences, and provide a platform for sharing ideas among friends? More importantly, how can brand planners use these insights to develop more effective brand communication? For Seekers, marketing communication is like a video game, and successful marketers will offer exciting, engaging, and even mesmerizing brand experiences.

Looking Ahead

As consumers deepen their involvement with online tools and mobile apps, new technologies are enabling marketers to create a more individually tailored experience for their customers, both in-store and online. An exciting development on the horizon is "programmatic creative," which doesn't just target a digital ad to a person at the right moment, but also allows marketers to build customized ads for individuals in real time![47] For example, Tennessee Tourism ran pre-roll video ads (promotional video messages that play before the main content) on sites across the web, but they tailored the ads people saw based on a dozen criteria (e.g. their geographic location; if they were foodies, golfers, outdoor enthusiasts, or rock-music fans). This process created more than 2,000 video ad possibilities. Snap recently acquired ad tech firm Flite as a means of gaining a foothold in this realm.

The stuff of consumer insight—needs and wants, thoughts, knowledge, attitudes, and responses—is uncovered through various kinds of research. These findings ultimately lead to brand communication strategies and plans. Before designing strategies, however, we will discuss methods of obtaining consumer insight, which we introduce in Chapter 9.

IT'S A WRAP

Dove The Beauty of a Campaign

This chapter underscores the importance of understanding the influences that affect consumer responses to advertising. Key to effective customer-focused advertising is staying sensitive to consumers and understanding how they think, act, and feel as well as to where they'll be able connect with the brand message.

The provocative copy in the Dove "Campaign for Real Beauty" challenges the audience to reconsider how they define beauty and to love their bodies, no matter what their age or shape. The campaign generated a huge buzz, but did it work to sell the product? According to Unilever, the campaign resulted in a 24 percent sales increase during the initial advertising period across the entire Dove brand.

The brand also fared well globally—in some places. When it was launched in the United Kingdom, sales of Dove Firming Lotion reportedly increased by 700 percent in the first seven months after the posters appeared. It generated a substantial press interest, with about 170 editorial pieces written in the first four months after the launch in Great Britain.

However, the Dove message did not resonate with all audiences. Ultimately, Dove created a localized campaign for the Taiwanese market inspired by the *Ugly Betty* television series when it was found that Taiwanese women didn't embrace the brand's "Real Beauty" philosophy.

The campaign radically changed the Dove brand image in the United States with its culturally relevant message. Overall, the Dove Self-Esteem Project has reached over 19 million young people to date in 138 countries around the world, and Dove is committed to reach 20 million more by 2020[48].

The definition of beauty portrayed in advertising really seems to be changing. When asked about the images in Dove ads, 76 percent said women in the ad are beautiful, and 68 percent said, "It made you think differently about the brand."

Advertising Age named the Dove's "Evolution" web video, which earned more than 6 million hits and lots of mentions in the national press, as one of its best nontelevision campaigns of the decade. In addition, the "Singin' in the Rain" campaign helped Dove become one of the top five hair brands in Canada.

Logo: Courtesy Janet Kestin; Nancy Vonk; Tim Piper; Mike Kirkland; Aviva Groll; Coby Shuman for Ogilvy & Mather, Toronto.

KEY OBJECTIVES SUMMARY

7.1. Explain how the consumer decision process works. The information-driven decision process involves five stages: need recognition, information search, evaluation of alternatives, purchase decision, and postpurchase evaluation. The paths approach to consumer decision making identifies a multitude of different routes that a consumer may take to reach a purchase decision.

7.2. Describe the cultural, social, psychological, and behavioral influences on consumer responses to marketing communication. The social and cultural influences on consumer decision making include norms and values, society and subcultures, social class, reference groups, age, gender, family status, education, occupation, income, and race. Psychological influences on consumers include perception, needs and wants, learning, and motivations.

7.3. Discuss targeting and how it differs from segmenting. In contrast to segmentation, which involves dividing a market into groups of people who can be identified as being in the market for the product, targeting identifies the group that would be the most responsive to an advertising message about the product. Segmenting and targeting use social/cultural, psychological, and behavioral characteristics to identify these critical groups of people, but targeting uses these data to build a profile of the ideal person to whom the marketing communication is directed.

7.4. List several characteristics that are used to segment markets and target consumers. Advertisers identify audiences in terms of demographics, psychographics, product-related behavior, and decision making. Demographic profiles of consumers include information on population size, age, gender and sexual orientation, education, occupation, income, family status, race, religion, and geography. Psychographic profiles include information on attitudes (activities, interests, and opinions) and lifestyles. Behavior profiles emphasize brand usage, as well as innovativeness and risk taking, and participation in trends and fads. Quantity of usage is an important characteristic of a profitable market. The relationship the consumer has with the brand in terms of use and loyalty is also important. Finally, the innovativeness of people in the group in terms of their willingness to try something new is another important behavioral characteristic.

KEY TERMS

acquired needs, p. 194
adoption process, p. 209
attitude, p. 205
brand communities, p. 193
cognitive age, p. 201
cognitive dissonance, p. 195
consumer behavior, p. 188
cool hunters, p. 208
core values, p. 189
corporate culture, p. 190

cultural cohort, p. 198
culture, p. 188
demographics, p. 199
designated marketing area (DMA), p. 204
diffusion, p. 209
discretionary income, p. 203
family, p. 193
household, p. 193
involvement, p. 187

lifestyle, p. 203
market segmentation, p. 197
microtargeting, p. 199
motive, p. 195
neuromarketing, p. 195
niche market, p. 197
norms, p. 189
perceived risk, p. 209
profiles, p. 199
psychographics, p. 204

reference group, p. 191
segmenting, p. 196
social class, p. 191
switchers, p. 209
target audience, p. 199
targeting, p. 198
trend spotters, p. 208
undifferentiated strategy, p. 196
usage, p. 209
values, p. 189

MyLab Marketing

Go to **www.pearson.com/mylab/marketing** for MyLab discussion questions (⚙) as well as the following assisted-graded writing questions:

7-1. What are the key behavioral influences on consumer behavior? For example, say you want to go out to eat on Friday. Discuss your decision about where to go in terms of behavioral factors.

7-2. Define targeting. How does it differ from segmenting? Explain how Dove approached the segmenting and targeting decision in its "Real Beauty" campaign. Discuss what makes this approach effective. Also discuss how this targeting can be made more relevant given the opportunities offered by interactive communication.

REVIEW QUESTIONS

7-3. In what ways does the culture in which you grew up affect your consumer behavior? Describe and explain one purchase you have made recently that reflects your cultural background.

7-4. What are reference groups? List the reference groups to which you belong or with which you associate yourself.

7-5. What is the difference between needs and wants? Give an example of something you have purchased in the past week that represents a need and another that represents a want.

⚙ **7-6.** What are your key demographic and psychographic characteristics? Build a profile of yourself and discuss how each one might be used in planning an advertising campaign targeted to someone like you.

⚙ **7-7.** What are the key steps in the product adoption process, and how do they relate to product purchases? Who do you know who might qualify as an early adopter? As a laggard? Profile those two people and discuss the key characteristics that make them different in their orientation to new ideas or products.

DISCUSSION QUESTIONS

⚙ **7-8.** Analyze the corporate culture at various agencies and clients. Start with the statement on www.ogilvy.com/About/Our-History/Corporate-Culture.aspx for an inside view of how this agency articulates its view of its own corporate culture. Then find at least one other agency or client website that refers to its corporate culture and compare that statement with Ogilvy's. (Look first at companies whose websites have been mentioned in this chapter or previous chapters.) Discuss where you would prefer to work and why.

7-9. We discuss inner- and outer-directed personalities in this chapter. Check out Reisman's theory (articles on websites, or *The Lonely Crowd*) and then write a profile for yourself and your best friend. Compare and contrast your orientation toward your peers. Also see https://susannabarlow.com/on-relationships/are-you-inner-focused-or-outer-focused/.

7-10. Consider the social factors that influence consumer decisions. Identify two demographic or psychographic factors that you think would be most important to each of these product marketing situations:

   a. Dairy product company (milk, cheese, or ice cream) offering an exclusive packaging design that uses fully degradable containers.

   b. A new SUV that is lighter in weight, runs on ethanol, and gets better gas mileage than the average SUV.

   c. An athletic clothing company that is sponsoring the next Pogopalooza, the world championship of extreme pogo.

⚙ **7-11.** What age-group category do you and your friends fit into? Gen Y? Millennial? There's always debate about the characteristics of these population groups, yet there are usually some general characteristics that help identify interests, attitudes, and behaviors. Develop a profile that fits yourself and your friends (who are in the same age group). Try to identify characteristics that generally represent this group.

7-12. Discuss the decision making involved in choosing your college:

   a. Interview two classmates and determine what influenced their decision to attend this school.

   b. How did you—and the people you interviewed—go about making this decision? Is there a general decision-making process that you can outline? Where are the points of agreement, and where did you and your classmates differ in approaching this decision?

   c. Draw up a target audience profile for students attending your college. How does this profile differ from another school in your same market area?

7-13. You are working on a new account, a bottled tea named Leafs Alive that uses a healthy antioxidant formulation.

The sale of bottled tea as well as healthy products is surging. Analyze your market using the following considerations:

a. What consumer trends seem to be driving this product development?

b. What cultural, social, psychological, and behavioral factors influence this market?

c. Plot the consumer decision process you think would best describe how people choose a product in this category.

d. Choose one of the VALS (www.sric-bi.com/vals) or the MONITOR's MindBase® groups that you think best describes the target market for this product. Explain your rationale.

TAKE-HOME PROJECTS

7-14. *Portfolio Project:* Choose two VALS and two MindBase categories. Find one print advertisement that appears to be targeted to people in each category. Explain why you think the ad addresses that audience. Do you believe that the categories are mutually exclusive? Can consumers (and ads directed to them) be classified in multiple categories? Why or why not?

7-15. *Mini-Case Analysis:* Review the chapter opening and closing story about Dove's "Real Beauty" campaign. How does this campaign reflect a cultural or social insight? What psychological insight helps explain the thinking behind this campaign? From what is presented in this mini-case, develop a profile of an individual member of this target audience.

TRACE North America Case

Multicultural Innovation

Read the TRACE case in the Appendix before coming to class.

7-16. From the case study and your own personal experiences in college, what factors do you believe most strongly influence Multicultural Millennials in their decision making?

7-17. What campaigns targeted to African Americans, Asian Americans, and Hispanic Americans are you aware of, and do you believe they are successful? Why or why not?

8

Strategic Planning

KEY OBJECTIVES

8.1 Explain the difference between objectives, strategies, and tactics in strategic planning as well as the three levels of planning and how they are connected.

8.2 Identify the key strategic decisions and explain why they are central to brand communication planning.

8.3 Demonstrate the purpose and role of account planning and how it is used in advertising and IMC.

In most cases, there is no one completely right way to do anything in advertising or brand communication, but if you understand how communication works, you may be able to identify the best strategy to accomplish the objectives most efficiently and effectively. This chapter explains the concept of strategic planning as it is used in business, marketing, and brand communication. In addition to targeting the right audience, which we discussed in Chapter 7, key planning decisions include identifying critical problems and opportunities, positioning or repositioning the brand against the competition, and making implementation (tactics) decisions. It also demonstrates the uses of account planning and explains its critical role in determining the consumer insights that lead to message and media strategies. The chapter is also designed to help you understand the broader strategic rationale behind integrated marketing communication (IMC) and advertising campaigns and how they advance the direction and mission of organizations.

MyLab Marketing

⭐ Improve Your Grade!

More than 10 million students improved their results using Pearson MyLabs. Visit **www.pearson.com/mylab/marketing** for simulations, tutorials, and end-of-chapter problems.

Campaign

"Eat Mor Chikin"

Company

Chick-fil-A

Agency

The Richards Group

Awards

Silver Effie Awards in Sustained Success Campaign and Restaurant Categories, Obie Hall of Fame (Outdoor Advertising Association of America), Silver Lion at Cannes International Advertising Festival, AdAge Marketer of the Year Runner-Up

Chick-fil-A Gets Love from Renegade Cows

Photo: Courtesy Chick-fil-A, Inc. Used with permission.

"Lose that burger belly." "Eat mor chikin." You gotta hand it to the cows. Those cows are udderly passionate about Chick-fil-A.

Although the renegade cows do not know how to spell, they sure know how to sell "chikin" sandwiches for Chick-fil-A. And their endearing personalities have helped them convince humans to make the switch from beef to chicken since 1995 in the award-winning "Eat Mor Chikin" campaign created by the Richards Group.

Chick-fil-A has developed a loyal fan base as passionate about the brand as its quirky cows. How did these cows moo-tivate such love?

Chick-fil-A started with a significant challenge: it had to persuade people to eat chicken sandwiches when everybody else in the world seemed to be eating hamburgers. Truett Cathy founded Chick-fil-A with the vision that his chicken sandwich company would be a leader in the quick-service restaurant industry. Chick-fil-A has become just that, in part by understanding how to put advertising to work to attract consumers' attention and their appetites.

The "Eat Mor Chikin" campaign is a great example that you do not have to be a big brand with millions of dollars to have great advertising. Chick-fil-A competes in the fast-food category, one of the largest and most competitive industries. To give you an idea about what it's up against, Chick-fil-A has 1,600 stores, and McDonald's has 33,000. It is outnumbered in store count and outspent in media by the likes of McDonald's, Burger King, and Wendy's.

Faced with these disadvantages in the marketplace, Chick-fil-A and its advertising agency set out to develop a brand campaign that would increase top-of-mind awareness, increase sales, and earn Chick-fil-A a spot in consumers' consideration list of fast-food brands. To do that effectively, the campaign positioned Chick-fil-A chicken sandwiches as the premium alternative to hamburgers.

At the heart of every piece of memorable advertising is a great concept. The really great ideas like Chick-fil-A's renegade cows have sticking power because they emotionally connect with the audience.

Agency founder Stan Richards said, "Cows have a national appeal and everybody empathizes with a cow because of their enlightened self-interest—by telling people to eat chicken, a simple idea that resonates with people."

The company couldn't outspend the competition. It couldn't even afford a national campaign on television, which is where most of its competitors were advertising. So it made a strategic decision to advertise where its competitors weren't: on billboards. Copywriters kept the idea simple and fun (after all, they are selling chicken sandwiches).

As the campaign has evolved over time, the agency created an integrated marketing campaign using social media, direct mail and ads, promotions, events, television, radio, the internet, clothing, and merchandise to build the reputation of the company that the fun-loving cows represent. Calendars have been so popular that production numbers have topped 2.4 million. Anyone brave enough to show up at one of the chain's restaurants dressed as a cow on the annual Cow Appreciation Day gets a free Chick-fil-A meal.

Chick-fil-A's "Eat Mor Chikin" campaign helped break the fast-food hamburger pattern. The witty use of Holsteins who hype consumers to "Eat Mor Chikin" instead of beef provided a bold brand personality that broke through industry clutter. The message and execution were simple, the cows were funny, the creative idea was unexpected, and the call to action was powerful.

In this chapter, you will learn the types of strategic decisions that planners make in the process of creating memorable brand communication that works. You will read about objectives, strategies, and tactics that help accomplish a client's goals.

You will also learn what it takes for companies such as Chick-fil-A to build brands that consumers love. Furthermore, you will learn that no matter how carefully brand communication is planned, effects cannot always be controlled, as illustrated by the 2012 crisis in which Chick-fil-A became the epicenter of a controversy after the owner stated the chicken chain's support of traditional marriage.

Did the charming cows successfully moo-ve consumers to eat more Chick-fil-A? Hoof it to the end of the chapter to see the results. (In 2016, after 22 years with the Richards Group, Chick-fil-A changed agencies, hiring McCann New York and Erich & Kallman.[1])

Sources: www.chick-fil-a.com; information courtesy of Mike Buerno, the Richards Group; "Winners Showcase," www.effie .org; "Chick-fil-A's Famous 'Eat Mor Chikin' Cows Moove into Popular Culture Promoting Chicken over Beef," press release, www.chick-fil-a.com/pressroom; www.mcdonalds.com; "Chick-fil-A Fast Losing Ground in Marriage Debate," July 26, 2012, www.adage.com.

8.1 Explain the difference between objectives, strategies, and tactics in strategic planning as well as the three levels of planning and how they are connected.

● **Principle**
Coming up with a big problem-solving idea in strategic planning is just as creative as coming up with a Big Idea for a brand communication campaign.

Pat Fallon (top) and Fred Senn were cofounders of Fallon Worldwide, the agency behind NBC, Holiday Inn Express, Travelers Insurance, Sony, and many other major brands.

What Is Strategic Planning?

What was the key idea that made the Chick-fil-A campaign so successful? Can you identify a strategy that jumps out at you? What about the Dove campaign that introduced Chapter 7? How would you describe the strategy that made it a winner?

What is strategy—and strategic planning? **Strategic planning** for IMC is the process of identifying a problem that can be solved with communication and then coming up with a great idea that solves that problem. Here's the mission of planning: identify a problem, determine **objectives** (what you want to accomplish with a message), decide on **strategies** (how to accomplish the objectives), and implement the **tactics** (specific activities that make the plan come to life). This process occurs within a specified time frame.

We talk a lot about creativity in this book, and we'd like to emphasize that strategic thinking is just as creative as coming up with a Big Idea for a brand communication campaign. Both processes involve searching for ideas to solve problems, whether they are found in marketing situations or communication challenges. Pat Fallon and Fred Senn, cofounders of the legendary agency Fallon Worldwide, explain that principle in their book *Juicing the Orange: How to Turn Creativity into a Powerful Business Advantage.* They have identified seven principles that link creative thinking and strategic planning to business results:[2]

1. *Always Start from Scratch* Simplify the problem. You know too much. There's a good chance that you know so much that you can't see how the problem could be solved in a fresh way.
2. *Demand a Ruthlessly Simple Definition of the Business Problem* Smart people tend to make things too complicated. Be a relentless reductionist. Einstein said, "Make things as simple as possible, but no simpler" (BrainyQuote, https://www.brainyquote.com/quotes/quotes/a/alberteins103652.html).
3. *Discover a Proprietary Emotion* The key component of any communication program is a powerful consumer insight that leads to a ruthlessly smart strategy executed brilliantly across all platforms. It all starts with the insight, which is the central truth of what you are going to say and how you are going to operate. Once you find an emotional truth, you can make it proprietary through execution.
4. *Focus on the Size of the Idea, Not the Size of the Budget* It's our credo that it's better to outsmart than outspend.
5. *Seek Out Strategic Risks* Understand the benefits of prudent risk. Great big ideas in the early stages are often scary ideas. When Darwin taught us about the survival of the fittest, he didn't mean the strongest. He meant that it's the most nimble—the quickest to adapt to a changing environment—who prosper both in nature and in a capitalist economy.
6. *Collaborate or Perish* This is more than "getting along"; it is about recognizing that the rules of engagement have changed. We live in an era in which victory goes to the best collaborators. This means teams from different disciplines and different corporate cultures will be working together. Teams that are aligned and motivated can make history.
7. *Listen Hard to Your Customers (Then Listen Some More)* Listening is often step number one on the road to understanding. Listening often yields that precious insight that gives you a competitive advantage; something your competitors have overlooked.

In her introduction to Part 2, Regina Lewis identified the key ideas that drove her consumer insight work for Dunkin' Brands and for Holiday Inn. For Dunkin', people loved the "everyday joe" image of Dunkin' and its coffee, a brand with which they could identify. For Holiday Inn, the challenge was to help a traveler feel at home and "stay you." Both created authentic meanings and met emotional needs. This chapter will look at how such strategic decisions are made by planners. We begin with Kristen Ewing's take on the strategic planning process in the Inside Story below.

Strategic planning for IMC is a part of planning conducted for the organization as a whole, which considers the broader, complex business environment. For the sake of simplification in this discussion, there are three levels of plans: the business plan, the marketing plan, and the brand communication/IMC plan, which includes direction for specific areas of marketing communication, such as advertising and public relations (Figure 8.1).

The Business Plan

Strategic planning is a process that gives direction to the entire organization. It starts with the overall business plan and then moves to functional areas of the company such as marketing.

THE INSIDE STORY

RPIE (Research, Planning, Implementation, Evaluation): A Realistic View

Kristen Ewing, *Public Relations, Carter Healthcare*

RPIE! RPIE! RPIE! It is the foundation for successful strategic plans. And yet, as we hustle to accomplish anything and everything in the professional world, RPIE gets left behind. Okay, that isn't quite true. RPIE isn't completely forgotten, just occasionally pushed aside. Money and time are often cited as reasons for this. Yes, both can throw a wrench into conducting all parts of RPIE, but to truly claim we are strategic communications professionals, RPIE cannot be forgotten.

This book provides you a wealth of information about RPIE to help prepare you for a journey in marketing communications. However, any professional will tell you the real world can be quite different from books and lectures. So, here are my real-world ramblings about RPIE.

Research

Research reminds us of being back in school and can often be dreaded. Too often, the bare minimum effort is given. Never should a basic Internet search be your only research. Always dive deeper into the research. Ask questions. It is through research you learn from the successes and failures of what came before.

Planning

The early stages of planning can be some of the most enjoyable. I have yet to find someone who doesn't love brainstorming because the word *no* is never allowed. Once the strategy and tactic are decided, though, planning can become somewhat tedious. Public relations professionals are counted on for anticipating every possible detail. While planning, never assume anything as a given. It is never good when you've planned on doing something only to be told it isn't possible at the last minute.

Implementation

Implementing strategies and tactics can be quite stressful. Will the event be successful? Will the release be read (and then published)? There are many variables we can't control that play a role in what we're implementing. However, if the planning was thorough, the stress should be minimal, and you will be confident as you implement your plan.

Evaluation

It can be difficult to provide return on investment for our tactics. Some are easy to provide results for, such as how many picked up the release and how many people attended an event. Others, such as gauging brand awareness, are more difficult to evaluate. As a professional, you should love this step because it shows your results to others. Evaluation also brings RPIE to a full circle. With appropriate research at the beginning, such as a survey gauging people's opinions of a brand, you can conduct research at the end with another survey to gauge how opinions changed. With pre- and post-research, you can show, with hard data (CEOs love numbers!), you were successful.

Each part of RPIE builds on what came before it. Without research, you will struggle to plan. Without a plan, you'll be randomly implementing tactics without an overall goal. With no evaluation, you'll struggle to prove success. As you journey through public relations, RPIE will be a block in your foundation for success.

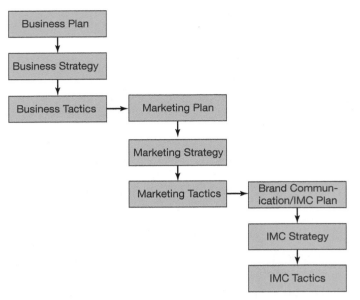

FIGURE 8.1

Planning from Top to Bottom

Planning involves coordinating a set of cascading objectives and strategies. Business objectives and strategies are achieved through planning at the level of marketing (and other marketing mix areas), and marketing objectives and strategies give direction to brand communication/IMC programs.

A marketing plan outlines objectives, strategies, and tactics for all areas of the marketing mix. A business plan is a snapshot of the company and how it intends to advance in the environment in which it operates.

External conditions, such as technological changes, have made companies obsolete, as Kodak found when the market died for its celluloid film. Forays into printers and online photo albums failed to revive the iconic brand, and it moved into bankruptcy in 2012. The recession that began in the United States in 2007 and picked up speed in subsequent years in Europe before moving on to Asia has affected almost every category of business. External factors are the framework in which business plans are created; they also present the challenges that may become the focus of strategic decision making in companies that either are threatened or see opportunities in such changes.

In larger companies, the business plan also directs the operations of **strategic business units (SBUs)**, which are fully functional organizations with their own competitors, marketing plans, and IMC/advertising campaigns. The business plan may take the form of a formal document given to potential investors. Figure 8.2 depicts the process for developing a business plan.

Mission Statement and Business Philosophy   A business plan begins with a description of the business itself—the history of the company, its products, the scope of its offerings, its corporate strengths, and its organizational structure and management team. A **vision statement** describes where the business is headed—it is usually an inspiring statement that points to the organization's ideal future. Raytheon, the maker of satellite and defense technologies, states its vision clearly on its website and on materials used in employees' everyday work. An organization's **mission statement** is derived from its vision and is a concise expression of the more practical goals, purpose, and policies of the business. A mission statement should be unique, focused, and differentiating. For example, the mission statement of the American Red Cross states that it "prevents and alleviates human suffering in the face of emergencies by mobilizing the power of volunteers and the generosity of donors" (American Red Cross mission statement, http://www.redcross.org/about-us/who-we-are/mission-and-values). Starbucks displays its mission statement in its corporate headquarters and at retail locations.

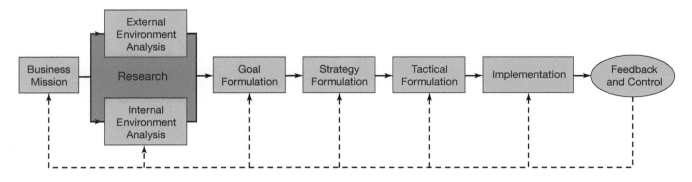

FIGURE 8.2

Steps in the Development of a Business Plan

The business planning process begins with a mission statement and moves through research, goal setting, strategy statements, identification of tactics, implementation processes, and controls (meeting the budget and quality standards, for example). The entire process is monitored through feedback.

Source: Philip Kotler and Kevin Lane Keller, *Marketing Management*, 13th ed., Upper Saddle River, NJ: Prentice Hall, © 2009: 48. Reproduced by permission of Pearson Education, Inc., Upper Saddle River, NJ.

The Starbucks mission statement also expresses the company's **business philosophy**, the fundamental principles that guide the operations of the business. For many companies, the primary business philosophy is simply to make a profit. However, a growing number of mission statements are including a **societal marketing** emphasis embodied in the **triple bottom line**, indicating the firm's commitment to enhancing its profits, its people, and the planet. This emphasis stems from the belief that what's good for a business should also be good for communities, employees, the environment, and society. Embedding social responsibility deep in the corporate mission, business plans, and operations not only guides business decisions, it also imbues the brand identity with integrity.

Photo: John Trax/Alamy Stock Photo

Starbucks displays its mission statement in its corporate headquarters and at retail locations to remind employees and customers of its commitment to inspiring and nurturing people and neighborhoods through their retail stores.

Research   Chapter 6 identified a number of research tools used in planning business decisions as well as marketing and brand communication programs. In business plans, it is particularly important to look both inside and outside the organization to identify strengths and weaknesses, both corporate and brand. Being able to foresee market changes, business opportunities, and technological breakthroughs determines a company's long-term success. Consider Apple's continued growth, which has been generated by innovative products such as the iPod, iPhone, iPad, and iTunes store, all of which focused on meeting consumer needs better than competitors. The Principled Practice feature about antismoking campaigns also provides insight about the role research plays in tracking consumer trends.

⬡ **Principle**
Embedding social responsibility principles in the corporate mission, business plans, and operations imbues the brand image with integrity.

Goals and Objectives   Business **goals**, which are long term and general, such as moving to a global strategy or achieving cost savings, provide direction to business plans. Often these plans are stated in terms of 5-year time frames. They also outline expectations for the financial side of the business.

The objectives for planning at this business level tend to focus on maximizing profit and **return on investment (ROI)**. ROI is a measurement that shows the degree to which the costs of conducting the business—the investment—are more than matched by the revenue produced in return. The revenue above and beyond the costs is where **profit** lies. A note about goals and objectives: both describe things you want to achieve, but goals tend to identify broad directions for the company (e.g., become a leading brand in Brazil), and objectives tend to be more specific and measurable (e.g., achieve 20% market share in Brazil within 1 year).

Strategies, Tactics, and Controls   At the business plan level, planning decisions are focused on research and development, operations, and sales and marketing. Strategies are plans designed to achieve the organization's goals and objectives. If the goal is to be the biggest maker of bicycles in your part of the country, strategies might involve buying other bike manufacturers, increasing the number of lines of bikes that you make, or energizing your regional sales staff. The tactics are specific activities that make the strategies come to life, such as designing a new bike for a specific niche market or developing new incentives for your sales force. Implementation consists of the decisions you need to make to actually design that new bike, including personnel (designers and engineers) as well as scheduling and budgeting.

Most companies operate with detailed budgets, audits, time sheets, and quality control procedures. They are some of the tools that assist with the control function of management and keep programs on strategy by tracking the effectiveness of strategic decisions and implementation programs. Controls are most effective when this information is fed back into the planning process and used to adjust future strategies. Below, Professor Wolburg describes how her research on cigarette smoking led to development of a marketing strategy that improved the effectiveness of advertising messages.

"Just Give Me My One Vice"

Joyce M. Wolburg, *Marquette University*

One day I asked my students to bring in samples of magazine ads to critique. One student showed two antismoking messages, which got the response, "Those ads make me so mad, they just make me want to light up a cigarette." I realized that if this reaction is common among other smokers, millions of dollars are wasted in campaign expenditures.

Using individual interviews among students, I discovered that smokers and nonsmokers had dramatically different views. Nonsmokers championed the ads—in fact, the more insulting the better. Smokers, on the other hand, were defiant and denied the health risks. "I am going to die from something someday, so why shouldn't this be my cause of death?" Some smokers also felt a sense of entitlement toward smoking. "All I'm doing is smoking. I'm not doing heavy drugs or robbing banks or murdering people. This is as bad as I get. Let me have my cigarette."

Psychologists have known for decades that when people are told to change their behavior, they are likely to dig in their heels and resist change because their freedom is at stake. My findings fit that theory perfectly. And because smokers took up the habit despite the many messages out there, antismoking messages must not work—or so the logic goes. They knew the health risks—"you would have to be a moron to not know that it kills"—but they didn't find the ads compelling. "There isn't an ad out there that would

get me to quit." Most figured they would quit smoking before it harmed their health, but they didn't count on how quickly they would become addicted.

I was convinced that antismoking messages were not connecting with students, and I began to wonder what convinced them to quit and how they did it. My next study found that the most common reason for quitting was a personal health scare; however, some quit because they no longer identified with smokers. Unfortunately, they thought quitting would be easy and weren't prepared for the challenge. Every student I interviewed made multiple attempts before they finally succeeded.

Every student also had a quit date in mind—"by my next birthday, by the time I graduate, by the time I get my first job, by the time I get married, by the time I have children." But they didn't have a plan for how to do it. One of the most common problems was not anticipating the situations that triggered smoking, and going out drinking was the most difficult.

Most students wanted to quit "cold turkey" because they saw it as a badge of honor. However, this strategy worked for only a few. One student beat the odds by meeting regularly with a physician's assistant because it gave him a sense of accountability. "I knew that if I smoked, I would have to tell him."

So, what does it all mean? Smokers won't quit unless they are ready, but campus support should be in place for those who are. Messages should use real examples of what worked and what didn't, not judgmental campaigns with scare tactics.

Sources: Joyce Wolburg, "College Students' Responses to Antismoking Messages: Denial, Defiance, and Other Boomerang Effects," *Journal of Consumer Affairs* 40, no. 2 (2006): 294–323; Joyce Wolburg, "Misguided Optimism among College Student Smokers: Leveraging Their Quit Smoking Strategies for Smoking Cessation Campaigns," *Journal of Consumer Affairs* 43, no. 2 (2009): 305–331.

The Marketing Plan

A **marketing plan** is developed for an SBU, brand, or product line. McDonald's, for example, may have a marketing plan for the corporate McDonald's brand, but there may also be marketing plans for individual product lines, such as the breakfast menu or the McCafé line. Marketing plans are evaluated annually. To a large extent, the marketing plan mirrors the corporate business plan, although the strategies are focused on an SBU or a specific brand rather than the larger organization or corporation. Figure 8.3 illustrates the strategic decisions found in a marketing plan.

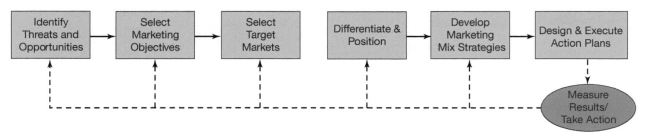

FIGURE 8.3

Steps in the Development of a Marketing Plan
A marketing plan begins with an analysis of the marketing situation in terms of strengths, weaknesses, opportunities, and threats. Setting objectives is the next step. Target markets are selected, and marketing strategies as well as action plans and specific executions of ideas and programs are developed. The plan is evaluated, and that information feeds back into the next generation of planning.

Step 1: Identify Threats and Opportunities A **situation analysis** is based on extensive market research that assesses the external and internal environments that affect marketing programs. It often begins with a **SWOT analysis**, which stands for strengths, weaknesses, opportunities, and threats. Strengths and weaknesses are internal to the company, and opportunities and threats are external. Strategic decisions attempt to leverage strengths to take advantage of opportunities and address weaknesses and threats that may hold the company back.

Step 2: Select Marketing Objectives At the marketing level, objectives tend to be focused on *sales* and **share of market**, measurements referring to the percentage of the category purchases that are made by the brand's customers. Sales objectives may operate annually, but they may also be quarterly or even weekly. Other objectives deal with specific areas of the marketing mix, such as distribution, where an objective might detail how a company will open a specific new territory or engage channel members in supporting a promotion (see Sunkist ad), and with brand relationship programs, such as frequent-flyer programs that drive loyalty and repeat business (see United Airlines ad).

J. Scott Armstrong, in his book *Persuasive Advertising*, wrote that objectives should be designed to have a good return on the brand communication investment. The objective, in other words, is sales and profits (or the equivalent for nonprofits) and should not be directed at the competition (i.e., increasing market share). He believes that is a mistake many marketing and marcom professionals make in writing their objectives.[3]

Step 3: Select Target Markets Assess consumer needs and wants relative to the product, segment the market into groups that are likely to respond, and target specific audiences and uncover insights about their thoughts and behaviors.

Step 4: Differentiate and Position Position the brand relative to the competition, which entails finding the brand's most important distinguishing features of interest to customers and communicating these features so that customers understand the brand's benefits relative to competing brands.

Step 5: Develop marketing mix strategies Based on the positioning strategy in step 4, develop marketing mix strategies such as selecting product design and performance criteria, pricing approaches, distribution decisions, and marketing communication.

Step 6: Design and Execute Action Plans Implementing the marketing mix could include product testing, working with designers on IMC elements, buying media, negotiating distribution agreements, and putting pricing and promotional plans into practice.

⬤ **Principle**
SWOT analysis is the process of finding ways to address a brand's weaknesses and threats and leverage its strengths and opportunities.

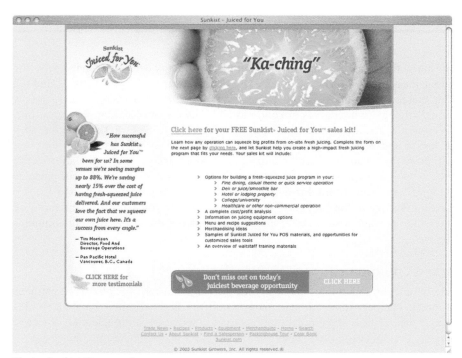

Photo: Sunkist Growers, Inc.

Sunkist's Business-to-Business "Ka-ching" ad targets members of the distribution channel and focuses on sales returns and an offer of a free sales kit.

"My SPAR": Letting Our Customers Lead

Daryl Bennewith, *Strategic Planning Director, TBWA Group, Durban, South Africa*

SPAR South Africa is one of the biggest chains of grocery stores in that country. Operating in a highly competitive environment, the brand must constantly evolve. From extensive research, we knew that SPAR continued to make consumers' life easier and more convenient and scored high in community involvement. However, were we becoming just another retail brand with the ever-present danger of becoming part of the clutter and just concerned with achieving targets and growing our bottom line?

So Where Could We Fight the Competition?

- Price?
- Quality?
- Freshness?
- Aspiration?
- Range?

In most of these areas, we did not have a competitive advantage and could not compete on purely rational aspects of shopping, and often consumers will perceive an attempt to do so as false. There is nothing unique about low prices! But to be in the game you obviously need to be price competitive.

Where Could We Have an Edge?

- Close connections with the customer
- Our business model and vision
- Service
- Convenience
- Employees' attitude
- Ownership
- Geographic locations

The problem is that retailers have in the past paid far too little attention to shoppers, but it also means there are tremendous opportunities to improve sales by understanding how to turn shoppers into customers. There must be no mistake; we have to capture the emotive brain before the thought process reaches the executive section.

How Do We Do That? We Had to Find Something That Made Us Unique

In SPAR's business model, every store is managed and run by the person who owns that store. It is not owned by some uncaring corporate entity (Figure 8.4). That means a closer connection to the customers and greater understanding of their needs.

This marketing analysis—and the marketing mix strategy derived from it—links the overall strategic business plan with specific marketing programs, including advertising and other IMC areas. For marcom managers, the most important part of the marketing plan is the discussion of the brand strategy, which gives direction to all brand communication programs. In addition, the *marketing mix strategy*, which includes decisions about the target market, brand position, product design and performance, pricing, and distribution as well as marketing communication, is important in planning brand campaigns. Product design and formulation decisions are sometimes responses to consumer trends, such as the increase in the number of packaged foods making high-fiber claims (think Fiber One with its expanded line of cereals and snack bars).

The SPAR story in the Matter of Practice feature lets you see inside the mind of a planner as he works through a series of strategic decisions involving positioning strategies for the SPAR brand.

The Brand Communication/IMC Plan

Brand communication planning operates with the same concern for objectives, strategies, and tactics found in business and marketing plans. It outlines all the communication activities needed to deliver on the business and marketing objectives in terms of communication objectives, strategies, tactics, timing, costs, and evaluation. Briefly, here are the marcom planner's goals:

- *Who?* Who are you trying to reach, and what insight do you have about how they currently think, feel, and act? How should they respond to your brand message?

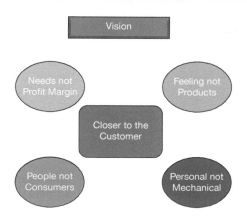

FIGURE 8.4
SPAR Planning Model

SPAR Planning Model

We need the magic that no other retail chain has. The magic that comes from each SPAR owner being an individual. The magic of SPAR being involved in the community. The magic of feeling at home when you walk in. We need the consumer to feel like SPAR is theirs.

As soon as you perceive something as being yours, your attitude toward that object changes. You now have a vested interest, you establish an emotional bond, and you develop a positive attitude. So could we instill those feelings in the SPAR brand?

"My SPAR" appeals directly to the emotional part of the brain. It will be our competitive positioning; we will have added the "feeling" part to the brain's brand-choice equation.

Our campaign started with a Facebook site (MySPAR) and print campaign where we appealed to people to tell us their unique stories of how SPAR made a difference in their lives. We chose some of the most endearing stories and converted them to television commercials using the actual people in the stories. It was a breakthrough in grocery advertising.

So what "My Spar" and its consumer stories did is turn the rational purchasing decision into an emotional one. It is a position far removed from the corporate face of our competitors.

It puts us one step ahead. And that's a great place to be.

Photo: Courtesy Daryl Bennewith, TBWA South Africa

"My Spar gave my little girl with muscular dystrophy the opportunity to shop with a 'baby trolley.' One of her first experiences of walking on her own."

Logo: Courtesy Daryl Bennewith

- **What?** What will you say to them? What directions from the consumer research are useful to the creative team?
- **Where?** How and where will you reach them? What directions from the consumer research are useful to the media team?

In general, a communication plan seeks to match the right audience to the right message and present the message in the right medium to reach that audience. If the marketing goal is to increase loyalty, for example, the brand communication plan would determine whether to use a frequency club, an advertising campaign, a sales promotion strategy, or all of the above. Such a plan typically includes a variety of marcom messages carried in different media and sometimes targeted to different audiences.

Earlier, we mentioned that there is a difference between a *strategy*, your plan to accomplish goals, and *tactics*, how you will execute and implement that plan. That's true of brand communication plans as well as marketing and business plans. In the discussion of message effects in Chapter 5, we introduced Armstrong's work on evidence-based principles and the four categories he used for strategies: information, influence, emotion, and exposure. His outline also included two other groups of tactics that are useful in making brand communication plans. He identified general tactics as focused on resistance, acceptance, message, and attention. In other words, tactics are often employed to lower resistance, create acceptance, deliver a message, or grab attention.[4]

Notice how these various levels of planning set up a cascade of goals and objectives. We said before that the marketing plan mirrors the corporate business plan and contains many of the

● **Principle**
A brand communication plan seeks to match the right audience to the right message and present the message in the right medium to reach that audience.

same components. What might be a more general goal at the business level, however, gets transformed into objectives at the marketing level because marketing has the task of designing the strategies that will deliver the business-level goal. The same thing happens between marketing and brand communication. The strategic decisions and communication objectives are designed to implement the marketing strategies.

As illustrated in Figure 8.1, the business and marketing plans provide direction to the brand communication (IMC) plan as well as to specific plans for specialist areas, such as advertising and other areas of marketing communication. This section provides a brief overview of brand communication plans. We will discuss IMC campaign plans in more detail in Chapter 16.

Plans for Marketing Communication Functions

Advertising, public relations, sales promotion, and other marcom areas all operate with their own plans, activities, and deadlines, drawn from the brand communication/IMC plan discussed above. They begin with the same strategic decisions found in a marketing or brand communication (IMC) plan, such as a communication situation analysis, SWOTs leading to the identification of a key (communication) problem, communication objectives, identification of a target audience, communication-based consumer insights, and analysis of the communication dimensions of the brand position.

The tactics section of these plans identifies specific activities that will be undertaken, such as a series of ads in key media scheduled at critical purchase times (e.g., back-to-school time and holidays). Three key elements—audience insight leading to a Big Idea, message strategy, and media strategy—are at the heart of communication planning and make up the key sections in these functional area plans.

8.2 Identify the key strategic decisions and explain why they are central to brand communication planning.

Key Strategic Decisions

Key strategic decisions that guide marcom plans include the analysis and statement of communication objectives, the target audience, brand position, and consumer insights. We'll also discuss brand communication strategy, which refers to the overall direction of the campaign—its focus and approach.

The Communication Objectives

After planners have examined the external and internal environments and defined the critical areas that need to be addressed, they can develop specific communication objectives to be accomplished during a specified time period. These objectives are formal statements of the goals of the advertising or other marketing communication. They outline what the message is designed to achieve in the long term and how it will be measured.

Remember from Chapter 5 the six categories in the Facets Model of Effects: perception, emotion, cognition, persuasion, association, and behavior. These effects can be used to identify the most common consumer-focused objectives. For example, here are some sample objectives for each category as well as sample ads and campaigns.

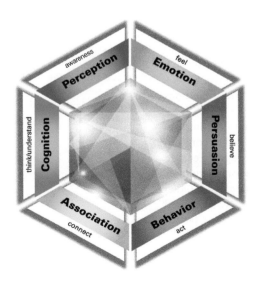

- *Perception Objectives* Grab attention; create awareness; stimulate interest; stimulate recognition of the brand or the message; create brand reminder.

  Examples: "1984" ad that launched the Apple Macintosh; Wendy's "BBQ 4 'Merica" campaign.

- *Emotion/Affective Objectives* Touch emotions; cue the psychological appeal; create brand or message liking; stimulate brand loyalty; stimulate desire.

  Examples: McDonald's "I'm Lovin' It" campaign; the "My SPAR" campaign.

- *Cognition Objectives* Deliver information; aid in understanding features, benefits, and brand differences; explain how to do or use something; counterargue; establish brand identity or cue the brand position; stimulate recall of the brand message; stimulate brand loyalty.

   Examples: The antismoking "Unsweetened Truth" campaign; Lean Cuisine's #WeighThis campaign.

- *Association Objectives* Establish or cue the brand personality or image; create links to symbols and associations; connect to positive brand experiences.

   Example: Old Spice's "What It Takes to Be a Man" campaign; Chick-fil-A's cows.

- *Persuasion Objectives* Stimulate opinion or attitude formation; change or reinforce opinion or attitude; present argument and reasons; counterargue; create conviction or belief; stimulate brand preference or intent to try or buy; reward positive or desired response; stimulate brand loyalty; create buzz or word of mouth; energize opinion leaders; create advocacy and referrals.

   Examples: The "Unsweetened Truth" campaign; Dove's "Campaign for Real Beauty."

- *Behavior Objectives* Stimulate trial, sample, or purchase; generate other types of response (coupon use, attendance, test drive, visit store or dealer, volunteering, sign up, call in, visit website, click, attend, participate); create word-of-mouth buzz; create advocacy and referrals.

   Examples: The Red Cross "Give blood. Give life" campaign; Buick's "24 Hours of Happiness Test Drive" campaign.

THE INSIDE STORY

Leadership in Management

Rachel Gallen, *Division Manager Beverage Distributors/E. & J. Gallo Denver, Colorado*

The complexity of management can be tricky to truly understand. I constantly get asked, "If you are not in the market selling each day, what exactly do you do?" Managing a marketing communication team is similar to coaching a sports team. First and foremost, recruiting and retaining players, also known as talent management, is what makes the organization run. Once you have the right team in place, you have to keep all your uniquely different players both inspired and motivated to beat the competition. The market is our playing field; competitive brands are our opponents. A company culture can be explained by the camaraderie and bond that comes with being part of a competitive team.

Leadership has been my strength since I was in elementary school. Whether it was in the classroom or on the sports field, getting a group to work together toward a common goal has been something that comes naturally to me. Figuring out how to develop each person who reports to me is a new challenge. On paper, my job is to ensure that we hit our sales and profit goals. But each day, that translates to figuring out what drives our team to beat the competition. Every manager has a style. I prefer to lead by example.

My team is in the middle of a launch of a new brand in a competitive category. The number one brand in this category is 30 times larger than our annual launch quota. Before the brand's launch meeting, I went into a few challenging accounts and made the presentation. The marketing team gives us sales tools and market data to be successful. However, real examples of objections, challenges, and successes from our market are what resonate the most with my team. After the marketing team presented, I walked through all the objections that I had encountered and how I overcame them. I summarized key lessons from the field to help prepare them for their presentations. My challenge to my team is to steal share. If the competition is doing it, we need to as well or better. The only way to be number one is to act like number one. As a team, we make the impossible seem possible.

The only way to win is to have everyone engaged toward our goals. Managing a team is incredibly rewarding. Like any sports team, we have some days where we play our A game, and then we have days that we learn how to be better for the future. If you are a leader, are results oriented, and have a confident personal presence, a career in sales and sales management could be a good fit for you. Good luck!

Gallen is a 2009 graduate of the University of Colorado. She was nominated to be featured here by Professor Bill Weintraub.

In addition, because managers are increasingly accountable for their IMC budgets, it is important that objectives be stated in quantitative terms whenever possible (e.g., increase brand awareness from 20 to 30 percent in six months). This practice allows a campaign's effectiveness to be determined and documented.

The Target Audience

As we discussed in Chapter 7, segmenting and targeting are important because a marketing communication strategy is based on accurately targeting an audience that will be responsive to a particular type of message, one that will deliver the objectives. Market segments are identified in marketing plans, but targeting audiences happens in brand communication plans.

The decision about the target audience (or audiences) is made possible because of a deep knowledge of consumers. In particular, this research-based knowledge identifies what makes specific groups of consumers different from people in other groups. These characteristics also identify how consumers are similar to others in ways that characterize a specific type of viewpoint or lifestyle. A peer-group strategy at the University of Florida addresses the problem of students' driving drunk, which is explained in the Inside Story on page 230.

Diversity and Empathy   There is more to targeting than just identifying and profiling a possible audience. How does the target audience relate to the brand, and how do marketing communicators relate to the target audience? Multicultural communication, in particular, demands an appreciation of diversity as well as the empathy that results from such an appreciation. To achieve that goal, agencies are adding multicultural specialists and are creating or buying firms that specialize in multicultural marketing.[5] These moves are in response to major brands demanding creative that better connects with their primary customers. For example, General Mills recently made headlines by saying it wanted the creative departments of its agency partners to be 50 percent women and 20 percent minorities.[6]

Professor Peggy Kreshel defines *diversity* as "the acknowledgment and inclusion of a wide variety of people with differing characteristics, attributes, beliefs, values, and experiences." That is the heart of the issue raised in *Madison Avenue and the Color Line* by historian Jason Chambers.

In advertising, diversity tends to be discussed primarily in terms of *representations of gender*, *race*, and *ethnicity in advertising content*, although, as Kreshel pointed out, diversity goes beyond the images used in ads:

> Who creates the ads we see? The industry's troubled, largely unsuccessful efforts to create a racially and ethnically diverse workplace tell part of the story. Minority-owned advertising agencies provide opportunities for diversity but are frequently viewed as being capable of speaking only to minority audiences. Women comprise the majority of the advertising workforce, yet an *Adweek* study a few years ago found only four female creative directors in the top 33 advertising agencies. We can only guess at the impact, knowing that creative directors are chiefly responsible for an agency's output.
>
> Content reflects those who create it and their perceptions of audiences. Advertisers' persistent emphasis on 18- to 34-year-olds, a group they view to be impressionable trendsetters who haven't yet formed brand loyalties, has occurred largely to the exclusion of other demographic groups. This preoccupation shapes our business (which constructs itself as youthful, rebellious, and cutting edge), media (where reality programming, the "entertainmentization" of news, and technological wizardry target 18- to 34-year-olds), and culture (reinforcing our celebration of the young, beautiful, and white).
>
> Similarly, marketers routinely define the Hispanic market primarily as "Spanish speaking." The richness and diversity of the many cultures that comprise that group—from Puerto Rico, to Mexico, to Central and South America—have been lost in the desire to construct a homogeneous market large enough to be economically viable. It is only recently that a conversation about the complexity of the Latino market—a complexity that goes beyond merely language or ethnic predilections—has begun to appear in the trade press.[7]

In recent years, major media firms have been sued and top agency executives have been fired for mishandling the gender equality issue.[8]

In recognition of the importance of this diversity issue, the American Advertising Federation (AAF) sponsors multicultural programs such as the Most Promising Minority Students and the AAF Mosaic Awards. The leader of those programs, Constance Cannon Frazier, is on this book's Advisory Board, and the work of some of the Most Promising Minority Students is featured in this book.

Brand Identity Strategy

A brand identity must be distinctive. In other words, it represents only one particular product within a category, and it needs to be recognizable and, therefore, memorable. Recognizing the brand means that the consumer knows the brand's identification markers—name, logo, colors, typeface, design, and slogan—and can connect those marks with a past brand experience or message.

To better understand how a brand can become an integrated perception, we propose an outline of the communication dimensions of branding using the same six effects we presented in the Facets Model of Effects in Chapter 5 and explain them in terms of different aspects of brand identity:

Advertiser's Brand Objective	*Consumer's Response*
Create brand identity	See/hear
Cue brand personality, liking	Feel
Cue brand position, leadership	Think/understand
Cue brand image	Connect
Create brand promise, preference	Believe
Inspire brand loyalty	Act/do

- **Brand Personality and Liking** Brand personality—the idea that a brand takes on familiar human characteristics, such as loving (Hallmark, Kodak), competent (IBM), trustworthy (Volvo, Michelin), or sophisticated (Mercedes, Hermes, Rolex)—contributes an affective dimension to the meaning of a brand. Green Giant, for example, built its franchise on the personality of the friendly giant who watches over his valley and makes sure that Green Giant vegetables are fresh, tasty, nutritious, and appealing to kids. Perceived warmth and competence are keys to building customer loyalty.[9] The point is to profile the brand as if it were a person, someone the target likes or respects, someone like Tom Hanks or Pink, for example.

- **Brand Position and Leadership** What does the brand stand for? As Jack Trout explained, "You have to stand for something," and it has to be something that matters to consumers.[10] Kodak is a classic example of a brand with a soul, one deeply embedded in personal pictures and memories. Hallmark's soul is found in the expression of sentiment. Starbucks created the high-end coffeehouse, and eBay owns the world of online auctions. Brand essence is also apparent when a brand dominates or defines its category. Category leadership often comes from being the first brand in the market, and with that comes an ownership position. ESPN, for example, owns sports information, and Silk is *the* soymilk drink. We'll talk more about positioning strategies in the section that follows.

- **Brand Image** Understanding brand meaning involves understanding the symbolism and associations that create a brand image, the mental impression that consumers construct for a product. The richness of the brand image determines the quality of the relationship and the strength of the associations and emotional connections that link a customer to a brand. Advertising researchers call this brand linkage.

- **Brand Promise and Brand Preference** A brand is sometimes defined as a promise because it establishes an expectation based on familiarity, consistency, and predictability. Believing the brand promise leads to brand preference and intention to buy. That's what has driven

Photo: Angela Weiss/Stringer/Getty Images

The singer-songwriter Pink brings high credibility to her spokesperson role, which helps generate awareness and positive buzz about Covergirl's products and programs.

Mistake #1: Drinking and Driving Drunk

Lisa Yansura, *Marketing Coordinator, Gragg Advertising, Kansas City Missouri, Formerly Adwerks Director, University of Florida*

Nightlife Navigators, a student-run organization at the University of Florida (UF), is leading the effort to end drunk driving by educating students about safe and affordable late-night transportation options in Gainesville, Florida. Nightlife Navigators is sponsored by the University of Florida's Student Government.

Nightlife Navigators approached Adwerks and asked us to help them launch their new website, www.nightlifenavigators.com. The website would include information on local bus routes, taxis, discussion boards, alcohol education, and other services for students. A graphic designer for Student Government created the logo, which looks like a neon bar sign.

On the launch date, Student Government and Nightlife Navigators would be on the UF campus giving out free food and distributing flyers, beverage koozies, and bottle opener key chains. SG representatives would be available to speak with students about the site and transportation options in Gainesville. To create buzz for the event, we ran full-page "Coming Soon" ads in local newspapers. Press releases were also issued to news outlets.

On the day of the event, hundreds of students received information about Nightlife Navigators. Additionally, the two largest newspapers in Gainesville, the *Independent Florida Alligator* and the *Gainesville Sun*, ran front-page stories regarding the event.

After the site launch, Adwerks created ads that would be placed in more than 50 restroom ad spaces in local bars and restaurants. Placement in these restaurants and bars was intended to reach students while they were out drinking and in need of a ride home.

The ads featured catchy headlines with various mistakes people tend to make when they're intoxicated, including performing karaoke, calling the wrong girl, going home with someone from the opposing team, and ordering shots for the entire bar. The subhead, found under the humorous images, reads, "At least you didn't drive"—the point being that we all do regrettable things when we drink, but one of the mistakes does not have to be drinking and driving.

Rather than using scare tactics or take a more serious approach as many anti–drunk driving campaigns do, Adwerks decided to take a more humorous approach that students can relate to instead of feeling like they're being lectured to.

Contributors to this campaign included Kelly Jack, who created the logo and the Adwerks team: account director Kaely Coon, senior account executives Lisa Yansura and Monica Moreno, art directors Larry Rosalez and Klara Cu, and junior account executives Monica Jones and Danielle Dennis.

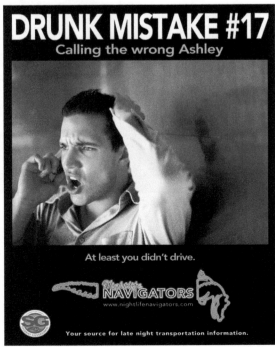

Photo: Adwerks

Photo: Adwerks

McDonald's to its position as a worldwide leader in the fast-food category. You know what to expect when you walk into a McDonald's anywhere in the world: quality fast food at a reasonable price.

- **Brand Loyalty** A personal experience with a brand can develop into a brand relationship, which is a connection over time that results in customers preferring the brand and buying it over and over. People have unique relationships with the brands they buy and use regularly, and that is what makes them brand loyal. The company's attitude toward its customers is another factor in loyalty.

To put it all together, a brand perception is created from different fragments of information, feelings, and personal experiences with a brand. You could say that a brand is an *integrated perception*;[11] in other words, all these different aspects of brand communication work together to create brand meaning. In the best of all worlds, these meanings would be consistent from one customer to another, but because of the vagaries of personal experience, different people may have different impressions of a brand.

Emotional branding is one way to anchor a brand perception. As we have said, emotion is a powerful tool in marketing communication, and brand liking leads to trust and loyalty. Branding expert John Williams explained, "Research shows that reason and emotions differ in that reason generates conclusions but not necessarily actions, while emotions more frequently lead to actions."[12] Brand liking is a powerful differentiator. The challenge to advertisers is to manage their communication efforts so the fragments fit together to form a coherent and integrated brand impression.

> ● **Principle**
> A brand is an integrated perception that includes fragments of information, feelings, and personal experience, all of which come together to give the brand meaning.

Photo: The Advertising Archives/Alamy Stock Photo

CLASSIC

A good example of creating a unique position in the soft drink market and a brand meaning that connects with its audience is the classic and long-running "UN-COLA" campaign used by 7UP.

Brand Positioning Strategy

We mentioned brand positioning in the previous list, but let's look at it in more depth. A **position** is how consumers define the product or brand relative to its competitors. A classic example of positioning is the 7Up campaign that used the term "UnCola" as a means of competing with category leaders Coke and Pepsi.

Planners may find themselves engaged in a new product launch, which allows them to develop a positioning strategy from scratch, but in most cases, they are dealing with a brand that has been on the market for some time. The questions then change. Is the current position working? Is it clear and focused, or does it need to be polished, clarified, or adjusted?

A position is based on two things. First, it is based on a particular feature or attribute; for example, Coke Zero is low calorie but tastes like regular Coke. The feature also can be

> ● **Principle**
> The goal of positioning is to locate a product in the consumer's mind that highlights its most valuable features and advantages relative to its competition.

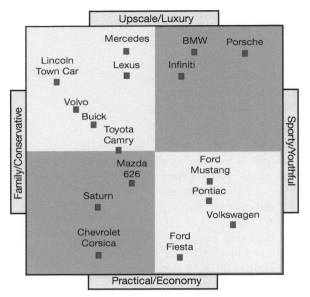

FIGURE 8.5
Perceptual Map
Perceptual maps illustrate the positions occupied by competitors relative to factors important to customers. These positions are determined by research into the perceptions of the target market.

🔴 **Principle**

Positioning identifies the features that make a brand different from its competitors and relevant to consumers.

Teaches Career Skills

High

Low ——————————————— **Elite** High

Low

FIGURE 8.6
US Armed Forces Positioning Map
Try this exercise. Review the three military ads on the next page. Using the dimensions provided on this blank perceptual map, where would you place each of the four branches of the US Armed Forces based on their advertising and your knowledge of them? What new messages could each branch create to improve its positioning in the minds of males age 17 to 24?

psychological, such as heritage (Hallmark: quality—"When you care enough to send the very best")[13] or leadership (regular Coke: "It's the real thing.").[14] Second, that feature must be important to the consumer.

A position also is based on some notion of comparison. Is the brand more expensive or less; is it a status product or a symbol of frugality; is it sporty, functional, safe, or risky? Walmart's position, for example, is encompassed in its slogan, "Always Low Prices." Positioning, then, is about locking the brand in consumers' minds based on some quality relevant to them where the brand stands out.

There's a reason we talk about "locating" a brand position. Many campaigns are designed to establish the brand's position by giving the right set of cues about these decision factors to help place the brand in the consumer's mind relative to the competition. If a position is a point in a consumer's mind, planners can map that; in fact, the way planners compare positions is by using a technique called a **perceptual map** that plots all the competitors on a matrix based on the two most important consumer decision factors. Perceptual mapping is a simple yet powerful tool for strategic thinking that combines brand, customer, and competitive factors. Figure 8.5 illustrates how positions can be mapped for automobiles.

The various branches of the US military recruit from the same primary customer base, mostly male 17- to 24-year-olds. Compare the positioning strategies of the Army, Navy, Air Force, and Marines as they represent themselves in their ads and consider their location on the perceptual map in Figure 8.6.

The US Armed Forces (Air Force, Army, Marines, Navy) conduct research with their target audience each year to learn what young men age 17-24 are most looking to gain from their work, and what aspects of service in the US military have the strongest appeal to them. They have discovered that "learning technical skills" that the recruits will be able to use after their time in the military is very important, and that "being part of something elite that they could be proud of" is also an important consideration.[15] Try the exercise featured in Figure 8.6.

Product Features and Attributes An initial step in crafting a position is to identify the **features** of the brand as well as those of the competition to determine where the brand has an advantage over its competitors. A marketer carefully evaluates the product's tangible features (e.g., size, color, design, price, and ease of use) and other intangible attributes (e.g., quality, status, value, fashion, and safety) to identify the dimensions of the product that are relevant to its customers and that make it different from its competitors.

An interesting twist on features developed when electric hybrid cars, such as General Motor's Volt, were introduced to the market. The standard miles-per-gallon (mpg) estimate of fuel efficiency was turned upside down with projections of 230 mpg for Volt and 367 mpg for Nissan's Leaf. Of course, these cars use very little gas as long as they are running on their batteries; gas is used only when the charge runs out. If you only use the car to run around town, theoretically you could get unlimited gas mileage.[16] So does this changing standard change consumer decision making as well as the marketing strategies of automakers?

Differentiation and Competitive Advantage Most markets involve a high level of competition. How does a company compete in a crowded market? It uses **product differentiation**, a strategy designed

Photo sources (top to bottom): U.S. Navy; Marine Corps Trademark Licensing Office; U.S. Air Force

In these three ads for the Navy, Marines and Air Force, can you perceive a difference in their positioning strategies? How do they communicate their differences in the style, copy, and graphics? Which do you think would be most effective recruiting volunteers from your generation? Why do you think that is so?

to focus attention on product differences that are important to consumers and that distinguish the company's product from that of its competitors. We refer to products that really are the same (examples include milk, unleaded gas, and over-the-counter drugs) as undifferentiated or **parity products**. For these products, marketers often promote intangible, or psychological, differences, particularly through branding.

The creation of a unique brand image for a product (think Swatch) is the most obvious way to differentiate one product from another. Internet-based Mozilla and Craigslist are small companies but big brands that are strong because they have the support of dedicated users. This strong customer-brand relationship reflects a leadership position—a brand that has defined or created its category. But it's not just hot Internet companies that have achieved this type of leadership. McIlhenny's Tabasco Sauce, which was launched in 1868, created and still dominates the hot sauce category.

A technique called **feature analysis** involves assessing a brand's features relative to competing products' features to identify where a brand has an advantage. Feature analysis is often accompanied by another tool, the **Fishbein multiattribute model**, which attempts to numerically estimate consumer preference based on their perception of features.[17] To use this tool, first identify the product category where your product competes (e.g., luggage, cars, cell phones). Then, make a chart of your brand and the competing products, identifying the relevant features important to your customers, as the following table illustrates. Based on opinion research with the target market, provide the rating that customers give to each brand on each feature (on a scale of: 1 = weak to 5 = strong) and also indicate how important each feature is to your customers (spreading 100 points between the features, indicating relative importance). In sum, this model considers how much your customers care about various features and how the various brands compare on these features.

Fishbein Multiattribute Model

Feature	*Importance to Customers* (sum = 100)	Brand Ratings (scale of 1 to 5)			
		Yours	*X*	*Y*	*Z*
Price	10	5	3	1	1
Quality	30	3	5	3	4
Style	20	4	2	5	2
Availability	10	4	4	2	1
Durability	30	3	4	4	5

Finally, for each brand, multiply each importance score by its rating, and add these multiples together to get a "weighted sum" for each brand. For example, your brand's total score would be calculated as $(10 \times 5) + (30 \times 3) + (20 \times 4) + (10 \times 4) + (30 \times 3) = 350$. In the same way, brand X = 380, brand Y = 340, and brand Z = 330. The model would predict preference for brand X because it received the highest overall total.

Using the two factors of importance and ratings, **competitive advantage** is found where (1) the product has a highly rated feature (2) in an area that is important to the target and (3) where the competition is weaker. Your brand in the preceding table would compete well on both price and style against X, on price and availability against competitor Y, and on price, style, and availability against competitor Z. Competitor X seems the most vulnerable on two features, price and style, but consumers don't rate these features to be as important as quality and durability, for which Brand X is rated highly.

According to the Fishbein multiattribute model, there are four possible strategies you might use to help your brand better compete in this marketplace. Let's assume the category in the above example is luggage.

1. **Improve your rating on a key feature.** You could improve customer perceptions of your brand's quality or durability (because those are the most important features to these luggage customers).
2. **Change the relative importance of a feature.** You may decide to develop a campaign that emphasizes the importance of price when buying luggage (because your brand is superior

Photo: shopics/Alamy Stock Photo

Listerine's Cool Mint product represents an effort to improve the brand's consumer ratings on an important product attribute—in this case, how the product tastes.

on that feature) by emphasizing the significant savings your brand offers that could help make the customer's overall trip more enjoyable.

3. **Demonstrate your advantage over a competitor on a key attribute.** Show a head-to-head comparison of your product versus a competitor. You might show that your brand actually outperforms brand X on the quality or durability feature and therefore customers should adjust their ratings of both brands. *Important*: If you name or show a competitor and make claims of superiority, you must be able to back up these claims with a study conducted by an outside, independent, and objective product testing service.

4. **Add an attractive new feature to your brand that competitors don't offer.** You might offer a free lifetime warranty on your luggage or include a tracking device on each bag as a standard feature. Choose a new feature that customers truly care about because as they include it in their decision process, you will receive a good rating, while your competitors will receive a "0" rating on that attribute.

An example of product turnaround built on knowledge of competitive advantages, disadvantages, and consumer performance is the launch of Cool Mint Listerine. Listerine's main competitor, Scope mouthwash, greatly outperformed Listerine on the attribute of taste, which was the number one feature preferred by consumers. To better compete with Scope, Listerine launched the Cool Mint product (with a new color similar to Scope's) to improve its taste perceptions.

Locating the Brand Position   Let's return now to the concept of a position to see how it is created. In addition to specific product attributes, a number of factors can be used to locate a position for a brand in consumers' minds, including the following:

- *Superiority Position* Jack Trout suggests that positioning is always easy if something is faster, fancier, safer, or newer.
- *Preemptive Position* Being first in the category often creates category leadership and dominance.
- *Value Position* Walmart's "Always Low Prices" is the epitome of offering good value for the money. Hyundai rode that position through the economic downturn and picked up market share faster than its competitors, passing both Honda and Ford to become the fourth-largest automaker in the world.[18]

● **Principle**
Strong brands are known for one thing. The test is, "What do you think of when you mention the brand's name?"

- *Psychological Position* Often brands are designed around nonproduct differences. For psychological positions, consider these examples: Volvo owns the safety position, Coke owns a position of authenticity for colas ("It's the real thing"), and Hallmark owns a quality position ("When you care enough to send the very best").
- *Benefit Position* How does the product help the consumer?
- *Usage Position* How, where, and when is the product used and who is using it?
- *Competitor's Strategy* How can the product go head-to-head with or move completely away from the competition?
- *Category Factors* Is the competition coming from outside the category, and, if so, how does the brand compare to these other categories, and how does that change the analysis of strengths and weaknesses?

As we've mentioned, the differences have to be distinctive to the brand as well as important to the consumer. The point is that strong brands become well known for one thing. When you think of Google or eBay, what's the first thing that comes to mind? (Google = search engine; eBay = online auctions.)

James Stengel, former global marketing chief at Procter & Gamble, has developed a new positioning approach that he calls "purpose-based marketing." He points to the company's Pampers brand, which moved from just keeping babies' bottoms dry to a higher purpose: helping moms nurture healthy, happy babies. The company created new programs offering parenting advice and conducted research on infant-related problems, such as sleeping, that led to product redesigns.[19]

Repositioning   Positions are difficult to establish and are created over time. Once established, they are difficult to change, as Kodak discovered with its ownership of the film category when the market moved to digital pictures. Category dominance is important, as Al Ries, one of the founders of the positioning concept, argues, but sometimes the category changes, and the brand has to change as well or get left behind. Al and Laura Ries recommend the difficult challenge of **repositioning** when the market changes or new targeting opportunities arise.

A campaign by Coke Zero to change its brand perception illustrates how positions define products in their users' minds. How many guys will admit that they are on a diet and drink Coke Zero? But Coke knows that 18- to 34-year-old males are a big cola-drinking market, and most of them preferred the taste of regular sugary sodas. Coca-Cola wanted to grow its market by convincing these men that Coke Zero tastes like Coke. Its agency, Crispin Porter + Bogusky, overcame the negative perception of a diet drink with an edgy campaign that used self-deprecating humor. The Big Idea was that Coke's legal department wanted to sue Coke Zero for taste infringement. The unconventional message not only changed guys' perception of Coke Zero's taste but also won a Silver Effie Award for its effectiveness.

We mentioned Kodak earlier, which is a fascinating study in positioning and repositioning, Kodak has always stood for pictures and over the years has owned the moment of capturing an image with a photo: "the Kodak moment." But Kodak also stands for film (think yellow box), and that was the reason for its marketplace problems as the camera industry moved to digital formats. Kodak's agency, Ogilvy, developed a repositioning strategy to adapt Kodak's position from "the Moment" to "the gallery," a place where pictures are kept.

Repositioning, in the view of the Rieses, can work only if the new position is related to the brand's core concept. They worried about Kodak's move and wondered if the link between the Kodak brand and film is too strong to stretch to digital products. In fact, the gallery position didn't work, and the changing environment, as well as public perceptions, was too problematic to overcome.

The principle in repositioning is to move ahead while at the same time retaining the brand essence. For an effective example, Ries and Ries point to IBM as a company that repositioned itself from a computer manufacturer to a provider of services. Even though the market for mainframe computers has been declining, they observe that the connection with IBM's brand essence is still there in IBM's new position as a global computer service company. An example comes from China, where IBM is marketing an urban-planning tool called Smart City that connects public services and infrastructure projects through information technology. IBM sees China, with its huge public sector and infrastructure projects, as a big market for its services.

The role of brand communication in a repositioning strategy is to relate the product's position to the target market's life experience and associations. A classic example of an effective repositioning campaign that retains the brand essence as it carves out a new location in consumers' minds is 7-Up, which is described in the Matter of Principle feature on the next page.

Consumer Insight and Account Planning

The concept of consumer insight, which we introduced in Chapter 7, is the last of our key strategic decisions. It may also be the hardest decision that planners make because it calls for solid research and thoughtful analyses that lead to, in many cases, unexpected conclusions about the direction the brand communication should take.

When we say **consumer insight**, what are we talking about? Larry Kelley and Donald Jugenheimer define and describe this special kind of insight as follows:

- "Understanding 'why' we behave the way we do"
- "Seeing and understanding clearly the inner nature of things"[20]

How, exactly, do we do that? What special skills are required for this type of seeing and understanding? Again, from Kelley and Jugenheimer:

- "Looking at things differently and seeing things intuitively"
- "Acute observation, deduction, penetration, and discernment"
- "Looking at relationships in a new and unique way"[21]

As Fallon and Senn outlined in one of their principles at the beginning of this chapter, the key to effective brand communication is finding a central emotional truth about a customer's relationship with a brand. Kelley and Jugenheimer, in their book on account planning, explained, "A true insight into consumer behavior will connect with the consumer at an emotional level." It will elicit a response, such as "that is exactly how I feel."[22]

As Regina Lewis[23] noted, consumer insights and the account planning function responsible for identifying them have transformed marketing research as well as communication planning. She calls for "deep insight into consumer minds and hearts." As we stressed in Chapter 4, it's not just about how people think. In Lewis's view, it's about consumer minds and hearts—their mental and emotional mind-sets.

When the Eight O'Clock coffee brand planners, for example, wanted to know more about Eight O'Clock's audience to better target their message, they used videotaped observational research to identify key insights into how people relate to coffee. Rather than a rosy sunrise, the tapes showed that it was a struggle to get moving. "In real life," the strategic planner concluded, "people stumble around, trying to get kids out of bed. Coffee is the fuel that gets them dressed, fed, and out the door." On other tapes, it also showed that coffee was the reward for mom after the kids are out the door. "I have my cup of coffee when the kids leave," one mom observed. "It's my first moment to take a breather. And it gives me energy."[24] Do you notice how many emotional truths emerged from this analysis?

Account Planning

Account planning analyzes the research to uncover consumer insights. Insight is what happens when the lightbulb goes off and the planner sees something in a new way. As in the Eight O'Clock coffee example, the planners struck gold by finding out that coffee is the fuel that gets adults, particularly moms, through the morning rush—and it's also the reward for surviving that busy routine. From this insight come clues about how and when to reach the target audience and what to say to her.

Account planning is the research and analysis process used to gain knowledge of the consumer that is expressed as a key consumer insight about how people relate to a brand or product. An **account planner**, then, is a person in an agency who uses a disciplined system to research a brand and its customer relationships to devise advertising (and other marketing communication) message strategies that are effective in addressing consumer needs and wants. Account planning agencies are based in research but focus on deriving meanings about consumers. Hall &

8.3 Demonstrate the purpose and role of account planning and how it is used in advertising and IMC.

The 7-Up Uncola Story: A Classic in Repositioning

Bill Barre, *Department of Journalism, Central Michigan University*

How do you turn what was originally a medicinal product (intended to cure hangovers) and then a mixer with whisky into a soft drink without changing anything about the product or its packaging?

If you said "magic," you'd be correct. But it's not the kind of magic you might think. This is branding magic. It's called positioning. And it created magical results for 7-Up in 1967, when the company repositioned the brand as the Uncola.

Preceding 1967, during the first 37 years that 7-Up was marketed, consumers didn't think of 7-Up as a soft drink, just as we don't think of club soda and tonic water as soft drinks. In 1967, a soft drink was a cola, and a cola was a soft drink.

Four people were in the room when the term "uncola" was first uttered. Three of them are deceased—Orville Roesch, 7-Up's ad manager; Bill Ross, creative director at JWT; and Bob Taylor, senior art director at JWT. Charlie Martell was the fourth person and just a young writer at JWT at the time of the meeting.

"I remember the meeting to this day," recalled Martell. "We realized that we had to be a lot more specific if we hoped to change people's minds about 7-Up. We had to find a way to pick up that green bottle (7-Up), pick it up mentally in consumers' minds, and move it over to here, where Coke and Pepsi were. And until we did that, anything we did that smacked of soft-drink advertising was going to be rejected by consumers."

The objective was clear, yet getting there proved to be completely perplexing. "They had to find a way to attach the word *cola* to 7-Up. Nobody had ever done that before. This was before the word *positioning* was even used in advertising and marketing," said John Furr, a management supervisor at JWT at the time.

Martell remembered that the strategy meeting started as it always started for 7-Up. "We got to talking about how to get somebody to move this green bottle from here to there. And I think Orville said something like we had to associate ourselves with the colas. And Bill Ross started talking about, 'Well, how about, maybe, we call ourselves the non-cola.' And Orville nodded. Thought that sounded good. And I chimed in with 'Maybe we could call it the uncola.' And everyone nodded and said that was an interesting thought. Didn't blow anybody away at that point. They filed it away in their collective consciousness. Few days later, came back and said, 'Maybe we just got something here.' Uncola—it did everything we had been wanting to do. In one word, it did it all. It positioned 7-Up as a cola, yet not a cola. We said, 'Hey . . . let's make some advertising.'"

Today, the 7-Up Uncola campaign is regarded as perhaps the classic example of brand repositioning. It's a classic example of how the right brand positioning can lead to marketing magic.

Partners, for example, has noted that with the new social media, the walls between private life and public life have been breached. (Check the company out at www.hall-and-partners.com.)

In case you're interested in account planning as a career, here is an actual job description for a vice president for global consumer insights for a major apparel company:

The role of the VP, Global Consumer Insights, is to create competitive advantage by delivering fact-based consumer/customer understanding and insights that facilitate speed and accuracy of strategic and tactical decision making across all critical parts of the organization—in short, turning data into Insights, and then into Action. The planner will accomplish this by placing consumers first, integrating their "voices" into the planning process, and creating sustaining value at the corporate and brand levels.

As the job description suggests, the account planning function develops the marketing communication strategy with other members of the client and agency team and guides its implementation in the creative work and media planning. Account planners don't design the creative strategy for a brand message because that is usually a team process with the participation of the creative people. Rather, the planner evaluates consumers' relationships with the brand to determine the kind of message to which they might respond. Ultimately, the objective is to help the creative team come up with a better idea, making their creative process easier and faster. Susan Mendelsohn, a leader in the US account planning industry and a member of this book's Advisory Board, explained the account planner's task as follows:[25]

1. Understand the meaning of the brand.
2. Understand the target audience's relationship to the brand.
3. Articulate communication strategies.
4. Prepare creative briefs based on an understanding of the consumer and brand.
5. Evaluate the effectiveness of the communication in terms of how the target reacts to it (so that planners can keep learning more about consumers and brand communication).

The Consumer Insight Process

Through the process of strategic and critical thinking, the planner interprets consumer research to find a key consumer insight that uncovers the relevance factor, the reason consumers care about a brand. Consumer insights reveal the inner nature of consumers' thinking, including such things as mind-sets, moods, motivations, desires, aspirations, and motives that trigger their attitudes and actions. One of this chapter's Inside Story features explained how a university student ad group sorted out significant consumer insights into drunk driving.

Research: Brand Intelligence   Insight begins with research. The objective is to puzzle out a key insight that will help move the target audience to respond to the message. **Insight research**, in other words, is basically about asking and listening and then asking more questions to probe deeper into thoughts, opinions, attitudes, desires, and motivations.

Planners use a wide variety of research tools to arrive at insights that lead to an intelligent strategic decision. In a sense, they are social anthropologists who are in touch with cultural and social trends and understand how these trends take on relevance in people's lives. To do that, the account planner is an *integrator* (who brings all the information together) and a *synthesizer* (who expresses what it all means in one startlingly simple statement).

Sally Reinman, worldwide market planner at Saatchi & Saatchi, wrote for this book in an earlier edition that research is more than numbers. She explained that research processes used to find insights are more varied than ever before. "To find these commonalities, I work with experts to learn the cultural meaning of codes and symbols that people use to communicate. The experts I work with include cultural and cognitive anthropologists, psychologists, interior decorators, and Indian storytellers." Her point was that anyone and any methodology that "can help me understand consumers and the consumer decision-making process is fair game."

Insights: The Fuel of Big Ideas   Advertising is sometimes thought to be *an idea* factory, but account planners look at advertising as *an insight factory*. As Mendelsohn says, "Behind every famously great idea, there is a perhaps less flashy, but immensely powerful insight."[26] Insights are the fuel that fires the ideas. Kelley and Jugenheimer describe this value as a "quality-of-life insight." They explain that it "identifies the intersection of the brand's benefit and the quality of life it provides to the consumer."[27]

Finding the "a-ha" in a stack of research reports, data, and transcripts, which is referred to as **insight mining**, is the greatest challenge for an account planner. The Account Planning Group association describes this process on its website (www.apg.org.uk) as "peering into nooks and

● **Principle**
The account manager is seen as the voice of the client, and the account planner is seen as the voice of the consumer.

● **Principle**
A great insight identifies the intersections between the interests of the consumer and the features of the brand.

crannies without losing sight of the big picture in order to identify a key insight that can transform a client's business."

Mendelsohn described insight mining as "a deep dive" into the meaning of a brand looking for "major truths." She explained that the planner engages in unearthing the relationship that a target audience has with a brand or product and what role that brand plays in their lives. Understanding the brand/consumer relationship is important because account planners are taking on the position of the agency's *brand steward.* As Abigail Hirschhorn, chief strategic planning officer at DDB, said, "Our work puts our clients in touch with the souls of their brands."[28]

How do you get started on finding these elusive insights? The account planning tool kit is made up of questions that lead to useful insights culled from research. Kelley and Jugenheimer recommend seven topics or questions you might ask to begin your search:[29]

- What is the product's reason for being?
- What is the product's history?
- How do consumers use the product?
- How do brand consumers see themselves?
- What are the untapped beliefs about the product?
- What are the barriers to using the product?
- What appears in category and brand advertising for the product?

Here is another set of questions that can lead to useful insights:

- What is a realistic response objective (perception, knowledge, feelings, attitudes, symbolic meanings, behavior) for this target group?
- What are the causes of their lack of response?
- What are the barriers to the desired response?
- What could motivate them to respond in the desired way?
- What is the role of each element in the communication mix to motivate them or remove a barrier?

Here's an example of how data analysis works. Imagine you are working on a cookie account. Here's your brand share information:

	2017 Share (%)	*2018 Share (%)*
Choco Nuts (your brand)	50	40
Sweet 'N Crunchy (your main competitor)	25	30

What's the problem with this situation? Obviously, your brand is losing market share, and your primary competitor is gaining share. As a result, one of your goals might be to use a marketing communication mix to drive higher levels of sales. But market share is influenced by a number of competitors and a simple sales goal is so broad that it would be difficult to determine whether communication is sufficient to solve the problem. Let's dig deeper and consider another set of data about household (HH) purchases in a year:

	2017 HH Purchases	*2018 HH Purchases*
Choco Nuts	4	3
Sweet 'N Crunchy	2.5	3

What problem can you identify here? It looks like your loyal brand users are reducing their purchases at the same time Sweet 'N Crunchy customers are increasing their purchases. If further investigation reveals that some of your customers are switching over to Sweet 'N Crunchy, you might choose a strategy to improve your product, convince people that your brand tastes better, and remind your loyal customers of the reasons they have preferred your brand.

When you combine the two pieces of information and think about it, another insight might explain this situation. Perhaps people are simply eating fewer cookies. If you determine this information to be true, the communication opportunity lies in convincing people to return to eating cookies. That is more of a *category sell* problem (bringing people back to eating cookies

Photo: Courtesy Domino's UK & Ireland. Used with permission.

Domino's has created competitive advantage in the pizza industry by making mobile ordering easier, a feature that its busy customers appreciate.

versus other snacks) than a *competitive sell* (attracting people to your brand instead of the competition). In the Choco Nuts example, it would take more research to know which situation applies here. Here's a summary of these two different strategic approaches.

	Competitive/Brand Sell	*Category Sell*
What?	Challenger brand	Leader brand
Who?	Loyal buyers	Medium/light/lapsed buyers
What effect?	Compare cookie brands	Compare against other snacks
Objective?	Increase share of wallet	Increase total category sales
Message?	"Our cookies are better than theirs"	"Cookies are better than candy or salty snacks"

The important dimensions account planners seek to understand in planning brand strategies include relationship, perceptions, promise, and point of differentiation. Most important to planners are clues about the brand's *meaning*, which is usually phrased in terms of the brand essence (core or soul), personality, or image and how that connects with consumers' lifestyles.

The Creative Brief

An important outcome of strategic research is a document called a **creative brief** or **communication brief**, which explains the main consumer insights and summarizes the basic strategy decisions. Although the exact form of this document differs from agency to agency and from advertiser to advertiser, the brief is an outline of the message strategy that guides the creative team and helps keep its ideas strategically sound. As the planner's main product, it should be clear, logical, and focused. Many agencies work alongside their clients on the brief, and some even ask them to commit to the strategy with their signature. Here is an outline of a typical communication brief (compiled from one contributed by Mendelsohn as well as from the creative brief outline developed by the Ogilvy agency and presented on www.ogilvy.com).

- *Problem* What's the problem that communication can solve? (establish position, reposition, increase loyalty, get people involved, increase liking, and so on)
- *Target Audience* To whom do we want to speak? (brand loyal, heavy users, infrequent users, competition's users, and so on)
- *Consumer Insights* What motivates the target? What are the "major truths" about the target's relationship to the product category or brand? What do consumers currently think and feel about the brand?

- *Brand Imperatives* What are the important features? What's the point of competitive advantage? What's the brand's position relative to the competition? Also, what's the brand essence, personality, or image? Ogilvy & Mather explained, "What is the unique personality for the brand? People use products, but they have relationships with brands."
- *Communication Objectives* What do we want customers to do in response to our messages? (perception, knowledge, feelings, symbolic meanings, attitudes and conviction, action)
- *The Proposition or Selling Idea* What is the single thought that the communication will bring to life in a provocative way?
- *Support* What is the reason to believe the proposition? Ogilvy & Mather explained, "We need to give consumers 'permission to believe'—something that allows them to rationalize, whether to themselves or others, what is in reality an emotionally driven brand decision. The support should be focused on the insight or proposition, the truths that make the brand benefit indisputable."
- *Creative Direction* How can we best stimulate the desired response? How can we best say it?
- *Media Imperatives* Where and when should we say it?

The brief is strategic, but it also should be inspirational. It is designed to ignite the creative team and give a spark to their idea process. A good brief doesn't set up limitations and boundaries but rather serves as a springboard. It is the first step in the creative process. Charlie Robertson, an account planner and brand consultant, likened the brief to a fire starter: "The match is the brief, the ignition is the inspiring dialogue [in the briefing], and the flare is the creative."[30]

Looking Ahead

Strategic consistency is the result of carefully researched marketing communication plans. The actual messages that bring the strategy to life are a result of strategic planning as well as creative thinking. Part 3 of this book will review the creative side of marketing communication beginning with Chapter 9, which continues the strategy discussion in terms of message strategy.

IT'S A WRAP

Cows Build Moo-Mentum for Chick-fil-A

Chick-fil-A and its advertising agency, the Richards Group, developed one of the most successful integrated brand campaigns in the fast-food industry, one that has been executed across all media over many years. The strategy is expressed in the line used by wacky cows who demand that we "Eat Mor Chikin" rather than hamburger.

After the initial rollout as a three-dimensional billboard, the long-running campaign has continued to evolve and make its way into every point of contact with the customer. It shows what can be accomplished when strategic choices are made about brand communication.

The iconic cows and their quirky antics have become such a key symbol of Chick-fil-A's marketing communication that they were recognized as one of America's most popular advertising icons in a public vote sponsored by *Advertising Week*. They even earned a spot on New York's Madison Avenue Advertising Walk of Fame.

Chick-fil-A's lighthearted, unconventional campaign has helped increase sales every year. Since the campaign's launch in 1995, sales have increased from just over $500 million to more than $6 billion in 2015. (Sales percentage increases beat the competition hoofs down.)

Oh yes, the campaign also won a herd of awards, including induction into the Outdoor Advertising Association of America's Obie Hall of Fame, a Silver Lion at the Cannes International Advertising Festival, and two Effie Awards, including one for its sustained success. That's one way to milk the cows for all they're worth, and that's no bull.

Logo: Courtesy Chick-fil-A, Inc. Used with permission.

8.1. **Explain the difference between objectives, strategies, and tactics in strategic planning as well as the three levels of planning and how they are connected.** Objectives are outcomes you want to achieve or accomplish; strategies are how you will accomplish the objectives; and tactics are the ways in which you implement the strategies, or the execution. The three-tiered process of strategic planning involves a set of cascading objectives and strategies. Business objectives and strategies as spelled out in a business plan are achieved through planning at the level of marketing (and other business areas, such as production), and marketing objectives and strategies give direction to a brand communication or IMC plan.

8.2. **Identify the key strategic decisions and explain why they are central to brand communication planning.** The key strategic decisions are setting communication objectives, targeting the audience, developing a brand strategy, and designing a brand positioning strategy. The objectives determine how the impact of the brand communication is to be measured; the target audience is identified that is most likely to respond to the brand messages in ways that will deliver on the objectives; the brand strategy reviews the critical dimensions of branding to either create or refine aspects such as brand identity, image, and personality; and the brand positioning strategy considers whether the brand position location needs to be established, refined, or repositioned. The brand strategy dimensions, including the position, connect with the target audience as expressed in the brand communication to the extent that consumer thoughts and emotions are understood.

8.3. **Demonstrate the purpose and role of account planning and how it is used in advertising and IMC.** Account planning matches the right message to the right audience and identifies the right media to deliver that message. The primary purpose of account planning is to use research to uncover consumer insights and then create a communication brief for the creative team that outlines how the insight gives direction to the message strategy and media strategy.

KEY TERMS

account planner, p. 237
account planning, p. 237
business philosophy, p. 221
communication brief, p. 241
competitive advantage, p. 234
consumer insight, p. 237
creative brief, p. 241
feature analysis, p. 234
features, p. 232

Fishbein multiattribute model, p. 234
goals, p. 221
insight mining, p. 239
insight research, p. 239
marketing plan, p. 222
mission statement, p. 220
objectives, p. 218
parity products, p. 234

perceptual map, p. 232
position, p. 231
product differentiation, p. 232
profit, p. 221
repositioning, p. 236
return on investment (ROI), p. 221
share of market, p. 223
situation analysis, p. 223

societal marketing, p. 221
strategic business unit (SBU), p. 220
strategic planning, p. 218
strategies, p. 218
SWOT analysis, p. 223
tactics, p. 218
triple bottom line, p. 221
vision statement, p. 220

MyLab Marketing

Go to **www.pearson.com/mylab/marketing** for MyLab discussion questions (⊛) as well as the following assisted-graded writing questions.

8-1. Discuss how the facets model of advertising effects can be used to structure a set of brand communication objectives.

8-2. Think of a product you purchased recently after seeing an advertisement. Which brand strategies can you discern in the advertising?

REVIEW QUESTIONS

8-3. Define objectives, strategies, and tactics and explain how they differ.

8-4. What information does a brand communication plan derive from the business plan or marketing plan?

8-5. What is a situation analysis, and how does it differ from a SWOT analysis?

⊛ **8-6.** Discuss the cascading concept in planning and setting objectives.

8-7. What are the key decisions involved in establishing a brand and planning brand strategy?

8-8. What is a position, and how is it established?

8-9. What is an insight, and how is it uncovered? What is insight mining?

8-10. What is account planning, and what does the account planner bring to a marketing communication plan?

⭐ **8-11.** The owners of the Vico brand of organic coconut water believe that it is the next big trend in the bottled water category. It uses the clear liquid inside young, green coconuts (not coconut milk, which is derived from pressing the coconut pulp). Healthy and natural, the product is popular in South America and is becoming a niche market in New York City and other cities with South American immigrant populations. Outline a preliminary situation analysis, objectives, targeting, positioning, and branding strategies. In each section, explain what other information you would need to fully develop this plan.

8-12. You are in a meeting about the strategy for an automotive client who is proposing a new upscale luxury version of an electric car. One of your team members says that positioning is an old strategy and is no longer useful for modern products because the market is so complex and changes so fast. Another person argues strongly that you need to understand the position in the consumer's mind before you can even begin to develop an advertising strategy. Discuss one side of this issue for the launch of this new product and develop your position to present and defend in a class debate.

8-13. *Portfolio Project:* Examine SUVs at the following websites: www.lexus.com, www.infiniti.com, and www.mercedes-benz.com. Based on what you find on these sites, compare the positioning strategies for these top-of-the-line SUV models. Analyze the product features, competitive advantage, and points of differentiation. Draw two perceptual maps that reflect your insights.

⭐ **8-14.** *Mini-Case Analysis:* Review the Chick-fil-A case that opened and closed this chapter. Assume you are working on this account and have been asked to pull together a presentation for the brand team for the next year of this campaign. What research would you recommend conducting to decide if the campaign should be continued or modified? What do you need to find out to make this decision?

Planning for Multicultural Communication

Read the TRACE case in the Appendix before coming to class.

8-15. Develop a creative brief based on what you believe an account planner would have developed. Keep it to one page.

8-16. Develop at least three business objectives and strategies, three communications objectives and strategies, and three media objectives and strategies based on the case study.

Connecting Heart and Soul

In the opening to Part 2, Regina Lewis, former vice president of insights for both Dunkin' Brands and InterContinental Hotels Group, said, "When a brand fails to convey a soul or essence that matches personal characteristics that consumers value, that brand lacks meaning. . . . On the other hand, when a brand becomes a badge that consumers are proud of displaying, that brand becomes interwoven into consumers' everyday lives."

That's true enough. In Part 2, you learned that understanding your audience is key to being able to understand how consumers think and behave.

But what should brand communicators do when they are faced with promoting products and ideas to audiences who are unlike themselves? Most likely, as a professional marketing communicator, most of what you'll be advertising will be to groups of which you're not a part.

Here are vignettes of two Effie Award–winning campaigns that effectively reached diverse audiences. Although they are outstanding examples of transcending multicultural boundaries

of race and ethnicity, communicators may face other challenges reaching diverse audiences related to sexual orientation, age, geography, and many other factors.

- Everybody knows about Oreo cookies, right? For generations, moms have bought Oreos as treats for their kids and have encouraged them to drink milk with the cookies. Kraft Foods aimed to increase Oreo cookie consumption in Hispanic households and discovered that unlike fully acculturated Hispanics and native-born Americans, immigrants were unfamiliar with the ritual of pairing cookies and milk. Kraft craftily recognized the well-loved Oreo ritual of "twist, lick, and dunk" as something that would need to be taught to immigrants if they were to share in the moments of family fun.

Kraft also realized that in the less acculturated Hispanic households, parents ask their children to help translate. The big idea of this campaign centered on taking advantage of the kids to transmit the message of the brand to their parents and build on the culturally held value of strong family ties.

Kraft brought the idea to life with its message, "To pull apart is to come together" (in Spanish: Separar es Unir). As kids pull the cookie apart, the family comes together to share the silly fun of eating Oreos.

Seen in a variety of media—television, radio, and consumer magazines—this emotional message resonated with the audience, who responded by consuming more Oreos. Although the sales data are confidential, the campaign exceeded all Kraft performance goals.

- To increase market share of the African American segment, Verizon worked with GlobalHue, the largest multicultural agency, to align the wireless company with something near and dear to the community: gospel music. Verizon sponsored "How Sweet the Sound," a nationwide competition to find the best gospel choir in the United States. Verizon approached this competition without a hard sell for its product by simply supporting and organizing the competition and offering substantial cash prizes.

The Verizon experience connects with the community through multiple media involving online, television, radio, newspaper, out-of-home, mobile, direct mail, and email. The competition increased Verizon Wireless sales 14 percent in cities where the program was hosted, and this success led Verizon to expand the competition in subsequent years to other cities around the country. GlobalHue was nominated as Multicultural Agency of the Year for its efforts.

Consider This

P2-1. Compare and contrast these two campaigns. What lessons can you learn from these cases that might help you communicate to diverse audiences?

P2-2. Explain how these campaigns work using the Facets Model of Effects. How do these campaigns help communicate brand meaning?

P2-3. Evaluate Kraft's strategy of reaching parents in less acculturated Hispanic households by linking the fun of the Oreo ritual with the valued relationship between parents and their children.

Sources: Laura Wentz, "Agency Hits: African-American Favorites," *AdAge*, January 4, 2010, 16; Effie Briefs, "How Sweet the Sound" and "Through the Voice of a Child," 2009, www.effie.org; Cameka Crawford, "Chicago-Based Choir Named 'America's Best Gospel Choir,'" January 10, 2013, www.news.verizonwireless.com.

3

PRINCIPLE
Great Creative Communicates a Truth about a Brand

Creativity and the Truth About Brands

Great creative in promotional communication looks easy. Just come up with a great visual and some snappy copy, and send it out to the world on several of the many communication delivery channels available today.

But consider this reality: great creative must communicate a truth about the brand that moves the organization toward a key goal, engage the hearts and minds of individuals both inside and outside of the organization in a way that aligns them with the brand, and accomplish all that within the context of the unique capabilities and limitations of a multiplicity of communication channels.

In short, creativity with a purpose demands 360-degree thinking and the ability to synthesize the Big Idea of a brand into a few words or stunning images that can't be ignored.

Great creative convenes, engages, intrigues, and inspires. Great creative inspires a conversation rather than merely disseminating information.

It rallies to action. It engages both the minds and hearts of fellow human beings.

Great creative is authentic. It is believable and provable as representative of enduring truths about the brand. It does not stretch the truth.

Great creative is disciplined in that it is designed to achieve a very specific outcome. Outcomes can inspire a purchase or a donation, increase attendance, raise awareness, or shape public opinion.

The creative palette of a good communication professional includes the core concept of the brand or organization and its mission and goals as well as the production toolbox and the message dissemination toolbox.

◄ MEG LAUERMAN is Director of University Communication Emeritus at the University of Nebraska-Lincoln.

The creative toolbox includes the obvious components of design, copy, visuals, and sound, and it can include more experiential components, such as taste, smell, and feel. The more a brand can be experienced through all senses, the more memorable it will be and the more loyalty it can generate. A brand that consistently delivers a great in-store or user experience delivers a powerful message that is unique to the brand.

Similarly, a brand that is centered around a cause often has the potential and power to engage the hearts and inspire the action of thousands.

On the analytical side, the creative palette includes the use of insights about the desired "audience" gained through research to best align the brand with the audience. The creative palette also includes insights on the media use habits of the audience and knowledge about how best to use each communication channel, such as social media, billboards, print ads, radio and television spots, direct mail, and email, to effectively reach the audience.

Great creative works from the inside out and the outside in. It is meaningful and believable to employees within the organization as well as to stakeholders, participants, customers, and members. It invites outsiders to join a strong community. It creates a loop of ongoing conversation and engagement.

Accomplishing great creative takes a team of individuals who understand design, the audience, the organization, and the production process for each communications channel, all working collaboratively.

There is nothing more freeing in the creative process than working with a strong singular brand, one that is unequivocally focused on one big idea, one that generates great content potential on an ongoing basis. Such a scenario often leads to memorable communications that last for years, if not decades.

There is nothing more frustrating than trying to communicate on behalf of an organization that does not have a core identity and clear goals. The identity and goals provide the road map for creative professionals to do their jobs effectively and artfully. Without that critical direction, most communication will be destined to be nothing more than hot air.

9

The Creative Side

9.1 Describe the role of creativity in integrated marketing communication.

9.2 Explain creative thinking and how you get the Big Idea.

9.3 Identify key message strategy approaches.

9.4 Define issues affecting the management of creative strategy and its implementation.

Effective marketing communication is successful because the right media deliver the right message to the right target audience at the right time. In Part 2, we explained how marketing communication works and how it's planned, and in Part 4 we'll consider the media and how a message is delivered. Here and in Chapters 10 and 11, we'll concentrate on how the message is created. It's important to keep in mind, however, that like two hands clapping, media and message need to work together to create effective communication. In fact, planning the message usually happens simultaneously with planning the media. And in many instances, communication across the disciplines of integrative marketing communication (IMC)—advertising, public relations, direct communication, and promotions—reinforce the message.

MyLab Marketing

⭐ **Improve Your Grade!**

More than 10 million students improved their results using the Pearson MyLabs. Visit **www.pearson.com/mylab/marketing** for simulations, tutorials, and end-of-chapter problems.

Campaign	Corporation	Agencies	Awards
#OptOutside	*REI*	*Venables Bell & Partners, Mediavest/Spark, Tool of North America, North Kingdom and Edelman*	*Best of Show at The One Show, Grand Prix and Gold Lion at the Cannes Lions festival*

REI Tells Customers to Take a Hike

Photo: Alex Milan Tracy/Associated Press

Take a hike. Really? Who in their right mind would have thought that a retail company would intentionally close its 143 stores and pay its 12,000 employees to skip work on the day after Thanksgiving, Black Friday, the busiest shopping day of the year? That's precisely what REI did. In a bold move that was either creative genius or pure madness, REI closed its doors and told customers to go outside and spend the day hiking or participating in outdoor activities away from the mall. Let's take a deeper look to see what drove the decision.

REI's mission is based on the notion that "being outdoors makes our lives better," according to Jerry Stritzke, president and CEO of REI. At the core, telling customers to go outside and skip shopping rings true to what the company stands for. It is an authentic, believable message. Make no mistake: REI wants customers to buy its gear, but not at the expense of the ultimate goal of enjoying the outdoors. Stritzke said that REI's "inviting America to #OptOutside with us because we love great gear, but we are even more passionate about the experiences it unlocks." Did you hear that? REI tapped into a basic truth. It's an inspiring message that resonated with consumers. Hundreds of state and national parks amplified the message by offering free admission.

One reason this idea captured the attention of customers and became the center of a lot of media focus is that REI zigged when others zagged. That is, all its competition did one thing (kept the stores open), and REI went another very memorable way. To execute the idea, REI offered a dedicated website, optoutside.rei.com, that recommended hiking trails and urged users to #OptOutside.

REI's brave move is notable because it illustrates a major change in the way successful companies connect with their customers. Charles Trevail, CEO at Omnicom's C Space, observed:

> REI's move signals a massive shift in the way companies are doing business and marketing themselves. The new reality is that as customers become more skilled at, and have better technology for, managing their many brand relationships, they will weed out or ignore companies that fail to sufficiently understand their needs and deliver value against them. This is the new consumerism—empowered, entrepreneurial, and enabled. REI's decision reflects its fundamental empathy for its customers, who have zero desire to stand in line for the best deal on a gorgeous fall Friday, when they could be hiking Mt. Moosilauke.

What was the outcome for REI? One would think it was greater brand awareness and credibility. See if the gamble on taking this outside chance paid off for REI in the It's a Wrap section at the end of this chapter.

Sources: REI Staff, "Thank You for Choosing to #Optoutside with Us," www.optoutside.rei.com, retrieved August 12, 2017; Charles Trevail, "Why REI's #OptOutside Is a Model for the Future of Marketing," November 3, 2015, www.adage.com; Judann Pollack, "REI's #OptOutside Takes Titan Grand Prix, Netflix 'House of Cards' Wins Integrated Grand Prix," June 25, 2016, www.adage.com; Micah Solomon, "REI Shocks Retail World by Closing for Black Friday, Paying 12,000 Employees to 'Opt Outside,'" October 27, 2015, www.adage.com; "Promo Jury at Cannes Gives Grand Prix to the Greatest Anti-Promotion of All Time," June 20, 2016, www.adage.com; Jack Neff, "REI and Swedish Tourism Win Promo and Direct Grand Prix for Taking Unusual Risks," June 20, 2016, www.adage.com; Paul Vercammen, "REI to Workers: Shun Black Friday and Instead Enjoy Blue Skies—With Pay!," November 30, 2015, www.cnn.com.

In this chapter, we look at the role of creativity and the Big Idea in IMC and discuss the process of creative thinking with the aim of showing how you can be a more creative thinker. Effective marketing communication is both an art in its creativity and a science in its strategy. This chapter shows you how the two dimensions come together as creative strategy—the logic behind the creative message. You will learn about a planning tool called a *creative brief*, which provides direction for the execution of the Big Idea, and strategies that effectively communicate your message and achieve the desired objectives.

9.1 Describe the role of creativity in integrated marketing communication.

What Is the Role of Creativity in IMC?

Simply put, **creativity** can be defined as the generation of fresh ideas and solutions to current problems or challenges.[1] The definition sounds simple, but creativity is complex and multifaceted, particularly in the digital age. Creativity is all around us: think about music, art, literature, and theatre. But you don't have to be an artist to be creative. Consider the invention of new products like electric cars or suitcases with wheels designed to meet a particular need. The ability to think like a problem solver and the courage to take risks and try something new are requisite skills for creativity.

As Meg Lauerman said in the part opening essay in the context of marketing communications, "Great creative must communicate a truth about the brand that moves the organization toward a key goal." Creativity has traditionally been associated with advertising, so this chapter will offer a heavy emphasis on advertising. We refer to the original products they produce as

● **Principle**
Creative strategy solves problems, and problem solving demands creative thinking. Both Big Ideas and Big Plans call for creative thinking.

the "creative," like Meg Lauerman did in the part opener when she described hallmarks of great creative. In fact, we often talk about "creatives" as the people who design ads. All agencies have copywriters and art directors who are responsible for developing the creative concept and crafting the execution of the idea. They often work in teams, are sometimes hired as a team, and may work together successfully for years. The account planner originally put the strategy together in the form of a creative brief, so that person may also be involved in providing both background and direction to the creative team. Because advertising creativity is a product of teamwork, copywriters, art directors, and social media and content directors work together to generate concept, word, and picture ideas. Video producers can also be part of the team for commercials and online content. The writing or design specialties of each team member come into play in the execution of the idea.

The **creative director** manages the creative process and plays an important role in focusing the strategy of ads and making sure the creative concept is strategically on target. Creative directors need to possess skills beyond creating static print ads or TV commercials; they need to understand how to engage consumers beyond adding a call to action in a commercial. The role of the creative director is evolving rapidly as these team leaders need to be familiar with **user experience (UX) design**, which involves the interactive conversation about the brand, such as how to engage viewers of ads with social media across platforms, ultimately integrating the marketing and creative direction.[2]

The creative team is expanding beyond writer/art director/creative director. Creativity isn't just about "ads" anymore. As the REI case demonstrates, no one in the IMC environment owns "creativity" exclusively. The success of REI's ultimate antipromotion is its Big Idea rather than specific ads with clever phrases and compelling images.

Anyone in the IMC process can generate fresh ideas and solutions. Those designing multiplatform campaigns also demonstrate creative ways to connect content with audiences. In the world of interactive media, the consumer is also often invited to participate in the creative activity. With the development of new crowdsourcing practices, marketers are finding ways to enlist the collective ideas of thousands to come up with great ideas. Doritos has held "Crash the Super Bowl" competitions that invite consumers to create ads to run during the Super Bowl. Even if consumers aren't directly part of the team, their blogs and other social media comments contribute real-time feedback and often shape and play a part in refining messages.

The ability to generate fresh ideas and solutions sometimes results in the creation of a new business as well as new products, as demonstrated in the Inside Story about Urban Decay Cosmetics.

The Art and Science of IMC

The art and science of marketing communication come together in the phrase *creative strategy*. A winning marketing communication idea must be both *creative* (original, different, novel, and unexpected) and *strategic* (right for the product and target and meeting the objectives). The message plan is a rational analysis of a problem and what's needed to solve that problem. This logic is built on a fresh insight that comes from research. The message itself translates the logic of the planning decisions into a creative idea that is original, attention getting, and memorable. Creative messages, such as REI's suggestion that its customers "OptOutside" during Black Friday, bring the strategy to life. It grabs attention and sticks in memory.

Professor Mark Stuhlfaut identified significant elements of creativity in advertising, which begin with novelty but include appropriateness as well as authenticity and relevance. Stuhlfaut adds that if it's creative, it is also often generative; in other words, it leads to other new ways of thinking.[3] Creative strategy goes beyond coming up with a novel idea; rather, it is about generating an idea that solves a communication problem in an original way. Stuhlfaut and Professor Margo Berman remind us that creativity is directed at achieving objectives. Creative strategy solves problems,[4] and problem solving demands creative thinking—the mental tool used in figuring things out. The twenty-first century has created a huge challenge for brand communication creatives who have to develop breakthrough messages that will not

Principle
Effective advertising is a product of both science (persuasion and logic) and art (creativity).

A Passion for the Business

Wende Zomnir, *Co-founder, Urban Decay,
Costa Mesa, California*

Being the creative force behind a brand like Urban Decay makes me responsible for cranking out great ideas. And in the 19 years I've been doing that, I've figured out a few things about how to generate creative ideas with which people connect. It begins with a passion for the business. Here are my seven principles about how to run a business creatively.

1. *Feel a passion for your brand.* Everyone in product development, design, public relations, merchandising, sales, and marketing at Urban Decay loves our makeup and deeply connects to our position as the counterculture icon in the realm of luxury makeup.
2. *Spot emerging trends.* Our best ideas don't start from analysts telling us what the trends are. My creative team and I talk about what kinds of colors, visual icons, textures, and patterns we are craving and start from there. Our job at Urban Decay is to lead graphically with our product design and formulation. We once launched a

volumizing mascara called Big Fatty and played off the connotations in the name, infusing the formula with hemp oil and wrapping the mascara vial in an Age of Aquarius–inspired print. Shortly after the product's release, a supplier to the cosmetics industry came in to show us a version of our own mascara, giving us a presentation on the coming trends. It's annoying, but when this happens, we know we're doing our job.

3. *Cultivate your inner voice.* You also need to develop a gut instinct for what will work. I thought that skulls were going to be huge because everyone in the office was craving them on T-shirts, shoes, key rings, and so forth. We decided to put them on our seasonal holiday compacts in 2005. And the same season that Marc Jacobs launched them, so did we. We had distributors begging us to sell them a version without the skull, but we stood firm and wouldn't change it because we knew it was right. And you know what? The same distributors who balked placed the biggest reorders and complained that we couldn't stock them fast enough.
4. *Check your ego.* Listening to that inner voice *is* something you can cultivate, but you've got to check your ego at the door to do it. That can be hard because being a creative leader means you've probably generated a lot of great ideas that work. So, you've got confidence in your concepts and your ability to deliver, but you have to be able to admit others have great ideas, too.

---

get lost in today's media explosion. As Professor Karen Mallia explains, in the Matter of Practice feature, we're in a second creative revolution that challenges creative thinkers to reimagine the way they work.

The next section focuses on developing the ability to think creatively and come up with Big Ideas and creative strategies that are innovative and entrepreneurial, relevant to a specific audience, and effective in helping audiences see brands and products in intended ways.

9.2 Explain creative thinking and how you get the Big Idea.

⬡ **Principle**
When advertising gives consumers permission to believe in a product, it establishes the platform for conviction.

Creative Thinking: How Do You Do It?

All the aspects of IMC—advertising, public relations, direct response and promotions—are creative idea businesses, but what do we mean by an idea? An **idea** is a thought or a concept in the mind. It's formed by mentally combining pieces and fragments of thoughts into something that conveys a nugget of meaning. Advertising creatives sometimes use the term **concepting** to refer to the process of coming up with a new idea, such as REI's idea to shut its stores on Black Friday. Big Ideas are also called **creative concepts**.

We have tried to define creativity and creative ideas, but to understand what it is, it may be helpful to think about what it isn't. What's the opposite of creative? In advertising, **clichés** are the most obvious examples of generic, nonoriginal, nonnovel ideas. An example of an industry

URBAN DECAY
beauty with an edge®

The distinctive feminine, dangerous, and fun personality of Urban Decay Cosmetics is seen in its packaging as well as its products' names, like Naked Palettes and shade names: "Smog," "Mildew," and "Oil Slick."

5. *Cherry-pick the best ideas.* Gut instinct is important, *but*—and this is big—even more crucial is being able to listen to all the ideas and sort out the junk. After you sort through everything, pick the very best concept, even if it's *not* your idea.

6. *Little ideas are important, too.* You've got to rally everyone behind your Big Idea, but realize that all those little ideas that prop up the big one are great, too. That's what makes so many of our products work in the marketplace: a big idea supported by little ideas—and the people who develop them.

7. *Be flexible.* My final important creative principle is flexibility. Knowing when to be flexible has resulted in some of the best work we've created here. While working on a body powder for summer that was to be impregnated with water for a cooling sensation on the skin, we ran into production problems. We wanted a powder, but I decided to add flavor instead. That edible body powder became a huge subbrand for us, spawning multiple flavors and generating huge amounts of press and revenue. The cooling powder would have been late, had quality control issues, and probably would have lasted a season.

Check out Urban Decay at www.urbandecay.com/, www.twitter.com/UrbanDecay, www.facebook.com/urbandecaycosmetics, and www.instagram.com/urbandecaycosmetics.

Zomnir (aka Ms. Decay) graduated from the University of North Texas, where she was a student of Professor Sheri Broyles.

Photo, logo: Courtesy Urban Decay Cosmetics. Used with permission.

whose advertising is immersed in clichés is hospitals: advertising conventions typically feature skilled doctors and caring nurses working together as teams in new high-tech buildings with amazing technology. In contrast, an innovative campaign for the Akron Children's Hospital used unscripted commercials featuring patients and their families who talk about how they are coping. The idea is that hospitals are dramatic places, and the challenge was to present the inherent drama in the hospital situation by focusing on real people. When the New York–based DeVito/Verdi agency was hired by the Mount Sinai hospital to also break away from the clichés, the agency drafted a list of commandments: no pictures of doctors, no smiling people, no fancy machinery, no overpromises about medical care, and no complicated medical terminology.[5]

To help you understand how creative people think about strategy and advertising ideas, consider the 12 tips offered in the Practical Tips box by Professor Tom Groth, whose students consistently win awards. They are suggestions about how professionals approach creative assignments, but they also provide you with a road map for your own personal growth as a creative person.

What's the Big Idea?

What we call a **Big Idea**, or a creative concept, becomes a point of focus for communicating the message strategy. The Marlboro Man campaign, with its connotation of western independence and self-reliance, is a Big Idea that has been worth millions, maybe billions, of dollars in brand

⬡ **Principle**
Big Ideas are risky because they are by definition new, unexpected, and untested.

The Second Creative Revolution: Magical Thinking Meets Bits and Bytes

Karen L. Mallia, *University of South Carolina*

Time was, if you had a clever headline, an arresting visual, and a memorable slogan, ta-da—you had an ad. Not anymore. You've no doubt seen many "ads" in the past few years that aren't really "ads" in the old-school sense: Burger King coupons delivered by "unfriending" Facebook friends, mobile apps from MasterCard and dozens more brands, brand content and publishing and experiences in every conceivable channel: from T-Mobile flash mobs in the United Kingdom to a "joy" coat from Cadbury—to say nothing of the videos that grew from them and criss-crossed the globe virally. You can even get messages (ads!) directly from your WIFI-enabled refrigerator. The Internet of Things will no doubt bring many more conversations between you and your possessions.

Now brand communication can be anything from sponsored tweets to a charmingly retro 30-second television spot. Increasingly, campaigns consist of media channels that are layered and interwoven in clever and complex ways. A good example of this is the groundbreaking Old Spice campaign you will read about in Chapter 10. Don Draper of *Mad Men* never imagined scripting, shooting, and airing ads responding to consumer comments for 56 straight hours, which is what the creative team, talent, and production crew did to make that "Responses" campaign.

Welcome to the second creative revolution. The entire process of making brand communication has undergone a massive shift the likes of which the industry hasn't seen since Bill Bernbach first paired copywriters and art directors into creative teams and launched the first creative revolution.

Coming up with radical brand ideas still calls for strategic and creative thinking, talent in art direction and writing, and the same passion and fearlessness and resilience. But now that creative is married to technology, it also means collaborating with the UX (user experience) designer, programmer, information architect, mobile developer, and countless others that [Mad Men's Sterling Cooper Advertising Agency] never envisioned.

Yet, despite changes bringing more and different talents into creative work and developing new kinds of messages for the latest digital toys, the underlying principles behind making brilliant work haven't changed much. Many core creative tenets are as true today as they were before we saw color television. It's important to know what truisms to hang on to—and to learn some radical new truths.

Enduring Creative Truths

- Great creative work starts with fresh insight, which comes from research. Insight comes from understanding people, products, and the relationship between them.
- Great creative work is built on a tight creative strategy, brilliantly executed.
- Great work is relevant—to its audience (not the whole world) and to the brand. It isn't art or stand-up comedy for its own sake.
- Great ideas are critical to great executions. In old-tech parlance, GIGO: garbage-in-garbage-out. Or, more explicitly, "you can't polish a turd." (See hundreds and hundreds of dull or stupid ads, forgettable taglines, and irrelevant celebrities to understand that no amount of hip typography and flashy gimmicks can mask the absence of a strong selling idea.)
- One execution is not an idea. Ideas are big, inspiring, and exciting and can have many iterations and live long lives. A one-off execution is as useless as yesterday's stale slang or moldy Starbucks.
- Every communication is a building block of brand image. Every ad, every video, every tweet, and every line of type either contributes to brand image or undermines it. The look and the voice convey as much as the concept.
- Great ideas often look obvious *after* they're conceived because they are the most perfect solution to the problem, but that doesn't make them easy to come by. What Edison said about inventing is equally valid for brand communication: it's 1 percent inspiration and 99 percent perspiration.

New Creative Truths

- Great work now takes a village, not just one or two geniuses. Creating for digital media requires diverse talents of more than just a writer and art director. Collaboration is key.
- The creative process doesn't flow like a waterfall, from step to step. It's *agile*, meaning that technology must be threaded and embedded throughout the creative process in order to develop great work. Digital is treated like an afterthought.
- In a 24/7 contact world, work is never done. Creative people live in constant beta, especially in a world where consumers can post on your Facebook page and deadlines are tighter.
- Scattershot brand communication is more dangerous than ever (see brand image).

In sum, if you want any career in this business, internalize all these truths and you are well on your way. If you want a creative career, beware. Although you need to be aware of every new campaign and media idea that others are doing, creative isn't about chasing the next big thing (like the quick-response code). It's grounded in a thorough understanding of the core tenets, great persuasive communication, and fluency with all the tools in your tool kit. Brilliant brand ideas are those that solve the client's problem in an engaging and unexpected way. Simple. (Not!)

Checklist for Killer Ads

Tom Groth, *University of West Florida*

Groth's ✓ list for killer ads.

Instructions:
1) **Do your ad**
2) **Go through this list.**
3) **Redo your ad.**
4) **Smile.**

1. A safe ad is a bad ad.

✓ Your goal isn't to blend in like elevator music. Many advertisers are afraid to "rock the boat."

✓ Safe advertising is liking waving at friends in the dark—you know it but they don't.

✓ If an ad doesn't scare you a bit . . . it's not much of an ad at all.

2. Make mistakes!

✓ Breakthrough creativity doesn't come from home runs . . . it comes from strike outs! *Winning* says something worked in the past. Don't be tempted to just repeat what worked before.

✓ Trial and error brings new answers. Trial and error opens doors instead of closing them.

3. What's your brand's "hook?"

"Ina-Gadda-Da-Vida . . . ."
"All Right Now . . ."
"Keep on rockin me baby . . ."

You may not know the lyrics—but you know the *hook*!

✓ **Decide exactly one thing in your ad that you want to stick in your prospect's mind.** It can be visual, verbal, musical . . . it's repetitive and sticks like glue in the mind.

✓ Many prospects buy what they know and it is just **one thing**—*the hook*! They remember *the hook* and buy *the hook.*

Which battery?	• Pink bunny battery or
	• Coppertop battery
Which tuna?	• Charlie the tuna or
	• Mermaid tuna.

✓ You need a sharp hook to catch the fish.

4. Leave something out.

"She gave you a big kiss for the birthday flowers. This year make it Diamonds. . . . . . . "

This open-ended headline let's the guy figure out its meaning.

✓ **Let the prospect "fill in the blanks."**

This *theatre of the mind* approach works for all media, not just radio.

It transforms a passive viewer into an active participant.

5. It's all about problem solving.

"Sales are falling!!! What are you going to do?"
"I'm gaining weight!!! What are you going to do?"

✓ It's all about problem solving—client's problems and prospect problems.

✓ If you can cleverly solve problems you'll never be unemployed.

6. Think "viewers" not "readers."

✓ **Is your promise visual?**

Do you read body copy? If you're under 30 your answer is probably . . . *rarely.*

✓ **Visuals offer instant gratification.**

Quick—show me! We are a visual culture. Images communicate at light speed and that's about all the time your ad has to get it's message across.

✓ **Become *visually literate*!** Sure you understand the language of visuals, but can you speak the language? It takes more than knowledge of the Creative Suite to be visually literate. It's time to learn that foreign language!

✓ **Agencies employ *Art Directors* not *Art Decorators*.** Your goal is **not** to make an ad look good. Your design must immediately make the brand's *significance shine through* as images and words combine in the viewer's mind.

7. Everything communicates.

✓ Does *everything* in your *advertisement* support your message? Yes, every last thing talks—your choice of fonts, props, wardrobe, colors, white space, talent, media, music, tone of voice etc . . .

✓ Choose wisely. Never just stick something into the ad.

✓ You cannot not communicate.

8. You're really different.

What is the answer to this math problem? $1 + 1 = \_\_$ Now imagine a math class where everyone in class comes up with a ***different*** answer yet everyone's answer is *right!*

✓ Unlike a math problem *creativity* recognizes that there are an unlimited number of answers to an advertising problem. They all can be *right* . . .or *wrong*!

✓ **There is only one of you.** Use your uniqueness to produce original answers that solve the toughest client and prospect problems.

9. "Good enough isn't good enough." –Jay Chiat

✓ Work hard. Resting is somehow very fatiguing.

10. The media is the message.

✓ Your media choice is a *creative* decision. Your ad in a newspaper communicates something quite different than the same ad in a magazine. Where you hang out says something about you.

11. Your prospect doesn't want your product, service, or brand.

✓ You better know what she wants.
  • a hug
  • to be admired
  • to be sexy
  • to quench a thirst

12. Ignorance is not bliss.

✓ **Don't play dumb.** Knowledge makes for killer ads.

Photo: Robert Landau/Alamy Stock Photo

CLASSIC

Coppertone Girl

Big ideas have the power to transform. Consider the Coppertone suntan lotion ads from the 1950s that showed a dog pulling down a little girl's bathing suit revealing a tan line and (gasp!) her bottom. Created by Joyce Ballantyne Brand, the Coppertone girl was modeled after the artist's three-year-old daughter. Outdoor boards featured a motorized dog and swimsuit bottom that moved up and down mechanically. This eye-catching work turned Coppertone from a small company in Florida to a national brand. Coppertone packaging features the iconic little girl and her dog to this day. Fun fact: three-year-old Jodie Foster made her acting debut in a Coppertone commercial in 1965.

equity over the years. It's ranked number three in *Advertising Age*'s Top 100 advertising campaigns of the twentieth century. Some other classic campaigns on the list include Smokey Bear, Volkswagen's "Think Small," Nike's "Just Do It," Avis's "We try harder," Clairol's "Does she or doesn't she?," and Apple Computer's "1984."[6]

Big Ideas can be risky because they are different and, by definition, untested. The "Whopper Freakout" campaign by Crispin Porter + Bogusky that featured video reactions of customers who ordered their Whoppers only to be told Whoppers had been taken off the menu (which was not really the case) was a risky strategy because it was so unexpected. The firm has had trouble with some of its other edgy ideas, such as the creepy Burger King. Thus, risky is good for edgy Big Ideas, but how far one should venture on the edge is a difficult question. Testing ideas is a good idea to reduce the chances of taking unnecessary risks.

Where do Big Ideas come from? As advertising legend James Webb Young, a founder of the Young & Rubicam agency, explained in his classic book on creative thinking, *A Technique for Producing Ideas*, an idea is a new or unexpected combination of thoughts. Young said, "The ability to make new combinations is heightened by an ability to see relationships."[7] An idea, then, is *a thought that comes from placing two previously unrelated concepts together*, as the classic Michelin ad campaign demonstrates by using a baby to convey the safety of Michelin's tires—a most unexpected and effective juxtaposition.

The ROI of Creativity

● **Principle**

An idea can be creative for you if you have never thought of it before, but to be truly creative, it has to be one that no one else has thought of before.

A Big Idea is more than just a new thought because in advertising it also has to accomplish something: it has a functional dimension. According to the DDB agency, an effective ad is *relevant* and *original* and has *impact*, which is referred to as *ROI of creativity*. That formula sounds like the way a businessperson would talk metaphorically about creativity in terms of "return on investment,"[8] but it has a different meaning here. According to DDB's philosophy, ideas have to be **relevant** and mean something to the target audience. **Original** means one of a kind; an advertising idea is creative when it is novel, fresh, unexpected, and unusual. Because it is novel, it is surprising and gets your attention. To be effective, the idea also must have **impact**, which means it makes an impression on the audience.

How do you know if your idea is creative? Any idea can seem creative to you if you have never thought of it before, but the essence of a creative idea is that *no one else has thought of it either*. Thus, the first rule is to avoid doing what everyone else is doing. In an industry that prides itself on creativity, **copycat advertising**—that is, using an idea that someone else has originated—is a concern.

The importance of originality may be obvious, but why is relevance important to an advertising Big Idea? Consider the award-winning California Milk Board campaign "Got Milk?" The consumer insight is that people drink milk with certain foods, such as cupcakes and cookies. If milk is unavailable to drink with those foods, people are—to say the least—frustrated. Thus, associating these products with milk is a highly relevant idea.

Likewise, why is impact important? We know that many advertisements just wash over the audience. An idea with impact, however, breaks through the clutter, gets attention, and sticks in memory. A *breakthrough ad* has stopping power and that comes from an intriguing idea, a Big Idea that is important, interesting, and relevant to consumers.

The Creative Leap

We all use different ways of thinking in different situations. For example, the term **divergent thinking** is used to describe a style of thinking that jumps around exploring multiple possibilities rather than using rational thinking to arrive at the "right" or logical conclusion. The heart of creative thinking, divergent thinking uses exploration (playfulness) to search for alternatives. Another term for divergent thinking is **right-brain thinking**, which is intuitive, holistic, artistic, and emotionally expressive thinking, in contrast to **left-brain thinking**, which is logical, linear (inductive or deductive), and orderly. How can you become a more creative thinker, someone who uses the right brain for divergent explorations?

First, think about the problem as something that involves a mind shift. Instead of seeing the obvious, a creative idea looks at a problem in a different way, from a different angle. That's referred to as *thinking outside the box*. It doesn't matter how dull the product might appear to be. There is always an opportunity to move it beyond its category limitations through a creative Big Idea.

Second, put the strategy language behind you. We talk a lot about strategy in this book (and will do more of that later in this chapter) with the goal of helping you gain a fuller understanding of the complexities and possibilities of marketing communication. Once you understand the many ways to communicate effectively, you can concentrate less on the academic descriptions and more on what you need to convey. In other words, use your common sense and creative gifts. Finding the brilliant creative concept entails what advertising giant Otto Kleppner called the *creative leap*[9]—a process of jumping from the rather boring business language in a strategy statement to an original idea. This Big Idea transforms the strategy into something unexpected, original, and interesting. Because the creative leap means moving from the safety of a predictable strategy statement to an unusual idea that hasn't been tried before, this leap is a *creative risk*.

A classic example of out-of-the-box thinking is Michelin's tire advertising, which is driven by the strategic idea that the tire is durable and dependable, language that would make quite a boring ad. The creative idea, however, comes to life in the long-running campaign that shows a baby seated in or near a tire. The visual is reinforced by the slogan "Because so much is riding on your tires." The creative concept "leaps" from the idea of a durable tire to the idea of protecting your family, particularly precious members like tiny children, by surrounding them with the dependability of a Michelin tire.

Dialing Up Your Creativity

How creative are you? You probably know people who are just naturally zany, who come up with crazy, off-the-wall ideas. Creative advertising people may be weird and unconventional, but they can't be totally

Photo: Agency: Goodby, Silverstein & Partners
Photo: Dan Escobar

The idea that some moments, such as when eating cupcakes and cookies, require a glass of milk is the creative concept behind the award-winning "Got Milk?" campaign. The creative concept is expressed in both words and pictures in this ad.

● **Principle**
A breakthrough ad has stopping power that comes from an intriguing idea.

Photo: Courtesy Michelin North America, Inc. Used with permission.

Michelin's dependability and durability surround and protect a car's precious cargo.

Leonardo DaVinci, Albert Einstein, and Georgia O'Keefe excelled in different fields, but all three qualify as creative geniuses.

How Creative Are You?

By Sheri Broyles, *University of North Texas*

Do you ever wonder whether you are creative? Does creativity have anything to do with your personality? Your personality is your own distinctive and consistent pattern of how you think, feel, and act. You may not be a creative genius, but still you may have creative abilities that can be nurtured and developed.

A current view of creativity suggests that the area of personality most related to creativity is how open you are to new experiences. According to researchers, how open you are to new experiences can be measured by survey questions that ask if you agree or disagree with statements like the following:

1. "I enjoy working on mind-twister-type puzzles."
2. "Once I find the right way to do something, I stick to it."
3. "As a child I rarely enjoyed games of make-believe."
4. "I enjoy concentrating on a fantasy or daydream and exploring all its possibilities, letting it grow and develop."

Which ones do you believe may predict a creative personality? Explain why. What can you do to expand your talents in those areas?

FIGURE 9.1
The Creative Personality

Source: Sheri J. Broyles, University of North Texas Department of Journalism, P.O. Box 311277, Denton, TX 76203, sbroyles@unt.edu. Also based on R. R. McCrae and P. T. Costa Jr., "Openness to Experience," in *Perspectives in Personality*, vol. 1, ed. R. Hogan and W. H. Jones (Greenwich, CT: JAI Press, 1985), 145–172.

eccentric. They still must be purpose driven, meaning they are focused on creating effective advertising that's on strategy. Figure 9.1 contains a mini-test to evaluate your own creative potential.

Coming up with a great idea that is also on strategy is an emotional high. Advertising creatives describe it as one of the biggest emotional roller coasters in the business world. One copywriter explained that when the ideas aren't flowing, you feel like fleeing the country. When it's a good idea, however, there's nothing better.

Ingvi Logason, owner of an award-winning agency in Iceland and a member of this book's Advisory Board, explains how he got the idea for a campaign for SORPA, a recycling center in Iceland. The project was to encourage people who were recycling to minimize the volume of their waste and, of course, recycle more. "The idea came from the unlikeliest source," he said.

⬡ Principle

To get a creative idea, you must leap beyond the mundane, formal business language of the strategy statement and see the problem in a novel and unexpected way.

After working on the problem for some time, "the idea came to me while channel surfing and stumbling on a specific scene in a film I had seen—*Fargo*," where the murderer is trying to dispose of a body by putting it into a tree shredder. Even though it has no correlation with recycling, the shredder, Logason said, "lit my lightbulb." The result was a humorous ad that received the highest likability score ever measured in Iceland and that led to an increase in waste brought in for recycling. According to Logason, "Inspiration for my ideas can almost always be traced to things I have done, experienced, seen, heard, or read." He concludes, "In a creative world it is important to try new things and live life like a discoverer."

Logason's "discoverer" is why we say that curiosity is the most important characteristic of creativity.[10] But what else is important? Research by the Center for Studies in Creativity in Buffalo, New York, has found that most people can sharpen their skills and develop their creative potential by understanding and strengthening certain personal characteristics. Research indicates that creative people tend to be independent, assertive, self-sufficient, persistent, self-disciplined, and curious, with a high tolerance for ambiguity. They are also risk takers with powerful egos that are internally driven. They don't care much about group standards and opinions and typically have inborn skepticism and strong curiosity. Here are a few other characteristics of creative people.

Principle
Getting a great advertising idea that is also on strategy is an emotional high.

- *Problem Solving* Creative problem solvers are alert, watchful, and observant and reach conclusions through intuition rather than through logic.
- *Playful* Creative people have fun with ideas; they have a mental playfulness that allows them to make novel associations.
- *The Ability to Visualize* Most of the information we accumulate comes through sight, so the ability to manipulate visual images is crucial for good copywriters as well as designers. They can see products, people, and scenes in the mind's eye, and they can visualize a mental picture of the finished ad while it is still in the talking, or idea, stage.
- *Open to New Experiences* As we said earlier, one characteristic that identifies creative people is that they are open to new experiences. Over the course of a lifetime, openness to experience may give you many more adventures from which to draw. Those experiences would, in turn, give a novelist more characters to write about, a painter more scenes to paint, and the creative team more angles from which to tackle an advertising problem.[11]
- *Conceptual Thinking* It's easy to see how people who are open to experience might develop innovative advertisements and commercials because they are more imaginative.[12] Such imagination led to a famous Nike commercial in which Michael Jordan and Larry Bird play an outlandish game of horse—bouncing the ball off buildings, billboards, and places that are impossible to reach.

The Creative Process: How to Get an Idea

Only in cartoons do lightbulbs appear above our heads from out of nowhere when a good idea strikes. In reality, most people who are good at thinking up new ideas will tell you it is hard work. They read, study, analyze, test and retest, sweat, curse, and worry. Sometimes they give up. The unusual, unexpected, novel idea rarely comes easily, and that's as true in science as it is in advertising.

The creative process can be portrayed as a series of steps. English sociologist Graham Wallas was the first to outline the creative process, but others followed, including Alex Osborn, one of the founders of the BBDO agency and the Creative Education Foundation.[13] Let's summarize this classic approach in the following steps:

Step 1. **Immersion** Read, research, and learn everything you can about the problem.

Step 2. **Ideation** Look at the problem from every angle; develop ideas and generate as many alternatives as possible.

Step 3. **Brainfag** Don't give up if—and when—you hit a blank wall.

Step 4. **Incubation** Try to put your conscious mind to rest to let your subconscious take over.

Step 5. **Illumination** Embrace that unexpected moment when the idea comes, often when your mind is relaxed and you're doing something else.

Step 6. **Evaluation** Does it work? Is it on strategy?

A structured creative exercise from Professor Linda Correll, who developed Creative Aerobics,[14] offers a method to help you unleash your creative potential. This four-step idea-generating process opens new doors and windows for ideas to enter your mind. To illustrate, think about finding a creative idea for a new brand of oranges. Here's how Creative Aerobics works:

1. *Facts* As a left-brain exercise, come up with facts about your product—an orange has seeds, is juicy, has vitamin C.
2. *New Names* Create new "names" for the product—a vitamin supplement, a kiss of sunshine.
3. *Similarities* Find similarities between dissimilar objects—both Florida sunshine and oranges suggest warmth, freshness, sunshine, the fountain of youth.
4. *New Definitions* Like creating a pun, creates new definitions for product-related nouns—peel (face eel, peel out), seed (seed money, bird seed), navel/naval (naval academy, contemplating one's navel), pulp (pulp fiction), C/see/si/sea (C the light).

Headlines derived from these idea starters might be "Seed money" (the money to buy oranges), "Peel out" (when your store is out of oranges), "Pulp fiction" (a story about an orange), and "C the light" (the orange is a low-calorie source of vitamin C), according to Correll.

Another specialized approach to creative problem solving involves **design thinking**, which stimulates innovation and solves complex problems through collaboration. This approach takes a broader view of creative problem solving, one that uses anthropological observation as well as innovation and teamwork environments.[15] Participants are encouraged to form teams of people of diverse skill sets and backgrounds. The five-part process asks the teams to empathize with the user, define the problem, ideate, create a prototype to solve the problem, and test the idea. Stanford University created an entire design school to spark creativity and collaboration in solving problems for innovators and entrepreneurs (www.dschool.stanford.edu). Design thinking can be applied to IMC contexts such as helping marketers understand how customers behave in their natural habitats, providing valuable insights about shoppers in a checkout line and stimulating innovation.

Brainstorming

As part of the creative process, some agencies use a thinking technique known as **brainstorming** where a group of 6 to 10 people work together to come up with ideas. One person's idea stimulates someone else's, and the combined power of the group associations stimulates far more ideas than any one person could think of alone. The group becomes an idea factory.

An example comes from David Droga, chairman of the award-winning Droga5 agency, who explained how his team came up with a tagline for a campaign for athletic-wear brand Puma.[16] After weeks of filling sweaty notebooks with half-baked ideas, the painful process ended with a great line for this very unusual company. You see, Puma champions "social" sports and the people who play them, everything from foosball to darts to karaoke to bowling—the kinds of sports you play with a drink in your hand. So what do you call highly competitive people in social sports? Then, at the point of giving up, someone on the team came up with "the after-hours athlete" and a slogan, as well as a position and name for the category, was developed.

The term *brainstorming* was coined by Alex Osborn, founder of the advertising agency BBDO and explained in his classic book *Applied Imagination*. The secret to brainstorming is to remain positive and defer judgment. Negative thinking during a brainstorming session can destroy the informal atmosphere necessary to achieve a novel idea. The role of the brainstorm facilitator is to encourage what the Idea Champions organization calls "the in-the-moment opportunities to spark the ever-mutating, collective genius of the group."[17] Read more about its brainstorming recommendations at www.ideachampions.com.

To stimulate group creativity against a deadline, some agencies have special processes or locations for brainstorming sessions with no distractions and interruptions, such as cell phones and access to email, and walls that can be covered with sheets of paper on which to write ideas. Some agencies rent a suite in a hotel and send the creative team there to get away and immerse themselves in the problem. When the GSDM agency was defending its prized Southwest Airlines account, the president ordered a 28-day "war room/death march" that had staffers working around the clock, wearing Rambo-style camouflage, and piling all their trash inside the building to keep any outsiders from rummaging around for clues to their pitch.

The following list builds on our previous discussion of creative thinking. It can also be used as an outline for a brainstorming session.

To Create an Original and Unexpected Idea, Use the Following Techniques:

- *What If?* To twist the commonplace, ask a crazy *what if* question. For example, what if wild animals could talk? What kind of personalities would they have? That question is the origin of Frontier Airlines' talking animals campaign.
- *An Unexpected Association* In **free association**, you think of a word and then describe everything that comes into your mind when you imagine that word. If you follow a chain of associations, you may come up with an idea that sets up an unexpected juxtaposition with the original word or concept. An ad for Compaq used a visual of a chained butterfly to illustrate the lack of freedom in competitors' computer workstations.
- *Dramatize the Obvious* Sometimes the most creative idea is also the most obvious. The MasterCard "Priceless" campaign ran its first commercial in 1997. It has expanded to more than 200 countries, building its success by meaningfully demonstrating a universal truth of the priceless things that money can't buy. The tagline, "For everything else, there's MasterCard"[18] creates positive feelings about the brand.
- *Catchy Phrasing* Isuzu used "The 205 Horsepower Primal Scream" for its Rodeo headline.
- *An Unexpected Twist* Silk suggests the unexpected in one of its headlines for dairy-free plant milk: "If you wonder how more plants fit into your life, it's in a glass."
- *Play on Words* Under the headline "Happy Camper," an ad for cheese showed a picture of a packed sport-utility vehicle (SUV) with a huge wedge of cheese lashed to the rooftop.
- *Analogy and Metaphor* Metaphors and analogies that by definition set up juxtapositions illuminate new patterns or relationships. Harley-Davidson compared the legendary sound of its motorcycles to the taste of a thick, juicy steak.
- *Familiar and Strange* Contrasting the familiar in an unexpected situation can create memorable images. UPS showed a tiny model of its familiar brown truck moving through a computer cord.
- *A Twisted Cliché* They may have been great ideas the first time they were used, but phrases such as "the road to success" or "the fast track" become trite when overused. But they can regain their power if twisted into a new context. The "Happy Camper" line was twisted by relating cheese to an SUV.
- *Twist the Obvious* Avoid the predictable, such as a picture of a Cadillac on Wall Street or in front of a mansion. Instead, use an SUV on Wall Street ("fast tracker") or a basketball hoop in front of a mansion ("slam dunk").
- *Exaggeration* Take a common situation or item and exaggerate it until it becomes funny (an unbreakable kiss with the lovers totally unresponsive to over-the-top attempts to break them apart).

To Prevent Unoriginal Ideas, Avoid or Work Around the Following:

- *The Look-Alike* Avoid copycat advertising that uses somebody else's great idea. Hundreds of ads for escape products (resorts, travel, liquor, and foods) have used the headline "Paradise Found." It's a play on "paradise lost" but still overused.
- *The Tasteless* In an attempt to be cute, a Subaru ad used the headline "Put it where the sun don't shine." It's an attempted twist on a cliché, but it doesn't work.

What Are Some Key Message Strategy Approaches?

9.3 Identify key message strategy approaches.

Creative thinking can be marshaled into a plan that helps focus the work. This section helps transform the thinking into action. It starts with a creative brief that identifies the most appropriate strategy to accomplish the goals of the organization, product, or idea.

The Creative Brief

The **creative brief** (or creative *platform*, *worksheet*, or *blueprint*) is the document prepared by an advertising account planner to summarize the basic marketing and advertising strategy described in Chapter 8. It gives direction to creative team members as they search for a creative concept, or Big Idea. Remember that we make a distinction between creative strategy and creative executions. **Creative strategy**, or **message strategy**, is *what* the advertisement says; **execution** is *how* it is said. This chapter focuses on creative strategy, and Chapters 10 and 11 explore the writing, design, and production of advertising executions.

The following outline summarizes the key points in a typical brief:

- *Problem* that can be solved by communication
- *Target audience* and key *insights* into their attitudes and behavior
- *Brand position* and other branding decisions, such as *personality* and *image*
- *Communication objectives* that specify the desired response to the message by the target audience
- *Proposition* or *selling idea* that will motivate the target to respond
- *Media considerations* about where and when the message should be delivered
- *Creative direction* that provides suggestions on how to stimulate the desired consumer response

Although a creative brief is terminology generally associated with advertising, public relations has a counterpart called a **Public Relations Plan**. The Public Relations Plan is typically based on a four-step process called the **public relations management process** that involves defining the problem or opportunity, programming (addressing key constituent publics, strategies, tactics, and goals), action, and evaluation.[19]

A Public Relations Plan is similar to the creative brief:

- Executive summary
- Communication process
- Background
- Situation analysis
- Message statement
- Audiences
- Key audience messages
- Implementation
- Budget
- Monitoring and evaluation

The creative brief and the public relations plan explain the thinking behind the creative ideas that emerge from the analysis of these elements. They aren't creative ideas, but they may touch on such execution or stylistic direction as the ad's **tone of voice**.

Different agencies use different formats, but most include these basic advertising strategy decisions. The point is that advertising planning—even planning for the creative side—involves a structured, logical approach to analysis. Other agencies may focus more on the intuitive, emotional message effects. The Crispin Porter + Bogusky agency, for example, designs advertising by looking for what it calls "tension points." Its brief asks planners to ask themselves, "What is the psychological, social, categorical, or cultural tension associated with this idea?"

The Road Crew social marketing campaign is an example of creative problem solving for a good cause. The problem was to get young men in Wisconsin small towns who drink and drive to use a ride service. The objective was to reduce the incidence of alcohol-related car crashes by 5 percent. The breakthrough creative concept was to use the idea of a road crew for a group of young partiers who needed a ride on their big night out.

The Road Crew campaign planning began with a creative brief:

- ***Why are we advertising at all?*** To create awareness for an evening alternative ride service.
- ***What is the message trying to do?*** Make the new ride service appealing to men so as to reduce the number of alcohol-related crashes.
- ***What are their current attitudes and perceptions?*** "My car is here right now. Why wait? There are few options available anyway. I want to keep the fun going all night long."

Photo: Courtesy of the Wisconsin Department of Transportation. Used with permission.

The Road Crew creators wanted to create a design in the spirit of the Harley-Davidson motorcycle image, realizing that members of the target audience were all Harley fans.

- *What is the main promise we need to communicate?* It's more fun when you don't have to worry about driving.
- *What is the key moment to which we tie this message?* "Bam! The fun stops when I need to think about getting to the next bar or getting home."
- *What tone of voice should we use?* The brand character is rugged, cool, and genuine. We need to be a "straight-shooter" buddy on the bar stool next to the target. The targets do not want to be preached to or told what to do. We need to communicate in a language to which they can relate. (Words like *program* may cause our audience to tune out.)

The creative brief summarizes the key strategic decisions that we identified in Chapter 8, such as message objectives, message targeting, and brand positioning, but they are interpreted in terms of creative strategy. Let's review them here as they apply to the Road Crew campaign.

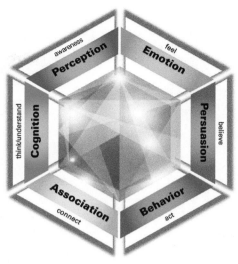

FIGURE 9.2
Facets Model of Effects

Message Objectives   What do you want the message to accomplish? What message objectives would you specify for the Road Crew campaign, for example, to meet the goal of reducing alcohol-related crashes by 5 percent? We introduced the concept of the *Facets Model of Effects* (Figure 9.2) in Chapter 5. Here is a review of some common message objectives that relate to the facets of effectiveness. Do any of them relate to the Road Crew goal of reducing alcohol-related crashes?

- *See/Hear* Create attention, awareness, interest, and recognition.
- *Feel* Touch emotions and create feelings.
- *Think/Understand* Deliver information, aid understanding, and create recall.
- *Connect* Establish brand identity and associations and transform a product into a brand with distinctive personality and image.
- *Believe* Change attitudes, create conviction and preference, and stimulate trust.
- *Act/Do* Stimulate trial, purchase, repurchase, or some other form of action, such as visiting a store or website.

We mentioned that the primary goal of the Road Crew campaign was to reduce the number of alcohol-related crashes. Other objectives involved creating awareness of the ride service program and positive attitudes toward it as well as establishing a cost-efficient level of rides in the first year of operations. To accomplish these objectives, the Road Crew team used fund-raising, solicited volunteers, and lined up other community support. The heart of the problem uncovered by the Road Crew research was a gap between *awareness* (don't drink and drive), *attitudes* (risky, scary, and potentially dangerous), and *behavior* (get someone else to drive). The campaign was designed to address this gap and encourage the target audience's behavior to change in accordance with their attitudes and awareness.

The creative team used the creative brief as the map to direct them as they created the campaign executions. The name "Road Crew" was the defining element of that campaign's Big Idea. It was supported with a slogan—"Beats driving"—that conveyed the benefit of the program in the language of the target audience. The logo was in the style of the Harley-Davidson logo. The Road Crew planners realized that a Big Idea that reflects the lifestyle of the target audience in appealing language and tone can motivate behavior and change attitudes, and Harley connects with the attitude of the young male audience the campaign wanted to reach.

Targeting   The target decision is particularly important in planning a message strategy. The target audience for the Road Crew campaign was identified as 21- to 34-year-old single men with a high school education and employed in blue-collar jobs. They were the primary target for the ride service because research found that this group is responsible for the most alcohol-related crashes, they kill more people than any other age group, and they themselves are most likely to die in an alcohol-related crash. What moves this group? Research found that many of these guys tended to worry about driving home drunk as the end of the evening approached and that this worry took the edge off an otherwise fun evening. The ride service made their evening more fun because it reduced their worry.

Photo: Zoran Milich/Contributor/Getty Images

Branding and Positioning The demands of the brand are also important considerations. Brand positions and brand images are created through message strategies and brought to life through advertising executions. Finding the right position is difficult enough, but figuring out how to communicate that position in an attention-getting message that is consistent across multiple executions and various media is difficult. The classic "Think Small" campaign that launched the VW Beetle is an example of advertising that created a powerful brand at the same time it carved out a unique position in a cluttered automobile market.

Brand communication creates symbols and cues that make brands distinctive, such as characters, colors, slogans, and taglines as well as brand personality cues. Geico's gecko and Frontier's talking animals are brand-savvy characters that make Mr. Clean, the Pillsbury Doughboy, and the Jolly Green Giant look way too earnest. The difference is that the new-age characters are ironic and even a little self-depreciating, and they speak to the ad resistance of today's consumers with irony and inner conflict.

The Harley-esque logo for the Road Crew campaign reflected the devil-may-care attitude of Harley riders. The connection with the Harley image made the Road Crew's do-good message more acceptable to the target audience.

Advertising and other forms of marketing communication are critical to create what brand guru Kevin Keller calls *salience*;[20] that is, the brand is visible and has a presence in the marketplace, consumers are aware of it, and the brand is important to its target market. In addition to brand salience—measured as *top-of-mind awareness*—another objective for branding and positioning campaigns is to create trust. We buy familiar brands because we've used them before and trust them to deliver on their promises. The Road Crew program, for example, would be a waste of time if the hard-partying young men in the target audience didn't think to call the limo service and trust it to be there to pick them up when they wanted to leave.

Photo: razorpix/Alamy Stock Photo

Translating Communication Objectives into Message Strategies

Once you have identified communication objectives, how do you translate them into strategies? Remember that there is no one right way to do brand communication; in most cases, there are a number of ways to achieve a communication objective. If you were creating advertising to increase the reservations for a hotel, for example, what would you emphasize: speed of check-in, size of the room, hair dryers, or mints on the pillow? Rather than tangible features like those, Sheraton decided to emphasize the emotional side of traveling and show people greeting one another. Because it's a global company, the greetings include hugs, bows, and kisses on both cheeks. The company believes that its customers worldwide like to be welcomed, appreciated, and made to feel at home.

Planners search for the best message design—the approach that makes the most sense given the brand's marketing situation and the target audience's needs and interests. Notice the use of the word *design*. The idea of design—as in **message design**—is not graphics; rather, it is problem solving. An interesting example of message design comes from Ben & Jerry's and illustrates the need to understand the consumer. The brand parent, Unilever, assumed that people ate more ice cream when it was sunny until it discovered social chatter that indicated otherwise. It found that people mentioned staying home and watching movies and eating Ben & Jerry's on rainy weekends. This insight helped Unilever design its messages.[21]

Choosing the Strategic Approach That Fits

What you want to say forms the foundation for the message design. How you say it is the strategic part. Given the multitude of ways to design a message, how do you identify strategic approaches that might work? First, let's review some simple ways to express a strategic approach—head and heart and hard sell or soft sell. We'll then look at some other models that get a little deeper into the complexities of message strategy.

Head and Heart   In the Facets Model of Effects, the cognitive objectives generally speak to the head, and the affective objectives are more likely to speak to the heart. Sometimes, however, a strategy is designed to inform the mind as it touches the emotions. For example, Procter & Gamble's "Thank You, Mom" campaign that ran in conjunction with the Rio 2016 Summer Olympic Games across 21 countries honored mothers in emotional videos that also mentioned products. Based on the insight that behind every athlete is an amazing mother, the emotional videos expressed athletes' gratitude and appreciation for their mother's everyday strength.[22] Of course, the everyday part connected to a product from Procter & Gamble, such as Pampers and Tide.

Another way to refer to head and heart strategies are hard-sell and soft-sell approaches. A **hard sell** is an informational message that is designed to touch the mind and create a response based on logic. The success of this approach is based on the assumption that the target audience wants information and will make a rational product decision. Consider this hard sell example for a car rental company: you can rent this car for less than any other rental company but only for a limited time, so hurry. It resonates with consumers' desire to save money.

A **soft sell** uses emotional appeals or images to create a response based on attitudes, moods, and feelings. The assumption with soft-sell strategies is that the target audience has little interest in an information search and will respond more favorably to a message that touches their emotions or presents an attractive brand image. A soft-sell strategy can be used for hard products. NAPA Auto Parts ran an emotional ad that showed a dog sitting at a railroad crossing, forcing a truck to brake hard to avoid hitting him as a train bears down on the scene. The slogan puts the heart-stopping visual story into perspective: "NAPA, because there are no unimportant parts."

But there are also examples of ads designed to stir emotions that didn't work because they are too manipulative or raised inappropriate emotions. It is possible to manipulate emotions in a way that viewers and listeners resent. For example, Nationwide insurance faced a backlash for airing a commercial during the Super Bowl in which a boy is killed. The commercial was designed to raise awareness of preventable childhood deaths, but audiences found the ad too sad, and they blasted Nationwide on social media. Fallout from the controversial spot led to the departure of the company's chief marketing officer.[23]

> **● Principle**
> Hard-sell informational messages lead to rational decisions; soft-sell emotional strategies create responses based on attitudes, moods, and feelings.

Sometimes, however, high emotion works. "This Is Your Brain on Drugs" is a public service announcement campaign that first ran in 1987 on behalf of Partnership for Drug-Free Kids (formerly Partnership for a Drug-Free America). The campaign appealed to the viewers' emotions based on the notion that using illegal drugs is both risky and uncool. In the original 30-second version, a man holding a frying pan said, "This is your brain," "This is drugs" (showing an egg), and "This is your brain on drugs," as he cracks the egg, which sizzles in the pan. "Any questions?" The message has made its way into popular culture and is credited by some studies as helping reduce drug use.[24]

Photo: Courtesy Partnership for Drug-Free Kids.™ Used with permission.

Systems of Strategies   Head and heart and hard sell or soft sell: all these terms refer to some basic, simple concepts. Creative strategy often is more complex, however. We'll look at two approaches that address other aspects of advertising strategy: Frazer's six creative strategies and Taylor's strategy wheel.

University of Washington professor emeritus Charles Frazer proposed a set of six creative strategies that address various types of message situations.[25] Although not comprehensive, these terms are useful to identify some common approaches to message strategy:

Frazer's Six Creative Strategies

Strategy	Description	Uses
Preemptive	Uses a common attribute or benefit, but brand gets there first—forces competition into "me too" positions.	Used for categories with little differentiation or new product categories.
Unique selling proposition	Uses a distinct difference in attributes that creates a meaningful consumer benefit.	Used for categories with high levels of technological improvement and innovations.
Brand image	Uses a claim of superiority or distinction based on extrinsic factors such as psychological differences in the minds of consumers.	Used with homogeneous, low-tech goods with little differentiation.
Positioning	Establishes a place in the consumer's mind relative to the competition.	Used by new entries or small brands that want to challenge the market leader.
Resonance	Uses situations, lifestyles, and emotions with which the target audience can identify.	Used in highly competitive, undifferentiated product categories.
Affective/anomalous (or ambiguous)	Uses an emotional, sometimes even ambiguous message to break through indifference.	Used where competitors are playing it straight and informative.

Depending on what needs to be communicated, message creators may want to employ one strategy or another to fit the particular situation. A contemporary twist on the concept of the unique selling proposition for a product is the idea that brand communicators could identify a unique story proposition that communicates what the brand is—in other words, its brand story.[26]

The preemptive strategy shows up in competitive advertising where one competitor tries to build a position or lay a claim before others enter the market. An example comes from the Coffee Wars between Starbucks and McDonald's that erupted when McDonald's announced its McCafé line of fancy coffees at lower prices. In anticipation of the McCafé advertising blitz, Starbucks began its first-ever branding campaign. Designed with burlap-sack backgrounds that are reminiscent of roasted coffee bags, the ads used hard-hitting headlines like "Starbucks or nothing. Because compromise leaves a really bad aftertaste" and "If your coffee isn't perfect, we'll make it over. If it's still not perfect, you must not be in a Starbucks." The campaign was designed to separate the Starbucks' experience from the mass-market approach of McDonald's and Dunkin' Donuts.

University of Tennessee professor Ron Taylor developed a process of analysis that offers a different framework for thinking about strategies. It divides strategies into the *transmission view*, which is similar to the more rational "head" strategies, and the *ritual view*, which is similar to the more feeling-based "heart" strategies. He then divides each into three segments: ration (rational), acute need, and routine on the transmission side and ego, social, and sensory on the ritual side.[27] In the Matter of Principle feature, he explains the principles behind this model as well as its application in a problem-solving context.

Strategic Formats

Even though advertising, and in a broader sense all brand communication, is a constant search for a new and novel way to express some basic truth, there are also some tried-and-true formats that have worked over the years. We'll talk about these options from a literary, psychological, and sales viewpoint.

Six Message Strategies in Six Minutes

Ronald E. Taylor, *University of Tennessee*

It's crunch time. You've got to generate several different message strategies to discuss with your boss for a new business pitch. She's meeting with a regional bottler who plans to add bottled water to her product line. Your boss wants to hear your ideas over lunch. The problem is that this bottled water is no different from all the other brands of bottled water.

You head out to meet your boss, a six-minute trip away from your office. You've got to enter the restaurant with the strategies in your head. You remember a strategy device from your advertising class in college: the six-segment strategy wheel (Figure 9.3). It was designed primarily to generate strategies, to create several to choose from. You remember that it had two broad divisions—transmission and ritual—and three segments under each division. You mentally work your way counterclockwise around the wheel to think about ways to promote the product:

1. *Ration Segment* Ration strategies are based on rational thought and logic. They represent the classic reason-why, product-focused message strategies. You think, "Brand X Water, the economical, convenient, portable beverage."

2. *Acute Need Segment* Acute need, or special need, strategies are based on consumers' unanticipated need for the product or service, like appliance repair or medical surgery, or special occasions, like the need for a tuxedo or dress for a formal occasion. But when do you have an acute need for water? When traditional supplies aren't available! "Stock up on Brand X Water for the hurricane season."

3. *Routine Segment* Routine strategies attempt to routinize everyday behavior. You remember that drinking multiple glasses of water a day is good for you, so you think, "Brand X Water, a great beverage with every meal every day."

You've moved down the left-hand side of the wheel, and the amount of time consumers spend deliberating on choices has been reduced in each segment. Now you are mentally crossing over the vertical line to the ritual, or emotional, side, and the importance of the item and emotional connection will increase as you move up the right-hand side of the wheel—and you're halfway to lunch with the boss:

4. *Sensory Segment* Sensory strategies are based on one of the five senses: sight, touch, hearing, smell, and taste. You think, "Refreshing, clear taste. Brand X Water."

5. *Social Segment* Many social strategies are based on establishing, maintaining, or celebrating relationships with others. You think, "Get noticed. Drink Brand X Water" or "Share Brand X Water with someone you love."

6. *Ego Segment* Ego strategies are based on images that consumers have of themselves. Brands say to consumers, "This is who you are." Active people who eat healthy foods and exercise regularly like reinforcement that they are doing the right thing. You think, "Brand X Water, the bottled water for people who care about their health."

The wheels are turning now. You've arrived at the parking lot and you start combining strategies:

- Serve refreshing (sensory) Brand X water to your family (social) every day (routine).
- Clear refreshment (sensory) in an unbreakable (ration), portable (ration) container.

Your boss is impressed with your ability to generate strategies. Most advertising professionals generate two or three and then do multiple executions within a single strategy, but you are not so limited. In fact, your boss has invited you to lunch again tomorrow to discuss the pitch for a national pizza chain. How many strategies can you generate?

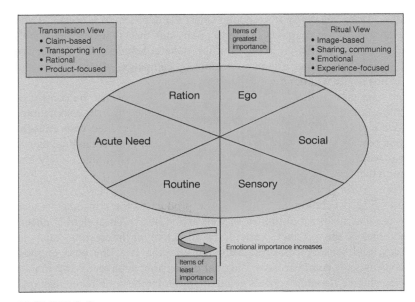

FIGURE 9.3
Taylor's Six-Segment Strategy Wheel

Source: Ronald E. Taylor, University of Tennessee, http://web.utk.edu/~retaylor/six-seg.htm.

Photo: SAUL LOEB/Getty Images

Tony the Tiger, the official mascot of Kellogg's Frosted Flakes, has helped convince consumers that "They're gr-r-reat!" since the brand character was created in 1952.

Lectures and Dramas Most promotional messages use a combination of two basic literary techniques to reach the head or the heart of the consumer: lectures and dramas.[28] A lecture is instruction usually given verbally. or it could be a demonstration using visuals. The speaker presents evidence (broadly speaking) and uses a technique such as an argument to persuade the audience. The advantages of lectures are many. They are relatively inexpensive to produce and are compact and efficient. A lecture can also deliver a dozen selling points in seconds, get right to the point, and make the point explicitly. In advertising, we use the phrase *talking head* to refer to an announcer who delivers a lecture about a product. This person can also be a celebrity spokesperson or an authority figure, such as a doctor or scientist.

Drama, however, relies on the viewer to make inferences about the brand. Usually, the drama is in the story that the reader has to construct around the cues in the ad. Through dramas, advertisers tell stories about their products; the characters speak to each other (Progressive insurance girl Flo), not to the audience. Like fairy tales, movies, novels, parables, and myths, advertising dramas are essentially stories about how the world works. They can be funny as well as serious. The Leo Burnett agency built a creative philosophy around "Inherent Drama," which describes the story lines built into the agency's archetypal brand characters, such as the Marlboro Man, Charlie the Tuna, the Jolly Green Giant, and Tony the Tiger.

Political advertising is a particular challenge in terms of how much information versus how much drama. In particular, the issue of negative advertising, which arouses emotions as well as counterarguments, is a topic of research, debate, and criticism. Professor Kathleen Hall Jamieson, who is known for her research on political advertising, said that the danger with negative advertising is its association with deception.[29] Marilyn Roberts reviewed the work of scholars on the topic and questions, "Does negativity in campaigns hurt the democratic process?" Even though scholars hold widely differing opinions, Roberts points out that "whether one views negativity as good, bad, or mixed, politics is about conflict." She concluded, "As interactive political advertising and blogs play a larger role in contemporary campaigns, the questions and concerns about the rise in negativity will not diminish."[30]

Although the impact of negative political advertising remains debatable, in the context of the plethora of news outlets, talk-show pundits, candidate surrogates, and so forth it sometimes seems as if the whole media environment, not just political advertising, is filled with untruths and negativity. An opinion piece in the *New York Times* observed, "We have entered an age of post-truth politics."[31] It is worth wondering what effect this negativity has on our society and our responsibility as communicators.

Psychological Appeals The psychological appeal of the product to the consumer is also used to describe a message that speaks to attitudes as well as the heart. An **appeal** connects with some emotion that makes the product particularly attractive or interesting, such as security, esteem, fear, sex, and sensory pleasure. Although emotion is at the base of most appeals, in some situations appeals can also have a logical dimension, such as saving money for retirement (relief based on knowledge). Appeals generally pinpoint the anticipated response of the audience to the product and the message. For example, if the price is emphasized in the ad, the appeal is value, economy, or savings. If the product saves time or effort, the appeal is convenience. Advertisers use a status appeal to establish something as a high-quality, expensive product.

Selling Premises   Advertising has developed a number of strategic approaches that speak to the head with a sales message. A **selling premise** states the logic behind the sales offer. A premise is a proposition on which an argument is based or a conclusion is drawn. To have a practical effect on customers, managers must identify the product's **features** (also called **attributes**) in terms of those that are most important to the target audience. A **claim** is a product-focused strategy based on a prediction about how the product will perform. Health claims on food products like cereal or oatmeal, for example, suggest that the food will be good for you. In a Blue Diamond Almond headline, the nuts were called a "superfood." The copy that followed supported the claim:

Ounce for ounce Blue Diamond® Almonds have more vitamin E than blueberries, more iron than spinach and 4× more fiber than broccoli, making them the supersnack of superfoods.

In other words, a rational, prospect-centered selling premise identifies a *reason* that might appeal to potential customers and motivate them to respond. Here is a summary of various types of rational customer-focused selling premises.

- A **benefit** emphasizes what the product can do for the user by translating the product feature or attribute into something that benefits the consumer. For example, a General Motors' electric car ad focuses on the product feature (the car doesn't use gas) and translates it into a benefit: lack of noise (no pistons, valves, or exhaust) and low mileage costs.
- A **promise** is a benefit statement that looks to the future and predicts that something good will happen if you use the product. For example, Dial soap has promised "round-the-clock protection" for decades: if you use Dial, you will feel more confident.
- A **reason why** emphasizes the logic behind why you should buy something, although the reason sometimes is implied or assumed. The words *because* and *reasons* call attention to a reason-why statement. For example, a multivitamin headline says, "Multiple Reasons to Take a Multi." The list that follows includes five points: immune health, heart health, bones and teeth, eye health, and energy.
- A **unique selling proposition (USP)** is a benefit statement that is both unique to the product and important to the user. The USP is a promise that consumers will get this unique benefit by using this product only. For example, an ad for a camera states, "This camera is the only one that lets you zoom in and out automatically to follow the action." The unique benefit can also apply to brands: Arla cream cheese tastes better because "Our ingredient list is shorter than their ingredient list."

Most selling premises demand facts, proof, or explanations to support the sales message. Proof statements that give the rationale, reasoning, and research behind the claim are used to substantiate the premise. The proof, or **substantiation**, needed to make a claim believable is called **support**. In many cases, substantiation calls for research findings. Volvo's longtime crash-safety position, which has been built over the decades, relies on the claim that 9 of 10 Volvos registered in the United States are still on the road.[32] With claims—and particularly with comparisons—the proof is subject to challenge by the competitor as well as industry review boards.

Other Message Approaches   In addition to the basic categories of selling premises, some common message formulas emphasize different types of effects. The planner uses these terms as a way to give direction to the creative team and to shape the executions. Here are some common formats.

- A **straightforward message**, which is factual or informational, conveys information without any gimmicks, emotions, or special effects. For example, the website for Gerber (www.gerber.com), expresses its commitment to "fostering healthy growth and development and helping establish healthy eating habits from Birth+ to Preschooler."[33]
- A **demonstration** focuses on how to use the product or what it can do for you, as the Mr. Clean character has illustrated for the Procter and Gamble products he represents.
- A **comparison** contrasts two or more products to show the superiority of the advertiser's brand. The comparison can be direct, with competitors mentioned, or indirect, with just a reference to "other leading brands." In the comparison approach, as with a demonstration, seeing is believing, so the objective is to show

● Principle
In the comparison approach, as with a demonstration, seeing is believing, so the objective is to build conviction.

CRAYON ON WALLS

Photo: SAUL LOEB/Getty Images

something that builds conviction. When people see two products being compared, they are more likely to believe that one is better than the other.

The Pepsi Challenge involved a blind taste test of sodas (Pepsi and Coca-Cola) by strangers who tried the products without knowing the brand names. Results showed that the tasters preferred Pepsi.[34] It also said something about the power of brand names.

- In a **problem solution message**, also known as **product-as-hero**, the message begins with a problem and then showcases the product as the solution. Many messages from pharmaceutical companies fall in this category. Bayer aspirin gets rid of your headache and other minor pain; Alka-Seltzer gives you relief from indigestion.
- **Humor** can be a useful creative strategy—using Progressive insurance's Flo as the star, for example—because it grabs attention and is memorable. Planners hope people will transfer the warm feelings of being entertained to the product. Recent research, however, found that funny commercials don't sell better than unfunny ones and that the funny ads that work best balance the humor with information and relevance.[35]
- The **slice-of-life message** is an elaborate version of a problem solution staged in the form of a drama in which "typical people" talk about a common problem and resolve it.
- In the **spokesperson** (also **spokes-character** or **brand icon**) or **endorser** format, the ad features celebrities whom we like (LeBron James), created characters (the Pillsbury Doughboy or the Geico gecko), experts we respect (the Maytag repairman or doctors), or someone "just like us" whose advice we might seek. An effective spokesperson brings liking and trust and speaks on behalf of the product to build believability. (The Federal Trade Commission rules make endorsers as well as advertisers liable for false or unsubstantiated claims, so spokespersons have to be very careful about what they say about any product they advertise.)
- **Teasers** are mystery ads that don't identify the product or don't deliver enough information to make sense, but they are designed to arouse curiosity. They are often used to launch a new product. The messages run for a while without the product identification, and then, when curiosity is sufficiently aroused, usually at the point when the product is officially launched, a concluding ad runs with the product identification. Think about movie trailers that are shown in theaters before the feature and are also available online, like the latest *Star Wars* and *Spider-Man* films. They're designed to stimulate your interest in attending those movies when they're released. Using the tools of social media, such as YouTube, Facebook, Instagram, and Snapchat, can stimulate interpersonal communication and heighten curiosity about a product as consumers piece together tidbits of information.

The use of celebrities as spokespersons, endorsers, or brand symbols is an important strategy because it associates the brand positively—or negatively—with a famous person and qualities that make that person a celebrity. Michael Jackson is credited with starting a new era of celebrity advertising when he signed a record-breaking $5 million contract with Pepsi in 1984. Before that time, celebrities were often reluctant to appear for a brand because they feared it might tarnish their image.

The luxury bag and luggage company Louis Vuitton is an icon, and its "LV" logo design is an easily identifiable brand logo on its products. But its brand communication is also iconic with a long list of eclectic celebrities. It has used Angelina Jolie shown floating on a Cambodian boat with a Louis Vuitton bag at her side, and another campaign featured Muhammad Ali and his grandson. Others include soccer great Pele, musician Keith Richards, Russian leader Mikhail Gorbachev, and even Lady Gaga, all iconic individuals on extraordinary journeys.[36] Pop superstars Selena Gomez and Taylor Swift have joined the list of endorsers for the French fashion house.[37]

Advertisers often worry about celebrities they have signed who might tarnish the brand's image. In 2013, for example, after being accused of making racist statements, Paula Deen lost her sponsorships with brands such as J.C. Penney, Sears, and Home Depot. Big celebrity crashes followed missteps by Lance Armstrong and Tiger Woods. Armstrong, the legendary Tour de France bike racer and founder of nonprofit organization LiveStrong, was also sponsored by a stable of big marketing names, including Nike, Nissan, and Anheuser-Busch, all of whom were dismayed when he faced doping charges and was stripped of his medals in 2012. One source estimates that golf star Woods lost between $23 million and $30 million in endorsements with companies such as Accenture and AT&T.[38] Temperamental stars, drug and driving arrests, assaults, and loose tongues are a nightmare for marketers. When swimmer Ryan Lochte, a 12-time Olympic medal winner, admitted to "exaggerating" about being robbed at gunpoint during the 2016 Summer Olympics in Rio de Janerio, his sponsors quickly distanced themselves from the bad publicity when they all ended their deals with him.[39] In an interesting twist, celebrity Sarah Jessica Parker dropped her relationship with her sponsor, Mylan N.V., maker of EpiPen, when the drug maker was accused of unnecessarily inflating the cost of its emergency allergy treatment, rendering it cost-prohibitive for many.[40] Parker appeared to be protecting her brand image.

Another aspect of celebrity effectiveness is their appeal or influence. There are a number of ways to measure such effectiveness. An **E score** is a system of ratings that measures the appeal of celebrities, athletes, and other newsmakers. A **Q score** is a measure of the familiarity of a celebrity as well as a company or brand. The Davie Brown Index measures a celebrity's awareness, appeal, and relevance as a brand image. It also evaluates the influence of the celebrity on buying behavior.

These scores are not just related to conventional celebrities. In social media, anyone can be a celebrity or at least attract a lot of followers. If you have a lot of followers, you may already have been scored in terms of your level of influence and identified as an "influencer." The website Klout is the dominant scorekeeper, but PeerIndex is another rating service for social networks. Scores range from 1 to 100, and the average score is in the high teens. A score in the 40s indicates a strong following.[41] Those with higher scores are the people whom marketers want to cultivate as brand advocates.

Matching Messages to Objectives

We talked earlier about message planning, including objectives, and then moved to a discussion of various types of message strategies. Now let's try to bring those two together. What types of messages deliver which objectives? If it's a credibility problem, for example, you might want to think about a testimonial, a demonstration of proof, a reason why, or even a news release with the built-in believability of a journalistic story. The Facets Model of Effects can be helpful in thinking through objectives and their related strategies.

- *Messages That Get Attention* To be effective, an advertisement needs to get exposure through the media buy and get attention through the message. Getting consumers' attention requires stopping power. Creative advertising breaks through the old patterns of seeing and saying things: the unexpectedness of the new idea creates stopping power. Messages that stop the scanning and break through the clutter can also be high in personal relevance, such as the Always "#LikeAGirl" online video. Intrusiveness is particularly important in cluttered markets. Many clutter-busting ads use multiple platforms and are intrusive, employing loud, bold effects to attract viewer attention—they work by shouting. Others use engaging, captivating ideas, curiosity/ambiguity, or mesmerizing visuals. Curiosity is particularly important for teaser strategies.

- *Messages That Create Interest* Getting attention reflects the stopping power of an advertisement; keeping attention reflects the ad's pulling power. An interesting thought keeps readers' or viewers' attention and pulls them through to the end of the message. One way to intensify interest is through curiosity, such as using a teaser campaign where the message unfolds over time. Ads that open with questions or dubious or ambiguous statements are designed to create curiosity.

- *Messages That Resonate* Ads that amplify the emotional impact of a message by engaging a consumer in a personal connection with a brand are said to resonate with the target audience, as illustrated by the University of Southern California–branded hospitals in a campaign that connected audiences with a message they could relate to, the USC fight song.

Photo: Copyright 2010 University of Southern California (USC) and Swanson Russell. Used with permission.

The University of Southern California's branded USC hospitals suffered from low awareness and preference in the crowded Los Angeles market. Swanson Russell, the agency working with hospitals, uncovered the insight that the hospitals' medical staff fought with the same fighting spirit as their athletic counterparts—just in a different arena. Building on this insight the "Fight On" campaign echoed the battle cry of USC's fight song and made the hospitals a household name by making the grit and courage of the medical staff the centerpiece of a campaign.

- ***Messages That Create Believability*** Advertising sometimes uses a credibility strategy to intensify the believability of a message. Using data to support or prove a claim is critical. The use of brand characters such as Colonel Sanders for KFC, who was a real person and the creator of the famous chicken recipe ("11 herbs and spices"), is designed to give consumers a *reason to believe* in a brand by cementing conviction.

- ***Messages That Are Remembered*** Not only do messages have to *stop* (get attention) and *pull* (create interest), but they also have to *stick* (in memory), which is another important part of the perceptual process. Most advertisements, such as the Smokey Bear campaign, are carefully designed to ensure that these memory traces are easy to recall. In Chapter 5, we explained that much of advertising's impact lies in its delayed effects; hence, memorability is a huge factor in effectiveness. Ads use catchy headlines, curiosity, and intriguing visuals to make this recall process as easy as possible and lock the message in memory.

- Repetition is used both in media and message strategy to ensure memorability. Jingles are valuable memorability devices because the music allows the advertiser to repeat a phrase or product name without boring the audience. Clever phrases are useful not only because they grab the consumer's attention, but also because they can be repeated to intensify memorability. Brand communication uses **slogans** for brands and campaigns, such as "Get Met. It Pays" (MetLife) or Nike's slogan, "Just Do It." **Taglines** are used at the end of an ad to summarize the point of the ad's message in a highly memorable way, such as Energizer's "Nothing outlasts the Energizer. It keeps going and going and going." In addition to verbal memory devices, many print and interactive messages and most television commercials feature a *key visual*. This visual is a vivid image that the advertiser hopes will linger in the viewer's mind. Color can be a memory cue. Wrigley's Doublemint gum uses green, and Juicy Fruit uses yellow.

- ***Messages That Touch Emotions*** Emotional appeals create feeling-based responses, such as love, fear, anxiety, envy, sexual attraction, happiness and joy, sorrow, safety and security, pride, pleasure, embarrassment, and nostalgia. Appetite appeal uses mouth-watering food shots to elicit feelings of hunger and craving. A more general emotional goal is to deliver a message that people like so as to create liking for the brand.

  Growing research suggests that music, such as instrumental scores, songs, jingles, and sonic brand signatures, can strengthen the emotional bond between brands and audiences and affect how consumers respond to the brand and communication. Given this evidence, music should be an integral part the creative work of the campaign rather than an afterthought, which it often is.[42]

- ***Messages That Inform*** Companies often use news announcements to provide information about new products, to tout reformulated products, or even to let consumers know about new uses for old products. The news angle, which is often delivered through news releases, is information focused. Informative ads and brochures that focus on features and attributes seek to create understanding about a product's advantages. Comparison ads are often heavy on information and used to explain a product's point of difference and competitive advantage. Attributes can be both tangible and intangible (Figure 9.4). The ads for Sunkist oranges and Tiffany's focus on tangible and intangible features.

- ***Messages That Teach*** People learn through instruction, so some advertisements are designed to teach, such as demonstrations that show how something works or how to solve a problem. Educational messages are sometimes designed to explain something, such as why it is important to brush your teeth or get involved in local politics. Learning also is strengthened through repetition. That's why repetition is such an important media objective.

- ***Messages That Persuade*** Persuasive messages are designed to affect attitudes and create belief. Strategies that are particularly good are *testimonials* and messages that generate word of mouth about the product. Endorsements by celebrities or experts are used to intensify conviction. Selling premises that focus on how the product will benefit the consumer, state a reason why, or explain a USP are persuasive, particularly if they provide proof or support. Torture tests, comparisons, and before-and-after demonstrations also are used to prove the truth of a claim. Conviction is often built on strong, rational arguments that use such techniques as test results, before-and-after visuals, testimonials by users and experts, and demonstrations to prove something. Celebrities, product placements, and other credibility techniques are used to give the consumer **permission to believe** a claim or selling premise.

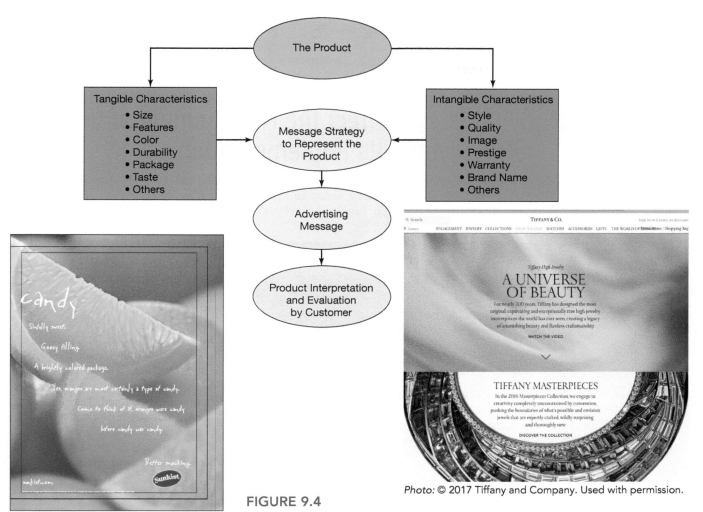

Photo: Sunkist Growers, Inc.

Photo: © 2017 Tiffany and Company. Used with permission.

FIGURE 9.4

Tangible and Intangible Product Attributes

The diagram illustrates the characteristics of tangible and intangible features. The Sunkist ad compares its oranges to candy, but in the comparison it identifies tangible product characteristics, such as flavor and color. The Tiffany ad uses intangibles: it associates the Tiffany brand image with luxury, beauty and flawless craftsmanship.

- *Messages That Create Brand Associations* The transformative power of branding, where the brand takes on a distinctive character and meaning, is one of brand communication's most important functions. *Image advertising*, in particular, is used to create a representation of a brand, an image in a consumer's mind, through symbolism. Advertising's role is to provide the cues that make these meanings and experiences come together in a coherent brand image. The Sunkist ad associated oranges with candy to convey the message of sweetness. An association message strategy delivers information and feelings symbolically by connecting a brand with a certain type of person or lifestyle. This link is often created through visuals. Some advertising strategies want you to identify with the user of the product or see yourself in that situation.

- *Messages That Drive Action* Even harder to accomplish than conviction is a change in behavior. It often happens that people believe one thing and do another. The Road Crew campaign was designed to overcome a gap between attitudes and behavior. Sometimes an advertising message can drive people to act by offering something free or at a discounted sales price. Sales promotion, for example, works in tandem with advertising to stimulate immediate action using sampling, coupons, and free gifts as incentives for action. Most ads end with a signature of some kind that serves to identify the company or brand, but it also serves as a **call to action** and gives direction to the consumer about how to respond, such as a toll-free phone number, website URL, or email address. Similar to the Road Crew campaign, another form of action is to discourage or extinguish actions, such as smoking, drug use, or driving drunk.

● **Principle**

A message needs to *stop* (get attention), *pull* (create interest), and *stick* (be memorable).

Ultimately, marketers want loyal customers who purchase and repurchase the product as a matter of habit or preference. **Reminder advertising**, as well as distributing coupons or introducing a continuity program (such as a frequent-flyer program), is designed to keep the brand name in front of customers to encourage their repeat business.

9.4 Define issues affecting the management of creative strategy and its implementation.

What Issues Affect the Management of Creative Strategy and Its Implementation?

We've talked about creative strategy and how it is developed as well as message strategies that deliver on these objectives. Let's now take a quick look at three management issues related to creative strategies: extension, adaptation, and evaluation.

Photo: Courtesy of Mastercard

Mastercard's "Priceless" campaign, introduced in 1997, demonstrates the concept of extendability, which means that the audiences have found the concept relevant over a period of time and in different media.

Extension: An Idea with Legs

One characteristic of a Big Idea is that it gives *legs* to a campaign. By that, we mean that the idea is strong enough to serve as an umbrella concept for a variety of executions in different media talking to different audiences. It can be endlessly extended. Extendability is a strength of Chick-fil-A, Geico's gecko, and Frontier's talking animals campaigns. The Mastercard "Priceless" idea is another outstanding example of a Big Idea that has been used over time and across many platforms. Extendability is what Stuhlfaut was referring to when he explained that creative thinking is *generative*.

Adaptation: Taking an Idea Global

The opportunity for standardizing the campaign across multiple markets exists only if the objectives and strategic position are essentially the same. Otherwise, a creative strategy may call for a little tweaking of the message for a local market or even major revision if there are cultural and market differences.

In the case where the core targeting and positioning strategies remain the same in different markets, it might be possible for the central creative idea to be universal across markets. Although the execution of this idea may vary from market to market, the creative concept works across all types of consumers. Even if the campaign theme, slogan, or visual elements are the same across markets, it is usually desirable to adapt the creative execution to the local market, as we explained in the discussion of cultural differences in Chapter 7.

An example of a difficult adaptation comes from Apple's series of "Mac vs. PC" ads that show a nerdy PC guy who can't keep up with the activities of a laid-back Mac guy. It uses delicate humor and body language to make subtle points about the advantages of the Mac system. In moving the campaign to Japan, Apple's agency TBWA/Chiat/Day wrestled with the fact that in Japanese culture, direct-comparison ads are considered rude. The Japanese version was tweaked to make the Apple more of a home computer and the PC a work tool, so the differences were focused more on place than on person.[43] The point is that cultural differences often require nuanced and subtle changes in ads if they are to be acceptable beyond the country of their origin.

Evaluation: The Go/No-Go Decision

How do you decide if the creative idea is strong enough to justify the expense of creating a campaign based on it? Whether local or global, an important part of managing creative work is evaluation, which happens at several stages in the creative process. Later we'll focus on evaluation of effectiveness, but we'll introduce some basics here to help you understand this important final step in the creative process.

A book on Bill Bernbach and the golden age of advertising, *Nobody's Perfect* by Doris Willens,[44] analyzed the brilliant advertising his creative team at DDB produced during the 1960s. In commenting on the book, positioning guru Al Ries observed that Bernbach was a true creative genius because he had the ability to sort good ideas from bad. Ries concluded, "It's a trait that's extremely rare."[45]

So nobody starts off being a Bernbach, but everyone can learn to be more critical about the brand messages they see. The first question to ask is, Is it on strategy? No matter how much the creative people, client, or account executive may like an idea, if it doesn't communicate the right message or the right product personality to the right audience at the right time, it is not effective.

However, as Alex Bogusky, formerly chief creative officer at Crispin Porter + Bogusky, said about the firm's over-the-top work (think the Burger King king), "I don't mind spectacular failure or spectacular criticism," because those ideas make headlines, which means everybody's talking about them. "There's so much advertising that nobody knows even exists," he added. "That's the stuff that I worry about making."[46]

Structural Analysis   The Leo Burnett agency has used an approach for analyzing the logic of the creative strategy that goes beyond just evaluating the strategy. The Burnett creative teams have used it to keep the message strategy and creative concept working together. This method, called **structural analysis**, relies on these three steps:

1. Evaluate the *power of the narrative* or story line (heart).
2. Evaluate the *strength of the product claim* (head).
3. Consider *how well the two are integrated*—that is, how the story line brings the claim to life.

Burnett creative teams check to see whether the narrative level is so high that it overpowers the claim or whether the claim is strong but there is no memorable story. Ideally, these two elements will be so seamless that it is hard to tell whether the impact occurs because of the power of the story or the strength of the claim. Such an analysis keeps the rational and emotional sides of an advertisement working together. It's important to test your ideas, and you'll learn about the tools to measure and predict their impact in Chapter 17.

A particular problem that Big Ideas face is that the message is sometimes so creative that the ad is remembered but not the brand. That's called **vampire creativity**, and it is one reason some advertisers shy away from really novel or entertaining strategies. That's also why it is important to test the effectiveness of the ad's creative features while still in the idea stage to determine if there is brand linkage and memorability.

Principle
Vampire creativity means the creative storyline overpowers the brand message.

Looking Ahead

This chapter is a brief review of creative thinking and message strategy. The next step in learning about the inner workings of the creative side is to move to the execution of message, both copy and design. We'll talk first about promotional writing in Chapter 10 and then visual communication in Chapter 11.

IT'S A WRAP

Taking the Outside Chance Pays Off

REI demonstrated an extraordinary empathy and commitment to its customers when it closed its stores and recommended that customers go outside and not shopping on Black Friday. The bold idea won the Best of Show at the One Show and a Grand Prix at the Cannes Lions International Advertising Festival. Even more important is that it was a big win for the brand.

About 1.4 million people heeded the message and played outside instead of going shopping. The effort generated a whopping 2.7 billion public relations impressions (more on that in later chapters).

The idea gained momentum. In the second year, 6,033,922 opted to spend the day outside and more than 500 organizations, including Subaru, partnered with REI, parks, and eco-friendly groups in the project.

John Hegarty, Bartle Bogle Hegarty founder and jury member of the competition, commended this award-winning work: "You should not be able to see where the advertising stops and the brand starts,"[47] he said. According to another jury member, the campaign broke new ground in part because REI "took the retail website and turned it into a place where you can discover parks. It grabbed you emotionally." Another jury member, Rob Reilly, global creative chairman for McCann Worldgroup, dubbed it "the greatest anti-promotion of all time" and said that #OptOutside "was just an amazing demonstration of a brand walking the talk."[48]

As students of IMC, we can learn a lot from REI, namely:

1. Zig when others zag. Be creative.
2. Have courage to execute bold ideas. Take risks.
3. Find an authentic voice for your brand. Stay true to the mission.
4. Know your customers. Empathize with them.
5. Products are more than things to buy. They add meaning to customers' lives.

Photo: Susan Montgomery/Shutterstock

KEY OBJECTIVES SUMMARY

9.1. Describe the role of creativity in integrated marketing communication. Creativity can be defined as the generation of fresh ideas and solutions to current problems or challenges. A winning marketing communication idea must be both *creative* (original, different, novel, and unexpected) and *strategic* (right for the product and target and meeting the objectives). In the context of marketing communications, creativity has traditionally been associated with advertising. Creative work in advertising is a product of a team that includes copywriters, art directors, social media directors, and video producers, all led by a creative director. In the contemporary media environment, creativity isn't just about ads anymore. Ideas that help solve communication problems can come from anyone in the process and from all IMC disciplines. The key to creativity is to connect content with audiences. In the world of interactive media, the consumer increasingly participates in the creative activity.

9.2. Explain creative thinking and how you get the Big Idea. An effective message makes a relevant connection with its audience and presents a convincing idea in an unexpected way that helps audiences see brands and products in intended ways. There is both a science (the way a message is persuasive, convincing, and relevant) and an art (the way a message is an unexpected idea). A Big Idea is a creative concept that makes the message attention getting and memorable. A typical creative process involves immersing yourself in background research; developing alternatives through ideation; getting past brainfag, where you hit the wall and can't come up with anything; and embracing illumination of the great idea.

9.3. Identify key message strategy approaches. A creative brief gives teams a plan to work from and identifies message objectives, targeting, branding, and positioning. Creative strategies are often expressed as appeals to the head, the heart, or both. More complex systems of strategies have been proposed by Frazer and Taylor. Creative strategy formats include lectures, dramas, psychological appeals, and selling strategies. Different formulas have evolved that deliver these strategies and guide the development of executions.

9.4. Define issues affecting the management of creative strategy and its implementation. Those working on the creative side of advertising must do so within the parameters of the business context. Some factors that have an impact on the development of creative strategy and its implementation are extension, adaptation, and evaluation. A concept is extendable if it can serve as an umbrella idea for other communication. A campaign is adaptable if the idea can be used in another context, such as a global application. Evaluation is a critical management issue because it is important to test whether a concept communicates the intended message to the target audience.

KEY TERMS

appeal, p. 268
attributes, p. 269
benefit, p. 269
Big Idea, p. 253
brainfag, p. 259
brainstorming, p. 260
brand icon, p. 270
call to action, p. 273
claim, p. 269
clichés, p. 252
comparison, p. 269
concepting, p. 252
copycat advertising, p. 256
creative brief, p. 262
creative concept, p. 252
creative director, p. 251
creative strategy, p. 262
creativity, p. 250

demonstration, p. 269
design thinking, p. 260
divergent thinking, p. 257
E score, p. 271
endorser, p. 270
evaluation, p. 259
execution, p. 262
features, p. 269
free association, p. 261
hard sell, p. 265
humor, p. 270
idea, p. 252
ideation, p. 259
illumination, p. 259
immersion, p. 259
impact, p. 256
incubation, p. 259
left-brain thinking, p. 257

message design, p. 264
message strategy, p. 262
original, p. 256
permission to believe, p. 272
public relations plan, p. 262
public relations management
  process, p. 262
problem solution message,
  p. 270
product-as-hero, p. 270
promise, p. 269
Q score, p. 271
reason why, p. 269
relevant, p. 256
reminder advertising, p. 274
right-brain thinking, p. 257
selling premise, p. 268
slice-of-life message, p. 270

slogans, p. 272
soft sell, p. 265
spokes-character, p. 270
spokesperson, p. 270
straightforward message,
  p. 269
structural analysis, p. 275
substantiation, p. 269
support, p. 269
taglines, p. 272
teaser, p. 270
tone of voice, p. 262
unique selling proposition
  (USP), p. 269
user experience (UX) design,
  p. 251
vampire creativity, p. 275

MyLab Marketing

Go to **www.pearson.com/mylab/marketing** for MyLab discussion questions (⬡) as well as the following assisted-graded writing questions:

9-1. What is an appeal? How do advertisements touch people's emotions? Discuss two techniques.

9-2. Find the campaign in this book that you think is the most creative.
- What is its Big Idea? How and why does it work?
- Analyze the ad in terms of the ROI formula for evaluating effective creative advertising.
- Re-create the creative brief that would summarize the message strategy.

REVIEW QUESTIONS

9-3. This chapter argues that effective brand communication is both a science and an art. Explain what that means and give examples of each.

⬡ **9-4.** How do various strategic approaches deliver on the objectives identified in the Facets Model of Effects?

9-5. Explain four types of selling premises.

9-6. What is a Big Idea, and what are its characteristics?

9-7. What does it mean when a creative director says that your idea needs to make a "creative leap"?

9-8. Describe the five steps in the creative process.

9-9. Explain how brainstorming is used in IMC.

9-10. List five characteristics of creative people. How do you rate yourself on those factors?

DISCUSSION QUESTIONS

⬡ **9-11** Divide the class into groups of 6 to 10 people and discuss this problem: *Your community wants to encourage people to get out of their cars and use alternative forms of transportation.* Brainstorm for 15 minutes as a group, accumulating every possible idea. How many ideas are generated?

Here's how to run this brainstorming group.
- Appoint one member to be the *recorder* who lists all the ideas as they are mentioned.
- Appoint another member to be the *moderator* and suggest techniques described in this chapter as idea starters.

- Identify a *cheerleader* to keep the discussion positive and find gentle ways to discourage critical or negative comments.
- Work for 15 minutes generating as many different creative concepts as your team can come up with, regardless of how crazy or dumb they might initially sound.
- Go back through the list as a group and put an asterisk next to the 5 to 10 ideas that seem to have the most promise.

When all the groups reconvene in class, each recorder should list the group's best ideas on the blackboard. As a class, pick out the three ideas that seem to have the most potential. Analyze the experience of participating in a brainstorming group and compare the experiences of the different teams.

9-12. The following are from actual brand communication campaigns. If you were involved in the go/no-go decision, what would you decide? For each idea, explain your analysis.

- You're assigned to develop a Super Bowl ad for the Groupon internet coupon website that advertises daily deals in local media. The company has been using a "Save the Money" campaign, with Hollywood stars talking about a cause they support and then connecting that to a deal they got off Groupon. So, what should you do for the Super Bowl? A colleague suggests using a star speaking about the plight of the Tibetan people and their culture, with pictures of snow-capped mountains and dancing children followed by a scene with the star in a Himalayan restaurant talking about what he saved on his meal. What do you think about this idea?
- Zappos, an online apparel retailer with a quirky, brash culture, has received a proposal from its agency. You are on the Zappos management team. The idea is to show naked models doing everyday things, such as jogging, playing Frisbee, hailing a cab, and riding a Vespa—all with censor bars strategically placed. Although using naked people to sell clothing is a little literal, the agency argues that it also is highly attention getting. What do you think?

TAKE-HOME PROJECTS

9-13. *Portfolio Project:* Find at least two newspaper or magazine advertisements that you believe are bland and unexciting. Rewrite them, first to demonstrate a hard-sell approach and then to demonstrate a soft-sell approach. Explain how your rewrites have improved the original ad. Also explain how the hard-sell and soft-sell appeals work. Which do you believe is the most effective for each ad? If you were a team of professionals working on these accounts, how would you go about evaluating

the effectiveness of these two ads? In other words, how would you test your intuitive judgment of which one works best?

9-14. *Mini-Case Analysis:* Summarize the creativity aspects of the REI "#OptOutside" effort. What makes this effort and its promotion creative? Brainstorm an idea for a new campaign that would extend the campaign's theme and develop this new Big Idea as a proposal to present to your instructor.

TRACE North America Case

Creative Multicultural Communication

Read the TRACE case in the Appendix before coming to class.

9-15. What was the Big Idea behind the "Hard to Explain, Easy to Experience" campaign?

9-16. How would you describe the campaign's message strategy?

10

Promotional Writing

KEY OBJECTIVES

10.1   Describe the writer's role in brand communication.

10.2   Name the types of brand communication writing.

10.3   Explain how to write for various media.

10.4   Identify some challenges that writers face.

In this chapter, you will learn about the role of promotional writing in marketing communications and how brands like Old Spice use multiple platforms to communicate their message and engage their customers. Words and pictures work together to produce a creative concept. However, the idea behind a creative concept in communication is usually expressed in some attention-getting and memorable phrase, such as "Curiously Strong Mints"[1] for Altoids. Finding these magic words is the responsibility of writers who search for the right way to warm up a mood or appeal to the audience. This chapter describes the role of the writer as part of this team and explains the practice of writing in advertising, public relations, and direct response in various types of media.

MyLab Marketing

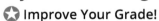 **Improve Your Grade!**

More than 10 million students improved their results using Pearson MyLabs.
Visit **www.pearson.com/mylab/marketing** for simulations, tutorials, and end-of-chapter problems.

Campaigns	**Company**	**Agency**	**Awards**
"The Man Your Man Could Smell Like," "Smellcome to Manhood"	*Old Spice/Procter & Gamble*	*Weiden+Kennedy, lead agency*	*Long-running Grand Effie and Gold Effie Awards in Beauty Products, Brand Experience, Media Innovation, Single Impact Engagement, Personal Care, and Sustained Success categories; Emmy for Outstanding Commercial*

Old Spice: Masculinity Delivered Ridiculously

Photo: Courtesy Procter & Gamble. Used with permission.

Photo: Courtesy Procter & Gamble. Used with permission.

In 2008, Old Spice appeared to be an aging deodorant brand, which had been eclipsed by its younger rivals. The following year Procter & Gamble (P&G), led by Weiden+Kennedy (the same agency that handles Nike), launched an aggressive, humorous campaign aimed at regaining its leadership position. The campaign, "What it

Photo: Courtesy Wieden + Kennedy. Used with permission.

takes to be a man," and its subsequent iterations show what it takes to be a great campaign and is literally a textbook case about how to engage with your audience through different kinds of writing and content.

Old Spice advertising is a good starting point for this chapter because it lets us see promotional writing through a lens of change. What worked to convince your grandfather to use Old Spice probably wouldn't persuade guys to use it now. You can see for yourself that a 1948 ad for Old Spice with the headline "Sail into Dad's Heart" and pictures of shaving lotions probably wouldn't cut it today to sell much shaving cream. Advertising has evolved to be much more complex than simply announcing that a brand of shaving cream is for sale, as the more recent "The Man Your Man

Could Smell Like" campaign proves. Let's take a behind-the-scenes look at what makes this award-winning campaign so effective.

P&G faced a significant challenge to protect Old Spice's share in the male body wash segment and boost sales amid fierce competition, particularly from Dove Men+Care body wash that was being introduced during the 2010 Super Bowl. Old Spice was perceived as a manly scent, not a feminine scent like other brands. P&G's research surprisingly revealed that women—not men—purchased 60 percent of men's body wash. The big idea driving the marketing communication: the campaign needed to spark conversations between men and women talking about a manly-scented body wash. If you want to "smell like a man," the choice is obvious: Old Spice.

Former NFL football tight end Isaiah Mustafa (remember the bare-chested guy on the horse?) brought the message to life with his hilarious and over-the-top delivery about manhood. Executing the idea in the digital age requires more than running an ad in a magazine or a commercial on television. P&G devised a strategy that involved using media in an innovative way, building buzz with social media and using YouTube, Facebook, Twitter, and the Old Spice website as well as television commercials to get people talking. Extending the campaign success, the brand offered a "response campaign" that showed "The Man Your Man Could Smell Like" responding in 180 videos to tweets and questions posed to him. Viewers responded to the interactivity and loved what they saw.

Old Spice's work is varied and evolving, and pieces are united by a simple brand promise: "masculinity delivered ridiculously." The infectious humor runs consistently throughout the award-winning campaign that has become a cultural phenomenon with edgy lines like: "The original. If your grandfather hadn't worn it, you wouldn't exist."

Some recent updates: "Smellcome to Manhood" challenges the Axe domination in the body spray category by using moms to tell the story of the spray as a symbol of transition from boyhood to manhood. Old Spice also created the videogame "Youland" to engage users. It uses your face and allows for personalization in the videogame as well as an appearance by Mustafa, who disappears after revealing he was only paid for "45 seconds of voice-over work." To continue to convince guys that Old Spice is cool, a new Old Spice Guy, Denver Broncos star linebacker Von Miller, was named to be the face of Old Spice's Hardest Working Collection. As they used to say on TV, stay tuned for the next installment.

Did Old Spice whip its competition? Turn to the It's a Wrap section at the end of the chapter to learn about the results and see if grandpa's brand is a big hit with the later generations.

Sources: "The Man Your Man Could Smell Like," Effie Awards published case study, Sept. 26, 2013, www.effie.org; Bruce Watson, "Smells Like Viral Advertising: Old Spice through the Ages," July 16, 2010, www.dailyfinance.com; "3 of the Most Successful Social Media Marketing Campaigns and Their Secrets to Becoming Viral," September 29, 2015, www.5thagency.com; John McCarthy, "Old Spice Lands You and Your Friends in a Nutty Retro Game Using Facebook," June 21, 2016, www.thedrum.com; Ad Age Staff, "Top Ad Campaigns of the 21st Century," January 12, 2015, www.adage.com; "Old Spice Names NFL Super Bowl MVP Von Miller as New Old Spice Guy to Represent the Legendary Performance of the Hardest Working Collection," August 23, 2016, http://news.oldspice.com/press-release/old-spice-names-nfl-super-bowl-mvp-von-miller-new-old-spice-guy-represent-legendary-pe, "Old Spice: The Scent of Success," https://effie.org/case_database/case/NA_2016_438329, retrieved August 14, 2017; www.effie.org/case_studies; Adweek Staff, "Old Spice: Smells Like a Commercial," August 24, 2010, www.adweek.com.

The Writer's Role in Brand Communication

10.1 Describe the writer's role in brand communication.

Writers in the different areas of brand communication have specialized skills. Advertising copywriting is a major job category. The ability to write well is equally critical for public relations and direct marketing. All these areas have specialists, but in some agencies and corporate departments, writers are expected to handle all different types of marketing communication. We'll begin with some general writing considerations and then discuss specific areas in more detail.

The Language of Brand Communication

The most important word selection in marketing communication is the brand or corporate name, and this responsibility can lie with the advertising department, corporate communication, or an outside branding consultant. Low-cost airline JetBlue was originally founded in 1999 as New Air, but its founders realized it needed a more distinctive name. They considered naming it Taxi and painting the planes yellow but backed off because of negative associations with New York City taxis and questionable service. JetBlue has been a good choice because it states the business (jet = airlines) as well as sky (blue) with its calming connotations.

There is a science to letters and sounds as well as words. Research has determined that letters with a hard edge, like T or K, suggest effectiveness (Kodak, Target, Tide); X and Z relate to science (Xcel, Zantac, Xerox); C, L, R, P, and S are calming or relaxing (Cialis, Lexus, Puffs, Revlon, Silk); and Z means speed (Zippo, Ziplock, Zappos.com). In the erectile dysfunction category, Lilly's drug Cialis is derived from *ciel*, the French word for "sky," and was chosen because it is a smooth, soft sound that connotes a sense of intimacy. In contrast, Pfizer's Viagra evokes the power of Niagara Falls.[2]

Many brand names are made up, but it's not just names that are created by marketing communicators. The "uncola" position was created for 7-Up, and more recently the True Value hardware chain has proclaimed itself "masters of all things hardwarian," a phrase that suggests mastery of a traditional art or skill.

A long-term brand or corporate identity effort, **slogans** have to be catchy and memorable. A distinctive catchphrase that serves as a motto for a campaign, brand, or company, it is used across a variety of marketing communication platforms and over an extended period of time. The award-winning and much-copied "What happens in Vegas stays in Vegas" is a tourism slogan permanently enshrined on the Madison Avenue Walk of Fame that hints at the pleasures you don't enjoy at home. "When it absolutely, positively has to be there overnight" helped separate FedEx from its competitors.[3]

The word **tagline** is often used to refer to a slogan, but technically it means a line at the end of an ad that wraps up the creative concept. It's more of a campaign theme than a brand slogan, so it is less enduring than a slogan and seldom positions the brand. For example, Motel 6 uses the tagline, "We'll leave the light on for you." Its slogan is "Lowest price of any national chain."[4]

The best slogans have a close link to the brand name: "With a name like Smucker's, it has to be good," "America runs on Dunkin'," "Ford Tough," and "Nothing runs like a Deere."[5]

Here's another characteristic of a good slogan: it is enduring. Classic slogans are rarely changed. A true classic, Maxwell House's "Good to the last drop," has been used since 1915, and Morton Salt's "When it rains, it pours" has been around since 1914. Avis's "We Try Harder" slogan, created by the DDB agency and its legendary copywriter Paula Green, has been used since 1962 and is a classic example of a slogan that communicates a position as well as a brand personality.[6]

The "Don't Mess with Texas"[7] antilitter slogan was by Austin-based GSD&M for the Texas Department of Transportation and has literally been talking trash for many years. The award-winning social-marketing campaign built around this slogan features billboards, print ads, radio and television spots, and a host of celebrities (Willie Nelson, Stevie Ray Vaughan, Matthew McConaughey, George Foreman, and LeAnn Rimes, among others) who take turns with the tough-talking slogan that captures the spirit and pride of Texans. One billboard, for example, warns, "Keep Your Butts in the Car." The Dontmesswithtexas .org website, where you can see all these ads, including the commercials, has also been featured by *Adweek* as a "Cool Site."

Photo: Gabbro/Alamy Stock Photo

The long-running "Don't mess with Texas" campaign has been talking trash since 1986.

Of course, slogans also have to be original, as Wisconsinites found out when the official state slogan was changed to "Live Like You Mean It." The state spent some $50,000 on the new slogan and then later discovered that it had been used as the tagline in a Bacardi Rum campaign.[8]

Unfortunately, many corporate slogans fall back into marketing language or clichés and come across as leaden ("Excellence through total quality" or "Where quality counts"). Wells Fargo, for example, uses "Together we'll go far," which is not distinctive, could be used by any company, and says nothing about Wells Fargo or its business. Accenture uses "High performance. Delivered." which is neither distinctive nor memorable. Consider the distinctiveness and memorability of the following slogans:[9]

TEST YOURSELF

Match the company with its slogan:[10]

1. Working together for patients
2. Imagination at work
3. A mind is a terrible thing to waste
4. See impossible
5. Where dreams come true
6. Melts in your mouth, not in your hands
7. Live mas
8. Just do it.
9. Diamonds are forever
10. Think different
11. When you care enough to send the very best
12. Shave time. Shave money.
13. That's powerful
14. The ultimate driving machine
15. The quicker picker upper
16. When it absolutely, positively has to be there overnight
17. Because I'm worth it
18. What can brown do for you?

A. Bounty
B. Bristol-Myers Squibb
C. Hallmark
D. BMW
E. Dollar Shave Club
F. Verizon
G. Disney
H. FedEx
I. L'Oréal
J. Taco Bell
K. UPS
L. Canon
M. Apple
N. De Beers
O. Nike
P. M&Ms
Q. United Negro College Fund
R. GE

Answers to Companies: 1:B Bristol-Myers Squibb; 2:R GE; 3:Q United Negro College Fund; 4:L Canon; 5:G Disney Parks; 6:P M&Ms; 7:J Taco Bell; 8:O Nike; 9:N De Beers; 10:M Apple; 11:C Hallmark; 12:E Dollar Shave Club; 13:F Verizon; 14:D BMW; 15:A Bounty; 16:H FedEx; 17:I L'Oréal; 18:K UPS

Study the slogans in the matching activity. Which ones did you get, and which ones stumped you? Which do you think are the best? Why?

Writers can increase the memorability of slogans with a variety of literary techniques. Here are some ideas.

- *Direct Address* "Have it your way"[11]; "Think small."
- *A Startling or Unexpected Phrase* Twists a common phrase to make it unexpected, as in the NYNEX campaign "If it's out there, it's in here" or the Perdue Farms tagline "It takes a tough man to make a tender chicken."[12]
- *Rhyme, Rhythm, Alliteration* Uses repetition of sounds, as in rhyme ("The best part of waking up is Folgers in your cup") and alliteration (M&Ms' "Melts in your mouth . . . not in your hands").[13]
- *Parallel Construction* Uses repetition of the structure of a sentence or phrase, as in Morton Salt's "When it rains, it pours."[14]

- *Cue the Product* Maxwell House's "Good to the last drop"; John Deere's "Nothing runs like a Deere"; Wheaties' "Breakfast of Champions"; "Beef. It's What's for Dinner."[15]
- *Music* "In the valley of the Jolly, ho-ho-ho, Green Giant."[16]
- *Double entendre* De Beers has used "A diamond is forever"[17] since 1938, and it works because two different meanings create connections with consumers: a diamond should last forever, and a diamond ring is a symbol of infinite love.
- *Combination* "It's your land, lend a hand," which is the slogan for Take Pride in America (rhyme, rhythm, parallel).
- *Keep Them Short* "Eat Mor Chikin" for Chick-fil-A.[18]

Writing Styles

Writing in brand communication can be formal or informal, personal or impersonal, and it uses all possible types of media. We'll discuss three types of promotional writing in this chapter: advertising, public relations, and direct response. All have some things in common, but their stylistics vary tremendously.

Advertising   In almost all situations, advertising has to win its audience, which is no small task given that it usually competes in a cluttered environment and the audience is generally inattentive and uninterested. For that reason, the copy should be as simple as possible; think "Eat Mor Chikin." Chick-fil-A's single line of copy is succinct and single-minded, meaning that it has a clear focus and conveys only one selling point.

Every word counts because both space and time are expensive. Ineffective or overused words and phrases—such as *interesting*, *very*, *in order to*, *buy now and save*, *introducing*, and *nothing less than*—waste precious space. The challenge of writing verbal diamonds in 140 characters predates Twitter; consider that the average outdoor board copy has always been around eight words.

● **Principle**
Effective copy is succinct, single-minded, and tightly focused.

Ad copy is usually written in a conversational style using real people language. The legendary David Ogilvy, founder of the advertising agency that bears his name, Ogilvy & Mather, explained his view many years ago of advertising as conversation:

> I always pretend that I'm sitting beside a woman at a dinner party, and she asks me for advice about which product she should buy and where she should buy it. So then I write down what I would say to her. I give her the facts, facts, facts. I try to make them interesting, fascinating, if possible, and personal—I don't write to the crowd. I try to write from one human being to another. . . . And I try not to bore the poor woman to death, and I try to make it as real and personal as possible.[19]

You can listen to David Ogilvy talking about his views on advertising on YouTube.

Copywriters try to write the way the target audience thinks and talks, often with personal language and direct address. For example, an ad for Trojan condoms makes a pointed argument on a touchy subject for its young, single-target audience. Combining headline with body copy, it reads as a dialogue:

> I didn't use one because I didn't have one with me.
> Get real.
> If you don't have a parachute, don't jump, genius.

Writing for print, video, audio, the internet, and social media demands that advertising copywriters apply styles appropriate to the media they employ and audience with which they communicate. The "Cool Not Cool" campaign has what Meg Lauerman calls in her essay that opened Part 3 the "power to engage the hearts and inspire the action of thousands," in this case, teens. Developing techniques to be able to effectively communicate in this way will be covered later in this chapter.

Public Relations   There are a variety of styles of writing used in public relations because that area uses so many different types of communication tools. Publicity, for example, is designed for news media and uses the basic stylistics of journalism. Corporate publications, such as newsletters and magazines, may be journalistic, but magazines may be more unconventional, with features about employees and moving personal stories. Public relations also produces

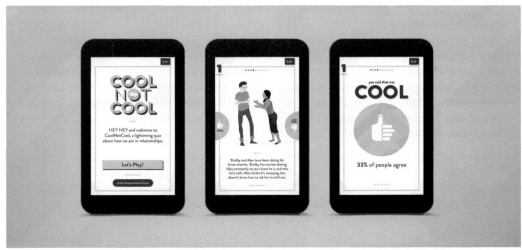

Photo: "That's Not Cool"® is a registered trademark of Futures Without Violence. Used with permission.

One in four teens in a relationship report that they have been called names, harassed, or put down by their partner through calls and texts, and that's not cool. Archrival partnered up with the Ad Council and Futures Without Violence to launch a mobile campaign as part of its "That's Not Cool" public service effort. With a focus on reaching teens, Archrival created an interactive game that helps teens identify inappropriate relationship interactions. Do you think the writing fits the audience?

corporate videos and news releases; again, the news releases and video news releases are more like television news, but the corporate videos may function more like films with action and dramatic stories. Public relations departments also produce brochures that can vary from informational to technical, depending on their audience. And public relations departments sometimes produce advertisements that may be created as part of a public relations campaign but also as corporate or advocacy point-of-view ads or a form known as *public service advertising*, which is developed in support of a good cause. So, public relations writers also need to know the stylistics of advertising writing. Knowing how to write effectively for the internet and social media is also an important tool for public relations professionals.

Direct Response   There are a number of media formats used in direct-response writing, everything from direct-mail letters and brochures to online social media and customer service or technical support. For that reason, the writing style can be more or less formal, depending on the target audience. On the other hand, the objective of many direct response efforts is to talk to individual customers or prospects using personalized messages (as much as possible) and direct address. It's about building a positive relationship with customers. Conversational style is more appropriate in the interactive forms that engage consumers one to one.

Strategy and Legal Imperatives

Common to all forms of brand communication are that it always has an objective and that it is designed to reach a particular audience, which means that even beautiful writing also has to make the strategy sing. If it doesn't move the audience and deliver on the objectives, it's not effective copywriting. That's true for all areas of promotional writing.

Not only does the writing have to be strategic, but the claims have to be tested and meet basic requirements of truth. The athletic shoe brand Skechers wound up paying $50 million to settle charges that its "toning shoes" language was using unfounded claims that the shoes would help consumers tone muscles and lose weight.[20] But sometimes it's hard for a writer to know what to do. Consider the following examples from the cereal market:

- Kellogg's was challenged by the Federal Trade Commission for advertising that children's attentiveness improved nearly 20 percent for those who ate Frosted Mini-Wheats compared to those who skipped breakfast. It's probably true that kids who eat breakfast pay more attention in school than kids who don't eat breakfast, but the commission said the numbers didn't support the claim.[21]

- Kellogg's Cocoa Krispies was challenged for bragging that the sugary cereal "helps support your child's immunity."[22]
- The Food and Drug Administration challenged Cheerios' long-running cholesterol-reduction claims: "You can lower your cholesterol 4 percent in six weeks." The agency allows the more general claim of reduced heart disease but doesn't allow specific rates of risk reduction, which it says is more appropriate for drugs. In defense of the Cheerios claim, General Mills responded that "the clinical study supporting Cheerios' cholesterol-lowering benefit is very strong." General Mills points to 25 years of clinical proof that Cheerios can help lower cholesterol and therefore is heart healthy.[23]

Are consumers being led astray by health claims on food packages, websites, and advertising? This problem concerns public relations as well as advertising. What is a writer to do if a marketing director asks for health claims? What kind of support would you like to see before you are comfortable writing this kind of copy?

10.2 Name the types of brand communication writing.

Types of Brand Communication Writing

We'll start with advertising copywriters because the other marketing communication areas also use advertising as part of their campaigns, and many of the advertising writing practices apply to all forms of promotional writing.

Advertising Copywriting

The person who shapes and sculpts the words in advertising is called a **copywriter**. *Copy* is the text of an ad or the words people say in a commercial. Copywriters begin with the strategy and creative brief. Then, working with an art director and perhaps a creative director, the creative team searches for Big Ideas in the form of magic words and powerful visuals that translate the strategy into a message that is attention getting and memorable. A truly great Big Idea will come to life in the interaction between the words and pictures, as illustrated by Nike's classic "Just Do It" campaign.

Although advertising is highly visual, words are crucial in the following four types of advertisements:

1. *Complex* If the message is complicated, particularly if it is making an argument, words can be more specific than visuals and can be read over and over until the meaning is clear.
2. *High Involvement* For a high-involvement product, meaning that the consumer spends a lot of time considering it, like purchasing a car, the more information, the better. That means using extensive copy.
3. *Explanation* Information that needs definition and explanation, such as how an electric car works, is best delivered through words.
4. *Abstract* If a message tries to convey abstract qualities, such as justice and quality, words tend to communicate these concepts more easily than pictures.

Photo: NIKE, Inc.

CLASSIC

"Just Do It" and the swish logo are so identifiable that they communicate even without the Nike name on the ad.

Love of Language A successful copywriter is a savvy marketer and a literary master, sometimes described as a "killer poet." Many copywriters have a background in English or literature. They love words and search for the clever twist, the pun, the powerful description, the punch, the nuance, and the rhyme and rhythm of speech. They use words that whip and batter, plead, sob, cajole, and impress. They know the meanings, derivations, moods, and feelings of words and the reverberations and vibrations they create in a reader's mind.

The Soul of a Copywriter

Nick Ciffone, *Creative Director, TBWA/Media Arts Lab*

As a copywriter, I've found advertising to be at the crossroads of business and art.

Good artists copy, great artists steal. (I stole this idea from Picasso, partially for the irony, but primarily because it's true.) To create, we must consume. Read Tolkien, Joyce, and Silverstein. Watch films during work. Listen to music during everything. Go to concerts, ones with small crowds. Go to foreign countries, ones with large crowds. Jump out of a plane. Ride a motorcycle. Put it all on black, all twenty dollars. Eat Wagyu beef when you don't have to pay for it. Talk to NFL athletes like friends, not famous people. Spend time with your parents and actually listen to them. Live somewhere different. Live with someone different. Take notes. Remember quotes. Remember people. Remember anything weird. So when a brand comes to you asking for a soul you have one of your own deep enough to reach into and share a little piece—for a lot of money.

And that's the business.

Nick Ciffone, a graduate of the advertising program at the University of Illinois, was nominated to be featured in this book by his professor, Peter Sheldon.

Volvo's campaign for its S90 luxury sedan generated a stirring atmosphere through a combination of words and images. The mini-story of the commercial and longer video features a writer seeking inspiration on a road trip. The writer travels across country in his Volvo as a narrator recites lines from Walt Whitman's poem "Song of the Open Road." The video flashes stunning images of the vehicle traveling through the outdoors and pairs them with Whitman's eloquent words, resulting in an elegant tone. The result is a fitting backdrop against which Volvo's message is superimposed: "Our idea of luxury." You can see "Song of the Open Road" on YouTube.

In addition to having an ear for the perfect phrase, copywriters listen to the way people talk and identify the tone of voice that best fits the target audience and the brand. It's critical to find the just-right word that communicates the intended meaning effectively. For example, real estate agents have found that certain words affect a house sale. For example, words with selling power include "beautiful," "move-in condition," "landscaping," and "starter home." Words that either stall a sale or lead to lower prices include "motivated," "handyman special," and "good value."[24]

Like poets, copywriters may spend hours, even days, crafting a paragraph. After many revisions, others read the copy and critique it. It then goes back to the writer, who continues to fine-tune it. Copywriters must have thick skins, as there is always someone else reading their work, critiquing it, and asking for changes. Versatility is a common trait of copywriters. They can move from toilet paper to Mack trucks and shift their writing style to match the product and the language of their target audience.

As Professor Karen Mallia has observed, copywriters can rejoice because the power of words remains strong even with new visual media. She said, "The power of words doesn't rest in their volume, but in their clever combination. In fact, the fewer the words, the more important every single one becomes—and the more critical copywriting talent becomes." The skill is to "distill a thought down to its most concise, precise, and unexpected expression. That's the reason the craft isn't about to disappear anytime soon, and great copywriters will always be in demand. Think 'Got Milk?' and 'think different' and see true mastery of the craft. Each tagline is just two words but rich in meaning and power."[25] Read Nick Ciffone's thoughts about the copywriter as artist in the Inside Story.

How to Write Effective Ad Copy The tighter the writing, the easier it is to understand and the greater its impact. Simple ads avoid being gimmicky, full of clichés, or too cute; they don't try too hard or reach too far to make a point. The following list summarizes some characteristics of effective copy.

- *Succinct* Use short, familiar words, short sentences, and short paragraphs.
- *Specific* Don't waste time on generalities. The more specific the message, the more attention-getting and memorable it is.

Photo: Courtesy Swanson Russell. Used with permission.

Hunger and food insecurity are year-round problems, especially in the summer when donations traditionally drop off. In response, Food Bank for the Heartland created Strike Out Hunger, an annual food drive that coincides with the College World Series in Omaha. The campaign created by Swanson Russell connected the two and—more importantly—connected Omahans with a way to give back to their community. Do you think this poster is effective? Why?

- *Personal* Directly address your audience whenever possible as "you" rather than "we" or "they."
- *Single Focus* Deliver a simple message instead of one that makes too many points. Focus on a single idea and support it.
- *Conversational* Use the language of everyday conversation. The copy should sound like two friends talking to each other, so don't shy away from incomplete sentences, thought fragments, and contractions.
- *Original* To keep your copy forceful and persuasive, avoid stock advertising phrases, strings of superlatives, brag-and-boast statements, and clichés.
- *News* News stories are attention getting if they announce something that is truly newsworthy and important. (In contrast, Post Shredded Wheat ran an ad with the headline "Beware of New" in which it bragged about its original recipe that it had been using for 117 years.)
- *Magic Phrases* Phrases that grab and stick add power and memorability. In comparing its paper towels with the cheaper competition, Bounty asked, "Why use more when you can use less?"
- *Variety* To add visual appeal, avoid long blocks of copy in print ads. Instead, break the copy into short paragraphs with subheads. In television commercials, break up monologues with visual changes, such as shots of the product, sound effects, and dialogue. The writer puts these breaks in the script, and the art director designs what they will look like.
- *Imaginative Description* Use evocative or figurative language to build a picture in the consumer's mind.
- *A Story—with Feeling* Stories are interesting and they have a structure that keeps attention and builds interest. Most important, however, is that they offer an opportunity to touch emotions. Connecting with a worthy cause, such as teaming with a nonprofit such as the "Strike Out Hunger" campaign, can connect people with passions.

To develop the right **tone of voice**, copywriters write to the target audience. If the copywriter knows someone who fits the audience profile, he or she may write to that person as if they were in a conversation, as the Trojan ad demonstrated. If the writer doesn't know someone, one trick is to go through a photo file, select a picture of the person who fits the description, and write to that person.

Humor is a type of writing that copywriters use to create entertaining, funny ads. The idea is that if the humor works, the funny copy will lend a positive aura to a brand. It's particularly important to master funny writing if you are trying to reach an audience that's put off by conventional advertising, such as young males.

A great example of humor in sports promotion, for example, is the "It's not crazy, it's Sports" campaign for ESPN. In one commercial, an average-looking guy with the name Michael Jordan walks up to a counter, greets a guy with a Michael Jordan sign in an airport, and claims a restaurant reservation—always faced with the disappointment of people who expect a different Michael Jordan. Check out these commercials on YouTube. The Practical Tips feature provides some suggestions on how to use humor in brand communication.

Grammar and Adese Copywriters also are attuned to the rules of grammar, syntax, and spelling, although sometimes they will play with a word or phrase to create an effect, even if it's grammatically incorrect. The Apple Computer campaign for the Macintosh that used the slogan "Think different" rather than "Think differently" caused a bit of an uproar in Apple's school market. That's why copywriters think carefully about playing loose with the language even if it sounds right.[26]

There are also some things copywriters try to avoid. Meaningless words (*really, very, a lot, pretty, nice*) or words made meaningless by overuse (*free, guarantee, opportunity*) are to be shunned in business writing and advertising.

So You Think You Want to Create a Funny Ad?

Fred Beard, *University of Oklahoma*

These parting words of British actor Sir Donald Wolfit should give anyone thinking of creating a funny ad second thoughts: "Dying is easy, comedy is hard."

Writing a funny, effective ad is especially hard when you consider that the ad must make people laugh at the same time it accomplishes an advertising objective: an increase in attention, recall, favorable attitudes, or an actual purchase. If you're still not deterred, keep in mind that funny ads work best when the following circumstances apply:

1. *Your goal is to attract attention.* Decades of research and the beliefs of advertising creative professionals match up perfectly on this one.
2. *Your goal is to generate awareness and recall of a simple message (think Aflac).* Most advertising creatives agree that humor works best to encourage recall of fairly simple messages, not complex ones.
3. *Your humor is related.* Did you ever laugh at an ad and forget what it was advertising? Creatives will tell you humor is a waste of money if it isn't related to a product's name, uses, benefits, or users.
4. *Your goal is to get the audience to like your brand.* Research shows people often transfer their liking of funny ads to the brand.
5. *You expect the audience to initially disagree with your arguments.* An ad's humor can distract people from arguments they disagree with, encouraging them to lower their perceptual defenses, accept the message, and be persuaded by it.
6. *Your target audience is men, especially young ones.* Creative professionals say younger male audiences respond best to humor, and research confirms men favor more aggressive humor.
7. *Your audience has a low need for cognition (NFC) or a high need for humor (NFH).* People with a low NFC don't enjoy thinking about things; they prefer emotional appeals like humor. People with a high NFH seek out humor. If your audience is low NFC and high NFH, you can't miss.
8. *You have good reasons for using the broadcast media.* By far, the majority of creatives believe humor works best in radio and television ads.
9. *You're advertising a low-involvement/low-risk product or service.* Academic researchers and creative professionals agree that funny ads seem to work best for routine purchases people don't worry about too much.
10. *Your humor is definitely funny.* Research shows if an ad's humor fails, not only will there be no positive outcomes, it could even produce negative responses.

Formulaic advertising copy is a problem that is so obvious that comedians parody it. This type of formula writing, called **adese**, violates all the guidelines for writing effective copy that we've been describing. It is full of clichés (as easy as pie), superlatives and puffery (best in class), stock phrases (buy now; free trial offer), and vague generalities (prices too low to advertise). For example, consider this copy; can you hear yourself saying something similar to a friend?

> Now we offer the quality that you've been waiting for—at a price you can afford. So buy now and save.

For more advertising clichés, check this website and vote for your favorite: www.thetoptens .com/most-overused-advertising-cliches. The pompous overblown phrasing of many corporate statements doesn't work. It doesn't get attention, it's not memorable, and it doesn't get read. We call it **your-name-here copy** because almost any company can use those words and tack a signature on the end. For example, a broadband service provider named Covad started off an ad as follows:

> Opportunity. Potential. These are terms usually associated with companies that have a lot to prove and little to show for it. But on rare occasion, opportunity can be used to describe a company that has already laid the groundwork, made the investments, and is well down the road to strong growth.[27]

It's all just platitudes and clichés, and any company could use this copy. It isn't attention getting, and it doesn't contribute to a distinctive and memorable brand image. That's always a

The Five Kinds of Days You'll Have as a Copywriter

Anastasia Guletsky, *Senior Copywriter and Content Strategist, Rise Interactive, Chicago*

When I talk to students about what I do as a copywriter, a lot of them will ask me to describe my average workday. I never know how to honestly answer that question because being a creative is anything but predictable. Instead of trying to come up with a representative model of what each day looks like, I like to break it down into the five different days that you'll experience as a copywriter wherever you go:

1. **The Flow.** I think that brainstorming and concepting with other creatives is one of my favorite things about being a copywriter. Developing that Big Idea behind a TV campaign, or even a single print ad, is what I live for. Everyone has his or her own brainstorm process, from think-tank meetings to going on a walk outside, but I find that playing improv comedy games gets me thinking in new directions.

2. **The Grind.** But not every day is spent on the noble pursuit of finding your Big Idea; brands still have their day-to-day marketing materials that you're responsible for. Think information-driven ads like direct mail, email creative, promotional print ads,

and so on. It's not the most glamorous writing, but the client expects those ads to be created nonetheless, and guess who's in charge of writing them?

3. **The Storm.** There will be days when your hard work is destroyed by the wrath of a fire-breathing monster lizard before your eyes, but just remember that it's not the end of the world. Whether it's a client or a creative director, your work is always subject to an endless stream of opinions and tweaks, and sometimes something even better will take form after you've picked up the pieces.

4. **The Hustle.** Demanding deadlines and tight turnarounds will have you working at a faster pace today, especially if you're pitching new business and trying to impress a prospective client. You're at the office until late at night perfecting every single detail of your work, and the pressure is on. Days like these will come once in a while, sometimes when you least expect it, but I find that any creative will thrive by being a real team player.

5. **The Friday.** Today makes "The Hustle" totally worth it. Happy hour, anyone?

risk with company-centered copy, which doesn't say much that relates to the customer's needs, wants, and interests.

Another type of adese is **brag-and-boast copy**, which is "we" copy written from the company's point of view with a pompous tone, similar to the Covad ad. Consider a print ad by Buick. The ad starts with the stock opening, "Introducing Buick on the move." The body copy includes superlatives and generalities, such as "Nothing less than the expression of a new philosophy," "It strikes a new balance between luxury and performance—a balance which has been put to the test," and "Manufactured with a degree of precision that is in itself a breakthrough."[28] Because people are so conditioned to screen out advertising, messages that use this predictable style are easy to ignore—or parody if you're a comedian.

There are great writers who, as David Droga, chairman of Droga5, said, "are skilled poets performing on a commercial canvas." Yet still there are adese, clichés, and brag-and-boast copy. As Droga said, "Writing bad copy is easy, which is why the majority of advertising feels disposable."[29] Our objective here is to help you develop sensitivity to the good—and bad—practices of copywriting.

To gain a better understanding of what it's like to be a copywriter, read the Day in the Life feature.

Public Relations Writing

Writing is a fundamental skill for public relations professionals. Like copywriters, public relations writers need to be able to write in various forms and styles across media platforms. Their work includes writing news releases, pitch letters, features, and op-ed pieces. They need to be able to communicate interactively on social media like Facebook, Twitter, Instagram, Snapchat, Pinterest, and other emerging apps. Some public relations professionals write speeches, make presentations, and create annual reports. They write for the internet.

Key to writing effectively in these many forms is writing simply in language the reader understands. It sounds easy, but in practice, it can be very challenging. Public relations professional, educator, and author Fraser Seitel offers some tips for success:[30]

- The idea must precede the expression. Identify what you want to communicate.
- Don't be afraid of the draft. Write and revise.
- Simplify, clarify.
- Write to a specific audience.

News Releases   A primary way to communicate public relations messages is through a **news release**. According to Seitel, a news release is the "single most important public relations vehicle."[31] News stories are written for both internal corporate media, such as newsletters and magazines, and for external media, such as newspapers and television stations. One way to distribute news releases broadly is via PR Newswire, a content distribution network that shares news with 10,000 global websites, 33,000 journalists, and 48 industry-specific Twitter feeds, reinforcing our contention that public relations writers need to be versatile and capable of writing for many different kinds of media. Just writing and distributing a news story is not sufficient; an editor of some media outlet needs to run the story. If the news story is not interesting, it will be ignored.

The primary criterion for a news story is newsworthiness. Editors judge news value based on such considerations as *timeliness* (something just happened or is about to happen), *proximity* (a local angle for local media), or *impact* (importance or significance). Announcements of new products, for example, are common publicity stories that are usually first presented internally in corporate publications and then follow in news releases for general media as well as specialized media where the product is relevant for a particular product category (groceries, medical procedures) or audience (mothers of infants, mountain bikers). Social media amplify the news.

For news stories, the traditional journalism "five W" form is followed, which means the release should lead with information that answers questions of who, what, why, when, where, and how. In other words, the first sentence clearly states the facts in such a way that the focus, as well as the importance of the news, is immediately obvious as the news release about Asteroid Day illustrates.

Video news releases are distributed to broadcast media with footage that explains the story. University research into global warming, for example, may be accompanied by stories such

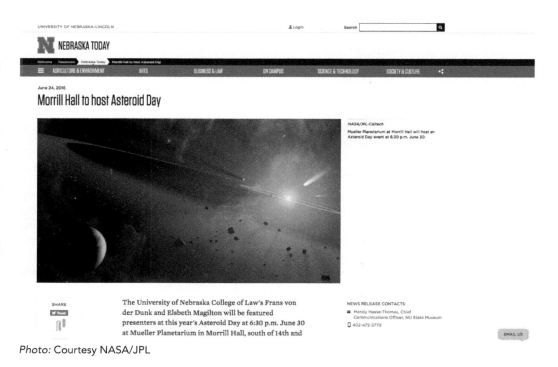

Photo: Courtesy NASA/JPL

as Arctic research that drew core samples for thousands-year-old ice to determine if there are identifiable changes in the atmospheric markers locked into the ice cores. There is no way local media would be able to develop the video footage on their own, but the university can facilitate the story, recognizing that television reporting is dependent on visual explanations of such complex issues and questions.

Features   Less reliant on news, **feature stories** focus on *human interest*. For example, stories about a United Airlines flight attendant who held a Guinness world record after a 63-year career appeared in corporate publications as well as in national media (*New York Times*, among many others), in local papers in the community where the 84-year-old lived (*Boulder Daily Camera*), and in Hawaii, where he started his career (*Pacific Business News*). Although the formats may differ slightly, news and feature stories are written for and distributed to print and broadcast media as well as the internet.

Social Media Opportunities   Good communicators in social media have the ability to create a direct relationship between a brand and consumers. They can distribute their content using the many tools of social media such as blogs, videos, newsletters, and personal comments, to name a few. In the context of marketing communication, the content distributed across the social media network helps users and the brand engage in a dialogue.

Direct-Response Writing

Direct-response messages are often longer and contain more explanation and detail than other forms of marketing communication. The message is wasted if it doesn't provide enough information and motivate the receiver to respond to it in some way. To be persuasive, messages must contain clear comparisons or details about relevant decision factors, such as price, style, and convenience.

Because direct-response messages can be individually targeted through technology, the more personalized the message, the better. For example, when a customer orders a book from Amazon.com, the company's system immediately suggests similar books. When an airline sends out promotional offers to its frequent flyers, these messages often show the number of miles traveled in the past year and the number of rewards earned year to date. It is obviously a personalized message and definitely attracts more attention.

Most important is that the message needs to counter consumers' reluctance to buy. Buying something through direct marketing has elements of risk because there is no salesperson or store to rely on for assistance and information. Most direct-response messages will include copy intended to put the buyer's mind at rest. Guarantees and warranties are important, but other strategies, such as testimonials, are used to reassure buyers about the company's reliability.

10.3 Explain how to write for various media.

Writing for Various Media

Different types of media have different styles, restrictions, and audiences. Writers adjust their presentation to accommodate the stylistic differences of the medium.

Basics of Writing for Print Media

The two categories of copy that print uses are display copy and body copy (or text). **Display copy** includes all elements that readers see in their initial scanning. These elements—headlines, subheads, call-outs, and taglines—usually are set in larger type sizes than body copy and are designed to get attention and to stop the viewer's scanning. **Body copy** includes the elements that are designed to be read and absorbed, such as the text of the ad message and captions.

We have suggested that ad copy should be succinct, but some respected copywriters, such as David Ogilvy and Howard Gossage, were successful in writing long copy ads that intrigued their audiences, building high levels of interest. Gossage, a legendary San Francisco adman, played with humorous ideas as well as words. One ad for Eagle Shirtmakers asked, "Is this your shirt?" A following line said, "If so, Miss Afflerbach will send you your [Eagle logo picture] label." The idea, which is explained in the body copy, is that Eagle makes shirts for various shirtmakers, so you can contact "Miss Afflerbach" for the official logo to add to your shirt. If you're interested in more of Gossage's tongue-in-cheek ads, check a collection compiled by the LA Creative Club at www.lacreativeclub.com/gossage.html or get his book *The Book of Gossage* from the Copy Workshop (www.adbuzz.com/copyworkshop_catalog.pdf).

The most common tools in the print writer's tool kit are listed here.

- *Headline* A phrase or a sentence that serves as the opening to the ad. It's usually identified by larger type or a prominent position, and its purpose is to catch attention. In a Corporate Angel Network "Cancer Patients Fly Free" ad, for example, the headline offers a relevant benefit to a particular audience.
- *Overlines and Underlines* Phrases or sentences that either lead into the headline or follow up on the thought in the headline are called overline and underlines, respectively. They are usually set in smaller type than the headline. The purpose of the **overline** is to set the stage, and the purpose of the **underline** is to elaborate on the idea in the headline; the underline also serves as a transition to the body copy.
- *Body Copy* The text of the ad is the body copy. It's usually smaller-sized type than the headline, overline, and underline and is written in paragraphs or multiple lines. Its purpose is to explain the idea or selling point.
- *Subheads* Used in longer copy blocks, **subheads** begin a new section of the copy. They are usually bold type or larger than the body copy. Their purpose is to make the logic clear to the reader. They are useful for people who scan copy, and they help them get a sense of what the copy says. Subheads are sectional headlines and are also used to break up a mass of "gray" type (or type that tends to blur together when one glances at it) into smaller blocks of copy.
- *Call-Outs* **Call-outs** are sentences that float around the visual. Usually, a line or arrow points to some specific element in the visual that a call-out names and explains. For example, Johnson & Johnson once ran an ad that used call-outs as the main pieces of the body copy. The head read, "How to bathe a mommy." Positioned around a picture of a woman are short paragraphs with arrows pointing to various parts of her body. These call-outs describe the good things the lotion does for feet, hands, makeup removal, moisture absorption, and skin softening.
- *Captions* A **caption** is a sentence or short piece of copy that explains what you are looking at in a photo or illustration. Captions aren't used very often in advertising because the visuals are assumed to be self-explanatory; however, readership studies have shown that, after the headline, captions have high readership.
- *Taglines* A short phrase that wraps up the key idea or creative concept and usually appears at the end of the body copy is called a tagline. It often refers back to the headline or opening phrase in a commercial.
- *Call to Action* A **call to action** encourages people to respond and gives information on how to respond at the end of an ad.

Display Copy The **headline** is a key element in print pieces. It conveys the main message so that people get the point of the message. In addition, the headline works with the visual to get attention and communicate the creative concept. This clutter-busting idea breaks through the competitive messages both in advertising and in surrounding articles. It comes across best through a picture and words working together, as the Wyoming Tourism ad illustrates. The headline, "Four Star Accommodations? Try Four Million." connects to a strong visual and body copy to invite the reader to visit Wyoming.

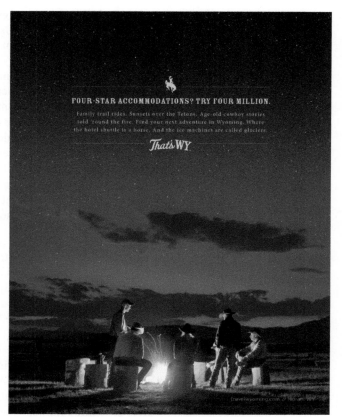

FOUR-STAR ACCOMMODATIONS? TRY FOUR MILLION.

Family trail rides. Sunsets over the Tetons. Age-old cowboy stories told 'round the fire. Find your next adventure in Wyoming. Where the hotel shuttle is a horse. And the ice machines are called glaciers.

That's WY

Photo: Courtesy Wyoming Office of Tourism, BVK and Andy Bardon Creative. Used with permission.

The headline, body copy, and visuals all work together as a unit to increase tourism to Wyoming.

People who are scanning may read nothing more, so beyond getting attention, writers want to at least register a point with the reader. The point has to be clear from the headline or the combination of headline and visual. That's particularly true with outdoor boards. In advertising, researchers estimate that only 20 percent of those who read the headline go on to read the body copy. So, for readers to take away anything from the ad, the message needs to be clear in the headline.

Headlines are often catchy phrases, but they also have to convey an idea and attract the interest of the audience. Tobler has won Effie Awards for a number of years for its clever headlines and visuals. For Tobler's Chocolate Orange, the creative concept showed the chocolate ball being smacked against something hard and splitting into orange-like slices. The headline was "Whack and Unwrap." The next year, the headline was "Smashing Good Taste," which speaks to the candy's British origins and to the quirky combination of chocolate and orange flavors. The headline and visual also tell consumers how to "open" the chocolate orange into slices: whack it.

⬤ Principle
Good headlines interrupt readers' scanning and grab their attention.

Agencies copytest headlines to make sure they can be understood at a glance and they communicate exactly the right idea. Split-run tests (two versions of the same execution) in direct-mail pieces have shown that changing the wording of the headline while keeping all other elements constant can double, triple, or quadruple consumer response. That is why experts, such as Ogilvy, state that the headline is the most important element.[32] A series of Good Housekeeping Seal of Approval ads use metaphors in the headlines to spark curiosity, such as "The Seal is like a push-up bra," followed by a copy line that explains that "it makes what you have a lot more noticeable."

Because headlines are so important, some general principles guide their development and explain the particular functions they serve.

- *Target* A good headline will attract only those who are interested; there is no sense in attracting people who are not in the market. Here's an example from a newspaper: "FARMERS: The Natural Resources District has cost-sharing available on fertilizer meters!" An old axiom is "Use a rifle, not a shotgun." In other words, use the headline to tightly target the right audience. That's true in advertising as well as in other publications.
- *Stop and Grab* The headline must work in combination with the visual to stop and grab the reader's attention. An advertisement by Range Rover shows a photo of the car parked at the edge of a rock ledge in Monument Valley with the headline "Lots of people use their Range Rovers just to run down to the corner."
- *Identify* In all brand communication, the headline should identify or suggest the company, product, or brand. The Big Idea also should be evident in the headline. That's true in magazine and news releases as well as advertisements.
- *Change Scanning to Reading* The headline should lead readers into the body copy or text. For readers to move to the text, they have to stop scanning and start concentrating. This change in mind-set is the reason only 20 percent of scanners become readers.

Headlines can be grouped into two general categories: direct action and indirect action. **Direct-action headlines** are straightforward and informative, such as "Keep Your Body Strong," which is one in a series of "Healthy People" posters for Johnson & Johnson. The copy associates the health of your body with the health of nature. It closes with a line that pulls these two thoughts together: "Your body is just like nature. Keep it strong with daily physical activity and bring your planet to balance." Notice how this structure of the message is consistent in the "Mind" and "Spirit" posters.

Direct-action headlines are highly targeted, but they may fail to lead the reader into the message if they are not captivating enough. **Indirect-action headlines** are not as selective and may not provide as much information as direct-action headlines, but they may be better at drawing the reader into the message and building a brand image.

Here are some common types of direct-action headlines.

- *Assertion* An assertion is a headline that states a claim or a promise that will motivate someone to try the product.
- *Command* A command headline politely tells the reader to do something.

Photos: Courtesy Michael Dattolico. Used with permission.

Michael Dattolico designed a series of posters for Johnson & Johnson to use in promoting its "Healthy People" initiative. These two advise you to keep "your mind flowing" and "your spirit pure."

A graduate of the University of Florida, Dattolico's work was nominated to be featured here by Professor Elaine Wagner.

- *How-to Heads* People are rewarded for investigating a product when the message tells them how to use it or how to solve a problem.
- *News Announcements* News headlines are used with new-product introductions but also with changes, reformulations, new styles, and new uses. The news value is thought to get attention and motivate people to respond.

Here are some common types of indirect-action headlines.

- *Puzzles* Puzzles are used strictly for their curiosity and provocative power. Puzzling statements, ambiguities, surprises, and questions require the reader to examine the body copy to get the answer or explanation. The intention is to pull readers into the body copy. Failure to engage the reader in the puzzle may result in a message that's ignored.
- *Associations* Headlines that use associations use image and lifestyle to get attention and build interest.

A headline for the Motorola Talk About two-way radio demonstrates the problem of bad reception: "Help, I Think I Need a Tourniquet!" That headline then draws us into the underline, which makes the point that if the reception isn't clear, the headline can sound like "Well, I think I'll eat a turnip cake!" This headline, which played with the similar sounds of words, and other curiosity-provoking lines are provocative and compel people to read on to discover the point of the message. Sometimes indirect headlines are called "blind headlines" because they give so little information. A **blind headline** is a gamble. If it is not informative or intriguing enough, the reader may move on without absorbing any product name information, but if it works as an attention getter, it can be effective.

Next to the headline, captions have the second highest readership. In addition to their pulling power, captions serve an information function. Visuals do not always say the same thing to every person; for that reason, most visuals can benefit from explanation. That's particularly true in images for news and feature stories. In addition to headlines, writers also craft the subheads that continue to help lure the reader into the body copy. Subheads are considered display copy in that they are usually larger and set in different type (bold or italic) than the body copy.

As we mentioned earlier, taglines are short, catchy phrases and particularly memorable phrases used at the end of an ad to complete or wrap up the creative idea. An ad from the Nike women's campaign used the headline "You are a nurturer and a provider. You are beautiful and exotic" set in an elegant script. The tagline on the next page used a rough, hand-drawn, graffiti-like image that said, "You are not falling for any of this."[33]

Body Copy   The body copy is the text of the message, and its primary role is to maintain the interest of the reader. It provides information, states the argument, summarizes the proof, and provides explanation. It is the information and, in the case of advertising, the persuasive heart of the message. You excite reader interest with the display elements, but you win readers over with the argument presented in the body copy. Consider the way the copy is written for award-winning Nike campaigns. Analyze the argument the copywriter is making and how the logic flows to a convincing conclusion. The Matter of Principle feature explains the logic and message strategy behind the Nike women's campaign, which focuses on self-awareness.

Two paragraphs get special attention in body copy: the **lead paragraph** and the **closing paragraph**. The lead, the first paragraph of the body copy, is another point where people test the message to see whether they want to read it. Notice in the beautifully crafted copy from the Nike women's campaign how the first lines work to catch the attention of the target audience: "A magazine is not a mirror."

Closing paragraphs in body copy and text serve several functions. Usually, the last paragraph refers back to the creative concept and wraps up the Big Idea. Direct-action messages usually end with a call to action with instructions on how to respond. A Schwinn bicycle ad that is headlined "Read poetry. Make peace with all except the motor car" demonstrates a powerful and unexpected ending, one that is targeted to its youthful audience:

Schwinns are red, Schwinns are blue.

Schwinns are light and agile too.

Cars suck. The end.[34]

An example of using a closing to contradict or confuse a point appeared in a 2013 New Balance ad that touted its dedication to a Made in America strategy, which it claims is a competitive advantage for its shoes. In small type at the very bottom of the full-page ad, the reader finds this statement: "1 of every 4 shoes we sell in the USA is made or assembled here." One would think that is a small claim for such a big ad.

Print Media Requirements   The media in the print category—from newspapers and magazines to outdoor boards and product literature—all use the same copy elements, such as headlines and body copy. However, the way these elements are used varies with the objectives for using the medium. Most newspaper advertising copy, for example, is straightforward and informative. The writing is brief, usually just identifying the merchandise and giving critical information about styles, sizes, and prices.

Magazines offer better-quality ad production, which is important for brand image and high-fashion brand communication. Consumers may clip and file advertising and publicity articles that tie in with the magazine's special interest as reference information. This type of magazine story can be more informative and carry longer copy than do newspaper ads. Publicity writers and copywriters also take care to craft clever phrasing for the headlines and the body copy, which, as in the Nike women's campaign, may read more like poetry.

The Principle of Truth

Jean Grow, *Marquette University*

It wasn't advertising. It was truth. We weren't selling a damn thing. Just the truth. And behind the truth, of course, the message was brought to you by Nike.
—Janet Champ, *Nike*

The creatives who produced early Nike women's advertising (1990–1997) were an amazing trio of women (Janet Champ, copywriter, and Charlotte Moore and Rachel Manganiello, art directors). Their work was grounded in the principle of truth, fueled by creativity, and sustained by nothing less than moxie.

"Nike in 1990 was not the Nike of today," Manganiello said. There was always this "political stuff about big men's sports. And, you know, [it was like we were] just kind of siphoning off money for women. So, in some ways we couldn't be as direct as we sometimes wanted to be." However, being direct and being truthful are not always the same thing. And truth for the Nike women's brand, and for themselves, was what these women aspired to.

Living the principle of truth and trusting their gut are what defined their work ethic and ultimately the women's brand. Moore explained, "I would posit that market research has killed a lot of advertising that was based on effective human dialogue, because it negates faith in intuition. Guts. Living with your eyes open."

To launch the women's brand within the confines of the male parent brand was no easy assignment. The creative team members began with their "gut" and with their "eyes open." They created campaign after campaign that moved the needle, but each time the approval process was a test of their principles, with meetings that were more than tinged with gender bias.

"We were almost always the only women in the room, and they killed the stuff because it scared them," said Champ. "But we always came back. And they let us do what we wanted, as long as we didn't 'sully' the men's brand, . . . and as long as women's products kept flying off the shelves, they were happy."

As time went on, their instincts and principles earned them respect. According to Champ, "We told them, pretty much, that we believed in it and they had

to run it and trust us, and they sighed, once again. They were soooooo tired of hearing me say that. And they ran it and they were *shocked* at what a nerve it touched."

In trusting their guts—in telling the truth—they created award-winning campaigns and exceeded marketing expectations. "As creative people," Moore said, "we had found our home and our voice, and we'd found the most fertile ground for the brand."

In the end, truth and the willingness to "trust your gut" are what make great brands and create fertile ground for others. When you consider the terrifically truthful Dove campaign, I suggest we owe a debt of gratitude to the women of early Nike women's advertising, who stood for truth years ago. I only wish we would see more truthful work. That, however, might take a truthful acknowledgment that women still make up less than a quarter of all advertising creative departments. In the end, truthful work depends on making a commitment to increasing the number of women in creative departments. To have guts. To live with one's eyes wide open.

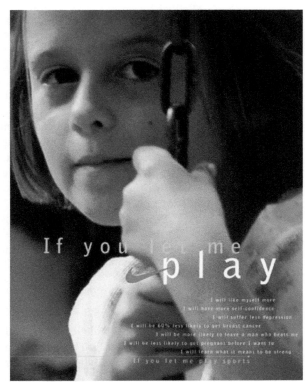

Photo: NIKE, Inc.

This ad from the "Let Me Play" campaign reflects Nike's strategy of talking to women about sports in a way that reflects their attitudes and feelings.

Directories that provide contact information, such as phone numbers and addresses, often carry display advertising. In writing a directory ad, copywriters advise using a headline that focuses on the service or store personality unless the store's name is a descriptive phrase, such as "Overnight Auto Service" or "The Computer Exchange." Complicated explanations don't work well in the Yellow Pages either because there is little space for such explanations. Putting information that is subject to change in an ad can become a problem because that directory is published only once a year.

Posters and outdoor boards are primarily visual, although the words generally try to catch consumers' attention and lock in an idea, registering a message. One of the most famous billboard campaigns ever was for a little shaving cream company named Burma-Shave. The campaign used a series of roadside signs with catchy, cute, and sometimes poetic advertising copy aimed at auto travelers. This campaign ran for nearly 40 years, from 1927 to 1963, until the national interstate system and fast cars made the signs obsolete.[35] Attesting to the cultural impact at the time, a set of signs is in the Smithsonian. On the Burma-Shave signs, the product was the hero:

When you lay	The hero
Those few cents down	Was brave and strong
You've bought	And willin'
The smoothest	She felt his chin—
Shave in town	Then wed the villain.
Burma-Shave	Burma-Shave

More recently, the city of Albuquerque used the Burma-Shave format to encourage drivers to reduce their speeds through a construction zone. The most important characteristic of writing for outdoor boards is brevity. Usually, a single line serves as both a headline and product identification. Often the phrase is a play on words. A series of black-and-white billboards in the Galveston-Houston area, recruiting priests for the Roman Catholic diocese, features a Roman collar with witty wording, such as "Yes, you will combat evil. No, you don't get to wear a cape." Others are more thoughtful: "Help wanted. Inquire within yourself." The copy must catch attention and be memorable. For example, a billboard for Orkin pest control showed a package wrapped up with the word "Orkin" on the tag. The headline read, "A little something for your ant."

Sometimes called **collateral materials** because they are used in support of a campaign, product literature—brochures, pamphlets, flyers, posters, and other materials—provides details about a product, company, or event. Product literature can be as varied as hangtags in new cars or bumper stickers. Taco Bell's little messages on its tiny taco sauce packages are an example of clever writing in an unexpected place with messages like "Save a bun, eat a taco" and "My other taco is a chalupa."

Typically, product literature is a heavy copy format or at least a format that provides room for explanatory details along with visuals; the body copy may dominate the piece. For a pamphlet with folds, a writer must also consider how the message is conveyed as the piece is unfolded. These pieces can range from a simple three-panel flyer to a glitzy multipage, full-color brochure.

Radio Messages and How to Write Them

Advertisers use radio to build brands because DJ endorsements and on-air chatter can help build trust. Radio can also remind consumers close to their time of purchase when advertising is most effective. Today, radio is no longer a medium that communicates only with mass audiences. It is distributed across multiple platforms—via streaming, HD, desktops, cars, MP3 players, and smartphones—and is capable of delivering enhanced personal interactivity to listeners through text messages, mobile apps, and time-shifting listening through podcasts.[36]

Ads and announcements that are broadcast on either radio or television are usually 15, 30, or 60 seconds in length, although 10- and 15-second spots may be used for brand reminders or station identification. This short length means that the message must be simple enough for listeners to grasp yet intriguing enough to prevent viewers from switching the station or skipping them altogether. That's why creativity is important to create clutter-busting messages that break through the surrounding noise and catch the listener's attention.

Radio is pervasive in that it surrounds many of our activities, but it is seldom the listener's center of attention and is usually in the background. Because radio is a transitory medium and listeners are often in the car or doing something else, the ability of the listener to remember facts (such as the name of the organization, addresses, and phone numbers) is difficult. That's why writers repeat the key points of identification information, such as a phone number or address. Radio urges the copywriter to reach into the depths of imagination to create a clutter-busting idea that grabs the listener's attention or a catchy tune that can be repeated without being irritating.

Radio's special advantage, referred to as **theater of the mind**, is that in a narrative format, the story is visualized in the listener's imagination. Radio writers imagine they are writing a play that will be performed before an audience whose eyes are closed. The writer has all the theatrical tools of voices, sound effects, and music but no visuals. How the characters look and where the scene is set come from their listeners' imaginations.

As an example of theater of the mind, consider a now-classic commercial written by humorist Stan Freberg for the Radio Advertising Bureau. The spot opens with an announcer explaining that Lake Michigan will be drained and filled with hot chocolate and a 700-foot mountain of whipped cream. The Royal Canadian Air Force will fly overhead and drop a 10-ton maraschino cherry, all to the applause of 25,000 screaming extras. The point is that things that can't be created in real life can be created by radio in the imagination of listeners.

Tools of Radio Writing   In radio advertising, the tools are the audio elements the copywriter uses to craft a commercial: voice, music, and sound effects. The most important element in radio is the human voice, which is heard in songs, spoken dialogue, and announcements. Most commercials use an announcer either as the central voice or at the closing to wrap up the product identification. The voices the writer specifies help listeners "see" the personalities in the brand message. Dialogue uses character voices to convey an image of the speaker: a child, an old man, an executive, and so forth. Writers specify voices for commercials based on the evocative qualities they contribute to the message. Jon Hamm of *Mad Men* fame was chosen as the voice of Mercedes-Benz. Former *Saturday Night Live* performer Jason Sudeikis has done voice work for Applebee's. Former *Friends* star Lisa Kudrow has done work for Yoplait yogurt. Do these choices fit the brand?

In radio, speaking style should match the speech of the target audience. Each group has its own way of speaking and its own phrasing. Teenagers don't talk like 8-year-olds or 50-year-olds. Spoken language is different from written language. We talk in short sentences, often in sentence fragments and run-ons. We seldom use complex sentences in speech. We use contractions that would drive an English teacher crazy. Slang can be hard to handle and sound phony, but copy that picks up the nuances of people's speech sounds natural.

Music is as important as the voice in radio writing. Music can trigger an emotional response. Using music and sonic logos consistently can strengthen brand recognition.[37] Music can be used behind the dialogue to create mood and establish the setting. Similar to movie scriptwriters, radio writers have a sense of the imagery of music and the role it plays in creating dramatic effects. Any mood, from that of a circus to a candlelit dinner, can be conveyed through music. The primary use of music is a **jingle**, which is a commercial in song. Radio writers understand the interplay of catchy phrases and "hummable" music to create little songs that stick in our minds. Anything consumers can sing along with helps them remember and get involved with the message.

Organizations can have a piece of music composed for a commercial or can borrow it from previously recorded songs. Numerous music libraries sell *stock music* that is not under copyright. In addition to customer-made jingles, many *jingle houses* create "syndicated" jingles made up of a piece of music sold to several different local advertisers in different markets around the country.

Folger's "The best part of waking up" offers an example of a contemporary jingle that can get you to sing along. One of the most famous jingles of all time was the song "I'd Like to Teach the World to Sing" produced for Coca-Cola in 1969 by its agency, McCann-Erickson. This jingle was an instant hit worldwide; it was later recorded as a pop song without the Coke reference and sold millions of copies. Called "Hilltop," the television commercial shows young people singing "I'd like to buy the world a Coke" on a hilltop in Italy. Surveys continue to identify it as one of the best commercials of all time. It is still run by Coke on special occasions, and the sheet music continues to sell years after the song was first written. The creation of the jingle

● Principle
Radio copywriters try to match their dialogue to the conversational style of the target audience.

Photo: Justin Sullivan/Getty Images

Folger's has differentiated itself from the competition in part with its jingle, "The best part of waking up."

was fictionalized and played a major role in the final episode of *Mad Men.*[38]

Sound effects are the icing on the radio message. The sound of seagulls, automobile horns honking, and the cheers of fans at a stadium all create images in our minds to cue the setting and drive the action. The classic Freberg "Lake Michigan" commercial for the Radio Advertising Bureau used **sound effects** to punctuate the imaginary event. The point is that radio can be more powerful than television in creating images in your mind. Sound effects can be original, but more often, they are taken from *sound-effects libraries* available on CDs or online.

The Practice of Radio Writing   The following guidelines for writing effective radio commercials address the distinctive characteristics of radio messages.

- *Keep It Personal* Radio has an advantage over print: the human voice. The copy for radio ads should use conversational language as if someone is "talking with" the consumer rather than "selling to" the consumer.
- *Speak to Listeners' Interests* Radio offers specialized programming to target markets. Listeners mostly tune in to hear music, but talk radio is popular, too. There are shows on health, pets, finance, politics—whatever interests people. Writers design commercials to speak to that audience interest and use the appropriate music and tone of voice.
- *Wake Up the Inattentive* Most people who are listening to the radio are doing something else at the same time, such as jogging, driving, or fixing breakfast. Radio messages are designed to break through and capture attention in the first three seconds with sound effects, music, questions, commands, or something unexpected.
- *Make It Memorable* To help the listener remember what you are selling, ads should mention the name of the product emphatically and repeat it. An average of three mentions in a 30-second commercial and five mentions in a 60-second commercial is recommended, as long as the repetition is not done in a forced or annoying manner. Copywriters use taglines and other key phrases to lock the product in consumers' memories.
- *Include Call to Action* The last thing listeners hear is what they tend to remember, so writers make sure the product is it. In radio, that's particularly important because there is no way to show a picture of the product or the label. Those last words communicate the Big Idea in a way that serves as a call to action and reminds listeners of the brand name.
- *Create Image Transfer* Radio messages are sometimes designed to link to other media such as television commercials and social media. Called **image transfer**, the visuals from the television version are re-created in a listener's mind by the use of key phrases and ideas from the television commercial.

Writers working on a radio commercial use a standard **radio script** format to write the copy to certain time blocks—all the words, dialogue, lyrics, sound effects, instructions, and descriptions. The instructions and descriptions are to help the producer tape the commercial so that it sounds exactly as the copywriter imagined. The script format usually has the source of the audio written down the left side, and the content—words an announcer reads, dialogue, and description of the sound effects and music—is written on the right. The instructions and descriptions—everything that isn't spoken—are typed in all-capital letters. You may also see a script written in paragraph form, with the instructions in parentheses.

Television/Video Messages and How to Write Them

Writers for television and other forms of video that often appear online on websites and mobile apps understand that it is the moving image—the action—that makes video so much more engaging than print. The challenge for the writer is to fuse the images with the words to present not only a creative concept but also a story, as the Old Spice commercials do so well.

⬢ **Principle**
The ability to touch our emotions and to show us things—to demonstrate how they look and work—make video highly persuasive.

One of the strengths of video, particularly television, is its ability to reinforce verbal messages with visuals or reinforce visuals with verbal messages. As Ogilvy's Peter Hochstein explained:

> The idea behind a television commercial is unique in advertising. The TV commercial consists of pictures that move to impart facts or evoke emotion, and selling words that are not read but heard. The perfect combination of sight and sound can be an extremely potent selling tool.[39]

Viewers watching a program they enjoy often are absorbed to a degree only slightly less than experienced by people watching a movie in a darkened theater. Storytelling is one way copywriters can present action in a television message more powerfully than in other media. Professor Eunjin (Anna) Kim and her research colleagues, S. Ratneshwar and Esther Thorson, have documented that narrative ads are more persuasive than nonnarrative ads. Their study concludes that "in creating narrative ads, advertisers in general should create narrative structures that (1) engender emotive response in terms of positive affect, (2) create a positive hedonic experience, (3) appear credible, and (4) communicate how consumers in the target audience can achieve their consumption goals by buying and using the advertised product/brand."[40]

To this end, effective television messages are written to maximize the dramatic aspects of moving images and storytelling, as the Matter of Practice feature explains about "the emotional pivot" in a story.

Dramatic stories with high emotion, as well as demonstrations, are just two of the techniques used in television advertising. Consider the following:

- *Action* Good television messages use the effects of action and motion to attract attention and sustain interest. Torture tests, steps, and procedures are all actions that are easier to present on television than in print.
- *Demonstration* Seeing is believing. Believability and credibility—the essence of persuasion—are high because we believe what we see with our own eyes.
- *Storytelling* Television is our society's master storyteller because of its ability to present a plot and the action that leads to a conclusion in which the product plays a major role.
- *Emotion* The ability to touch the feelings of the viewer makes television commercials entertaining, diverting, amusing, and absorbing. Real-life situations with all their humor, anger, fear, pride, jealousy, and love come alive on the screen.

Tools of Writing for Television/Video   Writers who work with video and television commercials have two primary tool kits: visual and audio. Both words and pictures are designed to create exactly the right impact. Because of the number of visual and audio elements as well as the many ways they can be combined, a television message is one of the most complex of all brand communication forms. It is also an ideal form for storytelling.

When we watch a commercial, we are more aware of what we're seeing than anything else. Copywriters keep in mind that visuals and motion, the silent speech of film, should convey as much of the message as possible. The visual can portray real or animated images, such a cartoon spokesperson like the Keebler cookie elves. **Animation** involves photographing successive drawings of images that give the illusion of motion. Emotion, which is the effect created by storytelling, is expressed convincingly in facial expressions, gestures, and other body language. Because television is theatrical, many of the copywriter's tools, such as characters, costumes, sets and locations, props, lighting, optical and computerized special effects, and on-screen graphics, are similar to those you would use in a play, television show, or movie.

As in radio, the three audio elements are music, voices, and sound effects, but they are used differently in television commercials because they are connected to a visual image. The writer may have an announcer speak directly to the viewer or engage in a dialogue with another person who may or may not be on camera. The writer writes the words they will say and blocks out on paper how this "talk" happens. A common manipulation of the camera-announcer relationship is the **voice-over**, in which an announcer who is not visible describes some kind of action on the screen. Sometimes a voice is heard **off camera**, which means you can't see the speaker and the voice is coming from the side, behind, or above.

How the Emotional Pivot Works in a Story

Charles Young, Founder and CEO, Ameritest

To investigate the power of emotional engagement in a video, we studied the structure of a six-minute film of Susan Boyle, who turned in a surprising 2009 performance on *Britain's Got Talent*. Employing the same research techniques we use to analyze television commercials, we found that this YouTube video is built on a standard dramatic structure that we commonly see in advertising, one that we call an "emotional pivot."

Good storytellers understand that with a pivot structure, the emotional impact is particularly strong because the valence of the emotion changes from initially negative to positive, which creates the strongest possible contrast between what the audience feels at the beginning of the story and what they feel at the end.

Here's how we identified the emotional pivot in the *Britain's Got Talent* video featuring a rather frumpy Scottish woman named Susan Boyle. Using a photo sort of still frames from the video, we track the flow of emotion throughout the six-minute video. In the graph, you can see strong negative emotions at the beginning of the video shown with strong spikes in the red line. That reflects the entrance onstage of this rather overweight and middle-aged Scottish woman. The rolled eyes and sideway glances of disbelief from the lead judge Simon Cowell reinforce this negative first impression.

Then toward the middle, the green (positive) line begins to rise rapidly, and the red (negative) line fades away as emotions turn, or pivot, on frame 18 as Susan begins to sing. As her beautiful voice fills the room, the judges and the audience are transformed.

Finally, positive emotions rise to a sustained, high volume of intensity for the rest of the video. It ends with the entire studio audience—and even one of the judges—on their feet, cheering wildly.

At the pivot point—the boundary between these two states of emotion—lies the most dramatic, brand-creating moment of this piece of film. So in frame 18, when Susan first begins to sing, we are able to pinpoint the actual moment of birth of a new star—or brand, in advertising terms.

In storytelling, that is the moment when a gap opens up in the mind of an audience, a break between what the audience expected to see and what just happened. The mind of the audience is forced to turn in a new direction. As their personal interpretations of the event are recalculated, audience members build a new mental model of reality to make sense of what they are seeing. Unexpectedly, the ugly duckling just turned into a swan!

Interestingly, when we tested a shorter version of the video with the "negative setup" removed, we found the emotional response to the singing was just as positive, but when we interviewed respondents, it was obvious that something was lost. This shorter version was much less likely to be rated as "unique," "involving," "entertaining," or "inspirational." In other words, changing the narrative to an uninterrupted flow of positive emotions diminished the impact. Ironically, the Susan Boyle story would be different—and she might not be a star—without Simon Cowell's display of cynicism at the beginning.

You can watch this video on YouTube. Search for "Susan Boyle I Dreamed a Dream."

Flow of Emotion®

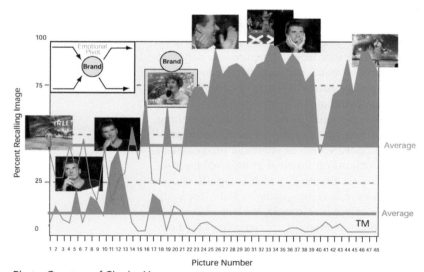

Photo: Courtesy of Charles Young

The Susan Boyle story is a classic example of an emotional pivot from negative to positive emotions.

Dialogue, both in radio and on television, is an interesting challenge for writers who try to keep the words natural and the interaction interesting. As you watch TV, notice the language that's used in the insurance commercials, for example. State Farm, Nationwide, Allstate, and Geico all take different approaches to selling their policies by creating situations viewers can relate to.

Music is as important in video as it is in radio. Music creates moods and heightens emotions. It has the potential to create a memorable aural signature for a brand. United Airlines has used Gershwin's "Rhapsody in Blue" consistently as an identifier. This music is woven throughout its promotional work—in commercials, the preflight video, and even the underground walkway at O'Hare International Airport. Sometimes music is background; at other times, the piece is the focus of the message.

Other creative tools that support the story line are the setting, casting, costumes, props, and lighting, all of which the writer must describe in the script. The setting, or **set**, is where the action takes place. It can be something in the studio, from a simple tabletop to a constructed set that represents a storefront or the inside of a home, or it can be a computer creation layered behind the action. Video shot outside the studio is said to be filmed **on location**, which means the entire crew and cast are transported somewhere away from the studio.

For many brand messages, the most important element is the people, who are called **talent**. Finding the right person for each role is called **casting**. People can be cast as follows:

- *Announcers* (either onstage or offstage), presenters, or introducers
- *Spokespersons* (or talking animals, such as Geico's gecko)
- *Character types* (old woman, baby, or police officer)
- *Celebrities,* such as Michael Phelps, LeBron James, Jennifer Aniston, and Lionel Messi

Depending on the characterizations in the commercial, costumes and makeup can be an important part of the story. Of course, historical stories need period costumes, but modern scenes may also require special clothing, such as golf outfits, swimsuits, or cowboy boots. Makeup may be important if you need to change a character from young to old. The writer must specify all these details in the script. The director usually manipulates the lighting, but the writer might specify special lighting effects in the script. For example, you might read "Intense bright light as though reflected from snow" or "Light flickering on people's faces as if reflecting from a television screen."

Writers might also specify the commercial's **pace**, or how fast or slowly the action progresses. Some messages are best developed at a languid pace; others work better when presented at an upbeat, fast pace. Research has found that the pace of television commercials has been steadily getting faster since the mid-20th century. Why do you suppose that might be?

Planning the Television Message   Writers must plan how long the message will be, what shots will appear in each scene, what the key visual will be, and where and how to shoot the commercial. Other key decisions the writer must consider are the length, number of scenes, and key frames. The common lengths of television commercials and announcements are 10, 15, 20, 30, and 60 seconds. The 10-, 15-, and 20-second lengths are used for reminders and product or station identification. The 60-second spot, which is common in radio, has almost disappeared in television because of the increasing cost of airtime. The most common length for a television announcement is 30 seconds. Promotional videos that run online can be any length, of course.

A commercial is planned in **scenes**—segments of action that occur in a single location. A scene may include several shots from different angles. A 30-second commercial usually is planned with four to six scenes, but a fast-paced commercial may have many more. Because television is a visual medium, the message is often developed as a **key visual** that conveys the heart of the concept. The **key frame** is the shot that sticks in the mind and becomes the image viewers remember when they think about the commercial.

Writers need to answer many questions when planning a television spot. How much information should there be in the commercial or announcement? Should the action be fast or slow? How intrusive should it be to catch people's attention?

Two documents are used to plan commercials: a television script prepared by the writer and a storyboard drawn by the art director. Similar to a radio script, a **television/video script** is the written version of the message. It contains all the words, dialogue, lyrics, instructions, and descriptions of the details we've been discussing—sets, costumes, lighting, and so forth. For television and other video, the script is written in two columns, with the audio on the right and the video on the left.

The key to the structure of a television script is the relationship between the audio and the video. The dialogue is typed as usual, but the instructions and labels are generally typed in all-capital letters. The video part of the script includes descriptions of characters, actions, and camera movements.

A **storyboard**, which is a visual plan or layout of the commercial, is drawn (by hand or on the computer) to show the number of scenes, composition of the shots, and progression of the action. The script information usually appears below the key images. Its purpose is to guide the filming. A **photoboard** uses photographic stills instead of art to illustrate the progression of images. It's created from the still photos or frames from the filming and is used to present to clients.

PANDA EXPRESS STORYBOARD - LOVE TAKES FIVE

GUY looks in the mirror and adjusts his hair

Pan across to GIRL (in another apartment) looking in the mirror and adjusting her hair the same way

GIRL picks up a pair of walking shoes from a group of five

GUY picks up a pair of running shoes from a group of five the same way

Now dressed for work, GUY gets on the number 5 bus

GIRL and GUY are on the same bus

GUY looks to his right at the GIRL on the same bus, she's looking down, reading the same book

GIRL looks at GUY, but he's looking down reading his book

GUY steps inside elevator and presses floor 5

GIRL steps out of adjacent elevator, just as GUY's doors are closing

View into GIRL's office

Camera move reveals GUY in nearby office

GIRL walks five dogs nearby the GUY running five miles

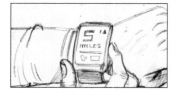
GUY's watch says "5 miles"

Establishing shot of Panda Express store

GIRL orders at the counter

Chef seasoning the wok

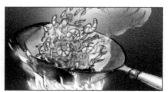
Beautiful wok toss of Five Flavor Shrimp

GIRL takes a bite

GIRL cracks open fortune cookie and holds the fortune "Your lucky number is five"

Fortune flies off her tray and lands on his

GIRL and GUY lock eyes and smile
VO: Some things are meant to be, together.

Hero shot of the dish
VO: New Five Flavor Shrimp.

End card, Couple sitting together
VO: Only at Panda Express.

Source: Courtesy Panda Restaurant Group and Bailey Lauerman Agency. Used with permission.

How to Write for the Internet: Online Media

The internet is more interactive than any mass medium. Not only do viewers initiate the contact, but they can respond as well. That makes the internet more like two-way (or multiple-way) communication, which is a major point of difference from other advertising forms. As a result, the internet writer is challenged to attract people to the brand and to manage a dialogue-based communication experience. In addition to targeting messages to audiences, organizations have to be prepared to listen and respond to those audiences. Writers also master the psychology of influence and understand how to get people talking across multiple devices and platforms. Websites and various social media that use the internet have the potential to be an echo chamber, repeating and reinforcing the brand message in various forms.

Internet writers create everything from catchy phrases for banners to copy that works like traditional advertisements, brochures, or catalogs. They also converse with the audience personally. Some forms of internet advertising look like more traditional ads, such as banners (usually across the top or down the side of the page), sidebar ads, and pop-ups. Email and video ads, as well as mobile ads on smartphones, all require variations of traditional copywriting techniques. Most of these formats end with a link to the sponsor's website where the user can participate in a more interactive brand experience.

⬤ **Principle**
To write great copy for the web, copywriters must think of it as an interactive medium and open up opportunities for dialogue with the consumer.

Websites   The challenges for those writing for the internet are to understand the user's situation and then design messages that fit their needs and interests. The web is an information medium, and users come to it, in some cases, for reference information—formats that look a lot like catalogs or even encyclopedias. Corporate or organizational websites are designed to provide information as well as image cues, so strategies that organize information and package it for easy accessibility are important. **Key words** are used to help *visitors* or *surfers* (rather than readers, listeners, or viewers) search for the site online as well as within the site for the information they need. Be mindful of the **user experience (UX)** because a good experience translates to higher conversion rates. Keeping web pages simple and visually appealing are hallmarks of good UX design. Users are looking for information quickly. If visitors to the site can't navigate easily or find information they need, chances are you'll lose them.

Some tips for writing for websites are as follows:[41]

- Call out important words.
- Use subheads to break up major copy blocks.
- Keep it simple.
- Convert paragraphs to bullet points.
- Limit your text links.
- Lead with the main message and then drill down.

- Keep it short.
- Scrolling is okay.

Creativity is also valued both to entice visitors and to keep them actively involved with the site. For example, the previously mentioned "Don't Mess with Texas" antilitter website invites visitors into the campaign with testimonials, letters, special events, and involvement programs in both English and Spanish. Celebrity selfies, an ad archive, art contests, and an education section all contribute to some good, clean fun. Check it out at http://dontmesswithtexas.org.

Blogs   One interactive form of communication on websites is a **blog**, which offers commentary and can serve many purposes, including promoting products and ideas. Blogs can be informational, help convey a brand personality through personal stories, and give news and industry updates, to name a few uses. Public relations practitioners find blogs attractive as a strategy for building relationships because they have the potential to credibility, foster goodwill, and a form positive reputation.[42] Writers need to think carefully about what they post, both in terms of content and style. Once the blog is on the internet, it's there to stay.

Internet Display Ads   Similar in some ways to traditional advertising, internet ads are designed to create awareness and interest in a product and build a brand image. Display ads range in format from simple all-type ads to rich media ads embedded with animation, sound, mouse-overs and drop-down boxes. In terms of creating interest, good copywriting works well in any medium, including the internet.

The most common form of online advertising is a small **banner ad** containing a little bit of text, images that grab attention, and perhaps motion and sound. To avoid being ignored, banners in this small format have to be creative to stand out amidst the clutter on a typical web page, and, similar to outdoor advertising, they have to grab the surfer's attention with few words. Effective banners arouse the interest of the visitor, who is often browsing through other information on the computer screen.

Sometimes banners provide brand reminder information only, like a billboard, but they usually also invite viewers to click on the banner to link to an ad or the advertiser's home page. The effectiveness of such efforts is monitored in part by the number of **click-throughs**. One mistake copywriters sometimes make is to forget to include the company name or brand in the banner or ad. Surfers should be able to tell immediately what product or brand the banner is advertising. Effective banner ads satisfy the need for entertainment, information, and context (a link to a product) and often use promotional incentives, such as prizes or gifts, to motivate visitors to click through to the sponsor's website[43] to drive action.

Native advertising blends promotional messages with other content. Usually online, this type of advertising is a hybrid, combining a promotional message and information to the point where its hard to categorize it as advertising, public relations, product placement, branded content, or anything else. The Invisalign brand paid to post its "Behind The Smile" message on the *New York Times* site. It gives a history of the smile, a payoff for reading the message, and then evolves into the technology of its product, clear aligners, the modern alternative to braces.

Photo: Courtesy of Align Technology

Native advertising is a hot, new term for a specific type of online advertising, but the concept really isn't that new. It is sponsored content. In other forms, it's known as advertorials (print) and infomercials (broadcast), which intertwine content with sponsorships. Writers of native advertising need to create the look and feel of the online publishing platform where the native ad runs. Twitter's Promoted Tweets and Facebook's Promoted Posts are other examples of native advertising. Using these forms can help boost exposure for messages. Like other sponsored content, native advertising should be labeled "promoted" or "advertising."

Social Media   In this complicated, fast-changing environment, there aren't a lot of rules for social media writers. In fact, marketing communication that uses text messaging and Twitter may even throw out the rules of spelling with vowel-free words. Twitter has its own microsyntax that is moving into popular culture with codes like "LOL," "OMG," and "#," the hashtag sign that means a searchable topic.[44] YouTube, Instagram, and Snapchat, Pinterest, and other platforms all offer opportunities to promote brands, although the focus of these efforts isn't on the writing. Mobile advertising is still in its infancy, and brands have yet to figure out how to target users effectively.

Megan Maisel, director of integrated media communications for the University of Texas MD Anderson Cancer Center, offers these tips for brand communicators in interactive media:[45]

* Define your audience and standardize your voice across all platforms.
* Measure and prepare to make changes quickly. What works today may not work in a month.
* Find the people stories. Share stories that you would be interested in sharing.
* Have clear calls to action. If you want your audience to do something (like a post, follow your page, or retweet), be explicit.
* Show some personality and have a sense of excitement.
* Sell one story several ways. Each social platform lets you engage your audience differently. Use the strengths of each one to make your message stand out.

Challenges Writers Face

10.4 Identify some challenges that writers face.

As discussed throughout this chapter, the writer's job is to find a memorable way to express the creative concept. A writer's talent will do no good if the audience cannot understand the "magic words." Understanding the words, as well as the creative idea, is particularly complicated in global brand communication.

Writing for a Global Brand

Language affects the presentation of the message. English is more economical than many other languages. That can create a major problem when the space for copy is laid out for English and one-third more space is needed for French or Spanish. However, English does not have the subtlety of other languages, such as Greek, Chinese, or French. Those languages have many different words for situations and emotions that do not translate precisely into English. Standardizing the copy content by translating the appeal into the language of the foreign market is fraught with possible communication blunders. It is rare to find a copywriter who is fluent in both the domestic and foreign language and familiar with the culture of the foreign market.

Headlines in any language often rely on humor, a play on words, or slang. Because these verbal techniques don't cross borders well, writers remove them from the international campaigns unless the meaning or intent can be re-created in other languages. For this reason, international campaigns are not literally translated word by word. Instead, a copywriter usually rewrites them in the second language. An ad for a Rome laundry shows how a poor translation can send the wrong message: "Ladies, leave your clothes here and spend the afternoon having a good time." When electronics giant Best Buy chose its Chinese name, it used "baisimai." The Mandarin pronunciation was close to the original. However, when the three Chinese characters used for the name are read together, they mean "Think it over a hundred times, before buying," hardly what you want consumers to do. Needless to say, the name failed, and ultimately, so did Best Buy's venture in China.[46]

The major distinction in cross-cultural communication is between **high-context cultures,** in which the meaning of a message can be best understood when contained within contextual

FIGURE 10.1
High- and Low-Context Cultures

cues, and **low-context cultures**, in which the message can be understood as it stands.[47] In Japanese, for example, a word can have multiple meanings. Listeners or readers will not understand the exact meaning of a word unless they clearly understand the context in which the word is used. In contrast, English is a low-context language; most of its words have clearly defined meanings that are not highly dependent on the words surrounding them. Figure 10.1 lists cultures from the highest to lowest context, with Japanese being the highest-context culture. This model helps explain the difficulties of translating brand messages into other languages.

Experience suggests that the most reasonable solution to the language problem is to use bilingual copywriters who understand the full meaning of the English text and can capture the essence of the message in the second language. It takes a brave and trusting international creative director to approve copy that he or she doesn't understand but is assured is right. A **back translation** of the ad copy from the foreign language into the domestic one is always a good idea, but it seldom conveys a complete cultural interpretation.

The most recent announcement on the global stage is the opening up of the internet to non-Roman letters, such as those used in Chinese, Korean, and Arabic. It's a challenge to develop translations for these languages so that a posting can be read in its original language as well as in Roman letter alphabets, but improved technology is making that possible.

Looking Ahead

The most important enduring principle is that in a Big Idea, the meaning emerges from the way the words and images reinforce one another. In this chapter, we've explored the practices and principles of promotional writing. In Chapter 11, we'll explain the important role of visual communication.

IT'S A WRAP

Scents-ational Success

This book explains and demonstrates principles and practices of effective marketing communication today. We are not only interested in ads that amuse us personally; we are also interested in ads that communicate effectively to achieve goals for the companies that sponsor them. Old Spice is a great example because it has demonstrated its effectiveness sufficiently to win the Grand Effie, the top prize in a competition that recognizes advertising and marketing communication that works, and a gold Effie in the category of sustained success as well as many other awards.

At the beginning of this chapter, you read that Procter & Gamble's Old Spice needed to fend off an attempt by Dove Men+Care to steal market share during its Super Bowl introduction. By using research and generating an insight that drove the campaign—Old Spice needed to involve men and women in a conversation about what a guy should smell like—Old Spice generated excitement with guys who were not current customers as well as the women who typically made most of the purchases of body wash. The tactic of using a hunk atop a horse captivated the audience (eye candy for the women and dry humor for the guys).

A far cry from what would have convinced your grandfather to buy Old Spice, this innovative interactive campaign effectively accomplished P&G's goals. Consider these statistics:

- Old Spice won more than 75 percent of the online buzz during the first three months following the campaign's launch.

- The YouTube videos received 10 million views from the launch in February to April. Six years later, one of the videos garnered more than 53 million views.
- The "Response" (viral video megahit Q&A interactive sessions with "The Man Your Man Could Smell Like") garnered more than 40 million views on YouTube at the end of the first week following its introduction.
- In one month, Twitter followers increased 2,700 percent, Facebook fans increased 60 percent (from 500,000 to 800,000), and Oldspice.com traffic increased 300 percent.

Becoming a cultural phenomenon, the campaign for "the manliest grooming product on the planet" generated an incredible amount of free PR. The six-month campaign resulted in 1.7 billion total impressions across traditional and online media outlets. Most important is that sales soared. From 2009 to 2015, Old Spice's sales of deodorants and body wash increased 51 percent.

Logo: Courtesy of Procter & Gamble. Used with permission.

KEY OBJECTIVES SUMMARY

10.1. Describe the writer's role in brand communication. In general, writers of marketing communication care about words and language as they develop messages. Although advertising, public relations, and direct response writing are different stylistically, all are bound by strategy and legal considerations. The goal of all types of writing is to communicate a memorable message that aligns with the strategy. Writers who have an ear for language create an authentic, credible voice and match the tone of the writing to the target audience or public.

10.2. Name the types of brand communication writing. Advertising copywriters, whose primary goal is to sell an idea, product, or image, aim to write succinct, single-minded copy that convinces a target audience to take some action. Words and pictures work together to shape a creative concept; however, it is the clever phrases and "magic words" crafted by copywriters that conjure understandable and memorable ideas. Public relations writers must be versatile and capable of writing in many different forms for a variety of purposes. They need to know journalistic conventions for writing news releases and features. They need to be able to develop relationships through social media. Above all, they use their skills to build positive relationships between brands and their publics. Depending on the objectives, direct-response writing uses a number of different formats, from direct-mail letters and brochures to online social media and customer service. In each format, the writing style needs to match the format and build a positive relationship.

10.3. Explain how to write for various media. The key elements of a print ad are headlines and body copy.

Headlines target the prospect, draw the reader's attention, identify the product, start the sale, and invite the reader to read on. Body copy provides persuasive details, such as support for claims, as well as proof and reasons why. Radio commercials are personal and play to consumers' interests. However, radio is primarily a background medium. Special techniques, such as repetition, are used to enhance retention. The three audio tools are voice, music, and sound effects. The key elements of television commercials and video are visual and audio. These media take advantage of motion and, to catch and maintain viewers' attention, use action, emotion, and demonstration to create messages that are intriguing as well as intrusive. Internet advertising is interactive and involving. Online advertising has primarily focused on websites and banners, although advertisers use forms that look more like magazine or television ads. Banners and other forms of online advertising have to stand out amid the clutter on a typical web page and arouse the viewer's interest. Native advertising is sponsored content most often found online, combining promotion with information to create a format that might interest users enough that they don't ignore it. Social media amplify the brand message and build personal relationships. Good writing is still good writing, even online.

10.4. Identify some challenges that writers face. Those who write for global brands face particular challenges because they need to make sure the message and creative ideas translate effectively in other cultures. Understanding the differences in language between high-context and low-context cultures is a prerequisite to effectively translating a brand across borders.

KEY TERMS

direct-action headline, p. 294
display copy, p. 292
feature stories, p. 292
headline, p. 293
high-context cultures, p. 307
image transfer, p. 300
indirect-action headline, p. 294
jingle, p. 299
key frame, p. 303

key visual, p. 303
key words, p. 305
lead paragraph, p. 296
low-context cultures, p. 308
native advertising, p. 306
news release, p. 291
off camera, p. 301
on location, p. 303
overlines, p. 293

pace, p. 303
photoboard, p. 304
radio script, p. 300
scenes, p. 303
set, p. 303
slogans, p. 282
sound effects, p. 300
storyboard, p. 304
subheads, p. 293

tagline, p. 282
talent, p. 303
television/video script, p. 303
theater of the mind, p. 299
tone of voice, p. 288
underlines, p. 293
user experience (UX), p. 305
voice-over, p. 301
your-name-here copy, p. 289

MyLab Marketing

Go to **www.pearson.com/mylab/marketing** for MyLab discussion questions (⚙) as well as the following assisted-graded writing questions.

10-1. What is the difference between a direct-action headline and an indirect-action headline? Find an example of each and discuss how it works.

10-2. Discuss the message characteristics of radio advertising. What does "theater of the mind" mean to a radio copywriter? What are the primary tools used by the radio copywriter?

REVIEW QUESTIONS

10-3. What qualities make a good tagline or slogan?

⚙ **10-4.** Discuss the differences in writing for advertising, public relations, and direct response.

⚙ **10-5.** Describe the various copy elements of a print ad.

10-6. What is adese, and why is it a problem in advertising copy?

10-7. What is the primary role of body copy, and how does it accomplish that?

10-8. One principle of print writing is that the headline catches the reader's eye but the body copy wins the reader's heart and mind. Find an ad that demonstrates that principle and explain how it works.

10-9. What are the major characteristics of television commercials? Describe the tools of writing for video.

10-10. Describe how internet advertising is written.

10-11. What are the major forms of writing for public relations professionals?

DISCUSSION QUESTIONS

⚙ **10-12.** Creative directors say the copy and art must work together to create a concept. Consider all the ads in this chapter and the preceding chapters and identify one that you believe best demonstrates that principle. Explain what the words contribute and how they work with the visual.

⚙ **10-13.** What do we mean by "tone of voice," and why is it important in advertising, public relations, and direct response? Find a magazine ad that you think has an appropriate tone of voice for its targeted audience (the readers of that particular magazine) and one that doesn't. Discuss your analyses of these two ads.

10-14. Select a product that uses a long-copy format in print. Examples are business-to-business and industrial products, over-the-counter drugs, and some car and appliance ads. Now write a 30-second radio and a 30-second television spot for that product. Present your work to the class along with an analysis of how the message design changed—and stayed the same—when you moved from print to radio and then to television.

10-15. Critique the following (choose one):

⚙ a. Jingles are a popular creative form in radio advertising. Even so, there may be as many jingles that you don't want to hear again as there are ones that you do. Identify one jingle that you really dislike and another one that you like. Analyze why these jingles either work or don't work and present your critique to your class.

b. Surf the web and find one banner ad that you think works to drive click-throughs and one that doesn't. Print them out and prepare an analysis that compares the two banner ads and explains why you think one is effective and the other is not. Present your critique to your class.

10-16. *Portfolio Project:* In the discussion questions at the end of Chapter 6, you were asked to consider the research needed for a new upscale restaurant chain that focuses on fowl—duck, squab, pheasant, and other elegant meals in the poultry category. Now your creative team is being asked to develop the creative package for the restaurant chain. Given this specialty category, the restaurant would be somewhat like a seafood restaurant. You have been asked to develop the creative package to use in launching these new restaurants in their new markets. Develop the following:

- The restaurant's name
- A slogan for the restaurant chain
- A list of five enticing menu items
- ⭐ A paragraph of copy that can be used in print to describe the restaurant
- ⭐ The copy for a 30-second commercial to be used in radio
- A news release announcing the opening of the restaurant

10-17. *Mini-Case Analysis:* Summarize the creative strategy behind the Old Spice campaign. Explain how the Big Idea works and how it is expressed in the copy. What makes the writing so engaging? Come up with an idea for another Old Spice "one-shot" ad and draft the copy.

Writing for a Multicultural Audience

Read the TRACE case in the Appendix before coming to class.

10-18. The case briefly discusses the tonality (voice) of the communications. Write a one-page direction to the creative team explaining what the tonality should be and giving rationale for your recommendation. Keep in mind the target audience and your client (TRACE).

11

Visual Communication

The arresting images of "Fearless Girl" communicated a cultural message about gender equality and the State Street brand that resonate with the company's stakeholders and the public. This chapter is about the visuals used in promotional communication, both how they are designed and what they contribute to the meaning of the brand. First we review some basic ideas about visual impact, both in print and video, and the role of the art director. Then we consider print art production and video production. We end with a discussion of the design of internet advertising.

MyLab Marketing

⭐ **Improve Your Grade!**

More than 10 million students improved their results using the Pearson MyLabs. Visit **www.pearson.com/mylab/marketing** for simulations, tutorials, and end-of-chapter problems.

Campaign
"Fearless Girl"

Organization
State Street Corp.

Agency
McCann New York

Awards
2017 Cannes Lions festival Titanium Grand Prix plus 3 Grand Prix awarded for Glass (addressing gender inequality), PR, and Outdoor categories

Picture This "Fearless Girl"

It's not quite clear where the expression "A picture is worth a thousand words" came from, and it really doesn't matter. What does matter is that it appears to ring true and has for centuries. Consider the impact of "Fearless Girl," and you'll think that a thousand words is an understatement.

Alone, with hands on hips and sporting a ponytail, "Fearless Girl" stands just over 4 feet tall and weighs about 250 pounds. That sounds a little chunky, but she's a bronze statue, so give her a break. She's caused a mighty stir, enticing the likes of US Senator Elizabeth Warren, singer/songwriter Cyndi Lauper, and billionaire businesswoman and founder of Spanx Sara Blakely to pose for pictures with her. Why, you ask?

This girl is all about delivering a powerful message about gender equality. Commissioned by State Street Global Advisors, the investment arm of Boston-based State Street Corporation, and created by sculptor Kristen Visbal, this statue was the brainchild of McCann senior art director Lizzie Wilson and senior copywriter Tali Gumbiner. They conceptualized the "Fearless Girl" as a public rela-

Photo: Rex Features/AP Images.

tions effort to spark a conversation about workplace gender diversity and encourage companies to recruit women to their boards. A plaque at the base of the statue says, "Know the power of women in leadership. SHE makes a difference." (SHE refers both to the subject of the statue and the NASDAQ ticker symbol of a State Street index fund.)

The placement and timing of the installation of the statue near the iconic Charging Bull on Wall Street in New York City on the eve of the International Women's Day march in March 2017 contributed brilliantly to the company's success in grabbing attention. "Fearless Girl" was originally granted a one-week permit by City Hall to reside on the street. The installation quickly trended on social media and became a viral sensation. The permit was extended for a year and there are ongoing efforts to make the statue's home permanent. One champion for extending its stay at its current location was US Representative Carolyn Maloney, who recognized the statue's symbolism of the resiliency of women.

Think about how visually compelling the statue is. "Fearless Girl" is brave, proud, and strong, and she's changed the cultural conversation about gender. After all, "Fearless Girl" stopped the "Charging Bull" in his tracks. By the way, Arturo Di Modica, the sculptor who created "Charging Bull," objected to the installation and wanted "Fearless Girl" to get out of his space and the bull's face because she was "attacking the bull." Well, at least she changed the meaning of the bull as art. Lawyers for the bull's sculptor said that the 50-inch-tall girl subverted the bull's meaning, which Di Modica defined as "freedom in the world, peace, strength, power and love." "Fearless Girl" makes the bull look more like a bully.

Richard Edelman, chief executive of PR giant Edelman, explained why it's important to connect with audiences and publics in cultural conversations: "It is harder to reach people through regular advertising nowadays—so brands have to be part of the 'cultural discussions that are taking place on social media.'"

"Fearless Girl" won the coveted Titanium Grand Prix, which is awarded for work from any category that is disruptive and irreverent, plus three Grand Prix trophies for separate categories of Glass (addressing gender inequality), PR, and Outdoor at the prestigious Cannes Festival. Judges noted that "Fearless Girl" demonstrated "culture-shifting creativity" that "transcended geography, language and culture" symbolizing the "hopes and ambitions for every little girl in the world." Also noteworthy is that the SHE fund increased by 374 percent, demonstrating that a Big Idea with a bold visual has the power to change conversations and build brands. Elisa Silva, SVP and director of client services at SS+K, summed up the impact: "The best ideas make us feel something deep in our bones, and 'Fearless Girl' really shook something loose in people. The statue did far more than it was intended to do, by sparking joy, outrage, and spirited debate that extended well beyond gender inequality."

To learn just how much impact this visual had plus see a picture of "Fearless Girl" and Wall Street's "Charging Bull," charge ahead to the It's a Wrap feature at the end of the chapter.

Sources: Jeff Green, "The Fearless Girl Is Worth $7.4 Million in Free Publicity for State Street," April 28, 2017, www .bloomberg.com; Tanya Dua, "'Fearless Girl Really Shook Something Loose': Why People Are Still Talking about the Wall Street Statue from a $2.5 Trillion Fund Manager," June 20, 2017, www.businessinsider.com; "Fearless Girl," https:// en.wikipedia.org/wiki/Fearless_Girl, last edited on August 15, 2017; E. J. Schultz, "McCann's 'Fearless Girl' Is Monday's Big Winner at Cannes," June 19, 2017, www.adage.com; Suzanne Vranica, "'Fearless Girl' Steals the Conversation," *Wall Street Journal*, June 20, 2017, R6; James Barron, "Wounded by 'Fearless Girl,' Creator of 'Charging Bull' Wants Her to Move," April 12, 2017, www.nytimes.com.

11.1 Define the role of visual communication.

What Is the Role of Visual Communication?

What makes "Fearless Girl" so visually remarkable? Does it grab your attention? How does the visual build brand personality? Is it interesting? Do you remember it? Isn't it amazing how powerful visuals gave life to an intangible object, a bank's index fund? If we consider a tangible product, say an ad for a Subaru, the same questions apply. Are the images attention getting, appealing, and memorable?

AN IMPERATIVE:
Respect the Dignity
of the Person

Edoardo Teodoro Brioschi, *Università Cattolica del Sacro Cuore, Milan, Italy*

I believe that there exist certain ethical principles that apply to business activities, and those include principles for marketing communication activities. Specifically, I'm concerned about the protection of the dignity of the person. A case in obvious conflict with this principle is the use in an advertisement of an image of a woman suffering from an illness: acute anorexia. That is the case in the "No-Anorexia No-l-ita" campaign for an Italian brand of youth apparel.

The woman presented in the ad is, in fact, practically a living skeleton. The message shows the image of a naked woman suffering from anorexia posing with her gaze turned to the observer. (The model is a 27-year-old French actress named Isabelle Caro, who is five feet five inches tall and weighs 70 pounds.) Both front and back views of her poses were used on outdoor boards and in the daily press during Milan fashion week as well as in other big cities, such as Rome and Naples.

The advertiser claimed that by presenting the images in this way, it sought to make specific reference to a drama experienced by young women: anorexia: "We want to keep young people informed about this terrible illness so that, by seeing the effects, the young will not take the same risk."

The body that self-regulates the advertising industry in Italy (Istituto di Autodisciplina Pubblicitaria [Italian Self-Regulation Institute]) examined the No-l-ita "No Anorexia" campaign and judged this message to be in conflict with its Code of Self-Regulation. It summoned the advertiser, Flash & Partners, producer of the No-l-ita brand, for a specific hearing to discuss the case.

As a number of experts testified, anorexia is a complex illness. It follows that, whatever the factor causing the pathology, the behavior at risk is not due to ignorance of its effect. Hence, the principle "If you know the results you will avoid them" is not valid. In fact, this pathology unfortunately derives from deep drives, probably including biochemical imbalances, which cannot be overcome or rectified by an advertisement that simply displays its devastating effects.

Therefore, this advertising was banned. In fact, the message in question uses the physical devastation of the naked body of a young woman for commercial purposes—for the purpose of marketing the firm's products—and in so doing, it offends her dignity and debases the personal and social drama caused by this type of pathology.

On this question, there was a more general observation by this jury, the highest judicial organ of the Italian Self-Regulation Institute. It notes that promotional campaigns dealing with such delicate areas as health and prevention call for extreme caution in their conduct, requiring scientific preparation and justifying a preventive screening by the bodies responsible for advertising self-regulation.

Visual Impact

A provocative outdoor board for the Italian women's apparel firm, No-l-ita, certainly got people's attention, but it also raised a furor in Italy because it showed shocking pictures of a naked anorexic woman. The image was shot by Oliviero Toscani, the former photographer/art director for Benetton, who stirred up emotions over his photos for that clothing brand by depicting a dying AIDS victim, death-row inmates, and a nun and priest kissing. In the Principled Practice feature, Professor Edoardo Brioschi examines the ethics of this image. The issue was only complicated several years afterward when the woman died.

The No-l-ita outdoor board had good intentions; it was designed to convey an antianorexic message. So what do you think? Should it have run? Should it have been taken down?

In effective advertising, both print and television, it's not just the words that need to communicate the message—the visuals communicate as well. And as the No-l-ita outdoor board illustrated, the image can be powerful, even shocking, and may inadvertently splash negative responses all over the brand.

In fact, visuals do some things better than words, such as demonstrate something. How would you demonstrate, for example, a sense of adventure found in discovering a new place?

If you could see Nebraska through my eyes, you would see untold stories.
In a vast, rugged range.
You would see ancient geography.
And you'd find a love for spontaneous adventure.
You would see a place of raw nature.
Filled with color and texture.
You would see yourself on a different planet.
Surrounded by natural ruins.
My name is Derek, and this is Toadstool Geologic Park through my eyes.

VisitNebraska.com

Photo: Courtesy Nebraska Tourism Commission and Bailey Lauerman. Used with permission.

This breath-taking visual for Nebraska Tourism grabs readers and invites them to take a leap and "Visit Nebraska."

⬡ **Principle**
The visual's primary function in an advertisement is to get attention.

Nebraska's "Visit Nebraska" campaign created this through strong illustrations and strong copy.

Even radio can evoke mental pictures through suggestive or descriptive language and sound effects. The effective use of visuals in advertising can be related to a number of the effects we have outlined in our Facets Model of Effects:

1. *Grab Attention* Generally, visuals are better at getting and keeping attention than words.
2. *Stick in Memory* Visuals persist in the mind because people generally remember messages as visual fragments, or key images that are filed easily in their minds, as the "Fearless Girl" demonstrates.
3. *Cement Belief* Seeing is believing, as the Subaru ad demonstrates. Visuals that demonstrate add credibility to a message.
4. *Tell Interesting Stories* Visual storytelling, such as was used in the quirky Altoids ads that play on the "Curiously Strong Mints" tagline, is engaging and maintains interest.
5. *Communicate Quickly* Pictures tell stories faster than words, as the "Fearless Girl" visual illustrates. A picture communicates instantly, whereas consumers have to decipher verbal/ written communication word by word, sentence by sentence, and line by line.
6. *Anchor Associations* To distinguish undifferentiated products with low inherent interest, brand communicators often link the product with visual associations representing lifestyles and types of users, as the "Fearless Girl" case demonstrates.

Photo: Courtesy Subaru of America and Toshi Oku.

Subaru demonstrates its "go-everywhere" capability in a single image.

In general, print designers have found that a picture in a print layout captures more than twice as many readers as a headline does. Furthermore, the bigger the illustration, the more the message grabs consumers' attention. Layouts with pictures also tend to pull more readers into the body copy; initial attention is more likely to turn to interest with a strong visual. People not only notice visuals but also remember the layouts with pictures more than those composed mostly of type. Both the believability factor and the interest-building impact of a visual story are reasons visuals are anchored so well in memory.

Photo: Chones/Shutterstock

Coca-Cola uses the brand's signature script and colors to create a unified visual identity.

Big Ideas that capture attention can be puzzling, funny, or shocking, like the No-l-ita billboard. Images are also used to help people remember the brand. Coca-Cola cans display consistent elements of design, underscoring the theme of unity. Attention, interest, memorability, believability—these factors help explain the impact of visual messages.

Brand Image and Position

The package design on the iconic Coke cans reflects the important role marketing communication plays in the creation of brand images and brand identity. Much of that contribution comes from the visual elements—the symbolic images associated with the brand and the elements that define the brand, such as the trademark and logo. A classic brand symbol, for example, is the target graphic used by the Target store. The association with the brand name is immediately clear, and the brand meaning—that Target is a store where you can go to get what you are looking for—also adds to the identity of the retailer.

A **logo**, which is the imprint used for immediate identification of a brand or company, is an interesting design project because it uses typography, illustration, and layout to create a distinctive and memorable image that identifies the brand. Think of the cursive type used for Coca-Cola, the block letters used for IBM, the apple with a bite out of it (in both rainbow stripes and white) for Apple computers, and NBC's peacock. Also check out the logo designs by Michael Dattolico and the captions, which explain his thinking about the objectives of the designs.

Brand icons are characters associated with a brand, such as Mr. Peanut, Uncle Ben, and Ronald McDonald. If they are effective, they become an enduring symbol of the brand. Initially, the character is designed to reflect the desired brand personality. The Jolly Green Giant is an imaginary and kind friend who encourages kids to eat their vegetables. Another example of a long-lasting icon is the Michelin man, representing the French company known for its tires and travel guides.

Logos and trade characters may need to be updated, as the Betty Crocker image has been a number of times. The trade magazine *Adweek* celebrates brand icons and annually inducts winners into its Madison Avenue Walk of Fame event every fall.

Package design is another area where brand image is front and center, as we mentioned with the newly designed Coca-Cola cans. Sometimes the brand link is in the shape of the packaging, as in the distinctive grandmotherly Mrs. Butterworth syrup containers or the appealing Panda Express packaging and advertising.

The package design also accommodates strategic elements with positioning statements, flags that reference current

SHOWCASE

BGB is a pretty standard landscaping company, but we wanted to give it a more Zen-like quality—clean, concise, a strong Asian influence in the circle, a groomed almost-bonsai tree, and the color red. Brought together, these elements offer a soothing company image to combat some of the negatives associated with landscaping (hard work and hassles!).

eMotion is a start-up company creating a product that utilizes the motion of a musical instrument and translates that into audible note variations. We wanted to capture both the "motion" of the musical notes in the logo and the emotion that all music embodies. The concept of the product captures a more fluid, rhythmic pairing of both the audible elements and movement of performance.

A graduate of the University of Florida advertising program, Michael Dattolico was nominated by Professor Elaine Wagner.

Logos: Courtesy Michael Dattolico. Used with permission.

Photo: Bloomberg/Contributor/Getty Images

Michelin Man has been used by Michelin since 1894 and his shape has evolved over time. He was slimmed down for the 100th anniversary to reflect smaller tires on modern cars.

campaigns, recipes, and pricing announcements as well as economic and popular culture events. The classic association between Wheaties and sports figures brings to life the brand's famous slogan, "Breakfast of Champions." See the parade of Wheaties stars on www.wheaties .com.

A brand position is often associated with words, such as the Avis "We Try Harder" slogan. Laura Ries, daughter of legendary Al Ries, one of the creators of the positioning concept, argues that one of the best ways to nail down a position is with a visual. She points to the universal recognition of the pink ribbon for the Komen Foundation, the contour bottle for Coke, the swoosh for Nike, and the Clydesdales for Budweiser, the King of Beers. Her ideas on how visuals play a more important role in marketing than words are explained in her iBook *Visual Hammer*. She explained that visuals are powerful "because they hold emotional power that sticks."[1]

Visual Storytelling

In visual storytelling, the images set up a narrative that has to be constructed by the reader or viewer. Visual storytelling is important to help viewers associate Folgers coffee with warm-hearted moments in a long-running campaign. One commercial, "Unpacked," tells a story about a couple who've just moved and are getting going in the morning, trying to

Photo: Courtesy Panda Restaurant Group and Bailey Lauerman Agency. Used with permission.

Sometimes, the American dream is made in a Chinese kitchen. Andrew and Peggy Cherng came to the United States in 1966 and soon opened their first restaurant. Now, Panda Express has nearly 1,800 stores in countries across the world. Bailey Lauerman's campaign featuring mouth-watering photos, along with clever packaging, has helped bring good food to its customers and good fortune to the company.

figure out where to start unpacking. It turns out that coffee is a pretty good place to start. The commercial ends with a jingle, "The best part of wakin' up is Folgers in your cup."[2] The story the visual tells may be about the product as hero, such as how effectively Bounty paper towels absorb spills. The point is that art directors design images that tell stories and create brand impressions.

Our ethics discussions in this book often focus on the appropriateness of an image and the story it tells about the brand. For example, an ad for Vaseline Intensive Care Lotion shows a conference room with a speaker and a group of businesspeople—both men and women—paying careful attention to the presentation. In the foreground is a happy woman in a business suit with her back to the speaker and her colleagues. Her legs are up on the table, and she's caressing them. She's also a black woman. The headline reads, "Nothing keeps you from handling your business." So, does Vaseline Intensive Care want us to know that if black women use their product, they become totally clueless in a business meeting? What appears to the creative team to be a dynamite visual may, on reflection, send a number of contrary messages.

Emotion and Visual Persuasion

We've talked about visual impact and the power of visual storytelling, but both come together in persuasive messages that are designed to touch the emotions and "move" the consumer to respond favorably to the brand. We know from Chapter 5 that emotion is a powerful factor in determining the persuasive effect of brand communication. We also know that emotional responses can be linked to moving visual images—moving, as in touch the emotions.

Mastercard's long-running "Priceless" campaign is a classic and demonstrates the power of a well-told story to create an emotional connection with the brand, even for something as abstract as a credit card. The trilogy tells the story of Badger the Dog, who got left behind on a family vacation. Viewers follow Badger as he makes his way back home, Of course, the commercial concludes with these now-classic lines: "There are some things that money can't buy. For your journey, there's Mastercard." Find it on YouTube and see how the visuals and music combine to make an emotional connection between the viewer and the brand.

Humor can be used to bind consumers with a brand. For example, the Volkswagen Tiguan Horses Laugh commercial juxtaposes horses that laugh as a background against which a frustrated guy tries to back his trailer into a parking place. They stop laughing when he shows up in a VW Tiguan with trailer assist that lets him demonstrate one of the car's key features. (Find it on YouTube, https://www.youtube.com/watch?v=U91Zp9wWS30.)

In many situations, emotion is the key driver of a prospect being "turned on" to a message. In the Matter of Principle feature, Professor Joe Tougas explores why emotionally loaded

Photo: Transcendental Graphics/Contributor/Getty Images

CLASSIC

Wheaties were first introduced in 1924, but it wasn't until 10 years later that the company realized the power of associating the health benefits of the brand with athletic performance. The famous "Breakfast of Champions" boxes have show-cased all kinds of winners, from Michael Jordan, with his record 18 boxes, to Tiger Woods and many Olympic stars, such as swimmer Michael Phelps and volleyball champion Misty May-Treanor.

● **Principle**

The power of visual storytelling enhances persuasive messages because visuals touch the emotions and move the consumer to respond favorably to the brand.

Save the Pandas! Save the Baby Seals! Save the Eagles! Save the Toads?

Joe Tougas, *Evergreen State College*

Messages about the importance of ecological preservation are often accompanied by stunning images of animals endangered by human activities. The images are carefully chosen to tug at our heartstrings—baby seals with large dark eyes, a panda mother with her pup, and a majestic eagle soaring in total freedom.

By combining the image with the verbal message, the author intends to motivate the viewer to very specific actions—sending a check to the sponsoring organization, calling members of Congress in support of a piece of environmental legislation, and so on. Such campaigns have been very effective in protecting endangered species and habitats.

The animals used in these campaigns tend to be "charismatic species" that most people find beautiful to look at or that easily trigger human emotions of sympathy or love. But does that mean that those species are more deserving of protection than the ugly or slimy ones—the toads and slugs of this world?

Changes in the climate and atmosphere have created a worldwide crisis for amphibians. Many species of toads and frogs are severely endangered. Are there reasons that people should care just as much about those ugly animals as we do about the beautiful ones?

The practice of using emotionally appealing images to promote a complex message illustrates a very general problem in communication strategy. When an organization decides to appeal to aesthetic values rather than moral, scientific, or political values, they are, in effect, choosing to persuade people to *do the right thing for the wrong reasons*.

Such an approach can be very successful but comes with a danger: once we have saved the eagles, we may feel justified in ignoring or undervaluing other species that are just as endangered and just as much at the mercy of human activities but that don't excite the same tender feelings.

Photo: silver-john/Fotolia

● Principle

The emotional hook of a visual engages the attention of a viewer and contributes to the depth of the memory traces left behind by the brand message.

visuals are particularly useful in certain types of environmental messages and maybe overlooked in other equally deserving causes.

Emotion is a "hook" that helps engage the attention of a viewer and contributes to the depth of the memory traces left behind by the brand message. The stronger the feelings elicited by a message, the more likely the viewer will find meaning in a message and link that meaningful experience to a brand. A visual can be the cue that turns on this brand linkage process.

As Charles Young, president of Ameritest and a member of this book's Advisory Board, explained, "It is the meaning of the emotions evoked by a particular string of images that is critical to the strategic brand-building process."[3] The Ameritest methodology is designed to identify those moments in a brand message that resonate emotionally for viewers, both negatively and positively. The Ameritest work over the years has determined a magnifier effect for emotionally engaging visuals that results in higher levels of liking. Emotional resonance delivered through visual content is particularly impactful. As the Ameritest researchers concluded in a study that identified this magnifier effect, prospects would be turned on to a brand more strongly when advertising was enhanced by emotional engagement with the surrounding context.[4]

Large or Small, Which Would You Choose? The Good, Bad and Ugly, Exposed

Amy Niswonger, *President, Ninth Cloud Creative & Little Frog Prints*

Having worked at both a boutique advertising/design firm as well as a large corporate design powerhouse, I can confidently say there are benefits to both. As a fresh new graduate, I was torn: which direction is right for me?

The smaller advertising firms certainly do have their benefits. As a young designer, I was able to wear multiple hats. I created ads, brochures, logos, billboards, and full marketing campaigns. Looking at my portfolio, I can confidently say, "That's my work." Stretched on a daily basis by my colleagues and creative director, I was entrusted to get the job done efficiently and effectively. I would be challenged to create unique successful solutions for my clients. Actively involved in a client-facing role, I pitched my ideas and backed up my concepts with research and reasoning. It was challenging but very rewarding. Now, look at the "bad and ugly," so to speak. The downside was that my clients were local, and some were regional but on a much smaller scale than if I had opted for a large design firm.

On the flip side, working at a corporate design firm also has its ups and downs. Huge international clients are in my personal portfolio. I am able to walk into many national retail stores and see projects that I contributed to. It's a great feeling of accomplishment. However, the downside is that I worked on a team that "did that," so only a tiny portion of the design is my own personal blood, sweat, and tears. Working on the same client for months at a time, I was sometimes overwhelmed by the level of detail that sometimes consumed my entire day, week, or even month.

Regardless, whichever direction is right for you, there are numerous benefits to both. You need to be happy in whatever direction you choose. At both positions, I had a sense of purpose, a responsibility to make my clients shine, whether it be a diamond in the rough or a Fortune 500 company. I was there to make it happen. The end result is "all good" because, let's face it, our job is to redesign the bad and the ugly.

Amy Niswonger is a creative director and professor who owns her own design studio. A graphic design and marketing graduate of Miami University in Oxford, Ohio, she was named a Most Promising Minority Student by the American Advertising Federation (AAF). She was nominated to be featured here by Connie Frazier, AAF chief operating officer.

What Are the Basics of Design?

11.2 Explain the basics of design.

Creating visual impact, as well as the visual brand identification elements, is the responsibility of the art director and designers. The art director is in charge of the visual look of the brand message, both in print and on television, and how it communicates mood, product qualities, and psychological appeals. The art director and copywriter team usually work together to come up with the Big Idea, but the art director is responsible for bringing the visual side of the idea to life.

Specifically, art directors make decisions about whether to use art or photography in print and film or animation in television and what type of artistic style to use. They are trained in graphic design, including art, photography, typography, the use of color, and computer design software. Although art directors generally design the ad, they may not create the finished art. If they need an illustration, they hire an artist. Newspaper and web advertising visuals are often **clip art** or **click art**, images from collections of copyright-free art that anyone who buys the clip-art service can use.

In addition to advertising, art directors may also be involved in designing a brand or corporate logo as well as packages, merchandising materials, store or corporate office interiors, and other aspects of a brand's visual presentation, such as shopping bags, delivery trucks, and uniforms. Graphic designer Amy Niswonger explains in the Inside Story how she views the working environment of graphic designers.

The Designer's Tool Kit

One of the most difficult problems that art directors—and those who work on the creative side of advertising—face is to transform a creative concept into words and pictures. As Meg Lauerman

Logos (top to bottom):
FedEx service marks used
by permission; Provided
courtesy of Frito-Lay
North America, Inc.;
Courtesy of NBC Universal
Media, LLC

⬤ **Principle**
For credibility, photography is a good medium.

noted in the Part 3 opening essay, the creative toolbox includes design, copy, visuals, and sound and sometimes more experiential components—taste, smell, and feel.

During the brainstorming process, both copywriters and art directors are engaged in **visualization**, which means they are imagining what the finished ad might look like. The art director, however, is responsible for translating the advertising Big Idea into a visual story. To do so, the art director relies on a tool kit that consists of illustrations or animation, photos or film shots, color, type, design principles, layout (print), and composition (photography, video, or film), among other visual elements.

Visual symbols are also fun and challenging for designers. Check out the following logos and see if you can find a symbolic message in designs with which you are probably very familiar. (FedEx has a white arrow between the E and X; there are two folks enjoying chips and a bowl of dip in the middle of Tostitos; and the peacock logo, with its full spectrum of colors, serves as a metaphor for NBC and its range of programming and technological capabilities.)

Illustrations and Photos   When art directors use the word *art*, they usually mean photographs and illustrations, each of which serves different purposes in ads. For instance, photography has an authenticity that makes it powerful. Most people believe that pictures don't lie (even though they can be altered). For credibility, then, photography is a good medium.

The decision to use a photograph or an illustration is usually determined by the advertising strategy and its need for either realism or fanciful images. Generally, a photograph is more realistic, and an illustration (or animation in television) is more fanciful. Illustrations, by definition, eliminate many of the details you see in a photograph, which can make it easier to understand their meaning because what remains are the "highlights" of the image. This ease of perception can simplify the visual message because it can focus attention on key details of the image. Illustrations also use artistic techniques to intensify meanings and moods, making illustrations ideal for fantasy (think about comic books and animated films). Photos convey a "seeing is believing" credibility. Photographs, of course, can also evoke an emotional response. For example, Patagonia demonstrates the outdoor clothing and gear in action and appeals to the reader's sense of adventure. "Visit Nebraska" invites travelers to see the beauty in the state.

It is also possible to manipulate a photograph and turn it into art, a technique that brought recognition to Andy Warhol, among others. This practice has become popular with the advent of the internet and the availability of easy-to-find digital images, some of which are copyrighted. That technique was used to create a political poster in 2008 and, at the same time, a legal nightmare for the artist, Shepard Fairey. Initially, Fairey claimed he found the original Obama photo using a Google Image search. The problem is that the iconic portrait with its social realism style was eventually found to have been constructed from a copyright-protected image taken by Mannie Garcia while on assignment for the Associated Press (AP), which claims ownership of the image and demanded credit as well as compensation. Garcia also believes he owns the copyright and supports Fairey's use of the image. Fairey claimed his use of the image follows the legal definition of fair use and doesn't infringe on AP's copyright.[5] Eventually, he admitted that he had used the AP image as a reference and was sentenced to two years of probation and 300 hours of community service.[6] Dilemmas like that face everyone who finds images online and wants to reuse them in marketing communication projects.

Another issue involving manipulated digitized images in a global environment revolves around the ability of

Photo: Courtesy Mikey Schaefer/Patagonia

This image from Patagonia showing climbers using its gear demonstrates how functional its clothing is.

Photo: Mannie Garcia/AP Photo

Photo: flab/Alamy Stock Photo

Recognized as one of the most important political images of recent years, the Obama "Hope" poster raises questions about fair use of manipulated images.

software programs, such as Photoshop, to manipulate specific content within a photo. Microsoft fell into a hole in 2009 when its website in Poland used a clumsy Photoshop application to turn a black man white. The original image had been used on Microsoft's US website and featured diverse genders and people of many colors. However, on the website based in Poland, where, presumably, there are fewer people of color, the artist chose to paste a white man's head on the body of a black man. Microsoft apologized, but the fiasco ran wild on news sites and blogs.[7]

The digital manipulation of photos of fashion models has been criticized as perpetuating unrealistic beauty standards by making women look too thin. The Dove campaign was created in part to expose how unnatural many of the "beautiful" images of women really are, as you read in Chapter 7.

Color   In addition to photos and illustrations, another important visual element that art directors manipulate is color. Color attracts attention, provides realism, establishes moods, and builds brand identity. Art directors know that print ads with color, particularly those in newspapers, get more attention than ads without color. Most ads—print, broadcast, and internet—are in full color, especially when art directors use photographs.

Color is particularly important in branding. Here's some compelling evidence: UPS uses a color called Pullman Brown to help identify and distinguish the delivery service from competitors like the US Postal Service and FedEx. Target, Nabisco, and Coca-Cola are associated with red; John Deere, Whole Foods, and BP with green; and IBM, Lowe's, and Pfizer with blue. McDonald's golden arches, Best Buy, Hertz, and Subway all use yellow. Nickelodeon, Crush, and Harley Davidson feature orange and black. Consistent use of a color can help a brand be memorable. Think about the meaning that is evoked when you think of your school's athletic colors.

In print, designers also use **spot color**, in which a second color in addition to black (a black-and-white photo or illustration with an accent color) is used to highlight important elements. The use of spot color is highly attention getting, particularly in newspaper ads.

Color also can help an ad convey a mood. Warm colors, such as red, yellow, and orange, convey happiness. Pastels are soft and often bring a friendly tone to a print ad. Earth tones are natural and no-nonsense. Cool colors, such as blue and green, are aloof, calm, serene, reflective, and intellectual. Yellow and red have the most attention-getting power. Red may symbolize alarm and danger as well as warmth. Black communicates high drama and can express power

Using Chinese Folk Arts in Promotional Designs

Qing Ma, *Zhejiang University City College, Hangzhou, China*

The formation of the colors of Chinese folk arts is based on traditional Chinese philosophy, which focuses on the inner experience of lifelike lingering charm and adorns serene, natural, simple, and deep artistic conception.

Many famous graphic designers in China tend to add indigenous elements, such as the elements of traditional Chinese ink painting and Confucianism, in their design works in order to give the advertisements natural and unrestrained artistic scenes.

This CD cover illustrates the theme of traditional Chinese instruments illustrated with high-quality bamboo. The design features a green bamboo shoot on the spine of the cover and bamboo drawings as a design feature with bamboo texture as background. In addition to colors, the freehand brushwork in traditional Chinese painting attracts the attention of Chinese customers.

"Red" has special meanings in the Chinese Lunar New Year. It means wealth, prosperity, and good luck when people celebrate the Spring Festival. For instance, the television animation advertisement "The Dance of Dragon" made by the Coca-Cola company uses the traditional Chinese figurine of an auspicious boy who is called "A Fu"; the figurine is usually made of clay and decorated with red color.

The red color and the traditional Chinese elements of fortune together set the tone for a happy new year in a Chinese northeastern village. The happy atmosphere made by the red color and lovely images caters to the taste and psychology of Chinese customers.

Another classic example of successful advertising by using appropriate designs is an advertisement for Hanfang, a Chinese health care company. A special blue background, which is usually used for making traditional Chinese blue printed cloth, is decorated with the patterns of some Chinese medicine and natural brushwork.

Photo: Courtesy of Qing Ma

The CD cover with its bamboo theme was screen printed with an illustration that brings a feeling of classical delicacy. The CD cover won an award at the Taiwan Straits bamboo arts competition for universities.

◉ **Principle**

Type has a functional role in the way it presents the letters in words so that they can be easily read, but it also has an aesthetic role and can contribute to the meaning of the message through its design.

and elegance. Notice that these color associations are culturally determined, and uses like those are common in Western countries but may not be effective in other cultures. White, for example, is the color of death in many Asian countries. Professor Qing Ma explains the use of color from Chinese folk arts in design in the Matter of Principle feature.

The use of black and white is also an important design choice because it lends dignity and sophistication to the visual, as the Nike ad illustrates. A historical effect can be created by shooting in black and white or by using a sepia tone, which can make the images look like old prints that have been weathered by time. When realism is important to convey in an ad, full-color photographs may be essential. Some products and ad illustrations just don't look right in black and white—pizza, flower gardens, and nail polish, for instance.

"Visit Nebraska" is Nebraska's campaign created to support tourism in a state that promises special moments in a surprisingly beautiful land. Created by Bailey Lauerman, each ad contains a narrative that paints the picture of an experience that is waiting to be discovered. The campaign was constructed without the use of a traditional headline or even a logo, with the desired result being the sense that there is a genuineness to the Nebraska experience. In each ad, the photography and copy work together to tell the story around the benefit of taking the time to slow down, enjoy one another, and soak up what Nebraska has to offer.

Typography Not only do art directors carefully choose colors, but they also specify the ad's **typography**, the appearance of the ad's printed matter. In most cases, good typesetting does not call attention to itself because its primary role is functional: to convey the words of the message. Type or lettering, however, also has an aesthetic role, and the type selection can, in a subtle or not-so-subtle way, contribute to the impact and mood of the message, as the Nike ads demonstrate.

Ad designers choose from among thousands of typefaces to find the right one for the ad's message. Designers are familiar with type classifications, but it is also important for managers and other people on the creative team to have some working knowledge of typography to understand what designers are talking about and to critique the typography and make suggestions. The many decisions an art director makes in designing type include the following:

Photo: Courtesy Nebraska Tourism Commission and Bailey Lauerman. Used with permission.

- The specific typeface, or **font**
- The way capitalization is handled, such as all caps, small caps, or lowercase
- Typeface variations that come from manipulating the shape of the letterform

Photo: Courtesy Nike, Inc.   *Photo:* Courtesy Nike, Inc.

The typography emphasizes Nike's "Just Do It" time-tested slogan. Notice that the trademark swoosh is so identifiable that the Nike name isn't even necessary.

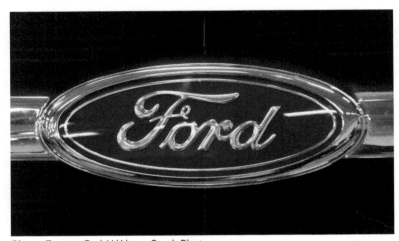

The Ford Motor Company logo has evolved since 1903.

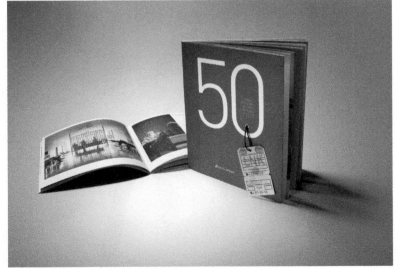

The Lincoln (Nebraska) Airport Annual Report effectively arranges elements of type and graphics to convey a message celebrating half a century of operation.

- The edges of the type block and its column width
- The size in which the type is set (vertical height)
- **Legibility**, or how easy it is to perceive the letters

Generally, logos are designed to last for a long time, but sometimes brands change the design and typography in an attempt to modernize the look, as Ford has done.

Design Principles, Layout, and Styles

The arrangement of the pieces in a print ad or video shot is called a layout, and it is governed by basic principles of design. Principles that designers use in layout include direction, dominance, unity, white space, contrast, balance, and proportion. The design has both functional and aesthetic needs: the functional side makes the visual message easy to perceive, and the aesthetic side makes it attractive and pleasing to the eye.

The design guides the eye by creating a visual path that helps the viewer scan the elements (direction). Dominant elements that are colorful or high in contrast (big versus small, light versus dark) catch the viewer's attention first. How all the elements come together is a function of the unity and balance of the design. Direction or movement is the way the elements are positioned to lead the eye through the arrangement. Simplicity is also a design principle, one that is in opposition to visual clutter. In general, the fewer the elements, the stronger the impact, an idea expressed in the phrase "less is more." Another saying is KISS, which stands for "Keep It Simple, Stupid."

Let's look at how these design principles are used in print layout and in the composition of a picture or photograph. For print messages, once art directors have chosen the images and typographic elements, they manipulate all the visual elements on paper to produce a layout. A **layout** is a plan that imposes order and at the same time creates an arrangement that is aesthetically pleasing.

Different layouts can convey entirely different feelings about a product. For example, look at the two ads for work boots. The ACG "Air Krakatoa" boot ad screams "waterproof!," signaling the boots' ability to stand up to the most serious weather conditions. In contrast, the ad for the Dunham boot looks like a work

Photo: Courtesy of New Balance Athletic Shoe, Inc.

The layout for the Dunham boot ad shown here speaks in a quiet voice about the beauty of nature. Even though it's a boot ad, it projects an elegance that reflects an appreciation for nature and a serene outdoor scene (footprints in the snow). The ACG "Air Krakatoa" ad with an asymmetrical layout uses spot color effectively in the copy. Notice how the layout "shouts," in contrast to the soft tone of voice of the Dunham boot ad.

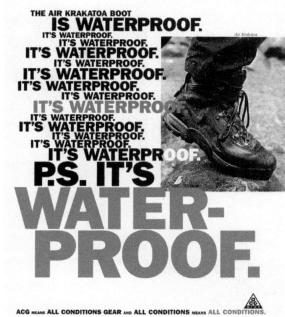

Photo: Courtesy of Nike, Inc.

of fine art. The difference between the two campaigns clearly lies with the visual impact that comes from the layouts as well as the imagery.

Here are some common types of layouts an art director might use. They apply to brochures and magazines as well as advertisements.

⬢ **Principle**
Design is usually improved by simplifying the number of elements. Less is more.

- *Picture Window* A common layout format is one with a single, dominant visual that occupies about 60 to 70 percent of the ad's space. Underneath it is a headline and copy block. The logo or signature signs off the message at the bottom.
- *All Art* The art fills the frame of the ad and the copy is embedded in the picture. The "Visit Nebraska" ads illustrate this type of layout.
- *Panel or Grid* This layout uses a number of visuals of matched or proportional sizes. If the ad has multiple panels all the same size, the layout can look like a windowpane or comic strip panel. The Dunham boot ad uses two side-by-side panels.
- *Dominant Type or All Copy* Occasionally, you will see layouts that emphasize the type rather than the art or even an all-copy advertisement in which the headline is treated as type art, such as the ACG ad. A copy-dominant ad may have art, but it is either embedded in the copy or placed in a subordinate position, such as at the bottom of the layout.
- *Circus* This layout combines lots of elements—art, type, and color—to deliberately create a busy, jumbled image. This layout is typical of some discount store ads or ads for local retailers, such as tire companies.
- *Nonlinear* This contemporary style of layout can be read starting at any point in the image. In other words, the direction of viewing is not ordered, as in the #OrangeChickenLove website for Panda Express on the next page.

These layout categories are functional, but there are also stylistic categories that designers will sometimes use to refer to their approach. Designers working with a layout problem that calls for a historical feeling, for example, might use design aesthetics from such periods as art nouveau, art deco, or modern or moderne. All of these were international styles popular in the late 19th century into the early to mid-20th century. Art nouveau uses flowing, curved lines reminiscent of vines and flowers. It was followed by art deco, which is much more linear and symmetrical. Modern design added an industrial, streamlined, and architectural quality to the elegance of art deco.

Photo: Courtesy Panda Restaurant Group and Bailey Lauerman Agency. Used with permission.

Other styles include postmodern, which is an eclectic primarily architectural design style that incorporates assemblages of elements from previous periods. Since then, we've seen the psychedelic art of the 1960s with its hippie images, followed by pop art, which turned everyday items, such as Andy Warhol's Campbell's Soup cans, into art.

Grunge design, which appeared in the 1990s, was a rejection of the niceties of traditional design. Its most recent incarnation is a contemporary style studied by graphic designer Nikki Arnell, who coined the term "Beautiful Messy" for this artfully hand-drawn design style that seems to reflect the millennial personality and style. The point of understanding these historical styles is that art directors often use them to communicate certain types of messages. There's nothing that says counterculture, for example, like a design in the psychedelic style.

The stages in the normal development of a print ad may vary from agency to agency or from client to client. Figure 11.1 shows the six-stage development of a Lincoln Marathon poster. This ad went through **thumbnail sketches**, which are quick, miniature preliminary sketches; **rough layouts**, which show where design elements go; **semicomps** and **comprehensives**, which are drawn to size and used for presentation either in-house or to the client; and **mechanicals**, which assemble the elements in their final position for reproduction. The final product that is used for actual production of the ad is a high-resolution computer file.

Composition

We've been talking about layout, which is a term used to describe how the elements in print (headline, art, tagline, and so on) are arranged. **Composition** refers to the way the elements in a picture are arranged (think a still-life painting) or framed through a camera lens (think a landscape photo or movie scene). Photographers and **videographers** (people who shoot a scene using a video camera) handle composition in two ways: (1) they may be able to place or arrange the elements in front of their cameras, and (2) they may have to compose the image by manipulating their own point of view if the elements can't be moved. In other words, they move around to find the most aesthetic way to frame an image that isn't movable, such as a scene or landscape, as well as to catch different lighting situations, such as bright sun and shade or shadow.

Similar to the way layouts are developed by using sketches, video images are also drawn and presented as **storyboards**, which are sketches of the scenes and key shots in a commercial. The art director imagines the characters and setting as well as how the characters act and move in the scene. The art director sketches in a few key frames the visual idea for a scene and how it is to be shot and how one scene links to the scenes that follow. In addition, the storyboard sketches also reflect the position and movement of the cameras recording the scene, a description of which is spelled out both in the script and on the storyboard.

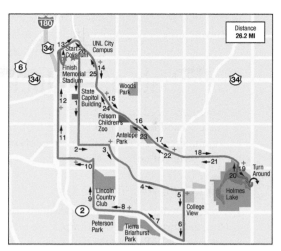

Source (bottom two images): Courtesy Lincoln Track Club and Bailey Lauerman. Used with permission.

FIGURE 11.1

Lincoln Marathon Creative Process

These images illustrate the evolution of an idea through its execution. Created by Bailey Lauerman, an Omaha firm, the work was inspired by this photograph of Abraham Lincoln and the marathon route traced on a map of the Lincoln Marathon. Juxtaposing the images in the rough sketch gave the artist a blueprint for the finished poster.

Environmental Design

Think about the last time you went to a sit-down restaurant versus your experiences in fast-food places. What's the difference in the way these spaces are designed both inside and outside? Think about the colors and surfaces and types of furniture. What do these design features say about the personality of the restaurant? How is a sit-down restaurant different in its design from a fast-food place?

Environmental design is entirely different from the usual marketing communication pieces. Remember that everything communicates, and that includes the design of the environment in which goods and services are offered for sale. Physical decisions about space and color and texture can communicate just as quickly as posters and signs.

The architectural design and interior ambiance of a store also contribute to its brand personality. If you have been in an Apple Store, you might remember some of the details of the environment that make the space different from, say, a department at Sears, not to mention a Nike or Patagonia store or a Tesla showroom. Nike stores have even been described as retail theater with displays and spaces that showcase not only the shoes and apparel, but also the sports with which they are associated.

11.3 Name the essentials of production for print media.

Essentials of Production for Print

Art directors need to understand print media requirements and the technical side of production because these factors affect both the look of the printed piece and its cost. Marketing communication managers also need to understand some of these basics so as to critique ideas and evaluate them in terms of cost and feasibility.

Print Media Requirements

Different media put different demands on the design and production of advertising. Newspapers and directories, for example, are printed at high speed on an inexpensive, rough-surfaced, spongy paper called **newsprint** that quickly absorbs ink on contact. Newsprint is not a great surface for reproducing fine details, especially color photographs and delicate typefaces. Most newspapers offer color to advertisers, but because of the limitations of the printing process, the color may not be perfectly in **registration** (i.e., all the color inks may not be aligned exactly, creating a somewhat blurred image).

Magazines have traditionally led the way in graphic print production because their glossy paper is a higher grade than newsprint. Excellent photographic and color reproduction is the big difference between newspapers and magazines. Magazine advertisements are also able to take advantage of more creative, attention-getting devices, such as pop-up visuals, scent strips, and computer chips that play melodies when the pages are opened. An Altoids ad that launched Altoids chewing gum, for example, ran in magazines with a novel print production technique. It showed a box of Altoids chewing gum on one page and a singed logo burnt onto the cartoon on the opposite page.

Out-of-home advertising takes many forms, from bus benches to kiosks and from blimps to projections. The most dominant forms are posters and outdoor boards, and the key to effective design is creating a dominant visual with minimal copy. Because billboards must make a quick and lasting impression from far away, their layout should be compact with a simple visual path. Here are some design tips.

- *Graphics* Make the illustration an eye-stopper.
- *Size* Images in billboards are huge; think of a 25-foot-long pencil or a 43-foot pointing finger. The product or the brand label can be hundreds of times larger than life.
- *Colors* Use bold, bright colors. The greatest impact is created by maximum contrast between two colors, such as dark colors against white or yellow. Special effects can be created by using textures and new inks, such as translucent, glow-in-the-dark, glitter, security or black light, and metallic colors.
- *Figure/Ground* Make the relationship between foreground and background as obvious as possible. A picture of a soft drink against a jungle background is hard to perceive when viewed from a moving vehicle at a distance. The background should never compete with the subject.
- *Typography* Use simple, clean, uncluttered type that is easy to read at a distance by an audience in motion. The industry's legibility research recommends avoiding all-capital letters, fanciful ornamental letters, and script and cursive fonts.
- *Product Identification* Focus attention on the product by reproducing the label or package at a huge size.
- *Extensions* Extend the frame of the billboard to expand the scale and break away from the limits of the long rectangle.
- *Shape* For visual impact, create the illusion of 3-D effects by playing with horizons, vanishing lines, and dimensional boxes. Inflatables create a better 3-D effect than most billboards can, even with superior graphics.
- *Motion* Add motors to boards to make pieces and parts move. Disk-like wheels and glittery things that flicker in the wind create the appearance of motion, color change, and images that squeeze, wave, or pour. Use revolving panels, called *kinetic boards*, for messages that change.

Photo: suwatpatt/Shutterstock

FIGURE 11.2
Line Art and Halftone Art
An example of a figure reproduced as line art (top) and as a halftone (bottom).

Print Art Reproduction

In general, there are two types of printed images: line art and halftones. A drawing or illustration is called **line art** because the image is solid lines on white background. Photographs, which are referred to as **continuous tones** or **halftones**, are much more complicated to reproduce because they have a range of gray tones between the black and white, as shown in Figure 11.2.

Printers create the illusion of shades of gray in converting photos to halftones by shooting the original photograph through a fine **screen**, which converts the image to a pattern of dots that gives the illusion of shades of gray: dark areas are large dots that fill the screen, and light areas are tiny dots surrounded by **white space**. The quality of the image depends on how fine the screen is. Newspapers use a coarse screen, usually 65 lines per inch (called a 65-line screen), whereas magazines use fine screens, which may be from 120 up to 200 or 300 lines per inch.

Screens are also used to create **tint blocks**, which can either be shades of gray in black-and-white printing or shades of color. A block of color can be printed solid, or it can be screened to

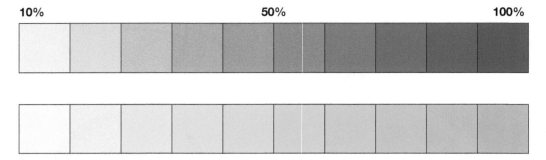

10%   50%   100%

FIGURE 11.3
Screen Values and Tint Blocks
The range of tint values that can be produced by different screens that represent a percentage of the color value.

create a shade. These shades are expressed as a range of percentages, from 100 percent (solid) down to 10 percent (very faint). Figure 11.3 gives examples of screens in color. A similar process is used with computer images, which are presented in pixels and measured in pixels per centimeter or pixels per inch (PPCM or PPI, respectively). Quality photos, for example, are generally presented in 300 PPI.

It would be impossible to set up a printing press with a separate ink roller for every hue and value in a color photo. How, then, are these colors reproduced?

Full-color images are reproduced using four distinctive shades of ink called **process colors** to produce **four-color printing**. These colors are *magenta* (a shade of pinkish purple), *cyan* (a shade of bright blue), *yellow*, and *black*. Printing inks are transparent, so when one ink overlaps another, a third color is created, and that's how the full range of colors is created. For example, red and blue create purple, yellow and blue create green, and yellow and red create orange. The black is used for type and, in four-color printing, adds depth to the shadows and dark tones in an image.

The process printers use to reduce the original color image to four halftone negatives is called **color separation**. Figure 11.4 illustrates the process of color separation.

Photo: Courtesy Nebraska Tourism Commission and Bailey Lauerman. Used with permission.

FIGURE 11.4
The Color Separation Process
These five photos illustrate the process of creating four-color separations: (A) Cyan plate. (B) Magenta plate. (C) Yellow plate. (D) Black plate. (*Note:* After cyan is added, there would also be combined plates showing cyan added first to yellow, then to magenta, and then to the combined yellow and magenta plates. These steps were left out to simplify the presentation.) (E) Finished art with all four process colors combined.

Digitization   If an ad is going to run in a number of publications, there has to be some way to distribute a reproducible duplicate of the ad to all of them. The duplicate material for **offset printing** is a slick proof of the original mechanical. More recently, **digitization** of images has been used to distribute reproducible images. That is also how computers now handle the color reproduction process. These digitized images can be transmitted electronically to printers across a city for local editions of national newspapers or by satellite for regional editions of magazines and newspapers, such as *USA Today*. Agencies also use this method for transmitting ad proofs within the agency network and to clients.

Digitization makes it possible to create some spectacular effects in out-of-home advertising. Some outdoor boards have become digital screens complete with changing and moving images. A new technique in transit advertising comes from Atlanta, where the city's buses are wrapping their sides with something called "glow skin." The ads use electroluminescent lighting to make the ads glow at night and appear to jump off the sides of the buses.

Binding and Finishing

Art directors can enhance their ads and other printed materials by using a number of special printing effects.

* *Die Cutting* A sharp-edged stamp, or die, is used to cut out unusual shapes. A common **die-cut** shape you're familiar with is the tab on a file folder.
* *Embossing or Debossing* The application of pressure to create a raised surface (**embossing**) or depressed image (**debossing**) in paper.
* *Foil Stamping* The process of **foil stamping** involves molding a thin metallic coating (silver or gold) to the surface of an image.
* *Tip-Ins* A **tip-in** is a separate, preprinted ad provided by the advertiser that is glued into a publication as the publication is being assembled or bound. Perfume manufacturers, for example, tip in samples that are either scratch-and-sniff or scented strips that release a fragrance when pulled apart.

3-D Printing

The latest printing technology innovation, which began making headlines in 2013, is 3-D printing, which doesn't mean images appear to jump off the page; rather, 3-D imaging processes are used to manufacture objects, such as iPad stands, jewelry, machine parts, or weapons and ammunition. A printer that looks like your desktop computer printer extrudes materials— plastics, even metal—to a specified size and shape, and some companies, such as Coca-Cola, Volkswagen, and Nokia, have used it as a marketing tool for their brands. Nokia released a 3-D printing kit that enables owners to customize phone cases.[8] Experts predict a new Industrial Revolution from this developing technology.

Essentials of Video Production

11.4 Identify the essentials of video production.

Where does an art director start when putting together a video for a commercial, a video news release, or some other kind of corporate film or video? Obviously, the first consideration is the nature of the image. The art director can arrange for filming on a constructed set or in a real location. The image is composed through the lens of the camera, just as it is for still images, but the difference—and the challenge—lies in the way the moving image takes shape. That's true for movies as well as for commercials and commercial videos used for a variety of promotional purposes.

Before we get too deep into this discussion, we should mention that the word *film* is not limited to the plastic material celluloid that once ran through a movie projector. The term has evolved to be used generically, even when it refers to video or digital production.

In addition to filming the scene yourself, another often cost-saving option is to use **stock footage**—previously recorded images, either video, stills, or moving film. Typical stock footage files include shots such as images from a satellite, historical scenes such as World War II battles, or a car crash. Animation, stop motion, and 3-D are other film production techniques that can be used instead of using stock footage or live filming.

Working within the framework of the creative strategy, art directors also create the look of the video or commercial. Watch the latest Super Bowl ads on YouTube to see how commercials vary in tone and appearance.

The art director can specify graphic elements, such as words, product logos, and still photos, computer generated right on the screen. A **crawl** is a set of computer-generated letters that appear to be moving across the bottom of the screen.

The big change has been the move from film to digital images. Some movies, such as *Star Wars: The Force Awakens* and *Star Wars: Episode 9*, were shot on film, but the trend in 21st-century moviemaking, as well as advertising, is to use digital technology. Sophisticated computer graphics systems, such as those used in the early days of digital filming to create the *Star Wars* and *Matrix* special effects, pioneered the making of artistic film and video. In the documentary *Side by Side*, Keanu Reeves takes you on a tour of this gee-whiz technology and its directors, such as Martin Scorsese and Steven Soderbergh.[9]

Computer graphic artists brag that they can do anything with an image. They can look at any object from any angle or even from the inside out. Computer graphics specialists use computer software to create, multiply, and manipulate video images. One creative video technique is called **morphing**, in which one object gradually changes into another. Photographs of real objects can change into art or animation and then return to life.

Filming and Editing

Most local retail commercials are simple and inexpensive, and they are typically shot and recorded at the local station. The sales representative for the station may work with the advertiser to write the script, and the station's director handles the taping of the commercial.

Creating a national television commercial is more complex and requires a number of people with specialized skills. The ad agency crew usually includes the copywriter and art director as well as the producer, who oversees the production and is responsible for the budget, among other things. The director, who is the person responsible for filming or recording the commercial, is usually someone from outside the agency. This person takes the art director's storyboard and makes it come to life.

The producer and director make up the core of the production team. The commercial's effectiveness depends on their shared vision of the final commercial and the director's ability to bring it to life as the art director imagined it. In the case of the "Cat Herders" commercial, the director was chosen by the agency because of his skill at coaxing naturally humorous performances from nonprofessional actors. In this commercial, he worked with real wranglers on their semiscripted testimonials about their work with kitties.

Productions and budgets vary. So do the responsibilities of the staff involved. Some local productions require that one person do more than one job on a production. Big budget productions can afford to have more specialized personnel. The following list summarizes the responsibilities of typical production personnel:

Who Does What in Production?

Copywriter	Writes the script, whether it contains dialogue, narrative, lyrics, announcements, descriptions, or no words at all.
Art Director	In television, develops the storyboard and establishes the look of the commercial, whether realistic, stylized, or fanciful.
Producer	Takes charge of the production, handles all production arrangements, finds the specialists, arranges for casting talent, and makes sure the expenses and bids come in under budget.
Director	Has responsibility for the actual filming or taping, including how long the scene runs, who does what, how lines are spoken, and how characters are played; in television, determines how the camera is set up and records the flow of action.
Cinematographer	Directs photography and is responsible for the camera crews and shooting the film.
Composer	Writes original music and sometimes the lyrics as well.

Arranger	Orchestrates music for the various instruments and voices to make it fit a scene or copy line. The copywriter usually writes the lyrics or at least gives the arranger some idea of what the words should convey.
Editor	Puts everything together toward the end of the filming or taping process; evaluates how to assemble scenes and which audio elements work best with the dialogue and footage.

The Process of Producing Videos and Commercials

Digital technology has replaced the analog process. With modern productions, images are recorded on hard drives, eliminating the use of film or videotape. Art directors work closely with editors, who assemble the recorded digital images to create the right pacing and sequence of images as outlined in the storyboard.

Filming Techniques   Animation is a filming technique that is often used in commercials. The technique of animation traditionally meant drawing images on acetate and then recording the images on film one frame at a time. Cartoon figures, for example, were sketched and then resketched for the next frame with a slight change to indicate a small progression in the movement of an arm or a leg or a facial expression. Low-budget animation uses fewer drawings, so the motion looks jerky. The introduction of computers has accelerated the process and eliminated some of the tedious handwork.

Animation is similar to illustration in print in that it abstracts images and adds a touch of fantasy and/or mood to the image. As Karl Schroeder, a copywriter with Nike and formerly at Coates Kokes in Portland, Oregon, explained about a project his Coates Kokes team worked on for a recycling center, "What was nice about it, when you consider that the spots needed to appeal to *everyone* who recycles in the area, was that it [animation] got us away from casting racially ambiguous, hard-to-pin-an-age-on talent."[10]

Animation effects can also be used to combine animated characters, such as Geico's little green gecko, with live-action figures or even with other animated characters. The famous Aflac duck was created as a collaboration between Warner Brothers and the Aflac agency, the Kaplan Thaler Group in New York. More advanced techniques, similar to those used in movies like *Avatar*, *Up*, and the *Shrek* series, create lifelike images and movement. Some animation software is so good that it not only creates lifelike images, but even adds realistic detail, such as hair on the animals. Current technology allows animation software to program not only characters, but also behaviors, allowing characters to interact with one another. Advergames (advertising branded products in videogames) offer amazing examples of animation.

A particular type of animation is **stop motion**, a technique used to film inanimate objects like the Pillsbury Doughboy, which is a puppet. The little character is moved a bit at a time and filmed frame by frame. The key decision about using animation techniques or, for that matter, other special effects is based on the question, does it tell the brand story better? In the case of the Pillsbury Doughboy, the investment seems to have paid handsome dividends in brand identity.

The technique used in stop motion is also used in **claymation**, which involves creating characters from clay and then photographing them one frame at a time. Both stop motion and claymation have been popular types of animation used by art directors who create advertising where fantasy effects are desired. Although new computer effects also are simplifying these techniques, sometimes these effects are costly.

3-D is a type of production that creates the illusion of depth using a special motion picture camera and projection hardware, as in the movies *Zootopia, Finding Dory,* and *Batman v. Superman: Dawn of Justice*. Viewers also have to wear special glasses. The 3-D technique has been around for many years, but only with the big success of the movie *Avatar* did it achieve wide popularity. 3-D is slowly moving to television and commercials.

Music and Action   Specifying the music is usually done as part of the copywriting; however, matching the music to the action is an art director or producer's responsibility. In some cases, as in high-production song-and-dance numbers, the music is the commercial. Other times, it is used to get attention, set a mood, or help tell a memorable story. Mastercard's commercial trilogy of

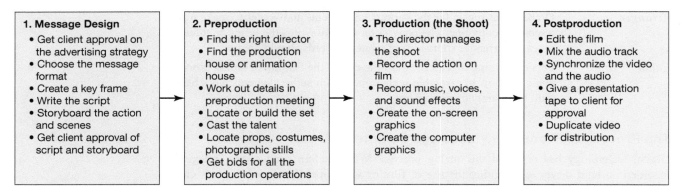

FIGURE 11.5
Video Production Process
In general, there are four steps in the production of a video after agreement is obtained on the message strategy.

Badger the Dog mentioned at the beginning of this chapter does a masterful job of employing music to enhance the storytelling.

The Production Process

For the bigger national commercials, the steps in the production process fall into four categories: message design, preproduction, the shoot, and postproduction. Figure 11.5 shows the steps in the process.

Preproduction The producer and staff first develop a set of **production notes**, describing in detail every aspect of the production. These notes are important for finding talent and locations, building sets, and working with the budget and estimates from specialists. In the "Cat Herders" commercial, finding the talent was critical. Some 50 felines and their trainers were involved in the filming. Because different cats have different skills, some were able to appear to be asleep or motionless on cue, whereas others excelled as runners or specialized in water scenes.

Once the bids for production have been approved, the creative team and the producer, director, and other key players hold a **preproduction** meeting to outline every step of the production process and anticipate every problem that may arise. Then the work begins. The talent agency begins casting the roles, while the production team finds a location and arranges site use with owners, police, and other officials. If sets are needed, they have to be built. Finding the props is a test of ingenuity, and the prop person may wind up visiting hardware stores, secondhand stores, and maybe even local recycling centers. Costumes must be made, located, or bought.

The Shoot The director shoots the commercial scene by scene but not necessarily in the order set down in the script. Each scene is shot, called a **take**, and after all the scenes in the storyboard have been shot, they are assembled through editing. The director records the commercial, and it is usually played back immediately to determine what needs correcting. Film, however, has to be processed before the director can review it. These processed scenes are called **dailies**, although dailies can now be available instantaneously with digital filming. **Rushes** are rough versions of the commercial assembled from **cuts** of the raw film footage. The director and the agency creative team, as well as the client representative, view them immediately after the shoot to make sure everything's been filmed as planned.

The film crew includes a number of technicians, all of whom report to the director. For both film and video recording, the camera operators are the key technicians. Other technicians include—and you've probably seen these terms in movie credits—the **gaffer**, who is the chief electrician, and the **grip**, who moves props and sets and lays tracks for the dolly on which the camera is mounted. The script clerk checks the continuity of the dialogue and other script details and times the scenes. A set is a busy, crowded place that appears at times to be total confusion and chaos.

The audio director records the audio either at the time of the shoot or, in the case of more high-end productions, separately in a sound studio. If the sound is being recorded at the time of shooting, a **mixer**, who operates the recording equipment, and a *mic* or *boom* person, who sets up the microphones, handle the recording on the set. In the studio, audio is usually recorded after the film is shot, so the video is synchronized with audio. Directors often wait to see exactly how the action appears before they write and record the audio track. However, if the art director has decided to set the commercial to music, the music on the audio track may be recorded before the shoot and the filming done to the music.

In some rare cases, an entire commercial is shot as one continuous action rather than individual shots edited together in postproduction. Probably the most interesting use of this approach is "Cog," an award-winning commercial for the Honda Accord that shows the assembly of pieces of the car piece by piece. It begins with a rolling transmission bearing and moves through valves, brake pedals, tires, the hood, and so forth until the car drives away at the end of the commercial. It's tempting to think it was created through computer animation, but the Honda "Cog" commercial was filmed in real time without any special effects. It took 606 takes for the whole thing to work—that's 606 run-throughs of the sequence! One of the most talked-about spots ever made, the publicity given to the commercial was probably even more valuable than an advertising buy. The "Cog" commercial won a Grand Clio (a creative award) as well as a Gold Lion at the Cannes Advertising Festival. Altogether, it picked up no fewer than 20 awards from various British and international organizations. The spot can be seen at www.ebaumsworld.com/flash/play/734.[11]

Postproduction   For film and video, much of the work happens after the shoot in **postproduction**, when the commercial begins to emerge from the hands and mind of the editor. The objective of editing is to assemble the various pieces of film into a sequence that follows the storyboard. Editors manipulate the audio and video images, creating realistic 3-D images and combining real-life and computer-generated images. The postproduction process is hugely important in video because so many digital effects are being added to the raw film/video after the shoot. In the "Cat Herders" commercial, Fallon could not film the cats and horses at the same time because of National Humane Society regulations. The director had to film the horses, background, and kitties separately. An editor fused the scenes together during postproduction, editing seamlessly to create the illusion of the elaborate cat drive.

Another goal of **video editing** is to manipulate time, which is a common technique used in commercial storytelling. Condensing time might show a man leaving work, then a cut of the man showering, and then a cut of the man at a bar. The editor may extend time. Say a train is approaching a stalled car on the tracks. By cutting to various angles, it may seem that the train is taking forever to reach the car—a suspense tactic. To jumble time, an editor might cut from the present to a flashback of a remembered past event or flash-forward to an imagined scene in the future. All these effects are specified by the art director in the storyboard.

The result of the editor's initial work is a **rough cut**, a preliminary edited version of the story that is created when the editor chooses the best shots and assembles them to create a story. After the revision and re-editing have been completed, the final version is created with the sound and video mixed together. The final version is usually distributed over the internet for local or national playback.

Web Design Considerations

11.5 Describe basic web design considerations.

Visuals are just as important on websites and in internet ads as they are in print ads and on outdoor boards. Photos on company websites are particularly important in terms of what they say about the corporate or brand image. Because websites are often created on the cheap, viewers may find themselves looking at product images that are fuzzy or confusing.

An article in the *Wall Street Journal*, for example, showed a baking company's unappetizing photos with a brownie baking pan that could be used as a roasting pan showing hunks of meat, prompting a customer to write in asking what connected brownies and bloody meat. Such photo flubs can eat into sales as well as hurt the company's image. As the founder of ProPoint Graphics, a presentation design firm, explained, "The images you use should reinforce your brand and message because in the end it is the pictures that your clients will remember."[12]

Web design includes creating ads that run on the web as well as the website itself. Banner ads are designed more like outdoor boards than conventional print ads because their small space puts intense requirements on the designer to make the ad communicate quickly and succinctly and yet attract attention and curiosity to elicit a click-through response. You can check out banner ads online at http://thelongestlistofthelongeststuffatthelongestdomainnameatlonglast.com/banner.html.

Designers know that web pages, particularly the first screen, should follow the same layout rules as posters. The graphics should be eye catching without demanding too much downloading time, and type should be simple, using one or two typefaces and avoiding all caps and letter-spacing, which can distort words. Because there is often a lot to read, organizing the information is critical. In terms of legibility, black type on a high-contrast background usually is best; all the design elements—type and graphics—should be big enough to see on the smallest screen.

What makes web design different from print designs is the opportunity to use motion, animation, and interactive navigation. Although attention getting, these tactics can also be irritating. Even in the highly visual online world, it's still important for the art and copy to work together to attract attention and build interest.

Usually, the illustrations are created by artists, but sometimes for low-budget projects, the illustrations and photos are obtained from clip-art services or, rather, click art, such as that provided by www.dreamstime.com or www.1StopPictures.com. Actually, any image can be scanned and manipulated to create a web image, which is causing copyright problems for artists and others who originally created the images, as explained with the Obama "Hope" poster story earlier in the chapter. Because of the magic of digitizing, web pages can combine elements and design styles from many different media: print, still photography, film, animation, sound, and games.

The combination of interactive navigation, live streaming video, online radio, and 360-degree camera angles creates web pages that may be more complex than anything you see on television, which is why ease of use is a factor in website design.

Web designers use a completely different toolbox than other types of art directors. Animation effects, as well as sophisticated navigation paths, are designed using software programs such as Silverlight, Director, Blender, and Squeak and nonlinear editing tools like Premier, FinalCut, and Avid. It's such a rapidly changing design world that it's difficult to keep track of the most recent innovations in web design software. The use of animation effects and streaming video has made websites look more like television and film.

For more examples of excellence in website design and reviews of the top websites, check out the following websites:

> www.webaward.org
> www.worldbestwebsites.com
> www.100bestwebsites.org
> www.topsiteslinks.com
> www.webbyawards.com
> www.clioawards.com
> www.oneclub.com

Action and Interaction

Web advertisers are continuing to find ways to bring dramatic action to the small screen to make the imagery more engaging. For example, Ford used a banner on the Yahoo! home page with the familiar Ford oval and a bunch of little black birds on a wire. Then three of the birds flew down to the middle of the page and started pecking at what looked like birdseed, uncovering an image of the new Explorer. The link read, "Click to uncover the next territory." Those who did click probably expected a pop-up image; instead, the page shook, the birds scattered, and a big red Ford Explorer drove up to the front of the screen, replacing most of the content. It was a surprising, highly involving, and effective announcement of the vehicle.

Because users can create their own paths through the website, designers have to make sure that their sites have clear **navigation**. Users should be able to move through the site easily, find the information they want, and respond. Navigation problems can really turn off viewers. Eye-tracking research (studies that use a camera to follow eye movement when looking at a page or screen) has found that if the navigation is cluttered or unclear, viewers will give up and move on to some other site.[13] Ideally, users who visit a site regularly should be able to customize the site to fit their own interests and navigation patterns.

Online video has also expanded the avenues for action on the small screen on minicomputers, tablets, and cell phones. Web video is becoming a new business opportunity for businesses that want to use videos to display their products. The secret is to plan these videos specifically for a small screen and not just try to use regular television or film images; the screen is just a fraction of the size of a television, and a lot of the detail in an image can get lost.[14]

If a site is well designed, people may want to interact with the organization sponsoring the site. For example, Texture/Media, a Boulder, Colorado, web design firm, created a seven-episode series over five months that detailed the journey of two men attempting to climb the MeruSharksfin summit in India for client Marmot Mountain Works. Called ClimbMeru.com, it chronicled the team's training and trip and hosted contest giveaways that helped gather information about Marmot's customers. Texture/Media's objective with its award-winning websites is to make the consumer a participant in its brand stories.

Looking Ahead

This chapter has focused on the impact of visuals and how to use them effectively in brand communication. To summarize, in most marketing communication media, the power to get attention lies primarily with the visual. Ideally, the visuals work with the words to present the creative concept. The excitement and drama in a television commercial are created through moving images, but it is an intriguing idea that grabs attention and remains in memory, particularly for larger-impact formats such as posters and outdoor boards.

This is the last chapter in Part 3 of our discussion on the design of the message. We introduced creative thinking and the creation of creative briefs and then discussed copywriting. In this chapter, we have provided you with a brief introduction to art direction and design. Next we discuss how messages are delivered, both to and from the target audience and other key stakeholders.

IT'S A WRAP

"Fearless Girl" Is Bullish on Women's Equality

You may have expected that a chapter on visual communication would feature an opening case study about some show-stopping visual advertising campaign like those produced by Geico, Allstate, or Apple. Arresting images are tools not only used by advertisers. This public relations effort demonstrates that visual elements are critically important to many aspects of brand communication. Would it have been as effective had the "Fearless Girl" been depicted some other way? Did the investment pay off for the sponsor, State Street? Is a picture worth a thousand words, or is it worth much more?

The answer to that last question is yes. According to Bloomberg.com, the investment produced marketing exposure equal to 28 percent of the firm's 2016 ad spending in the first 51 days following the statue's defiant appearance on March 7, 2017, on Wall Street. McCann reported in March that "Fearless Girl" generated lots of free media: nearly a million (958,923) tweets, 4,122 TV segments, 2,400 news articles, and 15,163 Instagram posts. That translates into traditional and social-media exposure generated by the brand valued between $27 million and $38 million. The publicity has raised awareness of the State Street brand and SHE fund. The firm saw the SHE fund average daily trading volume increase 385 percent following the installation of "Fearless Girl," and the fund assets rose 8 percent between March 6 and May 22. That's not bad for an investment of roughly $250,000, and that's not bad for a girl who's just over 4 feet tall.

Photo: Mark Lennihan/AP Images

11.1. Define the role of visual communication. Visual communication is important in brand communication because it creates impact: it grabs attention, maintains interest, creates believability, and sticks in memory. It also tells stories, delivers emotion, and creates brand images.

11.2. Explain the basics of design. The art director brings the visual side of an idea to life by creating visual impact as well as the visual brand identification in print, on video, and on the web. The designer's tool kit includes images, colors, and typography. The arrangement of all a print piece's elements in a layout gives the reader a visual order to the information being presented; at the same time, it is aesthetically pleasing and makes a visual statement for the brand. Principles that designers use in layout include direction, dominance, unity, white space, contrast, balance, and proportion. Composition is the way the elements in a picture are arranged, either through placement or by manipulating the photographer's point of view.

11.3. Name the essentials of production for print media. Art directors make different design choices depending on where the print brand communication happens: in a magazine, in a newspaper, out of home, on the web, or in a corporate publication such as an annual report. Illustrations are treated as line art, and photographs are reproduced through the halftone process by using screens to break down the image into a dot pattern. Full-color photos are converted to four halftone images, each one printed with a different process color—magenta, cyan, yellow, and black—through the process of color separation.

11.4. Identify the essentials of video production. Videos are planned using scripts and storyboards. Television commercials are shot live, shot on film or videotape, or created digitally. Videos can also be created by hand or digitally using animation, claymation, or stop action. There are four stages to the production of videos: message design (scripts and storyboards), preproduction, the shoot, and postproduction.

11.5. Describe basic web design considerations. Online brand communication can include ads and banners, but the entire website can also be seen as a promotional message. Art on web pages can be illustrations, photographs, still images, or moving images and may involve unexpected effects such as 360-degree images. When designers plan a web page, they need to consider navigation, or how people will move through the site. They also need to consider how to incorporate elements that allow for interaction between the consumer and the company that operates the site.

claymation, p. 335
click art, p. 321
clip art, p. 321
color separation, p. 332
composition, p. 328
comprehensives, p. 328
continuous tone, p. 331
crawl, p. 334
cut, p. 336
dailies, p. 336
debossing, p. 333
die-cut, p. 333
digitization, p. 333
embossing, p. 333

foil stamping, p. 333
font, p. 325
four-color printing, p. 332
gaffer, p. 336
grip, p. 336
halftones, p. 331
layout, p. 326
legibility, p. 326
line art, p. 331
logo, p. 317
mechanicals, p. 328
mixer, p. 336
morphing, p. 334
navigation, p. 338

newsprint, p. 330
offset printing, p. 333
postproduction, p. 337
preproduction, p. 336
process colors, p. 332
production notes, p. 336
registration, p. 330
rough cut, p. 337
rough layouts, p. 328
rushes, p. 336
screen, p. 331
semicomps, p. 328
spot color, p. 323
stock footage, p. 333

stop motion, p. 335
storyboards, p. 328
take, p. 336
thumbnail sketches, p. 328
tint blocks, p. 331
tip-in, p. 333
typography, p. 325
video editing, p. 337
videographer, p. 328
visualization, p. 322
white space, p. 331

MyLab Marketing

Go to **www.pearson.com/mylab/marketing** for MyLab discussion questions (⭐) as well as the following assisted-graded writing questions.

11-1. Discuss the aesthetic role of typography. Find an ad that illustrates how type can add meaning to the message.

11-2. One approach to design says that a visual image in an ad should reflect the image of the brand. Find a print ad that you think speaks effectively for the personality of the brand. Now compare the print ad with the brand's website. Does the same design style continue on the site? Does the site present the brand personality in the same way as the print ad?

REVIEW QUESTIONS

11-3. Explain in what ways visuals add impact to brand communication.

11-4. What are the responsibilities of an art director?

11-5. Compare the use of black and white, spot color, and full color in terms of visual impact.

⭐ **11-6.** List the design principles and explain each one.

⭐ **11-7.** What's the difference between line art and halftones?

11-8. What does the phrase *four-color printing* mean? What are the four process colors? What does the phrase *color separation* mean, and how does that work?

11-9. Explain the following video terms:
- Stock footage
- Morphing
- Animation
- Stop motion
- Claymation

11-10. Explain the four steps in the video production process.

11-11. Create a list of guidelines to use in designing a website.

DISCUSSION QUESTIONS

⭐ **11-12.** One of the challenges for designers is to demonstrate a product whose main feature cannot be seen by the consumer. Suppose you are an art director on an account that sells shower and bath mats with a new patented system that ensures that the mat will not slide (the mat's underside is covered with tiny almost microscopic suction cups that gently grip the tub's surface). Brainstorm some ways to demonstrate this feature in a television commercial. Find a way that will satisfy the demands of originality, relevance, and impact.

⭐ **11-13.** Choose one of the following design critique problems:

a. *Print:* What principles are most important in the design of a magazine ad? Collect two sample ads: one you consider a good example of effective design and one that you think is not effective. Critique the two ads and explain your evaluation based on what you know about how design principles work in layouts. Make suggestions for how the less effective ad could be improved.

b. *Television:* Find a television commercial that you thought was creative and entertaining. Then find one that you think is much less creative and entertaining. Analyze how the two commercials work to catch and hold your attention. How do the visuals work? What might be done to make the second commercial more attention getting? Compare and contrast the messages in the two commercials. You can also use online sources to find commercials, such as www.adcritic.com.

11-14. You have been asked to design a web page for a local business or organization (choose one from your local

community). Go to www.flickr.com and choose a visual to illustrate the website by trying to match the personality of the organization to a visual image. Then identify the primary categories of information that need to be included on the page. Develop a flowchart or map that shows how a typical user would navigate through the site. What other image could you find that might be used on inside pages to provide some visual interest to this business's online image? Now consider interactivity. How could this site be used to increase interactivity between this company and its customers? Create a plan for this site that includes the visual elements and a navigation flowchart.

⭐ **11-15.** You have a new client who has a new hand lotion for men, one that is designed to help men whose hands take a beating in their jobs. One of your colleagues, a photographer, believes that the only way to visualize the product and its use in an ad is through photography. Another colleague, an artist, argues that there are times when art is a much better way to illustrate a product than photography and that this production is a good example. Analyze the differences between using an illustration and using a photograph. What are their roles, and how do they create different types of effects? Are there certain product categories where you would want to use an illustration instead of a photograph and vice versa? Which would work best for this new product? Develop a quick presentation for your class that explains which approach you would use for this assignment.

TAKE-HOME PROJECTS

11-16. *Portfolio Project:* Select a product that is advertised primarily through print. Examples of such products are business-to-business and industrial products, school supplies, many over-the-counter drugs, and

some food items. Your objective is to develop a 30-second television spot for this product. Develop a creative brief (see Chapter 9). Elements of the creative brief should include: Identification of the problem, target audience, key insights, brand position, communication objectives, proposition or selling idea, media considerations, and creative direction. Brainstorm about ways to develop a creative idea for the commercial. Then write a script and develop a storyboard to present your idea for this product. In the script, include all the key decisions a producer and director would make.

11-17. *Mini-Case Analysis:* Summarize the creative strategy behind State Street's "Fearless Girl." Explain the critical elements of this public relations effort. How would you build on the success of "Fearless Girl"? What would happen if the conversation became more political? Is that good or bad for the brand? What would you advise State Street to do? Explain your thinking.

TRACE North America Case

Designing Multicultural Visual Communication

Read the TRACE case in the Appendix before coming to class.

11-18. Write a design memo that describes the "look" of the "Hard to Explain, Easy to Experience" campaign. What

elements would you make mandatory (e.g., typeface, colors), and which would you allow individual campuses to personalize in their own colors?

HANDS-ON CASE

Creative Coffee Wars Brewing

How many ads do you think you see in a day? Estimates vary wildly, running from a few hundred to several thousand. Although there seems to be no authoritative answer, you can safely assume it's a lot. Advertising is ubiquitous. It's everywhere, from logos on golf balls to product placements on television and place-based advertising on your phones. You see it on T-shirts and in magazines and even on the sides of buildings and in video games. In this message-filled world, it's a challenge to stand out from the competition. But some manage to stand out with outstanding creative.

In Part 3, we said that coming up with radical brand ideas calls for strategic and creative thinking, and McDonald's campaign to promote its McCafé coffee proves that point. Starting with a great concept and using the advertising tools of words and pictures, McDonald's launched its premium coffee in Seattle, Starbucks's hometown. The strategy involved recognizing a core value of Washingtonians, their affinity for the unpretentious, to challenge the coffee elitism represented by its arch-competitor.

Expanding this simple idea, McDonald's agency, DDB West, labeled McCafé's coffee "unsnobby" and created a campaign that touched the hearts and minds of consumers. It created memorable traditional outdoor transit signs and billboards proclaiming, "Large is the new grande." Another example, an outdoor tease, featured coffee beans scattered across the board. The outdoor reveal later showed the iconic "M" formed from the coffee beans and simple copy: "now serving espresso." No more fancy names or knowledge of foreign languages required.

McDonald's web microsite also played a part in the campaign. It invited visitors to get involved with the unsnobby theme by sending a coffee intervention in the form of a personalized Mad-Lib type of message to a friend. People could also play a game of HotShot Pinball on its site. While there, why not peruse the coffee menu? The site is simply a couple of engaging activities and a list of drinks. Need it be any more elaborate if the message is about a simple drink?

One element of the campaign included a 12-foot-tall inflatable coffee confessional housing McDonald's version of Dr. Phil, the Unsnobby Advisor, who dispensed advice in the form of "unsnobby" personal interventions.

What was Starbucks lovers' reaction to the coffee clash? Some bloggers claim the website was a waste of time. Others complained the campaign was anti-intellectual. Can people who like jazz and speak a foreign language still like McCafé, or are they, as McDonald's suggests, all snobby Starbucksonians?

In all, the campaign succeeded in getting people in the heart of Starbucks country to try McDonald's McCafé, overdelivering the trial goal by 173 percent. The campaign has since been rolled out nationwide with promising results. MarketWatch described the McCafé line as a cash cow for McDonald's.

The coffee wars have heated up, with competitors such as Starbucks, Dunkin' Donuts, and other fast-food chains entering the fray.

Consider This

P3-1. It's easy to see how McDonald's used words and pictures in some of its traditional advertising, like billboards.

Create a billboard to illustrate how you would use words and pictures to extend the "unsnobby" campaign for McDonald's.

P3-2. How does the McDonald's campaign make a relevant connection with its audience and sell its coffee in an unexpected way?

P3-3. McDonald's USA and Kraft teamed up for the retail launch of McCafé. How might you advertise McCafé packaged coffee? Create a storyboard for a commercial.

P3-4. Compare and contrast this campaign with Starbucks's approach. What is the Big Idea of both campaigns? Why and how do they work?

P3-5. If you were in charge of advertising for Starbucks, how would you respond to McDonald's?

Sources: Angela Moore, "Battle of the Beverages," April 21, 2010, www.marketwatch.com; Kevin Helliker, "Starbucks' Traffic Grows, Fueling Increase in Sales," *Wall Street Journal*, April 22, 2010, B2; Effie Briefs, "Unsnobby Coffee," www.effie.org; Jessica Wohl, "McCafé Coffee Campaign Shows How 'World's Best Mom' Gets through Hectic Day," January 15, 2016, www.adage.com.

4

PRINCIPLE
Media in a World of Change

We talked about creating messages in Part 3. In Part 4, we turn to the delivery of messages. We'll explore the changing media landscape and how companies use media to accomplish their objectives, but we'll also look at how consumers use traditional and new media to serve their own needs.

Push, Touch, Click, and Turn the Media World Upside Down

People consume media, as well as products and services, when they watch television, read publications, search for something on the internet, and use their cell phones to check for a store's location or hours. They push buttons, touch screens, click on links, and turn pages—electronic pages as well as paper. They are consumers of media, and their fingers are increasingly in control of the media relationship.

The media world has been experiencing incredible changes: from the dominance of traditional mass media to new online hybrid forms, from marketers' control of media placement to sharing control with consumers, and from media targeting consumers with messages to media engaging with consumers. To explore this dynamic media environment, two of this book's Advisory Board members, Larry Kelley and David Rittenhouse, share their thoughts on how the media world is evolving.

Morphing Media

A major change is the evolution that media have gone through as traditional media forms morph into digital formats and new functions. These changes have spawned a new vocabulary, including "native advertising," "programmatic buying," and the "internet of things." Kelley describes

◄ LARRY KELLEY is executive vice president and chief planning officer at Fogarty Klein Monroe and professor of advertising in the Jack J. Valenti School of Communication at the University of Houston.

it this way: "Media convergence is more than just providing content in a variety of forms. It is about the convergence of content, branding, and consumer engagement." *Convergence* is the definitive word in 21st-century media. He explains:

> Brands are now media, and media are now brands. It used to be that brands did something and that media said something. Now media and brands do something, say something, and engage with consumers. For example, Red Bull provides an energy drink, but it also publishes a magazine and engages with consumers through a variety of events. *Better Homes and Gardens* started as a magazine. Now it provides a variety of content and is now a brand of real estate agents. And it engages consumers through a variety of digital and physical sponsorships and events.

From Message Conduits to Consumer Connections

In his book on media, Kelley says that media are the conduits through which brand information is presented to audiences. But, he says, his approach has been modified by the digital revolution and now includes dialogue. In this new world, media actually make two-way communication possible: people to companies, companies to people, and people to people.

As a result, we need ways to describe new patterns of media use. Rittenhouse refers to "established" channels, such as broadcast, out of home, print, and even online search and display, in contrast to "emergent" channels, such as social, mobile, and online video. In this complex multimedia environment, we can see traditional targeted media and messages alongside consumer-generated media and messages. "Content is the creative" in social media, and this requires companies to operate much more as a service to their customers than traditional campaign-driven approaches.

And it's even more complex and interesting when planning across platforms. Rittenhouse describes media as physical/digital; in other words, digital layers are being added to physical content. So planners spread media activities across media as well as dive into them. This approach is being fueled by the rapid proliferation of smartphones and tablets through which consumers can access supplemental digital content or tap straight into an e-commerce environment from just about any physical marketing communication—from a print ad in a magazine, to product packaging, to an in-store display.

Kelley also points out that consumer engagement may be just as important as the delivery of a message using traditional push media. Media are all about connections—hooking up brands with people and people with information about brands—and the connection, if it's successful, will have high levels of experiential or emotional engagement.

How, then, do these media users connect with a brand while using media they choose and use to connect with others, including brands? People come in contact with a brand message in many different ways.

Multimedia, Multiplatform, and Multiuse

Yes, media consumers have always chosen television programs to watch, radio stations to listen to, and magazines to read, but in this environment, they are likely to be doing those activities on a computer or on a smartphone, and sometimes they're doing all those activities at the same time while texting a friend or playing a video game! Rittenhouse describes it as coviewing, using multiple media channels simultaneously. The key to surviving and thriving in this environment, according to Nathan Coyle of Domino Publishing, is to apply the integrated marketing approach to brand-building; that is, make sure your brand works across platforms, has "omnichannel" appeal across various types of media, and uses diversified initiatives built around a single coherent image and a unique set of benefits for customers.[1]

Photo: Reproduced with kind permission of Unilever PLC and group companies

▶ DAVID RITTENHOUSE is managing director at Neo@Ogilvy, the media arm of Ogilvy, where he plays a leading role in the agency's digital and demand generation media practice.

12

Media Basics

KEY OBJECTIVES

12.1 Explain how various media work in marketing communication and how the industry is organized.

12.2 Describe the key strategic media concepts.

12.3 Discuss why and how the media landscape is changing.

The lesson that the Axe campaign teaches about media is that smart marketing requires creative thinking about how to connect with the audience in this complex media environment. It also requires truly understanding major cultural trends, the attitudes of the audience, and the media they use. This chapter and Chapters 13 through 15 explain the media side of marketing communication—the story you don't see, that is, the backstory about how various ways to deliver a message are selected.

MyLab Marketing

⭐ **Improve Your Grade!**

More than 10 million students improved their results using the Pearson MyLabs. Visit **www.pearson.com/mylab/marketing** for simulations, tutorials, and end-of-chapter problems.

IT'S A WINNER

Campaign	Company	Agencies	Awards
"Axe: Find Your Magic"	*Unilever*	*72andSunny Amsterdam*	*Clio Awards Bronze Winner, Silver Epica Award, D&AD Wood Pencil Award*

Axe's Manifesto on Modern Masculinity

Photo: Christopher Gardiner/Shutterstock

Axe is the brand that became famous trying to help guys get ahead in the mating game. But a new campaign changed the game, declaring to men: "The magic isn't in the can, it's in you." Axe chose this message because it reflects emerging cultural definitions of masculinity, dating, and what it means to be attractive.

The campaign was fully integrated across several media—television, cinema, out of home, print, and display advertisements—and included a new Instagroom series, "designed to help inspire guys and give them the tools to achieve their own unique magic." These 15-second videos were designed to answer style and grooming questions that men search for most online, from how to style a mohawk to getting your tie just right.

"Masculinity today is going through seismic changes. More than ever, guys are rejecting rigid male stereotypes," said Matthew McCarthy, senior director of Axe & Men's Grooming for Unilever. "We've been part of guys' lives for decades, and Axe champions real guys and the unique traits that make them attractive to the world around them."

On the inspiration behind the "Find Your Magic" campaign, 72andSunny Amsterdam executive creative director Carlo Cavallone said: "Axe has always been at the forefront of culture. With Find Your Magic we're out to liberate guys . . . and empower them to be the most attractive men they can be—themselves." The message is that we all have our own "thing"—something special that makes us attractive to the world, whether it's your walk, your talk, your smile, or your style. It's your magic. 72andSunny also produced a short film that is a manifesto on modern masculinity. It, too, aligns the brand message with Unilever's Dove brand, which has been defying stereotypes and reinforcing the message of individual beauty in women for a number of years.

As a fully integrated campaign, Axe and John Legend are continuing the Axe Collective to elevate musicians and filmmakers and help them showcase their magic. Aspiring creators can visit Axe.com to learn more about a chance to be mentored by John Legend and to be featured at an event during SXSW or the Toronto International Film Festival.

The campaign was designed to play better with millennials and stand apart from prior Axe ads. But did it work? You will find more about the marketing effects of Axe's campaign at the end of the chapter in the It's a Wrap section.

Sources: www.forbes.com/sites/brandindex/2016/03/27/men-are-finding-the-magic-in-axes-new-campaign/#7b053a4f11b7; www.adweek.com/news/advertising-branding/ad-day-axe-gets-inclusive-remarkable-ad-thats-really-pretty-magical-168996; http://clios.com/awards/winner/13202; http://winners.epica-awards.com/2016/winners?medal=Silver; www.dandad.org/awards/professional/2016/film-advertising/.../axe-find-your-magic/; www.72andsunny.com/work/axe/find-your-magic; www.unileverusa.com/news/press-releases/2016/AXE-find-your-magic.html; Nat Ives, "Super Bowl Ad Review: Super Bowl Commercials Are Fun Again," February 7, 2016, http://adage.com/article/special-report-super-bowl/super-bowl-ad-review-super-bowl-commercials-fun/302579/.

12.1 Explain how various media work in marketing communication and how the industry is organized.

● **Principle**
All marketing communication messages, other than personal conversations, are carried by some form of media.

What Do We Mean by Media?

All marketing communication messages—other than face-to-face conversations—are carried by some form of media. When we talk about **media**, we are referring to *the way messages are delivered* to target audiences and, increasingly, back to companies as well as among audience members themselves. Media make up the *channel* step in the communication model (Chapter 5), conveying the message from the company or brand to its customers.

It's helpful to remember that the purpose for most media historically was to present news to the public, and advertising made presenting the news possible because it supported the costs of producing and distributing print or broadcast media. Of course, some revenue is derived from subscriptions, but in the United States, the bulk of the media revenue comes from advertising. As a result, over the years the word *media* has been associated with advertising, leading many to think that media are used only or primarily for advertising. Nothing could be further from the truth!

We know from the communication model presented in Chapter 5 that messages move through *channels of communication*. So, in this sense, media *deliver* messages. In traditional mass media, it is a one-way process from the source (the advertiser) to the receiver (consumers). In another sense, media are *interactive* because they offer opportunities for dialogue and two-way conversation. The media of marketing communication deliver messages to and from customers and move messages back and forth through channels. This two-way process expands the concept of delivery to include receiving and listening. Interactive communication is a hallmark of interactive marketing communication (IMC) programs that aim to build brand relationships, which is why this expanded view of media is so important to IMC planners.

For example, you may remember that in Chapter 6 we introduced the Icelandic lamb case study. In it, Ingvi Logason and his Reykjavík agency redefined the meaning of "advertising media." He said: "We created 'advertising' in the form of a series of traditional cooking shows designed to teach new and traditional recipes, but the shows would be only 40 to 90 seconds long. The execution of the campaign was ten cooking-show 'ads' that we strategically ran on various stations followed by viral distribution of the same micro-cooking shows through Facebook." He explained: "Sometimes the new way to present a message demonstrates creativity in the use of media as much as it does in the design of the message. The nature of creative ideas has changed with the development of new, more engaging media."

Media also offer opportunities for *engagement*, a media buzzword that refers to the captivating quality of media that the audience finds engrossing. Certainly, engagement can apply to television commercials and cinema advertising, but it can also be applied to print and internet ads—anything on which readers concentrate for some length of time. Media experts describe engagement as the closeness of fit between the interests of viewers and the relevance of the media content.[1] That is how media open the door of the critical "perception" step in the Facets Model of Effects that we introduced in Chapter 5. The principle of engagement is illustrated in sports marketing, such as ads and other events surrounding the Super Bowl, World Cup, and Olympic Games.

IMC and Media

In IMC programs, media are also *contact points* in that they *connect* a brand with the audience and ultimately *touch* their emotions as well as *engage* their minds. The difference between delivery and connection is significant. To deliver means "to take something to a person or place"; to connect means "to join together." Delivery is the first step in connecting: it opens the door to touching a customer in a meaningful way with a brand message. As a result of the digital revolution, the connection aspect has become even more important. This wording is not just semantics; the word *connection* changes the perspective of media planning. "Deliver" is a one-way concept; "connect" is a partnership. Laura Bright, a media professor at Texas Christian University, has explained that "brand messages are now brand conversations."[2]

All marketing communication areas, such as advertising, promotions, public relations, direct marketing, and events and sponsorships, use a variety of media to deliver messages to customers. IMC plans are *multiplatform* (use a variety of marcom areas), *multichannel* (use a variety of media), and *multitargeted* (engage a variety of stakeholders).

● **Principle**
IMC plans are multiplatform, multichannel, and multitargeted.

Effectiveness depends on coordinating all these efforts around some central concept, such as the brand position or, in the case of a campaign, the Big Idea. Larry Kelley and Donald Jugenheimer, who are authors of books on media and account planning, explain, "If all of these channels fail to deliver on the Big Idea you will have gaps in your communication plan, which will lead to a fragmented effort or a waste of money and resources."[3]

To get a picture of the scope of media, consider the following list:[4]

Internet Advertising	Billboards	Transit
Digital media	Newspapers	Direct mail
Television	Out-of-home	Radio online
Social networks	Branded entertainment	Cable online
Cable	Digital billboards	Digital transit
Alternative media	Mobile advertising	Digital in-store
Guerilla marketing	Television syndication	Movie theater advertising
Search engine advertising	Newspapers online	Satellite radio
Broadcast/cable product placement	Television online	Ambient media
Radio	In-store/point-of-purchase ads	Music product placement
	Native advertising	

Beyond conventional mass media like those listed here, IMC connection media also include direct personal experiences with events, salespeople, and customer service as well as word-of-mouth messages from people who influence us, all of which may become imbued with emotions leading to strong personal feelings about a brand.

Changes in the Media Industry

Media spending in 2015 finally passed its prerecession peak, with spending on mass media and integrated marketing tools surpassing $400 billion.[5] In addition, media spending has continued its move away from traditional outlets to vehicles that provide more feedback and accountability for the money spent, with internet advertising growing at 8 percent, the fastest growth rate of all media. TV advertising spending is projected to grow at about 3 percent through the early 2020s and will cede its status as the top media advertising vehicle. Together, television advertising and internet advertising are projected to account for close to 60 percent of total global advertising revenue. According to Deloitte's 2017 Media and Entertainment Industry Outlook, the rise of on-demand content (e.g., Netflix, Hulu) is challenging the traditional advertising model, pushing advertisers to explore other avenues for promoting their products.[6]

Consumer excitement surrounding the Internet of Things (IoT) and virtual reality (VR) devices has captured many advertisers' attention. In fact, the most searched marketing terms on Bing in 2016 were related to personal assistants and intelligent agents. Virtual and augmented reality came in second, and the term *artificial intelligence* was fourth on the list.[7]

New products called "wearables"—which includes smartwatches, fitness trackers, and virtual reality headsets—are becoming increasingly important to consumers because they interact seamlessly with their other devices and screens, giving their users a more personalized experience. The market for wearables is expected to triple in size to 245 million units by 2019, reflecting a shift to the "experience of things."[8] According to Venture Beat, 234 companies working on VR have already raised a total of $3.8 billion in capital, with a combined market value of $13 billion.[9]

How might IoT and VR be used in marketing communication? Consider these early efforts to create immersive, emotional connections with consumers:

- Mountain Dew partnered with Google and Tilt Brush to create an experience featuring National Basketball Association stars and local Toronto artists painting in Virtual Reality. The experience had 150 million views, said Adam Harter, vice president of marketing and cultural connections at Pepsi.[10]
- Luxury services in the airline and real estate industries are experimenting too. VR can allow prospects to experience business class or live like a king in a luxury apartment before handing over the cash.
- Audi, Jaguar, and Volvo released VR ads that simulate the experience of driving their cars. Coca-Cola has allowed consumers to virtually ride on Santa's sleigh; Nike captured Brazilian soccer player Neymar scoring for his national team, and even a cheese brand, Boursin, has taken viewers on a journey through a packed refrigerator.[11]

Successful virtual reality projects from *The New York Times*, *Vice*, and *Fox Sports* have paved the way for sponsorship opportunities, product placement, and immersive ads. One of the strong growth areas for VR is live content, which has often focused on sports. Turner Sports partnered with Oculus VR to live-stream sporting events like NCAA basketball to Samsung Gear VR users. "What better way to give people access than to put them in the live game itself," said Mark Johnson of Turner Sports. Offerings like these—content that isn't truly advertising but is backed by a brand—could further blur the line between traditional ads and consumer media.[12] Finally, gains in the accuracy of voice-activated digital assistants (e.g., Amazon's Alexa) are causing voice to replace screens as one of consumers' primary interfaces with the internet. This change has led to a wave of mergers and acquisitions, which is how large firms can rapidly add AI expertise to their strategies and operations.[13]

According to David Rittenhouse, a member of this book's Advisory Board, a more advanced use of artificial intelligence in marcom is to achieve bid optimization for programmatic ad buying (using software to purchase digital advertising placements). He said:

> My team has been testing the use of IBM's Watson technology (a learning algorithm) to make smarter bidding decisions on how much to bid for impressions in an auction. As an end-user, I can tell you that it works significantly better than a people-only model. It doesn't replace people (good for me, because I like being employed) but it improves some aspects of what people can do. For example, a programmatic media expert in my team cannot look in real-time, 24-hours-per-day, at how post-click conversion rates are correlated with bid amounts and then adjust bid amounts up or down with high precision (like thousands of a cent). The AI that we are using called Watson Bid Optimizer can. On the other hand, Watson Bid Optimizer can't run a campaign on its own. People are needed for nearly everything else, which is quite a lot.[14]

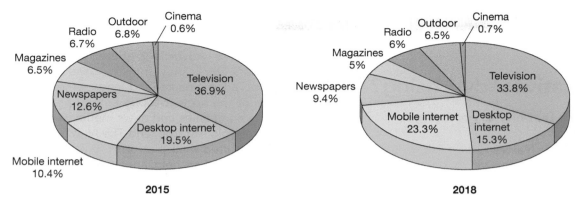

FIGURE 12.1

The Changing Media Landscape

Source: Based on Publicis ZenithOptimedia, *Advertising Expenditure Forecasts September 2016*, http://www.performics.com/executive-summary-advertising-expenditure-forecasts-september-2016/.

Figure 12.1 compares the size of the "ad spend" in the major media categories over time. What areas are growing or shrinking? Television continues to play a major role in media budgets simply because television reaches a huge audience. Nevertheless, spending on internet advertising surpassed TV in 2017. New forms of unmeasured media (digital media channels, such as search, mobile, display, and online video) are an exciting growth area but are difficult to track and represent in charts like this.

Media Types and Terms

The plural noun *media* is an umbrella term for all types of print, broadcast, out-of-home, and internet communication. The singular noun *medium* refers to each specific type (e.g., television is a medium). A **media vehicle** is a specific television program (*60 Minutes, The Simpsons*), newspaper (*The Washington Post, Chicago Tribune, El Nuevo Herald*), magazine (*Woman's Day, GQ*), or radio station or program (NPR's *All Things Considered*, Rush Limbaugh's talk show).

When a company "buys media," it is really buying access to the audiences of media vehicles. The form that those "buys" take is "space" (print, outdoor boards, internet) and "time" (radio and television). In addition to this basic media language, there are other ways to sort out the media landscape.

Size and Profile of Audience   Media, particularly those used in advertising, are referred to as **mass media**, the communication channels through which messages are sent to large, diverse audiences. A mass medium reaches many people simultaneously, and it uses some technological system or device to reach them (as opposed to personal communication). In contrast, the new computer-based media of the digital revolution are essentially personal, and messages are individually delivered.

The size of the audience is the reason we refer to radio and television as **broadcast media**: they cast their audio and visual signals broadly to reach mass audiences. In contrast, **niche media** are communication channels through which messages are sent to niche segments—identifiable groups of people with a distinct common interest, such as the Hispanic market. *Advertising Age* and *Adweek*, for example, are in a subsegment of the more general business magazine category. They reach the professional advertising industry niche. The distinction between mass and niche is not based necessarily on size. The *AARP Magazine*, for example, which targets those age 50 and over, is a niche publication, yet it is one of the world's largest-circulation magazines, with more than 38 million readers.[15]

Another term you'll see in media plans is **measured media**, which refers to the ability of media planners to analyze the cost of a media buy relative to the size of the medium's audience. Kantar/TNS is a media reporting service that tracks media consumption, performance, and value. The following categories identify the primary types of measured media:

- *Television* Network, cable, syndication, spot (local), Spanish language
- *Magazines* Consumer, business-to-business, Sunday, local, Spanish language

What Is Native Advertising?

Jooyoung Kim, Ph.D., *University of Georgia*

Native advertising is an interactive advertising placement strategy adopted by many marketers and publishers. Its main purpose is to cut through a highly cluttered online media environment and direct natural attention to the advertising that is relevant to the consumer interest at the moment of media use. By inserting native advertisements, broadly defined as "paid ads that are so cohesive with the page content, assimilated into the design, and consistent with the platform behavior that the viewer simply feels that they belong" (Interactive Advertising Bureau 2013, p. 3), advertisers think they may increase the opportunity for ad exposure and engagement. Becoming one of the hottest topics among practitioners, online companies and news media, such as Google, Facebook, Amazon, and *The New York Times*, have structured their platforms (both supply and demand side) to help advertisers effectively place native advertisements. This increasing interest in native advertising has also heightened critical concerns due to its potential to misguide and even deceive consumers by placing ads that are often indistinguishable from editorial content. However, with proper disclosure (i.e., ensuring that the media users can identify and know it is an advertisement) and placement that is consistent with the interest of consumers, a native advertisement can be viewed as relevant information that can actually be "welcomed" by media users who do not usually like the interfering experience from advertisements.

- *Radio* Network, national spot, local
- *Newspapers* National, local, Spanish language
- *Outdoor* Billboards
- *Freestanding inserts* Distributed primarily in newspapers

Metrics are available for traditional media either from the medium itself or from external auditing agencies, but these figures are much harder to find for new and nontraditional media because the auditing procedures for these new media have yet to be developed.

Notice that this traditional way of looking at consumers is based on seeing them as media audiences. Chapter 7 described consumers in other ways based on their personal characteristics and behaviors. Media planners also move away from the target audience mind-set and describe the audience as people. For example, Laura Bright has described targets in terms of their relationship to the brand: Strangers, Prospects, Customers, and Fans.[16]

Targeted and Interactive Conduits Another category of media refers to the way they transmit messages. Most mass media are defined by their audiences, and when they are used in brand communication, it is because they allow messages to be conveyed to people who fit certain demographic or psychographic categories. If you want to reach young men who like sports, for example, you might advertise in *Sports Illustrated* or on ESPN because their audiences match the profile of your target. In the Part 4 opening essay, Larry Kelley described these media as *conduits* because they deliver messages aimed at specific targets.

The placement of the message is an important factor in targeted media plans. For example, an example of tight targeting through specialized local media comes from the University of Florida, where the university's student advertising agency, Adwerks, developed a campaign for the university's student travel program based on posters and flyers that were designed to reach the student audience. The Adwerks team's objective was to increase sign-ups so as to meet the required number of participants. If trips that were close to full didn't reach a certain level of sign-ups, there was the potential for unhappy participants, creating a negative image for the program.

The internet, mail, and telephone are called **addressable media** because they are used to send brand messages to specific addresses, both geographic and electronic. They are particularly helpful in keeping in touch with current customers or with brand communities.

Online social media and mobile media are examples of **interactive media**, which allow conversations between companies and customers as well as between and among consumers. These messages are two-way in that they are carried to and from companies and consumer, and they require that both sides in the dialogue listen as well as speak.

Corporate versus Consumer Use of Media So far, we have been discussing media primarily from the viewpoint of companies and their brands. In the Part 4 opening essay, we mentioned that consumers as well as companies *use* media, and they use media for specific purposes. For example, companies want to reach certain targets so as to accomplish such objectives as building brand awareness, presenting brand information, and persuading people in the target market to change their attitudes. But just as important is that consumers use media for their own purposes. You may remember that we ended our discussion of the consumer in Chapter 7 by describing Seekers, who look for information, entertainment, and interaction. That's how they use media, and it affects how companies use media to communicate with them.

In other words, mass media may be good for delivering brand messages, but interactive media may be more useful for engaging consumers in a brand-related conversation, assuming that the conversation is relevant to their interests.

Paid, Owned, and Earned Media Recently, the media industry has begun separating media into three types of channels: **paid media, owned media,** and **earned media.** We'll use those categories to do a brief review of the variety of types of media available to brand communication planners. All of these will be discussed in more detail in this chapter and in Chapters 13 and 14, but here is an outline of these categories and the media included in them.

Paid, Owned, and Earned Media Categories

- **PAID MEDIA** are the traditional measured media, such as print and broadcast, where ad placements—both time and space—are bought by the company or organization. These "established" or "legacy" media channels are distinctive in that the advertising spending on them, as well as the size of their audiences, is tracked by media research services:
  - *Print* Newspapers, magazines, inserts, directories
  - *Broadcast* Radio, television, movie trailers
  - *Place based* Billboards, transit, kiosks, painted buildings and cars, movie trailers, event and sponsorship ads, stadium and aerial ads
  - *Online* Banner and display ads, search advertising
- **OWNED MEDIA** are channels that are controlled by the organization and that carry branded content, such as websites, direct-mail and email address lists, Facebook sites, blogs, public relations publications, company signage, and catalogs. In addition, we also include communication platforms that rely on one-on-one communication, such as personal sales or customer service:
  - *Corporate media* Stationery, signage, environmental design, delivery trucks, staff appearance, bags

Photo: Brooke Johnson, Writer; Travis Damon, Artwork.

SHOWCASE

TRIP, the Travel and Recreation Program at the University of Florida, is a student-run organization that plans and leads adventure and leisure trips for students and members of the Gainesville community. Our student Adwerks agency created the "Could Have Been" campaign with beautiful images from past trips. Playful headlines provided a sarcastic, but humorous, tone that spoke to our primary target of college students.

Adwerks director and account supervisor Lisa Yansura contributed this campaign on behalf of her University of Florida team: Kaely Coon, Jody Revels, Wendy Casorr, Becky Lazarus, Travis Damon, and Alli Schnur.

- *Branded media* Films (video or online) and webisodes, video games, books, events, apps, licensing and naming rights
- *Retail* Packaging, merchandising materials
- *Promotions and public relations* Literature and publications, annual reports, premiums and gifts, sales kits, training materials:
  Video Corporate and promotional videos—DVDs and streaming
  Publications Magazines, newsletters, annual reports, brochures
  Publicity Print, video, and online news releases; fact kits, photos and other graphics
  Events Displays and exhibits, speakers, information kits
  Brand reminders Premiums, gifts
  Out of home (OOH) Sign spinners, flash mobs
      Some owned media also open up the opportunity for interactivity:
- *Corporate interactive media* Kiosks, digital installations
- *Direct response* Mail, phone, online, catalogs
- *Personal contact* Personal sales, customer service—customer comment cards and surveys
- *Interactive public relations and promotions* Sampling, events, informational and media tours, news conferences, speeches, trade shows, guerilla marketing
- *Digital marketing* Email, websites and e-commerce, online catalogs, blogs, paid posts, social media accounts
- *Mobile marketing* Promotional messages sent to mobile phones and devices
- **EARNED MEDIA** are channels where brand communication is spread by outsiders, such as social media users or news media that carry publicity stories where the brand may be mentioned.
  - *Publicity* Hits and mentions in news media
  - *Word of mouth* Email, texting, buzz and viral communication, business-to-consumer-to-consumer influence
  - *Social media* Facebook, Twitter, LinkedIn
  - *Interest sharing* YouTube, Pinterest, Tumblr, Instagram, Snapchat, social games

We'll use this three-part classification system here but also use it to organize the media discussions in Chapters 13 and 14. The chart below summarizes these three media categories and how media professionals use them to make sense of the changing media landscape where media forms are converging, blurring, and changing their shapes. Instead of looking at media forms, paid, owned, and earned media are based on media functions.

Evaluating Paid, Owned, and Earned Media Use

Channel	Examples	Objective	Advantages	Limitations
Paid media: Brand pays to buy space or time	• Display and classified ads • Ads in out-of-home media • Ads on search sites	• Reach prospects	• Message control • Scale; can generate broad reach • Good brand reminder • Measurable	• Clutter • Lack of credibility • Low response rates • Indirect action
Owned media: A channel created and controlled by the brand	• Website • Blogs, Facebook page, Twitter account • Sponsored programs and events • Brand publications; literature	• Reach customers • Reach niche • Build brand relationships	• Message control • Cost efficiency	• Credibility • Difficult to scale up • Hard to measure
Earned media: Consumers and mass media control the mentions and comments about the brand	• Word of mouth • Viral communication • Social media • Publicity hits and mentions • Customer service	• Lets customers initiate contact • Engage in dialogue • Brand listens and responds	• Credible • Most engaging • Most persuasive	• Little brand control • Sometimes negative • Hard to measure

The Evolution of Media Forms and Functions

People in our contemporary society live in a world of media-delivered news, information, and entertainment that traditionally has been supported by advertising. Over several hundred years, media have evolved from print, to radio, then to television, and now to the internet. Newspapers, magazines, and posters provided the visual dimension of communication; radio added an audio dimension. Television enabled messages to be heard and seen with moving images.

Today, we have the internet, which has basically combined television and the personal computer, thus providing the added dimension of interactivity. But more than that, the internet has opened up unimagined new forms of social communication, and these new social media have also created new outlets for brand communication. We can summarize these changes in technology as eras:

- *The print era* Ink and print images reproduced as newspapers, magazines, and posters.
- *The broadcast era* Visual and audio information in the form of radio and television programs originally transmitted through airwaves but now also distributed by cable and satellite.
- *The digital era* Electronic information transmitted through the internet but, like broadcasting, now also distributed through cable and satellite. Saw the birth of corporate websites and e-commerce.
- *The social media era* Social networks connecting friends and contacts. Also where users can become publishers and generate their own content, some of which may be brand related.

Former advertising executive and now publisher Bruce Bendinger observed, "The printing press turned us into readers; the Xerox turned us into publishers; television turned us into viewers; the internet is turning us into broadcasters." The "Gangnam Style" phenomenon in 2012 was one of the first examples of how a YouTube video could become one of the most-watched videos of all time. The quirky song and dance (by South Korean performer Park Jae-sang, or Psy) was not only shared by South Koreans but also became a massive global hit, with some 7 million to 10 million viewers every day.[17]

It's useful to remember that this digital era is quite recent and its growth has been spectacular. The first website went online in 1991; the social networking sites of MySpace and Facebook went online in 2003 and 2004, respectively; and Twitter arrived in 2006. Photo and video-sharing applications such as Snapchat and Instagram exist almost entirely on mobile, and Instagram has already garnered 20 billion images since its launch in October 2010.[18] In contrast, the first newspaper ad appeared in the early 1700s, the first radio station went on the air in 1897, and television became popular in the United States in the 1940s and 1950s.

The point is that media have been and continue to be changing in form and function. This change is occurring rapidly, so it's difficult to keep up, let alone predict where we will be in five years or even one year. The media scene will probably never be settled, and it's certainly very dynamic.

Adaptation Every technological advance has threatened the older media whose managers feared their medium was on the edge of extinction. In fact, media have adjusted to their new circumstances by emphasizing what they do best: newspapers and magazines deliver information in depth, radio delivers music and other programs tailored to listeners' tastes, and television brings entertainment to the living room. The new media take on some of the characteristics and roles of the old at the same time that they add to the richness of the communication experience. Television, for example, has news shows and advertising that sound a lot like radio news programs, and both radio and television use news formats—and advertising—that they adopted from print.

A more dramatic shift, however, is occurring in the 21st century as computers and the internet personalize media and bring changes unlike any ever encountered in the history of media. Internet-based communication can do everything that the traditional media identified as their distinctive features and offers most of the communication dimensions of its media ancestors, but it also adds an interactive dimension.

The only "medium" that is even more multidimensional and interactive than the internet is personal selling, which also is a lot more expensive for commercial communication. A salesperson can not only show, tell, and interact but, most important, can also instantly create customized content.

● **Principle**
Every technological advance has threatened older media, and every new medium is launched in the footprints of its predecessor media.

How Consumers Mentally Engage with TV Ads

Jooyoung Kim, *University of Georgia*

The transformation of media into a digital platform means that the consumers can now "click" or "touch" the part of media interface easily whenever they want. This "touchability" of media interfaces means the brand touch points that were available only through traditional mass media can now be accessed anywhere the consumers are. This ubiquitous brand touchability has brought the consumers and brands nearly infinite ways to communicate among and between themselves. For advertisers, therefore, creating an advertisement which is more likely to be touched by consumers is becoming one of the key aspects that defines what an effective ad is. Here, "touch" can mean several things. It is generally an interaction or engagement a consumer makes with the advertisement. From the surface side, it can mean actual touching by a fingertip that can result in playing, liking, sharing, or calling. Considering these as behavioral engagement, what can be the mental side of engagement that might result in such engaging behaviors?

To identify the engagement dimensions of TV ads, my research team asked participants to rate a set of thirteen 2013 Super Bowl advertisements (e.g., Tide's "Miracle Stain," Audi's "Prom," M&M's "Love Ballad," and Budweiser's "Horse and Trainer Reunited"; you can watch the 2013 ads at http://superbowlcommercials .tv/2011-2020/2013) on variables potentially related to engagement used in earlier research such as involvement, presence, absorption, and attention. The results suggested that there are three distinct dimensions that initiate and maintain engagement when viewers are exposed to advertisements: Affective Captivation, Cognizance, and Resonance. The Affective Captivation dimension (e.g., "paid attention to the ad" and "was captivating") captures the emotional affective responses that viewers may harbor when exposed to advertisements. It is not just the affective state, but also the ability for the advertisement to captivate and grab the viewers' attentions that is critical in eliciting advertising engagement. The dimension of Cognizance (e.g., "noticed the message" and "understood the reasons") evaluates not just the cognitive processing of data, but the extent to which the advertisement was able to instigate active understanding of the narrative and the characters presented, through which the audiences can engage in mental simulation that puts themselves in the shoes of the characters presented in the ad. Following the narrative of the advertisement and mentally simulating one's self into the position of a character in the advertisement can lead to so-called transportation or the perception of actually being present in the advertisement. This perception is captured by the items of the Resonance dimension, which asks whether the individual felt as if he or she was "right there in the ad" or whether he or she "experienced the ad as if it were real."

Do you wonder who won the engagement war? It was Audi's "Prom" ad, whose composite engagement score was 5.42 (from the scale range of 1–7), closely followed by Budweiser's "Horse and Trainer Reunited" (5.30) and Tide's "Miracle Stain" (5.07). It's no wonder these ads were among the top 10 most popular ads during 2013 Super Bowl measured by USA Today's Ad Meter.

Photo: Kraay Family Farm, Home of the Lacombe Corn Maze Inc.

A Canadian family claimed a Guinness World Record for the largest quick-response code, which it created as a corn maze. The 15-acre corn maze includes this 7-acre QR-coded design.

Internet sites can quasi-create content by compiling customer online behavioral data from which information can be computed and patterns recognized. Then, the site can offer a selection of customer preferences (Amazon's suggested books) or provide predetermined answers to frequently asked questions.

In an interesting turnaround, print stories and ads can now carry **quick-response (QR) codes** and Snapcodes that let readers scan them to access additional information and websites via their smartphones. The media are learning from one another. A QR code is represented by a complex pattern that represents a unique location based on geographic coordinates and other data. Like bar codes, QR codes can be electronically scanned. However, you don't need a special reader to scan them; they can be scanned by smartphones. Is it worth it for companies to adapt to these rapid changes? Consider that 60 percent of US smartphone users between ages 13 and 34 now use Snapchat![19]

Convergence   Although new media tend to launch themselves by improving upon the forms of the media that preceded them, the older media also adapt by adopting some of the advances of new media. Nearly every media vehicle, for example, now has one or more (most have more) websites, which creates the **convergence** that Kelley described in the Part 4 opening essay.

Convergence makes it very difficult to categorize media. Is *The New York Times*' website a newspaper? Both *The New York Times* and *The Wall Street Journal* appear as online newspapers and also as online videos. They are not "print," but these new forms do carry news. So what do you call them? Media scholar Jugenheimer noted that "newspapers have websites, advertisements can be transmitted by e-mail, and television programs can be downloaded into iPods."[20] Furthermore, catalogs and radio are online, video is on computers, and cell phones and books are electronic.

Figure 12.2 diagrams this overlap of functions as print and broadcast media evolve into new digital forms. The point is that the old traditional form continues: there are still newspapers, magazines, and television programs that their audiences enjoy, and they continue to receive a large share of ad spending. At the same time, there are new digital forms that may do some of what a traditional medium does but also may open the door to new and expanded uses. For example, you can click on a link in an online news story and find additional background or related stories.

FIGURE 12.2
The Digital Overlap
With traditional media, such as print and broadcasting, adding online forms, the distinction between traditional and digital is less important than it used to be. The same promotional story can run in print, on television, and in online newspapers and streaming video.

Although we discuss convergence primarily as shape-shifting where traditional media take on characteristics of new electronic media, there's actually more to it than that. Kelley observes that promotional areas such as advertising and public relations are morphing together in integrated brand planning. Brand stewards and planners on both the corporate and the agency sides are working together to broaden the communication dimensions of brand relationships; and brand stewards may choose to bring conversations inside the company through corporate Facebook and Twitter accounts. At the same time, agency planners create the communication efforts that drive the dialogue to those sites. Finally, Kelley said that "media convergence is more than just providing content in a variety of forms; it is about the convergence of content, branding, and consumer engagement."[21] The brand, the message, and the media are all interwoven in contemporary media strategies.

The Contemporary Media Landscape   There have always been evolution and changes in the shape and forms of media; however, the speed of change has increased, as has the number of media available for use in brand communication, and that has created pressure for more coordination and integration. As Kelley said, "Everything is multiplatform." There's also been change in delivery systems from hardware—computers, hard drives, and dedicated machines, like game consoles—to "cloud marketing," where all the marketing efforts, programs, and even products live on the internet and can be downloaded to personal devices such as smartphones and tablets. Video games are moving in that direction and will leave game consoles behind.

The modern media landscape includes up to 200 television channels in some markets, a huge number of special-interest publications, millions of websites, and new and novel media forms that weren't even imagined just a few years ago, such as ads on conveyer belts at airports or brands stamped into the sand at the beach. The total number of commercial television stations in the United States grew steadily until 2005 and has plateaued at about 1,750 stations since then.[22] Despite the wide array of options, Nielsen reports that consumers consistently tune in to an average of just 17 channels.[23]

Media experts Kelley, Jugenheimer, and Kim Sheehan describe what has happened: "We have certainly seen the rise of new kinds of media. . . . The internet has led the way with a wide variety of media such as search-engine marketing, rich media, and streaming audio and video. Other media channels have come into play, including the iPod, cell phones, video games, and satellite radio."[24]

Kelley and colleagues also looked at existing media and how they have extended and adapted themselves to the lives of new media consumers. Point-of-sale media, for example, have been transformed "with opportunities appearing in seemingly every venue. Malls now have

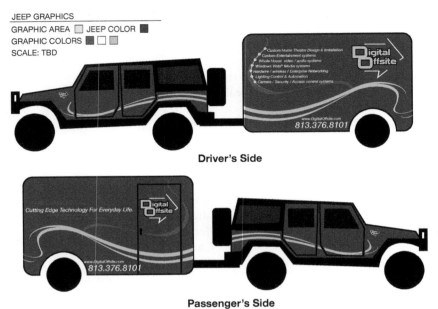

Driver's Side

Passenger's Side

Photo: Courtesy Michael Dattolico. Used with permission.

SHOWCASE

The Jeep graphics designed by Michael Dattolico for a technology client turned a vehicle into a moving billboard.

Michael Dattolico graduated from the advertising program at the University of Florida and was nominated to be featured here by Professor Elaine Wagner.

digital signs that show television commercials. In some major markets, buses contain television sets that are programmed to show a retail ad within a block or two of the retail establishment." And it's not just these new forms that add complexity to the media landscape. They added, "Ads are popping up in elevators, inside fortune cookies, and even on celebrity and wannabe-celebrity body parts."[25] As an example of the creative use of novel media, consider the Jeep trailer that Michael Dattolico designed as a painted brand image for one of his clients.

Key Media Players

In terms of jobs and career opportunities in media, there are professionals who both sell and buy media. It is important that you understand the difference. First let's look at the professionals who sell space or time in media.

- **Media salespeople**, also known as **media reps** (short for media representatives), work for a specific vehicle, such as a magazine or local television station, with the objective of building the best possible argument to convince media planners to use the medium they represent. Currently, media conglomerates dominate media sales. CBS, for example, created a coordinated ad-selling division, called CBS RIOT, which stands for "radio, internet, outdoor, and television." The new division was designed to serve primarily local markets and offers **cross-media** (also called **multichannel**) integrated deals. Disney reorganized its ad sales to deliver a similar cross-media ad sales program for its kids' media properties.
- Media **brokers** are people (or companies) who sell space (in print or online) and time (in broadcast) for a variety of media. If an agency wants to buy space in all the major newspapers in the West, for example, the agency's buyer could contract with a media rep firm whose sales reps and brokers handle national sales for all those newspapers. Working with a broker allows a media buyer to place a complex buy with one order.

On the buying side, media planners, buyers, and researchers work primarily for agencies, although they can also be found working for marketers who handle their own media work in-house. Their challenge is to determine the best way to deliver a message, which is called **media planning**. The job functions are as follows:

- **Media researchers** compile audience measurement data, media costs, and availability data for the various media options being considered by the planners.
- **Media planners** develop the strategic decisions outlined in the media plan, such as where to advertise geographically, when to advertise, and which type of media to use to reach specific types of audiences.
- **Media buyers** implement the media plan by contracting for specific amounts of time or space. They spend the media budget according to the plan developed by the media planner. Because media buyers are expected to maintain good media supplier relations to facilitate a flow of information within the fast-changing media marketplace, there should be close working relationships between planners and buyers as well as media reps so that media planners can tap this source of media information to better forecast media changes, including price and patterns of coverage.
- **Media-buying companies**, mentioned briefly in Chapter 2, are independent companies that specialize in doing media research, planning, and buying. They may be a spin-off from the media department in an advertising agency, but because they are independent companies, they work for a variety of clients. They consolidate media buying to get maximum discounts from the media for the volume of their buys. They then pass on some of this savings to their clients.

What Are the Fundamentals of Media Strategy?

12.2 Describe the key strategic media concepts.

Media often make up the largest single cost item in a marketing communication budget, especially for consumer goods and services. Procter & Gamble, for example, spent $10.1 billion on advertising worldwide in 2014, although its total promotional spending approached $18 billion.[26] (This later figure includes such marketing communication activities as sampling, direct mail, events, sales aids, and displays, among other programs.)

The Media Plan

The challenge that marketing communicators face is how to manage all the media opportunities and yet maximize the efficiency of budgets that are inevitably too small to do everything the firm would like to do to reach every current and potential customer. All this decision making comes together in a **media plan**, which identifies the optimal blend of media to use to deliver brand communication messages efficiently to a targeted audience. It is sometimes referred to as **connection planning** in that brand stewards working with media planners are trying to find ways to connect their brands to consumers' interests and lives, particularly to their customers, who, if they are happy with the brand experience, may become loyal to and advocate for the brand. The goal is to balance message impact and cost—maximizing impact while minimizing cost—while at the same time building an enduring brand relationship.

> **Principle**
> The goal of media planning is to maximize impact while minimizing cost.

The media plan is a subsection within a marcom plan and has its own objectives, strategies, and tactics. It is also developed in tandem with message planning, the topic of Chapter 9. Figure 12.3 shows these relationships but this time with an emphasis on media planning. We'll introduce some of the basic media planning concepts here but will explain these activities in much more detail in Chapter 15.

Key Strategic Media Concepts

This section is about the language of media. You will need to be familiar with these basic components in media strategy and planning to understand the review of media forms discussed in this chapter and in Chapters 13–15.

Media Mix   In most cases, a media plan will include more than one medium and therefore is called a *media mix*. This **media mix** is the way various types of media are strategically combined to create a certain kind of impact. For example, most consumers recognize the "Shot on iPhone" campaign, having seen one of Apple's 10,000-plus billboards across 25 countries showcasing

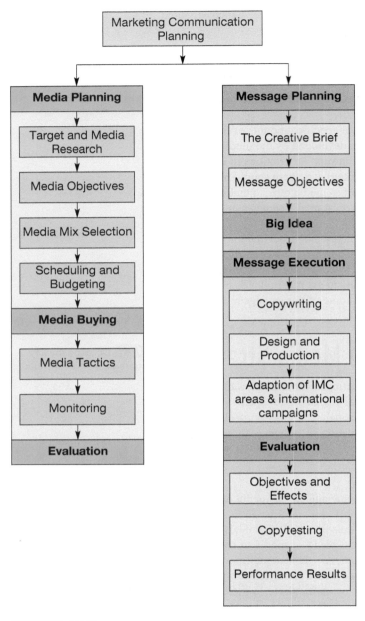

FIGURE 12.3

Brand Communication Planning

Media and message planning activities are interrelated and work in parallel.

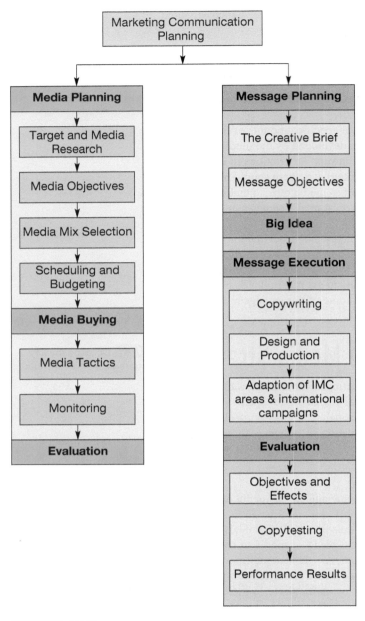 **Principle**

Media planners match the target audience with the audience of a particular medium.

the amazing photographs real people managed to shoot on their iPhones. The photos also appeared across newspapers, magazines, online, and in a set of 15-second TV commercials.[27]

Because of the breadth of IMC plans, the term **multiplatform** has become popular to describe multi-channel and multimarketing communication areas. In other words, in IMC plans, you will find, in addition to traditional measured media advertising, a variety of other tools being used, such as events and sponsorships, social media (such as Facebook and Twitter), branded entertainment (such as films or video games in which the brand is the hero), product placement, and guerilla marketing in addition to sales staff and channel promotions, training programs, publicity, and customer service.

Targets and Audiences One of the biggest challenges in developing a media plan is matching the advertiser's target audience with the audience of a particular medium. The same terms that we used to describe target audiences in Chapter 7 can be used to describe media audiences.

A major study by the Newspaper Association of America, for example, grouped media audiences into four useful categories by generation: traditionalists (born before 1946), baby boomers (born 1946–1964), Gen X (born 1965–1976), and Gen Y (born 1977–1994).[28] Since this study, millennials (born in the late 1990s into the first decade of the 21st century) have been commonly added to the list of media audiences categorized by generation. Dramatic differences are seen in the media experiences of these audience groups:

- Traditionalists grew up with newspapers, magazines, and radio (little or no television, no cell phone, no computers, no internet).
- Boomers, who are in their '50s, 60s, and 70s, always had those three types of media but also grew up with television (but still no cell phones, computers, or internet).
- Gen Xers, who are now in their 40s and 50s, grew up not only with the media of the preceding generations but also with tape recorders, Walkman portable radios, video games, VCRs, and cable television (still no cell phones, computers, or internet).
- Gen Yers, who are thirty-somethings, had all the above media, but also grew up with the computer, as well as satellite television, the internet, CDs, and cell phones (finally, we have a generation that grew up with computers and cell phones).
- Millennials have grown up with DVDs, TiVo, satellite radio, iPods, and smartphones and, more recently, have witnessed the introduction of iPads, Facebook, and Twitter. The marketing and ad industries are still learning about the next category of consumers: Generation Z.

The media planners' challenge is to know which media best reach which audiences, whatever their ages. In a classic example of targeting, the market for the launch of the iPod, for example, was a technologically sophisticated young adult. The target market also needed to have enough discretionary income to buy the product. That audience profile led initially to a target of innovators, people who are into cool gadgets and who love music. Where do you find those people? One place to start was with posters in subways and other urban sites. The campaign also used outdoor boards, print media, and television commercials in ways that would generate buzz. A key strategy was to get people talking about this new gadget. Eventually, the price dropped, and the market widened to include both college and high school students after the initial launch.

The Basis for the Buy

Decisions about which media to use are based on the profile of the audience that reads, views, listens, or visits a medium. Media sales reps provide their own data, but research by account planners and media researchers also uncovers media use patterns that help make these decisions.

Media planners use a variety of terms to identify and measure audiences. The terms are easy to confuse, so let's explain some here before we begin talking about specific characteristics of traditional media forms in Chapters 13–14.

- *Exposure* Media impact begins with **exposure**. We know from the discussion in Chapter 5 that the first step in making an impression is perception: you have to be exposed to a message before any other effect is possible. Exposure is similar to circulation for television in that it's a rough estimate of the number of households watching a program. However, just because a television is on doesn't mean anyone is paying any attention to the program, let alone the advertising that surrounds it.

    Media exposure is related to the idea of corporate and consumer *control* of media. In other words, companies may control the media buy, but they don't control what their target sees. In this cluttered media environment, consumers control what they read and watch, and media analysts recognize that with hundreds, maybe thousands, of media choices, control of media exposure now lies with the consumer. Exposure, in other words, doesn't equate to readership or viewership. At the most basic level of media planning, however, media planners still must estimate the number of exposures delivered by a media mix in putting together alternative versions of a media plan.

    > ● **Principle**
    > Exposure doesn't equate to readership or viewership; just because a television is on doesn't mean anyone is paying attention to it.

- *Impressions* An **impression** is one person's opportunity to be exposed one time to an ad in a specific vehicle. Impressions can be added up as a measure of the size of the audience either for one medium or for a combination of vehicles in a media mix.
- *Circulation* Impressions are different from **circulation** because impressions (at least in print) estimate the readership or the opportunity to be exposed rather than just the circulation, which refers to copies sold.
- *Gross Impressions* Circulation doesn't tell you much about the actual exposure of a print ad. A magazine may have a circulation of 1 million, and it might be read on average by 2.5 people per issue, so impressions for that issue would be 2.5 million. If the ad ran in three consecutive issues, the estimate of total impressions, called **gross impressions**, would be 7.5 million. Similarly, the number of viewers watching a program might be greater than the number of households reached because there may be more than one viewer watching and the commercial may be repeated several times in a program. Media planners add up all those watching and reading and multiply that number by the number of placements to estimate gross impressions for a media plan.
- *Ratings* Gross impression figures become very large and difficult to work with, which is why the broadcasting industry uses **ratings** (percentage of exposure), which is an easier measurement to work with because it converts the raw figure to a percentage of households. A television show having a rating of 20 means that 20 percent, or one-fifth, of all the households with televisions were tuned in to that program. Note that in the U.S., 1 rating point equals 1 percent of the nation's estimated 120 million television homes; that's why planners describe this program as having 20 **rating points**, or percentage points. A 20 rating is actually a huge figure because the fragmentation of cable has diversified television watching and made it very difficult to get 20 percent of the households tuned to any one program.
- *Share* A better estimate of impressions might also be found in a program's **share of audience**, which refers to the percent of viewers based on the number of sets turned on. The share figure is always larger than the rating because the base is smaller. For example, the 2015 Super Bowl, which at the time was declared the "most-watched television program ever," got a rating of 47 (47 percent of all households with television), but its share was 71, which means that 71 percent of all U.S. televisions turned on were tuned to the Super Bowl. The peak total audience was 120.7 million viewers.[29]

● **Principle**
The goal of most media plans is to reach as many people in the target audience as often as the budget allows.

Reach and Frequency   The goal of most media plans is to reach as many people in the target audience as often as the budget allows. **Reach** is the percentage of the media audience exposed at least once to the advertiser's message during a specific time frame. When we say that a particular media vehicle, such as the Super Bowl, has a wide reach, we mean that a lot of people are watching the program. When we say that it has a narrow reach, such as the *El Nuevo Herald*, we mean that a small percentage of the newspaper audience is reading that publication. The idea for the iPod launch was to initially target technologically sophisticated people who are also opinion leaders (whose thoughts on innovations like the iPod would influence many others).

Equally as important as reach is **frequency**, which refers to the number of times a person is exposed to an advertisement. There's a rule of thumb that you have to hear or see something three times before it makes an impact. That's the reason frequency of repetition is so important in many advertising campaigns. Different media have different patterns of frequency. Radio commercials, for example, typically achieve high levels of frequency because they can be repeated over and over to achieve impact. Frequency is more difficult to accomplish with a monthly magazine because its publication—and an ad's appearance in it—is much more infrequent than a radio broadcast.

Most media plans state both reach and frequency objectives, and the media mix is designed to accomplish both of those goals. You may remember the discussion in Chapter 6 of the lamb market in Iceland. The objective was to reposition lamb to meet the budget concerns of recession-stressed consumers. The campaign's media plan demonstrates how different media are chosen based on consumer use and the ability of the various media to deliver either reach or frequency.

Focus groups were used by the H:N Marketing Communication agency in Reykjavík to uncover key consumer insights about lamb, principally that consumers were not buying pricey prime lamb cuts and didn't know how to cook the more budget-priced cuts. In addition, Ingvi Logason's research found the following:

* The target group members are the largest consumers of television in the country.
* Close to 100 percent of the target group has high-speed internet access and are frequent users of the internet at work and at home.
* Iceland most likely has one of the highest penetrations of Facebook users in the world: 94 percent of the population in the age group of 25- to 40-year-olds (the lamb industry's target group) have Facebook accounts.

Logason explained that his agency created "an interactive media plan that would connect with our target group in settings where they could be engaged in the ads. We would connect with them on their leisure time where they worked, at home, and in social settings." Therefore, the plan used both television and Facebook. He explained: "The strength of self-dissemination and friend referrals on Facebook made sure the ad recipes traveled far and wide with the recommendation that the person posting the recipe liked it. A strong connection was created between viral ads, the lamb industry's website, and a Facebook group interested in lamb."

Traditional media, such as television, were also used, but the interactive media "allowed us to focus on reach in the television media buy while we were able to obtain high frequency through viral media." Additional activities included sponsoring television cooking shows, placing the product in television shows (cooking and other), and gathering various lamb recipes already online and linking them to the Facebook site. Logason reported that media measurements showed that the unorthodox media mix reached its target for both reach (mostly through television) and frequency (mostly through viral activities).

Intrusiveness   Because of the high level of commercial message clutter, companies in the past have valued creative ways of attracting attention to their messages. **Intrusiveness**—the ability of a medium to grab attention by being disruptive or unexpected—is the primary strategy for countering clutter. Kelley, in the Part 4 opener, pointed out that in the new media world, engagement will replace interruption. Still, most media use intrusiveness to some degree as a way to grab the attention of inattentive media consumers.

Media as well as messages vary in their degree of intrusiveness. The most intrusive medium is personal selling because the sales representative's presence demands attention. Likewise, a phone call is also demanding, and a loud voice or sound on television can be irritating.

The least intrusive media are print media because users choose when and to what extent to use these media and attend to them. Generally, the more intrusive a medium, the more it can be personalized but the more costly it is to use, which is why personal selling is so much more costly than mass media. Admittedly, the word *intrusive* has negative connotations. If a message is too disruptive or irritating, it may not help build a positive brand relationship.

There are ways to minimize the irritation level of intrusiveness. One is to choose media whose target audience is intrinsically interested in the product category. Research has shown that one of the benefits of specialized magazines is that readers enjoy learning about new products from the advertising. To have visibility without being intrusive is one of the reasons why product placements and events are popular. Giving customers opt-in or opt-out options for receiving brand information digitally means that when messages are sent, they are not unexpected and therefore are less likely to be seen as intrusive.

> ● **Principle**
> The more intrusive a medium, the more it can be personalized but the more costly it is to use.

Changing Patterns of Media Use

> **12.3** Discuss why and how the media landscape is changing.

Marketing communication media are in an incredible state of flux, partially because of the introduction of the computer and the internet, but also because of the way people choose to spend their time. Laura Bright identifies three factors driving these changes: (1) demassification and the trend to narrowcasting; (2) changes in media consumption, particularly multitasking, and (3) media models becoming consumer-centric.[30]

Consumer Use of Media

Consumers' use of media is changing as fast as the technology. It used to be that most American audiences were involved with three television networks, a newspaper, and one or two magazines. The modern media landscape includes hundreds of television channels, a huge number of special-interest publications, millions of websites, and new electronic media with content on-demand through the internet that enables dialogue, conversation, connection, and community. There are other trends as well:

- *Consumer Control* Rather than controlling media choices, consumers are much more in control of their own media and designing their own media landscapes, from video games to Twitter. The people formerly known as "audiences" are creating their own content, a practice we have referred to as *consumer-generated content*, such as the homemade videos and commercials seen on YouTube and personalized audio listening courtesy of the iPod and other MP3 players. Entertainment has become as much of a driving force for modern digital media as news was for traditional media.
- *Media-Driven Lives* A major change in consumer media use is the increase in media-driven lives. In their youthful days, the traditionalists' and baby boomers' lives were dominated by work and family activities. In contrast, more recent generations spend more time with media of all kinds, and those channels are more intertwined with their family, work, and leisure time.
- *Media Multitasking* People not only spend more time with media but also use more than one medium at a time. According to Nielsen, a whopping 86 percent of US smartphone owners say they use their devices as second screens while watching TV, and nearly half do it every single day.[31] Media users may sit at a computer searching for information, or they may be playing a video game at the same they are listening to an iPod and texting on their cell phones.
- *Social Media* Traditionally, most media involved a solitary experience, such as reading a paper or listening to radio, but another transformation is the creation of truly social media. First there were blogs, then MySpace and Facebook, and then Twitter, Instagram, and Snapchat, all of which made personal space public. The immediacy and intimacy of a phone conversation has exploded into millions of interactions via Twitter and other social media. (Think about it: If you tweet to your 1 million followers, are you broadcasting? You probably don't know the 1 million recipients, so has Twitter become a form of mass media?)

> ● **Principle**
> Entertainment is as much of a driving force for modern digital media as daily news was for traditional media.

Probably the biggest change is found in the increase in *interactive media*. We've always had interactivity in personal selling and direct marketing by telephone, but technological changes have forced traditional media to change their forms. Video game consoles continue to give new purpose to television screens, video game characters are appearing in a variety of advertising, and a TV's ability to display video game action is now a key factor in television purchasing. New technology has brought methods and devices for readers and viewers to participate in the creation of the message and initiate brand contact and to respond to advertisers. New mainly interactive media forms, such as social media (Facebook and Twitter), have opened up entirely new dimensions of interactivity that challenge brand stewards to keep up with their possibilities. We'll discuss this exciting new interactive world in Chapter 14.

Alternative Media Forms

If you want a fun and exciting career area, consider any of the myriad types of alternative or nontraditional media. We use the term *nontraditional media* to refer to media platforms and forms of contact other than traditional advertising media. For example, Olympian Nick Symmonds auctioned the right on eBay to tattoo a Twitter address tag on his shoulder. The winner was Milwaukee, Wisconsin–based advertising agency Hanson Dodge Creative. A new form of transit advertising in New York City is the face of MetroCards, the cards that regular riders of subways and buses use to pay their fare, which have been redesigned to allow space for small reminder brand ads.[32] And then there's the corn maze QR code shown earlier.

The point is that there are also other ways to present promotional messages besides traditional marketing communication. We'll briefly introduce a few of these media platforms, such as product placement, branded entertainment, word-of-mouth marketing, and guerilla marketing. Melissa Lerner, a specialist in new-media planning with Posterscope, a pioneering out-of-home media company, describes nontraditional media in the Matter of Principle feature as a creative opportunity for innovative thinkers.

Because teens are often the first to experiment with new media forms, the search for nontraditional media—that is, new innovative ways to reach target audiences—is particularly important for advertisers trying to reach the elusive youth market. In some ways, this search for innovative ways to deliver messages is just as creative as the message concepts developed on the creative side of advertising. That's why one of the principles of this book is that the media side can be just as creative as the creative side of advertising.

Product Placement   Technological trends as well as the changing patterns of consumer media use also affect media planning. For example, because of the difficulty of reaching targeted audiences with traditional media such as television, brands are increasingly showing up in movies, video games, and television programs. This practice is known as *product placement.*

For years, we have been exposed to **product placement**, in which a brand appears in an unskippable moment where viewers see brand information in a noncommercial, highly engaging way. With product placement, a company pays to have verbal or visual brand exposure in some other entertainment form. For example, in 2015, Mercedes-Benz paid movie producers to have their cars appear in 9 of the year's 31 top films, ranging from short cameos to scene-stealers. In the *Fast and Furious* series, two of the most important rituals involve Dodge muscle cars and Corona beer.[33] In the film *Martian*, a Vivo smartphone gets a cameo in the hands of NASA's public relations director Annie Montrose, an unlikely pairing considering Vivo is a Chinese brand. The phrase "Baskin-Robbins always finds out" was one of the funniest scenes in the *Ant Man* film. In *Skyfall*, Heineken paid a reported $45 million to replace the seemingly irreplaceable—as 007 skips his usual vodka martini for the Dutch beer.[34]

Product placement has become important because it isn't as intrusive as conventional advertising and audiences can't skip the ads as they can for television advertising using the remote control or a DVR. At the same time, it may make the product a star—or at least be associated with a star. Sometimes the product placement is subtle, as when a particular brand of aspirin is shown in a medicine chest or a character drinks a particular brand of beverage. In other cases, the brand is front and center. That happened with the prominent role of a BMW Z28, which became a star in the James Bond movie *The World Is Not Enough*. The movie placement, in fact, was the car's launch vehicle.

Television programs have also gotten into the product placement game. Both the Coca-Cola brand and the Ford Motor brand have been embedded into the successful talent show *American Idol*, and the Target bull's-eye has been seen as part of the action sets and props on *Survivor*.

Creative Use of Out-of-Home and Nontraditional Media

Melissa Lerner, *Vice President, Director, Client Delivery and Data, Posterscope*

As our society becomes increasingly mobile, out-of-home (OOH) nontraditional media helps advertisers make an impact on audiences at different times and locations throughout the day. Innovative media not only reach people while they are on the go, but also allow advertisers to intercept particular consumers via highly targeted messaging.

Nontraditional media include innovative emerging media and digital enhancements; place-based, branded environments; and guerilla executions. These new formats are often used in conjunction with traditional outdoor media. New technologies allow for consumer interaction in the outdoor environment.

Advertisers have recognized that successful OOH advertising is no longer passive. The shift from advertising "at" consumers to engaging "with" consumers is affording OOH platforms with unprecedented growth opportunities. See the figure for more details.

There is nothing better than working on a nontraditional media concept that comes to fruition and

Place/Affinity Based
Place-Based Broadcast:
Airport TV
In-Store TV/Radio
Mall TV
Physician/Pharmacy TV
Theater Radio

Affinity-Based:
Bar/Restaurant Media
Cinema
C-Store Media
College Media
Day Care Center Media
Gas/Service Station Media
Golf Media
Health Club Media
In-Flight Media
In-Office Building Media
In-School Media
In-Stadium Media
In-Store Media
Leisure Media
Physician Media
Ski Media
VIP Airline Lounge Media
Wild Posters

Alternative/Guerilla
Alternative:
Aerial Media
Custom Media
Event Sponsorships
Experiential Media
Interactive Kiosks
Naming Rights
Projection Media
Sampling
Specialty Media
Sports Sponsorship
Travel Affinity Sponsorships
New Technology

Guerilla Media:
Coffee Cups/Sleeves
Graffiti Murals
Mobile Media (e.g., AdVans)
Pizza Boxes
Street Teams
Umbrellas
Deli Bags

FIGURE 12.4

Nontraditional Media

New media specialist Melissa Lerner said that "clients are demanding more unique plans and ideas than ever before because impact and engagement help to become trendsetters in their respective industries." She described these projects as exciting, "never-done-before" campaigns.

generates exciting public relations and buzz within a marketplace.

Melissa Lerner graduated from Lehigh University with a degree in business and economics.

The greatest advantage of product placement is that it demonstrates product use in a natural setting ("natural" depending on the movie or program) by people who are celebrities. It's unexpected and, if it's an obvious use, may catch the audience when their resistance to advertising messages may be dialed down. It's also good for engaging the affections of other stakeholders, such as employees and dealers, particularly if the placement is supported with its own campaign.

The biggest problem is that the placement may not be noticed. There is so much going on in most movies that unless you can overtly call attention to the product, its appearance may not register.

A reverse product placement strategy was used by the watch brand Omega that appeared in the James Bond *Skyfall* movie starring Daniel Craig. To extend the association between the movie and the watch, which was a little hard to see despite Craig's glances at his timepiece, a frame from the movie showing Craig on top of a London building looking out over the city's rooftops was used in a two-page Omega magazine advertisement in upscale magazines.

A more serious problem occurs when there is not a match between the product and the movie or its audience. Another concern is that advertisers have no idea whether the movie will be a success or a failure as they negotiate a contract for the placement. What happens to the brand's image if the movie is a dud?

Another problem is an ethical one: when is a product placement inappropriate? For example, some pharmaceutical marketers have found that a product "plug" can be a way around the

Federal Drug Administration's requirements on the disclosure of side effects. Public policy critics warn that it's not just drugs; the problem exists for weapons, alcohol, tobacco, and gambling, among other product categories that raise social concerns. Product placement has been called "stealth advertising" by the Writers Guild of America, which argued that "millions of viewers are sometimes being sold products without their knowledge . . . and sold in violation of governmental regulations."[35] What do you think? Should there be more controls over product placement?

Branded Entertainment   Because media are being used more for entertainment, marketers are increasing their efforts to design **branded entertainment**. Similar to product placement, the use of the media of entertainment to engage consumers with brands is also referred to as **advertainment** or **branded media**, a topic we'll explore in more depth in Chapter 14.

An example of branded entertainment is Axe's production of an animated program, City Hunters. It took almost three years and more than 100 people on four different continents to produce the program. The creative team was composed of award-winning screenwriters, novelists, and creatives under the direction of the Catmandu Branded Entertainment company. The integrated launch campaign was a 360-degree promotional effort, and the show included the following:

- *Launch Parties* Celebrities and models depicted the show's characters.
- *Website* A dedicated website featured all of the show's information.
- *Text Messaging* Mating game tips were sent by the show's main character.
- *Interactive Billboards* Consumers could text a message that would change the image in the billboards.
- *In-Store Video Trailers* Special displays and flat screens were used to promote the show.
- *Sweepstakes* Prizes such as iPods were given away with a complete *City Hunters* season, merchandising, and so on.

Search and Mobile Marketing   In Chapter 5, we introduced the Seeker model, which recognizes that consumers are in control of not only their information search, but also how they want to be connected with an organization or brand. Because some 97 percent of consumers use computers to search for product and store information, marketing strategies are designed to assist in this process. Most (90 percent) of the search is done through search engines such as Google, Yahoo!, and Bing; however, consumers also use internet directory listings and do comparison shopping on review sites like Angie's List. Mobile search using cell phones is one of the fastest-growing media forms.[36] According to Google, more Google searches take place on mobile devices than on desktop computers in 10 countries, including the United States and Japan.[37]

For many companies, it means their communication programs have added *responding*, as well as *targeting*, to their brand communication strategies. Another new practice that responds to this increase in consumer control over the contact point is **search marketing**, which refers to the placement of online ads near topics of interest that people search for on their computers, tablets, or smartphones. These searches provide opportunities for highly targeted ads related specifically to the user's interests. *Search-engine advertising* is driven by these key words that consumers use in their search for information or entertainment.

In late 2016, mobile devices accounted for nearly half of all organic search engine visits in the United States, up from 33 percent in the last quarter of 2013. Mobile search is particularly relevant for local businesses because consumers use their mobile website for information, such as list of products and opening hours of the local business. A business's price list and phone number are also important features to include on its mobile website, according to consumers. In the United States, mobile search advertising expenditure passed desktop ad spend in 2015 and is expected to grow aggressively in the coming years. In 2016, about 62 percent of paid Google search clicks originated from mobile, with mobile phones accounting for nearly 40 percent of total clicks.[38]

There are also innovations in how cell phones are used by consumers as well as by marketers who want to send messages to them. The phone is the classic example of how media are shape-shifting as media functions converge. Telephones, of course, started as a hardwired home and office device connected by phone lines. With the development of satellite-based and broadband telecommunication, the cell phone has become the all-purpose personal communication tool. That means it has become an attractive medium for brand communication.

Mobile marketing is an exciting new platform for location-based messages that, among other uses, can reach consumers with a promotional message when they are in the neighborhood of a store. Both search and mobile marketing will be discussed in more detail in Chapter 14.

Word of Mouth   Because we recognize the power of personal communication in decision making, creative folks are challenged to come up with exciting new ways to generate buzz and convey brand messages through **word of mouth**. Buzz is important because it means that people are talking about a brand, and when it gets passed rapidly through a network of friends, we call it **viral communication**. This buzz may be the most important factor in consumer decision making because the recommendations of others are highly persuasive, more so than any advertisement.

Given the engaging work of its agency, Crispin Porter + Bogusky, Burger King is often lauded as the "king of buzz." Tia Lang, interactive director at Burger King, said, "Social media is very important in today's environment and we think generating buzz is a positive result in and of itself." She explained, "We have done some innovative campaigns that have helped lead to 20 consecutive quarters of positive sales."[39] Word of mouth and its importance to brand communication will also be discussed in Chapter 14.

Guerilla Marketing   Exciting and involving personal experiences are designed to reach people on the street and in public places through a practice known as **guerilla marketing**, which is a hot area of alternative marketing communication. At its most basic, people are employed in places with a lot of foot traffic—streets, malls, and plazas—to hand out sales materials, such as coupons, samples, or other leaflets. This place-based strategy can create unexpected personal encounters with a brand. Effective guerilla marketing uses surprise and curiosity to catch attention and create excitement as well as buzz about a brand.

The idea is to develop creative ways to reach people where they live, work, and walk to create a personal connection and a high level of impact. If it works, the encounter gets talked about, creating a buzz moment. Sears used computer-equipped Segways on Michigan Avenue in Chicago to launch its online layaway program. Microsoft used a team of "wire dancers" hung on a giant billboard on the side of a building for a Windows launch.

Photo: Directphoto Collection/Alamy Stock Photo

NBC's Bay Area station in San Francisco used this attention-getting guerilla marketing approach in local subway platforms.

Guerilla marketing is so much fun that it inspires creative people to come up with great ideas. More about matching wits than matching budgets, guerilla marketing has limited reach but high impact. Sometimes a guerilla marketing campaign will generate publicity that extends the impact.

Looking Ahead

We started and ended this chapter by noting that the media environment is going through a lot of shifts. This time is the most creative age in the history of commercial media. We talked about new, converging, and emerging media, with older media converging with new media and new forms being created faster than we can learn how to use them. This chapter also introduced the fundamentals and key concepts of media planning as well as the strategic decisions made by media planners. With this brief introduction to the basics of marketing communication media as well as the new, nontraditional, and changing forms of media, we turn to Chapter 13 for a review of traditional media—print, broadcast, and outdoor—and the characteristics that make them different from other media forms.

 Axe Cleans Up

Demonstrating another way to clean up, Axe has won many advertising awards over the years. The "Find Your Magic" campaign is no exception, winning a Clio Award, a Silver Epica Award, and a Wooden Pencil Award from D&AD. These sparkling efforts show the extent to which creative ideas can be applied to a variety of media and contexts, all to achieve the same effect—to sell the product.

Since the full campaign launched in January 2016, both Purchase Consideration and Ad Awareness showed a lift as measured by the YouGov BrandIndex. Among men, ad awareness peaked in the second half of February 2016 with a high of 25 percent, and purchase consideration increased to 20 percent. A shortened version of the ad appeared during that year's Super Bowl, further extending the message to more than 100 million people. Keith Weed, chief marketing and communications officer of Unilever, points to 76 million online views of Axe's "Find Your Magic" digital and Super Bowl ad as proof of the campaign's effectiveness. But what about sales? "It's still early days," he said, "but we see it as a success."

More broadly, ads that are progressive on gender issues just work better, Weed said, getting 12 percent better viewer involvement in tests on average than ads with stereotypical treatments. "I am encouraged by the overwhelmingly positive response the Axe message has received," said Matthew McCarthy, senior director of Axe and Men's Grooming at Unilever. "The Super Bowl is a great place to share this powerful stance on individuality and masculinity, and the scale allows us to bring more men and women into the conversation."[40]

Logo: 360b/Shutterstock

12.1. Explain how various media work in marketing communication and how the industry is organized. Media send and return messages to and from the company or brand and its customers; in other words, they make connections. Media deliver messages and offer opportunities for interaction; they also touch emotions, engage minds, and build brand relationships. Media have evolved technologically from print to broadcasting and now the internet. Marketing communication is evolving to include more internet-based media. Types of media include mass and niche media as well as addressable, interactive, and measured media. Key players both sell and buy media space and time; they include media salespeople and reps, media researchers, media planners, and media buyers.

12.2. Describe the key strategic media concepts. A media plan, which is prepared by a media planner, is a document that identifies the media to be used to deliver an advertising message to a targeted audience both locally and nationally. A media mix is the way various types of media are strategically combined in an advertising plan. Reach is the percentage of the media audience exposed at least once to the advertiser's message during a specific time frame, and frequency is the number of times a person is exposed to the advertisement.

12.3. Discuss why and how the media landscape is changing. Media use is changing, with consumers spending a lot more time with media and multitasking more as they are engaged with media. Media forms are also changing, with new ways to reach people being included in marketing communication plans, such as product placement, branded entertainment, search and mobile marketing, word-of-mouth marketing, and guerilla marketing.

KEY TERMS

addressable media, p. 352
advertisement, p. 366
branded entertainment, p. 366
branded media, p. 366
broadcast media, p. 351
brokers, p. 358
circulation, p. 361
connection planning, p. 359
convergence, p. 356
cross-media, p. 358
earned media, p. 353
exposure, p. 361

frequency, p. 362
gross impressions, p. 361
guerilla marketing, p. 367
impression, p. 361
interactive media, p. 353
intrusiveness, p. 362
mass media, p. 351
measured media, p. 351
media, p. 348
media buyers, p. 359
media-buying companies,
   p. 359

media mix, p. 359
media plan, p. 359
media planners, p. 359
media planning, p. 359
media reps, p. 358
media researchers, p. 359
media salespeople, p. 358
media vehicle, p. 351
mobile marketing, p. 367
multichannel, p. 358
multiplatform, p. 360
niche media, p. 351

owned media, p. 353
paid media, p. 353
product placement, p. 364
QR codes, p. 356
ratings, p. 361
rating points, p. 361
reach, p. 362
search marketing, p. 366
share of audience, p. 361
viral communication, p. 367
word of mouth, p. 367

MyLab Marketing

Go to **www.pearson.com/mylab/marketing** for MyLab discussion questions (⚫) as well as the following assisted-graded writing questions.

12-1. Discuss why product placement, branded entertainment, social and mobile marketing, and guerilla marketing became popular.

12-2. What qualities does an integrated campaign need to have in order to work well across multiple media platforms? How was the "Find Your Magic" campaign by Axe designed so it would be effective and self-reinforcing across a variety of media and contexts?

REVIEW QUESTIONS

12-3. Trace the evolution of media forms and explain how the new digital era is different from previous media environments.

12-4. Explain the roles of media salespeople, media planners, media buyers, and media researchers.

⚫ **12-5.** What is a media mix, and how does the mix differ for an IMC campaign?

12-6. What is the difference between reach and frequency?

12-7. Explain what is meant when we say IMC is multiplatform, multimedia, and multitargeted.

⚫ **12-8.** In what ways are consumer media patterns changing, and how does that affect marketing communication?

DISCUSSION QUESTIONS

⚫ **12-9.** What is the difference in perspective between how companies and consumers use media? Give an example from your own experience where these two perspectives either align or are at odds.

12-10. This chapter sets up a way to organize media in terms of paid, owned, and earned categories. Define each and explain how they are different. Give an example of each and explain why and when you would use that type of media.

12-11. You have been asked to help your family's restaurants rethink their media planning, which includes two upscale Italian restaurants and a small chain of five grilled panini sandwich shops. Is there any difference in how they might use traditional advertising versus the new online forms of brand communication? What media mix would you recommend for each type of restaurant? Explain the thinking behind your recommendations.

12-12. *Portfolio Project:* Collect three promotional messages from three different types of media. Analyze what you believe to be the target for each piece. Now analyze the medium in which each message appears. Research what you can about that media form to determine its audience. Compare your analysis of the targeting with the reach of the medium. Do you think they match? Explain why or why not.

12-13. *Mini-Case Analysis:* Reread the Axe story at the beginning of this chapter. What was the problem this brand faced, and how did that affect the media planning? What were the objectives of both the initial campaign and its follow-up? What was the Big Idea that drove the second campaign, and how did that affect the media mix? Do you think this effort was driven by reach or frequency? Considering all the new media reviewed in this chapter, what other media might Axe use in the next year of this campaign?

Multicultural Media

Read the TRACE case in the Appendix before coming to class.

12-14. Which medium do you believe would be most impactful in the "Hard to Explain, Easy to Experience" campaign? Why?

12-15. What target market insights led to the development of the "Hard to Explain, Easy to Experience" media plan?

13

Paid Media

KEY OBJECTIVES

13.1 Describe how marketers make effective decisions about advertising in published media, such as newspapers and magazines.

13.2 Explain the factors media planners consider when making place-based (out-of-home) media advertising decisions.

13.3 Explain how online advertising works.

The Aflac campaign has been successful because of its use of television to dramatize a funny situation where the Aflac duck tries to get the attention of people needing supplemental insurance. Television is a traditional medium for advertising messages; in fact, it's the dominant medium in terms of budget. However, the media world is huge and diverse. To organize this complex media environment, we are using the paid, owned, and earned categories that we mentioned in Chapter 12. This scheme moves the discussion from *channels*—many of which are changing their shapes and no longer true to their original forms—to *functions*.

Title
"The Search for the New Aflac Duck Voice"

Client
American Family Life Assurance Company (Aflac)

Agency
The Kaplan Thaler Group

Contributing Agencies
Digitas, MediaVest, Paine PR

Awards
Bronze Effie; Cannes Lion Winner

The Art of Laying an Egg and Making It Golden

Photo: American Family Life Assurance Company of Columbus (AFLAC)

What do an *Advertising* Age reporter, National Football League (NFL) player Dhani Jones, an Elvis impersonator, a civil engineer who wears duck costumes, a woman older than 90, actor Eddie Deezen, and three parrots have in common? Read on to find out.

In 1999, not many people knew about American Family Life Assurance Co. (Aflac), nor were they likely to be familiar with its primary service: supplemental workplace medical insurance, a type of insurance that is used by people to help cover the many loopholes and deductibles in their primary insurance coverage. In fact, the company had only a 10 percent brand awareness in a sea of competitors, including Geico, Allstate, Nationwide, and Met Life, to name a few.

Enter the duck in 2000, and things began to go swimmingly for Aflac. The long-running Aflac campaign featuring the quacking duck was the brainchild of New York's Kaplan Thaler Group. Almost all ads feature a white duck desperately screaming "Aflac!" at unsuspecting people who presumably need supplemental insurance. Alas, the duck's audience never quite seems to hear him. Ideal for television commercials, most of the ads contain a fair amount of slapstick, usually at the expense of the duck, whose memorable, exasperated-sounding voice originated with former *Saturday Night Live* cast member Gilbert Gottfried.

The campaign has been enormously successful, with brand awareness soaring to 94 percent in only three years. *Ad Age* named a commercial featuring the duck as one of the most recalled ads in the country, and online voters enshrined the icon on Madison Avenue's Advertising Walk of Fame.

The spokes-fowl is not without his problems, however. Actually, it was the voice behind the duck that laid an egg becoming a marketing disaster for Aflac, when Gottfried tweeted some insensitive comments following the earthquake and tsunami in Japan in 2011. Japan is home to 75 percent of Aflac's business. Aflac fired Gottfried immediately.

Not wanting to leave its icon speechless, Aflac moved to find a new voice for the duck. Within 24 hours of the Twitter incident, Aflac hatched a plan to invite the public to audition with its version of *American Idol*. Contestants flocked to the opportunity to compete for the unique job of being the duck's voice. More than 12,500 potential quackers tried out in six different cities across the United States and in online auditions, which brings us back to the question posed at the beginning of this case study: What do all those people have in common? They all auditioned to be *the voice*.

This campaign, which developed from an unplanned incident, offers an opportunity to examine how traditional and interactive media have become inexorably intertwined and critical to the success of brands. To be recognized and identified with Aflac, the duck must be seen and heard in some kind of video. Once the personality is established, the duck, because of "image transfer," can move to print, radio, and online, which, of course, he's done memorably. Furthermore, this campaign shows how quick and responsive brand managers must be to protect their brand reputation. Aflac has also spread its wings into social media with a Facebook 360 campaign that casts the brand's spokes-animal as a brave superhero in a comic-book-style video. This campaign reinforces the company's "One Day Pay" marketing message to consumers, which appears in a variety of other media in Aflac's $116 million annual budget.

Turn to the It's a Wrap section at the end of the chapter to learn more about how this effective campaign got consumers to know more about Aflac than its quack.

Sources: Rupal Parekh, "Hear the Voice of the New Aflac Spokesduck," April 26, 2011, www.adage.com; Maureen Morrison, "Aflac Goes on Duck Hunt to Find New SpokesQuacker," March 27, 2011, www.adage.com; Rupal Parekh, "Quacksmack: Ad Age's Rupal Parekh Tries Out to Be the Aflac Duck," April 10, 2011, www.adage.com; "The Search for the New Aflac Duck Voice," Effie Awards published case study (2012), www.effie.org; "Aflac Case Study," September 10, 2012, www.kaplanthaler.com; Adrianne Pasquarelli, "It's Aflac's Duck to the Rescue in New Facebook 360 Campaign: Animated Spot Will Be Supported by Instagram and Twitter Outreach," March 22, 2016, http://adage.com/article/digital/aflac-quacks-facebook-360-campaign/303223/.

This paid, owned, and earned approach also recognizes that media are interactive, not just targeted. Furthermore, it is inclusive and opens the door to discussions of media that are used in all the marketing communication areas, not just in advertising. To understand media planning in an integrated marketing communications (IMC) program, then, you need to have a broad understanding of all the various types of media used in brand communication.

This chapter will review the paid media category; in Chapter 14, we'll review owned and earned categories of media with a special focus on interactive media. Let's start with a review in this chapter of the traditional advertising media industries, sometimes called *legacy media*, which dominate the paid media category.

13.1 Describe how marketers make effective decisions about advertising in published media, such as newspapers and magazines.

Traditional Paid Media

What we are calling traditional advertising media include print, broadcast, out-of-home, and online media. Those are the major groups of the paid media category used in brand communication, and they usually demand a big share of the brand communication budget. They also play a huge role in creating brand visibility.

There are also specific media tools from the marketing communication areas of public relations, promotions, sales, and merchandising that are traditional in the sense that they've been around for a long time and are widely used. We'll introduce them in this chapter as well.

To review, paid media are used primarily in advertising. Advertisers pay a fee to media so as to present brand messages in their various vehicles—usually space and time in print, broadcast, out of home, or online. Paid media can provide wide reach, as in television audiences, or they can be tightly targeted, as in outdoor boards or magazines directed to small niche audiences.

Although the advertiser controls the size and timing of the message placement, it has no control over whether readers or viewers will notice the ad. All that's guaranteed is that the audience has the opportunity to be exposed in some way to the message. There also tends to be lots of *clutter*; think of all the ads in a magazine or in a television program. Clutter can lead to avoidance by the media user—turning the page, leaving the room when television ads come on, changing channels, or zipping through television ads.

Published Print Media

In Chapter 12, we looked at print media vehicles, including newspapers, magazines, brochures, and other printed surfaces such as posters and outdoor boards. Although magazines and newspapers especially have shifted some of their message delivery online, billions of dollars are still spent on traditional print media.

● **Principle**
Print media generally provide more information, rich imagery, and a longer message life than other media forms.

In terms of impact, print media generally provide more information, rich imagery, and a longer message life than broadcast media. Figure 13.1 details the pros and cons of each medium. It's an information-rich environment, so, in terms of our Facets of Effects Model, print media are often used to generate cognitive responses. If you want someone to read and understand something new, a magazine ad or brochure is useful because readers can take as much time as they need.

Consumers also find that reading a print publication is more flexible than watching or listening to broadcast because they can stop and reread, read sections out of order, or move

FIGURE 13.1
Pros and Cons of Each Form of Media

Medium	Pros	Cons
Newspapers	Short production time Local targeting Timely	Short-lived Limited readership (print) Low-resolution images
Magazines	High-resolution images Long lifespan Creative possibilities Can be targeted	Long production time Limited readership (print) Cluttered ad environment
Radio	Inexpensive Image transfer Can be targeted	Short life No feedback Messages often get skipped
Television	Can show demonstration Wide reach	Expensive Messages often get skipped
Out of home	Can be targeted High visibility	Wearout over time Limited message length
Online	Provides feedback Timely Can be interactive	Low response rates Cluttered ad environment May be annoying

Tsunami Disaster: The Inherent Value of Newspapers and Their Ads

Masaru Ariga, *Media Marketing Director, Dentsu, Tokyo, Japan*

The catastrophic earthquake and tsunami that hit northern Japan in 2011 and a series of nuclear-related anxieties that followed have apparently changed Japanese people's value system and behavior.

Inevitably, changes in the minds of consumers affect marketing. At Dentsu, an analysis was made of the changes in people's minds before and after the earthquake using "J-READ," a large-sample consumer database that enables time-series analysis.

Comparison with the 2010 and 2011 data indicates heightened concerns in areas such as energy, disaster prevention, and philanthropic activities. Undoubtedly, these are consequences of the Tohoku region earthquake.

This uplift of "disaster-related" awareness is seen more among those who are older, living in eastern Japan (which is closer to the epicenter), and women. This heightened interest was seen among housewives, conceivably because they found themselves in situations in which they needed to be concerned with such critical daily issues as food safety.

The Tohoku disaster also affected the way people perceive media. People experienced extreme states of mind when accurate and timely information was desperately needed. Analysis was made of the relations between the level of disaster-related awareness and people's evaluation of various media. Interestingly, only the perception of newspapers showed differences.

Those with high disaster-related awareness read newspapers longer and tended to better evaluate newspapers as a source of information. The evaluation of other media showed no such change. Having gone through situations where credible information was an absolute necessity, it may be that people came to realize the unique inherent value of newspapers.

Although attributes such as "can gain knowledge," "contents are credible," and "contains local information" were highly evaluated among all people, those with strong disaster-related awareness tended to also give higher evaluations to attributes such as "daily necessity," "usefulness in everyday life," "can track development in society," and "gain topics for conversation."

Likewise, those with higher consciousness tended to give higher evaluations to newspaper advertising. Interestingly, attributes for which there were wider gaps among people tended to gain high scores. Specifically, people in general highly evaluated "can understand what companies think," "get a feeling of familiarity with companies," and "ads are reliable." Those with higher consciousness were giving even higher ratings for these three particular attributes. These three attributes may represent the intrinsic value of newspaper advertising, which happened to be highlighted as a result of the social anxiety caused by the earthquake.

Marshall McLuhan once said, "The medium is the message." The fact that the value of newspaper ads extends beyond being a source of information about products and services to creating a positive impact on the evaluation of the companies themselves has implications for the strategic role that newspaper advertising can play in a marketing mix.

Masaru Ariga was in the first graduating class in 1992 from the IMC Master's program at Northwestern University; his undergraduate degree was from Waseda University in Tokyo.

through the publication at their own speed and on their own time. They can also save it and reread it. Because the print message format is less fleeting than broadcast and more concrete, people tend to spend more time with print and absorb its messages more carefully. Print can be highly engaging when targeted toward audiences that have a special interest in the publication's content, such as women and women's magazines.

Published Media: Newspapers

Newspapers' primary function is to carry news, which means that marketers with news to announce, such as a special sale or new product, may find newspapers to be a comfortable environment. Studies have consistently found that people consider many ads—that is, commercial information—to be news, too, and they read newspapers as much for the local ads as they do for the news stories. In fact, as Masaru Ariga found after the Japanese natural disaster, newspapers and their ads became of even more value.

⬢ **Principle**
A basic principle of newspaper publishing is that people read newspapers as much for the ads as they do for the news stories.

With more than 6,400 national and local papers in the United States, newspapers remain an important but primarily local medium. However, big dailies in the 500 largest markets account for only 1,300 of those papers, which means that most newspapers are small, and many of them are rural and suburban weeklies. Readers have been gradually moving online and away from print editions, but print versions remain important. National readership data from Nielsen Scarborough's 2015 Newspaper Penetration Report indicate that 51 percent of those who read a newspaper do so only in print, 5 percent read it on desktop only, 5 percent read it on mobile only, and 7 percent read it on both mobile and desktop.[1]

Another bit of good news is that consumers still consider newspapers to be a trusted and reliable source of information. Nielsen Scarborough also found that more than 169 million adults in the United States read a newspaper in a month—whether it be in print, on a website, or via mobile app. In total, newspapers reach 69 percent of the US population in a given month.[2]

● **Principle**
Readership is always larger than circulation for newspapers and magazines because they are often read by more than one person.

Other sources of revenue besides advertising include reader subscriptions and single-copy sales at newsstands. **Circulation** is the primary way newspapers' reach is measured and compared with the reach of other media. Readership is always larger than circulation because a newspaper is often read by more than one person.

As audiences have moved online for their news, major newspapers have responded to the challenge of retaining and engaging readers by providing well-designed news websites. Major newspapers' web traffic now far surpasses their circulation, and the number of website visitors and average minutes per visit have been rising for half of the top 50 papers. In response, newspapers have beefed up their digital ad offerings, and an estimated 25 to 30 percent of newspaper ad revenue is now coming from digital.

According to the Pew Research Center, "Gains in digital ad revenue, however, have not made up for the continued decline in print revenue. For the five companies that broke out digital vs. non-digital ad revenue for 2014–2015, non-digital ad revenue declined 9.9 percent, while digital's decline was less steep (−1.7 percent)."[3] These trends are affecting newspapers around the world as well. Global spending on newspaper print ads is expected to decline 8.7 percent to $52.6 billion in 2016. That would be the biggest drop since the Great Recession, when worldwide spending plummeted 13.7 percent in 2009.[4]

The primary characteristic of circulation is geography, whether the publication is national, regional, or local. The *Wall Street Journal* and *USA Today* are national newspapers and have the two highest circulations. Both have gone through major redesign programs to update their looks and appeal more to younger audiences. *USA Today* has been a design leader since it was launched, and now it's challenging the industry to keep up with its colorful design and format that better incorporates opportunities for advertisers to participate in print sponsorships.[5] The online *USA Today* page also has been redesigned to be more readable on phones and tablets.

Local media include large papers such as *The New York Times*, *Los Angeles Times*, *San Jose Mercury News*, and *The Washington Post*. Advertisers trying to reach a local market use newspapers because most newspapers (other than *USA Today* and *The Wall Street Journal*) are identified by the geography of the city or region they serve. *The New York Times* serves the New York region, but it also has a national circulation, particularly for its Sunday edition. Local papers are struggling to survive, but their readers still value them for their coverage of local politics, education, crime, sports stories, local events, church news, and local people features.

Decreasing subscriptions, however, have been a problem as readers have migrated to online versions and dropped their print subscriptions. Circulation revenues ($12.1 billion) are now estimated to be less than advertising revenues ($14.9 billion) by 2020.[6]

Photo: hakane/123RF

Traditional news outlets and periodicals have followed the lead of many businesses to design websites that can be easily accessed and read using a variety of platforms, and most importantly, on mobile devices.

We can't ignore the impact of the digital revolution on newspapers, with devoted readers wondering if their cup-of-coffee-and-morning-newspaper ritual is coming to an end. Major papers that have died include the *Rocky Mountain News*, *The Cincinnati Post*, *The Albuquerque Tribune*, and the *Oakland Tribune*. In 2009, Seattle's daily paper, the *Post-Intelligencer*, converted to an all-digital operation. The New Orleans *Times-Picayune* made headlines in 2012 as it tried to figure out a survival plan after seeing ad revenue drop more than 50 percent since 2005 at the same time publishing costs increased dramatically. The paper's solution was to experiment with a three-day-a-week publishing schedule, with the rest of the daily coverage appearing online. The demise of newspapers, should that happen, also impacts the profession of journalism and the coverage of local politics and community issues.

Industry Structure   Newspapers can be categorized according to their publication frequency, such as dailies, weeklies, and Sunday editions. Retailers like to place ads and press releases in daily newspapers because their **lead time** (the advance time needed to produce a publication) is short—just a few days. Food stores, for example, can change offers and pricing quickly depending on product availability. Local governments can also issue community announcements quickly.

Although newspapers go to a mass audience, they offer some **market selectivity**, which allows them to target specific consumer groups. Examples of market selectivity are special-interest newspapers (e.g., for coin collectors); ethnic editions, such as Spanish-language papers; special-interest sections (business, sports, and lifestyle); and special editions delivered to particular ZIP codes or zones. Newspapers' special-interest groups also include religious denominations, political affiliations, labor unions, and professional and fraternal organizations. For example, *Stars & Stripes* is the newspaper read by millions of military personnel. *The Wall Street Journal* and *Financial Times* are considered specialty newspapers because they concentrate on financial news.

Newspaper Advertising   Newspaper formats come in two typical sizes: broadsheet and tabloid. The broadsheet format—think any large metropolitan or national paper, such as *The New York Times* or *USA Today*—is typically 11 to 12 inches wide and 20 or more inches long. Tabloids are smaller and typically measure around 11 by 17 inches. Tabloids are popular in urban areas where readers may read them on buses or subways.

Newspaper advertising is sold based on the size of the ad space and the newspaper's circulation. The charges are published on a **rate card**, which is a list of the costs for advertising space and the discounts given to local advertisers and advertisers who make volume buys. National advertisers pay a higher rate as shown in this example from *The New York Times* rate card.

National Grocery Products

Nationwide Distribution	Sunday	Weekday
Open	$1,081	$927
5 pages / 630 column inches	981	843
10 pages / 1,260 column inches	964	828
20 pages / 2,520 column inches	944	813

New York Regional Distribution	Sunday	Weekday
Open	$976	$834
5 pages / 630 column inches	886	760
10 pages / 1,260 column inches	869	746
20 pages / 2,520 column inches	852	730

Most advertising sales are handled locally by the sales staff of the newspaper. Some chains centralize the sale of national advertising in their papers. There are also newspaper representatives (called "reps") who may sell space for many different newspapers, thus saving an advertiser or its agency from the need to make a multitude of buys to run a national or regional campaign in newspapers. The system is known as **one-order, one-bill**. The Newspaper National

Network (www.nnnlp.com) is a partnership of newspaper companies that place ads in news-papers across the country. Google has also gotten into this business, allowing advertisers to buy ads in daily newspapers through its website.

Until the 1980s, national advertisers shied away from using newspapers not only because of the buying problem, but also because each paper had its own peculiar size guidelines for ads, making it difficult to prepare one ad that would fit every newspaper. In the early 1980s, the American Newspaper Publishers Association and the Newspaper Advertising Bureau intro-duced the **standard advertising unit** system to solve this problem. The latest version of the standard advertising unit makes it possible for newspapers to offer advertisers a great deal of choice within a standard format. An advertiser can select from among standard ad sizes that will work in every newspaper in the country. There are 56 standard sizes for broadsheet newspaper advertising and 32 for tabloid-format newspapers. A full-page ad consists of all six columns of content, and the full depth of the page. In broadsheet format that's 21 inches, for a total of 132 column inches.

Another alternative that allows national advertisers to pay the local rate is cooperative (co-op) advertising with a local retailer. **Co-op advertising** is an arrangement between the adver-tiser and the retailer whereby the retailer buys the ad and the manufacturer pays half (or a portion, depending on the amount of space the manufacturer's brand occupies). This arrangement results in a pool of money in the United States that some have estimated to be in excess of $50 billion annually, much of which remains untapped at the end of every year because many individual retailers are unable or unwilling to tap into it. Co-op advertising has also filtered into the digital media space with an estimated $1.7 billion in available dollars. Co-op advertising is a great oppor-tunity for smaller businesses to extend their ad budgets, but Borrell Associates estimates that only 15 percent of local advertisers are currently participating in co-op advertising programs.[7]

Types of Newspaper Advertising   Three types of advertising are found within the local newspaper: retail/display, classified, and two types of inserts (magazine supplements and preprints). Most of them are found online as well as in the print form of the newspaper.

- *Display* The dominant form of newspaper advertising is **display advertising**. Display ads can be any size and can be placed anywhere in the newspaper except the editorial page. Dis-play ads can even be found in the classified section. Display advertising is further divided into two subcategories: *local* (*retail*) and *national* (*brand*). The Aflac ads are examples of national display for *The New York Times*. Advertisers who don't care where their display ads run in the newspaper pay the **run-of-paper (ROP) rate**. If they want more choice over the placement than the ROP rate, they can pay the **preferred-position rate**, which lets them select sections in which the ad will appear.
- *Classified* Two types of **classified advertising** are advertising by individuals to sell their personal goods and advertising by local businesses. These ads are arranged according to their interest to readers, such as "Help Wanted" and "Real Estate for Sale." Classified ads have represented approximately 40 percent of total newspaper advertising revenue in the past, but local online services, such as Craigslist, have almost destroyed newspaper classified advertising, adding to the bottom-line problems for local newspapers.
- *Supplements* Newspaper **supplements** are magazine-style publications inserted into a news-paper, especially in the Sunday edition, that are either syndicated nationally or prepared locally. Syndicated supplements, such as *Parade* and *USA Weekend*, are provided by an independent publisher that sells its publications to newspapers. These supplements also carry national advertising.
- *Preprints* Preprints are a type of supplement. **Freestanding inserts (FSIs)** are preprinted advertisements, such as the grocery or department store ads that are inserted into the news-paper. Also called **circulars**, FSIs range in size from a single page to more than 30 pages and are often printed elsewhere and then delivered to the newspaper. Newspapers charge the advertiser a fee for inserting a supplement. Next to local ads, preprints are the second largest revenue stream, with estimates of up to 70 percent of the Sunday newspaper revenues com-ing from preprints. Preprints, however, are threatened not only by a shift to online digital formats but also by a recent US Postal Service rate cut that makes it cheaper to mail certain types of national retail preprints.[8]

Photo: American Family Life Assurance Company of Columbus (AFLAC)

Photo: American Family Life Assurance Company of Columbus (AFLAC)

These examples of business-to-business newspaper display ads for Aflac ran in *The Wall Street Journal*. They address business managers with a message about making the supplemental insurance available to their employees.

Self-promotion, or **house ads**, is the type of advertising used by newspapers—and other media—to promote themselves. House ads in newspapers are usually set up in advance to help fill the layout where there is space left after the news stories and other ads have been placed. But newspapers may also use other media forms to promote themselves. London's *Guardian*, for example, used a two-minute commercial created by ad agency Bartle Bogle Hegarty based on retelling the *Three Little Pigs* as a modern news story. The highly creative television spot began with the Big Bad Wolf's death and then moved to a fast-paced accumulation of facts and speculation leading viewers through a fascinating introduction to the basics of news coverage. In addition to promoting the *Guardian*, the spot also drove a broader discussion of professional news coverage versus citizen journalism.[9]

Published Media: Magazines

Most American adults read at least one magazine per month, and they spend more time with magazines than with other print media. Similar to other mass media, magazines were hurt by the recession but seem to be slowly bouncing back. Ad spending in magazines is estimated to be stable at $16.8 billion per year through 2020. By 2020, digital ad revenue is expected to over-take print ad revenue in magazines ($9.2 billion and $7.7 billion, respectively). Similar trends are occurring in the trade magazine market: digital ad revenue will be $2.4 billion, surpassing print ad revenue's $2.3 billion.[10]

The more than 7,000 magazines published in the United States appeal to every possible interest. Total magazine readership grew to 1.75 billion people in 2015 across platforms, an increase of 6.2 percent. Most magazines aim at niche markets with a focus on a particular hobby, sport, age group, business category, or profession. These special-interest publications generally have small circulations, but there are exceptions. The number one magazine in terms of circulation is *AARP, The Magazine*, which is sent to all AARP members.

Color and quality of reproduction are the biggest strengths of magazines. They allow the advertiser's products and brand image to be presented in a format superior to the quality of newspapers. In general, media planners know that people tend to pay more attention to magazine advertising and stories than to television because they are concentrating more on the medium and the messages are generally more relevant to their interests. Readers also spend more time reading a magazine than they do reading a newspaper, so there is a better opportunity to provide in-depth information.

The Magazine Industry   The magazine industry hasn't suffered as much from the recession and changing media environment as newspapers, although, like most print media, it has been threatened by the digital revolution and the recession. A number of well-respected magazines have disappeared, but one of the most surprising was the announcement in 2012 that *Newsweek* would no longer appear in print, only online.[11] Despite the high risks associated with the magazine business, new publications continue to emerge, especially those that target business markets and growing market niches.

Magazine revenues come from advertising, subscriptions, and single-copy sales. According to the Magazine Publishers Association, advertising contributes 55 percent of magazine revenue and circulation 45 percent (subscriptions 32 percent; single-copy sales 13 percent).[12] Some publications, such as *People*, are more dependent on single-copy sales, which tend to be impulse buys. The reliance on single-copy sales was a problem during the recession.

Traditional delivery, called **controlled circulation**, is through newsstand purchases or home delivery via mail. These are measured media, and their circulation or sales can be determined. **Nontraditional delivery**, referred to as **uncontrolled circulation**, means that the magazine is distributed free to specific audiences. In addition to mail, other nontraditional delivery methods include hanging bagged copies on doorknobs, inserting magazines in newspapers (such as *Parade* magazine), delivering through professionals' offices (doctors and dentists), direct delivery (company magazines or those found on airplanes), and electronic delivery, which is being used by organizational and membership publications, such as university alumni magazines.

Meredith, the giant publisher of magazines such as *Better Homes & Gardens* and *Ladies Home Journal*, is searching for new revenue with custom publishing and multiplatform offerings for major marketers who are also its advertisers. For Kraft Foods, Meredith publishes Spanish-language magazines, designs Kraft's website, and coordinates weekly email blasts that feature recipe ideas. It also built Kraft's iFood Assistant, an app for cell phones that includes recipes, how-to videos, and shopping lists.[13]

Sophisticated database management lets publishers combine the information available from subscriber lists with other public and private lists to create complete consumer profiles for advertisers. These databases, combined with new technologies, have made personalized publishing a reality. For example, **selective binding** combines information on subscribers kept in a database with a computer program to produce magazines that include special sections for subscribers based on their demographic profiles. **Ink-jet imaging** allows a magazine such as *U.S. News & World Report* to personalize its renewal form so that each issue contains a renewal card already filled out with the subscriber's name, address, and so on. Personalized messages can be printed directly on ads or on inserts ("Mr. Jones—check out our new mutual fund today").

Satellite transmission, along with computerized editing technology, allows magazines to print regional editions with regional advertising. This technology also permits publishers to close pages (stop accepting new material) just hours before press time (instead of days or weeks, as in the past) so that advertisers can drop up-to-the-minute information in their ads.

Types of Magazines   The focus of audience interest is the main factor used when classifying magazines. The two main types of audiences that magazines target are consumer and business audiences. Consumer magazine advertising is directed at people who buy products for personal consumption. Examples are *Sports Illustrated*, *Time*, and *People*, which are general-interest publications.

Business magazines target business readers and include the following types of publications:

• *Trade magazines* are aimed at retailers, wholesalers, and other distributors; *Chain Store Age* is an example.

- *Industrial magazines* are aimed at manufacturers; *Concrete Construction* is an example.
- *Professional magazines* are aimed at physicians, lawyers, and other professionals; *National Law Review* targets lawyers, and *MediaWeek* targets advertising media planners and buyers.
- *Farm magazines* are aimed at those working in agriculture; *Farm Journal* and *Feed and Grain* are examples.
- *Corporate publications* are produced by companies for their customers and other stakeholders; airline magazines are good examples.

Photo: bibiphoto/Shutterstock

Advertisers look at the audience, geographic coverage, demographics, and editorial diversity of magazines as criteria for using them in a media plan.

Business magazines are also classified as vertical or horizontal publications. A **vertical publication** presents stories and information about an entire industry. *Women's Wear Daily*, for example, discusses the production, marketing, and distribution of women's fashions. A **horizontal publication** deals with a business function that cuts across industries, such as *Direct Marketing*.

In terms of vehicle selection, a number of factors influence how media planners fit magazines into their media mix:

- *Geography* The area covered may be as small as a city (*Los Angeles Magazine* and *Boston Magazine*) or as large as several contiguous states (the southwestern edition of *Southern Living Magazine*). Geographic editions help encourage local retail support by listing the names of local distributors in the advertisements. Most national magazines also offer a zone edition that carries different ads and perhaps different stories, depending on the region of the country.
- *Demographics* Demographic editions group subscribers according to age, income, occupation, and other classifications. Some magazines for example, publish a special "ZIP" edition for upper-income homes sent to subscribers who live in specific ZIP codes and who typically share common demographic traits, based primarily on income. *Time* sends special editions to students, business executives, doctors, and business managers.
- *Editorial Content* Each magazine emphasizes a certain type of editorial content. The most widely used categories are general editorial (*Reader's Digest*), women's (*Family Circle*), shelter (*House Beautiful*), business (*Forbes*), and special interest (*Ski*). *Ladies Home Journal* is experimenting with user-generated content by acquiring much of the content from posts on the magazine's website, its Facebook page, and other digital channels.[14]
- *Physical Characteristics* Media planners and buyers need to know the physical characteristics of a magazine because ads containing various elements of words and pictures require a different amount of space. The most common magazine page sizes are 8½ by 11 inches and 6 by 9 inches (*Reader's Digest*).

Media planners look for readership patterns that match their target audience and positioning strategy. *Ladies Home Journal* is one of the six magazines in the "women's service" category, which includes *Good Housekeeping*, *Woman's Day*, *Redbook*, *Better Homes and Gardens*, and *Family Circle*. Their positions are different relative to their readership. *Ladies Home Journal*, for example, reaches a "very mature" category whose average age is 56. In contrast, *Woman's Day* reaches a slightly younger audience (average age of 51) that could be characterized as mothers. It maintains a delicate balance as "the magazine my mother (and grandmother) depended on," without seeming old-fashioned. Going directly against competitor *Cosmopolitan*, *Glamour* is trying to reposition its audience (average 34 years) to younger women—millennials or Gen Yers.[15]

The patterns in the male magazine category are equally competitive and complex, ranging from what one *New York Times* writer describes as dudes to dandies—or, rather, lad magazines—(*Maxim*) to fashion (*GQ*). *Esquire* has maintained its "Man at his best" position and mix of well-written, general-interest articles. One aspect of its revival is its more web-like design with marginalia, small laughs, and jokes.[16]

Magazine Advertising   Advertising in magazines is generally highly targeted because most magazines are designed to reach consumers through their special interests. Magazine advertising benefits from much higher production values than in newspapers, and that makes them good for brand-image advertising. Because readers spend more time reading magazines than newspapers, the format is also good for long messages.

The emphasis on graphics encourages creativity, good design, and interesting production techniques, such as the see-through graphics in the Specialized Bike advertising below. The graphic elements are separated and printed on the front and back of a page. When you look at the ad, you see people in the foreground going about their business, but in the background, a faint image shows a daredevil bike rider jumping from one building to another or riding on a handrail going down the middle of a set of steps.

Like newspapers, magazine ad costs are based on the size of the ad and the circulation of the magazine. Although the format may vary from magazine to magazine, all magazines share some format characteristics. For example, the *back cover* and *inside front cover* are the most costly for advertisers because they have the highest level of exposure compared to all the other pages in a magazine. The *inside back cover* is also a premium position.

(front)

hold this page up to a light

Normally, the largest unit of ad space that magazines sell is the **double-page spread** (sometimes called "double truck"), in which an ad runs across two facing pages. A double-page ad must jump the **gutter**, the white space running between the inside edges of the pages, meaning that no headline words can run through the gutter and that body text is on one side or the other of the gutter. A page without outside margins, in which the ad's ink extends to the very edge of the page, is called a **bleed**. Magazines sometimes offer more than two connected pages (four is the most common number) that fold in on themselves. This kind of ad is called a **gatefold**. The use of multiple pages that provide photo essays is an extension of the gatefold concept.

Another popular format is a special advertising page or section that looks like regular editorial pages but is identified by the word "advertisement" at the top. Called **advertorials**, the content is usually an article about a company, product, or brand that is written by the corporation's publicity department. The idea is to mimic the editorial look so as to acquire the credibility of the publication's articles. Multiple-page photo-essay ads are more common in magazines such as *Fortune* and *BusinessWeek*; these magazines may present, for example, a 20-page special section for businesses in a foreign country.

Finally, a single page or double page can be broken into a variety of units called *fractional page space* (e.g., vertical half page, horizontal half page, half-page double spread, and checkerboard, in which an ad is located in the upper left and the lower right of a double-page spread).

Published Media: Directories

Directories are books like the Yellow Pages that list the names of people or companies, their phone numbers, and their addresses. In addition to this information, many directories publish advertising from marketers who want to reach the people who use the directory. Corporations, associations, and other organizations, such as nonprofits, also publish directories either in print or online that include members as well as other stakeholders. They are often provided as a service to members as part of an organizational communication program. Directory advertising is designed to get attention, communicate key information about the organization, reinforce the company's brand image and position, and drive behavior.

According to an article in the *Wall Street Journal*, print business phone directories are a $3 billion industry, and 40 percent of Americans consult one at least once a year. Although many view them as obsolete, usage is stronger among older consumers and in rural areas. Nevertheless, the industry is facing major changes and fighting for survival. Dex Media, Inc., which publishes more than 1,600 print directories in 42 states, has recently declared bankruptcy five times in seven years.[17]

A report by Thrive Analytics and the Local Search Association (previously known as the Yellow Pages Association) found that 62 percent of people used search engines as their first source of information about local businesses, compared to 27 percent for the online or print Yellow Pages, and that only 14 percent of people under age 29 described themselves as "extremely likely to use the yellow pages as a source of information."[18] Although search engines dominate for services like hotels, restaurants, and real estate, many consumers still turn to the print Yellow Pages to find plumbers, electricians, and roofers because they perceive these advertisers to be more trustworthy than firms that appear in online search results.

Broadcast Media: Radio

The reason advertisers like radio is that it is as close as we can come to a universal medium. Most every American listens to radio in some form, either over the air or streaming from internet-based services, such as Pandora or Spotify. Virtually every household in the United States (99 percent) has at least one radio, and most have multiple sets. And almost everybody listens to radio at some time during the day.

The overall radio advertising market in the United States is expected to remain relatively flat, increasing marginally from $17.8 billion in 2016 to $18.4 billion in 2020.[19] Radio's biggest advantage is that it is tightly targeted based on musical tastes (e.g., rock, country, and classical) and special interests (e.g., religion, Spanish language, and talk shows).

Broadcast media messages—both radio and television—are fleeting, which means they may capture attention for a few seconds and then disappear, in contrast to print messages,

⬤ **Principle**
Media planners use radio for tight targeting of narrow, highly segmented markets.

which can be revisited and reread. Radio is a talk-, news-, or music-driven medium where advertisements can also engage the imagination to create stories in the mind. In terms of our Facets of Effects Model, broadcast media are often more entertaining, using drama and emotion with audio to attract attention and engage the feelings of the audience. If done right, radio can engage the imagination more than other media because it relies on the listener's mind to fill in the visual element. Chris Thile's *Prairie Home Companion* is an example of radio stories.

The radio listening experience is unlike that of any other media, creating both challenges and opportunities for radio advertisers. It can be a more intimate experience because we tend to listen to it alone, particularly for people wearing headphones. In cars, where many people listen to radio, it offers advertisers something close to a captive audience. It's also relatively inexpensive both to produce commercials and to buy airtime. Check out the Radio Ranch website at www.radio-ranch.com for a look behind the scenes of radio commercial production.

● **Principle**
Radio advertising has the power to engage the imagination and communicate on a more personal level than other forms of media.

The Radio Industry   The United States has more than 10,000 commercial stations, and most of them, except for the new internet stations, have a limited geographical reach. In recent years, the radio industry's growth has been slow.

Radio is tightly targeted based on special interests (religion, Spanish language, and talk shows) and musical tastes. In other words, radio is a highly segmented advertising medium. About 85 percent of the radio stations are focused on music. Program formats offered in a typical market are based on music styles and special interests, including hard rock, gospel, country and western, top-40 hits, soft rock, golden oldies, and nonmusic programs, such as talk radio and advice, from car repair to finances to dating. Emerging trends in radio include more local ownership of stations, radio going entirely digital, a broader definition of radio that includes all things audio (traditional radio, digital radio, satellite, podcasting), and emphasis on radio as a moving-about medium which fits well with our more mobile society.[20]

Traditional radio stations are found on the AM/FM dial, and most serve local markets. Other options for radio listeners include public radio, cable and satellite radio, low-powered stations, and web radio. Stations with a broadcast range of approximately 25 miles are considered local stations. Regional stations may cover an entire state or several states. In addition to digital forms, which we'll discuss in Chapter 14, radio stations in the United States broadcast signals in several formats:

- *Cable Radio* Launched in 1990, **cable radio** technology uses cable television receivers to deliver static-free music via wires plugged into cable subscribers' stereos. The thinking behind cable radio is that cable television needs new revenue and that consumers are fed up with commercials on radio. The service typically is commercial free with a monthly subscription fee.
- *Satellite Radio* **Satellite radio** can deliver your favorite radio stations, regardless of where you are in the continental United States. Sirius and XM satellite radio introduced their systems in 2002. The two companies merged in 2007 as Sirius XM Radio and have some 31 million subscribers. For a monthly fee, the system allows you to access more than 150 channels.
- *Low-Power FM* If you're a college student, you may have a **low-power FM** station on your campus. These nonprofit, noncommercial stations serve a small market, with a reach of three to five miles.
- *Web Radio* Web radio provides audio files downloaded or streaming through a website called **netcasting**, which makes it possible to broadcast radio (and television) online. If the receiver is an iPod, smartphone, or other type of portable music player, the reception is called **podcasting**. Podcasting is possible because of the convergence of three technologies: an audio source (the radio station or music source, such as Spotify or Pandora), a web connection, and a portable media player or cell phone.
- *Public Radio Stations* **Public radio** stations are usually affiliates of National Public Radio (NPR) and carry much of the same programming, although they have to buy or subscribe to the NPR services. For that reason, some local public radio stations might carry a full range of NPR programming, whereas others that are less well funded may carry only a partial list of NPR programs. Public radio stations are considered noncommercial in that they rely

on listener support for most of their funding. In recent years, however, they have slowly expanded their corporate *sponsorship* messages or **underwriting**, which has increased along with the audience size because public radio is one of the few media that can deliver an audience of well-educated, affluent consumers.

Radio Advertising   The first radio commercials hit the air in 1922 in New York and advertised a real estate firm. These early ads were highly successful for many of the same reasons that keep radio popular today with advertisers. Media planners use radio to deliver a high level of frequency because radio commercials, particularly **jingles**, which are commercials set to music, lend themselves to repetition.

There are three types of radio buys: network, spot, and syndicated. Local advertising revenues account for approximately 75 percent. Network revenues are by far the smallest category, accounting for approximately 5 percent of total radio revenues. National spot advertising makes up the remainder. **Radio networks** are groups of affiliated stations. The network system produces programs and distributes them to their **affiliates**, who contract with the system. Some of the networks include ABC Radio, Clear Channel Communications, CNN Radio Network, the Fox Sports and Fox News networks, and others that deliver special-interest programming, such as talk radio. Let's review the categories of national radio buys.

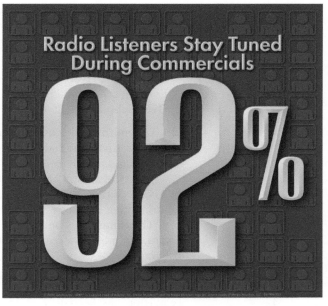

Photo: Courtesy of Arbitron, Inc.

Nielsen Audio (formerly Arbitron) is one of several major audience-rating services in the advertising industry. It estimates the size of radio audiences for more than 300 US markets.

- *Network Radio Advertising* Network advertising can be bought from national networks that distribute programming and advertising to their affiliates. A radio network is a group of local affiliates connected to one or more national networks through telephone wires and satellites. The five major radio networks are Westwood One, CBS, ABC, Unistar, and Clear Channel. The largest network by far is Clear Channel, with more than 1,200 stations. Many advertisers view network radio as a viable national advertising medium, especially for food and beverages, automobiles, and over-the-counter drugs.
- *Spot Radio Advertising—Both Local and National* Spot advertising lets an advertiser place an advertisement with an individual station rather than through a network. Thanks to the flexibility it offers the advertiser, **spot radio advertising** makes up nearly 80 percent of all radio advertising. In large cities, 40 or more radio stations may be available. Local stations also offer flexibility through their willingness to run unusual ads, allow last-minute changes, and negotiate rates. Buying spot radio and coping with its nonstandardized rate structures can be cumbersome, however. Although networks broadcast blocks of prerecorded national advertisements, they may also allow local affiliates open time to sell spot advertisements locally. (National media plans sometimes buy spots at the local level rather than through the network, so it is possible to have a national spot buy that only reaches certain markets.)
- *Syndicated Radio Advertising* Syndicated radio advertising is the original type of radio programming that plays on a large number of affiliated stations, such as the *TED Radio Hour*, Fox Sports Radio, *America Now*, and *This American Life*, which has a weekly audience of 2.2 million and is syndicated across 580 public radio stations. Program **syndication** has benefited network radio because it offers advertisers a variety of high-quality, specialized, and usually original programs. Both networks and private firms offer syndication. A local talk show may become popular enough to be "taken into syndication." Advertisers value syndicated programming because of the high level of loyalty of its audience.

Advertisers considering radio are most concerned with the number of people listening to a particular station at a given time. Radio audiences are grouped by the time of day when they are most likely to be listening, and the assumption is that different groups listen at different times of the day. Nielsen Audio (formerly known as Arbitron) divides a weekday into five segments called **dayparts** as follows:

- **Morning Drive Time:** 6–10 A.M.
- **Midday:** 10 A.M.–3 P.M.
- **Afternoon Drive:** 3–7 P.M.
- **Evenings:** 7 P.M.–midnight
- **Overnight:** midnight–6 A.M.

The **morning drive time** segment is the period when the most listeners are tuned in to radio. This drive-time audience is getting ready for work or commuting to work, and radio is the best medium to reach them.

As an illustration of the creative possibilities of radio, Allstate Insurance did a "Mayhem takeover" of radio stations across the nation during consumers' rush hour from 5 to 7 P.M., featuring their character "Mayhem" stepping in as DJ to recall "mayhemic moments" in history. The campaign won a Radio Mercury Award for Allstate and was a finalist for an Effie Award, but most of all, it helped the brand stand out among drivers in the saturated insurance category.[21]

Broadcast Media: Television

Television has become a mainstay of society, with 120 million TV homes in the United States. With 98 percent of American households having one or more television sets, television approaches the universality of radio. In more than half of US households, the television is on "most" of the time. The US television audience, however, is highly fragmented, tuning in to hundreds of different channels, plus online and alternative media, such as game consoles. Nielsen Media Research estimates that the average US household has a TV set on more than five hours a day.[22]

Coca-Cola's chief marketing officer Marcos de Quinto defended TV as providing the biggest bang for Coca-Cola's marketing buck. Coca-Cola's data showed its TV investment "returning $2.13 for every dollar spent on TV, compared with $1.26 for digital."[23]

● **Principle**
Television's dramatic impact comes from its moving images, as well as its emotional power.

With its drama and emotional impact as well as its moving images, television is primarily an entertainment medium. In-home theaters with their large-screen televisions are popular with viewers from all income levels.

But it's not just big screens. Through the magic of *video streaming*, programs can also be seen on computers, tablets, and smartphones. Television's use expanded with the introduction of the Wii, which makes the home television screen a facilitator in exercise programs as well as games. An estimated 63 percent of households in the United States will be equipped with an internet-connected TV device by 2019. As computers begin to use television screens to project their content, this cross-channel merger will open up entirely new uses for home televisions. MTV producers are experimenting with ways to put viewers in the director's set and let them control the camera and send singers into goofy scenarios.[24]

The economic model of broadcast television is generally based on an advertising-supported approach, at least for the traditional networks. The model relies on producing programs that attract a large audience advertisers want to reach. Advertising, plus revenue from the programs that are syndicated after they go off air, has supported network television since its beginnings, although that model is in serious trouble with the development of cable and the splintering of the viewing audience.

In this day of fragmented audiences, television is beholden to organizations like the NFL that can demand big fees for their programs. Football is one of the few programs that still draw huge audiences who watch the shows live, which explains why Fox, CBS, and NBC made a $28 billion deal with the NFL. The *Wall Street Journal* called the NFL "the League That Runs TV."[25]

Television advertising is embedded in programming, so most of the attention in media buying, as well as in the measurement of television advertising's effectiveness, is focused on the performance of various shows and how they engage their audiences. During the golden age of television in the 1950s and 1960s, the three networks virtually controlled the evening viewing experience, but that dominance has shrunk in recent years with the rapid increase in the number of cable channels. The following table shows **prime time** viewing over the years as well as the drastic drop in percentage of adults watching the leading shows during those years.

Years	(Percentage of Audience) Top Show
1952–1953	67 *I Love Lucy* (CBS)
1962–1963	36 *The Beverly Hillbillies* (CBS)
1972–1973	33 *All in the Family* (CBS)
1982–1883	26 *60 Minutes* (CBS)
1992–1993	22 *60 Minutes* (CBS)
2002–2003	16 *CSI* (CBS)
2007–2008	16 *American Idol* (Fox)
2008–2009	9.8 *American Idol* (Fox)
2009–2010	9.1 *American Idol* (Fox)
2010–2011	8.8 *American Idol* (Fox)
2011–2012	8.0 *Sunday Night Football* (NBC)
2012–2013	11 *NCIS* (CBS)
2013–2016	12 *Sunday Night Football* (NBC)

Source: Adapted from James Poniewozik, "Here's to the Death of Broadcast," *Time*, March 26, 2009, 62; Sergio Ibarr, "Fox Wins 5th Straight Season in Key 18–49 Demo," *TVWeek*, July 18, 2009, www.tvweek.com; Nellie Andreeva, "Full 2009–2010 TV Season Series Rankings," *Deadline Hollywood*, May 27, 2010, www.deadline.com; Nellie Andreeva, "Full 2010–2011 TV Season Series Rankings," *Deadline Hollywood*, May 27, 2011, www.deadline.com; Bill Garman, "Complete List of 2011–12 Season TV Show Ratings," May 24, 2012, www.tybythenumbers.zap2it .com; "Top 50 Most-Watched Shows of 2013–14," *Entertainment Weekly*, May 25, 2014; "Full 2014–15 TV Season Series Rankings: Football & 'Empire' Ruled," *Deadline Hollywood*, May 22, 2015, http://deadline.com/2015/05/2014-15-full-tv-season-ratings-shows-rankings-1201431167/; Michael Schneider, "These Are the 100 Most-Watched TV Shows of the 2015–16 Season: Winners and Losers," *IndieWire*, May 31, 2016, http://www.indiewire.com/2016/05/most-watched-tv-show-2015-2016-season-game-of-thrones-the-walking-dead-football-1201682396/.

Structure of the Industry   To better understand how television works, let's first consider its structure and programming options. The main types of television delivery systems include network, subscription (cable and satellite), pay programming, local and public television, and syndication.

As with radio, a **broadcast network** is a distribution system that provides television content to its affiliated stations. Currently, there are four national, over-the-air television networks in the United States: the American Broadcasting Company (ABC), the Columbia Broadcasting System (CBS), the National Broadcasting Company (NBC), and Fox Broadcasting, the newest entry. The big three networks' hold on the viewing audience dropped from 75 percent in 1987 to less than 30 percent in recent years. When Fox is included, networks still only capture less than half of the audience because of the rise of hundreds of cable stations, which have fragmented the audience.

● Principle
Cable programming has fragmented the television audience and makes it difficult for advertisers to reach a large, mass audience.

Network Television   With some 150 affiliates, **network television** sells commercial time to national advertisers for placement on programs that play throughout the network. Some time is left open for affiliates to fill with local advertising. Affiliates pay their respective networks 30 percent of the fees they charge local advertisers. In turn, affiliates receive a percentage of the advertising revenue (12 to 25 percent) paid to the national network. Advertising is the primary source of affiliate revenues. In addition to local affiliates, **independent stations** not affiliated with networks are found in local markets.

Costs for local advertising vary, depending on the size of the market and the demand for the programs carried. Most advertisers are local retailers, primarily department stores or discount stores, financial institutions, automobile dealers, restaurants, and supermarkets. National advertisers sometimes buy local advertising on a city-by-city or station-by-station basis, using **spot buys**. They do so to align the buy with their product distribution, to "heavy-up" a national schedule to meet competitive activities, or to launch a new product in selected cities.

Other forms of television service include the following:

- *Subscription Television* Subscription television is a delivery system that carries the television signal to subscribers either by cable or satellite. People sign up for television service and pay a monthly fee.

- *Cable Television* Network owners are under growing pressure as they lose customers to online services like Netflix. The **cable television** industry lost around 1 million subscribers in 2016, and almost no channel was untouched. Even popular sports like the NFL, the glue holding the cable bundle together, lost viewers.[26] In 2015, the top 13 pay-TV providers, including cable, satellite, and telecommunications companies, lost 385,000 subscribers, according to data from Leichtman Research Group, but these declines are gradual; at the end of 2015, pay TV still had more than 90 million customers.[27]

- *Public Television* Although many people still consider **public television** to be commercial free, the Federal Communications Commission (FCC) allows the approximately 900 Public Broadcasting System (PBS) stations some leeway in airing commercial messages, called program underwriting. PBS is an attractive medium for advertisers, however, because it reaches affluent, well-educated households. PBS has a refined image and PBS advertisers are viewed as good corporate citizens because of their support for noncommercial television. The FCC, however, says these messages should not ask for a purchase or make price or quality comparisons, which is why many placements are **program sponsorships**. Some PBS stations accept the same ads that appear on paid programming, but most PBS spots are created specifically for public stations. Some PBS stations will not accept any commercial corporate advertising, but they do accept noncommercial ads that are "value neutral"—in other words, ads that make no attempt to sell a product or service.

- *Satellite Television* **Satellite television** is similar to cable in that it's a competing delivery system. Direct broadcast television services became available in the United States in the 1990s. Dish Network and DirecTV provide the equipment, including the satellite dish, to access some 250 national and local channels. In addition to cable channels, satellite television also carries **superstations**, for example, WTBS-Atlanta, WGN-Chicago, and WWOR–New York. Satellite television is particularly useful for people who live in rural areas without local or over-the-air service. Satellite television has the potential to be a highly targeted medium in that it controls the delivery of programming and can target individual homes with *addressable ads.*

- *Syndication* An important revenue stream for networks and cable channels, such as HBO, that produce original programming is syndication. As in radio programming, television syndication refers to content providers that sell their programs to independent firms and other cable channels to replay as reruns. Some of the most popular first-run programs, such as *House* and *Law & Order*, are valuable properties and move quickly into syndication.

- *On-Demand Programming* **On-demand programming** is available to subscribers for an additional monthly fee. This type of programming offers movies, specials, and sports under such plans as Home Box Office, Showtime, and The Movie Channel. Pay networks do not currently sell advertising time.

Television Advertising   The first television commercial aired in 1941 when Bulova bought time on a New York station before a Major League Baseball game between the Phillies and Dodgers.[28] Television is used for advertising because it works like the movies: it tells stories, engages the emotions, creates fantasies, and can have great visual impact. Because it's an action medium, it is also good for demonstrating how things work. It brings brand images to life and adds personality to a brand. An example of the dramatic, emotional power of television comes from one of the greatest commercials of all time. Called "Iron Eyes Cody," the Ad Council's public service announcement was created as part of an environmental campaign. It shows a Native American man paddling a canoe through a river ruined by trash. A close-up shows a tear from his eye.

The first decision in using television is determining the ad's length, which is usually 10, 15, 30, or 60 seconds. The most common length is 30 seconds; for most advertisers, the 60-second spot is considered too expensive. The 10- and 15-second ad is like a billboard and simply announces that a program is "brought to you by [the advertiser]."

Long-form ads, which are of various lengths, are seen on late-night television, when the cost of broadcast time is much lower than at other times of day. High-end jeweler Cartier, for example, ran a cinematic three-minute ad in a **roadblock**—meaning that the ad ran on the traditional big three networks of ABC, CBS, and NBC at exactly the same time. *Advertising Age* speculated that this tactic would start a trend and increase demand for these long-form ads.[29]

Late-night **infomercials**, which can be program length, have been the venue for direct-response television, with its promise of how-to-do-it tools, vegetable cutters, and fitness equipment as well as get-rich investing. Tony Horton's brutal P90X fitness routine that has Sheryl Crow, former NFL quarterback Kurt Warner, and Representative Paul Ryan as fans has built its $400 million empire on television infomercials and exercise DVDs.[30]

A second decision is time availability. Similar to radio dayparts, television programs are slotted into time categories. The price of a commercial is based on the rating of the surrounding program (the rating is for the program, not the commercial). The price is also based on the daypart during which the commercial is shown. The following table shows the Television Standard Dayparts. The most expensive time block is prime time.

Standard Television Dayparts

Early morning	M–F 5–9 A.M.
Daytime	M–F 9 A.M.–4 P.M.
Early fringe	M–F 4–7 P.M.
Prime access	M–F 7–8 P.M.
	M–S 8–11 P.M.
	Su 7–11 P.M.
Late news	M–Su 11–11:30 P.M.
Late night	M–Su 11:30 P.M.–1 A.M.
Saturday morning	Sa 5 A.M.–1 P.M.
Weekend afternoon	Sa–Su 1 P.M.–5 P.M.

Although these time slots are important, media plans are vulnerable to the viewing behavior of consumers, who not only change channels but also change viewing times using time-shifting and zipping and zapping. Avoidance of advertising is easy to do with your handy remote control as follows:

- **Time-shifting** using a **DVR**, such as TiVo or the Dish Network Hopper, allows users to record favorite television shows and watch them whenever they like. The technology records the programming, letting users pause, do instant replays, and begin watching programs even before the recording has finished. The Bolt, a TiVo product, allows viewers to skip the entire commercial break.[31] Of course, on-demand services (e.g., Netflix) have further reinforced consumers' control over their viewing of commercial content.
- With DVR-recorded programs, consumers can **zip** past (fast-forward through) commercials completely or **zap** them by changing to another channel. These practices are forcing advertisers to rethink the design of their ads, recognizing that they only have a few moments to win the attention of button-happy viewers.

Advertisers and television executives are alarmed over the increasing popularity of time-shifting and zipping and zapping. It calls into question audience measurement numbers: if 20 percent of the audience is recording *American Idol* on Tuesday night only to watch it Saturday morning commercial free, are the ratings figures accurate? The DVR industry estimates that viewers zip past about 6 percent of television commercials—an estimated waste of some $5 billion in ad spending—and estimates that about 16 percent now will suffer that fate of commercials.[32] To further understand this pattern, TiVo has also announced that it is considering a service that will provide second-by-second data about which programs the company's subscribers are watching and which commercials they are skipping.

The ad-skipping debate continues in a battle between satellite television networks and networks over the ad-skipping Auto-Hop feature available on Dish, a practice that is well

Photo: Images courtesy of Keep America Beautiful, Inc.

CLASSIC

The "crying Indian" image from this famous commercial communicated a strong ecology message. The Native American man, played by Iron Eyes Cody, paddles his canoe up a filthy stream and sheds a tear as people in a speeding car throw trash out the window. To read about this "Keep America Beautiful" campaign, go to www.adcouncil.org and choose "Historic Campaigns" from the list on the left, and then scan down to the "Pollution: Keep America Beautiful" heading.

⬢ **Principle**
TV audiences have become very good at avoiding commercials unless the ads are intrusive or highly engaging.

Photo: Ethan Miller/Getty Images

DVR technology poses a challenge for advertisers because it enables consumers to bypass commercials.

established on home DVR systems, such as TiVo. The difference is that the skipping is being offered as a feature by Dish, which the networks say represents copyright infringement.[33]

In addition to choosing the length and time slot, a third decision determines the actual type of a television commercial in terms of whether it's a network participation, local spot, or sponsorship. Public service announcements are another type of commercial.

- *Participations* (*network*) Most commercials are sold as **participations**, where network advertisers pay for commercial time during one or more programs. The advertiser can buy any time that is available. This approach, which is the most common one used in network advertising today, provides a great deal more flexibility in market coverage, target audiences, scheduling, and budgeting. One problem that media buyers must negotiate is that the "time avails" (available time slots) for the most popular programs are often bought up by the largest advertisers or media-buying agencies, leaving fewer good time slots for small advertisers.

- *Spot Announcements (local)* The second form a television commercial can take is the **spot announcement**. Spot announcements are slots that appear in the breaks between programs, which local affiliates sell to advertisers who want to show their ads locally. Commercials are sold on a station-by-station basis to local, regional, and national advertisers. However, local buyers dominate spot television.

- *Sponsorships* In program **sponsorships**, the advertiser assumes the total financial responsibility for producing the program and providing the accompanying commercials. The *Hallmark Hall of Fame* program is an example of a sponsored program. Sponsorships represent less than 10 percent of network advertising. Sponsorship can have a powerful effect on the viewing public, especially because the advertiser can control the content and quality of the program as well as the placement and length of commercials. However, the costs of producing and sponsoring a 30- or 60-minute program make this option too expensive for most advertisers. Several advertisers can produce a program jointly as an alternative to single sponsorship. This plan is quite common with sporting events, where each sponsor receives a 15-minute segment.

- *Public Service Announcements* Public service announcements (PSAs) (PSAs) are spots created by agencies that donate their time and services on behalf of some good cause. PSAs are distributed to stations for local play based on the station's time availability. If time is available, PSAs run for free on radio and television stations. Check out the Ad Council's website (www.adcouncil.org) for a collection of these types of spots. The "Iron Eyes Cody" spot is an example of an Ad Council PSA.

● **Principle**
The television audience has become very good at avoiding commercials unless the ads are intrusive or highly engaging.

● **Principle**
Television advertising is tied to television programming, and the ad's effectiveness is determined by the popularity of the television program.

Target Audiences and Viewers   Targeting occurs by matching the programs with information about their viewership. For example, Comedy Central knows that its most important demographic is young men who see humor and comedy as essential to how they define themselves. Ralph Lauren announced for the first time that it would be a PBS television program sponsor when it signed on for the award-winning *Downton Abbey*. The Masterpiece Theater show's upscale setting and its tweedy jackets align perfectly with the Ralph Lauren brand image.[34]

Some programs are media stars and reach huge audiences. The Super Bowl is a good example. It has consistently broken records, with the 2015 Super Bowl (49) recognized as the most-watched program ever at 120.7 million viewers. Super Bowl 50 had 111.9 million TV viewers and 16.9 million tweets, and there were 27.6 million Super Bowl Tweets in 2017.[35] Other programs reach small but select audiences, such as the *NewsHour* on PBS. An overlooked television audience is the 50-plus boomer crowd. As younger viewers move to online venues, older people tend to stay loyal to their televisions, remote controls, and shows like *60 Minutes, NCIS,* and *Blue Bloods.*[36]

The Latino market is another audience group that is increasing in size and importance. Served primarily by Spanish-language programing through cable networks such as Univision, a new development is the partnership between ABC and Univision, which will create a 24-hour cable news channel that will broadcast in English. It will offer a blend of hard news and lifestyle programming along with an accompanying website.[37]

New Television Technology   New technology is having an impact on programming options as well as on distribution patterns and systems. Innovations, such as high-definition and interactive television, expand advertising opportunities.

- **High-definition television (HDTV)** HDTV is a type of television that delivers movie-quality, high-resolution images. All over-the-air stations broadcast their programming in an HDTV format. It's been a struggle, however, getting enough HDTV programming broadcast to build demand on the consumer side. As stations upgraded their equipment and moved to HDTV in 2009, the increased availability of HDTV programming made it necessary for consumers to upgrade to HDTV sets.
- **Interactive television** means you're watching your favorite program and a commercial comes on for a product that interests you. A button pops up on the screen that you can click with your remote, and you are asked questions about whether you want more information or a coupon or to give some other response. The technology requires that advertisers give their ads to a DVR service, such as TiVo, where codes are embedded. When the ad airs, the DVR boxes pick up the coding and turn on the interactive component for that subscriber. Axe used it to show young men how to use its body spray. The ad featured a motocross champion performing a motorbike stunt. While doing a backflip, the star ripped off his shirt and sprayed Axe from armpit to armpit. Viewers were then asked to go to a different channel to learn the move. Other features included videos and web pages that can be navigated by using the remote control.
- **Addressable television** allows companies to design and deliver ads to individual households based on consumers' interests, behavior, demographics, and readiness to buy. These ads arrive through Internet Protocol television (e.g., via a computer, phone, or Roku) and through set-top boxes (cable, satellite). For example, Viacom has partnered with Roku to use Roku's data to send tailored messages to custom audience segments that are viewing content on Roku devices and to better track digital viewing of its content. Addressable advertising now reaches 42 percent of homes and is expected to be in 74 percent of TV homes by 2020.[38]
- **3-D television** is coming to living rooms largely because of the popularity and innovations developed for 3-D movies. 3-D sets, as well as set-top boxes, are being tested by Japanese and Korean electronics rivals; Sony and ESPN are particularly focused on this new market.[39] British Sky Broadcasting is proposing a special 3-D television channel that will provide content for these new sets. In the United States, several Super Bowl ads have been filmed in 3-D.
- **Streaming video** is a process by which video programs—television, movies, YouTube creations, and even video games—are sent to computers and other electronic devices, such as smartphones and tablets. This practice has created a nightmare for television measurement services, which have been scrambling to estimate program viewing in these new media formats. In 2013, the ratings firm Nielsen announced that it had developed the technology to begin measuring viewership on these new broadband-enabled devices.

Out-of-Home Media

13.2 Explain the factors media planners consider when making place-based (out-of-home) media advertising decisions.

While many media have seen cutbacks and reductions in spending, out-of-home media has experienced resurgence. This is because it complements other media well (e.g., radio) and is well-suited to reach an ever-busy and on-the-go consumer marketplace.

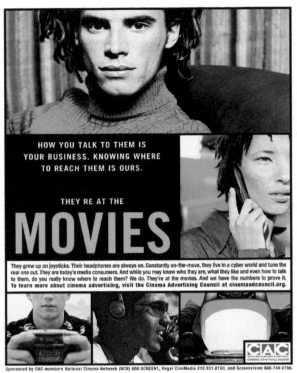

Photo: Courtesy Cinema Advertising Council

The Cinema Advertising Council is an organization devoted to advertising in movies. This ad was placed in *Advertising Age* to reach media buyers and remind them of the power of cinema advertising to target particular groups of moviegoers.

Movie Advertising

Movie theaters, particularly the large chain theaters, sell time at the beginning of their film showings for commercials, called **trailers**. Most of these trailers are previews advertising upcoming films, but some are national commercials for brands, ads for local businesses, PSAs, or other forms of sponsored programs.

Targeting is possible based on the appeal of the film, as the Cinema Advertising council argues in its "Movies" ad. Some films are for children (and their parents); others draw an audience that is heavily female; and action films, such as the *Matrix* series, draw more males. DVD, Blu-ray, Netflix, and other video distribution systems also place ads before their movies. The targeting strategy is the same as that for trailers, where the ad is matched to the film's audience.

The cost of placing a trailer is based on the number of theaters showing the spot and their estimated monthly attendance. Generally, the cost of a trailer in a first-run theater is about the same as the cost of a 30-second television spot in prime time. The reason trailers are valued by marketers is that they play to a captive audience with their attention on the screen, not reading or talking to other people. The attention level is higher for these ads than for almost any other form of commercials. But the captive audience dimension is also the biggest disadvantage of movie advertising because people resent the intrusion. They believe they paid for the ticket, so they shouldn't have to pay with their time and attention to watch commercials.

Movie giant Screenvision now offers a 20-minute preshow called *The Limelight* as a mobile app that lets viewers watch trailers, search for showtimes, and earn points toward free movie tickets and concession snacks. They can also play video games during the preshow, all of which is designed to engage viewers and create a more receptive environment for movie promotions.[40]

Video Game Advertising

Marketers and media planners have been frustrated trying to reach young people with traditional ads on mainstream media. That has led to an increased focus on unusual media that are clearly the province of young people, such as video games. Now a global multi-billion-dollar industry, the video game business is developing as a major new medium for advertisers to target 12- to 34-year-old males, although females are getting into the act as well, and the Wii U console is bringing in an older adult audience of both men and women with its sports and exercise programs. The iPad made the video game market mobile. Video games offer opportunities for advertising and also for product placement.

Marketing communication opportunities are mined both by creating online games and by placing products within games. For example, games feature paid product placements for Puma athletic shoes, Nokia mobile phones, and Skittles candies, among others. Volkswagen of America bought a placement in Sony Computer Entertainment's *Gran Turismo 3* car-racing game. Questions remain, however. For example, how are game players responding to ads in games, and when does it make sense to incorporate branded content in games? Are some brands more acceptable or appropriate than others?

A little bit of gaming history is in order. One of the first computer games, Pac-Man, was developed in 1980 and released for Atari in 1982. Adapted from an arcade game, the movement of the little round yellow big-mouth icon, which traveled a maze gobbling up cookies, was controlled with a joystick. Pac-Man had a spin-off breakfast cereal. Here's another piece of advertising trivia: in 1983, at age seven, Christian Bale of *Dark Knight* fame acted in a Pac-Man cereal commercial. You can find and watch this classic 1980s song-and-dance extravaganza on YouTube.

Outdoor:
8-Sheets
30-Sheets
Digital 30-Sheets
Bulletins
Digital Bulletins
Premiere Panels
Scaffolds
Spectaculars
Wallscapes
Street Furniture:
Bus Benches/Shelters
Phone Kiosks
Mall Displays
Newsstands/Racks
Sidewalk Displays
Urban Panels
Transit
Airport Media
Bus Media
Commuter Rail Media
Mobile Billboards
Subway Media
Truck-Side Media
Taxi
Digital Transit

Outdoor

NON-TRADITIONAL:
Place/Affinity Based
Alternative/Guerilla

Place/Affinity Based
Place Based Broadcast:
Airport TV
In-Store TV/Radio
Mall TV
Coffee Shop TV
Physician/Pharmacy TV

Affinity Based:
Bar/Restaurant Media
Cinema
C-Store Media
College Media
Day Care Center Media
Gas/Service Station Media
Golf Media
Health Club Media
In-Flight Media
In-Office Building Media
In-School Media
In-Stadium Media
In-Store Media
Leisure Media
Physician Media
Ski Media
VIP Airline Lounge Media
Wild Posters

Alternative/Guerilla
Alternative:
Aerial Media
Custom Media
Event Sponsorships
Experiential Media
Interactive Kiosks
Naming Rights
Projection Media
Sampling
Specialty Media
Sports Sponsorships
Travel Affinity
Sponsorships
New Technology

Guerilla Media:
Coffee Cups / Sleeves
Graffiti Murals
Mobile Media (e.g., Advans)
Pizza Boxes
Street Teams
Umbrellas
Deli Bags

FIGURE 13.2
Outdoor and Nontraditional Chart

SHOWCASE

Melissa Lerner, vice president at Posterscope, an out-of-home media company, developed this chart to illustrate the connections among outdoor, place-based media, and nontraditional, or alternative, media.

Source: Courtesy of Melissa Lerner

Place-Based Media

What we call **out-of-home media** or place-based media include everything from billboards to hot-air balloons. That means ads on public spaces, including buses, posters on building walls (barn roofs in the old days), telephone and shopping kiosks, painted and wrapped cars and semis, taxi signs and mobile billboards, transit shelters and rail platforms, airport and bus terminal displays, hotel and shopping mall displays, in-store merchandising signs, grocery store carts, shopping bags, public restroom walls, skywriting, in-store clocks, and aisle displays.

Even tall, highly visible grain silos have been recycled into huge Coke cans in Emporia, Kansas; a 50-foot-tall fiddle in Green Island, Iowa; and a beer can in Longmont, Colorado. And don't forget blimps and airplanes towing messages over your favorite stadium as well as inflatables that weave and wave in the wind at grand openings and other special events. Figure 13.2 is a depiction of the breadth of the outdoor and place-based media world.

Although total spending on out-of-home media is hard to determine because of the industry's diversity, this category is second only to the internet as the fastest-growing marketing communication industry. Why is it such a growth area? Out-of-home advertising's defining characteristic is that it is situational or **place-based media**: it can target specific people with specific messages at a time and place when they may be most interested. A sign at the telephone kiosk reminds you to call for reservations at your favorite restaurant, a sign on the rail platform suggests that you enjoy a candy bar while riding the train, and a bus card reminds you to listen to the news on a particular radio station. As mass media have decreased in impact, place-based forms, such as outdoor, have become more attractive to many advertisers as they try to reach a more "on the go" customer base.[41]

⬤ **Principle**
Out-of-home advertising is situational in that it targets people at specific locations.

Outdoor Advertising   Of the $9 billion spent on outdoor advertising in 2016, billboard ads accounted for approximately 60 percent; street furniture, such as signs on benches, transit ads, and alternative forms (e.g., cinema, shopping malls, wallscapes) brought in the rest. **Outdoor advertising** refers to billboards along streets and highways as well as posters in other public locations. The Outdoor Advertising Association sponsors the OBIE Awards for outstanding outdoor boards, such as those for the Cheyenne Mountain Zoo.

An advertiser uses outdoor boards for two primary reasons. First, for national advertisers, this medium can provide brand reminders to the target audience. A second use is directional; billboards are a primary medium when the board is close to or gives information about a company's location. The travel and tourism industries are major users of billboards directing travelers to hotels, restaurants, resorts, gas stations, and other services.

In terms of size and format, there are two traditional kinds of billboards, bulletins and posters, as well as digital billboards:

- The billboards you see along major highways are called bulletins, such as those for the Cheyenne Mountain Zoo. **Painted outdoor bulletins** range in size from 10 feet by 30 feet

Because of their size and graphics, billboards can make a dramatic statement, such as this OBIE Award–winning out-of-home media campaign for the Cheyenne Mountain Zoo in Colorado Springs.

Source: Outdoor Advertising Association of America

to 14 feet by 48 feet. Posters are generally about half the width of bulletins, at 10 feet by 22 feet, but can run as small as 5 feet by 11 feet. Vinyl is the material of choice for both bulletins and posters because it has a brighter appearance, UV defensive paint, and is much longer lasting than painted boards. Designers can add **extensions** to painted billboards to expand the scale and break away from the limits of the long rectangle. These embellishments are sometimes called **cutouts** because they present an irregular shape.

- *Digital and LED boards* are brightly lit plastic signs with electronic messaging. These signs come in a variety of sizes, colors, and brightness. **Digital displays** use wireless technology, which allows them to be quickly changed to reflect an advertising situation (a tire company could advertise all-weather tires during snowy conditions) or the presence of a target audience member. Melissa Lerner, vice president at Posterscope, said that "investments in digital pays off." She explained:

> Until recently, the outdoor landscape was dominated by large roadside billboards. OOH [out of home] is now experiencing a paradigm shift as static ad displays are being converted to digital units, and in the process becoming much more lucrative for media operators. For advertisers the conversion to digital, in addition to digital's lower production costs and shorter lead times, provides greater *availability*, *scalability*, and *flexibility* on content, as illustrated in Figure 13.3.

FIGURE 13.3

Melissa Lerner explains the ins and outs of using digital out-of-home media.

Digital OOH		
Availability	**Scalability**	**Flexibility**
High demand units now offer multiple faces, providing greater opportunity for advertisers seeking prime real-estate; however, this comes with a lower share of voice as total exposure decreases as the space is shared	Operators and advertisers can develop OOH networks for custom coverage, taking advantage of lower production costs and shorter lead times to optimize messaging across a custom network	Advertisers can now employ artwork in a range of formats, durations, and dayparts to optimize engagements and deployment of existing assets to reinforce impact and exposure, and drive efficiencies

Outdoor: An Effective Brand Communication Medium

James Maskulka, *Lehigh University*

In a recent campaign, the outdoor industry proclaimed, "Outdoor is not a medium. It's a large." In the contemporary view of outdoor, it is not just complementary but an integral part of a multiplatform advertising campaign and a viable alternative for establishing a brand's image, in addition to building brand awareness. Here are some tips on how to plan for and use outdoor advertising for maximum effectiveness.

1. *Frequency of Exposure* The successful execution of a transformational advertising strategy to build brand image requires frequent exposure over an extended time period—a primary benefit of outdoor.

2. *Brand Image Touch-Up* "Great brands may live forever," according to famous adman Leo Burnett, but even great brands may need image updating. This is the area where outdoor may have its greatest relevance to branding. Shifting a brand's image in response to changing consumer lifestyles guarantees that the brand remains relevant. The dynamic imagery of outdoor is an important tool in brand touch-ups.

3. *The Power of the Visual* Certain brand advertisers, such as those handling fashion and food, use visually driven creative as the brand's raison d'être. The campaigns must have consistent production values

from market to market, a benefit offered by national outdoor campaigns.

4. *A Friend in the Neighborhood* Rather than building a brand on attributes and differentiation, brands with strong philosophies and attitudes build on relationships with consumers. Outdoor delivers consistent exposure of brand personality cues to targeted customers who relate to the brand.

5. *Brand Image Buildup* The 30-day posting period is long enough so that these exposures can be seen as repositories of long-term brand image leading to favorable consumer attitude accumulation. It's like making a deposit in a bank and watching your wealth grow.

6. *Speaking the Language of Consumers* Brands increasingly serve as a form of consumer communication shorthand. The compact information of outdoor advertising matches consumers' limited processing time. To illustrate, a billboard combined with a vinyl-wrapped car and reinforced by a transit ad or a taxi poster reaches the time-starved consumer with much less investment in personal processing time.

7. *Clarity of Focus* Usually, the shorter the outdoor ad copy, the more effective the message. The outdoor message imposes a creative and disciplined brand communication lexicon that ensures ongoing reinforcement of the brand message.

8. *A Gigantic Canvas* Successful outdoor advertisers see billboards as "a gigantic canvas" on which the brand advertiser can create "mega art"[42] that links the brand with relevant icons and symbols. Some of the most important slogans and images in advertising have been captured on billboards.

Sources: Adapted from "Outdoor Advertising: The Brand Communication Medium," Outdoor Advertising Association of America special report, November 1999, www.oaa.org; Herbert Graf, "Outdoor as the Segue between Mass and Class," *Brandweek*, July 20, 1999, 19.

The key to the Digital Network is moving beyond a static single message or animated message rotated among others to developing a true communication channel, controlling the content (owned, earned, and paid), its distribution, and consequently the depth and breadth of audience connection.

Advertisers can purchase any number of units (75, 50, or 25 showings daily are common quantities). Boards are usually rented for 30-day periods, with longer periods possible. Bulletins are bought on an individual basis, usually for one, two, or three years.

The cost of outdoor advertising is based on the percent of population in a specified geographical area exposed to the ad in one day. It is typically based on a traffic count—that is, the number of vehicles passing a particular location during a specified period of time, called a **showing**. If an advertiser purchases a "100 showing," the basic standard unit is the number of poster boards in each market that will expose the message to 100 percent of the market population every day. If three posters in a community of 100,000 people achieve a daily exposure to 75,000 people, the result is a 75 showing. Conversely, in a small town with a population of 1,200 and one main street, one board may produce a 100 showing. As you can see, the number of boards required for a 100 showing varies with the size of the city.

Because of the very short time consumers are normally exposed to a traditional billboard message (typically, three to five seconds), the message must be short and the visual must be very attention getting. No more than 8 to 10 words is the norm. The Practical Tips feature identifies key features of outdoor media and provides suggestions on how to design effective attention-getting messages for this "gigantic canvas."

New and Novel Forms Innovation is important for the out-of-home industry, with some boards now equipped to run mini-movies and ads electronically. Another example of media convergence with video appearing as OOH media is the job search company Monster.com, which has been successful with trailers that replay as electronic signboard messages in public spaces. Some digitally enhanced outdoor boards can be hooked up to the web. Lerner explained, "At Out-of-Home communication agencies, we often plan new media concepts and generate exciting PR and buzz. Creative thinking is necessary to brainstorm and plan 'never-been-done before' campaigns."

In the Philippines, a green growing plant billboard has been created that protects the environment as it displays simple brand images, such as the iconic shape of a Coke bottle.[43] Another experiment in New York City's Herald Square used an electromagnetic dot display, a modern version of the old train station signs that flipped over to announce changes. This real-time display changes based on movements of passersby. If you jump, your dot matrix reflection will also jump.[44]

Another example of an unusual billboard with immense attention-getting power featured two live players on wires playing a game of (vertical) soccer in the Adidas "Football Challenge" outdoor board that captivated audiences in Japan. Imodium had another unique billboard, shown here.

Unique Uses for Billboards and Posters Posters may appear on the sides of buildings, construction sites, and even vehicles. In London, daily hand-lettered posters have been used for centuries to announce newspaper headlines. The walls of the subway, or Tube, stations in London are lined with posters advertising all kinds of products but particularly theater shows. The iPod was launched in London (and other places) with walls of posters that Tube riders encountered coming up or down the escalators. The walls were papered with the distinctive silhouetted images against neon backgrounds. The repetition of the images created a strong billboarding effect.

Photo: Work performed by DDB Latina Puerto Rico for Johnson & Johnson Puerto Rico. Chief Creative Director: Enrique Renta; Creative Director: Leslie Robles; Sr. Art Director: Luis Figueroa. Used with permission.

Imodium found a novel way to make use of the creative potential of outdoor advertising

Empty storefronts in prime downtown locations and major thoroughfares have become the latest venue for posting posters. With their large expanse of window space, abandoned retail stores became a frugal way to deliver a big message during the recession. Landlords may charge as little as $500 a month, in comparison to comparable spots on a billboard that might cost $50,000.[45]

Mobile billboards appear where their target audience is likely to be, such as at a large outdoor event. Because they are less common, the ads tend to be more memorable. 3-D billboards often contain unusual artistry that helps capture the attention and interest of passersby. Chick-fil-A's use of 3-D cows on billboards is a good example of this tactic. Special structures called **kiosks** are designed for public posting of notices and posters. Kiosks are typically located in places where people walk, such as a many-sided structure in a mall or near a public walkway, or where people wait. The location has a lot to do with the design of the message. Some OOH media serve the same function as the kiosk, such as the ad-carrying bus shelter.

Transit Advertising   Transit advertising is mainly an urban mass advertising form that places ads on vehicles such as buses and taxis that circulate through the community as moving billboards. Transit advertising also includes the posters seen in bus shelters and train, airport, and subway stations. Most of these posters must be designed for quick impressions, although people who are waiting on subway platforms or bus shelters often study these posters, so here they can present a more involved or complicated message than a billboard can. More recently, these walls have become the site for large-scale interactive digital advertising, such as the display along 60 feet of a corridor at New York's Columbus Circle station.

Another type of transit advertising is naming rights; by that, we mean that stations, for a fee, may carry the designation of a nearby business, such as Times Square Station at 42nd Street in New York, which refers to the *New York Times*. More recently, Barclays Center was added to the name of the Atlantic Avenue station in Brooklyn, which advertises both the new arena a block away and the giant international financial services company.[46]

There are two types of transit advertising: interior and exterior. **Interior transit advertising** is seen by people riding inside buses, subway cars, and taxis. These are primarily posters or car cards, sometimes with coupons or other forms of tear-off information that can be taken away. They can be designed like outdoor boards with simple messages, but because the riders are largely a captive audience, interior posters often carry more complex messages.

Exterior transit advertising is mounted on the side, rear, and top exteriors of these vehicles so that pedestrians and people in nearby cars see it. Even windows can be covered with see-through silk-screen images that carry commercial messages. Wraps started in 1993, when PepsiCo paid Seattle in return for permission to wrap six city buses with its logo.

Exterior transit advertising is reminder advertising; it is a frequency medium that lets advertisers get their names in front of a local audience who drive a regular route at critical times such as rush hour. *Painted vehicles* make up another type of transit advertising. More recently, drivers have been tempted to sign up to have their cars and trucks wrapped with ads. Some of them use striking graphics, such as the brand-image designs on the sides of many trucks, both long haul and delivery.

Event Advertising and Sponsorships
Ads at events are another type of OOH media. Think about the panels of ads in most stadiums: some are electronic, but many are printed posters. Ads also appear all over cars at races as well as on their

Photo: New York City/Alamy Stock Photo

This effect, which surrounds the entire car in a brand message for Tropicana, is called a train or bus wrap. Wraps can be used for either interior or exterior advertising.

driver's outfits. Companies pay huge fees as sponsors to get their logos in prominent positions. We discussed events and sponsorships in more detail in Chapter 4.

Online Advertising

13.3 Explain how online advertising works.

Internet advertising can be delivered to a website as a traditional display ad, just like those you see in a magazine, or it can be presented in a number of other formats, such as banner ads across the top or bottom of a web page. Spending on online advertising ($75 billion) has overtaken TV ad spending. Mobile ads are expected to receive over half of online spending dollars, and mobile video will be the fastest growing category.[47]

The greatest percentage of internet advertising is spent on large, established sites that operate as electronic publishers, such as www.nytimes.com, www.wsj.com, and www.espn.com, as well as on paid search, such as Google AdWords and Yahoo!'s Bing network. These media and search organizations have established reputations, and they know how to sell advertising, so they have been pioneers in the development of paid search.

Mobile is no longer a trend. It's now an integral part of everyday life for millions of consumers worldwide, and no other device is so ingrained in consumer behavior. On average, people in the United States spend three hours a day on their mobile devices.[48] With more than a billion users, Facebook has a lot of viewers whom advertisers would like to reach. The Facebook philosophy, however, seeks to protect its user experience of friends and conversations. To be true to its mission, it prizes subtle advertising and advocates using such ad forms as *sponsored stories* that look like Facebook posts. This philosophy tends to create tension with big advertisers as well as criticism.

The problem is that advertisers like General Motors would like a bigger presence on Facebook pages, and that, as well as the inability to prove advertising effectiveness, has been a big factor in marketer and investor reluctance to promote Facebook as an advertising platform. In response to the effectiveness issue, Facebook suggests measurement should focus not on "clicks," but rather on brand advertising image and relationship building.[49]

To capture more advertising dollars heading to mobile platforms, Facebook has been beefing up its "Audience Network," which lets marketers buy ads across the internet using Facebook's data. The company achieved sales in 2016 on its Audience Network of $1 billion (Facebook's total advertising revenue in 2015 was more than $17 billion).[50]

Google has been the most successful search engine at attracting advertising, even during the recession, leading in search engine advertising, display advertising, and mobile advertising.[51]

THE INSIDE STORY

Indian Villagers Advertise on Mobile Phones

Elisabeth Loeck, *University of Nebraska–Lincoln*

People in the remote Rampur-Mathura, India, village are using mobile phones to learn news about their community. Now local businesses are starting to use the network for advertising.

In the 20-kilometer radius that the news service reaches, Sunil Saxena, the program's founder, said that most people do not have access to television and cannot read newspapers. Mobile phones are the first device they can use to actually communicate information in a language they can understand. The trick will be figuring out how to make the service pay for itself. Advertising may be an answer.

Two reporters file audio stories from the community, which are distributed to 250 subscribers via their mobile phones. It costs 20,000 rupees a month to transmit the stories, but subscribers pay just 10 rupees a month for the service.

The network began running advertisements from local businesses in March 2010. In July, it began to charge 20 rupees a month for the exposure.

Kismet Ali and Lallan Idrieshia, mobile phone merchants in the village, used the network to advertise and saw an increase of 50 new customers from the exposure.

Saxena believes that their experiment with advertising proves that local businesses can be persuaded to use mobile phones as an advertising medium. If they can attract enough subscribers, they may in turn attract enough advertisers to support the network.

Note: In the summer of 2012, journalism and advertising students from the University of Nebraska–Lincoln traveled to India. Many had never traveled abroad before, and all came from different social and economic backgrounds. The project's goal was to tell stories about life in these rural villages of India.

Source: Courtesy of Elisabeth Loeck

Google also dominates the search ad industry and sells display ads, along with search ads, for thousands of sites. Google and Yahoo! bring in about $88 in revenue per person for their search engine users, whereas Facebook only makes about $15 per user, which helps explain Facebook's difficulty selling itself as an advertising medium.[52]

Digital media have benefited from innovations in interactivity that we call **rich media**, which means that viewers are able to participate in the ads or manipulate them by clicking or rolling over parts of the image. Viewers can also download streaming video or brand-related apps. Tablets, particularly the iPad, have taken advantage of the rich-media technology.

Although online advertising continues to be a hot topic at industry seminars, there are some critics who question its effectiveness. Michael Wolff, who blogs on Technology Review, says that people's behavior on the web and how they interact with advertising is different from traditional media. He charges that "the character of those ads themselves and their inability to command real attention has meant a marked decline in advertising's impact."[53]

Website Advertising

Small ads on other web pages that lure visitors to switch pages are called **banner ads**. Visitors can click on them to move to the advertised website, such as the one featured here in a series of animated banner ads for Zippo lighters. Banner ads are easy to create and are usually placed on a website featuring complementary products or related topics.

Display ads, like those in print, are larger than banners and include text and images in their designs. The design of other forms of display internet advertising is constantly changing as the industry advances. Some common, as well as novel, formats are the following:

- **Skyscrapers** are the extra-long, skinny ads running down the right or left side of a website. The financial site CBSMarketWatch.com, for instance, regularly runs this kind of ad. Response rates for skyscrapers, which began to be used aggressively by more companies in the early part of the twenty-first century, can be 10 times higher than for traditional banner ads.

- **Pop-ups** and **pop-behinds** burst open on the computer screen either in front of or behind the opening page of the website. Companies like Volvo and GlaxoSmith-Kline use these forms to present games and product information. However, they are seen as intrusive and annoying, so some internet advertisers have moved away from this format, and some computer software programs block them.

- **Micro-sites** or **mini-sites** are small websites that are the offspring of a parent website, such as the TDI Diesel site on the corporate VW site. For marketing purposes, the microsite may cover particular products, campaigns, events, or promotions. Micro-sites tend to be more tightly focused than their parent sites and may be transitory because the reason for the site might have a time frame and expire. Another variation allows advertisers to market their products on other branded websites without sending people away from the site they're visiting. General Motors, for example, has used a mini-site on the Shell Oil site that a viewer can access and enlarge later. This type of advertising generally gets a higher click rate than banners or display ads; the portal About.com estimates that 5 percent of the people who see the sites click on them.

Photo: Courtesy Zippo Manufacturing Company. Used with permission.

This series of banners for the Zippo lighter develops a message as the banners unfold. The message is a takeoff on the blackouts urban areas sometimes experience in the summer when electrical use is high. Do you think this series of banners would entice people to check out the Zippo website?

Online display advertising comes in many shapes and sizes.

Source: Courtesy MonetizePros. Used with permission.

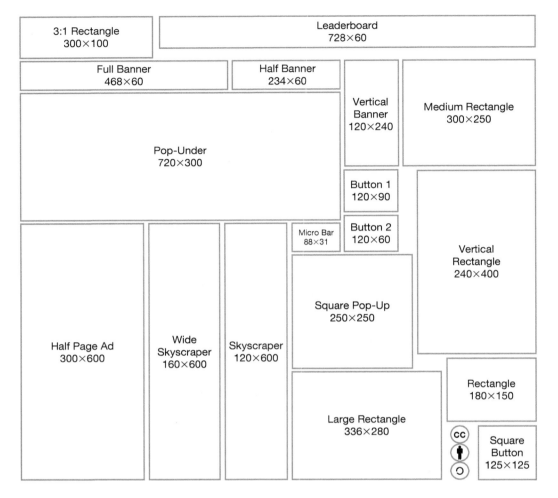

- **Superstitials** are thought of as the "internet's commercial" and are designed to work like television ads. When you go from one page on a website to another, a 20-second animation appears in a window.
- **Widgets** are tiny computer programs that allow people to create and insert professional-looking content into their personal websites and also onto their television screens. They include news notes, calculators, weather feeds, stock tickers, clocks, book or music covers, or other web gadgets that can be a brand-name promotional offer. It's a way to get a non-intrusive brand reminder ad on the desktop, website, or blog. Widgets also refer to mini-applications that pull content from some other place on the web and add it to your site. In addition to getting onto cell phone screens and social media pages, they also can monitor

The design of apps and products is increasingly using the UX process to develop useful interfaces.

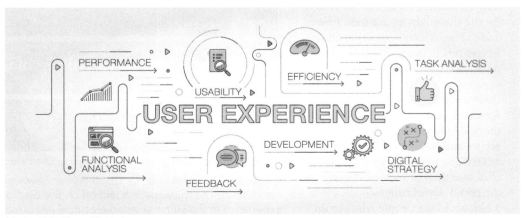

Photo: Enis Aksoy/Getty Images

contacts when someone clicks on the feature. Most recently, Yahoo! has created television widgets that allow access to content from new televisions by pushing a remote control button. The founder of Widgetbox.com classifies widgets as (1) self-expression tools (photos, clips, and games), (2) revenue generators on blogs (eBay categories and favorite DVDs or CDs from Amazon.com), and (3) site enhancement devices (news updates and discussion forums). A fourth type is a marketing communication message.

Designers of online ads, mobile apps, and products are increasingly turning to the processes and principles of User experience design (UX) and User interface design (UI) in order to maximize usefulness and accessibility to consumers, and to improve product websites so that visitors stay longer. The UX process originated in the field of ergonomics and focuses on the entire customer experience with a product or ad, and, as the figure shows, often includes field research, functional analysis, usability, and learning from customer testing and feedback. The UI process focuses on the look, feel, and layout of the ad or product interface and enhancing its attractiveness and interactivity with consumers. As the "Internet of Things" continues to expand into more areas of our lives, the interfaces we see on products, apps, and online ads are gradually converging, offering more human-centered, attractive, and intuitive designs wherever we go.

Photo: Pokki/Getty Images

The UI process focuses on designing an attractive look, feel, and layout of an ad or product interface.

While UX and UI help advertisers design good ad and website interfaces, their attractiveness can be further improved by using animation, games and contests, interviews with celebrities, or musical performances. Originally, Internet ads were jazzed up using relatively simple animation techniques to make elements move. New technologies provide even more active components. Research generally finds that the click-through rate nearly doubles when motion and an interactive element are added to a banner ad—and that's true for display ads as well.

Principle
The click-through rate nearly doubles when motion and an interactive element are added to a banner ad or to any form of online advertising.

Click-Throughs The measure of the success of an online ad or banner is the number of times viewers click on the link to check out the advertiser or the message. These clicks usually take viewers to the website of the advertiser or to some other special interesting feature.

Although online display ads were very popular when they first appeared and continue to be a major part of online advertising, across all ad formats and placements the **click-through** rate is 0.17 percent, which is less than 2 clicks per 1,000 impressions. The highest click-through rates occur in the technology, travel, and hospitality industries (average of 5 percent), and for these industries click-through is higher on smartphones than desktop computers.[54]

The difference in click-through response lies in the creativity and attention-getting power of the banner ad and where it is placed. The more related and relevant a site is to the brand, the more likely it will generate a higher level of click-throughs. Entertainment helps, too. For a collection of funny banners, check out www.valleyofthegeeks.com and notice the banner ads at the top of that site.

Principle
The more relevant a website is to the brand and the consumer, the more likely an ad will generate a higher level of click-throughs.

Pay-per-click is a type of online advertising that is driven by consumer search. The advertiser pays when a viewer clicks on an accompanying ad that takes them to the advertiser's site. Similar to search advertising, pay-per-click relies on key words that relate to a brand or product and bring the person searching to the product website. Each time a person clicks on your ad, you pay the negotiated click-through price.[55]

Online Video Ads Website visitors or viewers watching video downloads also confront a variety of online video ads. Because there are some 30 formats available, advertisers who want to use video are struggling to find the best platform for their ads. The most common are in a *preroll* format, which forces viewers to watch a video ad before viewing video clips. Other formats include interactive video ads that drop down over the screen and allow viewers to click for more information and videos that allow viewers to click on hot spots or buttons within the video to learn more about a product.

The lack of standardization means that agencies have higher production costs as they try to adapt to different delivery systems. A recent study led by the giant Paris-based agency Publicis with Microsoft, Yahoo!, CBS, and Hulu, the website portal for streaming television programming, as partners tested a number of these formats and concluded that the best way to deliver video ads is through an *ad selector*, a feature that offers a group of ads and invites viewers to choose one. The test found that consumers are more likely to watch and remember video ads if they are able to pick the ones they watch.[56]

Online Classified Ads A small part of the online advertising world is classified advertising, whether through local media websites or Craigslist. Classifieds are still used by local advertisers and organizations in newspapers but even more so on online sites. Previously the golden goose for local newspapers, the move to online "want ads" has been a big reason local newspapers are in trouble financially. Craigslist is a community exchange for people who either want to sell something or are looking for something. Its business model is to operate as a public service. It doesn't accept advertising but does charge for real estate listings and open-job postings.

Craigslist does have a problem with spammers who have automated the mass posting of ads, which has caused grief for customers and led to lawsuits by Craigslist. This included lawsuits against companies such as RadPad, who harvested content from Craigslist's site (a practice called "scraping") and sent unsolicited commercial emails to Craigslist users. Craigslist won a $60 million judgment against RadPad in 2017.[57] Other legal issues have surrounded its adult category, which carries explicit sexual service ads.[58]

Search Advertising

We introduced the concept of Seekers in Chapter 7. They become a potent force in marketing because they go online to search for information. People do hundreds of millions of searches a day on their computers, smartphones, tablets, and other electronic devices. Estimates for the percentage of internet advertising that goes to sites connected with search advertising range from 50 to 80 percent, which indicates how important the search function is for consumers and the marketers who are trying to reach them.[59]

The reason the consumer search function is so important is that it provides the marketer with an opportunity to position a brand message adjoining the list of sites (articles, blogs, and *Wikipedia* entries) that is compiled in response to a **key word** by search engines. This practice is called **search advertising** or **search marketing**.

Search providers, such as Google, MSN, Bing, and Yahoo!, auction off positions that let advertisers' ads be seen next to specific search results. Google AdWords is the leading platform available for search advertising, supplying most of Google's revenue each year. It functions on a "pay per click" basis; that is, advertisers only pay when their ad is clicked and the user is connected to their website. A benefit of online consumer searches is that they leave a trail of clues about products, features, and advertising approaches. This behavior can be mined for insights that lead to new products. To explore how this works, search the term "AdWords," and you will find dozens of sites by experts who help businesses construct their search marketing campaigns.

With a credit card and a few minutes, a small business owner can set up a link between his or her brand and a key word or key terms, such as "chocolate éclairs" or "real estate staging." It's the ultimate in brand linkage and interest association. Because consumers initiate the search,

⬢ Principle
Search marketing is important because it allows ads to be positioned on sites that are associated with keywords, which are topics of interest to the consumer doing the search. It is the ultimate in brand linkage and interest association.

the adjoining ads are not perceived to be as intrusive as other forms of advertising. In 2013, the Federal Trade Commission expressed concern that search engines would often bring up content that might not be identified as paid advertisements and laid out guidelines to help visitors more clearly distinguish ads from other types of information.

One development is Google's foray into *real-time search*, which not only produces the usual search results, but also lets Google supplement the results with updates posted each second on social media, such as Facebook and Twitter.[60] This mix of search and social media will only increase the speed with which brand messages spread and will challenge the ability of companies to monitor their brands' online presence.

The practice of maximizing the link between topics and brand-related websites is called **search optimization**. Companies try to affect their search engine rankings to drive more traffic to their websites. To have maximum visibility, they want their ads to appear as close to the top of the list as possible. An important first step for marketers in creating a viable website is getting it registered with popular search engines so that it shows up early on the list provided by the search engine.

Another type of consumer search using smartphones is based on a **quick-response (QR) code**, which is a type of two-dimensional bar code that uses a scannable matrix design of square dots. You see these and another version, "Snapcodes," in ads and articles, on packages, and the sides of buildings—even as a design in a corn maze (Chapter 12)—and anywhere a company wants to post this code as a scannable link to its website or Snapchat. It's one more way consumers can search for information using their mobile phones.

Online Advertising Sales

Selling online advertising space is complicated. Major sites, such as MSNBC.com and History.com, sell ads on their pages and charge premium prices because they are on high-traffic sites. Such ads can cost from $10 to $50 per thousand viewings, depending on the visibility of the position.[61] Advertisers and their media buyers get access to internet sites through providers such as DoubleClick, an internet advertising service owned by Google that places more than 100 billion online ads per month. DoubleClick provides reports on the placement and performance of these ads to both publishers and advertisers and also helps create ads and widgets. DoubleClick emphasizes the importance of building a web presence that is optimized for mobile, reporting that advertisers can double their mobile ad revenue if their mobile sites load in 5 seconds versus 19 seconds and that more than half of mobile site visits are abandoned if they take longer than 3 seconds to load.[62]

Middlemen companies act as brokers for online ad space that they aggregate across different sites and package as single buys, in effect setting up an ad network. These ad networkers offer less well designed sites and positions and may sell space for less than a dollar per thousand viewers. They are criticized for flooding the internet with cheap and sometimes tacky ads. Data-mining companies like Oracle's BlueKai and Nielsen's eXelate collect data on how visitors move around among sites and then sell access to advertising on groups of sites that attract similar visitors. This practice is similar to how local newspaper advertising can be purchased through group contracts and makes buying much more efficient.[63]

Google, Microsoft, and AOL have gotten into the ad sales business by setting up ad exchanges that allow advertisers to bid directly on available ad space on large groups of websites. In effect, they are cutting out the middlemen. Other big websites, such as ESPN, Turner Broadcasting, and *Forbes* magazine, have stopped doing business with the ad networks so as to gain better control over the quality of the content on their sites. The Online Publishers Association, which represents major publishers of web content, reported on a study that found that ads on portals, as well as ads bought from ad brokers, were significantly less effective than the ads that the premium sites offer. The idea is that the portals and ad networkers' ads may be cheaper, but they appear in formats that are less interesting and thus are less likely to connect with visitors.[64]

Digital Issues for Traditional Media

Print media as well as broadcast media have been struggling with competition from online media as well as decisions on how to support online versions of their own publications, particularly because tablets have made online print versions much more readable. Some newspapers and magazines have "bundled" subscriptions that include print, digital, and apps for smartphones and tablets. Others offer separate subscription rates for print, digital, or app packages.

In the realm of television, more and more cable customers are "cord-cutting," or moving away from television services that require a fixed contract and buying on-demand options instead. These on-demand options are called over-the-top content, which refers to audio, video, and other media content delivered over the internet without the involvement of a traditional provider such as cable or satellite TV. In pursuit of improved selection and lower costs, 385,000 people decided to cancel their standard TV packages in 2015 alone. This change explains the solid growth of streaming services such as Netflix (80 million subscribers), Hulu (12 million), CBS All Access (2 million), Showtime Anytime (2 million), and HBO Now (800,000).[65]

TV manufacturers have been involved in these trends as well. Samsung introduced an internet-connected TV that forces consumers to see display ads on its app menu screen if they want to use the sets' smart-TV features. Consumers must disconnect their TVs from the internet if they wish to avoid the ads, meaning that they won't be able to use streaming providers such as Netflix, Hulu, or Amazon Prime. Viewers have not been happy. On Reddit, home theater enthusiast said, "Free service plus ads, or paid service plus no ads—pick one, Samsung." Another user wrote, "Ads are a large reason why I ditched cable, the viewing experience wasn't worth the money with one-third of the broadcast time filled with ads."[66]

Looking Ahead

This chapter has provided an overview of paid advertising in traditional as well as new media. In truth, though, traditional media hardly exist anymore. An interview on public radio's NPR headlined "In a 24/7 World, What Is a Magazine?" began with this line: "It's hard to know what a magazine is these days." Is it paper? Is it a website? Martin Sorrell, head of WPP, the world's largest communication company (125 firms including Ogilvy & Mather and JWT advertising agencies), asked, "How do you define a newspaper or a magazine?" He observed, "I doubt free-to-air television or, in particular, newspapers and magazines, will ever be the same again."[67] That is one of the key points of change that Kelley pointed out in the Part 4 opener. He observed that all media, including the traditional ones, will have some type of digital and interactive component, and that will only make media selection more challenging.

Not only are these traditional media formats changing, but so are the ads that appear in them. CBS promoted its fall season with ads in the magazine *Entertainment Weekly* that contained video clips of its new programs. Similar to musical greeting cards, the technology used a flexible, thin plastic screen that was activated when the two-page ad was opened. The videos also included a Pepsi Max ad inside the CBS ad. An executive at Time Warner, publisher of *EW*, observed, "If we can efficiently put video into magazines, think about the possibilities it would open up."[68]

So let's move on to the exciting and equally fast-changing world of digital media, which are generating even more new opportunities for marketing communication. Chapter 14 will review the dynamic world of owned and earned media with its strong communication formats.

Aflac's Flap Ducks Disaster

He might not have a vocabulary beyond the word he knows best, "Aflac," but the duck has a voice that is essential to the brand awareness. The Kaplan Thaler Group succeeded in creating a campaign that led to a 94 percent awareness of Aflac and an increase of 55 percent in US sales during the first three years of the campaign, followed by double-digit growth in the following years. This campaign earned two gold Effie Awards for the duck who successfully communicated the brand personality as well as the honor of being voted one of the best-known brand icons.

When the duck's voice was silenced, the company and agency moved with lightning speed to restore it with a multiplatform communication effort, asking America to "answer the duck's call" at the aptly named Quackaflac.com website or the audition sites in six cities.

Aflac posted the job on Monster.com. When an existing media buy could not be canceled, Aflac ran a modified 2006 Aflac TV spot, "Silent Movie," featuring a silent duck that drove viewers to the Facebook page for more information and a chance to see a "Search for My Voice" video.

Finding this a golden-egg opportunity, the effort became news on CNN and CBS; in *Fortune*, *Newsweek*, and the *New York Times*; and on late-night entertainment shows, including Leno, Fallon, and Letterman. The search generated more than 70,000 media stories and 900 million media impressions. The efforts doubled positive brand and character social sentiment in six weeks, according to the agency.

Not only did the campaign create positive news for Aflac, but it also appears to have influenced sales. At the peak of the campaign, direct sales leads increased 80 percent. In the words of CNN's Wolf Blitzer, Aflac was able to "turn a gaffe into a gift."

And one lucky duck, Dan McKeague, was plucked from obscurity to be the winner of the *American Idol* of the insurance industry and arguably the world's most famous quacker.

Logo: American Family Life Assurance Company of Columbus (AFLAC)

KEY OBJECTIVES SUMMARY

13.1. **Describe how marketers make effective decisions about advertising in published media, such as newspapers and magazines.** Newspapers are great for announcements of news. They also provide local market coverage with some geographic flexibility plus an interaction with national news and the ability to reach shoppers who see the paper as a credible source. Magazines reach special-interest audiences who have a high level of receptivity to the message. People read them slowly, and they have long life and great image reproduction. However, magazines require long lead times, have a low level of immediacy and limited flexibility, and generally do not reach a broad mass market.

13.2. **Explain the factors media planners consider when making place-based (out-of-home) media advertising decisions.** Out-of-home media include everything from billboards to hot-air balloons. A common out-of-home medium is outdoor advertising, which refers to billboards along streets and highways as well as posters. Outdoor is a high-impact and directional medium; it's also effective for brand reminders and relatively inexpensive with a long life. Other forms of out-of-home media include on-premise signs, posters, and transit advertising. Movie theaters sell time for advertisements before their films. Marketing communication messages are also carried on discs, such as DVDs and Blu-ray, as well as in lobbies and other public spaces. Video games, whether played on dedicated consoles or computers or downloaded for small screens, such as smartphones, can carry advertising. Usually, the ads appear as banners at the top or bottom of the opening screen.

13.3. **Explain how online advertising works.** Online ads can be display ads, similar to those in print, or they can be banners across the top or bottom or on the sides. They can all be animated, and display ads can also include videos. Online classified ads have also become a big business. Search advertising means that ads appear on sites that appear when a user searches for a topic using a key word. Because this advertising is directed by consumer searches, it can be highly targeted to consumers' interests.

KEY TERMS

MyLab Marketing

Go to **www.pearson.com/mylab/marketing** for MyLab discussion questions (⭐) as well as the following assisted-graded writing questions.

13-1. A new radio station is moving into your community. Management is not sure how to position the station in this market and has asked you to develop a study to help make this decision. What key research questions must be asked, and what research methods would you recommend using to get more information about this market and the new station's place in it?

13-2. Describe search advertising and explain why it is becoming so important to marketers. What is a key word, and how does it function in search advertising?

REVIEW QUESTIONS

13-3. Explain how newspapers vary based on frequency of publication, format and size, and circulation.

13-4. Explain how newspaper readership is determined and measured and how readership differs from circulation.

⭐ **13-5.** What are the advantages of magazine advertising?

13-6. What is the greatest advantage of outdoor advertising? Of directory advertising?

13-7. How can radio be used most effectively, and what are the advantages and limitations of advertising on radio?

13-8. How can television be used most effectively, and what are the advantages and limitations of advertising on television?

13-9. What are trailers, and how are they used as an advertising form?

13-10. How can movie advertising be used most effectively, and what are its advantages and limitations?

13-11. What is a website, and how does it differ from other forms of advertising?

⭐ **13-12.** Define and describe a banner ad. Some experts say the effectiveness of banner ads is declining. Why would that be?

DISCUSSION QUESTIONS

13-13. You are the media planner for an agency handling a small chain of upscale furniture outlets in a medium-sized metro market that concentrates most of its advertising in the Sunday supplement of the local newspaper. The client also schedules display ads in the daily editions for special sales. Six months ago a new, high-style metropolitan lifestyle magazine approached you about advertising for your client. You deferred a decision by saying you'd see what reader acceptance would be. Now the magazine has shown some steady increases. If you were to include the magazine on the ad schedule, you'd have to reduce the newspaper advertising somewhat. What would be your recommendation to the furniture store owner?

13-14. You are a sales rep working for a college newspaper that has an online version. How would you attract advertising? One of your colleagues says there is no market for online advertising for the paper, but you think the paper is missing an opportunity. Consider the following questions in deciding whether online advertising for the paper makes sense. What companies would you recommend to contact? How can internet sites like your online newspaper entice companies to advertise on them? What competitive advantage, if any, would web advertising for your paper provide?

13-15. You are a major agency media director who has just finished a presentation to a prospective client in convenience food marketing where you recommend increasing the use of local radio and television advertising in spot markets. During the question-and-answer period, a client representative says, "We know that network television viewers' loyalty is nothing like it was 10 or even five years ago because so many people now turn to cable, DVRs, and the web. There are smaller audiences per program each year, yet television time costs continue to rise. Do you still believe we should consider commercial television as a primary medium for our company's advertising?" Another member of the client team questions whether broadcast is effective given the clutter on both radio and television with long commercial pods. "Why shouldn't we decrease our use of broadcast advertising?" How would you answer? Develop an argument either in support of increasing or decreasing the use of broadcast advertising for this client.

TAKE-HOME PROJECTS

13-16. *Portfolio Project:* You have been asked by the director of your school's student union to make a chart of all the traditional media serving your market to use in promoting the center's 50th-anniversary events. Develop a profile for each medium giving the key characteristics, such as type of programming (for broadcast), the type of audience reached, the products commonly advertised, and the appropriateness of this medium as an advertising vehicle for the center's special celebration. At the end of your media analysis, identify the top three that you would recommend and explain why.

13-17. *Mini-Case Analysis:* Aflac has been an award-winning campaign for years. How important do you think the "voice of the brand" is? Why not have multiple quacking ducks? Explain how its media use has contributed to its success. In particular, describe how the media mix has evolved. If you were a member of the team planning the next year's campaign, what other media might be useful?

TRACE North America Case

Multicultural Advertising Media

Read the TRACE case in the Appendix before coming to class.

13-18. In what ways do traditional advertising media contribute to the "Hard to Explain, Easy to Experience" campaign? Why?

13-19. How can online advertising be used in support of this campaign?

14

Owned, Interactive, and Earned Media

KEY OBJECTIVES

14.1 Explain what is meant by owned media that organizations control and manage.

14.2 Describe interactive owned media and explain why that interactive element is important.

14.3 Discuss what is meant by earned media and how organizations relate to brand discussions that are beyond their control.

14.4 Explain how multiplatform brand communication works and why it is important.

In this chapter, we'll review a wide variety of media forms and organize them into three categories: owned, interactive, and earned. Owned media are created and controlled by the organization. Interactive owned media include two forms: (1) media programs designed by the organization to unlock two-way communication between the brand and consumers and (2) social media, such as Facebook and Twitter.

The third category is called earned media. Historically, this category has been a public relations concept and refers to mentions in the news media. In this day of digital media, however, the concept of earned mentions has been expanded to include comments in social media. We'll talk about social media both as a type of interactive owned corporate medium in the sense that a company can have a Facebook page that creates a profile for a brand, similar to any user, and as an interactive earned medium where users engage in conversations that can be monitored for brand mentions.

IT'S A WINNER

Title	Client	Agency	Awards
"Survival Billboard"	Microsoft Xbox	McCann London	*One of the most-awarded campaigns of 2015, receiving several Cannes Lion Awards (5 Gold, 9 Silver, 6 Bronze); 6 Clio Awards; Clio Art Grand Prix; an Andy Award from The Advertising Club of New York; a London International Advertising Award; 9 Creative Circle Awards; 6 One Show Awards (including Best in Discipline); 2 Webby Awards; the AICP Next Awards 2016 Experiential top prize; a Yellow Pencil at D&AD Awards, 2016; and the Out of Home Grand Prize at New York Festival 2016*

Engaging Endurance

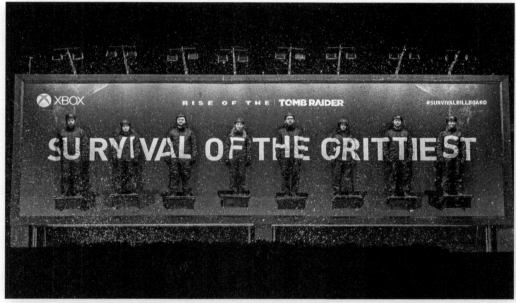

Photo: Courtesy McCann London

To help promote Microsoft Xbox's release of the latest game in the *Tomb Raider* series, eight contestants stepped up to survive 24 hours outdoors on a London billboard in November while extreme weather conditions were simulated and selected via real-time public voting. It was named "Survival of the Grittiest," and it became a gripping reality show that engaged people worldwide. Lara Croft is the video game's hero, and the event was designed to be a test of Croft-like grit and inner strength. The contestants faced blizzards, downpours, wind, and heat—all controlled by the public via a live stream. Viewers even gave up sleep to watch the billboard, supporting and speculating about the people on it. The winner, Adam, remained on the billboard for 20 hours 45 minutes and won the grand prize: a *Tomb Raider*–inspired holiday. Once the survivor was crowned, a wrap-up video was produced showing the highlights of the 24 hours, which was then promoted across key owned channels with paid support.

Lara Croft is an iconic video game character from *Tomb Raider* who first emerged on the scene in 1996. Today, games have better graphics and gameplay, but what has changed the most is their depth of story. Xbox knew it was important to let gamers know that Lara Croft was tougher, stronger, and grittier now and that the challenges she would face would be more profound. The game had intense competition from other games, such as *Fallout 4* and *Star Wars Battlefront*. McCann London and Dentsu Aegis Network teamed up to position *Rise of the Tomb Raider* as a title that sees Lara transform from hapless victim of circumstance to survivor. The team wanted to bring this storyline to life through a real-world challenge: the survival billboard. Eight contestants were elevated above central London to create the world's first human billboard. The campaign began with a recruitment phase, with lengthy "Terms & Horrible, Horrible Conditions," a humorous, disruptive attempt to discourage would-be contenders who didn't have what it takes from applying for the ultimate challenge on survivalbillboard.com.

The competition was streamed live on the survival billboard website as well as Twitch (the UK's second-biggest gaming site). In an interactive twist, viewers could vote for whatever weather condition they wished to unleash each hour through the microsite. McCann used print ads in a variety of papers that showcased "today's forecast" to ensure readers were aware of their ability to control the weather for the contestants. Check out the full story and case study on Vimeo and see how the campaign performed in the It's a Wrap feature at the end of the chapter.

Sources: "Xbox Survival Billboard: Case Study," *McCann London*, http://www.mccannlondon.co.uk/#!/case_study/xbox-survival-billbaord; Omar Oakes, "McCann and Microsoft's 'Survival billboard' wins another six Lions at Cannes," *Campaign*, June 25, 2016, http://www.campaignlive.co.uk/article/mccann-microsofts-survival-billboard-wins-six-lions-cannes/1400174; Duncan MacLeod, "Tomb Raider Survival Billboard wins again," *The Inspiration Room*, October 24, 2016, http://theinspirationroom.com/daily/2016/tomb-raider-survival-billboard/; "Xbox Case Study," *Newsworks*, http://www.newsworks.org.uk/write/MediaUploads/1%20Events%20Training/Awards/2016/Winners%20gallery/Microsoft_XBOX_case_study2.pdf; "Xbox: Survival Billboard," *Flux Broadcast*, http://fluxbroadcast.com/portfolio/xbox-survival-billboard/; "Grand Lia: Billboard," The Lia Awards, https://2016.liaentries.com/winners/index.cfm?id_medium=4&id_submedium=19&view=details&range=gp

14.1 Explain what is meant by owned media that organizations control and manage.

● **Principle**
Brand communication marshals a constellation of contact points to strategically present a consistent brand image.

Owned Media: We Own It, We Control It

Owned brand messages are delivered from a company to consumers through channels controlled by the company. These media represent a constellation of contact points that can be strategically designed to present a consistent brand image.

The biggest advantage of owned media is control, but there are other reasons to consider using this category of media. They are versatile and can be created for diverse audiences, contact points, and time frames. They can be used to address various objectives, but one of the most important is loyalty and the development of consumer-brand relationships. A limitation of owned media is that although you may own the publication or website, you have little or no control over consumer exposure to it. In other words, supplemental efforts are needed to drive traffic and get your audience to come to you. For that reason, some online programs, such as websites, are supported with offline traditional advertising.

The sections that follow are not inclusive. Rather, we compiled a variety of different ideas to inspire you to think broadly about brand communication opportunities.

Corporate Presence Media

By corporate media, we are talking about things you might not think of as media, such as the design of a building, or a delivery truck. But in integrated marketing communication (IMC) planning, we recognize that these things are important contact points that create the visual face of an organization or brand. How they present the brand image sends an important message.

Environmental Design   What a building looks like—both inside and outside—may reflect the image of the company and make a brand statement. Design, decor, and physical appearance send messages about the style and personality of the brand. Patagonia, for example, uses visual merchandising in its stores—rough wood surfaces, textiles, large outdoor posters, and lighting—to tell its story about its passion for the environment and ecologically sensitive outdoor sports. Other buildings merit recognition for their *visual branding*. The highly recognized Chrysler building in New York City, for example, is a classic skyscraper with its dramatic art-deco crown and spire. It often appears as a logo or graphic image that represents New York.

It's not only the exteriors that speak to corporate image; the interiors of buildings and public spaces also convey messages. For example, graphic designer Amy Niswonger has been following the redesign of McDonald's interiors and how it relates to brand image, She explains: "McDonald's is updating its image from kiddy classic to a destination for all ages. In the past few years, the company has achieved success both in updating its look and feel and expanding its target market without losing core customers." She asks how such a well-known look—the Golden Arches with the red-and-yellow color scheme and plastic interiors—can be accepted by customers. Her answer is that McDonald's immense brand equity makes it possible to update its interior design without taking a hit to its brand persona and hence to its market share.

Signage   Because they are a form of out-of-home media, retail and corporate signs are owned rather than paid. **On-premise signs** that identify stores have been with us throughout recorded history and are today the most ubiquitous form of brand communication. In this complex environment, an effective sign may be relatively simple, like McDonald's giant M, or more complex, like those found on the strip in Las Vegas, with their large illuminated and animated visual extravaganzas. Some on-premise signs also act like billboards. American Eagle Outfitters, for example, has a 15,000-square-foot sign above its Broadway store in New York City. The sign has 12 panels and operates 18 hours a day.

On the opposite end of the **signage** continuum are inexpensive forms, such as yard signs, bumper stickers, and buttons—the media of political campaigns. Yard signs are temporary and used by real estate agents as well as politicians. Although they can be tacky, yard signs are public statements and perform an important function either as a reminder or a motivation to action.

Appearance   You probably wouldn't list a uniform or a delivery truck as a communication media, but what comes to your mind when you think of a brown truck? "What can brown do for you?" UPS used that slogan to illustrate the power of a distinctive truck design that represents what UPS does best: deliver packages. Trucks can deliver messages as well as packages and products, however. That's why many companies with their own fleet of trucks insist that drivers keep the trucks clean and run them through car washes frequently.

The appearance, attitude, and conduct of staff, who in many businesses are the front line of customer contact, send other types of message, both positive and negative. That's why most companies have *training programs* for

Photo: Archimage/Alamy Stock Photo

Designer Amy Niswonger analyzes McDonald's new environmental design and concludes that "the customer inherently understands that the Big Mac is still the Big Mac; it's just served now in a hipper, cooler location."

Amy Niswonger is a graphic designer and professor who owns her own design studio. A graphic design and marketing graduate of Miami University in Oxford, Ohio, she was named Most Promising Minority Student by the American Advertising Federation (AAF). She was nominated to be featured here by Connie Frazier, AAF chief operating officer.

Photo: LouLouPhotos/Shutterstock

Out-of-home advertising, such as this on-premise sign from Las Vegas, is a highly creative medium as well as the second fastest growing medium after the internet. Every building—every store—needs a sign.

new employees. Training is reinforced by ongoing *employee relations* programs, usually run by either public relations or human resources. These programs keep staff informed and, to the degree they are critical to the success of promotional campaigns, on strategy in both their formal and informal stakeholder communication.

Branded Media

To take advantage of the value-added power of branding, companies find endless opportunities in media tools that bear the brand's name. The use of media of entertainment, for example, to engage consumers with brands is referred to as **branded entertainment**. The goal is to associate the brand with a fun, entertaining experience that creates positive feelings for the brand.

Film, Fun, and Games   Promotional video networks run sponsored programs and commercials, such as the channels you see in grocery stores, doctor's offices, and truck stops that distribute commercials by video or satellites on in-store televisions.

An exciting, emerging, and surging new media format is **branded videos**. These engaging video clips usually range in length from 3 to 12 minutes and are published under brands' names with the sole purpose of deepening relationships with customers and presenting a call to action. The longer formats offer brands the opportunity to develop a deeper emotional connection with viewers. You can view video shorts from H&M, BMW, Radio Flyer, and more on the brand websites or on sites such as www.shortoftheweek.com. Branded videos and live-streaming events can showcase behind-the-scenes footage, sneak peeks, product presentations, celebrity takeovers, live question-and-answer sessions, contests, raucous humor, or dramatic story telling. Similar to television programs with recurring episodes in a developing story, these **webisodes** created a new form of web advertising.

The most-engaging posts on Facebook in 2016 were all videos. Two of them were branded videos: Shell corraled celebrities to highlight the importance of alternative energy in a music video for "Best Day of My Life," and Kohl's brought a family presents and gift cards before the holidays.[1]

Meerkat and Periscope are two companies who enable brands to interact with audiences in real time through live-stream videos sent to their followers. Here are a few examples of what brands have done.[2]

* At SXSW, Twentieth Century Fox had some fun with fans, using Meerkat to live-stream its official launch of *The Simpson's* Kwik-E-Mart food truck.
* General Electric used drones equipped with Periscope on guided tours through remote facilities as a part of #Droneweek in 2016.
* Automaker Nissan streamed the unveiling of its 2016 Maxima model at the New York International Auto Show, which helped the automaker build buzz and extend its reach.
* Tony Hawk broadcast an impromptu skateboard performance in a backyard pool to his fans.
* J.C. Penney hosted Eva Longoria in its first Periscope live stream, who introduced fans to her new J.C. Penney bedding collection and answered their questions from an exclusive launch event held in Los Angeles.
* Taco Bell hosted a mock press conference about its new breakfast menu item and the associated "Breakfast Defector Day." The brand invited its fans to stop by Taco Bell on Cinco de Mayo to enjoy a free "Biscuit Taco."

Branded games, in addition to product placement and ads, can showcase a brand name—an actual video game that is designed around a brand experience. The game is created and owned by the company. Nissan created the GT Academy where drivers can compete in digital driving games in real Nissan sports cars. A multiplatform experience, the winners get to participate in a reality show format—think *Hunger Games*—with drivers competing live against one another in driving performance.[3]

In addition to films, other media carrying the brand name of a sponsor include events such as lecture series and exhibits. Samsonite has produced high-quality photographic desk diaries. Nestlé created a "Milkybar Kid to the Rescue" mass-market paperback for the children's market. We are attracted like magnets to opportunities to play, as the feature by Valerie Jones underscores.

The Serious Business of Play: Advertising in Video Games

Valerie Jones, *University of Nebraska–Lincoln*

Advertising has long tried to entertain. Making us laugh or making us cry helps cut through the clutter and make a brand memorable. But what about making us play?

The opportunity exists today to do much more than entertain an audience for 30 seconds. Brands can create and contribute to entertaining, engaging, interactive experiences for their audiences. One promising way to do that is through advergaming and in-game advertising.

If you hear the word *gaming* and automatically think of (1) casinos or (2) smelly teenage boys in a windowless basement surrounded by pizza boxes, think again. Gaming refers to video game play (on a computer, game console, or mobile phone or device), and the average gamer in the United States is 35, employed, and nearly as likely to be female as male (Entertainment Software Association, 2015). Genres of games cover the range from casual mobile games played a few minutes at a time to core console games that take months to master. Advergames are casual games designed specifically to feature products or brands, with the idea that entertaining the audience and enabling them to engage with the brand leads to brand preference and purchase intent. For example, Apple Jacks partnered with Cartoon Network to create a Rube Goldberg–style game featuring the cereal setting off the reactions, and Cartoon Network has continued featuring Apple Jacks games. The best-branded games are designed in such a way that removing the branding from them would take away from the fun and authenticity of the whole experience. (Think about Chipotle's scarecrow game.)

Because different genres of games attract different demographics of gamers, the type of integration between a brand and game depends on the goals and audience of the brand. Brands can have ads hard-coded into console games (think Burger King billboards in racing games) or rotating ads in computer games or internet-connected consoles (think display ads in *Bejeweled* rotating between Nordstrom and Kellogg or branded containers on cargo ships in *Splinter Cell* branded by IKEA in one level and Samsung in the next). Branding can even be integrated into the game (think of a character earning health points for drinking Snapple Green Tea or a new Disney-branded level). Value exchange ads are being used more and more, in which players engage with an ad (watch a video, install an app, play a custom mini-game) in exchange for exclusive content and rewards: a new level, a new item for the character, in-game currency, free game play time, and so forth.

Because gamers are engaged in play and having fun, it's important to consider that environment and the player's mind-set. Gaming is an immersive experience; there's little opportunity for multitasking if you want to advance to the next level. How can your brand add to the experience of a captive audience and do so in a way that also adds to your brand equity? How can your brand be the hero of the game, not the annoying intruder? With 42 percent of Americans regularly playing video games for three-plus hours/week, the value of being associated with play is a serious one to consider.

Sources: Entertainment Software Association, 2015; Internet Advertising Bureau, 2015.

Naming Rights   Another high-visibility area of branded media is **naming rights** for events and buildings. The objective is brand visibility, and the benefit to the organization or municipality is a hefty payment.

Naming rights dominate football bowl games, such as the Discover Orange Bowl and Chick-fil-A Bowl, and sports arenas, such as Citi Field in New York where the Mets play and CenturyLink Field (formerly Qwest field) in Seattle, which hosts both the NFL Seattle Seahawks and the Seattle Sounders soccer team. Heinz Field in Pittsburgh and Coors Field in Denver connect their towns with local companies, which makes a logical fit for the brand. Other names were not so well matched and encountered backlash, as when Candlestick Park in San Francisco was renamed 3Com Park, much to the dismay of local fans, and then became Monster Park after Monster Cable bought the 3Com rights.

Universities name buildings as well as classrooms, conference rooms, and academic programs after alumni and local leaders who give sizable donations. One of the most ironic examples comes from Harvard Law School, where the bathrooms in its Wasserstein Hall were named after benefactors. The Falik Men's Room was the gift of a bequest by William Falik, a lawyer and real estate developer with a sense of humor.[4]

⬤ **Principle**
Naming rights deliver high visibility for a brand and an association with an important gathering point, such as a sports arena or public building.

Photo: Tom Carter/PhotoEdit

Pepperidge Farm, with its consistent design and distinctive brand image, dominates cookie shelves because of the billboarding power of its consistent design across all the brand's variations.

● **Principle**
A package is the last ad a customer sees before making a purchase decision.

The Media of Retail

The retail store is a world of promotion. Packages proclaim brand identities, and merchandising materials attract attention and deliver motivating sales messages.

Packaging A package is both a container and a communication vehicle. In particular, it is the last ad a customer sees before making the decision to buy a brand, as the Pepperidge Farm shelf photo illustrates.

In an attempt to win over undecided consumers at the point of purchase, many manufacturers create innovative, eye-catching packages. Even if you can't afford a big advertising budget, you've got a chance to grab shopper attention if your product has a compelling image on the shelf. Although the industry has never developed a standard for measuring impressions from a shelf, advertisers are aware of the **billboarding** effect of a massed set of packages, a practice Pepperidge Farm uses to good effect. Once on the shelf at home or in the office, it is a constant brand reminder.

Packages can also deliver customer benefits. For example, recipes for Quaker Oats' famous Oatmeal Cookies, Nestlé's Tollhouse Cookies, Chex Party Mix, and Campbell's Green Bean Bake all started as promotional recipes on the product's packaging and turned into long-time favorites in homemakers' recipes. There is even a website for these classic recipes (www.backofthebox.com) that features more than 1,500 recipes found on packages.

Sometimes the package itself is the focus of the advertising, particularly if there is a new size or innovation, such as Coca-Cola's introduction of a new bottle made from plant materials that is more compostable than plastic.[5] Some packages, such as CD covers, can be artwork in and of themselves.

Merchandising Materials Merchandising materials are the media used in promotions for a store, product, or event. Manufacturers often provide brand-related window banners, posters, and freestanding displays. In addition to posters and banners, other media used by retailers include **shelf talkers** (signs attached to a shelf that give brand information and can also invite the consumer to take away some piece of information, such as a recipe or a coupon). **Point-of-sale (PoS) materials**—also called **Point-of-purchase (PoP) materials**—call attention to brands and provide a special reason to buy. Other store-based media include end-of-aisle displays, display cartons, banners, signs, and mechanical product and sample dispensers.

In terms of store-based merchandising, think about all the different materials in a Starbucks or McDonald's that carry the brand logo and maybe even other information: tray liners, table tents, coffee cups and sleeves, napkins, and coasters. Posters, signs, or other art are usually on the walls; sometimes art may be a part of the store's environmental design, but signs may also be used to announce special promotions. Bags and sacks—grocery bags, shopping bags, and other retail bags—are important brand PoP reminders. Even the stuffers that you find when you open up a pizza box delivered to your home are part of the merchandising program.

● **Principle**
Although the objective of point-of-purchase materials is to increase brand visibility, they also bring together all the elements of a sale, including the consumer, the product, and often price deals.

Department stores will sometimes have theme or seasonal promotions where they bring together related products and create settings in which to display them, such as beach parties or graduation celebrations. All these props and supporting signage become theme-related media for the merchandising event.

The objective may be to increase brand visibility, but merchandising programs are effective because they bring together all the elements of a sale—the consumer, the product, and money, often a price deal—at the same time. These PoP efforts are particularly important to motivate impulse buys.

The Owned Media of PR and Promotions

We mentioned promotions related to retail marketing, but there are a variety of promotional media that are used both in public relations and sales promotion programs. Here are a few of them.

Videos and Publications   Nearly all company videos for public relations purposes are available through corporate websites, but DVDs and flash drives are sometimes still distributed if the data or videos are extremely large. They remain tools for communicating in-depth information about a company or program. Monsanto, for example, posted video clips of testimonials from farmers using Monsanto products on YouTube and its website, hoping to attract customers, employees, and policy makers.

Companies produce huge amounts of publications and literature of various kinds. Corporate publications include books, magazines, newsletters, special reports, annual reports, catalogs, and collateral materials, such as brochures. They may be sent to key stakeholders as part of a corporate communication program. High-quality brochures are often produced for new car lines, universities, and high-end real estate developments.

Consider books, for example. They can be used as promotional tools and corporate reputation builders. A number of advertising and marketing communication agencies have published corporate history books, for example, that focus on the thoughts of their founders and the philosophies of their agencies. Examples are Crispin Porter + Bogusky and *Hoopla*, Leo Burnett's *Leo*, DDB's *Bill Bernbach Said,* and Ogilvy & Mather's *Ogilvy on Advertising*, among others.

But it's not just marcom agencies that produce books. A bank in Brazil presented 120 reasons why people should be customers of Banco Bradesco—one reason per page. The book is at the center of the bank's customer acquisition program.[6] Traditionally, books have been printed, but with the advent of simplified electronic publication, e-books are now being produced for phones, tablets, and e-readers.

Photo: Hoopla by Crispin Porter + Bogusky, Written by Warren Berger, Published by powerHouse Books

Publicity Media   Publicity, which was discussed in more detail in Chapter 3, is designed to encourage news media coverage. Press releases and video news releases are prepared news stories and features sent to print and television news media. Public relations offices assemble **press kits** that can contain such pieces as news releases, fact sheets, histories, maps, photos, artwork, and position papers, among many other collateral materials designed for different audiences and prepared, perhaps, in different languages. We think of press kits as being printed, but the pieces may also be on DVDs, flash drives, or online. Publicity is used to support all types of brand communication programs anywhere mass media coverage is useful to get information to the public.

Brand Reminders and Rewards   A **premium** is a tangible reward for a particular act, usually purchasing or repurchasing a product. Common premiums that reward behaviors are the loyalty cards, pens, and mints given away in restaurants. Events use T-shirts as well as an endless list of freebies, such as cups, caps, stuffed animals, and other souvenirs, most of which carry the brand's logo. These rewards are also brand reminders.

Premiums and prizes also recognize relationships. If you work on a Habitat for Humanity work site, for example, you may receive a T-shirt or

Photo: momo design/Shutterstock

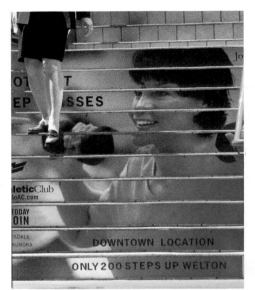

Photo: Jerry Cleveland/Getty Images

These painted stairs for the Denver Athletic Club in downtown Denver are an example of street-based guerilla marketing. It is also a captive ad because it is unavoidable for people approaching and walking up the stairs.

a cap, or maybe an energy bar. Premiums are also used as incentives to add value to a product or event. Examples of value-added premiums are the toys inside Cracker Jacks and an iPod given for taking a real estate tour.

Similar to premiums, corporate communication and public relations programs as well as high-end sales programs may use gifts. Industry data, for example, may be given to a business-to-business (B2B) prospect on a logo-decorated flash drive. Executive gifts, which are usually high-end expensive items, are used as special recognition for good B2B customers and sales contest winners. Sales programs often use competitions to increase excitement among the sales staff. The prizes can include big-ticket rewards, such as trips to resorts, beaches, and islands.

Place-Based Media We described out-of-home or place-based advertising in Chapter 13. Another type is street-based media, which create unexpected personal encounters with a brand, such as painted messages on streets.

In our discussion of *guerilla marketing* in Chapter 12, we mentioned that people on the street convey brand messages. People can be employed in places with a lot of foot traffic to hand out sales materials, such as coupons or samples. **Sign spinners**, or "human directionals," are hired by local businesses to stand on street corners with signs and banners that promote their stores or special marketing events. To get drivers' attention, they may appear in costumes or do little dance routines. For some, there is an art form in sign spinning, similar to break dancing, which calls for athletic prowess and dramatic moves in an involved choreography.

Another form of human media is the **flash mob,** which began as rehearsed groups of performers who show up in unexpected places and put on concerts and dances. Some flash mobs are for fun, but some are commercial. A classic commercial use of this crowd-based concept was the T-Mobile "Dance," where unassuming people walking through London's Liverpool Street Station seemed to spontaneously break out in a 400-person highly choreographed dance routine. Check out the video and the making of it on YouTube.

Photo: Courtesy of Nelson Bostock (T-Mobile UK)

One example of a flash mob employed as a street marketing technique is the T-Mobile "Dance" video that created a spectacle in London's Liverpool Station.

Owned but Interactive: Let's Talk

Interactive media are those forms that invite users to engage with or respond personally to the message. Some of them are similar to owned media in that the organization pretty much controls them, but the media format, such as email and Twitter, allows the organization to initiate communication with consumers, customers, and other stakeholders. Engagement beyond just exposure is the goal when organizations use interactive media. Some media, such as texting, are just naturally more interactive and thus more engaging than owned media.

There are also experiments with traditional media, such as television, that make it possible for viewers to interact with television messages through a set-top box or computer-accessible TV. Television is not just limited to viewing programs; it has become the center of the digital living room, with viewers enjoying new experiences such as games and exercise via their Wii players and other video games.

Corporate Interactive Media

A useful and sometimes exciting type of owned but interactive medium is the digital display that invites viewers to interact with data represented graphically on a screen in front of them on kiosks in public places and lobby walls.

Interactive electronic **kiosks** with liquid-crystal-display touch-screen computers, databases of information, full graphics, product photos, and online access are moving into the aisles in many stores—and malls—where they provide information about more products than the store can ever stock on its shelves. New kiosk advances add cameras, which, using facial-identity software, can estimate the user's age and gender, making it possible to do more customized responses.[7] Viewers can sometimes order merchandise directly from these kiosks.

Information that used to be provided in brochures, directories, and other publications can now be seen on **electronic walls** or **digital installations** in buildings, particularly in lobbies. Touch screens driven by extensive computer databases make these media forms interactive as users check out maps and calendars and delve into corporate history and product lines.

Direct-Response Media

We mentioned ordering directly from a kiosk. That's actually a type of direct marketing. The first marketing communication area to recognize the value of interactivity in brand communication was **direct-response marketing** (also called **direct advertising**). The traditional media of direct-response have been mail (letters, flyers, catalogs), phone, and now online messages, all of which have some kind of response device built into the message delivery.

Most direct-response programs are designed to generate transactions. The goal is to motivate customers to take action and place an order. Advances in digital technology made it possible to personalize messages and target tightly to prospects who are known to be interested. Even some advertising in print and television carries offers and reply forms to generate a sale.

The big technological changes that made personalized communication possible were online media combined with databases of consumer information. Such advances made it possible to target prospects based on their past behavior (what they bought, what sites they visited).

Technological innovations bring all kinds of new media into direct-response brand communication. WIFI-connected billboards can be interactive and create one-on-one brand communication opportunities. Tablet and smartphone users can interact with companies via electronic posters and quick-response (QR) codes, say in bus stops, that offer users free internet access to download apps, games, video ads, or coupons and may even lead to on-the-spot product sales. The Beneful dog food brand is using a 64-foot installation that, when it detects a passerby, presents a virtual dog that runs up to play a virtual game of chase or fetch. Viewers can customize the dog. The point is to demonstrate how the brand is associated with playing with a dog in real time, if not real life.[8]

Personal Contact Media

Employees and other stakeholders can deliver brand messages. When a friend, family member, or someone you respect tells you something about a brand, you are likely to believe it. That includes employees, who are often asked for their advice or opinions on a product or brand.

14.2 Describe interactive owned media and explain why that interactive element is important.

⬤ **Principle**
With interactive media, engagement is the goal.

⬤ **Principle**
Direct-response media are designed to generate a transaction without a salesperson by motivating a customer to take action and place an order.

The Day-to-Day Job in Digital Strategy & Planning

Sara Mahmood, *Digital Strategist-Ford Motor Company, Team Detroit*

Working on the Ford Motor Company business—one of the largest global automotive accounts—carries a lot of weight. Apart from a home, the car is the largest single purchase that a person makes. With so many models, features, and financing options, a lot goes into making a purchase decision and then taking care of that vehicle over its life span. My job is multifaceted because I focus on prospective and current owners within the digital landscape. I make the upfront exploring and shopping process as easy as possible for shoppers, digitally. I also keep prospective and current owners engaged with the brand by serving them compelling content through paid, earned, and owned media. I build positive sentiment through social networking, email marketing, and paid advertising. Assuming that people's digital experience with the brand is a good one, then over time they can become advocates and refer their network to the brand as well. I come up with underlying digital strategies that place the brand where people can see and connect with it online.

Because there are so many elements to my role, it's safe to say that no two days are the same. I'm always doing my best to stay ahead of the curve in terms of best practices and emerging digital media trends. I subscribe to a lot of online and print trade publications and attend as many professional knowledge-sharing events as I can. It's important to keep in mind that not every new practice makes sense for automotive. Staying connected with industry trends helps me figure out what trends the Ford brand should latch on to.

To accomplish my tasks, I work closely with a group of community managers. They deploy content and engage with followers on a day-to-day basis through owned social media accounts. Their insight, coupled with social listening data (from the analytics team), gives me a sense of what people are talking about within the social media landscape. I use these insights to insert the brand into social to fill people's needs for content and conversation. My analytics team helps me to numerically assess opportunities online and helps measure the impact of online content and conversations on brand reputation. Overall, digital strategists help shape how people view brands online. It is a great area for strong problem solvers to have high impact and shine.

A graduate of advertising and marketing communications plus supply chain management at Wayne State University, Sara Mahmood was named the Most Promising Rising Star by the American Advertising Federation in 2015.

Employee communication programs are designed to help employees convey strategic information through these critical personal conversations. Other important avenues for personal communication in business are found in sales and customer service operations.

Personal Sales In addition to conversation with employees, word-of-mouth communication can occur in more structured selling situations. Retail sales employees, for example, use personal communication to relay information about a product and give reasons to buy it. These reasons can be personalized to match the person and his or her interests. Salespeople in stores are trained to answer product questions and help customers find things.

In B2B marketing, sales reps often work from a scripted sales message to make sure they hit on the right selling points and convey the most important strategic information. They also are provided with sales kits that contain product specifications, photos, diagrams, and other information useful in decision making by business customers. More recently, all these data are available online and may be given to the prospect on a DVD or flash drive.

Similarly to press kits, **sales kits** are packets of information prepared to support personal sales efforts. A sales rep who covers a region or several states, for example, will carry along all the information needed to make a pitch to a prospective customer. Like press kits, sales kits can contain a variety of materials, but they also include such materials as selling strategies, presentation materials, information about the customer, profiles of the customer's market, and pricing charts. They can also appear in print, on flash drives, or online.

Similarily, media sales reps in advertising will have **media kits** that include profile information about the people who watch, listen, or read the medium along with numbers describing audience size and geographical coverage.

Training Materials   Another category of assembled information appears as **training materials** used to train B2B sales reps or other employees. Employee training materials may contain information about new projects, new products, or special promotions with presentation visuals, exercises, and background data. They can be in print, but most professional training sessions use PowerPoint slides and the materials may be distributed online or on a flash drive.

Customer Service   Another environment where personal communication is critical is in **customer service**, or **tech support** in the technology industries. Effective communication can cement customer satisfaction or dissatisfaction. What makes customer service different from other forms of commercial media is that customers can initiate the dialogue in person, by phone, or online. If it's a positive experience, customer service can strengthen the brand relationship; if it's negative, it can lead to or increase customer dissatisfaction with the product, brand, and company. Customer service is the front line of consumer attitude change about a brand experience.

> ● **Principle**
> If it's a positive experience, customer service can strengthen the brand relationship; if it's negative, it can lead to or increase customer dissatisfaction.

Traditional media used to elicit customer feedback are shoppers' surveys and comment cards. **Mystery shoppers**, a proactive form of customer service, are used to personally analyze and report on the shopping experience in a store. More recently, customer service is being driven by social media and cell phones.

Customer service is a specific department that handles questions and complaints, but it also refers to a company's attitude toward customers during these interactions. How the company behaves in solving a problem and the way the interaction is handled send some of the most impactful brand messages that customers receive.

General Motors, for example, set up special call centers with technical specialists who can help owners navigate through its MyLink and Cue systems. The call centers are fitted out with replicas of the cars and their "infotainment" center consoles. The tech support folks move from their cubicles to the consoles to walk customers through their problems. Mercedes-Benz uses a system that can link a driver's cell phone directly to its customer center for live help or to send a how-to-video loaded onto YouTube.[9]

Because customers have so many choices of brands and shopping outlets, how a company treats customers can be the major reason for choosing one over the others. Why has Southwest Airlines been so successful when competitors have faced bankruptcy? The primary reason is customer service.

Brand communication planners don't "manage" customer service in most companies, but they can monitor the messages that are being sent at this critical touch point and identify problems that might be undercutting a brand's communication strategy.

> ● **Principle**
> Brand communication planners don't manage customer service, but they can monitor the messages being sent and identify potential problems.

The importance of customer service as a contact point that delivers positive (or negative) brand experiences is reflected in a campaign by online retailer Zappos.com. This effort demonstrates to customers how its customer service representatives make it easy to order or return merchandise. Called "zappets," the puppet-like characters in the ads are based on actual Zappos.com employees, who the company calls its "customer loyalty team."

Interactive Promotional Media

We mentioned *events* earlier when we discussed owned media, saying that these media can be interactive environments used by both public relations and sales promotion to involve people personally in positive brand experiences. These brand-sponsored gatherings connect people who are customers, prospective customers, employees, suppliers, or other types of stakeholders.

Photo: Courtesy of Zappos. Used with permission.

Zappos.com celebrates its customer service representative in its "Happy to help. 24/7." campaign that reiterates the company's value propositions by showing how its employees—albeit in sock puppet form—interact with customers.

An interesting variation on interactive advertising is "live" or performance-based commercials for drip irrigation and treadle pump equipment found in rural areas of Africa and India where TV, radio, and/or newspaper ads do not reach. Traveling performers also present live infomercials about how to obtain banking services from mobile stages to a large and growing population of international brand-focused customers.[10]

Speeches, Conferences, and Tours   From the public relations side, speeches and informational tours are events that can generate questions and answers about an organization's programs, policies, and actions. An informational **tour** involves stakeholders in personally engaging situations. A grand opening for a new airport or concert hall, for example, may include tours with trained guides to explain the building's functions and design.

We won't spend a lot of time with news relations because that was covered in more detail in Chapter 3, but there are interactive publicity media that we should call to your attention. **News conferences**, for example, are designed as interactive experiences for the news media. Press representatives are invited to hear a spokesperson present information on some newsworthy topic or event and answer media questions. **Media tours** are a conference on wheels for media representatives that involve an itinerary and a traveling spokesperson. They may tour a location associated with a news topic, such as a new office or manufacturing plant that has achieved an award for its energy efficiency.

In addition to events, other types of promotional media engage people in interactive experiences. **Sampling**, for example, is a way for the consumer to try a product or service before buying it. The food-sampling tables at stores like Costco, for example, are staffed by people who prepare the food samples and provide information about the product and how to buy it as well as answer consumer questions.

Trade Shows, Displays, and Exhibits   A **trade show** is a promotional event where B2B companies within the same industry gather to present and sell their merchandise, demonstrate their products, and take orders. Displays and exhibits along with product literature and signage are the media used in these sales and meeting events. Booths are spaces that are designed to showcase the product and allow salespersons to speak personally to attendees.

A conference sponsored by an organization may be a named brand event. Apple's new product announcements, particularly when Steve Jobs was alive and the headliner, were highly anticipated by the computer and new technology markets. In addition to the event itself, there are usually myriad types of media used to publicize and support the event, such as name tags, programs, publicity materials, bags, and all kinds of take-home tchotchkes (samples, trinkets, souvenirs), to name just a few.

Displays and exhibits are important parts of sales promotion, events, and public relations programs. Displays include signage and booths, racks, and holders for promotional literature. A model of a new condominium complex, complete with a literature rack offering brochures about its development, is an example of a simple display. Exhibits tend to be larger than displays; they may have moving parts, sound, or video and usually are staffed by company representatives who deliver personal sales messages and demonstrate the product.

Owned Digital Media

We discussed how digital and online communication changed direct-response marketing, but that's true in all areas of brand communication. Let's review the evolution of this technology and how its various formats are used in brand communication.

Email   A product of an earlier time in online communication, email evolved from the days when we used to log on and off our computers and check messages in bursts. Some users still operate that way, but with newer technologies, many users are always online, with messages constantly streaming into their personal media. That has changed the function as well as the speed of online connections. In addition to speed, one of the attractive features of using email for brand communication is that it is inexpensive. All it takes is a list of email addresses and an

Using Social Media to Build Brand Communities

Benjamin Preston, *entrepreneur and marketing/communications professional, New York City*, Publicis Healthcare Communications Group

Since the dawn of social networking, organizations have been grappling with the best way to harness social media and existing digital networks. For years, businesses used a traditional media plan (media relations, email marketing, etc.) and treated social media as an add-on, like icing on the cake.

Since those early days of social media experimenting, some organizations have effectively developed media plans that maximize the impact of social media. These successes come from a radically new way of thinking that puts social at the center of any marketing plan.

As every year progresses, companies are finding bigger and more impactful ways to make viral content and establish stronger networks. Not surprisingly, their methods are all so vastly different. Most companies, like Dove or Red Bull, will perform public relations stunts that take advantage of the internet's addiction to novelty. Others, like Coca-Cola, create brand advocates through personalized experiences in hopes that their followers will create content that the brand can repurpose for its own usage.

The end goal of all these brands is the same: reach more people; make more money.

As I've moved from consumer to health care public relations, I've noticed a more authentic and beautiful way of using social media: brands creating networks that support their members. Unlike brands that seek attention to boost sales, these health care brands create communities on social media that support network members with various illnesses and disease.

For example, one brand that I've worked with established communities on several platforms that supported families and patients affected with multiple sclerosis (MS). The end result was a group of people exchanging experiences and advice that would improve the life of someone with MS—a beautiful sight. At the center of this life-changing dialogue was the disease, not the brand, in hopes that the lives of the members were affected for the best.

The takeaway? Social media will always evolve into something bigger, and as a public relations professional, you need to find a way to maximize your presence on social media to make a meaningful impact for those you try to reach.

internet connection. Constant Contact is an email service provider that distributes group emails and handles the back end of correspondence with prospective customers.

An example of a branded email effort is the announcement by Amazon of the Kindle Fire, which featured a contest to win the new device. Amazon users received emails with the announcement, photos, and product specifications as well as the contest information.

This interactive capability grew exponentially when smartphones began to act like mini-computers. The constant stream of information means that the inbox is now a river and that we can dip into it whenever we feel like it. What's different from earlier online media is constant connection. Contact with this river of information can be made through mobile phones, not just at a desk through a computer, as people fly through their daily activities.

Websites You're familiar with these terms, but let's review how the internet is shaping brand communication. A company's **website** is a communication tool that blurs the distinction between marketing communication forms, such as advertising, direct marketing, and public relations. It is the online face the organization presents to the world. In some cases, it looks like an online corporate brochure; it may also function as an online catalog or shopping site for **e-commerce**. Amazon.com and eBay are two good examples of internet-based e-commerce. Websites can also support promotional efforts, such as Guitar Hero's invitation to users to vote for their favorite smash hits. Benjamin Preston describes how social media have also been used to build networks to support customers' needs and interests.

E-commerce ventures are all over the web, but they serve an important consumer need in certain situations. For example, the web reaches people with specific interests. In fact, the internet is the ultimate niche medium in that people turn to it to find out about any topic that interests them.

For example, pungent Australian delicacy Vegemite and its similar uniquely flavored UK spread, Marmite, are hard to find by Aussies and Brits living away from home. Both products depend on websites to reach homesick fans. Marmite flaunts its distinctive taste with "love it" and "hate it" pages on Facebook and Twitter with humorous copy that reads: "Eat Marmite? You'd rather rip the wings off live chickens."[11]

The website can also be an information resource with a searchable library of stories and data about products, product categories, and related topics. In all cases, however, critical functions of a website are to create and support an organization's identity and reinforce the brand image and position.

● **Principle**

A website's critical functions are to support an organization's identity and reinforce the brand image and position.

Forrester Research has developed methods (e.g., social listening) for evaluating the brand-building function of websites. The company tracks effectiveness of website performance in terms not only of making a brand promise, but also of delivering easy-to-find and easy-to-use information.

Whether or not a website is effective depends on several factors. One is **stickiness**, and the other is its ease of **navigation**. A "sticky" website is one that is engaging: it encourages visitors to "stick around" instead of bouncing to another site because it is interesting and offers meaningful interactivity. The interest level is determined by what's "above the fold," to use a newspaper metaphor. Decisions about whether to leave or stay and investigate the site's content depend on what's visible without scrolling downward. Research has shown that most of the content "below the fold"—that you have to scroll down to see—has little or no impact.[12]

To increase its stickiness—in this case, its value to its customers—Campbell's Soup redesigned its cooking site based on consumer research that indicated cooks were interested in budget meals and recipes that move beyond the casserole. Within the site, www.CampbellsKitchen.com, visitors can search for dinner options by mood or flavor, such as chocolaty or cheesy, as well as standard menu categories. The site also has a seven-day meal-planning tool and a section about recipe substitutions and healthy alternatives.

Some people may find a marketer's website after doing a search using a search engine; others may come across the website address in some other communication, such as an ad or brochure, often with QR codes that link cell phone users directly to the website. Another way is to encounter a link on a related site, usually in the form of an ad with enough impact to entice the visitor to leave the original site and move to this new one. Internet strategists are keenly aware of the difficulty of enticing people to click through to a different website.

Blogs   More than 200 million digital essayists worldwide have created web **blogs** to talk about things that interest them.[13] Historically, bloggers used their blogs for creative expression and opinion pieces for a generally anonymous audience. Some are significant sources for online buzz. Although blogs sound like one-way communication tools, most of them also invite comments that are shared with other readers, stimulating conversations, if not debates, among them. Bloggers often have higher levels of credibility than ads or corporate websites.

Corporations use blogs to engage stakeholders of all kinds. Home Depot, for example, uses its "Apron Blog" on Facebook to post "how-to" information and design ideas as well as to showcase local community service projects conducted by employees.[14]

Corporate blogs are a way to keep employees and other stakeholders informed, but employees may also be encouraged to have personal blogs. Microsoft has several hundred staffers blogging on personal sites. Sales staffs have found that blogs are changing the sales process by making more experiences with a product available to prospects and keeping customers current with fast-changing technological trends.

A problem with blogs is that they are sometimes criticized as "stealth advertisers." **Paid posts**, where bloggers plug a product in return for cash or freebies from the company, have caught the attention of the Federal Trade Commission. On a blog for parents, for example, a blogger promoted a $135 embroidered baby carrier. The blogger admits the manufacturer sent the carrier free to the blogger. These endorsements are being addressed by new advertising guidelines that require bloggers to post "clear and conspicuous" disclosures that they have received compensation or freebies.[15]

"Socialtizing"   We've been talking in this section about media owned or controlled by a company or organization and used to generate interactions with its stakeholders. This last topic, social media, refers to the use of the media of social marketing as a promotional tool. We call this hybrid between advertising and corporate-driven social chatter **socialtizing**.

Facebook and Twitter, which you probably know well, are sites that allow users to share personal information with friends. A Facebook site can also be set up by a company to feature a brand with a brand profile just like any other member. There are over 65 million Facebook pages for businesses.[16]

Facebook marketers hope to make friends with interested consumers who visit their sites. Walmart has a corporate Facebook site with over 33 million followers, but it also encourages its 6,500 local stores to set up individual Facebook pages through its My Local Walmart program.[17]

Likewise, marketers can create a company account on Twitter, one that monitors brand references using a service that tracks news in real time as it searches, filters, and summarizes the huge flood of information appearing on Twitter every second. Marketers can also post brand-related videos on film and video-sharing sites, such as YouTube and Hulu.

Socializing provides information, but more importantly, it gets people talking about a brand and sharing their thoughts and experiences with a network of friends. The **network effect** describes the success of Facebook: "the more users a site attracts, the more others will want to use it, which creates a natural monopoly and a magnet for advertisers."[18] Services like Off-the-Wall software by Resource Interactive make it possible for companies to sell directly from their Facebook walls, which expands a social media presence into e-commerce. (See more at www.resource.com.)

To successfully place a brand within a communication environment like Facebook or Twitter, planners have to think strategically about the unique voice of the brand. *National Geographic*, for example, has a huge number of fans. But what should *National Geographic* sound like online? What should it say or not say? The company's mission is "to inspire people to care about the planet," and that's what drives its social media strategy. Do you think the example shown here embodies that mission? So *National Geographic*'s message strategy is to stay authentic by focusing on discussion topics that relate to and support its mission.[19]

The point is that every brand has a personality—caring and committed, off-the-wall zany, badass—and that needs to come through in online posts. Some brands use one person who knows exactly how to speak in the persona of the brand; others use a team of employees who know how to match dialogue to the brand personality. In all cases, these people need to "stay on brand" as they explore the give and take of social communication.

Grey Poupon used its elitist image to target Facebook fans with a sophistication test that lets them have their profiles checked to see whether they qualify as a taste leader to be a Grey Poupon user. The test looks at such factors as proper use of grammar on their Facebook pages, taste in art and restaurants, and books and movies selected to see if the fans qualify for membership in Grey Poupon's "Society of Good Taste."[20]

Experts recommend that a company have a plan for being present regularly on its social media sites—once or twice a day—and that the interactions be authentic and relevant both to the brand and its followers. Posts across various social media should be unique for each outlet because the sites are used in different ways by people with different interests. Scheduling and planning posts can be managed through tools such as Hootsuite and Tweetdeck that help manage all the social media outlets in a coordinated way.[21]

● Principle
The reason to use social media is to get people talking about a brand.

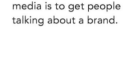
National Geographic
September 17, 2015 · 🌐

"A male may be attractive, but he doesn't deliver at the genetic level. In a way, it's false advertising," says biologist Judith Mank of peacocks, swans, and many other bird species—which boast colorful exteriors but don't pass on their gorgeous qualities.

Why Flashy Male Birds Aren't Really What They Seem
Among peacocks, swans, pheasants, and other birds, males' better looks don't necessarily mean better genes.
NEWS.NATIONALGEOGRAPHIC.COM

Photo: Photo courtesy Joel Sartore/National Geographic Creative. Text courtesy Patricia Edmonds. Used with permission.

National Geographic's mission is "to inspire people to care about the planet," and its social media posts are each designed to reinforce that mission and provide its followers with interesting and shareable content.

Research on Facebook usage provides interesting insights about how best to post on the social media site. For example, weekends are better than weekdays, and posts at 8 A.M. and before and after lunch are more likely to be shared than posts at other times.[22] Facebook itself provides ideas about how to increase engagement (comments, likes, sharing) on its site. It suggests that although touchy-feely conversations are okay, there are stronger responses from posts on topics relevant to the brand. Facebook finds that photos and videos generate the most sharing, which is more meaningful because it taps into the friend-of-a-fan network.[23]

● **Principle**
Organizations use social media to engage customers and create relationships as well as reach a network of people.

Marketers use these new social media tools to promote brands, engage customers, and create brand relationships, and most of these efforts are inexpensive compared with other forms of marketing communication. They are not only a point of connection—a digital touchpoint—but they also engage a "social web," a network of people connected through the social media site. Social media sites open up a new environment of conversation-based marketing communication, creating opportunities for entirely different forms of nearly instantaneous customer engagement with a brand.[24]

The movie *Hunger Games*, for example, was aggressively promoted through social networks, saving its Lionsgate marketing firm millions of dollars in conventional movie advertising. The art of movie promotion is increasingly moving to the web. One Lionsgate executive, Jon Feltheimer, predicted that movie studios will buy fewer TV ads and use more online promotion. The studio surveyed "The Hunger Games" moviegoers, said Feltheimer, and discovered that 55 percent of them obtained "the majority of the information about the movie" online.[25]

Given that social media generate individual posts, are the numbers of people reached through social media worth an organization's time? In an ideal world, if a brand has 100,000 fans on its e-commerce site and we assume that the median number of friends among adult Facebook users is 200, a brand post could *potentially* be shared with 20 million Facebook users. That's a lot of reach for one click.[26]

Mobile Marketing

Cell phones have become the medium of choice for many marketers. Not only can they run ads on them, but they can also send messages to people in their target market. **Mobile marketing** makes the cell phone a personal point-of-sale device with a strategy designed to contact people on the run. The Matter of Practice feature explains why this is such an attractive medium for advertisers.

Mobile messaging will continue to evolve. The tipping point for computer-based internet advertising came in 2004 when broadband access in homes passed 50 percent. The same is happening with mobile. Faster speeds allow for better viewing of mobile video content, streaming movies, TV, and advertising and bring mobile interactions closer to reality. But faster speeds will come at a cost. All major US wireless carriers have high-speed broadband networks, and new larger-screen mobile tablets and phones, while improving viewer experiences, gobble up larger swaths of expensive bandwidth.

The future of mobile devices is in their role of connecting users with products, services, and media in an unprecedented way. With branded mobile websites or apps, mobile users can access product information and make transactions anywhere and anytime. Mobile users can compare product prices in stores with offerings online, which not only creates a new shopping experience for consumers, but also intensifies the competition among different outlets, thus fundamentally transforming the retailing business. Mobile devices can serve as a bridge between the users and conventional advertising media. For example, mobile users can scan a QR code or key in a ** number from a magazine or billboard to access digital content right on their mobile device.

These innovative mobile uses help integrate mobile devices into the daily lives of users around the world and make mobile devices, using Marshall McLuhan's description, an indispensable extension of human beings.

Texting, for example, is a way marketers can contact customers and customers can contact companies. A real estate agent can send a text message to a client about a new listing, media can run instant polls, and organizations can text their members with announcements. The last example involves **group text messaging** software, which moves individualized communication into a form of mass communication.

Your Mobile Future

Michael Hanley, *Ball State University*
Hairong Li, *Michigan State University*

How "mobile" will your lifestyle be in the future?

Mobile phones are the most ubiquitous personal communication device in history and are the fastest growing delivery channel for advertising and IMC. How ubiquitous? There are more than seven billion people on Earth, and by 2020 there will be more than nine billion mobile subscriptions, two-thirds of those from smartphones. Half of all global internet users access the web through their mobile devices.

By 2018, US mobile advertising spending is projected to grow to nearly $60 billion and account for 70 percent of all digital ad spending. This explosive growth has prompted mobile marketing experts to label mobile phones the "fourth screen" of marketing, after movies, TV, and computers, and for good reason: the mobile device is the first wireless medium where traditional mass media—TV, radio, print, internet and cinema—can all be accessed.

Are the growth estimates for mobile advertising and promotions hype, reality, or both? To know, it's important to understand the scope of mobile users in the United States.

By mid-2015, there were more US mobile subscriptions than there were US citizens, because some people have multiple mobile phones. With the continued fragmenting of consumer media into smaller user-selected niches and the continued drop in advertising revenues by many traditional media segments, mobile devices have become an ideal platform for the delivery of personalized marketing messages.

But how will the future be different for a mobile-connected society? And how will that impact marketers as they try to target smaller and more mobile microaudiences?

The mobile phone is the communication device that most people say they could not live without. Always on, always available, always in touch—mobile devices provide a one-stop gateway to the information and entertainment we crave. As the sophistication of mobile apps, services, and websites evolves, we are becoming better shoppers, are more healthy, and are able to stay more constantly in touch with our friends and family.

Mobile devices are also becoming important gateways to other parts of our lives, allowing us to expand our me-time by using just-in-time purchasing of products and services; think Uber and Airbnb. Connected devices like wearables—think Apple Watch and Fitbit—medical sensors, smart homes, vehicles, and appliances—all part of the evolving Internet of Things that stay connected through smartphones—are just beginning to impact our mobile future.

For advertisers and marketers, the mobile channel offers these expanding message delivery options:

- Text messaging
- Internet of Things
- Search—keywords, images, and sound
- Games
- Music
- Location services, including geotargeting
- Photo and video sharing sites, like Pinterest and Mobli
- Video and audio streaming
- Mobile TV, free and subscription
- Mobile AM/FM radio, free (all smartphones have radio tuners built in)
- Social media—most users access through mobile devices
- Augmented reality (AR) and virtual reality (VR) applications

Hanley is coauthor of *Mobile Marketing Essentials* (2016).

But mobile marketing involves more than phone calls and text messages. The Mobile Marketing Association defines *mobile marketing* as the use of wireless media, primarily cellular phones and personal digital assistants (PDAs), such as RIM's BlackBerry. (PDAs evolved from early handheld digital tools that were used to keep track of schedules, contact lists, and personal reminder notes.)

The explosion in brand communication possibilities came with the introduction of the iPhone and a number of other smartphone makes and models. *Ad Age* said about the smartphone "It is a computer, a camera, a map, a compass, and, for a growing number, a wallet."[27] From a marketing perspective, smartphones can be used to check reviews, comparison shop, and even buy things.

Communication planners are interested in smartphones because they can be used in highly targeted mobile marketing strategies to deliver personal ads to folks on the go. A successful example uses a mobile ad campaign to promote Starbucks' green-tea natural energy-booster Refreshers beverages to its customers who are interested in this product. Using short messages and informative imagery as well as a coupon, the ads link to a store locator to find the nearest Starbucks location.[28]

Mobile marketers have found several important uses for smartphones, with search advertising claiming 49 percent of the advertising spending. Banner ads are next with 33 percent followed by messaging at 12 percent and video ads at 6 percent. Altogether, that totaled $2.6 million in 2012.[29]

A great example of what can be done with mobile advertising is Google, which won the Mobile Grand Prix award at Cannes with an ad that re-created the iconic "Hilltop" ad for Coca-Cola for the small screen. In addition to presenting "I want to buy the world a Coke," the mobile ad also lets viewers send a free Coke to friends anywhere in the world distributed via certain wired Coke vending machines. Essentially a B2B ad, Google is selling the creative capabilities of mobile advertising. Check out this fascinating ad at http://bit.ly/Lz4RAr.[30]

Another device in the mobile marketing space is the iPad, which energized the tablet market. It is a wireless tablet hybrid that has some of the capabilities of smartphones but also combines some of the features of a laptop or notebook computer as well as an e-reader (books, newspapers, magazines), a video viewer, and a video game player.

Marketers are finding gold in **branded apps** for cell phones, which are generally free but prominently linked to a brand. For example, REI has an app for snow reports. Apps that help travelers navigate their journeys lead in usage.

Apps that showcase the brand in a fun way are particularly popular. Zippo has a free virtual lighter for iPhones that looks and acts like a real lighter. You can jerk the phone to open or close the Zippo, and a little button lets you light it with a simple flick. The point is strictly brand identification, but there is a bit of utility in using a cell phone for that Zippo moment in concerts when people hold up their lights—in this case, images of a Zippo on their iPhones. It's almost a toy, but the engagement with the brand has made the Zippo app one of the more popular ones.

Other apps offer more utility. Banks, for example, let you check balances, pay bills, make transfers, and locate branches, and with the GPS navigation capability in some smartphones, the app can even plot a route. Kraft's app iFood Assistant, which is one of the few that comes with a price tag, provides recipes, cooking instruction videos, meal shopping lists, and store locators. Most new media provide apps that carry news feeds, some with a video. Even small stores can use apps for in-store customers that let them view merchandise or bypass the cash register and pay for their products on their mobile phones.

Although cell phone advertising is sometimes seen as an invasion of privacy, that puzzles marketers because, as *Advertising Age* reported, "it is very much a permission-based channel of communication."[31] As in other forms of advertising, the way to be less intrusive is to be more relevant and offer an option to **opt in**.

Principle

Through its geotargeting capability, mobile marketing can reach willing customers in the area with product and promotional news and announcements.

Mobile marketing can do more than point to a store's location. It can also make use of wireless communication (WIFI) combined with GPS locational devices to reach nearby customers with its *geotargeting* capabilities. A form of "push marketing," these opt-in devices increase engagement between brands and their fans.

If a cell phone user, for example, registers with a favorite store, that store can contact the user when he or she is in the neighborhood. These calls can announce special deals or invite the customer in for a taste test or some other type of promotion. The phones can also be used to contact a store. Pizza Hut and Papa John's customers, for example, can use their smartphones to place orders and, by dragging and dropping toppings onto virtual pizzas, can create their own personal pizza. Domino's features a simulated photographic version on its website that can be customized.[32]

Mobile marketing involves more than just cell phones; it also includes laptop computers and even portable game consoles as vehicles that can deliver content and encourage direct response within a cross-media communication program. Mobile marketing delivers instant messaging, video messages and downloads, and banner ads on these mobile devices.

Earned Interactive Media: Let's Listen

By earned, we mean media that carry mentions or stories about a brand, either through publicity, social media, personal contact, or word of mouth. The term *earned media* has been used in public relations to distinguish between paid advertising messages and unpaid brand mentions in the news media. Only in recent years has the word *earned* also been used to describe the way social media and word of mouth convey comments about brands.

The various media in the earned category carry conversations, complaints and criticisms, praise, and questions, all of which can, and should, be monitored by brand stewards. Most important is that they all impact the **brand reputation**, which is determined by what others say about the brand. That's a critical concept in IMC, and media strategies are particularly important in determining the strength of the brand's reputation as well as a positive impression.

Earned Publicity

We mentioned publicity in the owned media section when we discussed news releases and press kits prepared by an organization for the news media. Publicity also is an important type of earned media. In publicity, media-relations specialists seek to persuade media editors to carry stories about an organization or brand. These experts have no control over the media and can only hope that their stories are newsworthy and interesting enough to receive coverage.

When a story or significant parts of it appear in the media, the result is a **hit**. At another level, reporters may **mention** a company or brand in a story they are researching and writing. Because mentions can be either positive or negative, public relations specialists who monitor media coverage can only hope the mentions are positive. If they are negative, they may (and should) prompt a strategic response by the organization.

Because hits and mentions are not determined by the brand, they are seen as having higher levels of credibility than advertising and other forms of owned media. The reason is that publicity relies on an **implied third-party endorsement**—communication that is not initiated by the company. The medium and its reputation for credibility, which is based on its perceived objectivity, create a halo of respect for the message.

Word of Mouth

Interactivity starts with personal communication. That's why **word of mouth** has caught the attention of brand communication planners. The closer the medium is to a dialogue or the more users can generate or manipulate the content, the more the brand communication moves away from traditional advertiser-controlled one-way advertising. In the previous section, we talked about interactive media that organizations use to initiate interaction. In this section, we'll talk about the core of interactivity—personal conversation—and why it is important in brand communication.

A study of media use by syndicated research firm BIGresearch, which polled 15,000 consumers, found that the most influential form of communication is word of mouth. The finding was supported by other research that has found word of mouth to be the most important influence on consumer decision making—considerably more important than traditional media advertising.[33]

Rather than top down, word-of-mouth brand messages flow side to side, creating a network of shared brand experiences and impressions that interconnect within extended communication networks, both personal and professional. In other words, friends (and business colleagues) talk to friends, and each person has his or her own network of contacts through which messages can spread.

Buzz and Viral Communication   Brand communication planners have developed a growing respect for media that generate **buzz**—a cycle of word-of-mouth interactions, either personal or online, within a network of friends. The idea is to get people talking about a brand because we recognize that the most important factor in consumer decision making, next to personal experience with the brand, is the opinions of others.

One research finding is that buzz is best generated by disrupting common patterns of thinking; in other words, the idea is new and surprising.[34] One study found that whether the

14.3 Discuss what is meant by earned media and how organizations relate to brand discussions that are beyond their control.

● **Principle**
Earned media with their collection of brand mentions and comments give a reading on brand reputation; that is, they reflect what people say about the brand.

● **Principle**
When news media run a story or give a positive mention to a brand, a halo of respect for the message is created because of the perceived objectivity of the medium.

● **Principle**
The more interactive a medium and the closer it is to a dialogue, the more personal and persuasive the communication experience.

Photo: Courtesy of Eichborn AG and Jung von Matt/Neckar GmbH

Flies are the most unlikely of all media, but they were enlisted by a German publisher as a form of flying banners at the annual Frankfurt Book Fair.

information generates buzz is based on whether it's "interesting." But in face-to-face communication, the topics are more conversational and not as focused on "interesting" ideas. This research suggests that being interesting is more important for certain types of social media, but in personal conversation, the focus is more on top-of-mind personal experiences.[35] In other words, marketers should match the medium with the message in a word-of-mouth strategy.

The term **viral communication** describes the way a message spreads on the internet through interconnected networks of acquaintances. The spread of messages depends totally on consumers creating buzz through their own emails and social media chatter. Remember the numbers we quoted earlier about how one click to 100,000 Facebook friends who have 200 people in their network can lead to 20 million impressions? That's a great example of the power of viral communication.

What video content will spread worldwide? Companies such as Jukin Media analyze viral videos and help companies understand how to achieve maximum exposure and consumer engagement with their content. They use three genres for classification of the most successful clips: "cute," "fail," and "win." "Cute" is dancing toddlers and puppies or kittens. "Fail" includes wipeouts and schemes gone awry. "Win" is whatever affirms faith in humanity.[36]

A now-classic YouTube video that captured a lot of attention worldwide and went viral showed tiny advertising banners on flies that flitted around with their miniscule billboards at the annual Frankfurt Book Fair; the video was probably the ultimate in guerilla marketing. This Big Media Idea came from the German agency Jung von Matt. Search for "Amazing Fly Guerrilla Marketing" on YouTube to see how this idea got off the ground.

Business-to-Consumer-to-Consumer (B2C2C) Influence Some media plans are specifically designed to reach influential or early adopters whose opinions are valued by others. These strategies focus on finding the right individuals to deliver a message—that is, the best-connected people at the hub of an extended social network who will like a brand or brand message and promote it among the people they know.

Who are these people? It takes sophisticated sociographic networking mapping to find them, but generally they are described as community or fashion leaders, well-known experts, or people you turn to for advice.[37] This word-of-mouth marketing strategy is known as **brand advocacy** or **customer referral**. The idea is not just to create buzz, but to connect with influential, high-quality contacts who will spread the brand's story.

Japanese marketing communication giant Dentsu expresses this idea in its **B2C2C** concept, which we mentioned briefly in Chapter 13. On its face, it looks like a traditional model for top-down communication, but it goes beyond that. An expansion and modification of the traditional business-to-consumer (B2C) marketing concept, the Dentsu B2C2C strategy proposes that a marcom message may emanate from a business and then move to key customers and influencers who then talk about it with other consumers in the target market.

The important part of this model of word-of-mouth influence is the C2C aspect. Because of the interactive network, messages move back and forth between and among consumers. The messages may even recirculate back from consumers to key influential customers who are in touch with the business or maybe directly back to the business.

This model identifies not only how messages circulate, but also how influential people in the network make their opinions known and spread their influence. In Chapter 5, we talked about how influence moves through steps in the persuasion process. This B2C2C model illustrates the important role of a **brand advocate**—that key customer or stakeholder—who has positive things to share about a brand within a circle of friends and contacts. These earned mentions are critical. That's why organizations track social media conversations to identify these important interactions.

⬡ **Principle**
A B2C2C strategy is designed to move a message from a business to key influential customers who then talk about it with other consumers. Messages may use the same route to come back to the business.

Social Media Mentions

We introduced social media earlier as a platform an organization can use to insert its brands into friendship-based communication networks. However, at its core, the social media platform is online word of mouth that allows users to express themselves, interact with friends, publish their own content on the internet, and refer to brands and products they like. Social networks, such as Facebook, Instagram, Pinterest, and Tumblr, link people who share interests; LinkedIn connects business contacts.

Mostly, social media are about friends. That's why on Facebook, when you are invited to connect with people, you are asked to "friend" them. Users, including brands and brand fans, can create posts on their own Facebook site and can also post them on their friends "walls" as well as to other content sites.

Hairong Li, a Michigan State professor and contributor to this book, explained how certain characteristics of social media—personal content, user engagement, social relationships, and group dynamics—create social engagement that helps individuals, particularly young people, develop a sense of self. Li said that "sharing experience with others is integral to how we construct a coherent yet often fragmented sense of self in a networked society." According to Li, social media are all about relationships:

> Think about your friends in Facebook or MySpace. Some of them are people you first met in person and then continued that relationship online, and some are people with whom you are acquainted only online. Whether you've ever met them in person, some online acquaintances are close friends, some are merely random friends, and the rest are probably in between. Your relationships with these friends will affect how you respond to ads in social media. For example, a close friend of yours may post a comment about a new product she just bought and how she likes it. Wouldn't that make you think about the product after reading her comment?[38]

Digital conversations among friends create opportunities for researchers to get raw, unfiltered brand impressions from consumers, but how do we monitor these conversations? The Burson-Marsteller agency monitors earned media as it tracks the mentions of Global Fortune 100 companies on social media. In a sample month, the firm's Social Media Check-Up found that there are more than 10 million mentions of these 100 companies. The companies with the most mentions were HP, Ford, Sony, AT&T, Samsung, Toyota, Honda, Walmart, BP, and Verizon. The Check-Up discovered that only 70 percent of the companies respond to comments and posts. On average, more than 6,000 people were talking about each brand. On Twitter, however, 79 percent of the companies also had accounts and were attempting to engage users with retweets.[39]

Twitter or Microblogs   The concept of a blog with diary and essay postings was reinvented in miniature by **Twitter**, which permits posts of 140 characters or fewer. These mini-posts, called **tweets**, invite users to share their daily doings and immediate thoughts with *followers* of the **microblog**. Generally the followers are people known to the tweeter, although in the case of fans, they may approach the size and scale of a large mass audience. Actor Ashton Kutcher, for example, became the first to collect 1 million followers on Twitter, narrowly beating CNN's breaking news feed in a widely publicized race.[40]

Twitter posts are searchable based on their **hashtags**, which operate like keywords. **Tagging** by inserting a hash symbol (#) before a word in a tweet makes that word a category or topic that can be tracked. People tweeting about a brand or company will tag their post with the hash symbol plus the company name. Brand stewards and fans can follow the tag to see the stream of related mentions.

A hashtag backfire may also occur. Even if a company has good intentions, hashtags may not yield desired results. For example, McDonald's launched a marketing campaign around #McDStories to encourage customers to share fun, positive experiences. However, unsatisfied customers jumped on the hashtag and shared their negative experiences. Gap and American Apparel enraged victims of Hurricane Sandy when they used the #Sandy hashtag as an opportunity to promote themselves. The point is that brands can't assume that sponsored hashtags will generate the desired response.[41]

Twitter has become the medium of choice for complaints. Customers can spend many minutes on the phone waiting to talk to customer service—or get lost in the menu options—but Twitter messages are quick and easy. CitiBank, for example, has a Twitter address of @askCiti where customers can bypass the call center and get more immediate attention through the bank's social media operation. Plugged-in companies follow these tweets and are quick to respond, often with a telephone call, which beats waiting in a phone queue for a customer service person to answer.[42]

Advertising messages also can appear on Twitter as part of a user's stream of messages. A growing group of Tweeters have signed up to allow advertisers to send commercial messages under their name. Sometimes the ads are testimonials embedded in a person's regular stream of tweets (e.g., where to go to find M&Ms that can be customized or custom-label bottles of wine); others turn over their stream to an ad broker who inserts messages for brands and organizations, such as the Make a Wish Foundation.

A number of start-up companies are trying to match up brands and topics with influencers who are important within a topical community. As you can imagine, this practice is controversial, particularly if the commercial message is unacknowledged.

Reviews and Comments Movie reviews in newspapers have been around for years, but the development of social media has seen reviews pop up all over the web. Amazon features customer-contributed reviews of its books and other products. A secondary industry has even built up around paid reviews by ordinary people for e-commerce sites. An article on this practice observed that "consumer reviews are powerful because, unlike old-style advertising and marketing, they offer the illusion of truth."[43]

Angie's List has institutionalized the concept of local reviews by compiling trusted reviews of local businesses, such as dentists, plumbers, and landscapers. Through a national network of local websites, users subscribe to access the list. But the important dimension of Angie's List is that these service providers are reviewed and graded by consumers. The reviews are checked by staff and then compiled and posted on the list. Yelp is another social review and local search service. On both Angie's List and Yelp, advertisers can get preferred search position and extra listing space.

Another type of mention is the comments section that follows at the end of stories and blogs in online news media. If it's a business-related topic, it is important that these comments be monitored by brand stewards.

The Media of Sharing

Some may find it hard to believe that people talk about brands online, but they do. **Fan pages** exist for many brands where communities of people, usually loyal users, focus on or follow a favorite brand. Pepsi has some 8 million Facebook followers who contribute user-generated marketing materials, such as photos of Pepsi in interesting settings. Pepsi fans also get to see behind-the-scenes clips from commercials and other videos.[44]

Fans also share negative experiences and complaints as well as good brand experiences on some fan sites. There are even hate sites for some brands where critics gather to complain.

Procter and Gamble has set up an office in Silicon Valley to develop social networking sites for its many brands. Its Pringles fan page has more than 24 million global fans.[45] These advertisers use video clips, quizzes, downloadable gifts like ring tones and icons, and, of course, links to their own websites. Brand personalities, such as Geico's gecko, are particularly useful as featured characters with their own pages on Facebook.

Online Communities Fans are an example of an online **virtual community**, which is organized around a topic, brand, or shared interest. One example is the "smart USA" website, the official social networking site for "smart USA Insiders," the fans of smart cars.

Photo: Courtesy Mercedes-Benz

The smart USA Insider website enables owners and enthusiasts of the smart car in the United States to interact and stay connected with the smart brand and one another. The site allows members to create personal profiles and blogs, post videos and photos, participate in forum discussions, and join groups and list events. The site also gives members access to exclusive updates directly from smart USA, including occasional blog posts from smart USA's president. Check out the "smart USA insider" website (http://www.smartusainsider.com) and develop a profile of who you think might be a candidate for membership.

Brand communities are also ways to develop loyalty and strong brand relationships in partnership with the brand. The Harley Owner's Group (HOG) is probably the best known brand community and one of the biggest, with more than 1 million members. In addition to local groups, the HOG community is supported with its own website, www.hog.com.

Social media are international, and sites based on sharing are particularly important in Asian cultures. For example, Babytree is a Chinese-language site for parents of infants, with 50 percent of Chinese internet-using moms visiting the parent site. Rather than being an information site, Babytree functions more like a Facebook for parents, where a network of moms try to help themselves and one another, which is an interesting cultural difference from the US-based BabyCenter.[46]

Other sites that engage communities include *Flickr*, which is an online image and video management website; *YouTube*, the giant video posting service; and *Tumblr*, which is a blog-hosting platform where millions of users post their blogs, which get reposted as "tumblogs." *Instagram* is a photo-sharing social network that is known for its photo-editing capabilities. *Google+* invites viewers to share games and streaming images as well as photos, hangouts, and events. *SoundCloud* is a Facebook app that lets users share sounds, such as voices, musics, or other audio forms.

Pinterest, which is the third most popular social site after Facebook and Twitter,[47] allows users to pin images, videos, and other things that they find interesting to their pinboards. It's a sharing site in that images can be "repinned" and passed along to friends. But Pinterest offers more than personal online bulletin boards. An example of using Pinterest to make a point comes from England, where a video by Confused.com, a site known for price comparisons, posted a film of a woman in really tall heels who struggles to drive her car. It ends with contest information for viewers on how to win a pair of folding designer flat driving pumps by posting a picture of preposterous footwear.[48]

Marketers can join these online communities by buying ads or by posting images or blogs. Adidas, for example, sponsored an official soccer blog on Tumblr and was one of the first to advertise on the site.

Social games are the most popular type of shared-interest app on Facebook, which inspired Google+ to jump into this market. Facebook players spend, on average, about 45 minutes with a game. The Facebook-based *FarmVille*, created by online game marketer Zynga, was one of the first truly social games with a dedicated community of players who spend money on game currency they can use to buy virtual products. They also engage in business as they buy and sell things. Brands can enter into the game in various ways, but usually they participate by buying a location from which they, too, can do business.

FarmVille was followed by *Words with Friends*, another Zynga entry in the casual-game category, but one that is a hit on mobile phones. Some of these online video games charge for a download, but many bring in revenue from selling ads and sponsorships or selling products within the game. The next change will see "cloud" games that live on the internet and are streamed to computers or handheld devices.

Social media relationships offer opportunities for brand messages, particularly as people serve as viral marketing agents. Hairong Li points out that when you see movie trailers and album posters on the pages of your friends, they can be considered **user-generated ads**.[49] By user-generated ads, we mean content of commercial nature that is created or posted on the pages of users in social media.

Crowdsourcing   We mentioned **crowdsourcing** in Chapter 6 as a tool used by researchers for extended focus groups. That's also how the online encyclopedia *Wikipedia* was developed: by mobilizing a digital crowd to provide collective intelligence. In marketing, crowdsourcing can be used by shoppers to discover and select products as well as generate ideas for new products.

Slim Jim was an early user of crowdsourcing to engage its fans, who were invited to come up with a new name for the brand's community manager, resulting in "the Sultan of Snap." Fans are asked to decide what online projects the Sultan will take on as well as give feedback on videos and proposed and existing products.

Fab.com is a pioneer in crowd-sourced online retailing that promotes flash sales of whimsical, limited-edition items. The site's users have suggested and promoted such things as candy-colored typewriters, funny T-shirts, knitted hats for beards, and wild socks: bumblebee-striped, neon orange, and polka dots of all colors. Its fans even posted weird sock images on Pinterest and tagged them on Tumbler blogs.[50]

The site started by inviting design aficionados and influencers—found on design-related Facebook sites—to sign up. The strategy was to build an e-commerce design site through word of mouth. It tracked the ripple effect of sharing and discovered that each person who joined typically invited three friends to join as well. The site managers are devoted to metrics and continually chart customer sharing and orders.

Earned and Interactive Media Considerations

The opportunities brought to brand communication by word of mouth and social media are exciting. However, there are some things to think about in deploying media strategies in these new areas, such as dealing with negative communication and fake messages as well as estimating the true price of digital media messages.

Dealing with Negatives and Fakes   An unhappy customer is more than just one person's bad experience, particularly in retailing, because of the power of word of mouth. People share these experiences, and those conversations get passed on. Research has found that although 6 percent of unhappy shoppers will contact the store with their complaints, 31 percent will tell other people about the unhappy experience. Furthermore, half of the people in the study reported they have avoided a store because of someone else's negative experience. The study concluded that if 100 people have a bad experience, a retailer stands to lose between 32 and 36 current or potential customers.[51]

It's important for marketers to intervene in some way to turn the negative impression into a positive one. Tom Duncan, formerly a brand manager at a processed meat company, described his company's policy of sending a letter from the president to anyone with a complaint. Most people were so impressed that the company cared at the executive level that they said they would return as brand customers.[52] That was before the days of social media, but it does illustrate the importance of proactive strategies to deal with customer dissatisfaction.

Another problem is fake sites that can damage brand reputation. The internet in most Western countries is a wide-open system with little policing. That means fake Facebook pages gather likes, fake tweets gather followers, and false reviews bedevil consumer websites. Phony likes and paid reviews damage trust even if some brand supporter is behind the effort to puff up the brand's positive mentions, and they also undermine the credibility of the site, whether Facebook or Craigslist.[53]

Cheap but Not Free   We used a chart in Chapter 12 that showed the relative percent of brand communication media budgets dedicated to the internet. If you remember, it was a small part of the pie chart. The reason is that the charges for the use of digital media, particularly in the owned, interactive, and earned categories, are relatively low compared to media budget busters like television. At the same time, they don't have the reach that mass media like television have.

But that doesn't mean that digital media are free. Most of them demand resources, such as staffing, hardware and software systems, maintenance and operational support, and, perhaps, fees. In all cases, internet marketers must budget for the brand monitoring systems that cull mentions from the internet. These listening systems also need metrics to track volume and determine the level of the impact.

A word of caution is in order, however. Social media open up opportunities for those valuable referrals where one friend talks to another about a brand, but it's hard to know how much that happens. IBM, for example, tried to track these referrals from Facebook, Twitter, and YouTube on 2012's Black Friday (the day after Thanksgiving) and found that even though online sales increased 21 percent, just 0.34 percent came from referrals on social media.[54] However, many companies are finding ways to convert consumer buzz into positive actions. To catch the attention of its large social media following and introduce its new mobile ordering app, Taco Bell used an unusual tactic: it did a "blackout" for 72 hours and then turned off all Taco Bell social channels, including Twitter, Instagram, YouTube, Facebook, Tumblr, and even TacoBell .com. The fan and press inquiries earned 2 billion impressions for the company's message that the new way to Taco Bell is #OnlyInTheApp; in addition, more than 2.5 million customers downloaded the app as a result.[55] Taco Bell also won a Silver Effie Award for this campaign.

Multiplatform Brand Communication

14.4 Explain how multi-platform brand communication works and why it is important.

We've been talking about a mix of media that we've categorized first as owned and then as earned. You probably noticed that platforms such as public relations and promotions, but particularly interactive, were found in both of those big categories. That is because media forms are constantly changing shape and moving across what used to be commonly understood categories. TV was TV, print was print, and digital was digital. It wasn't that long ago that we would plan a television campaign or an out-of-home campaign with a message strategy dominated by the strengths of a primary medium, but no longer. Owned and earned aren't nice and neat, like media categories were in the simpler eras of media planning. It's a messy business.

Now we talk about how various media function, how these functions are interrelated, and how they can be used to extend each other's reach and impact. We use the word **platforms** to talk about big functions, such as public relations, promotions, and direct marketing, as well as big packages of media, such as print, broadcast, social media, viral media, search media, and mobile media. They are all platforms. **Multiplatform** media planning is complicated because sometimes the same types of POE media—paid, owned, and earned—are used in all these different areas.

One of the biggest differences in 21st-century media is that media planning now operates across not only a variety of media, but also across a multitude of platforms and marcom areas. The multiplatform use of blogs, linked social networks, and online communities (sports and celebrity fans, brand communities) as well as traditional media to engage customers and other stakeholders is designed to engage them personally and build brand relationships.

So let's end this chapter by talking about this bigger picture of media, particularly viral media and social media programs that are examples of more comprehensive approaches to POE planning. We'll put them in perspective with a closing note about multiplatform marketing.

● **Principle**
Conversation-based social media through such sites as Facebook and Twitter is word-of-mouth advertising on steroids.

Viral Marketing Programs

Viral marketing combines the marketing perspective with social media to create brand-focused viral communication strategies and campaigns. Designed to deliver a groundswell of opinion, buzz, or marketplace demand for a product, **viral marketing** initiates online communication to circulate a brand message among and between family, friends, and other contacts. It's word-of-mouth advertising on steroids.

Depending on public interest in the topic, this practice can distribute a message to an ever-widening network, and messages can flash across the internet like wildfire. Remember "The Diet Coke/Mentos Experiment" that resulted in a geyser of emails that exploded again and again around the internet? That viral message was watched by millions, and Mentos sales rose 15 percent. Check out the YouTube version of this story at www.youtube.com/watch?v=hKoB0MHVBvM.

Viral video technology has made it possible for interesting videos from a variety of sources (ads, films, YouTube) to be sent from one friend to another in a vast network of personal connections. Rhett & Link is a team of YouTubers who created a microsite, www.ilovelocalcommercials .com, to promote themselves as ad creators. Check out the site to see their self-promotion as well as some of their creations, all of which have been distributed as viral videos.

One of the first viral hits was Burger King's "Subservient Chicken," which helped launch the BK Broiler Chicken Sandwich. The silly costumed chicken would respond to commands to do things like tap dance or do exercises. It attracted millions of viewers who then shared the site with millions of their friends. Praised as possibly the most popular marketing website of its time, the site by Crispin Porter + Bogusky (CP+B) quickly registered half a billion hits in the first couple of weeks as well as a big increase in sales of Burger King's new chicken sandwiches. The strategy was to liven up Burger King's advertising, which was seen as boring, and give it a more edgy and fun image.

Photo: Amy Graves/WireImage for BWR Public Relations/Getty Images

With the line "Get chicken just the way you like it," Burger King's agency, Crispin Porter + Bogusky, launched the "Subservient Chicken" interactive video website for Burger King. Play with the "Subservient Chicken" and see if you think it is captivating. Why would it have been so popular at the time it was introduced?

Pepsi developed a character named Uncle Drew who brought Pepsi Max raves for the YouTube video that features basketball star Kyrie Irving. Irving was disguised as a sweatshirt-wearing, pot-bellied elderly man named Uncle Drew who is watching his nephew play a pick-up basketball game. To replace an injured player, Uncle Drew joins in and stuns watchers with his crossover dribbles, over-the-shoulder dunks, and three pointers. The video also shows the behind-the-scenes story about how Irving was transformed into the old guy. Check it out on Twitter with #uncledrew and on YouTube.

Viral communication has a dark side, too. Like the "hashtag backfire" mentioned earlier, a worry for planners is that viral messages can also spread negative stories or even be used to organize a boycott against a brand. As Simon Clift, Unilever's chief marketing officer, explained, "No matter how big your advertising spending, small groups of consumers on a tiny budget might hijack the conversation."[56] Negative word-of-mouth moves like a flash flood through the internet. It probably moves even faster than the fun stuff and can do immense damage to a brand's reputation.

In an ironic turn, the legendary Alex Bogusky, who retired from his former agency CP+B, became a supporter of the Center for Science in the Public Interest's campaign against sugary soft drinks. He created a parody four-minute animated film featuring a white polar bear family that looks a lot like the Coca-Cola bears. Shown guzzling soda and suffering the ill effects of too much sugar, the bears eventually dump their sodas. Designed as a viral video, the film drives viewers to a website, www.therealbears.org, where they get "the Unhappy Truth about Soda." Viewers are invited to share the video: "Facebook it. Tweet it. Pin it. Google+ it. Email the link to your friends and relatives. . . . Sharing is the only means we have to make sure the unhappy truth about soda gets out to the world."[57]

Social-Media Marketing

Similar to viral marketing, **social media marketing** mixes different kinds of media together in a strategy to drive consumer interaction and build widespread brand visibility and awareness. Brands can sometimes instigate the viral process, but there's no guarantee the word will spread, and the brand can certainly not control it.

Starbucks, named by *Fortune* magazine as one of its Top 10 Social Media Stars, makes creative use of its Facebook page. There you will find nearly 30 million fans talking about the company online and posting favorite photos of their lives with Starbucks. In addition to posts that mention the company, you'll also find deals and contests as well as discussions of Starbucks' community service activities. Users can manage their Starbucks account and send gifts to friends. But what really makes the site different is Starbucks' willingness both to display complaints from unhappy customers and to create a brand relationship program around their negative experiences. Check it out at www.facebook.com/Starbucks.

● **Principle**
Marketers who use social media recognize the value in conversations and customer relationship-building communication.

The reason these social networking sites are so attractive to marketers is that they engage the power of friendship-based influence. Because of these relationships, network members are more likely to respond to messages on the sites, including ads, if they are effective at becoming part of the social context. Social media also are good with local campaigns, particularly for small businesses. A limitation is that social media's posts and conversations may not convert prospects to customers as well as a more directly associated tool, such as search marketing.

Another aspect of social media and viral communication is that, for better or worse, these media mentions and viral videos can live forever. A well-liked YouTube video can be watched for years; likewise, a negative story, such as Bogusky's "The Unhappy Truth" video parody, can follow a brand forever.

Integration of Platforms

In his Part 4 opening comments, Larry Kelley said that people come in contact with a brand message in many different ways: due to the convergence of media platforms, content, branding, and consumer engagement. What that means is that brand communication today is more diverse and complex than ever before. Not only do brand messages move from one medium to another, but they start in one form, say print or TV, and wind up as a YouTube video that you can watch on your cell phone.

The Old Spice "The Man Your Man Could Smell Like" called attention to this shifting of platforms with a 30-second commercial featuring Isaiah Mustafa that moved from a television commercial during the 2010 Super Bowl to video-sharing websites, where it received more than 41 million viewers and won a Grand Prix at Cannes.

Another example of a multiplatform program comes from H&R Block, the tax preparation company that reached into the online tax filing space with a campaign that uses a Facebook page as well as a dedicated digital TV spot, blogs, a YouTube channel, apps, and widgets. An army of 1,000 tweeters respond to the "Ask a Tax Advisor" buttons on the H&R Block website as well as answer questions directly and "listen" in on topics being discussed on community forums. Realizing the growing importance of online services, the company hopes to maintain its presence with digital filers as well as support its stores and encourage filers to consult with its staff of professional tax experts both online and in stores.[58]

But we haven't seen anything yet. A *New York Times* article described new media forms, such as internet-connected glasses and wearable computers, not to mention voice-activated assistants like the iPhone's Siri or Microsoft's experiments with gesture-recognition computer programs. The idea is that computer-accessible instant information will become ubiquitous and the computers that drive these new media forms will be able to do much more than search on command.[59] Although these technological fantasies will open up unexplored and new opportunities in brand communication, we shouldn't fail to note that the media we have are also changing their shapes and that, too, opens up new opportunities.

Looking Ahead

This chapter has described the important developments in owned, interactive, and earned media. These new categories and new forms of media are changing the face of brand communication. Digital media in particular are bringing new forms of media as well as communication to brand message strategies. It is an exciting time to be a student in this field because the changes are happening at the fingertips of young people.

Chapter 15 will pull all these media channels and platforms together to explain how media planning and buying are managed but are also changing to meet the demands of this dynamic industry.

IT'S A WRAP

 **Xbox Wins**

The "Survival" billboard for Xbox is a great example of a how a firm can use traditional media to engage a lot of consumers in an interactive campaign and achieve tremendous earned media attention. Along with the attention that came with being one of the most awarded campaigns of 2015, "Survival" resonated with gamers and nongamers alike, creating widespread awareness and engagement. For example, the average "dwell time" for a good billboard is about eight seconds. The "Survival" billboard's was eight *minutes* (6,000 percent higher).

The event had 3.8 million views across the "Survival" Billboard website, Twitch, Facebook, YouTube, and syndicated partners, including Game and IGN, followed by 32,000 social media comments. Total impressions topped 46 million, with more than 50 media articles written, which was the equivalent of $6 million in earned media. To top it all off, Adam the railway engineer who won the top prize managed to also get a date with fellow contestant Eve, who came in third place. And that's something you can't measure!

Logo: Courtesy McCann London.

KEY OBJECTIVES SUMMARY

14.1. Explain what is meant by owned media that organizations control and manage. Owned media deliver brand messages through channels owned by the organization, such as (1) *corporate media*, which include environmental design, signage, and appearances;

(2) *branded media*, which include films and video games and using brand names on events and buildings; (3) *retail media*, such as packaging and merchandising materials; and (4) *public relations and promotional media*, which include videos and publications, publicity

media, brand reminders and rewards, and place-based media.

14.2. Describe interactive owned media and explain why that interactive element is important. Certain media that are owned are also interactive in that they permit the organization to interact with customers and other stakeholders, often in personal conversations or information exchanges initiated by customers. For example, (1) *corporate media* that are interactive include digital displays on kiosks or electronic walls; (2) *direct response* is the original interactive form of marketing, and its interactions are delivered via mail, phone, or digital forms; (3) personal contact includes personal sales and customer service; (4) interactive promotional media include speeches, conferences, tours, trade shows, events, displays, and exhibits; (5) digital media, of course, are interactive, but some of them allow more control by the organization, such as email, websites, blogs, and social media accounts for Facebook and Twitter; and (6) *mobile marketing* uses cell phones to deliver highly targeted messages to people on the go.

14.3. Discuss what is meant by earned media and how organizations relate to brand discussions that are beyond their control. Earned media are those that carry brand mentions or stories. Traditionally, earned referred to (1) *publicity* hits and mentions in news media. Today, it refers to additional areas: (2) *word of mouth*, another foundational area, includes buzz and viral communication as well as influential comments; (3) social media generates brand mentions on Facebook and Twitter as well as review sites; (4) the media of sharing describes communities as well as brand fan pages and social games; and (5) viral communication is the ultimate in online social communication spread through a network of friends.

14.4. Explain how multiplatform brand communication works and why it is important. Media forms are constantly changing shape and moving across what used to be commonly understood categories. Media categories don't hold, and media mixes are messy. So we talk about functions (owned and earned), marcom areas (corporate presence, public relations, promotions, and direct marketing, to name a few), and big packages of media (social media, viral media, search media, and mobile media). They are all platforms. Media planning now operates across not only a variety of media, but also across a multitude of platforms and marcom areas.

KEY TERMS

B2C2C, p. 428
billboarding, p. 414
blog, p. 422
brand advocate, p. 428
brand advocacy, p. 428
branded apps, p. 426
branded entertainment, p. 412
branded videos, p. 412
brand reputation, p. 427
buzz, p. 427
crowdsourcing, p. 431
customer referral, p. 428
customer service, p. 419
digital installations, p. 417
direct advertising, p. 417
direct-response marketing, p. 417
e-commerce, p. 421
electronic walls, p. 417

employee communication programs, p. 418
fan pages, p. 430
flash mobs, p. 416
group text messaging, p. 424
hashtags, p. 429
hits, p. 427
implied third-party endorsement, p. 427
kiosks, p. 417
media kits, p. 418
media tours, p. 420
mentions, p. 427
microblog, p. 429
mystery shoppers, p. 419
mobile marketing, p. 424
multiplatform, p. 433
naming rights, p. 413
navigation, p. 422

network effect, p. 423
news conferences, p. 420
on-premise signs, p. 411
opt in, p. 426
platforms, p. 433
paid posts, p. 422
point-of-sale (PoS) materials, p. 414
point-of-purchase (PoP) materials, p. 414
premium, p. 415
press kits, p. 415
sales kits, p. 418
sampling, p. 420
shelf talkers, p. 414
signage, p. 411
sign spinners, p. 416
social games, p. 431
social media marketing, p. 434

socialtizing, p. 423
stickiness, p. 422
tagging, p. 429
tech support, p. 419
texting, p. 424
tour, p. 420
trade shows, p. 420
training materials, p. 419
tweets, p. 429
Twitter, p. 429
user-generated ads, p. 431
viral communication, p. 428
viral marketing, p. 433
viral video, p. 433
virtual communities, p. 430
webisodes, p. 412
website, p. 421
word of mouth, p. 427

MyLab Marketing

Go to **www.pearson.com/mylab/marketing** for MyLab discussion questions (⚙) as well as the following assisted-graded writing questions.

14-1. Why is word of mouth becoming more important in brand communication programs?

14-2. Discuss multiplatform brand communication and how it is used.

REVIEW QUESTIONS

14-3. Explain the differences between owned and earned media. Give an example of each.

14-4. What are branded media, and why are they important?

14-5. Explain how interactive owned media differ from owned media. Give an example of interactive owned media and explain why the interactive element is important.

14-6. In the owned category, what are the media of personal contact?

14-7. What are the primary types of owned digital media? How are they used?

14-8. What is mobile marketing? Why is it important?

14-9. What are online communities, and how are they used in brand communication?

14-10. Discuss multiplatform brand communication and how it is used.

DISCUSSION QUESTIONS

14-11. Does your school have a naming rights program? Where do you see it operating on campus? Can you find out how much revenue was, or is, produced by this program? How does the association help or hinder the school or academic program's image?

14-12. This chapter used the *National Geographic* social media example to illustrate a brand personality online. Find another brand that uses YouTube to create a brand personality. Critique the blog's effectiveness.

14-13. Your small agency works for a local retailer (pick one from your community) that wants to make the most effective use of its tool kit of owned media. The retailer has very little money to use on advertising. Your agency team agrees that there might be more the firm could do to strengthen the media it controls. Brainstorm among yourselves and come up with a list of at least five ideas for making better use of these opportunities.

14-14. You are the media planner for a cosmetics company introducing a new line of makeup for teenage girls. Your research indicates that social media might be an effective medium for creating awareness about your new product line. How do you design a brand communication strategy that will reach your target market successfully using owned and earned forms of social media? What other media would you recommend using as part of this campaign, and why?

14-15. A new restaurant is planned that specializes in low-fat and low-carb healthy food. You have been asked to create a multiplatform campaign for the grand opening. Evaluate various media and platforms in terms of strengths and weaknesses for this marketing situation. Identify how well each connects with the people you think would be the target market for this restaurant. What more do you need to know to determine the appropriateness of these media ideas for this new restaurant? In your response, begin by stating your brand communication goals and your presumed target audience profile. Then put together your proposal for a multiplatform media mix for this restaurant.

TAKE-HOME PROJECTS

14-16. *Portfolio Project:* Collect online mentions for three major media outlets. Choose from such media as *The New York Times* (www.nytimes.com), *The Wall Street Journal* (http://online.wsj.com/home-page), FOX News (www.foxnews.com), ABC News (http://abcnews.go.com/), *The Washington Post* (www.washingtonpost.com), *USA Today* (www.usatoday.com), MSNBC (www.msnbc.msn.com), *The Huffington Post* (www.huffingtonpost.com), NPR (www.npr.org), and PBS (www.pbs.org). What is being said about each one? From what you find, develop a brand reputation profile for each.

14-17. *Mini-Case Analysis:* Microsoft's launch of the "Rise of the Tomb Raider" video game was successful due in part to the publicity surrounding its unique Survival Billboard event.

- What elements made the Survival Billboard so interesting to people?
- What parts of the campaign involved use of interactive, earned, or owned media?
- This was a low-budget campaign. How was it able to be so successful? What have you learned from this case?

TRACE North America Case

TRACE Multicultural Innovation

Read the TRACE case in the Appendix before coming to class.

14-18. Develop an idea that you believe would reach the TRACE target market of Multicultural Millennials (age 18–29) for these media types:

a. Owned Media

b. Owned but interactive media

c. Earned interactive media

d. Multiplatform brand communication

15

Media Planning and Negotiation

KEY OBJECTIVES

15.1 Discuss what is in a media plan and the role of media research in developing media plans.

15.2 Detail the four steps in media planning and explain their importance.

15.3 List the responsibilities of media buyers.

15.4 Explain current trends in media planning and buying.

As H:N knows, media planning is a problem-solving process. The problem is, how can media choices help meet the marketing and advertising objectives? The ultimate goal is to engage the target audience with the right message in the best possible way at the best possible time in the most efficient way possible. In this chapter, we review how a media plan is developed—how media planners set objectives and develop media strategies. We then explore the media-buying function and explain how media buyers execute the plan.

Title	Client	Agency	Awards
"Mottu Mars" *Mustache March*	*Icelandic Cancer Society*	*H:N Marketing Communication, Reykjavík*	*Icelandic ARA (most effective campaign of the year), Icelandic AAA (most interesting television ad of the year, public-interest category)*

A Hair-Raising Story about Men's Cancer

How can growing a mustache help save lives? Read on to learn how a campaign convinced a third of Iceland's male population to grow a mustache and grabbed their attention for an important cause.

Cancer is the cause of roughly one in every four deaths in the United States, with similar numbers in most of the Western European world. In Iceland, huge strides had been made educating women about the dangers of breast cancer and the importance of self-examination in between scheduled searches at the doctor's office. But when the talk turned to men and cancer, butt cheeks stiffened and mouths shut: male-related cancer was taboo. Everybody, especially males, avoided talking about cancer like the plague.

Past fund-raisers and awareness campaigns had been largely ineffective. As a result, the Icelandic Cancer Society needed and challenged our agency to come up with a knockout punch in the fight against male cancer.

Photo: Krabbameinsfélag/ Icelandic Cancer Society

We took the challenge and set out from day one to create the largest and most effective awareness campaign ever created in Iceland, establishing the following campaign objectives:

1. Raise money from individuals to use in the fight against male cancer.
2. Smash the taboo and break the silence—raise awareness of male cancer closer to the level set by the social awareness and discussion acceptance of female cancer.
3. Enlighten men on the importance of self-examination and understanding what to do.

4. Move the whole nation to participation (male cancer is not only an old man thing); do one of the following: give money, raise money on our website, sport a mustache, or do self-examination/get examination if needed.

To get people involved, we decided on an approach that took male humor to a place it had never been before. Being outrageously funny was a matter of life and death.

The starting point was to marry the long-held dream of every self-respecting man to grow and sport a mustache with a fully integrated (from a media standpoint) advertising campaign. We aimed to create a campaign that literally broke every rule in the book. We would get people talking, sharing, touching their body, laughing, poking, fondling their balls, viewing, searching, raising money, giving money, and growing mustaches all for the fight against cancer. The goal of the project was to make men comfortable enough with their own bodies that they would perform self-examinations to detect male-related cancer and seek medical assistance if needed. To reach the goal, the campaign aimed to do the following:

- Encourage men to sport a mustache in March, giving visual support for the fight against cancer and starting conversations.
- Set up a website where you could show your mustache and raise money through donors/sponsors.
- Create hilarious ads that would raise awareness, raise conversation, be shared online, and support mustache wearers relying heavily on television ads with light print.
- Follow up with strong public relations tactics, including interviews with cancer survivors, getting celebrity television and radio hosts to be screened for cancer at their doctor's office, working with anchormen on television sport shows to grow a mustache during March, and reporting on who was leading the online fund-raiser.
- Start the social media discussion by arming interested people with information and outrageously funny material to share online, stimulating more conversations where people shared personal and sometimes outrageous things.

March became Mustache March, with ads and public relations tactics generating online and face-to-face conversations. On Facebook, women urged other women to kiss only men with mustaches. People posted their mustache stories on YouTube. Everybody talked about organs they usually never talked about or, for that matter, admitted that they touched.

It was fun; it was sexy; it was—to be blunt—ballsy. Did it work to achieve the campaign goals? Go to the It's a Wrap feature at the end of the chapter to see.

This chapter-opening story was contributed by Ingvi Logason, principal at H:N Marketing Communications, Reykjavík, Iceland, and a member of this book's Advisory Board.

15.1 Discuss what is in a media plan and the role of media research in developing media plans.

How Are Media Plans Created?

Media planners are in the connection business. Their work connects brand messages with customers and other stakeholders, as the Iceland cancer case illustrates. They identify and activate the points of contact where brand messages touch consumers and engage their interest. The Iceland cancer campaign was multiplatform and multimedia, including traditional media, particularly print and outdoor, but also websites, internet videos, social media and viral marketing, a theatrical play, and party hosting. Notice that this media plan involved a lot more than advertising, which supports the point we made in Chapter 12 that all forms of marketing communication use media.

Engagement-making connections that resonate with the audience are the hallmark of effective marketing communication. Think about the Dove "Real Women" campaign in Chapter 7. But how do you find those points of engagement—the media that connect with the audience in a personal way as they go about their lives and talk to their friends?

Media Engagement Research

Some people believe media decisions are the hub in the advertising wheel because media costs are often the biggest element in the marketing communication budget. And if the right media aren't in play, it's like whistling in the dark because no matter how great the message, nobody sees or hears it.

Media Sources   Before planning can begin, media researchers gather all the information they can find on the media that might be used to engage the audience. Figure 15.1 and the list below illustrate the wide range of media information sources and the critical role media research plays in the overall advertising planning process.

- *Client Information* The client is a good source for various types of information media planners use in their work, such as demographic profiles of current customers (both light and heavy users), response to previous promotions, product sales and distribution patterns, and most importantly, the budget or how much can be spent on media. Geographical differences in category and brand sales also affect how the media budget is allocated. With consumer goods and services especially, rates of consumption can differ greatly from one region to another.
- *Market Research* Independently gathered information about markets and product categories is another valuable tool for media planners. Mediamark Research, Inc. (MRI), Scarborough (local markets), and Mendelsohn (affluent markets) are research companies that provide this service. This information is usually organized by product category (detergents, cereals, snacks, and so on) and cross-tabulated by audience groups and their consumption patterns. Accessible online for a fee, this wealth of information can be searched and compared across thousands of categories, brands, and audience groups. Although the reports may seem intimidating, they are not that difficult to use. Figure 15.2 is a page from an MRI report showing

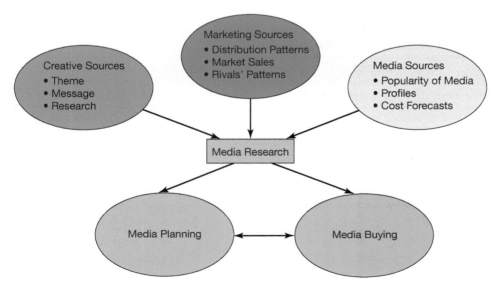

FIGURE 15.1
The Central Role of Media Research
Media planners look for data from creative, marketing, and media sources. All this information is used in both media planning and buying.

How to Read an MRI CrossTab

The CrossTab format is a standard research display format that allows multiple variables of related data to be grouped together. Below is a screen capture of a MEMRI[2] CrossTab, complete with explanations of key numbers. Please note that all the numbers are based on the 2004 Spring MRI study, and that the projected numbers (000) are expressed in thousands.

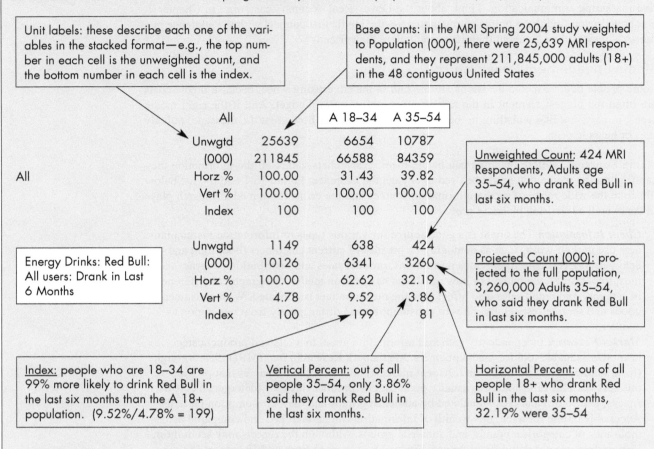

How the Numbers are Derived	
Unwgtd=424	The number of MRI respondents who meet the qualifications specified (in this case, A 35–54 who drank Red Bull in the last six months).
(000)=3,260	After applying each respondent's weight, the "(000)" value is the number of thousands of adults in the 48 contiguous United States represented by the MRI respondents who met the qualifications specified. Expressed in terms of individuals, this means 3,260,000 people.
Horz %=32.19	The percent calculated by dividing the "(000)" value in the cell by the "(000)" value in the base column=3260/10126=32.19%.
Vert %=3.86	The percent calculated by dividing the "(000)" value in the cell by the "(000)" value in the base row=3260/84359=3.86%.
Index=199	The percent calculated by dividing either the horz % in the cell by the horz % in the base row (62.62/31.43) or by dividing the vert % in the cell by the vert % in the base column (9.52/4.78). Either calculation generates the same result, because, when the horz % numbers and vert % numbers are expressed in terms of "(000)", the relationship is identical.

FIGURE 15.2
How to Read MRI CrossTabs
The MRI market research service provides information on 4,090 product categories and services, 6,000 brands, and category advertising expenditures as well as customer lifestyle characteristics and buying style psychographics.

Source: Courtesy of Mediamark Research Inc. All rights reserved.

how to read MRI data. Media planners use MRI data to check which groups, based on demographics and lifestyles, are high and low in category use as well as where they live and what media they use.

- *Competitive Advertising Expenditures* In highly competitive product categories, such as packaged goods and consumer services, marketers track how much competing brands spend on media compared to how much they are spending on their particular brand. This spending is called **share of voice**. In other words, marketers want to know which, if any, competing brands have louder voices (i.e., are spending more) than they do. For example, if the total spent on airline advertising last year was $200 million and $50 million of that was spent by United Airlines, United Airlines' share of voice would be 25 percent (50 divided by 200 = 25 percent). Most agencies recommend that a brand's share of voice be at least as high as its share of market. For a new brand, its share of voice obviously needs to be more than its share of market if it wants to grow.

- *Media Kits* The various media and their respective media vehicles provide media kits, which contain information about the size and makeup of their audiences. Although media-supplied information is useful, keep in mind that this is an "inside job"; that is, the information is assembled to make the best possible case for advertising in that particular medium and media vehicle. For that reason, outside research sources, such as media rep companies and the Nielsen reports, are also used. As discussed in previous chapters, Nielsen Media Research audits national and local television, and Arbitron measures radio. Other services, such as the Alliance for Audited Media (formerly known as Audit Bureau of Circulations), Simmons, and MRI, monitor print audiences, and Media Metrix measures internet audiences. All these companies provide extensive information on viewers, listeners, and readers in terms of the size of the audience and their profiles.

- *Media Coverage Area* One type of media-related information about markets is the broadcast coverage area for television. Called a **designated marketing area (DMA)**, the coverage area is referred to by the name of the largest city in the area. In this national market analysis system, every county in the United States has been assigned to a DMA. The assignment of a county to a DMA is determined by which city provides the majority of the county households' television programming. Most DMAs include counties within a 50- to 60-mile radius of a major city center. Even though this system is based on television broadcast signals, it is universally used in doing individual market planning.

- *Consumer Behavior Reports* We mentioned some of the consumer research sources in Chapter 7 that are used in developing segmentation and targeting strategies. They are also useful in planning media strategies. For example, media planners use such services as the PRIZM system, Nielsen's ClusterPlus system, and supermarket scanner data to locate the target audience within media markets.

The importance of media research stems not only from the large amount of money that's on the line but also from the sheer volume of data and information that media planners must gather, sort, and analyze before media planning can begin. Media research begins with collections of data about the readership and viewership of various media. Here's a quick summary of the key concepts and standard sources of the data.

Newspaper Readership   Over 60 percent of all US adults read at least one print newspaper each week. Only 5 percent of 18- to 29-year-olds often get news from a print newspaper, whereas about half (48 percent) of those 65 and older do.[1]

Newspaper readership tends to be selective, with a greater percentage reading specific sections rather than the whole paper. Business and professional newspapers, such as *Ad Age*, have particularly high readership levels. Newspapers measure their audiences in two ways: circulation and readership. Readership is always a larger number than circulation because when a paper is delivered to a home or office, it is often read by more than one person. This type of information facilitates the media planner's ability to match a certain newspaper's readership with the target audience. Agencies obtain objective measures of

A Certainly Uncertain Journey

Leo Wong, *Account Manager, Droga5, New York*

Deciding what you want do with your life at the age of 18 is no easy feat. Luckily enough, I decided early on that I wanted to pursue an advertising degree at the S.I. Newhouse School of Communications at Syracuse University focusing on the creative track.

It's off to being a copy-writer/art director, right? Nope! Although I passed all my portfolio classes with fly-ing colors, I soon realized that while I loved the creative thought process, I did not have the technical skills nor did I have an interest to learn them. On the other hand, I had some great internships in account management and sales that I thoroughly enjoyed because I was able to touch a little bit of everything and learn from different departments.

With that, I took my creative knowledge with me but actually started my career as an account executive at DigitasLBi working on eBay. As an account executive, I worked on all things digital for the e-commerce giant, from smart retargeting banner ads to online video, some social, and even print.

All was going swell in this position until an unex-pected staffing change moved me into media. I was really uncertain about this shift as I had never consid-ered this department nor really had any interest in it. But after some internal back and forth, I decided that it was a good opportunity for me to learn something new, so I thought of it as a "rotational program."

To my surprise, being an associate media planner on Taco Bell, assisting in buying and planning media, was an amazing experience! I was able to infuse my creativ-ity when working with millennial-focused media brands, like Pandora, Facebook, and ESPN, on how to effectively reach our target audience while also using my account management experience to stay on top of budgets, inser-tion orders, and ad trafficking. It was also a great oppor-tunity to learn about the ever-changing digital platform.

The moral of the story is that you need to keep an open mind, especially when you are starting your career. Don't confine yourself to what you think you may want to do. Be open to new experiences because you never know what you'll be able to learn. Even better, something may spark your interest and change your career path for the better!

Nominated by Constance Frazier, a member of this book's Advisory Board and chief operating officer of the American Advertising Federation (AAF), Wong is a graduate of Syracuse University's S.I. Newhouse School of Public Communications and a former student of Professor Brian Sheehan, a frequent contributor to this book. Wong was also named one of AAF's Most Promising Minority Students.

newspaper circulation and readership by subscribing to one or both of the following auditing companies:

- *Alliance for Audited Media* The Alliance for Audited Media is an independent auditing group that represents advertisers, agencies, and publishers. This group verifies state-ments about newspaper *circulation* and provides a detailed analysis of the newspaper by state, town, and county. Its members include only paid-circulation newspapers and magazines.
- *Scarborough* Scarborough is part of Nielsen's Local Insight Suite, which includes local measurements in 210 US markets, connecting media consumption, lifestyles, buying behavior, and attitudes (www.scarborough.com).

Magazine Readership   Reflecting challenges similar to the newspaper industry, magazine readership fell by almost 20 percent between 2012 and 2015.[2] Nevertheless, top magazines (e.g., *Better Homes and Gardens*, *National Geographic*, *Sports Illustrated*) have shown more resilience than newspapers. That is partly because magazines tend to have value to people and stay present long after they are distributed and partly because they have "pass-along" readership, where additional people read the magazine and see its advertisements. Magazine rates are based on the **guaranteed circulation** that a publisher promises to provide. Magazine circulation is the number of copies of an issue sold, not the readership of the publication (called "readers per copy").

Several companies attempt to verify the circulation of magazines along with the demo-graphic and psychographic characteristics of specific readers. As with newspapers, the

Alliance for Audited Media is responsible for verifying circulation numbers. Created in 1914, this group audits subscriptions as well as newsstand sales and also checks the number of delinquent subscribers and rates of renewal. Mediamark's MRI service is the industry leader in magazine readership measurement. MRI measures readership for many popular national and regional magazines (along with other media). Reports are issued to subscribers twice a year and cover readership by demographics, psychographics, and product use. The Simmons Market Research Bureau provides psychographic data on who reads which magazines and which products these readers buy and consume. Other research companies, such as Starch and Gallup and Robinson, provide information about magazine audience size and behavior.

Photo: Westend61 GmbH/Alamy Stock Photo

ESPN The Magazine was top ranked in 2016 with an audience of over 100 million.

One problem with these measurement services is the limited scope of their services. MRI, for example, has traditionally measured only about 210 magazines. That leaves media buyers in the dark regarding who is actually seeing their ads in magazines not covered by MRI's research. Without the services of an objective (outside) measurement company, advertisers must rely on the data from the magazines themselves, which may be biased. To address these and other measurement issues, the Association of Magazine Media introduced a new monthly system, Magazine Media 360, which measures audience engagement for digital, video, and print across desktop computers, mobile devices, and social media networks. Currently, 145 magazines representing 95 percent of magazine readership are participating.[3] When readership on all formats are added together, the rankings change. For example, in October 2016, *ESPN The Magazine* was top ranked with an audience of more than 100 million, due primarily to its strong web and mobile readership.

Another interesting change in magazine measurement is the move, which is supported by the Association of Magazine Media, to quantify the "experience" of reading the magazine rather than just the circulation and readers per copy. A pilot test of this concept found that the more engaged people were in the magazine experience, the more impact the advertising had.[4]

The Radio Audience The radio industry and independent research firms provide several measures for advertisers, including a station's **coverage**, which is similar to circulation for print media. It is simply the number of homes in a geographic area that can pick up the station clearly, whether those homes are actually tuned in or not. A better measure is station or program **ratings**, which measures the percent of homes actually tuned in to the particular station. Factors such as competing programs, types of programs, and time of day or night influence the circulation figure.

The Nielsen Audio Company estimates the size of radio audiences for more than 270 markets in the United States. It does so by working with a panel of more than 80,000 people in 48 markets across the United States who have agreed to wear a **portable people meter (PPM)**. These devices are about the size of a pager

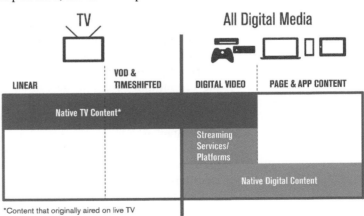

Source: Courtesy comScore. Used with permission.

Media measurement and analytics firm ComScore recently launched Xmedia, an audience measurement tool for TV content and digital media.

and measure exposure to media, including radio, television, cinema, and place-based digital media. Any station or signal picked up by the PPM gets credit, even if the person wearing the meter didn't pay attention.[5] The device has been found to be quite effective at predicting audience interest and has even led to format changes, such as when WRFF in Philadelphia switched from a Spanish-language talk-show format to alternative rock after new data revealed that rock music was more popular with the WRFF audience.

The Television Audience   A great number of advertisers consider television their primary medium. Can television deliver a target audience to advertisers effectively? What do we really know about how audiences watch television? Is it a background distraction? Do we switch from channel to channel without watching any single show? Or do we carefully and intelligently select what we watch on television? In an effort to estimate TV viewership, Nielsen uses TV set meters and sends millions of paper diaries to consumers in all 210 local television markets simultaneously in a period called **sweeps**. This normally occurs during the months of November, February, May, and July, and the data are used to set advertising rates and make program decisions.[6]

Television viewers are sometimes irritated by the intrusiveness of advertising and are not reluctant to switch channels or zip through commercials on prerecorded programs. Clutter is part of the problem advertisers face, and the audience has become very good at avoidance, unless the ads are intrusive or highly engaging. The Super Bowl is one of the few programs where viewers actually watch commercials. In fact, research has shown that on average, advertisers receive 54 percent higher brand recall from a Super Bowl ad than for ads run during prime time.[7]

Nielsen is the research company that dominates the television measurement industry. We introduced some of these measurement concepts in Chapter 12, but let's look at them again in the context of television research. **Exposure** is television's equivalent to circulation. Exposure measures households with sets turned on, a population referred to as **households using television (HUT)**. A HUT figure, however, doesn't tell you if anyone is watching the program. Remember from Chapter 12 that we defined an **impression** as one person's opportunity to be exposed one time to the advertising in a program. Like print, the impressions from television— the number of viewers exposed to a program—might be greater than the number of households reached because there may be more than one viewer watching and because the commercial may be repeated several times in a program or during a time period. We add all these impressions up and call them **gross impressions**.

For television programs, exposure is estimated in terms of number of viewers. The 2015 Super Bowl was watched by 115 million people, making it the most watched telecast ever.[8] Other forms of television viewing measurement, which we talked about in Chapter 12, include ratings and share. Ratings (percentage of exposure) are used because gross impression figures are so large. A rating of 10 means that 10 percent of HUT (homes using television) were tuned to the program carrying a brand's ad. Because one rating point equals roughly 1 percent of the 120 million homes in the United States, a 10 rating would be approximately 12 million households.

Another way to look at viewership is in terms of the share of the audience, which is based on the number of televisions turned on. The share is larger than a rating because the base figure (televisions turned on) is smaller than HUT. A rating of 10 for a Sunday night program might, for example, be a share of 20, which means that 20 percent, or one-fifth, of the 12 million televisions turned on were tuned to the program carrying the brand's ad. Nielsen continues to add to its PPMs in its top markets to track local viewing patterns.

Something not measured by all these metrics is the dedication of a program's superfans. When NBC proposed dropping *Chuck*, fans launched a campaign on Facebook, Twitter, and television blogs in defense of their favorite program. Realizing the significance of the attachment, Subway jumped in as an ally. To demonstrate the marketing power of ChuckTV.net, a consumer-generated campaign called "Finale & Footlong" urged fans to buy foot-long sandwiches from Subway to eat as they watched the season finale. The effort was successful, and NBC announced it would renew the show, although *Chuck* did eventually reach its end with the 2011–2012 season.[9]

FIGURE 15.3
Approximate Ad Prices for Premium Space in Major Media

ONLINE:		
Facebook	• $1 Million–$2 Million per Day	• In-Feed Video Ads
	• $500,000–$700,000 per day	• Home page takeover
YouTube	• $500,000 per day	• Home page advertising
	• $1 million	• Channel sponsorships
Yahoo!	• $450,000–$700,000 per day	• Home page takeover
	• $120,000 per day	• Banner ad, Yahoo News main page
AOL	• $150,000–$275,000 per day	• Banner ad, AOL main page
ESPN	• $200,000–300,000 per day	• Box banner ad, ESPN home page
Twitter	• $200,000 per day	• Promoted Trends
NewYorkTimes.com	• $120,000 per weekday	• "Push-down" ads, NYT home page
Vice Media	• $75,000 per day	• "Push-down" ads, Vice home page
Tumblr	• $20,000 per day	• Ads in users' feeds
Forbes	• $75–$100 per thousand impressions	• Welcome ad per visitor per day
StarGreetz	• $20,000–$100,000 per month	• Personalized video ads
Snapchat	• $750,000 per "brand story"	• Appears in "Stories" feed
Hulu	• $35 per thousand impressions	• In-stream video ads
Instagram	• $20 per thousand impressions	• Sponsored photo
Instagram	• $30 per thousand impressions	• Sponsored video
TELEVISION AND NEWSPAPER:		
NCAA men's basketball championship	• $1.5 million	• 30-second ad
Prime time broadcast TV	• $112,000	• 30-second ad in prime time
The Big Bang Theory	• $345,000	• 30-second ad
New York Times	• $50,000	• One full-color ad on front page
Broadcast TV	• $25 per thousand impressions	• 30-second ad
OUTDOOR:		
Times Square's largest billboard	• $2.5 million	• 4 weeks

Sources: "What It Costs: Ad Prices from TV's Biggest Buys to the Smallest Screens," *Advertising Age*, April 06, 2015, www.adage.com; Xander Becket, "The Cost of Advertising Nationally Broken Down by Medium," *WebpageFX*, January 13, 2016, www.webpagefx.com.

Do you ever wonder what it costs to place ads in premium space such as the largest billboard in Times Square or during a top-rated TV show? Figure 15.3 shows the approximate costs across a variety of traditional and online media.

Outdoor Viewership Outdoor advertising reaches people as they travel by a sign's site. The advertiser is interested in the percentage of the population of the total market (based on car or pedestrian counts) who, within a 24-hour period, are exposed to one or more boards carrying the brand message. A system called Geopath generates standard audience measurements for more than 1 million out-of-home media placements.

Traditionally, outdoor boards have been purchased and measured in terms of **showings**, which are estimates of the percentages of the population who had the opportunity to see the sign. These showings are usually stated as 25, 50, or 100 percent. The number of signs carrying the brand message is determined by the percentage of the audience that the media planner hopes to reach. A 50 showing, for example, means that 50 percent of the market's population was exposed to one or more of the outdoor brand messages in one day. Media plans still may refer to showings for outdoor media buys; to make it easier to compare the weight of the various media buys, however, the planners may convert this figure to something equivalent to rating points.

Online Audiences   Media planners are interested in estimates of the number of visits to a website, how much time was spent on the site, and the number of new and repeat visitors as well as supplemental information, such as more sophisticated analytics that are provided by ad-buying services and the sites themselves. Google and Yahoo! have built impressive models and ad-buying programs to help media planners. For ads and banners, data are collected about the number of click-throughs that moved the user from the ad to the advertisers' site.

Various types of software programs are available that can be integrated into the advertiser's information technology system that collect these types of usage data, which are then transmitted to companies that specialize in providing these measurement systems. Nielsen and comScore have digital ratings programs, as do Google, Microsoft, and Facebook. These systems record activity, but less is known about demographics, so the data are not as useful as planners might like. However, Snapchat introduced a program in 2017 that allows brands to buy its ads based on TV-style ratings from Nielsen and is opening up its ad platform to make ad buying easier. These moves helped establish the Snapchat platform and its ads as being on par with its digital rivals as well as traditional TV and help open doors for mobile television viewing via Snapchat. If it works, others are sure to follow.[10]

15.2 Detail the four steps in media planning and explain their importance.

Key Steps in Media Planning

The **media plan** is a written document that summarizes the objectives and strategies that guide how media dollars will be spent, primarily on the paid advertising media. The goal of a media plan is to find the most effective and efficient ways to deliver messages to a targeted audience. Media plans are designed to answer the following questions: (1) who (target audience), (2) what for (objectives), (3) where (the media vehicles used), (4) where (geography), (5) when (time frame), (6) how big (media weight), and (7) at what cost (cost efficiency). The first three are media objectives, and the others represent media strategies.

When integrated marketing communication (IMC) planners develop a media plan, they also take into consideration the media of all the marketing communication functions as well as consumer and target audience *contact points*. Contact points include exposure to traditional mass media as well as word of mouth, place-based media, in-store brand exposures, and the new interactive media.

Media planning is more than just choosing favorite media from a long list of media options. Traditional **measured media** are chosen on the basis of such metrics as gross rating points and cost per thousand, which are explained later in this chapter, but the new media lack similar metrics and are characterized more by such considerations as the quality of the brand experience, involvement, and personal impact. Old-line advertising media planners are intent on buying reach and frequency, but the problem is that many of their clients are looking for more effective outcomes, such as engaging experiences and brand-building relationships. Thus, the framework for making media-planning decisions is changing along with the list of media options. The media planner's job is also changing, as you can see in Heather Beck's A Day in the Life feature below.

What Do I *Do* as a Media Planner?

Heather Beck, *formerly Senior Media Planner, Melamed Riley Advertising, Cleveland, Ohio, and now photographer, Beck Impressions Photography*

People often ask me what it is that I *do* all day at work. There are 12 media planners in my office, and each of us would have a different answer to that question. But here's a general outline of a week's worth of work.

Monday morning there is a conference call involving everyone who works on an account. The client shares information such as sales numbers from the past week as well as budget changes or which markets are going to run a test campaign. The agency shares results from market research and the status of current projects. During the next couple of hours, I do *media research*—requesting and researching information from media sources for new projects.

It's lunchtime now! Once or twice a week, media reps either bring in a deli tray for the office or take us out for a lunch meeting to pitch their media products. It is the job of the media planner to do *media analysis*, by which I mean analyzing all the options and determining what is best for the client. So we don't let a nice lunch or fancy gift basket sway our judgment.

After lunch, I return phone calls and reply to emails. I spend the rest of the day gathering and organizing any information I have received and analyzing the data— that's when I do *media planning*. Actually, I do that all week long.

The rest of the week is similar. Tuesday morning conference calls are split up so that groups can talk specifics about their projects with their counterparts on the client side. It is the time to share detailed feedback. What works best in one market might not work well in another, so these results are essential in tailoring the media plans.

On Wednesday mornings, the agency has informal status meetings or conference calls on Thursday—that's a good time to check in with clients and do *evaluations* of our media plans. Then the day is spent finalizing projects.

Fridays are when all the agency players on an account put their projects together and determine the best way to do *presentations* of the results to clients. Another typical Friday task is to do *media buying*—that is, to place the planned media buys for the following week or month.

That's a generalized example of a typical week in the life of a media planner. Some days you might work until midnight, and other days you'll take long lunch breaks. It might seem like the same thing day to day, but the actual projects vary enough to keep it interesting and challenging. And if you need a break, you can always catch up on the latest issues of *Media Week* or *Ad Age*.

The four basic steps in media planning are targeting, setting media objectives, developing media strategies, and analyzing the metrics of a media plan.

Step 1: Target Audience

A key strategic decision, one that follows from the campaign plan, is identifying an audience for the brand message. In traditional media planning, based on targeting, the challenge is to select media vehicles (1) that are compatible with the creative executions and (2) whose audiences best match those of the brand's target audience. In other words, does the group of people who read this magazine, watch this television program, or see these posters include a high proportion of the advertiser's ideal target audience? If so, these media vehicles may be a good choice for the campaign, depending on other strategic factors, such as timing and cost.

The composition of households is particularly important in media planning, where many decisions are based on reaching households who subscribe to or view programs rather than individuals. That's because the media vehicles generally report their data and compute their impact (readers, users, or viewers) based on household estimates. So it's important to match the demographics with the household characteristics given for the media vehicle.

Media planners, for example, are unlikely to run ads for women's products on the Super Bowl, whose audience is skewed 56 percent male; instead, they buy time on the Oscars, which

Toyota Taps the Do-It-Yourself Community

Brian Sheehan, *Syracuse University*

The emergence of the internet has created innumerable online communities where like-minded people gather around their interests and passions. One such online community is the "do-it-yourself" crowd. They are people with an insatiable desire to know how things work: how they can install their own plumbing, rebuild their own computer, and fix their own car. For the launch of Toyota's new V-8 Tundra truck, Toyota realized that many of the full-sized truck buyers are the kind of people who want to do things for themselves and put their truck to the test. Many of them use their big trucks to haul big loads, trailers, or boats.

Toyota and its agency, Saatchi & Saatchi, saw an opportunity to match this audience with their media objective of connecting in-market truck buyers with credible, objective content about their cars. They did it by creating a unique partnership with HowStuffWorks .com (HSW). HSW is true to its name: it explains how everything works. Just put in your subject, and it will give you a detailed description of its inner workings. HSW does it so well it is able to rely on organic search to get to its audience, and it consistently ends up in the top 10 search results.

Toyota's agreement with HSW was a comprehensive package. There were the usual display ads tied to relevant content. For example, when someone typed in "How to Tow a Boat," HSW would give the answer while displaying an ad about Tundra's powerful, high-torque engine. There were 131 towing-related categories alone! If "How to Brake While Towing" was typed, the ad would be about the truck's huge rotors, which gave better braking performance. In addition, HSW created more than 100 pieces of specific Toyota-branded content per month for articles relating to Tundra as well as Toyota's Prius and Venza.

By tapping into a tight community with relevant, targeted advertising and content, Toyota was able to garner terrific online metrics and improve its image. After the campaign launched, display ad click-throughs, search engine traffic to Toyota.com, and time spent on the Toyota site all increased. In fact, traffic to the site was up 50 percent, and brand favorability shot up 40 percent.

The online space is noted for its fragmentation. Increasingly, the internet is dividing into communities of people who congregate around specialized websites, blogs, and insulated social networks. The marketers who succeed online will be the ones, like Toyota, who know how to embed their communications relevantly and seamlessly within the communities most disposed to using their products.

⬡ Principle

The tighter the focus on a target market, the easier it is to find appropriate media to deliver a relevant message.

has a much higher percentage of female viewers.[11] These kind of decisions make media planning both fun and challenging.

The breadth of the target, as defined in the marketing communication plan, determines whether the media planner will be using a broad mass media approach or a tightly targeted and highly focused approach. The tighter the focus, the easier it is to find appropriate media to deliver a relevant and focused message that connects with audience interests and engages them personally in a brand conversation.

As you can imagine, every media vehicle's audience is different and therefore varies regarding what percentage of its audience is in the brand's target audience. For example, Mercury Marine, which makes outboard boat motors, targets households that own one or more boats. It prefers to advertise in magazines where it can feature beautiful illustrations of its products as well as have room to explain the many benefits of its motors. Should it advertise in *Time* or *Boating* magazine? *Time* magazine reaches 3 million households, of which 210,000 have boats; in comparison, *Boating* has only 140,000 household subscribers. If you said *Time*, you're not being very cost efficient because even though that magazine reaches 70,000 more boat-owning households, it also reaches 2.8 million households that don't own boats. Mercury would have to pay to reach all readers, even those not in its target audience. By advertising in *Boating*, it can pretty well assume that subscribers either own a boat or at least are interested in boating.

The *Boating* story is an example of tight targeting to a *niche market*. In fact, the internet is the ultimate niche medium in that people turn to it to find out about any topic that interests them. The Matter of Practice feature explains how Toyota used online communication to tell a specific do-it-yourself community about the benefits of its full-size trucks.

In addition to information compiled by the team's media researchers, consumer insight research also is used to identify and analyze the target audience's media use patterns. Industry research helps. For example, research has determined a major shift in media use, with online media taking over from traditional media forms as the beginning spot in the search process. In a recent study, 81 percent of consumers said they conduct online research before making a purchase. 60 percent begin with search engines, and 61 will look at product reviews before making any purchase.[12] For larger purchases, people do their research online but prefer to actually buy the item in person.[13] That's good news for local retailers!

But even though search begins online—and that's true for business-to-business as well as consumer purchases—researchers say most customers still make purchase decisions using a combination of old media, new media, and old-fashioned conversations.[14]

A problem is that most consumers don't really know what influences them. (Just ask some of your friends how much advertising impacts what they buy. Most will probably say that "it doesn't" or "just a little.") For the launch of the Audi A3, the McKinley + Silver media team knew it needed an in-depth understanding of young males to develop a media plan that would work for this difficult-to-reach group. From research, it found that young males typically don't read or watch traditional media. They're busy and skeptical about commercial messages. The team came up with a profile of the target, which they described as "intelligent, independent, and innovative" and heavy users of new media. This target audience for this product category is made up of opinion leaders who influence their peers and who are not as interested in buying an entry-level car as they are in getting "what's next."[15]

A note about the changing dynamics of media planning is in order. This traditional approach to media that we've been describing is based on *exposures*, but newer approaches, particularly those coming from an IMC perspective, focus on *moments* when a message becomes a relevant brand experience. IMC planners have talked about consumer-based **moment of truth** for years, but now that concept is making its way into media planning. Procter & Gamble used the term FMOT, which refers to first moments of truth—the initial point of contact with a brand, say, is on a shelf; the second moment of truth is later when the product is used. But more recently, planners are focusing on what Google has called the **zero moment of truth**—the point when consumers search for information online or share brand experiences in a discussion with a friend. That moment typically precedes the first moment and hence the zero designation. As observed on a blog by the Location3 digital marketing agency, although advertising has always "exposed people to products before they see them in person, the Internet provides more in-depth communication about products."[16]

So you can see how this change in dynamics shifts the focus away from traditional targeting of households. Modern views of planning find ways to engage personally with consumers as individuals rather than as a member of a household at important moments when they are forming brand impressions. For example, companies can now target YouTube ads and ads in other environments to individuals based on their Google search histories.[17]

We also have mentioned in previous chapters that in interactive communication, the targeting concept expands to include consumer initiation of messages to friends as well as to the brand organization. All these new ways of looking at consumers are shifting the concept of targeting and have implications for how media planners look at their media opportunities. We'll say more about these changing perspectives as we continue to explain these more traditional approaches to media planning.

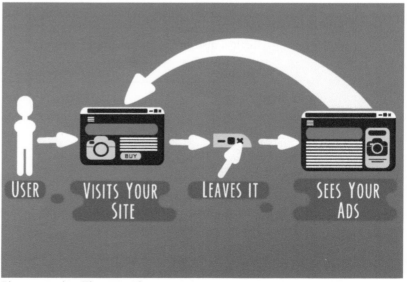

Photo: astephan/Shutterstock

Remarketing is a technique to increase engagement with online ads. It occurs when you see ads for products you've searched for previously next to your normal web activities.

Step 2: Communication and Media Objectives

Although creative decisions are sometimes made before media planning, this practice is changing. With the increasing variety of media options available, smart clients and agencies are having up-front cross-functional planning meetings that include creatives, media planners, and account executives. The media and message strategies are interdependent, so decisions in one area affect decisions in the other.

Marketing communication objectives, as you will recall, describe what a company wants target audiences to think, feel, and most importantly, do. **Media objectives** describe what a company wants to accomplish regarding the delivery of its brand messages and their impact on the target audience.

The communication objectives provide vital guidance to media planners. For example, why would brands want to spend some $4 million to advertise on the Super Bowl unless the buy fits with their brand communication objectives? On the other hand, the Super Bowl might make sense for brands that are building their images, launching new products, or want to use messages to shape public perceptions on a mass scale; after all, the event reaches well over 100 million viewers. Two advertisers illustrate reasons corporations might want to make the investment. Hyundai, for example, wanted to change its image from a maker of small, cheap cars to an upscale image, and Career Builder believed that its job search services would be appropriately communicated to a broad population as the United States came out of a recession.[18]

As we mentioned in Chapter 12, the two basic media objectives are reach and frequency. Let's consider how planners create strategies that deliver on those objectives.

The Frequency Objective   As we explained in Chapter 12, **frequency** refers to the repetition of message exposure. You should keep in mind that the frequency number for a media buy is actually the average number of exposure opportunities of those reached.

Because frequency is an *average*, it can be misleading. The range of frequency is often large: Some people see a particular brand message once, whereas others may see it 10 times within a given period. **Average frequency**, then, can give the planner a distorted idea of the plan's performance because all those people reached vary in the number of times they have the opportunity to be exposed to a message. New products or complex messages require more frequency so as to assist with consumer understanding and learning.

For these reasons, planners often use a **frequency distribution** model that shows the percentage of audience reached at each level of repetition. A **frequency quintile distribution analysis** divides an audience into five groups, each containing 20 percent of the audience. Employing media-usage modeling, it is then possible to estimate the average frequency for each quintile, as shown in the following table. For example, this table shows that the bottom 20 percent has an average frequency of 1, whereas the top 20 percent has an average frequency of 10. In this hypothetical distribution, the average frequency is 6.

Quintile	Frequency (Average Number of Exposure Opportunities)
Top 20% of universe	10
20%	7
20%	5
20%	3
Bottom 20%	1

If the media planner believes it is necessary that 80 percent of those reached should have an average frequency of 8, a more intensive media plan would be needed to raise the overall number of exposures—in other words, to shift the average from 6 to 8.

Effective Frequency   Because of the proliferation of information and clutter, there should be a threshold, or minimum frequency level, that produces some type of effect, such as a request for more brand information, a change in attitude toward the brand, or the most desired effect: purchase of the brand.

A standard rule of thumb is that it takes 3 to 10 exposures to have an effect on an audience. Obviously, this frequency range is extremely wide. The "right" frequency number

---

● Principle
Frequency is the first place to start when setting objectives for a media plan: set a frequency objective and then maximize reach at that frequency level.

is determined by several factors, including level of brand awareness, level of competitive "noise," content of the message, and sophistication of the target audience. Because so many different things can impact a response (i.e., an effect), audience response research is necessary. If the desired effect/response is not achieved, you may need to increase frequency of exposure or change the message. Research diagnostics, such as tracking studies, provide direction. The principle of **effective frequency** is that you add frequency to reach until you get to the level where people respond.

The Reach Objective   The percent of people exposed to a brand message one or more times within a specified period of time is called **reach**. A campaign's success is due in part to its ability to reach as many of the targeted audience as possible within a stated budget and time period. Consequently, many planners believe that reach is the most important objective and that it's the place to start when figuring out a media plan.

Using demographic and lifestyle data, planners can focus on reaching specific types of households (e.g., empty nesters, homes with two or more children under age 18, single-parent households, or households with incomes over $100,000) or individuals (males age 25–49 or people who rent). Such data enable planners to better match media profiles with the characteristics of the campaign's target audience.

Because most media reach large numbers of people who are not in the target market, however, most marketers are more interested in **targeted reach**, which is the percentage of a vehicle's audience that matches the brand's target market. An estimate of targeted reach can be developed assuming that the brand's target market can be identified in the vehicle's audience profile. Targeted reach is particularly important to calculate in order to estimate the amount of **wasted reach**, which is the number of people in the vehicle's audience who are neither customers nor prospects. We mentioned this problem in our discussion of network television, which is particularly susceptible to this criticism because of its mass audience.

Assessing the media for target audience opportunities is a major challenge for media planners. The evening news on television, for example, reaches a broad mass-market audience; if your target is women age 25 to 49, you have to consider the *targeted reach* of that news program. Obviously, both men and women watch news, so you know that your audience would probably be half or less of that, especially because you are targeting a specific age group. Maybe the evening news isn't a good option to reach this target because there would be so much waste. The outdoors, as discussed in Chapter 14, is a location-bound medium, and out-of-home media may be a more effective way to target this specified population.

Given the newer views of consumers not as targets but as participants in brand conversations, you can imagine that media planners are revising their views of reach as well. It's less about reach than about finding the appropriate way to connect. Susan Mendelsohn, a member of this book's Advisory Board, describes in the Matter of Practice feature what she calls vertical and horizontal reach, reflecting the difference between traditional mass media and online social media.

Media Waste   In the discussion of targeted reach, we mentioned waste as a result of targeting too wide of a target market. Actually, there are two sides to waste: both reach and frequency. The goal of media planning is to maximize media efficiency, which is to eliminate excessive overlap or too much frequency. Efficiency is therefore achieved by reducing **media waste**. Media professionals use their own experience, as well as audience research and computer models, to identify media efficiency. The point is that when additional media weight ceases to increase the response, it produces waste.

Writing Media Objectives   Given this discussion of the relationship between reach and frequency, it should be clear that usable media objectives would focus on those dimensions ideally including both factors. Here are some examples of media objectives.

1. Reach 60 percent of the target audience with a frequency of 4 within each four-week period in which the advertising runs.

Horizontal and Vertical Reach

Susan Mendelsohn, *President, Susan Mendelsohn Consultants*

What's more important in the current advertising climate, traditional vertical advertising, or horizontal social media reach?

Vertical advertising relies mainly on television, print, and radio to get the majority of its messages to potential consumers. Using this top-down model, advertisers attempt to motivate people to buy products by force-feeding messages and expecting the consumer to react. More recently, traditional vertical advertising has incorporated feedback loops so that consumers can have some say in how they respond to messaging and products, but consumers are not equal partners, and their input is minimal.

Enter the age of horizontal brand communication, where messages are targeted only to people who want them and advertisers encourage active participation of consumers via all forms of social media. Here, individual consumers become part of the advertiser's strategy to spread its message. Consumers feel empowered to make choices and shape the products and brands they use. Through the use of social media such as blogs, Twitter, and Facebook and the rise of smartphones, consumers are shaping the way information and products are being created, disseminated, and attended to.

In our fast-paced, information-overload world, successful advertisers need to incorporate both far-reaching vertical messaging and loyalty-building horizontal messaging in their communication plans. Both types of advertising approaches have advantages and disadvantages unique to themselves. Vertical advertising quickly and reliably gets its message out to mass audiences, even to those disinterested parties. The advertisers remain sovereign and have control over what is being said. Horizontal advertising requires that advertisers give up control in order to have the end user become part of the communication plan by passing information along. Using the horizontal paradigm, advertisers have become adept at listening and responding to consumers, although it can take much longer to build momentum for a product/message and requires more work to keep a dialogue going (unless the message is fortunate enough to go viral—a rare occurrence).

Both vertical and horizontal advertising play a significant role in the marketing mix. With the advent of consumer's use of technology in making purchases and affiliation decisions, vertical loop advertising can no longer exist in isolation but must embrace horizontal advertising to maximize message and brand effectiveness. One complements the other, and both are important.

2. Reach a maximum percentage of the target audience a minimum of five times within the first six months of advertising.
3. Reach 30 percent of the target audiences where they have an opportunity to interact with the brand and users of the brand.
4. Reach category thought leaders and influencers in a way that will motivate them to initiate measurable word of mouth and other positive brand messages.

The first of these objectives is the most common. It recognizes that you can seldom ever reach 100 percent of your target audience. It also acknowledges that a certain level of frequency will be necessary for the brand messages to been seen, heard, or read. The second objective would be for a product where the message is more complex; through research (and judgment), it has been decided that prospects need to be exposed to the message at least five times to be effective. In this case, frequency is more important than reach. Put another way, it is more important to reach a small portion of the audience five or more times and have them respond than it is to reach a major portion one or two times and have little or no response.

The third and fourth objectives deal directly with impact. To achieve these objectives, media buyers will have to find media vehicles and contact points, such as events and sponsorships, where interaction with the brand and its users is possible as opposed to using more passive media, such as traditional mass media. Notice that objective 4 is not measurable as stated.

Step 3: Media Strategies

Strategic thinking in media involves a set of decision factors and tools that help identify the best way to deliver the brand message. Regardless of whether a company spends a few hundred dollars on one medium or millions of dollars on a variety of media, the goal is still the same: to reach the right people at the right time with the right message. It's good to remember that there are always multiple ways to reach an objective; the difficult decision is deciding which way is the best. Specific **media strategies** are based on analyzing and comparing various ways to accomplish the media objectives and then selecting the approach that is estimated to be the most effective alternative.

Media Mix Selection   As you probably noted from our review of media in Chapter 13 and Chapter 14, media planners have a tremendous variety of media from which to choose, including all the owned and earned media as well as paid advertising. Traditional media planning, therefore, is a process of selecting advertising media to reach a certain audience and accomplish reach and frequency objectives. It attempts to match the advantages and limitations of the available media to the needs of the campaign strategy.

Most brands use a variety of targeted media vehicles, called a **media mix**, to reach current and potential customers. ESPN, for example, uses television, magazines, radio, and the internet as well as original programming on its own ESPN channel to promote its programs. Media mixes are used for a number of reasons. We mentioned earlier that you can rarely generate an acceptable reach level with just one media vehicle, so a reason for using a mix is to reach people not reached by the first or most important medium. Using a variety of media vehicles distributes the message more widely because different media tend to have different audience profiles. Of course, these different audience groups should generally fit within the brand's target market. Some people even reject certain media. Television advertising, for example, is considered intrusive, and internet advertising is irritating to some people. Other reasons for spreading the plan across different media include adding exposure in less expensive media and using media that have some attractive characteristics that enhance the creative message.

Still, the reason for choosing a particular medium or a set of media vehicles depends on the media objectives matched with the strengths of particular media. What media will best deliver what effects, and can you reinforce and extend those effects with a mix of media? Will the campaign deliver the desired return on investment (ROI)? If audience reach is an objective, television still reaches the largest audience; if frequency is important, radio may be the best media vehicle to use. Print and television are considered more trustworthy than other media, so they might be used by a media planner for a campaign that seeks to establish credibility for a brand or believability for a product claim.

The choice of media in the media mix is based on an analysis of their strengths and limitations and how those factors relate to a specific marketing situation. Figure 15.4 summarizes the various media we discussed in Chapter 13 and Chapter 14 in terms of their strengths.

An analysis of one industry's media mix choices presents an interesting argument about the logic of the media mix. The telecom industry (AT&T, Verizon, and Sprint) was critiqued by the firm BIGresearch and a team of media researchers from Northwestern University. Based on consumer research and a customized analytical model, the team was able to develop an idealized set of media allocations. In comparison to actual expenditures, the team concluded that the telecom industry overspends on television at the expense of others, such as the internet, radio, magazines, and outdoor. In particular, the consumer-based research determined an underuse of the internet based on amount of time, its ability to influence purchase, and its lower costs.[19]

Part of the problem is that in the past, media plans were dominated by one medium—a television-based campaign, for example. With media fragmentation and the diversity of consumer media use, these kinds of campaigns are rarely found anymore. Almost all are integrated with a wide variety of media, including social media and other online vehicles. As Laura Bright, media professor at Texas Christian University, explained, these "silo-driven campaigns" have given way to integrated campaigns focused on brand experiences rather than specific types of

FIGURE 15.4
Guide to Media Evaluation and Selection

	Strengths	*Limitations*
PAID MEDIA		
Print Advertising	• *Newspapers*: good for news announcements and comparison shopping; has positive consumer attitudes; good for reaching educated and affluent consumers; good for local market coverage; flexible in geography & scheduling	• *Newspapers*: short life span; clutter; limited reach for certain groups; poor production values
	• *Magazines*: High production values; targets consumers' interests—specialized audiences; receptive audience; long life span; format encourages creativity & good design; good for brand image messages; good for complex or in-depth messages	• *Magazines*: Long lead times—limited flexibility; lack of immediacy; high cost; may have limited distribution
	• *Directories*: Directional—tells where to find something in the local market; provides shopping information; trusted; inexpensive; good ROI; flexible in size, colors, formats but hard to change or update; long life	• *Directories*: Lack of flexibility in timing—can be a long time before a change can be made; competitive clutter and look-alike ads; low production quality
Broadcast Ads	• *Radio*: Pervasive; in most every home and car; reaches specialized target audiences in local market; reaches them at critical apertures (morning and evening drive time); can be timed to match consumer purchase cycles; offers high frequency; music (jingles) can be repeated more easily than other forms of advertising; good for reminder messages: flexible, easy to change; good for local tie-ins and promos; mental imagery can be highly engaging; audience less likely to switch channels when ads come on • *National television*: Pervasive; in almost every home; high level of reach; reaches a broad mass national audience although can be targeted by programs; high impact: has audio, video, motion; good for demonstration or drama; impresses other stakeholders, such as suppliers and franchisees • *Spot television*: Good for local & regional markets; good to "heavy up" in certain cities or regions where sales are higher or where strategy calls for increased emphasis	• *Radio*: Listener inattentiveness; may just be on in the background; lack of visuals; clutter; may have buying difficulties for local buys; lack of control: talk-show content is unpredictable and may be critical • *TV*: Clutter—cable offers a large number of channels; high production costs; wasted reach; inflexible—can't easily make last-minute changes; intrusiveness—audience resistance to advertising leads to avoidance and zipping and zapping
Place-Based Ads	• *Outdoor*: Good for local markets; directional; brand image and reminder; high impact—larger than life; less expensive; long life; place-based message for nearby businesses • *Posters and kiosks*: *Posters* can be dramatic and attention getting; sometimes in captive audience locations; *kiosks* are good for geographic messages; flexible and easy to update • *Transit*: *Interior* Good for captive audience; can present explanations; tear-offs & takeaways; *Exterior*: good for area markets; brand reminders	• Traffic moves quickly; can't handle complex messages—designs must be simple; may be easy to miss (depending on location); cluttered; some criticize outdoor ads as "polluting" the landscape; • *Posters and kiosks*: often cluttered environment; can't be complex message • *Transit*: low reach; hard to target; *Exterior Transit*: lacks the size advantage of other outdoor media

	Strengths	*Limitations*
	• *Movie trailers*: Captive audience; not highly targeted; less need for intrusiveness because captive audience; high impact if quality production values • *Event and sponsorship ads*: High-intensity environment; localtar geting unless televised; positive association with event	• *Movie trailers*: Audience resistance is high—hates being a captive audience; expensive; needs high-value production • *Event and sponsorship ads*: easy to ignore
Online Ads	• Good for hard-to-reach audiences, such as young males; inexpensive, particularly pay-per-click programs; with search marketing can be targeted based on viewer interest; generates dialogue; good messages can create buzz and go viral; can collect user information and track online behavior; engaging—high user involvement; real time	• Online ads should be consistent with other brand messages; cluttered; viewers may not notice ad or resent ad in social space; hard to measure impact
OWNED MEDIA		
Corporate Face	• Building design & interiors reflect organizational image; also bags, trucks & staff appearance; on-premise and other signs provide identification, directions	• Hard to change; hard to measure impact
Branded Media	• *Events, video games, films,* books, apps, etc., that carry brand name make brand visible in positive environment; can engage consumers in positive experiences—builds goodwill; *Branded apps* give something useful to user; widgets are reminders • *Naming rights* connect places to brand	• Hard to measure impact • Hard to measure impact or tie visibility to ROI
Retail Media	• *Package* delivers last message before purchase; billboard effect from multiple shelf facings; can reinforce brand image • *Merchandising* gets attention; increases in-store brand visibility; can tie in with special promotion	• Not easily changed; cluttered environment; hard to measure impressions; limited space for brand message • Can add clutter to store environment; retailer may not use them
PR & Promo Media	• *Publications* are under control of company; publications can be high quality, or inexpensive and quick to produce • *Videos* can present in-depth info, demonstrations, and tours • *Info and press kits* can be custom assembled for event or audience • *Speakers* and books can tell corporate story; speakers can explain and present a point-of-view • *Publicity* materials provide information to media • *Premiums and gifts*: provide brand reminders, reward behavior and reinforce relationships • *Training materials and sales kits*: teach employees and sales personnel about brand and focus them on message strategy • OOH: sign spinners, flash mobs	• Quality *publications, videos, books, gifts, & speakers* can have high cost per contact; limited reach; also hard to change • Inexpensive *premiums* can be seen as cheap trinkets; limited reach • *Publicity materials* may not reach or be used by news media • *Premiums* can be seen as cheap; limited reach; executive gifts are expensive • Sales force and employees may not follow the program; high cost per contact

(continued)

FIGURE 15.4
Guide to Media Evaluation and Selection (*continued*)

	Strengths	*Limitations*
OWNED & INTERACTIVE		
Corporate Interactive	• *Electronic installations* (walls) and *kiosks* allow users to find things and interact with information databases	• High cost per contact; hard to change
Direct Response	• *Direct-response* generates sales without intermediary; media can be mail, phone, print, broadcast, and online; can engage attention; can be personalized; builds in feedback • *Catalogs* can be highly targeted; trusted; attention getting; good visual sales tool; can provide in-depth information; convenient shopping	• *Direct*: Inexpensive per contact but low response rates; resistance to mail, email, and intrusive forms such as phone calls; depends on accurate database
Personal Contact	• *Personal sales* is more persuasive than mass media because one on one; sales messages can be tailored to consumer; personalized reason to buy; sales kits and scripts keep sales message strategically focused • *Customer service* delivers customer-initiated messages; high impact; adequacy of response leads to customer satisfaction or dissatisfaction with brand experience; represents the company's attitude to its customers; positive customer service can strengthen brand relationship; feedback through customer service, comment cards, & surveys can be used for ongoing customer research	• *Personal sales* is expensive per sales contact; salespersons need training; may not be strategically connected with marketing • *Customer service* is expensive per contact; representatives need training; the department may not be connected with marketing strategies; poor customer service leads to increased negative attitudes by customers
Interactive PR & Promos	• *News conferences and media tours* invite media to hear about—or see—something in person and respond with questions; the source's responses to the questions affect the credibility of the event • *Promotions*: Sampling, events, tours, and trade shows involve customers with a positive brand experience at a purchase point of contact; events create a sense of brand excitement	• If topic is not seen as newsworthy, media may not show up • Reach is small; hard to calculate ROI
Digital Marketing	• *Email and texting* can be used to generate one-to-one communication • *Websites* can provide in-depth content; can function as an online catalog and generate e-commerce; can be animated; may use streaming video; good for visual display; can demonstrate; inexpensive; flexible; easy to change • *Blogs* and mini-blogs (Twitter posts) are more personal; can stimulate responses • *Social media accounts*: Can establish brand profile on Facebook; can tweet Twitter messages to followers; fan pages create brand community; used to engage customers and strengthen brand relationships; entry into online communication networks; uses friendship-based patterns of influence	• Can be irritating, intrusive • *Website* may not match brand image; hard to track impact; navigation may be difficult; have to promote offline and online; keywords must be effective for search • *Blogs* may be seen as disguised advertising • *Social media* users have to find Facebook & Twitter feeds; consumer may resent commercial use of social media; hard to measure impact

	Strengths	*Limitations*
Mobile Marketing	• *Mobile marketing*: Can reach customers in the area of a store of promotion via a cell phone	• Reach is small; hard to calculate ROI; needs opt-in
EARNED INTERACTIVE		
Publicity	• *Hits* when a story is used by media; usually a positive impact; the story's impact increases because of its appearance in a credible 3rd-party medium • *Mentions* when a brand appears in a story; can be positive or negative	• Hard to monitor for brand depictions and impact; no control over media use of stories or comments in media investigations; hits and mentions can be counted but hard to know about impact on reader
Word of Mouth	• *Personal conversation*; also word of mouth using online media such as email and texting on cell phones • *Buzz* happens when people talking to one another spread the word about something; *viral* because it spreads through a web of interconnecting networks; posts that are "liked" can circulate rapidly within network; crowdsourcing lets fans generate and share brand-related ideas. • *B2C2C* generates influence by engaging thought and fashion leaders who become brand advocates	• Hard to measure impact; hard to monitor comments for brand or category mentions; organization can only initiate, can't control content or impact • Hard to control; hard to evaluate ROI
Social Media Mentions	• *Social media*, such as Facebook, Twitter, & LinkedIn, connect friends and family in conversational settings; energized word of mouth; brand mentions happen in a natural conversational setting	• Hard to monitor, particularly Facebook comments; hard to evaluate ROI; mentions can be negative
Media of Sharing	• Online virtual communities—brand fan clubs—gather around a mutual topic to share images and experiences; social games are played through apps • Crowdsourcing mobilizes a digital crowd to provide collective intelligence	• Sponsored brand fan clubs can be seen as corporate tools, but unsponsored fan clubs are under no brand control and can generate negative or erroneous information; hard to measure impact

media forms.[20] But even as we say that most media plans are multiplatform, another approach is to focus primarily on online media. The reason is that to connect with young markets, brands may find that the best way to reach this elusive group is through social or mobile media. Juicy Fruit, for example, created a "Sweet Talk" campaign that was launched as an app and supported on the brand's Facebook page.[21]

Media choices are sometimes designed to deliver the strategy of using one medium to deliver an audience to another medium or marketing communication tool. For example, mass media have frequently been used to promote special events and sales promotions. Likewise, mass media have been used to promote packaging, such as the famous Coca-Cola glass bottle. In 2013, Coke found that the bottles appealed to two different audiences with two radically different appeals and two entirely different sets of media usage: one is an older senior audience who respond to nostalgic messages and are heavy users of traditional media, and the other is a young audience for whom the glass bottles have a "cool" factor and are best reached through online and social media.

The emergence of the internet has intensified what you might call a two-step media platform. Print and broadcast, which are basically informative and awareness-building media forms, are often used to drive traffic to a brand's website, which is more interactive and experiential. The Frontier Airlines' "Web" ad is an example of this use.

Check out the web.

Get double miles, free DIRECTV® service and our guaranteed lowest fares when you book on our new web site*.

frontierairlines.com

*Book online by 6/15/06 and receive Free DIRECTV and double miles in our EarlyReturns® Mileage Program. Travel must be complete by 12/31/06.

Photo: Frontier Airlines. Used with permission.

This ad demonstrates the use of a creative print ad to drive traffic to a website.

Geographical Strategies   Another factor planners use in analyzing the target audience is geography. Are potential customers found all over the country, therefore calling for a national campaign, and does the client have the budget to afford such an extensive media plan? In most cases, the media plan will identify special regions or DMAs to be emphasized with a **heavy-up schedule**, which means that proportionately more of the budget is spent in those areas. The company's sales coverage area (i.e., geography) is a major factor used to make this decision. There's no sense advertising in areas where the product isn't available. Most national or regional marketers divide their market geographically. The amount of sales produced in each geographic market will vary, and marketers try to match advertising investments with the amount of forecasted sales or the sales potential.

To determine which geographical areas have the highest (and lowest) rate of consumption for a particular product category, marketers compute a **category development index (CDI)** for each market in which they are interested. Then they calculate a **brand development index (BDI)**, which estimates the strength of their brand in the various geographical areas. If General Mills were to bring out a new line of grits, for example, it wouldn't advertise nationally because most grits are consumed in the South.

A CDI is calculated for product categories. It is an index number showing the relative consumption rate of a product in a particular DMA or region as compared to the total universe (national or regional). A BDI is an index of the consumption rate of a brand in a particular market. The CDI tells you where the category is strong and weak, and the BDI tells you where your brand is strong and weak. CDI data can be found in industry and government sources, and BDI information is available through such services as Simmons and Scarborough as well as company data.

Different strategies are used to deal with these levels, and they have implications for the media mix and schedule. Planners typically don't make heavy allocations in weak sales areas unless strong marketing signals indicate significant growth potential. Conversely, strong sales markets may not receive proportional increases in advertising unless clear evidence suggests that company sales can go much higher with greater advertising investment. When there is a lot of competitive activity, a heavy-up strategy may be used to defend the brand's market share.

An example of geography affecting a media plan is found in local outdoor advertising. Local advertising is, by definition, geographic. But in the case of Bertucci's outdoor, the billboard's location is both near the restaurant and the baseball stadium.

Photo: Courtesy AdLab, College of Communication, Boston University

SHOWCASE

A billboard located at Boston's Kenmore Square above the Bertucci's restaurant is just two blocks from Fenway Park. Developed by the Boston University AdLab group, this billboard illustrates a message delivered at the right time and the right place.

Another change resulting from the digital revolution is that media plans are deemphasizing national campaigns and focusing on local connection points. Actually, we've had local media strategies all along, but media planners are looking at local marketing in the same way they are looking at consumers as initiators of brand contact rather than just targets. In a study of media planners' views of the changing dynamics of their field, Bright found that search advertising and mobile marketing are driving this trend.[22] Google has found that almost three-fourths of all online activity is related to local content, meaning that, for marketers, "local is no longer just a nice add-on option" and "more and more marketing is moving to the local level."[23] The term for this new emphasis on local marketing is **SoLoMo** (which stands for the convergence of social with local and mobile marketing), described as "the perfect storm of popular technologies and platforms that promises to deliver information you want where you are, usually via social apps."[24]

Scheduling Strategies   When should a potential customer be exposed to a brand message? Scheduling strategies are designed to identify the best times for consumers to come in contact with a brand message.

For many product categories, prospective customers have one or more ideal times or places at which they are most receptive to receiving and paying attention to a brand message. This ideal time/place is called an **aperture** and becomes an important factor in scheduling media placements. The goal is to know when the target is most likely to be involved and tuned in. Movies and restaurants advertise on Thursdays and Fridays, knowing these are the days when potential customers are planning for the coming weekend. Jewelry stores run special ads before Christmas, Valentine's Day, and Mother's Day. Ads for sporting goods, beer, and soft drinks pop up at athletic venues because sports fans are thinking about those products as they watch the game. Finding the right aperture is even more important with the new considerations of moments, brand engagements, and consumer connections.

Regardless of whether a company spends a few hundred dollars on one medium or millions of dollars on a variety of media, the goal is still the same: to reach the right people at the right time with the right message. If advertising budgets were unlimited, most companies would advertise every day. Not even the largest advertisers are in this position, so media planners manipulate schedules in various ways to create the strongest possible impact given the budget. Three scheduling strategies involve timing, duration of exposure, and continuity of exposure.

> **Principle**
> Advertising is most effective when it reaches the right people at the right time and place with the right message—in other words, finding the right aperture.

- *Timing Strategies: When to Advertise?* Timing decisions relate to factors such as seasonality, holidays, days of the week, and time of day. These decisions are driven by how often the product is bought and whether it is used more in some months than in others. Timing also encompasses the consumers' best aperture and competitors' advertising schedules. Another consideration is **lead time**, or the amount of time allowed before the beginning of the sales period to reach people when they are just beginning to think about seasonal buying. Back-to-school advertising is an example. Advertising typically starts in July or early August for a school calendar that begins in late August or September. Lead time also refers to the production time needed to get the advertisement into the medium. There is a long lead time for magazines, but it is shorter for local media, such as newspapers and radio.
- *Duration: How Long?* For how many weeks or months of the year should the advertising run? If there is a need to cover most of the weeks, advertising will be spread rather thin. If the amount of time to cover is limited, advertising can be concentrated more heavily. Message scheduling is driven by use cycles. For products that are consumed year-round, such as fast food and movies, advertising is spread throughout the year. In general, if you cannot cover the whole year, you should heavy up the schedule in higher-purchase periods. For example, movie marketers do most of their newspaper advertising on the weekends, when most people go to movies.

  Another question is, how much is enough? At what point does the message make its point? If the advertising period is too short or there are too few repetitions, the message may have little or no impact. If the period is too long, ads may suffer from **wearout**, which means the audience gets tired of them and stops paying attention.
- *Continuity: How Often?* **Continuity** refers to the way the advertising is spread over the length of a campaign. A **continuous strategy** spreads the advertising evenly over the campaign period. Two other methods to consider, pulsing and flighting, are shown in Figure 15.5.

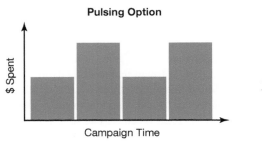

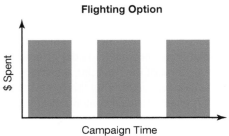

FIGURE 15.5
The Strategies of Pulsing and Flighting

A **pulsing strategy** is used to intensify advertising before a buying aperture and then to reduce advertising to lower levels until the aperture reopens. The pulse pattern has peaks and valleys, also called *bursts*. Fast-food companies such as McDonald's and Burger King often use pulsing patterns as they increase media weight during special promotional periods. Although the competition for daily customers suggests continuous advertising, they will greatly intensify activity to accommodate special events, such as new menu items, merchandise premiums, and contests. Pulsed schedules cover most of the year but still provide periodic intensity.

A **flighting strategy** is the most severe type of continuity adjustment. It is characterized by alternating periods of intense advertising activity and periods of no advertising, called a *hiatus*. This on-and-off schedule allows for a longer campaign. The hope in using nonadvertising periods is that the consumers will remember the brand and its advertising for some time after the ads have stopped. Figure 15.5 illustrates this awareness change. If the flighting strategy works, there will be a **carryover effect** of past advertising, which means consumers will remember the product across the gap until the next advertising period begins. The critical decision involves analyzing the *decay* level, the rate at which memory of the advertising is forgotten.

After a media schedule has been worked out in terms of what media will run when and for how long, these decisions are plotted on a **media flowchart**. Across the top is the calendar for the period of the campaign and down the side is the list of media to be used in this campaign. Bars are then drawn across the calendar that identify the exact timing of the use of various media. When the chart is complete, strategies such as pulsing and flighting are easy to observe. You can also see where reminder advertising in less expensive media (in-store signs, for example) may fill in between bursts and pulsing in more expensive media, such as television.

Size, Position, and Media Weighting Strategies   In addition to selecting the media mix, a media planner works with the creative team to determine the appropriate size and length of the message for each medium. This question of scope and scale applies to all media—even transit advertising, as the taxicab ad illustrates.

Media planners often use decision criterion called **weighting** to help them decide how much to budget (one term we have used is "heavy up") in each DMA or region and for each target audience when there is more than one. For example, if a media planner is advertising disposable contact lenses, there might be two target segments to consider: consumers who need help with their eyesight and the eye doctors who make the recommendations. You may recall the discussion in Chapter 1 of push and pull strategies, which is also relevant here. If the strategy is to encourage the consumer to ask the doctor about the product, the planner might recommend putting more emphasis on consumer publications to execute a **pull strategy** rather than focusing on professional journals for eye doctors or having sales professionals visit with these doctors, which would represent a **push strategy**. A weighting strategy might be to put 60 percent of the budget on consumers and 40 percent on doctors.

In the case of DMAs, weak markets may be given more than their share of media weight in the hopes of strengthening the brands in these markets, a practice known as *investment spending*. On the other hand, if competition is extremely heavy in a brand's strong markets, the strategy may be to give them more than their proportional share of media dollars to defend against competitors. Weighting strategies are also used in terms of seasonality, geography, audience segments, and the level of brand development by DMA.

Step 4: Media Metrics and Analytics

Like every other aspect of marketing communication, media plans are driven by questions of accountability. And because media decisions are based on measurable factors, identifiable costs, and budget limitations, media planners are engrossed in calculating the impact and efficiency of their media recommendations. With millions of dollars at stake, clients want data to justify media recommendations.

Photo: Tim Clayton/Contributor/Getty Images

This photo illustrates how transit advertising can be used to heavy up in a geographical area.

Impact: Gross Rating Points and Targeted Rating Points   Among the most important tools media planners use in designing a media mix using traditional media is a calculation of a media schedule's gross rating points and targeted rating points. As we've suggested, reach and frequency are interrelated concepts that, when combined, generate an estimate called gross rating points. **Gross rating points (GRPs)** indicate the weight, or efficiency, of a media plan. The more GRPs in a plan, the more "weight" the media buy is said to deliver.

To find a plan's GRPs, you multiply each media vehicle's rating by the number of ads inserted into each media vehicle during the designated time period and add up the total for the vehicles. For example, consider the data on the next page. If the plan delivered a household rating of 6 with eight insertions, the program *Survivor* would achieve an estimated 48 GRPs.

Once the media vehicles that produce the GRPs have been identified, computer programs can be used to break down the GRPs into reach and frequency (R&F) numbers. These R&F models are based on consumer media use research and produce data showing to what extent audiences, viewers, and readers overlap.

To illustrate how GRPs are determined and the difference in R&F from one media plan to another (using the same budget), look at the two media mixes that follow. Both are for a simple television media plan for a pizza brand. As you will remember from Chapter 13, a *rating point* is 1 percent of a defined media universe (country, region, DMA, or some other target audience description) of households unless otherwise specified. *Insertions* are the number of ads placed in each media vehicle/program within a given period of time (generally four weeks).

Using the same budget, the two different media mixes produce different GRP totals. A good media planner will look at several different mixes of programs that reach the target audience, figure the GRPs for each, and then break this calculation into R&F estimates for each plan. Because ratings are in percentages, the GRPs in both the plans in these tables indicate that they reach more than 100 percent. Of course, that is impossible, just as it's impossible to eat 156 percent of a pie. That is why these numbers are called *gross* rating points; they include exposure duplication. Nevertheless, knowing the GRPs of different plans is helpful in choosing which plan delivers more for the money budgeted.

How would computer models calculate reach and frequency numbers based on achieving 208 GRPs in plan A? The media mix model would estimate something close to the following: R = 35, F = 6.9. (Even though reach is a percent, industry practice is to not use the percent sign for reach numbers.) For plan B, where the number of GRPs is 176, the estimated R&F would be R = 55, F = 3.2.

Calculating GRPs for Plan A (R = 35; F = 6.9)

Program	*Household Rating*	*Insertions*	*GRPs*
Survivor	6	8	48
NCIS	4	8	32
The Voice	7	8	56
Sunday Night Football	9	8	72
		Total	208

Calculating GRPs for Plan B (R = 55; F = 3.2)

Program	*Household Rating*	*Insertions*	*GRPs*
Survivor	6	8	48
Empire	7	8	56
The Big Bang Theory	5	8	40
Thursday Night Football	4	8	32
		Total	176

How do you decide which is best? If a brand has a tightly targeted audience and wants to use repetition to create a strong brand presence, plan A might be a wise choice because it has a higher frequency (6.9 vs. 3.2). If, however, a brand has a fairly simple message where frequency is less important, a planner would probably choose plan B because it has significantly higher reach. The reason for the higher reach (55 vs. 35) with plan B, even though it has fewer GRPs, is that plan B has a much more diverse set of programs that attract a more diverse audience than plan A. But because plan B has a higher reach, it also has a lower frequency.

It is important to remember that GRPs are a combination of R × F. Due to budget constraints, reach increases and frequency decreases, and vice versa. Once experienced planners are given budgets, they generally have a good feel for how many GRPs those budgets will buy. The planning challenge is to decide whether to find a media mix with more reach or more frequency. That depends, of course, on media objectives.

The two media mixes shown previously are based on household rating points. For products that have a mass-market appeal, households are often used in targeting. However, for more specialized products, such as tennis racquets, sports cars, and all-natural food products, target audiences can be more narrowly defined. For example, let's say that those consuming the most natural food products are females, age 25 to 49, with a college degree; in addition, we know that they participate in at least one outdoor sport. That would be the target audience for most brands in this category. Therefore, when developing a media plan for a natural food brand, a media planner would be interested not so much in a media vehicle's total audience but in the percentage of the audience that can be defined as being in the campaign's target audience. Those not in the target are called waste coverage.

Because the total audience obviously includes waste coverage, the estimate of **targeted rating points (TRPs)** adjusts the calculation to exclude the waste coverage so that it more accurately reflects the percentage of the target audience watching a program. Once the waste coverage is eliminated, the TRPs are lower than the total audience GRPs. TRPs are, like R&F, determined by media usage research data, which is available from syndicated research services like MRI and from the major media vehicles themselves.

To illustrate the difference between household GRPs and TRPs, we'll use media plan A, shown previously. As shown below, the first column is household rating points, whereas the new second column shows targeted rating points, or the percent of homes reached that include a female, age 25 to 49, with a college degree and an affinity for at least one outdoor sport. The insertions remain the same, but the TRPs are greatly reduced, as you can see when you multiply targeted ratings by insertions. When the 80 TRPs are compared to the 208 household GRPs, you can see that 128 GRPs (208 − 80 = 128) were of little or no value to a natural food brand. The less waste, the more efficient the media plan.

Calculating TRPs for Plan A

Program	Household Rating	Targeted Rating	Insertions TRPs	Total TRPs
Survivor	6	3	8	24
NCIS	4	3	8	24
The Voice	7	3	8	24
Sunday Night Football	9	1	8	8
			Total	80

Another reason to tightly describe a target audience, especially in terms of lifestyle, is to take advantage of the many media vehicles—magazines, television programs and channels, and special events—that connect with various types of lifestyles. Examples of media that offer special interest topics are *Runners World*, which features topics of interest to runners; *This Old House*, the television program that describes home improvement and remodeling; *Self* magazine, which focuses on health and fitness; and *Budget Travel* for those looking for interesting but economical trips and vacations.

As important as ratings have been in traditional media plans, this computation may not be as important with individual contact media used by social and mobile advertising. It's the nature of the engagement rather than the breadth of the exposure that determines the effectiveness of the media impact.

New media plans also are substituting GRPs with something called **total audience impressions**, which are designed to better estimate the impact of an integrated campaign, including digital impressions as well as those delivered by measured media. Total audience impressions are derived from impression management efforts in public relations. Sophisticated programs are offered by companies such as comScore that provide validated impression reporting as well as comprehensive audience figures.[25] These new methods attempt to do a better job of estimating the impact of multiplatform campaigns.

Cost Efficiency   As mentioned earlier, one way to compare budgets with the competition is called *share of voice*. It sets the budget relative to your brand's and your competitors' market share. For example, if your client has a 40 percent share of the market, you may decide to spend at a 40 percent share of voice to maintain your brand's competitive position. To calculate this budget level, you need to find the total ad spending in your category as well as the share of market owned by your brand and your key competitors.[26] For example, if the category ad spending totals $10 million and you want your share of voice to be 40 percent, you would need to spend $4 million ($10 million × 0.40 = $4 million).

At the end of the planning process, after the media mix has been determined, the media planner will prepare a pie chart showing *media allocations*, a term that refers to allocating the budget among the various media chosen. The pie chart shows the amount being spent on each medium as a proportion of the total media budget. The pie chart visualizes the media mix and the relative importance, at least in terms of the budget, of each vehicle in the mix.

Although much of the discussion in this book has been focused on measured advertising media and their objectives, it's useful to note that the other IMC disciplines are also concerned about proving their efficiency. Public relations, for example, has established metrics comparable to those used in evaluating advertising media. In the Matter of Practice feature, Clarke Caywood explains how important it is to integrate not only media planning but also evaluations of efficiency comparing these other areas with advertising media planning. He also explains the concept of *earned media* in contrast to purchased (and measured) media.

Cost per Thousand, Targeted Cost per Thousand, and Cost per Point   Advertisers don't make decisions about the media mix solely in terms of targeting, geography, and schedule considerations. Sometimes the decision comes down to cold, hard cash. The advertiser wants prospects, not just readers, viewers, or listeners; therefore, advertisers compare the cost of each proposed media vehicle with the specific vehicle's ability to deliver the target audience.

Integrating Advertising and Public Relations Media Planning

Clarke Caywood, *Medill Graduate School, Northwestern University*

Ask advertising directors in a company or agency what profitable target media they have chosen for message delivery for their new corporate or product/service brand strategy, and they will probably give a list of traditional mass media advertising vehicles.

Then ask the public relations director in the same company or agency what the targeted media will be for the same program, and it will often be a list of news and feature story outlets.

In an integrated approach to media planning, the communication leaders should be targeting the same media to reach similar readers, viewers, and listeners. If not, the C-suite—chief executive officer, chief financial officer, and chief marketing officer—in the client company would want to know why not.

These newer models of media planning seem to be aligned with the growth of the large holding companies that contain advertising, direct database marketing, e-commerce, public relations, and now media-buying agencies where coordination and cross-functional planning are essential.

In the IMC program at Medill, we define integrated media planning as "coordinated research, planning, securing, and evaluation of all purchased and earned media." *Earned media* are used by marketing and public relations practitioners to differentiate paid media about a product, service, or company (advertising, promotions, direct mail, web ads, and so on) from positive or negative broadcast, print, and internet media articles and simple mentions about the product, service, or company. The term *earned* is used to avoid the term *free*, which accurately suggests the company does not pay the media for the placement, but "free" does not address that the publication of such stories requires hours of effort or years of experience by public relations professionals to persuade journalists to cover the product, service, or company for the benefit of their readers or viewers.

Just as selecting media for advertising has become a science and management art, the field of selection and analysis of earned media (including print, broadcast, and blogs) for public relations is now more of a science. Today, the existence of far richer database systems assists media managers who want to know which reporters, quoted experts, trade books, new publications, broadcasts, bloggers, and more are the most "profitable" targets for public relations messages. In other words, when we refer to *media planning*, we mean coordinating and jointly planning the earned media of public relations along with advertising and other purchased media.

Using the new built-in media metric systems, public relations directors can calculate return on investment on advertising versus public relations. With public relations, they can read and judge a range of positive, neutral, or negative messages as well as share-of-mind measures of media impact, advertising equivalency estimates, and other effectiveness indicators (see www.biz360.com).

Now, when the chief marketing officer and other C-suite officers ask the integrated agency directors of advertising, public relations, or IMC if the media are fully planned to reach targeted audiences, they can answer affirmatively.

The cheapest vehicle may not deliver the highest percent of the target audience, and the highest priced vehicle may deliver exactly the right target audience, so the selection process is a balancing act between cost and reach.

The process of measuring a target audience's size against the cost of reaching that audience is based on calculations of efficiency as measured by two commonly used metrics: cost per thousand and cost per point.

The term **cost per thousand (CPM)** is industry shorthand for the cost of getting 1,000 impressions. Marketers often prefer the CPM metric when their main goal is brand awareness and for smaller budgets. CPM is best used when comparing the cost of vehicles within the same medium (comparing one magazine with another or one television program with another). That is because different media have different levels of impact. To be more precise and to determine the efficiency of a potential media buy, planners often look at the **targeted cost per thousand (TCPM)**.

To calculate a CPM for a broadcast commercial, you need only two figures: the cost of an ad and the estimated audience reached by the vehicle. Multiply the cost of the ad by 1,000 and divide that number by the size of the broadcast audience. You multiply the cost of the ad by 1,000 to calculate a "cost per thousand."

In the case of print, CPMs are based on circulation or number of readers. *Time* magazine has a circulation of 4 million but claims a readership of 19.5 million. The difference between circulation and readership is due to what is called **pass-along readership**. In the case of *Time*, that means each issue is read by about five people. As you would suspect, media vehicles prefer that agencies use readership rather than circulation for figuring CPM because this method produces a much lower CPM. The procedures for calculating both CPM and targeted CPM are as follows:

- *Calculating CPM* In the following example, CPM is calculated based on *Time* readership and the price of a one-page, four-color ad, $240,000. Remember that you want to know what it costs to reach 1,000 readers:

$$CPM = \frac{Cost\ of\ ad\ \times\ 1,000}{Readership}$$

$$CPM = \frac{\$240,000\ \times\ 1,000}{19,500,000} = \$12.31\ CPM$$

- *Calculating TCPM* To figure the TCPM, you first determine how many of *Time*'s readers are in your target audience. For the sake of discussion, we'll say that only 5 million of *Time*'s readers fall into our target audience profile. As you can see from the following calculation, the TCPM greatly increases. That is because you still have to pay to reach all the readers, even though only about one-fourth of them are of value to you:

$$TCPM = \frac{Cost\ of\ ad\ \times\ 1,000}{Readers\ in\ target\ audience}$$

$$TCPM = \frac{\$240,000\ \times\ 1,000}{5,000,000} = \$48.00\ TCPM$$

- *Calculating Cost per Point* Now we'll look at how to determine **cost per point (CPP)**, which estimates the cost of reaching 1 million households based on a program's rating points. Divide the cost of running one commercial by the rating of the program in which the commercial will appear. If a 30-second spot on *NCIS* costs $320,000 and it has a rating of 8, the cost per rating point would be $40,000:

$$CPP = \frac{\$320,000}{8\ Rating} = \$40,000\ CPP$$

- *Calculating Targeted Cost Per Point* To figure the **targeted cost per point (TCPP)**, the rating points based on the target audience you want to reach, determine what percentage of the audience is your target. In the case of *NCIS*, we will estimate that half of the audience is our target. Thus, the overall rating of 8 is reduced to 4 (50% × 8 = 4 rating). Now we divide the one-time cost of $320,000 by 4 and find the TCPP is $80,000:

$$TCPP = \frac{\$320,000}{4\ target\ rating} = \$80,000\ TCPP$$

We can do this calculation to compare several different programs and identify those with lower costs.

CPMs have a wide range. A media planner may calculate a CPM of $40 to reach well over 100 million viewers of the Super Bowl. In contrast, in the example given earlier, iMapp.com might charge a CPM of $125 to reach a small but select group of eye doctors. iMapp is three times as expensive as the Super Bowl ad (not in real dollars but in CPM), but the higher CPM is justified because of the tight targeting. Media planners are constantly balancing cost with audience characteristics to decide if the media vehicle makes sense given the target audience size and characteristics.

What media would you buy with a $4.5 million budget? That's about what a 30-second Super Bowl ad costs. But consider what those funds would buy among the many online and social media choices available to media planners today:

- Feature your brand as a topic trend for 22 days on Twitter in the United States.
- Gain more than 6 million clicks on your search ads.
- Get your video viewed 50 million times on Facebook (3 seconds = 1 view).
- Have your ad on Snapchat for a solid week.[27]

Beyond CPM

As marketing communication spending online and on mobile have surged, additional metrics have emerged to help assess the effectiveness of messages on these platforms.

- *Cost per click (CPC):* CPC is the cost of digital advertising based on the number of clicks an ad receives. For example, if a $5 online ad gets 20 click-throughs, the cost is $0.25 per click. Google AdWords uses CPC pricing.
- *Cost per action (CPA):* CPA assesses a digital ad based on how many users click it and then take a certain action (e.g., sign up for your newsletter, download one of your white papers, make a purchase).
- *Cost per view (CPV):* Ad networks sometimes offer marketers the option of paying for an ad based on the number of times it is viewed on a website. CPV rates tend to be much lower than CPC rates.[28]

Media Optimization In our earlier discussion of media mix strategy, we looked at the efficiency of various media plans. Tools that help estimate the most optimum use of various media plans using computer models involve calculating the weight of a media schedule and optimizing the schedule for the greatest impact. These **optimization** techniques enable marketers to determine the relative impact of a media mix on product sales and optimize the efficiency of the media mix.

Generally, the models can create an unlimited number of media combinations and then simulate the response produced by each. For example, during the 2012 election, President Barack Obama's media strategists married data about viewing habits with personal information about voters the campaign wanted to reach in a program called "The Optimizer." Doing so allowed the campaign to direct messages with a high level of efficiency. The analytics department created a new set of ratings based on a model of targeted voters as opposed to broader media audience categories. After rating their likelihood to support the candidate, the strategists then worked backward to figure out how best to reach these individuals, whether online or through traditional media. It also identified voters who were unlikely to be reached by traditional campaign buys, including undecided voters who did not regularly watch news sources. Therefore, the campaign surprisingly bought more TV Land, the cable network that shows reruns, as well as late-night television than might have been expected.[29]

Using optimization models, the media planner can make intelligent decisions, given factors such as budget and timing. Optimization services include CPM Advisors (www.cpmadvisors .com), Aggregate Knowledge (www.aggregateknowledge.com), and Telmar (www.telmar.com).

The issue of media optimization, however, is bigger than just numbers and estimates of efficiency. It also involves questions of media overload and consumer irritation.

15.3 List the responsibilities of media buyers.

How Do Media Buying and Negotiation Work?

So far in this chapter, you've read about media plans and the key steps you would take to develop a media plan, and you've looked at some important big picture issues related to media planning. As you recall, the media plan is a recommendation that the client must approve before any further steps are taken. In fact, planning is only the first stage in advertising media operations. Once the plan directions are set, media buyers convert objectives and strategies into tactical decisions. They select specific media vehicles and negotiate with media companies for the time and space in media. A media buyer has distinct responsibilities, as outlined in Figure 15.6.

Media-Buying Basics

Media buying is a complicated process. The American Association of Advertising Agencies lists no fewer than 21 elements of a media buy for traditional media. The most important one, however, is matching the media vehicle to the strategic needs of the message and the brand. In addition to media selection, media negotiation makes the media plan come to life in a cost-effective way. In this section, we examine the most important buyer activities: providing information to media planners, selecting the media vehicles, negotiating costs, and monitoring the media performance and billing.

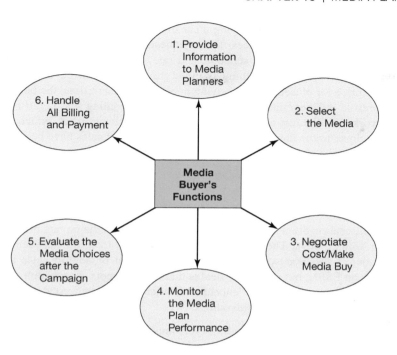

FIGURE 15.6
The Functions of a Media Buyer

Provide Inside Information   Media buyers are important information sources for media planners. They are close enough to day-to-day changes in media popularity and pricing to be an important source of inside current information. For example, a newspaper buyer discovers that a key newspaper's delivery staff is going on strike, or a magazine buyer's source reveals that the new editor of a publication is going to change the editorial focus dramatically. All these things can influence the strategy and tactics of current and future advertising plans.

⬡ **Principle**
Media buyers should be consulted early in planning because they are a good source of information on changes in media.

Select Media Vehicles   The media planner determines the media mix, but the buyer is responsible for choosing the specific media vehicles. Online media buying is usually handled through ad networks and the big portals. Online vehicles are also offering **programmatic buying**, which means that algorithms are used to purchase and place ads that target individual viewers, not just aggregated audiences based on their digital tracking data.[30] A word of caution is in order, however. Although programmatic buying can optimize the ad placement process and help brands achieve their goals, the marketers may not be sure *exactly* where their ads will appear online. Recent stories have emerged of companies surprised to find their brands appearing on offensive websites or next to offensive content (and being associated with it). There are tools and procedures available that allow companies to control where their ads appear; they simply need to use them.[31]

Armed with the media plan directives, the buyer seeks answers to a number of difficult questions as various media vehicles are considered. Does the vehicle have the right audience profile? Will the program's current popularity increase, stabilize, or decline? How well does the magazine's editorial format fit the brand and the message strategy (see the V8 example)? The answers to those questions bear directly on the campaign's success.

Photo: Courtesy Campbell Soup Company. Used with permission.

The physical characteristics of a magazine can affect its ability to deliver the desired message. For example, this V8 ad, which appeared in *Reader's Digest*, uses simple visuals and minimal copy to accommodate that magazine's small page size. *Reader's Digest* may not be the best choice for a complex ad.

Negotiate Costs   Just as a person buying a car often negotiates for the best price, so does a media buyer negotiate for the best prices. The key questions are whether the desired vehicles are available and whether a satisfactory schedule and rates can be negotiated. Aside from finding the aperture of target audiences, nothing is more crucial in media buying than securing the lowest possible price for placements. In buying network television time, the bulk of prime-time inventory is presold at a negotiated discount rate for the upcoming season during the **up-front market**. Networks sell the rest of their inventory in the **scatter market**, which means that the buys are made closer to the date.[32] Negotiations for up-front ad sales have become tougher and slower than in previous years as planners try to stretch their budgets around not only TV, but also social media, on-demand video, and mobile apps. The shift between the up-front and scatter markets is often cyclical because if advertisers pull back too far on up-front spending, they will end up paying up to 20 percent more for commercial time later in the year during the scatter market.[33]

Every traditional medium has a published rate card, but media buyers often negotiate special prices for volume buys. The buyer must understand the trade-off between price received and audience objectives. For example, a media buyer might be able to get a lower price for 30 commercials on ESPN, but part of the deal is that half the spots are scheduled with programs that don't reach the primary target audience. So the price may not be a good deal in the long run. Here are some other negotiation considerations.

- *Bargain for Preferred Positions* Media buyers must bargain for **preferred positions**, the locations in magazines and other print media that offer readership advantages (see Chapter 13). Imagine the value a food advertiser would gain from having its message located in a special recipe section that the homemaker can detach from the magazines for permanent use. How many additional exposures might that ad get? Because they are so visible, preferred positions often carry a premium surcharge, usually 10 to 15 percent above standard space rates.
- *Demand Extra Support Offers* With the current trend toward using other forms of marketing communication in addition to advertising, buyers often demand additional promotional support. These activities, sometimes called **value-added media services**, can take any number of forms, including contests, special events, merchandising space at stores, displays, and trade-directed newsletters. The "extra" depends on what facilities each media vehicle has and how hard the buyer can bargain.

Monitor Performance   A media buyer's responsibility to a campaign does not end with the signing of space and time contracts. The media buyer is responsible for tracking the performance of the media plan as it is implemented and afterward as part of the campaign evaluation. Buys are made in advance, based on forecasted audience levels. What happens if unforeseen events affect scheduling? What if newspapers go on strike, magazines fold, or a television show is canceled? Buyers must fix these problems.

Facebook, for example, faced a user revolt in 2013 by activist women who insisted the social media site should do a better job of finding and removing sites that glorify violence and abuse of women. The protests led a group of advertisers to withdraw their ads from Facebook.[34]

Underperformance and schedule problems are facts of life. Poorly performing vehicles must be replaced, or costs must be modified. Buyers also check the publication issues to verify whether advertisements have been placed correctly. Buyers also make every attempt to get current audience research to ensure that schedules are performing according to forecast. Media buyers are even found out "riding the boards," which means they check the location of the outdoor boards to verify that the client is receiving the outdoor exposure specified in the plan. Here are other responsibilities of media buyers.

- *Postcampaign Evaluation* Once a campaign is completed, the planner's duty is to compare the plan's expectations and forecasts with what actually happened. Did the plan actually achieve GRP, reach, frequency, and CPM objectives? Did the newspaper and magazine placements run in the positions expected? Such analysis is instrumental in providing guidance for future media plans.
- *Monitor Billing and Payment* Bills from the various media come in continuously. Ultimately, it is the responsibility of the advertiser to make these payments. However, the agency

Interactive Media Buying

Glenda Alvarado, *University of South Carolina*

Early 20th-century retail tycoon John Wanamaker is thought to have said, "I am convinced that about one-half the money I spend for advertising is wasted, but I have never been able to decide which half."

Advertising executives have struggled with this adage for years, inherently understanding that he was probably right, but there wasn't much that could be done about it. Traditional media buys are locked in a few days ahead of time and deciding which piece of the puzzle convinced a consumer to make a purchase is almost impossible.

Not so with digital and interactive media! All elements are adaptable at a moment's notice. A headline can be altered, an offer can be changed, and the location of the advertisement can be moved—all with the click of a mouse.

Digital and interactive media buys are usually made through an ad-serving company. Media executives can set limits on how many times a person is exposed to a message and receive regular updates on how each placement is performing. Detailed information on which sites are pulling consumers to a company, which version of a message is getting more hits, and what the return on investment for each ad has been are available in an Excel spreadsheet on a weekly, daily, or even hourly basis, if need be.

If the campaign goals or key performance indicators are not being met, buyers can negotiate with the placement company to gain better responses. This strategy is known as optimization and allows poor-performing advertising dollars to be more effectively allocated.

is contractually obligated to pay the invoice on behalf of the client. Keeping track of the invoices and paying the bills are the responsibility of the media buyer in conjunction with the accounting department.

So far, we've focused on buying for traditional media, but another complexity is the growth of online media, most of which call for entirely different media-buying techniques. The basis for the buy includes new measures such as click-throughs, and the data are monitored through services such as Nielsen Net Ratings and comScore. Google provides analytic data for search users (which includes visits to a site) as well as new or repeat viewers and time spent on the site. In a move to help advertisers untangle the complexity of marketing across multiple platforms, Nielsen launched its Total Content Ratings service in 2017, which consolidates all traditional, digital, and other TV/video viewing under one measurement system.[35] The Practical Tips feature provides additional ideas on how to buy interactive media.

In addition to negotiating, bargaining, buying, and monitoring the execution of a media plan, media buyers also have to deal with situations that crop up and complicate the planning. In effect, they are also troubleshooters. Buyers deal with the temporary snags in scheduling and in the reproduction of advertising messages that are sometimes unavoidable. Buyers must be alert for missed positions or errors in handling the message presentation and ensure that the advertiser is compensated appropriately when they occur. A policy of compensating for such errors is called "making good on the contract," known as **make goods**. Here are some of the common problems they may run into.

- *Program Preemptions* Special programs or news events sometimes interrupt regular programming and the scheduled commercials. In the case of long-term **program preemptions**, such as war coverage, buyers may have difficulty finding suitable replacements before the schedule ends.
- *Missed Closings* Magazines and newspapers have clearly set production deadlines, called **closings**, for each issue. Sometimes the advertising materials do not arrive in time. If the publication is responsible, it will make good. If the fault lies with the client or the agency, the publication makes no restitution.
- *Technical Problems* Technical difficulties are responsible for numerous goofs, glitches, and foul-ups that haunt the advertiser's schedule. **Bleed-throughs** (the printing on the back side of the page is visible and conflicts with the client's ad on the front side) and **out-of-register color** (full-color printing is made from four-color plates, which sometimes are not perfectly

aligned) for newspapers, torn billboard posters, broken film, and tapes out of alignment are typical problems.

The media buyer's life got even more complicated in 2010 with the live broadcast of the Academy Awards where E! Entertainment and Google worked feverishly to make real-time placements that would match the drama playing out onstage. The E! online channel was able to alter its Oscar-related ads within minutes to reflect not just the winners but also the content of the speeches, the onstage events, what the presenters were wearing, and other features of the coverage.[36]

Multichannel Buying (and Selling)

It should be clear from this review of media buyers' responsibilities that this job is challenging. Tom Carey, a retired Omnicom executive, observed that "service to clients is much about knitting together the multiple media choices and getting different companies—media, promotion, event marketing, public relations, etc.—to work together."[37]

A number of media services are available on the media side to help make buying for complicated media plans easier. Comcast and one of its media arms, NBC Universal, for example, promote their media opportunities using a multichannel plan that includes broadcast, cable, and the internet as well as original programming on its own channels. But the difference is that the media deals are packaged around a cause, such as the environment or wellness. Campbell Soup, for example, sponsored health segments on NBC's *The Today Show*. The idea is to match the media use of the target audience in all its complexity.

Newspapers have long offered simplified buys through such companies as Nationwide Newspapers, which can handle classified and display advertising in more than 21,000 newspapers. The Newspaper National Network is a trade association representing some 9,000 newspapers that also handles ad placement. In the digital world, DoubleClick's DART for Advertisers service helps advertisers manage online display and search marketing campaigns across online channels. All these services not only place ads but also provide performance data to help optimize a buy as well as report on the effectiveness of a marketer's specific plan.

On the other side of that coin is the *cross-media buy*, which is made easier by media companies that sell combinations of media vehicles in a single buy. This approach makes it easier to buy media across all of these platforms with a single deal rather than six phone calls. These **multichannel** deals are a result of media convergence. As content moves across these various forms of new media, so does advertising. Giant media groups, such as Viacom and Disney, are packaging "deals" based on the interests of the target audience. ESPN, for example, serves the sports market and can provide media integration that includes television, magazines, radio, and the internet. The media conglomerate Disney created a one-stop buying opportunity for advertisers targeting kids. To create this opportunity, Disney reorganized its ad sales staff to create one sales force for its various properties that reach children: two cable networks (Disney Channel and Toon Disney), kids' programming on ABC, Radio Disney, Disney.com, and *Disney Adventures* magazine.

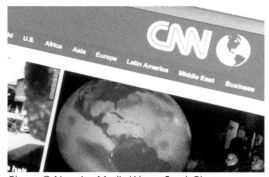

Photo: © Newsies Media/Alamy Stock Photo

CNN International illustrates an opportunity for marketers to obtain coverage across the globe.

Global Media Buying

Advertising practitioners can debate global theories of advertising, but one fact is inescapable: a true global medium does not currently exist, which means that global media plans have to piece together worldwide coverage using a variety of media tools. Television can transmit the Olympic Games around the globe, but no one network controls this global transmission. An advertiser seeking global exposure must therefore deal with different networks and different vehicles in different countries.

The definition of global media buying varies widely, but everyone agrees that few marketers are doing it yet. However, many are thinking about it, especially computer and other information technology companies that are being pursued by media such as AT&T. Today, the growth area is media buys across a single region. As media become more global, however, some marketers are beginning to make the leap across regions.

Satellite transmission now brings advertising into many homes, but its availability is not universal because of the *footprint* (coverage area of the satellite), technical limitations, and regulations of transmission by various governments. Satellites beam signals to more than one country in Europe, the Asian subcontinent, North America, and the Pacific, but they are regional, not global, in coverage. Despite its regional limitation, satellite transmission is still an enormous factor in the changing face of international advertising. For example, Sky satellite TV, with an audience spanning 32 countries across Europe and Russia, offers more than 370 English-speaking channels, giving advertisers the opportunity to deliver a unified message across the continent.[38]

The North American, European, Asian, and Latin American markets are becoming saturated with cable television companies offering an increasing number of international networks. Such broadcasters include the hugely successful Latin American networks of Univision and Televisa, whose broadcasts can be seen in nearly every Spanish-speaking market, including the United States. One of Univision's most popular programs, *El Chavo del Ocho,* is seen by over 90 million *daily* viewers in 16 countries.

In Europe, the rise of buying "centrals" came about with the emergence of the European Union and the continuing globalization of trade and advertising. *Buying centrals* are media organizations that buy across several European countries. Their growth also began with the development of commercial broadcasting and the expansion of media choices. These firms have flourished in an environment of flexible and negotiated rates, low inflation, and a fragmented advertising market. The buying centrals have nearly three-fourths of the media market in France, nine-tenths in Spain, and about two-fifths in Britain, Holland, Italy, and Scandinavia.

The important thing, however, is to be able to consider cultural implications in media use. For that reason, media planning and buying companies are also specializing or buying companies that know specific cultures, such as the Hispanic market in the United States and the Chinese market in Asia. Zenithoptimedia, for example, is a global media-buying company that has created ZO Multicultural, a multicultural unit that helps clients trying to reach ethnic markets.

Media Planning and Buying Trends

15.4 Explain current trends in media planning and buying.

Advertising experts have been proclaiming the demise of mass-media advertising for a number of years. It reached a high buzz level when Bob Garfield, an *Advertising Age* columnist, got industry-wide attention with his book *The Chaos Scenario*, in which he speculated about the media landscape in coming years when over-the-air network television is gone and everyone accesses their news, entertainment, and advertising any way they wish: television, phone, camera, laptop, game console, or MP3 player. His concept of "listenomics" emphasizes the importance of consumer-in-charge media choices.[39]

The truth is that the media landscape is dynamic and changing so fast that it's hard to keep track of how the media business is practiced. All these changes create new ways of operation and new opportunities for innovative media planners and buyers.

Unbundled Media Planning and Buying

We mentioned before the growth of media-buying services, such as the media megashop StarcomMediaVest, as separate companies that specialize in media buying. This shift in the way the media industry is organized is referred to as **unbundling media services**. It happens when an agency transforms its media department into a separate profit center, apart from the agency, that allows the media group to work for clients who may be competitors to some of those handled by the agency. Because these media-buying companies control the money, they have become a powerful force in the advertising industry, leading to a tug-of-war over control of planning.

Some of these media companies are now offering **consolidated services**, which means bringing the planning and buying functions back together. To take advantage of this consolidation argument, some media companies are also adding special planning teams for other related areas, such as events, product placement, internet marketing programs, and guerilla marketing programs. At this point, these big media companies begin to look more like traditional agencies.

Online Media Buying

A bigger threat to agencies than media-buying services comes from Google and Yahoo!, which, although not ad agencies, are making inroads into media buying and selling. Google is using its website to sell ads primarily to small advertisers and publishers who find Google AdWords and its Display Network to be cost-effective ways to reach targeted audiences across a variety of media. Google is betting that its expertise in search advertising, which matches ads to user interests, will give it an advantage over traditional ad media services.

New Forms of Media Research

As we mentioned earlier, one challenge media planners face is the lack of reliable audience research and measurement metrics for the new media. The traditional "measured" media with their CPMs were at least somewhat predictable in level of impact. But the metrics for online media—hits and clicks—don't really tell us much about impact. Comparing TRPs and clicks is like comparing apples and oranges.

Search advertising on the internet is also complicating things because, if it's successful, it steals viewers away from the original site. Does ESPN benefit when viewers leave its site to click on the banner ad for StubHub Ticket Center? How do you evaluate efficiency of the publisher's site? How about the search advertising? If one is a winner, does that automatically mean the other is a loser?

Viral marketing is equally difficult to measure, although YouTube is developing analytic data to help media planners assess the impact of the video-sharing site. Other companies, such as Visible Measures, Unruly Media, and Millward Brown's Link, provide viral monitoring services that assess the impact not only of YouTube but also of multiple online platforms. As such services mature, marketers will become smarter about selecting marketing communication messages with the most viral video potential.[40]

Another problem is that media research is based on each medium as a silo—separate studies for separate media. Most of the research services are unable to tell you much about the effectiveness of multiplatform media programs.

Looking Ahead

In Part 5, we'll review specific areas of marketing communication, such as public relations, direct response, sales promotion, and sponsorships—all of which are important aspects of multiplatform IMC programs. We'll end with a discussion of evaluation and wrap up the effectiveness theme that is so important in today's brand communication.

IT'S A WRAP

Having a Ball and Saving Lives

A mustache is the epitome of manhood—sexy and fun—and a fitting visual to grab attention for the fight against male-related cancer waged by the Icelandic Cancer Society.

The results were phenomenal. More than 9 out of 10 who experienced the campaign often said they were motivated to take action. More than 80 percent of the nation took part in Mustache March by giving money or spreading the conversation as a direct result of seeing the campaign. Slightly less than 40 percent of all grown men sported a dead-sexy mustache in the month of March (making Iceland look like an Eastern European country for a month). The campaign raised roughly $1.80 per inhabitant in Iceland, equivalent to a US charity raising $575,104,017. The Mustache March website was the fifth-most-visited site in all Iceland during the campaign.

Measured public relations media exposure was off the charts for the month with more than 13 prime-time television news stories. Countless television shows mentioned or had themes related to mustaches and cancer. More than 60 articles about the campaign appeared in major newspapers, resulting in lots of buzz. Mustache March measured 20 times the size of the next topic online in social media and regular online media, completely dominating the online forums for a whole month.

The biggest success was that 87 percent of all men said they would now talk freely about cancer and were more likely to seek a doctor's examination. And during the campaign month, more than 20 persons claimed that the campaign significantly affected their lives in a positive way because it motivated a visit to their doctor's office, where they were diagnosed with cancer and were receiving treatment.

Logo: Krabbameinsfélag/Icelandic Cancer Society

KEY OBJECTIVES SUMMARY

15.1. Discuss what is in a media plan and the role of media research in developing media plans. A media plan identifies how a brand can connect with its customers and other stakeholders in effective ways that resonate with the target audience. Media researchers gather, sort, and analyze the data used by media planners in making their planning decisions.

15.2. Detail the four steps in media planning and explain their importance. Step 1 identifies the media use patterns of the target audience and the times and places where they would be more receptive to brand messages. Step 2 states the media objectives in terms of reach and frequency. This step includes selecting the most appropriate media and developing a media mix that reaches the target audience in various ways. Step 3 is to develop media strategies that fine-tune the plan in terms of the reach/frequency relationship, geography, scheduling and timing, size and position in a media vehicle, and the way media vehicles are weighted in terms of their impact for this audience and brand situation. Step 4 is to use media metrics to analyze and predict the effectiveness (impact) and cost efficiency of the plan.

15.3. List the responsibilities of media buyers. Media buyers have inside information about the media industries that they feed back into the planning. Their responsibilities as buyers include providing information to media planners, selecting media vehicles, negotiating rates, monitoring the media plan's performance, evaluating the effectiveness of the media buy, and handling billing and payments.

15.4. Explain current trends in media planning and buying. The organization of the media industry is shifting as agencies unbundle their media services and as traditional media companies offer consolidated services, bringing their planning and buying functions together. Some media companies are also adding special planning teams for related areas, such as events, product placement, internet marketing programs, and guerilla marketing programs. Online media buying has been altered by a formidable new set of competitors such as Google and Yahoo!, who are leaders in search advertising. Another major challenge media planners face is the lack of reliable audience research and measurement metrics for the ever-expanding world of new media.

KEY TERMS

MyLab Marketing

Go to **www.pearson.com/mylab/marketing** for MyLab discussion questions (⭐) as well as the following assisted-graded writing questions.

15-1. What are some of the strategic considerations that determine the level of reach? Level of frequency?

15-2. The marketing management of McDonald's restaurants has asked you to analyze the aperture opportunity for its breakfast entrees. What kind of analysis would you present to management? What recommendations could you make that would expand the restaurant's nontraditional as well as traditional media opportunities?

REVIEW QUESTIONS

15-3. Explain the differences between media planning and media buying.

⭐ **15-4.** What is aperture, and how is it used in media planning?

15-5. How are gross impressions and GRPs calculated?

15-6. Explain the differences among continuous, flighting, and pulsing schedules.

15-7. Explain the differences between GRPs and TRPs. How are they used to estimate the impact of a media plan?

15-8. Explain the differences among CPMs, TCPMs, and CPPs. How are they used to estimate the cost efficiency of a media plan?

15-9. What do media buyers do?

DISCUSSION QUESTIONS

⭐ **15-10.** You have just begun a new job as a media planner for a new automobile model from General Motors. The media planning sequence will begin in four months, and your media director asks you what data and information you need from the media research department. What sources should you request? How would you use each of these sources in the planning function?

15-11. In performing an aperture analysis, choose one of the following products: video games (such as Nintendo),

men's cologne (such as Axe), computer software (such as Photoshop), or athletic shoes for aerobics (such as Reebok). For the brand you selected, analyze the marketing situation and give your intuitive answers to the following questions:

a. How does aperture work for this product?
b. Which media vehicles should be used to maximize and leverage the prospect's media aperture?
c. How can the timing and duration of the advertising improve the aperture opportunity?

TAKE-HOME PROJECTS

15-12. *Portfolio Project:* You have been asked to develop a media plan for a new reality show that you have created. Focus on the internet as a primary medium for this launch. Go to both www.google.com/adsense and https://advertising.yahoo.com/. Indicate how you would use the information provided by these sites in developing your media plan for this new reality television show.

15-13. *Mini-Case Analysis:* Outline the key decisions in the Icelandic men's cancer campaign. What were the media strategies that contributed to the success of this campaign? Using your analysis as a model, develop a proposal for a media plan for next year's follow-up campaign.

Planning and Buying Multicultural Media

Read the TRACE case in the Appendix before coming to class.

15-14. What media would you recommend to reach the TRACE target market of Multicultural Millennials (age 18 to 29)?

15-15. Based on TRACE's $100 million advertising budget, draw your own pie chart indicating the media you would select with a dollar figure attached to each medium.

HANDS-ON CASE

Making Milk Cool

"Got milk?" got consumer's attention. The campaign originated in 1993 to turn around a 15-year decline in milk consumption in California, and it did. Sponsored by the California Milk Processor Board (CMPB), the campaign urged consumers to buy more milk to pair with food like peanut butter and cookies by having them imagine what life would be like without enough milk. The campaign worked, winning a slew of major awards, including its recognition by *Advertising Age* as a Top 100 Advertising Campaign. More important is that sales increased. But one segment of the audience, teens, showed a troubling trend.

Research conducted by CMPB and its agency, Goodby, Silverstein & Partners (GSP), indicated that teens didn't think milk was so cool. In fact, 15 years of studies showed that teens' per capita consumption of milk dipped consistently. As kids age, they become more independent and tend to ignore Mom's advice to "drink milk." Other drinks like pop and sports drinks increasingly quench their thirst and absorb their money.

There's a significant amount spent marketing to the teen demographic. Packaged Facts, a market research firm, estimated that marketing products to teens exceeds $200 billion. More important than the potential profit to be made by increasing teen consumption is this question: if milk promotes good health, shouldn't teens be drinking it? That's a great idea, but it's hard to reach teens.

GSP accepted the challenge to connect to California teens in an attempt to shift their attitudes toward milk from uncool to cool. The objectives of the campaign were to engage teens to connect with and talk about milk, improve the image of milk, and ultimately get them to drink more of the white liquid.

How GSP connected with the teens offers a lesson in creative thinking in the brave new media world. Blogs revealed the importance of connecting online with teens and the influence of pop culture on their identities. This research also revealed that teens believed milk has lots of health- and self-image–related benefits, such as better teeth and stronger muscles.

What was GSP's Big Idea? It created a rock band called White Gold and delivered the milk message using "bizarre and random" humor. Looking at media as a way to engage consumers rather than interrupt their lives was key to the campaign's success.

Thinking like a band promoter and not like traditional advertisers, the agency produced musical magic, delivering the milk message through White Gold and the Calcium Twins. The band recorded an album and entered teens' digital social life through MySpace, Facebook, and Buzznet and on iTunes. Songs like "The Best I Can Give is 2%" deliver the important benefits-of-milk message. Television commercials featuring the band ran during shows like *American Idol*, *The Office*, and *Gossip Girl*. The band's website, WhiteGoldisWhiteGold.com, housed reviews, band history, discographies, and a music video. Poster-like full-page ads ran in *Rolling Stone*, *Seventeen*, and *Spin*. Hulu, Blinkx, and YouTube fed fans' online video viewing habits. The milk message was delivered to teens in ways they found palatable.

The new media world requires fresh thinking. Did the teens connect with the campaign's objectives? You bet they did. About 1.5 million views of White Gold music videos and an equal number of website views occurred in the first six months of the campaign. More than half of California teens were aware of White Gold, and nearly 9 out of 10 said that White Gold is "a fun and interesting way to learn about milk." White Gold–aware teens rated milk far higher than unaware teens, suggesting that White Gold successfully delivered the message to make milk cool.

Consider This

P4-1. What advice about media would you give to someone who wanted to market to teens?

P4-2. Describe the brand experience. How did this campaign combine the use of digital and traditional media? Was it effective?

P4-3. In what ways were the media choices for this campaign creative?

P4-4. Imagine you had this account. What would you plan for the next campaign? What media would you use?

Sources: Erik Sass, "Teen Market Grows to $208 Billion by 2011," June 27, 2007, www.mediapost.com; "White Gold Phenomenon Explodes on TV & Online," April 8, 2008, www.marketwire.com; Stuart Elliott, "California's Dairy Industry Takes Old Question to New Extreme," March 25, 2010, www.nytimes.com; Effie Briefs, "White Gold," www.effie.org; www.gotmilk.com.

5 PRINCIPLE
IMC and Total Communication

Hundreds of different communication activities deliver brand messages both formally through planned communication programs and informally through other activities. But it's not just the variety of messages that complicate a brand's presence. There is also a challenge from the changing environment in which brands live. For example, in 1998, Kodak was a huge global company and sold most of the photo paper and film bought worldwide. Three years later, it was struggling to stay alive in a digital world. Digital cameras and smartphones destroyed Kodak's brand vision as well as its business plan.

In Part 5, we describe how a collection of marketing communication platforms and tools can be coordinated as part of an integrated brand communication program. It also helps you see the two central questions that will guide the brand through a changing environment:

- *Effectiveness*—does it work?
- *Ethics*—is it right?

To help you understand how these principles and practices work to deliver effective brand communication, consider what Professor Tom Duncan, one of the early leaders in integrated marketing communication (IMC) education, has to say about IMC.

◄ TOM DUNCAN is the founder and director emeritus of the integrated marketing communication (IMC) master's program at the University of Colorado and an international consultant and speaker on IMC. He also established IMC as a master's program and MBA option at the Daniels School of Business at the University of Denver.

Building Brands, Brand Relationships, and Brand Equity

Because marketing communication functions have become so sophisticated and the media so fragmented, brand message clutter has significantly increased, making it more difficult and costly to manage. Companies are finding it increasingly difficult to reach prospects and retain current customers. Now add in all the emerging communication technologies that have empowered customers, facilitating their ability to talk about brands to each other as well as "talk back" to companies.

These changes have resulted in customers becoming more business savvy and at the same time having greater brand expectations than ever before. As these changes take place, competition becomes more intense, and top management demands more and more accountability and results from marketing communication expenditures.

The old marketplace motto "caveat emptor" (let the buyer beware) has become almost obsolete. A more accurate axiom today is "let the company beware." Recognizing this new marketing environment, smart companies have intensified their efforts to integrate their marketing communication and all other brand messages because that is the most cost-effective way to build brand relationships and brand equity.

Originally, IMC was about creating "one voice, one look" across all messages in a campaign. So the print ad "looked like" the television commercial, and the website matched the look of the outdoor advertising. We now know that a more effective approach to IMC has moved from this narrow "execution" focus to a much broader focus on branding and customer brand perceptions. IMC isn't just about advertising. Rather than just using advertising to sell products, companies now want to use everything that sends a message to create a coherent brand presence that leads to long-term brand relationships.

Although IMC has been around for many years, few understand the breadth—and depth—of this communication focus. Here are the basic premises behind effective IMC programs.

- IMC is not just advertising or public relations, and it's not just marketing communication; rather, it's everything a brand says and does. IMC involves the entire organization.

- IMC is a common sense ongoing process for managing brand perceptions and experiences as well as customer expectations about the brand.

- IMC planning delivers the brand essence (vision, position, personality, and image) in all marketing communication as well as at all brand contact points.

- IMC engages all stakeholders in meaningful and often interactive brand experiences.

- When these IMC best practices are applied, they lead to solid brand relationships, and that leads to enhanced brand equity.

The chapters in this part introduce you to the basic marketing communication principles. We tie everything up that has been presented in this book with a chapter on IMC, which reviews basic IMC principles and practices as well as the big picture of total brand communication. We also include a chapter to help you answer the question, does it work? Finally, we present issues related to ethics, social responsibility, and regulation and ask you to consider the question, is it right?

16

IMC Management

KEY OBJECTIVES

16.1 Discuss the eight key IMC concepts and explain why they are important.

16.2 Outline the key parts of an IMC campaign plan.

16.3 Identify the strategic decisions that underlie effective international marketing communication.

16.4 Explain what we mean by 360-degree communication program planning.

The Komen Foundation's "Pink Ribbon" campaign is an example of a simple promotional idea that captivates supporters and sponsors and involves them personally in building a successful breast cancer research organization. An award-winning integrated effort, the "Pink Ribbon" campaign illustrates how marketers in a hotly contested nonprofit marketplace make decisions about brand identity and communication. This chapter will bring together the basic IMC principles, many of which we have introduced in previous chapters. Then it will describe the formalities of planning for an IMC campaign, followed by an introduction to the challenges of managing a comprehensive integrated communication program.

MyLab Marketing

⭐ **Improve Your Grade!**

More than 10 million students improved their results using Pearson MyLabs.
Visit **www.pearson.com/mylab/marketing** for simulations, tutorials, and end-of-chapter problems.

IT'S A WINNER

Campaign	Organization	Agency	Awards
"I am Susan G. Komen for the cure."	*Susan G. Komen Foundation for the Cure*	*Burson-Marsteller's Proof*	*Multiple Halo Awards for Cause Marketing*

The Power of Pink

Source: Created by Burson-Marstellar, LLC d/b/a Proof Integrated Communications. Copyright, 2012 by Susan G. Komen.

Although you might not initially consider pink a fall color, think again. Everywhere you look in National Breast Cancer Awareness Month (October), you see pink. The National Football League's pink football equipment and pink-trimmed uniforms, Delta Airlines' pink plane, Panera Bread's Pink Ribbon Bagels, Avon's Pink Products, Yoplait's pink yogurt lids, KitchenAid's pink blenders, NASCAR's pink race cars, OtterBox's pink smartphone covers—you get the point.

Inspired by the success of red ribbons in raising awareness of AIDS, proponents of breast cancer awareness started using a pink ribbon as the symbol for its cause, which has evolved into one of the most successful charity brand identity campaign ideas ever. In 1991, the Susan G. Komen Foundation for the Cure, dedicated to educating women about breast cancer and finding a cure, was the first to distribute pink ribbons to breast cancer survivor participants in its "Race for the Cure" in New York City. Other groups with similar goals quickly adopted the pink ribbon.

The following year, leaders at the National Breast Cancer Awareness Month adopted the pink ribbon as its symbol. In 1993, Evelyn Lauder, a vice president of the Estée Lauder Companies, founded the Breast Cancer Research Institute and used the pink ribbon as its symbol as well.

What makes this campaign idea remarkable from a branding and integrated marketing communication perspective is the number of companies that have found synergy in joining an important cause as they promote their products. A *New York Times* reporter described the pinking of America as "multi-billion-dollar business, a marketing, merchandising and fund-raising opportunity that is almost unrivaled in scope." Behind this effort is a fascinating story of a brilliant marketing insight and sustained work to communicate the important cancer message.

Nancy G. Brinker, founder and CEO of the Susan G. Komen Foundation for the Cure, rebranded the disease from hopeless to hopeful in memory of her sister, who had died of breast cancer. Drawing on her career as a sales trainee at Neiman Marcus, Brinker made the message about cancer more optimistic, convincing people that there is hope for surviving the disease. That hope depended on educating women to get mammograms and investing in research about breast cancer. An annual event, "Race for the Cure," helps spread the positive message. Brinker replicated the message across the country by enlisting 121 affiliates to replicate the event, Komen's biggest revenue producer.

To fund the efforts to educate women and produce a cure, Brinker successfully enlisted a multitude of companies who found synergy in cobranding their products with a good cause, especially during October. She recognized the power of pink: to help companies associate their brand with a good cause. Companies generate goodwill for their brands and income to support the cause.

The ads featured on the opening page of this case study tell the stories of cancer survivors and the foundation. Much of the advertising in cause marketing features not only the charity, but its partnering companies as well.

Since 1982 Komen has raised more than $920 million for research and more than $2 billion for medical care. It now serves millions of cancer patients in over 60 countries. Is pink the color of success? Find out at the end of this chapter in the It's a Wrap feature.

Sources: Susan G. Komen website, ww5.Komen.org, downloaded August 30, 2017; Sam Borden, "A New Twist to N.F.L. Breast Cancer Awareness: A Pink Tutu," *New York Times*, October 5, 2012, www.nytimes.com; Natasha Singer, "Welcome, Fans, to the Pinking of America," *New York Times*, October 15, 2011, www.nytimes.com; Deborah Sweeney, "5 Companies Going above and beyond for Breast Cancer Awareness Month," *Forbes*, October 11, 2012, www.forbes.com; "OtterBox Promotes Strength in Numbers during Breast Cancer Awareness Month," *OtterBox*, October 4, 2012, http://media.otterbox.com/2012-10-04-OtterBox-Promotes-Strength-in-Numbers-During-Breast-Cancer-Awareness-Month; "Pink Ribbon," *Wikipedia*, www.wikipedia.org.

16.1 Discuss the eight key IMC concepts and explain why they are important.

Key IMC Concepts

Integrated marketing communication (IMC) is an important business concept as well as a set of principles and practices. It has been a major theme in this book, and we will use this chapter to summarize the basic principles and review the practices of IMC. We'll begin with the key concepts that separate IMC plans and programs from more traditional advertising and other marketing communication areas.

Stakeholders and Brand Relationships

● **Principle**
Interactive communication is the glue that joins brands and their stakeholders in respectful long-term relationships.

We start with stakeholders because a customer focus is critical in most IMC strategies. Although we say "customer," we are really referring to all the stakeholders who impact on that customer relationship. Relationship marketing, a concept that originated with public relations, shifts the focus from the objective of a one-time purchase to the maintenance of long-term involvement from and by all the firm's critical stakeholders, whether employees, distributors, channel members, agencies, investors, government agencies, the media, or the community.

Interactive and respectful communication is the link that connects brands and their key stakeholders and the glue that joins them in respectful long-term relationships. The possibility of authentic two-way communication has exploded with the development of digital technology and social media.

When Is Too Many Too Much?

Tom Duncan, *University of Colorado*

The question advertisers have to ask themselves when approving a plan that involves nontraditional media is whether they are using this tool effectively and with respect for consumers. Are advertisers trying to find every possible contact point they can identify, or are they creating logical associations that consumers will appreciate?

We are inundated with commercial messages from advertising of all sorts in all kinds of unexpected places that we routinely encounter. Message clutter is overwhelming every aspect of our daily lives.

Think about something as noncommercial as attending a symphony. You may find a new car in the lobby as well as promotional signs for any number of products—not to mention the symphony itself, which is promoting concerts and season subscriptions. Of course, there are ads in the program, but there may also be ads in the bathrooms and around the snack counter you visit at intermission. When you leave, you'll probably see more posters in windows adjoining the concert hall. You might even find a flyer tucked under the windshield wiper on your car.

There is a difference between "buying eyeballs" and delivering messages in a context that will intersect with a target audience's interests. Wilson Sporting Goods, for example, sponsors Tennis Camps by furnishing practice balls and making racquets available that participants can try for free. Even though the camp may be surrounded by Wilson, the message is relevant and the brand experiences are positive.

The point is that the less relevant the messages, the more irritating they become. Why is that a problem? The tipping point in impact is when the percentage of irrelevant messages is so high that people respond by tuning out *all* commercial messages—the relevant along with the irrelevant.

One reason TiVo became popular is because viewers can time-shift programs and zip through commercials. In what ways will consumers create defense mechanisms to protect themselves from nontraditional media that assault them in unwanted ways at inappropriate times?

How many messages can we surround them with before they rebel?

All stakeholders are critical in relationship marketing because they are communicators who can send either positive or negative messages about the brand. It is important to keep in contact with them, but it's even more important to set up relationship programs that invite two-way communication and let them initiate messages.

> **Principle**
> Brand relationships drive brand value.

Relevant messages delivered through media that drive positive experiences create value for consumers. This value adds up over time and emerges as loyalty—the ultimate goal of relationship marketing programs. Brand relationships are indicators of **brand value**—what a brand is worth both to the company and to its customers. Positive relationships underlie the financial value of a brand as well as its perceived value to customers. Negative impact, however, can come from mishandling the type and amount of messages directed to stakeholders, as the Matter of Principle feature explains.

> **Principle**
> Stakeholders overlap, and so do their messages.

It's important to remember that although we talk about stakeholders as if they were independent groups, in fact stakeholders may overlap. Employees, for example, are often customers as well as shareholders, and they often live in communities where the company is in business. It's important that a brand not say one thing to one stakeholder group and something opposite or contradictory to another—particularly not in this time of instant internet communication.

> **Principle**
> Receiving and responding to messages is as important as sending them.

The growth of **permission marketing**, a practice that invites consumers to sign up for messages, self-selecting themselves into a brand's target market, mirrors the shift from one-way to two-way communication. That's important as brands become more involved in social communication where online technology permits contacts that move beyond the frequently intrusive and unwanted forms of mass-media advertising.

Total Communication

Older views of IMC focused primarily on coordinating marketing communication, but as we mentioned in Chapter 1, we also believe that the marketing mix delivers messages. As long ago as 1976, Wayne DeLozier's marketing communication book treated all the marketing mix variables as communication variables.[1] How the product is designed and how it performs, where the brand is sold, and at what price—all of these marketing decisions send messages about the brand's position, quality, and image.

The brand consultant Interbrand released its 2016 Best Global Brands report ranking Apple and Google at the top. The report found that "a big part of what makes brands like Apple valuable is their cohesiveness as a connected business system." In other words, "Apple communicates with its customers through its hardware, software, and retail stores to deliver one consistent narrative."[2] The most important factor in integrated communication is a coherent brand concept that is expressed at every point of contact.

Media planning includes all the traditional as well as nontraditional media, but it is good to remember that in **360-degree communication** planning, there are other message delivery points in the way a company does business. A **total communication** program monitors all these sources of brand messages. Also remember that contemporary brand communication includes two-way as well as targeted strategies—receiving and responding to messages is as important as sending them.

Furthermore, consider that everything a brand does—and sometimes what it doesn't do— can send a message. You can't *not* communicate. Unintentional messages can arise from carelessly delivered brand experiences. For example, a long wait on a customer service help line or the inability of a company representative to answer a product safety question sends the message that the company doesn't value a customer's time or safety. Those messages can be more powerful—in a negative way—than anything said in the advertising. That's why it's necessary to monitor all marketing elements from a communication perspective.

Moving from Channels to Contact Points

The concept of **contact points** has redefined and broadened our understanding of media as a message delivery system. Contact points are the various ways a consumer comes in contact with a brand. As we proposed in Part 4, this view of media moves from traditional advertising media (print, broadcast, and outdoor) and the media of various marketing communication functions (press releases, events, promotional materials, and sponsorships) to experiential contacts that in previous advertising-dominated media plans weren't generally considered to be media, such as word of mouth and customer service.

These opportunities are found in a huge variety of vehicles, including everything from television to T-shirts and tweets on Twitter. The list is endless and can be identified only by studying the lives of customers to spot the points where they come in contact with a brand—or an opportunity for a brand experience or brand conversation. Every one of these varied vehicles can deliver a brand message, either positive or negative, whether planned and managed or not.

Contact point management, then, is the way marketing communication planners develop systems of message delivery, both to and from all key stakeholders. The objective is to maximize and leverage the good contact points and minimize the bad ones.

We also call them brand **touchpoints** because of the impact these personal experiences can have on stakeholder feelings about a brand. Consumers may receive information and impressions from a brand at a contact point, but a touchpoint is a brand experience that delivers a message that also touches emotions leading to positive and negative judgments. It has more emotional impact than a regular contact point. A *critical touchpoint*, then, is one that connects the brand and customer on an emotional level and leads to a yes-or-no decision about a purchase decision or a brand relationship.[3]

Sometimes referred to as experiential marketing, touchpoint strategies and programs use events and store design, among other means, to engage consumers in a personal and involving way. Some would argue that every brand contact is an experience; however, in experiential marketing, the goal is to intensify active involvement beyond the more passive activity of reading, viewing, and listening to traditional media. The idea is to connect with consumers in ways that create higher levels of emotional engagement that lead to brand liking as well as lasting bonds with a brand.

Message Synergy

When you combine stakeholders and contact points—all the messages delivered through all possible media to all key stakeholders—you have a bundle of messages. How do you manage

Sidebar Principles

● **Principle**
Everything a brand does, but also what it doesn't do, can send a message. You can't NOT communicate.

● **Principle**
Integrating the marcom tools is futile if contrary and more powerful messages are sent by other brand actions.

● **Principle**
Every part of the marketing mix—not just marketing communication—sends a message.

● **Principle**
IMC planning is designed to maximize and leverage the good contact points and minimize the bad ones.

● **Principle**
Touchpoints are contact points that touch our emotions.

● **Principle**
Synergy happens when all the messages work together to create a coherent brand perception.

Developing Your Personal Brand

Trent Walters, *Brand Management Principal, The Richards Group, Dallas, Texas*

In advertising, we often think of brands as something external: a promise offered by a company or service that ultimately makes a person's life better. But it is important to realize that people are brands just like companies and products are. Just think of the different celebrities out there, from movies and TV to sports and music. Each one is known for something, which is ultimately their personal brand. The same is true for you.

You as a person are a brand. And although you might not have attained celebrity status (yet), it is important for you to be sure that you build, develop, and maintain your personal brand, especially as you look toward a career in marketing communication. Every time you interact with someone, they get a taste of your personal brand. The way you talk, write, dress, carry yourself, and everything else you do gives others a perspective into "brand you."

Social media has allowed people to have so many more touchpoints with others than was ever possible before. At one time, a person's circle of influence was only large enough to include folks they personally came in contact with. With social media, today people can "personally connect" with thousands of people relatively instantly. That creates thousands of opportunities to either build up or break down your personal brand.

Ask yourself, "Are my personal brand touchpoints aligned? Does my Instagram profile represent the same person I profess to be during an interview? Does my Twitter handle contradict the person I claim to be in my cover letter? Do my social media pages truly convey that I am the type of person an agency wants to hire?" More people have access to your social media pages than you might think. And you can bet that employers are looking at them before they decide to bring you in. Be sure that your pages reflect your personal brand well.

A rule of thumb: use social media to display your well roundedness, cleverness, charm, whit, intelligence, and fun side. Do not use it to display your lack of judgment, crassness, or obnoxious, vulgar, and even profane sides. When in doubt, ask yourself, "Would I be comfortable if this post was on the front page of any major news site for all to see?" If the answer is still yes, post away.

Agencies are looking for fun, smart people who will represent their company and their clients well. Be sure that your personal brand lets them know you are a candidate who fits that bill.

Walters is a graduate of the University of North Texas, where he was selected by the American Advertising Federation to be one of its Most Promising Minority Students. He was nominated to be featured here by Professor Sheri Broyles.

all the meanings and points where inconsistency or confusion might arise? And why does that matter?

The point is that brand communication is not about single messages but rather about the impact of various impressions and brand meanings that evolve as the messages interact and reinforce one another. Remember the principle of synergy that proposes that $2 + 2 = 5$. In other words, messages that reinforce one another have a multiplier effect that not only cements a brand impression but also polishes and magnifies it. If you hear good things (or bad things) about a brand in advertising (but also in comments from friends) and what you hear corresponds to your experience with the brand, you are likely to become not just a customer but also a loyalist and perhaps even a brand fan.

At every point of contact with every stakeholder, the essence of the brand should be the same. Drivers, for example, look at cars and car safety differently, and so do car manufacturers, their suppliers and investors, and local community leaders. But the essence of a brand like Volvo must be consistent on its safety position. Strategic consistency drives synergy, and synergy drives the brand impression. Therefore, brand stewards and IMC planners are insistent on **strategic consistency**—the core or essence of the brand is clear in every message if messages are tailored to the particular interests of various stakeholders.

● **Principle**
Strategic consistency drives synergy.

A Brand Is an Integrated Perception

Message synergy is the basis for seeing a brand as an integrated perception. People automatically integrate brand messages and experiences—it's a natural process in perception—and that happens whether or not brand stewards try to manage the process. What do you think of when you think of Taco Bell, Mountain Dew, or Apple? Your impression will probably contain ideas about the brand's position in the market as well as images of the people you see using it and the messages you've heard articulated in media and mentions by people you know. How that stew of information and images comes together as an **integrated perception** is just the way we make sense of things, and that's how a brand impression is created. Perceptual integration works only if the pieces fit together.

Unified Brand Vision

There is an art and a science to IMC management. A successful brand is the product of both science—a complex system of planned and managed activities—and art—a vision of the essence of the brand in which all the pieces and parts fit together perfectly in a coherent brand perception.[4] The vision of the brand steward and how that unified vision is communicated to all the agents involved in the complex system of brand communication determines the effectiveness of a brand communication program.

In other words, marketing communicators are managing a multiplicity of brand activities and programs that are interrelated and that work well only to the extent that they work together. When they work together with a single **unified vision** of the brand, like a great symphony, the pieces and parts fit together perfectly, generating meaning and creating something of value.

Internal Integration

Brand management involves creating and monitoring a complex set of philosophies and activities. You can't be integrated externally if you are not integrated internally. A core brand strategy— a shared vision—drives the entire organization. **Cross-functional management** across department lines delivers unity of vision, which is the foundation for the consumer's integrated brand perception.

Brand Integrity

At the root of it all, if you look in the dictionary, you'll see that the word *integration* has the same Latin root as *integrity*. So you might conclude that an integrated brand is one that has **brand integrity**. It is more believable because what it says and does matches what others say about it. In other words, its brand reputation is supported by word-of-mouth comments, media stories, and testimonies from satisfied users. Being a good corporate citizen also adds trust to brand relationships and embellishes a brand's reputation.

This review of IMC's basic concepts also identifies a set of basic principles. We'll show how these principles are applied to IMC campaign planning and program management in the sections that follow. To summarize, the following are 14 principles that guide IMC:

1. Interactive communication is the glue that joins brands and their stakeholders in respectful long-term relationships.
2. Brand relationships drive brand value.
3. Stakeholders overlap; so do their messages.
4. Receiving messages is as important as sending them.
5. Every part of the marketing mix sends a message.
6. Integrating the marcom tools is futile if contrary and more powerful messages are sent by other brand actions.
7. Everything a brand does (and sometimes what it doesn't do) can send a message. You can't *not* communicate.
8. IMC planning is designed to maximize and leverage the good contact points and minimize the bad ones.
9. Touchpoints are contact points that touch our emotions.
10. Synergy happens when all the messages work together to create a coherent brand perception.

11. Strategic consistency drives synergy.
12. A brand is a unified vision (the art) and a complex system of message delivery and exchange (the science).
13. You can't be integrated externally if you are not integrated internally.
14. Integration leads to brand integrity.

IMC Campaign Planning

16.2 Outline the key parts of an IMC campaign plan.

One principle you have learned is that in marketing communication campaigns, a key objective is to create consistency among all the marcom tools and platforms. That's essentially a tactical approach, one focused on orchestrating consistent brand messages. In the Part 5 opener, Duncan referred to this approach as a "one voice, one look" strategy, which has always been a critical goal for campaigns. We now recognize, however, that although it's important to have strategic consistency based on the brand essence, there may be different message strategies for different audiences.

Stan Richards, founder of the Dallas-based Richards Group, explains the process his agency goes through in planning an integrated campaign. It's also the creative brief for what he calls **spherical branding**, which means that no matter what your angle of vision, the brand always looks the same.[5] We call it *360-degree planning*. Both refer to looking at a brand from all directions and points of view. Richards's brief outline is a good starting point for building a complete campaign plan:

- *Three-Part Positioning* Target audience? Competitors? Most meaningful brand benefit?
- *Brand Personality* Five to six words that define the brand's personality.
- *Affiliation* What club do you join when you adopt a brand?
- *Brand Vision* A statement of the brand's "highest calling."

What Is a Campaign Plan?

An IMC campaign is a complex set of interlocking, coordinated activities that has a beginning and an end. An IMC campaign plan is more complex than a traditional advertising or public relations plan because of the variety of marcom areas and stakeholders involved. An IMC plan outlines the objectives and strategies for a series of different but related marketing communication efforts that appear in different media, use different marketing communication tools, and convey different but complementary brand-consistent messages to a variety of stakeholders.

⬡ **Principle**
The more tools used, the harder it is to coordinate their efforts and maintain consistency across a variety of messages.

An IMC plan follows the same basic outline as an advertising plan. The difference, however, lies with the scope of the plan and the variety of activities involved in the effort. The more tools used, the harder it is to coordinate their efforts and maintain consistency across a variety of messages. The objective in IMC planning is to make the most effective and consistent use of all marketing communication functions and to influence or control the impact of other communication elements. Here is a typical outline:

I. Situation Analysis
   A. Background research
   B. SWOTs: strengths, weaknesses, opportunities, threats
   C. Key communication problem(s) to be solved

II. Key Strategic Campaign Decisions
   A. Objectives
   B. Targeting and engaging stakeholders
   C. Brand positioning strategy

III. Marcom Mix
   A. Platforms and objectives
   B. Synergy

IV. Message Strategy
   A. Key consumer and brand relationship insights
   B. Message direction
   C. Strategic consistency

  V. IMC Media and Contact Points
      A. Multimedia and multichannel
      B. Multiplatform
      C. Contact points, touchpoints, and critical touchpoints

  VI. Management and Campaign Controls
      A. Budgeting
      B. Evaluation of effectiveness

This outline is useful as a guide for a planning document, but more important is that it identifies the key strategic decisions that guide various sections of an IMC campaign plan. Consider the "Matter of Practice" story about the campaign to brand Billings, Montana, in Chapter 1. After reading about campaigns in this chapter, you should be better able to understand the strategy behind this community branding effort.

Situation Analysis

The first step in developing an IMC plan, just as in a marketing plan, is not planning, but *backgrounding*: researching and reviewing the current state of the business and gathering all pertinent information. After the research is compiled, planners try to make sense of the findings, a process sometimes referred to as a **situation analysis**. The goal for both advertising and IMC planning is to identify a problem that can be solved with communication. As Pat Fallon and Fred Senn explained in their *Juicing the Orange* list, you have to start by simplifying the problem (see Chapter 8). The information collection will probably be huge, but the problem statement zeros in on the most relevant concerns.

SWOT Analysis   The primary tool used to make sense of the information gathered and identify a key problem related to a brand or product is a **SWOT analysis**. The strengths and weaknesses are *internally focused*, and the opportunities and threats lie in the *external* marketing environment. In strategic planning, the idea is to *leverage* the strengths and opportunities and *address* the weaknesses and threats, which is how the key problems and opportunities are identified:[6]

- The *strengths* of a business are its positive traits, conditions, and good situations. For instance, being in a category leader is a strength. Planners ask how they can leverage this strength in the brand's communication.
- The *weaknesses* of a business are traits, conditions, and situations that are perceived as negatives. Losing market share is a weakness. If that is an important weakness, planners ask how they can or should address it with communication. Avis found a positive in a negative in its classic campaign when it positioned itself as number two, so "we try harder."
- An *opportunity* is an area in which the company could develop an advantage over its competition. Often, one company's weakness is another company's opportunity. Planners strive to identify these opportunities and leverage them in the brand's communication. That is a huge strategy for political campaign advertising.
- A *threat* is a trend or development in the environment that will erode business unless the company takes action. Competition and economic downturns are common threats. Communication planners ask themselves how they can address a threat if it is a critical factor affecting the success of the brand. McDonald's has promoted its healthy menu items to counter the perception of burgers as unhealthy choices.

     For the launch of Coke Zero, the strength of the brand lies with the Coca-Cola tradition as "the real thing." The opportunity existed to transfer that Coke magic to a calorie-free version of the flagship brand. The weakness is the association of diet drinks with women; Coke saw an opportunity in marketing to men. The threat lies with the perception that "diet drinks" have an unpleasant taste; the opportunity was to explain that Coke Zero tastes like regular Coke.

Key Communication Problems   The key word in the title of this section is *analysis*, or making sense of all the data collected and figuring out what the information means for the future success of the brand. Planners must analyze the market situation for communication problems that affect the successful marketing of a product as well as opportunities the marketing communication can create or exploit. Analyzing the SWOTs as well as the directions from the client and identifying key problems that can be solved with a brand message are at the heart of strategic thinking. An example of locating a timing opportunity is illustrated by Special K's "2-Week Challenge," which capitalized on consumers' goals to lose weight after the holidays.

IMC can solve only message-related problems such as image, attitude, perception, and knowledge or information. It cannot solve problems related to price, availability, or quality, although it can address the perception of these marketing mix factors. For example, a message can speak to the perception that the price is too high by focusing on a value strategy, or it can portray a product with limited distribution as exclusive. In other words, promotional messages can affect the way consumers perceive such marketing features as price, availability, and quality. The marketer's basic assumption—and success criteria—however, is that a campaign works if it creates the desired brand impression, influences people to respond, and separates the brand from the competition.

> ● **Principle**
> A campaign works if it creates the desired brand impression, influences people to respond, and separates the brand from its competition.

Campaign Strategy

Once the situation has been analyzed and the key problem or problems identified, planners decide a general statement of strategy. In other words, what is this campaign all about? The general strategy that guides a campaign can be described in several ways. For example, a strategy can focus on branding, positioning, countering the competition, or creating category dominance. In the case of the Susan G. Komen campaign, the "Pink Ribbon" idea was designed to quickly identify the nonprofit organization and its work in breast cancer research and to stake a claim to a distinctive brand vision.

Photo: Nadine Laubacher

The message strategy for the launch of Coke Zero used self-deprecating humor with a Big Idea that the Coca-Cola legal department wanted to sue Coke Zero for taste infringement.

Maybe the strategy is designed to change consumers' perception of the brand's price or price-value relationship. The strategy may also seek to increase the size of the market, or what marketers call **share of wallet**, the amount customers spend on the brand. Other marketing efforts might involve launching a new brand or a brand extension or moving the brand into a new market. Another common focus is the role and importance of the brand's competitive position and how to respond to competitors' messages. During the Great Recession, for example, a number of major brands, such as Dunkin' Donuts, Burger King, and Campbell's Soup, developed highly competitive advertising.

The important thing to remember, as marketing professor Julie Ruth explains,[7] is that planners have to first analyze the situation to arrive at a great strategy before racing ahead to think about tactics. So what's the difference between strategy and tactics? The decision to expand the market (strategy) by increasing share of wallet (objective) is implemented through promotional tactics ("buy four and get one free").

The situation analysis is the first step in developing the IMC campaign strategy. There are a number of related strategic decisions that follow from the situation analysis, and we'll discuss three of them here: *objectives*, *targeting*, and *brand position*.

Objectives   Given the huge amounts of money spent on brand communication, it is important for marketers to know what to expect from a campaign. Although a rule of thumb for advertising is that it should be single minded, we also know from Chapter 5 that multiple effects are often needed to create the desired impact, and that's particularly true in IMC planning. Some messages may use an emotional strategy whereas others are informational, but sometimes the message needs to speak to both the head and the heart. We mentioned in the discussion of the Coke Zero launch that customers needed to understand that the taste of Coke Zero was similar to regular Coke but that the message had to do it with a style and attitude that twenty-something males would like and find believable.

Although some objectives are tightly focused on one particular effect, others, such as brand loyalty, call for a more complex set of effects. To create brand loyalty, for example, a campaign must have both cognitive (rational) and affective (emotional) effects, and it must move people to repeat buying. That's one reason brand loyalty is considered a type of long-term impact developed over time from many experiences that a consumer has with a brand and brand messages.

Notice also that communication objectives may be important, even if they aren't focused directly on a sale. For example, Expedia.com, a travel consulting company, uses its campaigns as a way to draw attention to itself, create name recognition, and create understanding of the products and services it sells. The idea is that after brand awareness and understanding are created, the selling can start.

Every campaign must be guided by specific, clear, and measurable objectives. Effective campaigns use media to stimulate consumers and activate their responses. This diagram in Figure 16.1 by Melissa Lerner, vice president of an out-of-home media company, illustrates various types of impact that innovative media plans can deliver and how they can reinforce one another in an IMC plan.

We cannot overstate the importance of writing focused and measurable objectives. We say **measurable objectives** because that's how the effectiveness of a campaign is determined. A measurable objective has a starting baseline and a goal—the distance between those two points is what is measured. Determining the starting point is called **benchmarking**, which means the planner uses a comparable effort, such as a similar product or prior brand campaign, to predict a logical goal. A measurable objective includes five requirements:

Effective Campaigns—Stimulate and Activate

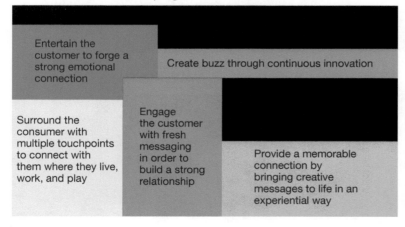

Entertain the customer to forge a strong emotional connection

Create buzz through continuous innovation

Surround the consumer with multiple touchpoints to connect with them where they live, work, and play

Engage the customer with fresh messaging in order to build a strong relationship

Provide a memorable connection by bringing creative messages to life in an experiential way

FIGURE 16.1

Out-of-Home Media Effects
Effective campaigns use media to stimulate consumers and activate their responses. This diagram by Melissa Lerner, vice president of an out-of-home media company, illustrates various types of impact that innovative media plans can deliver.

1. A *specific effect* that can be measured
2. A *time frame*
3. A *baseline* (where we are or where we begin)

4. The *goal* (a realistic estimate of the change the campaign can create; benchmarking is used to justify the projected goal)
5. *Percentage change* (subtract the baseline from the goal; divide the difference by the baseline)

A hypothetical objective, then, would read as follows: "The goal of this campaign is to move the target's awareness of Coke Zero's taste similarity with regular Coke from 18 to 23 percent within 12 months, an increase of 28 percent."

Targeting and Engaging Stakeholders   We introduced the concept of stakeholders in the IMC introduction in Chapter 1, but let's look a little deeper into this concept. The target in an IMC plan includes more than just consumers. As a reminder, the term *stakeholder* refers to any group of people who have a stake in the success of a company or brand. These potential audiences include all those who might influence the purchase of products and the success of a company's marketing program, as the table below shows. Employees are particularly important, and their support or *buy-in* for marketing communication programs is managed through an activity called **internal marketing**.

Based on research into consumers and customers as well as the involvement of other stakeholders, the targeting or engagement strategy identifies the most important audience groups. Research by account planners will help to flesh out the interests of these folks and provide critical insights. Account planning, with its strong emphasis on insights, has moved beyond its original advertising orientation and has become much more useful in IMC campaign planning. Insights into consumer, customer, and stakeholder relationships with the brand identify specific groups who might respond to brand messages. From these insights, a list of primary and secondary targets is built along with profiles of typical members of this group.

Types of Stakeholder Audiences

Corporate Level	Marketing Level	Marcom Level
Employees	Consumers	Target audiences
Investors, financial community (analysts, brokers, and the financial press)	Customers	Target stakeholders
	Competitors	Employees
	Market segments	Trade audiences
Government bodies and agencies	Distributors, dealers, retailers, and others in the distribution channel	Local community
Regulatory bodies		Media (general, special interest, trade)
Business partners	Suppliers and vendors, including agencies	Consumer activist groups
		General public
		Opinion leaders

As we mentioned in our list of principles, an important thing to remember is that people don't simply line up in one box or another. The fact of overlapping membership complicates message strategy and demands that there be a certain core level of consistency and integrity in all brand messages, both from a company and within stakeholder conversations.

Brand Strategy   Message consistency has to have a heart, core, soul, or DNA; in other words, it needs a central concept around which various messages can be unified. We refer to this central concept as *brand essence*, and it describes what makes the brand different and distinctive from all other brands in its product category. It tells consumers precisely what the brand stands for—what it means in the marketplace. It is the admission ticket to enter the minds of consumers in the battle for the mental marketplace.[8]

Red Bull is the energy drink; Coke Zero is the diet cola that tastes the same as the original cola. In some cases, perhaps most, the central core is the brand position—the statements about the core concept of Red Bull and Coke Zero are based on their positions. An example of a brand vision that reflects a core value comes from global marketer IBM, which expressed its support for world peace and world trade in this classic 1938 ad.

Photo: Courtesy of IBM Archives

IBM used this "World Peace" ad to demonstrate its commitment to world trade and the international marketing of its products in this ad campaign that ran on the eve of World War II.

There are times, however, when the brand position is adjusted for different markets. For example, if a brand is moving into a new country and represents a category of product that is new or unknown, the campaign strategy would need to be based on launching a category as well as a brand. In other markets, where the brand is well known, the brand strategy may be much more competitive, and the position is determined by the need to separate itself from other similar brands. Starbucks moving into India is an example of a new brand in a new category. Most of the world knows Starbucks, but coffee and the coffee shop environment may call for a different kind of message strategy, particularly in a solidly tea-based society.

Effective IMC plans lead to profitable long-term brand relationships. That's another dimension of the strategic decisions about the most profitable stakeholders to engage in brand communication. How do you engage them the first time, and how does the brand conversation continue and evolve? What are the links and connections in the relationship that must be built and protected?

The IMC Mix

The decision about which marcom tools to use in a campaign is based on an analysis of their strengths and weaknesses as well as consumer insights to determine how these functions can best be employed to meet the campaign's objectives. As we explained in Chapter 8, certain tools are better at delivering specific objectives. You use public relations, for example, to announce something that is newsworthy, whereas you use sales promotion to drive immediate action. Therefore, an IMC plan operates with a set of interrelated objectives that specify the strategies for all the different tools. Each area has a set of objectives. The following list presents the main IMC areas in terms of their primary effects:

- *Advertising* Reach wide audience through mass media; acquire new customers; establish brand image and personality; define brand position; identify points of differentiation and competitive advantage; counter competition; deliver brand reminders.
- *Public Relations* Announce news; affect attitudes and opinions; maximize credibility and likability; create and improve stakeholder relationships.
- *Consumer Sales Promotion* Stimulate behavior; generate immediate response; intensify needs, wants, and motivations; reward behavior; stimulate involvement and relevance; create pull through the channel; provide brand reminder.
- *Trade Sales Promotion* Build industry acceptance; push through the channel; motivate cooperation; energize sales force, dealers, distributors.
- *Point of Purchase* Increase immediate sales; attract attention at decision point; create interest; stimulate urgency; encourage trial and impulse purchasing.
- *Direct Marketing* Stimulate sales; create personal interest and relevance; provide in-depth information; create acceptance, conviction.
- *Sponsorship and Events* Build awareness; create brand experience, participation, interaction, involvement; create excitement.
- *Packaging* Increase sales; attract attention at selection point; deliver product information; create brand reminder.

* *Specialties* Reinforce brand identity; continuous brand reminder; reinforce satisfaction; encourage repeat purchase; reward loyal customers.
* *Guerilla Marketing* Intercept prospects where they work, live, and visit: create curiosity and excitement; provide opportunity for involvement; stimulate buzz.
* *Customer Service* Answer questions; solve customer problems; record complaints and compliments; turn bad customer experiences into positive experiences; listen to consumer perceptions and record feedback; notify appropriate departments of complaints and compliments; test-market communication strategies and copy points.

As you look over the list, think about what's required to launch a new product. In that situation, which tools would you select as the most appropriate? That's the type of thinking planners use at this point to initially decide which marcom tools would be most useful in meeting the campaign's objectives. Sometimes there might be a lead area, such as an event. The other areas provide support—for example, advertising, public relations, and direct marketing may be needed to get the word out; promotional materials are useful to reward people for getting involved; and specialties provide reminders. Other times, the campaign operates with a basket of tools—all of them important in their own way.

In times past, these functional areas were often little empires with their own ideas and programs. Sometimes the programs conflicted; for example, a special promotion might be planned at the same time as an event or big advertising campaign but with an entirely different theme. We refer to this approach as **silos**, which means they operated on their own with little concern for what the other areas were doing. They were jealous of their budgets and protective of their responsibilities. An example comes from the lack of connectivity between a company's retail and online customer shopping experience. A shoe shopper may see an online video and that leads her to a store to check out size and fit. From her mobile phone, she makes a purchase for a shoe color that was out-of-stock at the store. The company may have the customer's information filed in three different data silos even though the experience was based on a seamless experience in the shopper's eyes.[9]

IMC has sought to break down the walls between these functional areas and coordinate their activities with brand-focused, customer-based planning. The result is more consistency and synergy in message strategies.

Message Strategy

Chapter 9 explored the ins and outs of message strategy: how much to focus on rational or emotional messages, what message formats to use, and how to get a Big Idea that gets attention and sticks in memory. Those deliberations and their conclusions are written into the campaign plan. The message strategies are also matched to the different targeted stakeholders based on insights into what moves them.

Good Big Ideas are valued because they may be enduring, such as Frontier Airlines' talking animals. Furthermore, such ideas lend themselves to extendability, which means they "have legs." In other words, the idea is strong enough to serve as an umbrella concept for a variety of executions or mini-campaigns. The Matter of Practice feature explains how Frontier's animals can be endlessly extended.

Message strategy decisions support the overall campaign objectives and direction that we discussed earlier. For example, the campaign strategy might involve the long-term use of a celebrity spokesperson who becomes the face of the brand. This creates positive associations for the brand, and, to the extent that the celebrity is a superstar, the reputation of a winner is associated with the brand image.

For example, golf's Tiger Woods was one of the athletes whom Nike (as well as other brands, such as Accenture) signed as a spokesperson. The strategy disintegrated when Woods was caught up in a sex scandal. That event moved him from one of the most respected celebrity endorsers to a flawed figure with questionable integrity. His sponsors, including Nike and Accenture, among others, had to decide how to relate their brands not only to his longtime dominance of golf, but also to his loss of honor. It's not just the brand images that were threatened by Tiger's infidelities; economists estimate the loss to shareholders of his nine corporate sponsors as close to $12 billion.[10] And the same problem erupted with the legendary Tour de France winner Lance Armstrong, whose seven medals were taken away after officials determined

A Campaign with Legs (and Flippers)

Shawn Couzens, *Conceptual Engineer, AbbaSez,* and Gary Ennis, *Freelance Creative Director/Art Director, both former Creative Directors, Grey Advertising.*

When Frontier has something to sell—whether it's a new city, a website, or the frequent-flyer program—we let the animals deliver the message in a fun, humorous way. Certain characters are better suited for certain messages than others.

Flip, for example, is the lovable loser who never gets a break. For years, he's been dying to fly to a warm, tropical climate, such as Florida. But instead, he always gets sent to Chicago. That's been a recurring theme in several commercials. So, when Frontier expanded its service to Mexico, it was the perfect opportunity to build on Flip's story line—hence, "Flip to Mexico."

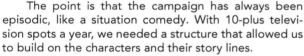

The point is that the campaign has always been episodic, like a situation comedy. With 10-plus television spots a year, we needed a structure that allowed us to build on the characters and their story lines.

If our base-brand campaign were a sitcom, *Flip to Mexico* would be a spin-off. The idea was to blanket a city with the "news" that Flip would quit unless he went to Mexico—and he needed the public's help to get there. We wanted the community to be an active participant in the story. To facilitate that, we launched a series of mock newscasts covering Flip's evolving story line. We hired "activists" to hold placards and distribute leaflets, and we created an elaborate underground website with lots of interactive content. We even involved real Frontier employees, like CEO Jeff Potter, to help blur the line between reality and fiction. Consumers enjoyed the

Photo: Courtesy Frontier Airlines. Used with permission.

interplay, and they happily rallied for Flip. The story really captivated the city of Denver. It was all over the news. And it deepened the bond between Frontier and the community at a time when other airlines were trying to eat into Frontier's home turf.

But it's no longer about just television, print, and radio. An idea has to perform across multiple platforms, and new media are a big part of that. Brands will have to find other ways to connect with consumers, like podcasts, interactive websites, YouTube contests, branded entertainment, product placement, long-format digital content, and more. Some brands are creating their own television shows or web channels with original programming. The media landscape will continue to change. What won't change is the need for talented writers and art directors who can think outside the parameters of traditional media and make the brand story relevant and entertaining across all these different media and formats.

A campaign is an evolving story, so you can't rest on your awards. When you launch a successful campaign and everyone likes it, you've set the creative bar pretty high. Everyone's waiting to see what you'll do next. Your job is to keep surprising them, keep raising the bar—because if you don't do it, someone else will.

There's a saying in the industry, "You're only as good as your last ad." It's kind of true. One week, you're being praised for an ad or campaign. But the next week, you have a new creative brief in your hand, and you have to prove yourself all over again.

that he had been actively blood doping during those competitions. Another big hit to the Armstrong reputation and image—as well as to his well-respected Livestrong cancer research foundation—was Nike's announcement that it would no longer use Armstrong as a celebrity figure in its advertising.

Another example of the strategic use of a celebrity, one that worked better than the Woods and Armstrong examples, is the humorous "Burn Some to Earn Some" opening story in Chapter 2. Peyton Manning is the deadpan manager of a convenience store who denies Gatorade to people who obviously aren't sweating.[11]

As we mentioned earlier, strategic consistency comes from the creative theme and the consistent presentation of the brand position and personality, even when different stakeholder groups receive different types of messages and interact with the brand in different ways. Consistency is a standard built into a carefully designed multiplatform and multimedia plan.

In most cases, the drive for brand consistency is a strategic need, but at other times, it reflects cost efficiency. IMC programs can be more effective because of their repetition, and this reinforcement creates more cost-efficient campaigns as well as more effective message strategies. Managers have learned that using multiple tools and channels in a consistent way is more profitable and builds longer-lasting customer relationships than relying on uncoordinated tools doing their own thing.

IMC Media and Contact Points

When most people think about media, they think about traditional mass media and advertising. Media planning in an IMC context does more than just deliver targeted messages; media also involve, engage, and connect consumers to the brand and to one another.

Multichannel and Multiplatform   On one level, media planning involves using media as planners have done for years: by employing all different types of traditional media, a practice identified as *multichannel* or *multimedia*. Media has become much more complex; one study estimated there are more than 200 options. It also estimated that what it calls omnichannel campaigns may include, on average, six platforms and 32 channels.[12] As DePaul University marketing professor Steve Kelly explained, "IMC tries to tie it all together. IMC is the goal of most marketers, but multichannel is what they actually do."[13]

We described media plans in Chapter 15, and all the information described in that chapter (e.g., media objectives, media selection and media mix, scheduling, and budgeting) appears in an IMC campaign plan.

When IMC planners think about media, they think about message delivery systems, and that includes all the media used in all the various marketing communication functions. We reviewed many of these in Chapter 14 under the title *multiplatform*. Direct response, for example, can appear in traditional media (print, with return forms to get more information about a brand or place an order, or infomercials on television) and also in letters mailed directly to the home or office, telemarketing (phone calls to the home or office), and in digital forms, such as email and Twitter. And Facebook makes it possible to order directly from that site.

For example, consider a Honda CR-V campaign in Iceland. The agency's owner, Ingvi Logason, described his agency's multimedia and multiplatform approach:

> The media emphasis had been on print with support from TV and the Internet. We shifted the emphasis to a 360° integrated approach where we focused, among other things, on media with large reach at the expense of high frequency. TV and interactive Web banners were at the forefront of the campaign with support from newspaper, radio, and event marketing. We also extended the traditional media with sponsorship of some big sports and cultural events that tied in with the car owners' lifestyles.[14]

An example of IMC multimedia planning comes from *The Today Show*, which launched a new recipe website and mobile application in sponsorship with Unilever. The "Cooking School" website contains previously aired segments of "Today's Kitchen" and streaming video webisodes as well as recipes, cooking tips, and promotions for Unilever brands such as Bertolli, Country Crock, Hellmann's, and Ragu. The recipes can be downloaded at home or to a mobile device. A smartphone app allows users to compile recipes and build shopping lists. The "Cooking School" partnership links mobile, online, and broadcast media.[15]

Contact Point Management   Another distinctive feature of IMC media plans is their emphasis on every important contact point, which can include a variety of experiential media as well as conventional media.

MATCH CR-V WITH YOUR MOBILITY

Photo: H:N Marketing Communications

The launch of the Honda CR-V in Iceland used digital media and promotional activities along with more traditional media.

Think about all the ways you come in contact with a brand message when you fly on an airline: reservations, check-in, baggage checking, the gate, the cabin attendants' and officer's messages over the loudspeaker, the seats and food and other cabin features, departure and arrival times, deplaning, and baggage again, not to mention customer service when you miss a plane or a bag gets lost.

Here's a case study of how one agency's "Contact Point Management" works: Tokyo-based Dentsu, which is the world's largest individual agency, has a strong IMC orientation, which shows up in the way Dentsu planners create IMC media plans. Dentsu's ContactPoint Management is a section in its IMC 2.0 model that identifies a wide diversity of contact points. Let's take a closer look at Dentsu's approach to IMC media planning.[16]

The objective of Dentsu's ContactPoint Management planning is to select the most effective contact points required to achieve the desired communication goals and to implement optimum integrated communication programs that eliminate waste. ContactPoint Management focuses on two strategies that are critical in delivering effective integrated communication:

1. *Identify the value contact points*, that is, the emotion-driving points at which or during which consumers come in contact with a brand.
2. *Move away from the traditional B2C model*, in which business targets a consumer with a message, *to a more interactive B2C2C model*, in which a business talks to consumers—particularly influential people, such as fashion leaders, who talk to other consumers. This approach uses mass media to stimulate interconsumer communications, or word of mouth, which delivers messages more persuasively.

Media selection recognizes that (1) contact points that work well must differ depending on the communication goal and (2) contact point effectiveness will differ from product category to product category and from target to target.

An example of how Dentsu manages a full set of brand contact points comes from an automotive campaign where two target audiences have been identified as a father (male, 50s) and a daughter (female, 20s). The communication objective is to position the new subcompact car model as "fun driving for grown men" and "a small cute model for young women."

The various contact points considered are evaluated and ranked using a proprietary contact point planning system called VALCON (Value Contact Point Tracer). Dentsu planners also have access to hundreds of media-related databases with vast volumes of contact point information to consult in this process. The final decisions about media usage are based on the roles and effects of the various media.

For the new subcompact, contact points were evaluated based on three objectives: their ability to launch a new product (recognition, build awareness), arouse interest (evaluation), and make the target feel like buying (intention, attitude). Here are the results by points assigned to various options.

	Father		Both		Daughter
Awareness	1. Newspaper				1. Train poster
	2. Out-of-home ads				2. Television ad
		3.	Direct mail	4.	3. Magazine ad
Interest	1. Car on display at event	3.	Car on streets	1.	
		4.	Television ad	2.	3. Automaker's website
		2.	Catalog	5.	
		5.	Newspaper insert	8.	4. Cars owned by friends
Intention	3. Car magazine story	2.	Catalog	1.	
		1.	Car on display	2.	
		6.	Test drive	3.	
					4. Television ad

As you can see, the plan calls for contact points that reach both audiences (television ads, catalogs, street media, newspaper inserts, and direct mail). Newspaper ads, out-of-home ads, the car on display at the dealer's showroom, and car magazine stories were added or emphasized for the "father" audience. For the "daughter" audience, magazine ads, a website, transit ads, radio ads, family word of mouth, and television ads were added. Here is how this complex media plan is diagrammed in terms of its effects.

	Recognition	*Evaluation*	*Attitude*
Father	Newspaper and out-of-home ads, car display at dealer		Car magazine stories
Both	Television ads, catalogs, street media, newspaper inserts, direct mail	Television ads, friends word of mouth	Catalog, car display at dealer, test drive
Daughter	Magazine and transit ads, website	Radio ads, family word of mouth	Television ads

Cross-Media Integration   Media selection also considers message needs. Here is where media planning and message planning intersect. Brand reminders, for example, are often found in television commercials and in out-of-home media. More complex information-laden messages are more likely to be found in magazines, direct mail, or publicity releases. If you want to stimulate immediate action, you might use daily newspapers, radio, or sales promotion.

The chief marketing officer at a digital media company reminds planners that "brand advertising is about telling a story, not just directing traffic." He calls for refocusing on media basics: "Interactivity has given us new options to tell a story, social media have given us tools to make it spread, and digital more broadly has forced advertisers to consider utility to the user." But he insists, "The basics persist—find paths to the consumers where you can get scale, buy attention, and repeat."[17]

The challenge is to create **cross-media integration**, which means the various media work together to create coherent brand communication. In traditional media, this synergistic effect is sometimes called *image transfer* and refers to the way radio, in particular, reinforces and re-creates the message in a listener's mind that was originally delivered by other media, particularly television.

An example of cross-media integration comes from the revitalization campaign for the *Atlantic Monthly* magazine. To reinforce its position as an intellectual leader, the campaign used the slogan "Think Again." To bring that idea to life, the campaign presented 14 of *Atlantic*'s most thought-provoking questions as 14 huge neon signs placed around New York City. At night, the creative team taped interviews with viewers as they wondered about the brightly lit messages. These videos, which showcased the personal, profound, and sometimes hilarious responses, were housed on a website and used as a hub for a debate of these great issues. So it was out-of-home marketing that created an event that turned into videos that enlivened a website (see http://vimeo.com/52209849). In this case, to quote media scholar Marshall McLuhan, the media became the message. Was it successful? The magazine saw a double-digit increase in readership, and the number of visitors to TheAtlantic.com increased by 27 percent over the previous year.

Management and Campaign Controls

To manage IMC, whether of a campaign or a program, a manager must keep up with an incredibly complex set of tasks. Sometimes the brand manager is able to keep track of everything, but another approach is to hire a consulting firm that specializes in managing big projects. The Inside Story describes how one consultant with a marketing communication background views his job.

In addition to keeping track of everything, all campaigns are designed to operate within a certain set of parameters, such as budgets, schedules, and evaluation. These controls keep the activities on track, on budget, and on strategy.

Budgeting and Scheduling   How much should an organization spend on a campaign? What a difficult decision that is. It depends on the organization, the area it serves (local or international), the time frame (a couple of weeks or months or a year), the stakeholders to be reached, and its

What in the World Is Marketing Portfolio Management?

Eric Foss, *Vice President, Consulting Services, North America, Pcubed, Ann Arbor, Michigan*

"Consulting services" in my title refers to the professional services my company, Pcubed, provides our clients, including a broad range of consulting services focusing on portfolio, program, and project management— hence the name, Pcubed.

My "marketing portfolio" focus is not unlike some IMC concepts that integrate advertising and marketing campaigns, programs, and activities—and then ties them to objectives of a specific program (e.g., a new product launch) or an organization (as with my retail client).

The goal remains consistent: *create the collaboration, transparency, and delivery rigor necessary to select the optimal mix of marketing and messaging initiatives that are aligned to marketing strategies.*

We focus on establishing collaboration and visibility not only to help drive effective marketing management but also to ensure that money spent on messaging and marketing is optimized to best achieve our objectives.

This foundation is necessary to measure effectiveness and return on investment.

I have worked across industries (e.g., aerospace and defense, technology, health care, and retail). I led a team on a major computer software firm's North American launch. A few years back, I partnered with the chief marketing officer and his team of vice presidents in the Dallas retail world to put together a marketing portfolio and help them more effectively identify and execute marketing programs.

Here's what the portfolio management concept means in practice:

- Creating a collaborative and dynamic decision-making model
- Aligning marketing programs to long-term marketing strategies and goals
- Integrating marketing activities with operations
- Balancing the independent needs of a broad group of stakeholders
- Maintaining visibility and oversight of a fast-moving portfolio of marketing initiatives, activities, and messaging
- Managing and measuring marketing and communication impact in the field
- Linking marketing spend to tangible outcomes

As a management consultant partnering with marketing leadership, the challenge is tailoring these concepts to fit the unique needs of an organization's marketing culture.

Foss graduated from the Department of Advertising at Michigan State University. He was nominated to be featured here by Professor Sandra Moriarty.

need for big, expensive media, such as television. In fact, all budgeting is dependent on a time frame or schedule.

A $50,000 budget will only stretch so far and probably will not be enough to cover the costs of television advertising in most markets. Microsoft, for example, used a $300 million ad blitz to launch its Windows 7 operating system in 2009, and the launch of Windows 8 in 2012 called for an even more massive budget from $400 million to over $1 billion. Windows 10 was described in one article as using a multi-million-dollar ad campaign for its launch in 2015.[18]

The budget determines how many stakeholders can be targeted, how many media and platforms the campaign can support, and the length of time the campaign can run.

Determining the total appropriation allocated to a campaign is not an easy task. Typically, a dollar amount is budgeted for marketing communication during the annual budget planning process. For major campaigns, the company or organization will decide on the overall budget level and apportion that out to campaigns and marcom programs as well as to various agencies and suppliers involved with the campaign or campaigns.

The big budgeting question at the marketing as well as marcom mix level is, how much do we need to spend? Let's examine five common budgeting methods used to answer that question.

- *Historical Method* Historical information is the source for this common budgeting method. A budget may simply be based on last year's budget, with a percentage increase for inflation or some other marketplace factor. This method, although easy to calculate, has little to do with reaching brand communication objectives.

- *Objective-Task Method* The **objective-task method** looks at the objectives for each activity and determines the cost of accomplishing each objective. For example, what will it cost to make 50 percent of the people in the market aware of this product or to extend a six-month plan to a year? This method's advantage is that it develops the budget from the ground up so that objectives are the starting point.

- *Percentage-of-Sales Method* The **percentage-of-sales method** compares the total brand sales with the total advertising (or marketing communication) budget during the previous year or the average of several years to compute a percentage. This technique can also be used across an industry to compare the expenditures of different product categories on advertising and marketing communication. For example, if a company had sales of $5 million last year and an advertising budget of $1 million, the *ratio* of advertising to sales would be 20 percent. If the marketing manager predicts *sales* of $6 million for next year, the ad budget would be $1.2 million. How can we calculate the percentage of sales and apply it to a budget? Follow these two steps:

1. $\dfrac{\text{Past advertising dollars}}{\text{Past sales}} = \%$ of sales

2. % of sales $\times$ Next year's sales forecast = New advertising budget

An example of this approach comes from Procter & Gamble. To illustrate the growth of Procter & Gamble's marketing spending in one particular year, a chart of all-inclusive marketing costs pegged 2012 outlays at around 16.5 percent of sales the previous year, or around $13.7 billion. In comparison, only $9.3 billion of that amount was for advertising spending, which incorporates only media and agency costs. Using the broader measure, Procter & Gamble's marketing as a *percent of sales* grew about a point from 15.5 to 16.5 percent, more than rebounding from a deep recession-related dip in 2009.[19]

- *Competitive Budgets* Analysis by competitive budgets uses competitors' budgets as benchmarks and relates the amount invested in advertising to the product's share of market. That suggests that the advertiser's share-of-advertising voice—that is, the advertiser's media presence—affects the share of attention the brand will receive and that, in turn, affects the market share the brand can obtain. A depiction of these relationships is

Share of media voice = Share of consumer mind = market share

Keep in mind that the relationships depicted here are only a guide for budgeting. The actual relationship between *share-of-media voice* (an indication of advertising expenditures) and **share of mind** or share of market depends to a great extent on factors such as the creativity of the message and the amount of clutter in the marketplace.

- *All You Can Afford* When a company allocates whatever is left over to marketing communication, it is using the "all-you-can-afford" budgeting method. It's really not a method, but rather a philosophy about advertising. Companies using this approach, such as high-tech start-ups driven by product innovation, don't value advertising as a strategic imperative. For example, a company that allocates a large amount of its budget to research and has a superior product may find that the amount spent on advertising is less important.

Photo: Courtesy Proctor & Gamble. Used with permission.

Charmin continues to emphasize softness in its international marketing. This cuddly bear was used in a campaign in Mexico. Notice that the ad is largely a nonverbal execution, which is easier to use for global campaigns than those with a lot of words.

Evaluation Advertising and other marketing communication agencies are creating tools and techniques to help marketers evaluate the efficiency and effectiveness of their marketing communication expenditures. The Interpublic Group, for example, a large marketing communication holding company, has created the Marketing Accountability Partnership to determine what marketers' dollars accomplish and how they can be better used. The issue of accountability is made more complicated by the growing use of global marketing.

16.3 Identify the strategic decisions that underlie effective international marketing communication.

International IMC Campaigns

Agencies involved with international campaigns need an international organizational structure as well. Organization depends on whether the client company as well as its agencies are following a **standardization** or a **localization** strategy. Some firms and their agencies exercise tight control, whereas others allow more local autonomy. All these approaches fall into three groups: tight central international control, centralized resources with moderate control, or a match of the client's organization. If the client is highly centralized, the agency account structure will be highly centralized.

Strategic Decisions   The problem of managing brand consistency limits most objectives to awareness and recall, two effective yet easily attainable marketing communication measures, although more specific objectives may be needed in individual markets. For example, a brand may be well known in one market, so its primary objective, then, is reminder. At the same time, it may be newly launched in another country, so the objectives there are awareness building and trial.

Positioning is one of the key strategic elements that brands usually try to keep consistent from country to country. Research is conducted to identify the problems and opportunities facing the product and its positioning strategy in each of its international markets, as the Charmin commercial about its softness illustrates. Particularly important is a good understanding of consumer buying motives in each market. That is almost impossible to develop without locally based consumer research. If analysis reveals that consumers' buying behavior and the competitive environment are the same across international markets, it may be possible to use standardized positioning throughout. The international consulting firm Accenture faced a strategic problem when Tiger Woods, the brand's longtime celebrity spokesperson, faced allegations of extramarital affairs. Much of Accenture's brand communication appears as images in airports, so the problem was to find universal imagery that continued to reflect the Accenture brand position. After testing a number of ideas, the decision was to use animals, such as an elephant, in unexpected and challenging situations. For example, one of the electronic displays shows an elephant balancing on a surfboard with text that reads, "Who says you can't be big and nimble?"[20]

Who says you can't be big and nimble?

To see how our research and experience can help you become a high-performance business, visit accenture.com
• Consulting • Technology • Outsourcing

accenture >
High performance. Delivered.

Photo: Courtesy of Accenture

Accenture's replacement campaign for its well-known celebrity, Tiger Woods, used animals that are less likely to make unfortunate headlines. Accenture's slogan "High Performance. Delivered." continued to be used in the new campaign depicting animals in challenging but semihumorous situations.

Setting the Budget   All the budgeting techniques apply in foreign markets. When preparing a single plan for multiple markets, many companies use an objective-task budgeting approach that entails a separate budget for each foreign market. (Remember that this approach looks at the objectives for each activity and determines the cost of accomplishing each objective.) This technique adds some flexibility to localize campaigns as needed. However, local practices also may affect the budget decision. Most notably, the exchange rate from country to country may affect not only the amount of money spent in a particular market but also the timing of the expenditures. The cost of television time in Tokyo is approximately twice what it is on US networks, and, rather than being sold during an up-front market every spring, Japanese television time is wholesaled several times during the year.

Central Control versus Local Adaptation   As noted previously, some marketers develop centralized global campaigns; others develop local campaigns in every major market. Most companies are somewhere in the middle. How are global campaigns created? International brand communication campaigns have two basic starting points: (1) success in one country and (2) a centrally conceived strategy. Planning approaches also include variations on the central campaign and bottom-up creativity:

- *Local Initiative* A successful campaign, conceived for national application, is modified for use in other countries. Wrigley, Marlboro, IBM, Waterman, Seiko, Philips, Ford, and many other companies have taken successful campaigns from one country and transplanted them around the world, a practice called *search and reapply.* When a local campaign is found to be successful, that campaign is taken to one or two countries that are similar to see how well the campaign works in these areas. If it is successful, use of the campaign is expanded and can eventually become the brand's primary international campaign. What is interesting about this strategy is that it provides additional motivation for local agencies. Although all local agencies want to do a good job to keep their local business, it is a major ego boost—not to mention the additional financial awards—when a local campaign is taken beyond its original country's borders.

  The Honda CR-V in Iceland is an example. As Logason explained, "Because of the effectiveness of the original campaign—both the insights behind the strategy and the idea of ownership of the 4×4 concept, which was so successful in Iceland—the campaign caught the eye of the global office, and it has been distributed and showcased globally to dealers in other markets as an example of strong, clever positioning."[21]

- *Centrally Conceived Campaigns* The second approach, a centrally conceived campaign, was pioneered by Coca-Cola and is now used increasingly in global strategies. Microsoft uses a centralized strategy for its Xbox video game system; because it was a new brand, a consistent marketing strategy was deemed to be essential. Although the centralization concept is simple, its application can be difficult. A work team, task force, or action group (the names vary) assembles from around the world to present, debate, modify (if necessary), and agree on a basic strategy as the foundation for the campaign. Cost is a huge factor. If the same photography and artwork can be used universally, this strategy can save thousands of dollars over each local variation.

- *Variations on Central Campaigns* Variations on the centrally conceived campaign also exist. For example, BBDO's many local agencies were used to adapt the creative ideas for all the markets served by DaimlerChrysler (now Chrysler after the company split). The office that develops the approved campaign would be designated the **lead agency** and would develop all the necessary elements of the campaign and prepare a standards manual for use in other countries. Because photography, artwork, television production, and color printing are costly, developing these items in one location and then overlaying new copy or rerecording the voice track in the local language saves money. However, because some countries, such as Malaysia, require that all campaign materials be locally produced, this approach gives direction to the message but still allows for local requirements to be met.

- *Bottom-Up Creativity* Sometimes a competition may be used to find the best new idea. For example, to extend McDonald's "I'm Lovin' It" campaign, McDonald's global chief marketing officer held a contest among McDonald's ad agencies all over the world. One winner, which became part of the international pool of ads, came from China, which has developed a lively creative advertising industry that produces edgy, breakthrough ads for young people. McDonald's strategy was not just to do the creative work in the United States, but rather to "Let the best ideas win."

Executing an International Campaign   The execution of a global campaign is usually more complex than a national plan. The creative may need to be reshot with local models and settings as well as language translation. Language is always a problem for a campaign that is dependent on words rather than visuals as the primary meaning carrier. A team of language experts may be needed to adjust the terms and carry over the meanings in the different languages. The Pepsi slogan "Come Alive," for example, was translated in Taiwan as "Pepsi will bring your ancestors back from the dead." KFC's "Finger Lickin' Good" slogan translated into Chinese as "Eat Your Fingers Off."

Product names can even be a problem. In Canada, Mercedes-Benz found that its GST model name is also the familiar initials of a tax commonly referred to in English as the "gouge and screw tax." But certain concepts, however, such as softness can cross ethnic and geographical boundaries, as the Charmin commercial illustrates. Government approval of television commercials can be difficult to secure in some countries. As advertisers move into international and global advertising, they face many of the same ethical issues that advertisers deal with in the United States, such as the representation of women and advertising to children, but they may also have to deal with questions about the Americanization or westernization of local cultures.[22] An example comes from a Nike ad used in China that showed LeBron James teaching moves to martial arts masters. Chinese officials banned it because they consider it insulting to national dignity.

It's not just government bans that can trouble message strategies. Social responsibility is taken seriously in some countries, and, with the internet and email, consumer concerns can create a huge issue. For example, an ad by fashion house Dolce & Gabbana showed a bare-chested man pinning a glamorous woman to the ground while his buddies looked on. Consumers in Spain, Italy, and the United States complained that the ad trivialized violence against women, and the many email complaints led the company to drop it.

The IMC Factor in International Campaigns To create a coherent brand impression on a global level requires both horizontal and vertical coordination. The vertical effort represents the coordination of the key planning decisions, such as targeting, positioning, objectives, strategies, and tactics, across all the various tools used in the communication program. The horizontal level requires coordination across all countries and regions involved in the plan.

● **Principle**
Global brand communication needs integration horizontally (across countries) and vertically through all the key strategic decisions.

Because of this complexity, it takes a dedicated manager to ensure that all the various marketing communication activities stay consistent with the brand and campaign strategy. IMC planners often use planning grids to plot strategic coordination of messages across countries and across marcom programs. The table below illustrates how such a grid might be constructed. The messages are plotted indicating how they may vary locally for different cultures as well as what brand elements are used, such as position or personality, to maintain consistency. Some companies sell not just one brand but a portfolio of subbrands or brand extensions, and the challenge is to maintain brand consistency across these different product lines in different countries. There may also be differences in the message strategy for different stakeholder groups. For each country, the planner describes the following brand message variations:

- Country-specific changes
- Audience-specific changes
- Brand consistency elements (the unchangeables)

Marcom Tool	*Country A*	*Country B*	*Country C*	*Country D*
Advertising				
Direct response				
Public relations				
Etc.				

16.4 Explain what we mean by 360-degree communication program planning.

Managing 360-Degree Communication Programs

Tom Duncan, one of the architects of IMC, explained that IMC practice originally focused on creating "one voice, one look" campaigns, but companies broadened that focus as they realized the need for greater consistency for all aspects of brand communication that lead to customer relationships.[23] That ongoing, multichannel, multiplatform, and multistakeholder approach to the practice of IMC is possible only if there is an organizational commitment to integrated communication programs.

A lesson you may have learned from our previous discussions is that IMC is a way of managing a brand with a singular vision of what the brand stands for. Unlike a short-term campaign approach, it is a philosophy that delivers total communication over the life of a brand. We are calling it *360-degree communication* because a unifying brand vision surrounds all the brand's interactions with all its stakeholders, a vision that must be shared by everyone involved with the brand. As Duncan said in the Part 5 opener, it's "not just advertising . . . it's everything a brand says and does." And that includes being a good corporate citizen.

Mission Marketing

Concern for social issues is increasingly important for for-profit companies because they want to be seen as socially responsible, and being a good citizen in actions as well as words is important in building and maintaining a positive brand reputation. Adopting a good cause and helping in its fund-raising and other community-oriented efforts is called **cause marketing**. For example, Target has donated a huge amount of money to its local communities as part of its community-caring effort. Another example of undergirding a program with a good cause is the website for Process for Progress, a credit card processing company that donates part of its profits to non-profit organizations.

Carol Cone founded the Cone agency, which specializes in cause marketing, and more recently started a consultancy called Carol Cone On Purpose, which focuses on company and brand purpose. Her mission is to link brands to causes for which people feel passion.[24] The Cone agency was behind the "Red" campaign, which supports women's heart health, as well as Yoplait's "Save Lids to Save Lives" and Avon's "Breast Cancer Crusade." Being a good corporate citizen is good for the bottom line. An article in *Advertising Age* explained the bottom-line importance of such strategies as "Companies do well by doing good."[25]

Professor Scott Hamula explained that "in addition to operating with a sense of social responsibility, marketers engage in philanthropy through cause marketing." The primary goals, he said, are "to help communities and nonprofit organizations while generating goodwill, positive word-of-mouth, and the hope that people will look more favorably on these brands when making their next purchase decision."[26]

Mission marketing is when a commitment reflects a company's core business strategy, as in Dove's "Real Women" campaign and Avon's support of breast cancer research.[27] It links a company's mission and core values to a cause that connects with its customers' interests. It is more of a commitment than cause marketing because it reflects a long-term brand-building perspective, and the mission becomes a point of passion for all stakeholders as well as the focal point for integrating all the company's marketing communication.

Mission marketing also contributes to synergy through what we identified earlier as brand integrity. The **integration triangle** in Figure 16.2 illustrates the gaps as well as the connections between the three key aspects of brand communication that must work together to create integration as well as integrity: (1) what the company or brand says about itself (*say*), (2) how the company or brand performs (*do*), (3) and what other people say about it (*confirm*). The point is that a brand fails as an integrated perception if there are gaps between what the brand says in its planned messages, what it does, and what others say about it.

Internal Integration

The problem of departmental *silos* with each marcom function going its own way is a barrier to integrated planning both at the marketer level and within agencies. According to Duncan, the solution is cross-functional management with a team of functional area representatives who coordinate their activities.[28] The Association of National

● **Principle**
360-degree communication is driven by a unifying brand vision that surrounds all the brand's interactions with all its stakeholders, a vision that must be shared by everyone involved with the brand.

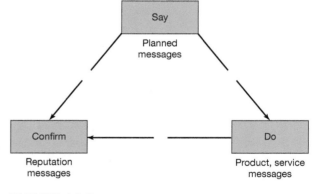

FIGURE 16.2
Integration Triangle
The "say-do-confirm" integration triangle explains how planned brand messages (say) are either reinforced or undercut by messages delivered by the product or service marketing mix (how well the brand and company perform). Reputation messages (what others say) are the ultimate test of the brand's integrity. When there are gaps between the say, do, and confirm messages, integration has failed.

Advertisers describes this organizational structure as "a team of colleagues who have the responsibility vision, understanding, and commitment to engage in a media-agnostic planning process."[29]

Another concern is coordinating all the agencies involved in creating the various brand messages. It's a particular problem facing holding companies with many distinctive agencies in their portfolio. As a way to better coordinate, for example, Dentsu Aegis Network US named Patrick Venetucci as the company's first president of operations and integration. Venetucci said that he'll "look to find commonalities among the agencies and 'more tightly align them with the markets, our clients, and with our competencies.'"[30]

Maurice Levy, CEO of the Paris-based Publicis Groupe holding company, contends that the giant company has suffered from a "silo mentality" that hurts clients. He asked, "How do we stop confusing clients with contradictory points of view coming from teams each defending their little piece of turf—to the detriment of the client's interests?"[31] More recently, he declined to call Publicis a holding company, preferring to use "a connected company."[32] Check out www.publicisgroupe.com to see how complex this problem can be for a large international agency.

The importance of the need for a shared vision was evident when the new chief executive at Ford realized that what the troubled car company needed after the auto meltdown around the start of the Great Recession was a unifying vision. To rally the troops, he had a motivating vision printed on laminated, wallet-size cards and given to the thousands of Ford employees. It proclaimed, "One Ford . . . One Team . . . One Plan . . . One Goal." The statement conveyed a strategy for returning Ford to its leadership position and undergirded the launch of the Ford Focus, the firm's first truly global car.[33]

To implement such a management effort, a cross-functional brand-focused team is created involving members from all the relevant parts of a company that interact with customers, with other stakeholders, and with outside agencies. Its members represent all the areas and tools that control contact points and brand interactions. This cross-functional team operates with a singular brand vision as it plans marketing communication, monitors its impact, and tracks consumer response.

Who is in charge of planning all these brand-building opportunities? One is the marketing and communication manager on the client side, such as Peter Stasiowski, who was featured in Chapter 1. But marketing communication managers work in partnership with agency managers who also provide guidance about such things as IMC strategies. Ed Chambliss, in the Matter of Principle feature, discusses how this partnership works as well as the qualifications needed to be an IMC manager, whether on the client side or the agency side. Check the website at the end of the feature for more information on the Phelps Group, a true IMC-focused agency.

An Organizational Case Study   An example of the organizational structure behind an IMC program comes from the Tokyo-based Dentsu agency, which has provided total communication service to its clients for decades.[34] But until the start of the twenty-first century, the agency was able to do multimedia coordination only at a one-voice, one-look level. New technology and a new management philosophy, however, created a new way of doing business.

To truly operate with an IMC orientation, Dentsu underwent a total reorganization and designed a comprehensive new IMC tool kit. Now the giant agency's employees have sophisticated tools to actually deliver on that total communication promise with a more advanced approach that Dentsu calls IMC 2.0. It defines IMC 2.0 as "an ongoing systematic process for creatively planning, producing, and evaluating brand communication that creates customer relationships, builds strong brands, and increases sales and profits."[35]

To engineer this turnaround, it first held an IMC audit, conducted by Duncan, to determine the agency's IMC strengths and weaknesses internally as well as in the eyes of key clients. Then it created an IMC Development Division with the mission of undertaking the IMC research-and-development arm. That division has some 90 to 100 staff members dedicated to basic research into IMC processes. The agency also created an IMC online site with more than 250 planning tools, models, and processes that can be used in IMC 2.0 projects. This portal also provides

Who's the Integrator Here, Anyway?

Ed Chambliss, *CEO, The Phelps Group*

I love smaller clients. I'm talking about clients who have little to no marketing department. Those clients who recognize the importance of integrated marketing communication (IMC) but don't know how to actually make it happen. They come to us and say, "Here—you be the integrator." That's because most smaller clients are smart enough to know they don't know everything, and that's why you hire a specialist—in this case, a specialist in IMC.

Over time, however, smaller clients become larger clients. And larger clients need in-house marketing departments, and marketing departments need marketing directors, and marketing directors need to be the integrators because, well, that's their job.

Which leaves a lot of marketing directors wondering, "If I'm the integrator, why should I hire an IMC agency? Why don't I just hire a bunch of agencies that are each 'best in breed' and then I'll integrate all of them myself?" Those are fair questions and ones that should be answered with other questions. To start, do marketing directors really know how to be integrators? That is, do they have the formal training in how to create an organization and processes that can orchestrate all the brand touchpoints, both outbound and inbound, across multiple suppliers? Or do they merely believe that integration

sounds like a great idea and think they can make it happen?

Chances are that the marketing director isn't one of the handful of trained IMC specialists out there. More likely, they're a specialist in one particular area of marketing communication who has been promoted into the "integrator" position. For these clients, hiring an IMC agency is a shortcut to integration. An IMC agency can advise the marketing director about how to best integrate the internal organization while doing all the external heavy lifting that true integration requires.

If the marketing director is trained in IMC, they'll already be asking these questions: "Are the 'best of breed' agencies I want to hire used to working in an integrated fashion? Or am I going to spend all my time trying to get them to understand that the overall puzzle is more important than just their one piece?"

That is where an IMC agency shines again. Whether a client hires us to do everything or just one particular type of work, they know that we understand the bigger picture. As one of my IMC-trained clients (who, by the way, hires us only for online work) says, "You guys get it. You understand the big picture. With other agencies, it's like explaining color to a blind man."

In the end, integration needs to happen, so a smart marketing director will assemble the team that has the best possible chance of making it a reality. If it works, the marketing director can take all the credit. But if integration doesn't happen, there's no credit to take, only blame.

For more about the Phelps Agency, check out www.thephelpsgroup.com.

Chambliss graduated from the University of Colorado Boulder with a master's degree in integrated marketing communication. He was nominated to be featured here by Professor Tom Duncan.

---

access to case studies, training modules, articles, and research on IMC. It registers more than 2,000 unique visits a day from Dentsu employees.

An IMC Planning Center with 350 people from a variety of media and marcom areas was established. The staff members assigned to this department are given intensive IMC training so that they have the skills to work in cross-functional IMC teams on client projects brought to them by various account groups. The agency's Brand Creation Center, an existing brand consulting group, was also integrated into the IMC Planning Center. Finally, each of Dentsu's 22 account groups has 5 to 10 embedded account planners who are trained in IMC practices. These planners help educate clients on the goals of IMC and establish a common language for planning.

It's a work in progress—and one that was complicated by the worldwide recession—but Dentsu's IMC executives and managers believed that the investment in reorganization was justified. The effort didn't come cheaply: Dentsu initially dedicated some 600 of its 4,500 employees to IMC development and client services.

Looking Ahead

We're near the end of this book. If you have any interest in working in marketing or marketing communication, what have you learned about integrated marketing communication that might help you in your career?

The industry is definitely moving in the IMC direction. A study by the Association of National Advertisers, for example, found that 74 percent of its members said they were using IMC for most or all of their brands. The association's CEO sees that as a call for "Renaissance Marketers" who understand the essentials of IMC. He describes them as "a new breed of holistic professionals who are system thinkers, customer-centric believers, innovators, and dreamers."[36] So there's definitely a job opportunity here. Does that sound like you?

Maybe you're even thinking about starting a business or going to graduate school and becoming a consultant. If so, it's important to understand that the concept of advertising has broadened to include almost everything that sends a brand message. If you go to work in marketing or marketing communication, you may be asked to help plan an IMC campaign or develop an IMC program. This chapter is your guide to IMC thinking and management practices.

This chapter started with IMC principles and then reviewed the development of IMC campaigns and the management of IMC programs. The objective is to drive consistency through all brand messages and experiences. It's cost-effective as well as more effective communication. Chapter 17 will continue this marketing communication journey with a discussion of evaluation—an important step in proving the effectiveness of IMC programs and campaigns.

IT'S A WRAP

Positively Pink

The "Pink Ribbon" campaign is arguably one of the most successful promotion efforts ever by cobranding a good cause with other brands. As you've read in this chapter, marketers can employ a variety of promotional techniques, and this campaign demonstrates the effectiveness of product tie-ins. Products and brands, such as Avon and Yoplait, that fit naturally with a cause, such as breast cancer awareness and research, can mutually benefit both the sponsors and the charity.

As we reported in the opening story, since its inception, the Susan G. Komen Foundation for the Cure has raised more than $2 billion for breast cancer care and more than $920 million for research and education.[37] But is it good business for the organization's partners?

Apparently it is. Yoplait, for instance, donates 10 cents for each pink yogurt lid to Komen, and since 1999, it has given more than $22 million. That's a lot of yogurt. New Balance's "Lace Up for the Cure" promotion donates 5 percent of retail sales of some of its pink shoes, guaranteeing Komen a minimum of $500,000 per year.

So there is potential to profit financially from such partnerships. What is harder to gauge is the value of the goodwill that product tie-in promotions create.

The former president of Old Navy, which produced pink Komen logo T-shirts, said that 5 percent of the purchase price goes to Komen. He said he did not expect big revenue for the shirts, but the association with the world's largest breast cancer charity generates abundant goodwill for the Old Navy brand plus several million dollars for the Komen cause.

Over time, Komen's work to improve women's chances to understand and survive breast cancer has garnered many awards, including many Halo Awards for Cause Marketing. As the "Pink Ribbon" campaign matures, it will be interesting to see how messaging develops so that the partnering companies' messages do not get lost in the pink dust.

Logo: The Running Ribbon is a registered trademark of Susan G. Komen.

KEY OBJECTIVES SUMMARY

16.1. Discuss the eight key IMC concepts and explain why they are important. IMC campaigns focus on *stakeholders.* The objective is to engage them in a meaningful relationship as well as target them for brand communication. It is a philosophy that monitors and manages all brand messages with all stakeholders at all contact points, not just the traditional marketing communication. In IMC, traditional advertising channels are expanded to include *contact points* that represent all the ways a consumer and other stakeholders come in contact with a brand. They all deliver messages and should be monitored if not controlled. *Message synergy* develops when all the messages from all contact points work together to present a coherent brand presence. Because people automatically integrate all the brand messages they receive, we refer to the way these diverse impressions come together as an *integrated brand perception.* Brand impressions are integrated on the basis of some core concept or brand essence, which is communicated throughout the organization as a *unified brand vision. Internal integration* means you can't be integrated externally unless you are integrated internally. In addition to a brand vision, that calls for an organization that creates and monitors all brand messages. *Brand integrity* means that what a brand says and does matches what other people say about it.

16.2. Outline the key parts of an IMC campaign plan. *Situation analysis* includes the background research, the SWOTs, and identification of the key communication problem(s). The *key strategic decisions* are objectives, targeting and engaging stakeholders, and the brand positioning strategy. The *marketing communication mix* includes selection of the platforms based on the objectives they can accomplish and how they lead to message synergy. The *message strategy* includes key consumer and brand relationship insights, overall message direction, and strategic consistency. *IMC media* consider multimedia, multichannel, and multiplatform *contact points.* The *management* of IMC campaigns uses *controls,* such as budgeting and evaluation.

16.3. Identify the strategic decisions that underlie effective international marketing communication. Marketing begins with a local brand, expands to a regional brand, and finally goes global. Advertising and marketing communication follow the same path. The biggest strategic decision involves how much of the marketing communication strategy is globalized or localized. Ultimately, such campaigns should be centrally controlled and centrally conceived. There should also be local applications and approval. In international as in all IMC campaigns, the challenge is to create brand consistency in all messages and customer experiences with the brand.

16.4. Explain what we mean by 360-degree communication program planning. Integration using 360-degree planning is both a way to develop campaigns that maximize consistency among all the marcom tools and a philosophy that monitors and manages all brand messages with all stakeholders at all contact points, not just the traditional marketing communication. The 360-degree marketing communication philosophy delivers total brand communication with a consistent vision for the life of the brand. 360-degree communication means that everything communicates: messages are delivered by every element of the marketing mix as well as every marcom message and brand experience.

KEY TERMS

360-degree communication, p. 484
benchmark, p. 490
brand integrity, p. 486
brand value, p. 483
cause marketing, p. 503
contact points, p. 484
cross-functional management, p. 486

cross-media integration, p. 497
integrated perception, p. 486
integration triangle, p. 503
internal marketing, p. 491
lead agency, p. 501
localization, p. 500
measurable objectives, p. 490

mission marketing, p. 503
objective-task method, p. 499
percentage-of-sales method, p. 499
permission marketing, p. 483
share of mind, p. 499
share of wallet, p. 490
silos, p. 493

situation analysis, p. 488
spherical branding, p. 487
standardization, p. 500
strategic consistency, p. 485
SWOT analysis, p. 488
total communication, p. 484
touchpoints, p. 484
unified vision, p. 486

MyLab Marketing

Go to **www.pearson.com/mylab/marketing** for MyLab discussion questions (⚫) as well as the following assisted-graded writing questions.

16-1. Explain cause marketing and mission marketing. How do they differ, and what do they contribute to an IMC program?

16-2. Outline the branding effort from Chapter 1 in terms of the sections of a standard campaign plan. From the case write-up reported in this chapter, is there anything missing?

REVIEW QUESTIONS

⚫ **16-3.** Explain the difference between planning an IMC campaign and planning a 360-degree total communication program.

16-4. What do we mean when we say that media planning in an IMC campaign plan moves from channels to contact points?

⚫ **16-5.** Why is a brand an integrated perception?

16-6. What are SWOTs, and how are they used strategically in analyzing a marketing situation?

16-7. What is cross-media integration, and why is it important?

16-8. What are two types of controls used in the management of an IMC campaign?

16-9. Explain how a global IMC program is more complex than an IMC program operated nationally.

16-10. What is internal integration?

DISCUSSION QUESTIONS

16-11. Choose a restaurant in your community and develop a campaign plan. What types of people does the restaurant target? Would you recommend that its advertising focus on price or image? What is (or should be) its image? Which media or marcom area should it use?

⚫ **16-12.** You have gotten a new assignment to be on a launch team for an upscale pen made in Switzerland under the brand name of Pinnacle. Its primary advantage is that it has an extremely long-lasting cartridge, one that is guaranteed to last for at least five years. The pen is available in a variety of forms, including roller ball and felt tip, and a variety of widths, from fine to wide stroke. Analyze the globalization or localization options for launching this pen first in Europe and then globally. What would your recommendation be on standardizing the brand communication?

16-13. You work for a large sporting-goods chain that would like to focus all its local philanthropic activities in one area. You believe the company could benefit from a mission marketing program. What should be in a proposal for the marketing vice president that explains

mission marketing? Why do you think a mission marketing project might work for the company?

16-14. Luna Pizza is a regional producer of frozen pizza. Its only major competitor is Brutus Bros. The following is a brief excerpt from Luna's situation analysis for the next fiscal year. Estimate the next year's advertising budgets for Luna under each of the following circumstances:

a. Luna follows a historical method by spending 40 cents per unit sold in advertising, with a 5 percent increase for inflation.

b. Luna follows a fixed percentage of projected sales method, using 7 percent.

c. Luna follows a share-of-voice method. Brutus, the primary competitive pizza brand, is expected to use 6 percent of sales for its advertising budget in the next year.

	Actual Last Year	Estimated Next Year
Units sold	120,000	185,000
$ sales	420,000	580,000
Brutus $ sales	630,000	830,000

TAKE-HOME PROJECTS

16-15. *Portfolio Project:* Compare the brand positioning and customer-focused content of three of the following corporate sites: www.accenture.com, www.ibm.com, www.nielsen.com, www.forrester .com, and www.strategicbusinessinsights.com.

Analyze the three sites you selected in terms of their brand vision and position as well as their commitment to a customer focus philosophy. What would you recommend to improve their online brand presence?

16-16. *Mini-Case Analysis:* How has the "Pink Ribbon" campaign built the reputation of the Susan G. Komen organization? Who does it target? What is its brand essence or core brand concept?

Explain how this campaign brings the brand's vision to life. What might you suggest to continue to improve the impact of this series of campaigns?

TRACE North America Case

Multicultural IMC

Read the TRACE case in the Appendix before coming to class.

16-17. How could you increase the consistency of the "Hard to Explain, Easy to Experience" campaign so that the overall impact was greater?

16-18. If you wanted to go global with this campaign, what would you need to learn about each new market before you ran the campaign?

17

Evaluating IMC Effectiveness

By this point, you should understand the potential power of brand communication. We've emphasized that effective campaigns do more than win awards for creativity. Their singular and number one purpose is to achieve the campaign's communication and marketing goals. As you will see in this chapter, there are many ways to evaluate the effectiveness of an integrated marketing communication (IMC) program. Companies evaluate the impact of the program's message, the performance of its individual IMC components, the power of the media that delivered the message, and the extent to which the IMC campaign's components worked in harmony to create changes in people's attitudes and behaviors. This chapter discusses the establishment of campaign objectives (against which campaign success can be evaluated) and examines the many types of effectiveness measurement that are possible.

IT'S A WINNER

Campaign	Company	Agency	Contributing Agencies	Awards
Metrics, Not Myths	*Adobe Systems*	*Goodby, Silverstein & Partners*	*Edelman Berland*	*Silver Effie Award, 2014; Webby Award, 2013*

Adobe Meets Marketing Myths with Measurement

When Adobe learned that professional marketers often feel angry about being undervalued by top management, it set out to change this perception by launching an integrated, attention-getting campaign for its new suite of end-to-end digital marketing and analytics products, called the "Adobe Marketing Cloud." Anchoring the campaign was the message that marketing isn't just "spin" or "BS," but instead can be measureable and impactful. Research into the question of marketing credibility revealed several major misconceptions and myths including, "There Is No ROI in Social Media," "You Can't Trust Marketers," and "Marketers Hate Big Data." Adobe also put the reputation of its analytics products on the line by sharing real-time updates on the effectiveness and results of the "Metrics, Not Myths" campaign.

MYTH Nº 1
"Marketing IS BS"
THAT'S BALONEY.
Marketing works, and we can prove it.
With Adobe® Marketing Cloud, you get a complete set of integrated solutions: analytics, social, advertising, targeting, and content management.
Go from data to insights faster than ever.
Metrics, not myths.
ADOBE & MARKETING
Follow us @AdobeMktgCloud

Photo: © 2017 Adobe Systems Incorporated. All rights reserved. Adobe and the Adobe logo are either registered trademarks or trademarks of Adobe Systems Incorporated in the United States and/or other countries.

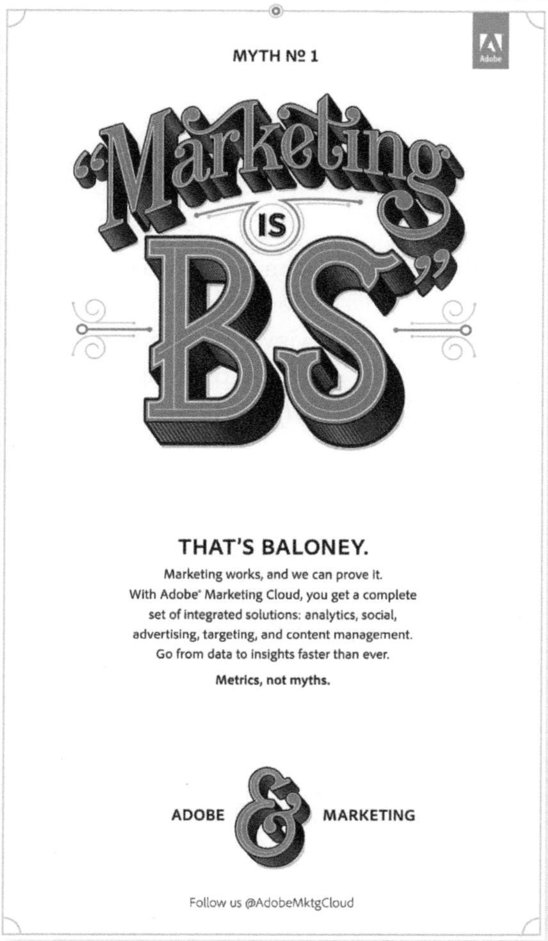

Campaign Objectives

Adobe is best known for its popular creative tools (e.g., Photoshop), so it faced a large hurdle gaining awareness and recognition for its new analytics tools in a very crowded ($77 billion) digital marketing industry. Adobe needed to transform itself from a creative company that "makes" to a marketing partner that "makes and measures." The campaign's purpose was to call out and then bust the myths of marketing. Why? It's because marketing overall has a perception problem. A study by Fournaise Marketing Group revealed that 73 percent of CEOs think marketers lack business credibility. According to an Adobe study called "The State of Online Advertising," 53 percent of consumers think most marketing is a bunch of BS. Building on these statistics, Adobe hired the Edelman Berland agency to help uncover more misperceptions about the marketing profession, focus on ways to dispel them, and develop a bold proclamation that placed Adobe squarely in the professional marketer's corner. By calling out marketing BS and offering certainty

instead of half-truths, Adobe wanted to become the trusted partner to deliver the confidence digital marketers desperately needed. Objectives included the following:

- Increasing direct inquiries by 20 percent.
- Significantly improving its perception among CEOs and consumers.
- Increasing overall awareness and engagement on social media (media and social sentiment, social engagement, community growth, and website traffic).
- Doubling its PTAT (People Talking About This) score of 5 percent.

Key Strategic Campaign Decisions

The campaign was integrated, blending together social media, PR, advertising, a website, a new app, and a video series to humorously challenge misconceptions and negative attitudes toward marketing while unveiling the new Adobe analytics products. The target audience was chief marketing officers and senior marketing decision leaders, so ads were placed with publications and sites such as the *New York Times*, *Wall Street Journal*, *Mashable*, and *Advertising Age*. Adobe spent an estimated $10 million on the campaign.

Message Strategy

The series was a mix of humorous ad-like videos, data-driven customer success stories, infographics, and light-hearted man-on-the-street takes of the consumer point of view on data and marketing. The videos were supported by paid social buys, which focused on spreading engagement with three videos—*BS Detector*, *The Slap*, and *The Robot*—that aligned with three myths—marketing is BS, social media is worthless, and marketers hate big data.

The coarse language used in the campaign was designed to reflect the frustration that professional marketers feel when their contributions are undervalued and they are told the impact of their work isn't measureable. It also followed a trend for marketing communication to use more common phrases and expressions. There was another reason: in an industry as active as digital media, which is cluttered with messages from both start-ups and heavyweights, Adobe needed its campaign to stand out from the crowd and gain attention and interest from busy professionals.

A key component of successful advertising and integrated marketing communications is evaluating the effectiveness of the communication. In this chapter, you will read about many ways to gauge effectiveness. Did Adobe's effort get the desired results, or was it just another pile of BS? Check out the It's a Wrap section at the end of the chapter to find out.

Sources: Stuart Elliot, "To Stand Out, Campaign for Adobe Gets Blunt," *The New York Times*, October 22, 2012, http://www.nytimes.com; "Adobe: Metrics, Not Myths," Effie Worldwide Case Database, 2014, https://effie.org; Talia Sinkinson, "Adobe's Product Launch Case Study: Stellar Strategies Adobe Is Using to Pump Up Visibility, Activate Audiences Online and Build a New Brand Story," *Bulldog Reporter*, May 23, 2014, https://www.bulldogreporter.com; "Project: Adobe Metrics, Not Myths," Edelman Digital, 2013, http://webby2013.edelmandigital.us; "Marketing is BS," Adobe Systems Inc., 2017, http://tv.adobe.com; Christine Beury, "The Ultimate Case Study: Part 2 – Off to a promising start," Adobe Digital Marketing Blog, November 4, 2012, https://blogs.adobe.com; "Adobe: Metrics not Myths," Adobe Systems Inc., https://blogs.adobe.com.

Brand Communication Impact: Did It Work?

What makes an IMC campaign effective? Is it that people like it? Is it that it moves people to take some kind of action? Or is it something else altogether?

17.1 Explain why it is important to evaluate brand communication effectiveness.

First Things First: The Campaign Objectives

Typically, a brand communication campaign has multiple objectives; for example, one (attitudinal) objective may be to change brand perceptions, and another (behavioral) objective may be to make people engage in some way with the brand. If we think about the Adobe introductory case, we recall that Adobe's IMC program was launched with a goal of getting the attention of marketing professionals and increasing awareness for the company's new suite of digital marketing and analytics products.

Regardless of the number of objectives a company sets for a campaign, it is critical that such stated objectives be established up front because they provide the all-important framework for evaluating whether a campaign was a success. Setting objectives—and establishing specific measures that will demonstrate success—make campaign evaluation possible. If, for example, Adobe stated that an objective of its IMC program was a 20 percent increase in the number of sales inquiries made by marketing professionals for its new product, at least one way in which its campaign would be evaluated would be automatically established. In using social media, in particular, clear campaign goals must be set. According to Jason Falls, founder of Social Media Explorer LLC, these goals can range from increasing the number of people actively participating in an online community to changing public sentiment from an existing level to a specific desired level. However, whatever the goals, they must be clear and specific and provide ways to measure the success of your marketing efforts.[1]

Are marketers pleased when great advertising contributes to sales increases? Of course they are! In the Matter of Practice feature, Charles Young, a member of this book's Advisory Board, describes a situation in which advertising has played an important role in sales for McDonald's.

> **● Principle**
> Campaign objectives and campaign evaluation work hand in hand. In the absence of clear campaign objectives, evaluation becomes a much murkier task.

The Campaign Purpose: Brand Building

To begin thinking about measuring IMC effectiveness, let's consider just one IMC component: advertising. Many executives believe that advertising works only if it produces sales. Syracuse University Professor Emeritus John Philip Jones, who has written many books and articles on the topic, estimates that of the $600 billion spent annually on advertising globally, only 41 percent—less than half—produces sales.[2] Jones contends that "advertising must generate an immediate jolt to sales before it can be expected to produce any further effect."[3]

Simon Broadbent, another leading figure in effectiveness research and originally a proponent of sales impact, however, came to realize that "long and deep" effects of advertising, or its brand-building effects over time, also are important.[4] Many other experts agree with this view, and it is the perspective supported here. A couple of reasons we support Broadbent's view follow.

First, determining advertising's impact on sales can be very difficult because of the impact of other environmental factors. Consider Amazon.com. Could a sales increase in a major northeastern city that is receiving holiday advertising truly be attributed to the advertising? Or could the sales gains be a result of horrible winter weather that is causing people to shop from their homes? It is extremely difficult to gauge the impact of different factors that may have contributed to revenue.

Second, sales simply are not the only reason brands advertise; rather, one of the major objectives of advertising is to create higher levels of brand awareness among consumers. An article in *Business 2.0* reported that an ad for the Six Flags amusement park was a smash success in viewer surveys—but that it must be deemed ineffective, regardless, because attendance at the company's 26 theme parks fell after the campaign instead of increasing. Is that response appropriate? It probably isn't. Perhaps the main reason people didn't come to the parks was an increase in gas prices. And if demonstrated brand awareness increases were in keeping with Six Flags campaign objectives, the campaign was successful.

It's our view that marketers intend their messages to accomplish a variety of goals. The goal of a nonprofit campaign may be to inform donors of how their donations are being spent; put another way, it may be to make donors more knowledgeable (and, one hopes, more engaged). The goal of a packaged goods team may be to build a brand relationship. And the goal of a hotel

> **● Principle**
> Brand communication can be deemed successful when set objectives—attitudinal, behavioral, or both—have been met.

> **● Principle**
> If you can't measure it, you can't manage it.

Can You Really Predict the Impact of Advertising on Sales?

Charles Young, *President, Ameritest*

We know from years of collecting and comparing ads that every player in the fast moving quick-service restaurant (QSR) category puts strong and weak ads on air each year—and that includes giants like McDonald's and Burger King. But how can you predict which ones will be effective or ineffective?

Our research company, Ameritest, constantly monitors commercials as they air, and we track ad quality using a proprietary system of metrics and analysis tools. From such data, we are able to measure, diagnose, and predict advertising effectiveness.

Importantly, in validating our commercial metrics, we recently asked the question, can we predict the sales that McDonald's reports to Wall Street? That is an important driver of the company's stock price.

In the QSR category, we collect data on all new television commercials during their first week of airing. For the five years from January 2007 to January 2012, we tested 1,292 QSR commercials—338 McDonald's ads and 954 competitive ads from 17 other major QSR brands. This validation to sales analysis, the largest ever conducted by a pretesting company, is based on 129,000 online consumer interviews—100 per commercial used in our standard analysis of all the commercials.

During this same time period, we collected the public sales figures that McDonald's reported to Wall Street for 62 consecutive months. The sales figures used included the change in same-store sales versus year ago for US sales.

To evaluate advertising quality, we looked at measures of executional quality and strategic message communication. Executional quality is a composite of three performance measures: attention-getting power, branding, and motivational impact. These measures were compared to competitive norms for this time period. Message communication was a variable that described which of nine possible strategic messages (taste, healthy, enjoyable place, and so on) were conveyed by each ad.

In building our sales validation model, we also included a sales momentum variable to describe other McDonald's marketing efforts (store remodels, menu changes) and a variable for the economic recession. Together, these two macroeconomic variables explained 22 percent of McDonald's sales growth.

When we added in the variable for advertising quality—combining executional impact and message communication—the predictive power of our sales validation model improved to 46 percent.

Given that our model did not even include advertising media spend data or other variables in the marketing mix, such as relative pricing, and so on, this finding is highly significant. It shows that a quarter of McDonald's sales growth—and its stock price—can be explained by the quality of its advertising creative.

So macroeconomic variables explain roughly a quarter of sales growth, ad quality explains a quarter, and ad spending yet another quarter, leaving all other variables to explain the rest. Clearly, advertising is the major force driving the growth of the McDonald's business.

This finding confirms not only that McDonald's ads generally are high in ad quality but also that television advertising had been a good investment for McDonald's over that five-year period.

company campaign may be to recruit new members for its frequent-traveler program. All these goals point to ways in which advertisements may serve campaign objectives—and therefore be effective—that are not reflected in sales numbers alone.

Rusty Duncan's Matter of Practice feature for a floor-covering firm is an example of a campaign that works on multiple levels. People like it and remember it, and that drives more people to purchase.

Because campaigns often have multiple objectives and because there are so many ways of measurement available in the IMC tool kit, there are multiple ways to assess the effectiveness of marketing communication campaigns. We discuss many of the more common ways of gauging campaign success in this chapter. That said, we also encourage all future marketers to know that new ways of measuring effectiveness are always possible.

Why Evaluation Matters

As we mentioned in Chapter 6, some evaluation of brand communication is informal and based on the judgment of experienced managers, and there is always a need for this. The important thing to recognize—very early in campaign planning stages—is that there also will be a need for multiple, formal evaluation mechanisms. As Professor Mark Stuhlfaut explains, evaluation

Standing Out in a Crowd Starts with Outstanding Ideas

Rusty Duncan, *COO and Partner, Insight Creative Group*

Photo: Courtesy Insight Creative Group. Used with permission.

"He freaking said yes!!!" That was the collective reaction by the small team at Insight Creative Group involved in pitching this out-of-home concept. We want the same thing most agencies do: creative outdoor that makes you pee yourself a little when you drive by. That is not always the case when selling flooring, but Bart (featured on the billboard and chief operating officer of Brewer Flooring Group) was feeling feisty this particular day. Bart understands that being creative and standing out in a crowded marketplace is important. We jumped on the opportunity to do what anybody would have done. Taking inspiration from the television show *Seinfeld*, we paralleled George Constanza's famous "Timeless Art of Seduction" pose with Bart, mirroring George's pose down to the toe stretch, but in the spokesman wardrobe Bart has sported for 10 years. The velvety lounge chair was replaced with rolls of carpet and carpet squares. Kramer was replaced with ICG art director and photographer Amy Nickerson. Then, veteran art director Brandon Anderson took it from there, creating the background and bringing his sketch to life. If this paragraph has a point, it's "keep pitching ideas," even to existing clients who you have worked with for nine-plus years. We are pretty fortunate to work with a client who understands the value of standing out. Bart has let us dress him in an adult onesie, hose him down with mustard and ketchup, put his face on carpet, and swim in all his clothes. You do things like that to be different and stand out because the brand benefits. Thanks, Bart, for taking another one for the team. Plus, you can't go wrong paying homage to the show about nothing.

"Look Ma, we went viral!" Like most things viral, it started with a post on Reddit. From there, the story was picked up by *Mashable*, sitting right next to a story about Instagram's controversial rebrand. Then, we got a nod from the venerable industry standard, *Adweek*. Then, suddenly the AV Club posted it, too. In total, the image of the billboard was viewed, shared, and commented on more than 1 million times.

It all started with the idea. Wait, let me back up. It started with episode 139 of *Seinfeld*, which gave us the idea to turn Bart into George. The entire process was quick and fun. Sketches got approved, photos were taken and the design followed. The result was loads of buzz, awareness, and increased sales for our client.

should be planned in to any campaign. That is not an onerous task when clear campaign objectives have been written, because evaluation can and should flow directly from those goals. But the inclusion of a "campaign evaluation phase" on the program time line is mandatory.

Structured evaluation not only determines the success of a campaign from an objective perspective, but also provides valuable feedback as brands plan campaigns for the future. Stuhlfaut's Matter of Principle feature builds on the idea of a cycle beginning and ending with research.

From the business perspective, formal evaluation of brand communication is a must. Why? The first reason is that the stakes in making an advertising misstep are high. By the time an average 30-second commercial is ready for national television, it has cost hundreds of thousands of dollars in production costs. If it is run nationally, its sponsor can invest several million dollars in airtime alone. The second reason is that advertising optimization—reducing risk by testing, tracking brand performance, and making changes where possible to increase the effectiveness of communication—helps ensure future success.

Experts in the IMC business put evaluation skills at the very top of the list of skills that will be needed in the communication industry over upcoming years. According to *Advertising Age*, a group of 75 ad industry leaders who met in New York City to brainstorm about the future of

Principle
The sheer costs of brand communication demand that it be evaluated so its effectiveness can be understood.

Completing the Cycle

Mark Stuhlfaut, *University of Kentucky*

So you've analyzed the market up and down, honed a strategic position, spent months creating the most attractive image, produced hard-hitting materials, placed ads in all the right media, stretched the budget, made sure everyone in your marketing chain is on message, and launched a tightly integrated communication campaign. It's time to sit back and enjoy the afterglow, right?

Not quite. You're job isn't finished until you've properly evaluated the results. Why? There are three very good reasons: (1) you need to find out what worked in the campaign, what didn't, and what could have worked better to solve any problems now; (2) a comprehensive evaluation provides valuable information that will serve as input for the next planning cycle; and (3) managers of marketing communication need to responsibly demonstrate the effectiveness of their efforts to clients and corporate management—you owe it to them to prove that their investment of resources in your programs and their trust in you were worth it.

Where do you start? A good beginning is to go back to the campaign's goals to see if they were met, which brings back the importance of having clear, measurable, and attainable objective statements.

What standards should you employ to know if you've succeeded? Sales data? They're one indicator, but too many intervening factors make tying marketing communication to sales figures difficult and not very meaningful. Therefore, other measures, such as the levels of awareness, comprehension, importance, and brand preference, are more useful for communication managers to determine whether the campaign was effective.

A thorough review takes more than a few quick surveys. Sure, you'll want to conduct quantitative and qualitative research to get feedback from consumers or customers. But you should also contact all the key stakeholders in the market—such as company sales personnel, distributors, dealers, editors, broadcasters, consultants, and other friendly third parties—to see if their communication needs were satisfied by the campaign. If you include these important people in your evaluation, you'll not only gain helpful information, but you'll also build strong relationships for the future.

The best evaluation techniques aren't something you add on to a campaign; they're something you build in to every phase of the process. Assess alternative positions early in the campaign's development. Compare different concepts in the rough layout stage. The earlier you test, the cheaper it is, and the better chance you have to get it right.

It's easy to say you don't have the time or the money to evaluate the campaign's elements. But consider the cost of not getting it right. The effort made to evaluate the effectiveness of the campaign before and after launch will pay off in the long run.

their field concluded that "the next-generation advertising exec will be a data geek with the soul of an artist, the business acumen of Warren Buffett and the storytelling skills of Don Draper."[5] That is due to the power big data will bring to IMC decision making.

How Evaluation Fits into the Stages of Brand Communication Testing

A complete understanding of the strength of your brand communication is accomplished through testing, monitoring, and measurement. This process is depicted in Figure 17.1, which illustrates how IMC planning is circular with evaluation being both a last step of one planning effort and the first step of the next effort.

In Chapter 6, we discussed message development testing; more specifically, we discussed how **concept testing**, **semiotic analysis**, and **pretesting** are used to make a campaign as strong as possible before it "goes live" in the marketplace. Ideally, the results of preliminary testing should be available before large sums of money are invested in finished work or in media buys. We also discussed monitoring buzz and tracking behavior while a campaign is running. Here, our focus will be on measurement: how we evaluate actual effects and results after a campaign effort has been completed.

17.2 Discuss the role campaign objectives play in the measurement of campaign success.

Evaluating the IMC Message

Once a campaign is over, how do we find out whether brand communication was effective? How do we know whether the messaging "worked"? Questions about impact are critical and must be addressed. If they are not and there is no proof that a campaign worked, companies may be tempted to make the mistake of cutting communication spending that is driving their business. To put it another way, in the absence of proof that IMC efforts have made a brand stronger, brand managers who are under pressure to cut spending could put a stop to the very IMC efforts that are allowing them to remain competitive. Also, in a scenario in which an IMC program is not having positive effects on attitudes or behaviors, brand managers need to know that so they can improve on their campaigns moving forward.

As we discussed earlier in this chapter, any attempt to measure the impact of brand messaging by looking only at sales numbers poses challenges. Therefore, the impact of brand messaging typically is measured in terms of its communication effects—the mental responses to a message (such as increased awareness or a change in brand perceptions) that serve as **surrogate measures** for sales impact. Positive postcampaign changes in measures such as brand awareness, knowledge of what a brand offers, liking of a brand, and intent to purchase a brand suggest that an advertising message or some other form of brand communication is making a positive contribution to an eventual brand purchase. Many other measures for which we hope to see increases as a result of brand communication are also important and will be included in our discussion below.

When campaigns don't work, a very important role of postcampaign message testing involves understanding what went wrong. Some messages might confuse the audience, others might fail to get people's attention, and still others might fail to resonate with consumers. In these situations, campaign message evaluation must bring the issues to light. In some cases, brand messages lack credibility and can even have a negative impact. For example, when a publicity release for the *God of War II* video game actually featured a deceased goat, animal rights groups were incensed.[6] Other consumers likely were offended as well. Again, a brand manager must know not only that this situation has happened, but also exactly why and how. Solid campaign evaluation measurements tell us precisely what a campaign has and has not accomplished.

Table 17.1 groups key message effectiveness measures and then matches them to the types of research questions that are used to determine effectiveness. We use the word *ad* throughout the table, but the questions are relevant for all IMC tools used in a given campaign.

Experts in Message Evaluation

Many research companies in addition to some large agency research departments specialize in measuring the various dimensions of effectiveness described in Table 17.1. The most successful of these companies have conducted so many tests that they have developed **norms** for common product and service categories. To put it another way, after a campaign runs, these companies can look at a client's changes in key measures (e.g., increases in brand awareness or intention to purchase) and compare them to changes achieved by other campaigns of comparable budget. Norms allow brand and agency leaders to determine whether a particular campaign message has performed above or below the category average in terms of "moving the needle" on items such as those listed in the table.

Most large measurement companies also have developed diagnostic methods that identify the strong and weak aspects of an IMC campaign. These methods are important because, as we

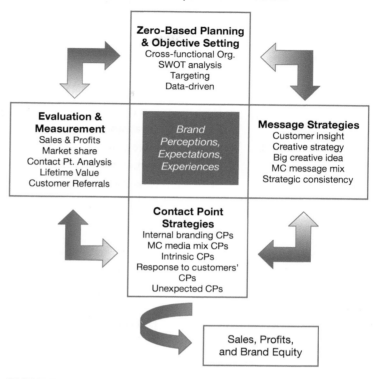

IMC Brand Optimizer Model

FIGURE 17.1

IMC Brand Optimizer Model

This IMC model created by Professor Tom Duncan illustrates that evaluation is a circular process: IMC plans start by gathering information and move through the various steps in the planning process to come back to the last step in the process, which is again gathering information. This time, however, information is gathered to determine what worked and what didn't. That information feeds back into the process, and the organization learns from the results.

TABLE 17.1 **Effectiveness Research Questions**

Effect	*Research Questions*
Perception	
Awareness/noticed	Which ads do you remember seeing?
	Which ads were noted?
Attention	What caught your attention?
	Did the ad stand out among the other ads and content around it?
	What stood out in the ad?
Recognition (aided)	Have you seen this ad/this campaign?
	Sort elements into piles of remember/don't remember.
Relevance	How important is the product message to you? Does it speak to your interests and aspirations?
Emotional/affective	What emotions did the ad stimulate?
	How did it make you feel?
Liking/disliking	Do you like this brand? This story? The characters (and other ad elements)?
	What did you like or dislike about the brand? The ad?
Desire	Do you want this product or brand?
Cognition	
Interest	Did you read/watch most of it? How much?
	Did it engage your interest or curiosity?
	Where did your interest shift away from the ad?
Comprehension/confusion	What thoughts came to you? Do you understand how it works? Is there anything in the ad you don't understand? Do the claims/product attributes/benefits make sense?
	Do you have a need for this brand or can it fulfill a need for you?
Recall (unaided)	What happened in the commercial? What is the main message? What is the point of the ad?
Brand recall/linkage	What brand is being advertised in this ad?
	[In open-ended responses, was the brand named?]
Differentiation	What's the difference between Brand X and Y?
Association	When you think of this brand, what (products, qualities, attributes, people, lifestyles, etc.) do you connect with it?
	Do you link this brand to positive experiences?
Personality/image	What is the personality of the brand? Of whom does it remind you? Do you like this person/brand personality?
	What is the brand image? What does it symbolize or stand for?
Self-identification	Can you see yourself or your friends using this brand?
	Do you connect personally with the brand image?
Persuasion	
Intention	Do you want to try or buy this product/brand?
	Would you put it on your shopping list?
Argument/counterargument	What are your reasons for buying it? Or for not buying it—or its competing brand(s)? How does it compare to competitors' brand(s)?
	Did you argue back to the ad?
Believability/conviction	Do you believe the reasons, claims, or proof statements?
	Are you convinced the message is true? The brand is best?
Trust	Do you have confidence in the brand?
Behavior	How many people actually did buy, try, call, send, click, visit, attend, inquire, volunteer, donate, advocate, or whatever the desired action?
	What is the rate of change?

discussed above, understanding what worked and what did not work is what makes us able to make campaigns better over time.

Below is a list of a few of the more prominent communication evaluation companies and the types of tests and measurements they provide. Of course, new entrants (often working with new technology) and mergers cause this list of firms to change quite frequently.

- *Ameritest* Brand linkage, attention, motivation, communication, flow of attention and emotion through the commercial
- *Ipsos ASI* Recall, attention, brand linkage, persuasion (brand switch, purchase probability), communication
- *Millward Brown* Branding, enjoyment, involvement, understanding, ad flow, brand integration, feelings about ad, main standout idea, likes/dislikes, impressions, persuasion, new news, believability, relevance
- *PwC* Support and benchmarking techniques to help to establish quality communication from assessment through delivery and evaluation
- *TNS Global* Brand choice, brand power (in the mind and in the market), motivations driving brand choice
- *GfK* Advertising planning, advertising optimization (testing of communication across channels), monitoring of ongoing effectiveness of brand communication
- *Sapient* Advanced analytics, storytelling across digital channels

Also, major online companies, such as Google, provide myriad tools for online campaign evaluation that include everything from straightforward analytic tools that measure site traffic or key word search results to more complex tools that allow marketers to create experiments. In such experiments, for example, a campaign might appear to some consumers but not to others so that its impact on consumer attitudes may be clearly assessed. Companies such as MetrixLab use a tagging technology to know how many times people are exposed to a campaign and then measure how heavily exposed consumers and lightly exposed consumers differ in their intent to try a brand.

Message Evaluation Techniques

Now that we understand the broad role of campaign evaluation—through which we learn not only whether an IMC campaign met its objectives but also how it may have failed to deliver results—we can examine the most common research techniques used. Different types of measurement are required because brand managers are likely to set different objectives for different types of campaign messages. For example, Adobe expected its television and print ads to increase buzz as well as inquiries about its new analytics products among marketing professionals, and it expected its website to help transform Adobe's image from a creative company that "makes" to a marketing partner that "makes and measures." To begin, we'll expand on the role of communication tracking research, which initially was mentioned in Chapter 6.

Tracking Studies   Communication **tracking studies** are conducted from the time a campaign is launched until after it has concluded. They involve the collection of information from random samples of consumers who live in markets where they were exposed to a campaign. Companies differ in their exact time lines for data collection; in a best-practice scenario, however, information is collected from consumers two weeks after a campaign is launched, six weeks after a campaign is launched, and then at regular intervals between that point and the point at which the campaign concludes. Tracking studies are relevant to this chapter's campaign evaluation discussion because those measures collected at the conclusion of a campaign cycle are analyzed particularly closely by brand managers. It is through analyzing these measures that brand managers not only determine campaign impact, but also determine whether the campaign's core message has the staying power to be used for another cycle.

Of the research questions listed in Table 17.1, those focusing on campaign recall, recognition, comprehension, and relevance are staples of communication tracking surveys. It is imperative that consumers understand the message because they may become disengaged if they have to puzzle out its meaning.

Tracking surveys also include specific questions about how consumers perceive the personality of the brand (has the campaign reinforced the personality the brand team seeks to build?), self-identification with the brand (do consumers feel the brand is "a brand for me"?),

FIGURE 17.2
Tracking Brand Response

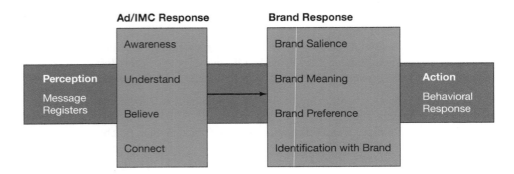

purchase intent, and purchase rate. If a campaign did not cause consumers to feel increased affinity with the brand or increase their likelihood of buying it, IMC campaign effectiveness is certain to come under question. At its most basic level, a brand tracker includes the components shown in Figure 17.2.

Scanner Analysis Still another common component of posttest evaluation is **scanner research**. Many retail outlets, especially drugstores, discount stores, and food stores, use electronic scanners to tally up purchases and collect consumer buying information. When you shop at your local Safeway, for example, each product you buy has an electronic bar code that conveys the brand name, the product code, and its price. If you are a member of Safeway's frequent-buyer program and have a membership card that entitles you to special promotional offers, the store can track your purchases.

Photo: Dmitry Kalinovsky/Shutterstock

Scanner research reads the information from a shopper's identification card and records that along with product information. Many retail outlets use electronic scanners to track sales among various consumer groups.

Scanner research is also used to see what type of sales spikes are created when certain ads and promotions are used in a given market. Both the chain and the manufacturers of the brands are interested in such data. The regional Safeway system may decide to establish a consumer panel so that it can track sales among various consumer groups. In this instance, you would be asked to join a panel, which might contain hundreds of other customers. You would complete a fairly extensive questionnaire and be assigned an ID number. You might receive a premium or a discount on purchases for your participation. Each time you make a purchase, you also submit your ID number. Therefore, if Safeway runs a two-page newspaper ad, it can track actual sales to determine to what extent the ad worked. Various manufacturers who sell products to Safeway can do the same kind of testing. The panel questionnaire also contains a list of media that each member reported using so that media performance can also be evaluated.

Single-Source Data **Single-source data** are obtained by measuring various media/marketing exposure, purchase behavior, and loyalty for the same individual or household. Such data may include data from loyalty card purchases, scanner data, TV or cable set-top boxes, personal people meters, and household demographics. As you might imagine, these data are very helpful to advertisers who wish to detect the effects of their IMC campaigns among consumers. Single-source data companies, such as Nielsen, arrange to have test commercials delivered to a select group of households within a market to compare changes in behavior to a control group of households. The purchasing behavior of each group of households is then collected by scanners in local stores. Because brand communication is the only manipulated variable, the method permits a fairly clear reading of cause and effect.

Syracuse University Professor Emeritus John Philip Jones, who spent many years at J. Walter Thompson, has used single-source data from the firm combined with Nielsen television viewing data to prove that advertising can cause an immediate impact on sales. His research has found that the strongest campaigns can triple sales, whereas the weakest campaigns can actually cause sales to fall by more than 50 percent.[7]

Although fairly expensive, **single-source research** can produce dependable results. Brand communication is received under natural conditions in the home, and the resulting purchases are actual purchases made by consumers. Drawbacks are that single-source research is better for short-term immediate sales effects and that it doesn't capture other brand-building effects very well.

Memory Tests   Memory tests are based on the assumption that brand communication leaves a mental residue with the person who has been exposed to it; in other words, the audience has learned something. One way to measure IMC effectiveness, then, is to contact consumers who were exposed to the campaign and find out what they remember. Memory tests fall into two major groups that you may remember reading about previously: recognition tests and recall tests.

One way to measure memory is to show a magazine advertisement, for example, to people and ask them whether they remember having seen it before. This kind of test is called a **recognition test**. In a **recall test**, respondents who have read the magazine are asked to report what they remember from the ad about the brand. In tests, the interviewer may go through a deck of cards containing brand names. If respondents say, "Yes, I remember seeing an advertisement for that brand," the interviewer asks the interviewees to describe everything they can remember about the ad. Obviously, a recall test is more rigorous than a recognition test.

Similarly, new television commercials are often run during the Super Bowl. The evening after the game, interviewers may make thousands of random phone calls until they have contacted about 200 people who were watching the program at the exact time a particular commercial appeared. The interviewer then asks a series of questions, such as the following:

1. Do you remember seeing a commercial for any SUVs?
2. *If No* Do you remember seeing a commercial for the Jeep Wrangler? (memory prompt)
3. *If Yes to Either of the Above* What did the commercial say about the product? What did the commercial show? What did the commercial look like? What ideas were brought out?

The first type of question is called an **unaided recall** question because the particular brand is not mentioned. The second question is an example of **aided recall**, in which the specific brand name is mentioned. The answers to the third set of questions are written down verbatim. The test requires that the respondent link a specific brand name—or at least a specific product category—to a specific commercial. This type of test sometimes is called a **brand linkage test**. The long-running Pacific Life campaign is a good example of a visual that could serve as a strong and memorable brand message.

Inquiry Tests   **Inquiry tests**, a form of action response, measure the number of responses to an advertisement or other form of brand communication. The response can be a call to a toll-free number, an email or website visit, a coupon return, a visit to a dealer, an entry in a contest, or a call to a salesperson. Inquiry tests are the primary measurement tool for direct-response communication, but they also are used to evaluate advertisements and sales promotions when the inquiry is built into the message design. Inquiry tests also may be used to evaluate the effectiveness of alternative advertisements using a split-run technique in magazines, where there are two versions of the magazine printed, one with ad A and the other with ad B. The ad (or direct-mail piece) that pulls the most responses is deemed to be the most effective.

Photo: Courtesy Pacific Life Insurance Company. Used with permission.

Pacific Life uses an image of a leaping whale to reflect its image of a confident insurance company that excels in its market. Is it effective? Does it work?

17.3 Describe the key ways in which campaign evaluation is conducted.

Evaluating the Performance of Various IMC Tools

As we know from Chapters 1 and 5, IMC synergy exists when all campaign components work together to create a solid and understandable brand meaning. The overarching campaign impact is strongest when the right mix of IMC tools is used. Therefore, before overarching campaign synergy is measured, evaluation usually is conducted on a tool-by-tool basis. In other words, brand managers determine whether each element of the IMC mix (e.g., public relations efforts or a website) individually achieved its desired objectives. They may employ internal data, or they may examine results from an outside research organization, such as Gallup & Robinson or Millward Brown. Either way, as was mentioned earlier in this chapter, the important things to remember in planning an evaluation program are that brand managers must think about evaluation up front and that specific objectives must be set for every IMC tool used in the mix.

Advertising may be the most visible IMC tool; however, other brand communication tools, such as sales promotions and online messages, may be better at achieving the objective of getting people to respond with an immediate purchase. Public relations can be particularly strong at building credibility. Whatever its objective, each IMC tool that is employed in a campaign must be evaluated to understand whether it has achieved its goals. Most IMC tools have their own metrics through which their performance is measured at a campaign's close. As shown in Melissa Lerner's media effects model shown in Figure 16.1, effective media campaigns activate consumer response on a number of levels, an idea underscored by this book's Facet Model of Effects. Therefore, evaluation methods should be chosen so that marketers can assess a range of effects and objectives.

In an integrated plan, we must use the best tool to accomplish a desired effect and then measure success in achieving that effect accordingly. In Table 17.2, the main effects are located in the first column, with a collection of surrogate measures identified in the second column (this list is not inclusive; it's just a sample). The last column lists the communication tool or tools that may be most appropriate for achieving the objective. Below, we explain in more detail how a few IMC tools are measured in terms of their effectiveness.

Advertising

How do you describe effective advertising? You've been watching it for most of your life. An examination of Table 17.2 shows that advertising has the potential to be particularly effective in accomplishing a number of objectives, such as increased brand awareness and improved brand image. It also can be a useful tool for providing brand reminders to the customer and encouraging repurchases.

The most common **posttesting**, or campaign evaluation, technique used to evaluate advertising is the tracking study, which was described earlier in this chapter. Whether a campaign runs for six weeks or six months, the measures taken at its close—and for several weeks beyond—are closely scrutinized by company and agency leaders to determine whether the campaign can be deemed a success. Communication tracking studies represent very large investments on the part of marketers; that said, given the cost of creating advertising, thorough campaign evaluation represents money well spent.

Public Relations

Public relations practitioners typically track the impact of a public relations campaign in terms of successful **output** (e.g., how many news releases led to stories or mentions in news stories) and **outcome** (attitudinal or behavioral change due to the impact of materials produced). To put it another way, to get a comprehensive picture of the impact of public relations, practitioners have evaluated process (what goes out) and outcome (effect on the target audience).

Output evaluation might be conducted by asking specific questions. How many placements (news releases that ran in the media) did we get? How many times did our spokesperson appear on talk shows? How much airplay did our public service announcements receive, or how much and what kind of buzz are tweets generating? The results are presented in terms of counts of minutes, mentions, or retweets.

TABLE 17.2 **Message Effectiveness Factors**

Key Message Effects	Surrogate Measures	Communication Tools
Perception	Exposure	Advertising media; public relations; point of purchase; digital
	Attention	Advertising; sales promotion, packaging; point of purchase
	Interest	Advertising; sales promotion; public relations, direct; point of purchase; digital
	Relevance	Advertising; public relations; direct; point of purchase; digital
	Recognition	Advertising; public relations; packaging; point of purchase; specialties
Emotional/Affective	Emotions and liking	Advertising; sales promotion; packaging; point of purchase; digital
	Appeals	Advertising; public relations; sales; events/sponsorships
	Resonate	Advertising; public relations; events/sponsorships
Cognition	Understanding	Advertising; public relations; sales; direct; digital
	Recall	Advertising; sales promotion; public relations; point of purchase; specialties
		Advertising; public relations; packaging
Association	Brand image	Advertising; public relations; events/sponsorships; digital
Persuasion	Attitudes	Advertising; public relations; direct; digital
	Preference/intention	Advertising; public relations; sales; sales promotion; digital
	Credibility	Public relations
	Conviction	Public relations; sales; direct
	Motivation	Advertising; public relations; sales; sales promotion; digital
Behavior	Trial	Sales promotion; sales; direct; point of purchase; digital
	Purchase	Sales promotion; sales; direct; digital
	Repeat purchase	Advertising; sales promotion; sales; direct; specialties; digital

Outcomes, on the other hand, are usually measured in terms of changes in public opinion and relationship tracking. Ongoing public opinion tracking studies ask other questions. Has there been a change in audience knowledge, attitudes, or behavior? Can we associate behavioral change (e.g., product trial, repeat purchase, voting, or joining) with the public relations effort?

The search for methods to tie public relations activities to bottom-line business measures, such as return on investment (ROI), is like the quest for the Holy Grail. Public relations practitioners would like to demonstrate ROI because that would provide even more support for the importance of public relations effects. A surrogate ROI measure can be based on shareholder value, which can be seen as a company or brand's reputation capital. For example, research conducted on companies with the most effective employee communication programs has determined that they provide a much higher total return to shareholders. In addition, web-based analytical tools are making it possible to connect earned media results to online business goals, such as the generation of website traffic, sales leads, revenue, and donations for nonprofit organizations.[8]

Although some still argue that not all the value of public relations programs is measurable,[9] others claim that it is possible to increase the use of metrics to determine the impact a public relations campaign is having on consumer engagement, especially in the digital arena. According to Lee Odden, CEO of TopRank Online Marketing, "Linking, bookmarking, blogging, referring, clicking, friending, connecting, subscribing, submitting inquiry forms and buying all are engagement measures at various points in the customer relationship."[10] Mark Story, of the Arkansas Department of Human Services, advocates using new ways to measure performance and consumer engagement.[11] Objectives and the metrics for measuring success must be established up front; only then are public relations professionals truly capable of campaign evaluation.

Consumer, Trade, and Point-of-Purchase Promotions

Sales promotion managers for packaged goods and other products that use distribution channels need to evaluate both the impact of consumer (or end-user) promotions and promotions targeted at retailers and other channel members. You will recall that sales promotion is a set of techniques that prompts consumers, sales representatives, and the trade to take immediate action. At the most basic level of evaluation, managers require proof of promotion execution, such as copies of store ads and pictures of in-store displays. One responsibility of the sales force is to conduct store checks to verify that stores are doing what they promised. At the most important level of promotion evaluation, however, the behaviors and types of involvement that promotions are designed to create must be measured.

Promotions that contain a response device, such as coupons, have a built-in evaluation measure. Beyond response and redemption rates, however, brand managers often also measure consumer awareness of promotions, sales force participation in promotions, and various appropriate forms of online consumer reaction. What is measured depends on promotional objectives.

Overall, the efficiency of a sales promotion can be evaluated in terms of its financial returns more easily than can the impact of advertising. We compare the costs of a promotion, called a **payout analysis**, to the forecasted sales generated by the promotion. A **break-even analysis** seeks to determine the point at which the total cost of a promotion exceeds the total revenues generated, identifying the point where the promotion was not productive. Figure 17.3 depicts this analysis.

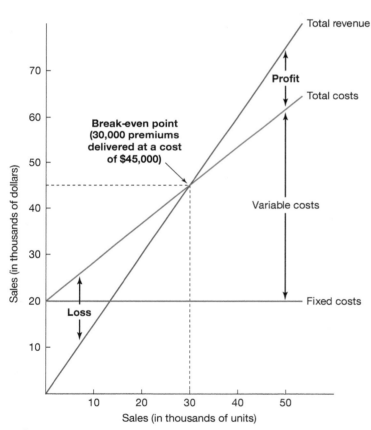

FIGURE 17.3

A Sales Promotion Break-Even Analysis

At the break-even point, where 30,000 premiums are delivered at a cost of $45,000, the sales revenues exactly cover but do not exceed total costs. Below and to the left of the break-even point (in the portion of the diagram marked off by dashed lines), the promotion operates at a loss. Above and to the right of the break-even point, as more premiums are sold and sales revenues climb, the promotion makes a profit.

Source: Diagram by Melissa Lerner, a partner at EnPlay, an out-of-home media company.

Direct Marketing   The primary objective of direct-marketing communication is to drive a transaction or generate some other type of immediate behavioral response, such as a donation or visit to a dealer. What makes this marketing communication tool so attractive to marketers is that response is so easily measurable. Some advertisements request direct response via a toll-free number, a mail-in coupon, a website or email address, or an offer embedded in the body copy. Instead of depending on consumers' memories, measures of a message's persuasive abilities, or some other indirect indication of effectiveness, the advertiser simply counts the number of viewers or readers who either buy a product or take some other action (e.g., request additional information). In this way, direct marketing mechanisms are the easiest IMC tools to evaluate in terms of message efficiency and in terms of return on marketing investment.

Evaluation of Digital IMC Components   Many IMC efforts, whether advertising, public relations, or other campaign elements, are conducted not only offline but also online. Some digital performance indicators are website traffic volume, such as **page views** or the simple number of visitors to a site. Banner advertising and other ads are evaluated using **click-through rates**, as mentioned in Chapter 13; however, one thing the industry has learned is that this form of advertising is decreasing in effectiveness. Pop-up banners, in particular, can get more attention than banner ads, but they are also seen as more irritating.

Instead of click-through rates, some advertisers use a metric of **cost per lead** that records how well a click-through generates prospects, an attempt to get at ROI. A more important metric, however, is **conversion rate**, which is the percentage of people who complete a desired action, such as playing a game, signing up for a newsletter, or buying something. Of course, online sales also are an important measure of digital effectiveness.

The most important thing to understand in considering evaluation of online efforts is that although websites used to be the primary digital properties for connecting with targets and the place where the most digital interaction was happening, that no longer is true. Today, digital communication is multichannel (e.g., desktop, mobile, tablet, outdoor display) and multiplatform (social sharing, paid digital media like banners, email, consumer reviews, video sharing, music, games, and much more). According to Melissa Read, director of marketing analysis and strategy at Sapient, "We think of this world and the experience consumers have with it as an **ecosystem** of digital properties. The consumer journey in discovering, considering and purchasing products from brands happens inside and outside of this ecosystem, as it also includes offline touch points, such as the in-store experience and **experiential marketing**."[12] When she says "experiential marketing," Read is referring to all the other ways consumers experience a brand.

So, in addition to evaluating digital efforts through looking at conversion rates (e.g., the rate of shift from information seeking to trial usage) and sales, experts are now evaluating digital campaign components in terms of their ability to generate awareness and consideration—measures that used to be applied only to traditional media—as well. Consumers no longer see themselves as bouncing back and forth between traditional and digital worlds as they make commitments to brands, so we must attempt to understand myriad influences that digital efforts may be having on the way they think and feel.

Evaluating the Performance of Media Vehicles

17.4 Explain how the performance of media vehicles is evaluated.

Brand communication has little chance to be effective if no one sees it. Analyzing the effectiveness of the media plan is yet another important part of campaign evaluation. Did the plan actually achieve reach and frequency objectives? Did the newspaper and magazine placements run in the positions expected and produce the intended Gross Rating Points (GRP) and cost-per-thousand levels? In other words, did brand managers get what they paid for?

Media Optimization

When a brand manager optimizes the mix of IMC tools used, the resulting brand perception becomes stronger. One of the biggest challenges in media planning is media efficiency—getting the most for the money invested. As we explained in Chapter 15, media planners operate with computer models of **media optimization** that are used in making decisions about media selection, scheduling, and weights (amount of budget). Models are always theoretical, so one important benefit of campaign evaluation is that the actual performance of a plan can be compared with the results projected by the media planner's model. The goal of media optimization is to optimize the budget—to get the most impact possible with the least expenditure of money. When we compare actual media reach and frequency, for example, with projections, our findings allow us to fine-tune our spending for the future to be as efficient as possible.

Evaluating Exposure

For major campaigns, agencies do post-buy analyses, which involve checking the media plan against the performance of each media vehicle. As mentioned above, a critical question is whether campaign reach and frequency objectives were obtained.

Verifying the audience measurement estimates is a challenge. Media planners are working sometimes with millions of dollars, and they can't afford to get it wrong. For print, services such as the Alliance for Audited Media (formerly known as Audit Bureau of Circulations), Experian Simmons (formerly known as SMRB), and Mediamark provide data. Likewise for broadcast, Nielsen provides audience monitoring. Media planners use these estimates up front to develop a media plan, and media buyers use them later to verify the accumulated impact of the media buy after the campaign has run. As we use the word *impact*, however, an important point must be clarified: when impact is judged by media audience measures, those numbers must be viewed with caution. Just because audience members have been exposed to marketing communication does not mean they have paid attention to it, and media professionals must always keep that at the top of their mind.

As media choices and, thus, their jobs become more and more complex, media planners are being asked to prove the wisdom of their recommendations in areas where the data they use are sometimes suspect or unreliable, particularly if there are problems with the media measurement companies' formulas and reporting systems. Nielsen, for example, has been subject to much questioning of its television ratings. Online measurement systems certainly remain imperfect, even though media agencies such as MindShare have made vast progress in recent years.

Vehicle-by-Vehicle Evaluation

To better understand the obstacles encountered in media evaluation, let's first look at a few areas where media performance is hard to estimate: out-of-home media, digital media, and alternative media. Then we will review some traditional media evaluation techniques.

Photo: Mikael Karlsson/ Alamy Stock Photo

This outdoor board by Mothers Against Drunk Driving (MADD) reinforces the organization's message to drivers on the roads. Research based on traffic counts does not account for the emotional impact of messages like these.

Out-of-Home Media As you would expect, accurately evaluating the mobile audience for outdoor advertising is challenging. Traffic counts can be reviewed, but the problem is that traffic does not equal exposure. Just because a car drove by a board doesn't mean that the driver or passengers actually saw it.

To address this issue, Traffic Audit Bureau for Media Measurement, Inc., has created the TAB visibility research program, which uses eye-tracking technology to determine how a billboard's format and angle to the road affect the likelihood that it will be noticed. TAB out-of-home measures even take into account the speed limits of roads on which signs are placed.

So, although outdoor advertising continues to present measurement challenges, progress is being made to better understand its impact. In particular, evaluation experts are seeking to move beyond traffic counts to understand the emotional impact of billboards.

Digital Media Until recently, the measures of effectiveness used to evaluate offline campaigns did not seem to transfer well to the online world. It used to be that digital tracking was tough and offline tracking was stronger in showing the relationship between IMC spend and results. Today, however, this scenario has changed. Web-analytic firms are developing much more sophisticated evaluation programs. As Read said, "We have people who study digital analytics and are experts at telling stories about the consumer journey with both offline and online data."[13] That said, some obstacles to establishing clear measures of digital media effectiveness do remain and will be discussed later in this chapter.

Alternative Media Alternative media programs, such as word of mouth, social media, and guerilla marketing campaigns, are even harder to evaluate, and media planners continue to search for reliable indicators of exposure numbers and buzz from these new sources that equate to the performance measures for traditional media. Research company Millward Brown designed a metric for online word of mouth to track and analyze sentiments expressed on social networks, blogs, and chat rooms.[14] Procter & Gamble created TREMOR, which develops buzz campaigns and is also used to design analysis techniques to track measurable business results for word-of-mouth campaigns. Another interesting experiment was conducted by Boston University college students and the Mullen ad agency using Twitter to get near-instantaneous feedback on how viewers were reacting to Super Bowl ads. This project was designed "to use a new medium to comment on an old medium," according to Mullen's chief creative officer.[15] However, as with mobile media, obstacles to clear measurement of alternative media effectiveness remain.

Newspaper Readership Measurement   For newspapers and other traditional media, assessment is more straightforward. As we introduced in Chapter 13, newspapers measure their audiences in two ways: **circulation**, or number of subscribers, and **readership**, or number of readers. These same measurements are revisited in postcampaign evaluation. Agencies obtain objective measures of newspaper circulation and readership by subscribing to one or both of the following auditing companies: the Alliance for Audited Media, an independent auditing group, and Scarborough Research, which provides local data for almost 80 of the nation's largest cities.

Magazine Readership Measurement   As was also mentioned in Chapter 13, magazine rates are based on the **guaranteed circulation** that a publisher promises to provide as well as figures for their **total audience**, or total number of readers.

Postcampaign evaluation requires verification of the circulation of magazines along with the demographic and psychographic characteristics of specific readers. As for newspapers, the Alliance for Audited Media is responsible for verifying magazine circulation numbers. MRI verifies readership for many popular national and regional magazines (along with other media) and also covers readership by demographics, psychographics, and product use. Experian Simmons provides psychographic data on who has read which magazines and which products these readers buy and consume. Still other research companies, such as Gallup & Robinson, provide information about magazine audience size and behavior.

Measuring the Broadcast Audience   A station's **coverage**, which is similar to circulation for print media, and station or program **ratings** (as delivered by Nielsen Audio) are revisited by marketers after a campaign to ensure that the radio medium delivered. For television, Nielsen data help advertisers understand the audience that a campaign actually reached. Again, *ratings* along with *shares*, **households using televisions (HUT)**, and **gross impressions** are revisited so that a comparison of anticipated and actual audience delivery can be conducted. The effect that advertising can have on an entire nation's tourism industry is revealed in a study described in the Matter of Practice feature by Jami Fullerton and Alice Kendrick.

Now that we have discussed some details of how the performances of individual IMC tools and media are gauged, we will examine key challenges involved in overall IMC campaign evaluation in the next section. Some key concerns revolve around how results from traditional and new media can be integrated and how their combination affects the results of the overarching campaign.

IMC Campaign Evaluation Challenges

17.5 List some of the key challenges faced in evaluating IMC effectiveness.

Most IMC campaigns use a variety of tools and media to reach and motivate customers to respond. The major challenge in overall program evaluation is to pull everything together and look at the big picture of campaign performance (components' synergistic performance) rather than the individual pieces and parts.

As companies move from an evaluation mind-set that only considers measures such as impressions to one that looks closely at conversion rates and consumer engagement, they are getting closer to a true measure of overarching campaign success. These better metrics, when combined with important metrics collected in ongoing brand tracking studies, should give marketers a more complete picture of campaign performance. That said, exactly which metrics companies choose to combine for evaluation and how those metrics are weighted with regard to their individual importance differs from brand to brand and remain an area of intense debate.

Measuring ROI

Advertisers continue to improve how they measure **brand communication ROI**, which compares the costs of creating and running communication versus the revenue it generates; however, because the dollar impact of communication is difficult to measure, so is this cost-to-sales ratio.

Cuban Tourism Advertising: A Key to Improved Diplomatic Relations?

Jami Fullerton,
Oklahoma State University

Alice Kendrick,
Southern Methodist University

Cuba is a top tourist destination in the Caribbean, where hundreds of thousands of Canadians, Europeans, and other world travelers—but not Americans— enjoy Cuban beaches, rum, and cigars every year.

On December 17, 2014, US President Barack Obama and Cuban President Raul Castro simultaneously announced plans to initiate diplomatic relations between the two countries after several decades of a US-imposed travel and trade embargo with Cuba. Five months prior to the historic announcement, we conducted an online experiment among US citizens about their views toward Cuba and their interest in traveling to Cuba, before and after they viewed a 30-second television commercial that the Cuba Ministry of Tourism was running in other countries. The study provided a snapshot of Americans' attitudes toward Cuba during a time when travel to the communist-ruled, Caribbean island nation was forbidden.[*]

Our study involved a representative sample of 321 US adults from 49 states. Only nine of our subjects had traveled to Cuba before, but we asked all of them to imagine that the travel ban had been lifted and Americans were free to visit their island-nation neighbor.

One of the first questions attempted to gauge US top-of-mind perceptions of Cuba. We asked US respondents to write three words that initially came to their mind when they thought about Cuba. The most frequently mentioned were the three C's: Cigars, Communism, and Castro. Initially, respondents were somewhat ambivalent about traveling to Cuba (4.09 on a 7-point scale), but after seeing the "Autentica Cuba" tourism commercial,[**] Americans' interest in travel to Cuba increased significantly.

But the commercial appeared to do more than heighten travel interest. Attitudes toward the Cuban government and Cuban people also increased significantly after viewing the ad, a finding that suggests the "bleed-over effect" of tourism advertising was at work. The bleed-over effect, first demonstrated in a 2008 study of Australian citizens' views toward the United States and US tourism advertising,[***] refers to tourism ads' potential not only to increase interest in travel, but also to improve attitudes toward the country being advertised. In the case of Cuban diplomatic relations, this point could be important.

Given the attractive climate, short travel time, and the relative strength of the US dollar, Americans, if given the opportunity through the lessening of travel sanctions, will likely be eager to visit the island. If the United States becomes a market for Cuban tourism and Cuba promotes tourism to their country through advertising in US media, not only will prospective American visitors learn about Cuba, but millions of US citizens who may never visit also will see the beauty and diversity of the country.

Face-to-face interaction with people in other countries, such as study abroad or vacation travel, is considered a gold standard in international relationships. President Obama mentioned this concept in his 2014 speech when he spoke of the "power of people-to-people engagement" and how American values are best represented by the American people. Given that point, our research suggests that loosening vacation travel restrictions to Cuba should further improve diplomatic relations between publics in the two countries. Further, mediated public diplomacy, such as the commercial produced by the Cuban government, has been shown to be a valuable asset in shaping public opinion. Therefore, Cuban tourism ads may play an important public diplomacy role in coming years as well.

[*]Alice Kendrick, Jami Fullerton, and Sheri Broyles, "Would I go? US Citizens React to a Cuban Tourism Campaign," *Place Branding and Public Diplomacy* 11 (2015), 249–262.

[**]The Autentica Cuba commercial can be viewed at http://vimeo.com/26323429.

[***]J. Fullerton, A. Kendrick, and G. Kerr, "Australian Student Reactions to US Tourism Advertising," *Place Branding and Public Diplomacy* 5, no. 2 (May 2009): 141–150.

ROI is easier to calculate for direct marketing and sales promotions (because the impact of these tools can be isolated and verified) than for the campaign overall.

One question related to ROI concerns how much spending is too much. That is, how do you determine whether you are overadvertising or underadvertising? The best way to answer this question is to use **test marketing**; in this approach, a campaign is launched in several different but matched (similar) cities at different levels of media activity. Then a comparison of the campaign results (sales or other kinds of trackable responses) in the different markets helps brand managers determine the appropriate levels and types of media spending.

Even though test marketing helps brand managers assess ROI, however, time is a factor as well. We mentioned in the beginning of this chapter that there is a debate about advertising's ability to impact short-term sales results as well as long-term branding.

University of Southern California professor Gerard Tellis reminded us that advertising not only has **instantaneous effects** (consumer responds immediately) but also **carryover effects** (delayed impact).[16] Any evaluation of campaign effectiveness therefore needs to be able to track both types of effects over time. So, even when test markets are established, brand analysts face a challenge in determining just how long they continue to compare results in markets after the campaign has concluded, which means that ROI measures can remain subjective.

The Synergy Problem

Another challenge with evaluating campaigns—particularly IMC campaigns—is estimating the impact of synergy. Intuitively, we know that multichannel communication with messages that reinforce and build on one another will have more impact than will single messages from single sources; however, that can be difficult to prove. As Bob Liodice, CEO of the Association of National Advertisers, said, "There is no single, consistent set of metrics that transcends discipline-centric measurements."[17]

If the campaign planning is well integrated, which means that each specialty area cooperates with all others in message design, delivery, and timing, there should be a **synergistic effect**. In other words, the overall results are greater than the sum of the individual functional areas if used separately.

A number of studies have attempted to evaluate IMC impact by comparing campaigns that use two or three tools to see what is gained when more message sources are added to the mix. For example, an experimental study in the *Journal of Advertising* found that people respond to an ad very differently if it is accompanied by positive vs. negative publicity about the brand.[18] In another study, the Radio Ad Effectiveness Lab reported that recall of advertising is enhanced when a mix of radio and internet ads are used rather than just website advertising alone.[19] A *Journal of Advertising Research* article considered the interaction of four factors: unified and consistent communication, strategic consistency in targeting (different messages for different audiences), database communication, and relationship programs.[20] Such studies of both the platforms and the components of IMC are beginning to tease out the effects of synergy, but they are a long way from perfect evaluation of the effects of a total communication program.

The most common way of measuring a campaign's total impact is the brand tracking approach mentioned previously. As various ingredients in the campaign are added and taken away, changes in tracking study results can show the effects and help identify what combinations of marketing communication tools and media work best for a brand. In other words, the brand manager looks at tracking study results over time, as tools and media used vary, and asks if the brand became stronger on critical dimensions of the image, such as personality and positioning cues, because of the campaign.

A final complication in evaluating the synergy of programs is the need to consider other messages and contact points beyond the brand communication campaign. Brand experiences, such as those involved with customer service and word of mouth, may be even more important than the planned communication campaign. The Principled Practice feature by Professor Keith Murray demonstrates how these unconventional message effects can have an important impact on the brand.

According to Murray in his analysis of the impact on the United Airlines brand by one unfortunate brand experience with a broken guitar, three points are dramatized:

1. Key management decisions count for a lot. Crafting and fostering a superb product—in the case of United, creating a great customer service and experience—involve the provision of a real, tangible, palpable reality that the customer can and does detect and enjoy. No amount of promotion hype can compensate for an inferior product offering.
2. Social media are not to be ignored or taken lightly by the firm. Social media messages, which are inherently powerful to begin with in conveying useful information to current and prospective customers, take on an even greater influence in the absence

of competing counterpart information from the firm itself through mass media and other paid sources. To disregard the impact of social media is to make a huge management error.

3. Managing the brand involves more than just having a good promotion strategy. Guarding the brand as well as the image of the firm generally involves an integrated management strategy whereby promotion decisions are called on to (1) support sound management and product-related practices (e.g., offer good customer service to begin with and attentive customer service in its absence) and (2) deploy a comprehensive range of promotion strategies, including fostering favorable social media (and responding to it when it happens), not just ignoring the negative messages that come along. The most successful carriers strive to manage their media exposures as much as they pay attention to their service operations. Evidence of that can be amply seen by the volume of negative clips posted by patrons of struggling, relatively unprofitable carriers compared to hardly any negative postings for the more exemplary ones (e.g., Southwest).

Digital Challenges

Marketers face several challenges when capturing the success of digital marketing communication efforts. First and foremost, marketers often want to skip straight to digital measurement without having a clear sense of their business objectives. At its core, digital IMC is about connecting with a target audience and getting them to do something valuable. So marketers must remind themselves to start their digital measurement planning with the desired business outcomes in mind.

Second, marketers must develop the right digital **key performance indicators**, which tell us whether or not digital communications are driving the business toward success. A measure of success can be direct, such as a product purchase, or it can be indirect, such as viewing a product podcast (which suggests that product purchase will happen eventually). Either way, success indicators must be succinctly defined.

Finally, digital communication evaluation must be phrased in a way and in a language that broader business leaders can understand. Due to the range of digital properties that can be measured and the range of key performance indicators that can be captured, reporting communication performance can become quite complex quickly. So digital evaluation experts must keep returning to the business objectives that were set initially and communicate in those terms. According to Read, "Reporting to executive-level audiences is not about showing clicks or views or time spent on digital properties; rather, it is about helping them understand how these things contributed to the broader business goals that they care about—like product sales, customer retention, cross-sell and up-sell."[21]

One final reminder is that digital marketing metrics and the processes that capture them are still in their infancy. This fact was starkly revealed in 2016 when both Facebook and Twitter revealed that they had unintentionally inflated viewership numbers for videos and advertisements appearing on their social networks. In a string of announcements, Facebook admitted that its calculations on viewership and engagement had been inaccurate. This news caused marketers to lose confidence in Facebook's published metrics, but Twitter's errors resulted in advertisers paying more money than they should have. Due to such mishaps, Facebook and others in the industry have begun third-party measurement audits of digital platforms by independent firms such as the Media Rating Council.[22]

International Challenges

International brand communication is difficult to evaluate because of market differences (e.g., language, laws, and cultural norms) and the acceptability of various research tools in different countries. There also may be incompatibilities among various measurement systems and data analysis techniques that make it difficult to compare the data from one market to similar data from another market. An international communication program definitely should focus, at least initially, on pretesting because unfamiliarity with different cultures, languages, and consumer behaviors can result in major miscalculations.

After a campaign has concluded, international evaluation is critical yet difficult. One thing that complicates international campaign evaluation is that countries may have had very different

Can a Broken Guitar Really Hurt United?

Keith Murray, *Bryant University*

It's been a YouTube hit and made the email rounds for a long time—the "United Breaks Guitars" video. It's the story of a musician who made a trip on United Airlines (UA) and was compelled to "check" his Taylor guitar as baggage—which is how UA came to be vulnerable to the charge that, in the handling of it, it damaged the instrument. When asked to make it right—to pay for fixing the Taylor guitar—UA declined.

The musician, Dave Carroll, responded by writing a ballad about the experience and posting it on YouTube. A lot of people viewed the clip; it's catchy and tells the story in an amusing way. People have sent it to their friends, and friends have sent it to their friends, which has led now to literally millions of people seeing it. You can see the video and a CBS report about the incident on YouTube.

So was UA smart to ignore this incident? In other words, did UA really "save" the $1,200 it would have taken to fix the guitar in the first place?

It seems clear that UA might have been shortsighted. If you "do the numbers," you come to the conclusion that UA may have paid a much higher price than it realized.

The following table shows how much money might have been—and is still being—lost by UA from 8 million people (in 2010) seeing the YouTube clip and deciding *against* using UA. It gives various levels of impact from 1 to 10 percent. It also compares the percent of this lost revenue against UA's sales revenue in 2008.

What the calculations show is compelling. If only 1 percent of those who learned of the broken Taylor guitar were affected by the story, UA only lost somewhere between $30 million and $60 million. However, if the negative influence is higher, UA could arguably have forgone as much as half a *billion* dollars, or about 3 percent of its annual sales. In any case, all these figures stand in stark contrast to the $1,200 asked for by Mr. Carroll in the first place.

That gets to the real point of the story: if UA (or any company) has a flawed system to handle and remedy customer complaints—in other words, if UA has customer service "issues" that produce unsatisfactory results for customers—it can pay a very high price for its poor service. And the damage is exponential because the average person tells about 10 people about a bad brand experience, all of which has a chilling effect on patronage by those who hear such tales of woe.

These numbers show the huge impact of failure to pay attention to customer complaints and service system problems. Can one little broken Taylor guitar—and all the other little failures each day—affect a mammoth company like United Airlines? You bet.

Number of $500 Trips Not Taken in a Year	Percent of Viewers Influenced by YouTube Videos to Not Patronize UA in a 12-Month Period			
	1%	2%	5%	10%
One trip	$30 million	$60 million	$150 million	$300 million
% 2008 revenue	0.15	0.31	0.78	1.56
Two trips	$60 million	$120 million	$300 million	$600 million
% 2008 revenue	0.31	0.63	1.56	3.13

starting points (precampaign measurements) with regard to brand awareness, affinity, and the real audience behind the HUT metrics. So, although the campaign can be analyzed in terms of global impact, analysis still must be conducted on a country-by-country level as well. Also, consumers in different countries approach rating scales differently; in parts of Asia, for example, consumers may think that to give a brand a low score on a 1-to-7 scale is less than respectful, so scores that are reported are inflated.

A final challenge in international IMC evaluation lies in the fundamental communication challenges that all multinational companies experience. Getting managers across countries "on the same page" as to how evaluation measures can and should be interpreted is not an easy task.

17.6 Detail ways to determine if a campaign met its objectives.

Back to the Big Picture: Did the Campaign Work?

The ultimate measure of campaign performance is the answer to one seemingly simple question. Did the campaign achieve the objectives that were set at the very beginning of the planning process? Because a planning process can be imperfect, this question is not always so simple.

A model of effects can be developed for a specific campaign and used to drive not only the planning of the effort, but also the evaluation of its effectiveness. For example, one of the goals of a ski resort is to lock in revenue as early as possible. In advance of the ski season, when tasked with the objectives of keeping recent pass holders loyal as well as bringing in competitive pass holders, Vail Resorts introduced its innovative Colorado Pass Club (CPC) and marketed it with biweekly emails full of promotions, offers, and discounts exclusively for pass holders and promotions that ranged from dining and ticket events to discounted lodging and gear. These efforts were supported by radio spots and a special CPC website. What were the results? The number of total season passes sold for the ski season increased 12 percent, and this increase was generated despite a historically low snowfall and a struggling economy. Pass holders loved the brand relationship-building efforts, and so did Vail Resorts.

Remember Adobe's BS campaign at the beginning of the chapter? Adobe used a variety of platforms and media to reach professional marketers with an arresting message that directly spoke to one of the primary challenges they face. Below are two more examples from the campaign. This campaign received a great deal of attention, but did it meet its objectives of visits, inquiries, and sales? You can find out in the It's a Wrap section at the end of the chapter.

Adobe's Marketing Cloud product is designed to help marketers measure outcomes from their campaigns. These ads were developed after Adobe learned of the frustrations of marketing managers, and the integrated campaign included Adobe showing customers the results and effectiveness of this campaign using the Marketing Cloud software.

Photos: © 2017 Adobe Systems Incorporated. All rights reserved. Adobe and the Adobe logo are either registered trademarks or trademarks of Adobe Systems Incorporated in the United States and/or other countries.

Connecting the Dots: Tying Measurement Back to Objectives

Competent brand communication managers return to the campaign objectives—all the various desired effects that were stated up front—and then adequately and realistically measure the campaign's performance against those objectives. Here's an example that demonstrates how evaluation methods should be matched to the original campaign objectives.

Effie Award–winner UPS wanted to reposition itself by broadening its package delivery image.[23] Although UPS dominated ground delivery, it lost out to Federal Express in the overnight and international package market. UPS knew from its customer research that to break out of the "brown and ground" perception, the company had to overcome the inertia of shipping managers who use UPS for ground packages and FedEx for overnight and international. The company also had to shift the perception of senior executives from a company that handles packages to a strategic partner in systems planning. From these insights came three sets of objectives that focused on breaking through awareness, breaking the inertia trance, and breaking the relevance trance.

Here's how the campaign performed on those objectives. Notice the mix of perception, image, and behavioral measures. Also notice that measurement of success was made possible by the presence of baseline and benchmark measures that had been collected in the past; in the absence of such data, it is very difficult for a brand manager or agency to point to significant increases or "wins."

Objective 1: Breaking through Awareness

- Awareness of the Brown campaign outpaced *all* past UPS advertising measured in the 10-plus-year history of its brand tracking study.
- Among those aware of the campaign, correct brand linkage to UPS was 95 to 98 percent across all audiences (compared to a historical average of 20 to 40 percent for past UPS advertising).
- "What Can BROWN Do for You?" has taken hold in popular culture. For instance, the tagline was mentioned in the TV shows *Saturday Night Live* and *Trading Spaces*.

Objective 2: Breaking the Inertia Trance

- With shipping decision makers, the brand showed steady and significant gains in key measures like "Helps my operation run more smoothly," "Dynamic and energetic," and "Offers a broad range of services."
- International shipping profitability increased 150 percent, and overnight volume spiked by 9.1 percent after the campaign ran. The targeted companies' total package volume increased by 4.39 percent.
- From the start of the campaign in March to the year-end, annual ground shipping revenue grew by $300 million.
- The campaign was a hit in terms of response, with a 10.5 percent response rate and an ROI of 1:3.5. In other words, every $1 spent on the campaign generated $3.50 in revenue.

Objective 3: Breaking the Relevance Trance

- For the first time in the 10-plus-year history of the brand tracking study, UPS leads FedEx in all image measures among senior-level decision makers. All significant brand image measures continued upward.
- Among senior decision makers, the biggest gains were in key measures like "For people like me," "Acts as a strategic partner to my company," "Helps in distribution and supply chain operations," and "Provides global competitive advantage."
- At the start of the campaign, annual nonpackage (supply chain) revenue was approximately $1.4 billion. By the end of the year, nonpackage revenue had almost doubled to $2.7 billion. This revenue increase unquestionably represents IMC program success.

The "What Can Brown Do For You" campaign successfully repositioned UPS within the shipping industry as a versatile provider of a wide array of business services. That allowed UPS to further strengthen this positioning through two follow-up campaigns, "We ♥ Logistics" and

Evaluation doesn't just happen at the end of a campaign or after the ad is run. It has to be planned into the campaign from the very beginning by the team responsible.

Photo: Rawpixel.com/Shutterstock

"United Problem Solvers." All these efforts have been designed to support UPS's broader strategy of capturing a greater share of more profitable business services, such as providing temperature-sensitive medical shipping for hospitals and pharmacies and helping brick-and-mortar retailers handle the logistics of e-commerce shipping and returns.[24]

Looking Ahead

Beyond connecting the objectives and the measurements, advertisers continue to search for methods that will bring all the metrics together and efficiently and effectively evaluate brand communication effectiveness. A Florida agency, Zimmerman Advertising, has positioned itself specifically on that issue. Through its "Brandtailing" program, it measures all its initiatives based on ROI success yet also promises to deliver long-term brand building as well as short-term sales.

The leading global public relations and communications firm Burson-Marsteller uses what it calls an "Evidence-Based Approach to Communications." According to its website, this approach is designed as a "scientific approach to communications, driven by data at the beginning, the middle and the end." Also, the site states that "by using Evidence-based tools for benchmarking at the beginning of a program and measuring effectiveness at the end, clients can demonstrate a positive communications ROI."[25] This message certainly meshes with what we have presented as true, "best-practice" IMC throughout this chapter.

Ultimately, the goal is to arrive at holistic, cross-functional metrics that are relevant for integrated communication, a task undertaken by Dell Computers and its agency DDB. Given Dell's direct-marketing business model, the company had extensive call and order data in its database. DDB helped organize the collection of detailed marcom information, which made it possible to begin linking orders to specific marcom activities. This new marcom ROI tracking system made it possible for Dell to recognize a 3 percent gain in the efficiency of its marketing communication. As the metrics system became more sophisticated, it also began to move from a reporting and metrics evaluation engine to a strategic tool providing deeper insights into consumer behavior.[26]

Many pieces are still missing in the evaluation of complex IMC programs. Research think tanks are struggling to find better ways to measure consumers' emotional connections to brands and brands' relationships with their customers[27] and how marketing communication messages affect those connections and relationships. But let's end with an inspirational video called "Life Lessons from an Ad Man." It's a little old, but Rory Sutherland makes several good points in an entertaining manner about how marketing communication can increase the intangible value consumers ascribe to brands. See it at www.ted.com.

Metrics, Not Myths: Adobe Systems

Adobe

No more "BS"

At the beginning of the chapter, you read about Adobe's efforts to launch its Marketing Cloud products into the digital metrics market using a provocative campaign that challenged marketing myths. Now you'll find out about its effectiveness.

On the day the campaign launched, traffic to the Marketing Cloud website was up nearly 10 times. Within the first three days, Adobe generated more than 2,200 social media mentions and drove 1.1 million views of the campaign's video series. By the end of the first week, Adobe garnered more than 60 media placements with top-tier outlets such as *CNBC*, the *New York Times*, *Mashable*, and *Forbes*. Over the course of the campaign, Adobe:

- Generated 96 million views of its Metrics Not Myths video series.
- Experienced a 45 percent increase in direct sales inquiries.
- Received more than 5,000 mentions of "Adobe Marketing Cloud" on social media channels and nearly unanimous positive/neutral sentiment of the "#MetricsNotMyths" Twitter hashtag.
- Exceeded its goal to drive site visits to its digital marketing pages by 206 percent.
- Grew its Facebook community by more than 40 percent.
- Achieved five times its objective of engagement with a 30 percent PTAT (People Talking About This) score.
- Had double-digit increases for Adobe in the digital marketing space on every brand-tracker category.

Figure 17.4 reflects how well the "sales funnel" worked for the campaign.

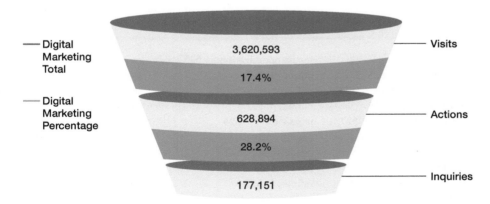

FIGURE 17.4
Adobe "Metrics Not Myths" Campaign Outcomes

The success of the "Metrics, Not Myths" campaign shows that the conversation among marketing professionals regarding the effectiveness of digital marketing was long overdue. The message resonated well with professional digital marketers looking to go "from zeros to heroes" within their organizations. Adobe exceeded its objectives for the campaign on every metric and earned the company mind share, market space, and a new stream of revenue in the digital marketing category. And that's no BS.

17.1. Explain why it is important to evaluate brand communication effectiveness. Marketing communication evaluation is used to test, monitor, measure, and diagnose the effectiveness of IMC messages. Without campaign evaluation, marketers cannot know whether IMC efforts had any impact; they also do not know how to improve on their current campaign.

17.2. Discuss the role campaign objectives play in the measurement of campaign success. Campaign objectives set the stage for measurement. Based on objectives, companies can determine exactly what to measure and which tools to use to evaluate campaign success.

17.3. Describe the key ways in which campaign evaluation is conducted. Campaign evaluation is conducted using tracking studies, scanner analyses, and single-source research, among other methods. Campaign research also is conducted for various IMC tools (e.g., digital) specifically and to understand the wisdom of media choices.

17.4. Explain how the performance of media vehicles is evaluated. One of the biggest challenges in media planning is media efficiency—getting the most for the money invested. For major campaigns, agencies do postbuy analyses, which involve checking the media plan against the performance of each media vehicle. A critical question is whether campaign reach and frequency objectives were obtained. Just because audience members have been exposed to marketing communication does not mean they have paid attention to it, and media professionals must

always keep that in the top of their mind. Each media vehicle has its own metrics and means of assessing performance. Newspapers and other traditional media have fairly straightforward metrics: readership, circulation, coverage, ratings, and gross rating points. However, media performance is more difficult to estimate for out-of-home media, digital media, and alternative media. However, media planners have developed innovative new technological means of assessing even these.

17.5. List some of the key challenges faced in evaluating IMC effectiveness. Key challenges relate to difficulties in assessing monetary return on campaign investment. Also, building communication programs that span many types of traditional and digital media, not to mention different cultures, requires special team-building skills and analytical talents.

17.6. Detail ways to determine if a campaign met its objectives. Competent brand communication managers return to the campaign objectives—all the various desired effects that were stated up front—and then objectively measure the campaign's performance against those objectives. A good campaign assessment should compare pre-campaign and post-campaign measures of perception, image, consumer preferences, and behaviors. Measurements of success are only possible if past baseline and benchmark measures are present. If these measures or data are not available, it is very difficult for a brand manager or agency to point to significant changes to these key metrics due to an IMC campaign.

aided recall, p. 521
brand communication ROI, p. 527
brand linkage test, p. 521
break-even analysis, p. 524
carryover effects, p. 529
circulation, p. 527
click-through rates, p. 524
concept testing, p. 516
conversion rate, p. 525
cost per lead, p. 524

coverage, p. 527
(digital) ecosystem, p. 525
experiential marketing, p. 525
gross impressions, p. 527
guaranteed circulation, p. 527
households using television (HUT), p. 527
inquiry tests, p. 521
instantaneous effects, p. 529
key performance indicators, p. 530

media optimization, p. 525
norms, p. 517
outcome, p. 522
output, p. 522
page views, p. 524
payout analysis, p. 524
posttesting, p. 522
pretesting, p. 516
ratings, p. 527
readership, p. 527
recall test, p. 521

recognition test, p. 521
scanner research, p. 520
semiotic analysis, p. 516
single-source data, p. 520
single-source research, p. 521
surrogate measures, p. 517
synergistic effect, p. 529
test marketing, p. 528
total audience, p. 527
tracking studies, p. 519
unaided recall, p. 521

MyLab Marketing

Go to **www.pearson.com/mylab/marketing** for MyLab discussion questions (⬤) as well as the following assisted-graded writing questions.

17-1. What is a tracking study, and how is it used?

17-2. Historically, marketing experts have found the evaluation of traditional media to be easier than the evaluation of digital media. How is that changing?

REVIEW QUESTIONS

17-3. Why is the setting of campaign objectives important?

17-4. Why is campaign measurement becoming more important than it used to be?

17-5. What is single-source research, and how do scanner data relate to it?

17-6. What is media optimization, and how do we evaluate how close we are to achieving it?

17-7. Why is an IMC campaign difficult to evaluate?

17-8. What are some challenges posed by evaluating digital efforts in particular?

DISCUSSION QUESTIONS

17-9. Most clients want a quick and easy answer to the question of whether an IMC program works. Advertising professionals, however, tend to believe that a sales-only approach to evaluation is not appropriate. Why do they think that way? If you were helping an agency prepare for a presentation on its campaign results, what would you suggest the agency say to explain away the idea that you can evaluate a campaign with a single sales measure?

17-10. You are hiring a research consulting company to help a client evaluate the effectiveness of its communication efforts. One of the consultants recommends using focus groups to evaluate their effectiveness. Another consultant says that focus groups aren't very effective for campaign evaluation and recommends other measures. Which viewpoint do you believe is most insightful? For campaign evaluation purposes, is qualitative or quantitative research used most often?

17-11. Explore the websites of two IMC evaluation companies, such as Ameritest (www.Ameritest.net), Ipsos ASI (www.ipsos.com), Millward Brown (www.millwardbrown.com), or Sapient (www.sapient.com), and compare the services they offer. If you were looking for a company to evaluate a campaign for recall, which one would you prefer? Why? What if you were looking for a company to evaluate a campaign for digital impact? Why?

TAKE-HOME PROJECTS

17-12. *Portfolio Project:* Put together a portfolio of 10 ads for a set of product categories targeted to a college audience. Set up a focus group with participants recruited from among your friends and ask them to look at the ads. In a test of unaided awareness, ask them to list the ads they remember. Identify the top-performing ad and the bottom ad in this awareness test. Now ask the focus group participants to analyze the headline, the visual, and the brand identification of each of these two ads. How do the two ads compare in terms of their ability to get attention and lock the brand in memory?

17-13. *Mini-Case Analysis:* Reread the chapter-opening story about Adobe's Marketing Cloud software. Explain what is meant when we say the point of this campaign is to change the relationship these professionals had with the Adobe brand. How did this campaign succeed in that objective? How was effectiveness determined? If you were on the marketing team and were asked to develop a broader set of evaluation tools, what would you recommend and why?

TRACE North America Case

Evaluating Campaign Effectiveness

Read the TRACE case in the Appendix before coming to class.

17-14. If you worked for TRACE, how would you pretest this campaign prior to using it across the country?

17-15. What methods would you use to conduct concurrent and posttesting of the campaign?

17-16. If you worked for TRACE, how would you evaluate the success of the "Hard to Explain, Easy to Experience" campaign in the market year to year?

18

Social Impact, Responsibility, and Ethics: Is It Right?

With a huge potential to make a significant impact on society, brand communicators shoulder the responsibility for choosing what products and ideas they want to advertise, what messages they communicate, and how they want to communicate them. In this chapter, you'll explore the impact of brand communication on society, study ongoing debates about the power of communication, and examine issues related to social and ethical responsibility. Finally, you will learn about some key legal and regulatory processes that ensure that harmful communication is minimized.

Campaign	Company	Agency	Awards
Social Media	*TOMS*	*N/A*	*2015 Next Generation Award, Harvard T. H. Chan School of Public Health; 2013's "Five Best Communicators in the World, USA Today; Keynote Speaker, SXSW Interactive, 2014*

Sole Purpose: Selling Shoes with a Soul

Photo: Tiffany Rose/Contributor/WireImage

Photo: Adrian Lourie/Alamy Stock Photo

Chances are that you own a pair of TOMS shoes or know someone who does. If you do, you might want to know more about their backstory. It's an inspiring account about a man on a mission who hopes to see a future of social-minded businesses and consumers. And no, his name isn't Tom.

Chronicled in his *New York Times* best seller, *Start Something That Matters*, and on the TOMS website, it is the story of Blake Mycoskie, founder and chief shoe giver of TOMS. A college dropout, Mycoskie started several businesses, including a campus laundry and an outdoor advertising company, before he created the concept for TOMS and the idea of One for One, a business model the helps a person in need for every product purchased.

Photo: Ali Bura fi/Associated Press

Ever the entrepreneur and free spirit, 29-year-old Blake revisited Argentina in 2006 after having first seen the country with his sister as a participant on the CBS reality show *Amazing Race* (and losing the top $1 million prize by a mere four minutes). During the second visit, he immersed himself in the culture, learning how to tango, play polo, and drink the national wine. He also wore the national shoe, the *alpargata*, a soft, canvas shoe sported by nearly everyone in the country.

While in Buenos Aires, he met an American woman who volunteered with a small group of people on a shoe drive, helping get shoes to kids who lacked them. He toured several villages, which heightened his awareness of the poverty of so many children. An idea began to form in his head. Instead of creating a charity to provide shoes, why not create a *for-profit* business to help provide shoes?

Taking the first step, he came up with a novel concept: sell a pair of shoes today and give a pair tomorrow. And what should he name his new company? "Shoes for a Better Tomorrow" soon morphed into "Tomorrow's Shoes" and then into "TOMS" that you know today. Mycoskie's initial goal was to sell 250 pairs of shoes so that he could send 250 pairs to children in Argentina.

Publicity played a large role in the success of TOMS. What Mycoskie thought would be a short article by the *Los Angeles Times* fashion writer turned up on the front page, and orders poured in. By the end of the day, he'd sold 2,200 pairs of shoes, which was a bit of a problem because he didn't even have 200 pairs on hand.

Nonetheless, success grew by leaps and bounds as *Vogue, People, O, Time,* and *Elle* ran other stories. Photographers snapped pix of celebrities like Tobey Maguire, Kiera Knightley, and Scarlett Johansson wearing their TOMS. Upscale retailers like Nordstrom insisted on carrying the brand. By the end of the summer, more than 10,000 pairs of TOMS had been sold.

By 2011, TOMS had an annual growth rate of 300 percent and had given away 10 million pairs of shoes. Today TOMS has stepped beyond shoes. It now is in the business of distributing pairs of glasses or medical treatments in exchange for sunglasses sold. It distributes clean water for coffee, and TOMS Roasting launched in Whole Foods stores and TOMS's own cafés. TOMS Bag Collection help kits ensure the safe birth of babies in areas of need.

This case provides important lessons for those concerned with creating and promoting a business and the social impact of the work. According to Mycoskie, a third of the revenue has come from direct-to-consumer sales via the website, and virtually no money was spent on traditional advertising. Instead, 5 million social media followers spread the word.

The power of the story at the heart of the communication is critical. According to Mycoskie, your success depends not on your experience or degrees or who you know. You need to have a memorable story and know your mission. As we've stated repeatedly in this book, companies can no longer rely solely on traditional ad campaigns. In this fragmented media world, people gather information about brands from a multitude of sources, following people on Twitter feeds and blogs, watching Hulu, and surfing iPads, to name a few. Consumers are smart enough to learn and check comments about brands and products online.

You've got to know what business you are in if you are a brand communicator. As Mycoskie said, "We weren't selling shoes; we were selling the promise that each purchase would directly and tangibly benefit a child who needed shoes." As the company grew more successful, Mycoskie realized that it wasn't only the successful production of shoes that mattered. Instead, it was the high he got from starting things and doing the unexpected, like creating a new business model for selling shoes and helping others and then venturing first into the coffee business—and reconnecting with his mission of improving lives.

To learn more about the social impact of TOMS, turn to the It's a Wrap feature at the end of the chapter.

Sources: www.toms.com; Blake Mycoskie, "The Founder of TOMS on Reimagining the Company's Mission," *Harvard Business Review*, January–February 2016, www.hbr.org; Blake Mycoskie, 2011, *Start Something That Matters* (New York: Random House, 2011); Jessica Weiss, "TOMS Sets Out to Sell a Lifestyle, Not Just Shoes," July/August 2013, www.fastcompany.com; "TOMS shoes," *Wikipedia*, last modified August 22, 2017, www.wikipedia.org.

What Is the Social Impact of Brand Communication?

18.1 Name and discuss the key debates related to the social impact of brand communication.

As we've repeatedly said in this book, at its core, effective brand communication is about building brand integrity and a trustworthy reputation. Brands take on meaning when consumers see that all areas of marketing communication about the brand are consistent and authentic. Communicators want the recipients of their messages to feel positive about the brand but not at the expense of doing what is right both ethically and legally.

The TOMS story is a good example of communicating authentically with its key audience. The campaign teaches us that messages do not necessarily need to be entertaining to be effective, but they need to tell compelling messages that resonate with their audiences. TOMS appeals to consumers who want to buy shoes and join the company in improving lives.

Most communication about brands is either neutral or positive, meaning that brand stewards recognize that their product, service, or organization has an obligation to benefit society in some way. They value their brand's duty to demonstrate **social responsibility**. Examples of companies that aspire to be socially responsible with their brands are plentiful.[1] As you've just read, TOMS donates a pair of shoes to a child in need for every pair of its shoes that are sold. Premium ice-cream maker Häagen-Dazs, a brand known for its all-natural ingredients, fittingly created a campaign to help find a solution to the mysterious disappearance of honeybees. General Electric's "Ecomagination" campaign focuses on using renewable energy and reducing carbon emissions.

The profession also seeks to do good. The Ad Council (www.adcouncil.org) is a professional organization whose mission is to make a difference in society through communications programs about significant public issues. You can see the Ad Council's public service announcements, like the Smokey Bear work created to prevent wildfires, at www .psacentral.org.

These examples provide evidence that most brand professionals strive to do good. Brand managers work hard to protect the integrity of their brands and make sure the communication about the brand is consistent. One problem with brand consistency occurs when there are ethical questions about practices that undercut the brand, as explained next.

What Are the Key Debates about the Social Impact of Marketing Communication?

Marketing communication, particularly advertising, sometimes draws criticism for its social impact, so much of the discussion that follows is focused on advertising because of its high visibility. We review some of the debates related to advertising's role in society from the perspectives of advertising as an institution and as an applied practice. Our intention is to review the criticisms, but understand that we believe that advertising is a good force in society and in our economy even though it may sometimes be used in ways that generate concern.

Public relations also plays a major role in a brand's demonstration of social responsibility, and you've already read some about that in Chapter 3. Developing a positive relationship between the client and its audiences is the core of the public relations profession, and demonstrating the ability to have a positive social impact is a way to accomplish that goal.

Read the Inside Story by Mary Nichols, founder of Karmic Marketing based in Portland, Oregon, for an example about how she helped a small nonprofit organization in that city increase its donations—and its good relationship with the community. Farmers Ending Hunger (FEH) lines up farmers to donate crops to the Oregon Food Bank and then organizes transportation for the crops. Her work for FEH received the People's Choice Award by SoMe, a national organization that honors the best social media projects and campaigns in the United States.

Sprinkled throughout this book are "Principled Practice" boxes that emphasize the importance of social and ethical responsibility. The following are some of the key social responsibility issues that fuel debates.

Can Advertising Create Demand?   Some critics charge that advertising causes **demand creation**, which results when an external message drives people to feel a need or want, sometimes unnecessarily. A 2009 Harris Poll indicated that two-thirds of Americans believed ad agencies were at least partially to blame for the economic crisis in 2008 because they caused people to buy things they couldn't afford.[2] Others reject this notion. Does advertising create demand for products people don't need? Has advertising convinced you to buy products you don't need? Why would consumers buy an expensive Porsche when a stripped-down version Kia would provide the same ability to transport them from point A to point B?

Let's start the discussion by considering deodorants. Did you know that no one used deodorants much before 1919? People didn't worry about having body odor. An ad for a new product, Odorono (a great name, and it's still being used, by the way), targeted women because everyone assumed that men were supposed to emit bad odors and that women would be the more likely users of the product. The launch ad in *Ladies' Home Journal* so offended readers that about 200 people canceled their subscription. The ads were effective, however. Sales for

Farmers Ending Hunger

Mary Nichols, *Founder and Chief Community Builder, Karmic Marketing*

Oregon—the state that wins awards for healthy lifestyles and fit people—has some other statistics that aren't so wonderful. Oregon is the number one state in the country for food insecurity for children, it's the third-hungriest state in the nation, and one in five Oregonians is on food stamps.

When I was asked to help with the organization's marketing, the first thing I did was create a set of realistic objectives that included building awareness, getting more donations, and building relationships with current and new donors through social media. We also wanted to increase the Facebook fan base, gather data on donors from our online donation program, create an email list database, and upgrade the website to better describe Farmers Ending Hunger (FEH) and our Adopt-an-Acre program.

Adopt-an-Acre was the Big Idea that demonstrated how far donations go in addressing the food crisis. Adopting one acre (a $250 contribution), for example, feeds pancakes to 2,300 families of four; adopting two acres ($500) feeds fresh vegetables for one day to 1,000 families.

To help FEH with its lack of visibility, we created a new easy-to-use website (www.farmersendinghunger.com).

A customer relationship management system was integrated into the site to capture donor information as well as set up recurring monthly donations.

We started cross promoting other like-minded organizations and supporters in all our Facebook posts. We realized that not all target donors were on Facebook, so we also sought personal contact at the biggest farmers' markets in Portland.

At the markets, we got other vendors to donate vegetables, and we created a "Build your own Mr. Potato Head" as a children's activity. While the kids were occupied, we told their parents about FEH and encouraged them to donate. We took photos of the kids who wanted to be photographed and encouraged parents to go to our Facebook page, "like" it, and download the photos.

We also attended the Nike Farmers' Market, earning approval to be on the Nike Global Giving website, where all employee donations are matched by the company.

Recognition, such as the *Portland Monthly* "Light a Fire," *Willamette Week* Give Guide, and the SoMe award, earned media stories. In terms of quantifiable results, we increased Facebook followers by more than 310 percent, added 1,500 email subscribers (versus none a year ago), earned 45 media feature stories, and, best of all, saw an increase of more than 48 percent in donations versus the previous year.

This organization inspires me—and I like to think I helped a little in dealing with the hunger crisis in Oregon.

Logo: Mary Nichols, Founder and Chief Community Builder, Karmic Marketing

---

the deodorant rose 112 percent.[3] Did advertising make women buy something they didn't even know they needed? Was that a bad thing?

If you think it doesn't happen today, think about Unilever's Axe product. Axe pioneered the new category of body spray for men in 2002. Did guys know before 2002 that they needed scented body spray? Is it a good thing that advertising entices people to buy products like deodorants and body sprays? Can such advertising improve consumers' lives?

Companies often conduct significant research to find out what consumers want before they launch new products. If people do not want the products being marketed, they do not buy them. Advertising may convince people to buy a product—even a bad one—once. If they try the product and don't like it, they won't buy it again. (Ask your friends who owned the defective Samsung Galaxy Note 7 phones.) In this day and digital age, word spreads fast, and their friends won't buy it either. So, to some extent, advertising creates demand. At the same time, it is important to remember that audiences may refuse to purchase the product if they don't feel a need for it.

● **Principle**
If people do not want the products being marketed, they do not buy them.

Does Advertising Mirror Social Values or Shape Them? Another important debate about advertising's role in society questions the limits of its influence. At what point does advertising cross the line between reflecting social values and creating them? Professionals believe they are

Within the Curve of a Woman's Arm
A frank discussion of a subject too often avoided

Photo: David M. Rubenstein Rare Book & Manuscript Library

CLASSIC

A. J. Walter Thompson ad for Odorono deodorant was so startling that readers begged the Ladies' Home Journal *to stop running the ad. It was considered disgusting then, but how do you see it now?*

reflecting the values of their society. Critics argue that advertising has repeatedly crossed this line, influencing vulnerable groups, such as children and young teenagers, too strongly.

For example, do ultrathin models in advertising cause young women to have eating disorders, as some have claimed? Although it is probable that the images women and girls see influence them in some ways, it's difficult to say that these images directly and solely cause the problem because many factors in a person's environment potentially influence eating choices. Some research, however, supports the view that advertising is partly to blame; advertising may contribute to the problem. What do you think?

Can advertising manipulate people's choices? Critics of advertising argue that it can create social trends and has the power to dictate how people think and act. They believe that even if an individual ad cannot control behavior, the cumulative effects of nonstop television, radio, print, internet, and out-of-home and social media can be overwhelming. Others contend that effective brand communication spots trends and then develops messages that connect target audiences with the trends. In other words, if people are interested in achieving healthy lifestyles, you will see ads that use health appeals as an advertising strategy. In this way, advertising mirrors values rather than sets them. Do you agree with that argument?

This shape-versus-mirror debate is the most central issue we address in considering advertising and public relations' role in society. What drives consumers to behave or believe as they do? Is it promotional communication, or is it other forces? Why do women buy cosmetics, for example? Are they satisfying a deep cultural need for beauty, or were they manipulated by advertising to believe in the hope that cosmetics offer? Women can even purchase a product by the cosmetics company Philosophy called Hope in a Jar. Or have their families and friends socialized them to believe they look better with makeup than without? Like the lesson we learned in the TOMS story, we need to consider what is really being sold: shoes, improving lives, or both? And what are the cultural forces that underlie the decision? It's complicated to decipher. Advertising and societal values are interwoven, so the answer to the debate may simply be that advertising both mirrors and shapes values.

Does Advertising Cause People to Be Too Materialistic?   The years since the 1960s are notable for the rise of a materialistic consumer culture in the Western world, and some argue that it is overly commercialized, too materialistic. Consider the Nike Zoom LeBron Soldier 10iD basketball shoe, which costs more than $180. Do we need these shoes that can be customized? Who will buy them? Did advertising create this culture, or does it simply reflect a natural striving for the good life?

Some argue that advertising heightens expectations and primes the audience to believe that the answer is always a product. If you have a headache, what do you do? You take a pill. The pill may actually make your headache vanish. What is left unsaid by an advertisement is that you might get rid of the headache just as easily by taking a nap, drinking less alcohol or more water, or taking a walk to relieve stress. Nobody pays for ads to tell you about free alternatives. Consumers, however, are not always passively doing what advertisers tell them. As we have said, they have the power to refuse to buy what is being sold if they think about it.

Should Some Audiences Be Protected from Advertising?   Marketing to youth is one of the most controversial topics in the industry. One reason advertising to children attracts so much attention is that children are seen as vulnerable. Children do not always know what is good for them and what is not. Concerned adults want to make sure that they protect impressionable minds from exploitative marketers. (A similar argument is made regarding older adults, who, some fear, are vulnerable to scams and other unscrupulous techniques.) They want to help children learn to make good choices. Do you think that is a valid argument? Are children highly impressed by advertising? How should marketing to vulnerable audiences be regulated? Who gets to decide what's good for these audiences?

A current issue that's being addressed relates to selling soft drinks, candy, and food with high fat and sugar content to children. Recognizing that obesity among youth is a major health problem, the Council of Better Business Bureaus launched the Children's Food and Beverage Advertising Initiative to help 10 major corporations set guidelines to cut down on junk-food advertising. The companies, which are responsible for producing almost two-thirds of the food and drink advertising for children under 12, include General Mills, McDonald's, Coca-Cola, PepsiCo, Hershey, and Kellogg. Marketing alcohol to black teens is another important issue because of the use of rappers like Ice-T to promote malt liquors and the dozens of pages of alcohol ads that appear in black youth–culture magazines such as *Vibe*. A Georgetown University study stirred a national controversy when it reported that the alcohol beverage industry is marketing far more heavily to African American young people than to others in that age group.[4]

You'll read more about the important issue of advertising to children in the regulation section of this chapter.

What Are the Key Debates and Issues about Brand Communication Practices?

Next we'll give you a checklist of issues that can have a negative impact on brands if the communication does not align with the brand image or respect the audience.

Does Brand Communication Fairly and Accurately Portray People?   Stereotypes are a big issue, as are other problems, such as cultural relevance and honesty.

• *Diversity and Stereotypes* Athletic blacks, feeble seniors, sexy Italians, smart Asians: you're probably familiar with these and other examples of stereotypes. A **stereotype** is a representation of a cultural group that emphasizes a trait or group of traits that may or may not communicate an accurate representation of the group. Sometimes the stereotype is useful (athletes are fit) and aids communication by using easily understood symbolic meanings, but sometimes the stereotype relies on a characteristic that is negative or exaggerated and, in so doing, reduces the group to a caricature. That is the problem with portraying older adults as all being absentminded or feeble, for instance.

 Here's another example. Think about sports teams like the Washington Redskins, Kansas City Chiefs, and Cleveland Indians. Critics claim these sports names and images reduce Native Americans to a caricature and claim that racial and ethnic groups are stereotyped in their promotions. Do you believe these team names and logos represent negative stereotypes, and, if so, what should be done about them when millions of dollars have been invested in building these brands?

 The issue of stereotyping also raises the shape-versus-mirror question. For example, stereotyping women as sex objects is a practice that is deeply embedded in our culture. Using such strategies also makes advertising a participant in shaping and reinforcing that cultural value.

 Intentionally or not, communicators choose how they portray people in their ads. Even the absence of a particular group of people, such as seemingly invisible older adults, communicates a message. If they are not included, are they important?

 Portraying groups negatively can damage brand relationships with consumers. Marketers who see their audiences in stereotypical ways can also hinder their efforts to communicate effectively. Cohort groups, like millennials, are not homogenous, and marketers need to approach them not as a monolithic group but through segmentation based on a number of attributes like age, culture, and income.[5] Reducing millennials to stereotypes—such as they aren't loyal and have short attention spans, they only shop online, and they are cheap—fails to recognize buying differences that call for different marketing strategies.

• *Cultural Differences in Global Advertising* In the global economy, advertisers seek worldwide audiences for their products. As they do so, they sometimes make mistakes overlaying their worldview on that of another culture without thinking about the impact of the message.

Respecting a Muslim Perspective

Robert Meeds, *California State University, Fullerton*

Nearly one-fourth of the world's population and almost 50 countries are Muslim, which makes advertising to Muslims an essential part of the marketing mix for global brands. In addition to the Arab League countries of the Middle East and Africa, many large non-Arab countries such as Indonesia, Turkey, Iran, and Bangladesh are also predominantly Muslim. With such diverse worldwide Muslim audiences, advertisers are wise to adapt to local markets and sensibilities.

Similar to Christmas and the winter holidays in Western countries, the holy month of Ramadan is a major annual shopping (and therefore advertising) event. Gift retailers, tourism companies, and even car dealers and home appliance retailers all compete for Muslim consumers' attention during this high-spending holiday time. And even though Ramadan includes daily fasting from sunrise to sunset for observant Muslims, restaurants and grocery stores also have promotions for Iftar (the evening breaking of the fast where large groups of friends and family gather for elaborate meals and celebrations).

In most Muslim countries, you will see a mix of standardization and localization approaches to advertising for global brands. Localized advertising approaches may include photos or illustrations of models in traditional local attire, or ads may feature specific regional items, such as McDonald's Halloumi Muffin sandwich (halloumi is a dense, salty cheese popular throughout the Mediterranean and Arab regions). And although not an Islamic consideration, another localized approach to advertising commonly seen in Arab countries is to flip the layouts of ads and use an "S" eye-flow approach instead of an "inverted S" eye flow approach often seen in Western ads. That's because Arabic is a language that reads from right to left instead of left to right.

The Islamic concepts of halal and haram are important for advertisers to keep in mind because they govern diet, behavior, and all matters of daily life in Islam. Halal is an Arabic word that means something is permitted; haram means something is forbidden. In many Muslim countries, it is not legal to advertise products such as alcohol that are considered haram, even if the products can be legally sold. Although not all Muslims agree on everything that is halal or haram, most advertisers try to avoid running ads that the more conservative members of Muslim societies might find offensive. As such, you typically won't see ads featuring scantily clad models or creative concepts based on risqué double entendres. And in the more conservative Muslim countries, ads including pictures of Muslim women can also be considered haram.

For these reasons, many advertisers play it safe with their marketing in Muslim countries and run informational campaigns that focus on the product rather than emotional campaigns that may not translate well or be consistent with the cultural values of the audience.

Concerns about the homogenization of cultural differences are expressed as **marketing imperialism** or **cultural imperialism**. These terms are used to describe what happens when Western culture is imposed on others, particularly Middle East, Asian, and African cultures. Some Asian and Middle Eastern countries are critical of what they see as America's materialism, disrespectful behavior toward elders, and appeals to sex. They worry that **international advertising** and media will encourage their young people to adopt these viewpoints.

Consider that respect for culture and local customs is so important that insensitivity to local customs can make an ad completely ineffective. Customs can be even stronger than laws. When advertising to children age 12 or older was approved in Germany, for example, local customs were so strong that companies risked customer revolt by advertising. In many countries, naming a competitor in comparative advertising is considered bad form.

See the Matter of Principle box by Robert Meeds, who writes about the importance of understanding the Muslim culture.

- *Sex Appeals and Body Image* Advertising that portrays women (or men) as sex objects is considered demeaning and sexist, particularly if sex is not relevant to the product. Sometimes ads use sex appeals that are relevant, such as Victoria's Secret ads. The ethical question, then, is, when is sexy is too sexy? Transit authorities in two Canadian cities decided that Virgin Mobile's ads were too racy for the public and asked the company to pull risqué ads from bus shelters that showed embracing couples and invited viewers to "Hook up fearlessly."[6]

Playing on consumers' insecurities about their appearance presents advertisers with a classic ethical dilemma because self-image advertising can be seen as contributing to self-improvement, but sometimes such advertising is questionable because it leads to dangerous practices. Some critics charge that women place their health at risk to cultivate an unrealistic or even unhealthy physical appearance. Supermodels don't always project healthy portrayals of women. Do you think advertising sends this message?

The same problem of physical appearance exists for men, particularly young men, although the muscular ideal body may not lead to the same health-threatening reactions that young women face unless men resort to steroids to attain this image. The standard of attractiveness is a sociocultural phenomenon that both mirrors and shapes our ideals. Responsible advertisers have therefore begun using models of more normal size and weight as a way to reduce the pressure on young people. The "Dove Campaign for Real Beauty" that you read about in Chapter 7 defies the notion that women need to be thin to be beautiful. Lane Bryant, the plus-size retailer, is also shattering stereotypes by tackling issues related to body shaming, trying to make it an unacceptable form of discrimination with its "Shine On" campaign and #ThisBodyIsMadeToShine.

- *Poor Taste and Offensive Advertising* Although certain ads might be in bad taste in any circumstance, viewer reactions are affected by such factors as sensitivity to the product category, timing (e.g., if the message is received in the middle of dinner), and other circumstances, such as whether the person is alone or with others when viewing the message. Some television ads, for example, might not bother adults watching alone but would make them uncomfortable if children were watching.

Nationwide suffered a severe backlash from offended viewers who reacted negatively to a depressing commercial about preventable injuries that lead to childhood death that aired during the Super Bowl. The depressing commercial didn't match the fun environment of the game.

Also, some ads become offensive in the wrong context. Advertisers and media outlets must try to be sensitive to such objections. Outraged advertisers, including Applebee's, General Mills, and Kraft, pulled ads from Fox News Channel's *Glenn Beck* program after the host called President Barack Obama a "racist" with a "deep-seated hatred for white people." They didn't want their brands to be associated with such disparaging remarks.

Sometimes messages are just plain offensive, no matter in what context they appear. A GoDaddy commercial that offended many was pulled from the Super Bowl after viewers saw the sneak preview and complained that the advertiser appeared to be promoting puppy mills. GoDaddy took swift action and pulled the commercial.

We all have our own ideas about what constitutes good taste. Unfortunately, these ideas vary so much that creating general guidelines for good taste in advertising is difficult. Different things offend different people at different times. In addition, taste changes over time. What was offensive yesterday may not be considered offensive today. The Odorono ad offended people in 1919, but would it today? By today's standards, that advertisement seems pretty tame. Today's questions of taste center on the use of sexual innuendo, nudity, vulgarity, and violence. What about the Axe ads for male body sprays? Do you find them offensive or in good taste?

An ad can be offensive to the general public even if the targeted audience accepts it, which is the point behind the Axe ads. Brand communicators would be wise to conduct research to gauge the standards of taste for the general population as well as the specific target audience. If they fail to do so, they risk alienating potential consumers. Some might argue that any publicity is good publicity and that offensive advertising calls attention to your product in a memorable way. However, over time, it may damage a brand's precious reputation.

● **Principle**
Good taste is a difficult standard to apply because different things offend different people at different times.

Is Communication Honest and Transparent? Even though most advertisers and public relations professionals try to create messages that communicate fairly and accurately, communicators need to understand what is not considered acceptable so that they can avoid unethical and even illegal behavior. Advertising claims are considered to be unethical if they are false, misleading, or deceptive. In the drive to find something to say about a product that will catch attention and motivate the audience to respond, advertisers sometimes stretch the truth. **False advertising**, which is a type of misleading advertising, is simply a message that is untrue. Misleading claims, puffery, comparative advertising, endorsements, and product demonstrations are explained next.

● **Principle**
Advertising claims are unethical if they are false, misleading, or deceptive.

- *Misleading Claims and Puffery* Consumers have sometimes been targets of unfair, deceptive, or fraudulent practices in the marketplace. Misleading claims in weight-loss advertising or burying hidden costs such as shipping fees are examples of types of issues that arise. Volkswagen, for instance, promoted "clean diesel" in its vehicles, claims that were later discovered to be untrue. To protect consumers from misleading claims and promote competition, the **Federal Trade Commission (FTC)**, a government regulatory body, helps regulate these unfair practices. In the Volkswagen case, the FTC sought a court order seeking compensation for consumers who'd bought or leased the diesel cars based on false claims that the cars were low emission.[7] The scandal cost the company about $20 billion to settle lawsuits and recall nearly 11 million vehicles worldwide.[8] The harm done to the brand in the loss of trust can't be measured by a dollar amount.

  Misleading claims are not just a problem in the United States. Makeup company L'Oreal accused its rival Christian Dior of misleading consumers with its ad featuring Natalie Portman wearing Christian Dior mascara. It charged that the ad had been digitally retouched and that consumers would unrealistically believe that they, too, could have spectacularly long lashes. Britain's Advertising Standards Authority banned the ads.[9]

  Not all exaggerated claims are considered misleading. **Puffery** is defined as "advertising or other sales representations, which praise the item to be sold with subjective opinions, superlatives, or exaggerations, vaguely and generally, stating no specific facts."[10] Campbell Soup, for example, has used the slogan "M'm!, M'm!, Good!," which is vague and can't really be proven or disproven. It's a classic example of puffery, generally deemed to be of little concern to regulators looking for false or misleading claims because it is so innocuous.

  Obviously exaggerated "puffing" claims are legal, so the question of puffery is mainly an ethical one. According to the courts, consumers expect exaggerations and inflated claims in advertising, so reasonable people wouldn't believe that these statements ("puffs") are literal facts. One noted advertising scholar, the late Ivan Preston, a former member of this book's Advisory Board, dedicated his professional life to studying puffery and misleading advertising. He found the original "proof" that no one believes puffery or what those literal claims imply: a British common law case in 1602 declared it as so obvious that no evidence was needed. However, empirical evidence on the effectiveness of puffery is mixed. Some research suggests that the public might expect advertisers to be able to prove the truth of superlative claims, and other research indicates that reasonable people do not believe such claims. This issue is particularly important when advertising to vulnerable audiences such as children who might not know the difference between fact and opinion.

- *Comparative Advertising* We're used to seeing advertisers take on their competition in an ad: Macintosh versus Microsoft, Dunkin' Donuts versus Starbucks, Campbell's Soup versus Progresso. Although it is perfectly legitimate to compare a marketer's product favorably against a competitor, regulations govern the use of **comparative advertising** if it can be challenged as misleading.

  Advertisers face the common threat that competitors will misrepresent their products. Although no one expects a competitor to be totally objective, advertisers have legal recourse to object to unfair comparisons. Law in the United States permits awards of damages from an advertiser who "misrepresents the nature, characteristics, qualities, or geographic origin in comparative advertising." In 2010, a New York court granted Weight Watchers International a temporary restraining order against Jenny Craig, claiming that Jenny Craig's advertising made deceptive claims about its success rate.[11]

  Advertisers who engage in comparative advertising know that research in support of their competitive claims must be impeccable. The Dunkin' Donuts ad compares its coffee to Starbucks and backs up its claim with a national taste test.

  Under the law, companies/plaintiffs are required to prove five elements to win a false-advertising lawsuit about an ad making a comparative claim:

  1. False statements have been made about either product.
  2. The ads actually deceived or had the tendency to deceive a substantial segment of the audience.
  3. The deception was "material" or meaningful. In other words, the plaintiff must show that the false ad claim is likely to influence purchasing decisions.

Photo: B Christopher/Alamy Stock Photo

Photo: Kevin Wheal/Alamy Stock Photo

Photo: Ian Dagnall/Alamy Stock Photo

Some companies compare themselves to their competitors directly in advertising. Others distinguish themselves from the competition visually and with a slogan. For example, FedEx's slogan, "When it absolutely, positively has to be there overnight" was created to set it apart from UPS and the US Postal System. The vehicles display the competitors' distinctive logos.

4. Falsely advertised goods are sold in interstate commerce.
5. The suing company has been or likely will be injured as a result of the false statements, either by loss of sales or by loss of goodwill.

In addition to the federal laws, consumers also may rely on state laws governing unfair competition and false ad claims if the consumer is the victim of a false comparative claim.

- **Endorsements and Demonstrations** A popular advertising strategy is the use of a spokesperson who endorses a brand. That's a perfectly legal strategy unless the endorser doesn't actually use the product. An **endorsement** or **testimonial** is any advertising message that consumers believe reflects the opinions, beliefs, or experiences of an individual, group, or institution. However, if consumers can reasonably ascertain that a message does not reflect the announcer's opinion, the message isn't an endorsement and may even be misleading.

Consider the billboard of President Obama wearing a Weatherproof-brand jacket during his visit to the Great Wall of China. The company put the image on its website for a time and promoted "the Obama jacket" until the White House asked that the company take down the billboard. It claimed the ad was misleading because Weatherproof never received approval or an endorsement from the president.[12]

The increasing prominence of digital media raises another ethical dilemma. Is it acceptable for company representatives to pose as consumers or pay bloggers to post endorsements as customer reviews online? The Word of Mouth Marketing Association says no. Its ethics code[13] explicitly prohibits consumers from taking cash from manufacturers, suppliers, or their representatives for making recommendations, reviews, or endorsements unless full disclosure

Photo: KB4 WENN Photos/Newscom

Weatherproof, an apparel company, stirred up controversy with its Times Square billboard showing President Obama wearing what looked to be one of its jackets. Do you think this was a misleading use of a public image?

is provided. Do you think it was ethical that Ford loaned 100 bloggers its new Fiesta[14] to drive and presumably chat about on the internet? If so, under what conditions? When Kim Kardashian West and her sisters praise products on social media, are those testimonials or advertisements? The FTC is struggling to define which are paid brand endorsements and identify them as ads.[15] The FTC requires that payments made to online influencers in exchange for positive reviews need to be disclosed. We'll probably see lots more examples of **blogola**, also referred to as flogging (sponsored conversations), in the future.[16]

Federal regulations require that endorsers be qualified by experience or training to make judgments, and they must actually use the product. If endorsers are comparing competing brands, they must have tried those brands as well. Those who endorse a product improperly may be liable if the government determines there is deception.

Product demonstrations in television advertising also must not mislead consumers. This mandate is especially difficult for advertisements of food products because such factors as hot studio lights and the length of time needed to shoot the commercial can make the product look unappetizing. Think about the problems of shooting ice cream under hot lights. Because milk looks gray on television, advertisers often substitute a mixture of glue and water. The question is whether the demonstration falsely upgrades the consumers' perception of the advertised brand. The FTC evaluates this kind of deception on a case-by-case basis.

One technique some advertisers use to sidestep restrictions on demonstrations is to insert disclaimers, or "supers," which are verbal or written words in the ad that indicate exceptions to the advertising claim made. You've probably seen car commercials that start with beauty shots of the product. Suddenly, the message is less clear; for several seconds, five different, often lengthy disclaimers flash on the screen in tiny, eye-straining type, including "See dealers for details and guaranteed claim form" and "Deductibles and restrictions apply."

- *Native Advertising and Branded Content* Native advertising has emerged as a form of digital communication as marketers and publishers seek new ways to engage audiences. Native advertising is similar to news, features, entertainment, and other items that surround it. An ethical problem arises if the consumer can't tell the difference between advertising and other content. The FTC requires transparency: a promotional message shouldn't mislead the audience to believe that it is anything other than an ad. That is, if it is likely to be confusing to a consumer, the message should carry a prominent disclaimer that it is an advertisement. Branded content, often used in native marketing, places the brand in the content. For example, Facebook defines branded content as "any post—including text, photos, videos, Instant Articles, links, 360 videos and Live videos—from media companies, celebrities or other influencers that features a third party product, brand or sponsor."[17] Facebook allows branded content to be posted only if its content policies are followed, such as a requirement that the content must be tagged as branded content. The FTC created Endorsement Guides designed to make sure that truth-in-advertising is the guiding principle and that endorsements are honest and not misleading. Someone reading a glowing review online should know, for instance, if the endorser is being paid to tout the product.
- *Fake News* Examples of fake news—hoaxes, propaganda, and disinformation—are not hard to find. In 2011, the *Los Angeles Times* ran an exposé about a water commission that hired a public relations firm to produce fake news. In June 2016, the FTC charged a Florida weight loss supplement marketer of defrauding consumers by hacking their email accounts and sending messages to consumers that appeared to come from friends and family. The messages

directed consumers to fake news sites that deceptively promoted the products.[18] The FTC has the authority to stop these deceptive practices. Creating false stories clearly runs counter to the Public Relations Society of America Code of Ethics that advocates preserving the free flow of unprejudiced information. The 2016 presidential election stirred controversy, with critics claiming that inaccurate and misleading stories disseminated on social media swayed voters' choices and calling for more regulation both from the government and Silicon Valley.

What Are Some Product-Specific Issues Related to Social Responsibility?   Marketers need to consider carefully what they choose to produce and advertise. Some key areas of concern include controversial products, unhealthy or dangerous products such as alcohol and tobacco, and prescription drugs. The decision to produce the product lies with the marketing department and the company's business objectives, but advertising is frequently in the spotlight because of its visibility.

- **Controversial Products** Before an agency can create an ad for a client, it must consider the nature of the client company and its mission, marketing objectives, reputation, available resources, competition, and most importantly, product line. Can the agency and its staff members honestly promote the products being advertised? What would you do if you were a writer for an agency or public relations firm that has a political client you don't support? Several agencies have resigned from profitable tobacco advertising accounts because of the medical evidence about the harm cigarettes cause. In cases where the agency works on a controversial account, there are still ethical ways to approach the business.

  Marketing communication reflects the marketing and business ethics of its clients and, because of its visibility, sometimes gets the blame for selling controversial, unsafe, or dangerous products. For example, products that were once considered not suitable to advertise, such as firearms, gambling, hemorrhoid preparations, feminine hygiene products, pantyhose and bras, laxatives, condoms, and remedies for male erectile dysfunctions, have become acceptable, although advertising for them may still be offensive to some people.

  Some products are controversial for political reasons or because of environmental issues. Oil companies, for example, have been criticized for their practices and are constantly trying to prove their role as good corporate citizens.

- **Unhealthy or Dangerous Products** One way to make ethical decisions is to choose the route that minimizes potential harm. Because there has been so much negative publicity about the health effects of eating a steady diet of heavily processed food, food companies, particularly fast-food producers such as McDonald's and Wendy's, have reacted to charges of culpability in the nation's obesity problem. McDonald's slimmed down Ronald McDonald, added

> **● Principle**
> The ethics of selling a controversial or unsafe product lies with the marketing department; however, marketing communication may be criticized because it is the visible face of marketing.

Ronald McDonald is slimmer and more active than originally to help convey the importance of making healthier choices.

Photo: Dennis Jones/Getty Images

healthier choices to its menu, and moved away from using cholesterol-causing saturated fats when making french fries. Disney launched efforts to serve healthier food in its theme parks as an effort to improve the diets of children. Wendy's reduced the amount of trans fats it uses for cooking.[19]

One of the most heated advertising issues in recent years has been about tobacco advertising. Although Congress passed a law that banned cigarette advertising on television and radio starting in 1971, that did not resolve the issue. Proponents of the ban on cigarette advertising argue that because cigarettes have been shown to cause cancer as well as other illnesses, encouraging tobacco use promotes sickness, injury, or death for the smoker and those inhaling secondhand smoke. They argue that further restricting advertising on those products would result in fewer sales and fewer health problems for the United States as a whole.

Opponents of advertising bans counter with the argument that prohibiting truthful, non-deceptive advertising for a legal product is unconstitutional and a violation of their rights to free speech. They believe that censorship is more of a problem than advertising a legal product even if it is unhealthy.

In an effort to reduce smoking by youth, the Master Settlement Agreement signed in 1998 by forty-six states' attorneys general and tobacco manufacturers established a set of restrictions on tobacco advertising, marketing, and promotional programs or activities. For example, it prohibits or restricts the use of cartoon characters; direct and indirect targeting of youth; billboards, transit ads and other outdoor advertising not in direct proximity to a retail establishment that sells tobacco products; and product placements in entertainment media. The restrictions also stipulated that $150 million be provided to fund antismoking ads.

In recognition of the growing public concerns about cigarette marketing, tobacco companies have voluntarily curbed their advertising and pulled ads from magazines with high levels of youth readership and from most outdoor billboards. Most major tobacco companies also run antismoking ads aimed at teenagers. Philip Morris has virtually stopped advertising and shifted its budget to events and other promotions that reach its customers rather than trying to use advertising to reach new customers.

Banning tobacco advertising is not unique to the United States. Many other countries have even stronger restrictions against such advertising. A near-total advertising ban in the United Kingdom took effect in early 2003, and similar restrictions were launched in the European Union (EU) two years later. Canada and New Zealand have banned tobacco advertising, and Australia and Malaysia have prohibited nearly all forms of it.

The ethics of advertising liquor is another concern. The biggest issue for the spirits industry is charges of advertising to underage drinkers. Liquor executives contend that they follow voluntary advertising guidelines to avoid images and time slots that appeal to kids. That stance has been hard to keep, however, because every major brand is trying to win over young consumers.

The Distilled Spirits Council, a trade organization representing producers and marketers of distilled spirits sold in the United States, offers a model for industry self-regulation. Its Code of Responsible Practices encourages members to follow the guidelines set forth in the code when promoting their products (available at www.discus.org/responsibility/code).

The beer industry has also been the target of strong criticism. Although it is unlikely that beer advertising will be banned, some companies sensitive to public opinion have initiated proactive programs that educate and discourage underage drinkers.

- *Prescription Drugs* In 1997, the US government loosened its controls on pharmaceutical advertising. As a result, the amount of prescription drug advertising has skyrocketed, with the US pharmaceutical industry spending $6 billion on advertising prescription drugs in 2016, according to Kantar Media, a media monitoring and measuring firm.[20] Although these print and television ads have proven very successful in terms of increased sales, various consumer groups, government agencies, and insurance companies have been quite critical of them.

Some doctors claim that they are being pressured to write prescriptions inappropriately because their patients are influenced by the drug ad claims. Other doctors say they appreciate that the advertising has caused consumers to become more active in managing their own health and more informed about their drug options.

In recent health care reform efforts, some lawmakers targeted the pharmaceutical industry sector because they believe these ads contribute to the high cost of health care.[21] As part of the reform, health insurance companies are required to spend at least 80 percent of the premiums they receive on medical care, not on overhead, advertising, or other costs.[22] For guidelines pertaining to advertising prescription drugs, see the US Food and Drug Administration's website at www.fda.gov/Drugs/ResourcesForYou/Consumers/PrescriptionDrugAdvertising/default.htm.

Communicators' Ethical Responsibilities

18.2 Describe the ethical responsibilities that brand communicators bear.

By now, you are familiar with many of the ethical and social issues facing marketing communication. How does it involve you? This section will give you a better understanding about what we mean by ethics and provide some decision-making tools as you encounter ethical dilemmas.

Ethics are the "shoulds" and "oughts" of behavior—the "right thing to do." Defining what is right can be challenging. What one person says is right isn't always what others believe appropriate. Ethics and morals are closely related, but they are not synonymous. **Morals** are frameworks for right actions and are more the domain of religion and philosophy. Examples of moral systems are the Ten Commandments from the Judeo-Christian religious tradition and the Buddhists' Eightfold Path. These moral systems provide a framework for behavior.

Although ethics reflect what is right and wrong, the difficulty lies in making choices from equally compelling or competing options. How should you behave when the answer is unclear? We know that doing the right thing is ethical, but it's sometimes hard to know what the right thing is. Sometimes there's no one right answer. Consider, for example, this situation. You are a graphic designer. You want to use a picture you found on the internet, and you don't want to copy it unethically. How much do you have to change the digital picture before it becomes your own?

Consider the case of Italian clothing maker Benetton, which created a controversy several years ago with an ad featuring a photo of a priest kissing a nun and another of an emaciated AIDS victim at the moment of death, attended by his distraught family. Is it riveting? You bet it is. Professor Fred Beard suggested that few people inside or outside advertising would argue that the presentation of a potentially offensive message is always morally wrong. He asks some hard ethical questions about "shockvertising," which has grown as advertisers learned that controversy attracts attention. Should advertisers care if they offend people?

Here are some questions Beard wrote that illustrate how complicated the decision is and help you decide if the ads crossed the line:[23]

- Is it inherently wrong to present words and images that will undoubtedly offend most people if the goal is to draw attention to humanitarian issues and problems?
- Does it make a difference if the goal of widely offensive advertising is solely to sell products?
- Do people have a right not to see ads that offend them? Because some media, such as television and outdoor advertising, are more intrusive than others, does the medium make a difference?
- What do advertising codes of ethics say about audience offense? Are advertisers professionally and morally obligated to follow them?
- To whom do advertisers owe the most responsibility—their own organizations and stakeholders, society, consumers, other advertising professionals?

The Matter of Principle feature by Professor Kim Sheehan explores ethical issues embedded in Corporate Social Responsibility campaigns that pair charitable organizations with brands. Do you think pinkwashing is ethical? Does it enhance the brand?

Personal and Professional Ethics

Ethical decisions are usually complex and involve navigating a moral maze of conflicting forces: strategy versus ethics, costs versus ethics, effectiveness versus ethics, and so on. They demand the ability to do what ethicists call "moral reasoning."[24] In the end, if you are a responsible professional making a decision about a strategy or an execution tactic to be used in an advertisement, you must be aware of industry standards as well as ethical questions that underlie the core issues we have discussed in this chapter.

Corporate Social Responsibility and Pinkwashing

Kim Sheehan, *University of Oregon*

Partnering with a charitable organization is arguably an easy decision for brands to make. Brands earn accolades and possibly increased sales from consumers who see brands as sharing the values of the charitable organization. The organizations gain increased awareness and in most cases donations from partnering brands. These communications campaigns are called corporate social responsibility, or CSR, campaigns.

Many brands eagerly partner with charities that fund breast cancer awareness and research (such charities include the Susan G. Komen Foundation and the Breast Cancer Research Foundation). Almost all Americans believe that breast cancer research is a critical cause that corporations should support, and 75 percent of Americans intend to purchase a breast cancer–related product or service during October, which is Breast Cancer Awareness Month. Partnering with breast cancer charities has few risks of alienating potential consumers, compared to causes working to end societal challenges such as HIV/AIDS or poverty.

CSR advertising promoting relationships between brands and breast cancer charities generally use the iconic pink ribbon to symbolize both breast cancer awareness and the search for a cure. The Susan G. Komen Foundation began distributing pink ribbons at the end of its fund-raising athletic event, the Race for the Cure, in 1991: the color pink was selected for breast cancer awareness as a distinctly feminine color. Cosmetics giant Estee Lauder helped popularize the pink ribbon in 1992. Today, the pink ribbon is one of the most widely recognized symbols in the United States. However, the use of the pink ribbon is not licensed or regulated, so any company can use the pink ribbon on any type of product. Because of that, brands *that display the pink ribbon can be associated with increased risks of breast cancer, such as wine and cosmetics, or are otherwise unhealthy for society, such as guns and fast food.*

Additionally, CSR ads do not need to provide specific information about brands' donations to breast cancer causes. When consumers purchase products with pink ribbons, they often assume that a portion of that purchase will be donated to breast cancer awareness, which may or may not be true. A company's actual donation may also be tiny relative to their profits.

The growth in concerns over inappropriate use of the pink ribbon has led to the framing of the phenomenon as pinkwashing. Pinkwashing is the practice of using the color pink and pink ribbons that communicate that a brand is much more involved in the fight against breast cancer than the brand actually is.

Brands participating in CSR campaigns should communicate several aspects of the relationship clearly. First, brands should name the partner charity. Second, brands should identify the specific mechanism for donating funds, whether funds are based on a percentage of a consumer's purchase or are a one-time donation to the charity. Finally, if possible, brands should provide links to a website where more details on the relationship can be found so that consumers make well-informed choices about the products they buy.

More important is that personal judgment and moral reasoning rest on an intuitive sense of right and wrong, a moral compass that tells you when an idea is misleading, insensitive, too over the top, or too manipulative. Then you need the courage to speak up and tell your colleagues. Does the Benetton advertising pass your personal standards for good advertising? Similarly, an edgy Mountain Dew ad that elicited criticism for its perceived racism and making light of violence toward women may have worked for its teenage male audience, but is that a good reason for bringing such criticism to the brand?

Professionals in advertising by and large see themselves as ethical people. However, polls indicate that the public tends to see them differently. In a recent Honesty and Ethics Poll conducted by the Gallup organization, advertising practitioners ranked near the bottom, with nurses, pharmacists, and doctors at the top.[25] Advertising practitioners ranked slightly ahead of car salespeople, telemarketers, members of Congress, and lobbyists at the bottom. That poll suggests the public is not persuaded that advertising professionals are guided by ethical standards. Read the Matter of Practice feature by Steve Edwards and begin to think about how you might improve society with your life's work.

Determining what constitutes ethical behavior happens on many levels. Individually, advertisers call on their own moral upbringing. The various marcom industries provide codes of

Advertising Gets No Respect!

Steve Edwards, *Southern Methodist University*

Why is the profession of advertising ranked just above being a used-car salesman on surveys of ethical practices? Why should you care? Advertising has tremendous power to shape our attitudes about our world and ourselves, inform people of important ideas, and change behavior. Yet advertising students will graduate and get jobs paying less than students in finance, accounting, marketing, or engineering. Why?

Advertising surrounds us and is accessible everywhere and, as with anything that is plentiful, is undervalued. If you have water flowing from the tap, let it flow. But if you were in a desert with a single bottle of water, that same resource becomes precious.

People tend to underestimate the effects of advertising on themselves while overestimating its effects on others. And although consumers enjoy the information or entertainment advertising provides, they underestimate the knowledge and skills needed to advertise effectively and thus devalue the profession.

Professions are strong to the degree that (1) they are identified and differentiated by their specialized knowledge, (2) they educate new members, and (3) they make the value of their knowledge/work clear to the wider society. Think about why doctors are well respected.

Strengthening the profession of advertising starts with you. Become an advocate for the field. Start by (1) developing an understanding of how advertising affects society both positively and negatively, (2) being able to define the specialized knowledge of advertising that others have not studied, and (3) educating others about the power of the industry.

Specifically, pay attention to the economic versus social effects of advertising. Criticisms of advertising often focus on specific ads that encourage socially undesirable behaviors (overconsumption in general or underage drinking), target impressionable children, or stereotype certain societal groups. Anticonsumerist organizations, such as *Adbusters.org*, promote "buy nothing day" and offer social criticism of advertising using spoof ads. However, people rarely think of the importance of communication messages focused on hygiene, poverty, AIDS, obesity, recycling, alcoholism, literacy, and so on, but it is through advertising that we learn about such things.

It is also through advertising that consumers learn that BMW is "The Ultimate Driving Machine" or that the Toyota Prius "helps save gas and helps the environment." The choices we make as consumers are based on the fundamental values we deem important. And yes, advertising, along with other large societal institutions (e.g., religion or government), helps set or reinforce an agenda for what we as a society value. But it is due in part to advertising that consumers are educated about products in the marketplace and, by making purchase decisions, can force companies to improve products or lower prices to compete.

Advertising is a powerful force and should be respected, but advocates are needed.

Where are you in this debate about the value of advertising? Do you see yourself as an advocate or a critic? If you were at a party, could you defend yourself as a student of advertising, perhaps even an advertising professional?

---

ethics and standards of self-regulation to help guide practitioners. The government helps regulate marcom practices through legal means.

Professional Codes of Ethics Industry standards can provide help with a decision about ethical behavior. Many professions write a **code of ethics** to help guide practitioners toward ethical behavior; organizations doing so include the American Association of Advertising Agencies, the Public Relations Society of America, and the Word of Mouth Marketing Association. Professional ethics are often expressed in a code of standards that identifies how professionals in the industry should respond when faced with ethical questions. Codes of ethics can be helpful to guide your actions. However, they are broad statements and are not intended to explain what you should do in every circumstance you encounter.

In an effort to help advertisers build consumer trust and brand loyalty in a global and digital economy, the Institute for Advertising Ethics created eight Principles and Practices for Advertising Ethics, which emphasize the importance of transparency and the need to conduct business and relationships with consumers in a fair, honest, and forthright manner (Figure 18.1).[26] The Principles and Practices for Advertising Ethics was the result of a collaboration of the American

FIGURE 18.1
Institute for Advertising
Ethics's Principles and
Practices for Advertising
Ethics

Principles and Practices for Advertising Ethics
Institute for Advertising Ethics

Principle 1

Advertising, public relations, marketing communications, news, and editorial all share a common objective of truth and high ethical standards in serving the public.

Principle 2

Advertising, public relations, and all marketing communications professionals have an obligation to exercise the highest personal ethics in the creation and dissemination of commercial information to consumers.

Principle 3

Advertisers should clearly distinguish advertising, public relations and corporate communications from news and editorial content and entertainment, both online and offline.

Principle 4

Advertisers should clearly disclose all material conditions, such as payment or receipt of a free product, affecting endorsements in social and traditional channels, as well as the identity of endorsers, all in the interest of full disclosure and transparency.

Principle 5

Advertisers should treat consumers fairly based on the nature of the audience to whom the ads are directed and the nature of the product or service advertised.

Principle 6

Advertisers should never compromise consumers' personal privacy in marketing communications, and their choices as to whether to participate in providing their information should be transparent and easily made.

Principle 7

Advertisers should follow federal, state and local advertising laws, and cooperate with industry self-regulatory programs for the resolution of advertising practices.

Principle 8

Advertisers and their agencies, and online and offline media, should discuss privately potential ethical concerns, and members of the team creating ads should be given permission to express internally their ethical concerns.

Sources: University of Missouri School of Journalism and American Advertising Federation. An expanded version of the "Principles and Practices for Advertising Ethics with Commentary" is available at www.aaf.org and www.rjionline.org.

Advertising Federation, the Reynolds Journalism Institute, and the University of Missouri School of Journalism.

The Public Relations Society of America offers an example of a code of ethics for those in that profession (Figure 18.2). You can see the entire code of ethics at https://www.prsa.org/aboutprsa/ethics/codeenglish#.WEYtDpKISCY.

International Standards and Codes   Standards of professional behavior are not found only in the United States and other Western countries. Singapore, for example, has an ad code specifically designed to prevent Western-influenced advertising from impairing Asian family values. Malaysia's requirement that all ads be produced in that country not only keeps that country's advertising aligned with its own standards and cultural values, but also cuts back dramatically on the number of foreign ads seen by its public. Advertisers who violate the ethical code of conduct

FIGURE 18.2
The Public Relations
Society of America Code
of Ethics

PRSA Member Statement of Professional Values

This statement presents the core values of PRSA members and, more broadly, of the public relations profession. These values provide the foundation for the Member Code of Ethics and set the industry standard for the professional practice of public relations. These values are the fundamental beliefs that guide our behaviors and decisionmaking process. We believe our professional values are vital to the integrity of the profession as a whole.

ADVOCACY

We serve the public interest by acting as responsible advocates for those we represent. We provide a voice in the marketplace of ideas, facts, and viewpoints to aid informed public debate.

HONESTY

We adhere to the highest standards of accuracy and truth in advancing the interests of those we represent and in communicating with the public.

EXPERTISE

We acquire and responsibly use specialized knowledge and experience. We advance the profession through continued professional development, research, and education. We build mutual understanding, credibility, and relationships among a wide array of institutions and audiences.

INDEPENDENCE

We provide objective counsel to those we represent. We are accountable for our actions.

LOYALTY

We are faithful to those we represent, while honoring our obligation to serve the public interest.

FAIRNESS

We deal fairly with clients, employers, competitors, peers, vendors, the media, and the general public. We respect all opinions and support the right of free expression.

Source: Courtesy of the PRSA. Used with permission.

in Brazil can be fined up to $500,000 or imprisoned for up to five years. This punishment would certainly prompt an advertiser to be careful.

In the Netherlands, industry members have encouraged the formation of an "ethical office" to oversee all agencies, advertisers, and media. That office is responsible for reviewing advertisements to ensure that they comply with the Dutch Advertising Code and general ethical principles. In Swedish advertising agencies, an executive known as the "responsible editor" is trained and experienced in marketing law; that editor reviews all advertisements and promotional materials to ensure that they are legally and ethically acceptable.

Why and How Is Brand Communication Regulated?

18.3 Discuss how advertising is regulated.

Although it would be ideal if individuals and companies always made socially responsible choices and everyone could agree that those choices resulted in proper actions, sometimes that does not occur, and regulatory or legal action is needed. The company may decide it is acceptable to advertise certain products, for example, and the government may decide otherwise.

FIGURE 18.3
Advertising Review and
Regulation

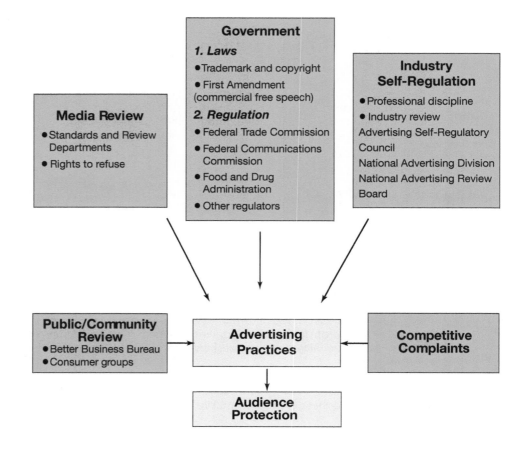

Various systems are in place to monitor the social responsibility of advertising and other brand communication, including laws, government regulatory bodies, professional oversight groups, and industry self-regulation. Figure 18.3 identifies the organizations with oversight responsibility for advertising and groups them in terms of five specific categories: government, media, industry, public or community groups, and the competition. Let's examine each of those systems.

Brand Communication's Legal Environment

Making laws and enforcing them are domains of government. Congress makes laws related to advertising, and regulatory agencies in the executive branch of the federal government enforce those laws. The following list summarizes important advertising legislation, most of which shows the growing authority of regulatory bodies, such as the FTC, to regulate advertising:

- *Pure Food and Drug Act (1906)* Forbids the manufacture, sale, or transport of adulterated or fraudulently labeled foods and drugs in interstate commerce. Supplanted by the Food, Drug, and Cosmetic Act of 1938; amended by the Food Additives Amendment in 1958 and the Kefauver-Harris Amendment in 1962.
- *Federal Trade Commission Act (1914)* Establishes the commission, a body of specialists with broad powers to investigate and to issue cease-and-desist orders to enforce Section 5, which declares that "unfair methods of competition in commerce are unlawful."
- *Wheeler-Lea Amendment (1938)* Prohibits unfair and deceptive acts and practices regardless of whether competition is injured; places advertising of foods and drugs under FTC jurisdiction.
- *Lanham Act (1947)* Provides protection for trademarks (slogans and brand names) from competitors and also encompasses false advertising.
- *Magnuson-Moss Warranty/FTC Improvement Act (1975)* Authorizes the FTC to determine rules concerning consumer warranties and provides for consumer access to means of redress, such as the "class-action" suit. Also expands FTC regulatory powers over unfair or deceptive

acts or practices and allows it to require restitution for deceptively written warranties costing the consumer more than $5.

- *FTC Improvement Act (1980)* Provides the House of Representatives and the Senate jointly with veto power over FTC regulation rules. Enacted to limit the FTC's powers to regulate "unfairness" issues in designing trade regulation rules on advertising.
- *Telemarketing and Consumer Fraud Act and Abuse Protection Act (1994)* Specifies that telemarketers may not call anyone who requests not to be contacted. Resulted in the Telemarketing Sales Rules.
- *Do-Not-Call Registry Act (2003)* Authorizes the FTC to implement and enforce a do-not-call registry.

Federal legislation has focused on many areas of advertising, ranging from establishing requirements for those who send unsolicited commercial email (CAN-SPAM Act) to cigarette labeling and advertising (Federal Cigarette Labeling and Advertising Act of 1966) and fair packaging and labeling. Providing a comprehensive list of all the statutes affecting advertising law is not our purpose; however, brand communicators should be aware that the federal government and the FTC, in particular, provide oversight to ensure that advertising is fair.

In this section, we examine two pivotal areas of case law—trademarks and copyright protection and the First Amendment—as they pertain to advertising and other areas of marketing communication.

Trademark and Copyright Protection   A **trademark** is a brand, corporate or store name, or distinctive symbol that identifies the seller's brand and thus differentiates it from the brands of other sellers. A trademark can be registered through the Department of Commerce, which gives the organization exclusive use of the mark, as long as the trademark is maintained as an identification of a specific product. Registered trademarks enjoy more legal protection than those that are not registered. Under the Lanham Trademark Act of 1947, the **US Patent and Trademark Office** of the Department of Commerce protects unique trademarks from infringement by competitors.

Even an audio trademark is protected, as a case in the EU illustrates. A distinctive audio sound based on the noise of a cock crowing and the way it was represented in Dutch had been registered with the EU's trademark office. When this sound trademark was used by a different company, the first company sued for trademark infringement.

A recent trademark issue is protection for **uniform resource locators (URLs)**, which are internet domain names. URLs need to be registered to be protected just like any other trademark. They are issued on a first-come, first-served basis for any domain name not identical to an existing brand name.

A **copyright** gives an organization the exclusive right to use or reproduce original work, such as an advertisement or package design, for a specified period of time. The **Library of Congress** controls copyright protection. Copyrighting of coined words, phrases, illustrations, characters, and photographs can offer some protection from other advertisers who borrow too heavily from competitors. Commonly used designs or symbols, however, cannot be copyrighted, nor can ideas be copyrighted. For a copyright to be obtained, a work must be fixed in a tangible medium. Copyright infringement can occur when a product is used in an ad without proper permission. A sweet example is the maker of Peeps, those marshmallow chicks and bunnies, which sued American Greetings for using pictures of Peeps without authorization.[27]

Brand Communication and the First Amendment   The most basic federal law that governs advertising and other forms of marketing communication is the First Amendment to the US Constitution, which states that Congress shall make no law "abridging the freedom of speech, or of the press."

How have courts applied the First Amendment to advertising? First Amendment protection extends to **commercial speech**, which is speech that promotes commercial activity. However, that protection is not absolute and is often restricted. The US Supreme Court generally applies a different standard to commercial speech than it does to other forms of speech, such as that enjoyed by the press and filmmakers, because the conditions are different for different forms of speech.

Protection of advertising as commercial speech has varied over the years. In 1980, in conjunction with its ruling on *Central Hudson Gas and Electric v. Public Service Commission of New York*, the Supreme Court established a test that determines to what extent the government can restrict advertising. This decision also stipulated the degree to which advertising is considered commercial speech, although a more recent Supreme Court decision in 2010, *Citizens United v. Federal Election Commission*, enhanced the free speech rights of corporations, particularly for political speech.

A number of cases have attempted to change the common view of advertising as commercial speech. Most notably, the Supreme Court struck down a Massachusetts law that restricted tobacco advertising. Free speech advocates applauded the decision, while critics of tobacco companies lamented it. Although no one expects advertising to have the same constitutional protection of free speech that is given to individuals, courts throughout the United States are narrowing the gap.

The Supreme Court permits some restrictions on commercial speech. For example, it has held that false or misleading commercial speech can be banned. Even truthful commercial speech can be restricted if the government can prove that the public good demands such restrictions.[28]

Have you wondered why politicians can get away with unfounded attacks against their opponents? The "truth in advertising" standard does not apply to political advertising. Candidates' statements and advertisements are considered "political speech," which is protected by the First Amendment, and candidates can get away with distorting facts. It is legal for candidates to lie. In fact, if broadcasters choose to run any candidates' ads, the Federal Communications Act requires the station to air commercials even when they know they contain false information.[29] The reason lies in a belief that voters have a right to uncensored information.

Except for political communication, the Supreme Court has essentially ruled that only truthful commercial speech, not misleading or deceptive statements, is protected. Because the nation's courts continue to reinterpret how the First Amendment applies in different cases, advertisers need to keep close track of legal developments.

International Laws and Regulations As advertisers, agencies, and media become more global, it will be imperative for the players to understand local laws in the countries in which they operate. Marketing practices, such as pricing and price advertising, vary in their legal and regulatory restrictions.

Some product categories, such as over-the-counter drugs, are particularly difficult to work with because regulations about their marketing and advertising are different in every country. Advertising for certain types of products is banned. The United Arab Emirates forbids tobacco advertisements. In January 2017, France joined Australia in the ban requiring tobacco products to be sold in plain packaging. In Hong Kong, outdoor display advertising of tobacco products is banned. Malaysia has banned most forms of tobacco advertising, including print, television, radio, and billboards.

There also are differences in the legal use of various marketing communication tools. A contest or promotion might be successful in one country and illegal in another. Different laws and self-regulatory codes about direct marketing exist in different EU countries. For example, France requires an opt-in clause to a mailing or questionnaire asking permission to add the customer's name to a mailing list.[30] Germany prohibits companies from making unsolicited telephone calls and faxes to consumers. Nestlé lost the Kit Kat trademark in the European Union because the company did not prove that the Kit Kat shape had acquired distinctiveness in every EU member state.[31] Because of the difficulty in complying with widely varying laws, international advertisers often work with either local agencies or with international agencies that have local affiliates and experts who know the local laws and can identify potential legal problems.

The Regulatory Environment

In addition to specific legislation that affects the practice of marketing communication, there are also government bodies that oversee the application of these laws and establish standards and regulations that marketers must meet. The FTC is the primary body that oversees marketing communication, but a number of other agencies are also involved in regulating the messages sent to consumers, as summarized in the following list:

Specialized Government Agencies That Affect Advertising

Agency	*Effect on Advertising*
Federal Trade Commission (www.ftc.gov)	Regulates credit, labeling, packaging, warranties, and advertising
Food and Drug Administration (www.fda.gov)	Regulates packaging, labeling, and manufacturing of food and drug products
Federal Communications Commission (www.fcc.gov)	Regulates radio and television stations and networks
US Postal Service (www.usps.gov)	Controls advertising by monitoring materials sent through the mail
Bureau of Alcohol, Tobacco, Firearms and Explosives (www.atf.gov)	Division of the US Department of Justice that regulates advertising for alcoholic beverages
US Patent and Trademark Office (www.uspto.gov)	Oversees trademark registration to protect against patent infringement
Library of Congress (www.loc.gov)	Provides controls for copyright protection

In addition to the FTC, the **Food and Drug Administration (FDA)** and the **Federal Communications Commission (FCC)** are dynamic components of the regulatory environment. Let's look in more depth at their missions and the type of practices they regulate.

FTC Established by Congress in 1914 to oversee business, the FTC is the primary agency governing the advertising industry. Its main focus with respect to advertising is to identify and eliminate ads that deceive or mislead the consumer. Some FTC responsibilities include the following:

- *Unfairness* Initiate investigations against companies that engage in unfair competition or deceptive practices.
- *Deception* Regulate acts and practices that deceive businesses or consumers and issue cease-and-desist orders where such practices exist. **Cease-and-desist** orders require that the practice be stopped within 30 days; an order given to one firm is applicable to all firms in the industry.
- *Violations* When the FTC finds a violation of the law, such as a deceptive or unfair practice, it mandates (1) a cease-and-desist order, (2) an affirmative disclosure, or (3) corrective advertising.

Specifically, the FTC oversees false advertising, and in recent years, that oversight has focused on health and weight-loss business practices, 900 telephone numbers, telemarketing, and advertising that targets children and the elderly. The FTC hosts the National Do Not Call Registry to help citizens keep from receiving unwanted telemarketing calls. The FTC monitors the ratings system and the advertising practices of the film, music, and electronic games industries. Periodically, it issues progress reports to Congress on youth-oriented entertainment advertising to make sure that ads for products with potentially objectionable content—primarily violent or sexual content—are not seen on media targeted to youth. The FTC's reports to Congress cover advertising on television and websites as well as print media.

The existence of a regulatory agency such as the FTC influences advertisers' behavior. Although most cases never reach the FTC, advertisers prefer not to risk long legal battles with the agency. Advertisers are also aware that competitors may complain to the FTC about a questionable advertisement. Such a move can cost the offending organization millions of dollars.

The FTC revised its guidelines governing testimonial advertisements, bloggers, and celebrity endorsements in October 2009 for the first time since 1980. These guidelines toughen rules for endorsements and testimonials by requiring that the results touted by endorsers are likely to be typical. The revisions also now cover bloggers, who must disclose any free products or other compensation they get in exchange for their endorsements.[32] Updates are available at www.ftc.gov/opa/reporter/advertising/index.shtml.

FDA   The FDA is the regulatory division of the US Department of Health and Human Services that oversees package labeling, ingredient listings, and advertising for food and drugs. It also determines the safety and purity of foods and cosmetics. In particular, the FDA is a watchdog for drug advertising, specifically in the controversial area of direct-to-consumer ads for prescription drugs. Its job is first to determine whether drugs are safe and then to see that these drugs are marketed responsibly. Marketing includes promotional materials aimed at doctors as well as consumers.

For pharmaceutical companies, advertising is a commercial free speech issue, and the industry has brought pressure on the FDA to make direct-to-consumer advertising rules for prescription drugs more understandable, simpler, and clearer.

FCC   The FCC, formed in 1934 to protect the public interest in broadcast communication, can issue and revoke licenses to radio and television stations. The FCC also has the power to ban messages, including ads, that are deceptive or in poor taste. The agency monitors only advertisements that have been the subject of complaints and works closely with the FTC to eliminate false and deceptive advertising. The FCC takes actions against the media, whereas the FTC is concerned with advertisers and agencies.

Other Regulatory Bodies   In addition to the FTC, the FDA, and the FCC, most other federal agencies that regulate advertising are limited to a certain type of advertising, product, or medium. We have already discussed the Patent Office and the Library of Congress and their roles in protecting copyrights and trademarks. Let's now look at other key regulatory agencies.

- *Bureau of Alcohol, Tobacco, Firearms and Explosives* The **Bureau of Alcohol, Tobacco, Firearms and Explosives** within the Treasury Department regulates deception in advertising and establishes labeling requirements for the liquor industry. This agency's power comes from its authority to issue and revoke annual operating permits for distillers, wine merchants, and brewers. Because there is a danger that public pressure could result in banning all advertisements for alcoholic beverages, the liquor industry strives to maintain tight controls on its advertising.
- *US Postal Service* The **US Postal Service** regulates direct-mail and magazine advertising and has control over the areas of obscenity, lotteries, and fraud. To give you an idea of the magnitude of the US Postal Service's responsibility, *Direct Marketing News* reported that the estimated spending on direct mail in 2016 was $47 billion, even in a period of declining spending on the medium.[33] Consumers who receive advertisements in the mail that they consider sexually offensive can request that no more mail be delivered from that sender. The postmaster general also has the power to withhold mail that promotes lotteries. Fraud can include a number of questionable activities, such as implausible, get-rich-quick schemes.
- *States' Attorneys General* The National Association of Attorneys General seeks to regulate advertising at the state level. Members of this organization have successfully brought suits in their respective states against such advertising giants as Coca-Cola, Kraft, and Campbell Soup. More recently, numerous attorneys general have led the way against the tobacco industry and have supported the advertising restrictions discussed earlier.

The Impact of Regulation

In our discussion of issues, we mentioned several that have spurred governmental regulation, such as children's advertising, deception, and claim substantiation. In this section, we discuss these regulations in terms of the government agencies taking responsibility for them.

The FTC and Children's Advertising   Developing responsible advertising aimed at children is a critical issue. The FTC and other governmental agencies have gotten involved with the regulation of marketing to children.

After a 1978 study found that the average child viewed more than 20,000 television commercials per year, a heated debate ensued. One side favored regulation because of children's inability to evaluate advertising messages and make purchasing decisions. The other side opposed regulation, arguing that many self-regulatory mechanisms already existed and that the proper place for restricting advertising to children was in the home.

In response, the FTC initiated proceedings to study possible regulations of children's television. Despite the FTC's recommendations, the proceedings did not result in new federal regulations until 1990. In the interim, self-regulation in the advertising industry tried to fill this void.

The National Advertising Division (NAD) of the Council of Better Business Bureaus, Inc., set up a group charged with helping advertisers deal with children's advertising in a manner sensitive to children's special needs. The Children's Advertising Review Unit, established in 1974, evaluates advertising directed at children under the age of 12.

In 1990, Congress passed the Children's Television Advertising Practice Act, which placed 10.5-minute-per-hour ceilings for commercials in children's weekend television programming and 12-minute-per-hour limits for weekday programs. The act also set rules requiring that commercial breaks be clearly distinguished from programming, barring the use of program characters to promote products.

Advocates for children's television continue to argue that many stations made little effort to comply with the 1990 act and petitioned the FCC to increase the required number of educational programs to be shown daily. In 1996, broadcasters, children's advocates, and the federal government reached an agreement requiring all television stations to air three hours of children's educational shows a week.

Responding to issues emerging in the digital environment, the Children's Online Privacy Protection Act grants parents control over what information websites can collect from their children. The FTC issued the Children's Online Privacy Protection Rule in 2000 and revised it in 2013, requiring websites and online services to provide parents with direct notice of their information practices and get parental consent before collecting information from children.

Regulating Deception   Ultimately, advertisers want their customers to trust their products and advertising, so many take precautions to ensure that their messages are not deceptive, misleading, or unreasonable. **Deceptive advertising** is intended to mislead consumers by making claims that are false, by failure to make full disclosure of important facts, or both. The current FTC policy on deception contains three basic elements:

1. *Misleading* Where there is representation, omission, or practice, there must be a probability that it will mislead the consumer.
2. *Reasonableness* The perspective of the "reasonable consumer" is used to judge deception. The FTC tests reasonableness by looking at whether the consumer's interpretation or reaction to an advertisement is reasonable.
3. *Injurious* The deception must hold the probability of material injury. Here, "material" is defined as "affecting consumers' choice or behavior regarding the product or service." In other words, the deception is likely to influence consumers' decision making about products and services.

This policy makes deception difficult to prove because the criteria are rather vague and hard to measure. It also creates uncertainty for advertisers, who must wait for congressional hearings and court cases to discover what the FTC will permit.

The Problem of In-Advertising Disclosure

Keith Murray, *Bryant University*

How many meaningful messages can one 30-second commercial effectively provide viewers? This question points to an interesting problem in marketing and communication because it addresses a big issue in advertising—or at least *focuses attention on* a big problem in advertising—but one hardly anyone seems to notice.

Have you ever viewed, say, a TV commercial that displays what you might call a lot of small-type-size, frequently fleeting bursts of "fine print"? You know what I mean: a lot of words that remain fixed—or fly—across the screen that are almost impossible to read, understand, or comprehend much of their intended meaning? That's what's called in the advertising business *in-advertising disclosure* or, to use another term for the same concept, affirmative disclosure.

What Is an "In-Advertising Disclosure"?

Fundamentally, an in-ad disclosure is any type of communication that modifies, diminishes, qualifies, limits, or restricts the description, the applicable audience, or the terms of the offer being made such that without the disclosure the viewer of the commercial might otherwise be misinformed, mislead, or worse yet, deceived. Research data indicate that about half of all TV broadcast commercials have one or more affirmative disclosures, either in print or verbal context; hence, it is easy to see that this issue is not a particularly isolated or exceptional one. An understanding of why it's a contentious issue in the field—especially in broadcast advertising—is critical for marketing and advertising professionals to understand and appreciate.

Two Kinds of In-Advertising Disclosure

Typically, advertising disclosures represent two somewhat different types of messages within the commercial. On the one hand, an affirmative disclosure can represent information that the sponsoring firm wants you, for one reason or another, to be aware of, but doesn't have time, space, or specific interest to communicate one or more of the important ideas or information points in the more dominant, obvious part of the commercial message. However, without the in-ad disclosure, certain commercials might easily be viewed as potentially misleading—say if the model of car visibly shown in the commercial is different than the one being featured in the body of the advertisement, or a special price is only for certain customers, or that the attractive financing terms are only available to a specific, limited set of buyers.

A second type of in-ad disclosure is one that is mandated, typically by Congress, the Federal Trade Commission, the Federal Drug Administration, or some other governmental agency. In this context, public policy makers have promulgated the requirement that certain informational or warning messages need to be included in a commercial message, with the primary purpose to serve a particular public interest when it comes to certain product categories, terms, or offers.

Why Are In-Ad Disclosures a Problem?

So, one asks, what's the big deal about using affirmative disclosures in commercial broadcast communications?

Regulating Substantiation   An area of particular concern to the FTC in determining misleading advertisement is **claim substantiation**. The advertiser should have a reasonable basis for making a claim about product performance or run the risk of an FTC investigation. Food claims, such as those focused on calories or carbohydrates, must be supported by research about nutrition, as demonstrated by the SlimFast ad.

Consequently, an advertiser should always have data on file to substantiate any claims it makes in its advertisements. Also, this research should ideally be conducted by an independent research firm.

The FTC determines the reasonableness of claims on a case-by-case basis. In general, the FTC considers these factors:

- *Type and Specificity of Claim* For example, Computer Tutor claims you can learn the basics of using a computer by simply going through the company's three-CD set.
- *Type of Product* FedEx promises a certain delivery time, regardless of weather, mechanical breakdown, and so forth. This product has a great many uncontrollable variables compared to Heinz ketchup, which the company promises will be "thick."
- *Possible Consequences* A website that claims it is secure can cause serious damage to its customers if, in fact, it is not.

That's a good question with a somewhat complicated answer. When it comes to broadcast disclosures—and really disclosures in television or radio advertising—fine-print advertising is particularly problematic. The reason it's especially troublesome is because one party (i.e., the advertiser) almost completely controls the opportunity and practical ability of the other party (i.e., the viewer, prospective buyer, or message recipient) to see, understand, appreciate, and adequately weigh the merits of the qualifying details about the commercial. Indeed, there are at least five substantial flaws associated with a disclosure, and it is instructive to briefly consider each in turn to understand how advertisers can—and do—restrict the impact of in-ad disclosures. One or more of the five following realities is almost always true about affirmative disclosures in a broadcast advertising context:

1. Disclosures are fleeting; the fine-print "copy" content is not visually shown on a television monitor for very long, making what is presented difficult to read by the average viewer. In general, the average television viewer's reading comprehension rate is in the range of about 150 words per minute (WPM). It is not unusual—indeed, it is typical—for disclosure copy shown on the screen to require reading comprehension rates anywhere from 5 to 200 *times* the average viewer's effective WPM rate.

2. Disclosures are hard to read and are almost always composed of small, hard to view type, hence the term *fine print*.

3. Disclosures are obscured by other distractions, like an in-motion scene or a complex, distracting background.

4. Disclosures are almost always written in technical, or "legalese," terminology, and are almost never presented in a dramatic, compelling way.

5. Disclosures are shown at a time in the commercial when the viewer is least likely to be paying attention—in the final seconds of the commercial messages when viewership and audience attention is lowest.

   In the end, affirmative disclosure is controversial for several reasons:

- Affirmative disclosures serve to potentially influence and distort what is communicated in a principle commercial message.
- In-advertising disclosures potentially pose a formidable ethical dilemma in the field of marketing and advertising. The presence of disclosures in a commercial raise the question of whether it's acceptable—ethical, really—to plan to unduly exaggerate the attractive aspects of the stated offer and, in effect, confuse, mislead, or, more drastically, deceive the prospect with an unrealistic offer.
- There's the question of whether government information regulations really serve the interests of consumers. When mandated disclosure requirements technically are fulfilled by compliant advertisers but have little practical, expected impact on consumers as a result of such a perfunctory disclosure process, the critical question is whether government-mandate warnings and disclosures are effective at all in the service and interests of consumers.

Interesting Follow-Up Assignments for Advertisers-in-the-Making

Hunt on YouTube or record "off-air" programming that has commercials with affirmative disclosures in them. Check out [A] how many ways the disclosures one finds exhibit the problems noted above and [B] in what ways the interests or ethical obligations of the ad sponsor are potentially compromised.

- ***Degree of Reliance*** Business-to-business customers depend on the many claims made by their vendors. Therefore, if XPEDX (yes, that's how it's spelled), a manufacturer of boxes and other packages, claims in its ad that it can securely deliver any size product, it had better deliver.
- ***Type and Accessibility of Evidence*** The type of evidence could range from testimonials from satisfied customers to complex product testing in multiple laboratories. It could be made available through a toll-free number request or online.
- ***What Substantiation Is Reasonable*** What do experts in this area believe is reasonable proof of a claim?

Remedies for Deception and Unfair Advertising   Common sources of complaints concerning deceptive or unfair advertising practices are competitors, the public, and the FTC's own monitors. After the FTC determines that an ad is deceptive, the first step in the regulation process is to issue a **consent decree**. The FTC notifies the advertiser of its finding and asks the advertiser to sign a consent decree agreeing to stop the deceptive practice. Most advertisers do sign the decree to avoid the bad publicity.

Duracell was forced to modify one of its ads after Energizer complained that the ad inferred that Duracell CopperTop batteries would last three times longer than other heavy-duty and

Photo: Courtesy of SlimFast. Used with permission.

The disclaimer in the SlimFast ad indicates the conditions under which the consumer can snack and lose weight. In case you cannot read the fine print, it says: "Individual results may vary. Based on the SlimFast Plan (a reduced-calorie diet, regular exercise, and plenty of fluids). Check with your doctor if nursing, pregnant, under 18, or following a doctor prescribed diet."

super-heavy-duty batteries. The ad didn't mention Energizer by name, but Energizer charged the ad was "false and misleading" because consumers would think the comparison was with other alkaline batteries, such as Energizer. In fact, the CopperTop does not last longer than other alkaline batteries. The ad was modified with a disclaimer.[34]

It is important for students of advertising to understand the legal ramifications of deceptive and unfair advertising. Under some circumstances, the FTC holds advertisers and their agencies accountable. Essentially, an agency is liable for deceptive advertising along with the advertiser when the agency is an active participant in the preparation of the ad and knows or has reason to know that it is false or deceptive.

If a complaint seems justified, the commission can follow several courses of action:

- ***Cease-and-Desist Orders*** When an advertiser refuses to sign a consent decree and the FTC determines that the deception is substantial, the FTC issues a cease-and-desist order. The process leading to the issuance of a cease-and-desist order is similar to a court trial. An administrative law judge presides. FTC staff attorneys represent the commission, and the accused parties are entitled to representation by their lawyers. If the administrative judge decides in favor of the FTC, the judge issues an order requiring the respondents to cease their unlawful practices. The advertiser can appeal the order to the full five-member commission.

- ***Corrective Advertising*** The FTC may require **corrective advertising** when consumer research determines that an advertising campaign has perpetuated lasting false beliefs. Under this remedy, the FTC orders the offending organization to produce messages for consumers that correct the false impressions the ad made. The purpose of corrective advertising is not to punish an advertiser but to prevent it from continuing to deceive consumers. The FTC may require a firm to run corrective advertising even if the campaign in question has been discontinued.

    A landmark corrective advertising case is *Warner-Lambert v. FTC*. According to the FTC, Warner-Lambert's campaign for Listerine mouthwash, which ran for 50 years, had been deceiving customers, leading them to think that Listerine could prevent or reduce the severity of sore throats and colds. The company was ordered to run a corrective advertising campaign, mostly on television, for 16 months at a cost of $10 million.

    After the Warner-Lambert corrective campaign ran its course, 42 percent of Listerine users continued to believe that the mouthwash was being advertised as a remedy for sore throats and colds, and 57 percent of users rated cold and sore throat effectiveness as a key reason for purchasing the brand.[35] These results raised doubts about the effectiveness of corrective advertising to change impressions and have affected recent court decisions.

- ***Consumer Redress*** The Magnuson-Moss Warranty-FTC Improvement Act of 1975 empowers the FTC to obtain consumer redress when a person or a firm engages in deceptive practices. A judge can order any of the following: cancellation or reformation of contracts, refund of money or return of property, payment of damages, and public notification.

Media Review of Advertising

The media attempt to regulate advertising by screening and rejecting ads that violate their standards of truth and good taste. Most networks have a standards and practices department that screens every ad and gives approval before the ad can run. Each individual medium has the discretion to accept or reject a particular ad. For example, some magazines do not accept tobacco and liquor ads, and many magazines and television stations do not show condom ads. The major television networks craft their own standards and guidelines.

The First Amendment gives any publisher the right to refuse to publish anything the company does not want to publish, which sometimes creates battles between media companies and advertisers. For example, some billboard companies in Utah refused to run billboards for a Wasatch Beer company brand named Polygamy Porter. The brand's slogan "Why have just one!" and headlines such as "Take Some Home for the Wives" were deemed offensive to the state's Mormon population. A similar brouhaha arose when the state's Brighton Ski Resort promoted its four-person lifts with a billboard during the Salt Lake City Olympics that read, "Wife. Wife. Wife. Husband." The billboard company that banned the beer ads received letters both for and against its stand, which highlights the difficulty of such decisions.

Self-Regulation

Rather than wait for laws and regulatory actions, responsible advertisers take the initiative and establish individual ethical standards that anticipate and even go beyond possible complaints. Such a proactive stance helps the creative process and avoids the kinds of disasters that result from violating the law or offending members of society.

Advertisers practice three types of self-regulation: self-discipline, industry self-regulation, and self-regulation by public and community groups.

Self-Discipline   An organization such as an advertising agency exercises self-discipline when it develops, uses, and enforces norms within its own practices. Self-discipline starts with the individuals in the agency or organization. It is each person's responsibility to recognize ethical issues and be intentional about his or her behavior. We hope that this chapter will help you think about making choices that you deem the right thing to do in your career.

Virtually all major advertisers and advertising agencies have in-house ad review procedures, including reviews by agency and client attorneys. These employees help ensure that work is legal. Typically, the attorneys are concerned with how claims are phrased and substantiated. Are the claims verifiable? Do research and data prove the truth of the claims? Is there anything in the wording that could be misinterpreted or misleading? Is there anything deceptive in the visual images?

Several US companies (e.g., Colgate-Palmolive, General Foods, and AT&T) have their own codes of behavior and criteria that determine whether advertisements are acceptable. Companies without such codes tend to have informal criteria that they apply on an ad-by-ad basis. At a minimum, advertisers and agencies should have every element of a proposed ad evaluated by an in-house committee, lawyers, or both.

Industry Self-Regulation   When the development, use, and enforcement of norms come from the industry, the term used is *industry self-regulation*. In the case of both advertisers and advertising agencies, the most effective attempts at pure self-regulation have come through industry groups, such as the Advertising Review Council and the Better Business Bureau (BBB).

In 1971, several professional advertising associations, in conjunction with the Council of Better Business Bureaus, established the National Advertising Review Council, now known as the Advertising Self-Regulatory Council (ASRC), which negotiates voluntary withdrawal of national advertising that professionals consider deceptive. NAD of the Council of Better Business Bureaus and the National Advertising Review Board (NARB) are the two operating arms of the Advertising Self-Regulatory Council.[36] Neither is a government agency.

NAD is made up of people from the field of advertising. It evaluates complaints submitted by consumers, consumer groups, industrial organizations, and advertising firms. NAD also does its own industry monitoring. After NAD receives a complaint, it may ask the

FIGURE 18.4

Consumers or groups submitting a complaint to NAD and NARB go through this process. The ultimate power of NAD and NARB is the threat of passing the claim to the FTC. Usually, cases are settled before that point.

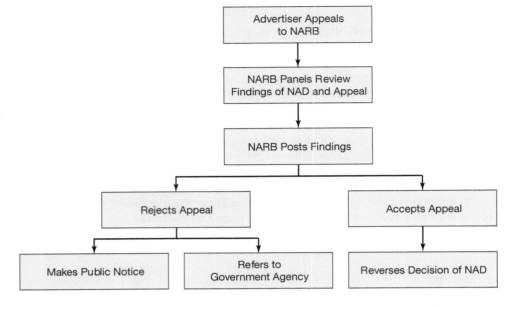

advertiser in question to substantiate claims made in the advertisement. If that substantiation is deemed inadequate, NAD representatives ask the advertiser to change or withdraw the offending ad. When a satisfactory resolution cannot be found, NAD refers the case to NARB.

NARB is a 50-member regulatory group that represents national advertisers, advertising agencies, and other professional fields. When the advertiser appeals a case to NARB, it faces a review panel of five people: three advertisers, one agency person, and one public representative. This NARB panel reviews the complaint and the NAD staff findings and holds hearings to let the advertiser present its case. If the case remains unresolved after the process, NARB can (1) publicly identify the advertiser and the facts about the case and (2) refer the complaint to the appropriate government agency, usually the FTC. Although neither NAD nor NARB has any real power other than threatening to invite government intervention, these groups have been effective in controlling cases of deception and misleading advertising. Figure 18.4 summarizes the NARB appeal process.

Self-Regulation by Public and Community Groups The advertising industry voluntarily involves nonindustry representatives, such as the BBB or the media, in the development, application, and enforcement of norms. Local and consumer activist groups represent two ways in which self-regulation occurs in this manner:

- *Local Group* At the local level, self-regulation that has been supported by the BBB (www.bbb.org) functions much like the national regulatory agencies and also provides local businesses with advice concerning the legal aspects of advertising. Approximately 250 local and national bureaus made up of advertisers, agencies, and media have screened hundreds of thousands of advertisements for possible violations of truth and accuracy. Although the BBB has no legal power, it receives and investigates complaints and maintains files on violators. It also assists local law enforcement officials in prosecuting violators. The ease with which the BBB can be accessed on the internet has prompted businesses to be more careful about complying with its standards.

- *Consumer Activist Group* Consumer groups of all kinds monitor advertising practices. The Action for Children's Advertising group follows the practices of advertisers who market to children and will file complaints with industry boards or regulatory agencies about advertisements they consider questionable. The consumer group Public Citizen inspired the FDA to require warnings on print ads for certain types of nicotine products. Groups that are focused on media literacy also review the performance of advertisers. For example, the Cultural Environment Movement is a nonprofit coalition of independent organizations and individuals that focuses on fairness, diversity, and justice in media communication.[37]

Making a World of Difference

Gandhi's quote inspires greatness: "Be the change that you wish to see in the world." Following in gigantic footsteps, Mycoskie has done that in his own way in the 21st century. He continues his mission to improve lives through innovation and an entrepreneurial spirit. Consider the difference he's making with his company in 70 countries:

- TOMS has given more than 60 million pairs of shoes to children in need since 2006.
- TOMS Eyewear, launched in 2011, has helped restore sight to more than 400,000 people in 13 countries.
- TOMS Roasting Co., launched in 2014, has provided more than 335,000 weeks of safe water in six countries to support the creation of sustainable water systems.
- TOMS Bag Collection, started in 2015, provides an entire line of bags reflecting the styles and textiles where the company gives shoes, sight, and water. The purpose of this segment of the business is to help provide training for skilled birth attendants and distribute birth kits containing items for the safe delivery of babies. As of 2016, TOMS had aided more than 25,000 mothers.

Mycoskie and his company have won a world of accolades, including the prestigious 2009 Award for Corporate Excellence (ACE) from the US secretary of state. *People Magazine* featured Mycoskie in its "Heroes Among Us" section, and Bill Gates featured TOMS shoes in his *Time* article "How to Fix Capitalism."

Some critics claim that by giving away shoes (and eyewear and water and birth kits) TOMS is treating the symptom of the much deeper problem of poverty. Is the problem a lack of shoes or a lack of jobs and opportunity? Nonetheless, Mycoskie and his company are showing their way of forging new pathways—in business and promotion—that have the result of making a world of difference. And he's demonstrating how to do well by doing good.

Logo: Peter Horree/Alamy Stock Photo

KEY OBJECTIVES SUMMARY

18.1. Name and discuss the key debates related to the social impact of brand communication. To some extent, brand communication creates demands for products; however, the power of promotional efforts to do that is hard to measure. The shape-versus-mirror debate is a central issue in considering advertising's role in society. Critics of advertising tend to believe that it has the power to shape social trends and the way people think and act; advertising professionals tend to believe that it mirrors values rather than sets them. In fact, advertising and society's values are probably interactive, so the answer may simply be that advertising both mirrors and shapes values. Whether or not advertising causes society to become overcommercialized relates to the criticism that buying products appears to be the solution to every problem. Counterarguments emerge from the position that consumers can make intelligent choices about what they need.

18.2. Describe the ethical responsibilities that brand communicators bear. All brand communicators have a social responsibility to make good ethical choices. At the root of ethical behavior is the individual decision maker's set of moral values. When faced with a dilemma of equally compelling choices, advertising and public relations professionals can consult their personal values, professional codes of ethics, and international standards of ethical behavior to guide their moral decision-making.

18.3. Discuss how advertising is regulated. In a complex society, there is usually not one answer to what constitutes "right" behavior. Regulatory agencies help enforce advertising standards. Several governmental bodies help regulate advertising:

- The FTC is the agency concerned primarily with identifying and eliminating deceptive advertising.
- The FDA oversees advertising related to food and drugs.

- The FCC monitors advertising broadcast by radio and television stations.
- Other regulatory bodies with some advertising oversight include the Bureau of Alcohol, Tobacco, Firearms and Explosives; the US Postal Service; the Patent and Trademark Office; the Library of Congress; and the states' attorneys general offices.

In addition to governmental oversight, advertising is also self-regulated. Individuals working in the field need to act responsibly to make ethical and legal choices. Advertising agencies have in-house ad review procedures and legal staff that monitor the creation of advertising. The industry has a number of bodies that review advertising, such as the Advertising Self-Regulatory Review Council, the National Advertising Division of the Better Business Bureau, and the National Advertising Review Board. Other bodies include the various media review boards, competitors who are concerned about unfair advertising that might harm their brands, professional organizations such as the Public Relations Society of America, and public and community groups that represent either local or special-interest groups.

KEY TERMS

blogola, p. 550
Bureau of Alcohol, Tobacco, Firearms and Explosives, p. 562
cease-and-desist order, p. 561
claim substantiation, p. 564
code of ethics, p. 555
commercial speech, p. 559
comparative advertising, p. 548
consent decree, p. 565

copyright, p. 559
corrective advertising, p. 566
cultural imperialism, p. 546
deceptive advertising, p. 563
demand creation, p. 542
endorsement, p. 549
ethics, p. 553
false advertising, p. 547
Federal Communications Commission (FCC), p. 561

Federal Trade Commission (FTC), p. 548
Food and Drug Administration (FDA), p. 561
international advertising, p. 546
Library of Congress, p. 559
marketing imperialism, p. 546
morals, p. 553
puffery, p. 548

social responsibility, p. 541
stereotype, p. 545
testimonial, p. 549
trademark, p. 559
uniform resource locators (URLs), p. 559
US Postal Service, p. 562
US Patent and Trademark Office, p. 559

MyLab Marketing

Go to **www.pearson.com/mylab/marketing** for MyLab discussion questions (⚙) as well as the following assisted-graded writing questions.

18-1. Define ethics. How do you determine what is ethical? If you are called on to make a decision about the promotion of an event for one of your clients, where does the ultimate consideration lie? What questions would you ask?

18-2. A pharmaceutical company has repackaged a previously developed drug that addresses the symptoms of a scientifically questionable disorder affecting approximately 5 percent of women. Although few women are affected by the "disorder," the company's advertising strategy is comprehensive, including dozens of television, radio, and magazine ads. As a result, millions of women with symptoms similar to those of the disorder have sought prescriptions for the company's drug. In turn, the company has made billions of dollars. What, if any, are the ethical implications of advertising a remedy to a mass audience when the affected group is small? Is the company misrepresenting its drug by conducting a "media blitz"? Why or why not?

REVIEW QUESTIONS

18-3. Explain the debate over whether advertising shapes or mirrors society. If you were to take a side in this debate, which side would you choose?

⚙ **18-4.** What do you consider the most pressing ethical issues facing brand communicators? Explain.

18-5. Explain how trademarks and copyrights are legally protected and why the First Amendment is important to advertisers.

18-6. In addition to the FTC, what other governmental bodies are involved in regulating advertising practices?

DISCUSSION QUESTIONS

18-7. The Dimento Game Company has a new basketball video game. To promote it, "Slammer" Aston, a professional basketball star, is signed to do the commercial. Aston is shown in the commercial with the game controls as he speaks these lines: "This is the most challenging court game you've ever tried. It's all here—zones, man-to-man, pick and roll, even the alley-oop. For me, this is the best game off the court." Is Aston's presentation an endorsement? Should the FTC consider a complaint if Dimento uses this strategy? What would you need to know to determine if you are safe from a challenge of misleading advertising?

18-8. Zack Wilson is the advertising manager for the campus newspaper. He is looking over a layout for a promotion for a spring break vacation package. The headline says, "Absolutely the Finest Deal Available This Spring—You'll Have the Best Time Ever If You Join Us in Boca." The newspaper has a solid reputation for not running advertising with questionable claims and promises. Should Zack accept or reject this ad? Take one side of this issue and write a short one- to two-page position paper explaining your viewpoint. In a class discussion, determine how many of your classmates agreed or disagreed with your view.

TAKE-HOME PROJECTS

18-9. *Portfolio Project:* Check the websites of three big-name companies, such as the following:

- McDonald's (www.mcdonalds.com)
- Avon (www.avon.com)
- Ben & Jerry's (www.benjerry.com)
- Starbucks (www.starbucks.com)
- Body Shop (www.thebodyshop.com)
- Target (www.target.com)
- Häagen-Dazs® (www.haagendazs.us)

Write a two- to four-page report on their efforts to be socially responsible. How is the company's social responsibility position reflected in its advertising?

18-10. *Mini-Case Analysis:* Imagine that you are now working for Starbucks. What does the company do that provides evidence that it is socially and environmentally responsible? What other ways can you think of for the company to expand these efforts?

TRACE North America Case

Multicultural Ethics and Issues

Read the TRACE case in the Appendix before coming to class. Then answer the following questions:

18-11. Does the "Hard to Explain, Easy to Experience" campaign communicate its brand message of innovation without using ideas, words, or images that are offensive or insensitive to the target audience?

18-12. Give an example that demonstrates how the TRACE campaign is socially responsible.

18-13. What evidence in this case leads you to believe that the advertising team that created this campaign understood Multicultural Millennials? Can you add any additional insights?

HANDS-ON CASE

Authentically Green?

Increasingly, companies are attempting to align themselves with good causes, such as showing that they're caretakers of the environment. You may be familiar with "Ecomagination," a strategy created by General Electric to drive innovation and growth of earth-friendly environmental solutions. It pledged $1.5 billion investment in research and development of green technologies toward this effort, such as using wind energy, recovering wastewater, and exploring the use of compressed natural gas for vehicles. Read about Häagen-Dazs's efforts to solve the mystery of disappearing honeybees and Dawn's efforts to help save wildlife. You don't have to look far to see examples of other corporations that are engaged in work to help sustain the environment.

Often criticized for the harm some of the ingredients do to the environment, corporations producing household cleaners are, well, trying to clean up their act.

The green niche is a fast-growing segment of the $2.7 billion market for household cleaning products. In 2008, the Clorox Company, a century-old company known for its not-so-environmentally-friendly products, such as bleach, Pine-Sol, and Formula 409, launched a line of ecofriendly products it called Green Works in part to take advantage of this opportunity. The products contain 95 percent natural plant- and mineral-based biodegradable cleaning ingredients. Packaging can be recycled, and the products are not tested on animals. The Sierra Club even endorsed it, although that relationship has now ended. Green Works products received a seal from the Environmental Protection Agency's program Design for the Environment, which recognizes and promotes green chemistry and the health of humans and the environment. (You might want to review the FTC's Green Guides at www.ftc.gov, which are designed to help companies make green claims that customers can understand.)

Sales for Clorox Green Works products soared to $53 million in 2009. By 2012, though, they fell to $32 million. Do you wonder why? There are two reasons: the overall market has slowed down, and competition has increased, according to Packaged Facts, a source of market research on consumer goods.

In the Part 5 opener you read about building brands, brand relationships, and brand equity. As a marketer, you should build and maintain distinctive brands that your customers love. Capitalizing on social trends can be good business and can connect your company with good causes that make consumers feel good about your brand. It can also backfire if they do not find the marketing to be sincere or they find the products inferior.

Some critics vented their opinions about Green Works on blogs and other venues:

- This isn't green; it's greenwashing. How sincere can the Clorox Company be when it sells not only green products, but also other products that are highly toxic and environmentally unfriendly?
- Green isn't something a company is because it develops a new product line. Rather, it's about changing the inside culture of a company.
- Can Green Works truly claim it's green on its labels when there are no industry standards defining "natural cleaners"?

Do you think Green Works is authentically green?

Consider This

P5-1. After reading about Green Works in the case and on the internet, do you think this product line is a believable attempt by Clorox to improve the environment? Why or why not?

P5-2. Does Green Works represent an attempt to mirror a trend in society or create one?

P5-3. Had you been the product manager, would you have put the Clorox name on the Green Works products, as the company did? Explain your decision.

P5-4. Do you think that green marketing is an enduring movement? Why or why not?

Sources: http://ge.ecomagination.com; www.greenworkscleaners.com; www.environmentalleader.com; Jane L. Levere, "In an Overhaul, Clorox Aims to Get Green Works Out of Its Niche," April 21, 2013, www.nytimes.com; Jack Neff, "Consumers Don't Believe Your Green Ad Claims, Survey Finds," September 16, 2013, www.adage.com; "Green Household Cleaning and Laundry Products in the U.S.," 3rd ed., March 13, 2015, www.packagedfacts.com.

TRACE*
American Advertising Federation Competition

▲ PHIL WILLET

The following case was written by Phil Willet when he was an assistant professor of advertising in the College of Journalism and Mass Communications at the University of Nebraska–Lincoln. Professor Willet was the faculty adviser to the National Student Advertising Competition team that won the 2012 American Advertising Federation National Student Advertising Competition. The competition is the oldest and largest advertising competition in the United States.

Trace North America: Multicultural Innovation

Hard to Explain, Easy to Experience:
To Be Understood and Appreciated by the Target Audience,
TRACE Has to Be Experienced

The challenge for the 2012 NSAC is to develop a fully integrated marketing campaign to help TRACE build awareness and lasting favorability among African American, Hispanic, and Chinese Millennial consumers in the United States. The campaign should focus on the TRACE innovation theme and ultimately lead to increased market share across this multicultural target.

The Problem

The demographic landscape of the United States is changing. Now more than ever, larger populations of multicultural individuals are present and fully integrated into all parts of American society. As such, building a market share in the African American, Hispanic, and Chinese Millennial markets is absolutely necessary. TRACE recognizes the need to connect with these audiences and will do so by generating increased awareness about its innovative brand.

Research

What we learned about Multicultural Millennials:

Foundation

"People don't buy what you do, people buy why you do it."

This quote, from former advertiser Simon Sinek, is relevant to our challenge of increasing brand awareness in the Multicultural Millennial market. Naturally, our first step was to discover exactly *why* TRACE makes vehicles.

---

* TRACE CAR CO. is a fictitious brand created by the author. This case is based on the actual case created by the University of Nebraska–Lincoln for the 2012 American Advertising Federation National Student Advertising Competition.

Brand Promise

The TRACE brand aspires to provide customers with innovative ideas for the joy of everyday driving. The target audience expresses its aspiration to make daily life vital and energetic by adding spice or edge and TRACE delivers innovative ideas to its customers.

TRACE lives, breathes, and implements innovation into every aspect of its company. *For customers to buy TRACE, they have to "buy" that TRACE is innovative.*

The target demographic must believe that TRACE adheres to its brand promise. The foundation of our research and the communication model was to observe how the target market relates to innovation and its importance in their lives.

Objectives and Methods

The University of Nebraska–Lincoln research team conducted 311 quantitative surveys, 35 video interviews, 30 written interviews, 10 dealership interviews, 5 test drive interviews, and 4 multicultural focus groups to find out the following:

1. What does innovation mean to Millennial Hispanics, Chinese, and African Americans?
2. What are the similarities and differences between these target markets?
3. How do the target markets want to see themselves in advertising?
4. What factors influence the car buying process?
5. How do the target markets feel about TRACE and its main competitors?

Research Insights

Chinese American

- Place heavy emphasis on education, work, and family
- Are sensitive to prestige
- Favor luxury auto advertising

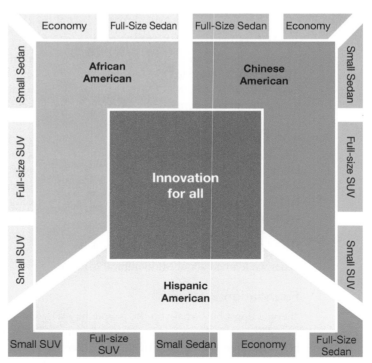

ABOVE: This model demonstrates the parallels between TRACE, the target markets, and innovation. At the core of the model is innovation, surrounded by the three target markets. This layer represents what the audiences associate with innovation. We connected their associations to TRACE's five core models, composing the outer layer. This gave us a basis for positioning each model for the three markets.

Hispanic American

- Focus on technological aspects of vehicles
- View features as more important than brand image
- Favor commercials that are especially creative or humorous

African American

- Female spouse or family member makes most purchasing decisions
- Loyal to brands they have grown up with
- Favor humorous advertising

Key Combined Insights on the Target Audiences:

- They have strong bonds with family. Family is *key* for big purchase decisions, typically accompanying the target markets to the dealership.
- They want to see themselves in advertising more often, being portrayed in a positive and professional light.
- They are youthful, price conscious consumers.
- Decisions rely *heavily* on brand experience.
- They associate with others based on interests more often than ethnicity.

Strategy

What we want to say and reason to believe

Our Proposition: To be understood and appreciated by the target audience, TRACE has to be experienced.

Reason to Believe: Once the target markets know more about TRACE and its innovative features, they will realize that it is the intelligent choice. Features that the targets find innovative include Brake Override Technology, Vehicle Dynamic Control, and Continuously Variable Transmission. Once the markets experience these innovations, they will find them valuable in their purchasing decisions. *Driving a TRACE can't be explained; it must be experienced.*

"Ever since having so much space in my new TRACE, I have been inspired to make some changes."
—Alisha, 21

Alisha drags chair across classroom, away from group of students. Other students look confused.

Closeup of desk chair as it is moved across the floor. "SCREEECH!"

Classmates have confused expressions while Alisha looks relaxed in her moved desk.

Panning of TRACE. MUSIC: "Countdown"—Beyoncé
VOICEOVER: "The new TRACE is big on space but small on price. It's innovation that's . . ."

Wide shot of the TRACE: " . . . but easy to experience."

TRACE Logo including the "Hard to Explain, Easy to Experience" and "Innovation for All" tags.
MUSIC: fade out
Alisha looks relaxed in her moved seat. ". . . hard to explain . . ."

Creative Executions

The television spots pair a vehicle and its features with a specific demographic in the target audience. A character in each of the spots has experienced a TRACE feature and has been inspired to make changes in their life to reflect these innovations.

Because TRACE is an innovative company, we wanted our print campaign to share that spirit of innovation. We created ads that feature members of the target market and use new tactics, which include foldout pages and peel-off stickers. The creative format will drive home our idea that TRACE's innovations are hard to explain but easy to experience.

Promotions and Public Relations

In addition to the print and television, the "Hard to Explain, Easy to Experience" creative team created point-of-purchase dealership displays, interactive walkways, in-window outdoor displays with the ability to post to Facebook Timeline, out-of-home theater displays, and elevator wraps. Public relation efforts included post-recycled playgrounds with an innovative playground Web application and multicultural scholarships.

Media

Our $100MM media plan will go a long way in helping us reach multicultural Millennials.

Objectives

- Nationwide: Maintain 70 percent reach with an average frequency of 3 throughout the year
- Spot Markets: Achieve 85 percent reach with an average frequency of 4 during targeted months
- Generate buzz through outdoor, digital, and traditional advertising integration

Strategies

- Pulse media by maintaining a yearlong national presence with extra emphasis placed in strategic areas at strategic times. TRACE sales data from 2010 and 2011 was also used in these decisions.
- April–May to launch campaign and coincide with May's typically high car demand

In-Window Outdoor
In-window outdoor technology creates an interactive storefront display to allow consumers to interact with TRACE's history and its Facebook Timeline page. Individual screens reflect real-time footage of people interacting with TRACE vehicles correlating to a specific year in TRACE history. The selected year determines what is reflected in the window. For example, if they select the year 1934, a black-and-white display of a TRACE from that year will appear. Consumers can then take photos of themselves with the vehicles and share the photos to their own Facebook Timeline profiles.

- August–September to coincide with the launch of new models and higher-than-average car demand
- December because it historically ranks first or second in car-buying volume for TRACE
- March because it historically ranks first or second in car-buying volume for TRACE and to finish the campaign on a strong note
- Target the top 10 markets in population for each of the three segments (total of 16 markets with the overlap)

Tactics

Media buys are based on each of the target audiences' media usage and lifestyle. While some vehicles are geared toward one of the target markets, others can be used for all three.

Overview

The April 2013–March 2014 "Hard to Explain, Easy to Experience" campaign will use an optimized combination of traditional and nontraditional media to maximize our reach to three target markets as well as generate buzz around the TRACE brand.

Evaluation

We will explore several tactics to measure the effectiveness of our campaign.

Concurrent and posttesting will be conducted to reaffirm the achievement of our objectives during the campaign. Concurrent testing will take place at three-month intervals during the campaign to measure the level of effectiveness. Concurrent testing will include tracking studies of telephone interviews, e-mail interviews, surveys, and product audits. Surveys will accompany these methods to provide a view of the campaign's effectiveness.

In order to have a better idea of the target market's foot traffic into TRACE dealerships, each dealership will keep a database on all multicultural Millennials that enter a dealership and express interest in the cars.

Posttesting will occur directly after the complete run of the campaign and will measure several factors, including recognition, recall, attitudes, awareness, and sales. Recognition tests will prove most valuable for evaluating brand awareness and lasting favorability among the target market.

Summary

The success of the "Hard to Explain, Easy to Experience" campaign will be determined by its primary goal of driving multiculturals to the dealership to experience TRACE's innovation. The car-buying process is a major and somewhat complicated decision. We believe the better educated the consumer, the more likely TRACE can fulfill its brand promise of "Innovation for all."

University of Nebraska-Lincoln NSAC Agency

Account Services: Hans Christensen, Account Supervisor; Kevin McCaskill, Account Supervisor; Calvin Drey, Account Planner/Project Manager/PR; Michelle Pineda, Account Coordinator/ Project Manager/PR; Paul Henderson, Account Planner; Chelsey Wahlstrom, Account Planner/ PR; Zee Chiweshe, Account Planner/PR; Jana Schneider, Account Planner/PR; Ashley Turner, Account Planner.

Media Services: Sara Smits, Media Director; Bingjie Zhao, Media Planner; Tayler Thomas, Account Planner/Media Planner/PR; Megan Homolka, Copywriter/Media Planner.

Creative: Landon Stahmer, Creative Director; Rance Ristau, Project Manager; Nolan Gauthier, Copywriter; Tim Obermueller, Copywriter; Russell Troxel, Copywriter; Dana Oltman, Art Director; Dennis Bukowski, Art Director; Maddie Jager, Art Director; Dylan McCaugherty, Interactive Designer/Writer; Abby Meyer, Film.

GLOSSARY

3-D television Television programs that have been filmed using technology that creates the illusion of depth, which is the third dimension—the other two being width and height.

360-degree communication The practice of looking at a brand from all directions and all points of view using a brand vision that surrounds all the brand's interactions with all its stakeholders.

A

Account executive A person who acts as a liaison between the client and the agency.

Account management People and processes at an ad agency that facilitate the relationship between the agency and the client.

Account planner The person responsible for the strategy and its implementation in the creative work.

Account planning A process of using research to gain information about the brand in its marketplace, the consumer's perspective, or both, and to use that research to contribute directly to advertising development.

Account services The account management function of an agency, which acts as a liaison between the client and the agency.

Acquired needs A driving force learned from culture, society, and the environment.

Active publics Those people who communicate and organize to do something about an issue or situation.

Added value A marketing activity, such as advertising, that makes a product more appealing or useful.

Addressable media Media, such as mail, the internet, and the telephone, that carry messages to identifiable customers or prospects.

Addressable television Television technology that permits the signal to be personalized to a home.

Adese Formula writing that uses clichés, generalities, stock phrases, and superlatives.

Adoption process Buying behavior that reflects the speed with which people are willing to try something new.

Advertainment A form of persuasive advertising in which the commercials look like TV shows or short films, and provide entertainment as opposed to high levels of information.

Advertisement A notice about a product (good, service, or idea) that is designed to get the attention of a target audience.

Advertiser A person or organization that initiates the advertising process.

Advertising Paid nonpersonal communication from an identified sponsor using mass media to persuade or influence an audience.

Advertising agency An organization that provides a variety of professional services to its client, who is the advertiser of a product.

Advertising department An advertising department operates within an organization to use a variety of IMC tools to achieve its goals (revenue, profits, market share, goodwill, donations, earned media).

Advertorials An advertising page or special segment that looks like regular editorial pages but is identified by the word "advertisement" at the top; the content is often about a company, product, or brand and written by the organization's public relations department.

Advocacy A type of advertising that communicates a viewpoint.

Advocacy advertising A type of corporate advertising that involves creating advertisements and purchasing space to deliver a specific, targeted message.

Affective response A response caused by or expressing feelings and emotions.

Affiliates A station that contracts with a national network to carry network-originated programming during part of its schedule.

Agency networks Large conglomerations of agencies under a central ownership.

Agency of record An advertising agency that manages the business between a company and the agencies it has contracts with.

AIDA A hierarchy of effects identified as Attention, Interest, Desire, and Action.

Aided recall When one can remember an idea after seeing a cue.

Animation A film or video technique in which objects or drawings are filmed one frame at a time.

Annual report A financial document legally required of all publicly held companies.

Aperture The ideal moment for exposing consumers to an advertising message.

Appeal An advertising approach that connects with some need, want, or emotion that makes the product message attractive, attention getting, or interesting.

Argument A cognitive strategy that uses logic, reasons, and proof to build convictions.

Art director The person who is primarily responsible for the visual image of the advertisement.

Association The process used to link a product with a positive experience, personality, or lifestyle.

Attention Concentrating the mind on a thought or idea.

Attitude A learned predisposition that we hold toward an object, person, or idea.

Attribute A distinctive feature of a product.

Average frequency The average number of times an audience has an opportunity to be exposed to a media vehicle or vehicles in a specified time span.

Awareness The degree to which a message has made an impression on the viewer or reader.

B

B2C2C A model of communication that begins with messages from a business (B) directed to key influential consumers (C) who then communicate with other consumers (C).

Back translation The practice of translating ad copy into a second language and then translating that version back into the original language to check the accuracy of the translation.

Bandwagon appeals The idea that people respond to popular causes and ideas and want to join up or adopt a trendy viewpoint.

Banner ad Small, often rectangular-shaped graphic that appears at the top of a web page.

Behavioral targeting The practice of identifying groups of people who might be in the market for a product based on their actions—particularly the patterns of their online behavior.

Beliefs A term related to a person's cognitive processing—how they arrive at a position, viewpoint, or decision based on their knowledge, attitudes, and opinions.

Believability The extent to which a marketing communication message is accepted as true.

Benchmarking Comparing a result against some other known result from a comparable effort.

Benefit Statement about what the product can do for the user.

Big Idea A creative idea that expresses an original advertising thought.

Billboarding The practice of massing a set of packages with a consistent design to create visual impact on a shelf.

Bleed A full-page ad with no outside margins—the printed area extends to the edge of the page.

Bleed-throughs In printed communication, the image on one side of a sheet of paper can be seen on the other, usually because the ink has thoroughly saturated the paper.

Blind headline An indirect headline that gives little information.

Blog A regularly updated web page that includes text, hyperlinks, videos, and/or photographs, and is written in an informal style.

Blogola Company representatives who pose as consumers or paid bloggers who post endorsements as customer reviews online without the sponsorship being made known to readers, also known as flogging.

Body copy The text of the message.

Brag-and-boast copy Self-important copy that focuses on the company rather than the consumer.

Brainfag In creative thinking, this is the point where concentration ceases to produce ideas because of mental fatigue and the mind closes down.

Brainstorming A creative thinking technique using free association in a group environment to stimulate inspiration.

Brand A name, term, design, or symbol that identifies the goods, services, institution, or idea sold by a marketer.

Brand advertising An advertising strategy that focuses on creating an image or perception of a brand.

Brand advocacy A word-of-mouth strategy that uses customer referrals to create buzz and connect with influential contacts who will spread information about the brand.

Brand advocate A key customer or stakeholder who communicates positive information within a circle of friends or contacts.

Brand communication All the various marketing communication messages and brand experiences that create and maintain a coherent brand concept or image.

Brand communities Groups of people devoted to a particular brand, such as the Harley Owners Group (HOG) for Harley-Davidson.

Brand content A form of advertising that generates interesting, informative, or entertaining content as a way to promote a particular brand.

Brand development index (BDI) A numerical technique used to indicate a brand's sales within a particular market relative to all other markets where the brand is sold.

Brand equity The value associated with a brand; the reputation that the brand name or symbol connotes.

Brand extension Use of an established brand name with a related line of products.

Brand icon A character used to represent the brand.

Brand identity Unique characteristics of a product within a product category.

Brand image A special meaning or mental representation created for a product by giving it a distinctive name and identity.

Brand integrity A brand is more believable because what it says and does matches what others say about it.

Brand journalism Developing and publishing interesting and well-written stories about a company that make readers want to know more about the company and its products.

Brand licensing A partner company rents the brand name and transfers some of its brand equity to another product.

Brand linkage test A research method that asks viewers to link a specific brand or product category to a specific commercial.

Brand linkage The extent to which an advertising message is connected to the brand and locked into the memory of people who see the message.

Brand loyalty The degree of attachment that a customer has to a particular brand as expressed by repeat sales.

Brand management An organizational structure that places a manager or management team in charge of a brand's total marketing efforts.

Brand name The part of the brand that can be spoken, such as words, letters, or numbers.

Brand personality The image projected by a brand that often resembles characteristics of people.

Brand position The location a brand occupies in consumers' minds relative to its competitors.

Brand promise Communication that sets expectations for what a customer believes will happen when the product is used.

Brand relationship Communication aimed at delivering reminders about familiar brands and building trust.

Brand reputation What other people say and think about a brand.

Brand steward A person who manages a brand's marketing and communication.

Brand transformation A brand's meaning is more valuable than the products, goods, or services it represents.

Brand value Enhanced meaning of a brand that adds worth to products and services.

Branded apps A software program mounted on a cell phone, computer, or social networking page that contains information sponsored by or related to a brand.

Branded entertainment Programs, such as the Hallmark Hall of Fame, that are sponsored by a particular brand.

Branded media This refers to forms of entertainment media that are owned by an organization and used to create high levels of engagement with a brand.

Branded videos Informative, educational, or entertaining videos created by marketers that are designed to engage with audiences and connect them to a brand in a more relevant and trustworthy way than traditional advertising.

Break-even analysis A type of payout plan that seeks to determine the point at which the total cost of the promotion exceeds the total revenues, identifying the point where the effort cannot break even.

Broadcast media Communication vehicles such as television and radio that deliver audio, video, or other messages to a dispersed audience.

Broadcast network A national group of affiliated stations through which programming and advertising are distributed.

Brokers People or companies who sell space (in print) or time (in broadcast) for a variety of media.

Bureau of Alcohol, Tobacco, Firearms and Explosives The law enforcement agency in the US Department of Justice that regulates advertising of alcohol and tobacco products.

Business philosophy The fundamental principles that guide the operations of the business.

Business-to-business (B2B) advertising Targets other businesses.

Business-to-business (B2B) market Organizations that produce products for use by other businesses in their operations or for resale to consumers.

Buzz Gossip created by people over a popular interest in something.

C

Cable radio A technology that uses cable television receivers to deliver static-free music via wires plugged into cable subscribers' audio systems.

Cable television A form of subscription television in which the signals are carried to households by a cable.

Call centers Facilities with banks of phones and representatives who call prospects (outbound) or answer customer calls (inbound).

Call to action A concluding line that tells people how to buy the product.

Call-out A block of text separate from the main display copy and headline where the idea is presented.

Campaign A comprehensive advertising plan for a series of different but related ads that appear in different media across a specified time period.

Captions Text that explains what is happening in a corresponding photo or illustration.

Carrot mob A technique used by environmentalists to reward companies that support green marketing.

Carryover effect A measure of residual effect (awareness or recall) of the advertising message some time after the advertising period has ended.

Casting Finding the right person for the role.

Catalog A multipage direct-mail publication that shows a variety of merchandise.

Category development index (CDI) A numerical technique that indicates the relative consumption rate in a particular market for a particular product category.

Cause marketing Sponsoring a good cause in the hope that the association will result in positive public opinion about the company.

Cease-and-desist order An FTC remedy for false or deceptive advertising that requires an advertiser to stop its unlawful practices.

Channel marketing Advertising and promotion efforts directed at members of the distribution channel.

Channel markets The members of a distribution chain, including resellers or intermediaries.

Channel of communication The media through which an advertisement is presented.

Channel of distribution People and organizations involved in moving products from producers to consumers.

Channels Media or companies such as local newspaper or radio stations that transmit communication messages from the advertiser to the audience and from consumers back to companies.

Circulars Preprinted advertisements ranging in size from a single page to more than 30 pages that are often printed elsewhere and supplied to a newspaper, where they are inserted between sections.

Circulation The number of copies sold.

Claim A statement about the product's performance.

Claim substantiation The reasonable basis for making an assertion about product performance.

Classified advertising Commercial messages arranged in the newspaper according to the interests of readers.

Claymation A stop-motion animation technique in which figures sculpted from clay are filmed one frame at a time.

Clichés Generic, nonoriginal, non-novel ideas.

Click art See Clip art.

Click-through rates A method of measuring the effectiveness of online advertising by dividing the number of times the ad was presented on a website by the number of times it was clicked on by viewers.

Click-through The act of clicking on a button on a website that takes the viewer to a different website.

Clip art Generic, copyright-free art that can be used by anyone who buys the book or service.

Closing Represents the last date to send an ad to production.

Closing paragraph The last paragraph of body copy in an ad that sums up the selling message, usually ending with a call to action.

Clutter The excessive number of messages delivered to a target audience.

Co-op advertising Also called cooperative advertising; an arrangement between a retailer and manufacturer in which the manufacturer reimburses the retailer for all or part of the retailer's advertising costs.

Cobranding A product offered by two companies with both companies' brands present.

Code of ethics The rules and standards for a system of socially responsible professional practice.

Cognition How consumers respond to information, learn, and understand.

Cognitive dissonance A tendency to justify the discrepancy between what you receive and what you expected to receive.

Cognitive learning When advertisers want people to know something new after watching or hearing a message.

Cold call Contacts that are made to leads that have not been qualified as interested; also includes cold calls made by telemarketers to random phone numbers.

Collateral materials Brochures and other forms of product literature used in support of an advertising, public relations, or sales promotion effort.

Color separation The process of splitting a color image into four images recorded on negatives; each negative represents one of the four process colors.

Comarketing Programs through which manufacturers partner with retailers in joint promotions.

Commercial speech Our legal right to say what we want to promote commercial activity, as defined by the First Amendment.

Commission system The procedures through which advertising agencies are paid a commission for placing ads—buying time and space—on behalf of their clients.

Communication brief A strategy document that explains the consumer insight and summarizes the message and media strategy.

Community relations The relationship that an organization has with the people who live in the areas where it operates.

Comparative advertising A message strategy that explicitly or implicitly compares the features of two or more brands.

Comparison An advertising strategy that compares two or more brands.

Competitive advantage Features or benefits of a product that let it outperform its competitors.

Compiled list In database marketing, a list that is created by merging several lists and purging duplicate entries.

Composition The art of arranging the way the elements in a photograph are positioned.

Comprehension The process by which people understand, make sense of things, and acquire knowledge.

Comprehensives A layout that looks as much like the final printed ad as possible.

Concept testing When a simple statement of an idea is tried out on people who are representative of the target audience in order to get their reactions to the Big Idea.

Concepting Creating a Big Idea.

Conditioned learning Learning through association by connecting a stimulus to a reward through repeated exposure to a stimulus that eventually leads to the reward.

Connection planning Another way to refer to media planning, but in this approach the emphasis is on engagement and two-way communication opportunities.

Consent decree A formal FTC agreement with an advertiser that obligates the advertiser to stop its deceptive practices.

Considered purchase Buying something after gathering and evaluating information.

Consolidated services Company action of bringing planning and buying functions together.

Consumer behavior The process of an individual or group selecting, purchasing, using, or disposing of products, services, ideas, or experiences to satisfy needs and desires.

Consumer-generated content Advertising created by consumers for a brand.

Consumer insight Planning conclusions and decisions about why people behave as they do based on solid consumer research and thoughtful analyses of the findings.

Consumer market Selling products to a general (non-business) audience.

Consumer relations The manner in which a business communicates and interacts with the public to build positive relationships with consumers to ultimately gain and retain customers.

Consumer research A type of market research that identifies people who are in the market for a product.

Consumer research panel Information provided by an ongoing group of carefully selected people interested in a particular topic or product category.

Contact points The media, as well as other places and ways, where a consumer engages in a brand experience.

Content analysis Research that analyzes articles, news stories, and other printed materials for themes and positive or negative mentions of a brand or company.

Contest A form of promotion that requires participants to compete for a prize or prizes based on some sort of skill or ability.

Continuity Even, continuous advertising over the time span of the advertising campaign.

Continuity program A program designed to encourage loyalty and repeat purchases.

Continuous strategy A media strategy that spreads the advertising evenly over a period.

Continuous tone Images that have a range of tones from white to black and all the shades of gray in between.

Controlled circulation Publications that are distributed, usually free, to selected individuals.

Convergence Because of the digitization of media forms, specialized media, such as newspapers and television, are becoming more alike in their content and how they are delivered online.

Conversion rates In sales, changing a prospect into a customer.

Conviction A particularly strong belief that has been anchored firmly in one's attitudes.

Cool hunters People who specialize in spotting trends.

Copycat advertising Using some other brand's creative idea.

Copyright The owner or creator of certain types of original works who has the sole right to reproduce and distribute the work.

Copytesting Evaluating the effectiveness of an ad, either in a draft form or after it has been used.

Copywriter The person who writes the text for an ad.

Core values Underlying values that govern a person's (or a brand's) attitudes and behavior.

Corporate advertising A type of advertising used by firms to build awareness of a company, its products, and the nature of its business.

Corporate culture The values and attitudes that shape the behavior of an organization and its employees.

Corporate identity advertising Promotional method aimed at enhancing or maintaining a company's reputation in the marketplace.

Corporate image A perception of a company that its stakeholders create in their minds from messages and experiences with the company.

Corporate relations Relations between a corporation and the public involving an organization's image and reputation.

Corporate social responsibility Programs designed to create a platform of good citizenship for corporations and other organizations.

Corrective advertising An FTC directive that requires an advertiser to run truthful ads to counter deceptive ads.

Cost per lead Record of how well a click-through generates prospects.

Cost per point (CPP) A method of comparing alternative media vehicles on the basis of what it costs to deliver 1,000 readers, viewers, or listeners; the cost of an advertising unit (30-second TV or radio spot, for example) per 1,000 impressions.

Cost per thousand (CPM) The cost of exposing each 1,000 members of the target audience to the advertising message.

Coupons Legal certificates offered by manufacturers and retailers that grant specified savings on selected products when presented for redemption at the point-of-purchase.

Coverage The degree to which a particular advertising medium delivers audiences within a specific geographical area.

Crawl Letters that move across the bottom of the screen.

Creative As a noun, creative is the product that demonstrates originality. In advertising, it also refers to the person who produces the work.

Creative boutique An advertising agency that specializes in the creative side of advertising.

Creative brief The document that outlines the key strategy decisions and details the key execution elements.

Creative concept A Big Idea that is original, supports the ad strategy, and dramatizes the selling point.

Creative director The person responsible for managing the work of the creative team.

Creative strategy The determination of the right message for a particular target audience, a message approach that delivers the advertising objectives.

Creativity The use of the imagination or original ideas, especially in the production of an artistic work. Creativity in IMC seeks to solve a communication problem in a unique and memorable way that will have long-lasting impact, work with less media spending, and build customer loyalty.

Credibility The believability or reliability of a source of information.

Crisis management Management of people and events during times of great danger or trouble.

Cross promotion A type of cooperative marketing program in which marketers use associations between complementary brands to create a joint promotional program.

Cross-functional management A practice that uses teams to coordinate activities that involve different areas in and outside a company.

Cross-media integration The practice of using a variety of media and messages that work together to create a coherent brand impression.

Cross-media See Multichannel.

Crowdsourcing Aggregating the wisdom of internet users in a type of digital brainstorming that collects opinions and ideas from a digital community.

Cultural cohort A segment of customers from multiple countries who share common characteristics that translate into common wants and needs.

Cultural imperialism Imposing a foreign culture on a local culture; usually referred to as the impact of Western culture, products, and lifestyles on a more traditional culture.

Culture The complex whole of tangible items, intangible concepts, and social behaviors that define a group of people or a way of life.

Customer referral A form of brand advocacy, this practice seeks to involve satisfied customers in spreading the message about a brand.

Customer satisfaction The degree to which there is a match between the customer's expectations about a product and the product's actual performance.

Customer service The process of managing customers' interactive experiences with a brand, particularly those experiences based on complaints or requests for information or service.

Cut An abrupt transition from one shot to another.

Cutouts Irregularly shaped extensions added to the top, bottom, or sides of standard outdoor boards.

D

Dailies Processed scenes on film that a director reviews to determine what needs correcting.

Data mining Sifting through and sorting a company's computer database records to target customers and maintain relationships with them.

Databases Lists of consumers with information that helps target and segment those who are highly likely to be in the market for a certain product.

Daypart The way the broadcast schedule is divided into time segments during a day.

Debossing A depressed image created on paper by applying heat and pressure.

Deceptive advertising Advertising that misleads consumers by making claims that are false or by failure to fully disclose important information.

Decode The interpretation of a message by a receiver.

Delayed effects An advertisement's impact occurs at a later time (than its time of delivery).

Demand creation An external message creates a want or need.

Demographics Human traits such as age, income, race, and gender.

Demonstration An advertising strategy that shows how the product works.

Designated marketing area (DMA) Households in each major U.S. metropolitan area, or TV or radio broadcast coverage area.

Design thinking A human-centered methodology focused on developing innovations to solve problems. It involves collaborating across disciplines to develop solutions that integrate the needs of people, the possibilities of technology, and the requirements for business success.

Diaries In advertising research, consumers record their consumption activities, including media use.

Die-cut Using a sharp-edged stamp to cut irregular shapes in printed materials.

Differentiation An advertising strategy that calls to the consumer's attention the features that make a product unique or better than the competition.

Diffusion Adoption of new ideas based on Everett Rogers' Diffusion of Innovations theory.

(Digital) ecosystem All the digital experiences consumers have with a brand.

Digital displays Outdoor advertising that uses digital technology to create an image.

Digital installations These are touchscreen formats, such as kiosks and electronic walls, that carry promotional messages and organizational content.

Digitization Converting art into computer-readable images.

Direct action Immediate response to advertising, such as completing an order form and sending it back by return mail.

Direct-action headlines Straightforward headlines that say what they mean without trying to be clever.

Direct advertising A form of direct marketing, this is an advertising platform that delivers messages directly to a receiver without an intermediary such as traditional media or sales staff.

Direct mail A type of direct marketing that sends the offer to a prospective customer by mail.

Direct marketing (DM) A type of marketing that uses media to contact a prospect directly and elicit a response without the intervention of a retailer or personal sales.

Direct-response advertising A type of marketing communication that achieves an action-oriented objective as a result of the advertising message.

Direct-response communication A type of promotional message that motivates an immediate response usually leading to a purchase without the intermediary impact of a retailer or sales representative.

Direct-response marketing A multichannel form of marketing that connects sellers and customers directly rather than through an intermediary, such as a retailer.

Directional advertising Tells people where to go to find goods and services.

Discretionary income The money available for spending after taxes and necessities are covered.

Display advertising Sponsored messages that can be of any size and location within the newspaper, except the editorial page.

Display copy Type set in larger sizes that is used to attract the reader's attention.

Distribution In marketing, the channel of distribution describes the route a product takes moving from its manufacturer to the customer.

Distribution chain The companies involved in moving a product from the manufacturer to the customer.

Divergent thinking In creative thinking, people trying to come up with a creative idea are advised to move away from logical thinking (inductive, deductive) and look for unexpected ideas by making mental jumps and creative leaps.

Double-page spread An advertisement that crosses two facing pages in a magazine.

DVR A digital video recorder that allows users to record television shows and watch them whenever they like, a practice called time-shifting.

E

E score A system of ratings for celebrities, athletes, and other newsmakers that measures their appeal.

E-commerce Selling goods and services through electronic means, usually over the internet.

Earned media Free publicity generated through promotional efforts other than paid media, often resulting from public relations or social media.

Effective frequency A planning concept that determines a range (minimum and maximum) of repeat exposures for a message.

Effects The type of impact delivered by an advertisement or other marketing communication.

Electronic walls A digital installation that is often found in lobbies and carries corporate information accessed through touch screens.

Embossing The application of pressure to create a raised surface image on paper.

Emotional appeals Message strategies that seek to arouse our feelings.

Employee communication programs Information and training programs for employees that help them deliver brand messages strategically.

Employee relations Relations between the company and its workers.

Encode The creation of a message in words and pictures by a source.

Endorsement Any advertising message that consumers reasonably believe reflects the opinions, beliefs, or experiences of an individual, group, or institution.

Endorser A person who testifies on behalf of the product (goods, service, or idea).

Engagement Advertisement that gets and holds the attention of its audience.

Ethics A set of moral principles that guide our actions.

Ethnographic research A form of anthropological research that studies the way people live their lives.

Evaluation Rigorous analysis of completed or ongoing activities to determine their effectiveness and efficiency.

Evaluative research Research that determines how well the ad or campaign achieved its goals.

Event marketing Creating a promotion program around a sponsored event.

Execution The different variations used to represent the message of a campaign.

Experiential marketing Marketing strategies and events that connect a brand and a prospective customer in a personal and involving way.

Experimental research Scientific research in which an investigator controls most of the key variables in order to study the impact of manipulating one or more—changing the product's price or the type of appeal in an ad, for example.

Expert panel A type of research that involves obtaining the opinions from a group of people who are recognized as experts in the area being studied.

Exposure The opportunity for a reader, viewer, or listener to see or hear an advertisement.

Extensions Embellishments to painted billboards that expand the scale and break away from the standard rectangle limitations.

Exterior transit advertising Advertising posters that are mounted on the sides, rear, and tops of vehicles.

Extranets Networked computer systems that can be accessed by authorized outside users, enabling businesses to securely exchange information over the internet.

F

False advertising Advertising that is misleading or simply untrue.

Family Two or more people who are related by blood, marriage, or adoption and live in the same household.

Fan pages Chat rooms and other websites where brand loyalists share stories about a favorite brand.

Feature analysis A comparison of your product's features against those of competing products.

Feature story In the media, these are human-interest stories, in contrast to hard news.

Features A product attribute or characteristic.

Federal Communications Commission (FCC) A U.S. government agency that regulates broadcast media and can eliminate ads that are deceptive or offensive.

Federal Trade Commission (FTC) An independent agency of the US government that works to promote consumer protection and prevent fraudulent, deceptive, and unfair business practices.

Fee system A compensation tool for advertisers requiring that client and agency agree on an hourly fee or rate or negotiate a charge for a specific project.

Feedback Information about reactions to a good, service, or idea that is used as a basis for improvement.

Financial relations Communications with the financial community.

Fishbein multiattribute model A means of estimating consumer evaluation of a set of marketplace choices that uses a combination of three components: key attributes, weights of key attributes, and consumer ratings of products on those attributes.

Flash mob A sudden and conspicuous gathering of people in public places generated by viral e-mail messages, telecommunications or social media.

Flighting strategy An advertising scheduling pattern characterized by a period of intensified activity called a flight, followed by a period of no advertising called a hiatus.

Focus group A group interview led by a moderator.

Foil stamping A commercial printing process that applies metallic foil to the surface beneath.

Font A set of printable or displayable characters in the same style, pitch, and spacing.

Food and Drug Administration (FDA) A US government agency responsible for protecting the public health by ensuring the effectiveness and safety of medications, biological products, medical devices, and the nation's food supply.

Four Ps The marketing mix, which includes the product (design and performance), price (value), place (distribution), and promotion (marketing communication).

Four-color printing A printing process that replicates the full color of a photograph although it only uses four colors of ink.

Free association Getting a new idea by creating a juxtaposition between two seemingly unrelated thoughts—usually done by describing everything that comes into your mind when you are given a word to think about.

Freestanding insert (FSI) Preprinted advertisement placed loosely in the newspaper.

Frequency distribution A media planning term describing exactly how many times each person is exposed to a message by percentage of the population (reach).

Frequency program A type of continuity program designed to encourage repeat purchases.

Frequency quintile distribution analysis A media planning analysis technique that divides a target audience into five equal-sized groups, each containing 20 percent of the audience, and establishes an average frequency of exposure for each of these segments (also called quintile analysis).

Frequency The number of times an audience has an opportunity to be exposed to a media vehicle or vehicles in a specified time span.

Friendship focus groups Group interviews with people who know one another and have been recruited by the person who hosts the session, which is usually held in that person's home.

Fulfillment The back-end operations of direct marketing, which include receiving the order, assembling the merchandise, shipping, and handling returns and exchanges.

Full-service agency An agency that provides clients with the primary planning and advertising services.

Fund-raising (or development) The practice of raising money by collecting donations, sometimes called development or strategic philanthropy.

G

Gaffer Chief electrician on a film shoot.

Game A type of promotional sweepstakes that encourages customers to return to a business several times in order to increase the chances of winning.

Gatefold Four or more connected pages that fold in on themselves.

Gatekeepers Individuals who have direct relations with the public such as writers, producers, editors, talk-show coordinators, and newscasters.

Goals Long-term business directions and decisions that can be measured and evaluated.

Goodwill A positive attitude about a company among the general public.

Grip Individual who moves the props and sets on a film shoot.

Gross impressions The sum of the audiences of all the media vehicles used within a designated time span.

Gross rating points (GRPs) The sum of the total exposure potential of a series of media vehicles expressed as a percentage of the audience population.

Group text messaging Software that makes it possible to deliver individualized online communication through a mass distribution system.

Guaranteed circulation Publications such as magazines guarantee to their advertisers that a certain number of copies will be sold or distributed to subscribers.

Guerilla marketing A form of unconventional marketing, such as chalk messages on a sidewalk, that is often associated with staged events.

Gutter The white space, or inside margins, where two facing magazine pages join.

H

Halftones (Continuous tone): Image with a continuous range of shades from light to dark.

Hard sell A rational, informational message that emphasizes a strong argument and calls for action.

Hashtags Mashed-together phrases marked with a hash symbol (the pound sign) that indicates what topic the Twitter tweet addresses.

Headline The title of an ad; it is display copy set in large type to get the reader's attention.

Heavy-up schedule In media planning, a schedule can be designed that spends proportionately more of the budget in certain key ways, such as season or geography.

Hierarchy of effects A set of consumer responses that moves from the least serious, involved, or complex up through the most serious, involved, or complex.

High involvement Perceiving a product or information as important and personally relevant.

High-context culture The meaning of a message is dependent on context cues.

High-definition television (HDTV) A type of television set that delivers movie quality, high-resolution images.

Hits The number of times a website is visited.

Holding companies One or more advertising agency networks, as well as other types of marketing communication agencies and marketing services consulting firms.

Horizontal publication Publications directed at people who hold similar jobs.

House ad An ad by an organization that is used in its own publication or programming.

House list A compilation of a company's past customers or members.

Household All those people who occupy one living unit, whether they are related or not.

Households using television (HUT) A measure of households using TV.

I

Idea A thought or product of thinking.

Ideation The process of creating an idea.

Illumination The point when a new idea strikes.

Image transfer When the presentation in one medium stimulates the listener or viewer to think about the presentation of the product in another medium.

Immersion Gathering information and concentrating your focus on a problem.

Impact The effect of the message on the audience.

Implied third-party endorsement When the media endorse a product and the public finds it credible.

Impression In media planning, one person's opportunity to be exposed to an advertising message.

In-depth interview One-on-one interview using open-ended questions.

In-house agency An agency within an advertiser's organization that performs all the tasks an outside agency would provide for the advertiser.

Inbound telemarketing Incoming calls initiated by the customer.

Incubation A step in the ideation process, when you turn your attention elsewhere and let your subconscious play with a problem.

Independent stations Local stations unaffiliated with a national network.

Indirect action Delayed response to advertising such as recalling the message and later in the store selecting the brand.

Indirect-action headlines Headlines that aim to capture attention, although they might not provide much information.

Infomercial Infomercials are extended TV commercials that use the techniques of direct response communication to make an offer to viewers who are prospects for the brand.

Ingredient branding Acknowledging a supplier's brand as an important product feature.

Ink-jet imaging A printing process that allows a mailer, such as a magazine, to personalize its content for the reader.

Inquiry tests Evaluation that measures the number of responses to a message.

Insight mining Finding some nugget of truth in a stack of research findings that leads to a key understanding of how consumers feel, think, or behave.

Insight research Intelligence about consumer behaviors, thoughts, opinions, attitudes, desires, and beliefs that come from asking probing questions and carefully listening to and analyzing the answers.

Instantaneous effects Immediate responses to advertising and other marketing communication, as opposed to delayed or carryover impact.

Institutional advertising A type of corporate advertising that focuses on establishing a corporate identity or viewpoint.

Institutional markets Usually nonprofit organizations, such as hospitals, government agencies, or schools, that buy products to use in delivering their services.

Integrated marketing communication (IMC) The practice of unifying all marketing communication efforts so they send a consistent brand message to target audiences.

Integrated perception The process of synergy creates a coherent brand impression—a perception of a brand—from a multitude of messages, mentions, and personal experiences.

Integration In marketing communication, integration means every message is focused and works together to present a coherent impression of a brand.

Intention A preference that motivates consumers to want to try or buy a brand.

Interactive communication Personal conversations between two people.

Interactive media Communication channels that involve two-way communication with users and in which the outputs depend on a user's inputs. Websites and video games are two common types of interactive media.

Interactive television A television with computer capabilities.

Interest Activities that engage the consumer.

Interior transit advertising Advertising posters that are mounted inside vehicles such as buses, subway cars, and taxis.

Internal marketing Providing information about marketing activity and promoting it internally to employees.

International advertising Advertising designed to promote the same product in a number of countries.

Intranets Networked systems of electronic communication, especially a private network, that allow employees to be in touch with one another from various locations.

Intrusive Marketing communication messages that intrude on people's perception in order to grab attention.

Intrusiveness Techniques used by messages and media to grab attention by being disruptive or unexpected.

Involvement The intensity of the consumer's interest in a product.

Issue management The practice of advising companies and senior management on how public opinion is coalescing around certain issues.

J

Jingles A short slogan or verse designed to be easily remembered and set to music.

K

Key frame An image from a commercial that sticks in the mind and becomes the visual that viewers remember when they think about the commercial.

Key performance indicators Identifying the most reliable factors that drive effectiveness and business success.

Key visual Image that conveys the heart of the concept.

Key words A word or phrase typed into a search engine to finds websites relevant to a certain topic.

Kiosks Multisided bulletin board structures designed for public posting of messages.

Knowledge structure See Network of associations.

L

Layout A drawing that shows where all the elements in the ad are to be positioned.

Lead agency In international marketing, the agency that develops the campaign.

Lead generation The identification of prospective customers.

Lead paragraph The first line or paragraph of the body copy that is used to stimulate the reader's interest.

Lead time Production time; also time preceding a seasonal event.

Leads The identification of potential customers, or prospects.

Left-brain thinking Logical, linear, and orderly thought; inductive or deductive.

Legibility How easy or difficult a type is to read.

Library of Congress The largest library in the world, with millions of books, recordings, photographs, newspapers, maps, and manuscripts in its collections. It is the main research arm of the US Congress and the home of the US Copyright Office.

Licensing The practice whereby a company with an established brand "rents" it to another company.

Lifestyle The pattern of living that reflects how people allocate their time, energy, and money.

Lifetime customer value An estimate of the revenue coming from a particular customer (or type of customer) over the lifetime of the relationship.

Line art Art in which all elements are solid, with no intermediate shades or tones.

Lobbying A form of public affairs involving corporations, activist groups, and consumer groups who provide information to legislators in order to get their support and to get them to vote a certain way on a particular bill.

Local advertising Advertising targeted to consumers who live within the local shopping area of a store.

Localization A strategy in international advertising that adapts the message to local cultures.

Logo A distinctive brand mark that is legally protected.

Low involvement Perceiving a product or information as unimportant.

Low-context cultures The meaning of a message is obvious without needing a sense of the cultural context.

Low-power FM Nonprofit, noncommercial stations that serve a small area market, such as a college campus.

Loyalty program A program designed to increase customer retention by rewarding customers for their patronage.

M

Make goods Compensation that media give to advertisers in the form of additional message units. These are commonly used in situations involving production errors by the medium and preemption of the advertiser's programming.

Market An area of the country or a group of buyers.

Market research A type of marketing research that investigates the product and category, as well as consumers who are or might be customers for the product.

Market segmentation The process of dividing a market into distinct groups of buyers who might require separate products or marketing mixes.

Market selectivity When the medium targets specific consumer groups.

Marketer The company or organization behind the product.

Marketing Business activities that direct the exchange of goods and services between producers and consumers.

Marketing communication (marcom) The element in the marketing mix that communicates the key marketing messages to target audiences.

Marketing imperialism Marketing practices that result in imposing foreign cultural values on a local culture with different values and traditions.

Marketing mix A blend of four main activities: designing, pricing, distributing, and communicating about the product.

Marketing plan A written document that proposes strategies for using the elements of the marketing mix to achieve objectives.

Marketing research Research that investigates all elements of the marketing mix.

Marketing services This includes a variety of suppliers hired by marketers, such as researchers and various types of marketing communication agencies.

Mass media Communication channels, such as newspapers or television, used to send messages to large, diverse audiences.

Measurable objectives The effectiveness of brand communication is determined by how well it meets its objectives, which must be specific, clear, and measurable in terms of a starting baseline and a goal.

Measured media Media used in advertising that are evaluated by auditing companies that track performance data, such as circulation, readership, and viewership.

Mechanicals A finished pasteup with every element perfectly positioned that is photographed to make printing plates for offset printing.

Media The channels of communication that carry the ad message to target audiences.

Media buyer Specialists who implement the media plan by contracting with various media for placement of an advertisement.

Media buying companies Firms and agencies that are hired to negotiate the best media rates and purchase the media for a marketing campaign, such as slots of time for radio or television commercials or ad space in newspapers, magazines, or websites.

Media flowchart A planning document that shows how the media plan will run in terms of the scheduling of the various media used.

Media kit Also called a press kit, a packet or folder that contains all the important information for members of the press.

Media mix Selecting the best combination of media vehicles, nontraditional media, and marketing communication tools to reach the targeted stakeholder audiences.

Media objective Goals or tasks a media plan should accomplish.

Media optimization The best use of various communication methods to promote the company.

Media plan A decision process leading to the use of advertising time and space to assist in the achievement of marketing objectives.

Media planners Media specialists who develop the strategic decisions outlined in the media plan.

Media planning The way advertisers identify and select media options based on research into the audience profiles of various media.

Media relations Relationships with media contacts.

Media reps Media salespeople who sell media time and space for a variety of media outlets.

Media research The process of gathering information about all the possible media and marketing communication tools available to be used in a marketing communication plan.

Media researchers The specialists who gather information about media audiences and performance.

Media salespeople People who work for a specific medium and call on media planners and buyers in agencies to sell space or time in that medium.

Media strategy The decisions media planners make to deliver the most effective media mix that will reach the target audience and satisfy the media objectives.

Media tour A traveling press conference in which the company's spokesperson travels to different cities and meets with the local media.

Media vehicle A single program, magazine, or radio station.

Media waste Wasted efforts in media buying come from targeting too wide of a target market (reach) or buying too many exposures (frequency).

Media-buying companies An offshoot of the media-buying function in full-service agencies, these companies become freestanding agencies that specialize in buying media for clients and other agencies.

Mental rehearsal Visualization of imagined actions that is the predecessor to the behaviors with which the advertiser hopes the consumer will feel comfortable and familiar.

Mention The direct identification of a brand or marketing campaign by traditional news or media organizations, including social media, blog posts, and online forums. Often used in assessing earned media.

Message The words, pictures, and ideas that create meaning in an advertisement.

Message design The communication approach that makes the most sense given the brand's marketing situation and the target audience's needs and interests.

Message strategy The determination of the right message for a particular target audience that delivers the advertising objectives.

Metaphors A figure of speech in which a term or phrase from one object is associated with something entirely different to create an implicit comparison.

Micro-sites Small websites that are offspring of a parent website.

Microblog A small blog—Twitter, for example.

Microtargeting The practice of using vast databases of personal information to predict attitudes and behavior of selected groups.

Mini-sites Smaller websites that exist on a marketing partner's site permitting viewers to click on the mini-site for additional information without leaving the original website.

Mission marketing Linking the mission of the company to a good cause and committing support to it for the long term.

Mission statement A business platform that articulates the organization's philosophy, as well as its goals and values.

Mixer The individual who operates the recording equipment during a film shoot.

Mobile marketing The use of wireless communication to reach people on the move with a location-based message.

Moments of truth The moments in time when a message is particularly relevant to a consumer and becomes an engaging media experience.

Morals The framework for separating right from wrong and identifying good behavior.

Morning drive time On radio the day part that reaches people when they are commuting to work.

Morphing A video technique in which one object gradually changes into another.

Motivation An unobservable inner force that stimulates and compels a behavioral response.

Motive An internal force—like the desire to look good—that stimulates you to behave in a particular manner.

Multichannel An advertising plan that uses several different forms of media, such as TV, print, radio, and online.

Multiplatform In IMC planning, multiple functional areas and tools, such as public relations and sales promotion, are used to deliver messages and create brand interactions, a practice referred to as multiplatform communication.

Mystery shoppers A proactive form of customer service, unidentified shoppers are asked to personally analyze and report on their experiences shopping in a store.

N

Naming rights The practice of allowing brand names to be associated with buildings and events in order to create brand visibility.

Native advertising Sponsored content that matches the form, feel, and function of the neighboring publication's editorial content but is paid for by an advertiser and is intended to promote the advertiser's product.

Navigation The action of a user moving through a website.

Needs Basic forces that motivate you to do or to want something.

Netcasting The action or practice of broadcasting a program over the internet, such as a podcast.

Network of associations The linked set of brand perceptions that represent a person's unique way of creating meaning.

Network effect The impact of shared information through an online communication network creates a multiplier effect.

Network television Television networks are central broadcasting companies with affiliated stations in local markets that run programming provided by the network.

Neuromarketing The brain-science approach investigating how consumers think.

News conferences Presentations by an organization of news announcements through a meeting where reporters are also invited to ask questions.

News release Primary medium used to deliver public relations messages to the media.

News value The quality of information that makes it of interest to news editors based on such considerations as timeliness, proximity, impact, or human interest.

Newsprint An inexpensive paper with a rough surface, used for printing newspapers.

Niche market Subsegments of the general market which have distinctive traits that may provide a special combination of benefits.

Niche media Communication channels used to reach audience segments defined by a specialized interest, such as ethnicity or profession.

Noise Anything that interferes with or distorts the advertising message's delivery to the target audience.

Nongovernmental Organization (NGO) Any nonprofit organization operating on a local, national, or international level.

Nonprofit advertising Advertising programs used by nonprofit organizations, such as charities, associations, and hospitals.

Nontraditional delivery Delivery of magazines to readers through such methods as door hangers or newspapers.

Norms Simple rules that each culture establishes to guide behavior.

O

Objective The goal or task an individual or business wants to accomplish.

Objective-task method Budgeting approach based on costs of reaching an objective.

Observation research Qualitative research method that takes researchers into natural settings where they record people's behavior.

Off camera In television, a voice that is coming from an unseen speaker.

Offer A direct marketing tool that provides potential customers with an item's information, description, terms of sale, and often an incentive for quick action in buying.

Offset printing A printing process that prints an image from a smooth-surface chemically treated printing plate.

On location Commercials shot outside the studio.

On-demand programming A form of subscription television that allows subscribers to receive special programming for a fee.

On-premise signs Signage that identifies stores.

One-order, one-bill When media companies buy newspaper advertising space for national advertisers and handle the rate negotiation and billing.

Opinion leaders Important people who influence others.

Opt in (Opt out) In e-mail advertising (and direct mail) consumers agree to be included or not included in the list.

Optimization Computer modeling that helps media planners determine the relative impact and efficiency of various media mixes.

Original Unique and the first of its kind.

Out-of-home media All advertising that is displayed outside the home, from billboards, to blimps, to in-store aisle displays.

Out-of-register color When the four colors used in full-color printing are not perfectly aligned with the image.

Outbound telemarketing Telemarketing sales calls initiated by the company.

Outcome Evaluation techniques that determine the effect of communication on the target audience.

Outdoor advertising Advertising on billboards along streets and highways.

Output In public relations evaluation, the number of press releases and contacts that led to stories or mentions in news stories.

Overlines Text used to set the stage and lead into the headline of copy.

Owned media Media channels controlled by the organization and that are used to carry branded content.

P

Pace How fast or slowly the action progresses in a commercial.

Package goods Products sold for personal or household use.

Page views The number of times a website is visited.

Paid media Marketing efforts that involve a paid placement of a commercial message into traditional or digital media.

Paid posts The practice of using bloggers who plug a product in return for incentives such as cash or freebies.

Painted outdoor bulletins A type of advertisement that is normally created on-site and is not restricted to billboards as the attachment.

Parity products Products so similar to each other that competitors are readily substitutable. Examples include milk, unleaded gas and over-the-counter drugs; also known as undifferentiated products.

Participant observation A research method in which the observer is a member of the group being studied.

Participations An arrangement in which a television advertiser buys commercial time from a network.

Pass-along readership The view that a magazine, although only bought by one consumer, may actually be read by several; difference between circulation and readership.

Payout analysis A comparison of the cost of a promotion against the forecasted sales generated by the promotion.

Payout planning A way to evaluate the effectiveness of a sales promotion in terms of its financial returns by comparing the costs of the promotion to the forecasted sales of the promotion.

Perceived risk The relationship between what you gain by making a certain decision and what you have to lose.

Percentage-of-sales method A budgeting technique based in the relationship between the cost of advertising and total sales.

Perception The process by which we receive information through our five senses and acknowledge and assign meaning to this information.

Perceptual map An analytical technique that plots the mental positions held by consumers of a set of competitors on a matrix.

Performance incentive A form of agency compensation that pays agencies on their ability to develop marketing communication that achieves certain goals agreed upon with the client.

Permission marketing A method of direct marketing in which the consumer controls the process, agrees to receive communication from the company, and consciously signs up.

Permission to believe Credibility building techniques that increase consumers' conviction in making decisions.

Personal sales Face-to-face contact between the marketer and a prospective customer.

Personal selling Face-to-face contact between the marketer and a prospective customer that intends to create and repeat sales.

Persuasion Trying to establish, reinforce, or change an attitude, touch an emotion, or anchor a conviction firmly in the potential customer's belief structure.

Photoboards A mockup of a television commercial that uses still photos for the frames.

Pitch letter A letter to a media outlet that outlines a possible story idea that the PR person would like to provide.

Place-based media Out-of-home media that carry ads and other promotional messages in public spaces.

Platforms Functions or areas of marketing communication such as public relations or direct marketing.

Podcasting Making digital recordings of broadcasts available for downloading to a computer or mobile device.

Point of differentiation The way a product is unique from its competitors.

Point-of-purchase (PoP) materials In-store merchandising materials that use such promotional materials as aisle displays, shelf signs, and window posters to feature a brand and its promotional offer.

Point-of-purchase Also called point-of-sale, these are materials that call attention to a brand in a store and provide a special reason to buy.

Point-of-sale materials See Point-of-purchase

Pop-ups and pop-behind Types of ads that burst open on the computer screen either in front of or behind any page of a website.

Portable people meter (PPM) An audio measurement device developed by Nielsen that is carried throughout the day by its individual panelists across the United States. The PPM measures how many people are exposed or listening to individual radio stations and television stations, including cable television.

Position A brand location in the consumer's mind relative to competing brands based on the relative strengths of the brand and its competitors.

Positioning The way in which consumers perceive a product in the marketplace.

Postproduction In TV production, assembling and editing the film after the film has been shot.

Posttesting research A type of research that uses a number of methods to evaluate the effectiveness of a program after it has been implemented.

Posttesting Research conducted after a message or campaign has run that seeks to determine the effectiveness of the communication effort.

Predictive dialing Technology that allows telemarketing companies to call anyone by using a trial and error dialing program.

Preference Favorable positive impression of a product that leads to an intention to try or buy it.

Preferred positions Sections or pages of print media that are in high demand by advertisers because they have a special appeal to the target audience.

Preferred-position rate Charges by media for space or time that are in high demand because they have a special appeal to the target audience.

Premium A tangible reward received for performing a particular act, such as purchasing a product or visiting the point-of-purchase.

Preprints Advertising circulars furnished by a retailer for distribution as a free-standing insert in newspapers.

Preproduction The process of outlining every step and decision to be made in the production process in a set of production notes that are compiled from a preproduction meeting with the creative team, producer and other key participants.

Press conference A public gathering of media people for the purpose of establishing a company's position or making a statement.

Press kits Packets of information provided to reporters that contain such materials as press releases, fact sheets, histories, maps, photos, and other corporate information.

Pretesting Evaluative research of finished or nearly finished ads that leads to a go/no-go decision.

Price copy A term used to designate advertising copy devoted to information about the price and the associated conditions of a particular product.

Price deal A temporary reduction in the price of a product.

Primary research Information that is collected from original sources.

Prime time Programming on TV that runs between the hours of 8 P.M. and 11 P.M.

Pro bono Situation in which all services, time, and space are donated.

Problem solution message A message strategy that sets up a problem that the use of the product can solve.

Process colors Four basic inks—magenta, cyan, yellow, and black—that are mixed to produce a full range of colors found in four-color printing.

Producer A person, company, or country that makes, grows, or supplies goods or services for sale. Also, a person who oversees the production and delivery of an agency's work.

Product A good, service, or idea created to satisfy a business or consumer need or want.

Product differentiation A competitive marketing strategy that tries to create a competitive difference through real or perceived product attributes.

Product placement The use of a brand name product in a television show, movie, or event.

Product-as-hero A form of the problem-solution message strategy.

Production notes A document that describes in detail every aspect of a commercial's production.

Profiles A composite description of a target audience using personality and lifestyle characteristics.

Profit The difference between the amount earned and the amount spent in buying, operating, or producing something.

Program preemptions Interruptions in local or network programming caused by special events.

Programmatic buying Media buying based on huge amounts of behavior tracking data and the algorithms that permit targeting individuals, not just aggregated audiences.

Projective techniques A psychoanalytic research technique that asks respondents to generate impressions to gather insights about consumers and brands.

Promise Found in a benefit statement, it is something that will happen if you use the product.

Prospecting In database marketing, this is the process of identifying prospects based on how well they match certain user characteristics.

Prospects Potential customers who are likely to buy the product or brand.

Psychographics All psychological variables (especially activities, interests, and opinions) that combine to describe our inner selves and help explain consumer behavior.

Psychological pricing A strategy that tries to manipulate the customer's purchasing judgment.

Public affairs Relations between a corporation, the public, and government involving public issues relating to government and regulation.

Public communication campaigns Social issue campaigns undertaken by nonprofit organizations as a conscious effort to influence the thoughts or actions of the public.

Public opinion People's beliefs, based on their conceptions or evaluations of something, rather than on fact.

Public radio A network of radio stations that use public broadcasting material usually provided by National Public Radio (NPR).

Public relations A management function enabling organizations to achieve effective relationships with various publics in order to manage the image and reputation of the organization.

Public relations management process A four-step process that defines the problem or opportunity, programming, action, and evaluation.

Public relations plan The document that summarizes the basic strategy for public relations efforts.

Public service advertising A type of advertising that is developed for a good cause, usually pro bono.

Public service announcements (PSAs) A type of public relations advertising that deals with public welfare issues and typically is run free of charge.

Public television Broadcast TV stations that generally function based on donations rather than commercial advertising.

Publicity Information that catches public interest and is relayed through the news media.

Publics All groups of people with which a company or organization interacts.

Puffery Advertising or other sales representation that praises a product or service using subjective opinions, superlatives, and similar techniques that are not based on objective fact.

Pull strategy A strategy that directs marketing efforts at the consumer and attempts to pull the product through the channel.

Pulsing strategy An advertising scheduling pattern in which time and space are scheduled on a continuous but uneven basis; lower levels are followed by bursts or peak periods of intensified activity.

Push strategy A strategy that directs marketing efforts at resellers, where success depends on the ability of these intermediaries to market the product, which they often do with advertising.

Q

Q score A measure of the familiarity of a celebrity, as well as a company or brand.

Qualitative research Research that seeks to understand how people think and behave and why.

Quantitative research Research that uses statistics to describe consumers.

Quick-response (QR) codes A type of matrix barcode that is machine-readable and contains information about the item to which it is attached. Recent versions include Snapcodes, Spotify Codes, and Facebook's Messenger Codes.

R

Radio network A group of local affiliates providing simultaneous programming via connection to one or more of the national networks.

Radio script A written version of a radio commercial used to produce the commercial.

Random sample The type of research sample requiring that each person in the population being studied has an equal chance of being selected to be in the sample.

Rate card A list of the charges for advertising space.

Ratings, rating points Percentage of population or households tuned to a program.

Reach The percentage of different homes or people exposed to a media vehicle or vehicles at least once during a specific period of time. It is the percentage of unduplicated audience.

Readership The number of readers of print media.

Real-time marketing Marketing activities performed "in the moment" that determine an appropriate or optimal approach to a particular customer at a particular time and place.

Reason to believe Supporting or proving an advertising claim intensifies believability.

Reason why A statement that explains why the feature will benefit the user.

Rebate A sales promotion that allows the customer to recover part of the product's cost from the manufacturer in the form of cash.

Recall People remember seeing an ad and what the ad said.

Recall test A test that evaluates the memorability of an advertisement by contacting members of the advertisement's audience and asking them what they remember about it.

Receiver The audience for an advertisement.

Recognition An ability to remember having seen something before.

Recognition test A test that evaluates the memorability of an advertisement by contacting members of the audience, showing them the ad, and asking whether they remember having seen it before.

Reference group A group of people that a person uses as a guide for behavior in specific situations.

Referrals When a satisfied customer recommends a favorite brand.

Refund An offer by the marketer to return a certain amount of money to the consumer who purchases the product.

Registration The way the various color inks align in four-color printing.

Relationship marketing The ongoing process of identifying and maintaining contact with high-value customers.

Relevance The message connects with the audience on a personal level.

Relevant Ideas that mean something to the target audience.

Reliability In research, reliability means you can run the same test over again and get the same results.

Reminder advertising An advertising strategy that keeps the brand name in front of consumers.

Repositioning Developing a new position for the product as the marketing environment changes.

Reputation management The trust stakeholders have in an organization.

Reseller Intermediaries in the distribution channel, typically wholesalers, retailers, and distributors who buy products from manufacturers and then resell them to the ultimate user.

Resonance A message that rings true because the consumer connects with it on a personal level.

Response list In direct marketing, a list that is compiled of people who respond to a direct-mail offer.

Retail advertising A type of advertising used by local merchants who sell directly to consumers.

Retainer Agency monthly compensation based on an estimate of the projected work and its costs.

Return on investment (ROI) Return on investment means that the costs of conducting the business should be more than matched by the revenue produced in return.

Rich media Digital media with multiple formats that allows viewer participation in the presentation of the content.

Right-brain thinking A type of divergent thinking that is intuitive, holistic, artistic, and emotionally expressive.

Roadblock Running a television commercial on all the networks at exactly the same time.

Rough cut A preliminary edited version of the commercial.

Rough layouts A layout drawn to size but without attention to artistic and copy details.

RPIE Research, Planning, Implementation, and Evaluation.

Run-of-paper (ROP) rate In newspaper advertising, a rate based on a location that is at the discretion of the publisher.

Rushes Rough versions of the commercial assembled from unedited footage.

S

Sales kits Packets of information used by media representatives and other types of sales personnel.

Sales promotion Marketing activities that add value to the product for a limited period of time to stimulate consumer purchasing and dealer effectiveness.

Sample In research, a subset of the population that is representative of the key characteristics of the larger group.

Sampling Allowing the consumer to experience the product at no cost.

Satellite radio Subscription radio programming delivered by satellite to receivers anywhere in the continental United States.

Satellite television Subscription television programming delivered by satellite to locations with satellite dishes.

Satellite transmission A delivery system for television, telephone, radio, and internet communication via satellite between a transmitter and a receiver at different locations on Earth.

Scanner research Research that tracks consumer purchases and compares the marketing communication received by the consumer's household.

Scatter market Most prime-time television advertising is presold; however, the remaining inventory is sold during a period, called the scatter market, which is closer to the date of a program's scheduled run.

Scenes Segments of action that occur in a single location.

Screen Used to convert continuous tone art to halftone by shooting the image through a fine screen that breaks the image into a dot pattern.

Search advertising Advertising that adjoins keyword content on websites.

Search marketing Marketing communication strategies designed to aid consumers in their search for information.

Search optimization The practice of maximizing the link between topics that consumers search for and a brand-related website.

Secondary research Information that already has been compiled and published.

Segmenting Dividing the market into groups of people who have similar characteristics in certain key product-related areas.

Selective attention The process by which a receiver of a message chooses to attend to the message.

Selective binding A database-driven publishing technique that combines information on subscribers with a printing program in order to present special ads, content, and promotional sections based on subscribers' demographic profiles.

Selective perception The process of screening out information that doesn't interest us and retaining information that does.

Self-liquidator A type of mail premium that requires a payment sufficient to cover the cost of the item.

Selling premise The sales logic behind an advertising message.

Semicomps A layout drawn to size that depicts the art and display type; body copy is simply ruled in.

Semiotic analysis A qualitative research method designed to uncover layers and types of meaning.

Semiotic testing Assessing consumers' understanding and interpretations of the signs, symbols, objects, and intended meaning in a communication vehicle.

Set A constructed setting in which the action of a commercial takes place.

Share of audience The percent of viewers based on number of sets turned on.

Share of market The percentage of the total market in a product category that buys a particular brand.

Share of mind The extent to which a brand is well known in its category.

Share of voice One brand's percentage of advertising messages in a medium compared to all messages for that product or service.

Share of wallet The amount customers spend on the brand.

Shelf talkers Signs or coupons attached to a shelf that customers can take away for information or discounts.

Showing The percentage of the market population exposed to an outdoor board during a specific time.

Sign spinners A form of "human directional," these are people who hold signs and banners that promote stores or special marketing events.

Signage A type of out-of-home media, retail and corporate signs are owned by the organization.

Silos Programs and departments that operate on their own with little coordination with other promotional efforts.

Single-source data Data collected using single-source research, which combines scanner data and cable viewing data to determine the relationship between television advertising and sales.

Single-source research A test that is run after an ad campaign is introduced that shows a causal relationship between marketing communication and sales.

Situation analysis The first section in a campaign plan that summarizes all the relevant background information and research and analyzes its significance.

Skyscrapers Extra-long narrow ads that run down the right or left side of a website.

Slice-of-life message A type of problem-solution ad in which "typical people" talk about a common problem.

Slogans Frequently repeated phrases that provide continuity to an advertising campaign.

Smartphones High-end cell phones, such as the BlackBerry or iPhone, with computing and photographic capabilities that can access the internet, as well as perform traditional telephone functions.

SMCR model A communication model that identifies the Source, Message, Channel, and Receiver.

Snapcodes A customizable form of a QR code created within Snapchat to help people access material or follow other users.

Social class A way to categorize people on the basis of their values, attitudes, lifestyles, and behavior.

Social games Like a computer game except it's played with friends—an example is FarmVille and Second Life.

Social learning People learn by watching others.

Social media Interactions between people via electronic communication that enable users to create and share content and network in virtual communities.

Social media marketing Marketing strategies that take advantage of the interactivity found on social media, such as Facebook and My Life.

Social responsibility A corporate philosophy based on ethical values.

Socialtizing This is the practice of using social marketing media as a promotional tool.

Societal marketing A business philosophy that describes companies whose operations are based on the idea of socially responsible business.

Soft sell An emotional message that uses mood, ambiguity, and suspense to create a response based on feelings and attitudes.

SoLoMo An emphasis on local marketing, which takes advantage of the convergence of social, local, and mobile marketing.

Sound effects Lifelike imitations of sounds.

Source credibility Belief in a message one hears from a source one finds most reliable.

Source The sender of a message, the advertiser.

Spam Unsolicited or undesired electronic messages.

Speakers' bureau A public relations tool that identifies a group of articulate people who can talk about an organization.

Specialty advertising Free gifts or rewards requiring no purchase and carrying a reminder advertising message.

Spherical branding A form of 360° degree planning that means that no matter what your angle of vision, the brand always looks the same.

Spokes-character A created or imaginary character who acts as a spokesperson.

Spokesperson A message strategy that uses an endorser, usually someone the target audience likes or respects, to deliver a message on behalf of the brand.

Sponsorships (cause or event) An arrangement in which a company contributes to the expenses of a cause or event to increase the perceived value of the sponsor's brand in the mind of the consumer.

Spot announcements Ads shown during the breaks between programs.

Spot buy Broadcast advertising bought on a city-by-city basis rather than through a national buy.

Spot color The use of an accent color to call attention to an element in an ad layout.

Spot radio advertising A form of advertising in which an ad is placed with an individual station rather than through a network.

Stakeholders Groups of people with a common interest who have a stake in a company and who can have an impact on its success.

Standard advertising unit A standardized system of advertising sizes in newspapers.

Standardization In international advertising, the use of campaigns that vary little across different cultures.

Stereotype The process of positioning a group of people in an unvarying pattern that lacks individuality and often reflects popular misconceptions.

Stickiness Ad messages that hold the audience's interest long enough for the audience to register the point of the ad; also refers to the amount of time a viewer spends on a website.

Stock footage Previously recorded film, video, or still slides that are incorporated into a commercial.

Stop motion An animation technique in which inanimate objects are filmed one frame at a time, creating the illusion of movement.

Storyboard A series of frames sketched to illustrate how the story line will develop.

Straightforward message A factual message that focuses on delivering information.

Strategic business unit (SBU) A division of a company focused on a line of products or all the offerings under a single brand name.

Strategic consistency Messages vary with the interest of the stakeholder but the brand strategy remains the same, projecting a coherent image and position.

Strategic philanthropy Philanthropy involves contributions of time, resources, or money to a good cause—it's strategic when it is aligned with an organization or brand's mission.

Strategic planning The process of determining objectives, deciding on strategies, and implementing the tactics.

Strategic research All research that leads to the creation of an ad.

Strategy The design or plan by which objectives are accomplished.

Streaming video Moving images transmitted online.

Structural analysis Developed by the Leo Burnett agency, this method evaluates the power of the narrative or story line, evaluates the strength of the product or claim, and considers how well the two aspects are integrated.

Subheads Sectional headlines that are used to break up a mass of "gray" type in a large block of copy.

Subliminal Refers to messages transmitted below the threshold of normal perception so that the receiver is not consciously aware of having seen it.

Subscription television Television service provided to people who sign up for it and pay a monthly fee.

Substantiation Providing support for a claim, usually through research.

Superstations Independent but high-power television stations.

Superstitials Short internet commercials that appear when you go from one page on a website to another.

Supplements Syndicated or local full-color advertising inserts that appear in newspapers throughout the week.

Supply chain The network of suppliers who produce components and ingredients used by a manufacturer to make its products.

Support The proof or substantiation needed to make a claim believable.

Surrogate measures Mental responses to a message that may predict eventual sales impact.

Survey research Research using structured interview forms that ask large numbers of people exactly the same questions.

Swag A type of freebie—gifts and promotional knickknacks—given to people who attend events as brand reminders.

Sweeps In television programming, these are quarterly periods when more extensive audience data are gathered.

Sweepstakes Contests that require only that the participant supply his or her name to participate in a random drawing.

Switchers Television viewers who change channels.

SWOT analysis An analysis of a company or brand's strengths, weaknesses, opportunities, and threats.

Syndication This is where local stations purchase television or radio shows that are reruns or original programs to fill open hours.

Synergistic effect Evaluation that seeks to determine if the sum of the individual promotional efforts is greater than if the areas are used separately.

Synergy The principle that when all the pieces work together, the whole is greater than the sum of its parts.

T

Tactic The specific techniques selected to reflect the strategy.

Tagging In Twitter, a technique of marking a keyword by inserting a hash symbol (#).

Taglines Clever phrases used at the end of an advertisement to summarize the ad's message.

Take Each scene shot for a commercial, sometimes done repeatedly for the same scene.

Talent People who appear in television commercials.

Target audience A segment of a target market to whom promotional messages are aimed.

Targeted cost per point The practice of estimating the rating points specifically for the target audience specified in the plan.

Targeted cost per thousand (TCPM) The cost to expose 1,000 likely consumers of a product to an ad message.

Targeted rating point (TRP) The practice of adjusting a television program's rating points to more accurately reflect the percentage of the target audience watching the program.

Targeted reach The practice of identifying key characteristics of the target population to better match media audience profiles.

Targeting Breaking a business or consumer market into segments and then concentrating marketing efforts on one or more segments whose needs and desires most closely match a company's product or service offerings.

Teaser A message strategy that creates curiosity as the message unfolds in small pieces over time.

Tech support A form of customer support, this is the practice of hiring people who can provide assistance to customers in solving problems using technology.

Telemarketing A type of marketing that uses the telephone to make a personal sales contact.

Television/video script The written version of a television commercial specifying all the video and audio information.

Test marketing An evaluation method that launches a campaign in several different (but matched or similar) markets but with different levels of media activity or different message alternatives.

Testimonial See "endorsement."

Texting Text messaging, or texting, refers to the practice of sending a brief message between mobile phones or other computer devices connected to a phone network.

Theater of the mind In radio advertising, the story is visualized in the listener's imagination.

Think/feel/do model A model of advertising effects that focuses on the cognitive, emotional, and behavioral responses to a message.

Thumbnail sketches Small preliminary sketches of various layout ideas.

Tie-in promotion Preprinted ads that are provided by the advertiser to be glued into the binding of a magazine.

Time-shifting Using digital video recorders (DVRs) to record television programming for playback at some other time.

Tint blocks A screen process that creates shades of gray or colors in blocks.

Tip-ins Preprinted ads that are provided by the advertiser to be glued into the binding of a magazine.

Tone of voice Ad copy is written as a conversation or an announcement and the voices carry emotional cues.

Total audience impressions Rather than using GRPs (gross rating points), media planners use total audience impressions, which better estimate the total impact of an integrated campaign, including impressions from digital and new media, as well as measured media.

Total audience In magazine research, this is a technique used to determine the total number of readers.

Total communication The practice of monitoring and managing all sources of brand communication.

Touchpoints The contact points where customers interact with the brand and receive brand messages.

Tour Tours of a facility, building, or some other space are used to provide engaging informational experiences for stakeholders.

Town hall forums Meetings within an organization as part of an internal marketing program to inform employees and encourage their support.

Tracking studies Studies that follow the purchase of a brand or the purchases of a specific consumer group over time.

Trade deal An arrangement in which the retailer agrees to give the manufacturer's product a special promotional effort in return for product discounts, goods, or cash.

Trade show A gathering of companies within a specific industry to display their products.

Trademark When a brand name or brand mark is legally protected through registration with the Patent and Trademark Office of the Department of Commerce.

Traffic department People within an agency who are responsible for keeping track of project elements and keeping the work on deadline.

Trailers Advertisements shown in movie theaters before the feature.

Training materials Information assembled to use in training sessions for sales representatives and other employees and stakeholders.

Transformation Creating meaning for a brand that makes it a special product, one that is differentiated within its category by its image.

Trend spotters Researchers who specialize in identifying trends and fads that may affect consumer attitudes and behavior.

Trial Trying a product is usually the first step in making a purchase.

Triple bottom line A concept of corporate social responsibility that seeks to broaden the goals and impact of businesses to include social and environmental responsibilities. It is often presented as 3P's: profit, people, and planet.

Tweets A short comment of 280 characters made by Twitter users.

Twitter An online social networking site that makes it possible for users to share "tweets," short messages limited to 280 characters.

Typography The use of type both to convey words and to contribute aesthetically to the message.

U

Unaided recall When one can remember an idea all by oneself.

Unbundling media services Media departments that separate themselves from agencies, becoming separate companies.

Uncontrolled circulation Publications that are distributed free usually in racks in high-traffic areas.

Underlines Text used to elaborate on the idea in the headline and serve as a transition into the body copy.

Underwriting In public broadcasting, a sponsor contributes funds to pay for the cost of the programming.

Undifferentiated strategy A view of the market that assumes all consumers are basically the same.

Unified vision A vision of what the brand stands for that is shared by all stakeholders.

Uniform resource locators (URLs) Internet domain names that are registered and protected.

Unique selling proposition (USP) A benefit statement about a feature that is both unique to the product and important to the user.

United States Patent and Trademark Office (USPTO) The US federal agency that reviews and assesses applications for trademarks and patents.

United States Postal Service (USPS) An independent agency of the US federal government responsible for providing postal service to households and businesses across the nation.

Up-front market Most prime-time television advertising is pre-sold with negotiated discount rates for the upcoming season.

Usage Categorizing consumers in terms of how much of the product they buy.

User experience (UX) design Taking into account various aspects of a user's interactions with a system, such as usability and accessibility, to improve how viewers engage with products, social media platforms, apps, and websites.

User-generated ads Promotional copy on personal websites developed by the site's owner to promote a product, service, viewpoint, or cause.

User interface design (UI) Design of the space where interactions between humans and machines occur (such as computers, home appliances, and apps), with a focus on maximizing usability and the user experience.

UX An abbreviation for user experience, which refers to a person's emotions and attitudes about using and interfacing with a particular product, system, or service.

V

Validity The research results actually measure what they say they measure.

Value added, value-added media services A marketing or advertising activity that makes a product—or a media buy—more valuable.

Value billing A practice by marketers of paying agencies for creative and strategic ideas, rather than for executions and media placement.

Values The source of norms; values are not tied to specific objects or behavior, are internal, and guide behavior.

Vampire creativity Big ideas that are so powerful that they are remembered but the brand is not.

Vertical publications Publications targeted at people working in the same industry.

Video editing Processing of recorded video to improve its final presentation; may include time manipulation and sound additions.

Video news releases Contain video footage that can be used during a television newscast.

Videographer Person who shoots images with a video camera.

Viral communication Word-of-mouth, or buzz, that gets passed rapidly through a network of friends.

Viral marketing A strategy used primarily in web marketing that relies on consumers to pass on messages about a product.

Viral video The practice of sending interesting videos digitally from a variety of sources, such as ads or YouTube, to friends and colleagues in a vast network of personal connections.

Virtual communities A social network of individuals sharing common interests, ideas, and goals over the internet.

Vision statement A statement that communicates what the company or organization aspires to become.

Visualization Imagining what the finished copy will look like.

Voice-over A technique used in commercials in which an off-camera announcer talks about the on-camera scene.

W

Wants Motivations based on desires and feelings.

Wasted reach Advertising directed at a disinterested audience that is not in the targeted audience.

Wearout The point where the advertising gets tired and there is no response or a lower level of response than at the advertising's launch.

Webisode Web advertisements that are similar to TV programs with a developing storyline.

Website A set of interconnected web pages on the internet that represent information collected by a person or organization.

Weighting In media planning, decision criteria are used to determine the relative amount of budget allocated to each medium.

White space Areas in a layout that aren't used for type or art.

Widgets Tiny computer programs that allow people to create and insert professional-looking content into their personal websites, as well as their computers, and other electronic media screens.

Word association A projective research technique that asks people to respond with the thoughts or other words that come to mind when they are given a stimulus word.

Word of mouth Free advertising that comes from people talking about a product.

Word of mouth Informal oral or written communication between consumers, normally about a brand. Also known as "buzz," it may be positive or negative in nature.

Word-of-mouth communication Messages delivered by friends, family members, or other important people who influence your opinions and impressions.

Y

Your-name-here copy Pompous writing used in corporate communication that contains generic claims that do not differentiate the company.

Z

Zap Changing channels when a television commercial comes on.

Zero moment of truth The point in the consumer buying cycle when consumers search for information online or share brand experiences with a friend.

Zip Fast forwarding past commercials in a previously recorded program.

ENDNOTES

PART 1

[1] Rance Crain, "Lee Clow on How a Holistic View Can Stave off Brand Extinction," December 7, 2015, www.adage.com.
[2] Don Schultz, "The Future of Advertising or Whatever We're Going to Call It," *Journal of Advertising*, July 11, 2016, 1–10.
[3] Alexandra Buell, "Maurice Levy Talks About the Publicis Reorganization, Succession and P&G Review," December 3, 2015, www.adage.com.

CHAPTER 1

[1] Anupreeta Das and Emily Glazer, "Beauty Brands, Waiting for Suitors," *Wall Street Journal*, August 3, 2012, B1.
[2] Tom Duncan and Sandra Moriarty, *Driving Brand Value: Using Integrated Marketing to Manage Profitable Stakeholder Relationships* (New York: McGraw-Hill, 1998).
[3] Graham Robertson, "How to Be a Great Brand Leader: Do Absolutely Nothing," February 10, 2016, www.adage.com.
[4] Nathalie Tadena, "More Agency Reviews Expected This Year, Study Finds," July 5, 2016, www.wsj.com.
[5] Kate Maddox, "Microsoft Tops the List of Most Valuable B-t-B Brands," June 8, 2016, www.adage.com.
[6] Thomas Hazlett, "The iPhone Turns Five," *Wall Street Journal*, June 27, 2012, A17.
[7] Tom Duncan and Frank Mulhern, eds., *A White Paper on the Status, Scope and Future of IMC*, University of Denver, March 2004, 10.
[8] Giep Franzen, "The Complex World of Organization Branding," *Advertising and IMC Principles and Practice*, 9th ed. (Upper Saddle River, NJ: Prentice Hall, 2012).
[9] Giep Franzen and Sandra Moriarty, *The Science and Art of Branding* (Armonk, NY: M. E. Sharpe, 2009).
[10] Rachel Feintzeig, "I Don't Have a Job. I Have a Higher Calling," *Wall Street Journal*, February 25, 2015, p. B1.
[11] Max Willens, "What Does Your Brand Sound Like?," October 22, 2014, www.adage.com.
[12] Charles Young, personal correspondence, June 15, 2015.
[13] Sandra Moriarty and Giep Franzen, "The I in IMC: How Science and Art Are Integrated in Branding," *International Journal of Integrated Marketing Communication* 1, no. 1 (Spring 2009): 29.
[14] Fareed Zakaria, "Why America's Obsession with STEM Education Is Dangerous," March 26, 2015, www.washingtonpost.com.
[15] Allie Rees, "Don't Hate on Valentine's Day: Relationship Marketing in 2015," February 15, 2015, www.MediaPost.com.
[16] Emma Hall, "Volvo Will Try to Reinvent Auto Marketing With New Strategy," December 16, 2014, www.adage.com.
[17] Suzanne Vranica and Jens Hansegard, "IKEA Discloses an $11 Billion Secret," *Wall Street Journal*, August 10, 2012, B1.
[18] WPP, "2018 BrandZ Top 100 Most Valuable Brands," June 8, 2016, www.wpp.com.
[19] Angela Doland, "Branding Lessons from China's Alibaba," September 24, 2014, www.adage.com.
[20] Sarah Yager, "Doritos Locos Tacos," *Atlantic*, July/August 2014, 94.
[21] E. J. Schultz, "Coming to Grocery Stores: 'Got Milk?' Branded Food," May 22, 2015, www.adage.com.
[22] Andy Frawley, "ROI Is Dead. A New Metric Is Needed for Customer Relationships," March 4, 2015, www.adage.com.
[23] Gord Hotchkiss, "The Messy Part of Marketing," April 7, 2015, www.mediapost.com.
[24] Joe Mandese, "Publicis' Levy: Marketing Risks Being 'Uberized,'" February 15, 2015, www.mediapost.com.
[25] Ad Age Staff, "What Will Win at Cannes," June 15, 2015, www.adage.com.
[26] Brendan Snyder, "LGBT Advertising: How Brands Are Taking a Stance on Issues," March 2015, www.thinkwithgoogle.com.

CHAPTER 2

[1] Jerry Della Femina, "Scotch for Dessert: An Ad Man's Spirited Memoir," July 24, 2010, www.npr.org.
[2] Lesley Bielbym, "The 'A' Word—Does Advertising Still Exist?," April 22, 2016, www.adage.com.
[3] Marc Johns, personal correspondence, June 23, 2015.
[4] David Bell, "Inspiration for Advertising Ethics: An Interview with David Bell," American Academy of Advertising, Myrtle Beach, SC, March 15, 2012.
[5] Stephen Fox, *The Mirror Makers: A History of American Advertising and Its Creators* (New York: Vintage Books, 1985); "Advertising History Timeline," *Advertising Age*, 2005.
[6] Bill Bernbach interview, *Printer's Ink*, January 2, 1953, 21.
[7] Christopher Zara, "AT&T, Comcast among Biggest US Advertisers," January 20, 2015, www.ibtimes.com.
[8] Angela Doland, "How Japan's Dentsu Climbed to the Top of the Agency World," May 5, 2015, www.adage.com.
[9] Tim Peterson, "Amazon Assembles Creative Training Program for Ad Agencies," December 10, 2014, www.adage.com.
[10] Based on Ad Age's 2017 Agency A-List, January 23, 2017, www.adage.com.
[11] David Rittenhouse, personal correspondence, June 8, 2015.
[12] Parekh Rupal, "Agency of the Year: Crispin Porter & Bogusky," January 19, 2009, www.adage.com.
[13] Alexandra Bruell, "It's Not Just Cyclical: Industry Change Is Driving Marketing Giants to Review Media Agencies," May 12, 2015, www.adage.com.
[14] Tom Goodwin, "Specialization Was a Mistake: How Agencies Can Restructure for the Future," April 14, 2015, www.adage.com.
[15] Malika Toure, "McCann Worldgroup's Harris Diamond Is Ad Age's 2015 Agency Executive of the Year," January 26, 2015, www.adage.com.
[16] David Beals, "Keeping the Commission System Would Have Benefited No One," April 15, 2016, www.adage.com.
[17] "Pay-for-Performance Starts to Gain Steam," January 29, 2012, www.adage.com.
[18] Jeremy Mullman and Natalie Zmuda, "Coke Pushes Pay-for-Performance Model, April 27, 2009, www.adage.com.
[19] Matt Iliffe, "The Future of Your Agency Is Not with Creative—It's with Creative Culture," December 12, 2014, www.adage.com.
[20] Bob Garfield, "Bob Garfield's 'Chaos Scenario,'" August 6, 2009, www.npr.org.
[21] Todd Wasserman, "Grand Marketer of the Year '05: Jim Stengel, Procter & Gamble," http://www.adweek.com/brand-marketing/grand-marketer-year-05-jim-stengel-procter-gamble-94475/. Retrieved Sept. 24, 2017.
[22] Bradley Johnson, "What You Need to Know about the Global Ad Market," December 8, 2014; www.adage.com, Wayne Friedan, "Broadcast TV Advertising Forecast to Continue Early 2015 Decline," April 13, 2015, www.mediapost.com.
[23] Queenie Wong, "Video Advertising on Facebook and Other Social Media on the Rise," *Naples Daily News*, June 8, 2015, 2B.
[24] "ANA Survey: 52% of Marketers Will Ask Agencies to Lower Internal Costs," April 2, 2012, www.adage.com.
[25] Alexandra Bruell, "The Ad Agency of the Future Is Coming. Are You Ready?," May 2, 2016, www.adage.com.

CHAPTER 3

[1] Public Relations Society of America, http://apps.prsa.org/AboutPRSA/PublicRelationsDefined/, retrieved July 20, 2017.
[2] US Bureau of Labor Statistics, "Occupational Outlook Handbook," December 17, 2015, http://www.bls.gov/ooh/media-and-communication/public-relations-specialists.htm.
[3] Ronn Torossian, "The Biggest PR Crises of 2016 So Far (and What Brands Can Learn From Them)," March 16, 2016, www.Forbes.com.

4 Matt Egan, "5,300 Wells Fargo Employees Fired over 2 Million Phone Accounts," September 9, 2016, www.money.cnn.com.

5 Lindsay Stein, "United Airlines' Consumer Perception Plunges to Lowest Level in Decade," *Advertising Age*, April 13, 2017, www.adage.com.

6 Claire Atkinson, "Rubenstein: PR Maestro," *Advertising Age*, October 11, 2004, 46.

7 Pranay Gupte, "Integrity, Not Image Fixing, Is 'Real' Public Relations," *New York Sun*, February 8, 2005, www.rubenstein.com/files/NY_Sun.pdf.

8 Public Relations Society of America, http://apps.prsa.org/AboutPRSA/PublicRelationsDefined/, retrieved July 20, 2017.

9 Tom Duncan and Sandra Moriarty, *Driving Brand Value: Using Integrated Marketing to Manage Profitable Stakeholder Relationships* (New York: McGraw-Hill, 1997).

10 Jack Ewing and Hiroko Tabuchi, "VW Settles Diesel Emissions Case in U.S., Clearing Just One Financial Hurdle," June 28, 2016, www.nytimes.com.

11 Claire Stammerjohan et al., "An Empirical Investigation of the Interaction between Publicity, Advertising, and Previous Brand Attitudes and Knowledge," *Journal of Advertising* 34 (2005): 55–67.

12 Thomas L. Harris, APR, Fellow PRSA, plankcenter.ua.edu, retrieved July 26, 2017.

13 "The Page Principles," www.awpagesociety.com/site/the-page-principles, retrieved July 26, 2017.

14 www.haagendazs.us/about/news/haagendazsloveshoneybees/, retrieved July 26, 2017.

15 Thomas L. Harris, *Value-Added Public Relations: The Secret Weapon of Integrated Marketing* (Lincolnwood, IL: NTC Business Books, 1998).

16 "2016 Edelman Trust Barometer," January 17, 2016, www.edelman.com.

17 Sandra Moriarty, "IMC Needs PR's Stakeholder Focus," *AMA Marketing News*, May 26, 1997, 7.

18 Fraser P. Seitel, *The Practice of Public Relations*, 13th ed. (Boston: Pearson, 2017), 10.

19 Lindsay Stein, "How Public Relations Is Earning Its Place in 2016," January 11, 2016, www.adage.com.

20 Seitel, *Practice of Public Relations*, 73.

21 John Paluszek, personal communication, August 3, 2009.

22 Rupal Parekh, "The Implosion of Lance Armstrong's Endorsement Empire: $30 M and Counting," October 19, 2012, www.adage.com.

23 Jonathan Salem Baskin, "CMOs Go Beyond a PR Plan to Prepare for an Inevitable Product Crisis," March 8, 2010, www.adage.com.

24 Stein, "How Public Relations Is Earning Its Place."

25 Seitel, *Practice of Public Relations*, 173.

26 Lisa Belkin, "Moms and Motrin," *New York Times*, November 17, 2008, www.nytimes.com.

27 Mark Suster, "If It Didn't Happen on Twitter It Didn't Really Happen. Here's Why," November 13, 2012, www.bothsidesofthetable.com.

28 "A Legacy of Giving and Service," July 21, 2017, https://corporate.target.com/corporate-responsibility.

29 "Dawn Expands 4-Year Commitment to Wildlife Rescue with $1 Million Donation and New Documentary Series Featuring Rob Lowe," July 16, 2013, http://www.businesswire.com/.

30 Jack Neff, "Dawn's Wildlife Rescue Efforts Shine in Gulf Coast Oil Spill," May 4, 2010, www.adage.com; Leslie Kaufman, "Ad for a Dish Detergent Becomes Part of a Story," *New York Times*, June 15, 2010, www.nytimes.com.

31 Kiley Skene, "A PR Case Study: Red Bull Stratos," *News Generation*, March 14, 2014, www.newsgeneration.com; Dave Thier, "Felix Baumgartner's Jump Proves the Power of Publicity Stunts," October 15, 2012, www.forbes.com.

32 Thomas Harris, "iPod, Therefore iAm," *ViewsLetter*, September 2004, 3.

33 Seitel, *Practice of Public Relations*, 322–323.

34 Christopher Klein, "The First Macy's Thanksgiving Day Parade," November 26, 2014, www.history.com.

35 Sherman, Erik, "Steve Jobs' Rules for Public Relations," May 21, 2014, www.slate.com.

36 Leander Kahney, "What Apple Product Launches Say about Tim Cook's Leadership," March 22, 2016, www.cultofmac.com.

37 Seitel, *Practice of Public Relations*, 191.

38 "7 Public Relations Trends to Watch in 2015," *PRNews*, December 19, 2014, www.prnewsonline.com; Brooke W. McKeever, "#PRin2016: What to Watch for in 2016 and Beyond (Nonprofit Trends)," January 28, 2016, www.prsay.prsa.org; Greg Beaubien, "A Forecast of 2016 Marketing Trends," *Public Relations Tactics*, December 2, 2015, www.prsa.org; Amit Jain, "Emerging Models of PR Measurement," *PR Week*, July 16, 2014, www.prweek.com.

39 Jack Neff, "REI and Swedish Tourism Win Promo and Direct Grand Prix for Taking Unusual Risks," June 20, 2016, www.adage.com.

CHAPTER 4

1 Stephanie Gleason, "Fuller Brush Goes into Chapter 11," *Wall Street Journal*, February 23, 2012, B8; napavalleyregister.com/news/local/st-helena-man-buys-fuller-brush-gives-it-napa-home/article_4de1cff2-e693-11e2-af9d-001a4bcf887a.html.

2 Avon Press Release, February 16, 2017, www.media.avoncompany.com.

3 Amway Press Release, February 8, 2017, www.globalnews.amway.com.

4 Lina Younes, "Put and End to Junk Mail," February 26, 2009, https://blog.epa.gov/blog/2009/02/put-an-end-to-junk-mail/. Retrieved September 17, 2017.

5 Montgomery Ward website, August 8, 2015, www.wards.com, downloaded.

6 FTC infographic, "10 Years of Do Not Call," www.consumer.ftc.gov/articles/0372-10-years-do-not-call-infographic. Retrieved September 17, 2017.

7 Teresa Day, "How Direct Sellers Are Leveraging New Technology." *The Ultimate Social Business Model*, Special Supplement to *The Wall Street Journal* by *Direct Selling News*, June 24, 2011, 18.

8 Arlene Gerwin, "Sale Promotion Planning," in *The Power of Point-of-Purchase Advertising: Marketing at Retail*, 3rd Ed., ed. Robert Liljenwall (Washington D.C.: Point-of-Purchase Advertising International, 2008), 63.

9 Gerwin, "Sale Promotion Planning," 63.

10 James O'Toole, "J. C. Penney Offers Kids Free Haircuts," *CNN Money*, September 10, 2012, www.money.cnn.com.

11 Paul Ziobro, "Target Site Goes Down as Buyers Swarm Sale," *Wall Street Journal*, April 20, 2015, B1.

12 Jill Stravolernos, "78 Percent of Americans Get Coupons from Newspapers," *Boulder Daily Camera Business Plus*, January 11, 2010, 8; John Waggoner, "Consumers Open Wallets, but Not for New Stuff," *USA Today*, May 19, 2009, www.usatoday.com, B1.

13 Jack Loechner, "Digital Coupons Becoming Core Promotional Element," February 17, 2016, www.mediapost.com.

14 Suzanne Vranica, "NBC Universal Tees Up Cause-Related Shows," *Wall Street Journal*, October 19, 2009, B4.

15 Angela Doland, "How a Sponsorship Deal Sparked an Uproar Against China's Baidu," January 19, 2016, www.adage.com.

16 Ashley Rodriguez, "Lowe's Gives Away Glow-in-the-Dark Cat Hats during March Madness," *Advertising Age*, March 27, 2015, www.adage.com.

17 Yahoo! Inc.

18 Ashley Rodgriguez, "Best Practices: How to Create a Rewards Program That Really Works," *Advertising Age*, June 17, 2015, www.adage.com.

19 Gerwin, "Sale Promotion Planning," 63.

20 "Cultivating Comprehensive Data Privacy throughout Your Organization," TRUSTe Whitepaper, September 12, 2012, www.truste.com, 1.

21 Fatemeh Khatibloo, "Personal Identity Management" (Cambridge, MA: Forrester Research, September 30, 2011).

22 Belinda Luscombe, "Using Business Savvy to Help Good Causes," *Time*, March 28, 2011, 65.

23 Kara Swisher, "Silicon Valley, the Long View," *Wall Street Journal*, June 4, 2012, R6.

24 Natasha Singer, "More Companies Are Tracking Online Data, Study Finds," *New York Times*, November 12, 2012, www.nytimes.com.

25 David Rittenhouse, personal correspondence, September 14, 2012.

26 Giles D'Souza and Joseph Phelps, "The Privacy Paradox: The Case of Secondary Disclosure," *Review of Marketing Science* 7, no. 4 (2009), bepress.com/romsjournal/vol7/iss1/art4.

CHAPTER 5

1 Ennis Higgins, "Conversations with David Ogilvy," in *The Art of Writing Advertising* (Chicago: Advertising Publications, 1965).

[2] Claude E. Shannon and Warren Weaver, *The Mathematical Theory of Communication* (Urbana: University of Illinois Press, 1949).

[3] Tim Peterson, "How Twitter's New Ad Format Will Get People Tweeting about Its Advertisers," January 5, 2016, www.adage.com.

[4] Elihu Katz and Paul Lazarsfeld, *Personal Influence* (New York: Free Press, 1955).

[5] Dennis DiPasquale, personal communication, June 7, 2012.

[6] "Burson-Marsteller Global Social Media Check-Up 2012," July 17, 2012, www.businesswire.com.

[7] Harley Manning and Kerry Bodine, *Outside In: The Power of Putting Customers at the Center of Your Business* (Cambridge MA: Forrester Research, 2012), 22.

[8] Stephanie Strom, "McDonald's Introduces Screen Ordering and Table Service," November 17, 2016, www.adage.com.

[9] Demetrios Vakratsas and Tim Ambler, "Advertising Effects: A Taxonomy and Review of Concepts, Methods, and Results from the Academic Literature," Marketing Science Institute Working Paper (Cambridge, MA: Marketing Science Institute, 1996), 96–120; Thomas Barry and Daniel Howard, "A Review and Critique of the Hierarchy of Effects in Advertising," *International Journal of Advertising* 9, no. 2 (1990): 429–435; Michael Ray, "Communication and the Hierarchy of Effects," in *New Models for Mass Communication Research*, ed. P. Clarke (Beverly Hills, CA: Sage, 1973), 147–175; Thomas Barry, "The Development of the Hierarchy of Effects: An Historical Perspective," *Current Research and Issues in Advertising* 10, nos. 1–2 (1987): 251–295.

[10] Ray, "Communication and the Hierarchy of Effects"; Richard Vaughn, "How Advertising Works: A Planning Model," *Journal of Advertising Research* 20, no. 5 (1980): 27–33; Richard Vaughn, "How Advertising Works: A Planning Model Revisited," *Journal of Advertising Research* 26, no. 1 (1986): 57–66.

[11] Gergely Nyilasy and Leonard Reid, "Agency Practitioner Theories of How Advertising Works," *Journal of Advertising* 38, no. 3 (Fall 2009): 86.

[12] Sandra Moriarty, "Beyond the Hierarchy of Effects: A Conceptual Model," *Current Issues and Research in Advertising* 1 (1983): 45–56.

[13] J. Scott Armstrong, *Persuasive Advertising: Evidence-Based Principles* (New York: Palgrave Macmillan, 2010), 25.

[14] Ivan Preston, "The Association Model of the Advertising Communication Process," *Journal of Advertising* 11, no. 2 (1982): 3–24.

[15] Charles Young, "The Essence of an Ad," Ameritest Research Reports, May 2012, www.ameritest.net.

[16] Mike Azzara, "Al Yenta: It Matches Your Press Release to the Journalists Who'll Want It," December 1, 2016, www.mediapost.com's AI Insider.

[17] Ann-Christine Diaz, "Geico's New Campaign Is Really Unskippable," February 29, 2016, www.adage.com.

[18] Tom Duncan and Sandra Moriarty, *Driving Brand Value: Using Integrated Marketing to Manage Profitable Stakeholder Relationships* (New York: McGraw-Hill, 1997).

[19] Young, "The Essence of an Ad."

[20] "Best Ad of the Year? Texas Pol's Wife Makes Hilarious Appeal to Voters," October 27, 2016, www.FoxNews.com.

[21] Katie Ford, "Top 5 Takeaways from Cause Marketing Forum," June 4, 2012, www.causemarketingforum.com.

[22] Erik du Plessis, *The Advertised Mind* (London: Kogan Page, 2005), 4.

[23] Marilyn Roberts, "Does Negative Political Advertising Help or Hinder Citizens?," in Sandra Moriarty, Nancy Mitchell, and William Wells, *Advertising & IMC: Principles and Practice*, 9th ed. (Upper Saddle River NJ: Prentice Hall, 2012), 117.

[24] Ann-Christine Diaz, "Behind the Music: Coca-Cola Sings a Whole New Tune with 'Taste the Feeling,'" January 22, 2016, www.adage.com.

[25] Jon D. Morris et al., "The Power of Affect: Predicting Intention," *Journal of Advertising Research*, May/June 2002, 7–17.

[26] Russell I. Haley and Allan L. Baldinger, "The Copy Research Validity Project," *Journal of Advertising Research*, April/May 1991, 11–32.

[27] Kevin Claveria, "How to Engage Millennials for Customer Insight and Marketing," August 12, 2016, www.Visioncritical.com.

[28] Ann-Christine Diaz, "Tearjerker about Hard-Working Mom and Her Boy Shows What's Really Important for Chinese New Year," February 9, 2016, www.adage.com.

[29] Kathy Delaney, "How Brands Should Be Marketing Wellness to Women," September 12, 2016, www.adage.com.

[30] Tom Krisher, "GM's Ads Aren't Getting the Job Done," *Boulder Daily Camera*, August 1, 2012, 11A.

[31] David Stewart and David Furse, *Television Advertising: A Study of 1000 Commercials* (Lexington, MA: Lexington Books, 1986).

[32] Thomas J. Page Jr., Esther Thorson, and Maria Papas Heide, "The Memory Impact of Commercials Varying in Emotional Appeal and Product Involvement," in *Emotion in Advertising*, ed. Stuart J. Agrees, Julie A. Edell, and Tony M. Dubitsky (New York: Quorum Books, 1990), 255–281.

[33] Charles E. Young, "Co-Creativity," Ameritest Reports, January 2008, www.ameritest.net, 1.

[34] Ann Marie Barry, "Perception Theory," in *The Handbook of Visual Communication*, ed. Ken Smith et al. (Mahwah, NJ: Lawrence Erlbaum Associates, 2005), 23–62.

[35] Charles E. Young, *Branded Memory* (Seattle: Ideas in Flight, 2011): 62.

[36] Gerard Tellis, *Effective Advertising: Understanding When, How, and Why Advertising Works* (Thousand Oaks, CA: Sage, 2004), 183–184; Grant McCracken, "Culture and Consumption: A Theoretical Account of the Structure and Movement of the Cultural Meaning of Consumer Goods," *Journal of Consumer Research* 13 (June 1986): 71–84.

[37] Young, *Branded Memory*, 52.

[38] Preston, "The Association Model of the Advertising Communication Process"; Ivan Preston and Esther Thorson, "Challenges to the Use of Hierarchy Models in Predicting Advertising Effectiveness," in *Proceedings of the 1983 American Academy of Advertising Conference*, ed. Donald Jugenheimer (Lawrence: University Press of Kansas, 1983), 27–33.

[39] David Ogilvy, *Confessions of an Advertising Man* (New York: Dell, 1963), 119; American Advertising Federation Advertising Hall of Fame, www.advertisinghalloffame.org/members.

[40] Candice Choi, "Kellogg Used 'Independent Experts' to Promote Cereal," *Naples Daily News*, November 24, 2016, 18A.

[41] Keith O'Brien, "Supersize," *New York Times Magazine*, May 4, 2012, 44–48, 78, 81.

[42] Charles E. Young, "Essence of an Ad," Ameritest Research Reports, May 2012, www.ameritest.net. Retrieved September 25, 2017.

[43] Jack Loechner, "Internet of Things Offers Opportunity for Customer Loyalty Programs," September 19, 2016, www.Mediapost.com.

[44] "Davos Man Needs His Image Polishing," *Economist*, January 25, 2011, www.economist.com.

[45] Dave Fiore, "Designing a New Creative Dojo for the Brave New Agency," May 2, 2016, www.adage.com.

[46] Charles Young, "Imaging the Four Types of Brand Memory Tags in Restaurant Advertising, 2007," Ameritest/CY Research, April 2007, www.ameritest.net, 15.

[47] Richard Cross and Janet Smith, *Customer Bonding: Pathway to Lasting Customer Loyalty* (Lincolnwood, IL: NTC Business Books, 1995), 54–55.

[48] Erik du Plessis, *The Advertised Mind: Ground-Breaking Insights into How Our Brains Respond to Advertising* (London: Millward Brown, 2005), 4.

[49] John Philip Jones, *When Ads Work: New Proof That Advertising Triggers Sales*, 2nd ed. (New York: Lexington Books, 2007); Louise Marsland, "How Much Advertising Actually Works?," SAMRA Convention 2006 News, March 15, 2006, www.bizcommunity.com.

[50] Young, *Branded Memory*, 4.

CHAPTER 6

[1] "Research for R.O.I.," Communications Workshop, Chicago: DDB, April 10, 1987.

[2] "Social Is the New Normal for Travel Marketers," *eMarketer*, June 5, 2012, www.emarketer.com.

[3] Julia Chang, "More Than Words," *Sales and Marketing Management*, September 2006, 14.

[4] Emily Steel, "Marketers Find Web Chat Can Be Inspiring," *Wall Street Journal*, November 23, 2009, B8.

[5] "Twilight of the Twinkie?," *Wall Street Journal*, January 14–15, 2012, C4.

[6] Stephanie Clifford, "Social Media Are Giving a Voice to Taste Buds," *New York Times*,

July 30, 2012, http://www.nytimes.com/2012/07/31/technology/facebook-twitter-and-foursquare-as-corporate-focus-groups.html.

[7] Kalia Strong, "4 Ways to Use Pinterest for Market Research," *Search Engine Watch*, May 10, 2012; www.searchenginewatch.com, Amber Wallor, "How Local Businesses Can Do Research and Gain an Edge with Pinterest," *SmartBlog on Social Media*, May 7, 2012, www.smartblogs.com.

[8] Ann Marie Barry, "Perception Theory," in *The Handbook of Visual Communication*, ed. Ken Smith, Sandra Moriarty, Gretchen Barbatsis, and Keith Kenney (Mahwah, NJ: Lawrence Erlbaum Associates, 2005), 23–62.

[9] Ilan Brat, "The Emotional Quotient of Soup Shopping," *Wall Street Journal*, February 17, 2010, B6.

[10] Batman, Warner Brothers (1989).

[11] "Hoover Fails to Shake Off Free Flights Horror," *Marketing Week*, May 1, 1997, http://www.marketingweek.com/1997/05/01/hoover-fails-to-shake-off-free-flights-horror/.

[12] Joseph Herbert Appel, *The Business Biography of John Wanamaker: Founder and Builder* (New York: Macmillan, 1930).

[13] DDB North America, July 9, 2016, http://ddbnorthamerica.com/category/lifestylestudy/, accessed.

[14] Sandy Moriarty, Nancy Mitchell, William Wells (2012), "Cheesy Fun. It's Not Just for Kids," in *Advertising and IMC Principles and Practices*, 9th ed. (Upper Saddle River, NJ: Prentice Hall), 161–162.

[15] Steve Lohr, "Computers That See You, Read You and Even Tell You to Wash," *New York Times*, January 2, 2011, 1.

[16] Emily Glass, "The Eyes Have It: Marketers Now Track Shoppers' Retinas," *Wall Street Journal*, July 12, 2012, B1.

[17] Gina Chon, "To Woo Wealthy, Lexus Attempts Image Makeover," *Wall Street Journal*, March 24–25, 2007, A1.

[18] Sue Shellenbarger, "A Few Bucks for Your Thoughts?," *Wall Street Journal*, May 18, 2011, D3.

[19] Shellenbarger, "A Few Bucks for Your Thoughts?"

[20] Based on Dr. Bryan Gross, personal communication, June 17, 2016.

[21] Leigh Ann Steere, "Culture Club," *Print*, March/April 1999, 4–5.

[22] Shay Sayre, *Qualitative Methods for Marketplace Research* (Thousand Oaks, CA: Sage, 2001), 31.

[23] Dana Mattioli, "Lululemon's Secret Sauce," *Wall Street Journal*, March 22, 2012, B1.

[24] Russell W. Belk, ed., *Highways and Buyways: Naturalistic Research from the Consumer Behavior Odyssey* (Provo, UT: Association for Consumer Research, 1991).

[25] Sayre, *Qualitative Methods for Marketplace Research*, 20.

[26] Ellen Byron, "Seeing Store Shelves through Senior Eyes," *Wall Street Journal*, September 14, 2009, B1.

[27] Antonio Regalado, "McCann Offers Peek at Lives of Low-Income Latins," *Wall Street Journal*, December 8, 2008, B6.

[28] Regina Lewis, personal communication, November 21, 2006.

[29] Larry Soley, "Projective Techniques for Advertising and Consumer Research, *AAA Newsletter* 6, no. 2 (June 2010): 1, 3–5.

[30] Emily Eakin, "Penetrating the Mind by Metaphor," *New York Times*, February 23, 2002, www.nytimes.com.

[31] Sandra Yin, "New or Me Too," *American Demographics*, September 2002, 28.

[32] Mendelsohn, personal communication.

[33] Jim Edwards, "Victory Dance for the Vain: A Reporter Goes 'Under,'" *Brandweek*, October 3, 2005, 23.

[34] Robin Couler, Gerald Zaltman, and Keith Coulter, "Interpreting Consumer Perceptions of Advertising: An Application of the Zaltman Metaphor Elicitation Technique," *Journal of Advertising* 30, no. 4 (Winter 2001): 1–14; Eakin, "Penetrating the Mind by Metaphor"; Daniel Pink, "Metaphor Marketing," *Fast Company* 14 (March 31, 1998): 214, www.fastcompany.com; HBS Division of Research (Feb 22, 2000), The Mind of the Market Laboratory, "ZMET," www.hbs.edu.

[35] Greenbook Research Industry Trends Report, http://insightinnovation.org/wp-content/uploads/2015/05/2015GRITweb.pdf, 2015.

[36] Tim Perzyk and George Slefo, "Twitter Turns 12,000 Users into Quick-Research Panel for Marketers," *Advertising Age*, June 8, 2016, http://adage.com/article/digital/twitter-launches-insiders/304351/.

[37] Morrison, Maureen, "Last Call for Marketers? Snapchat Users to Pass Both Twitter and Pinterest This Year," *Advertising Age*, June 8, 2016.

[38] Karl Weiss, personal communication, August 10, 2012.

CHAPTER 7

[1] Valentina Zarya, "Dove Is Back at It with Another Inspirational Ad," *Fortune*, June 28, 2016, http://fortune.com/2016/06/28/dove-my-beauty-my-say/; Katie Dupere, "Dove's New Campaign Challenges How the Media Portrays Women in Sports," July 26, 2016, http://mashable.com/2016/07/26/dove-women-in-sports/#1_2kgtdAjqqt; http://www.dovehaveyoursay.com/, accessed October 7, 2016.

[2] Milton Rokeach, *The Nature of Human Values* (New York: Free Press, 1973).

[3] Wagner A. Kamakura and Jose Afonso Mazzon (1991), "Value Segmentation: A Model for the Measurement of Values and Value Systems," *Journal of Consumer Research* 18 (September): 201–218.

[4] Sam Schechner, "European Consumers Tighten Their Belts," *Wall Street Journal*, August 6, 2012, A14; "Consumers Are Saving More and Spending and Borrowing Less," Harris Poll news release, June 26, 2009, www.harrisinteractive.com.

[5] Marieke deMooij, "How Advertising Works Cross-Culturally," in *Advertising Principles and Practices*, 8th ed., ed. Sandra Moriarty, Nancy Mitchell, and William Wells (Upper Saddle River, NJ: Prentice Hall, 2009), 549.

[6] Michael Bush, "Dove Finds Perfect Match in China's 'Ugly Betty,'" *Advertising Age*, adage.com, May 26, 2009.

[7] Dave Taylor, "The Odd World of the Cult of Apple," *Boulder Daily Camera*, January 7, 2009, 9.

[8] Rose M. Kreider and Jonathan Vespa (2014), "The Historic Rise of One-Person Households: 1850–2010," https://www.census.gov/content/dam/Census/library/working-papers/2014/demo/paa2014kreider-vespa.presentation.pdf; Statistica, "The Rise of the American 1-Person Household," https://www.statista.com/chart/1415/the-rise-of-the-american-one-person-household/, accessed July 21, 2017.

[9] *The 2015 Consumer Expenditure Survey*, Bureau of Labor Statistics, http://www.bls.gov/cex/, http://www.bls.gov/cex/2015/aggregate/cucomp.pdf, accessed November 23, 2016; *Eric Klinenberg, "Solo Nation:* American Consumers Stay Single," *Fortune*, January 25, 2012, http://fortune.com/2012/01/25/solo-nation-american-consumers-stay-single/; Eddie Yoon and Michelle Stacy (2015), "The Billion-Dollar Opportunity in Single-Serve Food," *Harvard Business Review*, https://hbr.org/2015/10/the-billion-dollar-opportunity-in-single-serve-food.

[10] Susan Mendelsohn, private e-mail, September 20, 2009.

[11] Eugene Schwartz, *Breakthrough Advertising* (Stamford, CT: Bottom Line Books, 2004), 4.

[12] Ann Marie Barry, "Perception Theory," in *The Handbook of Visual Communication*, ed. Ken Smith et al. (Mahwah, NJ: Lawrence Erlbaum Associates, 2005), 23–62.

[13] David Brooks, "The Segmentation Century," *New York Times*, May 31, 2012, www.nytimes.com.

[14] Bryan Walsh, "America's Food Crisis and How to Fix It," *Time*, August 31, 2009, 31–37; Paul Kaihla, "Sexing Up a Piece of Meat," *Business 2.0*, April 2006, 72–74.

[15] Meta S. Brown, "Big Data Analytics and the Next President: How Microtargeting Drives Today's Campaigns," *Forbes*, May 29, 2016.

[16] Dana Mattioli and Miguel Bustillo, "Can Texting Save Stores?," *Wall Street Journal*, May 9, 2012, B1.

[17] Harley Manning and Kerry Bodine, *Outside In: The Power of Putting Customers at the Center of Your Business* (Cambridge, MA: Forrester Research, 2012), 124.

[18] Fry, Richard. "Millennials Overtake Baby Boomers as America's Largest Generation," Pew Research Center, April 25, 2016, http://www.pewresearch.org/fact-tank/2016/04/25/millennials-overtake-baby-boomers/.

[19] Tamar Lewin, "If Your Kids Are Awake, They're Probably Online," *New York Times*, January 20, 2010, www.nytimes.com.

[20] MCorp Consulting, "Insights and Influence in 140 Characters or Less . . . ," *Touchpoint*

Insights, October 2009, http://blog
.mcorpconsulting.com; Mickey Meeco,
"What Do Women Want? Just Ask," *New York Times*, October 29, 2006, 29.

[21] "Graduate Degree Attainment of the U.S. Population," Council of Graduate Schools, July 2009, http://cgsnet.org/ckfinder/userfiles/files/ DataSources_2009_07.pdf; Aimee Heckel, "Layoffs Hitting Men Hardest," *Boulder Daily Camera*, October 25, 2009, D1; Richard Stengel, "The American Woman," *Time*, October 26, 2009.

[22] Alan Kirkpatrick, "Creating Equity," *Bylines* (CU-Boulder's School of Journalism and Mass Communication alumni publication), Spring 2009, 15.

[23] Andy Kiersz, "Here Are Some of the Demographic and Economic Characteristics of America's Gay Couples," *Business Insider*, June 27, 2015, http://www.businessinsider.com/ census-data-on-gay-households-2015-6.

[24] Bob Witeck, personal communication, August 10, 2012.

[25] Data computed from "Current Population Survey: A Joint Effort between the Bureau of Labor Statistics and the Census Bureau— Annual Social and Economic Supplement," 2011, https://www.census.gov/programs- surveys/cps/data-detail.html.

[26] Binyamin Appelbaum, "Where Wealth Declined Most," *New York Times*, June 11, 2012, www.nytimes.com.

[27] Nathaniel Popper and Tara Bernard, "In Era of Cheap Money, Consumers Are Shut Out," *New York Times*, June 8, 2012, www.nytimes.com.

[28] Laurie Burkitt and Bob Davis, "Chasing China's Shoppers," *Wall Street Journal*, June 15, 2012, B1.

[29] "Fast Facts on U.S. Hispanics," *Advertising Age 2012 Hispanic Fact Pack*, supplement to *Advertising Age*, July 24, 2012, 38.

[30] R. Thomas Umstead, "BET: African- Americans Grow in Numbers, Buying Power," *Multichannel News*, January 26, 2010, www.multichannel.com.

[31] Sabrina Tavernise, "Whites Account for Under Half of Births in U.S.," *New York Times*, May 17, 2012, www.nytimes.com.

[32] Taverniese, "Whites Account for Under Half of Births in U.S."

[33] "Country of Birth," *Advertising Age 2009 Hispanic Fact Pack*, supplement to *Advertising Age*, July 27, 2009, 39.

[34] Jack Neff and Emily York, "ANA Urges Marketers: We Must Be the Ones to Lead the Country Out of Recession," *Advertising Age*, November 9, 2009, www.adage.com.

[35] D'Vera Cohn and Andrea Caumont, "10 Demographic Trends That Are Shaping the U.S. and the World," Pew Research Center, March 31, 2016, http://www.pewresearch. org/fact-tank/2016/03/31/10-demographic- trends-that-are-shaping-the-u-s-and-the-world/; Besheer Mohamed, "A New Estimate of the U.S. Muslim Population," Pew Research Center, January 6, 2016, http://www .pewresearch.org/fact-tank/2016/01/06/a-new- estimate-of-the-u-s-muslim-population/.

[36] "Mohammad Now Top Male Name in England, World," *NPR Morning Edition*, September 17, 2009, www.npr.org.

[37] Richard Stengel, "The Responsibility Revolution," *Time*, September 21, 2009, 38–40.

[38] "Segment Details," Claritas MyBestSegments, https://segmentationsolutions.nielsen.com/ mybestsegments/Default.jsp?ID=30&pageName =Segment%DEtails, accessed January 16, 2017.

[39] Associated Press, "Designers Target Toddlers Who Have $10,000 to Spare," August 13, 2012, www.cnbc.com.

[40] Clair Cain Miller, "Google and F.T.C. Set to Settle Safari Privacy Charge," *New York Times*, July 10, 2012, www.nytimes.com.

[41] Dana Mattioli, "On Orbitz, Mac Users Steered to Pricier Hotels," *Wall Street Journal*, January 26, 2012, A13.

[42] Kate Stein, "Shop Faster," *New York Times*, April 16, 2009, www.nytimes.com.

[43] Everett Rogers, *Diffusion of Innovations*, 3rd ed. (New York: Free Press, 1983).

[44] Sandra Moriarty, Nancy Mitchell, and William Wells, *Advertising and IMC Principles and Practices*, 9th ed. (Upper Saddle River, NJ: Prentice Hall, 2012), 97–98.

[45] "How to Target Facebook Ads," https:// www.facebook.com/business/a/online-sales/ ad-targeting-details, accessed December 1, 2016; "Ad Targeting," https://business.twitter. com/en/targeting.html, accessed December 1, 2016; "YouTube Targeting: Precision Targeting at Scale," https://static.googleusercontent.com/ media/www.youtube.com/en//yt/advertise/ medias/pdfs/targeting-onesheeter-en.pdf, accessed December 1, 2016.

[46] Don Schultz, personal communication, August 12, 2012.

[47] Mike Shields, "The Process of Making Digital Ads Is Gradually Starting to Become More 'Programmatic,'" *Wall Street Journal*, December 22, 2016, http://www.wsj.com/ articles/the-process-of-making-digital- ads-is-gradually-starting-to-become-more- programmatic-1482404400; Kurt Wagner, "Snap Has Acquired an Ad Tech Company Called Flite," *Recode*, December 19, 2016, http://www.recode.net/2016/12/19/14010630/ snap-flite-ad-tech-aquisition.

[48] "Dove is Helping Young People Build Body Confidence and Self-Esteem," https:// brightfuture.unilever.com/stories/485841/ Dove-is-helping-young-people-build-body- confidence-and-self-esteem.aspx, accessed August 8, 2017.

CHAPTER 8

[1] Patrick Coffee,"Chick-fil-A Breaks with The Richards Group, Sends Work to McCann and Erich & Kallman," July 21, 2016, http:// www.adweek.com/agencyspy/chick-fil-a- breaks-with-the-richards-group-sends-work-to- mccann-and-erich-kallman/113431.

[2] Pat Fallon and Fred Senn, *Juicing the Orange: How to Turn Creativity into a Powerful Business Advantage* (Boston: Harvard Business School Press, 2006).

[3] J. Scott Armstrong, *Persuasive Advertising: Evidence-Based Principles* (New York: Palgrave Macmillan, 2010), 16.

[4] Armstrong, *Persuasive Advertising*, 16, 25.

[5] Suzanne Vranica, "Ad Firms Heed Diversity," *Wall Street Journal*, November 29, 2010, B7.

[6] Sapna Maheshwari, "Brands to Agencies: Diversify or Else," *New York Times*, September 30, 2016, http://www.nytimes.com/2016/10/01/ business/brands-to-ad-agencies-diversify- or-else.html?_r=0.

[7] Peggy Kreshel, "What Is Diversity and Why Is It Important?" in Sandra Moriarty, Nancy Mitchell, and William Wells, *Advertising & IMC Principles and Practice*, 9th ed. (Upper Saddle River, NJ: Prentice Hall, 2012), 201.

[8] Jeremy Barr, "New York Times Seeks Dismissal of Lawsuit Alleging Discrimination in Ad Sales: Department Denies That Institutional Gender Inequality Exists at Company," *Advertising Age*, August 2, 2016, http:// adage.com/article/media/york-times-asks- discrimination-case-dismissed/305293/?utm_ source=mediaworks&utm_medium= newsletter&utm_campaign=adage&ttl= 1470773878; "Saatchi Chairman Kevin Roberts Resigns after Gender Comments: Stepping Down on Sept. 1," *Advertising Age*, August 3, 2016, http://adage.com/article/media/york- times-asks-discrimination-case-dismissed/305293/ ?utm_source=mediaworks&utm_medium= newsletter&utm_campaign=adage&ttl= 1470773878.

[9] Chris Malone, "Customer Loyalty: Warmth, Competence Are Key," *Forbes*, September 1, 2010, http://www.forbes.com/2010/09/01/ marketing-brands-loyalty-bp-mcdonalds- burger-king-tropicana-tylenol-cmo-network .html.

[10] Jack Trout, "Branding Can't Exist without Positioning," *Advertising Age*, March 14, 2005, 28.

[11] Giep Franzen and Sandra Moriarty, *The Science and Art of Branding* (Armonk, NY: M. E. Sharpe, 2009), 5.

[12] John Williams, "Emotional Branding: What's Love Got to Do with It? Plenty!," April 16, 2008, www.entrepreneur.com.

[13] Hallmark Cards

[14] Coca-Cola Company

[15] J. Walter Thompson and the NPD Group, *United States Marine Corps Attitude and Awareness Tracking Study, Summary Report and Findings—Male*, JWT internal report, 1998.

[16] Carl Bialik, "New Vehicles Leave MPG Standard Behind," *Wall Street Journal*, August 26, 2009, A12.

[17] William L. Wilkie and Edgar A. Pessemier, "Issues in Marketing's Use of Multi-attribute Attitude Models," *Journal of Marketing Research* 10 (November 1973): 428–441.

[18] Nick Bunkley, "With Low Prices, Hyundai Builds Market Share," *New York Times*, September 22, 2009, www.nytimes.com.

[19] Suzanne Vranica, "Veteran Marketer Promotes a New Kind of Selling," *Wall Street Journal*, October 31, 2008, B4.

20 Larry Kelley and Donald Jugenheimer, *Advertising Account Planning: Planning and Managing an IMC Campaign*, 3rd ed. (Armonk, NY: M. E. Sharp, 2015), 72.

21 Kelley and Jugenheimer, *Advertising Account Planning*, 72.

22 Kelley and Jugenheimer, *Advertising Account Planning*, 72.

23 Regina Lewis, panel member on "A Creative Brief That Breathes," American Academy of Advertising Annual Conference, March 15–18, 2012, Myrtle Beach, SC.

24 Joe Ruff, "Research Goes beyond Focus Groups," *Denver Post*, December 6, 2004, 2E.

25 Susan Mendelsohn, personal communication, January 8, 2004.

26 Susan Mendelsohn, personal communication, January 8, 2004.

27 Kelley and Jugenheimer, *Advertising Account Planning*, 80.

28 Quoted in Laurie Freeman, "Planner Puts Clients in Touch with Soul of Brands," *Advertising Age*, February 8, 1999, www.adage.com.

29 Kelley and Jugenheimer, *Advertising Account Planning*, 73.

30 Charlie Robertson, "Creative Briefs and Briefings," in *How to Plan Advertising*, 2nd ed., ed. Alan Cooper (London: Thomson Learning and the Account Planning Group, 2004), 62.

CHAPTER 9

1 Thomas Vogel, *Breakthrough Thinking: A Guide to Creative Thinking and Idea Generation* (Blue Ash, OH: HOW Books, 2014), 15.

2 George Penston, "The Creative Director Role (As We Know It) Will Not Exist in 10 Years," *Advertising Age*, August 29, 2016, www.adage.com.

3 Mark Stuhlfaut, "How Creative Are We? The Teaching of Creativity Theory and Training," *Journal of Advertising Education* 11, no. 2 (Fall 2007): 49–59.

4 Mark Stuhlfaut and Margo Berman, "Pedagogic Challenges: The Teaching of Creative Strategy in Advertising Courses," *Journal of Advertising Education*, Fall 2009, 37.

5 Andrew Newman, "No Actors, Just Patients in Unvarnished Spots for Hospitals," *New York Times*, May 4, 2009, www.nytimes.com.

6 "Top 100 Advertising Campaigns," *Advertising Age*, March 29, 1999, www.adage.com.

7 James Webb Young, *A Technique for Producing Ideas*, 3rd ed. (Chicago: Crain Books, 1975).

8 Jerri Moore and William D. Wells, *R.O.I. Guidebook: Planning for Relevance, Originality and Impact in Advertising and Other Marketing Communications* (New York: DDB Needham, 1991).

9 Thomas Russell and Glenn Verrill, *Kleppner's Advertising Procedure*, 14th ed. (Upper Saddle River, NJ: Prentice Hall, 2002), 457.

10 Tevor Guthrie, "Sometimes It's Better to Study Dolphin Brains Than Advertising," *Advertising Age*, July 17, 2012, www.adage.com.

11 Sheri J. Broyles, "The Creative Personality: Exploring Relations of Creativity and Openness to Experience," unpublished doctoral dissertation, Southern Methodist University, 1995.

12 Broyles, "The Creative Personality."

13 Graham Wallas, *The Art of Thought* (New York: Harcourt, Brace, 1926); Alex F. Osborn, *Applied Imagination*, 3rd ed. (New York: Scribner's, 1963).

14 Linda Conway Correll, "Exercise Your Creative Muscles," in Sandra Moriarty, Nancy Mitchell, and William Wells, *Advertising and IMC Practices and Principles*, 10th ed. (Upper Saddle River NJ: Prentice Hall, 2012), 232.

15 Melissa Korn and Rachel Silverman, "Forget B-School, D-School Is Hot," *Wall Street Journal*, June 7, 2012, B1.

16 David Droga, "Sweating Ad Copy Like 'Mad Men,'" *Wall Street Journal*, June 11–12, 2011, C12.

17 Idea Champions, "The 10 Personas of a Really Effective Brainstorm Facilitator," March 30, 2012, www.ideachampions.com.

18 MasterCard Worldwide.

19 Frazer P. Seitel, *The Practice of Public Relations*, 13th ed. (New York: Pearson, 2017), 86–87.

20 Kevin Keller, *Strategic Brand Management*, 3rd ed. (Upper Saddle River, NJ: Prentice Hall, 2008), 76–81.

21 Lucy Aitken, "More Data Is at the Heart of Everything," *Warc*, August 22, 2016, www.warc.com.

22 O&G Launches "Thank You, Mom" Campaign for Rio 2016, April 27, 2016, https://www.olympic.org/news/p-g-launches-thank-you-mom-campaign-for-rio-2016.

23 Ashley Rodriguez, "Nationwide CMO Exits in Wake of 'Dead Boy' Super Bowl Ad," *Advertising Age*, May 6, 2015, www.adage.com.

24 Steve Smith, "This Is Your Brain on Drugs: How Drug Public Service Announcements Have Changed over the Years," September 29, 2015, www.medicaldaily.com.

25 Charles Frazer, "Creative Strategy: A Management Perspective," *Journal of Advertising* 12, no. 4 (1983): 36–41.

26 Tom Altstiel and Jean Grow, *Advertising Creative: Strategy, Copy, Design*, 4th ed. (Los Angeles: Sage, 2017), 43.

27 Ron Taylor, "A Six Segment Message Strategy Wheel," *Journal of Advertising Research*, November–December 1997, 7–17.

28 William Wells, "How Advertising Works," speech to the St. Louis American Marketing Association, September 17, 1986.

29 Kathleen Hall Jamieson, *Packaging the Presidency: A History and Criticism of Presidential Campaign Advertising*, 3rd ed. (New York: Oxford University Press, 1996); Kathleen Hall Jamieson, *Dirty Politics; Deception, Distraction, and Democracy* (New York: Oxford University Press, 1992).

30 Marilyn Roberts, "Does Negative Political Advertising Help or Hinder Citizens?," in Sandra Moriarty, Nancy Mitchell, and William Wells, *Advertising & IMC: Principles and Practices*, 9th ed. (Upper Saddle River NJ: Prentice Hall, 2012), 117.

31 William Davies, "The Age of Post-Truth Politics," *New York Times*, August 24, 2016, www.nytimes.com.

32 Stuart Schwartzapfel, "Real 'Mad Men' Pitched Safety to Sell Volvos," *New York Times*, March 5, 2012, 13.

33 https://www.gerber.com/why-gerber/whygerber. Retrieved August 13, 2017.

34 Larry Alton, "3 Highly Memorable Product Demos That Made Their Brand," *Inc.*, February 29, 2016, www.inc.com.

35 Jack Neff, "Funny TV Ads Don't Sell Better Than Unfunny Ones," *Advertising Age*, July 13, 2012, www.adage.com.

36 Christina Binkley, "Behind the Choice of a Luxury-Bag Pitchman," *Wall Street Journal*, June 7, 2012, D3.

37 "Stars in Louis Vuitton," *InStyle*, http://www.instyle.com/celebrity/stars-wearing-louis-vuitton. Retrieved August 13, 2017.

38 Darren Rovell, June 18, 2010, www.CNBC.com.

39 Matt Bonesteel, "Ryan Lochte Loses All Four Commercial Sponsors after Rio Olympics Incident," August 11, 2016, www.washingtonpost.com/.

40 Andrea Mandell, "Sarah Jessica Parker Cuts Ties with EpiPen," *USA Today*, August 26, 2016, www.usatoday.com.

41 Stephanie Rosenbloom, "Got Twitter? You've Been Scored," *New York Times*, June 26, 2011, www.nytimes.com.

42 "What We Know about Using Music in Advertising," *Warc*, June 2016, www.warc.com.

43 Goeffrey Fowler, Brian Steinberg, and Aaron Patrick, "Mac and PC's Overseas Adventures," *Wall Street Journal*, March 1, 2007, B1.

44 Doris Willens, *Nobody's Perfect: Bill Bernbach and the Golden Age of Advertising* (self-published using Amazon's CreateSpace, 2009).

45 Al Ries, "Advertising Could Do with More of Bernbach's Genius," *Advertising Age*, July 6, 2009, www.adage.com.

46 Janet Forgrieve, "Ad Agency's Colo., Fla. Offices on Same Team," *Rocky Mountain News Rocky Business*, March 8, 2007, 6.

47 Judann Pollack, "REI'S #Optoutside Takes Titanium Grand Prix, Netflix 'House of Cards' Wins Integrated Grand Prix, Jury Awarded Work that Tapped into the Cultural Zeitgeist," June 25, 2016, www.adage.com.

48 Jack Neff, "REI and Swedish Tourism Win Promo and Direct Grand Prix for Taking Unusual Risks, Outdoor Retailer Closed Black Friday, While Tourist Group Invited World to Call Random Swedes," June 20, 2016, www.adage.com.

CHAPTER 10

1 Wrigley Company

2 Tom Murphy, "Drug Brand Search Extends from A to Z," *Boulder Daily Camera*, January 18, 2008, 9A.

3 Al Ries, "Sound Advice for Creating a Slogan: Forget Words for a Lasting Impression,

Think Beyond the Written Word," *Advertising Age*, July 6, 2016, www.adage.com.

[4] Laura Ries, "Slogans vs. Taglines: What is Your Brand's Battlecry?" *Advertising Age*, November 11, 2015, www.adage.com.

[5] *Slogans:* The J.M. Smucker Company; Dunkin' Brands, Inc.; Ford Motor Company; John Deere

[6] *Slogans:* Maxwell House Coffee; Morton Salt Consumer Products

[7] Texas Department of Transportation

[8] Gail Collins, "Come Visit. Live Life. Eat Cheese," *New York Times*, April 25, 2009, www.nytimes.com. *Slogan:* Bacardi Limited.

[9] Wells Fargo Bank N.A.; Accenture PLC, www.accenture.com

[10] (2) United Negro College Fund; (6) Mars Inc.; (9) Hitachi, Ltd; (10) Apple Inc.; (16) FedEx Corporation; (18) UPS

[11] Burger King Corporate Office

[12] NYNEX; Perdue Farms

[13] Folgers Coffee Company; Mars Inc.

[14] Morton Salt Consumer Products

[15] Maxwell House Coffee; John Deere; General Mills

[16] B&G Foods Inc.

[17] De Beers UK Limited

[18] Chick-fil-A Inc.

[19] Ennis Higgins, "Conversations with David Ogilvy," in *The Art of Writing Advertising* (Chicago: Advertising Publications, 1965), 85.

[20] Brent Kendall, "Skechers to Pay $50 Million to Settle Ad Suit," *Wall Street Journal*, May 17, 2012, B3.

[21] Federal Trade Commission, "Kellogg Settles FTC Charges That Ads for Frosted Mini-Wheats Were False," April 20, 2009, http://ftc.gov/opa/2009/04/kellogg.shtm.

[22] Bruce Horovitz, "Critics Blast Kellogg's Claim That Cereals Can Boost Immunity," *USA Today*, November 2, 2009, www.usatoday.com.

[23] Tiffany Hsu, "FDA Warns General Mills over Cheerios Cholesterol Claims," May 12, 2009, www.latimesblogs.latimes.com.

[24] Sanette Tanaka, "A Motivated Seller by Any Other Name . . . ," *Wall Street Journal*, October 5, 2012, M4.

[25] Karen Mallia, "Practice: Where Is Creative Headed?" in Moriarty, Sandra, Mitchell, Nancy, and William Wells, *Advertising and IMC Principles and Practices*, 10th ed. (Boston: Prentice Hall, 2015), 246.

[26] Yumiko Ono, "Sometimes Ad Agencies Mangle English Deliberately," *Wall Street Journal*, November 4, 1997, B1.

[27] Covad Communications Group, Now MegaPath

[28] Buick-Chrysler

[29] David Droga, "Sweating Ad Copy Like 'Mad Men,'" *Wall Street Journal*, June 11–12, 2011, C12.

[30] Frazer P. Seitel. *The Practice of Public Relations*, 13th ed. (Boston: Pearson, 2017), 313–314.

[31] Seitel, *The Practice of Public Relations*, 317.

[32] David Ogilvy, *Ogilvy on Advertising* (New York: Vintage, 1985).

[33] Joan Voight, "Nike: Goodby, Wieden Equals On Branding, Brand Marketing," November 17, 1997, www.adweek.com/brand-marketing/nike-goodby-wieden-equals-branding-41737/.

[34] *Encyclopedia of Major Marketing Campaigns*, © 2007 Thomson Gale, www.encyclopedia.com/marketing/encyclopedias-almanacs-transcripts-and-maps/pacific-cycle-inc.

[35] J. J. Sedelmaier, "The Motion-Graphic Ads of Burma-Shave: 1927–1963." *Print*, printmag.com, May 8, 2012.

[36] RAB, "Radio's Role in Today's Media Landscape," September 25, 2016, www.rab.com.

[37] WARC Best Practice, "What We Know ABOUT Using Music in Advertising," *Warc*, June 2016, www.warc.com.

[38] Jay Moye, "Coke's 'Hilltop' featured in Final Scene of 'Mad Men,'" May 18, 2015, www.coca-colacompany.com.

[39] Peter Hochstein, "Ten Rules for Making Better Radio Commercials," Ogilvy & Mather's *Viewpoint*, 1981.

[40] Eunjin Kim, S. Ratneshwar, and E. Thorson, "Why Narrative Ads Work: An Integrated Process Explanation," *Journal of Advertising*, 46(2) (2017): 283–296.

[41] Tom Altstiel and Jean Grow, *Advertising Creative: Strategy, Copy, Design*, 4th ed. (Los Angeles: Sage, 2017), 278.

[42] Lisa Lundy, "Five Steps to Build Relationships with Bloggers," August 29, 2016, www.instituteforpr.org.

[43] Blessie Miranda and Kuen-Hee Ju-Pak, "A Content Analysis of Banner Advertisements: Potential Motivating Features," Annual Conference Baltimore, Association for Education in Journalism and Mass Communication, August 1998.

[44] Jenna Wortham, "Coining Terminology for Life on the Web," *New York Times*, May 6, 2012, 3.

[45] Mark Renfree, "6 Tips for Influential Writing on Social Media," *PR News*, January 22, 2015, www.prnewsonline.com.

[46] Jerry Clode, "Five Tips to Avoid Brand Name Blunders in China," *WARC*, August 2016, www.warc.com.

[47] Edward Hall, *Beyond Culture* (Garden City, NY: Anchor Press/Doubleday, 1976).

CHAPTER 11

[1] Laura Ries, "Repositioning 'Positioning': Connect with Consumers with a Visual Hammer, Not Verbal Nails," *Advertising Age*, March 12, 2012, www.adage.com.

[2] The Folger Coffee Company, http://folgers2.votigo.com/folgers-jingle-history.

[3] Charles Young, "The Essence of an Ad," Ameritest Special Report, 2011, 1–2.

[4] Todd Cunningham, Amy Shea, and Charles Young, "The Advertising Magnifier Effect: An MTV Study," Ameritest Research Report, 2006, 15–16.

[5] Shepard Fairey, "Obama Poster Artist in Legal Battle with AP, Makes Major Admissions in Case," *Editor & Publisher*, October 16, 2009, www.editorandpublisher.com; "Protecting AP's Intellectual Property: The Shepard

Fairey Case," Associated Press, October 20, 2009, www.ap.org/prights/fairey.html; "The Shepard Fairey–AP Case: A Clearer Picture," *Los Angeles Times*, November 1, 2009, www.latimes.com.

[6] Chad Bray, "Artist Gets Probation in Dispute over 'Hope,'" *Wall Street Journal*, September 7, 2012, www.wsj.com.

[7] Kunur Patel, "Lessons from the Microsoft Photoshop Fiasco," *Advertising Age*, August 31, 2009, www.adage.com.

[8] Ann-Christine Diaz, "How Coke, W, Nokia and Others Use 3D Printing in Marketing," August 29, 2013, www.adage.com.

[9] A. O. Scott, "Finding Drama in Newfangled Filmmaking," *New York Times*, August 30, 2012, www.nytimes.com.

[10] Karl Schroeder, "Metro Recycling in Stop-Motion Animation," *Advertising & IMC: Principles & Practices*, 10th ed. (Boston, Pearson, 2015), 293.

[11] Stuart Elliott, "Is That Honda Commercial Real?," *New York Times Direct*, June 10, 2003, NYTDirect@nytimes.com; "Honda's Cog Does It Again, Taking the Grand Clio," *AdForum Alert*, May 19, 2004, www.adforum.com.

[12] Barbara Haislip, "Picture (Not) Perfect," *Wall Street Journal*, May 21, 2012, R7.

[13] Laura Ruel and Nora Paul, "Eyetracking Points the Way to Effective News Article Design," *Online Journalism Review*, March 13, 2007, www.ojr.org.

[14] Heather McWilliams, "Zooming in to Web Video," *Business Plus*, March 5, 2007, 3.

PART 4

[1] Sara Guaglione, "'Domino' CEO Nathan Coyle on the Importance of a Multiplatform Brand," *Media Post*, January 27, 2017, http://www.mediapost.com/publications/article/293900/domino-ceo-nathan-coyle-on-the-importance-of-a-m.html.

CHAPTER 12

[1] Erwin Ephron, "Engagement Is Many Different Things," *Admap*, April 2006, 41–42; Joe Mandese, "Medialink," *Admap*, April 2006, 10; "Sports Ad Spending Roars Back," *Sports Business Journal*, May 2–8, 2011, 1; "McDonald's Unveils Sponsorship Plans for London 2012 Olympic Games," press release, July 20, 2011; "McDonald's Announces Eight-Year Extension of Top Olympic Sponsorship through 2020," press release, January 13, 2012; Stephanie Clifford, "An Online Game So Mysterious Its Famous Sponsor Is Hidden," *New York Times*, April 1, 2008, www.nytimes.com; Olympic Marketing Fact File 2012, International Olympic Committee, www.freedownloadb.com.

[2] Laura Bright, "Media Planning Education in 2012 and Beyond," American Academy of Advertising, Myrtle Beach, SC, March 15–18, 2012.

[3] Larry Kelley and Donald Jugenheimer, *Advertising Account Planning: Planning and Managing an IMC Campaign*, 2nd ed. (Armonk, NY: M. E Sharpe, 2011), 160.

4 Yeusung Kim and Sheetal Patel, "Teaching Advertising Media Planning in a Changing Media Landscape," *Journal of Advertising Education*, Fall 2012, 21.

5 Publicis Group's ZenithOptimedia, *Advertising Expenditure Forecasts*, December 2015, https://www.zenithmedia.com/product/advertising-expenditure-forecasts-december-2015/.

6 Deloitte, "Digital Democracy Survey," April 2016, https://www2.deloitte.com/us/en/pages/technology-media-andtelecommunications/articles/digital-democracy-survey-generational-media-consumption-trends.html.

7 Laurie Sullivan, "Bing Search Reveals 2017 Trends," MediaPost Search Marketing Daily, January 5, 2017, http://www.mediapost.com/publications/article/292246/bing-search-reveals-2017-trends.html.

8 "Wearables Market to Be Worth $25 Billion by 2019," CCS Insight, *Wearables Forecast, Worldwide, 2015–2019*, http://www.ccsinsight.com/press/company-news/2332-wearables-market-to-be-worth-25-billion-by-2019-reveals-ccs-insight.

9 Dean Takahashi, Venture Beat, "The Landscape of VR Is Complicated—with 234 Companies Valued at $13B," October 2015, http://venturebeat.com/2015/10/12/the-landscape-of-vr-is-complicated-with-234-companies-valued-at-13b/E.

10 "Will Virtual Reality Experiences for Brands Rival Super Bowl Ads?" by Marty Swant, *AdWeek* October 18, 2016, http://www.adweek.com/news/technology/will-virtual-reality-experiences-brands-rival-super-bowl-ads-174105.

11 "Virtual reality: the next big thing in advertising?" by Justina Crabtree, *CNBC*, Aug 22, 2016, http://www.cnbc.com/2016/08/19/virtual-reality-the-next-big-thing-in-advertising.html.

12 Steve Peterson, "The Future of Virtual Reality: Marketing and Advertising," *[a]listdaily*, November 10, 2016, http://www.alistdaily.com/digital/future-virtual-reality-marketing-advertising/.

13 Mike Azzara (February 16, 2017), "AI M&A Gathers Momentum," *Media Post: AI Insider*, accessed February 25, 2017, http://www.mediapost.com/publications/article/295349/ai-ma-gathers-momentum.html.

14 David Rittenhouse (Ogilvy Japan), personal correspondence, January 7, 2017.

15 AARP Media Sales Kit, December 27, 2016, http://advertise.aarp.org/.

16 Bright, "Media Planning Education."

17 Wayne Arnold, "Beyond 'Gangnam Style': Why Korea Is a Pop Culture and Products Powerhouse," *Advertising Age*, November 28, 2012, www.adage.com.

18 "The History of Social Networking," *Digital Trends*, May 14, 2016, http://www.digitaltrends.com/features/the-history-of-social-networking/#ixzz4TUSjSbWi.

19 "Here's a Secret Secondary Use for Snapchat," by Kia Kokalitcheva *Fortune*, May 13, 2016, http://fortune.com/2016/05/13/snapchat-qr-code-reader/.

20 Donald Jugenheimer, *Advertising and IMC Principles and Practice*, 9th ed. (Upper Saddle River, NJ: Prentice Hall, 2012), 330.

21 Larry Kelley, personal communication, July 12 and 20, 2012.

22 "Number of commercial TV stations in the United States from 1950 to 2016," Statista, 2017, https://www.statista.com/statistics/189655/number-of-commercial-television-stations-in-the-us-since-1950/.

23 "Changing Channels: Americans View Just 17 Channels Despite Record Number to Choose From," *Nielsen Newswire*, May 6, 2014, http://www.nielsen.com/us/en/insights/news/2014/changing-channels-americans-view-just-17-channels-despite-record-number-to-choose-from.html.

24 Larry Kelley, Donald Jugenheimer, and Kim Sheehan, *Advertising Media Planning*, 3rd ed. (Armonk, NY: M. E. Sharpe, 2012), 7.

25 Kelley, Jugen, and Sheehan, *Advertising Media Planning*, 9.

26 Jack Neff, "P&G Will Keep Hiking Ad Spend amid Soft Sales: More Cuts Coming Too, Some Targeting Massive $18 Billion Promotion Budget," April 26, 2016, http://adage.com/article/cmo-strategy/pg-hiking-ad-spend/303731/.

27 "Why Apple is rebooting its 'game-changer' billboard ads," by Lara O'Reilly, *Business Insider*, Feb. 3, 2016, http://www.businessinsider.com/why-apple-is-re-running-its-shot-on-iphone-ad-campaign-2016-2.

28 Newspaper Association of America, "The Source: Newspapers by the Numbers 2006," January 2007, 3–4, www.naa.org.

29 "Super Bowl 49 watched by 114.4M, sets U.S. TV viewership record," by John Breech, Feb 2, 2015, *CBS Sports*, https://www.cbssports.com/nfl/news/super-bowl-49-watched-by-1144m-sets-us-tv-viewership-record/.

30 Laura F. Bright (2011), "Media Evolution and the Advent of Web 2.0," Chapter 2 in *Handbook of Research on Digital Media and Advertising*, edited by Matthew S. Eastin, Terry Daugherty and Neal M. Burns (Information Science Reference, Hershey, PA).

31 "Advertising and Audiences: State of the Media," *Nielsen Reports: Media*, May 12, 2014, http://www.nielsen.com/us/en/insights/reports/2014/advertising-and-audiences-state-of-the-media.html.

32 Stuart Elliott, "A Bet (and Tattoo) on an Olympian," *New York Times*, July 4, 2012, www.nytimes.com; Matt Flegenheimer, "M.T.A. Opens Front of MetroCard to Advertising," *New York Times*, July 18, 2012, www.nytimes.com.

33 "Furious 7: Dodge, Corona Return for Starring Roles," by Abe Sauer, *Brandchannel*; April 6, 2015, http://www.brandchannel.com/2015/04/06/furious-7-dodge-corona-return-for-starring-roles/.

34 "Show Me the Money: The World of Product Placement," by Terry O'Reilly; *CBC Radio: Under the Influence*, http://www.cbc.ca/radio/undertheinfluence/show-me-the-money-the-world-of-product-placement-1.3046933.

35 N. E. Marsden, "What TV Is Really Selling," *Washington Post*, October 30, 2009, www.washingtonpost.com.

36 Beth Bulik, "Layering in Local," "Smart Strategies for Local Marketing," and "Location, Location, Location: Search, Social," *Ad Age Insights*, October 1, 2012, 3, 5.

37 "Building for the next moment," *Google Inside AdWords*, May 05, 2015, https://adwords.googleblog.com/2015/05/building-for-next-moment.html.

38 "Mobile search - Statistics & Facts," *Statista*, August 2016, https://www.statista.com/topics/2479/mobile-search/.

39 Michael Bush, "What's the Next Marketing Platform? How to Measure Success? Ad Age's Media Mavens Answer the Big Questions," *Advertising Age*, December 9, 2009, www.adage.com.

40 Tim Nudd, "Axe Is Bringing Its Great 'Find Your Magic' Commercial to the Super Bowl," *AdWeek*, January 28, 2016, http://www.adweek.com/news/advertising-branding/axe-bringing-its-great-find-your-magic-commercial-super-bowl-169249; Jack Neff, "How Dove and Axe Got Into Alignment, and Why They Still Need Digital Specialists," *Advertising Age*, July 5, 2016, http://adage.com/article/cmo-strategy/unilever-sweed-gender-ads-solving-digital-woes/304793/.

CHAPTER 13

1 Pew Research Center, "State of the News Media 2016," June 2016, accessed October 6, 2017, https://assets.pewresearch.org/.

2 "Newspapers Deliver Across the Ages," December 15, 2015, http://www.nielsen.com/us/en/insights/news/2016/newspapers-deliver-across-the-ages.html.

3 Michael Barthel, "Newspapers: Fact Sheet," Pew Research Center's Journalism Project, June 15, 2016, http://www.journalism.org/2016/06/15/newspapers-fact-sheet/.

4 Suzanne Vranica and Jack Marshall, "Plummeting Newspaper Ad Revenue Sparks New Wave of Changes," *Wall Street Journal*, October 20, 2016, http://www.wsj.com/articles/plummeting-newspaper-ad-revenue-sparks-new-wave-of-changes-1476955801.

5 Jason Del Rey, "In USA Today Redesign, Hope for a New Canvas for Web Advertisers," *Ad Age*, September 13, 2012, www.adage.com.

6 "US Online and Traditional Media Advertising Outlook, 2016–2020," *MarketingCharts*, June 14, 2016, http://www.marketingcharts.com/traditional/us-online-and-traditional-media-advertising-outlook-2016-2020-68214/.

7 "Report: Billions in Local 'Co-Op Advertising' Funds Left Unspent Annually," *Marketing Land*, August 13, 2015, http://marketingland.com/report-billions-in-co-op-advertising-funds-left-unspent-each-year-138671.

8 Alan Mutter, "Twin Threats Peril Preprint Newspaper Ads," *Reflections of a Newsosaur*, August 29, 2012, www.newsosaur.blogspot.com.

9 Tim Nudd, "The Spot: High on the Hogs," *Adweek*, May 8, 2012, www.adweek.com.

[10] "US Online and Traditional Media Advertising Outlook, 2016–2020," *MarketingCharts*, June 14, 2016, http://www.marketingcharts.com/traditional/us-online-and-traditional-media-advertising-outlook-2016-2020-68214/.

[11] Jerry Schwartz, "*Newsweek* Axes Print Magazine," *Boulder Daily Camera*, October 19, 2012, 2A; Christine Haughney and David Carr, "At *Newsweek*, Ending Print and a Blend of Two Styles," *New York Times*, October 18, 2012, www.mediadecoder,blogs.nytimes.com.

[12] *2009–2010 Magazine Handbook* (New York: Magazine Publishers Association, 2009), 17.

[13] Emily Steel, "Meredith Builds Up a Sideline in Marketing," *Wall Street Journal*, February 25, 2010, B6.

[14] "*Ladies' Home Journal* Lets Readers Write the Magazine," *Advertising Age*, January 8, 2012, www.adage.com.

[15] "*Ladies' Home Journal* Lets Readers Write the Magazine"; Stuart Elliott, "Ad Campaign Will Encourage People to Love People,'" *New York Times*, September 11, 2012, www.mediadecoder.blogs.nytimes.com; Stuart Elliott, "*Woman's Day* Turns 75 While Looking Forward," *New York Times*, September 16, 2012, www.nytimes.com; Stuart Elliott, "*Glamour* Campaign Tries to Claim a Generation," *New York Times*, September 9, 2012, www.nytimes.com.

[16] David Carr, "How *Esquire* Survived Publishing's Dark Days," *New York Times*, January 22, 2012, www.nytimes.com.

[17] Anne Kadet, "Yellow Pages Hang on in Digital Age," *Wall Street Journal*, June 17, 2016, http://www.wsj.com/articles/yellow-pages-hang-on-in-digital-age-1466157601; Tom Corrigan, "Yellow-Pages Publisher Hibu Files U.S. Bankruptcy Case," *The Wall Street Journal*, August 5, 2016, http://www.wsj.com/articles/yellow-pages-publisher-hibu-files-u-s-bankruptcy-case-1470422933.

[18] Jason Peaslee, "Are The Yellow Pages Dead?" *Thrive Analytics*, January 10, 2014, http://www.thriveanalytics.com/blog/?p=220.

[19] "US Online and Traditional Media Advertising Outlook, 2016–2020," *MarketingCharts*, June 14, 2016, http://www.marketingcharts.com/traditional/us-online-and-traditional-media-advertising-outlook-2016-2020-68214/.

[20] "The Future of Radio: Seven Important Trends," September 1, 2016, http://www.medialifemagazine.com/future-radio-seven-important-trends/.

[21] "When Big Clients Go Local—Target, Allstate Win Big," *Inside Radio*, April 20, 2016, http://www.insideradio.com/free/when-big-clients-go-local-target-allstate-win-big/article_bf20168e-06ce-11e6-a868-07228a9d0b09.html; "Allstate Mayhem Radio Takeover," Effie Worldwide Case Database; https://www.effie.org/case_studies/case/ME_2016_438489.

[22] Ron Winslow, "Watching TV Linked to Higher Risk of Death," *Wall Street Journal*, January 12, 2010, D1.

[23] Brian Sheehan, "Long Live Reach: Buying Eyeballs Still Works If It's Done Right," January 13, 2017, *Advertising Age*, http://adage.com/article/guest-columnists/long-live-reach-buying-eyeballs-works/307490/?utm_source=daily_email&utm_medium=newsletter&utm_campaign=adage&ttl=1484866330?utm_visit=633885.

[24] John Jurgensen, "Reinventing the Music Video," *Wall Street Journal*, May 6, 2011, D1.

[25] Matthew Futterman, Sam Schechner, and Suzanne Vranica, "NFL: The League That Runs TV," *Wall Street Journal*, December 15, 2011, B1.

[26] "Cord-Cutting Forces Cable Networks to Make Hard Choices," *Advertising Age*, December 29, 2016, http://adage.com/article/cmo-strategy/cord-cutters-dropping-cable-force-networks-make-hard-choices/307314/?utm_source=mediaworks&utm_medium=newsletter&utm_campaign=adage&ttl=1483649165?utm_visit=263079.

[27] Oriana Schwindt, "Pay TV Industry Loses 385,000 Cord-Cutters In 2015; A 'Slow Decline, Not a Tailspin,'" *International Business Times*, March 10, 2016, http://www.ibtimes.com/pay-tv-industry-loses-385000-cord-cutters-2015-slow-decline-not-tailspin-2334232.

[28] Bob Lodice, "10 Events That Transformed Marketing," *Advertising Age*, January 18, 2010, www.adage.com.

[29] Brian Steinberg, "Cartier's Three-Minute Gem Extends Demand for Longer Spots," *Advertising Age*, March 7, 2012, www.adage.com.

[30] Andrew Martin, "The Fitness Revolution Will Be Televised (after Leno)," *New York Times*, March 29, 2011, 1.

[31] Steven Perlberg, "TiVo Touts Ad-Skipping in Image Revamp: The TiVo Bolt Skips over Entire Commercial Pods at Once," *Wall Street Journal*, November 3, 2015, http://www.wsj.com/articles/tivo-touts-ad-skipping-in-image-revamp-1446570469.

[32] Paul Bond, "The Growing Use of DVRs," *Hollywood Reporter*, April 28, 2009, http://hollywoodreporter.com.

[33] Brian Stelter, "Battle over Dish's Ad-Skipping Begins as Networks Go to Court," *New York Times*, May 24, 2012, www.nytimes.com.

[34] Marisa Guthrie, "Ralph Lauren to Sponsor PBS' 'Masterpiece,' Create Special 'Downton Abbey' Ads," *Hollywood Reporter*, September 10, 2012, www.hollywoodreporter.com.

[35] John Breech, "Super Bowl 49 watched by 114.4M, sets U.S. TV viewership record," CBS Sports, February 2, 2015, https://www.cbssports.com/nfl/news/super-bowl-49-watched-by-1144m-sets-us-tv-viewership-record/; Nelson Granados, "Super Bowl Game, Ads, and Half-Time Show Invade Social Media," *Forbes*, Feb 6, 2017, https://www.forbes.com/sites/nelsongranados/2017/02/06/super-bowl-game-ads-and-half-time-show-invade-social-media/#e92e6f37c9dc.

[36] "Boomer TV," *AARP Magazine*, June 2012, 7.

[37] Arian Campo-Flores and Sam Schechner, "Disney's ABC, Univision Mull News-Channel Launch," *Wall Street Journal*, February 7, 2012, B1; Christopher Stewart and Arian Campo-Flores, "Univision, ABC to Start News Channel—in English," *Wall Street Journal*, May 8, 2012, B1.

[38] Jason Lynch, "Study Projects Addressable TV Advertising Will Double by 2018: Marketers Can Reach Specific Demographics," *AdWeek*, November 17, 2016, http://www.adweek.com/news/television/study-projects-addressable-tv-adverting-explode-popularity-2018-174674; "Say Yes to Addressability: A Guide to Precise TV Targeting," 2016 Report, Video Advertising Bureau, accessed January 20, 2017, http://www.thevab.com/wp-content/uploads/2016/11/VAB-Addressability-Report.pdf; Keach Hagey, "Nielsen to Include Set-Top-Box Data in Ratings for First Time," *Wall Street Journal*, April 4, 2016, http://www.wsj.com/articles/nielsen-to-include-set-top-box-data-in-ratings-for-first-time-1459764001; Jon Lafayette, "Viacom Makes Addressable Advertising Deal with Roku: Programmer Looks to Cash in on Over-the-Top Viewing," *B&C*, April 28, 2016, http://www.broadcastingcable.com/news/currency/viacom-makes-addressable-advertising-deal-roku/156021.

[39] Daisuke Wakabayashi, "Sony Pins Future on a 3-Revival," *Wall Street Journal*, January 7, 2010, A1; Suzanne Vranica, "Marketers Face Zooming Costs as ESPN Launches 3-D Channel," *Wall Street Journal*, June 10, 2010, B1.

[40] Tanzina Vega, "An Upgrade for the Show before the Show," *New York Times*, April 5, 2012, www.nytimes.com.

[41] Janet Morrissey, "Look Up: In the Digital Age, Billboards Are Far from Dead," *New York Times*, September 4, 2016, www.nytimes.com.

[42] *The Signage Sourcebook* (South Bend, IN: Signage Foundation, 2003).

[43] Rhodina Villanueva, "Country's 1st Plant Billboard Launched," *Philippine Star*, June 24, 2011, www.philstar.com.

[44] Sayaa Weissman, "Cool Stuff: TNT Electromagnet Dots Billboard," *Digiday*, July 20, 2012, www.digiday.com.

[45] Stephanie Clifford, "As Storefronts Become Vacant, Ads Arrive," *New York Times*, May 12, 2009, www.nytimes.com.

[46] David Dunlap, "New Territory for Ads, with a Moving Target," *New York Times*, September 16, 2012, www.cityroom.blogs.nytimes.com.

[47] http://www.marketingcharts.com/traditional/us-online-and-traditional-media-advertising-outlook-2016-2020-68214/; eMarketer, "Average Time Spent per Day with Major Media by US Adults," June 2016, (accessed October 6, 2017), www.emarketer.com.

[48] eMarketer, "Average Time Spent per Day."

[49] Shayndie Raice, "Facebook Combats Criticism over Ads," *Wall Street Journal*, June 13, 2012, 13B; Geoffrey Fowler, "Facebook: One Billion and Counting," *Wall Street Journal*, October 5, 2012, B1; Tanzina Vega and Stuart Elliott, "At Ad Week, the Vital Role of Digital Marketing," *New York Times*, October 2, 2012, www.nytimes.com; "Big Spenders Push Ad Line, but Facebook Holds Ground," *Advertising Age*, May 27, 2012, www.adage.com.

[50] Mike Shields, "Facebook Planning to Shut Down Its Ad Exchange," *The Wall Street*

Journal, May 25, 2016, http://www.wsj.com/articles/facebook-planning-to-shut-down-its-ad-exchange-1464199840.

[51] Amir Efrati, "Google Near Ad Triple Crown," *Wall Street Journal*, September 20, 2012, B7.

[52] Fowler, "Facebook."

[53] Michael Wolff, "The Facebook Fallacy," *Technology Review*, May 22, 2012, www.technologyreview.com.

[54] "Display Advertising Clickthrough Rates—Smart Insights Digital Marketing Advice," *Smart Insights*, April 26, 2016, http://www.smartinsights.com/internet-advertising/internet-advertising-analytics/display-advertising-clickthrough-rates/.

[55] Rosalind Gray, "Catching New Customers," *Costco Connection*, February 2012, 23.

[56] Suzanne Vranica, "Element of Choice Draws in Online Viewers," *Wall Street Journal*, February 4, 2010, B11.

[57] "Craigslist Garners $60 Million Judgment against Radpad in Scraping Dispute," by Jeffrey Neuburger, *Proskauer New Media and Technology Law*, April 17, 2017, http://newmedialaw.proskauer.com/2017/04/17/craigslist-garners-60-million-judgment-against-radpad-in-scraping-dispute/.

[58] Brad Stone, "Craigslist Expands Legal Battle against Spammers," *New York Times*, October 8, 2009, http://bits.blogs.nytimes.com.

[59] Esther Thorson, personal communication, April 20, 2009; Abbey Klaasen, "The State of Search Marketing: 2009," *Advertising Age*, November 2, 2009, www.adage.com.

[60] Brad Stone, "Google Adds Live Updates to Results," *New York Times*, December 8, 2009, www.nytimes.com.

[61] Emily Steel, "Pricing Tensions Shake Up Web Display-Ad Market," *Wall Street Journal*, September 21, 2009, B6.

[62] "The need for mobile speed: How mobile latency impacts publisher revenue," *DoubleClick*, September 2016, https://www.doubleclickbygoogle.com/articles/mobile-speed-matters/.

[63] Emily Steel, "Target-Marketing Becomes More Communal," *Wall Street Journal*, November 5, 2009, B10.

[64] Emily Steel, "Web Sites Debate Best Values for Advertising Dollars," *Wall Street Journal*, August 13, 2009, B7.

[65] Brandon Katz, "Digital Ad Spending Will Surpass TV Spending for The First Time in U.S. History," *Forbes*, September 14, 2016, http://www.forbes.com/sites/brandonkatz/2016/09/14/digital-ad-spending-will-surpass-tv-spending-for-the-first-time-in-u-s-history/#33bbff2d6959.

[66] George Slefo, "Samsung Smart TVs Force Ads onto Menu Screen," *Advertising Age*, December 21, 2016, http://adage.com/article/digital/samsung-smart-tv-update-forces-ads/307246/.

[67] Martha Woodroof, "In a 24/7 World, What Is a Magazine?," NPR, August 30, 2009, www.npr.org; Suzanne Vranica, "WPP Chief Tempers Hope for Ad Upturn," *Wall Street Journal*, September 21, 2009, B1.

[68] Theresa Howard, "CBS, Pepsi Max Put Video in Some Magazine Ads," *USA Today*, August 19, 2009, http://usatoday.com.

CHAPTER 14

[1] Rebecca Hia, "Brands Tap into Emotion for the 5 Most Engaging Facebook Posts of 2016," *Advertising Age*, December 22, 2016, http://adage.com/article/digital/brands-engaging-facebook-posts-2016/307274/.

[2] Seth Fiegerman, "The Most Creative Uses for Meerkat, SXSW's Hottest App," *Mashable*, March 15, 2015, http://mashable.com/2015/03/15/meerkat-uses/#NsnhR7C2UGqJ; Ross Benes, "Ad Tech's Biggest Winners and Losers in 2016," *Digiday*, December 22, 2016, http://digiday.com/platforms/ad-tech-winners-losers/; Jayson DeMers, "5 Visual Marketing Trends That Will Dominate 2016," *Forbes*, December 30, 2015, http://www.forbes.com/sites/jaysondemers/2015/12/29/5-visual-marketing-trends-that-will-dominate-2016/#54797733b3e2.

[3] Karl Greenberg, "Nissan Expands GT Academy for 2012," *Marketing Daily*, May 7, 2010, www.mediapost.com.

[4] Elie Mystal, "True Story: Harvard Law Sells Naming Rights to Its New Bathrooms," *Above the Law*, February 1, 2012, www.abovethelaw.com.

[5] Chris Herring, "Coke Bottle Is Part Plant," *Wall Street Journal*, January 25, 2010, B7.

[6] Eric Pfanner, "Old Medium Dusted Off," *International Herald Tribune*, July 9, 2007, 11.

[7] Evan Ramstad, "Big Brother, Now at the Mall," *Wall Street Journal*, October 9, 2012, B6.

[8] Lisa Lacy, "Beneful Lets People Play with Digital Dogs," *ClickZ*, May 7, 2012, www.clickz.com; Spencer Ante, "Billboards Join Wired Age," *Wall Street Journal*, February 4, 2011, B10.

[9] Jerry Bennett and Mike Ramsey, "Drivers Seek Help with Techie Cars," *Wall Street Journal*, October 5, 2012, B8.

[10] "The Infomercial Comes to Life in India's Remotest Villages," by Eric Bellman, *The Wall Street Journal*, June 10, 2009, https://www.wsj.com/articles/SB124458376269599545; "Traveling Tellers, With Electronic Gear, Take Banking to Rural India," by Vikas Bajaj, *The New York Times*, September 29, 2011, http://www.nytimes.com/2011/09/30/business/global/teller-atm-hybrid-takes-banking-to-rural-india.html?mcubz=1.

[11] Rachel Pannett, "Aussie Delicacy Vegemite Loses Some of Its Savory Appeal," *Wall Street Journal*, May 10, 2012, A1.

[12] Evan Hessel and Taylor Buley, "How to Know Your Web Ad Is Working," *Forbes*, April 29, 2009, www.forbes.com.

[13] "Buzz in the Blogosphere: Millions More Bloggers and Blog Readers," *Nielsen Newswire*, March 8, 2012, http://www.nielsen.com/us/en/insights/news/2012/buzz-in-the-blogosphere-millions-more-bloggers-and-blog-readers.html.

[14] "Top 10 Social Media Stars," *Fortune*, May 7, 2012, http://money.cnn.com/.

[15] Douglas MacMilan, "Blogaola: The FTC Takes on Paid Posts," *Business Week*, May 19, 2009, www.businessweek.com; N. E. Marsden, "What TV Is Really Selling," *Washington Post*, October 30, 2009, www.washingtonpost.com.

[16] "Facebook Starts 2017 With 65 Million Local Business Pages," by David Kaplan, *GeoMarketing*, Feb 2, 2017, http://www.geomarketing.com/facebook-starts-2017-with-65-million-local-business-pages.

[17] "Total number of Walmart stores in the United States from 2012 to 2017, by type," *Statista*, https://www.statista.com/statistics/269425/total-number-of-walmart-stores-in-the-united-states-by-type/.

[18] James Stewart, "When the Network Effect Goes into Reverse," *New York Times*, August 17, 2012, www.nytimes.com.

[19] Andy Sernovitz, "How National Geographic Uses Social Media to Get Fans Talking," *SmartBlog on Social Media*, May 4, 2012, www.smartblogs.com.

[20] Elizabeth Olson, "Grey Poupon Ups the Ante on Assuming an Elite Image," *New York Times*, September 22, 2012, www.nytimes.com.

[21] Stacy Nunnally, "Dos and Don'ts: Scheduling Social Media Activity," *Nashville Business Journal*, May 9, 2012, www.bizjournals.com.

[22] Dan Zarrella, "5 Questions and Answers about Facebook Marketing," *Dan Zarrella blog*, January 14, 2011, www.danzarrella.com; Nunnally, "Dos and Don'ts."

[23] "Facebook to Brands: You're Posting Stuff Wrong," *Advertising Age*, May 6, 2012, www.adage.com.

[24] Al Ries, "We're So Quick to Crown Social-Media Successes That We Forget What They're Actually Based On," *Advertising Age*, May 6, 2012, www.adage.com.

[25] Ronald Grover, "'Hunger Games' Success Spells Trouble for TV Ads," *Reuters*, May 4, 2012, www.reuters.com.

[26] Brandon Bornancin, "Off the Wall Overview and Capabilities," *Resource Interactive*, 2009, slide no. 29, www.slideshare.net/BrandonBornancin/off-the-wall-by-resource-interactive; "6 New Facts about Facebook," by Aaron Smith, *Pew Research Center: FactTank*, February 3, 2014, http://www.pewresearch.org/fact-tank/2014/02/03/6-new-facts-about-facebook/.

[27] Michael Learmounth, "Mobile Marketing Fact Pack 2012," *Advertising Age Mobile Fact Pack*, August 20, 2012, 1.

[28] Rimma Kats, "Starbucks Taps Mobile Advertising to Boast Product Awareness," *Mobile Marketer*, September 11, 2012, www.mobilemarketer.com.

[29] "Mobile Ad Spending," *Advertising Age Mobile Fact Pack*, August 20, 2012, 6.

[30] Kunur Patel, "Google Wins Inaugural Cannes Mobile Grand Prix," *Advertising Age Mobile Fact Pack*, August 20, 2012, 22–23.

[31] Michael Bush, "Texting Trumps Talking in U.S., Just Not as Ad Platform," *Advertising Age*, February 18, 2010, http://adage.com/article/digital/digital-texting-trumps-talking-ad-platform/142180/.

32 Julie Jargon, "Domino's IT Staff Delivers Slick Site, Ordering System," *Wall Street Journal*, November 24, 2009, B5.

33 Joe Mandese, "Simultaneous Research Study Reveals Consumers Buzz Most over Word-of-Mouth, Not Ads," *MediaPost Publications*, January 19, 2007, http://publications.mediapost.com.

34 Steve Knox, "Why Effective Word-of-Mouth Disrupts Schemas," *Advertising Age*, January 25, 2010, www.adage.com.

35 "Matching the Medium with the Message in Word-of-Mouth Marketing," *Knowledge @ Wharton*, April 11, 2012, www.knowledge.wharton.upenn.edu.

36 "How Jukin Media Built a Viral-Video Empire," by Jamie Lauren Keiles, *The New York Times Magazine*, December 27, 2016, http://www.nytimes.com/2016/12/27/magazine/how-jukin-media-built-a-viral-video-empire.html.

37 "The Buzz Starts Here: Finding the First Mouth for Word-of-Mouth Marketing," *Knowledge @ Wharton*, March 4, 2009, www.knowledge.wharton.upenn.edu.

38 Hairong Li, quoted in Sandra Moriarty, Nancy Mitchell, and William Wells, *Advertising & IMC: Principles and Practice*, 9th ed. (Upper Saddle River, NJ: Prentice Hall, 2012), 397–398.

39 "HP, Ford, and Sony Top Social Mentions List of Brands," *Search Engine Watch*, August 3, 2012, www.clickz.com.

40 Brandon Griggs and John Sutter, "Oprah, Ashton Kutcher Mark Twitter 'Turning Point,'" *CNN*, April 18, 2009, www.cnn.com.

41 Elizabeth Mitchell, "Republicans' #areyoubetteroff Hashtag Backfires When Twitter Responds 'Yes,'" *PR News*, September 7, 2012, www.mediabistro.com; https://blog.loginradius.com/2015/04/hashtag-fails/; Kashmir Hill, "#McDStories: When a Hashtag Becomes a Bashtag," January 24, 2012, *Forbes*, http://www.forbes.com/sites/kashmirhill/2012/01/24/mcdstories-when-a-hashtag-becomes-a-bashtag/#5dddab6193f4.

42 Suzanne Kapner, "Citi Won't Sleep on Customer Tweets," *Wall Street Journal*, October 5, 2012, C1.

43 David Streitfeld, "The Best Reviews Money Can Buy," *New York Times*, August 26, 2012, 1, 6.

44 Pringles Facebook page, https://www.facebook.com/PringlesUS/?brand_redir=39910168890.

45 Jack Neff, "P&G Embraces Facebook as Big Part of Its Marketing Plan," *Advertising Age*, January 25, 2010, www.adage.com.

46 "Five Questions with Babytree CEO Allen Wang," *Advertising Age*, August 23, 2012, www.adage.com.

47 Sean Ludwig, "Pinterest Now the Third Most Popular Social Network after Facebook & Twitter," *VB(Venture Beat)*, April 5, 2012, www.venturebeat.com.

48 "U.K. Pinterest Contest Highlights Dangers of Driving in Heels," *Advertising Age*, April 22, 2012, www.adage.com.

49 Steven M. Edwards, Hairong Li, and Joo-Hyun Lee "Forced Exposure and Psychological Reactance: Antecedents and Consequences of the Perceived Intrusiveness of Pop-up Ads," *Journal of Advertising* 31, no. 3 (2002): 83–95.

50 Natasha Singer, "Learning to Chase Online Word of Mouth," *New York Times*, May 26, 2012, www.nytimes.com.

51 "Beware of Dissatisfied Consumers: They Like to Blab," *Knowledge @ Wharton*, March 8, 2006, www.knowledge.wharton.edu.

52 Tom Duncan, personal conversation, January 5, 2013.

53 Somini Sengupta, "Facebook's False Faces Undermine Its Credibility," *New York Times*, November 12, 2012, www.nytimes.com.

54 "Overheard," *Wall Street Journal*, November 27, 2012, C10.

55 Taco Bell: Taco Bell Blackout, 2016 Effie Silver Award, Case Study, https://www.effie.org/case_studies/case/NA_2016_441130.

56 Jack Neff, "Lever's CMO Throws Down the Social-Media Gauntlet," *Advertising Age*, April 13, 2009, www.adage.com.

57 Natalie Zmuda, "Alex Bogusky Takes on Coca-Cola, Soda Companies," *Advertising Age*, October 9, 2012, www.adage.com.

58 Beth Bulik, "Army of Tweeting Tax Pros Leads H&R Block Social Push," *Advertising Age*, January 4, 2010, www.adage.com.

59 Claire Miller, "Google Wants to Join the Party, Not Crash It," *New York Times*, October 14, 2012, www.nytimes.com.

CHAPTER 15

1 "Pathways to news," by Amy Mitchell, Jeffrey Gottfried, Michael Barthel, and Elisa Shearer, *Pew Research Center*, July 7, 2016, http://www.journalism.org/2016/07/07/pathways-to-news/.

2 Mathew Ingram, "Print Readership Is Still Plummeting, and Paywalls Aren't Really Helping," *Fortune*, June 1, 2015, http://fortune.com.

3 Leslie Kaufman, "Magazines Get a Way to Measure Their Reach across Media Platforms," *New York Times*, September 29, 2014; Leslie Kaufman, "Magazines Get a Way to Measure Their Reach Across Media Platforms," *New York Times*, September 29, 2014, www.nytimes.com; "Magazine Media 360° is . . ." *MPA: The Association of Magazine Media*, September 2, 2017, http://www.magazine.org/magazine-media-360.

4 "Northwestern University Reader Experience Study Tool Kit," Magazine Publishers of America, December 12, 2012, www.magazine.org.

5 "Nielsen to Increase Portable People Meter Sample Size by 10% across 48 Radio Metro Areas," December 21, 2016, http://www.nielsen.com/us/en/press-room/2016/nielsen-to-increase-portable-people-meter-sample-size-by-10-percent-across-48-radio-metro-areas.html; "Did the Portable People Meter Destroy Radio?," *Makegood*, October 23, 2014, http://www.the-makegood.com/2014/10/23/did-the-portable-people-meter-destroy-radio/.

6 "TV Ratings," *Nielsen*, http://www.nielsen.com/us/en/solutions/measurement/television.html.

7 Chris Smith, "Could a Super Bowl Commercial Really Be Worth $10 Million? Surprisingly, Yes," *Forbes*, January 16, 2015, http://www.forbes.com/sites/chrissmith/2015/01/16/could-a-super-bowl-commercial-really-be-worth-10-million/#31491d177276.

8 "Super Bowl 50 Draws 111.9 Million TV Viewers, 16.9 Million Tweets," February 8, 2016, www.Nielsen.com.

9 Sandra Gonzalez, "'Chuck' Series Finale React: Were You Satisfied with the Ending?," *Entertainment Weekly*, January 27, 2012, www.popwatch.ew.com; Emily Bryson York, "Subway Caught Up in Fan Effort to Save NBC Series 'Chuck,'" *Advertising Age*, April 27, 2009, www.adage.com.

10 Christopher Heine, "Snapchat Is Now Selling Ads Against Nielsen's TV-Like Ratings System," *AdWeek*, January 24, 2017, http://www.adweek.com/digital/snapchat-now-selling-ads-against-nielsens-tv-ratings-system-175733/; Seb Joseph, "Snapchat Is Opening Up Its Ad Platform Ahead of Its Planned IPO," *Business Insider*, January 31, 2017, http://www.businessinsider.com/snapchat-opens-up-ad-platform-ahead-of-its-planned-ipo-2017-1.

11 Jack Neff and Rupal Parekh, "Dove Takes Its New Men's Line to the Super Bowl," *Advertising Age*, January 5, 2010, www.adagecom.

12 Kimberlee Morrison, "81% of Shoppers Conduct Online Research Before Buying," *AdWeek*, November 28, 2014, http://www.adweek.com/digital/81-shoppers-conduct-online-research-making-purchase-infographic/.

13 "Customers Like to Research Online but Make Big Purchases in Stores, Says New Retailer Study," *Forbes*, May 25, 2016, https://www.forbes.com/sites/forbespr/2016/05/25/customers-like-to-research-online-but-make-big-purchases-in-stores-says-new-retailer-study/#565604c2244b.

14 "9 Things to Know about Influencing Purchasing Decisions," *ConversionXL*, March 19, 2012, www.conversionxl.com.

15 "Audi: The Art of the Heist, Effie Awards Brief of Effectiveness, 2006, www.edwardbouches.comwp-content/uploads/2012/01/art-of-heist.pdf.

16 Alex Porter, "FMOT vs. ZMOT: A Conversation with Morgan McAlenney," Location3, May 4, 2011, www.location3.com.

17 Garrett Sloane, "Advertisers Can Now Target YouTube Ads Based on People's Google Search Histories," *Advertising Age*, January 20, 2017, http://adage.com/article/digital/advertisers-target-youtube-ads-based-search-histories/307614/.

18 Tom Van Riper, "Super Bowl Ads: A Whole New Ballgame," *Forbes*, January 13, 2010, www.forbes.com.

19 Chrissy Wissinger, "Prosper MediaPlanIQ: Telecom Companies Need to Reallocate Ad Expenditures," BIGresearch press release, February 5, 2009, www.bigresearch.com.

20 Laura Bright, "Media Planning Education in 2012 and Beyond," American Academy of Advertising 2012 Conference, Myrtle Beach, SC, March 15–18, 2012.

21 "Sweet Talk," *Evolution Bureau*, accessed September 17, 2012, www.evb.com.

22 Bright, "Media Planning Education."

23 Beth Bulik, "Layering in Local," *Smart Strategies for Local Marketing*, Ad Age Insights Report, October 1, 2011, 3.

24 Beth Bulik, "Location, Location, Location: Search, Social," *Smart Strategies for Local Marketing*, Ad Age Insights Report, October 1, 2011, 7.

25 "Validated Campaign Essentials," comScore, October 21, 2012, www.comscore.com.

26 Carla Lloyd, "Modern Media Planning," in *Strategic Media Decisions*, 2nd ed., ed. Marian Azzaro (Chicago: Copy Workshop, 2008), 183–184.

27 "What the Cost of a Super Bowl Ad Can Buy Online," Digiday, January 30, 2015, http://digiday.com/platforms/cost-super-bowl-ad-can-buy-online/.

28 Kantar Media, "A Guide to Online Advertising Rates," January 20, 2014, http://www.kantarmedia.com/us/thinking-and-resources/blog/a-guide-to-online-advertising-rates.

29 Jim Rutenberg, "Secret of the Obama Victory? Rerun Watchers, for One Thing," *New York Times*, November 12, 2012, www.nytimes.com.

30 Tanzina Vega, "The New Algorithm of Web Marketing," *New York Times*, November 18, 2012, www.nytimes.com.

31 Pagan Kennedy, "How to Destroy the Business Model of Breitbart and Fake News," *New York Times*, January 7, 2017, https://www.nytimes.com/2017/01/07/opinion/sunday/how-to-destroy-the-business-model-of-breitbart-and-fake-news.html; Joel B. Pollak, "Fake News Plus Fascism: New York Times Urges Boycott of Breitbart," Breitbart, January 8, 2017, http://www.breitbart.com/big-government/2017/01/08/new-york-times-aims-breitbart-misses-badly/.

32 Suzanne Vranica, "CBS, ABC Win Higher Rates," *Wall Street Journal*, June 13, 2012, B8.

33 Joe Flint and Suzanne Vranica, "Television-Ad Spending Shows Signs of Revival," *Wall Street Journal*, April 17, 2016, http://www.wsj.com/articles/television-ad-spending-shows-signs-of-revival-1460885403; Brian Steinberg, "Upfront Ad Sales Negotiations Tougher, Slower Than Predicted," *Variety*, June 2, 2016, http://variety.com/2016/tv/news/2016-tv-upfront-advertising-1201787798/.

34 Monica Hesse, "Activist discusses campaign to pressure Facebook on pages that denigrate women," *The Washington Post*, May 30, 2013, https://www.washingtonpost.com/lifestyle/style/activist-discusses-campaign-to-pressure-facebook-on-pages-that-denigrate-women/2013/05/30/9e66617e-c963-11e2-9f1a-1a7cdee20287_story.html?utm_term=.cc84c6e8554f.

35 Wayne Friedman, "Nielsen Releases 'Limited' Total Content Ratings," *MediaPost*, January 27, 2017, http://www.mediapost.com/publications/article/293920/nielsen-offers-limited-release-of-total-content.html?utm_source=newsletter&utm_medium=email&utm_content=leftcolumn&utm_campaign=100028.

36 Emily Steel, "Web Sites Target Oscars Fans; Ads Will Reflect Show Events," *Wall Street Journal*, March 4, 2010, B7.

37 Terry Stephan, "You've Come a Long Way, Baby," *Northwestern*, Winter 2012, 18.

38 http://www.skyeurope.tv/.

39 Bob Garfield, *The Chaos Scenario* (Nashville, TN: Stielstra, 2009).

40 Ken Mallon and Duncan Southgate, "Where Digital Marketing Is Heading in 2010 (Part I)," *Advertising Age*, December 29, 2009, www.adage.com.

CHAPTER 16

1 Wayne DeLozier, *The Marketing Communications Process* (New York: McGraw-Hill, 1976), flyleaf.

2 Adrianne Pasquarelli, "The Power of Cohesive Branding: Why Apple Wins," *Advertising Age*, October 17, 2016, www.adage.com.

3 Tom Duncan and Sandra Moriarty, "How Integrated Marketing Communication's 'Touch Points' Can Operationalize the Service-Dominant Logic," in *The Service-Dominant Logic of Marketing*, ed. Robert Lusch and Stephen Vargo (Armonk, NY: M. E. Sharpe, 2006), 240.

4 Giep Fanzen and Sandra Moriarty, *The Science and Art of Branding* (Armonk, NY: M. E. Sharpe, 2009).

5 Stan Richards, "It's Been a Rocket Ride," *Dallas Business Journal*, April 7, 2006, www.dallas.bizjournals.com.

6 Tom Duncan and Sandra Moriarty, *Driving Brand Value: Using Integrated Marketing to Manage Profitable Stakeholder Relationships* (New York: McGraw-Hill, 1997).

7 Julie Ruth, "Implementing Strategy for Success," *AAA Newsletter*, June 2010, 5–6.

8 Franzen and Moriarty, *The Science and Art of Branding*, 88.

9 Darin Archer, "Making the Holiday Shopping Experience Seamless," *Advertising Age*, December 6, 2016, www.adage.com.

10 Bill Lindelof, "Tiger's Fall Cost Sponsors $12 Billion," *Boulder Daily Camera*, December 29, 2009, 3C.

11 "AmEx Plans Jerry Seinfeld-Meets-Superman Internet Show," *Advertising Age*, February 4, 2004, www.adage.com.

12 Tanya Gazdik, "ANA Finds 'Brand Activation' Approaching 60% of Marketer Budgets, Eclipses Advertising," April 20, 2016, mediapost.com.

13 Steve Kelly, personal communication, January 11–13, 2010. Used with permission.

14 Ingvi Logason, "Match CR-V to Your Lifestyle," in Sandra Moriarty, Nancy Mitchell, and Bill Wells, *Advertising and IMC Principles and Practice*, 9th ed. (Upper Saddle River, NJ: Prentice Hall, 2012), 532–534, 556.

15 Elaine Wong, "Unilever Signs On as Sponsor of *Today Show*'s 'Cooking School,'" *Brandweek*, January 12, 2010, www.brandweek.com.

16 "Dentsu Launches Next-Generation Communication Planning System IMC ver.2.0ˢ," Dentsu press release, April 13, 2006; "Integrated Communication by Use of ContactPoint Management®," PowerPoint presentation, Tokyo, November 2006; presentations at IMC consulting visits by Tom Duncan and Sandra Moriarty with Dentsu, Tokyo, Japan, April and November 2006.

17 Troy Young, "It's Not the Impression That Counts. It's What You Do with It," *Advertising Age*, January 19, 2010, www.adage.com.

18 Todd Bishop, "First Windows 8 Ad Touts 'Reimagined' Operating System," October 14, 2012, www.geekwire.com; Tom Warren, "Microsoft reportedly spending over $1 billion on Windows 8 marketing blitz," *The Verge*, October 12, 2012, www.theverge.com; Mary Jo Foley, "Microsoft kicks off Windows 10 ad campaign," *ZD Net*, July 20, 2015, www.zdnet.com.

19 "P&G to Slash $10 Billion in Costs over Five Years," *Advertising Age*, February 23, 2012, www.adage.com.

20 Emily Steel, "After Ditching Tiger, Accenture Tries New Game," *Wall Street Journal*, January 14, 2010, B1.

21 Logason, "Match CR-V to Your Lifestyle," 532–534, 556.

22 Katherine Frith and Barbara Mueller, *Advertising and Societies: Global Issues* (New York: Peter Lang, 2002).

23 Tom Duncan, "The Evolution of IMC," *International Journal of Integrated Marketing Communication* 1, no. 1 (Spring 2009): 17.

24 "Carol Cone On Purpose," Conscious Issue 04: Powerful Voices, January 4, 2017, purposecollaborative.com; Paul Holmes, "Carol Cone Launches New Firm 'On Purpose,'" November 17, 2015, www.homesreport.com.

25 Nick Bartle, "Finding the Real Bottom Line," *Advertising Age*, January 27, 2010, www.adage.com.

26 Scott Hamula, quoted in Sandra Moriarty, Nancy Mitchell, and Bill Wells, *Advertising and IMC: Principles and Practice*, 9th ed. (Upper Saddle River, NJ: Prentice Hall, 2012), 561.

27 Duncan and Moriarty, *Driving Brand Value*.

28 Duncan, "The Evolution of IMC."

29 Bob Liodice, "Essentials for Integrated Marketing: As More Power Shifts to Consumers, Need Grows for Common Metric and 'Renaissance Marketers,'" *Advertising Age*, June 9, 2008, www.adage.com.

30 Lindsay Stein, "Amid Acquisition Surge, Dentsu Aegis U.S. Names Its First President for Operations and Integration," *Advertising Age*, October 14, 2016, www.adage.com.

31 Aaron Patrick, "Publicis Chief Seeks Unity Within," *Wall Street Journal*, July 12, 2006, B3.

32 Larissa Faw, "New Approach At Publicis Group: 'Sapient Inside,'" March 22, 2016, www.mediapost.com.

33 Bill Vlasic, "Ford's Bet: It's a Small World After All," *New York Times*, January 10, 2010, www.nytimes.com.

34 Tom Duncan and Sandra Moriarty, "How One Agency Re-Organized to Walk the New IMC Talk," *Admap*, September 2007, 35–38; Thomas Duncan, "IMC and Branding: Research

Propositions," *International Journal of Integrated Marketing Communications* 1, no. 1 (Spring 2009): 17–23.

35 IMC consulting visit by Tom Duncan and Sandra Moriarty with Dentsu, Tokyo, Japan, January 2006.

36 Liodice, "Essentials for Integrated Marketing."

37 Susan G. Komen website, ww5.Komen.org, downloaded August 30, 2017.

CHAPTER 17

1 Jonathan Crowe, "Defining Audience Engagement: What Marketers Talk About When They Talk About Engagement," *OpenView Labs*, August 21, 2012, http://labs .openviewpartners.com/defining-audience-engagement/#.WbRsdiMrJaV.

2 "Worldwide Ad Spending Growth Revised Downward: Annual Gains in Worldwide Ad Spending Will Hover around 6% throughout the Forecast Period," *eMarketer*, April 21, 2016, https://www.emarketer.com/Article/ Worldwide-Ad-Spending-Growth-Revised-Downward/1013858; Louise Marsland, "How Much Advertising Actually Works?," *SAMRA Convention 2006 News*, March 15, 2006, http://www.bizcommunity.com/ Article/196/119/9593.html.

3 John Philip Jones, *When Ads Work: New Proof That Advertising Triggers Sales*, 2nd ed. (Armonk, NY: M. E. Sharpe, 2007), xvii.

4 Simon Broadbent, *When to Advertise* (Henley-on-Thames, UK: Admap Publications, 1999).

5 Natalie Zmuda, "Marketing Quant 101: Universities Gear Up for Data Talent Crunch," *Advertising Age*, March 18, 2013, www.adage .com.

6 "10 Massive Advertising Campaign Failures," *CNBC: Media*, February 17, 2011, www.cnbc .com/id/41624240/page/3.

7 Jones, *When Ads Work*, p. 214.

8 Institute for Public Relations, "Using Web Analytics to Measure Impact," email release, February 15, 2010.

9 Eric Webber, "You Can't Quantify Everything," September 9, 2008, www.adage.com.

10 Crowe, "Defining Audience Engagement: What Marketers Talk About When They Talk About Engagement."

11 Mark Story, "A View on Skills for the PR Professional of Tomorrow," January 13, 2009, http://www.markstory.me/2009/01/13/a-view-on-skills-for-the-pr-professional-of-tomorrow/.

12 Melissa Read, personal communication, March 13, 2013.

13 Read, personal communication.

14 Brian Morrissey, "New Campaign Metric: Social Chatter," *Adweek*, January 27, 2010, www.adweek.com.

15 Chris Reidy, "Locals Plan Twitter Experiment on Super Bowl Ads," *Boston Globe*, January 30, 2009, www.boston.com.

16 Gerard Tellis, *Effective Advertising* (Thousand Oaks, CA: Sage, 2004), 6.

17 Bob Liodice, "Essentials for Integrated Marketing: As More Power Shifts to Consumers, Need Grows for Common Metric

and 'Renaissance Marketers,'" *Advertising Age*, June 9, 2008, www.adage.com.

18 Claire Stammerjohan, Charles M. Wood, Yuhmiin Chang, and Esther Thorson, "An Empirical Investigation of the Interaction between Publicity, Advertising, and Previous Brand Attitudes and Knowledge," *Journal of Advertising* 34, no. 4 (December 2005): 55–67.

19 "Unaided Advertising Recall Significantly Higher with Mix of Radio and Internet," *Research Brief*, February 23, 2007, www .centerformediaresearch.com.

20 Dong Lee and Chan Park, "Conceptualization and Measurement of Multidimensionality of Integrated Marketing Communication," *Journal of Advertising Research* 47, no. 3 (September 2007): 222–236.

21 Read, personal communication.

22 Gavin O'Malley, "Facebook Reassures Advertisers, Undergoes MRC Audit," *Media Post*, February 10, 2017, http://www.mediapost .com/publications/article/294963/facebook-reassures-advertisers-undergoes-mrc-audi. html; Lindsay Stein, "ANA Calls for Facebook Metrics to Be Audited and Accredited," *Advertising Age*, September 29, 2016, CMO Strategy RSS, http://adage.com/article/cmo-strategy/ana-calls-facebook-metrics-audited-accredited/306096/; Tim Peterson, "Twitter Overcharged Video Advertisers due to Error in its Android App," *Marketing Land*, December 23, 2016, http://marketingland.com/twitter-overcharged-video-advertisers-due-error-android-app-201750.

23 2004 Effie Brief provided by UPS and the Martin Agency.

24 Laura Stevens, "UPS Launches New Ad Campaign: 'United Problem Solvers' Slogan Emphasizes Services to Businesses," *Wall Street Journal*, March 8, 2015, http://www.wsj .com/articles/ups-launches-new-ad-campaign-1425838722.

25 Burson-Marsteller, "Introducing Evidence-Based Communications," The Burson-Marsteller Blog, www.burson-marsteller. com/bm-blog/introducing-evidence-based-communications/.

26 Marlene Bender and Art Zambianchi, "The Reality of ROI: Dell's Approach to Measurement," *Journal of Integrated Marketing Communications* 2006: 16–21.

27 Jack Myers, "Jack Myers' Weekend Think Tank: Can the Rules of Research Change?," *MediaPost Publications*, January 5, 2007, http://publications.mediapost.com.

CHAPTER 18

1 Bob Liodice, "10 Companies with Social Responsibility at the Core," *Advertising Age*, April 19, 2010, www.adage.com.

2 Harris Poll, "Majorities of Americans Lay at Least Some Blame for Economic Crisis on Media and Advertising Agencies for Causing People to Buy What They Couldn't Afford," *Harris Interactive*, April 15, 2009, www.harrisinteractive.com.

3 Charles Goodrum and Helen Dalrymple, *Advertising in America: The First 200 Years* (New York: Harry N. Abrams, 1990).

4 Center on Alcohol Marketing and Youth, "Exposure of African-American Youth to Alcohol Advertising," June 19, 2003, http:// www.camy.org/_docs/resources/reports/ archived-reports/exposure-aa-youth-full-report.pdf.

5 Mindy Pankoke, "Three Stereotypes to Avoid when Marketing to Millennials," *Advertising Age*, September 16, 2016, www.adage.com.

6 Anna Mehler Paperny, "Virgin Ads Too Sexy for Calgary, Mississauga Transit," *Globe and Mail*, January 8, 2010, www.theglobeandmail .com.

7 E. J. Schultz, "FTC Charges Volkswagen with Deceptive Advertising," *Advertising Age*, March 29, 2016, www.adage.com.

8 William Boston, "Volkswagen Shake-Up Meets with Investor Skepticism," *Wall Street Journal*, November 18, 2016, www.wsj.com.

9 Suzan Clarke, "Agency Bans Dior Mascara Ad Featuring Natalie Portman," *ABC News*, October 25, 2012, abcnews.go.com.

10 Herbert J. Rotfeld and Kim B. Rotzoll, "Is Advertising Puffery Believed?," *Journal of Advertising* 9, no. 3 (1980): 45.

11 Noreen O'Leary, "Weight Watchers Wins 1st Round vs. Jenny Craig, *Adweek*, January 21, 2010, www.adweek.com.

12 Stephanie Clifford, "Coat Maker Transforms Obama Photo into Ad," *New York Times*, January 6, 2010, www.nytimes.com.

13 Word of Mouth Marketing Association, "Ethics Code," September 21, 2009, www .womma.org/ethics/code.

14 Eric Tegler, "Ford Is Counting on Army of 100 Bloggers to Launch New Fiesta," *Advertising Age*, April 20, 2009, http://adage.com.

15 Sapna Maheshwari, "Endorsed on Instagram by a Kardashian, but Is It Love or Just an Ad?" *New York Times*, August 30, 2016, www .nytimes.com.

16 Josh Bernoff, "When and How to Pay a Blogger," *Advertising Age*, May 26, 2009, http://adage.com.

17 "Branded Content on Facebook: Our Updated Policy and a New Tool," March 30, 2017, www.facebook.com/business/news/branded-content-update, retrieved September 9, 2017.

18 Hank Schultz, "FTC Cites Another 'Fake News' Weight Loss Marketing Scheme," June 7, 2016, www.nutraingredients-usa.com.

19 Bruce Horovitz, "Wendy's Will Be 1st Fast Foodie with Healthier Oil," *USA Today*, June 8, 2006.

20 Bruce Horovitz and Julie Appleby, Kaiser Health News, "Prescription Drug Costs Are Up; So Are TV Ads Promoting Them," March 16, 2017, www.usatoday.com.

21 Theresa Howard, "Push Is On to End Prescription Drug Ads Targeting Consumers," *USA Today*, August 10, 2009, www.usatoday .com.

22 Jeffrey Young, "Health Care Reform Rebates for Health Insurance Costs Rolling In," *Huffington Post*, July 16, 2012, www.huffingtonpost.com.

23 Fred Beard, "Brilliant or Offensive Advertising?" In Sandra Moriarty, Nancy Mitchell, and William Wells, *Advertising &*

IMC: Principles and Practice, 10th ed. (New York: Pearson, 2015), 72.

[24] Philip Patterson and Lee Wilkins, *Media Ethics: Issues and Cases*, 6th ed. (Boston: McGraw-Hill, 2008).

[25] "Honesty/Ethics in Professions," December 2–6, 2015, www.gallup.com.

[26] Institute for Advertising Ethics, "Principles and Practices," March 17, 2011, www.rjionline.org/institute-for-advertising-ethics.

[27] Tom Spalding, "Peeps Maker Sues Greeting Card Firm," *USA Today*, October 7, 2009, www.usatoday.com.

[28] Chris Adams, "Looser Lip for Food and Drug Companies?," *Wall Street Journal*, September 17, 2002, A4.

[29] Amy Sullivan, "Truth in Advertising? Not for Political Ads," *Time*, September 23, 2008, www.content.time.com.

[30] dbt, "Database and Internet Solutions," January 31, 2010, www.dbt.co.uk.

[31] "Nestle Loses EU Kit Kat Trademark," *Warc*, December 19, 2016, www.warc.com.

[32] Federal Trade Commission, "FTC Publishes Final Guides Governing Endorsements, Testimonials," October 5, 2010, www.ftc.gov/opa/2009/10/endortest.shtm.

[33] Ginger Conlon, "2016 Will Be a Growth Year in Marketing Spending," *Direct Marketing News*, February 2, 2016, www.dmnews.com.

[34] Jack Neff, "Duracell Agrees to Modify Robo-War Duck Ad," *Advertising Age*, February 6, 2002, www.adage.com; Daniel Golden and Suzanne Vranica, "Duracell's Duck Ad Will Carry Disclaimer," *Wall Street Journal*, February 7, 2002, B7.

[35] John J. Burnett, "Gays: Feelings about Advertising and Media Used," *Journal of Advertising Research*, January–February 2000, 75–86.

[36] Maureen Morrison, "NARC Nixed as Industry Opts for Name Change," *Advertising Age*, April 23, 2012, www.adage.com.

[37] Roy F. Fox, "Hucksters Hook Captive Youngsters," *Mizzou*, Summer 2002, 22–27.

INDEX